Hydraulics and Its Applications

˙DRAULICS AND ITS APPLICATIONS

BY

A. H. GIBSON,

D.SC., ASSOC. MEM. INST. C.E., MEM. INST. MECH. E., F.R.S.E.

Professor of Engineering in the University of St. Andrews,
University College, Dundee

SECOND EDITION, REVISED AND ENLARGED.

NEW YORK
D. VAN NOSTRAND COMPANY
25 PARK PLACE
1919

First Published -   -   1908.
Second Edition -   -   1912. *Reprinted* 1919.

Printed in Great Britain.

PREFACE

WERE water a perfectly non-viscous, inelastic fluid, whose particles, when in motion, always followed sensibly parallel paths, Hydraulics would be one of the most exact of the sciences.

But water satisfies none of these conditions, and the result is that in the majority of cases brought before the engineer, motions and forces of such complexity are introduced as baffle all attempts at a rigorous solution.

This being so, the best that can be done is to discuss each phenomenon on the assumption that the fluid in motion is perfect, and to modify the results so obtained until they fit the results of experiment, by the introduction of some empirical constant which shall involve the effect of every disregarded factor.

It is worth while here impressing on the student of the science that, apart from these experimentally-deduced constants, his theoretical results are, at the best, only approximations to the truth, and may, if care be not taken in their interpretation, be actually misleading.

On the other hand, it may be well to answer the criticism of those who would cavil at such theoretical treatment, by pointing out that the results so obtained provide the only rational framework on which to erect the more complete structure of hydraulics.

In the following pages an attempt has been made to consider the science, and its application to the design of Hydraulic Machinery, in a manner suitable for a student who has some initial knowledge of mechanics.

While written primarily with the needs of a student in view, it is, however, hoped that the book may prove of value to such as are actively engaged in the practice and profession of Hydraulic Engineering. Although it has not been attempted to elude the largely imaginary difficulties of a mathematical treatment involving some knowledge of the Differential and Integral Calculus, the knowledge of this subject which is necessary for a thorough grasp of the greater part of the book is very slight.

Where, as in some few paragraphs, a somewhat more extended

mathematical knowledge is required, the work is such as may safely be left by all but the more advanced student of the subject.

In the section devoted to Hydraulic Machinery, it has not been attempted to deal in any way exhaustively with the subject, and only such machines have been illustrated or described as are typical of their class, represent good modern design, and illustrate some definite principle of construction. For many of these illustrations the Author is indebted to the manufacturers, and while reference has been made to these in the text, he would take this opportunity of thanking them collectively for the help which they have so courteously tendered.

As was essential, reference has been freely made to the minutes of the proceedings of the various English and American societies, and to the English and German technical press, as well as to standard works on the subject. Of these the Author is particularly indebted to the Councils of the Institution of Civil Engineers, the Institution of Mechanical Engineers, the American Society of Civil Engineers, the *Zeitschrift des Vereins deutscher Ingenieure*, *The Engineer*, and *Engineering*.

The greatest debt of all is, however, owing to the teachings and published papers of his old professor and some time chief, Osborne Reynolds. Old students of the Professor will readily recognise to what extent any slight merit which the book may possess is due, directly or indirectly to the influence of one to whom the science of Hydraulics owes so much.

In conclusion the Author would tender his thanks to Mr. S. Chapman, to Mr. E. Magson, and to Mr. C. H. Lander and Mr. F. Pickford, of the Manchester University, each of whom has revised a portion of the proof, and to whose kindly criticism and suggestion the book owes much.

A. H. GIBSON.

MANCHESTER,
February, 1908.

PREFACE TO SECOND EDITION

SINCE the first edition of this work appeared, a great deal of work has been done on the experimental side of Hydraulics, and as far as possible such work has been noted in the present edition.

The book has been practically rewritten. Much of the original matter has been re-arranged; some has been deleted; and considerable additions have been made to almost every section, particularly to those dealing with flow over weirs, through pipes, and in open channels; with methods of gauging such flows; and with the mechanical applications of Hydraulics. A chapter dealing with wave motion has been added, as have articles dealing, among other subjects, with the flow of fluids other than water, the admixture of fluids in pipes, and the interaction of passing vessels.

Such errors as have been noticed in the first edition have been corrected, and the Author would thank those readers whose kindness and courtesy in intimating these, has made their elimination largely possible.

A. H. GIBSON.

DUNDEE,
  October, 1912

CONTENTS

SECTION I.

CHAPTER IV.

CHAPTER V.

CHAPTER VI.

CHAPTER VII.

CONTENTS

CHAPTER VIII.

CHAPTER IX.

CHAPTER X.

CONTENTS

CONTENTS

LIST OF SYMBOLS AS GENERALLY ADOPTED THROUGHOUT THE BOOK

Where, for any reason, this notation has been departed from, special notice is given.

v .. .. Linear velocity in feet per second.

u .. .. ,, ,, ,, ,,

v_r .. .. Relative ,, ,, ,,

w .. .. Tangential ,, ,, ,, $\left.\begin{array}{l}\text{in case of a turbine or}\\\text{centrifugal pump.}\end{array}\right\}$

f .. .. Radial ,, ,, ,,

f . .. Coefficient of friction (in pipe flow).

ω . .. Angular velocity in radians per second.

r . .. Radius in feet.

$\left.\begin{array}{l}d\\D\end{array}\right.$ .. .. $\left.\right\}$ Pipe diameters in feet.

$\left.\begin{array}{l}A\\a\end{array}\right.$ .. .. $\left.\right\}$ Areas in square feet.

l .. .. Length in feet.

m .. .. Hydraulic mean depth.

i .. .. Slope of a channel.

$\left.\begin{array}{l}h\\H\end{array}\right.$ .. .. $\left.\right\}$ Head in feet of water.

p .. .. Pressure—usually in lbs. per square foot.

W .. .. Weight of 1 cubic foot of water = 62·4 lbs.

g .. .. 32·2 feet per second per second.

ρ . .. Density of water = $W \div g$.

Q .. . Quantity in cubic feet per second.

μ .. .. Coefficient of viscosity.

η .. .. Efficiency.

U .. .. Work done.

HYDRAULICS AND ITS APPLICATIONS

SECTION I.

CHAPTER I.

Introductory—Historical *Résumé*—Physical Properties of Water—Density—Compressibility—Cohesion—Adhesion—Capillarity—Surface Tension—Viscosity.

INTRODUCTORY—PHYSICAL PROPERTIES OF WATER.

ART. 1.—HYDROMECHANICS.

THE science which deals with liquids at rest or in motion may be divided into two branches: **Hydrostatics,** which deals with the equilibrium of liquids at rest; and **Hydrodynamics,** which deals with the problems connected with their motion. The term **Hydraulics** is usually broadly applied to that portion of the latter branch which deals with the motion of water in so far as this is of importance in the problems brought directly under the notice of the engineer.

A knowledge of the fundamentals of Hydrostatics is, however, so essential to a thorough grasp of the principles of Hydrodynamics, and is of such direct importance to the hydraulic engineer, that a treatise on Hydraulics would not be complete without some preliminary treatment of this branch of the subject.

The origin of the science is of great antiquity, and no attempt will be made to give a detailed historical *résumé* of its growth. Some few of the principles of Hydrostatics were enunciated by Archimedes (B.C. 250), and it is a remarkable fact that for 1,800 years from this date—until the time of Stevinus, Galileo, and Torricelli—practically no further progress was made.

The construction of the elaborate series of aqueducts and of service pipes for supplying Rome with water indeed shows that the Romans possessed some knowledge of the properties of water when at rest and

H.A.　　　　　　　　　　　　　　　　　　　　　　　B

when in motion in pipes and open channels, but we have no record that this knowledge was based on any quantitative laws.

A treatise by Stevinus, written about 1585, would appear to follow historically that of Archimedes. In this the method of obtaining the pressure of a liquid on the sides and base of a containing vessel was first demonstrated.

Galileo, in a treatise published in 1612, discussed the Hydrostatic Paradox and also the flotation of bodies in water.

Shortly afterwards Torricelli made an important investigation into the behaviour of a jet when issuing vertically from an orifice, while, since the middle of the seventeenth century, numerous investigators have been at work deducing by experimental observation and theoretical reasoning the laws governing the various manners of motion of liquids, and applying these laws to the development of the science of Hydraulics. Of these experimentalists perhaps Mariotte, Bernoulli, and D'Alembert, with Poiseuille, Darcy, and Bazin in France; Rankine, Froude, Osborne Reynolds and James Thomson in England; Eytelwein, Weisbach, and Hagen in Germany; Venturi in Italy, with Francis and Hamilton Smith in America, are most worthy of note.

In spite, however, of all the work which has been so ably accomplished by these and other observers, Hydraulics cannot yet be classed as an exact science. The laws governing many of its phenomena are still imperfectly understood, and the difficulties—chiefly analytical—to be overcome before all the disturbing factors can be taken fully into account are very great. In such cases, experience, based on the results of experiment, forms the only safe guide. In other cases, however, the deductions of theory are found to be perfectly in accord with observed phenomena, and an attempt will be made in the course of this work to indicate to what extent our knowledge of the forces controlling any phenomenon is sufficiently accurate and comprehensive to enable theory to be an exact guide, and where, on the other hand, theory, based on insufficient data, is only useful as indicating in what direction a true solution is to be found.

ART. 2.—PHYSICAL PROPERTIES OF WATER.

In its pure state, water is an almost colourless, transparent, odourless liquid, and one of the best solvents to be found in Nature. Its maximum density occurs at 4° C., or 39·1° F., and under atmospheric pressure it freezes at 32° F. and boils at 212° F. The freezing point is lowered, and the boiling point raised by an increase in pressure, the opposite being true of a reduction of pressure. The specific gravity at maximum density is unity, and the specific heat varies slightly with temperature, increasing from 1·000 at 32° F. to 1·013 at 212° F.

The latent heat of fusion of ice at 32° F. is about 142 B.T.U., while the latent heat of evaporation at 212° F. is 966·6 B.T.U.

Weight of Water.—Authorities differ as to the precise value of the weight at maximum density, the lowest value given being about 62·379 lbs. per cubic foot and the highest 62·425 lbs. The latter value—that of Rankine—is commonly adopted as being most nearly correct. The following table, calculated from Rankine's formula, gives the weight per

Temp. Fahr.	Weight per cubic foot.	Temp. Fahr.	Weight per cubic foot.	Temp. Fahr.	Weight per cubic foot.	Temp. Fahr.	Weight per cubic foot.
32°	62·42	80°	62·23	130°	61·56	180°	60·55
40°	62·42	90°	62·13	140°	61·37	190°	60·32
50°	62·41	100°	62·02	150°	61·18	200°	60·07
60°	62·37	110°	61·89	160°	60·98	210°	59·82
70°	62·31	120°	61·74	170°	60·77		

cubic foot at different temperatures. At 212° F. values by different experimenters vary from 59·56 lbs. to 59·84 lbs. Above this temperature the exact values are not so well known and are unimportant to the engineer. For the purpose of all calculations relating to Hydraulics it is sufficiently accurate to take the weight per cubic foot at 62·4 lbs., more especially as the water with which the engineer has to deal is never perfectly pure, but contains more or less of the soluble salts. Unless otherwise stated, the above value will be adopted throughout this treatise.

The density of sea water varies slightly with the locality, but is about 1·026 times that of fresh water. Its weight, at the temperatures commonly met with in practice, may be taken as 64·0 lbs. per cubic foot.

Compressibility.—Water is very slightly compressible, the compressibility varying with the temperature and with the amount of air in solution. When pure, the decrease in volume δV, due to an increment in pressure δP, of one atmosphere, decreases from ·0000518 to ·0000412, as the temperature increases from 32° F. to 140° F. (Grassi).

This gives values of the bulk modulus K, which equals $-\dfrac{\delta P}{\dfrac{\delta V}{V}}$, varying from 284,000 to 356,000 lbs. per square inch under this temperature variation. As the temperature is further increased the modulus K diminishes to 319,000 lbs. per square inch at 212° F. Its values, over the range of temperatures experienced in practice, are as follow [1] :—

Temp. F.°	32°	40°	50°	60°	70°	80°	90°
K (lbs. per square inch)	284,000	295,000	303,000	311,000	319,000	328,000	335,000

The mean value may be taken in round numbers as 300,000 lbs. per square inch or 43,200,000 lbs. per square foot.

The compressibility is so slight that in all practical calculations concerning water at rest or in a state of steady motion it may be assumed to be an incompressible fluid. In certain important phenomena, however, notably those involving a sudden initiation or stoppage of motion, this compressibility becomes an important, and often the predominating factor, and in the treatment of such cases the above mean value of K will be adopted.

In such cases it should be noted that it is the ratio of the bulk modulus to the density of a fluid which forms the true criterion of its compressibility or elasticity, as it is this ratio which governs the wave propagation on which such phenomena depend. In this respect air is only about eighteen times as compressible as water.

At ordinary temperatures and pressures, water is capable of dissolving about 2 per cent. of its own volume of air. As the temperature is raised part of this is liberated. The volume in a saturated solution under a pressure of one atmosphere is approximately as follows[2] :—

Temp. F.°	32°	40°	60°	90°	120°	150°
Percentage volume of air in solution	2·88	2·56	2·10	1·78	1·62	1·49

At a given temperature the volume of gas absorbed is sensibly independent of the pressure, so that the weight absorbed is proportional to the pressure. Any reduction in pressure tends to liberate part of the air, and

[1] From Landholt and Bornstein. Grassi, "Annales de Chimie et Physique," 1851, vol. 31, p. 437, gives results which are in close agreement with these.

[2] A. Winkler, "Zeits. f. Phys. Chemie," 1892, vol. 9, p. 171, and Bohn and Bock, "Wied Ann.," 1891, vol. 48, p. 319.

the hissing which is so often noticeable in jet pumps and injectors, or where water is escaping at high velocities past the restricted area of a valve seat, is due to the reduction of pressure and subsequent liberation of bubbles of air, which occurs under these circumstances. The trouble which is experienced in keeping the air vessels on the delivery side of a pump charged is due to the facility with which water dissolves gases under high pressures.

Ice Formation.—In still water, under normal conditions, when ice is formed this exists as a surface layer. In very cold climates, in addition to existing in the ordinary surface form, ice is found in the form of anchor ice and of frazil. **Anchor ice** consists of an agglomerated mass of coarse crystals clinging to the bed of the channel and formed there by loss of heat by radiation, the cooling of the bottom thus produced causing ice to form. This can only occur with a clear sky and where the surface ice— if any—is transparent. Surface ice will in general effectually prevent its formation. It is usually found in rapid streams, where surface ice cannot form.

Frazil consists of fine spicular ice crystals floating in the water and formed by slight supercooling below 32° (probably about ·001° being sufficient). This adheres to the surface ice and to the anchor ice, and may finally choke up the stream. In engineering work frazil ice is particularly objectionable, as it adheres to the racks and strainers and to the gates of a turbine, and if, due to exposure to air, these are slightly supercooled, freezes into one solid mass.

In common with all other liquids, water also possesses the properties of **Cohesion, Adhesion,** *and* **Viscosity.**

Art. 3.—Cohesion

is that property of a liquid, or solid, which enables neighbouring molecules to resist any stress of the nature of a tension. **Adhesion** is that property which enables it to adhere to a solid body with which it may be in contact. Thus a drop of water exhibits cohesion in its hanging together, and adhesion in virtue of its clinging to a solid body, the force of gravity being overcome both by cohesion and by adhesion. Both phenomena are due to molecular attraction, cohesion between neighbouring molecules of the liquid, and adhesion between those of the solid and liquid. A consideration of the molecular theory of matter indicates that if a is the distance between any two molecules, their mutual attractive force is approximately equal to $\dfrac{k}{a^6}$; and it follows that a rise in temperature, by increasing the molecular distance, diminishes both cohesion and adhesion.

Their relative values vary for different combinations of solid and liquid, the adhesive force being greater than that of cohesion when the liquid wets the solid and *vice versâ*. Also the adhesive force, unlike that of cohesion, is found to vary largely with the time of contact, increasing within limits as this is increased.

That water, under suitable conditions, may exist in a state of tensile stress may be shown in many ways, and experiments [1] show that this may attain considerable proportions. For example, Achard and Gay-Lussac each obtained values of about 1,024 lbs. per square foot, while Dufour [2] succeeded in raising water, in the spherical state and exposed to atmospheric pressure, to a temperature of 356° F. without boiling. Since this corresponds to a vapour pressure of 132 lbs. per square inch, the cohesion must have attained this value for rupture not to have taken place. This high value is probably due to the absence of dissolved air at this temperature.

With water in bulk, the great difficulty in demonstrating cohesion is to get it into such a state that it may be exposed to a direct tensile stress over any appreciable area.

The method of rupture, as it commonly occurs, may be likened to that of a sheet of paper by a tear extending from one edge. Could the water be brought into such a state that its rupture was similar to that of the same sheet of paper when pulled directly into two parts, the effect of cohesion would be more strikingly apparent. Such an action, however, involving the simultaneous rupture over any appreciable area, is extremely difficult to procure except where the water exists in the state of a film, and on this account the effect of cohesion on the behaviour of water in bulk is negligible. Its importance to the engineer is then confined to its effects as shown in the phenomena of capillarity and surface tension.

That the idea of cohesion is not incompatible with the exceeding mobility of the particles of water may be indirectly demonstrated by the behaviour of two iron surface plates when brought into contact. Here, if the plates are clean, the resistance to sliding of one over the other is very small, while the force necessary to overcome cohesion and to separate the plates by normal motion is surprisingly great.

---

[1] For an account of some experiments on cohesion, see a paper by Osborne Reynolds in "Proceedings of the Manchester Literary and Philosophical Society," 1880—1.

[2] Maxwell's "Heat," p. 259.

The phenomenon known as **Capillarity**, which appears in the tendency of a liquid to rise or fall from its normal level in a tube of fine bore, according as the liquid does or does not wet the tube, would appear to be due to cohesion and adhesion; while it is probable that cohesion between the surface molecules of a liquid gives rise to **Surface Tension**, the property of a liquid which gives it the appearance of having an elastic skin at its surface of separation from a gas, or from any other liquid. Experiment shows that the tension in any such surface film is everywhere the same, and that the tension across any imaginary line in the surface is normal to that line. Also the tension is independent of the curvature of the surface; decreases with an increase in temperature; is constant for a given temperature, for the surface of separation of any particular liquid and gas, or of any two given liquids; and for any given liquid and solid in the presence of air, the angle of inclination, a, of the surfaces is constant.

Thus, for water and glass at a temp. of 68° F.   .   . $a = 25° 32'$
      for mercury and glass .   .   .   .   . $a = 128° 52'$
while the surface tension, expressed in pounds per foot run of the line of contact, and at the above temperature, has the following values (from Quincke's experiments) : —

    For water and air   .   .   . $T = ·005548$ lbs. per foot
    For mercury and air .   .   . $T = ·03698$,,

No satisfactory explanation of the precise nature of surface tension has been formulated. Beyond doubt, however, it is a molecular phenomenon, and is inseparable from that of cohesion, the intensity of the one probably determining that of the other.

Many theories have been educed to explain the phenomena of capillarity. Of these, the two which have been most generally accepted are due respectively to Poisson and Young. Briefly outlined, the former assumes that when a liquid wets a plate the attraction between the layer of molecules in intimate contact with the plate and the plate itself is greater than the intermolecular attraction of the liquid. The molecular motion of the molecules forming the surface film is thus reduced, while in consequence of their greater freedom, that of the molecules immediately distant from this film is increased. The density of this secondary layer of fluid is thus reduced below the normal, and the resultant upward pressure of the surrounding fluid causes it to rise up the plate until a state of statical equilibrium is attained between the cohesive forces and the action of gravity on the supported fluid.

Where a liquid does not wet the plate, the density of this secondary film is increased by the molecular action between the plate and fluid, with a consequent fall in the surface level in the immediate neighbourhood of the plate. That this variation of density actually occurs has been indirectly proved in other ways, while results obtained by the application of this theory are amply confirmed by experiment.

The second theory attributes the phenomena to the action of a series of surface tensions, which are assumed to exist at every surface of contact of any liquid or gas with any solid, and also at the surface of contact of any liquid with any other liquid, or with a gas. Thus at the common line of intersection of a solid, liquid, and gas, *i.e.*, at the line passing through P (Fig. 1) and perpendicular to the plane of the paper, three surface tensions, of intensity T_{as}, T_{al}, and T_{ls} per unit length of this line, are in existence. For equilibrium then, their directions and magnitudes will be

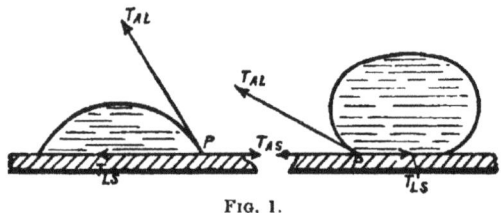

Fɪɢ. 1.

related according to the ordinary laws of statical equilibrium. Thus for contact with a plane surface we have—

$$T_{as} = T_{ls} + T_{al} \cos a,$$

and the angle a will be acute or obtuse according as $T_{as} - T_{ls}$ is positive or negative.

If $T_{as} = T_{ls} + T_{al}$, $a = 0$ and for this, and all greater relative values of T_{as}, the fluid will immediately spread to cover the surface, the effect being as though the liquid were pulled outwards in every direction by the tension T_{as}, the resultant of the tensions T_{ls} and T_{al} being insufficient to resist this motion. On the other hand if $T_{as} - T_{ls}$ is negative, cos a is negative and the angle a is obtuse. If $T_{ls} - T_{as} = T_{al}$, $a = 180°$, and the liquid, if in sufficiently small masses, assumes the spherical state.

On these assumptions, justified in so far as the results obtained by their application go, the various phenomena of capillary action easily lend themselves to mathematical treatment.

Rise of Liquid in a Capillary Tube.—Let h be the height of the liquid in the tube, of diameter d feet, and let w be the weight of unit volume of the liquid. Here h is measured to a horizontal plane tangential to the curved surface at the top of the column (Fig. 2). Let $V =$ the (small) volume of liquid above this plane.

The height of the column when in a state of equilibrium may be deduced from the principle of virtual work,[1] *i.e.*, by equating the work done against gravity in any small vertical displacement of the column, to that done by the surface tensions.

If δx is this displacement we have, for equilibrium

$$(T_{ls} - T_{as})\, \pi\, d\, \delta x + w\, \delta x \left\{ \frac{\pi\, d^2 h}{4} + V \right\} = 0$$

$$\therefore h = \frac{4}{w\, d}(T_{as} - T_{ls}) - \frac{4\, V}{\pi\, d^2}$$

But $T_{as} - T_{ls} = T_{al} \cos a$

$$\therefore h = \frac{4\, T_{al} \cos a}{w\, d} - \frac{4\, V}{\pi\, d^2} \qquad (1)$$

In general V is very small, so that without sensible error (1) may be written

$$h = \frac{4\, T \cos a}{w\, d} \qquad (2)$$

Similarly it may be shown that the vertical rise or fall between two parallel plates at a distance d apart $= \dfrac{2\, T \cos a}{w\, d}$ (3)

Fig. 2.

It is with the former case of capillary action that we are chiefly concerned in hydraulics, as affecting the accuracy of measurements of pressure in a liquid, when these depend upon the height of a supported column of the liquid. Thus with a piezometer, in which pressure is measured by means of a water column, the artificial elevation of the pressure column by capillary action at about 68° F. is given by

$$h = \frac{4 \times \cdot005548 \cos 25°\ 32'}{62 \cdot 4\, d}\ \text{feet.}$$

---

[1] More simply, it may be considered that the whole weight of the supported column is carried by the surface films, and that this weight is equal to the vertical component of the surface tension. This leads, as before, to the equation

$$\pi\, d\ .\ T \cos a = w\, \frac{\pi\, d^2}{4}\, h,$$

$$\therefore h = \frac{4\, T \cos a}{w\, d}$$

With liquid in its spherical state we have $2\, \pi\, r\, T = \pi\, r^2\, p$, or $p = \dfrac{2\, T}{r}$, giving p, the excess of internal over external pressure. Thus with small values of r a comparatively small value of T may be accompanied by a large value of p.

If d be measured in inches, this artificial elevation in inches is given by

$$h = \frac{\cdot 04624}{d} \text{ inches.}$$

In the case of a mercury column, taking the specific gravity of mercury to be 13·596, we have $\cos a = - \cdot 6276$

$$\therefore h = - \frac{4 \times \cdot 03698 \times \cdot 6276 \times 144}{62 \cdot 4 \times 13 \cdot 596 \, d} \text{ inches}$$

$$= - \frac{\cdot 01576}{d} \text{ inches}$$

where d is measured in inches.

The negative sign here indicates that the surface of the mercury column is depressed below the level corresponding to the statical pressure alone. The following table gives values of h at 68° F. corresponding to various tube diameters.

DIAMETER OF TUBE IN INCHES.

		·02	·04	·06	·08	·10	·125	·15	·20	·25	·30	·50
h in inches	Water in glass tube . .	2·312	1·156	·771	·578	·462	·370	·308	·231	·185	·154	·092
	Mercury in glass tube .	·788	·394	·263	·197	·158	·126	·105	·079	·063	·053	·032

Evidently then, tubes of small bore—below about ·3 in. internal diameter—are not advisable for use in such pressure-measuring apparatus, especially where small pressures are to be measured, except where the difference of height in two similar tubes is used to indicate the pressure. Here the effects of capillarity, being the same for each tube, neutralise each other. Again, since the specific gravity of mercury is 13·596, the proportional error introduced by neglecting capillarity in the case of a mercury column will be $\frac{13 \cdot 596 \times \cdot 01576}{\cdot 04624} = 4 \cdot 63$ times that introduced with a water column, and will be in the opposite direction.[1]

The effect of surface tension in liquid in motion may be strikingly shown by allowing two jets of water, moving steadily in the same straight

[1] Lack of space prevents any further investigation into the properties of surface films. These are, however, except in so far as they affect the stability of jets, only of slight importance in hydraulics. For further information the reader is referred to any textbook of physics or hydrostatics, or to the article on Capillary Action in the " Encyclopædia Britannica."

ine and in opposite directions, to meet. No splash occurs, but a perfectly clear and steady circular film of water is produced in a plane
perpendicular to that of the jets, while under favourable circumstances
the diameter of this may be extended to some feet before it breaks up
into a series of detached drops.

Art. 4.—Viscosity.

Every known fluid offers a resistance, analogous to friction, to the
relative sliding motion of any two adjacent layers, and the physical
property of the fluid to which this is due is termed **Viscosity.** This
property—only noticeable when the
fluid is in motion—is the cause of
all so-called fluid friction and gives
the fluid the appearance of being able
to withstand a shear stress between
adjacent layers.

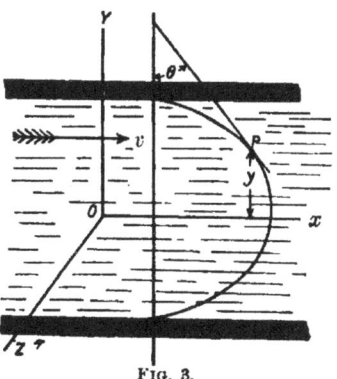

FIG. 3.

The magnitude of this shear or
distortive stress over any plane is proportional to the rate of distortion,
and hence to the rate of change of
velocity with space perpendicular to
the plane. Thus if co-ordinate axes
OX, OY, OZ (Fig. 3) be taken at
some point O of a stream, and if f_s be
the distortive stress accompanying
relative motion of adjacent layers in a direction parallel to the axis of
x, the velocity in this direction at any point P, distant y from that axis,
being denoted by v, and if the velocity in the direction of OZ is zero, we
have, at the point P

$$f_s \propto \frac{dv}{dy} \tag{1}$$

If a curve, having ordinates representing values of v, be plotted on a
base parallel to OY, and if θ be the angle which the tangent to the
curve at P makes with this base line, the values which f_s adopts as y
varies will be represented to scale by the corresponding values of
tan θ.

Putting $f_s = \mu \dfrac{dv}{dy}$, the coefficient μ is termed the **Coefficient of Viscosity**

The value of this coefficient varies with different fluids, and varies with temperature for any particular fluid.

For water, experiments by Poiseuille indicate that it follows the law

$$\mu = \frac{\cdot 00003716}{\cdot 4712 + \cdot 01435\ T + \cdot 0000682\ T^2}$$

where T is in degrees F., and the corresponding value of the distortive stress f_s is given in pounds per square foot. Using the Fahrenheit scale and taking the poundal and the foot as units of force and space, the formula becomes

$$\mu = \frac{\cdot 001197}{\cdot 4712 + \cdot 01435\ T + \cdot 0000682\ T^2}$$

With the pound, foot, and degree Centigrade as units we get

$$\mu = \frac{\cdot 00003716}{1 + \cdot 03368\ T + \cdot 000221\ T^2}$$

while using the poundal, foot, and degree Centigrade this becomes

$$\mu = \frac{\cdot 001197}{1 + \cdot 03368\ T + \cdot 000221\ T^2}$$

In C. G. S. units, the unit of force being taken as the weight of 1 gramme, and the temperature in degrees Centigrade, we have

$$\mu = \frac{\cdot 0000181}{+ 1\ \cdot 03368\ T + \cdot 000221\ T^2}.$$

The following table indicates the values of μ for water corresponding to different temperatures, f_s being expressed in pounds per square foot.

Temperature.		μ.
Fahrenheit.	Centigrade.	
$32°$	$0°$	$\cdot 00003716$
$50°$	$10°$	$\cdot 00002735$
$68°$	$20°$	$\cdot 00002109$
$86°$	$30°$	$\cdot 00001685$
$104°$	$40°$	$\cdot 00001376$
$122°$	$50°$	$\cdot 00001150$
$140°$	$60°$	$\cdot 00000971$

[1] Expressed dimensionally we have $\mu = f_s \div \dfrac{a\,v}{dy} = \text{stress} \div \dfrac{\text{vel.}}{\text{space}} = \text{stress} \times \text{time}$

But $\text{stress} = \dfrac{\text{force}}{\text{area}} = \dfrac{\text{mass} \times \text{acceleration}}{\text{area}} = \dfrac{M \times V}{L^2 \times T} = \dfrac{M}{LT^2}$.

$\therefore \mu$ is of dimension $\dfrac{M}{LT^2} \div \dfrac{1}{T} = \dfrac{M}{LT}$.

Experiments by Hauser indicate that above 32° F. the viscosity of ater, in addition to varying with temperature, also increases very ightly with an increase in pressure, and this would appear to be borne ut by the critical velocity experiments of Messrs. Barnes & Coker at ie McGill University. It may be noted that whereas with liquids the iscosity decreases with an increase in temperature, with gases the reverse . the case. Researches by Dr. Grindley and the author show that in the ise of air the viscosity is independent of the pressure, and, if temperatures re measured in degrees Centigrade, increases with the temperature according to the law

$$= \{355\cdot3 + 1\cdot168\ T - \cdot00248\ T^2\} \times 10^{-9} \text{ ft. lb. sec. units, or}$$

pproximately

$$\mu = \{358 + \cdot932\ T\} \times 10^{-9} \text{ ft. lb. sec. units}$$

etween the limits of temperature 0° C. and 100° C.[1]

This is as might be inferred from the kinetic theory of fluids, for layers ! fluid moving with different velocities are continually interchanging iolecules by diffusion. Thus the more rapidly moving layers are connually losing momentum by interchange with the slower layers, and a intinually applied force is necessary to maintain this state of motion. ince the diffusivity increases with an increase of temperature both in quids and gases, it would be expected that in both cases the viscosity ould increase with temperature.

It is, however, extremely probable that cohesion plays a great part in roducing viscosity in liquids, and while in gases the molecules exert rces on each other by collision only, so that here diffusivity is the aportant factor in producing viscosity, in liquids the greater cohesion lower temperatures more than counterbalances the diminished diffusivity id hence increases the viscosity.

Since the interchange of molecules will be proportional to the area er which such interchange takes place, the resistance to distortion will proportional to this area. Evidently then if eddies are formed in the urse of a stream of fluid, since the area over which interchange of omentum may take place is greatly increased, the viscous resistance to otion will also be increased.

Viscosity, being a physical property of a fluid, is independent of the locity of translation of its particles, and where motion takes place in irallel straight lines, the resistance to motion can be directly inferred om a knowledge of the viscosity. If eddies are formed, however, the

[1] " Proc. Roy. Soc.," vol. 80 A., 1908, p. 114.

motions and forces involved are of such complexity as to prevent an attempt at a solution from *à priori* reasoning based solely on a knowledge of the physical properties of the fluid.

Although from the definition of viscosity, the stresses in different fluids under similar circumstances of motion will be proportional to their values of μ, yet in comparing the effects of viscosity in modifying such motion, it is the ratio of these stresses to the inertia of the fluid which must be taken into account. Thus the determining factor is $\mu \div \rho$. (Cf. p. 71.) From this point of view air is a much more viscous fluid than water, as will be seen from the following figures.

		32° F.	60° F.	100° F.
μ ft. lb. sec. units	air	35.5×10^{-8}	37.2×10^{-8}	39.6×10^{-8}
	water	37.2×10^{-6}	23.0×10^{-6}	14.0×10^{-6}
ρ i.e., weight per cub. ft. $\div g$	air	25.1×10^{-4}	23.8×10^{-4}	22.1×10^{-4}
	water	1.938	1.936	1.925
$\dfrac{\mu}{\rho}$	air	14.15×10^{-5}	15.61×10^{-5}	17.91×10^{-5}
	water	1.92×10^{-5}	1.19×10^{-5}	$.727 \times 10^{-5}$
Ratio of values of $\dfrac{\mu}{\rho}$	$\left\{\dfrac{\text{air}}{\text{water}}\right\}$	7.37	13.1	24.6

From these it appears that at 60° F. the relative effect of viscosity in modifying the motion is practically thirteen times as great in the case of air as in the case of water.

The energy absorbed in overcoming viscous resistance in any fluid motion finally appears in the form of heat which is dissipated by conduction and radiation.

CHAPTER II.

Hydrostatics—Principles—Pressure Intensity—Transmissibility of Pressure—Atmospheric Pressure—Pressure Gauges—Resultant Pressure—Centre of Pressure—Equilibrium of Floating Bodies—Metacentric Height—Oscillations of Ships—Strength of Pipes and Cylinders.

ART. 5.—HYDROSTATICS.

COMMONLY, any substance which, at ordinary temperatures, possesses in a marked degree the property of accommodating itself to the shape of any vessel into which it may be placed, is termed a *fluid*.

Fluids may be divided into two classes; gases and liquids; according as they are easily, or with difficulty, compressible.

Definition of a Perfect Fluid.—By a perfect fluid we mean a substance such that the pressure exerted by it on any surface with which it may be in contact is everywhere normal to that surface.

The laws governing the action and reaction, and generally the statical equilibrium, of such a fluid may be easily deduced from theoretical considerations. Before, however, extending these laws to the case of such a fluid as water, it becomes necessary to determine to what extent this differs, in its essentials, from our conceptions of a perfect fluid.

From the above definition it follows that with a perfect fluid any action of the nature of friction between solid and fluid is impossible, since this would necessitate the action of some force tangential to the surface. It follows that there can be no frictional resistance to the motion of a solid body through the fluid, or to the steady motion of the fluid through any pipe or channel having solid boundaries, and that in consequence any portion of the fluid may be separated from any other portion by a force however small, if applied for a sufficient length of time. Further, the perfect fluid is incapable of existing in a state of tension.

Such a conception is useful, although no such substance as a perfect fluid is known in Nature. All known fluids, in virtue of their properties of cohesion and viscosity, offer some resistance of the nature of friction to the motion of any solid surface with which they may be in contact.

Evidently then the laws governing the behaviour of a perfect fluid when in motion, are not applicable, without some modification, to water; nor are the laws governing its statical equilibrium applicable to that of water in cases where, as when under the influence of capillary action, the effect of cohesion is great. When dealing, however, with water in bulk, impregnated as it usually is with air in solution, the effect of cohesion may be neglected, and when at rest water may be considered as satisfying the essential condition of a perfect fluid, viz., that it exerts a normal pressure on all surfaces with which it may be in contact. All the laws governing the statical equilibrium of a perfect fluid, depending as they do solely on this property, can then be applied to that of water, and are included among the principles of Hydrostatics.

Art. 6.—Pressure at a Point.

The average pressure intensity over any area A equals the total pressure P on the area divided by the area, or equals $\frac{P}{A}$. If the pressure varies from point to point of the area, and if this be divided into a large

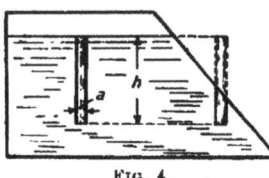

number n of small areas δA, the pressure on any one of these containing a given point being δP, then the limiting value to which the ratio $\frac{\delta P}{\delta A}$ tends, as n is made infinitely large, is taken as the pressure intensity—or more shortly the pressure— at the point under consideration.

Fig. 4.

The units in which pressure intensity is measured depend on those of force and space.

In English practice the unit is usually the pound per square inch, or per square foot. In the metric system of units the usual unit is the kilogramme per square centimetre.

These units are connected by the relationship that 1 kilogramme per square cmm. = 14·223 lbs. per square inch.

Art. 7.—In a Liquid at Rest, the Pressure Intensity is everywhere the same at the same Depth, and is the same in all Directions.

The truth of the first of these propositions may be seen by considering the equilibrium of a small vertical column of the liquid of cross sectional area a and having its base at the depth h below the surface (Fig. 4) Wherever this column is taken in the liquid its weight will be the same and must be balanced by the vertical upward pressure on the base, which will therefore be the same. Since the sectional area of the column is unaltered, it follows that the pressure intensity on the base must every-where be the same.

If W is the weight of unit volume, or the intrinsic weight of the liquid, the weight of the column $= W\,a\,h$.

If p is the pressure intensity at a depth h, the upward pressure on the base $= p\,a$.

$$\therefore\ p\,a = W\,a\,h.$$
$$\therefore\ p = W\,h.$$

The pressure of still water against the sides or bottom of any vessel is then simply due to the "head," or height of the level of the free surface of the water above the point considered. Each square foot of the surface at a depth h may be considered as supporting a column of water of 1 square foot cross sectional area, and of height h, and therefore of weight $62\cdot4$ h lbs.

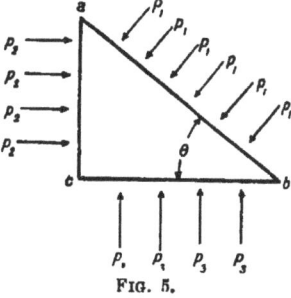

FIG. 5.

∴ Pressure per square
foot, per foot of head $= 62\cdot4$ lbs.
Pressure per square
inch, per foot of head $=\quad\cdot433$ lb.
∴ Head equivalent to a pressure of 1 lb. per square inch $= 2\cdot308$ feet.

The second of the above propositions may be deduced by considering the equilibrium of a triangular prism of the liquid of unit length having its edges horizontal, and its ends perpen-dicular to the sides. If $a\ b\ c$ (Fig. 5) be a cross section of the prism, $a\ c\ b$ being a right angle and $b\ c$ being horizontal, and p_1, p_2, p_3 be the mean intensities of pressure on the sides $a\ b$, $a\ c$, $c\ b$, we have for equilibrium, resolving parallel to the sides $b\ c$ and $c\ a$,

$$p_2\,ac = p_1\,ab\,\sin\theta$$
$$p_3\,cb = p_1\,ab\,\cos\theta + W\,\frac{ac\ cb}{2}.$$

Putting $ac = ab\,\sin\theta$; $bc = ab\,\cos\theta$, we get

$$p_2 = p_1$$
$$p_3 = p_1 + \frac{W}{2}\,ab^2\,\sin\theta\,\cos\theta.$$

If now the sides of the prism be indefinitely diminished $p_1, p_2,$ and p_3 become, in the limit, the pressure intensities at the same point, but in different directions. Also ab^2, being of the second order of small quantities, will vanish, so that in the limit

$$p_1 = p_2 = p_3.$$

_H.A.

C

It follows from these theorems that the free surface of still water is a surface of equal pressure, and that all equipotential surfaces in the fluid are parallel to this. This surface is not plane, but is everywhere normal to the direction of the force of gravitation, and therefore to the direction of a plumb line.

ART. 8.—TRANSMISSIBILITY OF PRESSURE IN A FLUID.

If a pressure be applied to the surface of a fluid, this pressure is transmitted equally to all parts of the fluid. This may be seen by considering a closed vessel filled with water, and fitted with a piston of area A, to which a force P is applied, producing a pressure intensity at this point of $P \div A$. Considering any other area A of the surface, the two may be supposed connected by a cylinder of the fluid, having imaginary boundaries (Fig. 6).

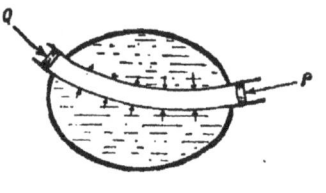

FIG. 6.

Suppose piston P to be displaced through a small distance x. Then in virtue of the incompressibility of the fluid, Q will be displaced through the same distance. Also, since the reaction of the cylinder walls is everywhere perpendicular to the direction of motion of the contained fluid, no work is done against this reaction, and in consequence the work done by $P =$ work done on Q. Since the areas and displacements of P and Q are the same, the pressure intensities over their surfaces, introduced by the action of the external forces, must also be equal. The total pressure intensity at either P or Q will then be obtained by adding to the pressure produced by the force P, that due to the weight of the liquid. Altering the plane of the pistons at P and Q will evidently not affect the pressure intensity on either surface.

This property is taken advantage of in many hydraulic machines, notably in Bramah's Hydraulic Press, and in machines of a like type.

In the Hydraulic Press, illustrated diagrammatically in Fig. 7, water is forced by means of a small pump F, whose plunger has an area a, into the cylinder C of the press whose area is A. Neglecting friction, a force P, applied to the plunger of the force pump, will then produce a pressure intensity of $\dfrac{P}{a}$ in the pump and press cylinder, and hence a force of $Q = P\dfrac{A}{a}$ on the press plunger. A particular case of the transmissibility of pressure is found in the transmission of the pressure of the atmosphere on the surface of water to every part of its depth. Thus the pressure intensity at any depth h is strictly that due to the weight of the superposed water, together with the atmospheric pressure.

Atmospheric Pressure.—The pressure of the atmosphere varies from day to day at the same place, and from place to place at the same time. Its mean value at sea level is about equivalent to that at the base of a mercury column 30 inches in height, or 14·7 lbs. per square inch. This is equivalent to the pressure at the base of a water column of approximately 34 feet in height, and this is usually taken as the height of the water barometer. Thus the true pressure intensity at a depth h below the free surface of water is given by 62·4 $(h + 34)$ lbs. per square foot.

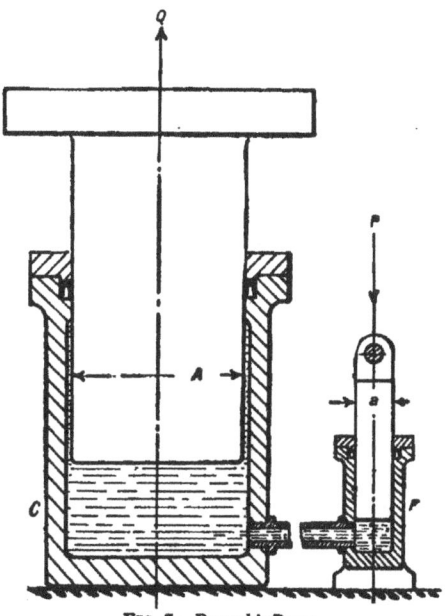

FIG. 7.—Bramah's Press.

In most hydrostatic problems, however, it is the pressure in excess of that due to the atmosphere which is required, so that the pressure at a submerged point is commonly taken as being that due to the head of water alone.

ART. 9.—PRESSURE GAUGES.

The most accurate method of measuring the difference between the pressure at any point in the length of a pipe and that of the atmosphere, is by means of a piezometer or manometer in which the difference is measured by the height of a column of liquid supported by the excess pressure. Where the difference of pressure is not more than one or two pounds per square inch, this liquid may conveniently be water, when the pressure difference is given by $h \div 2·31$ or ·433 h lbs. per square inch,

h being measured in feet.   Fig. 8 A and **B**, shows such a gauge fitted to a
pipe conveying respectively air—in A—and water—in B.   O in each
case marks the zero of the scale, and, in B, *h* measures the pressure at

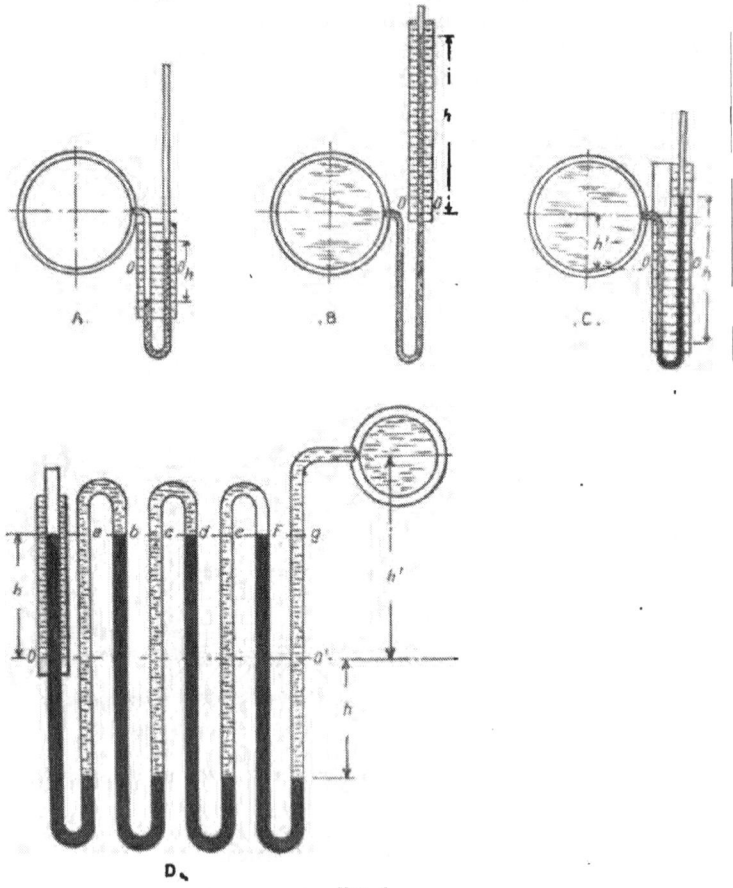

FIG. 8.

the centre of the pipe, from which the pressure at any other point may
be calculated from purely statical considerations.   If the pressure is so
great as to give an inconveniently long column of water, mercury (specific
gravity 13·596) may be used as shown in Fig. 8 C.   If $O O$ is the common

level of the mercury columns with no water in the pipe, the pressure at the centre of the pipe under the conditions shown is that due to a column of mercury h feet high, minus that due to a column of water of height $h' + \frac{1}{2} h$ feet, and is therefore equal to $13{\cdot}596\, h - {\cdot}5h - h' = 13{\cdot}096\, h - h'$ feet of water. Where the pressure is in excess of 100 feet of water, such a gauge gives an inconveniently long mercury column and a type of gauge in which a large range of pressures may be recorded on a comparatively short scale is shown in Fig. 8 D. This consists of a series of n U tubes connected as shown, the lower half of each being filled with mercury and the upper half with water. If this gauge be coupled up to a pipe, and if $O\,O'$ be the common level of the surfaces of separation of mercury and water when the connecting tube is full of water, but with atmospheric pressure in the main, and if O be taken as the zero of the scale, the pressure in the main corresponding to a recorded height of h feet is $2\,n \times 12{\cdot}6\, h + h - h' = (25{\cdot}2\,n + 1)\, h - h'$ feet of water. This follows since the pressure at b = pressure at a = atmospheric pressure + pressure due to a column of mercury $2\,h$ feet high − pressure due to a column of water $2\,h$ feet high, so that the pressure at $b = 2 \times 12{\cdot}6\, h$ feet of water above the atmosphere. Again, pressure at d = pressure at c = pressure at $b + 2 \times 12{\cdot}6\, h$ feet of water = $4 \times 12{\cdot}6\, h$ feet of water above the atmosphere. Similarly pressure at $f = 6 \times 12{\cdot}6\, h$, and at $g = 8 \times 12{\cdot}6\, h = 2\,n \times 12{\cdot}6\, h$ feet of water.

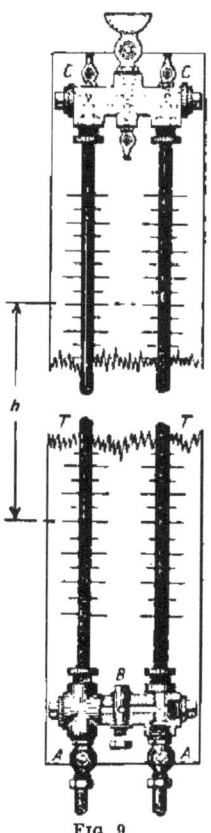

FIG. 9.

Differential Gauges.—Where it is required to determine the difference of pressure at two points in the length of a pipe conveying water, some form of differential gauge is commonly used. Such a gauge is shown in Fig. 9. Here the tubes $A\,A$ are coupled up to the required points in the pipe, the water from which partially fills the branches TT of the inverted U tube. If the difference of pressure is moderately large, the upper portion of this tube contains air, and the difference of level of the free surfaces then gives the difference in pressure in feet of water.[1] An air cock is provided at C, by which air may be pumped into or withdrawn from the tubes; so that whatever the mean pressure in the pipe, the free surfaces of the columns may be brought to a convenient height on the gauge scales. For very small pressure differences the upper part of the U is filled with some liquid whose specific gravity is slightly less than that of water. Gasoline (specific gravity approx. ·71); kerosene (specific gravity approx. ·8); toluene (methyl-

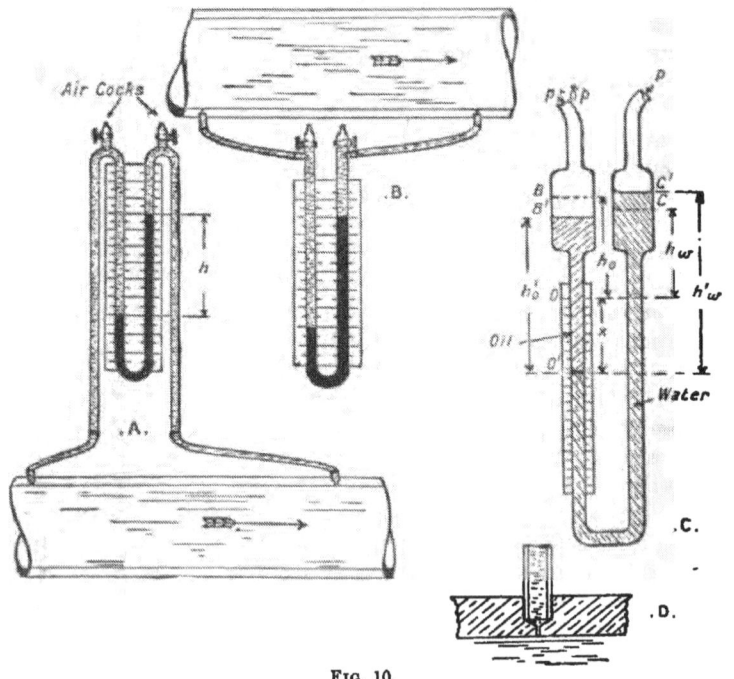

Fig. 10.

benzene, specific gravity approx. ·87); or sperm oil, are suitable liquids for this purpose. If S is the specific gravity of this liquid, and h is the difference of level of the surfaces of separation in the two tubes, the difference of pressure is that due to the difference in the weights of two columns, one of water and the other of this secondary liquid, and is

[1] Actually, the difference between the pressures produced by a column of water and one of air, each of the same height h. Owing to the small specific gravity of air the weight of the latter may, however, be safely neglected, except where the pressure in the pipe is very great.

therefore such as would be produced at the base of a column of liquid of specific gravity $1 - S$. This gives a difference of pressure of $(1 - S) h$ feet of water, and the gauge reading is thus multiplied in the ratio $1 \div 1 - S$, as compared with that of a simple water gauge recording the same difference of pressures. This multiplying factor will be termed the "gauge coefficient" in future, and will be denoted by C. The three-way cock at B allows of any air in the connecting pipes being readily expelled, and allows the quantity of air or of oil in the upper part of the tubes to be regulated as required.

A second type of gauge, in which the gauge fluid is heavier than water, is shown in Fig. 10 A or B. If the pressure difference is large, mercury may be used in the gauge, in which case if h is the difference of level, the difference of pressure equals $(13 \cdot 596 - 1) h = 12 \cdot 596 h$ feet of water, and the gauge coefficient $= \cdot 0794$. If the pressure difference is small, a mixture of carbon tetrachloride and of gasoline with a specific gravity of $1 \cdot 25$ gives a gauge whose coefficient is $1 \div (1 \cdot 25 - 1) = 4$.

A type of differential gauge which is useful for measurements of air flow is shown in Fig. 10 C, and consists of a U-tube whose branches are enlarged at their upper ends. Water is poured into one and some lighter fluid (specific gravity S) into the other leg of the tube. Let a and A be the sectional area of the small and large portions of the tubes. If 0 is the zero of the scale reading, let O, B and C be the levels of the surface of separation of oil and water and of the free surfaces when the latter are exposed to atmospheric pressure, and let O', B', C' be these levels when the pressure difference at the free surfaces is δp, these pressures being respectively p and $p + \delta p$.

Then
$$p + h'_w = p + \delta p + Sh'_o$$
$$\therefore \delta p = h'_w - Sh'_o$$

But $h'_o = h_o + x - x \dfrac{a}{A} = h_o + x \left(1 - \dfrac{a}{A} \right)$.

And $h'_w = h_w + x + x \dfrac{a}{A} = h_w + x \left(1 + \dfrac{a}{A} \right)$.

$$\therefore \delta p = h_w + x \left(1 + \dfrac{a}{A} \right) - S \left\{ h_o + x \left(1 - \dfrac{a}{A} \right) \right\}$$
$$= x \left\{ \dfrac{a}{A} (1 + S) + 1 - S \right\}.$$

As compared with a simple water gauge, the coefficient in such a gauge is $1 \div \left\{ \dfrac{a}{A} (1 + S) + 1 - S \right\}$.

By using two fluids of specific gravity S' and S, such as a mixture of alcohol and water of specific gravity, say ·85, and kerosene of specific gravity, say ·82, the coefficient becomes $1 \div \left\{\dfrac{a}{A}(S' + S) + (S' - S)\right\}$.

Thus in the latter case taking $\dfrac{a}{A} = \tfrac{1}{16}$, the coefficient becomes 7·43, while with water and kerosene in the same tube the coefficient is 6·1.

Errors of Fluid Differential Gauges.—Any error made in estimating the specific gravity of one of the fluids in a differential gauge will lead to an error in the gauge coefficient, and this error will be proportionately greater the larger the coefficient. Where the heavier fluid is water, an error of one-tenth of 1 per cent. in the estimation of S will lead to the following percentage errors in the value of C.

Assumed value of C.	2	5	10	20
Per cent. error in the estimation of C . .	·10	·40	·90	1·9

In a gauge which may be required to record under widely differing pressures, an appreciable error may be introduced, unless allowance is made for the different compressibilities of the two fluids. In such a gauge as is shown in Fig. 9, where air and water are the fluids, the gauge reading is usually taken as giving the true pressure difference in feet of water, although, strictly speaking, this is the difference between the pressures due to this same height of columns of air and of water. At atmospheric pressure the error thus introduced is negligible, but at higher pressures it may become important, as indicated in the following table.

Mean pressure in pipe.		Specific gravity at 50° F.		C.	Per cent. error.
Lbs. per square inch above atmosphere.	Feet of water.	Water.	Air.		
0	0	·99969	·00125	1·00125	·125
14·7	34	·99974	·00250	1·0025	·25
44·1	68	·99983	·00375	1·00375	·375
88·2	136	·99998	·00750	1·0075	·75
176·4	272	1·00027	·01500	1·0150	1·5
352·8	544	1·00085	·03000	1·030	3·0

The percentage error is smaller where two liquids are used, owing to the smaller difference in their compressibilities, although with toluene and water (specific gravity of toluene ·866 at 50° F.—compressibility ·000079 per unit volume per atmosphere) the error amounts to 1·02 per cent. at 20 atmospheres pressure and to 0·5 per cent. at 10 atmospheres pressure. With kerosene—compressibility ·0000696 at 60° F.—as the gauge fluid, this error would be correspondingly less. A variation of temperature, by altering the relative specific gravities of the two fluids, may alter the gauge coefficient appreciably, as indicated below. The values of C are the gauge coefficients for a gauge using water in connection with the particular fluid.

Temp. °F.	Specific gravity (mean).				C.		
	Water.	Sperm oil.	Toluene.	Kerosene.	Sperm oil.	Toluene.	Kerosene.
40°	1·000	·8872	·8709	·8115	8·85	7·73	5·30
50°	·9997	·8836	·8660	·8079	8·58	7·45	5·20
60°	·9990	·8800	·8611	·8026	8·32	7·19	5·06
70°	·9980	·8764	·8562	·7940	8·08	6·95	4·84

Over such a range of temperatures, the percentage error, corresponding to a temperature range of 10° F., has a mean value of 2·4 per cent. with sperm oil, 2·8 per cent. with toluene, and 2·4 per cent. with kerosene, its magnitude increasing with the temperature. With water and mercury, the coefficients of expansion are so nearly identical that the error caused by this effect is practically negligible.

Slight differences in the bores of the tubes and in their degree of cleanliness also affect the readings by altering the form of the meniscus, while where oil and water are used, the attraction between oil and glass causes it to act in the gauge as though its specific gravity were higher than is actually the case. In view of these facts, it is not sufficient to calculate the gauge coefficient from a knowledge of the specific gravities alone if the gauge is required for accurate work, and the only satisfactory way is to calibrate it against a head of water under the same conditions as to pressure and temperature as are likely to be experienced in use.

In order that a piezometer may give an accurate record of the pressure in a pipe containing water in motion, it is important that the surface of the latter should be smooth in the neighbourhood of the piezometer opening, and especially important that any burr or roughness produced on the pipe wall by the drilling of the latter should be removed. Where a pipe is of small bore, and where the pressure is to be measured at a point at some distance from one end, this is a matter of some difficulty, and in such a case a hole should be drilled at one operation through both walls of the pipe. The entering hole may then be plugged up and the second hole which, with care, will be found to be free from any burr, may be used as the pressure opening. Such an opening should be small—one-thirty-second of an inch will usually be found to be ample, the connection appearing as shown in Fig. 10 D.

The point of attachment of the pressure tubes to the main is immaterial, the free surfaces or surfaces of separation in the gauge rising to the same height whether the point of attachment is at the highest or lowest point of the main.[1]

Where a continuously recording gauge is to be used, the possibilities of a single pressure opening becoming choked render it advisable to adopt the arrangement shown in connection with a Venturi meter in Art. 196.

ART. 10.—RESULTANT PRESSURE AND CENTRE OF PRESSURE OF A SUBMERGED AREA.

If p denote the mean pressure intensity over a small element of area δA, the total pressure on this element will be given by $p \, \delta A$ and the total pressure on the whole submerged area will be the sum of all these small normal pressures, and will be represented by $\Sigma \, p \, \delta A$.

The resultant of all these elementary forces is termed the Resultant Pressure on the area, while the point in which the line of action of this resultant meets the area is termed the Centre of Pressure.

If the Centre of Gravity—or centroid—of an element δA, be at a depth x below the free surface of the liquid, the total pressure on the whole submerged area will thus be given by

$$\Sigma \, W x \, \delta A.$$

If $\bar{x}$ be the depth of the centroid of this area it can be easily shown that $\Sigma \, x \, \delta A = \bar{x} \, \Sigma \, \delta A = \bar{x} \, A$.

$$\therefore \quad \Sigma \, W x \, \delta A = W A \, \bar{x},$$

i.e., the total pressure on a single face of any submerged area is equal to the area multiplied by the depth of its centroid below the free surface and by the intrinsic weight of the fluid.

Example 1.—Calculate the total pressure on the internal curved surface of an hemispherical bowl of radius r, placed with its diametrical plane horizontal, and just filled with water.

Here $\bar{x} = \dfrac{r}{2}$; $A = 2 \pi r^2$.

$$\therefore \quad \text{Total pressure} = 62 \cdot 4 \times 2 \pi r^2 \times \frac{r}{2} = 62 \cdot 4 \pi r^3 \text{ lbs.}$$

[1] Confirmed experimentally by Messrs. Marx, Wing & Hoskins. "Trans. American Soc. Civil Engineers," 1898.

In this case the resultant pressure will, for equilibrium, be vertical and equal to the weight of the water;

$$\therefore \text{ Resultant pressure} = 64\cdot2 \times \frac{2}{3}\pi\, r^3 \text{ lbs.}$$

In the case of a plane surface, such as a dock gate, the total pressure on a face will be the same as the resultant pressure, both being normal to the face.

Example 2.—In the dock gate shown in Fig. 11, the width of gate being 20 feet, the depth of the centroid of the submerged portion on the right-hand side is 5 feet, and on the left-hand side is 2 feet. The areas of these submerged surfaces are 200 feet and 80 feet respectively, so that the total pressures, and also the resultant pressures on the two faces, are $5 \times 200 \times 62\cdot4 =$ 62,400 lbs. and $2 \times 80 \times 62\cdot4 =$ 10,000 lbs. The resultant of the two pressures will then be a single force of $62{,}400 - 10{,}000 = 52{,}400$ lbs. acting from right to left. The magnitude of the resultant pressure intensity, and of its distribution over the gate are indicated in Fig. 11. Here the pressure intensity at any depth is indicated by the horizontal distance between the surface of the gate and the straight lines $A\,C$ and $F\,G$. The resultant pressure at any depth is then to the left, and is represented by the horizontal width of the shaded area. Evidently at all points below the lower surface level, the resultant pressure intensity will be constant, since the pressure intensity increases at equal rates on both sides of the gate. The resultant force to the left per foot run of the gate is represented by the shaded area.

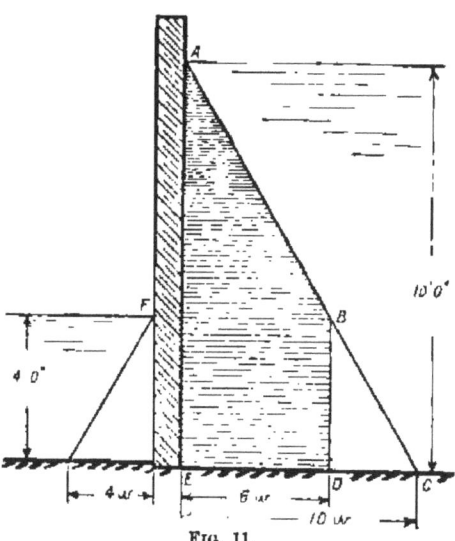

Fig. 11.

The determination of the position of the Centre of Pressure of an area is the same as that of the line of action of the resultant of a series of statical forces each normal to the surface under consideration. Referring this to rectangular co-ordinates $O\,X$ and $O\,Y$ (Fig. 12) of which $O\,X$ is vertical and $O\,Y$ in the surface, we have, taking moments about these axes and representing the co-ordinates of the Centre of Pressure by $X\,Y$,

$$\Sigma\,(p\,\delta\,A\,\cos\theta)\,X = \Sigma\,(p\,\delta\,A\,\cos\theta\,x) \quad (1)$$
$$\Sigma\,(p\,\delta\,A\,\cos\theta)\,Y = \Sigma\,(p\,\delta\,A\,\cos\theta\,y) \quad (2)$$

writing $p = W\,x$ these become

$$\Sigma\,(W\,\delta\,A\,\cos\theta\,x)\,X = \Sigma\,(W\,\delta\,A\,\cos\theta\,x^2) \quad (3)$$
$$\Sigma\,(W\,\delta\,A\,\cos\theta\,x)\,Y = \Sigma\,(W\,\delta\,A\,\cos\theta\,x\,y) \quad (4)$$

Here θ is the angle between the tangent plane to the surface at the point $(x\,y)$ and the plane $X\,O\,Y$. It follows that $\Sigma\,(\delta\,A\cos\theta)$ is the projection of the surface on this plane. Call this A', and let $\bar{x}',\bar{y}'$, be the co-ordinates of the centroid of this projection on the reference plane.

Then (3) becomes

$$W\,A'\,\bar{x}'\,X = W\,\Sigma\,(\delta\,A\cos\theta\,x^2)$$

$$\therefore X = \frac{\Sigma\,(\delta\,A\cos\theta\,x^2)}{A'\,\bar{x}'}\tag{5}$$

Similarly

$$Y = \frac{\Sigma\,(\delta\,A\cos\theta\,xy)}{A'\,\bar{x}'}\tag{6}$$

It follows that the centre of pressure of any curved surface has the same co-ordinates as that of its projection on the plane of reference.

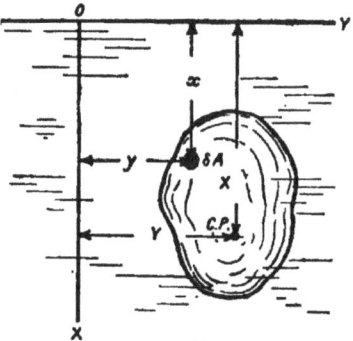

FIG. 12.

Example.—The centre of pressure of the curved surface of a hemisphere having its diametrical plane vertical, and immersed with its upper edge in the surface of the water, is at the same depth as that of the vertical diametrical plane.

Since $\Sigma\,(\delta\,A\cos\theta\,x^2)$ is the moment of inertia of the projection of the surface, about the axis $O\,Y$, expression (5) may be written

$$X = \frac{A'\,k'^{\,2}}{A'\,\bar{x}'} = \frac{k'^{\,2}}{\bar{x}'}$$

where k' is the radius of gyration about the axis $O\,Y$ of the projection of the surface on the plane $X\,O\,Y$.

In the case of the hemispherical surface just considered—radius r—

$$\bar{x}' = r \qquad A' = \pi\,r^2$$

$$A'\,k'^2 = \frac{\pi\,r^4}{4} + \pi\,r^2\cdot r^2 = \pi\,r^2\left\{\frac{5}{4}\,r^2\right\}$$

$$\therefore X = \frac{5}{4}r.$$

Where the surface is plane, the axes $O\,X$, $O\,Y$ may be taken in the plane itself, when $\theta = 0°$, and the above expressions reduce to

$$X = \frac{A\,k^2}{A\,\bar{x}} = \frac{k^2}{\bar{x}}$$

$$Y = \frac{\Sigma\,(x\,y\,\delta\,A)}{A\,\bar{x}},$$

here A is the area and k its radius of gyration about the axis $O\,Y$ in
he surface, x now being the distance of the centroid of the area from the
urface, measured in the plane of the area.[1]

In the case of a rectangle, having its side b in the surface, and its side
inclined at an angle θ to the vertical,

$$A\ k^2 = \frac{1}{12}\,bd^3 + \frac{bd^3}{4} = bd\left(\frac{d^2}{3}\right)$$

$$\bar{x} = \frac{d}{2}$$

$$\therefore\ X = \frac{2}{3}\,d,$$

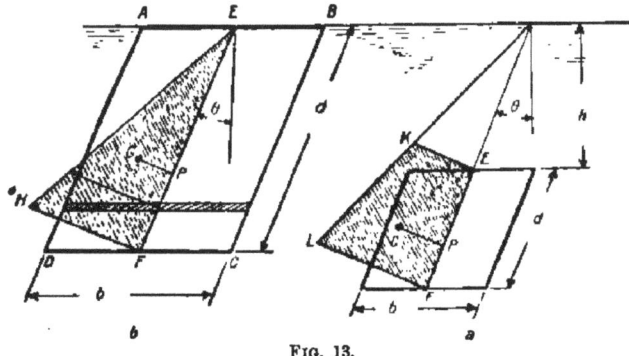

FIG. 13.

$i.e.$, whatever the inclination, the C. P. is on the median line at a point
distant $\frac{2}{3}$ the length of the rectangle from the surface.

Where the upper edge of the rectangle is horizontal and at a depth h
below the surface (Fig. 18 a)

$$k^2 = \frac{d^2}{12} + \left(h\sec\theta + \frac{d}{2}\right)^2$$

$$\bar{x} = h\sec\theta + \frac{d}{2}$$

$$\therefore\ X = \frac{\dfrac{d^2}{12} + \left(h\sec\theta + \dfrac{d}{2}\right)^2}{h\sec\theta + \dfrac{d}{2}}$$

[1] If k_1 is the radius of gyration of the figure about an axis in its plane parallel to the surface
and passing through its C. G. we have $k^2 = k_1^2 + \bar{x}^2$, so that the distance of the C. P. below
the C. G. is $X - \bar{x} = \frac{k^2}{\bar{x}} - \bar{x} = \frac{k_1^2}{\bar{x}}$.

Where the plane of the rectangle is vertical $\theta = 0°$ and the abov:
becomes

$$X = \frac{\dfrac{d^2}{12} + \left(h + \dfrac{d}{2} \right)^2}{h + \dfrac{d}{2}}$$

From the form of this result it is clear that as h increases, X become:
more nearly equal to $\left(h + \dfrac{d}{2} \right)$ i.e., the Centre of Pressure approaches mor:
nearly to the centroid of the area.

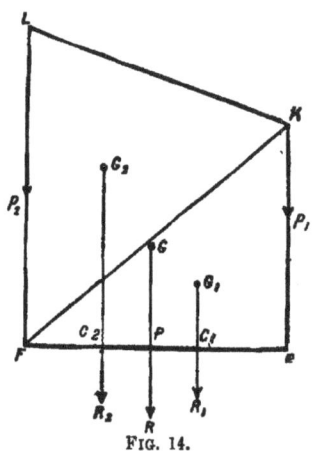

FIG. 14.

The position of the Centre of Pressure
may, in some instances, be deduced by
elementary methods.

E.g., Parallelogram with base in surface (Fig. 13 b). Divide the surface int:
a series of elementary horizontal strip:
of equal width. The pressure on each i:
proportional to its distance from the
surface, and will be represented by the:
ordinate of the triangle $E F H$ erected
on the strip and perpendicular to the
area as shown. This triangle may be
taken to represent the load diagram.
The single resultant of this load wil:
pass through the C. G. of the load area:
will be perpendicular to the surface; and
will therefore cut the median line $E F$ at

a distance from E equal to $\dfrac{2}{3} E F$, i.e., at P.

If the upper edge of the parallelogram be at a depth h below the
surface, the load diagram will now be a quadrilateral $E K L F$, such that
$L K$ when produced meets $F E$ produced in the surface.

If $E K = p_1$ and $F L = p_2$, considering the pressure per unit width, we
may divide the load area into two, $E K F$ and $F K L$ (Fig. 14).

The resultant of first   is $R_1 = \dfrac{p_1}{2} . E F = \dfrac{p_1}{2} b.$

„   „   „ second is $R_2 = \dfrac{p_2}{2} . E F = \dfrac{p_2}{2} b.$

This varying pressure may then be replaced by two single forces R_1
and R_2, acting through the C. G'. G_1 and G_2 of the two load areas, *i.e.*, at
points distance $\frac{1}{3} E F$ from E and F respectively.

The resultant of these will pass through P, where

$$\frac{C_1 P}{C_2 P} = \frac{R_2}{R_1} = \frac{p_2}{p_1},$$

$i.e.$, the Centre of Pressure divides the middle third of the median line in the inverse ratio of the pressures at the two ends.

The magnitude of the resultant $R = \frac{p_1 + p_2}{2} . b.$

Taking moments about F we have

$$\frac{p_1 b^2}{3} + \frac{p_2 b^2}{6} = R . F P. \qquad \therefore 2 p_1 + p_2 = \frac{6 R . F P}{b^2}.$$

$$\therefore \frac{2 R}{b} + p_1 = \frac{6 R . F P}{b^2}. \qquad \therefore p_1 = \frac{2 R}{b^2} \left\{ 3 F P - b \right\}$$

$$\therefore p_2 = \frac{2 R}{b^2} \left\{ 2 b - 3 F P \right\}.$$

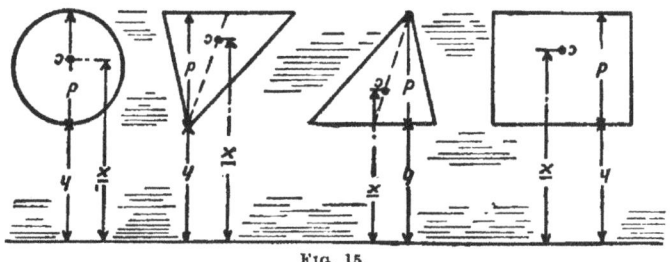

FIG. 15.

If $F P = \frac{E F}{3}$, then $p_1 = 0.$

If $F P = \frac{2 E F}{3}$, then $p_2 = 0.$

$I.e.$, when the resultant acts through either extremity of the middle third of $E F$, the pressure at one end is zero.

For both p_1 and p_2 to be positive, the C. P. must lie within the middle third. Wherever the pressure intensity varies uniformly across a surface as in this case, this deduction holds true. One particular case, of great importance to the hydraulic engineer, occurs in a masonry dam or retaining wall exposed to water pressure on one side. Here the pressure across any horizontal joint varies uniformly, and in order that the jointing material should not be exposed to a tensile stress the C. P. of each joint should lie within its middle third.

The following table gives the position of the centre of pressure in some cases of frequent occurrence in practice (Fig. 15 A, B, C, D). The

distances d, h and $\bar{x}$, are measured in the plane of the figure in eac
case.

Figure.	A	B	C	D
$\bar{x}$	$\frac{2}{3}\left\{\dfrac{3h^2 + 3hd + d^2}{2h + d}\right\}$	$\dfrac{6h^2 + 4hd + d^2}{6h + 2d}$	$\dfrac{6h^2 + 8hd + 3d^2}{6h + 4d}$	$h + \dfrac{d^2}{16h}$

Art. 11.—Equilibrium of Floating Bodies.

When a body is freely floating in a liquid, the conditions of equilibriu.
may be inferred by imagining the body removed and the space occupie.
by it to be filled with the liquid. The reactions of the surroundin.

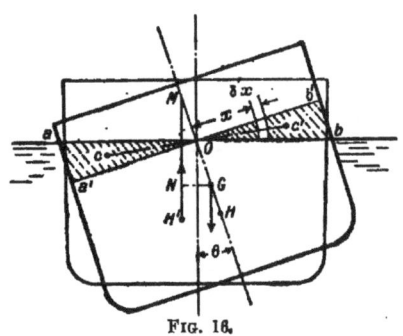

Fig. 16.

liquid will be unaltered by the change, the whole being still in equilibrium, and it is clear that the resultant pressure of the surrounding liquid is vertically upwards, and is equal to the weight of the displaced liquid, and also that the line of action of this resultant pressure passes through the Centre of Gravity of the displaced liquid. It follows that for equilibrium the weight of the floating body is equal to the weight of the liquid which it displaces, and that the Centres of Gravity of the body and of the displaced liquid are in the same vertical line.

The Centre of Gravity of the displaced liquid is called the **Centre of Buoyancy.**

Stability of Equilibrium.—If a floating body be slightly displaced from its equilibrium position so that the line joining the C. G. and the Centre of Buoyancy is no longer vertical, the forces now acting may tend to restore the body to its original position; to move it still further from that position; or to maintain it in equilibrium. In the first case the equilibrium is said to be stable; in the second, unstable; and in the third, neutral.

Let G (Fig. 16) be the C. G. of the floating body; H the Centre of Buoyancy when in the equilibrium position; and H' the C. B. in the displaced position shown. Through H' draw a vertical $H'M$ to meet HG in M.

The weight of the body now acts vertically downwards through G, and the equal force of buoyancy vertically upwards through H', each of these forces being equal to W, the weight of the body, and together forming a couple whose arm is GN, the perpendicular from G on to $H'M$.

Obviously if M is above G this couple tends to restore the body to its equilibrium position, so that the equilibrium is stable, unstable, or neutral, according as M is above, below, or coincides with G.

If the angle of displacement $= \theta$, the magnitude of the righting moment $= W \cdot GN = W \cdot GM \sin \theta$.

As θ is increased the position of the intersection M of the verticals through H and H' will in general move and will approach or recede from G. The point M, for an infinitely small angle of displacement, is called the **Metacentre** of the body, and the distance GM is called the **Metacentric Height**.

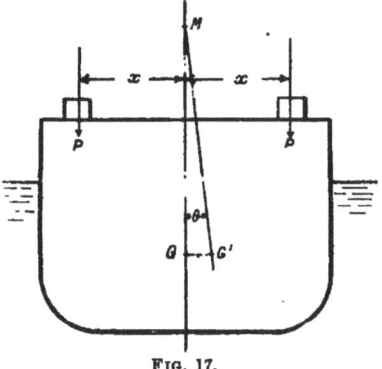

FIG. 17.

Evidently in ship design it is of the highest importance that the metacentre should be above G, under all conditions of loading and under any circumstances of rolling.

The height GM may be determined experimentally by placing two equal weights P at equal distances x from the centre line of the vessel, when floating on an even keel and in its equilibrium position.

Let W be the weight of the vessel, including the weights P.

Then if both weights be moved through a distance δx to the right, the C. G. of the vessel will move through a distance GG' (Fig. 17) where

$$G'G = \frac{2P}{W} \cdot \delta x.$$

Also GG' will be parallel to the direction in which P is moved, i.e., will be perpendicular to GM, since if any portion of a body be moved in a given direction, the C. G. of the whole moves in the same direction.

If θ be the angle of heel produced by this shift of the weights

$$GG' = GM \tan \theta.$$

$$\therefore \ G\,M = G\,G' \cot \theta = \frac{2\,P}{W} \cdot \delta\,x \cot \theta.$$

θ may be measured by noting the change in inclination of a long pend-
lum as the weights are moved. The experiment should be repeated f
different values of $\delta\,x$, measured both to the right and to the left, and
curve may then be drawn on an angle base, showing values of $G\,M$. I
exterpolation the value of $G\,M$ in the limit when $\theta = 0$ can then i
determined.

Since the righting couple $= W \cdot G\,M \sin \theta$, this equals $2\,P\,\delta\,x$ cos
so that the same experiment enables us to draw the Stability Cur-
showing the value of this righting couple for different angles of heel.

If the small masses be moved about, the weight, and therefore t
volume of water displaced r
maining constant, the locus
the Centre of Buoyancy
termed the Surface of Bu
ancy. Since, for equilibriu
the vertical through the C. I
must pass through the C. G
and since for small displac-
ments, the line joining tw
successive positions of th
C. B. is parallel to the surfac-
it follows that the tange:
plane to the surface of buo
ancy at the C. B. is parallel to the water surface, and therefore that th
vertical through the C. G. of the body is normal to the surface of buo
ancy. In other words, any curve of buoyancy $H_1\,H_2\,H_3$ is an involu
of the corresponding curve of metacentres $M_1\,M_2\,M_3$ (Fig. 18).

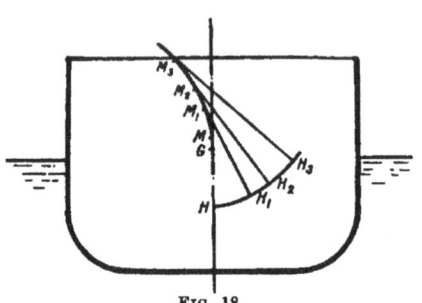

FIG. 18.

In general in the case of a ship, owing to the fact that the under wate
contours are not symmetrical about an amidships section, as they ar
about a longitudinal section, the vertical through the centre of buoyanc
in the displaced position will not intersect the line $H\ G$, since the C. B
is now displaced in a different plane from that of the rotation of the boat
By projecting the verticals through the successive centres of buoyanc
on to two vertical planes, one running fore and aft, and the other perpen
dicular to this, we get one series of intersections on each plane, and thu
get two metacentric heights, the first for pitching displacements (Fig. 19
and the other, previously obtained, for rolling displacements.

The latter is in general, for the ordinary type of ship, by far the mor nportant, although the stability in a longitudinal direction may be seriously affected by the flooding of one or more watertight compartments. n the case of vessels of the submarine type, the longitudinal stability ecomes of the greatest importance, lack of such stability causing tendency to dive suddenly.

The metacentric height for >re and aft displacements nay be experimentally deter- nined just as for rolling lisplacements.

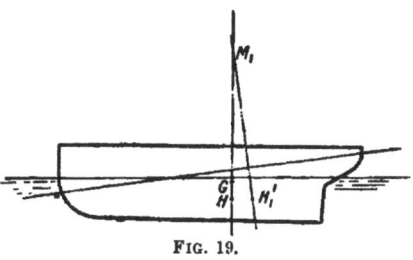

FIG. 19.

The position of the meta- entre may be determined theoretically as follows, if the ositions G and H of the 3. G. of the vessel and of the centre of buoyancy are known.

Let A = area of section of vessel made by the plane of water line, or plane of flotation.

„ K = radius of gyration of this area about a longitudinal axis through its Centroid.

„ V = volume of water displaced by vessel.

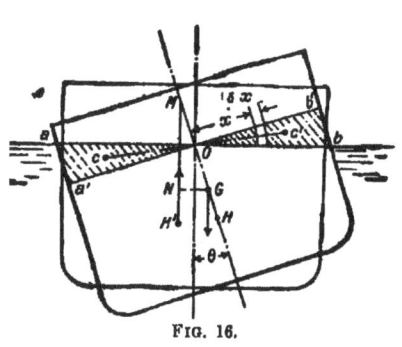

FIG. 16.

Let G, H, H', M, have the meanings previously attached to them.

„ O be the elevation of the line of intersection of the planes of flotation in the equilibrium and displaced positions (Fig. 16).

Then if a small angular displacement θ be given to the vessel, the volume displaced, being proportional to the weight of the vessel, does not change.

∴ Volume of wedge $a\,o\,a'$ = volume of $b\,o\,b'$,

Again if y be the depth, perpendicular to the paper, of any element δx of the wedge at a distance x from o, the volume of this element $= y\,x\,\theta\,\delta x$.

∴ Volume of wedge $a\,o\,a' = \theta \int_0^a x\,y\,d\,x$

∴ Since volume displaced is unaltered we have

$$\theta \int_o^a x\, y\, d\, x = \theta \int_o^b x\, y\, d\, x$$

and for this to be true the axis through O must pass through the centroi of the water line section. Also, due to the immersion of the wedge $a\,o$ and the emersion of $b\,o\,b'$, we get an upward force of buoyancy tran ferred from C. G. of wedge $b\,o\,b'$ to that of $a\,o\,a'$, or since if $w = wt$ of cubic foot of water, the moment of buoyancy due to the immersion of a element of the wedge as shown is $w.\ x^2.\ \theta.\ y\ \delta x$.

∴ Moment of buoyancy of $\left.\begin{matrix} \\ \end{matrix}\right\}$ $= w\ \theta \int_{-b}^a y\ x^2\ d\ x$
wedges $a\,o\,a'$ and $b\,o\,b'$

$$= w\ \theta\ A\ K^2$$

But by the transference of the wedge of water, the centre of buoyance is moved parallel to $c\ c'$; c and c', being the C. G³. of the wedges; throug a distance $H\ H'$, where $H\ H'$. $V\ w = w\ \theta\ A\ K^2$ (as before).

$$\therefore\quad H\ H' = \frac{A\ K^2}{V}\ \theta.$$

Also, if θ is small $\dfrac{H\ H'}{H\ M} = \theta$ very nearly.

$$\therefore\quad H\ M = \frac{A\ K^2}{V}.$$

Knowing $H\ M$, and determining $G\ M$ experimentally, $H\ G$ can $l\epsilon$ determined, from which, if the position of H is known, that of G may then be found. H may in general be determined with comparative ease since the contours of a vessel at various levels, and hence the volume displaced between these levels, are usually accurately known. The problem then simply resolves itself into finding the C. G. of these volume by taking moments about the water line.

Art. 12.—Time of Oscillation of a Rolling Ship in Still Water.

When a floating body is freely oscillating, the resistance of the water being neglected, its motion is similar to that of a pendulum except that the body does not now oscillate about a fixed axis.

Just, however, as in the case of a pendulum, the righting couple is proportional to the sine of the angle of displacement, so that the time of a complete double oscillation is given—as in the case of a pendulum—by

$$T = 2\ \pi \sqrt{\frac{\text{Moment of inertia of body about axis of oscillation}}{g \times \text{righting moment for unit angle of displacement.}}}$$

As the displacement increases, the curve, to which the plane of flotation is everywhere tangent, is known as the Curve of Flotation, and evidently in rolling the motion of the body is exactly the same as if an imaginary curve of flotation fixed in the vessel were to roll on a fixed horizontal surface. The position of the instantaneous axis of oscillation may then be determined by noting that since the weight of the vessel and the buoyancy, both vertical, are the only forces acting on the body, the C. G. of the vessel must move vertically, if at all, so that the instantaneous axis is in the horizontal line through G (Fig. 20). Again since the curve of flotation rolls on a horizontal surface, the instantaneous centre must also be in the vertical through the centre of flotation F, i.e., the axis is at O, the point of intersection of G O and F O. For small oscillations O will sensibly coincide with G.

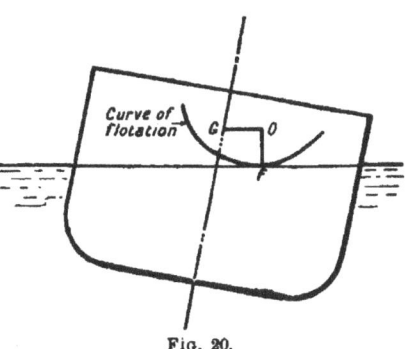

Fig. 20.

If k = radius of gyration of a body of weight W about an axis through its C. G., and if m = metacentric height for rolling displacements, the equation of motion may be written

$$\frac{d^2 \theta}{d t^2} \cdot \frac{W k^2}{g} + W m \sin \theta = 0$$

or for small displacements

$$\frac{d^2 \theta}{d t^2} \cdot \frac{W k^2}{g} + W m \theta = 0$$

from which we get $T = 2 \pi \sqrt{\dfrac{k^2}{g m}}$, the relation given above.

Although a certain unknown mass of water will move along with the vessel, increasing the inertia of the moving mass without increasing the restoring couple and thus tending to increase the time of oscillation, yet in practice very close agreement is found between the calculated and experimental periods.

E.g. In the Devastation, the calculated time was 7 secs.[1]

,, experimental ,, 6·75 secs.

[1] These are the times of a single oscillation.

E.g.　In the Monitor (U.S.N.) calculated time was 2·5 secs.
　　　　　　　　　　　" experimental　　" 2·7 secs.

Froude, experimenting on ships fitted with and without bilge keels, found that the effect of the keel is to extinguish the oscillations more rapidly, but that the effect on the period of rolling is very slight, the average difference produced by the addition of these keels being about 6 per cent. Also the extinctive effect is greater when the ship is moving than when stationary.

The effect of an increase in the metacentric height is to stiffen the vessel and to diminish the period of the oscillation, while any increase in its radius of gyration tends to increase the period. Too great stiffness is inadvisable because of the tendency of the forces brought into play to strain the vessel, and it is often advisable in the case of a cargo vessel to arrange the cargo so that its heavier portions are as near to the skin of the vessel as possible. This increases the radius of gyration, and thus the period of rolling, without seriously affecting the stability.

The metacentric height in the case of merchant ships varies of course with the loading, but when fully loaded is usually between 1½ and 4 feet. For small vessels, such as tugs and torpedo boats, it varies from about 1 to 2 feet.

Art. 13.—Strength of Pipes and Cylinders.

This will be briefly discussed as being of great importance to the hydraulic engineer.

In a thin pipe the stress over the whole thickness of metal may be taken as being sensibly uniform, and by considering a section made by a diametrical plane we see that the force per unit length of pipe tending to rupture it across this plane $= 2\,r\,p$, where

　　　　　$r =$ pipe radius in inches.

　　　　　$p =$ internal pressure in lbs. per square inch.

If　　　$t =$ thickness of pipe in inches and $f =$ stress per square inch in metal, we have the force resisting rupture along this plane $= 2\,f\,t$.

$$\therefore \text{ for equilibrium } f = \frac{p\,r}{t} \text{ or } t = \frac{p\,r}{f}.$$

For steel or wrought-iron pipes this rule is sufficiently accurate, and here the working value of f varies from 7,500 to 8,500 lbs. per square inch for wrought iron, and 10,000 to 12,000 lbs. per square inch for steel,

---

[1] For an investigation into the action of bilge keels see a paper by Dr. G. H. Bryan. "Trans. Inst. Naval Architects," 1900. Also by G. H. Baker, " Trans. Inst. Naval Architects," 1912.

ncreasing with the size of pipe. In a riveted pipe the efficiency of the riveted joint must be taken into account in determining this thickness. This may be taken at about 55 per cent. for single and 70 per cent. for double riveting. A minimum thickness of about $\frac{3}{16}$ inch should be adopted to allow for any reduction by corrosion.

Where the pipes are to be exposed to considerable pressure, and especially when made of cast iron, the distribution of pressure over the

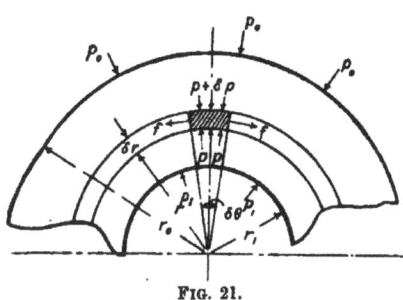

walls is not so simple, those fibres of the metal nearer the centre being more heavily stressed than those further removed. In this case consider the equilibrium of a portion of an elementary ring of metal concentric with the pipe, having inner and outer radii r and $r + \delta r$, and subtending an angle $\delta \theta$ at the centre (Fig. 21). Let the radial pressure on the faces

FIG. 21.

of this element be p and $p + \delta p$, and the circumferential stress in the metal be f.

Then, for equilibrium of this element we have

$$(p + \delta p)(r + \delta r)\,\delta \theta - p\,r\,\delta \theta + f\,\delta r\,\delta \theta = 0 \qquad (1)$$
$$\therefore \ r\,\delta p + p\,\delta r + f\,\delta r = 0$$

or
$$r\,\frac{\delta p}{\delta r} = -f - p. \qquad (2)$$

Again, if we assume that the plane ends of the pipe remain plane during extension, we get the further condition that

$$p - f = \text{constant} = 2\,A. \qquad (3)$$

Combining this with (2) we have, in the limit :—

$$r\,\frac{d p}{d r} + 2\,p = 2\,A$$

or
$$r^2\,\frac{d p}{d r} + 2\,p\,r = 2\,A\,r \qquad (4)$$

$$\therefore \ \frac{d(p\,r^2)}{d r} = 2\,A\,r.$$

Integrating this expression we get

$$p\,r^2 = A\,r^2 + B$$
$$\therefore \ p = A + \frac{B}{r^2} \qquad (5)$$

and, from (3)
$$f = -A + \frac{B}{r^2}. \qquad (6$$

Assuming, as is generally permissible in practice, that when $r = r_0$, i.e., at the outer circumference, $p = o$, and putting $p = p_1$ when $r = r_1$, i.e., at the inner circumference, we get on substituting,

$$\begin{cases} A = p_1 \left\{ \dfrac{r_1^2}{r_1^2 - r_0^2} \right\} \\[2mm] B = p_1 \left\{ \dfrac{r_0^2\, r_1^2}{r_0^2 - r_1^2} \right\} \end{cases}$$

Substituting these values in (6) we have

$$f = p_1 \frac{r_1^2}{r^2} \left\{ \frac{r^2 + r_0^2}{r_0^2 - r_1^2} \right\} \qquad (7$$

Evidently this will have its maximum value when $r = r_1$, i.e., at the inner circumference, and at this point.

$$f_{(max.)} = p_1 \frac{r_1^2 + r_0^2}{r_0^2 - r_1^2} \qquad (8$$

This may be written

$$r_0 = r_1 \sqrt{\frac{f + p_1}{f - p_1}}. \qquad (9$$

The value adopted for the working stress f varies with the pipe diameter, and with cast-iron pipes increases gradually from about 2,000 lbs. per square inch in a 2-inch pipe to 3,000 lbs. per square inch in an 8-inch pipe, and 3,500 lbs. per square inch in a pipe or cylinder of 24 inches diameter.

The following table indicates the thickness of cast-iron pipes and cylinders for heavy pressures, as calculated on the above assumption.

Pipe diameter in inches.	Working pressure, lbs. per square inch.		
	750	1000	1120
2	$\frac{1}{2}$	$\frac{3}{4}$	$\frac{7}{8}$
3	$1\frac{1}{16}$	$1\frac{5}{16}$	$1\frac{1}{8}$
4	$1\frac{13}{16}$	$1\frac{1}{8}$	$1\frac{3}{8}$
5	$\frac{29}{32}$	$1\frac{5}{16}$	$1\frac{9}{16}$
6	$1\frac{3}{32}$	$1\frac{7}{16}$	$1\frac{23}{32}$
8	$1\frac{5}{32}$	$1\frac{11}{16}$	$1\frac{13}{32}$
10	$1\frac{13}{32}$	$2\cdot0$	$2\frac{5}{16}$
12	$1\frac{13}{32}$	$2\frac{5}{16}$	$2\frac{21}{32}$
16	$2\frac{5}{32}$	$2\frac{15}{16}$	$3\frac{13}{32}$
20	$2\frac{5}{8}$	$3\frac{9}{16}$	$4\frac{1}{8}$
24	$3\frac{1}{32}$	$4\frac{1}{8}$	$4\frac{3}{4}$

Collapsing Pressures of Cylindrical Pipes.—The sudden discharge of water from a hydraulic pipe line, such as may follow a burst at its lowest point, may, unless special provision be made, lead to the production of a partial vacuum in the pipe and thus give rise to an effective external collapsing pressure which is increased by the pressure of the earth filling in the case of a buried pipe. Very few reliable experiments are available as to the effect of such pressures on pipes of large diameter. R. T. Stewart[1] as the result of experiments on steel lap-welded tubes of diameters ranging from 3 to 10 inches concluded that if the length of the pipe is greater than 6 diameters the collapsing pressure p_c is given by

$$p_c = 1000 \left(1 - \sqrt{1 - 1600 \frac{t^2}{D_o^2}}\right) \qquad \text{if } p_c \text{ is less than } 580,$$

$$\text{or } \text{,,} \frac{t}{D_o} \text{ ,, } \text{ ,, } \cdot 023,$$

while $p_c = 86670 \frac{t}{D_o} - 1386$, for higher values of p_c or of $\frac{t}{D_o}$.

Here p_c is in pounds per square inch; $t =$ thickness in inches; $D_o =$ outside diameter in inches. If slightly distorted, later experiments[2] on 10-inch pipes with thicknesses of ·15 to ·20 inch indicate that the collapsing pressure p_c' is approximately given by

$$p_c' = \frac{\cdot 098 \ (p_c - 50)}{(x - \cdot 874)^{1\cdot 25}} + 50.$$

Where $p_c =$ collapsing pressure for corresponding circular pipe.
$x =$ ratio of maximum to minimum outside diameter.

Examples.

1. In a hydraulic press the ram is 10 inches and the pump plunger 1 inch diameter, the leverage for working the pump 16 to 1. What is the velocity ratio of the pump handle and ram? Actually a force of 30 lbs. exerts a pressure of 44,000 lbs. on the press table. What is the efficiency?

Ans.: 1,600; 91·7 per cent.

2. A dock gate is 12 feet broad and 14 feet deep, and the water rises 12 feet on one side and 9 feet on the other side above its lower edge. Find the resultant pressure and centre of pressure for each side of the gate and find the magnitude and position of the resultant of these.

[1] "Trans. Am. Soc. Mech. Eng.," 1906, p. 730.
[2] "Trans. Am. Soc. Mech. Eng.," 1907, p. 123.

Ans.: 53,914 lbs.; 3,870 lbs.; centres of pressure 4 feet; 1 foot from lower edge.

Single resultant 50,544 lbs. at 4·20 feet from lower edge.

3. A rectangular sluice gate, 5 feet broad and 6 feet deep, having its upper edge at a depth of 4 feet, is inclined at 45° to the vertical and admits water to an empty penstock. The sluice is lifted by a force applied parallel to its plane. Determine the necessary magnitude of this force if the coefficient of friction between gate and guides is ·12.

Ans.: 1,375 lbs.

4. A circular conduit, 6 feet diameter, which just runs full, is fitted with a sluice, and it is required to balance this about a horizontal axis. Show that this axis should be placed 2 feet 3 inches above the bottom of the conduit.

5. A vertical wall, 10 feet high and 3 feet thick, is exposed to water pressure on one side. What is the maximum depth of water in order that the lowest joint should not be anywhere under tension? Weight of masonry per cubic foot = 170 lbs.

Ans.: 6·26 feet.

6. A battleship weighs 13,000 tons. On filling the ship's boats on one side with water—this weighing 60 tons and its mean distance from the centre of the boat being 30 feet—the angle of displacement of a plumb line is 2° 16′ (tan θ = ·0396). Determine the metacentric height for rolling displacements.

Ans.: 3 feet 6 inches.

7. Show that a solid cylinder of length l, radius r, and specific gravity s, floating with its axis vertical, is in stable equilibrium if

$$r > l \sqrt{2 s (1 - s)}.$$

8. A single-riveted steel pipe, 30 inches internal diameter, is exposed to a head of 450 feet of water. Taking f = 12,000 lbs. per square inch, and the efficiency of the joints = 60 per cent., what should be its thickness?

Ans.: t = ·407 inch = $\frac{13}{32}$ inch.

9. A cast-iron pressure pipe, 4 inches diameter, is exposed to a pressure of 1,100 lbs. per square inch. Taking f = 2,800 lbs. per square inch, what is the requisite thickness?

Ans.: t = 1·032 inch = $1\frac{1}{32}$ inch.

10. The mean pressure over the horizontal section of a dam is 5 tons per square foot. The centre of pressure over this section is at a point

istant $\frac{3}{4}$ of its width from the down-stream edge. Determine the maximum and minimum pressures on the section.

Ans. $\begin{cases} \text{Maximum} = 8\cdot75 \text{ tons per square inch.} \\ \text{Minimum} = 1\cdot25 \quad ,, \quad ,, \quad ,, \end{cases}$

11. It is proposed to subject the lower 9 feet of a wall 17 feet high and 5 feet thick, weighing 150 lbs. per cubic foot, to water pressure. Determine the centre of pressure on the lowest horizontal section.

Ans.: At a distance from the centre of the section = 7·14 inches.

SECTION II

CHAPTER III.

Motion of Viscous Fluids—Stream Line and Eddy Motion—Vortices—Conditions regula▨▨
the two modes of Motion--Reynolds's Researches—Critical Velocity in Parallel Pipes—▨
Converging Pipes—Motion of a Fluid—Equations of Motion—Flow against Visc▨
Resistance — Between Parallel Plates — Through Circular Tube — Genesis of E▨▨
Formation.

ART. 14.—MOTION OF VISCOUS FLUIDS.

WHEN a rigid body moves, the motion at any point in its mass can b▨
accurately determined once the motions of any three points, not in th▨
same straight line, are fixed. In this case, when the boundary condition▨
are known, the determination of the internal motion is simple. But wit▨
a fluid such as water the motion of the mass of fluid as a whole does no▨
necessarily give the internal motion. While giving the mean motion, i▨
does not fix the absolute motion of each particle of the fluid relatively t▨
any fixed point. This is quite apart from intermolecular motion, whic▨
gives rise to diffusion in a mass of water even when apparentl▨
motionless.

By the earlier experimentalists the motion of water in mass was im▨
perfectly understood. On the assumption of a motion simple an▨
analogous to that of a rigid body, it was impossible to reconcile th▨
results experimentally obtained by many observers, while the very trans-
parency, or uniform opacity of most fluids made it impossible to see th▨
internal motion. Probably the first indication of there being more tha▨
one kind of fluid motion was obtained from the appearance of the fre▨
surface of flowing water. Where not otherwise disturbed this may hav▨
two appearances, corresponding to different modes of motion. In the on▨
objects are reflected from the surface without distortion, while in th▨
other an irregular motion of the surface may be noted, and reflection i▨
accompanied by distortion. Where motion occurs in a passage havin▨
solid lateral boundaries, however, even this indication is absent, and the
introduction of floating particles of solid matter does not help to any
extent in showing the nature of the action which is taking place.

Matters remained in this state for many years, and it was left for

Osborne Reynolds, by his method of colour bands,[1] to prove conclusively that the motion in a mass of water may be of two kinds ; to make clear the simplicity of the one, and the complexity of the other ; and to demonstrate the reasons for, and the laws governing each kind of motion.

The conclusions to be drawn from Professor Reynolds's experiments are as follows :—firstly, we may have a continuous **steady** motion of the particles, in which the motion at a fixed point always remains constant ; and secondly, we may have **unsteady** or **eddy** motion, when the motion at any fixed point varies according to no definite law. This is due to the formation of eddies or vortices in the fluid.

Introducing the idea of **stream lines**, *i.e.*, of imaginary lines in the fluid, such that at any point the direction of motion is tangential to the line, it

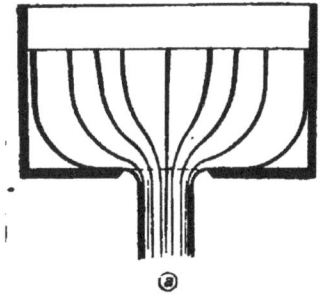 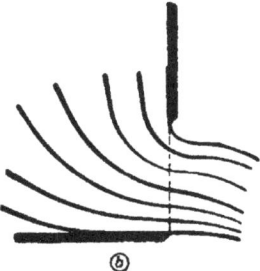

FIG. 22.

follows that in steady motion these stream lines become fixed, and this type of motion is therefore known as **stream line motion**. Certain properties of these stream lines are of interest. They must always have a continuous curvature, except where the motion is zero, since to cause an infinite change of curvature, an infinite force acting perpendicular to the direction of curvature would be necessary. It follows that in steady motion a fluid will always move in a curve round any sharp corner, and that the stream lines will be tangential to any such boundaries, as indicated in Fig. 22 *a* and *b*, in which the general form of the stream lines for steady flow out of two forms of orifice are shown. With a very viscous fluid, an approximation to this infinite force may be introduced by the effect of cohesion, and the radius of curvature may then become very small. This has been clearly

[1] For a full account of this method of investigating the two manners of motion of water see a paper by Osborne Reynolds, " Phil. Trans. Royal Society," 1883.

shown in a series of experiments by Dr. Hele Shaw[1], who, by producing flow between two parallel glass plates at an extremely small distance apart produced a state of affairs in which viscosity was the predominating factor. In ordinary cases, however, this is not so, and the effect of the inertia of the fluid is more marked than that of cohesion. On this account it is always necessary for easy flow to design any pipe or passage for conveying fluids with curves having as gradual a curvature as possible.

If the stream line be imagined to form the axis of a tube of finite sectional area having imaginary boundaries, and such that its area, at different points in its length, is inversely proportional to the velocity at those points, this is known as a stream tube.

If the motion at a fixed point varies, and if it is still possible to find a definite motion for these points such that the motion of the fluid relative to the points may remain constant, the latter may be reduced to steady motion by considering the motion relative to these moving points. The fluid may then be said to have a continuous, steady, but unequal motion.

In almost all the cases of fluid motion which are of practical importance in hydraulics, the motion is found to be unsteady.

ART. 15.—VORTICES.

A mass of fluid, rotating about some axis in the fluid itself and forming a closed circuit, is termed a vortex or eddy. This axis may be straight, curved, or may return on itself, in which latter case we have a vortex ring. Where a vortex of the former type is formed, it may be shown that the motion is unstable unless the ends of the axis are in contact with some solid surface. A stable vortex, whether with a rectilinear or a circular axis, may be projected through the surrounding fluid with surprisingly small loss of energy.

An instance of this may be found in the case of the ordinary smoke ring, or of a similar vortex ring in water. If this vortex ring be coloured by the admission of aniline dye to the generating box, and if the ring be then projected through a tank of clear water, it is seen to travel with a motion of uniform rotation about its circular axis through the surrounding liquid, its outer layers moving, relatively to the axis, in the opposite direction to that of its own motion of translation. Relatively to the surrounding water the motion at the outer layers is very small, so that

---

[1] "Trans. Inst. Naval Architects," 1897—8, 1900.

the vortex moves through the surrounding fluid with a resistance almost akin to rolling friction. This accounts for the small resistance experienced. The surrounding water is displaced in a direction at right angles to that of the ring's translation, and thus, with a ring moving horizontally, waves are produced on the surface of the water.

That the relative motion between the outer layers of the vortex and the surrounding water is very small is shown by the slowness with which the coloured water of the ring diffuses.

An attempt to propel a solid sphere of approximately the same size and mass as the ring through the fluid by means of a sudden blow, shows very forcibly the relative loss of energy as compared with that of vortex motion.

The whole subject of the translatory motion of vortices is fraught with difficulty, and no attempt will be made here to discuss this motion analytically. The following may be taken as a partial explanation of the reason of this translation. Consider a vortex ring at the instant of formation. The velocity at the interior of the aperture is greater than that outside; the pressure inside is therefore less than that outside; and in consequence the ring begins to contract. The effect of this contraction of the aperture is to set up motion in the surrounding fluid, which, combined with the cyclic motion inseparable from vortex production, increases the velocities in front of, and decreases those behind the ring. This sets up a difference of pressure at similar points before and behind the ring, which urges the latter forward with an increasing velocity. A limit to this velocity is reached when the velocity within the aperture approximates to that without.[1]

The mass of fluid forming a vortex has the property that its momentum is unaffected by its angular motion, just as the momentum of a fly-wheel in any direction is unaltered by the fact of the wheel itself rotating about its own axis, the momentum of the mass in any direction being equal to the mass multiplied by the resolved part of the velocity of its mass centre in that direction.

When a stream of fluid flows past an immersed solid, at all but the slowest velocities eddies are formed in the rear of the solid, which, however, are not of the type already described, in that the motion is not now cyclic, the mass comprising an eddy being composed partly of fluid flowing around the edges of the solid and partly of fluid drawn from its rear face. As a consequence of this there is a continual backward

[1] For an extension of this idea and for an investigation into the motion of vortices, consult a paper by Mr. W. M. Hicks, "Phil. Trans. Royal Society," 1881, p. 161.

flow towards the central portion of this face, to make good the loss of
fluid abstracted by the eddies at its sides, the state of affairs being
represented in Fig. 23 A.

Where the body extends from the surface to the bottom of the stream,
so that the motion is sensibly in two dimensions, the eddy formation is a
discontinuous process. In such a case eddies may be formed either

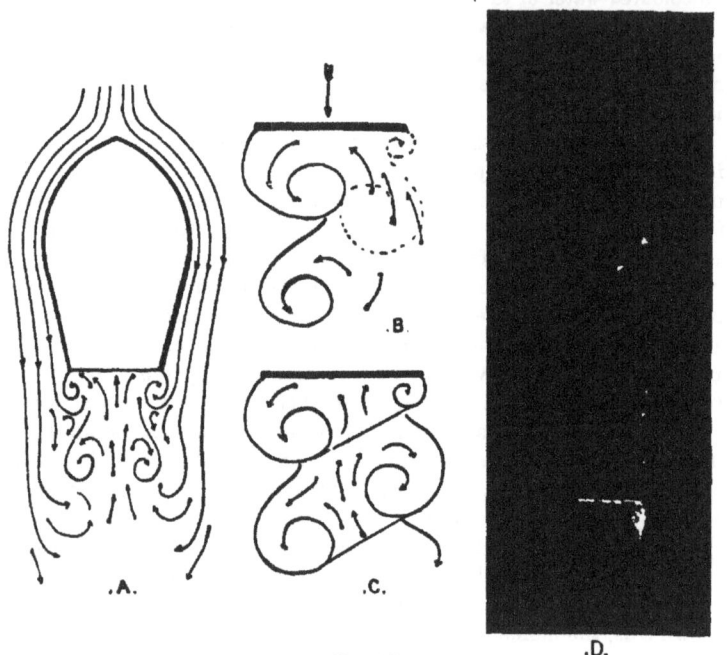

Fig. 23.

simultaneously at each edge, or alternately at the two edges of the body,
as shown in Fig. 23 B.

The eddies as first formed are small, and gradually grow until sufficiently large to impede the rearward flow in the wake which is necessary to
feed them. They then break away and join the procession of eddies
forming the boundary of the wake.

When formed in three dimensions, eddies may be produced either
continuously or discontinuously. In the former case they are at different
stages in their growth at different points of the perimeter of the body, and

ppear in the wake as a spiral (Fig. 23 C). This type of vortex formation is usually found in the rear of a plate, normal or slightly inclined to the current. If the plate be inclined to the current at an angle exceeding about 30° the formation becomes discontinuous, as indicated in Fig. 23 D,[1] which shows the eddies formed behind a square plate inclined at 40° to the stream. In this type of motion two spirals are formed from the sides of the plate and are linked together to form a chain of eddies by a sheet of fluid flowing from the trailing edge of the plate.

From the manner of eddy formation it is evident that the pressure on the rear surface of the body in a current of fluid will be less than normal, and subject to a periodic variation, the period depending on the time of formation of an eddy and so on the shape and dimensions of the body and on the velocity of flow.

If the body is supported so as to be capable of vibration, and the period of eddy formation synchronises, or nearly so, with that of its natural vibration, oscillations are set up which may become very large. This effect may often be noted where a flexible bough dips into a steady stream. On account of this action, current meters, in which the pressure on a stationary flat plate is taken as a measure of the velocity, are not satisfactory.

Art. 16.—Conditions regulating the Two Manners of Motion.

Several conditions combine to determine whether in any particular instance the motion of water shall be steady or unsteady. Osborne Reynolds[2] came to the conclusion that the conditions tending to stability and steadiness of motion are :—

(1) An increase in viscosity.

(2) Converging solid boundaries.

(3) Free (exposed to air) surfaces.

(4) Curvature of the path, with the greatest velocity at the outside of the curve.

And that the conditions tending to instability and unsteadiness of motion are :—

(1) A decrease in viscosity.

(2) Solid (rigid tangentially) boundaries in general and particularly diverging solid boundaries.

(3) A stream of fluid flowing through fluid at rest.

[1] Tech. Report, Aviation Committee, 1911—12.
[2] " Phil. Trans. Royal Society," 1883.

(4) Curvature with the greatest velocity at the inside of the curve.

(5) Greater density of the fluid.

Experiments carried out at McGill University show that an increase in pressure also tends to stability of motion.

The effect of solid boundaries in producing instability would appear to be due rather to their tangential than their lateral stiffness. One very remarkable instance of this effect of boundaries possessing tangential stiffness, however small this may be, occurs when a film of oil is allowed to form on the surface of water. Here the oil film exerts a small but appreciable tangential constraint, with the result that motion which was originally stable becomes unstable.

This results in the formation of eddies below the surfaces of the oil and water, and the energy which was originally imparted by the action of the wind to form and maintain stable wave motion is now applied to the institution of this eddy motion, with the well-known result as to the stilling of the waves.

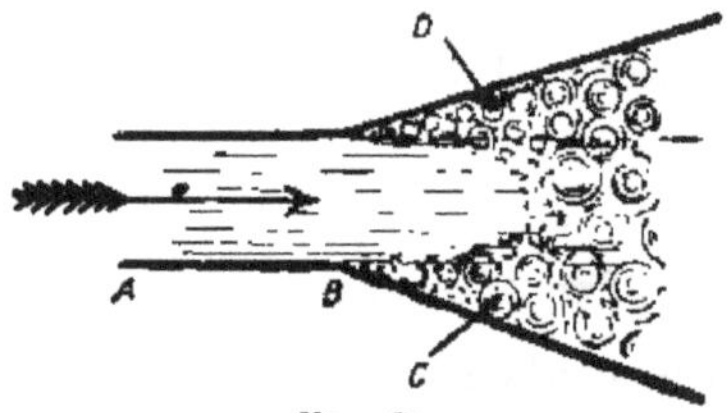

FIG. 24.

Where one stream of liquid is in contact with a second stream moving with a different velocity, the common surface of separation is found to be in a most unstable condition. Reynolds showed this by allowing the two liquids, Carbon Bisulphide and water, to form a horizontal surface of separation in a long horizontal tube. The tube was then slightly tilted so as to produce a relative axial motion of the fluids, when it was found that for extremely small values of the relative velocity the motion was unstable.

In this manner may be explained why diverging boundaries are a cause of instability. In such a case as that shown in Fig. 24, the motion from A to B in the parallel portion of the channel may be perfectly steady, depending on the dimensions of the channel and the velocity of flow. On leaving B, however, at any but the smallest velocities the water appears to be projected in the form of a core of the same dimensions as the channel, through the mass of dead water at C and D. Here all the conditions necessary for instability are present.

This instability attending the relative motion of fluids of different density affords an explanation of the interesting phenomenon known as "deadwater," which is sometimes noticed when a ship encounters a surface layer of fresh water, overlying the denser sea-water. Under such circumstances the resistance to motion is greatly increased. The phenomenon has been investigated by V. W. Ekman (Norwegian Polar Expedition Researches, 1893, No. 15), who found that the resistance is due

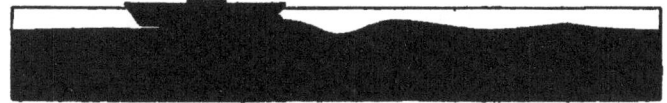

FIG. 25.

to the formation and maintenance of a train of waves at the surface of separation of the fluids, as shown in Fig. 25.

More recent experiments[1] tend to show that the foregoing conclusions as to the effect of curvature of the path in affecting the manner of motion are not justified, and that, as shown at the impact of a steady jet on a plane surface, at the efflux of a jet from a sharp-edged orifice, and in motion in a free vortex, curved motion with the velocity greatest at the inside, not at the outside of the curve, tends to steady motion. Generally speaking, wherever the velocity of flow is increasing and the pressure diminishing, as in the case where lines of flow are converging, there is an overwhelming tendency to steady motion. In a tube with converging boundaries, it is this which leads to steadiness of flow, and it is because this effect is sufficiently pronounced to overcome the tendency to sinuous motion which all solid boundaries, of whatever form, produce, that the motion in such tubes is steady for very high velocities of flow.

ART. 17.—CRITICAL VELOCITY.

The experiments by which Professor Reynolds demonstrated the nature of the two modes of motion of water were carried out on glass tubes of various diameters up to 2 inches, and about 4 feet

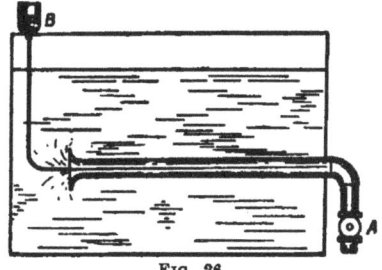

FIG. 26.

6 inches long. These were fitted with bell-mouth entrances, and were immersed horizontally in a tank of clear water having glass sides (Fig. 26). In carrying out the experiment the water in the tank is allowed to come absolutely to rest, and the valve A is then slightly

[1] By the Author, "Memoirs, Manchester Lit. and Phil. Soc.," Vol. 55, 1911, No. 13.

opened, allowing water to flow slowly through the tube. A little water, coloured with aniline dye, is introduced into the mouthpiece through a fine tube supplied from the vessel B.

At first this coloured water is drawn out into a single stream tube,

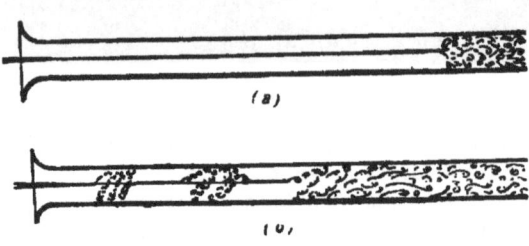

(a)

(b)

FIG. 27.

extending through the whole length of the tube, as shown in Fig. 26, the whole appearing to be motionless unless a slight motion of oscillation is given to the water in the supply tank, when the stream line sways gently from side to side, but without in the least losing its definition. As the valve A is further opened the velocity through the tube increases, and the stream tube is drawn out more and more, still retaining its definition

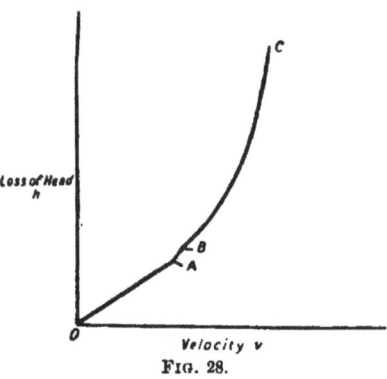

FIG. 28.

until at a certain velocity eddies begin to be formed intermittently near the end of the tube more remote from the mouthpiece (Fig. 27 a).

The formation of these eddies is very clearly denoted and is accompanied by the almost instantaneous diffusion of the colour band. As the velocity is still further increased the point of initiation of eddy motion advances towards the mouthpiece, this point being fixed for any one velocity. Finally the motion throughout becomes unsteady (Fig. 27 b).

Any initial disturbance of the water tends to reduce the velocity at which the motion changes from steady to sinuous, and which is termed the Critical Velocity.

Having determined the nature of the two manners of motion possible in a parallel pipe, and the existence of a " critical velocity," below which the motion is steady, and above which it is unsteady, Reynolds determined the law of resistance in the two cases and the points at which the change takes place, by measuring the loss of head accompanying different velocities of flow. On plotting a curve showing velocities and losses of head (Fig. 28) it was found that up to a certain velocity, for any given tube, these points lie on a straight line passing through the origin of co-ordinates. Above this velocity, the points lie more or less on a smooth curve, indicating that the loss of head is possibly proportional to r^n.

To test this, and if so to determine the value of n, the logarithms of the loss of head and of the velocity were plotted (Fig. 29), since if

$$h = k v^n$$

$\log h = \log k + n \log v$ which is the equation to a straight line, inclined at an angle θ to the axis of $\log r$ (where $\tan \theta = n$), and cutting off an intercept $= \log k$ on the axis of $\log h$.

It was then found that with velocities increasing between each pair of experiments, the plotted points lie on a straight line up to a certain point A, the value of θ for this

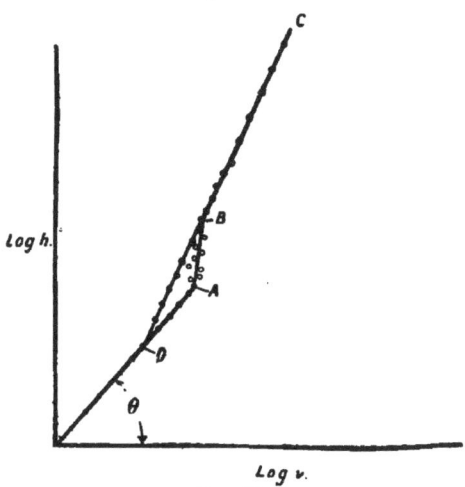

FIG. 29.

line being 45°. Up to this point n is unity and h is proportional to v. At A, which marks the *higher* critical velocity, or the point at which motion, initially steady, becomes sinuous, the law suddenly changes and h increases very rapidly. The relation between h and r, however, follows no definite law, until the point B is reached, where the velocity is about 1·3 times that at A. Above this point a perfectly definite law holds, the plotted points from B to C and onwards lying on a straight line.

The angle of inclination θ of this line varies with the material and surface of the pipe, but is constant for any one pipe.

With a lead pipe, $\tan \theta = 1·722$, so that here the law of resistance above the critical point is $h \propto v^{1·722}$.

When the velocities are decreased between each pair of experiments, it is found that the plotted points follow the straight line C B D to its intersection D with D O, indicating that eddies once initiated do not die out until the velocity is reduced to that corresponding to D. The velocity at D, which is less than that at A, is termed the *lower* or *true* critical velocity.

For velocities between D and A the motion, if steady, is unstable. and any initial disturbance will produce eddy motion which will no: die out.

A consideration of the part of the log h, log v, curve between A and B. shows that here the value of n is greater than before A or after B, and that with motion of this intermittently unsteady or unstable type the increased resistance accompanying an increase in velocity is greater than even when the motion is altogether sinuous. This would appear to be due to the fact that within this range of velocities eddies are being initiated in the tube, and the loss of head in the tube is due, not only to the actual resistance to motion, but also to the absorption of energy in eddy formation. After B is passed the eddies fill the whole length of tube, and the loss of head is then simply due to resistance to motion through the tube, i.e., to the maintenance, as opposed to the initiation, of eddy motion.[1]

As a result of his experiments, Reynolds concluded that the critical velocity is inversely proportional to the diameter d of the pipe, and is given by the formula

$$v_c = \frac{1}{b} \cdot \frac{P}{d}.$$

where b is a numerical constant.

„ $P \propto \dfrac{\text{viscosity}}{\text{density}}$, and therefore depends on the temperature of the water.

If t = temperature in degrees centigrade, then for water the value of P is given by

$$P = \frac{1}{1 + \cdot 03368\, t + \cdot 000221\, t^2}.$$

[1] Messrs. H. T. Barnes and E. G. Coker, " Proc. Roy. Soc.," vol. 74, determined the critical velocity by allowing water to flow through the given tube, which was jacketed with water at a higher temperature. A delicate thermometer indicated the temperature of the discharge water at exit. So long as the motion is steady, the transmission of heat through the water takes place entirely by conduction and is extremely slow, so that the thermometer gives a steady reading practically identical with that in the supply tank. Immediately the critical velocity is attained, however, the temperature of discharge increases rapidly and the change from steady to unsteady motion is manifested by a sudden jump of the mercury thread of the thermometer.

Thus when $t = 32°$ F. $= 0°$ C. . . . $P = 1.$
  „ „ $t = 62°$ F. $= 16\frac{1}{2}°$ C. . . . $P = $ ·616.
  „ „ $t = 100°$ F. $= 37\frac{3}{4}°$ C. . . . $P = $ ·385.
  „ „ $t = 212°$ F. $= 100°$ C. . . . $P = $ ·1523.
If the unit of length is 1 metre . . . . $b = $ 48·79.
  „ „ „ „ 1 foot . . . . $b = $ 4·06.

This gives the higher C. V. at which steady becomes eddy motion.

Exactly the same formula, but with a different numerical coefficient, was found to hold for the lower (true) C. V. at which eddy becomes steady motion.[1]

Here if the unit of length is 1 metre . . . . $b = 278.$
  „ „ „ „ „ 1 foot . . . . $b = 25·8.$

E.g., with water at 10° C. —50° F.—

        Motion is steady if $v\,d < $ ·029
          „   unstable if $v\,d\; {> \atop <}\; {·029 \atop ·182}$
          „   turbulent if $v\,d > $ ·182

the unit of length being 1 foot.

More recent experiments,[2] carried out on glass tubes by the colour band method, show that by taking the greatest care to eliminate all disturbance at entry to the tube, values of the higher critical velocity considerably greater than (up to 3·66 times as great as) those given by the above formula may be obtained. The probability is, in fact, that there is no definite *higher* critical velocity, but that this velocity always increases with decreasing disturbances. It is very doubtful, moreover, whether the Reynolds law is strictly true for diameters much in excess of those (up to about 2 inches) covered by his experiments.

ART. 18.—CRITICAL VELOCITY IN A CONVERGING TUBE.

The numerical constants involved in the case of the stability of motion in flow through a parallel tube have been accurately determined, but not in the case of a converging or a diverging tube. At sufficiently low velocities we know that the motion is steady in any case, but in converging or diverging tubes the angle of inclination of the sides has a great influence on the velocity at which stable becomes unstable motion.

---

[1] "Phil. Trans. Roy. Soc.," 1883. Also "Scientific Papers," Osborne Reynolds, vol. 2, pp. 51—103. This coefficient was obtained from experiments in which the resistance to flow at different velocities was measured.

[2] Ekman, "Arkiv. för Matematic, Ast. och Fys," 1910. Band 6, No. 12.

The exact effect of altering this inclination is still unknown, except that increasing the angle of divergence rapidly diminishes the stability, while in converging tubes stability of motion rapidly increases with the angle of convergence. At all ordinary velocities in fact, the motion in tubes or nozzles having more than a few degrees of convergence may be considered as being steady. Experiments by the author [1] on pipes having sides converging uniformly at an angle θ gave the following results. The critical velocities were obtained in the usual way, by plotting the logarithmic homologues of loss of head and of velocity at the contracted section, noting the point at which the index of v suddenly changes. As the motion at the entrance to the larger pipe was in every case unsteady, owing to the bends and irregularities in the supply pipe, these values mark the lower critical velocity at which eddy motion settles down into non-sinuous or stream-line motion.

Values of θ.	5°.	7¼°.	10°.	15°.
C. V. feet per second—				
At large section (3-inch diam.) . .	1·5	1·94	2·44	3·25
„ throat (1½-inch diam.) . .	6·0	7·76	9·77	12·9
„ point where diam. is 2¼ inches .	2·7	3·45	4·34	5·73

The temperature of the water in these experiments was $57\frac{1}{2}°$ F. The lower critical velocity in a parallel pipe of the same mean diameter (2¼ inches) at this temperature is 0·133 feet per second, while in a 3-inch and a 1½-inch pipe it is respectively 0·10 and 0·20 feet per second, the higher critical velocities being respectively 0·86, 0·65, and 1·29 feet per second. Should the ratio of higher to lower critical velocities have the same value in a conical pipe as in a parallel pipe, this would mean that in the case of a 1½-inch jet discharged from a converging nozzle with steady flow in the supply pipe, the critical velocity would have the following values—

Value of θ.	5°.	7¼°.	10°.	15°.
C. V. (higher), feet per second . .	39·0	50·4	63·5	83·8

and this would explain the glassy appearance of the high velocity jet leaving the nozzle of a Pelton wheel. Further experiments are, however

[1] "Proceedings, Roy. Soc. B.," vol. 83. 1910. p. 376.

needed to settle this point and also to determine how, with the same values of θ but with different inlet and outlet diameters, the critical velocity depends on the latter factor.

ART. 19.—MOTION OF A FLUID.

The motion of any particle of fluid acted upon by external forces and by its own weight may be considered from two points of view. In the first, by equating the work done on the mass to the increase of energy in the potential, pressure, and kinetic form, together with the loss by dissipation, as by internal friction, which converts mechanical energy into heat, we get an expression for the velocity in terms of the applied forces. With steady motion of a non-viscous fluid this method is always applicable.

Where a mass of fluid has unsteady—sinuous—motion, however, the impossibility of determining the kinetic energy possessed by its eddies in virtue of their rotation renders the application of the energy equation impossible, and it becomes necessary to consider the motion from the point of view of the production of momentum, since the momentum of the fluid forming a vortex is unaltered by its motion of rotation.

With unsteady motion, moreover, of a viscous fluid, the magnitude and direction of the forces—including those due to viscosity—acting at any particular point become indeterminate, so that the molecular motion at the point is then indeterminate, and the general equations of motion become in general impossible of application. Even in the case of the steady motion of a viscous fluid, these, when stated in terms of the viscosity, become so unwieldy that, except in one or two particular cases, e.g., those of steady flow between parallel plates or through a circular pipe, they are unfitted for application to the solution of any practical problem, although where so applicable the solution becomes perfectly accurate.

A simplification of these equations may be obtained by neglecting the effect of viscosity—i.e., assuming the liquid to be a perfect fluid—and it is in this form that they are usually stated. Evidently the solution of any such equation can only be made to apply to the results of any given problem by the introduction of some constant obtained by experiment which itself has the effect of modifying the solution so as to take into account the effect of viscosity, and it is to this extent that hydraulics is to be considered an experimental science. If it were possible in every case to apply the equations of motion in full, the science would become exact.

The equations in full are deduced in the following pages, and the terms involving viscosity are afterwards eliminated, so as to give the form usually stated for a non-viscous incompressible fluid.

Afterwards, in considering the motion of fluids, it will be assumed that with uniform steady motion the distribution of pressure is unaffected, so that the pressure at any point is the equivalent of the hydrostatic pressure due to its depth. This appears from the general equations of motion. Also the further assumption is made, that if the moving particles have the acceleration which they would have if acted upon by their external forces alone—i.e., if independent of the surrounding particles—the pressure throughout is uniform. Thus, in a jet falling freely through the atmosphere under the action of gravity, the pressure throughout is sensibly uniform and equal to that of the atmosphere.

The principles on which the following demonstrations are based may be briefly indicated, and are as follow :—

The Principle of Linear Momentum.—The rate of change of the component of the linear momentum of any system in any direction is equal to the parallel component of the applied forces.

The Principle of Angular Momentum.—The rate of change of the component of angular momentum of a system about any axis is equal to the moment of the applied forces about that axis.

The Principle of the Conservation of Energy.—The sum of the kinetic and potential energies of any system is constant, except for the effect of such dissipative forces as friction which convert mechanical energy into heat.

Art. 20.—Equations of Motion for a Viscous Fluid.

Taking a fixed point O in the fluid as the origin of co-ordinates, let OX, OY, OZ be three co-ordinate axes, and let u, v, w be the components of the velocity of a particle parallel to these three axes. $u, v,$ and w, will be supposed finite and continuous, and, since they vary with the position of the particle and the time, are functions of x, y, z, and t.

The velocity of a particle may be considered from two points of view. Considering any fixed point, the velocity of successive particles as they pass that point may vary, and since x, y, z are now constant, the rates of variation parallel to the three axes are represented by the partial differentials $\frac{\partial u}{\partial t}$, etc. For steady motion these are separately zero.

If, however, we consider the variation of velocity of any one particle as moves from point to point of its path, since this now also includes the riation of x, y, z with t, its components will now be represented by $\dfrac{d\,u}{d\,t}$:., and are the components of the true acceleration of the particle. lese are not necessarily zero for steady motion.

If then a particle moves from a point $(x,\,y,\,z)$ to a second point $+\,\delta x;\,y+\delta y;\,z+\delta z)$ in time $\delta\,t$, its change of velocity $\delta\,u$ is given

$$\delta\,u = \frac{\partial\,u}{\partial\,x}\,\delta\,x + \frac{\partial\,u}{\partial\,y}\,\delta\,y + \frac{\partial\,u}{\partial\,z}\cdot\delta\,z + \frac{\partial\,u}{\partial\,t}\cdot\delta\,t$$

id in the limit

$$\frac{d\,u}{d\,t} = \frac{\partial\,u}{\partial\,x}\cdot\frac{d\,x}{d\,t} + \frac{\partial\,u}{\partial\,y}\cdot\frac{d\,y}{d\,t} + \frac{\partial\,u}{\partial\,z}\cdot\frac{d\,z}{d\,t} + \frac{\partial\,u}{\partial\,t} \quad (1)$$

But from the definitions of u, v, w, we have

$$u = \frac{d\,x}{d\,t} \quad : \quad v = \frac{d\,y}{d\,t} \quad : \quad w = \frac{d\,z}{d\,t}$$

$$\therefore \quad \frac{d\,u}{d\,t} = u\frac{\partial\,u}{\partial\,x} + v\frac{\partial\,u}{\partial\,y} + w\frac{\partial\,u}{\partial\,z} + \frac{\partial\,u}{\partial\,t} \quad (2)$$

milarly

$$\frac{d\,v}{d\,t} = u\frac{\partial\,v}{\partial\,x} + v\frac{\partial\,v}{\partial\,y} + w\frac{\partial\,v}{\partial\,z} + \frac{\partial\,v}{\partial\,t} \quad (8)$$

id

$$\frac{d\,w}{d\,t} = u\frac{\partial\,w}{\partial\,x} + v\frac{\partial\,w}{\partial\,y} + w\frac{\partial\,w}{\partial\,z} + \frac{\partial\,w}{\partial\,t} \quad (4)$$

Next consider an elementary parallelopiped in the fluid bounded by lges $\delta\,x$, $\delta\,y$, $\delta\,z$ (Fig. 30). For ntinuity of motion the difference tween the amounts of fluid which ›w into and out of its faces during me $\delta\,t$ must be equal to the increase in the mass which they close. Expressing this analytilly, we get the equation of ntinuity.

Now the mass of fluid entering ross the face $O\,B$ in time $\delta\,t = u\,\delta\,y\,.\,\delta\,z\,.\,\delta\,t$.

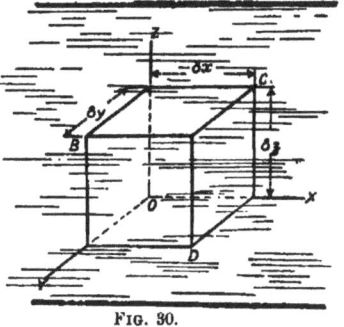

FIG. 30.

And the mass of fluid leaving ross the face $C\,D$ in time $\delta\,t = \rho\,u\,\delta\,y\,.\,\delta\,z\,.\,\delta\,t + \dfrac{\partial}{\partial\,x}(\rho\,u)\,\delta\,x\,.\,\delta\,y\,.\,\delta\,z\,.\,\delta\,t.$

$\therefore$ Gain across these faces $= -\dfrac{\partial}{\partial\,x}(\rho\,u)\,\delta\,x\,.\,\delta\,y\,.\,\delta\,z\,.\,\delta\,t.$

$\therefore$ Total gain

$$= -\left\{ \frac{\partial}{\partial x}(\rho\, u) + \frac{\partial}{\partial y}(\rho\, v) + \frac{\partial}{\partial z}(\rho\, w) \right\} \delta x . \delta y . \delta z . \delta t.$$

But the mass contained at time $t = \rho\, \delta x . \delta y . \delta z.$

and   „   „   „   „ $t + \delta t = \left(\rho + \frac{\partial \rho}{\partial t} . \delta t \right)$

$$\delta x . \delta y . \delta z.$$

$\therefore$ Gain in time $\delta t = \frac{\partial \rho}{\partial t} . \delta t . \delta x . \delta y . \delta z.$

Equating these expressions for the gain, we have

$$\frac{\partial \rho}{\partial t} + \frac{\partial (\rho\, u)}{\partial x} + \frac{\partial (\rho\, v)}{\partial y} + \frac{\partial (\rho\, w)}{\partial z} = 0$$

from which, if ρ is constant, i.e., if the fluid is incompressible, we have

$$\frac{\partial u}{\partial x} + \frac{\partial v}{\partial y} + \frac{\partial w}{\partial z} = 0$$

as the equation of continuity for an incompressible fluid.

In the case of a gas ρ is not constant, but we may have $\frac{\partial \rho}{\partial t} = \text{const}$ in which case we have regular motion in the gas.

Now if the stresses in a viscous fluid (which follows the same stress stra law as an elastic solid) be represented by the notation $p_{xx},\ p_{xy},\ p_{yz},$ e where each of these symbols denotes a stress on the plane perpendicular the axis of co-ordinates represented by the first suffix, in the direction the second suffix, so that, for example, the stress p_{xy} is a stress on plane perpendicular to $O\,X$, in the direction $O\,Y$, and is therefore tangential stress on this plane, the relations holding between the varie stresses for equilibrium are given by the following equations.[1]

$$p_{xx} = -p - \frac{2}{3}\mu \left(\frac{\partial u}{\partial x} + \frac{\partial v}{\partial y} + \frac{\partial w}{\partial z} \right) + 2\mu \frac{\partial u}{\partial x}$$

$$p_{yy} = -p - \frac{2}{3}\mu \left(\frac{\partial u}{\partial x} + \frac{\partial v}{\partial y} + \frac{\partial w}{\partial z} \right) + 2\mu \frac{\partial v}{\partial y}$$

$$p_{zz} = -p - \frac{2}{3}\mu \left(\frac{\partial u}{\partial x} + \frac{\partial v}{\partial y} + \frac{\partial w}{\partial z} \right) + 2\mu \frac{\partial w}{\partial z}$$

$$p_{xy} = p_{yx} = \mu \left(\frac{\partial v}{\partial x} + \frac{\partial u}{\partial y} \right)$$

$$p_{yz} = p_{zy} = \mu \left(\frac{\partial w}{\partial y} + \frac{\partial v}{\partial z} \right)$$

$$p_{zx} = p_{xz} = \mu \left(\frac{\partial u}{\partial z} + \frac{\partial w}{\partial x} \right)$$

---

[1] Stokes on "Theories of the internal friction of fluids in motion and of the equilibrium an motion of elastic solids"; also Lamb's "Motion of Fluids," p. 219, or "Hydrodynami

ere $p = -\dfrac{p_{xx} + p_{yy} + p_{zz}}{3}$, and $\mu =$ Coefficient of Viscosity.

But, considering the elementary volume $\delta x \cdot \delta y \cdot \delta z$, we see that the al force acting on this volume, due to any variation of stress on opposite es of the volume in the direction $O X$, is

$$\left\{\frac{\partial p_{xx}}{\partial x} + \frac{\partial p_{yx}}{\partial y} + \frac{\partial p_{zx}}{\partial z}\right\} \delta x \cdot \delta y \cdot \delta z.^{1}$$

So that if an external force, having a component X per unit mass in is direction, also act on the element, we have

$$\left.\begin{array}{c}\text{Total force on element} \\ \text{in direction } O X\end{array}\right\} = \left[\left(\frac{\partial p_{xx}}{\partial x} + \frac{\partial p_{yx}}{\partial y} + \frac{\partial p_{zx}}{\partial z}\right) + \rho X\right]$$
$$\delta x \cdot \delta y \cdot \delta z.$$

$$\left.\begin{array}{c}\text{iis equals mass} \times \text{acceleration} \\ \text{of element in direction } O X\end{array}\right\} = \rho \cdot \delta x \cdot \delta y \cdot \delta z \times \frac{d u}{d t}.$$

$$\therefore \ \rho X + \left(\frac{\partial p_{xx}}{\partial x} + \frac{\partial p_{yx}}{\partial y} + \frac{\partial p_{zx}}{\partial z}\right) = \rho \frac{d u}{d t}.$$

Similarly, considering the accelerations in directions $O Y$ and $O Z$, we get

$$\rho Y + \left(\frac{\partial p_{xy}}{\partial x} + \frac{\partial p_{yy}}{\partial y} + \frac{\partial p_{zy}}{\partial z}\right) = \rho \frac{d v}{d t} \qquad (9)$$

$$\rho Z + \left(\frac{p_{xz}}{\partial x} + \frac{\partial p_{yz}}{\partial y} + \frac{\partial p_{zz}}{\partial z}\right) = \rho \frac{d w}{d t}$$

95, p. 508. In this discussion, p_{xx}, etc., are reckoned positives when tensions, while p, as is mmon in hydrodynamical problems, is reckoned positive when a compression. This ounts for the negative sign before p in (7).

[1] This may be proved as follows. The difference of normal stress on the faces $O B$ and D (Fig. 30A) $= \dfrac{\partial p_{xx}}{\partial x} \delta x.$

$\therefore$ Difference of normal force on these faces $= \dfrac{\partial p_{xx}}{\partial x} \delta x$. $y \cdot \delta z.$

Also the difference of tangential stress in the direction X, on the faces $O C$ and $B D = \dfrac{\partial p_{yx}}{\partial y} \delta y$, while the ultant force due to these tangential stresses in this direc- ion $= \dfrac{\partial p_{yx}}{\partial y} \cdot \delta x \cdot \delta y \cdot \delta z.$

Similarly the tangential stresses on the faces $O D$ and C in the direction $O X$ give rise to a resultant force $\dfrac{p_{zx}}{\partial z} \delta x \cdot \delta y \cdot \delta z.$

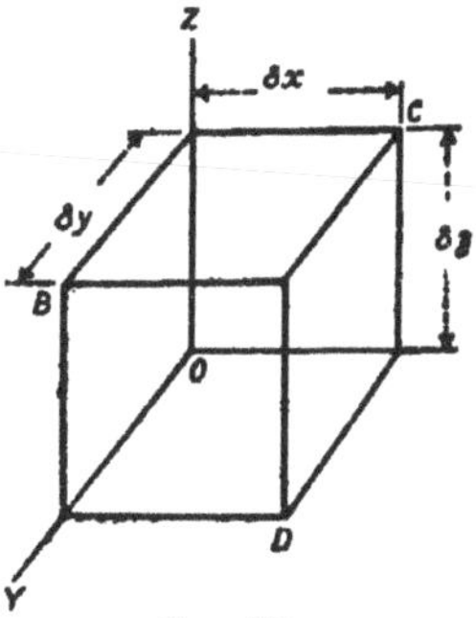

FIG. 30A.

These include all the forces due to variation of stress across the element, which have a omponent in the direction $O X$. Summing these, we get the resultant force in the direction t increasing x. Similarly for the forces in the directions $O Z$ and $O Y$.

Differentiating the equations (7) and (8), so as to obtain the value $\frac{p_{xx}}{\partial x}$, etc., in the case of a viscous fluid, and inserting the values obtained in equations (9), the first of these becomes

$$\rho X - \frac{\partial p}{\partial x} - \frac{2}{3}\mu\frac{\partial}{\partial x}\left(\frac{\partial u}{\partial x} + \frac{\partial v}{\partial y} + \frac{\partial w}{\partial z}\right) + 2\mu\frac{\partial^2 u}{\partial x^2}$$
$$+ \mu\left(\frac{\partial^2 u}{\partial y^2} + \frac{\partial^2 v}{\partial x.\partial y}\right) + \mu\left(\frac{\partial^2 w}{\partial x.\partial z} + \frac{\partial^2 u}{\partial z^2}\right) = \rho\frac{d u}{d t}.$$

From the equation of continuity we have

$$\frac{\partial u}{\partial x} + \frac{\partial v}{\partial y} + \frac{\partial w}{\partial z} = 0$$

Also $\frac{\partial^2 u}{\partial x^2} + \frac{\partial^2 v}{\partial x\,\partial y} + \frac{\partial^2 w}{\partial x\,\partial z} = \frac{\partial}{\partial x}\left(\frac{\partial u}{\partial x} + \frac{\partial v}{\partial y} + \frac{\partial w}{\partial z}\right) = 0.$

So that the equations become

$$\rho\frac{d u}{d t} = \rho X - \frac{\partial p}{\partial x} + \mu(\nabla^2 u)$$
$$\rho\frac{d v}{d t} = \rho Y - \frac{\partial p}{\partial y} + \mu(\nabla^2 v) \qquad (1$$
$$\rho\frac{d w}{d t} = \rho Z - \frac{\partial p}{\partial z} + \mu(\nabla^2 w)$$

where ∇^2 denotes the operator $\left(\frac{\partial^2}{\partial x^2} + \frac{\partial^2}{\partial y^2} + \frac{\partial^2}{\partial z^2}\right).$

The terms involving μ in these equations are complex, and for purpose of practical application to hydraulic problems are usually neglected. this is done, the equations of motion for a non-viscous, incompressible fluid become

$$\rho\frac{d u}{d t} = \rho X - \frac{\partial p}{\partial x}$$
$$\rho\frac{d v}{d t} = \rho Y - \frac{\partial p}{\partial y} \qquad (1$$
$$\rho\frac{d w}{d t} = \rho Z - \frac{\partial p}{\partial z}$$

or, writing $\frac{d u}{d t}$ in terms of $\frac{\partial u}{\partial x}$, etc., from equation (2), and dividing throughout by ρ

$$X - \frac{1}{\rho}\frac{\partial p}{\partial x} = u\frac{\partial u}{\partial x} + v\frac{\partial u}{\partial y} + w\frac{\partial u}{\partial z} + \frac{\partial u}{\partial t}$$
$$Y - \frac{1}{\rho}\frac{\partial p}{\partial y} = u\frac{\partial v}{\partial x} + v\frac{\partial v}{\partial y} + w\frac{\partial v}{\partial z} + \frac{\partial v}{\partial t} \qquad (1$$
$$Z - \frac{1}{\rho}\frac{\partial p}{\partial z} = u\frac{\partial w}{\partial x} + v\frac{\partial w}{\partial y} + w\frac{\partial w}{\partial z} + \frac{\partial w}{\partial t}$$

the Eulerian equations of motion.

Here the axes of co-ordinates have been taken to coincide with the principal axes of stress. If, however, these are transferred, exactly similar equations are obtained.

In the case where gravity is the only external force acting on the fluid, $X = o$, $Y = o$, and $Z = -g$, g acting in the opposite direction to that of z increasing.

So far, the equations are applicable to motion of any kind, whether steady or unsteady, but in their present form are not obviously useful for the solution of any practical problem. So long as the motion is sinuous and irregular nothing further can be done with them.

Art. 21. — Application to Stream Line Motion.

If, however, the fluid be moving with definite stream line motion, these equations can be considerably simplified. Suppose a particle moving with stream line motion from O, in the direction OS (Fig. 31), with velocity V_s, the space OS being δs. The direction cosines of

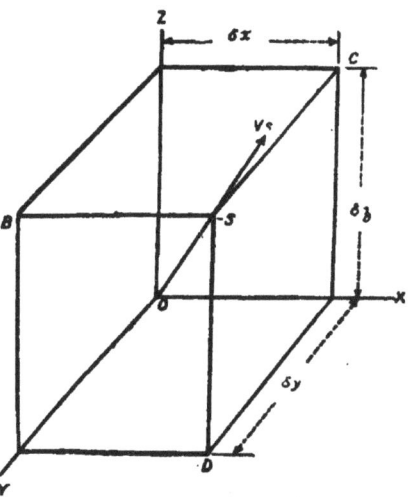

FIG. 31.

this motion in the directions OX, OY, OZ, are $\dfrac{d\,x}{d\,s} \cdot \dfrac{d\,y}{d\,s} \cdot \dfrac{d\,z}{d\,s}$.

Also

$$\begin{cases} \dfrac{d\,x}{d\,s} = \dfrac{u}{V_s} = l \\[2mm] \dfrac{d\,y}{d\,s} = \dfrac{v}{V_s} = m \\[2mm] \dfrac{d\,z}{d\,s} = \dfrac{w}{V_s} = n \end{cases}$$

Again, geometrically we get

$$V_s{}^2 = u^2 + v^2 + w^2 \tag{13}$$

And
$$V_s = l\,u + m\,v + n\,w. \tag{14}$$

For stream line motion, and with only gravity acting, the general equations (12) may then be written

$$-\frac{1}{\rho}\frac{\partial p}{\partial x} = \frac{\partial u}{\partial t} + V_s\left(l\frac{\partial u}{\partial x} + m\frac{\partial u}{\partial y} + n\frac{\partial u}{\partial z}\right)$$

$$-\frac{1}{\rho}\frac{\partial p}{\partial y} = \frac{\partial v}{\partial t} + V_s\left(l\frac{\partial v}{\partial x} + m\frac{\partial v}{\partial y} + n\frac{\partial v}{\partial z}\right)$$

$$-g - \frac{1}{\rho}\frac{\partial p}{\partial z} = \frac{\partial w}{\partial t} + V_s\left(l\frac{\partial w}{\partial x} + m\frac{\partial w}{\partial y} + n\frac{\partial w}{\partial z}\right) \qquad (15)$$

Now $\left(l\frac{\partial u}{\partial x} + m\frac{\partial u}{\partial y} + n\frac{\partial u}{\partial z}\right) = \frac{dx}{ds}\cdot\frac{\partial u}{\partial x} + \frac{dy}{ds}\cdot\frac{\partial u}{\partial y} + \frac{dz}{ds}\cdot\frac{\partial u}{\partial z}$

$$= \frac{du}{ds}$$

$$\therefore \quad -\frac{1}{\rho}\frac{\partial p}{\partial x} = \frac{\partial u}{\partial t} + V_s\frac{du}{ds}$$

$$-\frac{1}{\rho}\frac{\partial p}{\partial y} = \frac{\partial v}{\partial t} + V_s\frac{dv}{ds} \qquad (16)$$

$$-g - \frac{1}{\rho}\frac{\partial p}{\partial z} = \frac{\partial w}{\partial t} + V_s\frac{dw}{ds}$$

Multiplying these equations respectively by l, m, and n, and adding gives

$$-ng - \frac{1}{\rho}\left(l\frac{\partial p}{\partial x} + m\frac{\partial p}{\partial y} + n\frac{\partial p}{\partial z}\right) = l\frac{\partial u}{\partial t} + m\frac{\partial v}{\partial t} + n\frac{\partial w}{\partial t} + u\frac{du}{ds}$$

$$+ v\frac{dv}{ds} + w\frac{dw}{ds}. \qquad (17)$$

From (14) we get $\frac{\partial V_s}{\partial t} = l\frac{\partial u}{\partial t} + m\frac{\partial v}{\partial t} + n\frac{\partial w}{\partial t}.$

From (13) we get $\frac{dV_s^2}{ds} = 2\left(u\frac{du}{ds} + v\frac{dv}{ds} + w\frac{dw}{ds}\right),$

Also $\qquad\qquad l\frac{\partial p}{\partial x} + m\frac{\partial p}{\partial y} + n\frac{\partial p}{\partial z} = \frac{dp}{ds}.$

$\therefore$ Substituting, equation (17) becomes

$$-ng - \frac{1}{\rho}\frac{dp}{ds} = \frac{\partial V_s}{\partial t} + \frac{1}{2}\frac{d}{ds}(V_s^2)$$

or, since $n = \frac{dz}{ds}$

$$-g\frac{dz}{ds} - \frac{1}{\rho}\frac{dp}{ds} = \frac{\partial V_s}{\partial t} + \frac{1}{2}\frac{d}{ds}(V_s^2),$$

or,

$$\frac{d}{ds}\left(\frac{p}{\rho} + \frac{V^2}{2} + gz\right) = -\frac{\partial V_s}{\partial t}.$$

If W = weight of unit volume of the fluid, $W = \rho g$, so that the equation may be written

$$\frac{d}{ds}\left(\frac{p}{W} + \frac{V_s^2}{2g} + z\right) = -\frac{1}{g}\frac{\partial V_s}{\partial t}. \qquad (18)$$

Integrating this we get $\dfrac{p}{W} + \dfrac{V_s^2}{2g} + z = -\dfrac{1}{g} \int \dfrac{\partial V_s}{\partial t} . ds$ (19)

In steady stream line motion, the velocity at any fixed point remains constant, so that $\dfrac{\partial V_s}{\partial t} = 0$, and the equation then becomes

$$\frac{p}{W} + \frac{V_s^2}{2g} + z = \text{constant.} \qquad (20)$$

This equation holds throughout any particular stream line, but the constant varies from one stream line to another. When all stream lines start under the same conditions, as in the case of a flow from a small orifice in the base of a vessel, the constant is the same throughout.

ART. 22.

By an algebraic transformation, we may obtain from the general equations of motion an equation giving the rate of increase of kinetic energy, which becomes equal to the sum of two terms.[1] The first is the rate of increase of kinetic energy due to work done by the stresses, and the second has been called the rate of increase of kinetic energy in the form of heat. It follows that the u, v, w, which have been defined as the component velocities at the point O, must strictly also take into account, and include these heat motions. From this point of view we may say that if the heat motion dissipated by radiation and conduction is equal to the relative molecular motion, the motion as a whole is steady. If, however, the relative molecular motion is greater than that dissipated in this way, we have eddies formed.

ART. 23.—FLOW AGAINST VISCOUS RESISTANCE.

' · resistance to steady motion of a fluid through a pipe or channel is simply due to the viscosity of the fluid, and not to any actual slip at the boundary of solid and fluid if the adhesive force at the boundaries is sufficiently great to overcome the shear in the fluid at these points. That this is true, at all events in the case of water at pressures slightly above atmospheric, may be shown by immersing a glass tube horizontally in water and introducing a drop of aniline dye to the bottom of the tube. If now water be allowed to flow through the tube, the coloured matter in contact with the side will not be removed so long as the motion remains steady. Directly the motion becomes unsteady, however, rapid diffusion takes place and the colouring matter at once disappears. It follows from

---

[1] Phil. Trans. Roy. Soc., A., Vol. 186, 1894, p. 123. Reynolds Sci. Papers, II., p. 535.

this that with steady motion the resistance is independent of the natur, of the solid surface. With unsteady motion on the other hand, ther would appear to be an actual interchange, by the breaking down of adhesion, of molecules in intimate contact with the boundaries (Arts. 1 and 67), and since any such interchange will be greater as the rougl ness of the surface increases, and will vary with the material of the pip it might be inferred that resistance to unsteady motion will depend on the state and material of the surface, and will increase as its roughne increases.

ART. 24.—STEADY FLOW BETWEEN HORIZONTAL PARALLEL PLATES.

Take OX, OY, OZ, co-ordinate axes in the fluid (Fig. 32). Let th direction of motion be parallel to the axis of x, and the plates perpe dicular to that of y. Sup pose the boundaries in th direction of OZ to be in finitely distant, so as not t affect the motion, and neg lect the effect of gravity. Let $2h$ = distance betweer plates, and let OX bisect this distance.

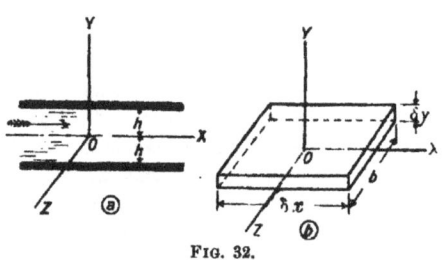

FIG. 32.

Let u, v, and w denote velocities of flow in direc tions OX, OY, OZ. Then $v = 0$, ∴ if p is the intensity of norma pressure on any plane perpendicular to OX we have $\frac{dp}{dy} = 0$. The variations of velocity and pressure in the direction OZ may be neglected since the boundaries in this direction and therefore the points at which the pressure may be zero, are at an infinite distance.

It follows that $\frac{dp}{dz} = 0$, so that on any plane perpendicular to OX the intensity of normal pressure is uniform.

The tractive—or shear—force on any plane perpendicular to OY and of area A is $\mu \frac{du}{dy} \cdot A$, where μ = coefficient of viscosity (Art. 4).

The difference of tractive force on the two faces of a stratum of thick ness δy, and of area A (Fig. 32 b), is thus given by

$$\frac{d}{dy} \left\{ \mu \frac{du}{dy} \cdot A \right\} \delta y = \mu \frac{d^2 u}{dy^2} A \, \delta y,$$

.e., by the rate of change of this force with respect to y, multiplied by the change in y.

But if b is the width of the stratum, and δx its length, the area of each end $= b \, \delta y$, while its area $A = b \, \delta x$.

Also, since for equilibrium the difference of traction on the two faces of the stratum is equal to the difference of normal pressures on the two ends,

$$b \cdot \delta y \cdot \frac{d p}{d x} \cdot \delta x = \mu \frac{d^2 u}{d y^2} \cdot A \, \delta y = \mu \frac{d^2 u}{d y^2} \cdot b \, \delta x \, \delta y$$

$$\therefore \quad \frac{d p}{d x} = \mu \frac{d^2 u}{d y^2} .^1$$

Integrating this expression, we get

$$u = C + B y + \frac{1}{2 \mu} \cdot y^2 \cdot \frac{d p}{d x}, \text{ where } C \text{ and } B \text{ are constants.}$$

Since the motion is symmetrical about the axis of x, *i.e.*, is the same for equal positive and negative values of y, the term involving the first power of y must vanish, since this would change sign with y, so that $B = 0$.

Again for uniformity of flow $\frac{d p}{d x}$ is constant, while, assuming no slip at the boundaries, we have $u = 0$ for $y = \pm h$.

Determining the constant C, so that these boundary conditions are satisfied, we get

$$u = - \frac{1}{2 \mu} \left\{ h^2 - y^2 \right\} \frac{d p}{d x}$$

i.e., the pressure diminishes as x increases. Evidently, too, from the form of the equation the curve of velocities is a parabola.

The flux over unit width of the plates is given by

$$\int_{-h}^{h} u \, d y = - \frac{2}{3} \frac{h^3}{\mu} \cdot \frac{d p}{d x}$$

If the measurements are taken in pounds, feet, and seconds, the volume per second in cubic feet, Q, is given by

$$Q = \frac{2}{3} \frac{h^3}{\mu} \cdot \frac{d p}{d x}.$$

---

[1] This may be deduced directly from the general equations of motion, p. 62, for since $v = 0$; $w = 0$; $\frac{d u}{d t} = 0$; equations (10) reduce to

$$\frac{\partial p}{\partial x} = \mu (\nabla^2 u).$$

Since $\frac{d p}{d y} = 0$; $\frac{d p}{d z} = 0$; $\frac{d u}{d x} = 0$; $\frac{d u}{d z} = 0$, this becomes $\frac{d p}{d x} = \mu \frac{d^2 u}{d y^2}$.

If $p_1 - p_2 =$ fall of pressure between two points at a distance l apart this becomes

$$Q = \frac{2}{3} \frac{h^3}{\mu} \cdot \frac{p_1 - p_2}{l}.$$

The maximum velocity occurs at the axis, where $y = 0$, and equals $\frac{1}{2\mu} \cdot h^2 \cdot \frac{dp}{dx}$.

The mean velocity $= \dfrac{\text{flux over a section}}{\text{area of section}} = \dfrac{Q}{2 h} = \dfrac{1}{3\mu} h^2 \dfrac{dp}{dx}$

$$\therefore \frac{\text{Maximum velocity}}{\text{Mean velocity}} = \frac{3}{2}.$$

The shear stress on the boundaries is given by

$$\mu \frac{du}{dy} = y \frac{dp}{dx} = h \cdot \frac{p_1 - p_2}{l}.$$

ART. 25.—STEADY FLOW THROUGH A CIRCULAR PIPE.

Suppose the pipe to be horizontal, and, neglecting the effect of gravity, assume the flow to be produced by a uniform difference of pressure head along its length. Let the axis of x be the axis of the tube, and let a be its radius. Using the same notation as in the preceding example, and assuming the velocity everywhere parallel to $O\,X$, we have $v = o$, $w = o$.

$$\therefore \frac{dp}{dy} = 0 \,;\, \frac{dp}{dz} = 0, \text{ as in the previous case.}$$

The tangential stress, or tractive force per unit area, on a plane perpendicular to a radius $= \mu \dfrac{du}{dr}$.

Hence for a cylindrical shell concentric with the pipe, of length δx and having inner and outer radii r and $r + \delta r$, the difference of the tangential force on the inner and outer surfaces will be $\dfrac{d}{dr} \left\{ 2 \pi r \cdot \delta x \cdot \mu \dfrac{du}{dr} \right\} \delta r$, and this must be balanced by the difference of normal pressure on the two ends of the shell.

Since $\dfrac{dp}{dr} = o$, the pressure intensity p at any point of the section is uniform.

$$\therefore \; 2 \pi r \cdot \delta r \cdot \frac{dp}{dx} \cdot \delta x = \frac{d}{dr} \left\{ 2 \pi r \cdot \delta x \cdot \mu \frac{du}{dr} \right\} \delta r$$

$$\therefore \; \frac{d}{dr} \left\{ r \frac{du}{dr} \right\} = \frac{dp}{dx} \cdot \frac{r}{\mu}.$$

Integrating, we get

$$u = \left\{ \frac{1}{4\,\mu}\frac{d\,p}{d\,x} \right\}\, r^2 + A \log r + B. \qquad (1)$$

Since the velocity at the axis, where $r = o$, cannot be infinite and since $\log o = \text{inf.}$, $A = o$.

Determining B, so that $u = o$ when $r = \pm\, a$, i.e., for no slip at the boundaries, gives

$$u = -\,\frac{1}{4\,\mu}\cdot\frac{d\,p}{d\,x}\cdot\left\{ a^2 - r^2 \right\} \qquad (2)$$

So that the flux through the pipe, which equals

$$\int_0^a u\,.\,2\,\pi\,r\,d\,r = \frac{\pi\,a^4}{8\,\mu}\cdot\frac{d\,p}{d\,x}\ \text{cubic feet per second.}$$

Writing $\dfrac{d\,p}{d\,x}$ as $\dfrac{p_1 - p_2}{l}$ where p_1 and p_2 are the pressure intensities at a distance l apart, along the axis of the pipe, we have

$$Q = \frac{\pi\,a^4}{8\,\mu}\cdot\frac{p_1 - p_2}{l}\ \text{cubic feet per second.}$$

The maximum velocity is obtained by putting $r = o$ in equation (2) and equals $\dfrac{p_1 - p_2}{4\,\mu\,l}$. a^2 feet per second.

$$\text{The mean velocity} = \frac{Q}{\text{area of section}} = \frac{p_1 - p_2}{8\,\mu\,l}\,.\,a^2\ \text{feet per second. (3)}$$

$$\therefore\ \ \text{Maximum velocity} = 2\ \text{(mean velocity)}.$$

On equating expressions (2) and (3) it is readily shown that the filament of mean velocity is found at a radius ·707 a.

From equation (2) we see that the curve of velocities across a diameter is a parabola, and

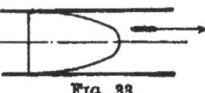

Fig. 33.

that the surface of velocities for the pipe will be a paraboloid of revolution (Fig. 33).[1]

If $\bar{v}$ = mean velocity, we have $p_1 - p_2 = \dfrac{32\,\mu\,l\,\bar{v}}{d^2}$, Poiseuille's form of the equation. (Arts. 63 and 64.)

The shear stress at the boundary is given by

$$\mu\,\frac{d\,u}{d\,r} = \frac{r}{2}\cdot\frac{d\,p}{d\,x} = \frac{a}{2}\cdot\frac{p_1 - p_2}{l}. \qquad (4)$$

---

[1] For a curve showing the variations in velocity for stream line flow through a two-inch pipe, see a paper by Morrow, "Proc. Roy. Soc.," vol. 76, 1905.

Art. 26.—Steady Flow through a Circular Tube, assuming Slip at the Boundaries.

If we assume slip at the boundaries of a circular tube, some assumption must be made as to the magnitude of the slip before any determination of the pressure fall along the tube can be made. Assuming, as seems rational, that the velocity at the boundaries is proportional to the tangential stress $u \left(\dfrac{d\,u}{d\,r} \right)_{r=a}$, we have if $u' =$ velocity at boundaries, then

$$u' \propto \mu \left(\frac{d\,u}{d\,r} \right)_{r=a} \text{ or } \quad u' = - k \left(\frac{d\,u}{d\,r} \right)_{r=a} = \frac{k\,a}{2\,\mu} \cdot \frac{d\,p}{d\,x} \quad \text{from (4), Art. 25.}$$

Using this to determine B in equation (1), Art. 25, and proceeding as before, we finally get

$$Q = \frac{\pi\,a^4}{8\,\mu} \left\{ 1 + \frac{4\,k}{a} \right\} \frac{p_1 - p_2}{l} \text{ cubic feet per second.}$$

Art. 27.—Genesis of Eddy Formation.

The reason for the sudden change from steady to sinuous motion in a pipe at the critical velocity is not clear. It has been suggested that the change takes place when the shear stress, accompanying the varying rate of flow across the pipe, becomes greater than that which the liquid is capable of withstanding. That this theory is untenable is clear if it be remembered that in viscous flow through a pipe the maximum shear occurs at the boundaries, and has the value $\dfrac{r}{2} \dfrac{d\,p}{d\,x}$ (p. 69). For the theory to hold, this shear stress must have the same value in any pipe for the initiation of eddy motion, so that $r \dfrac{d\,p}{d\,x}$ must be constant.

But $r \dfrac{d\,p}{d\,x} = - \dfrac{8\,\mu\,Q}{\pi\,r^3} = - \dfrac{8\,\mu\,\bar{v}}{r}$ (p. 69), and therefore the critical velocity should vary directly as the radius of the pipe. This result is directly opposed to the results of observations, experiments indicating that this velocity is inversely proportional to the radius.

The law governing the position of the critical point was inferred by Reynolds from a consideration of the general equations of motion for a viscous fluid.

Here the first equation of (9), p. 61, is

$$\rho\,X + \left(\frac{\partial\,p_{xx}}{\partial\,x} + \frac{\partial\,p_{yx}}{\partial\,y} + \frac{\partial\,p_{zx}}{\partial\,z} \right) = \rho \left\{ u \frac{\partial\,u}{\partial\,x} + v \frac{\partial\,u}{\partial\,y} + w \frac{\partial\,u}{\partial\,z} + \frac{\partial\,u}{\partial\,t} \right\}.$$

Also for continuity we have

$$\frac{\partial u}{\partial x} + \frac{\partial v}{\partial y} + \frac{\partial w}{\partial z} = 0$$

$$\therefore \quad u\frac{\partial u}{\partial x} + u\frac{\partial v}{\partial y} + u\frac{\partial w}{\partial z} = 0.$$

Adding this to the right-hand side of the above equation, this becomes

$$\rho \left\{ 2 u\frac{\partial u}{\partial x} + \left(v\frac{\partial u}{\partial y} + u\frac{\partial v}{\partial y} \right) + \left(w\frac{\partial u}{\partial z} + u\frac{\partial w}{\partial z} \right) + \frac{\partial u}{\partial t} \right\}$$

$$= \rho \left\{ \frac{\partial (u\,u)}{\partial x} + \frac{\partial (u\,v)}{\partial y} + \frac{\partial (u\,w)}{\partial z} + \frac{\partial u}{\partial t} \right\}$$

So that the equation may be written

$$\rho X + \left\{ \frac{\partial}{\partial x} (p_{xx} - \rho\,u\,u) + \frac{\partial}{\partial y} (p_{yx} - \rho\,u\,v) \right.$$
$$\left. + \frac{\partial}{\partial z} (p_{zx} - \rho\,u\,w) \right\} = \rho \frac{\partial u}{\partial t},$$

the left-hand side of this equation expressing the force producing the acceleration $\frac{\partial u}{\partial t}$, in the direction $O\,X$. Taking this to be the direction of mean flow in a tube, and neglecting the external force ρX, and $(p_{xx} - \rho\,u\,u)$, which simply marks the variation in the direction of flow, we are left with two terms which represent the variations in directions at right-angles to this. Since these involve the shear on parallel layers of the fluid, it is probable that the conditions involving steady or sinuous motion depend in some definite manner on these terms, and since, in a parallel tube, terms in y and z are similar and symmetrical if the effect of gravity be neglected, we may consider any one of these, and note how any variation in this may affect the conditions of flow.

Considering the term $\frac{\partial}{\partial y} (p_{yx} - \rho\,v\,u)$, substituting from equation (8), p. 60, this may be written

$$\frac{\partial}{\partial y} \left\{ \mu \left(\frac{\partial v}{\partial x} + \frac{\partial u}{\partial y} \right) - \rho\,v\,u \right\}.$$

The first of these terms involves the coefficient of viscosity μ, and is of the nature $\mu \times \frac{\text{velocity}}{\text{space}} = \frac{\mu V}{L}$, while the second is of the nature ρV^2. It was inferred then, that since the relative value of these terms probably determines the critical velocity, the latter will depend on the relation $\frac{\mu}{\rho V L}$.

Putting $L = \frac{d}{k}$ where d is the diameter of pipe, experiments were devoted to determining whether the critical velocity v_c was given by $\dfrac{k}{\rho}\dfrac{\mu}{\eta}$. These experiments conclusively justified the inference and led, as previously indicated (p. 54), to the formula

$$v_c = \frac{1}{b} \cdot \frac{P}{d}$$

where P is proportional to $\mu \div \rho$ and b is a numerical constant.

CHAPTER IV.

Bernoulli's Theorem — Elementary Proof — Experimental Verification — Applications — Converging Flow — Loss due to sudden change in Section of a Stream — Special Cases — Gradual Enlargement of Section — Change of Pressure across Stream Lines — Vortex Motion — Forced Vortex — Free Vortex — Compound Vortex.

ART. 28.

Bernoulli's Theorem.—The theorem expressed in the equation $\frac{p}{W} + \frac{V^2}{2\,g} + z =$ constant, is commonly known, from its discoverer, as Bernoulli's theorem.

It expresses the fact that the total energy of the fluid per lb. in any stream tube is constant. The three terms denote (1) the pressure energy per lb. $\frac{p}{W}$; (2) the kinetic energy per lb. $\frac{V^2}{2\,g}$; (3) the potential energy per lb. z, where z is the height above some datum to be fixed for any particular problem. The significance of the second and third of these terms is obvious, but some difficulty is often experienced in grasping the precise significance of the first, or pressure energy term. If p be the pressure intensity in pounds per square foot, and W the weight per cubic foot, the expression $\frac{p}{W}$ gives the height in feet of a column of water which would produce the statical pressure "p."

Now, if water is compressed in a cylinder fitted with a movable piston its pressure is enormously increased by an extremely small movement of the piston. Exactly the same thing would occur if some elastic solid, such as indiarubber, were compressed in the cylinder, and, just as with rubber, so with the water, the work done on the substance during compression would be returned during a slow retrograde motion of the piston.

Since, due to an increase in pressure of p lbs. per square foot, the proportional decrease in the volume of water is given by

$$\frac{\delta V}{V} = \frac{p}{31 \times 144 \times 10^4} = \frac{p}{K}$$

∴ Work expended per cubic foot in compressing water to this pressure $= \frac{p}{2} \cdot \frac{p}{K} = \frac{p^2}{2\,K}$, and this amount of work is stored in the water, in virtue

of its elasticity, and would be given out during expansion. If, in the
cylinder in question, the piston were fixed, and the water allowed to escape
through a small nozzle, the kinetic energy of the issuing jet would equal
the above expression, while the pressure would, with the removal of the
first few drops of water, fall to that of the atmosphere.

The amount of energy thus stored in the water per lb. in virtue of its
elasticity is $\dfrac{1}{2}\dfrac{p^2}{K\,W}$ foot lbs., and if water were a perfectly incompressible
fluid, so that $K = \infty$, would be zero. But this is not what is meant in
hydraulics by the pressure energy of water.

Suppose, however, the piston pressed home with a continuous pressure
of p lbs. per square foot, while the water escapes from the cylinder. The
work done on the water per cubic foot is now p foot lbs., and per
is $\dfrac{p}{W}$ foot-lbs.

The pressure of the water is exactly the same as before, but now, as
long as the piston is moving, the water is capable of doing work, in
virtue of this pressure, at the rate of $\dfrac{p}{W}$ foot lbs. per lb., and this is what
is meant by the pressure energy.

The idea of pressure energy only becomes applicable when we have a
continuous supply of water under pressure, as is the case, for example, in
the supply pipes of an hydraulic power company. Here a continuous
supply of pressure water is pumped into the mains, with a velocity which
is in general so low that the kinetic energy is negligible. The potential
energy is also in general negligible, so that it is in virtue of the pressure
energy alone that the water is capable of doing work. If, however, the
pumps are stopped and the accumulators disconnected, the withdrawal of
a very few cubic feet of water from the mains will reduce the pressure to
that corresponding to the statical head at any point, and the capacity for
doing work to almost zero.

Or consider an element of a stream tube of weight W, at a depth h
below the free surface, and at a height z above some datum. Its potential
energy is $W\,z$ foot lbs., while, in virtue of its position, its pressure energy
is $W\,h$, its pressure "p" being $W\,h$.

Removed from its connection with the surrounding mass of fluid, which
guarantees the permanence of the pressure conditions for a finite period,
the potential energy is unaltered, but its available pressure energy is
now practically zero—absolutely zero in the case of a perfectly incompressible fluid.

ART. 29.—ELEMENTARY PROOF OF BERNOULLI'S THEOREM.

Making the assumption that the fluid is non-viscous, and therefore exerts
ly normal forces on any bounding surface, the proof of this theorem is
sily deduced. Consider the element—length δs—of a stream tube in
ch a fluid, the only forces tending to produce motion of this element

ing its own weight and the normal pres-
res of the surrounding fluid (Fig. 34).
Let its cross sectional area at the top be
$ + \delta a$," and at the bottom "$a$," the pres-
re intensities at the top and bottom being
$- \delta p$ and p respectively. Let the average
rmal pressure on the sides of the element
q. Actually q will lie between p and
$- \delta p$.
This normal pressure will have an un-
.lanced component $q \cdot \delta a$ along the axis,
id, since the fluid is non-viscous, the only
:ect of this pressure in producing motion
the direction of the axis will be due to
is component.
Let the direction of the axis make an
igle θ with the vertical.

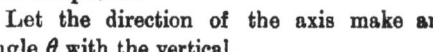

FIG. 34.

Then the magnitude of the resultant of forces on top and bottom faces of element, in the direction of its motion $= \begin{cases} (p - \delta p)(a + \delta a) - p a \\ = p \, \delta a - a \, \delta p. \end{cases}$

Resultant of normal pressures on sides of element in same direction $= - q \, \delta a.$

The only other force acting on the element is its weight, and the
solved part of this in the same direction

$$= \left\{ W \left(a + \frac{\delta a}{2} \right) \delta s \cos \theta \right\}$$

Resultant force in direction of motion $= p \, \delta a - a \, \delta p - q \, \delta a + W \left(a + \frac{\delta a}{2} \right) \delta s \cdot \cos \theta$

$$= \text{mass} \times \text{acceleration}$$

$$= \frac{W \left(a + \frac{\delta a}{2} \right) d s}{g} \times \frac{d v}{d t} \quad \text{where } v = \text{velocity} \text{ of element.}$$

Putting $q = p - k \, \delta p$, and neglecting small quantities of the second
der, we get

$$\frac{W a \, \delta s}{g} \cdot \frac{\delta v}{\delta t} = W a \, \delta s \cos \theta - a \, \delta p \qquad (1)$$

But $r = \dfrac{\delta s}{\delta t}$ and $\delta s \cos \theta = -\delta z$, z being measured vertically upw_, and δz being the difference of level of the two ends of the element.

$\therefore$ Equation (1) becomes $\dfrac{W}{g} \cdot v\, \delta v = -W\, \delta z - \delta p$

or $\qquad \dfrac{W}{g} r\, \delta v + W\, \delta z + \delta p = 0.$

When δs, δp, are indefinitely small we get, in the limit, on integra::

$$\dfrac{W}{g} \cdot \dfrac{v^2}{2} + W z + p = \text{constant}$$

or $\qquad \dfrac{v}{2g} + \dfrac{p}{W} + z = \text{constant.}$

ART. 30.

Since r is the velocity along a stream line, any attempt to apply this equation to the motion of a mass of fluid by taking v as the mean velocity of the mass will obviously lead to error unless the square of this mean velocity, multiplied by the mass itself, is equal to the sum of the squares of the various stream tube velocities, each multiplied by the mass contained in its own stream tube; and this is only true when all the stream lines are parallel and have the same velocity, and when, in consequence, no internal work is being performed against viscosity.

While this state of affairs is never accurately realised in the case of the motion of water in pipes or open channels, yet the equation may be made to apply to such cases by the introduction of a term involving losses of energy due to viscous resistance.

E.g., if the suffixes (1) and (2) refer to two successive positions of a particle of viscous fluid, we may say that

$$\dfrac{p_1}{W} + \dfrac{v_1^2}{2g} + Z_1 = \dfrac{p_2}{W} + \dfrac{v_2^2}{2g} + Z_2 + {}_1H_2,$$

where ${}_1H_2$ represents this loss of energy between the positions and (2).

Where we have turbulent motion between (1) and (2), this equation may still be usefully applied, ${}_1H_2$ now including the loss of energy in eddy formation. Applying this to the case of flow through a pipe or channel of varying area, it is usual to assume that the equation still holds when v_1 and v_2 are the mean velocities of flow in the direction of the axis at the two sections (1) and (2).[1]

[1] In the case of flow in a straight pipe with the transverse curve of velocities in the form of a semi-ellipse, the actual kinetic energy of flow parallel to the axis is about 2 per cent. greater than the value computed from the mean velocity, when the latter has a value of 5 feet per second.

Vhere the flow changes from steady to unsteady between (1) and (2)
term $_1H_2$ will then include the kinetic energy due to motion in
ections perpendicular to the axis of the pipe.

ART. 31.—EXPERIMENTAL VERIFICATION OF BERNOULLI'S THEOREM.

The apparatus shown (Fig. 35) consists of a horizontal passage having
allel vertical sides of plate glass, the first half forming a converging,
1 the second half a diverging channel. The passage connects two
ervoirs, A and B, and pressure tubes are erected at frequent intervals.

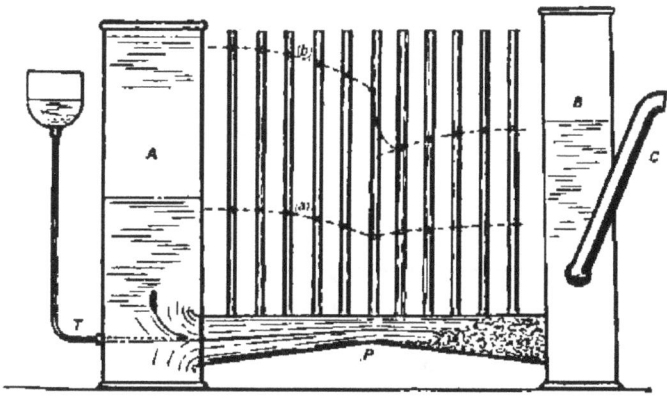

FIG. 35.

Water is fed into the tank A, which is of large area compared with the
ssage, and is led away by the overflow C. By suitable regulation of the
w into A, and of the height of the overflow C, the velocity of flow
·ough the channel and the pressure at any point may be regulated as
quired. Aniline dye may be introduced into the incoming stream of
ter by means of the capillary tube T.

At very low speeds the motion throughout the passage is steady, and
curve joining the tops of the pressure columns is as shown in (a).
any point to the right of the throat the pressure head will be less than
it at the corresponding point to the left, because of viscous resistance,
that, since the velocity head is the same at the two points, the total head
less on the right.

As the velocity is increased, the first indication of unsteady motion is

provided by an occasional eddying of such colour bands as get below
horizontal through the lowest point of the throat.

The velocity at which this occurs depends on the angle of diver.
of the sides of the passage. As the velocity is increased this unst
motion extends to the whole of the water in the diverging portion of
passage, the motion in the converging part being uniformly ste
The pressure curve now appears as shown in (b), and is discontinuo
the throat.

On plotting the energy curve, $\frac{p}{w} + \frac{v^2}{2g} + z = y$, the curve show

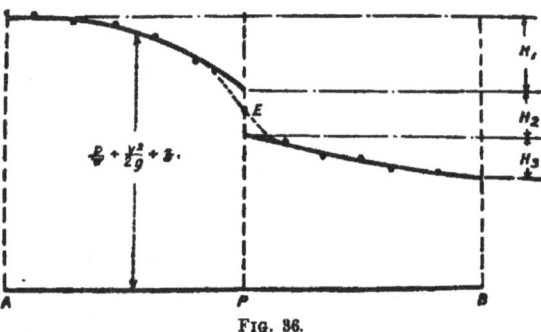

FIG. 86.

Fig. 86 is obtained, and shows very clearly the magnitude of
various losses.

Drawing smooth curves between the plotted points from A to P
from P to B, it will be noted that the observed point E at P lie
neither of these curves. In the figure, H_1 represents loss of head, du
viscous resistance between A and P: H_2, the loss due to eddy forma
at the throat; and H_3, the loss due to viscous resistance and to
formation between P and B. Evidently from the position of E and
form of the curve P B, almost the whole energy of eddy formatio
absorbed at and within a very small distance of the throat. With sp
below the critical velocity $H_2 = O$ and $H_1 = H_3$ (approx.).

With speeds exceeding the critical, H_3 becomes less or greater t
H_1, depending on the velocity, as, with fairly low velocities, the ed
formed at the throat die out to some extent before reaching B, th
kinetic energy being transformed into available pressure energy and th
reducing H_3. At suitable velocities indeed H_3 may be negative, indicat

,hat the energy rendered available by the dying out of eddy motion is more than equal to that absorbed in overcoming viscous resistance after the throat is passed.[1]

With high velocities, however, the process of eddy formation goes on after the throat is passed, part of the available pressure energy being expended to this end, and H_3 is in consequence increased. At a suitable velocity, a balance is obtained between the energy absorbed from P to B in eddy formation and that made re-available by the dying out of eddies, and in this case H_3 will equal H_1.

In every case, however, the head loss $(H_2 + H_3)$ is greater than H_1, and experiments show very clearly that, while it is possible to change pressure head to velocity head without appreciable loss of energy, it is impossible to change velocity head to pressure head by the reverse operation without loss, except at velocities too low to be considered in practice.

This is one important factor in the difference between the efficiencies of centrifugal pumps and turbines.

ART. 32.—FLOW IN CONVERGING CHANNELS. RADIAL FLOW.

Where flow takes place in a converging channel, the motion is steady, and, neglecting viscosity,[2] the energy throughout any stream tube is constant, so that

$$\frac{p}{W} + \frac{v^2}{2g} + z = \text{constant.}$$

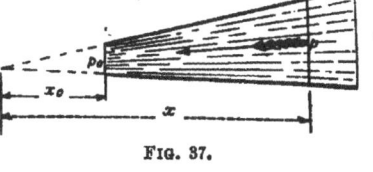

FIG. 37.

But for continuity of flow, if $A =$ area of channel at some point where the velocity is v,

$$A v = \text{constant} = A_0 v_0$$

where A_0 and v_0 are the area and velocity at some point distant x_0 from the point of convergence of the boundaries (Fig. 37).

Putting $A = k x$ we have $v = \dfrac{x_0 v_0}{x}$, and if z is constant, i.e., if the stream lines are horizontal,

$$\frac{p}{W} + \frac{x_0^2 v_0^2}{2 g x^2} = c \qquad (1)$$

[1] Since the velocity across the section is unequal, the K. E. ($\Sigma(m v^2)$) is greater than $M v^2$ where v is the mean velocity. Thus the equalisation of the velocities tends to increase the apparent, though not the actual, K. E.

[2] For the viscous resistance in a converging channel, see "Phil. Mag.," July, 1909, p. 25.

$$\therefore \frac{p}{W} = c - \frac{x_0^2 \, v_0^2}{2 \, g \, x^2}.$$

But from (2) $\frac{p_0}{W} = c - \frac{v_0^2}{2 \, g}$

$$\therefore \quad c = \frac{p_0}{W} + \frac{v_0^2}{2 \, g}$$

$$\therefore \frac{p - p_0}{W} = \frac{v_0^2}{2 \, g} \left\{ 1 - \frac{x_0^2}{x^2} \right\} \text{ feet of water.}$$

This applies to flow through a converging channel having parallel upper and lower boundaries and to the case of (inward) radial flow towards a centre. The result gives the fall in pressure between two points radially distant x and x_0 from the origin, and may be applied to flow in an inward flow radial turbine. Since with outward flow between diverging boundaries the motion is unsteady, Bernoulli's equation ceases to hold, so that the formula is inapplicable to the case of a radial (outward flow) turbine.[1]

In the case of flow through a circular converging pipe or nozzle $A = k \, x^2$.

$$\therefore v = \frac{x_0^2 \, v_0}{x^2}, \text{ and assuming } s \text{ constant}$$

we have
$$\frac{p}{W} + \frac{x_0^4 \, v_0^2}{2 \, g \, x^4} = c.$$

As before
$$c = \frac{p_0}{W} + \frac{v_0^2}{2 \, g}$$

$$\therefore \frac{p - p_0}{W} = \frac{v_0^2}{2 \, g} \left\{ 1 - \frac{x_0^4}{x^4} \right\} = \frac{v_0^2}{2 \, g} \left\{ 1 - \frac{A_0^2}{A^2} \right\}.$$

It follows that if a pipe of area A suffer a contraction of section to a and if p_A and p_a are the corresponding pressures and V_A the velocity at entrance to the pipe

$$\frac{p_A - p_a}{W} = \frac{V_A^2}{2 \, g} \left\{ \left(\frac{A}{a} \right)^2 - 1 \right\} \text{ feet.}$$

$$\therefore V_A = \sqrt{ \frac{2 \, g \, (p_A - p_a)}{W \left\{ \left(\frac{A}{a} \right)^2 - 1 \right\} } } \text{ f. s.}$$

This enables the velocity of flow and the discharge to be obtained from a measurement of $\frac{p_A - p_a}{W}$, the difference of pressures in feet of water at

[1] Steady motion is, however, possible with radial outward flow without solid boundaries. This is shown when two equal and steady vertical jets impinge directly on each other. Here a circular disc of water with radial outward flow and having perfectly steady stream-line motion, as may be shown by the introduction of colour bands, is produced.

he entrance and throat of the pipe. The Venturi meter (Art. 196) depends directly on this principle for its action.

An interesting phenomenon accompanying radial outward flow is noticed if a plate on which a jet is impinging normally be brought gradually nearer to the orifice, until a point is reached where the escaping stream touches both plate and nozzle (Fig. 38).

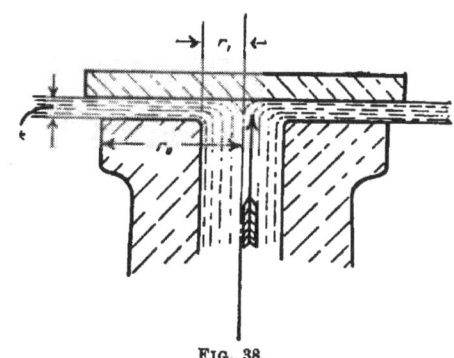

Let r_1, p_1, v_1, a_1, be the radius, pressure, velocity, and area of the issuing stream at the exit from the orifice and at the commencement of its flow between the plate and the nozzle.

FIG. 38.

Let r_0, p_0, v_0, and a_0 represent similar quantities at the point of escape of the stream into the atmosphere.

Then

$$\begin{cases} a_1 = 2\,\pi\,r_1\,t, \text{ where } t = \text{thickness of the escaping stream.} \\ a_0 = 2\,\pi\,r_0\,t. \\ v_0 = v_1\dfrac{a_1}{a_0} = \dfrac{v_1\,r_1}{r_0}. \\ p_0 = \text{atmospheric pressure.} \end{cases}$$

Neglecting frictional and eddy losses between (1) and (0), we have

$$\frac{p_1}{W}+\frac{v_1^2}{2\,g} = \frac{p_0}{W}+\frac{v_0^2}{2\,g} = \frac{p_0}{W}+\frac{v_1^2}{2\,g}\cdot\frac{r_1^2}{r_0^2}$$

$$\therefore\ \frac{p_0 - p_1}{W} = \frac{v_1^2}{2\,g}\left\{1-\left(\frac{r_1}{r_0}\right)^2\right\} \qquad (1)$$

Since r_1 is less than r_0, $p_0 - p_1$ is positive, and the pressure at (1) is less than atmospheric. It follows that since the pressure between ( ) and (0) is everywhere less than atmospheric, while that on the corresponding portion of the outer face of the plate is atmospheric, there will be a resultant force tending to force the plate up to the orifice.

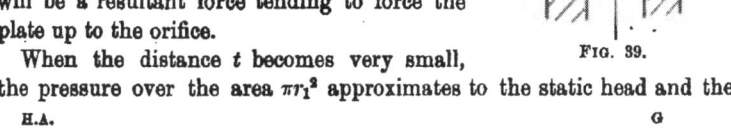

FIG. 39.

When the distance t becomes very small, the pressure over the area πr_1^2 approximates to the static head and the plate is forced away from the orifice, so that an intermittent action is set up, the plate vibrating to and from the orifice, but never being driven far away.

The ball-nozzle (Fig. 39), designed to give a thin evenly distributed discharge from a fire hydrant, acts on exactly the same principle.

Here a cage is fitted to prevent the loss of the ball on the first impact of the jet.

Art. 33.—Loss due to the Sudden Enlargement of Cross Section of a Stream.

Whenever the cross section of a pipe or channel increases abruptly, the water, on passing the enlargement, is thrown into a state of unsteady

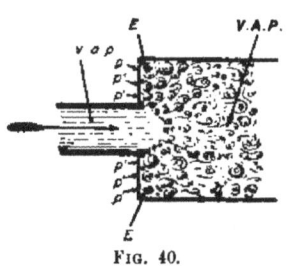

FIG. 40.

motion, with a consequent loss of available energy. If the mean velocities before and after passing the enlargement are known the equations of momentum may be applied to determine the magnitude of this loss.

For, consider the case of flow through a horizontal pipe (Fig. 40), suffering a sudden change of area from a to A.

Let p and v be the pressure and mean velocity immediately before the change of section.

Let P and V be the pressure and mean velocity in the large pipe when the motion has steadied after impact.

Let p' be the mean pressure on the end of the pipe at EE.

Neglecting frictional effects, which will be small, the forces tending to produce a change of momentum in the direction of flow between the sections at which p and P are measured are:—

(1) the pressure over the area at $p = pa$.[1]

(2) „   „   „   „   „ $EE = p'(A - a)$.

(3) „   „   „   „   „ at $P = PA$.

∴ The force producing change of momentum in the direction of motion $= \{p\,a + p'(A - a) - P\,A\}$ lbs.   (1)

This must equal the change of momentum per second in the direction of this force

$$= \frac{W\,A\,V^2}{g} - \frac{W\,a\,v^2}{g} = \frac{W}{g}\{A\,V^2 - a\,v^2\}.$$ (2)

---

[1] The pressure p being measured at the mean depth of the section.

The assumption is commonly made that the pressure p' over the face EE is uniform, and is sensibly equal to p. Although the actual distribution and magnitude of this pressure probably vary with the ratio of the areas and relative position of the two branches, and with the velocity, we have not sufficient experimental data to frame any definite law connecting the two. The above assumption, however, appears to be fairly well justified by the results of such experiments as are to hand, and making use of this we have, on combining equations (1) and (2)

$$(p - P)\,A = \frac{W}{g}\{A\,V^2 - a\,v^2\} \tag{3}$$

Also for continuity of flow $A\,V = a\,v \therefore v = \dfrac{A\,V}{a}$

$$\therefore \qquad (p - P)\,A = \frac{W}{g}\left\{1 - \frac{A}{a}\right\} A\,V^2. \tag{4}$$

If now $H' = $ loss of head due to shock at the enlargement, we have

$$\frac{p}{W} + \frac{v^2}{2\,g} = \frac{P}{W} + \frac{V^2}{2\,g} + H' \tag{5}$$

$$\therefore \qquad \frac{p - P}{W} + \frac{V^2 A^2}{2\,a^2\,g} - \frac{V^2}{2\,g} = H' \tag{6}$$

Substituting for $\dfrac{p - P}{W}$ from (4) we get

$$H' = \frac{V^2}{2\,g}\left(\frac{A}{a} - 1\right)^2 \tag{7}$$

$$= \frac{v^2}{2\,g}\left(1 - \frac{a}{A}\right)^2 \tag{8}$$

$$= \frac{(v - V)^2}{2\,g} \tag{9}$$

Writing m for $\dfrac{A}{a}$, relations (7) and (8) become:—

$$H' = \frac{V^2}{2\,g}(m - 1)^2 \tag{10}$$

$$= \frac{v^2}{2\,g}\left(1 - \frac{1}{m}\right)^2 \tag{11}$$

Recent experiments by the author[1] indicate that the percentage loss increases slightly with the ratio of enlargement, and in pipes with the same ratio of enlargement is greater the smaller the pipe.

Denoting the ratio of enlargement by m, and the smaller diameter by d, the loss at a sudden enlargement for values of m between 2 and 12,

[1] "Trans. Roy. Soc. Edinburgh," vol. 48, 1911, p. 97.

and for pipe diameters ranging from ·50 inch to 6 inches, can be expressed. within narrow limits, by the relationship—

$$\text{loss of head} = \frac{102\cdot5 + \cdot25m - 2\cdot0d}{100}\left\{\frac{(v_1 - v_2)^2}{2g}\right\}\cdot\text{feet.}$$

The following table shows the results obtained by the use of the formula against those experimentally obtained :—

Diameters of pipes.	Value of m.	Loss expressed as percentage of $\frac{(v_1 - v_2)^2}{2g}$.	
		Experimental.	By formula.
·65 to 2·15 inches	10·96	103·5	103·9
·50 „ 1·5 „	9·0	102·8	103·7
1·0 „ 3·0 „	9·0	102·1	102·8
1·5 „ 3·0 „	4·0	101·7	100·5
2·0 „ 3·0 „	2·25	99·2	99·1
3·0 „ 6·0 „	4·0	97·5	97·5
4·0 „ 6·0 „	2·25	92 (approx.)	95·0

ART. 34.—LOSS IN PIPES AND PASSAGES WITH A GRADUALLY INCREASING CROSS-SECTION.

The loss of head accompanying a gradual enlargement of section would naturally be expected to be less than that experienced at a sudden enlargement of section between the same initial and final areas. T· determine the extent to which this conclusion is justified a somewha: extended series of experiments on such pipes was recently carried out by the author.[1]

Circular Pipes with Uniformly Diverging Boundaries.—Calling θ the angl· of conicity of a pipe, the following table, as also Fig. 41, shows the mea: of the results obtained.

Loss of Energy expressed as a Percentage of $\frac{(v_1 - v_2)^2}{2g}$, the Theoretical Loss at a Sudden Change of Velocity from v_1 to v_2.

Value of θ	180°.	90°.	60°.	40°.	20°.	10°.
Pipe diameters in inches. ·65 to 2·15	103·5	...	...	...	...	...
·50 „ 1·50	102·8	102·6	102·8	82·0	45·0	16·6
1·0 „ 3·0	102·1	104·1	101·3	80·8	44·0	...
1·5 „ 3·0	101·7	111·1	120·5	101·7	42·5	17·5
2·0 „ 3·0	99·2	112·1	...	88·7	41·9	18·6

[1] " Proc. Roy. Soc. A.," vol. 83, 1910. " Trans. Roy. Soc. Edinburgh," vol. 48, 1911, p. 97.

From these it appears that as θ is diminished from 180° the loss increases, attains a maximum value for some value of θ in the neighbourhood of 65°, and afterwards diminishes rapidly with θ until θ is about 5° 30′. This value gives a minimum loss of approximately 13·5 per cent. Any further diminution in θ is accompanied by an increased loss owing to the large value of the wall friction in pipes of the comparatively great length accompanying such small values of θ. The value of θ giving rise to the

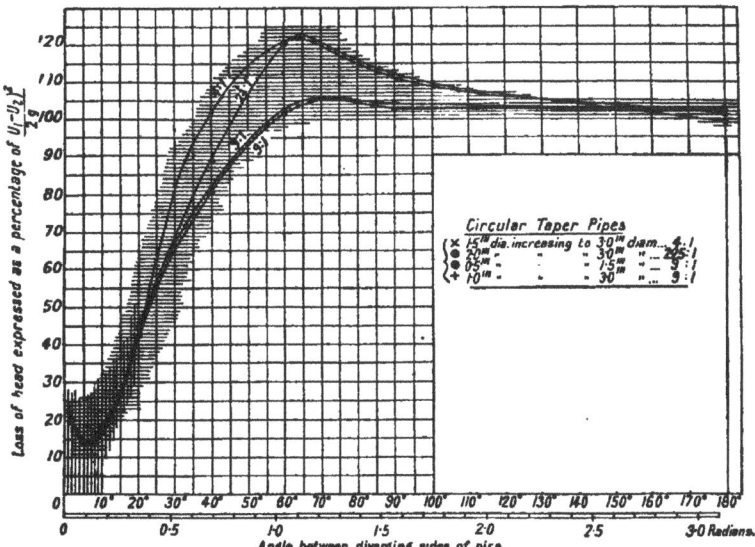

FIG. 41.—Loss of Head in Circular Taper Pipes.

same loss as is experienced with a sudden change of section, varies from 41° to 60°, being slightly greater for a given area-ratio the larger the pipes, and, for a given mean diameter, increasing in an irregular manner with the area-ratio. Its mean value over the range of ratios considered is approximately 50°, and where, in the design of hydraulic machinery, it is necessary for this value to be exceeded, a sudden enlargement of section gives a more efficient transformation of energy than does a uniformly tapering pipe. For values of θ between 7·5° and 35° the loss may be expressed with a fair degree of accuracy by the relationships—

$$\text{loss} = \cdot 0110 \; \theta^{1\cdot 22} \frac{(r_1 - r_2)^2}{2g} \text{ feet, where } \theta \text{ is in degrees,}$$

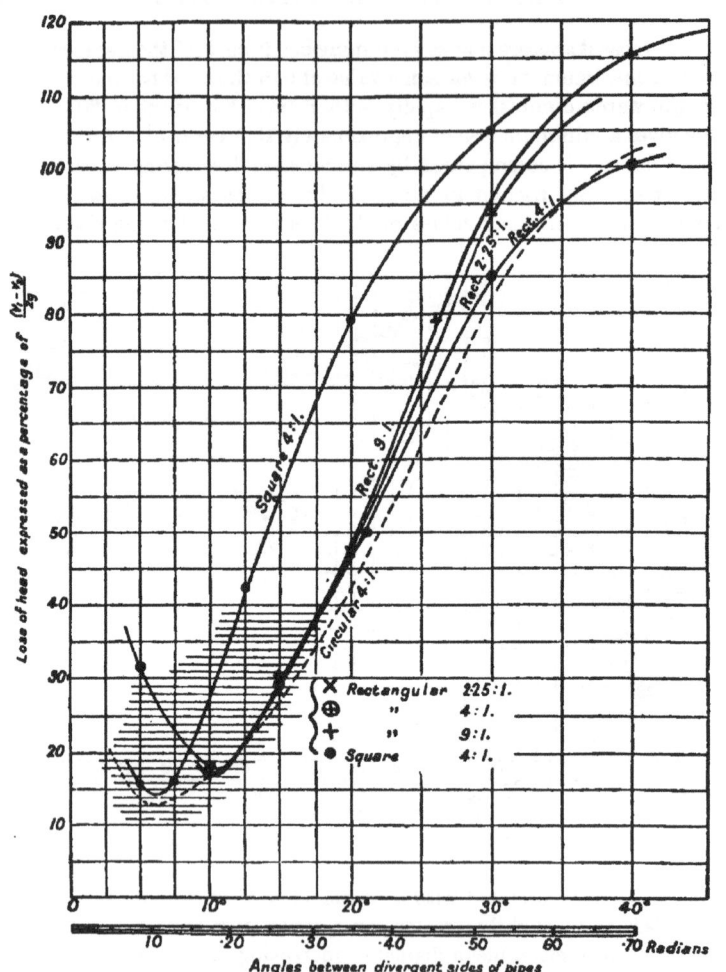

FIG. 42.—Percentage Loss of Head in Straight Taper Pipes of Square and Rectangular Section.

or

$$\text{loss} = 3\cdot50 \left(\tan\frac{\theta}{2}\right)^{1\cdot22} \frac{(v_1 - v_3)^2}{2g} \text{ feet.}$$

This latter relationship becomes of importance in the design of trumpet-shaped pipes to give a minimum loss of energy.

Rectangular Pipes with Uniformly Diverging Boundaries.—Three sets of rectangular pipes were examined, these having one pair of sides parallel and 1·329 inch apart in every case. The areas of the small and of the large ends of these pipes were, in the case of the pipes having area-ratios of 4 : 1 and 9 : 1, identical with those of the circular taper pipes having the same ratios of enlargement.

The results of the means of the experiments on these pipes are plotted in Fig. 42. From these it appears that the percentage loss is very approximately the same for all ratios of enlargement between 2·25 : 1 and 9 : 1 for values of θ between 10° and 40°, and that it varies but little with the dimensions of the pipe. The minimum loss is obtained when θ is approximately 11°, the percentage loss under these circumstances being about 17·5 per cent. As θ is increased the loss increases rapidly, and attains a value of 100 per cent. when θ is between 31° and 40°, the value of this critical angle being less with the smaller ratios of enlargement and with the pipes having the smaller mean sectional areas. For values of θ between 10° and 35°, the only values of any use in practice, the loss can be expressed with a fair degree of accuracy by the relationships—

$$\text{loss} = ·0072\ \theta^{1·40}\ \frac{(v_1 - v_2)^2}{2g}\ \text{feet, where } \theta \text{ is in degrees.}$$

$$= 5·30 \left(\tan\frac{\theta}{2}\right)^{1·40}\frac{(v_1 - v_2)^2}{2g}\ \text{feet.}$$

Experiments on rectangular pipes having an enlargement ratio of 9 : 1, and having θ respectively 40°, 50°, and 90°, showed corresponding losses of 115, 122·3, and 119 per cent. This indicates a maximum loss when θ is approximately 70°, or when it has sensibly the same value as gives maximum loss in the corresponding circular pipe.

Pipes of Square Section with Uniformly Diverging Boundaries.—Five pipes, having a smaller section 1·329 inch square and a larger section 2·658 inches square and with θ respectively 5°, 7·5°, 12·5°, 20°, and 30°, were examined, the results being plotted in Fig. 42. The percentage loss is a minimum for a value θ in the neighbourhood of 6°, practically the same as for a circular pipe, and has a value of about 14·5 per cent.

Trumpet-Shaped Pipes.—From à priori reasoning it would appear that when the initial and final areas and the length of a pipe are fixed, the loss of head may be reduced by making the pipe trumpet shaped, the angle of divergence of its sides being least where the velocity is greatest and vice versâ. To test this point several pipes were examined, these being designed so as to make either the retardation $\left(\dfrac{d\ v}{d\ t}\right)$ constant, the change of velocity per unit length of pipe $\left(\dfrac{d\,v}{d\,x}\right)$ constant, or the loss

head per unit length of pipe $\dfrac{d(v^2)}{d\,x}$, constant. The latter pipes were foun:
to be the more efficient, the saving, over a straight taper pipe of th
same length ranging from 20 per cent. to 60 per cent. and being great.
the shorter the pipe.

In a rectangular pipe of length l, satisfying this condition and havin
one pair of sides parallel, if the half-breadths at the small and the lar;
ends are respectively y_1 and y_2, the half-breadth y, at a distance x from t:
small end is given by

$$\frac{1}{\sqrt[4]{y}} = \frac{1}{\sqrt[4]{y_1}} - \frac{x}{l}\left(\frac{1}{\sqrt[4]{y_1}} - \frac{1}{\sqrt[4]{y_2}}\right), \quad [1]$$

while in a circular pipe whose smaller and larger radii are r_1 and r_2, th
radius at a distance x from the small end is given by

$$\frac{1}{\sqrt[4]{r^5}} = \frac{1}{\sqrt[4]{r_1^5}} - \frac{x}{l}\left(\frac{1}{\sqrt[4]{r_1^5}} - \frac{1}{\sqrt[4]{r_2^5}}\right).$$

Where the length of pipe is great, or the ratio of areas small, the
curves thus formed may, at the smaller end of the pipe, diverge at an
angle less than that ($6°$ in a circular pipe and $11°$ in a rectangular pipe
giving minimum loss, and in such a case the pipe would be made to

---

[1] The loss in a straight taper pipe whose angle of divergence is θ is proportional to $\delta\,(v)^2$ an:
very sensibly to θ^n or to $\left(\tan\dfrac{\theta}{2}\right)^n$ where $n = 1.40$ for a rectangular pipe. Hence in a leng:
δx of a trumpet-shaped rectangular pipe, over which the mean angle is θ, the loss :
presumably proportional to $\delta\,(v)^2\left(\dfrac{d\,y}{d\,x}\right)^{1.40}$ or to $\dfrac{d\,(v^2)}{d\,x}\cdot\left(\dfrac{d\,y}{d\,x}\right)^{1.40}\cdot\delta x$ where y is the half
breadth of the pipe and where x measures the distance of the element under consideratio:
from some datum point on the axis of the pipe.

But in such a pipe $v^2 \propto y^{-2}$,

$$\therefore \text{ loss in length } \delta x = \frac{d}{d x}(y^{-2})\left(\frac{d y}{d x}\right)^{1.4}\delta x.$$

For this to be constant per unit length

$$\frac{d}{d x}(y^{-2})\left(\frac{d y}{d x}\right)^{1.4} = \text{constant},$$

or

$$y^{-3}\left(\frac{d y}{d x}\right)^{2.4} = \text{constant},$$

$$\therefore \frac{d y}{d x} = k\,y^{1.25},$$

$$\therefore \int\frac{d y}{y^{1.25}} = \int_{x_1}^{x} k\,d x,$$

$$\therefore y_1^{-.25} - y^{-.25} = K\,(x - x_1).$$

If the origin from which x is measured be taken at the small end of the pipe, where th diverge uniformly at this best angle up to a point where its straight sides would intersect the calculated curved sides.

If, on the other hand, the length of pipe is small or the ratio of areas large, the calculated curves may, towards the larger end of the pipe, diverge at an angle greater than that giving a loss equal to that at a sudden enlargement.

In such a case a more efficient pipe is obtained by enlarging the pipe to its final section by a sudden enlargement at the point at which the angle of divergence becomes equal to this critical value.

A still more efficient pipe is obtained if, from the point at which the angle of divergence becomes equal to the critical angle, the section is enlarged gradually, the best angle of divergence being found to vary but slightly in such circumstances and in any cases likely to be found in practice, being approximately 20° for a rectangular pipe, and 10° for a circular pipe.

Compound Pipes and Passages.

The loss of head in a pipe whose section increases gradually from A_1 to A_3, and which then suffers a sudden enlargement of area to A_2 (Fig. 43), is approximately equal to the sum of the separate losses which would be experienced in the taper portion of the pipe and at the sudden enlargement,

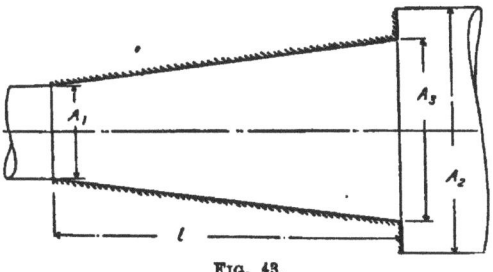

FIG. 43.

if these were independent of each other. By reducing the angle of

half-breadth is y_1, $x_1 = 0$, and if l be the length of the pipe, and if y_2 be the half-breadth at the larger end, $x_2 - x_1 = l$, and

$$K = \frac{1}{l}\left\{ y_1^{-\cdot 25} - y_2^{-\cdot 25}\right\}.$$

$$\therefore y^{-\cdot 25} = y_1^{-\cdot 25} - \frac{x}{l}\left(y_1^{-\cdot 25} - y_2^{-\cdot 25}\right)$$

In a circular pipe $n = 1\cdot22$, while $r^2 \propto y^{-4}$, so that

$$\frac{d}{dx}(y^{-4})\left(\frac{dy}{dx}\right)^{1\cdot22} = \text{constant.}$$

Proceeding as above, this gives

$$y_1^{-1\cdot 25} - y^{-1\cdot 25} = K(x - x_1),$$

and on the same assumptions as before

$$K = \frac{1}{l}\left\{ y_1^{-1\cdot 25} - y_2^{-1\cdot 25}\right\}.$$

divergence of the first portion of such a tube, the sudden enlarge ment of section and the accompanying loss is made greater, but the loss in the diverging portion is reduced in a double degree, since not only is the numerical coefficient expressing such loss as a percentage of $(v_1-v_3)^2/2g$ diminished, but A_3 is diminished at the same time, and thus the factor v_1-v_3 is also diminished. A diminution in the angle of divergence therefore causes a rapid diminution in this portion of the loss, which may, or may not, be counter-balanced by the loss at the sudden enlargement of section. Owing to the comparatively low velocities at the large end of the pipe, however, except in pipes whose length is comparatively very short, and whose ratio of enlargement is small, this latter loss is comparatively small and the total loss is a minimum with a pipe—straight or curved—whose angle of divergence— actual or effective—is little, if any, greater than that giving minimum loss in the diverging portion of the pipe alone.

It thus becomes possible to design a pipe—often with a considerable reduction in length—in which the boundaries are straight, and in which the loss is still appreciably less than in a straight taper pipe giving the full enlargement of section with the best possible value of θ.

The total loss of head in such a pipe (shown in Fig. 43) is theoretically equal to

$$K\frac{(v_1-v_3)^2}{2g}+\frac{(v_3-v_2)^2}{2g}\text{ feet}$$

where K is obtained from the curves of Figs. 41 and 42. As $\dfrac{v_3}{v_1}=\dfrac{A_1}{A_3}$ while $\dfrac{v_2}{v_1}=\dfrac{A_1}{A_2}$, where A represents the corresponding area this becomes

$$\frac{v_1^2}{2g}\left\{K\left(1-\frac{A_1}{A_3}\right)^2+\left(\frac{A_1}{A_3}-\frac{A_1}{A_2}\right)^2\right\}\text{ feet,}$$

or

$$\frac{(v_1-v_2)^2}{2g}\left[\left(\frac{A_2}{A_2-A_1}\right)^2\left\{K\left(1-\frac{A_1}{A_3}\right)^2+\left(\frac{A_1}{A_3}-\frac{A_1}{A_2}\right)^2\right\}\right]\text{ feet.}$$

In a rectangular pipe whose breadth increases uniformly from b_1 to b_3 in a length L,

$$b_3=b_1+2L\tan\frac{\theta}{2}$$

$$=b_1+L\theta\text{ (approximately) where }\theta\text{ is in angular measure,}$$

so that $A_3=A_1+L\theta$, and the above expression becomes

loss =

$$\frac{(v_1-v_2)^2}{2g}\left[\left(\frac{b_2}{b_2-b_1}\right)^2\left\{K\left(1-\frac{b_1}{b_1+L\theta}\right)^2+\left(\frac{b_1}{b_1+L\theta}+\frac{b_1}{b_2}\right)^2\right\}\right] \qquad (1)$$

'he corresponding expression for circular pipes is

$$\text{loss} = \frac{(v_1 - v_2)^2}{2g} \left[\left(\frac{r_2^2}{r_2^2 - r_1^2} \right) \left\{ K \left(1 - \frac{r_1^2}{\left(r_1 + \frac{L\,\theta}{2} \right)^2} \right)^2 + \left(\frac{r_1^2}{\left(r_1 + \frac{L\,\theta}{2} \right)^2} - \frac{r_1^2}{r_2^2} \right)^2 \right\} \right]$$

(2)

Differentiating these expressions with respect to θ, the value of θ and
ence of b_3 or r_3, giving minimum loss of head, may be obtained. As,
owever, K varies with θ, the resulting expression becomes extremely
umbersome, and the best value is more easily obtained by trial of a few
alues of θ and the corresponding values of K. Handled in this way a
olution is readily obtained.

The following table shows values of θ giving minimum loss of head in
uch a pipe, along with the corresponding loss of head in the pipe, and
ⁿ a straight taper pipe of the same length and with the same initial
nd final areas.

	Ratio of areas.	Value of θ giving minimum loss.	Length of pipe (inches).	Value of θ in straight taper pipe of same length.	Loss of head expressed as a percentage of $\frac{(v_1 - v_2)^2}{2g}$	Loss of head expressed as a percentage of the loss in straight taper pipe.
Rectangular Pipes.	9 : 1 {Sections ·59 inch × 1·329 inch and 5·315 inches × 1·329 inch}	10° 20′ 10° 40′ 11° 00′ 11° 45′	17·95 8·81 6·49 4·08	15° · 30° 40° 60°	16·2 15·3 16·2 20·3	54·9 16·0 14·2 ...
	4 : 1 {1·329 inch square to 1·329 inch × 5·315 inches}	10° 20′ 11° 00′ 12° 00′ 12° 45′ 15° 30′	15·15 11·30 7·45 5·48 3·45	15° 20° 30° 40° 60°	15·6 15·3 18·2 23·0 29·4	53·8 32·6 22·0 21·1 ...
	2·25 : 1 {1·329 inch square to 1·329 inch × 2·99 inches}	10° 40′ 13° 20′ 15° 40′	6·30 3·10 2·29	15° 30° 40°	15·2 22·8 28·2	51·5 26·8 25·2
Circular Pipes.	9 : 1 ·50 inch diam. to 1·50 inch diam.	7° 10′ 11° 00′	3·80 1·87	15° 30°	13·6 18·2	52·3 27·2
	4 : 1 1·50 inch diam. to 3·0 inches diam.	7° 00′ 13° 30′	8·57 2·80	10° 30°	12·7 20·8	73·5 22·2
	2·25 : 1 2·0 inch diam. to 3·0 inches diam.	7° 00′ 15° 00′	5·71 1·87	10° 30°	13·4 24·3	72·5 35·2

By this method of construction the loss may be reduced in favourable
ircumstances to about 90 per cent. (in rectangular pipes) and to about

96 per cent. (in circular pipes) of the minimum possible loss in
uniformly tapering pipe undergoing the full enlargement section. In
designing the pipe
from A_1 to A_3 with
curved boundaries, the
loss may be still further
reduced. In the
majority of cases
occurring in practice,
however, the addi-
tional trouble of cal-
culation and cost of
template will not be
counterbalanced by

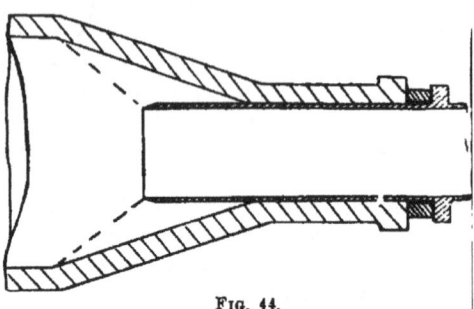

Fig. 44.

the slight increase in efficiency which they render possible.

Effect of projecting Smaller Pipe into Space bounded by Diverging Walls—
For the purpose of examining this effect, a thin sleeve of inter
diameter ·90 inch and external diameter 1·0 inch was prepared and use
inside the various 1-inch pipes, as shown in Fig. 44.

The results of the experiments are as follow :—

Percentage Loss of Head.			
Value of θ . . .	40°	60°	90°
Taper pipe without sleeve . . .	80·8°/₀	101·3°/₀	104·1°/₀
Projecting pipe with diameters ·90 inch and 3 inches . .	Pipe projecting— ·50 inch . 98·0°/₀ 1·00 inch . 108·0°/₀	Pipe projecting— ·25 inch . 104·5°/₀ ·50 inch . 107·2°/₀ 1·00 inch . 112·0°/₀	Pipe projecting - ·25 inch . 107·7

In every case the effect of the projection is to increase the loss, the
effect being greater the greater the length of the projection and also the
less the angle of divergence of the conical sides. The loss is, in fact,
greater in every case than would be experienced if the pipe walls were
tapered off from the extremity of the projecting pipe, as shown by the
dotted lines in the sketch

ART. 35.—Loss due to Sudden Contraction of Area of a Stream.

When water flowing along a channel or through a pipe meets with a dden contraction of the area of the pipe, as shown in Fig. 45, we also t a loss of energy which is due, not directly to the contraction of the ream, but to the subsequent re- llargement which always takes place. The stream, after passing the con- action, suffers a further diminution area, and for a short distance ils to fill the pipe, afterwards re- :panding as shown.[1] Up to the con-

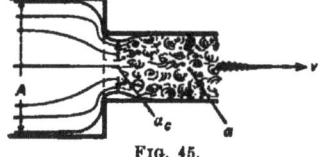

FIG. 45.

acted section the loss is solely that due to simple viscous resistance.

If A represents the larger stream area

,, a ,,   ,, smaller   ,,

,, a_c ,,   ,, *vena contracta*

', v and v_c representing the velocities at these sections, the loss of energy ue to this enlargement is approximately

$$\frac{(v_c - v)^2}{2\,g} \text{ ft. lbs. per lb.}$$

Writing C_c for $\frac{a_c}{a}$, the above may be expressed in the form

$$\frac{(v_c - v)^2}{2\,g} = \left(\frac{1}{C_c} - 1\right)^2 \frac{v^2}{2\,g} = F\,\frac{v^2}{2\,g}$$

Here F is called the coefficient of hydraulic resistance, and can only be etermined experimentally.

A series of experiments carried out by the author on the apparatus hown in Fig. 45, having a value of $m = 10.96$, and having pipe diameters f 2·15 inches and ·65 inch, gave a mean value of ·600 for C_c, over a ange of values of v from 1·35 to 8·69 feet per second. The value iminished from ·610 with the lowest to ·587 with the highest of these elocities. Experiments on a 6-inch pipe, contracting respectively to 3-inch and to a 4-inch pipe, give in the former case a value of $F = 7.87$ ($C_c = ·595$), and in the latter case $F = 1.0$ ($C_c = ·692$).

If C_c has the value ·586, the loss $= ·50\,\frac{v^2}{2\,g}$. This is approximately he value of C_c, where the area A is so large as not to affect the stream

[1] This action may occur even though the pipe is full of water, the space shown empty in ig. 46 being now occupied by dead water which takes no part in the flow through the pipe.

line production, and gives the loss usually found where a pipe is led ‹
of a reservoir by means of a sharp-edged junction.

ART. 36.—LOSS CAUSED BY A DIAPHRAGM IN A PARALLEL PIPE.

Much work in this direction has been done by Weisbach, to whom ·
following experimental results are due.

With a diaphragm having an aperture a leading from a reservoir
large area into a pipe of area A (Fig. 46), calling the loss $\left\{\dfrac{A}{C_c\,a} - 1\right\}^2$ ·

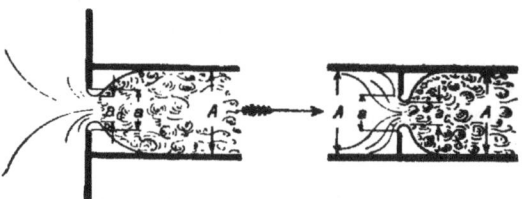

FIGS. 46 and 47.

$= F\dfrac{v^2}{2\,g}$, the following values were obtained. Here $C_c\,a = $ area o
vena contracta.

$\dfrac{a}{A}$	·1	·2	·3	·4	·5	·6	·7	·8	·9	1·0
C_c	·616	·614	·612	·610	·607	·605	·603	·601	·598	·5%
F	231·7	50·99	19·78	9·612	5·256	3·077	1·876	1·169	·734	·4%

With a diaphragm inserted in a pipe of area A (Fig. 47) the following
values were obtained.

$$\text{Loss} = \left(\frac{A}{C_c\,a} - 1\right)^2 \frac{v^2}{2\,g} = F\frac{v^2}{2\,g}.$$

$\dfrac{a}{A}$	·1	·2	·3	·4	·5	·6	·7	·8	·9	1·0
C_e	·624	·632	·643	·659	·681	·712	·755	·813	·892	1·00
F	225·9	47·77	30·83	7·80	3·753	1·796	·797	·29	·06	·00

A formula connecting the area of the *vena contracta* with that of the
aperture in the diaphragm, in terms of the relative area of pipe and of
aperture, is given by Rankine, and is

$$C_c = \frac{a_c}{a} = \frac{\cdot 618}{\sqrt{1 - \cdot 618 \frac{a^2}{A^2}}}$$

Thus when $a = A$, $C_c = 1$.

,, a is very small, C_c has the limiting value $\cdot 618$.

The effect of the portion of the pipe before the orifice is to produce a
closer approximation to parallelism of the stream lines, and in consequence a *vena contracta* of larger area is obtained, with a reduced after-
enlargement, and hence less loss than where this constraint is absent.

ART. 37.—CHANGE OF PRESSURE ACROSS STREAM LINES.

If water be moving with stream line motion, these stream lines being
curved, the pressure varies from one stream
tube to another. This change in pressure
may be determined by considering the equilibrium of an elementary column of fluid of
sectional area δa (Fig. 48), having its axis radial,
and resting with its two ends in two stream
tubes, whose pressures are p and $(p + \delta p)$
respectively. The centrifugal force on the
column is balanced by the difference of
pressure on the two ends and we have, for
equilibrium,

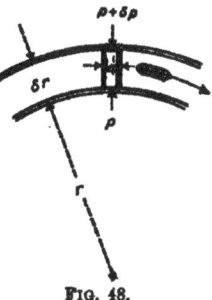

FIG. 48.

$$W \cdot \delta a \cdot \delta r \cdot \frac{v^2}{g\,r} = \frac{d\,p}{d\,r} \cdot \delta r \cdot \delta a$$

$$\therefore \frac{W\,v^2}{g\,r} = \frac{d\,p}{d\,r}$$

ART. 88.—VORTEX MOTION. PRESSURE IN A ROTATING LIQUID.

Where a mass of liquid moves as a whole with vortex motion, this may
occur in either of two ways.

The first is seen when a vessel containing water is rapidly rotated, or
when the contained water is stirred so as to make it rotate as a solid
body, the velocity increasing with the radius. Such a vortex is termed
a Forced Vortex.

The second is seen when water flows through a hole in the bottom of

a vessel.   Here a vortex is usually formed naturally, some initial distur-
ance of the water determining the direction of rotation, although in th·
northern hemisphere the earth's rotation
would itself tend to cause a rotation in
an anti-clockwise direction as viewed
from above.   This is termed a **Free
Spiral Vortex.** The water moves spirally
towards the centre with stream line
motion, so that, neglecting viscosity, its
energy per unit mass is everywhere the
same. If, while the mass is rotating,
the orifice be plugged, the motion
becomes one of simple rotation in
horizontal planes, and forms a **Free
Cylindrical Vortex.**

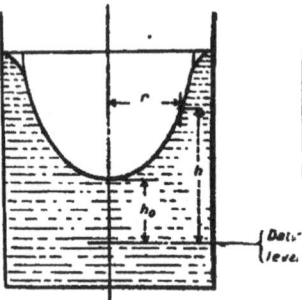

Fig. 49.—Forced Vortex:

Forced Vortex Motion.—Since the angular velocity w is constant, w·
have at any radius r, $v = w\,r$.   (1

The increase in pressure radially is given by

$$\frac{d\,p}{d\,r} = \frac{W}{g} \cdot \frac{w^2\,r^2}{r} = \frac{W}{g} w^2\,r.$$

Integrating between the limits r_1 and r_2 we have

$$\frac{p_1 - p_2}{W} = \frac{w^2}{2\,g}(r_1^2 - r_2^2).$$ (

If $p = p_0$ where $r = o$,

$$\frac{p - p_0}{W} = \frac{w^2}{2\,g} \cdot r^2$$

or, putting $\frac{p}{W} = h$ (Fig. 49),

$$h - h_0 = \frac{w^2}{2\,g} \cdot r^2 \quad \therefore \quad h = h_0 + \frac{w^2\,r^2}{2\,g}$$

which is the equation to a parabola.

Since the pressure at any point is that equivalent to the column of
water supported at the point, it follows that all surfaces of equal pressure
including the free surface of the vortex, form paraboloids of revolution
having the axis of rotation as their common axis.   Near the sides of the
vessel the liquid lags owing to viscosity, and here the surface level will
fall below that of the paraboloid.

Free Cylindrical Vortex Motion.—Here, since we have stream line
motion, the equation $\frac{p}{W} + \frac{v^2}{2\,g} + z = $ constant, holds.

∴ in any horizontal plane $\frac{p}{W} + \frac{v^2}{2g} =$ constant.

Differentiating,

$$\frac{1}{W} \cdot \frac{d\,p}{d\,r} + \frac{v}{g} \cdot \frac{d\,v}{d\,r} = 0. \tag{1}$$

Introducing the condition for rise in pressure across a stream tube, viz., $\frac{d\,p}{d\,r} = \frac{W\,v^2}{g\,r}$, this becomes

$$\frac{v^2}{g\,r} + \frac{v}{g}\frac{d\,v}{d\,r} = 0$$

$$\therefore \frac{d\,v}{d\,r} + \frac{v}{r} = 0, \text{ or } -\frac{d\,r}{r} = \frac{d\,v}{v}.$$

Integrating we get $\log_e r + \log_e v =$ constant $= B.$

$$\therefore v\,r = \text{constant} = e^B = B_1.$$

$$\therefore v = \frac{B_1}{r} \tag{2}$$

i.e., in a free vortex the velocity varies inversely as the distance from the axis of rotation.

It follows that the increase of pressure with radius is identical with that in inward radial flow.

Thus if p_1, v_1, r_1, are the attributes of a point in the same horizontal plane as p, v, r,

$$\frac{p - p_1}{W} = \frac{v_1^2}{2\,g}\left\{1 - \frac{r_1^2}{r_2^2}\right\} \tag{3}$$

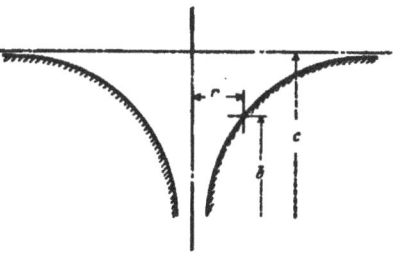

FIG. 50.—Free Vortex.

Putting $\frac{p}{W}$ constant in Bernoulli's equation we get the equation to the curve of equal pressure, that is $\frac{v^2}{2\,g} + z =$ constant $= C$, and substituting for v in terms of r from (2) we have

$$\frac{B_1^2}{2\,g\,r^2} + z = C$$

$$\therefore C - z = \frac{B_1^2}{2\,g\,r^2}$$

the equation to a hyperbolic curve of the nature $y\,x^2 = A$, and which is asymptotic to the axis of rotation and to the horizontal through $z = C$ (Fig. 50).

A Free Spiral Vortex may be considered as a case of cylindrical vortex and radial motion combined in the required proportions, since in each case the velocity is inversely proportional to the radius. The angle between the stream line and the corresponding radius vector at any point will then be constant, and the stream lines will form a series of equiangular or logarithmic spirals. The difference of pressure between any two points may then be found by adding the pressure differences due to the two methods of flow taken separately.

Strictly this should only be applied to cases of inward flow, since outward flow causes instability.

In a free spiral vortex formed under normal conditions, the surface resistances tend to prevent the attainment of such high velocities near the centre of rotation as are indicated by the preceding analysis. In consequence the actual values of $C - z$ for small radii are less than those calculated. The following observations by the author on the surface profile of such a vortex, produced by the discharge from a circular cylindrical vessel 2 feet in diameter under a constant head of 9 inches bear out this point.

Radius inches.		12.	10.	8.	6.	4.	3.	2.	1.
$(C - z)$ inches. Orifice 1 inch diameter	observed . . .	·0	·02	·05	·08	·13	·19	·40	1·?
	calculated $(C - z) = \dfrac{1·71}{r^2}$		·02	·03	·05	·11	·19	·43	?·?
$(C - z)$ inches. Orifice 1·5 inch diameter	observed . . .	·00	·03	·06	·13	·26	·43	1·06	?·?
	calculated $(C - z) = \dfrac{3·82}{r^2}$		·04	·06	·11	·24	·45	·95	3·?

Since the velocity varies inversely as the radius, and since this velocity cannot be infinite at the axis where $r = o$, an air column is essential at the centre of a free vortex. When this air column cannot be maintained, we get a combination of a forced vortex—at and near the axis—and a free vortex at points further removed (Fig. 51).

If a be the radius at which the two surface curves intersect, the depth of the central depression below the general level of the surface may be shown to be given by $\dfrac{w^2 a^2}{g}$ feet.

This is termed a **Compound Vortex**, and the state of affairs there existing is of importance in its application to the theory of the flow of water in a centrifugal pump fitted with a Vortex Chamber. Here the water in the impeller forms a forced vortex with outward radial flow, while when free of the vanes an approximation to a free spiral vortex is formed, and the pressure increases as the velocity diminishes outwards.

Certain properties of the free vortex are of interest. If a film of oil be formed on the surface, owing to its density being less than that of water this at once approaches the axis of rotation and disappears down the funnel of the vortex. The same thing happens to any small floating body. If of moderate dimensions, however, the portion nearer the axis of rotation is in a region of higher velocity than those portions further removed, and a series of frictional forces is thus called into play, acting on the body, which forces are greater as the points at which they act are nearer the axis of rotation. The effect of this is to produce a rotation of the body about some point near its outer edge, and away from the centre of the vortex. The body may be thus alternately attracted to and repelled from this centre, the action being repeated as long as the vortex is in existence.

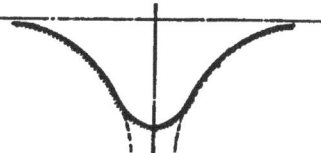

FIG. 51.—Compound Vortex.

A large floating body destroys the funnel in its upper part, and, if air is prevented from entering through the exit, in the lower part also.[1] Since in the floating body $v \propto r$, while in the liquid $v \propto \dfrac{1}{r}$, this, by friction, tends to destroy the vortex motion of the upper layers of liquid, and, by viscosity, also of the lower layers.

The formation of a vortex in a discharging vessel increases the time of discharge by diminishing the effective area of the orifice, and by reducing the inclination of the issuing particles to the plane of the orifice. Experiments by the author showed that when discharging water under heads varying from 8 to 12 inches in a free spiral vortex, the coefficient of discharge was sensibly independent of the head and had a value ·287 for a 1-inch orifice and ·178 for a 1½-inch orifice. When no vortex formed, the coefficient was ·62.

EXAMPLES.

(1) In a 12-inch Venturi meter the throat diameter is 4 inches. Taking C to be constant $= ·982$, determine the difference of head at the entrance and throat when discharging

[1] For a full account of such phenomena, a paper by the author—"Memoirs, Manchester Lit. and Phil. Soc.," 1911—may be consulted.

$$(a) \ 100$$
$$(b) \ 500 \ \Bigg\} \ \text{gallons per minute.}$$
$$(c) \ 1{,}000$$

N.B.—1 gallon = 10 lbs.

Answer. (*a*) Vel. = ·340 *f. s.* — ·149 feet.

(*b*) „ = 1·701 *f. s.* — 3·73 feet.

(*c*) „ = 3·402 *f. s.* — 14·92 feet.

(2) Inward radial flow takes place between two parallel circular plates 3 feet diameter and 6 inches apart. Discharge takes place through an orifice 18 inches diameter in the centre of the lower plate. Neglecting viscous resistances, determine the pressure at the entrance when 1,000 cubic feet per minute pass the plates, assuming the pressure at the edge of the discharge orifice to be atmospheric.

Answer. ·585 feet of water = ·254 lb. per square inch.

(3) If in the previous example the plates are fitted with vanes and rotate at 400 revolutions per minute, determine the difference of pressure at inlet and outlet due solely to the production of a forced vortex.

Answer. 46·04 feet of water = 20 lbs. per square inch.

(4) Taking the above (2) and (3), as an example of an inward radial flow turbine, determine the total pressure drop between inlet and outlet.

Answer. 46·62 feet of water.

(5) A centrifugal pump has an impeller 12 inches internal, 24 inches external diameter and runs at 800 revolutions, discharging into a vortex chamber where a free vortex is formed. If the outer diameter of the vortex chamber is 3 feet, determine the rise in pressure due to the vortex motion

(*a*) in the wheel;   (*b*) in the vortex chamber.

Neglect all losses and assume a perfectly efficient vortex chamber.

Answer. (*a*) 81·9 feet of water.

(*b*) 60·6 „   „

(6) A flat cylindrical disc, 18 inches diameter, keyed on to the lower end of a 3 inch vertical shaft serves as a hydraulic footstep bearing. Its lower face is plane and bears against radiating ribs cast in the pressure cylinder, while its upper face carries a series of radial ribs which bear against the plane upper lid of the pressure cylinder. Thus water above the disc rotates with the disc, while the water below is at rest. The upper and lower sides are in free communication around the periphery of

the disc. Determine the resultant upward pressure on the shaft at a speed of 400 revolutions per minute.

Answer. 844 lbs.

(7) A pipe 4 inches diameter is suddenly enlarged to 6 inches diameter. Determine the consequent loss of energy per lb. of water with a velocity of flow in the small pipe of 6 feet per second.

Answer. ·173 foot lb. per lb.

CHAPTER V.

Flow from a small Orifice—Coefficients of Contraction, Velocity and Discharge—Suppressed Contraction- Borda's Mouthpiece—Sharp-edged Orifice—Converging Mouthpi-·—Bell-mouthed Orifice—Diverging Outlet—Velocity of Approach—Time of empty:. Reservoir—Submerged Orifice—Form of Jets.

Art. 39.—Flow from a Small Orifice.[1]

If. an opening be made in the side or base of a tank containing water. the introduction of a few drops of aniline dye shows that steady stream line motion is set up in the mass of fluid, these stream lines convergin: towards the orifice from every side. At the boundary of the issuin: jet the stream lines are, as already explained (Art. 14), tangenti.

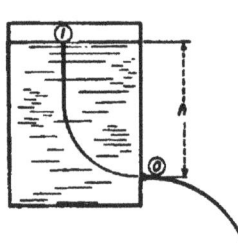

to the edges of the orifice, and with a sharp-edged orifice the general stream line motion is as shown in Fig. 22. It follows that, after passing the plane of the orifice, the section of the jet gradually diminishes, and its boundaries do not become parallel until some finite distance from the orifice. The section at which the jet becomes parallel is termed the *vena contracta*, or contracted vein, and with a small circular orifice is at a distance from the orifice equal to about ·498 times the diameter.

Fig. 52.

Now suppose a particle of weight w lbs. to travel along a stream line from the surface to the orifice and on to the *vena contracta* (Fig. 52). Since the motion is steady, the energy throughout is constant (neglecting viscosity); and if we suppose the surface area to be large, so that the surface velocity may be neglected, when in the surface its kinetic energy is zero. If the orifice is at a mean depth h below the free surface, and if its level be taken as datum, the potential energy of the particle is wh foot lbs., while its pressure energy is zero, its pressure being that of the atmosphere which is taken as datum pressure.

[1] By a small orifice we mean one whose dimensions are small in comparison with the head of water above its centre, so that at any point in its area the head may be taken as equal to that at its centre without sensible error. The subject-matter of Arts. 39—46 refers to such orifices

Immediately after passing the orifice, its potential energy is zero, so that if we can determine its pressure energy, its kinetic energy and therefore its velocity may be inferred. Now on passing the orifice the jet is exposed to atmospheric pressure, and if the pressure is the same throughout its pressure energy is zero. If the jet is parallel this condition is satisfied,[1] but so long as its boundary is curved the centrifugal action of the outer layers necessitates an increase in pressure along the radius of curvature towards the centre of the jet. It follows that in the plane of the orifice, and up to the *rena contracta*, the pressure in the interior of the jet is greater than that of the atmosphere.

The distribution of pressure and of velocity across a horizontal diameter in the plane of the orifice is substantially as shown in Fig. 53. With free lateral contraction, the velocity at the centre of the jet varies from ·62 to ·64 $\sqrt{2\,g\,h}$, while with lateral contractions suppressed this velocity is about ·69 $\sqrt{2\,g\,h}$ (Bazin).

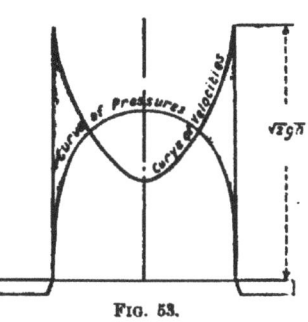

FIG. 53.

At the *vena contracta*, however, the pressure across the jet is uniform and atmospheric,[1] the pressure energy at the orifice having been converted into kinetic energy, with a consequent increase in velocity from orifice to *rena contracta*.

The pressure energy at the *rena contracta* then is zero, the potential energy is zero, while the kinetic energy is $\dfrac{v^2}{2\,g}$ ft. lbs. per lb.

Denoting the surface by the suffix $(_1)$, and the *rena contracta* by the suffix $(_0)$, we have

$$w\left[\frac{p_0}{W} + \frac{v_0^2}{2\,g} + z_0\right] = w\left[\frac{p_1}{W} + \frac{v_1^2}{2\,g} + z_1\right]$$

$$\text{where } p_1 = p_0 = 0; \; z_0 = 0; \; v_1 = 0$$

$$\therefore \quad \frac{v_0^2}{2\,g} = z_1$$

$$\therefore \quad v_0 = \sqrt{2\,g\,z_1} = \sqrt{2\,g\,h} \text{ ft. per sec.}$$

i.e., theoretically the velocity of efflux at the *rena contracta* is the same as

---

[1] Even in a parallel jet the pressure in the interior will be greater than atmospheric because of the surface tension. The magnitude of this excess pressure, in feet of water, is given by $h' = \dfrac{2\,T}{d\,W}$, where T is the surface tension in lbs. per foot and d is the diameter in feet

if the particles had fallen freely through a height h feet under the action of gravity.

The truth of the above theorem was demonstrated by Torricelli[1] who showed that a vertical jet of fluid would rise very approximately to the free level in the vessel from which it was supplied.

Due, however, to the viscosity of the liquid, to surface tension, and to the resistance of the air, the velocity is always slightly less than this theoretical value, and is given by $C_v \sqrt{2 g h}$, where C_v is called the **Coefficient of Velocity**. The value of C_v can only be determined experimentally, but with a sharp-lipped orifice increases with h from about ·96 to ·994. Weisbach gives the following values for an orifice of ·083 feet diameter :—

h feet . .	·066	1·64	11·5	56·0	838
C_v . . .	·959	·967	·975	·994	·994

At the *vena contracta* the stream lines for the first time become parallel and perpendicular to the cross section of the stream, so that if a_c be the sectional area of the *vena contracta* in square feet, the volume discharged per second $= C_v \sqrt{2 g h} \times a_c$ cubic ft. If a is the area of the orifice, the ratio $\dfrac{a_c}{a}$ is termed the **Coefficient of Contraction**, and is denoted by C_c. The discharge is thus given by $C_c\, C_v \sqrt{2 g h} \times a = C \sqrt{2 g h} \times a$ cub. ft. sec.

Here C is termed the **coefficient of discharge**.

These coefficients vary with the head h; with the area of the orifice; and with the shape of the orifice and its position.

The following table, giving values of C, abridged from Hamilton

Head from centre of orifice in feet.	Square Orifices; lengths of side of square in feet.				
	·02	·04	·07	·12	·20
·4	—	·643	·628	·616	—
·6	·660	·636	·623	·613	·605
1·0	·648	·628	·618	·610	·605
6·0	·623	·612	·607	·605	·604
20·0	·606	·604	·602	·602	·602
100·0	·599	·598	·598	·598	·598

[1] De motu gravium naturaliter accelerato (1643).

Head above centre of orifice in feet.	Circular Orifices; diameters in feet.				
	·02	·04	·07	·12	·20
·4	—	—	·628	·612	—
·6	·655	·630	·618	·609	·601
1·0	·644	·623	·612	·605	·600
6·0	·618	·607	·602	·599	·598
20·0	·601	·599	·597	·596	·596
100·0	·593	·592	·592	·592	·592

Smith's "Hydraulics," indicates the nature of these variations. In each case the orifice had full contraction, had free discharge into air, and the inner face of the plate in which the orifice was formed had sharp corners, so that the escaping jet only touched these inner edges.

More recent experiments throw some doubt on the assumption, based chiefly on the work of Smith, that the coefficient decreases up to a head of 100 feet, under which head it has a constant value of ·592 for all diameters from ·5 inches to 12 inches. Among these may be quoted those of *Messrs. Judd and King* at the Ohio State University,[1] which were carried out on orifices of diameters $\frac{3}{4}$ inch, 1 inch, $1\frac{1}{2}$ inches, 2 inches, $2\frac{1}{2}$ inches, under heads varying from 4 to 93 feet. The results showed a very small change in the coefficient for an increase of head. The following are from tests on the 2-inch orifice :—

Head in feet . . .	5·00	9·08	17·80	23·24	36·12	47·02	57·70	69·99	92·01
Coefficient of discharge	·6084	·6083	·6080	·6083	·6082	·6088	·6081	·6080	·6080

Experiments by *H. J. Bilton*[2] indicate that if an orifice is less than about 2·5 inches diameter perfect contraction is impossible, the degree of imperfection becoming more marked as the diameter decreases. This is true however high the head. For orifices of greater diameters the contraction appears to be complete and constant for heads above about 17 inches, attaining a value ·598. Smaller orifices likewise have a "critical" head, greater than 17 inches, above which the contraction is constant but

[1] *Engineering News*, New York, September 27, 1906.
[2] *Engineer*, June 19, 1908.

greater than ·598.   The coefficient is the same for a given orifice under a given head, whatever be the direction of discharge.   The following table give the essential results of these experiments :—

Diameter of orifice in inches . .	0·15	0·2	0·25	0·3	0·4	0·5	0·6	0·75	1·0 and over
Normal coefficient of discharge .	0·631	0·630	0·628	0·627	0·624	0·621	0·618	0·613	—
Critical head in inches	65	55	45	32	25	22½	20	18	1?

COEFFICIENTS OF DISCHARGE FOR STANDARD CIRCULAR ORIFICES.

Head in inches.	Diameter of Orifice in Inches.						
	2½ and over.	2	1½	1	¾	½	¼
45 and over	0·598	0·599	0·603	0·608	0·613	0·621	**0·628**
22	—	—	—	—	—	**0·621**	0·638
18	—	—	—	—	**0·613**	0·628	0·643
17	**0·598**	**0·599**	**0·603**	**0·608**	0·614	0·625	0·645
12	0·600	0·601	0·606	0·612	0·618	0·630	0·653
9	0·604	0·606	0·612	0·619	0·623	0·637	0·660
6	0·610	0·612	0·618	0·626	0·632	0·643	0·669
3	—	—	—	0·640	0·646	0·657	0·680
2	—	—	—	—	—	0·663	0·683

The critical heads and the corresponding normal coefficients are in bold figures.

T. P. Strickland,[1] from experiments on sharp-edged orifices of 1 inch and 2 inches diameter, deduces the formula $C = ·5925 + \dfrac{·018}{\sqrt{h \cdot d^{\frac{1}{2}}}}$ where d is the diameter in inches and h the head in feet.

With a rectangular orifice, the coefficient is rather greater than with a square orifice of the same area, and generally increases with the ratio of the perimeter to the area of an orifice.

Suppressed Contraction.—Any interference with the free production of stream lines, such as occurs, for example, where the depth of water above the orifice is too small, or where this is near the sides or bottom of a tank

[1] "Proc. Inst. C.E.," vol. 181, p. 531.

s indicated in Fig. 22 b, curtails the full flow to the orifice, and tends to revent the full contraction of section at the *vena contracta*. In any such ase the value of C_c and of C will be greater than indicated above, the rue values being entirely dependent on the circumstances governing the ow to the orifice.

From experiments on a rectangular orifice, ·177 feet long and ·089 feet ride, in which the contraction could be suppressed on part or the whole f the perimeter by means of flat plates perpendicular to the plane of the rifice and ·22 feet long, *Bidone* educed the formula

$$C = ·608 + ·0925\ x,$$

vhere x is the fraction of the peri- neter over which the contraction is suppressed. For circular orifices

$$C = ·608 + ·079\ x.$$

With this device, however, contrac- ion of section takes place at the inner edges of the baffle plates, and when the orifice is entirely surrounded this simply forms a Borda's mouthpiece running full (p. 113) with C about ·75.

Experiments by *Lesbros* on a vertical orifice, ·656 feet square, showed mean values of the coefficient, for heads between 1·5 and 10 feet, in the ratios 1·00, 1·082, 1·043, 1·116, according as the contraction was un- affected, suppressed at the lower edge, at one side, and at the lower edge and sides, and thus agree fairly well with Bidone's results.

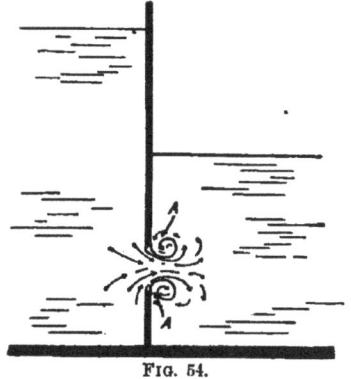

FIG. 54.

Where an orifice is made in the thick side of a vessel, or is fitted with an external pipe so that the jet, after springing clear of its inner edges, again touches the sides of the orifice before escaping, or where fitted with re-entrant mouthpiece, the physical conditions governing the flow are entirely changed, and the coefficients assume new values. Thus the coefficient of contraction may vary from ·5 to 1·0 under different condi- tions of working, with the same size of orifice and the same head. There is, however, nothing mysterious about this change—it is governed entirely by the conditions of flow, and, as will be seen, may be predeter- mined with some exactitude when those conditions are known.

Submerged Orifices.—If an orifice discharges below the surface of the water in a second vessel instead of into the air, this has the effect of in- creasing the pressure against which discharge takes place, and thus of reducing the effective head, and also of slightly reducing the value of ᴛ coefficient of discharge.

The reduction of the coefficient of discharge is probably a second.:t effect of the eddy formation which occurs in the dead water surroundi־; the jet at A and B, Fig. 54, the dead water comprising the eddy project:: into the stream and reducing its effective area.

In the sketch (Fig. 55), if the suffix $(_1)$ refer to the free surface in ; upper vessel and suffix $(_0)$ to the *vena contracta*, we have, neglect:- viscosity,

$$\frac{p_1}{W} + \frac{r_1^2}{2g} + z_1 = \frac{p_0}{W} + \frac{r_0^2}{2g} + z_0.$$

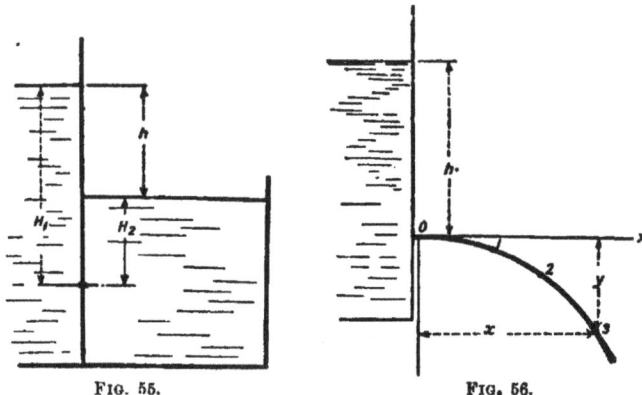

FIG. 55.   FIG. 56.

Taking the datum level at the centre of the orifice, and assuming ᴛᴧᴇ area at the surface in the upper vessel to be large, we have

$$p_1 = 0; \ r_1 = 0; \ z_0 = 0; \ z_1 = H_1; \ \frac{p_0}{W} = H_2$$

$$\therefore \ H_1 - H_2 = \frac{v_0^2}{2g} \ \text{feet}$$

$$\therefore \ v_0 = \sqrt{2g(H_1 - H_2)} = \sqrt{2gh,}$$

where h = difference in level of the free surfaces on the two sides of the orifice.

ART. 40.—EXPERIMENTAL DETERMINATION OF THE COEFFICIENTS.

(1) **Coefficient of Velocity, for an Orifice in a Vertical Plate.**—Keeping h constant, mark on a flat board parallel to the plane of the jet, points 1, 2, 3, 4, etc., by means of a set square, these points marking as nearly as

ossible the centre of the jet.   Draw a smooth curve through the points,
and draw the horizontal OX through O (Fig. 56).   Taking any point on
the curve we get, if v is the velocity of efflux, measuring horizontal
distances from the *vena contracta*,

$$x = v\,t;\ y = \frac{1}{2}\,g\,t^2$$

$$\therefore\ v = \frac{x}{t} = \frac{x}{\sqrt{\dfrac{2\,y}{g}}} = \sqrt{\frac{g\,x^2}{2\,y}}.$$

But $\dfrac{v}{\sqrt{2\,g\,h}} = C_v.$ $\qquad\qquad \therefore\ C_v = \sqrt{\dfrac{x^2}{4\,y\,h}}.$

If the issuing jet make an angle a with the horizontal, then, the origin
of co-ordinates being taken at the *vena contracta*,

$$x = v\cos a\,.\,t;\ y = \frac{1}{2}\,g\,t^2 - v\sin a\,t.$$

Since $v\sin a\,t = x\tan a$, on substituting for t^2 we get:

$$y + x\tan a = \frac{g\,x^2}{2\,v^2\cos^2 a}$$

$$\therefore\ v = \sqrt{\frac{g\,x^2\sec^2 a}{2\,(y + x\tan a)}}.$$

Then $C_v = v \div \sqrt{2\,g\,h}.$ If a is not known, if a second pair of values
x_1, y_1, are measured, we get

$$v = \sqrt{\frac{g\,x_1^2\sec^2 a}{2\,(y_1 + x_1\tan a)}},$$

and from these two equations a may be calculated.

A second method of determining the coefficient of velocity is to allow a
jet of water to escape from
an orifice in the vertical side
of a tank supported on knife
edges (Fig. 57), the level of
the water in the tank being
maintained constant by the
influx of a vertical stream.
The position of a pointer
fixed to the tank is noticed
before the orifice is opened,
and when the jet is allowed
to escape, this pointer is

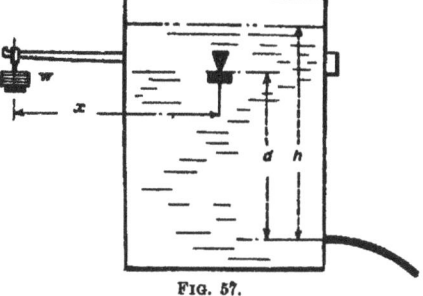

FIG. 57.

brought back to the same mark by means of the weight W, placed at a
leverage x.

The weight of water w leaving the vessel per second is determined weighing. Then if v be its mean velocity in a horizontal direction, momentum per second leaving the tank in this direction $= \dfrac{w\,v}{g}$. T produce this flux of momentum a constant horizontal force of magnit $\dfrac{w\,v}{g}$ lbs. must be impressed on the jet, a force which can only be due to otherwise unbalanced pressure on the side of the tank opposite to the orif.

We have then, taking moments about the knife edge:—

$$W\,x = \frac{w\,v}{g}\,.\,d \quad \text{where } d = \text{depth of orifice below knife edge}$$

$$\therefore \quad v = \frac{W}{w}\,.\,g\,.\,\frac{x}{d}\ \text{feet per second}$$

$$\therefore \quad C_v = \frac{W\,g\,x}{w\,d\,\sqrt{2\,g\,h}}.$$

This method is only suitable for experiments on a small scale. A th method, which has been applied very successfull consists in measuring the actual velocity at sever points in the cross section of the *vena contracta* b means of a Pitot Tube (Arts. 68, 101). If then v the velocity at any radius x, the total discharge $=$

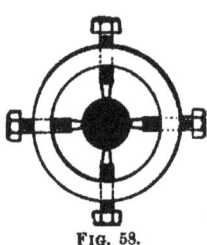

FIG. 58.

$\displaystyle\int_0^r 2\,\pi\,v\,x\,dx$ cubic feet per second. If a curve plotted having as abscissæ the values of x and ordinates the corresponding values of $2\,\pi\,x\,v$, th area under this curve will represent the dischar per second, from which the mean velocity may be obtained by dividing the area of the jet.

(2) The **coefficient of contraction**, C_c, may be measured by using a ri (Fig. 58), surrounding the jet at the *vena contracta*, and fitted wi micrometer measuring screws, which may be adjusted until just touchin its surface.[1]

(3) The **coefficient of discharge**, C, may be determined directly b measuring the quantity Q in cubic feet discharged per second from th orifice a, under a head h.

Then $$C = \frac{Q}{a\,\sqrt{2\,g\,h}}.$$

[1] For a sketch of a contraction gauge, and for experiments on the measurements of th coefficients in the case of a large jet forming part of a Pelton Wheel installation, see a pap by W. R. Eckhart, "Proc. Inst. Mech. Engineers," 1909—10. Also *Engineering*, January 1 1910, p. 59.

Art. 41.

Theoretically we may always calculate the flow from an orifice in the side or bottom of a vessel, by equating the flux of momentum across the plane of the orifice per second to the unbalanced statical pressure on the opposite vertical side in the one case, and to weight of the unbalanced column of water in the other, *i.e.*, by expressing the fact that the total unbalanced force in the direction of flow is taken up in producing this flow. With an ordinary opening in the side or bottom of a vessel, however, the calculation of this unbalanced force is impossible, since, due to the fact that there is stream line motion along the face containing the

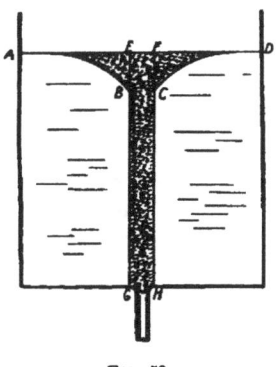

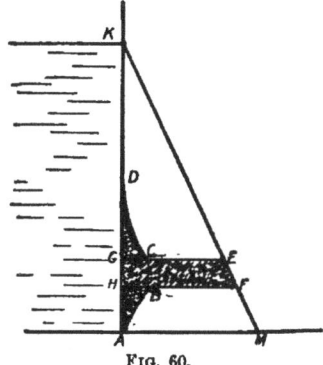

Fig. 59.   Fig. 60.

opening, giving the water kinetic head, the pressure head at any point in this face is less than that simply due to the statical head at that point by an amount which is indeterminate.[1] The resultant unbalanced pressure is therefore in this case indeterminate. In the case of an opening in the flat, horizontal bottom of a vessel, the pressure over this face is not uniform, since the kinetic head is greatest near the orifice, the distribution of pressure being as represented in Fig. 59, where the ordinates from the base to the curve *A B C D* measure the pressure on the base.

When the orifice *G H* is closed, the pressure on *G H* is that represented by the shaded area *E F H G*, but when open the unbalanced pressure becomes that represented by the whole shaded area *A B G H C D*.

Similarly in the case of an opening in the vertical side *A K* of a vessel (Fig. 60). Here the area *G E F H* represents the pressure on *G H*

---

[1] Since part of the head produces acceleration towards the point.

when the orifice is closed, while the horizontal distances between the lines

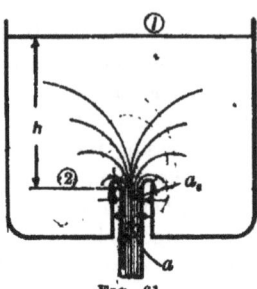

FIG. 61.

$K M$ and the curves $A B$ and $C D$ measure the pressures on the side of the vessel with an issuing jet. The shaded area then represents the unbalanced pressure, which is to be equated to the outflow of momentum per second from the orifice.

By returning the mouthpiece for some distance into the vessel, as in the **Borda mouthpiece** (Fig. 61), this flow over the face containing the orifice is prevented, and the pressure on this face now approximates to that due to the statical head alone. The equations of momentum can therefore be easily applied.

ART. 42.—BORDA'S MOUTHPIECE.

Let a be the area of the orifice and a_c the area of the stream as soon as it has assumed a parallel cylindrical form, i.e., at the *vena contracta*. Let h be the depth of this point below the surface. If the suffixes (₁) refer to the surface and (₂) to the *vena contracta*, we have, neglecting viscosity,

$$\frac{p_1}{W} + \frac{v_1^2}{2\,g} + z_1 = \frac{p_2}{W} + \frac{v_2^2}{2\,g} + z_2.$$

Also $p_2 = p_1 = 0$; $z_1 - z_2 = h$; $v_1 = 0$ if surface area is large,

$$\therefore \quad v_2^2 = 2\,g\,h.$$

Mass carried away per second $= \dfrac{W}{g} \cdot a_c\, v_2$.

$\therefore$ Momentum carried away per second $= \dfrac{W}{g} \cdot a_c\, v_2^2$.

This momentum is produced by a force equal to the weight of a column of water of area a and of height h (approximately).

$$\therefore \quad \text{Force producing motion} = W\,a\,h \text{ lbs.}$$

$$\therefore \quad W\,a\,h = \frac{W}{g} \cdot a_c\, v_2^2$$

$$= \frac{W}{g} \cdot a_c \cdot 2\,g\,h$$

$$\therefore \quad a_c = {\cdot}5a,[1]$$

[1] Actually $v_2^2 = C_v^2 \times 2\,g\,h$, so that $\dfrac{a_c}{a} = \dfrac{1}{2\,C_v^2}$. The coefficient of contraction for the Borda running full is modified in a similar manner.

.*e.*, the coefficient of contraction in the case of a Borda's mouthpiece, where the effluent stream does not touch the sides of the mouthpiece, is one half.

Borda's Mouthpiece running full.—With a vertical Borda, where the water in the vessel is initially quite steady, the issuing jet after becoming parallel does not again come into contact with the sides of the mouthpiece. If, however, the water in the vessel be agitated, the jet, after contracting to form a *vena contracta*, again expands to fill the mouthpiece (Fig. 62). This is termed running full as opposed to running freely as in the previous case. The issuing motion is now turbulent, not steady as is the case with a free Borda. It is worthy of note that under no circumstances

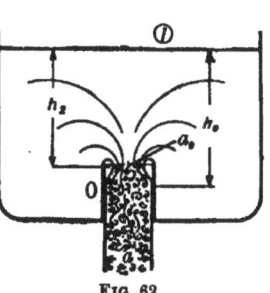

FIG. 62.

with a free Borda, or indeed with any jet having non-sinuous motion, is any splash produced on meeting a solid surface. With sinuous motion splashing always occurs.

We now get a loss of head due to the expansion of the stream from a_c to a after contracting, so that

$$\frac{p_1}{W} + \frac{v_1^2}{2g} + z_1 = \frac{p_0}{W} + \frac{v_0^2}{2g} + z_0 + \text{loss due to expansion.}$$

The loss due to expansion (Art. 33) $= \dfrac{v_0^2}{2g}(m-1)^2,$

where $m = \dfrac{a}{a_c}$

$\therefore \quad \dfrac{p_1}{W} + \dfrac{v_1^2}{2g} + z_1 = \dfrac{p_0}{W} + \dfrac{v_0^2}{2g}[(m-1)^2 + 1] + z_0$

But $p_1 = 0$ and $v_1 = 0$. Also $z_1 - z_0 = h_0$.

$\therefore \quad \dfrac{p_0}{W} + \dfrac{v_0^2}{2g}[(m-1)^2 + 1] = h_0.$ (1)

Now equating the momentum passing the section at O per second, to the force producing it, we get

$$W a h_0 - p_0 a = \frac{W}{g} a v_0^2$$

$$\therefore \quad h_0 - \frac{p_0}{W} = \frac{v_0^2}{g}$$

But $h_0 - \dfrac{p_0}{W} = \dfrac{v_0^2}{2g}[(m-1)^2 + 1]$ from (1)

$\therefore \quad$ Equating these values we get $\dfrac{(m-1)^2 + 1}{2} = 1$

$$\therefore \quad (m-1)^2 = 1 \quad \text{or } m = 2,$$

i.e., the coefficient of contraction at the neck in a Borda's mouthpiece running full is one half.

If the jet discharges into the atmosphere so that $p_0 = 0$ we have

$$v_0^2 = g\,h_0, \text{ so that } v_0 = \frac{\sqrt{2\,g\,h}}{\sqrt{2}} \text{ (approximately)},$$

i.e., the velocity of discharge is $\dfrac{1}{\sqrt{2}}$ times the velocity when flowing free, and since the area of full jet = 2 (area of free jet).

$\therefore$ Quantity flowing per second from full Borda $\left. \right\} = \sqrt{2}$ (quantity from free Borda).

The coefficient of discharge from such an orifice is thus equal to $\sqrt{2}$ times the coefficient for a free Borda mouthpiece and therefore to

$$\frac{1}{C_v^2 \sqrt{2}}. \text{ Taking } C_v = \cdot 975 \text{ this would make } C = \cdot 745.$$

Experiments by H. J. Bilton[1] on such mouthpieces, $2\frac{1}{2}$ diameters in length, gave the following values for C, no variation of C with head being noted for heads as low as 6 inches :—

Diameter (ins.).	$\frac{1}{8}$	$\frac{1}{4}$	$\frac{3}{8}$	$\frac{1}{2}$	$\frac{3}{4}$	1	$1\frac{1}{2}$	2	$2\frac{1}{2}$
C	·91	·87	·85	·88	·81	·79	·77	·76	·75

The difference between the calculated and experimental values of C is due to the fact that the area at the *vena contracta* is actually greater than ·5 a because of the effect of viscosity in modifying the equation of momentum. Eddy loss at the re-expansion of the stream is consequently reduced with a corresponding increase in discharge.

Denoting the contracted section by the suffix $(_2)$ we have

$$\frac{p_2}{W} + \frac{v_2^2}{2\,g} + z_2 = \frac{p_0}{W} + \frac{v_0^2}{2\,g} + z_0 + \text{loss due to expansion.}$$

But loss due to expansion $= \dfrac{v_0^2}{2\,g}(2-1)^2 = \dfrac{v_0^2}{2\,g}$ (Art. 33)

Also $v_2 = 2\,v_0,$

$$\therefore \quad \frac{p_0 - p_2}{W} = \frac{4\,v_0^2 - 2\,v_0^2}{2\,g} + (z_2 - z_0)$$

[1] "Victorian Inst. of Engineers," April 1, 1908.

$$\therefore \quad \frac{p_0 - p_2}{W} = \frac{v_0^2}{g} + (z_2 - z_0).$$

Again $v_0^2 = g\, h_0$,

$$\therefore \quad \frac{p_0 - p_2}{W} = h_0 + z_2 - z_0.$$

In a horizontal mouthpiece $z_2 = z_0$,

$$\therefore \quad \frac{p_0 - p_2}{W} = h_0 \text{ feet,}$$

i.e., the gain of pressure from ($_2$) to ($_0$) is equal to a head of h_0 feet.

If the jet issues into the atmosphere $p_0 = 0$.

$$\therefore \quad \frac{p_2}{W} = -h_0 \text{ feet.}$$

Or the pressure at ($_2$) is less than that of the atmosphere by an amount equivalent to a head h_0 of water.

This reduction of pressure at section ($_2$) explains why the velocity at this point, and hence the discharge, is greater with a full Borda than with one running free. The conditions from the surface to the section at ($_2$) are exactly the same whether the mouthpiece runs full or free, but in one case the jet is discharging at this point against atmospheric pressure, while in the other case this pressure is in part removed.

.The effect is then substantially the same as if the free Borda were subjected to an additional head h_0.

The theoretical limit of this h_0 is 34 feet, but practically, the liberation of dissolved air as the pressure falls, prevents the formation of anything approaching an absolute vacuum.

Art. 43.—Sharp-edged Orifice in a flat Plate, with External Tube.

With an external tube of the same diameter as the orifice, the effluent stream, after forming a *vena contracta*, always re-expands to fill the tube (Fig. 63).

In this case, as already explained, the coefficient of contraction cannot be theoretically deduced by an application of the equations of momentum. Its value is probably about ·62, but almost certainly varies with the head and size of orifice. The final area of the jet $= a$, so that the coefficient of velocity is the same as the coefficient of discharge. This coefficient varies with the size of orifice, with the length of tube, and probably to some extent with the head. Experiments by Weisbach gave the following values of C_v, for tubes having a length equal to about three diameters :—

Diameter (feet).	·032	·066	·098	·131
C_v	·843	·832	·821	·810

The value of C_v was found to vary with the length of the tube approximately as follows :—

Length ÷ diameter .	1·0	3·0	10·0
C_v	·88	·82	·78

If suffixes ($_0$) and ($_2$) refer to outlet and to *vena contracta*, since we have

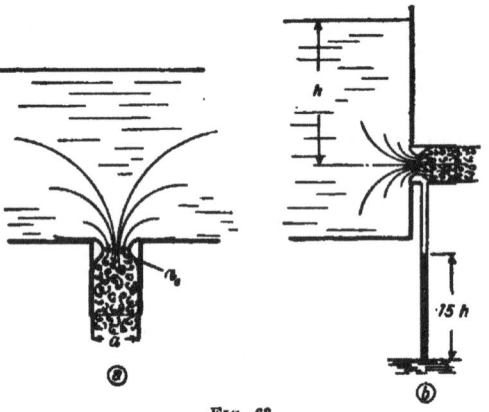

FIG. 63.

no loss of head from the surface to the section at ($_2$) we get

$$h = \frac{p_2}{w} + \frac{v_2^2}{2g} \qquad (1)$$

Again, since the only loss of energy between section ($_2$) and the outlet, neglecting friction, is that due to the enlargement of section from a_c to a, i.e.,

$$\frac{v_0^2}{2\,g}\,(m-1)^2, \qquad\qquad \text{where } m = \frac{a}{a_c},$$

we have $\quad h = \dfrac{p_2}{W} + \dfrac{v_2^2}{2\,g} = \dfrac{v_0^2}{2\,g}\,\{1 + (m-1)^2\,\}$ $\qquad\qquad$ (2)

Writing $v_0 = C_v \sqrt{2\,g\,h}$ we get $\dfrac{1}{C_v^2} = m^2 - 2\,m + 2$ $\qquad$ (3)

Giving C_v its mean observed value, ·825, this makes $m = 1\cdot 685$ $= \dfrac{1}{\cdot 594}$ while giving $\dfrac{1}{m}$ the value ·62, as observed for a similar orifice without the external tube, it makes $C_v = \cdot 852$. The difference between this value and ·852 is probably due to the loss due to expansion being somewhat greater than indicated above. Assuming this loss to be given by $k\dfrac{v_0^2}{2\,g}\{\,m-1\,\}^2$, *cf.* Art. 88, and introducing this into equation (2), equation (3) becomes

$$\frac{1}{k}\,C_v^2 = m^2 - 2\,m + 1 + \frac{1}{k}$$

while giving C_v and $\dfrac{1}{m}$ the values ·825, and ·620, this makes $k = 1\cdot 25$.

If, in equation (1), we substitute $m\,C_v\,\sqrt{2\,g\,h} = m\,v_0$ for v_2 this becomes $\dfrac{p_2}{W} = h\,(1 - m^2\,C_v^2)$,

and giving C_v and m the values ·825 and $\dfrac{1}{\cdot 62}$ we have $\dfrac{p_2}{W} = -\cdot 763\,h$.

This agrees very closely with the observed value of $\dfrac{p_2}{W}$, which is approximately $-\cdot 75\,h$.

If then an orifice be made in the mouthpiece, at the *vena contracta* (Fig. 63 b), a tube coupled to this and having its lower end open and in water will support a column of height approximately ·75 h. Theoretically, this will hold until ·75 h = height of the water barometer = 34 feet, *i.e.*, until $h = \dfrac{34}{\cdot 75} = 45\cdot 4$ feet. The effect then of adding the external mouthpiece is to reduce the pressure on the discharge side of the orifice, and so to increase the effective head, and therefore the velocity of discharge. For continuity of flow it is essential that the pressure at the *vena contracta* should be greater than absolute zero (− 34 feet of water), so that a short outlet tube will not run full under a head greater than about 40 feet.

If a diverging tube be placed at the discharge end of the mouthpiece or indeed at the outlet from any pipe fed by the mouthpiece, the pressure at the *vena contracta* will, so long as this is greater than the absolute zero, be reduced, and the discharge thereby increased if this outlet runs full.

This follows since the pressure difference at the *vena contracta* and at the outlet increases with the ratio of the velocities and hence of the areas. If however the final area of the tube be so large that the pressure at the *vena contracta* is reduced to absolute zero (— 34 feet of water), continuity of motion becomes impossible and the diverging tube ceases to run full. Even with a moderate ratio of areas the angle of divergence of the sides θ (Fig. 64 b) should not exceed 16° (Venturi), while the maximum effect is obtained with an angle of about 6°, the diameter increasing from 1 to 1·8 in a length = 9 diameters.

The same increased discharge may be obtained, within limits, by the substitution of a parallel discharge pipe of greater area than the discharge orifice.

Roman law recognised the latter fact, and prohibited the attachment of pipes of greater diameter than the aperture provided at the reservoir, for a distance of 50 feet. The possibility of a partial evasion of the law by the application of a conical frustrum at the open end of the pipe was, however, not apparently perceived.

Sharp-edged Orifice with Converging Mouthpiece.—If a conical converging pipe be fitted external to the orifice, with its larger diameter equal to that of the orifice, the coefficients of velocity and of discharge at exit depend on the angle of convergence.

The following values are taken from experiments by Castel, and indicate that a maximum discharge is to be obtained when the angle of convergence is about 13°·20′.

Diameter of mouthpiece = ·61 inches.

Angle of Convergence.	0°·0′	1°·36′	3°·10′	5°·26′	7°·52′	10°·20′	12°·4′	13°·24′	14°·28′	16°·36′	21°·0′	29°·58′	40°·20′	4°·′
C_v	·830	·866	·894	·924	·931	·950	·955	·962	·966	·971	·971	·975	·980	··
C	·829	·866	·895	·920	·929	·938	·942	·946	·941	·938	·918	·896	·869	··

Diameter = ·787 inches.

Angle of Convergence.	2°·50′	5°·26′	6°·54′	10°·30′	12°·10′	13°·40′	15°·2′	18°·10′	33°··
C_v	·906	·930	·938	·953	·957	·964	·967	·970	··
C	·910	·928	·938	·945	·949	·956	·949	·939	··

The mean of three experiments[1] on a large rectangular converging mouthpiece under a head of 9·6 feet gave a value of $C = ·981$. In this mouthpiece the length was 9·6 feet; the large end 2·4 × 3·2 feet; and the small end ·044 × ·623 feet, opposite faces enclosing angles respectively of 11°·38′ and 15°·18′.

ART. 44.—BELL-MOUTH ORIFICE.

With a bell-mouth orifice (Fig. 64 *a*) having a curvature approximately the same as that of the natural stream lines, the pressure over the walls of the mouthpiece will be zero; the coefficient of contraction, unity; and the only loss of head, that due to viscosity. Here $C_c = 1$; $C_v = ·975$ (experimental);

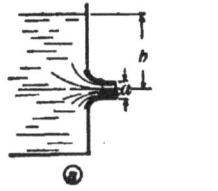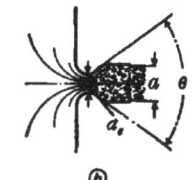

FIG. 64.

$$\therefore \quad C = ·975$$

Since $v = ·975 \sqrt{2 g h}$; $\dfrac{v^2}{2 g} = ·95 h$

∴ loss of energy due to this type of mouthpiece = ·05 h

$$= ·05 \frac{v^2}{2 g} \text{ ft. lbs. per lb. (approximately).}$$

Experiments by Weisbach indicate that the general proportions of such a mouthpiece should be as shown in Fig. 65, the sides of the mouthpiece making an angle of 67° with the plane of the orifice at a point distant about $\dfrac{d}{10}$ from that plane.

Bell-mouth Orifice with Diverging Outlet.—If a diverging pipe be fitted to the bell-mouth as shown in Fig. 64 *b*, so long as this pipe runs full the pressure at the throat is reduced just as at the *vena contracta* in the previous forms of mouthpiece. The effect of the adjutage is therefore to increase the velocity of flow through the throat, and hence the discharge. The loss of energy due to the divergence may be calculated as in the previous case.

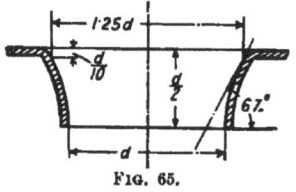

FIG. 65.

---

[1] "Practical Hydraulics," Downing, 1861. By Lespinasse et Languedoc.

Art. 45.—Velocity of Approach.

Where the surface area of a vessel is not so large as to allow of the velocity of approach of the water to an orifice being neglected, if the suffixes $(_1)$ and $(_2)$ refer to the surface and to the *vena contracta* respectively, we have

$$\frac{p_1}{W} + \frac{v_1^2}{2\,g} + z_1 = \frac{p_2}{W} + \frac{v_2^2}{2\,g} + z_2.$$

Putting $p_1 = 0$ and $p_2 = 0$, we have

$$\frac{v_2^2}{2\,g} = \frac{v_1^2}{2\,g} + z_1 - z_2$$

$$= \frac{v_1^2}{2\,g} + h \qquad (h = \text{head over orifice})$$

$$\therefore \ v_2^2 = 2\,g\,h + v_1^2.$$

Here v_1 is the velocity of approach.

In words, the kinetic energy at efflux is equivalent to the potential energy at the surface, together with the kinetic energy due to the velocity of approach.

The statical head which would give the same velocity of efflux is now

$$H = \left[h + \frac{v_1^2}{2\,g} \right] = h + h'.$$

So that the effect of the velocity of approach in increasing the outflow is theoretically the same as that of an additional head h' where $h' = \dfrac{v_1^2}{2\,g}$.

If $\dfrac{a_c}{A}$ be the ratio of the *vena contracta* and surface areas, we have

$$v_1 = v_2 \frac{a_c}{A},$$

$$\therefore \ v_2^2 = 2\,g\,h + v_2^2 \frac{a_c^2}{A^2} = \frac{2\,g\,h}{1 - \dfrac{a_c^2}{A^2}}$$

i.e., the effective head is increased in the ratio $\dfrac{1}{1 - \dfrac{a_c^2}{A^2}}$.

The discharge is therefore increased in the ratio $\dfrac{A}{\sqrt{A^2 - a_c^2}}$

$$= \frac{1}{1 - \dfrac{a_c^2}{2\,A^2}} \text{ (approximately)}.$$

ART. 46.

Time of emptying a Vessel through a small, freely discharging Orifice.— (1) Suppose the surface area A of the vessel to be uniform and large compared with the area a of the orifice.

Let $v =$ velocity of efflux at any instant, and h the height of free surface above the *vena contracta* at the same instant.

Now assuming that $v = c_v \sqrt{2 g h}$, we have, since

$$\frac{\text{velocity of fall of surface}}{\text{velocity of efflux}} = \frac{a_c}{A}, \text{ that}$$

$$\text{velocity of surface} = -\frac{d h}{d t} = C_v \frac{a_c}{A} \sqrt{2 g h} \qquad (1)$$

$$\therefore \quad C_v \frac{a_c}{A} \sqrt{2 g} \cdot d t = -\frac{d h}{\sqrt{h}} \qquad (2)$$

Integrating between any two limits of height h_1 and h_2 we get the time $t_2 - t_1 = t$, necessary to lower the surface through the distance $h_1 - h_2$.

$$\therefore \quad C_v \frac{a_c}{A} \sqrt{2 g} \cdot t = 2 \left\{ h_1^{\frac{1}{2}} - h_2^{\frac{1}{2}} \right\}$$

$$\therefore \quad t = \frac{2 A}{C_v a_c \sqrt{2 g}} \left\{ h_1^{\frac{1}{2}} - h_2^{\frac{1}{2}} \right\} \qquad (3)$$

If C be the coefficient of discharge for the orifice the time will then be given by

$$t = \frac{2 A}{C a \sqrt{2 g}} \left\{ h_1^{\frac{1}{2}} - h_2^{\frac{1}{2}} \right\} \qquad (4)$$

EXAMPLE.

With Borda's mouthpiece running freely

$$t = \frac{2 A}{\cdot 51 a \sqrt{2 g}} \left\{ h_1^{\frac{1}{2}} - h_2^{\frac{1}{2}} \right\}.$$

Time of emptying a Reservoir of varying Cross-section, by small freely discharging Orifice.— Here A is no longer constant but will be a function of h, so that equation (1)

$$-\frac{d h}{d t} = \frac{C a}{A} \sqrt{2 g h}$$

may be integrated if A is an integrable function of h.

EXAMPLE I.

Reservoir with uniformly varying cross-sectional Area.— Let $k D =$ area of reservoir at the orifice.

Then $A = k(D + h)$,

and $-k \int_{h_2}^{h_1} \left(\dfrac{D+h}{\sqrt{h}} \right) dh = C \int_{t_2}^{t_1} \left(a\sqrt{2g} \right) dt$,

$$\therefore\ t_2 - t_1 = t = \frac{k}{C} \left[\frac{2D\left(h_1^{\frac{1}{2}} - h_2^{\frac{1}{2}}\right) + \frac{2}{8}\left(h_1^{\frac{3}{2}} - h_2^{\frac{3}{2}}\right)}{a\sqrt{2g}} \right]$$

Where $C =$ coefficient of discharge.

Example II.

Hemispherical Bowl—Radius r—emptied through Hole in the Bottom.

Here $A = \pi\{r^2 - (r-h)^2\} = \pi\{h^2 - 2rh\}$

$$\therefore \int_{h_2}^{h_1} \frac{A}{\sqrt{h}}\, dh = \pi \int_{h_2}^{h_1} \left(h^{\frac{3}{2}} - 2r\,h^{\frac{1}{2}} \right) dh$$

$$= \pi \left\{ \frac{2}{5}\left(h_1^{\frac{5}{2}} - h_2^{\frac{5}{2}} \right) - \frac{4}{8}\,r\left(h_1^{\frac{3}{2}} - h_2^{\frac{3}{2}} \right) \right\}$$

$$\therefore\ t_2 - t_1 = t = \frac{\pi}{C} \left[\frac{\frac{2}{5}\left(h_1^{\frac{5}{2}} - h_2^{\frac{5}{2}} \right) - \frac{4}{8}\,r\left(h_1^{\frac{3}{2}} - h_2^{\frac{3}{2}} \right)}{a\sqrt{2g}} \right]$$

Where the lower limit of height is less than about four times the diameter of the orifice, a vortex with an air core, is usually formed with the effect that the area of discharge is reduced (Art. 38).

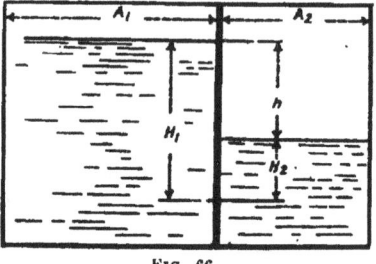

FIG. 66.

Time of Discharge from a Submerged Orifice. — If two vessels whose surface areas are A_1 and A_2 (Fig. 66) are connected by an orifice of area a, and if at any instant H_1 and H_2 are the heights of their free surfaces above the level of the orifice, we have, neglecting viscosity, and assuming

$$v = \sqrt{2g(H_1 - H_2)} = \sqrt{2gh}$$

Velocity of surface $A_1 = v \cdot \dfrac{a}{A_1}$; velocity of $A_2 = v\,\dfrac{a}{A_2}$

$$\therefore\ -\frac{dh}{dt} = C\sqrt{2gh} \cdot a \cdot \left\{ \frac{1}{A_1} + \frac{1}{A_2} \right\}$$

$$\therefore \quad t_2 - t_1 = t = \frac{2}{C\left\{\frac{1}{A_1} + \frac{1}{A_2}\right\} a \cdot \sqrt{2g}}\left\{h_1^{\frac{1}{2}} - h_2^{\frac{1}{2}}\right\}$$

where $C =$ coefficient of discharge.

Where the upper surface remains at the same level we have the state of affairs which holds during the filling of a canal lock through a submerged orifice in the lock gate. The upper surface is in effect now of infinite area, so that putting $A_1 = \infty$ in equation (1), we get the time of filling the lock.

$$\therefore \quad t = \frac{2A_2}{C a \sqrt{2g}}\sqrt{H_1 - H_2}.$$

With submerged orifices the value of C is about ·61, diminishing slightly with an increase in the effective head $H_1 - H_2$.

ART. 47.—FORM OF JET.

Where a jet issues from an orifice in the horizontal base of a vessel, its sectional area gradually diminishes as the velocity increases, until it finally breaks up into a series of detached drops. With a circular orifice this is the most noticeable feature. With any other form of orifice, however, the jet after escaping suffers a continuous change in the form of its cross section. This is due to the effect of the tension of its surface film, which tends in the first place to bring the jet into the circular form. The inertia of the particles of water causes this effect to be slightly overdone, so that a continual alteration and realteration of section takes place, the jet finally—if sufficiently large in diameter and of sufficient height—settling down into a circular section. The action is periodic and approximately isochronous, and consequently with a steady jet the section at any fixed point is constant.

Where a jet escapes from an orifice in the vertical side of a vessel a second disturbing factor now affects its form, for since the velocities of efflux at points on a vertical diameter of the orifice increase with the depth, the trajectories of any two particles situated in the same vertical plane will intersect if produced.

This has the effect of narrowing the jet in the direction of its depth, and, by the consequent impact of particles, causing it to become wider in a horizontal direction. Surface tension prevents dispersion of the stream, and brings the diverging particles back towards the axis of the jet and in a horizontal plane. The consequent impact causes the jet to become narrower in a horizontal direction and increases its depth, and a continual succession of such reactions produces a continual state of change of section along its length. The action is periodic and approximately isochronous and consequently, with a steady jet, the points at which the cross section is of the same general shape as the orifice are relatively stationary With a circular orifice, the section varies from an ellipse with major axis horizontal near the *rena contracta* to the same with major axis vertical. With a polygonal orifice of n sides the section ultimately becomes a star of n points, these points having thickened extremities. The angular points either coincide in direction with those of the orifice or intersect

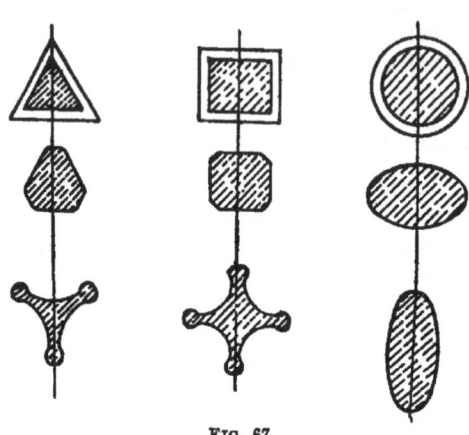

FIG. 67

a corresponding face, always being symmetrical with respect to the orifice. Fig. 6 illustrates the general form taken by the jet from a triangular, square, or circular orifice, the upper section in each case being at, and the second slightly past the *rena contracta*, and the lower giving the star form assumed by the jet.[1]

Fig. 68 shows the form taken by a stream issuing from a sharp-edged rectangular notch. The effect of the impact of converging particles is here strongly marked. The cross sections at various points on the jet are indicated in the figure.

EXAMPLES.

(1) A circular orifice 1 square inch in area is made in the vertical side of a large tank. If the jet fall vertically through $1\frac{3}{4}$ feet while moving horizontally through 5 feet, at the same time discharging 16 gallons per minute, determine the horizontal force on the tank.

Answer. 1·286 lbs.

(2) If the tank of the preceding example is suspended from knife edges

---

[1] For further information, a paper by Lord Rayleigh ("Proceedings, Royal Society," vol. 71) should be consulted.

; feet above the level of the orifice, and if, when the head of water in the
ank is 4 feet, the discharge is 205 lbs. per minute, while a weight of

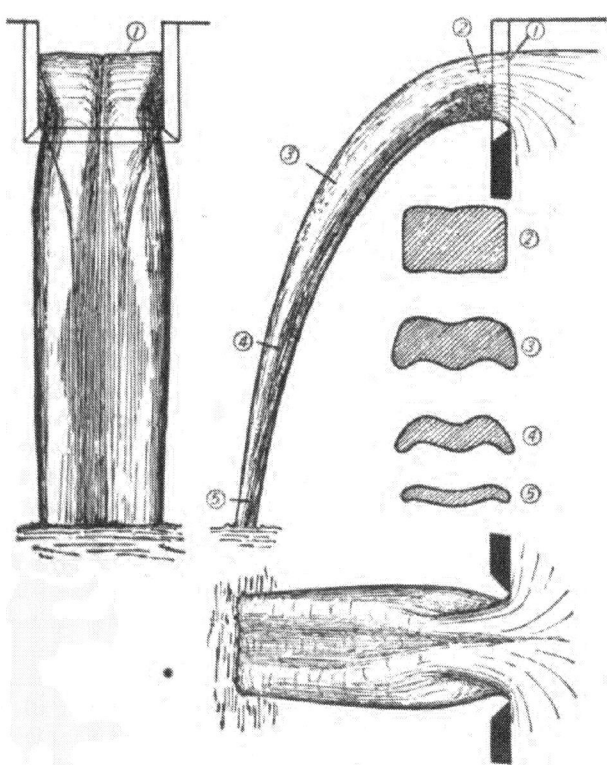

Fig. 68.

8·35 lbs., with a horizontal leverage of 1 foot, is required to keep the tank
vertical, determine the coefficients of velocity, contraction, and discharge.

Answer. $C_v = ·98$; $C_c = ·638$; $C = ·625$.

(3) A boat, having jet propulsion, moves at 10 miles per hour. The
water leaves the nozzles with a relative velocity of 40 feet per second. If
1,500 lbs. per second are passed through the pumps, determine the propelling force on the vessel.

Answer.   1,180 lbs.

CHAPTER VI.

ART. 48.—LARGE ORIFICES.

WHERE an orifice is large, except where formed in the horizontal base of a vessel the assumption that the mean velocity over its whole area is sensibly equal to that at its centre of area is no longer true, and it becomes necessary to take account of the variation of velocity at different depths in its plane. As in the case of a small orifice a *vena contracta* is formed of approximately the same sectional shape as the orifice, and depending for its magnitude on the shape, dimensions, and head above the latter, and on the circumstances governing the formation of stream lines in the approaching vein.

In the usual theoretical discussion of the flow from such an orifice the two fundamental assumptions on which the theory is based are themselves false and quite misleading, and while the results obtained are not without value as forming the basis of useful empirical formulae, the treatment cannot be looked upon as scientific.

Briefly outlined, the method consists in assuming that at all points at the same depth in the plane of an orifice the velocity of efflux is the same, being that corresponding to the head of water above the point, and that the direction of flow at each point is perpendicular to the plane of the orifice.

Calculating the discharge over a small element δa of the area, i.e., $\sqrt{2gh} \cdot \delta a$ and summing such discharges over the elements which go to make up the whole area, gives what is termed the theoretical discharge $\int \sqrt{2gh} \cdot \delta a$, and this, when multiplied by an empirical constant termed the coefficient of discharge, gives the true discharge.

Fig. 53, which indicates roughly how the velocity at the orifice varies at different points in the cross section, sufficiently shows the error involved in the first, while a consideration of the stream line formation hows the error of the second assumption. Fig. 69 indicates how he velocity perpendicular to the orifice varies, and how it differs from the heoretical velocity $\sqrt{2\,g\,h}$, as given by the horizontal ordinates of the arabola $m\,n\,q$. Here the actual velocity is represented in elevation and lan by the corresponding ordinates of the curves $a\,c\,b$, and a' $' a''$.

The solid represented in plan ind elevation by the shaded areas will then represent to scale the volume discharged per second; while the solid bounded by the plane of the orifice; the perpendiculars an, bq, $a'\,p'$, $a''\,p''$; and the curved surface of the parabola, represented by $n\,p\,q$, will represent to the same scale the theoretical discharge. The ratio of these volumes thus gives the coefficient of discharge.

In spite of the recognised fallacies embodied in the method of treatment outlined above, the difficulties encountered in a rigorous treatment are so many and the results obtained so cumbrous, that we are still compelled to fall back on the more simple, though inaccurate, formulae, together with these experimentally deduced coefficients.

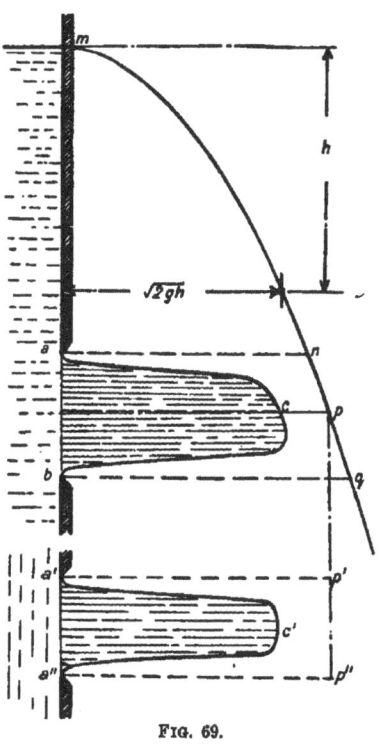

FIG. 69.

The assumptions, however, become more rational if the state of affairs at the *vena contracta* be considered instead of at the orifice. Here we may assume with some reason that the flow is everywhere perpendicular to the cross section of the stream, and that the pressure throughout is sensibly uniform and equal to that of the atmosphere, so that, except for the retarding effect of the atmosphere at the boundaries, the velocity at any point in this section, at a depth h, below the free surface in the vessel, is sensibly equal to $\sqrt{2\,g\,h}$. The more important cases of flow will now be considered on this assumption.

Art. 49.—Large Vertical Rectangular Orifice, neglecting Velocity of Approach.

Let H' = height of free surface above top of *vena contracta*.
„ b = breadth of orifice.
„ d = depth „
„ b' = breadth of *vena contracta* } assumed to be a rectangle.
„ d' = depth „ „

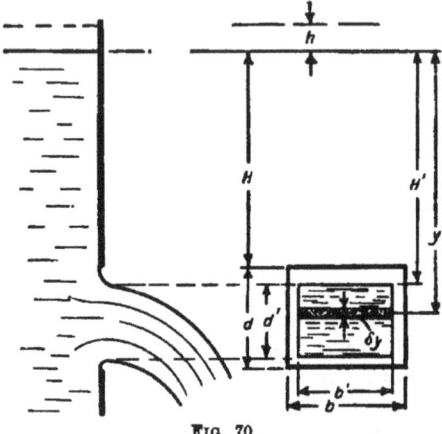

FIG. 70.

Consider the flow over any element of the *vena contracta* at a depth y below the free surface, and having an area $b' \, \delta y$ (Fig. 70).

The velocity at this depth $= C \sqrt{2 g y}$ feet per second.

∴ Flow over this area per second $= C_v \, b' \, \delta y \sqrt{2 g y}$, c.f.

Integrating this expression, and giving y the limits $H' + d'$ and H' we get the flow over the whole area.

$$\therefore Q = C_v \, b' \sqrt{2 g} \int_{H'}^{H' + d'} \sqrt{y} \, d y = \frac{2}{3} C_v \, b' \sqrt{2 g} \left[y^{\frac{3}{2}} \right]_{H'}^{H' + d'}$$

$$= \frac{2}{3} C_v \, b' \sqrt{2 g} \left\{ (H' + d')^{\frac{3}{2}} - H'^{\frac{3}{2}} \right\} \qquad (1)$$

The difficulty of obtaining accurate measurements of b', H' and d' now arises, since these vary with, but do not bear a fixed ratio to b, H, and d, while experimental evidence as to the precise nature of the variation is wanting. The best way out of the difficulty appears to be to write

$$C = C_e \frac{b' \left\{ (H' + d')^{\frac{3}{2}} - H'^{\frac{3}{2}} \right\}}{b \left\{ (H + d)^{\frac{3}{2}} - H^{\frac{3}{2}} \right\}}$$

where $H =$ depth of top of orifice below the free surface. This then gives us

$$Q = \frac{2}{3} C b \sqrt{2g} \left\{ (H + d)^{\frac{3}{2}} - H^{\frac{3}{2}} \right\} \qquad (2)$$

The reason for this substitution is that the value of C in this formula has been determined with some accuracy for various types of orifice and for different heads.

Formula (2) is that obtained by the inaccurate process of reasoning outlined at the beginning of this article, for, assuming that the flow through any element $b \, \delta y$ of the orifice is the same as that through the corresponding element of the *vena contracta* of area $b' \dfrac{d'}{d} \cdot \delta y$, and that this flow is therefore given by $C b \, \delta y \sqrt{2g \, y}$, where C has the same value for each element, and therefore for the whole area, we have

$$Q = C b \sqrt{2g} \int_{H}^{H + d} \sqrt{y} \cdot dy$$

$$= \frac{2}{3} C b \sqrt{2g} \left[(H + d)^{\frac{3}{2}} - H^{\frac{3}{2}} \right]$$

Comparing this with the simple formula

$$Q = C b d \sqrt{2g \left(H + \frac{d}{2} \right)},$$

obtained by considering the head over the section as sensibly equal to that at its centroid, we see that the two values of Q are in the ratio $\dfrac{2}{3} \dfrac{(H + d)^{\frac{3}{2}} - H^{\frac{3}{2}}}{d \sqrt{H + \dfrac{d}{2}}}$. For values of H greater than $\dfrac{d}{2}$ the difference

amounts to less than 1·0 per cent., so that for all larger values of H, the simpler formula is to be preferred.

The velocity of approach may be taken into account by increasing the head by an amount h as explained on p. 120, thus making the effective head $= H + h$.

Then $Q = \dfrac{2}{3} C b \sqrt{2g} \left[(H + h + d)^{\frac{3}{2}} - (H + h)^{\frac{3}{2}} \right]$ \qquad (2)

H.A.   K

As is clear from the expression assumed above for the value of C, this is not a constant, but varies both with the depth of the water and with the dimensions of the orifice, and can only be determined by experiment.

With sharp-edged orifices, and a free discharge into air, the values of C for a square opening are very approximately as given below (Hamilton Smith).

Head above centre of orifice in feet.	Length of side of square in feet.			
	·40	·60	·80	1·0
·6	·601	·598	—	—
1·0	·603	·601	·600	·599
3·0	·605	·604	·603	·603
6·0	·604	·603	·602	·602
10·0	·603	·602	·602	·601
20·0	·601	·601	·601	·600
100·0	·598	·598	·598	·598

For vertical rectangular orifices the value of C varies with the ratio of the width b to the depth d.

The following table gives the value of the coefficient for orifices 1 foot wide :—

Head in feet from centre of orifice.	Values of d in feet.						
	$\frac{1}{8}$	$\frac{1}{4}$	$\frac{1}{2}$	$\frac{3}{4}$	1·0	1·5	2·0
1·0	·632	·632	·618	·612	·606	·626	—
3·0	·627	·627	·615	·610	·605	·614	·619
6·0	·615	·615	·609	·604	·602	·606	·610
10·0	·606	·603	·601	·601	·601	·601	·602
20·0	·602	·601	·601	·601	·601	·601	·602

ART. 50.—FLOW THROUGH A CIRCULAR ORIFICE.

Let H = depth of centre of orifice (Fig. 71).

„ R = radius of orifice.

„ r = „   „ vena contracta.

Then the area of an elementary strip taken in the *vena contracta* at a distance y from the centre, as shown, is $2 x \delta y$.

The head over the element $= H - y$,

$\therefore$ Flow over this element $= \sqrt{2 g (H - y)} \times 2 x \delta y$

$\therefore \quad \delta Q = 2 \sqrt{2 g} \times \sqrt{(r^2 - y^2) (H - y)} \, \delta y$.

For convenience in integrating, expand $\sqrt{H - y}$ by the Binomial Theorem, *i.e.*, put

$$\sqrt{H - y} = \sqrt{H} \sqrt{1 - \frac{y}{H}} = \sqrt{H} \left\{ 1 - \frac{y}{2 H} - \frac{y^2}{8 H^2} + - \text{etc.} \right\}$$

$$\left(\text{since } (1 - x)^n = 1 - n x + \frac{n (n - 1)}{2} x^2 - \text{etc.} \right)$$

Now put $y = r \cos \theta$.

Then $\qquad \dfrac{d y}{d \theta} = - r \sin \theta$.

$\therefore \quad \delta y = - r \sin \theta \, \delta \theta$,

and $\quad \sqrt{r^2 - y^2} = \sqrt{r^2 (1 - \cos^2 \theta)}$

$\qquad\qquad = r \sin \theta$.

So that $\delta Q = 2 \sqrt{2 g H} \left\{ - r^2 \sin^2 \theta \right.$

$\left. \left(1 - \frac{r \cos \theta}{2 H} - \frac{r^2 \cos^2 \theta}{8 H^2} + - \text{etc.} \right) \right\} \delta \theta$.

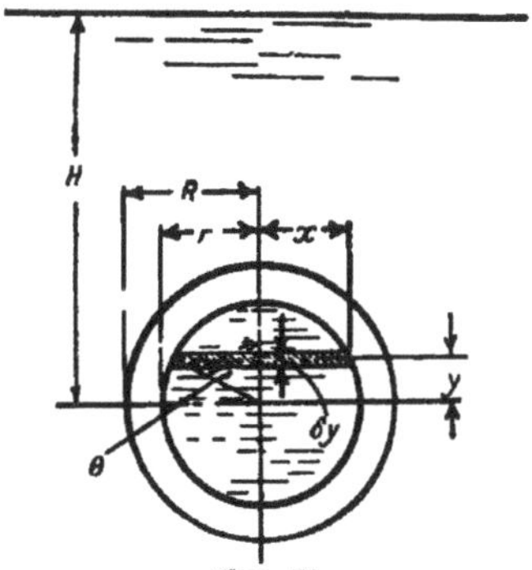

Integrating this expression and giving the limits π and o, since these are the values of θ corresponding to the values $+ r$ of y, we get, on introducing C_v, the total flow Q over the whole section.

FIG. 71.

$$\therefore \quad Q = 2 C_v \sqrt{2 g H} \int_0^{\pi} r^2 \sin^2 \theta \left(1 - \frac{r \cos \theta}{2 H} - \frac{r^2 \cos^2 \theta}{8 H^2} + - \text{etc.} \right) d \theta$$

$$= C_v \pi r^2 \sqrt{2 g H} \left\{ 1 - \frac{1}{32} \frac{r^2}{H^2} + - \text{etc.} \right\}$$

the succeeding terms being negligible.

If C be the coefficient of discharge for the orifice, then since $C_v = \dfrac{r^2}{R^2}$ we may write

$$Q = C \pi R^2 \sqrt{2 g H} \left\{ 1 - \frac{1}{32} \frac{r^2}{H^2} \right\}$$

As in the case of a rectangular orifice, the coefficient in general decreases as the orifice increases and also as the head increases.

K 2

The following table gives the approximate values of C for circular orifices (Hamilton Smith) :—

Head above centre of orifice (feet).	Diameter of orifice in feet.			
	·40	·60	·80	1·0
1·0	·597	·595	·593	·591
2·0	·599	·597	·596	·595
4·0	·598	·597	·597	·596
6·0	·598	·597	·596	·596
10·0	·597	·596	·596	·595
20·0	·596	·596	·595	·594
100·0	·592	·592	·592	·592

ART. 51.—SUBMERGED ORIFICES.

If the water level on the discharge side is above the highest point of the opening we get a submerged orifice.

Let H_1 = depth of water above upper edge of orifice on the incoming side, in feet.

Let H_2 = similar depth on discharge side.

Then the effective depth at all points in the orifice is the same, viz., $H_1 - H_2$ (p. 108).

∴ Theoretical velocity of efflux = $\sqrt{2 g (H_1 - H_2)}$ ft. sec.

∴ Quantity per second through orifice = $C A \sqrt{2 g} \sqrt{H_1 - H_2}$ where A is the area of the orifice.

Taking into account the velocity of approach, v_1, the effective head will now be $H_1 + h - H_2$ feet, where $h = \dfrac{v_1^2}{2 g}$, and the discharge will be given by

$$Q = C A \sqrt{2 g} \sqrt{H_1 + h - H_2} \text{ cub. ft. sec.}$$

The value of C for a submerged orifice may be taken as being about 1 per cent. less than its value for the same orifice under the same effective head, and when discharging freely into air.

Hanbury Brown[1] gives the following as being approximate values of C for sluices and regulator openings in masonry piers :—

[1] " Irrigation," Constable & Co., London, 1907.

Ordinary lock sluices . . . . . . $C =$ ·62

Small regulator openings with shallow water . . ,, ·57

Regulator openings up to 6 feet wide with recesses⟩ ,, ·62
  in the piers . . . . ∫

Ditto between 6 feet and 13 feet wide . . . ,, ·72

Ditto above 13 feet wide ⤫ ⤫ ⤫ ⤫ ⤫ ⤫ ,, ·82

Regulator openings up to 6 feet wide with straight⟩ ,, ·72
  and continuous piers . . . . . ∫

Ditto between 6 feet and 13 feet wide . . . ,, ·82

Ditto above 13 feet wide . . . . . . ,, ·92

A series of experiments[1] on a submerged orifice 4 feet square through a wooden bulkhead 3·75 inches thick, with various forms of entry, gave the following values of C:—

—	Form of entrance.	Values of C.		
		Max.	Min.	Mean.
a	Square corners	·625	·605	·61
	Contraction sup-⟩on bottom . . .	·665	·625	·64
b	pressed by means⎱of guides curved ,, ,, and one side	·735	·675	·69
c	to arcs of ellipses, so as to gradually ,, ,, and two sides	·825	·757	·78
d	divert the incom-ing stream . ∫on all four sides . .	·970	·919	·95

In every case the minimum value of C was obtained with a mean velocity of flow ranging from 1·9 to 2·3 feet per sec., the velocities of flow ranging from approximately 1·0 to 4·0 feet per sec.

The experiments were extended by the addition of tubes of lengths ·62, 1·25, 2·50, 5·0, 10·0, and 14·0 feet on the discharge side of the orifices, and the curves of Fig. 72 denote to what extent these affected the discharge.

For the tubes having square corners at the entrance, the coefficient of discharge increases at first almost directly as the length of tube increases, then at a gradually decreasing rate until the length "L" of the tube becomes between 3 and 3·5 times the side of the square. For lengths

[1] " Bulletin of the University of Wisconsin," No. 216. Engineering Series, vol. 4, No. 4.

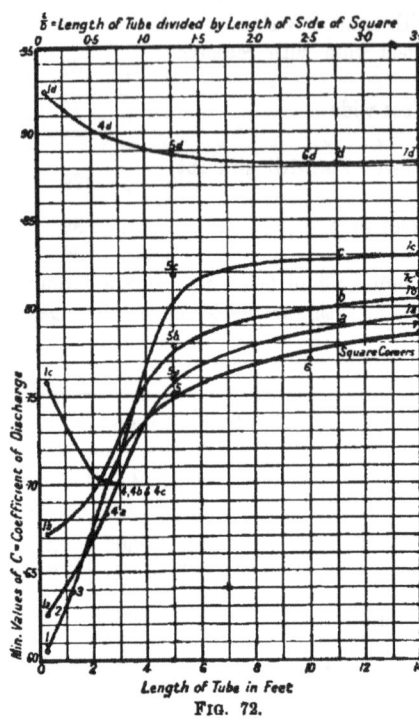

$\frac{L}{D}$ = Length of Tube divided by Length of Side of Square

Min. Values of C = Coefficient of Discharge

Length of Tube in Feet

FIG. 72.

less than about **5** fe
observations showed a
upstream current locate
at the upper side of th
tube, this reducing th
effective discharge are.
This effect was found t
become less marked a
the velocity was increase.
For greater lengths of out
let tube this current wa
absent, and the condition
permitted the formation
a region of less tha
normal pressure at ti
vena contracta (p. 117). I
n represents the numbe
of sides on which the con
traction is suppressed, the
following relationships giv
the minimum values
C within about **2** pe
cent. :—

For $L \div D \leqq 0.1$;
$$C = .605 + .019 \, n^2.$$

For $L \div D \geqq 3.0$; $C = .786 + .0055 \, n^2.$

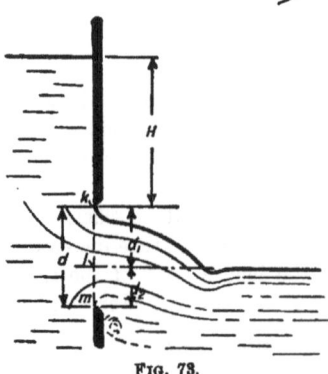

FIG. 73.

Partially Submerged Orifice (Fig. 73).—
Here the portion of the orifice l
below the normal water level on th
discharge side, may be considered as
a submerged orifice, while the portion
$k \, l$ above this level may be looked up
as discharging freely into air, the
quantity passing each portion bein
calculated separately on these assump
tions.

Thus in a rectangular orifice of
breadth b and depth d, having a hea
of water on the supply side $= H$ abov

he top of the orifice, with free discharge over a depth d_1, and submerged over the remainder d_2 of its depth we have

Discharge over depth $d_1 = Q_1 = \dfrac{2}{3}\, C_1\, b\, \sqrt{2\,g}\, \left\{ (H + d_1)^{\frac{3}{2}} - H^{\frac{3}{2}} \right\}$

,,   ,,   ,, $d_2 = Q_2 = C_2\, b\, d_2\, \sqrt{2\,g}\, (H + d_1)^{\frac{1}{2}}.$

$\therefore$ Total discharge $Q = Q_1 + Q_2 = b\, \sqrt{2\,g}$

$$\left[\frac{2}{3}\, C_1\, \left\{ (H + d_1)^{\frac{3}{2}} - H^{\smile} \right\} + d_2\, C_2\, (H + d_1)^{\frac{1}{2}} \right]$$

If $C_1 = C_2 = C$ we get

$$Q = C\, b\, \sqrt{2\,g}\, \left[(H + d_1)^{\frac{1}{2}} \left\{ \frac{2}{3}\, (H + d_1) + d_2 \right\} - \frac{2}{3}\, H^{\frac{3}{2}} \right]$$

If $h =$ the head equivalent to the velocity of approach, the formula becomes

$$Q = C\, b\, \sqrt{2\,g}\, \left[\begin{array}{l} (H + d_1 + h)^{\frac{1}{2}} \left\{ \frac{2}{3}\, (H + d_1 + h) + d_2 \right\} \\[1ex] \qquad - \frac{2}{3}\, (H + h)^{\frac{3}{2}}. \end{array} \right]$$

The difficulty in exactly estimating d_1 and d_2, and the undulatory motion of the surface which is usually found in a partially submerged orifice, renders this a most unsatisfactory method of estimating the flow of a stream.

The coefficients so far given only apply where the jet is wholly submerged or where discharge takes place freely into the air. If the issuing stream, instead of springing clear of the orifice adheres to its face, the formation of a true *vena contracta* is prevented and we have an abnormal increase in C. Thus if the jet is discharging freely into air, and if the level on the discharge side is allowed to rise, at some point before the level reaches that of the notch sill the discharge ceases to be free and a sudden increase in the value of C results. As d_2 increases, C resumes its normal value.

From a scientific point of view the above treatment, due to Dubuat, is not satisfactory. A rational treatment would require to take into account the distribution of pressures and velocities in the issuing stream, and from the nature of the case would lead to results too cumbersome for practical application.

ART. 52.—LAW OF COMPARISON FOR ORIFICES.

Similar orifices are such as may be represented by the same drawing to different scales. If similarly situated, the free water surface will be represented by the same line, whatever the scale of the drawing.

If the scale ratio for any two orifices, *i.e.*, the ratio of an two corresponding linear dimensions, is S, the ratio of the areas corresponding elements of the orifices will be S^2, while if similarly situated with respect to the water surface, their depths are proportion to S.

That the value of C may be expected to be very approximate the same for two such similar orifices was shown by Professor James Thomson[1] in a discussion of which the following is a brief résumé.

Consider two similar and similarly situated particles of fluid (1) and (2). The masses of these and their weights are in the ratio of the volumes, so that we have $w_1 = S^3 w_2$.

Now if these particles are to trace out paths which shall be similar, corresponding forces acting upon them must have the same ratio, and it follows that this ratio must be the ratio of their weights since this is fixed. Apart from the forces due to the statical pressure corresponding to the depth of the particle, which are proportional to its depth multiplied by its area, and therefore follow the required law, the only other forces are those due to centrifugal action and to the effect of viscosity. Neglecting the latter,[2] and terming F the centrifugal force, we have

$$\frac{F_1}{F_2} = \frac{w_1 v_1^2}{r_1} \cdot \frac{r_2}{w_2 v_2^2} = S^3 \cdot \frac{r_2}{r_1}\left(\frac{v_1}{v_2}\right)^2$$

But if the paths of the particles are similar, $r_1 = S r_2$,

$$\therefore \frac{F_1}{F_2} = S^2 \left(\frac{v_1}{v_2}\right)^2$$

It follows as a necessary condition that $\left(\frac{v_1}{v_2}\right)^2 = S$ and this condition will evidently be fulfilled if $\left(\frac{v_1}{v_2}\right)^2 = \frac{h_1}{h_2}$, *i.e.*, if $v^2 = 2 g h$, and if all corresponding particles are similarly situated with respect to the free surface. In such a case, the paths of all corresponding particles being similar, the contractions of the two jets will also be similar and the values of C will become identical. A simple ratio thus connects the relative discharge of the two orifices.

[1] "British Association Report," 1876, p. 243.

[2] Since the force introduced by viscosity $= \mu \frac{d v}{d s}$ per unit area, we have, if P is this force

$$\frac{P_1}{P_2} \propto (S)^2 \cdot \frac{d v_1}{d v_2} \cdot \frac{d s_2}{d s_1} \propto \left[(S)^2 \cdot \sqrt{S} \cdot \frac{1}{S}\right]$$ if $v_1 = \sqrt{2 g h_1}$, so that $\frac{P_1}{P_2} \propto (S)^{\frac{3}{2}}$. Viscosity therefore tends to prevent exact similarity of flow, unless $\frac{\mu_1}{\mu_2} \propto (S)^{\frac{3}{2}}$.

In two triangular notches having the same value of θ, we have two similar and similarly situated orifices, so that $\dfrac{Q_1}{Q_2} = \left(\dfrac{H_1}{H_2} \right)^{\frac{5}{2}}.$

ART. 53.—FLOW OVER NOTCHES AND WEIRS.

Where the free surface on the supply side is below the level of the upper edge of an orifice, this is termed a notch, and, if of large dimensions, a weir.

The theoretical treatment for flow over such notches follows exactly similar lines to that for flow through large orifices, and is subject to the same erroneous assumptions. The errors in-volved in assuming that the velocity of efflux perpendicular to the plane of the notch, at the notch, at any depth h, is propor-tional to $\sqrt{2\,g\,h}$, is indicated in Fig. 74, where the horizontal ordinates of the parabola $m\,n\,q$ show the theoretical velocity at any depth below the free surface of the still water at S, while the ordinates of the curve $a\,n\,c\,b$ denote the actual velocities in

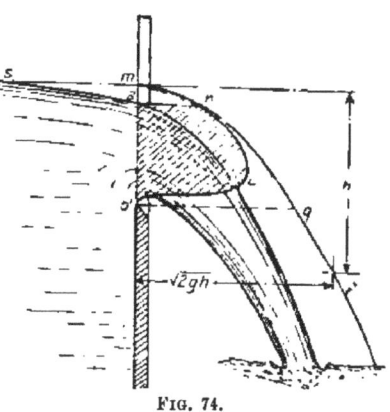

FIG. 74.

this direction in the plane of the notch. The coefficient of discharge will then be equal to the ratio of the volumes represented in elevation by the shaded area $a\,n\,c\,b$ and the area $m\,n\,q\,b$.

The fact that owing to the curvature of the stream lines the pressure over a cross section is nowhere uniform, renders a rigorous treatment impossible, and the next best method is to consider the state of affairs in the plane of the notch.

An examination of the contour of the escaping stream shows that in the plane of the notch its upper surface is lower than the free surface at a point a short distance up-stream where the motion is steady.

This fall from s to a (Fig. 74) is essential if the surface filaments are to have the required velocity of efflux at the notch, and since their motion is approximately perpendicular to the plane of the orifice and is unaffected save by the resistance of the air, their velocity may be taken as sensibly equal to $\sqrt{2 g (a\, m)} = \sqrt{2 g\, H'}$ (Fig. 75).

In general H' is approximately equal to $\cdot 14\, H$, where $H =$ height of water measured to still water level, above the crest of the notch or weir, so that $(H - H') =$ depth of water at crest in feet.

Art. 54.—Theoretical Formulae for Flow over Weirs.

Rectangular Weirs (Fig. 75).—Let $b =$ length of weir in feet.

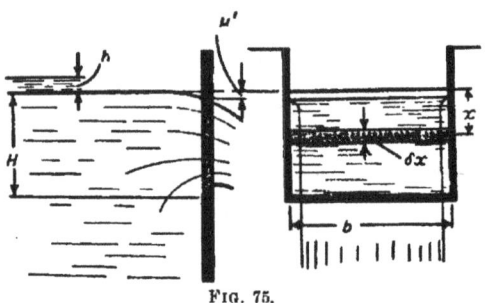

Consider the flow across any element of area $b\,\delta x$, in the plane of the weir, at a depth x below the still water surface of the supply.

The volume passing this element per second $= \delta Q = C' b\, \delta x\, \sqrt{2 g x}$ cub. ft. per sec.

Integrating this expression and giving x

FIG. 75.

the upper and lower limits H and H', and assuming that C' has the same value for each element, we have

$$Q = \frac{2}{3} C' b \sqrt{2 g} \left\{ H^{\frac{3}{2}} - H'^{\frac{3}{2}} \right\} \text{ cub. ft. per sec.} \qquad (1)$$

The value of this coefficient C' has not been experimentally determined, so that the formula in its present form cannot be applied to determine the discharge in any practical case. If, however, we write

$$C' \left\{ H^{\frac{3}{2}} - H'^{\frac{3}{2}} \right\} = C\, H^{\frac{3}{2}}$$

the formula becomes

$$Q = \frac{2}{3} C b \sqrt{2 g}\, H^{\frac{3}{2}} \text{ cub. ft. per sec.} \qquad (2)$$

and the value of this coefficient is known with fair accuracy for different values of H.

Formula (2) may be deduced with less reason by assuming the depth of water in the plane of the notch to be H, i.e., neglecting the fall from still water level, and assuming that the velocity of the surface filaments is zero, and therefore by integrating the expression $\delta Q = C b\, \delta x\, \sqrt{2 g x}$

between the limits H and 0. It might also be deduced from equation (2) of p. 129 by writing $H = 0$; $d = H$.

The value of C, in addition to varying with the breadth and depth of the weir, varies largely with its position with respect to the sides and bottom of the approach channel. Where the sides of this channel are so far removed as not to affect the contraction of section at either side of the weir, this is said to have two end contractions, while where the channel is of the same breadth as the weir, the latter has no end contractions, and is termed a *Suppressed Weir*. The bottom contraction is also affected by the nearness of the sill of the weir to the bottom of the channel of approach and by the inclination of the weir face.

Where the "*nappe*," or falling sheet of water, comes into contact with the top or down-stream face of the weir, as shown in Figs. 80 and 88, a further and in general irregular variation takes place in C. In what immediately follows, only those weirs will be considered in which the *nappe* springs clear of the crest and discharges freely into the air, the crest being vertical, narrow in comparison with the head, and having a sharp upstream edge.

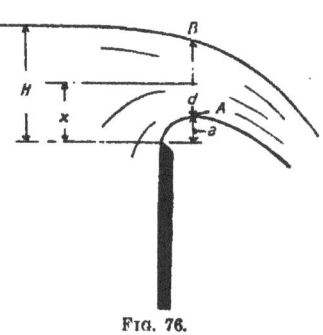

FIG. 76.

Boussinesq's Theory.—A theoretical treatment of the flow over a suppressed weir, which is of much interest, is due to *Boussinesq*.

Let H = depth above sill.

,, a be the amount by which the arched under side of the vein rises above the sill. (Assumed, and verified by Bazin, to be a definite fraction (·13) of H) (Fig. 76).

At the vertical section, at which a is a maximum, let d be the vertical thickness of the vein.

If we assume that, over this section, the stream lines are portions of concentric circles and are normal to the section, and also assume that there is no loss of energy up to this section we have the conditions obtaining in free vortex flow and as in that case, if r is the radius of curvature of any stream line, $v r$ is constant.

Consider any filament, x above the sill, of velocity v, and radius r.

Let v_a = vel. at A; v_b = vel. at B.

Then $v_a = \sqrt{2 g (H - a)}$; $v = \sqrt{2 g (H - a)} . \dfrac{r_a}{r_a + x - a}$

$$\therefore \ Q = b \int_a^{d+a} \sqrt{2\,g\,(H-a)} \cdot \frac{r_a}{r_a + x - a} \cdot dx$$

$$= b \sqrt{2\,g\,(H-a)} \cdot r_a \log \frac{r_a + d}{r_a}$$

Let $r_a = n\,d$

Then $Q = b \sqrt{2\,g\,(H-a)} \cdot n\,d \log \left(1 + \dfrac{1}{n}\right)$

And since $\left(\dfrac{r_b}{r_a}\right)^2 = \left(\dfrac{v_a}{v_b}\right)^2 = \dfrac{H-a}{H-a-d}$

$$\therefore \ d = (H - a) \left\{ \frac{2\,n+1}{(n+1)^2} \right\} \ [1]$$

$$\therefore \ Q = b \sqrt{2\,g} \left\{H - a\right\}^{\frac{3}{2}} \left[\frac{n\,(2\,n+1)}{(n+1)^2} \log\left(1 + \frac{1}{n}\right) \right]$$

But for permanence of *régime* the flow will adjust itself until the discharge is a maximum, and in this case $\dfrac{d\,Q}{d\,n} = o.$

On differentiating [2] this gives $\dfrac{2\,n+1}{3\,n+1} = \log_e\left(1 + \dfrac{1}{n}\right)$

or $n = \cdot 8814$ $\left(\log\,(1 + \dfrac{1}{n}) = \cdot 7581\right)$

$$\therefore \ Q = b \sqrt{2\,g}\,(H-a)^{\frac{3}{2}} \left\{ \frac{\cdot 8814 \times 2 \cdot 7628}{(1 \cdot 8814)^2} \right\} \times \cdot 7851$$

$$= b \sqrt{2\,g}\,H^{\frac{3}{2}} \left\{1 - \frac{a}{H}\right\}^{\frac{3}{2}} \times \cdot 522.$$

Taking $a \div H = \cdot 13$ this becomes

$$Q = \cdot 423\,b \sqrt{2\,g}\,H^{\frac{3}{2}}$$

$$= 3 \cdot 39\,b\,H^{\frac{3}{2}} \ \text{c. f. s.}$$

a value in very close agreement with results experimentally.

[1] $\left(\dfrac{r_b}{r_a}\right)^2 = \left(\dfrac{n+1}{n}\right)^2 = \dfrac{H-a}{H-a-d}$

$$\therefore \ d = (H - a) \left\{ 1 - \left(\frac{n}{n+1}\right)^2 \right\}$$

$$= (H - a) \left\{ \frac{2\,n+1}{(n+1)^2} \right\}.$$

[2] $\dfrac{d\,Q}{d\,n} = K \left[\dfrac{n\,(2\,n+1)}{(n+1)^2} \cdot \dfrac{n}{n+1} \left(-\dfrac{1}{n^2}\right) + \log\left(1 + \dfrac{1}{n}\right) \right.$

$$\left. \left\{ \frac{(n+1)^2\,(4\,n+1) - n\,(2\,n+1)\,2\,(n+1)!}{(n+1)^4} \right\} \right]$$

$$\therefore \ 2\,n+1 = \log\left(1 + \frac{1}{n}\right) \left\{(n+1)\,(4\,n+1) - 2\,n\,(2\,n+1)\right\}.$$

$$= (3\,n+1)\,\log_e\left(1 + \frac{1}{n}\right).$$

ART. 54a.—EXPERIMENTAL RESULTS AND FORMULAE.

Adopting the base formula $Q = K b H^{\frac{3}{2}}$ cub. ft. per sec., where $K = \frac{2}{3} \sqrt{2 g}\, C$, many experiments have been carried out to determine the value of K. Of these, perhaps those of Francis, Fteley and Stearns, Smith, Bazin, and Williams are the most reliable.

Francis,[1] in a preliminary series of experiments carried out in 1848 and 1851, assumed the formula $Q = K b H^x$, and found x to vary slightly with the head, having a mean value 1·47.

In his later experiments, however, carried out in 1852, he adopted, for convenience, the constant value 1·5, and determined the corresponding values of K.

From these experiments, carried out on weirs from 8 to 10 feet long, and with heads ranging from ·62 to 1·56 feet, he deduced the empirical formula

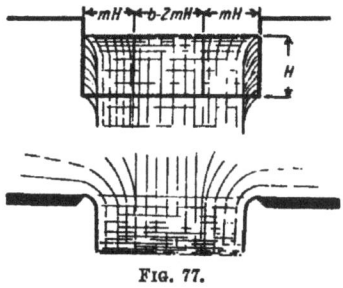

FIG. 77.

$$Q = 3\cdot33 \left(b - \frac{n}{10} H \right) H^{\frac{3}{2}} \text{ cub. ft. per sec.}$$

for the flow over a sharp-edged rectangular notch, where $n = 2$, 1, or 0, according as the stream has 2, 1, or 0 end contractions, the bottom contraction being free in every case.

Thus for two end contractions $Q = 3\cdot33\,(b - \cdot2\,H)\,H^{\frac{3}{2}}$ c.f.s.

„   one   „   contraction $Q = 3\cdot33\,(b - \cdot1\,H)\,H^{\frac{3}{2}}$ c.f.s.

„   no   „   „ $Q = 3\cdot33\,b\,H^{\frac{3}{2}}$ c.f.s.

That this formula, though empirical, has a rational basis may be seen if we consider the state of affairs in a long and shallow notch having two end contractions (Fig. 77).

If the notch is sufficiently broad, a certain section in the middle will have stream lines which, as seen from above, are parallel, while the two end sections have stream lines which suffer an amount of curvature depending on their distance from the ends. The distance over which this curvature extends is found to be approximately $m\,H$, where $m = 1\cdot5$.

---

[1] Lowell Hydraulic Experiments (New York, 1883).

This end contraction evidently diminishes the discharge by an amoun:
which is constant for a given depth, and it is reasonable to assume that :
therefore diminishes the effective breadth of the notch by an amoun:
which is also constant for a given depth, and which depends only on th:
depth. The law of its variation with the depth has not been accurate.
determined, but it was assumed, as appears to be approximately true, that
the diminution in effective length is directly proportional to the dep:b
and that the effective length is therefore equal to $(b - n k H)$ where n is
the number of contractions and k is a constant to be determined
experimentally. Francis then assumed (though not on theoretica:
grounds) that the discharge from notches of equal effective length varie:
according to a constant power of the depth, so that the formula
became [1]

$$Q = K \{ b - n k H \} H^x.$$

Though neither of the assumptions made is quite correct, yet if x b:
given the value 1·5, K the value 3·33, and k the value $\frac{1}{10}$, they lead to
results closely in accord with experiment.

In general the Francis formula is suitable for use for all heads above
6 inches where the bottom contraction and end contractions, if any, are
free, and where the length of crest is greater than three times the head.

Even where the ratio of length to head is less than three, the formula
gives fairly accurate results, the discharge as calculated being always
slightly less than observed. Recent experiments at Cornell University [2]
on a suppressed weir 6·56 feet wide and with heads ranging from 2·0 to
4·85 feet give mean results 98·4 per cent. of those calculated by its use,
and indicate its reliability for heads up to 5 feet.

For perfect contractions Francis specifies a distance to side of approach
channel $= 2 H$, and a depth below the weir crest $= 3 H$, and states that
a reduction of the bottom clearance to $2 H$ and of the side clearance to
H increases the flow by about 1 per cent.

Effect of the Velocity of Approach.—As in the case of a submerged
orifice, the fact that the stream has kinetic energy in virtue of its velocity
of approach to the weir may be taken into account, and correction made
for this by adding to the measured head H a supplementary head h,
where $h = \frac{v^2}{2 g}$. Here v is the velocity of approach, and is necessarily the

---

[1] A formula of this form was suggested by Boyden in 1846.
[2] "Trans. Am. Soc. C.E.," vol. 44, p. 397. The maximum variation from Francis's formula, viz., 4 per cent., occurred with 2·64 feet head.

computed mean velocity over the whole section of the approach channel. But the distribution of velocity over this section is not at all uniform, the filaments nearer the surface and nearer the centre having a velocity greater than the mean, depending on the depth, width, and surface condition of the channel. The particles which suffer the least change in their direction of motion on passing the weir are thus those which have a velocity of approach greater than the mean, and since the velocity of approach in these particles has a greater proportional effect in increasing the flow past the weir than in those which approach its plane in a more oblique direction, the effective velocity of approach will be greater than that corresponding to the calculated head h. Most experimenters, therefore, put the effective head as equal to $H + a\, h$, where a has some value greater than unity, and write

$$Q = K\, b\, (H + a\, h)^{\frac{3}{2}} = K\, b\, D^{\frac{3}{2}}.$$

Francis, however, allows for the velocity of approach by putting $H + h$ and h as his limits of integration in formula (1) of this article, and thus gets

For a suppressed weir $\quad Q = 3 \cdot 33\, b \left\{ (H + h)^{\frac{3}{2}} - h^{\frac{3}{2}} \right\}$

With one end contraction $Q = 3 \cdot 33\, (b - \cdot 1H) \left\{ (H + h)^{\frac{3}{2}} - h^{\frac{3}{2}} \right\}$

With two end contractions $Q = 3 \cdot 33\, (b - \cdot 2\, H) \left\{ (H + h)^{\frac{3}{2}} - h^{\frac{3}{2}} \right\}.$

In using Francis's formula, care should be taken to apply the correction in this manner.

The value of $h = \dfrac{v^2}{2\, g}$ is determined by approximation. Thus Q is first determined from the measured H, and this value of Q is used to determine v from the known area of the channel.

The second approximation to the true value of Q, obtained by inserting the value of h thus found, in the expressions given above, is always sufficiently near for all practical purposes.

Since in this formula we have $D^{\frac{3}{2}} = \left\{ (H + h)^{\frac{3}{2}} - h^{\frac{3}{2}} \right\}$

$$\therefore\quad D = \left\{ (H + h)^{\frac{3}{2}} - h^{\frac{3}{2}} \right\}^{\frac{2}{3}}.$$

Expanding this as a series and omitting all terms containing a small quantity of the second order, we get

$$D = H + h - \frac{2}{3}\sqrt{\frac{h^3}{H}} = H + a\, h, \text{ where } a = 1 - \frac{2}{3}\sqrt{\frac{h}{H}}$$

Fteley and Stearns,[1] from experiments on suppressed weirs 5 ar' 19 feet long, and with heads ranging from ·07 to 1·60 feet, and als from a discussion of Francis's results, obtained the formula for a sr- pressed weir

$$Q = 3·31\ b\ H^{\frac{3}{2}} + ·007\ b \text{ cub. ft. per sec.}$$

For a weir with end contractions, b is to be replaced by $(b - ·1\ n\ H$ The velocity of approach is to be allowed for by putting the effective hea $= H + a\,h$, where

$a = 1·5$ for a suppressed weir.

$a = 2·05$ for a weir having two end contractions.

These are mean values. Actually the experiments showed that a varis with H, as shown approximately in the following table :—

Depth of channel of approach below crest.	Suppressed weir—channel 5 feet wide, depth on crest in feet.					
	·2	·4	·6	1·0	1·5	2·0
·5	1·70	1·53	1·52	1·48	—	—
1·0	1·87	1·79	1·71	1·61	1·52	—
1·7	1·66	1·68	1·60	1·54	1·46	1·38
2·6	1·51	1·49	1·47	1·48	1·38	1·33

Hamilton Smith,[2] from experiments by Fteley and Stearns, Francis and self, with weir lengths from ·66 up to 19 feet, heads up to 2 feet altered Francis's formula so as to take a correction $H + a\,h = D$, for the velocity of approach, giving a the values 1·4 for a contracted, and 1·33 for a suppressed weir.

Then $Q = 3·29 \left\{ b + \dfrac{D}{7} \right\} D^{\frac{3}{2}}$ for a suppressed weir.

$Q = 3·29\ b\ D^{\frac{3}{2}}$ for one end contraction.

$Q = 3·29 \left\{ b - \dfrac{D}{10} \right\} D^{\frac{3}{2}}$ for two end contractions.

Smith also suggests determining v, and therefore h, by measuring the surface velocity in the approach channel, the ratio of surface velocity t mean velocity being usually approximately equal to a.

Bazin,[3] from his own experiments on suppressed weirs from 1·65 to

1 "Trans. Am. Soc. C.E.," 1883, pp. 1—118.
2 Hamilton Smith, "Hydraulics," pp. 99 and 137.
3 "Annales des Ponts et Chaussées," 1898, 2me trimestre.

6·56 feet long, and with heads ranging from ·17 to 1·97 feet, and also from an examination of the results of Fteley and Stearns, deduced the formula

$$Q = \left\{ \cdot405 + \frac{\cdot00984}{H} \right\} b \sqrt{2 g} \; H^{\frac{3}{2}} \text{ c.f.s.}$$

for a weir with no velocity of approach. For a weir with velocity of approach, the effective head $= H + 1\cdot69\, h$, and on substituting for h in terms of the depth of approach channel Bazin finally gets

$$Q = \left\{ 1 + \cdot55 \left(\frac{H}{P+H} \right)^2 \right\} \left\{ \cdot405 + \frac{\cdot00984}{H} \right\} b \sqrt{2 g} \; H^{\frac{3}{2}} \text{ c.f.s.}$$

Approximately, for heads from 4 inches to 1 foot we have

$$Q = \left\{ \cdot425 + \cdot21 \left(\frac{H}{P+H} \right)^2 \right\} b \sqrt{2 g} \; H^{\frac{3}{2}} \text{ cub. ft. per sec.}$$

correct within about $2\frac{1}{2}$ per cent. In these formulae $P =$ height of the weir crest above the bed of the approach channel. All dimensions are in feet. Expressing the formula in the form $Q = K\, b\, H^{\frac{3}{2}}$, the following values of K are deduced from Bazin's experimental results :—

Head in feet, $H.$	Height of notch sill above channel bed, in feet.				
	·66 ft.	1·00 ft.	1·50 ft.	2·00 ft.	5·00 ft.
·164	3·667	3·686	3·610	3·604	3·593
·230	3·652	3·598	3·561	3·550	3·529
·656	3·850	3·667	3·555	3·501	3·406
1·050	—	3·823	3·661	3·555	3·394
1·575	—	—	3·796	3·655	3·394
1·969	—	—	3·877	3·733	3·422

The following table shows the ratio of the velocity-of-approach correction applied by various experimenters for a suppressed weir.

Bazin.	Fteley and Stearns.	Smith.	Francis.
1·0	·887	·787	depends on $h \div H.$

This large difference is, however, more apparent than real, as the larger velocity corrections are compensated by smaller weir coefficients. Actually

H.A.   L

the final agreement is, in general, fairly close, as is shown by the following table, which shows the comparative values of Q per foot of crest length for a suppressed weir :—

Length.	Height of crest.	Head.	Velocity of approach.	Francis.	Fteley and Stearns.	Bazin.	Smith—Francis.
10 ft.	2 ft.	1·0 ft.	1·15 f.s.	1·00	1·015	·985	1·018
10 ,,	4 ,,	1·0 ,,	·68 ,,	1·00	1·001	1·010	1·002
10 ,,	4 ,,	4·0 ,,	3·53 ,,	1·00	1·050	1·050	1·115

It may be shown that neglect to allow for the velocity of approach will lead to an error which may amount to 6 per cent. where A (the area of approach channel) $= 2\ b\ H$, but is reduced to ·7 per cent. if $A = 6\ b\ H$. and to ·25 per cent. if $A = 10\ b\ H$. Thus with a suppressed weir it is in general important that this should be taken into account, while with two end contractions it is usually unnecessary.

Braschmann's formula :

$$Q = \left\{ \cdot 3838 + \cdot 0386\ \frac{b}{B} + \frac{\cdot 00174}{H} \right\}\ b\ \sqrt{2\ g}\ H^{\frac{3}{2}}\ \text{c.f.s.}$$

the dimensions being in feet, is much used in Germany. Here B is the width of the approach channel. The formula only applies to rectangular weirs with two end contractions and free bottom contraction, and agrees well with that of Francis, where $B \overset{=}{>} 4\ b$.

The following values of C were determined by Professor Dwelshauvers-Devy, of Liège, from experiments on a small rectangular notch 2·593 inches wide, and with heads varying from ·4 to 4·8 inches,[1] with no velocity correction :—

Head in inches.	·4	·5	·6	·8	1·0	1·5	2·0	2·5	3·0	4·0
C	·629	·622	·618	·6125	·609	·6042	·6029	·6023	·6021	·6021

Recent experiments on a sharp-crested weir 2·505 feet long, height of crest 8·05 feet, and contractions suppressed[2] showed that over a range of

---

[1] " Proceedings Inst. Civil Engineers," vol. 94, p. 333.

[2] " Bulletin of the University of Wisconsin," No. 216, p. 283.

heads from ·3 to 1·7 feet the variation from the formula of either Francis or Bazin in no case exceeded 1·7 per cent., while the variation from the Hamilton Smith formula increased steadily from ·7 per cent. with ·3 foot head to 7·9 per cent. with 1·7 feet head.

Discharge over a Curved Weir.—Where a curved weir has a large radius of curvature, and discharges radially inwards, the discharge per foot run may be expected to be but slightly less than the discharge over a straight weir under the same head.

An extreme case of the curved weir with inward or outward flow is found in the case of flow over the upper edge of an open vertical stand pipe.

Experiments carried out at Cornell University [1] on a series of such pipes of diameters 2, 4, 6, 9, and 12 inches with outward flow, show that, if D is the diameter in feet, for heads less than ·028 $D^{1.04}$ the flow is similar to that over a sharp-crested weir, while for heads greater than ·107 $D^{1.08}$ the flow becomes similar to that of a jet.

The discharge for weir flow is given by the formula

$$Q = 8 \cdot 8 \; D^{1 \cdot 29} \; H^{1 \cdot 29} \quad \text{cub. ft. per sec.}$$

$$= 2 \cdot 01 \left\{ l \, H \right\}^{1 \cdot 29} \quad \text{,, \quad ,,}$$

Here l is the length of the crest, l and H both being in feet.

For jet flow the discharge is given by

$$Q = 5 \cdot 7 \; D^2 \; H^{0 \cdot 53} \quad \text{c.f.s.}$$

$$= C \, A \, \sqrt{2 g} \; H^{53} \quad \text{c.f.s.}$$

where A is the area and $C = \cdot 905$.

In similar experiments on pipes of 6·9, 10·1, 13·7, 19·4, and 25·9 inches outside diameter, with flow radially inwards,[2] the discharge was given by

$$Q = K \, l \, H^{1 \cdot 42} \quad \text{cub. ft. per sec.}$$

where K has the following values :—

Diameter of weir (inches).	6·9	10·1	13·7	19·4	25·9
Value of K . . .	2·93	2·94	2·97	2·99	3·03

These constants hold for heads up to one-fifth of the diameter of the weir.

[1] " Proc. Am. Soc. C.E.," 1906, p. 479.
[2] H. J. F. Gourley, " Proc. Inst. C.E.," vol. 184, 1910—11, pt. 2, p. 297.

Effect of a Change in Head on the Discharge from a Rectangular Weir.

Since $\quad Q = K H^{\frac{3}{2}}, \quad \therefore \quad \dfrac{dQ}{dH} = 1\cdot 5\, K\, H^{\frac{1}{2}},$

$$\therefore \quad \delta Q = 1\cdot 5\, K\, H^{\frac{1}{2}}\, \delta H, \quad \text{and } \dfrac{\delta Q}{Q} = 1\cdot 5\, \dfrac{\delta H}{H},$$

i.e., the proportional change in Q is $1\cdot 5$ times that in H.

Effect of Inclination of Weir Face.

As might be expected from its effect on the crest contraction, a:

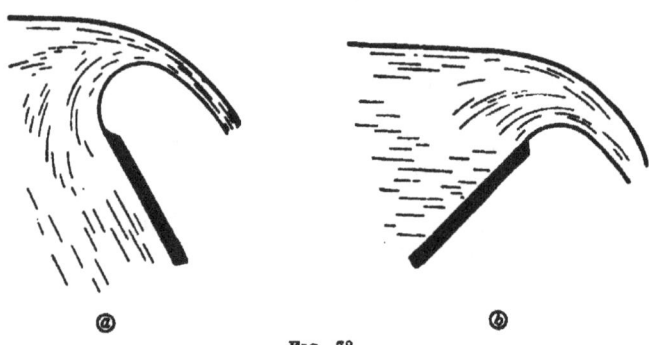

Fig. 78.

up-stream inclination of the weir face (Fig. 78 *a*) reduces, while a down-stream inclination (Fig. 78 *b*) increases, the discharge.

Bazin obtained the following comparative results with inclined weirs :—

Direction of inclination.	Up-stream.			Weir, vertical.	Down-stream.				
Slope : horizontal distance given first . . .	1 to 1	2 to 3	1 to 3	0	1 to 3	2 to 3	1 to 1	2 to 1	4 to 1
Relative discharge . .	·93	·94	·96	1·00	1·04	1·07	1·10	1·12	1·0

The maximum discharge was obtained with a down-stream inclination of 7 to 4.

Professor G. S. Williams, in experiments on weirs with a down-stream inclination of 1 to 1, obtained a mean comparative increase of 7·2 per cent. with a crest height of 6·65 feet, and of 8·8 per cent. with a crest height of 11·25 feet. The heads in these experiments ranged from ·5 to 4 feet.

Effect of a Sloping Apron on the Down-stream Side of a Sharp-crested Weir.

If such a weir, having a vertical up-stream face and a sharp crest is fitted with a sloping apron on the down-stream side, the discharge is increased to an extent which depends on the slope of the apron. *Bazin*, experimenting on such weirs having heights of 1·64 and 2·64 feet and with heads ranging from ·3 to 1·5 feet, deduced the approximate formula $K = \dfrac{3 \cdot 85}{S^{12}}$ for values of the slope S between 1 and 12.

Effect of Rounding the Up-stream Edge.

A slight rounding of the up-stream edge, by diminishing the contraction

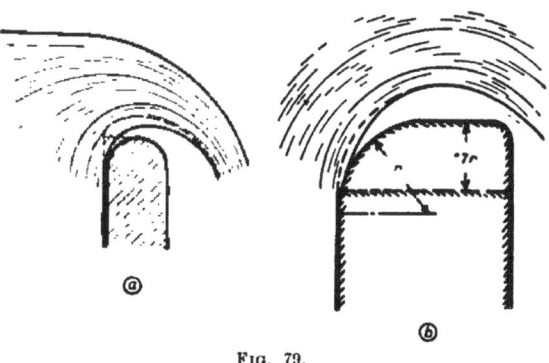

Fig. 79.

of section as indicated in Fig. 79 a, always causes an increased discharge. Messrs. *Fteley and Stearns*, from experiments with crest radii up to 1 inch, found that, so long as the *nappe* was fully aerated, the effect of the rounding was to increase the effective head by h', where $h' = \cdot 7 \ r$ (Fig. 79 b).

Effect of Clinging Nappe.

The experiments of Bazin showed very clearly the importance of taking into consideration the particular form assumed by the *nappe*.

If discharging freely, with free admission of air underneath, such a *nappe* is said to be fully aerated. In a suppressed weir discharging between the walls of a discharge channel of its own width, the *nappe* will remain in contact with these walls, and tends to eject the air enclosed in the underlying space. For free aeration it is necessary for air holes to be provided in these wing walls.

If no provision is made for such an air supply, a partial-vacuum is

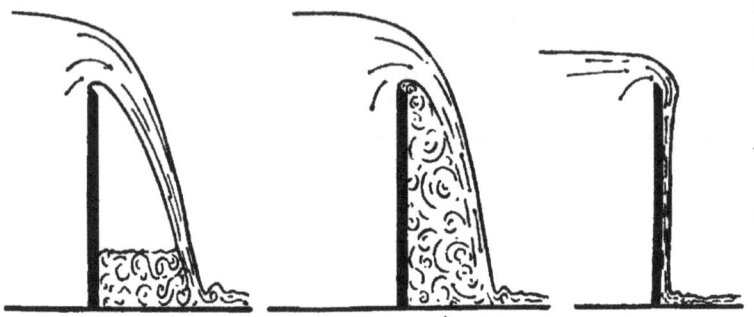

FIG. 80.—Depressed, Drowned, and Clinging Nappes.

produced beneath the *nappe* ; the latter is said to be depressed, and the discharge is increased (Fig. 80 *a*).

In an extreme case of the depressed *nappe* the whole of the air behind the *nappe* may be ejected, when this space is occupied by a turbulent eddying mass of water which does not itself join in the general motion of the *nappe*. The latter is then said to be drowned or wetted underneath (Fig. 80 *b*).

With very low heads the *nappe* may adhere to both crest and down-stream face of weir (Fig. 80 *c*).

Bazin gives the following as the relative discharges from a thin-edged weir 2·46 feet high and with a head of ·656 foot under different *nappe* conditions :—

Nappe.	Relative discharge.
Free discharge into air with full aeration	1·000
Nappe depressed with partial vacuum beneath . . .	1·060
Nappe wetted underneath ; down-stream water level ·42 foot below crest	1·148
Nappe adhering to down-stream face	1·279

Except with a freely discharging *nappe* the state of affairs is very unstable. Any pulsation in the stream flow, any floating body piercing the *nappe* and allowing admission of air, or even a sudden gust of wind, blowing the *nappe* into contact with the weir face may totally alter the conditions of flow, and no attempt should be made to use a weir, except when discharging freely, as a measuring device.

For steep down-stream slopes where the *nappe* tends to break free from the apron, the discharge is increased by the partial vacuum formed beneath the *nappe*. As this slope becomes flatter the conditions approach those for a horizontal crest, while for slopes of 3 to 1 the discharge is approximately the same as for a thin-crested, freely discharging weir.

ART. 54b.—TRIANGULAR NOTCH.

Let H be the head of water above the vertex P of the notch (Fig. 81), H being measured to the level of the still water surface behind the notch. Let $B =$ breadth of notch at height H.

Then assuming the velocity of efflux at any depth x to be given by $\sqrt{2 g x}$, a formula for the discharge can be deduced as for the rectangular notch.

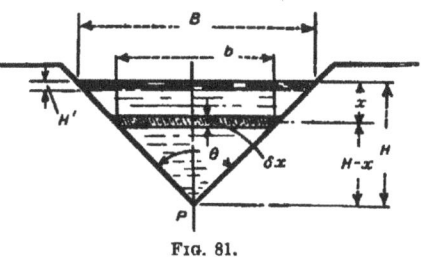

FIG. 81.

Thus the area of an element of the area at a depth x and of width δx is $b \, \delta x = B \cdot \dfrac{H - x}{H} \cdot \delta x.$

$\therefore$ Flow over this element

$$= \delta Q = B \sqrt{2 g x} \cdot \frac{H - x}{H} \cdot \delta x \text{ c.f.s.} \tag{1}$$

$$\therefore Q = C' B \sqrt{2 g} \int_{H'}^{H} \left(1 - \frac{x}{H}\right) x^{\frac{1}{2}} \, dx$$

$$= C' B \sqrt{2 g} \left[\frac{2}{3} \left\{ H^{\frac{3}{2}} - H'^{\frac{3}{2}} \right\} - \frac{2}{5} \left\{ H^{\frac{3}{2}} - \frac{H'^{\frac{5}{2}}}{H} \right\} \right]$$

$$= C' B \sqrt{2 g} \left[\frac{4}{15} H^{\frac{3}{2}} - H'^{\frac{3}{2}} \left\{ \frac{2}{3} - \frac{2}{5} \frac{H'}{H} \right\} \right] \tag{2}$$

To get this into a form available for practical use we must write

$$C' \left[\frac{4}{15} H^{\frac{3}{2}} - H'^{\frac{3}{2}} \left\{ \frac{2}{3} - \frac{2}{5} \frac{H'}{H} \right\} \right] = \frac{4}{15} C H^{\frac{3}{2}},$$

So that $C = C' \left\{ 1 - \left(\frac{H'}{H} \right)^{\frac{3}{2}} \left(2 \cdot 5 - 1 \cdot 5 \frac{H'}{H} \right) \right\}.$

Equation (2) then becomes

$$Q = \frac{4}{15} C B \sqrt{2 g} H^{\frac{3}{2}} \tag{3}$$

the formula obtained by integrating the expression (1) between the limits H and 0.

Putting $\frac{B}{2} = H \tan \frac{\theta}{2}$, where θ is the angle included between the sides of the notch, this becomes

$$Q = \frac{8}{15} C \sqrt{2 g} \tan \frac{\theta}{2} H^{\frac{5}{2}} \tag{4}$$

$$= 4 \cdot 28 C \tan \frac{\theta}{2} H^{\frac{5}{2}} \tag{5}$$

The coefficient C here includes both variables C' and H'. Since the ratio $\frac{B}{H}$ is constant for any one notch, it is to be expected that the value of C with different heads will be more nearly constant than in the case of a rectangular notch. Experiments by *Professor James Thomson*[1] indicate that this is so, the value increasing very slightly as the head diminishes. With a right-angled notch the variation was less than 1 per cent. under a range of heads from 2 inches to 7 inches, while with a notch having sides inclined at 2 horizontal to 1 vertical ($\tan \frac{\theta}{2} = 2$) the value of C increased by about 2 per cent. as the head was reduced.

As the result of these experiments Professor Thomson estimated the mean value of C for a right-angled notch as ·598, thus giving a discharge

$$Q = 2 \cdot 536 H^{\frac{5}{2}} \text{ cubic feet per second.}$$

With a notch having side inclinations of 2 to 1 ($\tan \frac{\theta}{2} = 2$), the mean value of C was found to be ·618, making

$$Q = 5 \cdot 29 H^{\frac{5}{2}} \text{ cubic feet per second,}$$

while as the angle is still further increased, C appears to approach a limiting value ·620.

[1] "British Association Report," 1861, p. 351.

With these wide-angled notches the value of C, however, fluctuates between much wider limits than in the case of the right-angled notch and this renders the former type not so suitable for measuring purposes.

Thomson's formula for a right-angled notch may be written in the form

$$Q = \cdot 305 \, H^{\frac{5}{2}} \text{ cub. ft. per minute}$$

where H is the head in inches.

A series of very careful experiments has been carried out by *Mr. James Barr*,[1] on such notches, with heads up to 10 inches. The chief results of these are shown graphically in Fig. 82, where curves C, A, and

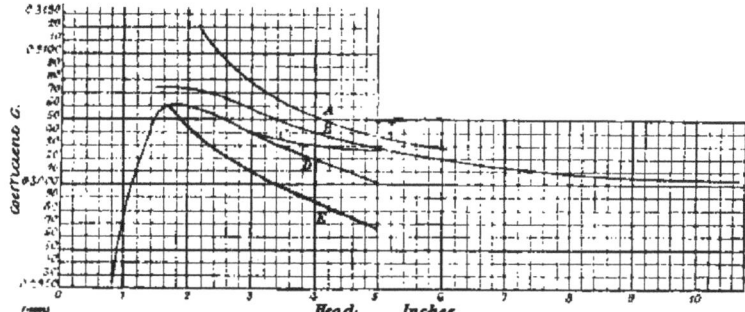

FIG. 82.—Value of Coefficient C in $Q = CH^{\frac{5}{2}}$ c.f.m. for a Right-angled Notch.

B respectively represent the results obtained on a notch with an extremely fine edge, on one with a crest $\frac{1}{12}$ inch broad, and on one with a crest $\frac{1}{16}$ inch broad. In these experiments the approach channel was 4 feet wide, and the depth of the floor of the channel below the vertex of the notch was 2 feet.

To find the effect of the width of the channel of approach upon the discharge, false sides made of wood were placed in the flume. They extended the full depth of the flume, and for a distance of 8 feet up-stream.

Two sets of experiments were made, in one of which a head of 3 inches was maintained and in the other a head of 4 inches. Fig. 83 gives the results. They show that in order that the flow may be independent of the channel width, the latter must be at least eight times the head.

A sheet of zinc 36 inches broad and 42 inches long was used as a

---

[1] *Engineering*, April 8 and 15, 1910.

temporary floor to investigate the effect of the depth of the channel :
approach upon the discharge. The results are given in Fig. 84, which show
that the presence of the floor produces a slight diminution in the discharge,
and that this effect disappears when the channel depth is about three

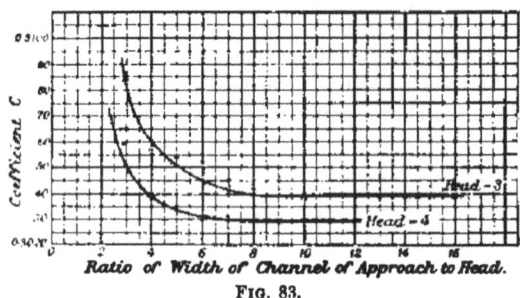

Ratio of Width of Channel of Approach to Head.

FIG. 83.

times the head with a 3 inch head and about four times the head with a
4 inch head.

Experiments were also made in which the head was varied. For the
results given in E (Fig 82) the floor was maintained level with the vertex

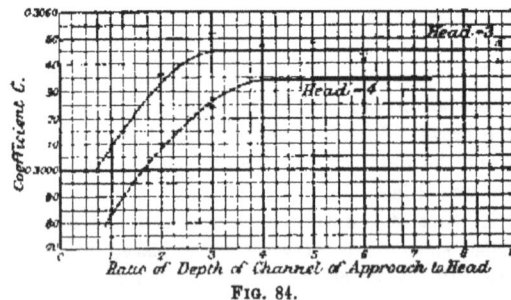

Ratio of Depth of Channel of Approach to Head

FIG. 84.

of the notch, and it was at a depth 6 inches below the vertex for the
results given in D (Fig. 82).

By coating the up-steam face of the weir plate with coarse emery the
discharge was increased by 2·4 per cent. with a 3 inch head and by 1·7
per cent. when the head was 4 inches.

The results of the whole series of experiments are in extremely close
accord with those previously obtained by Professor Thomson.

While suffering from the disadvantage that only small quantities of water are passed with a comparatively high head, the triangular has the advantage over the rectangular notch where the flow is very variable, that with either large or small heads it is equally easy to take accurate measurements of the head, while with the rectangular notch with very low heads this is practically impossible.

On allowing for the velocity of approach, equation (4) becomes

$$Q = \frac{8}{15} C \tan\frac{\theta}{2} \cdot \sqrt{2\,g} \left\{ (H + h)^{\frac{5}{2}} - h^{\frac{5}{2}} \right\} \text{ cub. ft. per sec.}$$

Here h may be taken as $1\cdot4\,\dfrac{v^2}{2\,g}$, where $v =$ velocity of approach.

In using the notch, care should be taken that the sides are equally inclined to the vertical.

Variation of Discharge with Head.

Since
$$Q = K\,H^{\frac{5}{2}}$$

$$\therefore \quad \frac{d\,Q}{d\,H} = 2\cdot5\,K\,H^{\frac{3}{2}}$$

$$\therefore \quad \frac{\delta\,Q}{Q} = 2\cdot5\,\frac{\delta\,H}{H}$$

It follows that a small change in, or error in estimating H, produces $2\cdot5$ times the percentage change or error in Q.

Art. 54c.—Trapezoidal Notch (Fig. 85).

Let b be the bottom breadth of the notch. Let θ be the inclination to the vertical, of the sides.

The notch then becomes equivalent to a rectangular notch of breadth b,

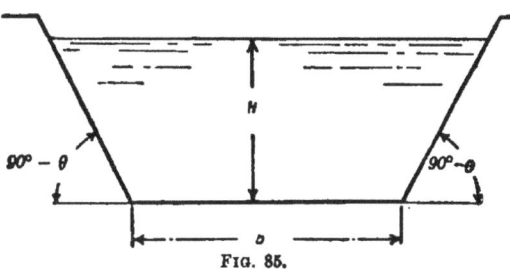

Fig. 85.

together with a triangular notch having an angle $2\,\theta$ between its inclined sides, and the discharge Q due to a head H is obtained by adding the values of Q, as calculated for two such notches.

$$\therefore \quad Q = \sqrt{2g} \left\{ \frac{2}{3} b \, C_1 \, H^{\frac{3}{2}} + \frac{8}{15} C_2 \tan \theta \, H^{\frac{5}{2}} \right\} \tag{1}$$

Assuming $C_1 = C_2 = C$ this becomes

$$Q = C \sqrt{2g} \, H^{\frac{3}{2}} \left\{ \frac{2}{3} b + \frac{8}{15} H \tan \theta \right\}. \tag{2}$$

Francis's formula for a rectangular notch shows that the two end contractions reduce the effective breadth by $\cdot 2 \, H$, and the discharge by an amount

$$\cdot 2 \, H \times \frac{2}{3} C \sqrt{2g} \, . \, H^{\frac{3}{2}} = \frac{2}{15} C \sqrt{2g} \, . \, H^{\frac{5}{2}}.$$

If then the ends of the weir, instead of being vertical, are inclined outwards so that the added area counterbalances the increased contraction of section of the stream, the coefficient K in the formula $Q = K b H^{\frac{3}{2}}$ should be independent of the head.

For this to be so we have

$$\frac{2}{15} C \sqrt{2g} \, . \, H^{\frac{5}{2}} = \frac{8}{15} C \sqrt{2g} \tan \theta \, H^{\frac{5}{2}},$$

so that $\tan \theta = \frac{1}{4}$, or the sides are to be inclined outwards with a slope of 1 in 4. This is termed a **Cippoletti** [1] **Weir.**

From his own experiments and those of Francis, on heads from 3 to 24 inches, *Cippoletti* made $Q = 3 \cdot 367 \, b \, H^{\frac{3}{2}}$ cub. ft. per sec., the Francis velocity correction being used.

Experiments by *Messrs. Flinn and Dyer* [2] on weirs having sill lengths of from 3 feet to 9 feet, and heads from $\cdot 3$ foot to $1 \cdot 25$ feet, gave, as the mean of thirty-two experiments, $K = 3 \cdot 283$. In this formula, however, the velocity correction of Hamilton Smith (effective head $= H + 1 \cdot 4 h$) was used. Had the Francis correction been applied this coefficient would have been in close accord with that of Cippoletti.

If $C_1 = \cdot 623$ (Francis mean value) and $C_2 = \cdot 593$ (Thomson's value for a right-angled notch), the inclination of the sides becomes 1 to 4·2. Experiments by *J. C. Stevens* [3] on weirs having lengths of 6 inches and of 1, 2, and 3 feet, with side inclinations of 1 to 4, and with heads ranging from $\cdot 08$ foot to $\cdot 8$ foot, indicate that for small lengths, the discharge is

[1] First described by C. Cippoletti. See " Giornale del Genies Civiles," 1886.
[2] "Trans. Am. Soc. C.E.," vol. 32, 1894, pp. 9—33.
[3] *Engineering News*, New York, August 18, 1910, p. 171.

greater than is given by the formula, the error increasing as the length is diminished. For lengths less than 3 feet the side inclinations should apparently vary as follows :—

Length of weir (feet)	·5	1·0	2·0	3·0
Cotan θ . . .	4·25	4·2	4·1	4·0

ART. 55.—SUBMERGED WEIRS.

Where the water on the down-stream side of a weir rises above the level of the sill we get a submerged weir.

If H_1 and H_2 (Fig. 86) be the heights of the free surfaces above the sill of a rectangular weir, the flow over the upper part of the section, of a depth $H_1 - H_2$, may be considered as a free discharge into air, and that over the lower part, of depth H_2, as a discharge through a submerged orifice.

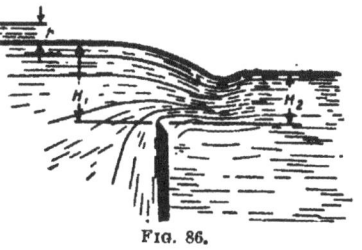

FIG. 86.

Thus for the upper portion $Q_1 = \dfrac{2}{3} C_1 b \sqrt{2 g} (H_1 - H_2)^{\frac{3}{2}}$

,, ,, lower ,, $Q_2 = C_2 b \sqrt{2 g} H_2 (H_1 - H_2)^{\frac{1}{2}}$

If we assume $C_1 = C_2 = C$, we have for the total flow

$$Q = C b \sqrt{2 g (H_1 - H_2)} \left\{ \frac{2}{3} (H_1 - H_2) - H_2 \right\}$$

$$= C b \sqrt{2 g (H_1 - H_2)} \left\{ \frac{2}{3} H_1 + \frac{1}{3} H_2 \right\}.$$

Taking into account the velocity of approach, we have

$$Q_1 = \frac{2}{3} C_1 b \sqrt{2 g} \left\{ (H_1 - H_2 + h)^{\frac{3}{2}} - h^{\frac{3}{2}} \right\}$$

$$Q_2 = C_2 b \sqrt{2 g} H_2 (H_1 - H_2 + h)^{\frac{1}{2}}$$

$$\therefore \quad Q = C b \sqrt{2 g (H_1 - H_2 + h)} \left\{ \frac{2}{3} (H_1 - H_2 + h) + H_2 \right.$$

$$\left. - \frac{\frac{2}{3} h^{\frac{3}{2}}}{(H_1 - H_2 + h)^{\frac{1}{2}}} \right\}$$

As a very close approximation we have

$$Q = C\, b\, \sqrt{2g\,(H_1 - H_2 + h)}\; \left\{ \frac{2}{3}\,(H_1 + h) + \frac{1}{3}\,H_2 \right\}.$$

The value of C varies with the ratio $\dfrac{H_2}{H_1 + h}$, and can only be deduced by experiment.

The following mean values are obtained from the results of experiments by Francis, and by Messrs. Fteley and Stearns :—

Francis.—Depth of water at sill ·85 to 2·3 feet.[1]

Ratio $\dfrac{H_2}{H_1 + h}$	·00	·1	·3	·5	·7	·9
C . . .	·628	·625	·606	·594	·594	·596

Messrs. Fteley and Stearns.[2]

$\dfrac{H_2}{H_1 + h}$	·1	·3	·5	·7	·9
C . .	·630	·605	·590	·585	·595

Redtenbacher makes $C_1 = ·57$ and $C_2 = ·62$ in the above formula. while *Pestalozzi* also makes C_2 equal to ·62 and makes C_1 vary from ·534 to ·566, diminishing as the ratio of H_2 to H_1 increases. It is indeed to be expected that C_2 will be greater than C_1, since owing to eddy formation behind the weir the pressure on the discharge side of the crest will be less than that corresponding to the assumed statical head $H_1 - H_2$, thus giving rise to an increased discharge over the lower portion of the stream.

The difficulty of obtaining accurate values of H_1 and H_2, combined with

---

[1] Suppressed weir 22·2 feet long. " Trans. Am. Soc. C.E.," vol. 12.

[2] Suppressed weir 5 feet long. Values of H_1 from ·3 to ·8 foot. Crest 3·2 feet from bottom of channel. " Trans. Am. Soc. C.E.," vol. 12.

The results of experiments on submerged weirs 1 foot and 2 feet long, with two end contractions, are given in *Engineering News*, New York, August 18, 1910, p. 174.

the fact that H_2 is in a continual state of change owing to the undulatory motion of the surface, renders the submerged weir very unsatisfactory as a means of measuring the flow of water.

The above discussion of submerged weir flow is due to Dubuat, and is admittedly unsatisfactory from a scientific point of view. The difficulties in the way of a more rational investigation of the problem based on the

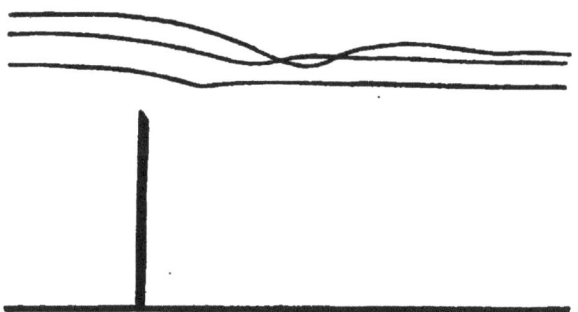

FIG. 87.—Surface Curves in Neighbourhood of Submerged Weirs.

variations of pressure and velocity in the stream are, however, extremely great, as will be realised from a study of Fig. 87.

These curves show the profile of the stream as measured by the author in the neighbourhood of such a weir, under different heads.

Bazin gives the empirical formula

$$Q = C \left\{ 1{\cdot}05 + {\cdot}21\, \frac{H_2}{P} \right\} \sqrt[3]{\frac{H_1 - H_2}{H_1}} \, . \, b \, \sqrt{2\,g} \, . \, H_1^{\frac{3}{2}} \text{ c.f.s.}$$

where C is the coefficient in the formula

$$Q = C\, b \, \sqrt{2\,g} \, . \, H_1^{\frac{3}{2}} \text{ c.f.s.}$$

for flow over a similar weir freely discharging under the head H_1, and where P is the depth of the approach channel below the weir crest.

ART. 56.—BROAD-CRESTED WEIRS.

Experiments by Bazin indicate that in general the *nappe* will clear the crest of a sharp-edged weir if this is of less width than $\cdot 5\,H$. For widths between $\cdot 5\,H$ and $\cdot 66\,H$ the condition is unstable, and any variation in the flow will cause the *nappe* to cling or to break free, with a corresponding variation in the discharge, while for widths greater than this the *nappe* clings to the crest in every case.

More recent experiments by G. S. Williams indicate that the ratio of crest width w to head, at which the *nappe* springs clear, depends on the head and is usually less than ·5, as shown in the following table :—

Crest width (feet)	·48	·93	1·65
Head at which *nappe* becomes clear (feet)	1·5	2·5	(*Nappe* not clear when $H = 4$ feet.
Ratio of $w : H$.	·32	·38	< ·41

Where the crest is sufficiently wide to cause adherence of the *nappe*.

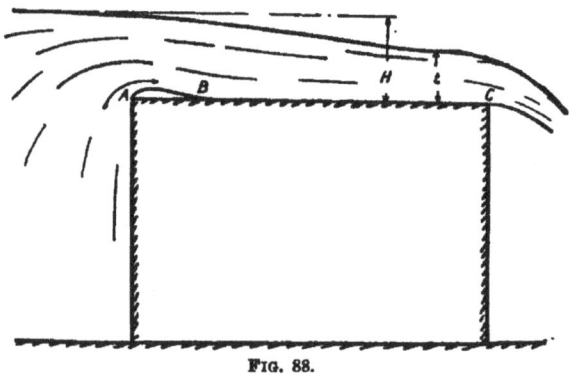

Fig. 88.

the weir is termed broad-crested. In such a weir the stream springs clear of the crest at its up-stream edge A and again makes contact at B, as in Fig. 88, so that the discharge is reduced by the friction offered by the surface from B to C. An increase in the head diminishes the length of this portion of the surface, but increases the velocity of flow, so that some one particular head will give the minimum loss due to this cause, and will give a maximum coefficient of discharge. As the width of crest is increased the friction loss increases and the coefficient of discharge in consequence decreases.

Bazin experimenting on flat-crested weirs having crest widths ranging from ·164 foot to 6·56 feet, and with heads from ·25 foot to 1·5 feet, found that where the *nappe* adheres to the top but not to the down-stream face of such a weir, the discharge may be expressed by

$$Q = K' \, b \, H^{\frac{3}{2}}, \text{ where } K' = K \left\{ \cdot 70 + \cdot 185 \, \frac{H}{w} \right\}.$$

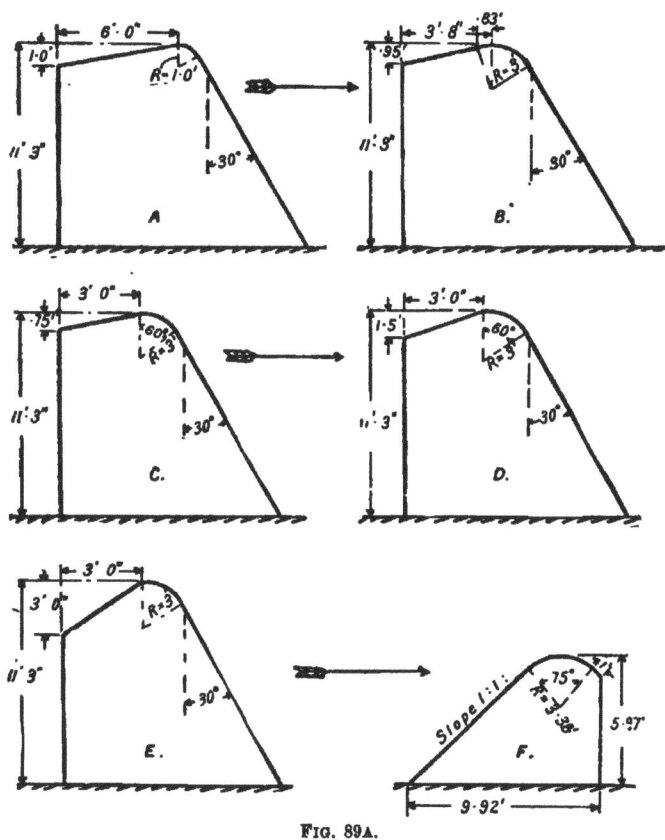

FIG. 89A.

Here K is the coefficient for the corresponding thin-crested weir, as calculated from Bazin's formula.

For wider crests, and for heads greater than 1·5 feet, this formula gives rather low results, while if applied to the Francis formula, the results are much too low for crest widths greater than 8 feet and for heads greater than 1 foot.

. An examination by the author, of experiments by G. S. Williams[1] on such weirs, with widths ranging from ·48 foot to 16·3 feet and with heads from ·5 foot to 4·0 feet, shows that, adopting the Francis formula, the discharge is given within about 3 per cent. for all widths and heads, so long as

$$w > 2\,H, \text{ by writing } K' = K \left\{ \cdot 75 + \cdot 1 \sqrt{\frac{H}{w}} \right\}.$$

Fteley and Stearns, using crest widths of from 2 to 10 inches, and heads

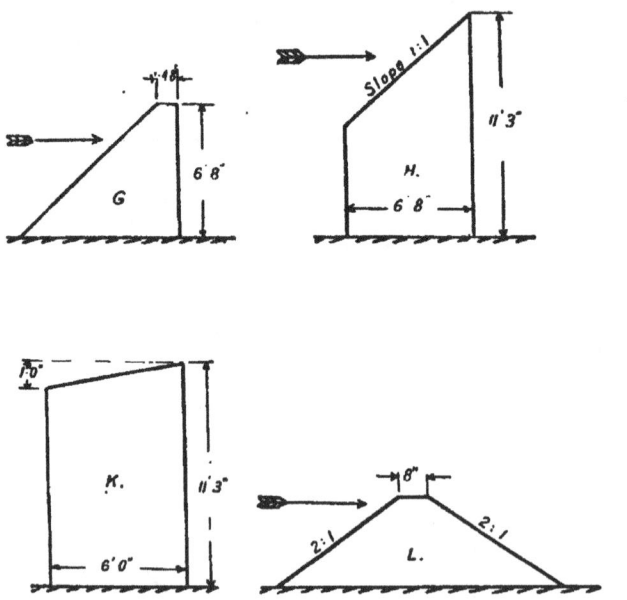

Fig. 89B.

from ·116 to ·894 feet, deduced the formula $Q = K\,b\,(H + k)^{\frac{3}{2}}$, where $k = \cdot 2016 \sqrt{(\cdot 807\,b - H)^2 + \cdot 2146\,b^3} - \cdot 1876\,b$, and K is the coefficient for a thin-crested weir.

The most reliable experiments on flow over broad-crested weirs and dams are those by Bazin[1] and those carried out at Cornell University between 1898 and 1904 under the supervision of Professor G. S. Williams.[1] In the latter experiments which were made for the United States Geological

[1] For a full discussion of these results, as well as those of Bazin, see " Water Supply and Irrigation," Paper No. 200, U.S. Geological Survey ; " Weir Experiments, Coefficients and Formulas," by R. E. Horton. Also see " Rafter," " Trans. Am. Soc, C.E.," vol, 44, 1900.

Survey and for the United States Board of Engineers on Deep Waterways the weirs were 16 feet in length and heads up to 4 feet were used. The Cornell experiments were by far the more extensive, and the chief results of these are shown by the following tables and the diagrams of Fig. 89 A, B, and C. On all weirs having vertical down-stream faces the *nappe* was fully aerated. In the weirs with inclined down-stream faces no air was admitted under the *nappe*.

RECTANGULAR FLAT-CRESTED WEIRS.

Values of K' in formula, $Q = K' b H^{\frac{3}{2}}$.

H (feet).	Values of w.							
	0·48 ft.	0·93 ft.	1·65 ft.	3·17 ft.	5·89 ft.	8·98 ft.	12·24 ft.	16·30 f.
0·5	3·01	2·76	2·73	2·66	2·61	2·61	2·61	2·61
1·0	3·24	3·01	2·93	2·70	2·67	2·66	2·65	2·64
1·5	3·33	3·19	3·03	2·73	2·69	2·67	2·67	2·65
2·0	3·33	3·29	3·08	2·73	2·68	2·67	2·66	2·65
3·0	3·33	3·33	3·12	2·71	2·65	2·64	2·62	2·61
4·0	3·33	3·33	3·15	2·69	2·63	2·61	2·60	2·59

COMPOUND WEIRS (A TO F). FIG. 89A.

H (feet).	A.	B.	C.	D.	E.	F.
0·5	3·21	3·10	3·22	3·23	3·23	3·23
1·0	3·42	3·27	3·35	3·46	3·46	3·27
1·5	3·54	3·38	3·44	3·61	3·64	3·40
2·0	3·55	3·44	3·47	3·68	3·75	3·46
3·0	3·30	3·48	3·48	3·75	3·87	3·87
4·0	3·14	3·51	3·48	3·81	3·96	3·65

From experiments on weirs of ogee cross section (A to F), the formula

$$K' = \left\{ 3·62 - ·16 (s - 1) \right\} H^{\frac{1}{20}}$$

was found to give the coefficient with reasonable accuracy. Here s is the slope of the up-stream face.

Example : $s = 2 : 1$; $H = 4.0$; $\therefore K' = 3.46 \times 4\frac{1}{10}$; $\log 4\frac{1}{10} = .0301$; $\therefore K' = 3.46 \times$ $1.0716 = 3.70$.

This formula holds for weirs with an up-stream slope more than from 3 feet to 4·5 feet broad, and with a down-stream radius (above from 2 feet

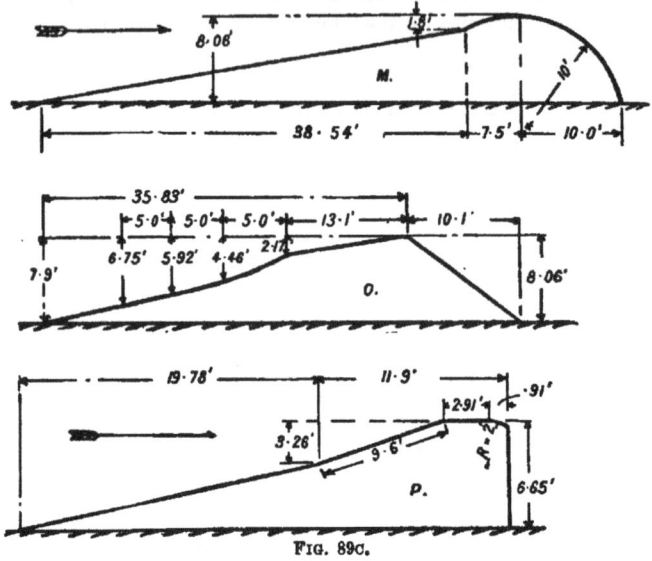

FIG. 89c.

to 3 feet) great enough to retain the *nappe* in contact, and yet not so large as to simulate a broad, flat crest.

TRAPEZOIDAL AND TRIANGULAR WEIRS (G TO L).　FIG. 89B.
Type G.

Up-stream Slope.	1 to 1.	2 to 1.		3 to 1.	4 to 1.	5 to 1
Crest Width (feet).	·48	·33 [1]	·66 [1]	·66 [1]	·66 [1]	·66 [1]
Head (feet). ·5	3·22	3·35	3·22	3·64	—	3·31
1·0	3·57	3·68	3·44	3·82	3·44	3·33
1·5	3·59	3·88	3·59	3·83	3·46	3·34
2·0	3·60	3·77	3·66	3·69	3·48	3·35
3·0	3·58	3·68	3·68	3·55	3·48	3·38
4·0	3·55	3·70	3·70	3·55	3·48	3·39

[1] " Rafter," crest height = 4·7 feet.

Types H to L.

Head (feet).	H.	K.	L.
·5	3·53	3·47	3·14
1·0	3·59	3·46	3·42
1·5	3·64	3·45	3·52
2·0	3·65	3·42	3·61
3·0	3·68	3·35	3·66
4·0	3·61	3·29	3·66

COMPOUND WEIRS (M to P). FIG. 89c.

Head (feet).	M	N [1]	O	P
·5	3·21	2·91	3·65	3·06
1·0	3·21	3·16	3·63	3·05
1·5	3·20	3·33	3·61	3·04
2·0	3·16	3·42	3·56	3·11
3·0	3·06	3·51	3·45	3·20
4·0	3·01	3·58	3·38	3·27

From a consideration of these various tables it appears that with dams having an ogee cross section, or having an up-stream slope, the discharge usually increases according to some higher power of the head than the 1·5th. Recent gaugings of the flow over large dams of these types[2] indicate that this power may attain a value as high as 1·75, though it usually lies between 1·50 and 1·65.

Effect of Condition of Nappe, on Discharge over wide, flat-crested Weirs.

Just as with a thin weir the *nappe* from a wide-crested weir may either spring clear of the down-stream face, be depressed, or be drowned. A simple depression of the *nappe* has, however, little effect on the discharge, slightly increasing it for low heads and diminishing it for high heads. If the *nappe* is drowned the effect is very slight so long as the stream

---

[1] Type N is identical with M, but with the addition of a 12 inch × 12 inch timber baulk on its crest.

[2] *Engineering News*, New York, September 29, 1910, p. 321.

clings to the crest over its whole width. In some cases a mass of turbulent water separates the *nappe* from the weir crest. Under such circumstances Bazin found that the discharge is the same as from a thin weir with drowned *nappe*, and is given by

$$Q = K' \, b \, H^{\frac{3}{2}}, \text{ where } K' = K \left\{ \cdot 878 + \cdot 128 \, \frac{P}{H} \right\},$$

P being the depth of the approach channel below the weir crest, and K being the coefficient for a thin-crested weir freely discharging under the same head.

Art. 57.—Rational Formula for Flow over broad-crested Weirs.

As was first pointed out by *Dr. W. C. Unwin*, a rational formula for flow over a weir of this type may be deduced if the crest be assumed to be so wide that the filaments form a parallel stream of thickness t (Fig. 88) before leaving the crest, and that in this stream the pressure at any point is that statically corresponding to its depth. We then have the velocity at the surface and at every point in this stream $= \sqrt{2 \, g \, (H - t)}$, while $Q = b \, t \, \sqrt{2 \, g \, (H - t)}$.

The value of t will adjust itself to give a maximum discharge, and this theoretical value for maximum flow may be determined by equating $\frac{d \, Q}{d \, t}$ to zero. This gives $t = \frac{2}{3} \, H$, and substituting this value, we get $Q = \cdot 385 \, b \, \sqrt{2 \, g} \, H^{\frac{3}{2}}$ as the maximum possible discharge. Writing this in the usual form $Q = \frac{2}{3} \, C \, b \, \sqrt{2 \, g} \, H^{\frac{3}{2}}$, we get $C = \cdot 578$, and $K = 3 \cdot 087$.

This method of treatment becomes more rational if account be taken of the fact that in a parallel stream flowing in an open channel, the distribution of velocity over any vertical is not uniform, being a maximum at or near the surface and a minimum at the bottom.

Experiments show that the ratio of the mean velocity over the section of such a stream to the maximum surface velocity, while varying with the depth, width, and roughness of the bottom of the channel, lies between the limits ·82 and ·87 for such surfaces and depths as are common on the crest of such weirs, this ratio increasing with the depth of water.

Assuming, as is practically the case, that the maximum surface velocity in the case of the weir is equal to $\sqrt{2 \, g \, (H - t)}$, the mean velocity will equal $k \sqrt{2 \, g \, (H - t)}$, and the discharge will be given by

$$k \cdot K \cdot b H^{\frac{3}{2}} = 3 \cdot 087 \ kbH^{\frac{3}{2}} = K'bH^{\frac{3}{2}} \text{ cub. ft. sec.}$$

Thus corresponding to the values ·82 and ·87 of k, the values of K become 2·53 and 2·69.

The validity of this formula receives remarkable confirmation from the results of the tests on such weirs at Cornell (p. 163), where for all heads between ·5 foot and 4 feet, and for all crest widths greater than 5 feet the values of K' lie between 2·59 and 2·69.

A sloping crest increases the discharge, as does any rounding of the up-stream corner. The effect of this rounding is not so pronounced as with a thin-crested weir, diminishing as the crest width increases and also as the head increases. Fteley and Stearns, experimenting on a crest 4 inches wide, with radii of one-fourth, one-half, and one inch respectively, found the effective head to be increased in the ratio $\left\{ 1 + \frac{\cdot 41 \ R}{H} \right\}$, this correction being applicable for heads of not less than ·17 and ·26 feet on weirs with radii of one-fourth and one-half inch respectively.

Bazin's experiments on crests having widths of 2·62 and 6·56 feet, heads from ·25 foot to 1·50 feet, with an up-stream crest radius of 4 inches, showed a mean increased discharge of 13·5 per cent. with the narrower and 10 per cent. with the broader crest, while the United States Deep Waterways experiments on a weir 22 feet wide, with 6 : 1 slope on each face, showed an average increase of 2 per cent. with an up-stream edge rounded to a radius of 4 inches. Experiments on weir B, Fig. 89A, showed that a rounding of the up-stream edge to a radius of 4 inches increased the discharge by about 4 per cent. at the higher heads. The condition of the crest as regards roughness is found not to influence the discharge by more than about 2 per cent.

ART. 58.—RISE IN SURFACE LEVEL PRODUCED BY A WEIR.

A dam or weir is usually placed across a stream with the idea of rais-ing the surface level and increasing the depth of water up stream. The distance to which this effect may be felt is sometimes considerable (see Art. 89), and can only be determined when the rise in level in the neighbourhood of the dam is known. This may be obtained if the dis-charge of the stream before the introduction of the dam is known (since this discharge will be unaffected by the presence of the dam) by equating this, in cubic feet per second, to the flow over a dam of the required length b and under a head H.[1] This determines H, and therefore the total rise in level when the height of dam is given. Thus if $h = $ mean depth of water before the introduction of the dam, and if $h_d = $ height of dam,

we have
$$Q = \frac{2}{3} C b \sqrt{2 g} H^{\frac{3}{2}}$$

$$\therefore \quad H = \left\{ \frac{1 \cdot 5 Q}{C b \sqrt{2 g}} \right\}^{\frac{2}{3}} \text{feet,}$$

$$\therefore \quad \begin{array}{l} \text{Rise in surface level} \\ \text{produced by the dam} \end{array} \Big\} = h_d + H - h$$

$$= h_d - h + \left\{ \frac{1 \cdot 5 Q}{C b \sqrt{2 g}} \right\}^{\frac{2}{3}} \text{feet.} \tag{1}$$

The same reasoning applies to the case of a submerged weir thrown across a stream, or to the rise in level produced by the erection of bridge piers in the stream (Art. 91).

ART. 59.—Use of the Weir as a Water Measuring Appliance.

The standard sharp-edged weir having a free discharge, or, for small quantities, the right-angled triangular notch, are the only types for which the coefficients have been determined with sufficient accuracy to admit of use for accurate measurement of flow without previous calibration.

For accurate measurement the following are essentials :—

1. Sharp-edged weir sill, fixed so as to be incapable of vibration, having its face vertical and perpendicular to the direction of the stream, and, if rectangular, having its sill horizontal.

2. Clear discharge into air, no adherence of vein to weir face.

3. Weir long in proportion to its depth, i.e., $b > 3 H$.

4. H small in comparison with the depth of the approach channel, and sectional area of vein ($b H$) not greater than $\frac{1}{4}$ that of this channel in a weir with end contractions, or not greater than $\frac{1}{3}$ its area with a suppressed weir.

5. Suitable channel of approach. This should be as long and of as uniform section as possible so as to allow of the motion becoming steady before reaching the weir. The length should, if possible, exceed 30 H, this ratio being increased where the length of weir is largely in excess of 3 H. In Bazin's experiments the length of supply channel was 49·2 feet with a maximum head of 1·97 feet and a maximum weir length of 6·56 feet, giving a length $= 25 H$. In Messrs. Fteley and Stearns' experiments the length

---

[1] This velocity may be determined by current meter or float observations. See Arts. 98—101.

was 12 feet with a head of 1·60 feet, screens being used above the weir to equalise the velocity. Where a length approximating to 30 H is impossible, one or more perforated diaphragms should be placed across the stream so as to steady the motion as far as possible.

6. Accurate determination of the head H. To measure H, water should if possible be run off by an auxiliary channel until exactly level with the notch sill. This level may be determined with great accuracy by observing the reflection at the surface in the immediate neighbourhood of the sill, since the absence of any curvature of the surface at this point, indicated as it is by non-distortion of reflected objects, shows that the correct level has been obtained. This level may then be read off, either for rough work on a graduated staff fixed vertically in the bed of the stream some 6 or 7 feet above the weir, or on a hook gauge (Fig. 153), the point of which is adjusted until exactly in the surface.

A preferable method consists in driving a stake into the bed of the stream above the weir until its upper end is below the level of the sill. This carries a short vertical wire, which may be filed down, until, as shown by straight edge and level, its point is exactly level with the sill. The water level may then be adjusted with great accuracy until this point is exactly in the surface when this level may be read off on the hook gauge also adjusted until its point is in the surface.

When the weir is discharging steadily, the head can be determined, either by direct reading of the graduated staff or by taking the reading on the hook gauge when its point is again adjusted so as to be in the surface. Care should be taken when using the graduated staff that allowance is made for the increase in height over the up-stream face of the staff, and the decrease over the down-stream face, due to the piling up of the water which occurs at a solid obstacle. For accurate work, measurements of the head taken in a flowing stream are inadmissible. Quite apart from the disturbance produced by any immersed object in such a stream, the nature of its flow which is seldom, if ever, perfectly steady, and the action of the wind, produce oscillations of its surface which seriously affect the possibilities of even approximately accurate results. To reduce the effect of such oscillations and to avoid the disturbance caused by the presence of the gauge, observations should be taken in a pit from 18 inches to 2 feet square, in communication with the main stream through a pipe one or two inches in diameter, opening out flush with the bed of the approach channel, and perpendicular to the direction of flow. This was the method adopted by Bazin, the pit being situated about 16·5 feet above the weir.

By this means, using a hook gauge fitted with adjusting screw and vernier, results accurate to $\frac{1}{50}$ of an inch may be easily obtained, and with practice the possible error may be reduced to about $\frac{1}{200}$ of an inch. Note should always be made of the effect of capillary action in raising the apparent height of the surface at the hook.

Where it is impossible to stop flow past the weir for this preliminary work, a vertical staff fixed near the weir face on its down-stream side may be graduated by straight edge and level, to give heights above the sill in the neighbourhood of the surface. These heights may then be transferred by means of a straight-edge and level to the measuring staff, or may be used to give the datum level to which to adjust the zero reading of the hook gauge.

In selecting a formula for use in any particular case, it should be remembered that that of Francis gives accurate results for weirs with perfect bottom contractions and with heads above 6 inches. The formulæ of Smith, Fteley and Stearns, and Bazin are better for very small heads, or where the bottom contraction is imperfect, this element tending to decrease the discharge being included in the larger velocity-of-approach correction. Under such circumstances Bazin's formula is probably most reliable.

Although in expert hands the method of measurement by weirs will give results which may be relied upon as correct within about 2·0 per cent., this degree of exactitude is not to be expected with any but the most careful measurements and consideration of the special conditions of each case.

Art. 60.—Time of Emptying a Vessel through a Large Orifice.

If the orifice be situated in the horizontal base of the vessel, the formulae relating to the time of discharge are the same as those for a small orifice (p. 121), except that now the effect of the velocity of approach is to be taken into account. Thus if a_c = area of *vena contracta* and A that of the vessel we have the velocity of efflux corresponding to a head H, given by

$$v = C_v \sqrt{\frac{2 g H}{1 - \frac{a_c^2}{A^2}}}$$

$$\therefore \; - \frac{dH}{dt} = C_v \frac{a_c}{A} \sqrt{\frac{2 g H}{1 - \frac{a_c^2}{A^2}}} \tag{1}$$

$$\therefore \; \frac{C_v a_c \sqrt{2 g}}{A \sqrt{1 - \frac{a_c^2}{A^2}}} \, dt = - \frac{dH}{\sqrt{H}} \tag{2}$$

And on integrating we have, if $t = t_2 - t_1$, the time necessary to lower he surface through the distance $H_1 - H_2$,

$$t = \frac{2\sqrt{A^2 - a_c^2}}{C_v\, a_c\,\sqrt{2g}}\left\{H_1^{\frac{1}{2}} - H_2^{\frac{1}{2}}\right\}$$

$$= \frac{2\sqrt{A^2 - a_c^2}}{C\,\sqrt{2g}}\left\{H_1^{\frac{1}{2}} - H_2^{\frac{1}{2}}\right\} \tag{3}$$

where C = coefficient of contraction for the orifice.

With an orifice in the vertical side of a vessel the effect of the variation of velocity at different depths in the orifice must be considered.

Thus with a large rectangular orifice of depth d, the rate of discharge at the instant when the head of water above the upper edge is H feet, is given by

$$Q = \frac{2}{3}\, C\, b\, \sqrt{2g}\left[(H + d)^{\frac{3}{2}} - H^{\frac{3}{2}}\right] \text{ cubic feet per second}$$

$$= 5\cdot76\, C\, b\left[(H + d)^{\frac{3}{2}} - H^{\frac{3}{2}}\right] \text{ cubic feet per second,}$$

and the velocity of fall of the surface $\left(-\dfrac{dH}{dt}\right)$ is therefore equal to

$$\frac{Q}{A} = \frac{5\cdot76\, C\, b}{A}\left[(H + d)^{\frac{3}{2}} - H^{\frac{3}{2}}\right] \text{ feet per second.}$$

Thus equation (1) above becomes

$$-\frac{dH}{dt} = \frac{5\cdot76\, C\, b}{A}\left[(H + d)^{\frac{3}{2}} - H^{\frac{3}{2}}\right]$$

and on integrating this between the required limits, the time occupied in lowering the surface through any required distance may be found.

Time of lowering the Level in a Reservoir through a Rectangular Notch.— With the usual notation, the volume discharged per second with a head H behind the notch is given by

$$Q = K\, b\, H^{\frac{3}{2}} \text{ cubic feet.}$$

$\therefore$ At this instant we have the velocity of the free surface in the reservoir given by

$$-\frac{dH}{dt} = \frac{K\, b\, H^{\frac{3}{2}}}{A}$$

Integrating this, the time ($t_2 -$ seconds, to lower the level through a distance $H_1 - H_2$ feet, is given by

$$t_2 - t_1 = t = \frac{2A}{K\, b}\left\{\frac{1}{H_2^{\frac{1}{2}}} - \frac{1}{H_1^{\frac{1}{2}}}\right\} \text{ seconds.}$$

EXAMPLES.

(1) A lock, 1,000 square feet area, is filled through a submerged orifice 3 feet long by 2 feet deep. The depth of water above the centre of this is initially 19 feet on the outside and 7 feet on the inside. Assuming a coefficient of discharge of ·61, determine the time occupied in filling the lock if the outside level remains constant.

Answer. 236 seconds.

(2) Assuming the level on the lower side of the above lock to remain constant, determine the time of emptying the lock, the sluice being the same size as on the entry side.

Answer. 236 seconds.

(3) Using Francis' formula, determine the discharge over a rectangular notch 36 inches long, and with heads of 3, 6, and 12 inches.

(a) With no side contractions

(b)   ,,   one ,,   ,,

(c)   ,,   two ,,   ,,

		Head.		
		3 inches.	6 inches.	12 inches.
Answer.	a	1·25 c.f.s.	3·53 c.f.s.	10·0 c.f.s.
	b	1·24 c.f.s.	3·47 c.f.s.	9·66 c.f.s.
	c	1·23 c.f.s.	3·41 c.f.s.	9·38 c.f.s.

(4) A submerged weir, 10 feet long, has a depth of water on the up-stream side of 17 inches, on the down-stream side of 9 inches. The velocity of approach = 1·96 feet per second. Assuming the head equivalent to this velocity of approach to be given by $h = 1·4 \dfrac{v^2}{2\,g}$, determine the discharge in cubic feet per minute. Assume $c = ·592$.

Answer. 3,090 cubic feet per minute.

(5) Show that in a triangular right-angled notch, discharging from a tank of sectional area A square feet, the time of lowering the surface level from H_1 feet to H_2 feet above the vertex of the notch is given by

$$t = \frac{1\cdot25\ A}{C\ \sqrt{2\ g}} \left\{ \frac{1}{H_2^{\frac{3}{2}}} - \frac{1}{H_1^{\frac{3}{2}}} \right\} \text{ seconds,}$$

nd taking $C = \cdot593$ determine the time of lowering the surface level of ₁ tank of 500 square feet sectional area from a depth of 1·5 feet to 1·0 eet above the vertex of the notch.

Answer. $t = 60$ seconds.

(6) Find the time required to empty a swimming bath through a flat ;rating in the bottom of the deep end.

Depth of water at deep end   =   6 feet.
     ,,   ,,   shallow end =   3 feet.
Length of bath   = 80 feet.
Breadth   = 30 feet.

Area of grating = 2 square feet.   Coefficient of discharge ·65.

Answer.   596 seconds.

(7) Two cylindrical tanks A (5 feet diameter) and B (10 feet diameter) ₁re connected by a short pipe 4 inches diameter with bell-mouth inlet. ₁t the beginning the level in A is 10 feet and in B is one foot above the ·entre line of the pipe.   In what time will the surface levels be the ₁ame?

Answer.   138 seconds.

CHAPTER VII.

ART. 61.—FLUID FRICTION.

WHENEVER a liquid flows over a solid surface, or when a submerged plane moves in the direction of its length through a liquid, a resistance to motion is experienced. This is commonly termed fluid friction, and should not be confused with the wave-making resistance which is experienced owing to the formation of surface waves, when a partially submerged body is in motion.

Though initially due to viscosity, the laws governing fluid friction are usually very different from those of simple viscous resistance, because of the fact that except at extremely low speeds the motion of the fluid becomes unsteady, eddies are formed, and the energy absorbed in fluid friction now chiefly consists of the energy of formation of these eddies. This energy is finally absorbed in overcoming the viscous resistance of the fluid at points remote from the surface at which the eddies are generated.

As previously indicated, the laws of fluid friction for a liquid for steady and unsteady motion are widely different.

With **Steady Motion—Stream-line Motion** :—

(1) The frictional resistance is directly proportional to the velocity.

(2) Is sensibly independent of the pressure in the fluid.

(3) Is directly proportional to the area of the wetted surface if this is large, i.e., if the resistance is not sensibly affected by the acceleration of the fluid at the leading edges of the surface.

(4) Is independent of the nature of the wetted surface.

(5) Is directly proportional to the viscosity of the fluid, and so varies greatly with temperature.

These laws may be most easily verified by experiments on the flow of water through capillary tubes.

With **Unsteady or Eddy Motion** :—

(1) The frictional resistance varies with a higher power of the velocity than the first, and is usually approximately proportional to V^2.

(2) Is independent (within wide limits) of the pressure in the fluid.

(3) Where a submerged plane moves through still water, the resistance s not proportional to the area of the surface, but, per unit area of the surface, decreases as the length of the latter increases, and approaches a ower limiting value. In the case of flow through a pipe, the length is usually such as to allow of this limiting constant value being attained, so that here the frictional resistance does become practically proportional to the area of the wetted surface.

(4) Varies with the nature of the wetted surface.

(5) Varies only slightly with temperature, but is proportional to some power of the density of the fluid, usually slightly less than the first. It is usually assumed to be directly proportional to the density.

By far the most important series of experiments to determine the resistance to the motion of submerged planes, are those carried out in 1872 by Mr. Froude, at Torquay. Here a series of flat boards, having differently prepared surfaces, were held vertically and suspended from a carriage which was driven at an uniform speed, and were thus towed endwise through the still water in a large basin. The carriage was fitted with a dynamometer and automatically recorded the velocity and resistance of the board. These boards were $\frac{3}{16}$ inch wide, 19 inches deep, and varied in length from 1 foot to 50 feet. The top edge was submerged to a depth of $1\frac{1}{2}$ inches and the boards were fitted with a cut-water, the resistance to this being determined separately. In these experiments Mr. Froude determined that—

(1) The resistance varies greatly with the condition of the surface, the resistance for boards 50 feet long at a velocity of 10 feet per second being with a coating of

Varnish or smooth paint of such composition as is found on the bottom of iron ships . .	·250 lbs. per sq. ft.	
Tinfoil	·246 ,,	,,
Fine sand	·405 ,,	,,
Calico	·470 ,,	,,
Sand of medium coarseness	·488 ,,	,,

(2) The resistance is proportional to v^n, where

n {
(a) depends on the surface,
(b) decreases, up to a certain limit, with an increase in length,
(c) is sensibly independent of the velocity.

(3) The total resistance increases with the length, though the resistance per square foot decreases as the length increases.

Writing: Resistance $= f S v^n$

Length of surface	2 feet				8 feet				20 feet				50 feet			
	A	B	C	D	A	B	C	D	A	B	C	D	A	B	C	D
Value of n	2·00	1·95	2·16	2·00	1·85	1·94	1·99	2·00	1·85	1·93	1·90	2·00	1·83		1·83	2·00
Mean resistance in lbs. per square foot	·41	·38	·30	·90	·325	·314	·278	·625	·278	·271	·262	·534	·250		·246	·488
Resistance per square foot over last foot in lbs.	·390	·370	·295	·730	·264	·260	·263	·488	·240	·237	·244	·465	·226		·233	·456

Here *A* refers to varnished surfaces, or to the painted surface of an iron ship.

   ,, *B* ,, surfaces coated with paraffin wax.

   ,, *C* ,, ,, ,, tinfoil.

   ,, *D* ,, ,, covered with sand of medium coarseness.

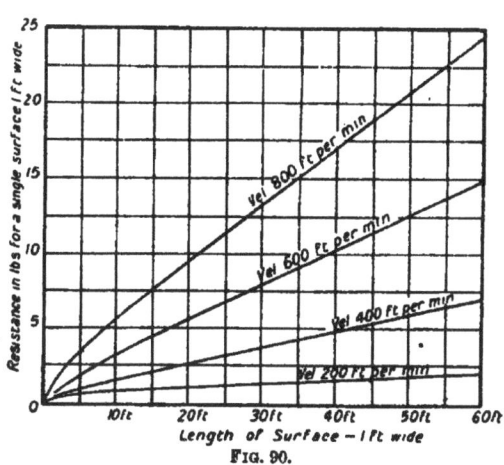

Fig. 90.

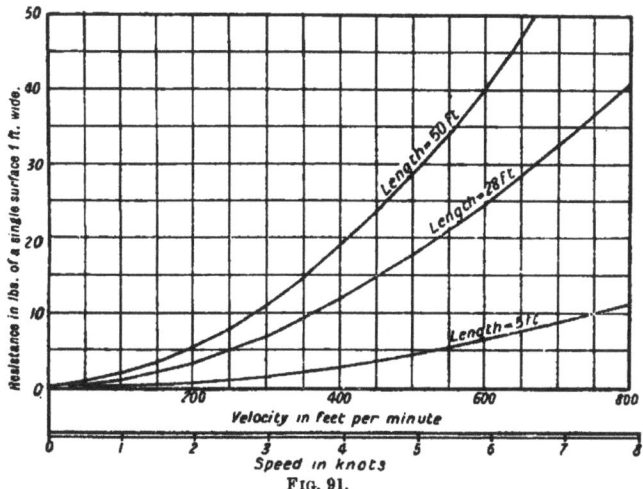

Fig. 91.

where S = area of surface, it was found that

f
- (a) depends on the surface.
- (b) decreases with an increase in length, becoming approximately constant when the length is large.
- (c) is independent of the pressure.
- (d) is proportional to the density of the fluid and diminishes very slightly as the temperature increases.

H.A.

N

The fact that the resistance per square foot over the aft part of the surface is less than at a point nearer the prow may be explained as follows.[1] The first portion of the surface, in passing through the water, experiences resistance, and communicates motion, in its own direction, to the water. The succeeding portion of the surface is then in contact with a body of water having a smaller relative velocity, and hence producing a smaller resistance per unit area, while it would appear that the velocity of the accompanying current increases until at some point in the surface a balance is obtained between the amount of energy given to the

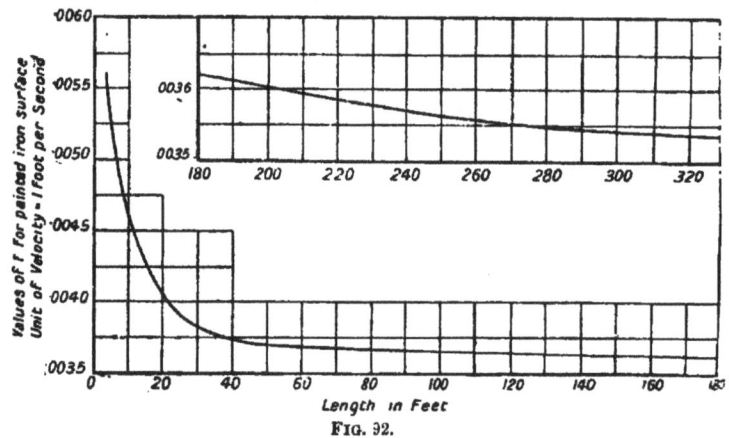

FIG. 92.

accompanying stream per second, and the energy dissipated by eddy formation in the surrounding fluid and in producing motion of a greater volume of this water against viscous resistances. After this point is reached, the velocity of the accompanying current and the resistance per square foot of surface remain approximately constant. It will be noted that the mean resistance per square foot of area diminishes very slightly for lengths above 50 feet.

A short *résumé* of Mr. Froude's results is given on p. 176, these particular experiments being carried out at a velocity of 10 feet per second.[1]

Curves (Figs. 90 and 91) have been prepared from the results of these experiments, and show respectively the resistance with length at constant speed, and with speed for a given length, for a varnished or painted iron surface. In Fig. 92 values of f in the formula, Resistance $= f S v^n$, have

---

[1] From the British Association Report, 1874.

been plotted from the experimental results for a painted iron surface for lengths up to 50 feet, and the curve thus obtained has been produced to give approximate values for lengths up to 330 feet.

The results may thus be extended for application to the determination of the frictional resistance of vessels of great length. For ships, the value of n may be taken as 1·83, and the following table indicates results obtained by exterpolation from the above curve :—

	Length in feet.	50	100	200	300
Values of f	With the unit of velocity = 1 foot per sec.	·00371	·00361	·00356	·00353
	With the unit of velocity = 1 knot = 1·69 foot per sec.	·00968	·00941	·00929	·00922

The following values of f are given by J. Hamilton[1] :—

Length in feet.	Iron bottom (painted).	Copper sheathing.	
		Smooth.	Rough.
200	·00944	·00943	·01170
300	·00923	·00930	·01152
400	·00910	·00926	·01140
500	·00904	·00926	·01136

Art. 62.—Disc Friction.

The resistance to the rotation of a disc in water at high speeds is of importance in the design of centrifugal pumps and turbines, the energy expended in overcoming such resistances amounting in the case of some high-speed pumps to as much as 15 per cent. of the total energy given to the shaft.

Theory of Disc Resistance.

Assuming the resistance of an elementary ring of mean radius r and of radial width δr to be given by $f . 2 \pi r \delta r . v^n$, where f is a coefficient of

[1] " Inst. Naval Architects," March, 1898.

friction and v is the velocity of the element,[1] then if ω is the angular velocity of the disc in radians per second $r = \omega r$, and the moment of the resistance $= 2\,\pi f\,\omega^n\,r^{n+2}\,\delta r$. Then the moment of resistance of the two faces of a disc having a radius of R feet

$$= 4\,\pi f\,\omega^n \int_0^R r^{n+2}\,d\,r \text{ foot lbs.}$$

$$= \frac{4\,\pi f\,\omega^n}{n+3}\,.\,R^{n+3} \text{ foot lbs.}$$

Assuming the resistance of the edge of the disc to follow the same law, and therefore to be given by $2\,\pi b\,.\,f\,\omega^n\,R^{n+2}$, where b is the breadth in feet, the total moment of disc resistance, M, will be given by

$$M = 2\,\pi f\,\omega^n\,R^{n+2}\left\{\frac{2\,R}{n+3} + b\right\} \text{ foot lbs.}$$

Effective Radius.—Writing the resisting moment as

$$\frac{4\,\pi f\,\omega^n}{n+3}\,.\,R_1^{n+3} \text{ foot lbs.,}$$

where R_1 is the effective radius of the disc, i.e. the radius of an infinitely thin disc giving the same resistance, then

$$R_1^{n+3} = R^{n+3} + \frac{(n+3)\,b\,R^{n+2}}{2}$$

$$\therefore\quad R_1 = R\left\{1 + \frac{(n+3)\,b}{2\,R}\right\}^{\frac{1}{n+3}}$$

$$= R\left\{1 + \frac{b}{2\,R}\right\}$$

if b is small compared with $2\,R$.

Dr. W. C. Unwin has carried out a series of experiments on discs 10, 15 and 20 inches diameter rotating inside a casing whose side clearance could be varied from 1·5 inches to 6 inches.[2] The maximum speed attained in these experiments was about 470 revolutions per minute. More recent experiments by A. Ryan and the author have extended these speeds up to 2,200 revolutions per minute on discs of 9 and 12 inches diameter.[3]

In the apparatus used in the latter experiments a horizontal, motor-driven shaft carries the disc to be tested. The shaft passes through easily fitting bushes in the sides of a casing surrounding the disc, as shown in Fig. 93.

[1] The friction per square foot at a velocity v feet per second is, from this definition, $f\,v^n$ lbs.

[2] "Proc. Inst. C.E.," vol. 80, 1885, p. 221.

[3] "Proc. Inst. C.E.," vol. 179, 1909–10, pt. I.

The casing is prevented from rotating, and its tendency to rotate, which is equal to the resistance to rotation of the disc, is measured by weights applied to a hanger on the one side, and by a light spring balance supporting the other side of the casing. A long, light pointer attached to the casing and work-ing over a graduated scale serves to magnify the readings of this balance. The two parallel sides of the casing are provided with adjustable plates with different surfaces, and are separated by a series of cast-iron rings 18 inches in internal diameter, these form-ing the body and enabling the side clearance to be varied at will from $\frac{1}{8}$ inch to $2\frac{1}{8}$ inches.

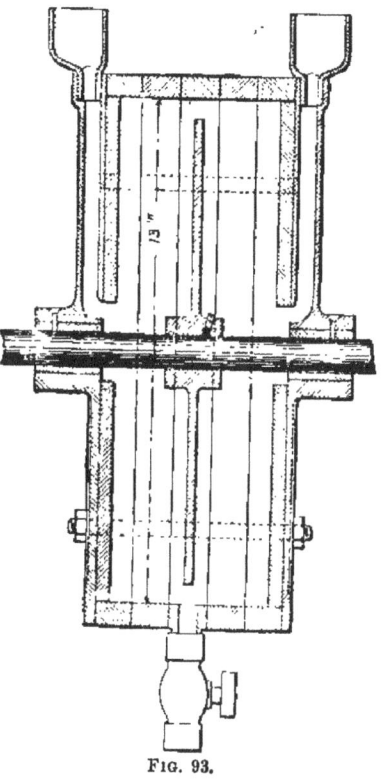

Fig. 93.

Six plain discs in all were examined, these being either 9 inches or 12 inches in external diameter and about 0·2 inch thick. They were formed of polished brass, of rough cast-iron, and of rough cast-iron painted and varnished. The surface of the rough cast-iron discs was left as received from the foundry, except that all outstanding roughness was dressed off. These would be considered excellent castings and had a comparatively smooth skin. After being used they received two coats of quick-drying varnish-paint, and were then used for the third series of experiments. Each disc is carried on a central boss $1\frac{1}{4}$ inches in diameter and $\frac{3}{4}$ inch deep.

The results throughout were very consistent, and there is no reason to suspect an error of more than about 2 per cent. in those of any series.

Variation of Disc Resistance with Temperature.—As it was recognised that it would be impossible to carry out a series of experiments without some variation in the mean temperature of the water, preliminary experiments were made to determine how such a variation affected the resistance.

A possible law of such variation may be deduced from purely theoretical considerations, the only assumptions made being that the resistance of each element of the rotating surface is proportional to the same power n of its velocity, and to some power of the viscosity μ, and of the density w of the fluid, both of which vary with temperature.[1]

On this assumption it may be shown that the resistance, other things being equal, is, as in the case of pipe flow, probably proportional to $\mu^{2-n} w^{n-1}$, where n is that power of the velocity to which the resistance at constant temperature is proportional.

For the purpose of determining the temperature variation three sets of experiments were carried out, using respectively a 12-inch brass disc in a machine-ironed casing, with $1\frac{1}{8}$ inch clearance; the same disc in a rough cast-iron casing, with $\frac{1}{8}$ inch clearance; and a 12-inch disc with radial vanes $\frac{1}{4}$ inch deep and with $\frac{3}{8}$ inch side clearance, in a painted and varnished casing. The values of n were determined in each case from a second set of experiments carried out as nearly as possible at constant temperature, all the results being corrected to 65° F. by an application of the foregoing hypothetical formula. This involves the method of successive approximation for finding the true value of n, but as the temperature corrections were small (never above about $2\frac{1}{2}$ per cent., and generally very much less) the first approximation, differing as it did from the true value by not more than 1 per cent., was in general sufficiently accurate. In this way the following values were obtained :—

Series A.

12-inch brass disc in smooth casing . . . . $1\frac{1}{8}$ inch clearance, $n = 1.785$

Series B.

12-inch „ „ „ rough cast-iron casing . . $\frac{1}{8}$ „ „ , $n = 1.840$

Series C.

12-inch „ „ with radial vanes . . . . . $\frac{3}{8}$ „ „ , $n = 1.930$

The results of the temperature-variation experiments are then as follows :—

Series A.—1,400 revolutions per minute.

Temperature ° F. .	65	72	74	80	95	100	109	113	128	140
Resisting moment (foot lbs.) .	3·279	3·203	3·194	3·117	3·002	2·986	2·920	2·894	2·803	2·701
Ratio to moment at 65° F. .	1·000	0·977	0·973	0·950	0·915	0·910	0·890	0·883	0·855	0·825

[1] By the theory of dimensions. The method is applied to pipe flow on p. 198.

SERIES B.—1,175 revolutions per minute.

Temperature ° F. . .	65	78	98	104	115	133	159
Moment (foot lbs.) . .	2·480	2·394	2·249	2·257	2·175	2·105	2·010
Ratio to moment at 65° F.	1·00	0·965	0·908	0·910	0·877	0·850	0·810

SERIES C.—1,050 revolutions per minute.

Temperature ° F. . . .	60	76·5	100	132·5
Moment (foot lbs.) . . .	6·460	6·377	6·215	6·138
Ratio to moment at 65° F. .	1·003	0·989	0·963	0·950

In addition to these, a number of experiments by Dr. W. C. Unwin on a disc having $n = 1·85$ are available. These are as follows:—

Temperature ° F. .	41·2	53·0	70·4	130·5
Resistance . . .	0·1215	0·1149	0·1112	0·1003

For the sake of comparison the whole of the foregoing results have been plotted in Fig. 94 against the curves representing the relationship,

$$\text{Resistance at } t° \text{ F.} = \text{Resistance at } 65° \text{ F.} \times \left\{ \frac{\mu}{\mu_{65}} \right\}^{2-n} \cdot \left\{ \frac{w_t}{w_{65}} \right\}^{n-1},$$

for corresponding values of n. From these it appears that the theoretical curves fit the experimental results remarkably closely, quite sufficiently closely indeed to justify the adoption of this formula.

To render the series more complete the theoretical curves for $n = 1·9$ and $n = 2·0$ have also been added.

The results show that the resistance diminishes with an increase in temperature, the amount of the variation with a given temperature-difference increasing as the temperature diminishes and also as n diminishes. Its value in the neighbourhood of 65° F. with a polished brass disc ($n = 1·8$) is about one-third of 1 per cent. per degree Fahr. When $n = 1·9$ this falls to one-seventh of 1 per cent. per degree Fahr., and when $n = 2·0$ it becomes inappreciably small.

Experimental Results.

The main results of the experiments are given in the table opposite: In this the values of n were obtained from curves representing logarithms of the resisting moments in foot lbs., plotted as ordinates against logarithms of the revolutions per minute. Speeds varying between 450 and 2,200 revolutions per minute were used for the determinations.

From these results it is apparent that in no case does n attain a value

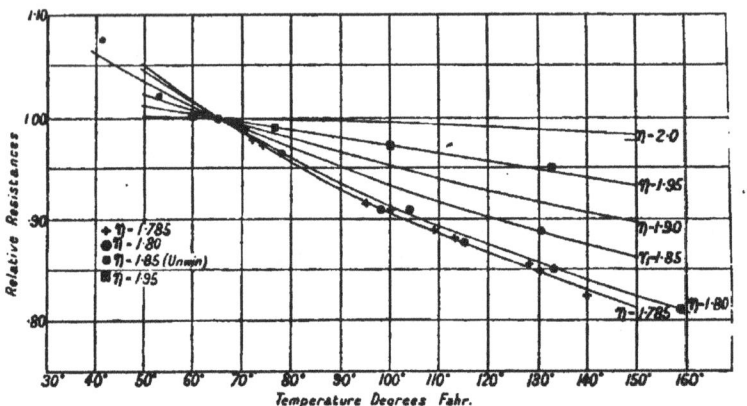

Fig. 94.—Variation of Disc Resistance with Temperature.

so high as 2, its maximum value, even with a rough cast-iron disc, being only 1·915. A comparison of these results with those of Dr. Unwin shows that in every case the values of n obtained by the latter experimenter, at speeds between 67 and 350 revolutions per minute, are higher than those obtained by the author at these greater speeds. The following table indicates the different values obtained with various discs :—

VALUES OF "n" WITH SMOOTH CASING.

—	Polished brass disc.	Painted and varnished cast-iron disc.	Rough cast-iron disc.
Unwin, 10 inch . .	1·85	1·94	2·00
Author, 12 inch . .	1·79	1·797	1·808
,, 9 inch . .	1·88	1·83	1·85

From this it would appear that n is not a constant for all speeds, but diminishes slightly as the speed increases.

RESULTS OF EXPERIMENTS.

		Side clearance.	Value of "n."	Value of "f."	Moment in foot lbs. at 1,500 revolutions per minute.	Friction in lbs. per square foot at an *average* speed of	
						10 feet per sec.	50 feet per sec.
		Inches.					
Polished brass disc 12 inches in diameter	Rough cast-iron casing	1/8	1·800	0·00409	3·772	0·260	4·72
		5/8	1·800	0·00422	3·890	0·268	4·86
		1 1/8	1·810	0·00414	3·950	0·269	4·98
		1 5/8	1·800	0·00432	3·981	0·274	4·99
		2 1/8	1·800	0·00474	4·367	0·301	5·46
	Painted cast-iron casing	1/8	1·792	0·00360	3·119	0·222	3·92
		5/8	1·797	0·00359	3·251	0·226	4·07
		1 1/8	1·810	0·00356	3·396	0·231	4·27
		1 5/8	1·800	0 00359	3·308	0·228	4·14
		1/8	1·816	0·00346	3·311	0·227	4·22
	Smooth metal casing	5/8	1·809	0·00373	3·459	0·239	4·40
		1 1/8	1·785	0·00438	3·772	0·267	4·70
		1 5/8	1·772	0·00421	3·428	0·251	4·37
		2 5/8	1·766	0·00471	3·750	0·278	4·78
Ditto 9 inches diameter	Painted casing	5/8	1·830	0·00342	0·9053	0·232	4·12
Rough cast-iron disc 12 inches in diameter	Rough cast-iron casing	5/8	1·912	0·00300	4·385	0·247	5·31
		1 1/8	1·915	0·00301	4·457	0·250	5·40
		1 5/8	1·912	0·00297	4·345	0·244	5·25
		2 1/8	1·915	0·00302	4·467	0·251	5·42
	Painted cast-iron casing	5/8	1·798	0·00428	3·886	0·270	4·85
		1 1/8	1·807	0·00426	4·018	0·273	5·00
		1 5/8	1·813	0·00424	4·098	0·278	5·11
		2 1/8	1·813	0·00416	4·018	0·273	5·02
	Rough cast-iron casing with two concentric baffles 1/2 inch deep on each side	5/8	1·883	0·00337	4·365	0·261	5·38
		1 1/8	1·883	0·00337	4·365	0·261	5·38
Ditto 9 inches diameter	Painted casing	5/8	1·850	0·00372	1·099	0·263	5·15
Painted and varnished cast-iron disc 12 inches diameter	Rough cast-iron casing	5/8	1·850	0·00353	3·959	0·249	4·90
	Painted cast-iron casing	5/8	1·795	0·00361	3·232	0·236	4·05
		1 1/8	1·798	0·00374	3·354	0·234	4·21
Ditto 9 inches diameter	Painted casing	5/8	1·830	0·00340	0·8995	0·224	4·26
		Clearance over vanes.					
12-inch brass disc with four radial vanes on each face, in painted casing	Vanes 1/2 inch deep	1/8	1·910	0·00903	13·00	0·730	15·77
		5/8	1·910	0·01067	15·35	0·861	18·60
	Vanes 1/4 inch deep	3 3/8	1·950	0·00668	11·22	0·598	13·74
			1·950	0·00687	11·56	0·615	14·14

Power absorbed in Disc Resistance.—Since the resisting moment is given by $\dfrac{4\,\pi f\,\omega^n}{n+3}\,R_1{}^{n+3}$ foot lbs., the work absorbed in overcoming this resistance is given by $\dfrac{4\,\pi f\,\omega^{n+1}}{n+3}\,R_1{}^{n+3}$ foot lbs. per second

$$= \frac{4\,\pi f\left(\dfrac{\pi\,N}{30}\right)^{n+1}}{550\,(n+3)}\,R_1{}^{n+3}\ \text{horse-power.}$$

The following table indicates the magnitude of the horse-power absorbed at 1,500 revolutions and at 2,000 revolutions per minute, in a few typical cases with a $\frac{3}{8}$ inch side clearance :—

HORSE-POWER ABSORBED.

—	12-inch polished brass disc.		12-inch rough cast-iron disc.		12-inch painted cast-iron disc.		9 inch polished brass disc, in painted casing.	12-inch brass disc with four radial vanes $\frac{1}{8}$ inch deep on each face, in painted casing.
	In rough cast-iron casing.	In painted casing.	In rough cast-iron casing.	In painted casing.	In rough cast-iron casing.	In painted casing.		
H.P. at 1,500 revolutions	1·11	0·928	1·25	1·11	1·13	0·923	0·258	4·38
H.P. at 2,000 revolutions	2·49	2·07	2·9	2·49	2·57	2·06	0·581	10·12

Effect of Roughness in Surface of Disc.—The table on p. 187 shows comparative values of the resistance at 1,500 revolutions per minute as affected by disc roughness, the resistance of a polished brass disc being taken as unity for each type of casing.

From these results it appears that at this speed the resistance of a polished brass and of a painted cast-iron disc are practically identical. At still higher speeds the resistance of the painted disc becomes proportionately greater than that of the polished disc if the interior of the casing is rough, and becomes proportionately less at lower speeds. In a painted casing, however, the relative resistances are the same for all speeds. The relative resistances of a rough cast-iron disc and of one made of polished brass depend largely on the clearance, the roughness of the casing, and the speed. In a rough cast-iron casing at 1,500 revolutions per minute the resistance of a rough disc varies from about 1·12 times to 1·03 times that of a polished disc, as the clearance varies from $\frac{3}{8}$ inch to $2\frac{1}{2}$ inches, while in a smooth painted casing the ratio varies from 1·195 to 1·22.

It may be taken that in a rough cast-iron casing a rough cast-iron disc gives about 10 per cent. greater resistance at this speed than one which is polished, and that in a painted casing this is increased to about 20 per cent. greater resistance.

Owing, however, to the higher value of n in the case of a rough disc in a rough casing, its resistance increases more rapidly with an increase in

COMPARATIVE RESISTANCES WITH VARIOUS DISCS.

—	Polished brass disc.	Painted and varnished cast-iron disc.	Rough cast-iron disc.
12-inch disc in rough cast-iron casing . ⅝ inch clearance, 1¼ ″ ″, 1⅝ ″ ″, 2½ ″ ″	$n = 1\cdot80$ { 1·00, 1·00, 1·00, 1·00	$n = 1\cdot85$ { 1·017, —, —, —	$n = 1\cdot91$ { 1·115, 1·130, 1·090, 1·025
12-inch disc in painted and varnished casing . ⅝ inch clearance, 1¼ ″ ″, 1⅝ ″ ″	$n = 1\cdot80$ { 1·00, 1·00, 1·00	$n = 1\cdot80$ { 0·994, 0·988, —	$n = 1\cdot80$ { 1·195, 1·148, 1·220
9-inch disc in painted and varnished casing with ⅝ inch casing	1·00 $n = 1\cdot83$	1·006 $n = 1\cdot83$	1·222 $n = 1\cdot85$

speed than does that of a polished disc. In a smooth casing their relative resistances are practically independent of the speed.

Effect of Roughness in the Surface of the Casing.—The comparative results obtained with the three surfaces at 1,500 revolutions per minute are tabulated on p. 188, the resistance in a painted and varnished casing being taken as unity for each type of disc.

From these results it appears that with such clearances as are found in practice the effect of a roughness of the casing in increasing the resistance is as great as that of the roughness of the disc—in fact, a painted or polished disc in a rough casing gives, within about 2 per cent., the same resistance as a rough disc in a painted casing. The relative effect of the roughness of the casing is more pronounced with a smooth than with a rough disc.

Effect of a Variation in the Clearance of the Casing.—The comparative results as affected by the side clearance between the disc and casing are given in the Table on p. 189, the resistance in each case being expressed as a multiple of that obtained with the minimum clearance adopted with the particular disc and casing under consideration. The speed was 1,500 revolutions per minute throughout.

From these results it appears that in practically every case the minimum resistance is obtained with the minimum clearance, and that relative increased resistance with an increase in side clearance is much more marked with a smooth than with a rough disc. With a rough cast-iron disc indeed, and with clearances from $\frac{5}{8}$ inch to $2\frac{1}{8}$ inches, the

RESISTANCES WITH VARIOUS SURFACES.

Type of disc and clearance.	Relative Resistances.		
	With painted and varnished casing.	With smooth metal casing.	With rough cast-iron casing.
12-inch polished brass disc ($\frac{1}{4}$ inch clearance	1·00	1·06	1·21
$\frac{5}{8}$,, ,,	1·00	1·06	1·20
$1\frac{1}{8}$,, ,,	1·00	1·08	1·13
$1\frac{5}{8}$,, ,,	1·00	1·04	1·20
$2\frac{1}{8}$,, ,,	1·00	1·00	1·165
12-inch painted and varnished cast-iron disc with $\frac{5}{8}$ inch clearance .	1·00	—	1·22
12-inch rough cast-iron disc . ($\frac{5}{8}$ inch clearance	1·00	—	1·13
$1\frac{1}{8}$,, ,,	1·00	—	1·11
$1\frac{5}{8}$,, ,,	1·00	—	1·06
$2\frac{1}{8}$,, ,,	1·00	—	1·11

resistance appears to vary very little with the clearance, whether with a rough or a smooth casing. One rather peculiar feature of the results obtained with a smooth disc in a smooth casing, and to a smaller extent with the rougher discs and with the rougher casing, is worthy of note. This is,.that as the clearance is increased from $\frac{1}{4}$ inch, the resistance at first increases, then diminishes, attaining a minimum value with a clearance of about $1\frac{5}{8}$ inch, and afterwards appears to increase rapidly as the clearance is increased to $2\frac{1}{8}$ inches. The following is offered as a possible explanation of this phenomenon :—

In considering the simple theory of disc-resistance it is tacitly assumed that the water dragged around with the disc travels in concentric paths, each particle remaining at a constant distance from the axis of the disc. In a closed casing and with side clearances so small as to lead to a non-sinuous motion of the water this would be the case ; the index n would be unity, and the resistance would be due to simple viscous shear of successive layers of the fluid. Under such conditions the resistance would decrease as the clearance was increased, until the latter became so large that sinuous motion was set up. With any clearance large enough to satisfy practical requirements, however, the motion is sinuous, and disc-resistance is modified by the fact that the water nearest the disc is thrown radially outwards by centrifugal force, so that a circulatory current is set up, this passing radially outwards along the face of the

COMPARATIVE RESISTANCES WITH VARYING SIDE CLEARANCE.

Side clearance . . . . . inches	⅛	⅝	1⅛	1⅝	2⅛
12-inch polished brass disc in painted casing .	1·00	1·04	1·09	1·06	—
The same in smooth metal casing . . .	1·00	1·05	1·14	1·03	1·13
The same in rough cast-iron casing . .	1·00	1·03	1·05	1·06	1·16
12-inch painted and varnished cast-iron disc in painted and varnished casing . .	—	1·00	1·04	—	—
12-inch rough cast-iron disc in painted and varnished casing	—	1·00	1·03	1·06	1·03
The same in rough cast-iron casing . .	—	1·00	1·02	0·99	1·02
The same in rough cast-iron casing with two concentric baffles, ¼ inch deep and 5 inches and 10 inches in diameter, on each side .	—	1·00	1·00	—	—

disc and inwards over the sides of the casing. Due to this current, energy is wasted, firstly from friction at the sides and outer periphery of the casing, and secondly, from the formation of eddies caused by the relative motion of the radial outward and inward currents.

Considering only the first of these causes, it would appear that the resistance should increase steadily with an increase in the side clearance and surface area of the casing; but with a very small clearance it is probable that the circulatory current is only slightly apparent, and that as the clearance is increased its magnitude, and the loss of energy which it involves, will at first increase rather rapidly. A further increase in the clearance, by giving more room to the currents, diminishes their relative velocity at a point midway between the disc and the casing, and it is conceivable that there will be some definite clearance for which the reduction in the eddy loss due to this relative motion may exactly counterbalance the loss due to an increased area of the surface of the casing. As the clearance is further increased the impact loss will diminish until the effect of surface friction becomes the all-important factor in producing the resistance.

To determine whether, by the use of concentric circular baffles fixed to the casing, the circulating currents might be localised so as to reduce their effect, two series of experiments were carried out with two such baffles in position on each side of the casing; these baffles consisted of rings respectively 5 inches and 10 inches in diameter and projecting $\frac{1}{2}$ inch. The clearance between the casing and the disc was $\frac{5}{8}$ inch in one series and $1\frac{1}{2}$ inch in the other. The results showed that while in the first case the resistance was unaltered by the baffles, in the second case it was reduced by about 2 per cent.

Effect of Radial Vanes on the Disc.—In turbines and centrifugal pumps having impellers of the open-vaned type, or having balancing discs fitted with shallow radial vanes, it has usually been assumed that the increased resistance over that obtaining with plain discs is negligible. To test this a brass disc, 12 inches in diameter, was provided with four radial vanes on each face. Two series of experiments were carried out, one with vanes $\frac{1}{4}$ inch deep, and the second with $\frac{1}{2}$ inch vanes.

The results of these experiments, as compared with those carried out on plain discs, are given below.

The surprisingly high value of the resistance with these vanes is doubtless due to loss of energy in eddy formation behind the trailing edges of the vanes.

EFFECT OF RADIAL VANES.

		Relative resistances at 1,500 revolutions per minute.
Painted casing with $\frac{1}{2}$ inch side clearance	Plain disc	1·00
	„ Vanes $\frac{1}{4}$ inch deep	3·60
	„ „ $\frac{1}{2}$ „ „	4·17
Painted casing with $\frac{5}{8}$ inch side clearance	Plain disc	1·00
	„ Vanes $\frac{1}{4}$ inch deep ($\frac{5}{8}$ inch side clearance) .	3·56
	„ „ $\frac{1}{2}$ „ „	4·72

Effect of a Variation in Disc Diameter.—As indicated on p. 180, similar discs of different diameters and having clearances proportional to their radii, would have resistances proportional to the $(n + 3)$ power of these radii.

In the following Table the results from a series of 9-inch discs in a painted cast-iron casing with $\frac{5}{8}$ inch side clearance, and running at 1,500 revolutions per minute, are compared with those obtained from similar 12 inch discs with similar (0·825 inch) side clearance, the latter results being obtained by interpolation from those obtained experimentally with $\frac{5}{8}$ inch and with $1\frac{1}{8}$ inch clearance. As the same casing was used throughout, the radial clearance was not, however, similar in the two cases, being respectively $\frac{1}{2}$ inch and 2 inches.

The results show that the resistances in these experiments are proportional to the $(n + x)$ power of the radii, where x, instead of being equal

EFFECT OF A VARIATION IN DIAMETER.

	Diam.	Ratio of effective radii.	Value of "n."	Mean value of "n."	Moment at 1,500 revs. per min.	$\left(\frac{\text{Diam.}}{\text{ratio}}\right)^{n\,+\,x}$	Moment ratio.	Ratio of the last two columns.
Polished brass disc	Inches. 9	1·326	1·830	1·813	Foot-lbs. 0·9053	3·89	3·66	1·063
	12		1·797		3·311			
Painted cast-iron disc	9	1·317	1·830	1·812	0·8995	3·77	3·63	1·040
	12		1·795		3·263			
Rough cast-iron disc	9	1·317	1·850	1·824	1·099	3·78	3·54	1·069
	12		1·798		3·890			

to 3, has the values 2·782, 2·765 and 2·741 in the respective series. From the last column of the Table it appears that the resistance of the smaller disc is approximately 6 per cent. greater than would be the case if x were equal to 3, i.e., if the radial clearance were proportional to the radius, so that a given increase in radial clearance would appear to have approximately the same effect as a corresponding increase in side clearance.

Results of Dr. Unwin's Experiments.—For the sake of comparison the main results of these are given in the following Table. In them the speed varied between 66 and 350 revolutions per minute, and for the values here given the virtual radius of the disc was 0·8488 foot.

From the Table it appears that although the differences between these values of "f" and "n" and those obtained by the author are in some cases large, the values of the friction per square foot as calculated for the two speeds in every case agree fairly closely.

Average values of f and n, which will be sufficiently near for all

RESULTS OF DR. UNWIN'S EXPERIMENTS.

	Side clearance.	Value of "n"	Value of "f."	Friction in lbs. per square foot at a *Mean* velocity of	
				10 Feet per sec.	50 Feet per sec.
	Inches.				
Polished brass disc — Smooth metal casing . .	1½	1·85	0·00286	0·2018	3·955
	3	1·85	0·00296	0·2093	4·100
	6	1·85	0·00326	0·2299	4·703
Casing coated with rough sand	3	1·95	0·00271	0·2436	5·600
Painted and varnished cast-iron disc in smooth metal casing	3	1·94	0·00254	0·2200	4·970
	6	1·94	0·00269	0·2331	5·260
Rough cast-iron disc in smooth metal casing	1½	2·00	0·00213	0·2129	5·320
	3	2·00	0·00227	0·2273	5·680
	6	2·00	0·00243	0·2432	6·080
The same covered with fine sand in same casing	3	2·05	0·00306	0·3395	9·160
The same covered with coarse sand .	1½	1·91	0·00729	0·5874	12·690
	3	1·91	0·00790	0·6376	13·790
	6	1·91	0·00887	0·7153	15·450

practical calculations, are given in the following Table.   These values have been determined by a consideration of Dr. Unwin's results at low speeds and the author's at high speeds.

AVERAGE VALUES OF "f" AND "n."

	Mean velocity.	Polished brass disc.		Painted and varnished cast-iron disc.		Rough cast-iron disc.	
		f	n	f	n	f	n
	Feet per second.						
Smooth casing	10	0·0031	1·85	0·0026	1·94	0·0023	2·00
	20	0·0033	1·84	0·0029	1·91	0·0027	1·96
	30	0·0035	1·83	0·0032	1·88	0·0032	1·91
	40	0·0037	1·82	0·0035	1·84	0·0037	1·86
	50	0·0039	1·80	0·0037	1·80	0·0042	1·81
Rough cast-iron casing	10	0·0029	1·92	0·0027	1·97	0·0026	2·00
	20	0·0033	1·89	0·0029	1·94	0·0027	1·98
	30	0·0037	1·86	0·0031	1·91	0·0028	1·96
	40	0·0041	1·83	0·0033	1·88	0·0029	1·93
	50	0·0044	1·80	0·0035	1·85	0·0030	1·91

One or two points which have been brought out by the foregoing investigation would appear to deserve special note in connection with the design of pumps and turbines.

All clearances, side and radial, should be cut down to the absolute minimum compatible with freely-running surfaces.   That this point needs emphasizing will be evident from a consideration of Fig. 806, which is taken from examples of modern high-speed pumps by makers of repute. The manner in which the disc resistance might be reduced without any accompanying drawback is indicated by dotted lines.

The internal surfaces of all casings should be finished off as smoothly as possible and should be coated with a hard varnish paint or enamel. The same applies to the surfaces of the discs.   It would appear, further, that very little is to be gained by machining and polishing a smooth-cast surface as compared with simply painting and varnishing it.

CHAPTER VIII.

Pipe flow—Experimental Formulae—Darcy—Hagen—D'Aubuisson—Prony—Eytelwein—Weisbach—Kutter—Rational formula for pipe flow—Reynolds—Unwin—Lawton—Thrupp—Tutton—Values of f and C for various pipes—Fire hose—Resistance with oil—Sand—Mean velocity—Distribution of velocity—Measurement of discharge—Pitot tube—Relation of pipe diameter to volume discharged—Gradual and sudden stoppage of motion in an uniform pipe—Water hammer.

ART. 68.—PIPE FLOW.

ONE very important effect of fluid friction is experienced in the resistance to the flow of water through a pipe. This resistance can only be overcome by a gradual fall of pressure in the liquid, in the direction of motion, and, reasoning from analogy to the resistance experienced by a plane surface moving through water, it might be inferred that, with sinuous motion, the total resistance R would equal $f\,S\,v^n$,

where $\begin{cases} f \text{ depends chiefly on the surface of the pipe and to a smaller} \\ \quad \text{extent on viscosity.} \\ S = \text{area of wetted surface.} \\ n \text{ depends on the pipe surface, and is approximately equal to 2.} \end{cases}$

Putting A = sectional area of pipe in square feet.

,, P = length of perimeter of pipe.

,, $p_1 - p_2$ = fall in pressure in lbs. per square foot over a length l feet of pipe.

This becomes

$$(p_1 - p_2)\, A = f\, P\, l\, v^n$$

$$\therefore \quad p_1 - p_2 = f\frac{P}{A} \cdot l\, v^n. \tag{1}$$

Here $\dfrac{A}{P} = \dfrac{\text{area}}{\text{perimeter}}$ is termed the **hydraulic mean depth**[1] and is commonly denoted by m, so that (1) may be written

$$p_1 - p_2 = \frac{f\, l\, v^n}{m}. \tag{2}$$

In the case of a circular pipe $m = \dfrac{\pi r^2}{2\,\pi\,r} = \dfrac{r}{2} = \dfrac{d}{4}$, so that, if in

---

[1] If the mass of water in the pipe be imagined as distributed over a horizontal surface of the same area as the walls of the pipe, its depth will then be the same as the hydraulic mean depth for the pipe.

addition we express $p_1 - p_2$ as a difference h of head in feet of water, equation (2) becomes

$$h = \frac{f \, l \, v^n}{62 \cdot 4 \, m} = \frac{f' \, l \, v^n}{d}. \tag{3}$$

The analogy between the two cases is, however, not exact, in that, while with a solid moving through a large body of water any disturbance set up at the surface may be propagated over any unknown distance, becoming less marked as the distance from the solid increases and finally dying out altogether, any such disturbance in a pipe has a strictly limited range of extension, but is in general communicated to the whole mass of water in motion.

Where the motion through the pipe is everywhere steady, it is entirely governed by the law of simple viscous resistance and the conditions are accurately stated by the formulae of p. 69. Thus Poiseuille (1845), experimenting on tubes of very fine bore (between ·02 and ·10 millimetres), found the resistance to motion to be directly proportional to the velocity, and to the pipe length, and inversely to the square of the diameter, and deduced the law (see p. 69):—

$$\text{loss of pressure} = \frac{32 \, \mu \, l \, v}{d^2}.$$

Many experimental researches have been carried out from time to time to determine the law of resistance with sinuous or unsteady motion, and it is now proposed to consider the results of these somewhat in detail.

Probably the most complete series of experiments is that of Darcy, who in 1857, experimenting on cast-iron pipes having diameters ranging from ·5 inch to 20 inches, and lengths of 110 yards, concluded that the resistance is proportional to the length and to the square of the velocity and is inversely proportional to the diameter. Thus expressed, the law becomes

$$h = \frac{v^2 \, l}{c^2 \, d}$$

c being a constant for any one type of surface.

It was found, however, that this formula was not strictly applicable to all diameters of pipe, since, as d increases, the resistance diminishes according to a slightly higher power of d than the first. Darcy found that, within the range of his experiments, keeping c a constant, this exponential value of d might be replaced by $\left\{ \dfrac{d}{1 + \dfrac{1}{12 \, d}} \right\}$, and thus obtained the law

$$h = \frac{v^2 \, l}{c^2 \, d} \left\{ 1 + \frac{1}{12 \, d} \right\} \qquad (4)$$

{ where d = diameter of pipe in feet.
  „ v = velocity in feet per second.
  „ h = head loss expressed in feet of water.

Assuming, with Darcy, that the loss is proportional to the kinetic energy of the stream, and replacing d by its value $4 \, m$, the above becomes

$$h = f \left(1 + \frac{1}{12 \, d} \right) \frac{l \, v^2}{2 \, g \, m} \qquad (5)$$

$\left(\text{where } f = \frac{2 \, g}{c^2} \right)$, in which form the equation is often stated.

Darcy's experiments, carried out on C. I. pipes, gave, in round numbers, the following values of the coefficient f.

{ For clean and bare metal surfaces . . . $f = \cdot005$.
  For old and incrusted . . . . . . $f = \cdot010$.

Hagen (1854) deduced from experiments by Bossut, Couplet, and Dubuat the formula—

$$h = \frac{f \, l \, v^{1\cdot75}}{d^{1\cdot25}} \qquad (6)$$

but did not discover any law of variation of these indices or of the coefficient f, with the surface or diameter of the pipe. Most of the other formulae deduced by the earlier experimentalists are merely modifications of the formula—

$$h = \frac{f \, l \, v^2}{2 \, g \, m}$$

or, to put it in the form adopted by De Chezy—

$$v = C \sqrt{\frac{m \, h}{l}}. \qquad (7)$$

The more important of these are stated below, and for ease of comparison have been reduced, where possible, to one of these forms. Where the original formula did not contain the factor $2 \, g$, in introducing this the value 64·4 has been adopted, and other numerical factors altered correspondingly. Dimensions throughout are in feet.

Thus, *D'Aubuisson*, *Prony*, and *Eytelwein* assumed that the resistance to motion is composed of two parts, one due to simple frictional resistance at the boundaries and proportional to the velocity, and the second due to eddy production and proportional to v^2. The constants a and b in the formula—

$$h = \frac{l}{2\,g\,m} \left\{ b\,v + a\,v^2 \right\}$$ (8)

where $f = a + \dfrac{b}{v}$, were then determined on this assumption.

These values were as follows :—

—	a.	b.
D'Aubuisson .	·00670	·00121
Prony. . .	·00684	·00112
Eytelwein . .	·00549	·00144

Weisbach, on the other hand, assuming the first part of the resistance proportional to $v^{\frac{3}{2}}$, obtained the formula—

$$h = \frac{f\,l\,v^2}{2\,g\,m}, \text{ where } f = \cdot00360 + \frac{\cdot00429}{\sqrt{v}}.$$ (9)

Adopting the same formula, *Bazin* put $f = \cdot00294 \left(1 + \dfrac{\cdot3736}{d} \right)$, while *Kutter* and *Ganguillet* put

$$f = 64\cdot4 \left\{ \frac{1 + \left(41\cdot6 + \dfrac{\cdot00281\,l}{h} \right) \dfrac{N}{\sqrt{m}}}{\dfrac{1\cdot811}{N} + 41\cdot6 + \dfrac{\cdot00281\,l}{h}} \right\}^2$$ (10)

where N is a coefficient depending on the roughness of the pipe surface and varying from ·010 to ·019, its value for clean cast-iron or asphalted pipes being ·013, for new riveted pipes ·014, and for old pipes ·019.

These formulae, excepting that of Kutter, neglecting as they do any variation in resistance produced by a variation in the physical condition of the pipe surface, are obviously only of value where the experimental conditions can be reproduced. Moreover the fundamental assumption in the formulae of D'Aubuisson, Prony, and Eytelwein, as to the resistance depending on two powers of the velocity, has been clearly demonstrated to be unsound by Reynolds. This since in every case where the logarithms of the resistances and velocities have been plotted these are found to lie on accurately straight lines (p. 53).[1]

[1] True at all events for the range of velocities common in practice. See also Saph and Schoder, "Trans. Am. Soc. C.E.," Vol. 51, 1903.

Kutter's formula, introducing as it does a roughness coefficient N, has a much wider range of application, and gives much more consistent results than those previously mentioned, from Hagen to Weisbach. This formula however, assumes the resistance to be always proportional to v^2, whereas experiment indicates that for smooth surfaces the power of the velocity is always less than the second, and we are led to the conclusion that none of these formulae, while giving good results within their own particular range of application, can be looked upon as representing the general state of affairs in pipe flow.

Art 64.

A rational law of resistance to pipe flow, applicable to either steady or unsteady motion, was first evolved by Professor Osborne Reynolds. This is deduced on the assumptions that the resistance to flow along any small element of the pipe depends on the diameter, length, and surface condition of the element; on the viscosity and density of the fluid; and on the mean velocity of flow through the element; and also that it depends on some power of each of these factors.

This being so we may write

$$\delta p = k \cdot d^x \cdot \mu^y \cdot \rho^z \cdot v^n \cdot (\delta l)^a, \tag{1}$$

where δp = pressure difference in lbs. per square foot at two points δl ft. apart along the pipe.

„ d = pipe diameter in feet.

„ μ = coefficient of viscosity of the fluid under the temperature conditions obtaining in the pipe.

„ δl = length of element of pipe in feet.

„ ρ = density of the fluid.

„ v = mean velocity of flow in this element in feet per second.

„ k = is a numerical coefficient.

Although the expression contains no term directly marking the effect of the roughness of the pipe surface, this effect is included in the terms μ^z and v^n. This will be seen if it be granted that the effect of the roughness in increasing the resistance to flow is due to loss of available energy in eddy production, the eddies being formed by the sudden deflexion of particles of fluid in close proximity to the walls.

The mass of fluid thus affected will be greater as the roughness increases and as the velocity of flow increases, and will also depend directly on its density, while the loss of energy per unit mass will depend on the velocity. It follows that the effect of a variation in the roughness will be felt in the factors involving both ρ and v, and that the values of the indices z and n of these expressions as determined for equation (1) will implicitly involve the effect of the roughness.

If [M], [L], and [T] be the fundamental units of mass, length, and time, (1) may be expressed dimensionally as

$$\left[\frac{M}{L\,T^2}\right] = k\,[L]^z \cdot \left[\frac{M}{L\,T}\right]^y \cdot \left[\frac{M}{L^3}\right]^z \cdot \left[\frac{L}{T}\right]^s \cdot [L]^a$$

and since experiment shows that the resistance to flow is, other things being equal, directly proportional to the length, $a = 1$.

Inserting this value the equation becomes

$$[M] \cdot [L]^{-1} \cdot [T]^{-2} = k \cdot [M]^{x+y} \cdot [L]^{z-y-3z+s+1} \cdot [T]^{-(y+n)}.$$

Equating indices of like quantities we get

$$x - y - 3z = -2 - n;\ y + z = 1;\ y = 2 - n,$$

from which we have

$$\begin{cases} x = n - 3 \\ y = 2 - n \\ z = n - 1 \end{cases}$$

The formula then becomes

$$\delta p = g\,h\,\rho = K\,r^{n-3}\,\mu^{2-n}\,\rho^{n-1}\,v^n \cdot l \qquad (2)^1$$

If i represents the loss of head in units of length of a water column per unit length of pipe, so that $i = \dfrac{h}{l}$, i is called the hydraulic gradient of the pipe, and gives the slope at which this would need to be laid in

---

[1] A similar rational law may be deduced for the flow of compressible fluids by writing $\dfrac{p_m}{c\tau}$ for ρ in equation (1). Here τ is the absolute temperature of the gas, while c is the constant obtained from the relationship $p\,V = c\,\tau$. We then get

$$\delta p = \frac{k\,\mu^{2-n}\,\tau_m^n\,l}{d^{3-n}}\left(\frac{p_m}{c\tau}\right)^{n-1} \cdot = \frac{A\,p_m^{n-1} \cdot \tau m}{B^n \cdot d^{3-n}} \cdot l$$

An examination, by the author, of the results of experiments on the flow of air through pipes, by several experimenters, and with diameters ranging from ·125 in. to ·98 feet—velocities from 10 to 40 feet per second, confirms the assumptions made in deducing this formula ("Phil. Mag.," March, 1909). From these experiments the following values of n have been deduced :—

						$n.$
Small lead pipe,	·125 in. in diameter		...	...	...	1·28
Lead pipe,	2·16 ins.	,,	...	...	...	1·77
Cast-iron pipe	5·9 ,,	,,	...	...	...	1·81
	7·87 ,,	,,	...	...	...	1·78
	11·8 ,	,,	...	...	...	1·77

while $A = 125 \times 10^{-6}$; $B = 6 \cdot 60.$; if δp is measured in lbs. per sq. ins.

Below the C. V. $n = 1$, and the formula becomes $\delta p = \dfrac{k\,\mu\,r_m\,l}{d^2}$ indicating that the pressure drop is now independent of the absolute pressure in the pipe—a result verified by the experiments.

order to give the required flow without any external head. Evidently i
is independent of the units used, and the formula may now be written

$$i = \frac{B^n \cdot P^{3-n} \cdot r^n}{A \cdot d^{3-n}}$$ (3)

where P is proportional to $\frac{\mu}{\rho}$ and has the value

$$P = \frac{1}{1 + \cdot 03368 \, t + \cdot 000221 \, t^2} \text{ (p. 12),}$$

and A and B are constants.

The values of these constants have been determined and

if the units are feet and degrees centigrade $\begin{cases} A = 1 \cdot 93 \times 10^6 \\ B = 36 \cdot 9 \end{cases}$

,,   ,,   ,, metres and degrees centigrade $\begin{cases} A = 67 \cdot 7 \times 10^6 \\ B = 396 \end{cases}$

The formula is found to hold, with fair accuracy, for all velocities above
or below the critical points by a suitable substitution for n.

Reynolds gives the following mean values of n for velocities above the
critical, those for cast iron being deduced from Darcy's results

		n.
Lead pipe	. . . .	1·79.
Varnished pipe	. . . . . .	1·82.
Glass pipe	. . . . . .	1·79.
New cast iron	. . . . . .	1·88.
Old incrusted C. I.	. . . . .	2·00.

Below the C. V., $n = 1$ for all surfaces, and the formula becomes

$$h = \frac{B}{A} \cdot \frac{P \, l \, v}{d^2} .$$

Poiseuille's formula $h = \frac{p_1 - p_2}{g \, \rho} = \frac{32 \, \mu \, l \, v}{g \, \rho \, d^2}$, the head being expressed
in centimetres of water and the units in the C. G. S. system, becomes,
on transforming to the metre as the unit of length, $h = \frac{278}{47 \cdot 7 \times 10^6} \cdot \frac{v \, P}{d^2}$

$= 5 \cdot 83 \times 10^{-6} \frac{v \, P \, l}{d^2}$. This is identical with the Reynolds formula on
substitution for the constants A and B.

If $n = 2$, the term containing P and involving the temperature
becomes unity, and therefore for old and incrusted pipes the resistance is
independent of the temperature, and the formula becomes

$$h = \frac{B^2}{A} \frac{v^2 \, l}{d}$$

$$= \cdot 000709 \, \frac{l \, v^2}{d} \text{ feet of water.}$$

Comparing this with the simplified form of Darcy's formula

$$h = \frac{f\,l\,v^2}{2\,g\,m} \text{ or } \frac{4\,f\,l\,v^2}{2\,g\,d}$$

we have coincidence if $\cdot000709 = \dfrac{4\,f}{64\cdot4}$,

i.e., if $f = \cdot0114$,

which is the value given by Darcy's formula for rough pipes $7\frac{1}{8}$ inches diameter.

It will be noted that in the general formula, the sum of the indices of d and v is always 3.

Variation of Resistance with Temperature.

From the form of equation (3), it appears that if n is less than 2, the resistance depends on the temperature, and varies as P^{2-n}. Experiments by the Author on the resistance of rotating discs (p. 181) indicate the accuracy of this deduction, and this is substantially confirmed by experiments by Mr. Mair[1] on a brass pipe, $1\frac{1}{2}$ inches diameter $(n = 1\cdot79)$. The relative resistances as experimentally obtained and as calculated are as follow:

Temperature Fahrenheit °		56°	90°	160°
Relative resistances. .	experimental	1·00	·87	·74
	calculated	1·00	·90	·77

For values of n in the neighbourhood of 2 the effect of temperature variation is very small. When $n = 1\cdot8$, the resistance alters about one-third of one per cent. per degree Fahrenheit, while when $n = 1\cdot9$ the change is one-seventh of one per cent. per degree Fahrenheit.

It is worth noting in passing, that while with sinuous motion the difference between the discharge at 5° and 35° centigrade is negligible, below the C. V. the discharge at 5° centigrade is only one-half that at 35° centigrade under the same head.

Other Exponential Formulae.—On applying the Reynolds formula in its original form to the results of other experiments, it is found to be somewhat lacking in adaptability, while experience tends to show that in the particular case where $n = 2$ the resistance does not, as indicated, vary inversely as the first, but as a slightly higher power of the diameter.

---

[1] " Proc. Inst. C.E.," vol. 84, 1886, p. 424.

Professor Unwin, neglecting the small effect of temperature change at velocities above the critical, wrote this formula in the form

$$h = \cdot\frac{f\, l\, v^n}{d^x}$$

and deduced values for f, n, and x, from the results of experiments made by many different observers, and on pipes ranging in diameter from 2 inches to 48 inches.[1] He found that x is always greater than unity, increasing with the diameter between the limits 1·127 and 1·390.

The following are Unwin's mean values for f, n, and x.

Surface.	Size of pipes examined.	f (in foot units).	x.	n
Wrought iron .	1¾ ins. diam.	·000351	1·210	1·75
Asphalted pipes .	10 ins. to 48 ins.	·000395	1·127	1·85
Riveted wrought iron . .	10 „ to 26 „	·000405	1·390	1·87
New cast iron .	3 „ to 20 „	·000334	1·168	1·95
Cleaned cast iron	3 „ to 12 „	·000378	1·168	2·00
Incrusted cast iron	2 „ to 9 „	·000685	1·160	2·00

G. M. Lawford,[2] comparing the latter formula with many recorded observations of more recent date, states that by writing the formula in the form

$$h = k \cdot \frac{\cdot0254\, l\, v^{1\cdot87}}{2\, g\, d^{1\cdot127}},$$

and by giving k the following values, the necessity for altering the value of x with increasing diameter is obviated, while the formula gives good results for asphalted pipes of all diameters from 3 inches to 48 inches.

Diameter of pipe.	k.	Diameter of pipe.	k.	Diameter of pipe.	k.
3 ins.	2·081	18 ins.	·904	33 ins.	·806
6 „	1·486	21 „	·880	36 „	·797
9 „	1·220	24 „	·858	39 „	·778
12 „	1·062	27 „	·839	42 „	·765
15 „	·964	30 „	·823	45 „	·754
				48 „	·744

[1] "Industries," 1886, vol. 1, p. 51 and *seq.*
[2] "Proceedings Inst. Civil Engineers," vol. 153, p. 297.

A further modification of the Reynolds formula, proposed by *Thrupp*,[1] is given by

$$h = \frac{C^n v^n l}{m^x} \text{ where } m = \frac{d}{4}.$$

The following are values of C, x, and n for pipes of various materials,

Surface.	n.	C.	x.
Lead	1·75	·00522	1·085
Smooth wrought iron.	1·80	·00479	1·170
Riveted „ „ .	1·825	·00567	1·235
New cast iron . .	1·850	·00535	1·240
„ „ „ . .	2·00	·00675	1·260

and for pipes of between 2 and 15 inches diameter the formula gives good results. For wrought iron pipes of less than 2 inches diameter a correction should be applied by writing

$$x + a \sqrt{\frac{b}{m}} - 1 \text{ for } x, \text{ where } a = \cdot0324 ; \ b = \cdot07.$$

Tutton, adopting the Thrupp formula, as a result of an examination of approximately 1,000 experiments by various observers obtained the following mean values for n, C, and x.

Surface.	Diameters (feet).	n.	C.	x.
Wood. . . .	1·05 to 6·00	1·96	·00775	1·295
New W. I.. . .	·40 to 4·00	1·82	·0072 to ·00532	1·129
Asphalted pipes .	·40 to 4·00	1·82	·00787 to ·00605	1·129
New C. I. and cement-coated pipes .	·27 to 2·00	1·96	·00793 to ·00636	1·295
Old C. I. pipes. Lightly tuberculated . . .	·08 to 4·00	1·96	·0115 to ·00757	1·295
Heavily tuberculated . . .		1·96	·0322 to ·0125	1·295

[1] Society of Engineers, 1887.

For the sake of comparison, the values of f, x, and n, in the formula $h = \dfrac{f\,l\,v^n}{d^x}$, as obtained by Unwin, Thrupp, and Tutton are given in the following table.

VALUES OF f, x, AND n IN FORMULA $h = \dfrac{f\,l\,v^n}{d^x}$.

—	x			n			$f \times 10^6$		
Material of Pipe.	Thrupp.	Tutton.	Unwin.	Thrupp.	Tutton.	Unwin.	Thrupp.	Tutton.	Unwin.
Lead	1·085	—	—	1·75	—	—	475	—	—
Wood . . .	—	1·295	—	—	1·96	—	—	439	—
Asphalted pipes .	—	1·129	1·127	—	1·82	1·85	—	446 to 706	35.
Plain wrought iron .	1·170	1·129	1·210	1·80	1·82	1·75	341	347 to 606	351
Riveted wrought iron	1·235	—	1·390	1·825	—	1·87	445	—	405
New cast iron .	1·240 1·260	1·295	1·168	1·85 2·00	1·96	1·95	354 261	300 to 458	334
Cleaned cast iron .	—	—	1·168	—	—	2·00	—	—	378
Old lightly tuberculated cast iron	—	1·295	1·160	—	1·96	2·00	—	426 to 945	685
Old heavily tuberculated cast iron	—	1·295	—	—	1·96	—	—	1120 to 7250	—

While these exponential formulae are more complicated than the old formula of the De Chezy type, the increased accuracy rendered possible by their use more than counterbalances any inconvenience in handling. With the exception of the Kutter formula, which is exceedingly cumbrous to handle without the aid of specially prepared tables, this inconvenience is indeed more apparent than real since the formulae are in a form suitable for logarithmic or slide-rule calculation.

In many cases, however, it is convenient to be able to express resistance to flow in the forms

$$h = \frac{f\,l\,v^2}{2\,g\,m},\ \text{or}\ v = C\,\sqrt{m\,i},$$

and to enable this to be done without sacrificing accuracy, the values of
f and of C have been calculated from the mean results of the exponential
formulae of Unwin, Tutton, and Thrupp, showing, within the range of
velocities common in practice, their variation with v and with the pipe
diameter, in pipes of different types.

These values, given in the following tables, may be relied upon to give
reasonably accurate results with pipes well laid and jointed.   The internal
fouling of a pipe due to corrosion and tuberculation, by increasing the
roughness of its walls and by reducing its effective area, will generally
reduce the effective value of f considerably after a few years' use, and
allowance should be made for this in computing the diameter necessary
to maintain a given discharge.

With a small iron pipe under unfavourable circumstances, tuberculation
may cause f to attain ten times its original value within as many years'
use.   In wooden pipes, on the other hand, no corrosion takes place, and
f is usually slightly less for an old than for a new pipe.

Experiments carried out by Herschell, on riveted pipes consisting
of alternate large and small rings, with projecting rivet heads, and
which were coated with asphaltum, gave values of f in the formula
$h = \frac{f\,l\,v^2}{2\,g\,m}$, for a $3\frac{1}{2}$ feet diameter pipe, ranging from ·00675 with a
velocity of 1 foot per second, to ·0055 with a velocity of 6 feet per second.
With a similar 4-feet pipe, f varied from ·00675 to ·0056 with the same
range of velocities.

After four years' use, the latter pipe gave values of f ranging from ·0085
to ·0065 with the same range of velocities.

Experiments[1] on a bare riveted pipe with butt joints and 6 feet in
diameter, when new gave $f = $ ·0052 for all velocities from 1 to 4 feet per
second.   After two years' use the values of f were found to range from
·0139 at ·5 feet per second to ·00975 at 1 foot per second, and ·00618 at
4 feet per second.

J. Duane, as a result of experiments on a new 48-inch riveted main of
length 5,992 feet, obtained a value of $f = $ ·00858 in the same formula
with a velocity of 2·28 feet per second.   After seven years, considerable

---

[1] "Transactions American Society Civil Engineers," 1898 and 1900.

tuberculation was found to have taken place on the interior surface of the pipe, and a second series of experiments gave $f = \cdot 00698$.

MEAN VALUES OF f AND C, IN FORMULAE $h = \dfrac{f\,l\,v^2}{2\,g\,m}$ AND $v = C\sqrt{m\,i}$.

LEAD. (From Thrupp's Exponential Formula.)

Velocity, feet per second.			Diameter (inches).			
			1.	2.	3.	4.
2	{	f c	·00793 90	·00747 93	·00721 94·5	·00705 95·5
4	{	f c	·00660 99	·00622 101·5	·00600 103·5	·00586 105
6	{	f o	·00603 103·5	·00568 106·5	·00549 108·5	·00535 109·5
8	{	f o	·00563 107	·00530 110	·00512 112	·00500 113·5
10	{	f c	·00530 110	·00500 113·5	·00482 116	·00471 117

WOOD. (From Tutton's Results.)

Velocity, feet per second.			Diameter (inches).					
			6.	12.	18.	24.	36.	48.
2	{	f c	·00841 87·5	·00686 97	·00607 103	·00560 107	·00496 113·5	·00456 119
4	{	f c	·00817 89	·00667 98·5	·00590 105	·00543 109	·00483 116	·00442 120·5
6	{	f c	·00805 89·5	·00657 99	·00581 105·5	·00535 109·5	·00475 116·5	·00436 121·5
8	{	f c	·00797 90	·00650 99·5	·00575 106	·00530 110	·00470 117	·00431 122·5

ASPHALTED PIPE. (From Exponential Formulae of Tutton and Unwin.)

Velocity, feet per second.			Diameter (inches).						
			6.	9.	12.	18.	24.	36.	48.
2	{	f	·00657	·00623	·00601	·00570	·00550	·00521	·00503
		c	99	102	103·5	107	108	111	113·5
4	{	f	·00585	·00555	·00535	·00507	·00489	·00468	·00447
		c	105	108	109·5	112·5	115	117	120
6	{	f	·00550	·00520	·00502	·00476	·00459	·00435	·00420
		c	108	111·5	113·5	116·5	118·5	121·5	124
8	{	f	·00521	·00495	·00477	·00453	·00436	·00415	·00399
		c	111·5	114	116	119·5	121·5	124·5	127·5
10	{	f	·00506	·00480	·00463	·00439	·00423	·00401	·00387
		c	113	116	118	121	123·5	127	129

BARE WROUGHT IRON. (From Exponential Formulae of Thrupp, Tutton and Unwin.)

Velocity, feet per second.			Diameter (inches).						
			3	6	12	24	36	48	60
2	{	f	·00612	·00543	·00482	·00427	·00400	·00380	·00367
		c	102·5	109	116	123·5	127·5	130	132
4	{	f	·00530	·00471	·00417	·00370	·00347	·00329	·00319
		c	110	117	124	131·5	136·5	140·5	142
6	{	f	·00487	·00434	·00384	·00341	·00319	·00303	·00292
		c	115·5	122	129·5	137	142	146	148·5
8	{	f	·00459	·00408	·00361	·00321	·00300	·00285	·00275
		c	119	125·5	132	141·5	147	151	153·5
10	{	f	·00437	·00388	·00344	·00306	·00285	·00272	·00262
		c	121·5	129	137	145	151	154	157

Riveted Wrought Iron or Steel Pipes. (From Thrupp and Unwin.)

Velocity, feet per second.		Diameter (inches).					
		12	24	36	48	60	72
2	f	·00615	·00495	·00437	·00400	·00372	·00351
	c	102	114	121·5	127·5	131·5	137
4	f	·00553	·00445	·00393	·00358	·00333	·00316
	c	108	120	128	132·5	138	143
6	f	·00520	·00419	·00369	·00338	·00315	·00297
	c	111·5	124	132·5	137	143	147·5
8	f	·00496	·00400	·00352	·00322	·00300	·00294
	c	114	127·5	135·5	141·5	147	151
10	f	·00481	·00388	·00342	·00312	·00291	·00275
	c	116	129	136·5	143·5	148·5	153·5

New Cast Iron. (From Exponential Formulae of Thrupp, Tutton and Unwin.)

Velocity, feet per second.		Diameter (inches).						
		3	6	9	12	18	24	36
2	f	·00691	·00588	·00535	·00500	·00455	·00425	·00387
	c	96·5	104·5	109·5	113·5	119·5	123·5	129
4	f	·00654	·00556	·00505	·00473	·00430	·00403	·00367
	c	99	108	113	117	122·5	127·5	133
6	f	·00635	·00539	·00490	·00459	·00417	·00390	·00356
	c	100·5	109	114·5	119	124·5	129	134·5
8	f	·00617	·00525	·00479	·00447	·00407	·00380	·00346
	c	102	111	117	119·5	125·5	130	136

CLEANED CAST IRON. (From Unwin.)

At all Velocities.	Diameter (inches).						
	3	6	9	12	18	24	36
f	·00770	·00685	·00640	·00609	·00569	·00541	·00505
c	91·5	97	100·5	103	106·5	109	113

OLD, LIGHTLY TUBERCULATED CAST IRON. (From Tutton and Unwin.)

Velocity, feet per second.		Diameter (inches).						
		3	6	9	12	18	24	36
2	f	·0147	·0126	·0115	·0108	·00983	·00921	·00835
	c	66	71·5	75·5	77·2	81	83·7	88
4	f	·0146	·0125	·0113	·0106	·00965	·00905	·00825
	c	66·3	72	76	77·7	81·5	84·1	88·5
6	f	·0145	·0124	·0112	·0105	·00958	·00897	·00817
	c	66·6	72·3	76·4	78·2	82	84·5	89
8	f	·0144	·0122	·0111	·0104	·00950	·00890	·0810
	c	67	72·6	76·8	78·7	82·4	85·0	89·5

A series of experiments by Freeman [1] on the flow through fire hose, give the following mean values of f, at velocities ranging from 10 to 30 feet per second.

Unlined linen hose . . . $f = ·0084$
Smooth rubber lined hose . $f = ·0044$

It is probable that at such velocities as are common in practice, viz., about 100 feet per second, these values would become about ·0080 for the unlined, and ·0040 for the rubber-lined hose.

ART. 65.

Since the velocity in a pipe is inversely proportional to $\sqrt{f}$ an error in the assumed value of f will only lead to approximately half the percentage error in v, and hence in the calculated discharge. Still, since the physical condition of a pipe surface, and any deviation from straightness

[1] "Transactions American Society Civil Engineers," 1889, p. 303.

of the pipe vitally affect the resistance, and since the determination of the relative physical condition of two surfaces, even though of the same material, is a matter of the greatest difficulty, no pipe flow formula is to be relied upon as giving the discharge corresponding to a given loss of head, with any great degree of accuracy in a proposed pipe line. The difficulty in exactly reproducing the conditions of the experiments from which the formulae have been deduced prevents this, and the engineer who prognosticates to within 10 per cent. the discharge from a pipe under given pressure conditions has every reason to be satisfied with his choice of constants.

Velocities Adopted in Practice.—In water supply systems the mean velocity of pipe flow usually ranges from 3 feet to 6 feet per second. In the pipe lines forming the supply and discharge mains of power installations such velocities are often exceeded, velocities up to 10 feet per second being common where such pipe lines are comparatively short, and velocities up to 15 feet or even 20 feet per second being adopted in exceptional circumstances where the available head is great and the length of pipe line comparatively small.

Art. 66. Friction with Fluids other than Water.

Very little is known as to the loss of head accompanying the flow of liquids other than water. With crude oils the loss of head is very heavy owing to the great viscosity. Attempts have been made to reduce this loss of head by the addition of some 10 per cent of water. This reduces the loss considerably but the discharge takes the form of an emulsion from which the water is removed with difficulty. By using a pipe having rifled grooves along its walls, centrifugal action keeps the heavier water in contact with the walls, and reduces both emulsification and loss of head. Tests made by the Southern Pacific Railroad Co.,[1] give the following values of C in the formula $v = C \sqrt{mi}$.

8-in. plain pipe conveying oil	...	...	...	$C = 5\cdot46$
8 ,, ,, ,, ,,	90 % oil and 10 % water			$C = 7\cdot11$
8 ,, rifled ,, ,,	90 % oil and 10 % ,,			$C = 65$
8 ,, pipe ,,	water only	...	...	$C = 113$
8 ,, plain ,, ,,	oil	...	...	$C = 3\cdot76$
8 ,, rifled ,, ,,	90 % oil and 10 % water			$C = 79$
8 ,, pipe ,,	water only	...	...	$C = 100$

Water Charged with Sand.—When a stream of water flows over a mass

---

[1] *Engineering News*, New York, June 7, 1906. *Engineering Record*, May 23, 1908.

of loose material which may be carried in suspension, at moderate velocities of flow the material is rolled along the bottom of the pipe or channel, with comparatively great loss of head.   As the velocity increases, at a certain point, depending on the size and weight of the particles, these are picked up and carried in suspension in the water.   Experiments on sand, having grains varying from ·16 m.m. to ·75 m.m. in diameter show that for a 1-inch pipe this velocity is about 3·5 feet per second, while for a 3-inch pipe it is about 4 feet per second, and for a 32-inch pipe about 9 feet per second.[1] With grains of approximately uniform size the minimum resistance is attained with this velocity. With grains of widely varying size the minimum resistance is attained with a velocity somewhat less than is necessary to pick up the larger grains. With fine sand the additional loss of head is about 25 per cent. of that due to the water alone, for each 1 per cent. of added sand. For velocities higher than are necessary to cause suspension, the proportion of solid matter which may be carried is approximately independent of the velocity. Experiments show that the proportion of sand to water may exceed 50 per cent.   Where a sand ejector is used this proportion depends largely on the form of ejector.[1] This is on similar lines to the ordinary jet pump, and is situated at the bottom of the sand hopper, the sand being carried into suspension by means of a number of small water jets surrounding the inlet to the ejector

Mixtures of Water and Air.—See Art. 189.

Art. 67.—Variation of Velocity over the Cross-Section of a Cylindrical Pipe.

Experiments show that with sinuous motion through a pipe the velocity of flow is much greater at the centre than near the walls. From experiments on pipes with diameters ranging from 8 inches to 19 inches Darcy deduced the formula

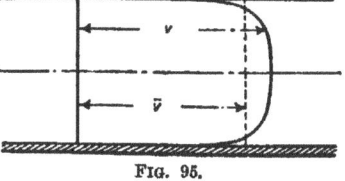

FIG. 95.

$$v = v_{max} - \frac{k}{a} x^{\frac{3}{2}} \sqrt{i} \quad . \quad (1)$$

as giving the velocity v at any radius x of a pipe of radius a. When the unit of length is the metre, $k = 11·3$, and when the foot, $k = 20·4$. The volume of the solid of

---

[1] "Transactions American Society Civil Engineers," Vol. 57, 1906.

revolution (Fig. 95), whose height represents the velocity at any radius, is given by

$$\int_0^a 2\,\pi\,xv\,dx$$

$$\therefore \text{ mean height} = \frac{2\,\pi \int_0^a xv\,dx}{\pi\,a^2}$$

Substituting for v from equation (1) we have

$$\text{mean velocity, } \bar{v} = v_{max} - \frac{4}{7} k \sqrt{ai}.$$

$$\therefore \left(\frac{x}{a}\right)^{\frac{3}{2}} = \frac{4}{7}$$

$$\therefore x = \cdot 689\,a$$

giving the radius at which the velocity is equal to the mean over a cross-section.

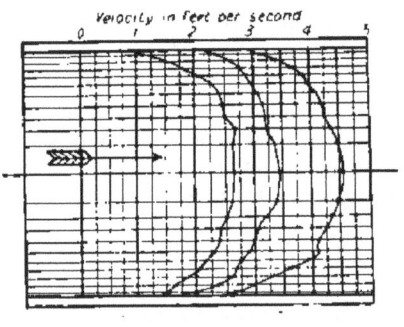

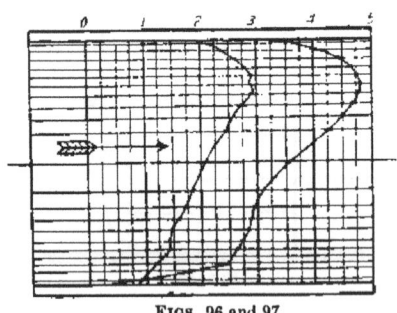

Velocity in feet per second

FIGS. 96 and 97.

More recent experiments by Bazin[1] on a cement pipe 2·63 feet diameter, and by Messrs. Williams, Hubbell, and Fenkell[2] on cast iron asphalted pipes having diameters of 12″, 16″, 30″, and 42″, indicate that the curve of velocities is very nearly an ellipse to which the pipe walls are tangential. Calling u the minimum velocity at the walls, and V the maximum velocity at the centre, the equation to the curve would then be

$$\frac{x^2}{a^2} + \left(\frac{v-u}{V-u}\right)^2 = 1.$$

The volume of the solid of revolution bounded by this curve is equal to

$$\pi\,a^2 u \times \tfrac{2}{3}\,\pi\,a^2\,(V-u)$$
$$= \pi\,a^2\,\bar{v}$$

$$\therefore \bar{v} = u + \tfrac{2}{3}\,(V-u).$$

[1] "Mem. de l'Académie des Sciences," xxxii. 1897.
[2] "Proc. Am. Soc. C. E.," vol. xxvii., 1901, p. 314.

The mean velocity occurs at a radius $x = \cdot75\,a$.

Messrs. Williams, Hubbell, and Fenkell found the surface velocity to be practically one-half that at the centre,[1] in which case the mean velocity is ·83 times the maximum. The ratio was found to increase with the mean velocity. Figs. 96 and 97 show velocity curves obtained on the 30-inch pipe respectively on the straight and at a bend in these experiments.

The results of Bazin's experiments can be represented very approximately by the formula

$$v = V - k \left(\frac{x}{a}\right)^3 \sqrt{ai}$$

where k has a mean value, with the foot as unit, of 38, though a more accurate formula is

$$v = V - 38 \left\{ \left(\frac{x}{a}\right)^3 + 1\cdot29 \left(\frac{x}{a}\right)^2 \left(1 - 1\cdot1 \frac{x}{a}\right)^2 \right\} \sqrt{a\,i}$$

The mean results of these experiments gave $u = \cdot51\,V$; $\bar{v} = \cdot855\,V$; and showed the mean velocity to be attained at a radius ·74 a.

Assuming $\bar{v} = C\sqrt{mi} = \cdot707\,C\sqrt{ai}$, from Bazin's simpler formula assuming $x = \cdot74\,a$, we have

$$\bar{v} = V - 15\cdot4\sqrt{ai}$$

$$\therefore \frac{V}{\bar{v}} = 1 + \frac{21\cdot8}{C}$$

The value $\bar{v} = \cdot855\,V$, thus corresponds to a value of $C = 128$. It is indeed to be expected that as here indicated, the ratio of mean to maximum velocity will vary with the diameter and surface conditions of the pipe, both of which affect C. Experimentally the ratio is found to range from ·79 to ·86, increasing with the diameter and smoothness of the pipe, the following table indicating how, from Bazin's simple formula, this ratio varies with C or with the value of f.

C	80	90	100	110	120	130	140
f	·0105	·0079	·0064	·0053	·0045	·0038	·0033
$\bar{v} \div V$	·785	·804	·820	·834	·846	·857	·865

[1] See the discussion on surface velocity on p. 215.

Other experiments have been carried out by Cole[1] and by Morrow[1] from which, together with those already quoted, it may be concluded that in gauging the discharge of a pipe by means of a Pitot tube (p. 218), the mean of observations at a radius varying from ·69 a in small, to ·75 a in large pipes, will give the mean velocity directly, while the mean of observations at the centre of the pipe when multiplied by a constant varying from ·79 to ·86, with an average value of ·84, will also give the mean velocity with a fair degree of accuracy.

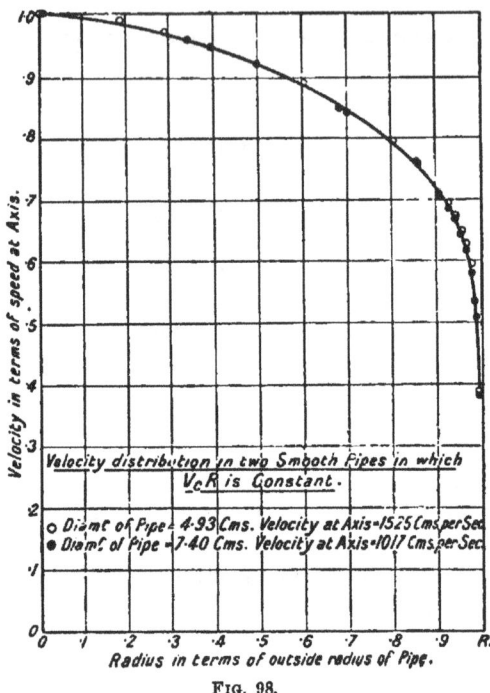

Experiments by R. Threlfall,[3] on the flow of air through gas pipes from 6 to 36 inches diameter, indicate that here the radius of the circle of mean velocity is about 0·775 of the pipe radius, though in one case of a gas main, 15¾ inches diameter, the radius of mean velocity was about ·9 of the pipe radius.

FIG. 98.

The ratio of mean to maximum velocity in these experiments was very constant over a wide range of velocities—22 $f.s.$ to 41 $f.s.$—and had the mean value 0·873.

Recent experiments by Michael Longridge[4] on air flow through a 16-inch pipe at velocities ranging from 77 to 210 feet per second showed that the ratio of mean to maximum velocity varied by less than 1¼ per

[1] "Trans. Am. Soc. C. E.," 1902, vol. 47, pp. 63—276.
[2] "Proc. Roy. Soc.," 1905, vol. 76, p. 205.
[3] "Proceedings Institute Mechanical Engineers," 1904.
[4] "Engineer's Report of Brit. Engine and Boiler Insurance Co., Ltd., for 1910," p. 92.

cent. from its mean value 0·921. The radius of mean velocity in these experiments was ·80 of the pipe radius.

Surface Velocity.—Since the Pitot tube, with which velocities are invariably measured, cannot be used to determine velocities at points nearer to the wall than the radius of its orifice, the manner in which the velocity varies at points very near the wall is difficult to determine with any degree of accuracy. By producing the curve obtained by plotting velocities across the pipe, the earlier experimenters concluded that the surface velocity was approximately one-half the maximum velocity. More recent experiments by Morrow on a pipe 2 inches in diameter, and by Stanton[1] on the flow of air through pipes of 5 and 7·4 cmm. diameter, however, indicate that the velocity of the film in actual contact with the wall is zero, even with sinuous flow, and that the velocity at first increases very rapidly as the centre of the pipe is approached. The film of fluid in the immediate neighbourhood of the wall appears to be moving with steady viscous flow, this state of viscous flow merging almost imperceptibly into that of sinuous flow, the thickness of the film undergoing rectilinear motion being extremely small.

In the latter experiments a Pitot tube having an orifice only ·25 millimetre deep was used. In rough pipes (resistance proportional to τ^2) the velocity curve was found to be similar from the centre to within 3 millimetres of the walls, for all velocities, and to be a parabola, having the equation

$$v = V_c - A\ r^2.$$

For smooth pipes the curve was also parabolic up to a radius of 0·8 a. For exact similarity of the curves over the whole range of radii, it is necessary that the central velocities should be inversely proportional to the pipe diameters. Fig. 98 shows velocity curves obtained in these experiments.[2]

ART. 67 A.—MIXING OF ADJACENT LAYERS DURING FLOW OF LIQUID IN PIPES.

From the fact that the velocity near the centre of a pipe is much greater than near the walls, it is evident that there must be a continual admixture of the faster moving liquid with those more slowly moving particles nearer the walls ahead of it. Thus the particles of a column of the fluid, originally of unit length, will, at any subsequent time, be

---

[1] " Proc. Roy. Society," A., vol. 85, 1911, p. 366.

[2] In the above formula V_c is the velocity at the centre of the pipe.

found to be distributed over a length greater than that which they originally occupied. This matter is of some importance in connection with oil transmission pipe lines, through which from time to time different grades of oil are to be pumped, and in which it is desirable to know the probable volume of contaminated oil likely to follow a change over from grade to grade.

In experiments on a wooden pipe line conveying water and consisting of a length of 13,200 feet of 10-inch pipe in series with 47,500 feet of 16-inch pipe,[1] aniline dye or bran was admitted for a measured time to the intake, and the discharge from a relief valve on the 10-inch pipe, situated 12,700 feet from the intake, and from the outlet from the 16-inch pipe, was carefully watched for the appearance and disappearance of the colouring matter or bran. With the dye the exact instant of appearance and disappearance, particularly the latter, could not be determined with any very great accuracy, but the time of passing the relief valve was apparently about one minute greater than the time of admission. As the mean velocity was 582 feet per minute, this means that the mixing had extended over a length equal to $58,200 \div 12,750 = $ 4·6 per cent. of the distance traversed. The bran apparently took eighteen minutes longer than the time of admission to pass the outlet from the 16-inch pipe, indicating an admixture over about 8·5 per cent. of the distance traversed. Experiments carried out with colouring matter on a 4-inch and a 6-inch pipe line at Cornell[2], conveying water at velocities ranging between about ·9 and 4·5 feet per second showed that the admixture extended over a mean distance equal to about 13·3 per cent. of the distance traversed in the 6-inch pipe, and 11 per cent. of this distance in the 4-inch pipe. Both these pipes were spiral riveted, but the 4-inch pipe had an asphalted surface. On the whole it would appear that the percentage distance for similar pipes diminishes with an increase in diameter, and for pipes of the same diameter increases with the roughness, apparently varying little with the mean velocity.

Experiments by the Standard Oil Co.[3] on the admixture of oil of different grades in a 6-inch pipe line, 24 miles long, showed that with light amber oil, specific gravity ·79, displacing heavy black oil, specific gravity ·85, with a mean velocity of flow of about 4 feet per second, the length of admixture was between 8·5 and 12·1 per cent. of the distance travelled, while, where the heavy displaced the light oil, the length was only ·44 per cent. Similar experiments on an oil-pipe line 210 miles long between

[1] J. L. Campbell, *Engineering News*, August 27, 1908, p. 227.
[2] *Cornell Civil Engineer*, Dec. 1911, p. 122, by Prof. E. W. Schoder.

Morgantown and Millway, with light oil displacing heavy oil, showed a length of admixture varying from 10 to 12 per cent.

Art. 68.—Measurement of Pipe Discharge.

The volume actually discharged by a pipe may be determined approximately in several ways.

(1) The most accurate method is that of collecting and weighing the quantity discharged in a definite time, but this is impossible with any but the smallest of pipes.

(2) The mean velocity may be computed from a knowledge of the hydraulic gradient and of the diameter and internal condition of the pipe by an application of one or other of the formulae of Art. 65. Where these data can be accurately obtained an error not exceeding 10 per cent. may be expected, with pipes ranging from 3 inches to 6·0 feet in diameter. The hydraulic gradient may be obtained by observing the difference in the free level of the columns in two

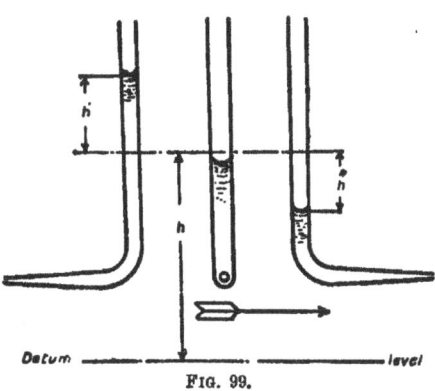

FIG. 99.

piezometers, or pressure tubes, placed at a known distance apart, or by the use of one of the types of differential gauge described in Art. 9.

(3) The velocity·may be deduced from Pitot tube observations, this being used to give the velocity at the centre, or at the radius of mean velocity (p. 214), or at a series of radii across the pipe. In the first case the mean velocity is approximately ·84 times that observed. In the third case the mean velocity is given by

$$\bar{v} = \frac{1}{\pi a^2} \int_0^a 2\pi v r \, dr,$$

where a is the pipe radius, and r the velocity at radius r, the integration being performed graphically. (See p. 110.)

The **Pitot tube** consists of a tube of fine bore bent at right angles (Fig. 99), having both ends open, and so arranged that while one leg remains vertical, the other may be rotated so as to point either up, down, or across stream thus placing the plane of its orifice either at right angles to or parallel to the direction of flow.

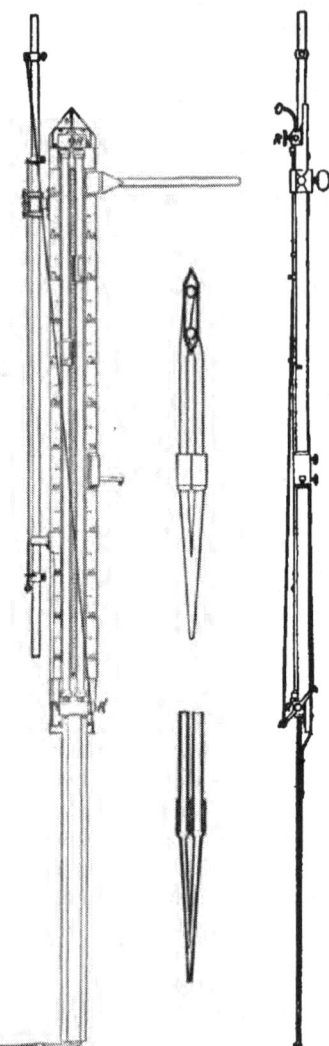

When pointed up-stream, the statical pressure immediately inside the entrance to the tube must balance the statical head of water outside together with the pressure equivalent to the velocity head, so that if h' feet be the height of water in the tube above the free service level when turned up-stream, we have $h'=kv^2\div 2g$, where k is a constant very approximately equal to unity.

Similarly, if turned down-stream, and if h'' is now the depression in the tube, we should have $h''=k'\ v^2\div 2g$.

Theoretically, with the orifice pointing across the stream, the level inside the tube should indicate h, the statical head alone. Owing, however, to eddy formation and to a consequent reduction of pressure at the orifice, the level inside the tube is slightly less than h.

When turned down-stream, eddy formation also affects the reading h'', giving this a lower value than the theoretical, while even when pointing up-stream the reading h' is only accurate when the tube is of very fine bore, and is given a conical form so as to divert the oncoming stream with a minimum of disturbance. For this reason, the tube should be calibrated by observations in water moving with known velocities. Otherwise, even with a well-constructed apparatus, an error of about 5 per cent. is possible, the calculated being greater than the actual velocity.

FIG. 100.—Pitot Tube.

The instrument as improved and used by Darcy and Bazin for stream measurements[1] is shown in Fig. 100. It consists essentially of two tubes, one drawn to a point and facing up-stream, and the other straight and with an opening at its lower end whose plane is parallel to that of motion of the stream. The air in both tubes is partially exhausted so as to bring the water columns to a convenient height on the scale. A

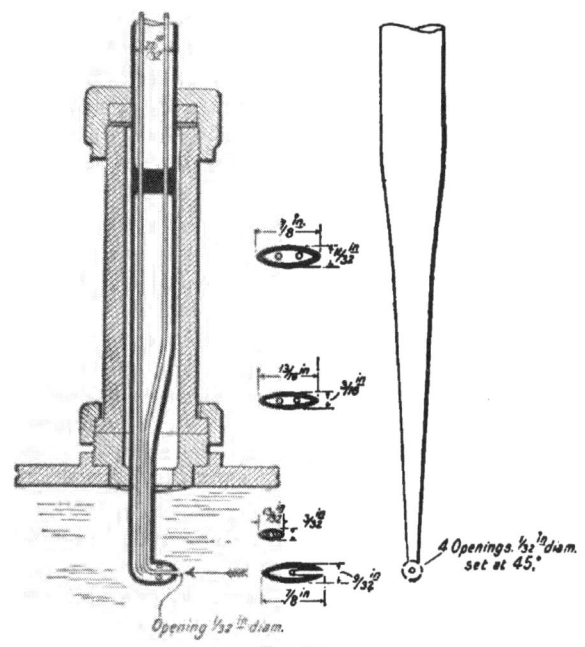

FIG. 101.

cock R' is provided by which the columns may be simultaneously isolated from their orifices. The instrument may then be removed to a convenient position and the readings taken at leisure. Darcy and Bazin rated this meter in flowing water by surface floats, and also by observing the velocity at many points in a cross section and comparing the mean so obtained with the known mean velocity; and in still water by taking readings from a boat towed with a known mean velocity. The respective mean values of C, in $v = C \sqrt{2g h'}$ (h' being the difference in the

[1] Darcy and Bazin, " Recherches hydrauliques," 1865.

heights of the two columns) as thus obtained were 1·006, ·993, and 1·084.

In modern types of the Darcy tube the static pressure is taken from a series of small openings in the walls of a tube held parallel to the current, and by this method, using extremely small openings, the effect of eddy formation is greatly reduced. Such a tube, as used for pipe flow work by Professor G. S. Williams,[1] is shown in Fig. 101. Here the statical pressure is transmitted through four openings, each $\frac{1}{31}$ inch diameter, while the impact orifice itself is $\frac{1}{16}$ inch diameter. The tube was manipulated through a stuffing-box in the wall of the pipe, this permitting the orifice to be adjusted to any required radius.

The tube shown in Fig. 101 was rated in two different ways. By moving it at a known speed through still water in a circumferential trough, of approximately 12 feet diameter and of 72 square inches cross sectional area, the mean value of C was ·926, while using it to determine the velocity at the centre of a 2-inch pipe whose discharge was caught and weighed, on the assumption that the central velocity was 1·33 times the mean velocity the mean value of C was found to be ·895. The values obtained by this second method may reasonably be expected to be lower than those obtained by the first method, since the velocity at the section of the pipe containing the statical pressure orifices is of necessity greater than in the plane of the orifice, and the pressure as recorded by the static column will consequently be less than in the latter place. This effect will be more marked the greater the ratio of the cross section of the tube to that of the pipe, and unless calibrated in a pipe of approximately the same dimensions as that in which it is to be used, the results of such ratings can only be approximate.

On the whole it would appear preferable for pipe work to use a simple Pitot tube to measure the impact pressure, and to obtain the static pressure from an orifice in the pipe walls at the same level as, and in the plane of, the impact orifice. Using the tube in this manner C is found to be very sensibly equal to unity.

When used for measuring the velocity of flow in an open jet the necessity for the static pressure tube vanishes, and under such circumstances the point of a stylographic pen has been found to give good results as the impact branch of the tube.[2]

(4) The velocity may be obtained by Venturi meter (Art. 196), when for

---

[1] See "Proc. Am. Soc. C.E.," vol. 27.

[2] For the description of a Pitot tube for high velocity jet work see a paper by W. E. Ekman, "Proc. Inst. Mech. Eng.," 1909—10.

fairly large pipes an error not exceeding 1·5 per cent. is to be expected. With small pipes, one of the other types of meter described in Art. 196 may be used.

(5) A chemical method of determining the discharge is described by F. Van Iterson.[1] A given weight per minute of sodium thiosulphate being introduced into the pipe, a sample of the discharge is taken at some point nearer the exit, and the quantity of chemical present is measured. The chemical being diluted in proportion to the volume of discharge, a measure of the latter is obtained. The sample is titrated with standard iodine, starch being used as an indicator. Several cocks arranged at different points on the circumference of the pipe should be used for withdrawing the samples, so as to obtain as far as possible a fair sample of the mixture. This method has been used with success for determining the discharge of sewage pumps at La Haye.

Where a colourless discharge is expected, coloured liquid may be introduced into the pipe in known quantities, and the colour of the discharge compared with that of standard admixtures. The method is, however, only to be looked upon as giving approximate results.

ART. 69.—Relation of Diameter of Pipe to Quantity Discharged.

With rough pipes, since $Q = \dfrac{\pi\, d^2}{4} . v$, and since the loss of head H in any length l is given by

$$H = \frac{v^2}{2\,g}\left\{\frac{f\,l}{m}\right\}$$

$$\therefore \quad v = \sqrt{\frac{2\,g\,H\,m}{f\,l}}$$

$$\therefore \quad Q = \frac{\pi\,d^2}{4}\sqrt{\frac{2\,g\,H\,d}{4\,f\,l}} = \frac{\pi}{4}\sqrt{\frac{2\,g\,H}{4\,f\,l}} . d^{\frac{5}{2}}$$

$$\therefore \quad Q = C'\sqrt{\frac{H}{l}} . d^{\frac{5}{2}}, \text{ where } C' = \sqrt{\frac{g}{2\,f}} . \frac{\pi}{4}.$$

For smooth pipes, the loss of head is proportional to a lower power of the velocity than the second, and to a power of the diameter slightly different from the first, i.e.,

$$H = k\,\frac{v^n\,l}{d^x}$$

---

[1] *Le Génie Civil*, Paris, vol. 44, p 411.

$$\therefore \quad v = \left(\frac{H \, d^x}{k \, l} \right)^{\frac{1}{n}}$$

$$\therefore \quad Q = C' \left(\frac{H}{l} \right)^{\frac{1}{n}} \cdot d^{2 + \frac{x}{n}}$$

Professor Unwin gives coefficients for formulae deduced by Hagen, which for clean cast iron pipes make

$$Q = C \left(\frac{H}{l} \right)^{\frac{1}{2}} d^{2 \cdot 54}$$

C' having the value 41·9.

In experiments carried out by M. Vallot, Q was found to be proportional to $d^{2.65}$

ART. 70.—INITIATION AND STOPPAGE OF MOTION IN A PARALLEL PIPE.

(a). **Gradual Stoppage.**—Neglecting the effect of the elasticity of the water, and thus assuming that during acceleration or retardation in a pipe line, the velocity throughout the pipe is uniform at any instant, if a retardation $-\dfrac{d\,v}{d\,t}$ be produced in any way, as by the gradual closing of a valve at the outlet to the pipe, or by the retardation of a plunger giving motion to the water column, the rise in pressure behind the valve or piston due to this retardation will be given by

$$p' \, a = - \frac{w}{g} \cdot l \cdot a \cdot \frac{d\,v}{d\,t}$$

$$\therefore \quad p' = - \frac{w\,l}{g} \cdot \frac{d\,v}{d\,t} \qquad \text{lbs. per square foot . (1)}$$

where "l" is the length, and "a" the sectional area of the column in square feet. The minus sign is used since $\dfrac{d\,v}{d\,t}$ being an acceleration, is itself negative if the motion is being retarded. This pressure difference at the two ends of the pipe is superposed on that due to steady flow with the velocity obtaining at the given instant. Thus if the loss of pressure from entrance to exit, due to steady flow with velocity v feet per second, is $\dfrac{w v^2}{2g} \left(1 + \dfrac{fl}{m} \right)$ lbs. per square foot, and if v and $\dfrac{d\,v}{d\,t}$ are respectively the velocity and the acceleration at a given instant, the pressure at the valve will be less than the statical pressure under conditions of no flow, by an amount

$$\frac{w}{g} \left\{ l \frac{dv}{d\,t} + \frac{v^2}{2} \left(1 + \frac{fl}{m} \right) \right\} \text{ lbs. per square foot.}$$

A general expression for the pressure changes, accompanying changes of velocity in a pipe line may be obtained from Bernoulli's equation. If at any point in the pipe the acceleration is $\dfrac{d\,v}{d\,t}$, the force per pound

necessary to produce this acceleration is $\dfrac{1}{g}\dfrac{d\,v}{d\,t}$, and the work done by

this force while motion takes place through a small distance $\delta\,x$ is

$\dfrac{1}{g}\cdot\dfrac{d\,v}{d\,x}\cdot\delta x.$

Similarly, if the work done against frictional resistances is expressed as

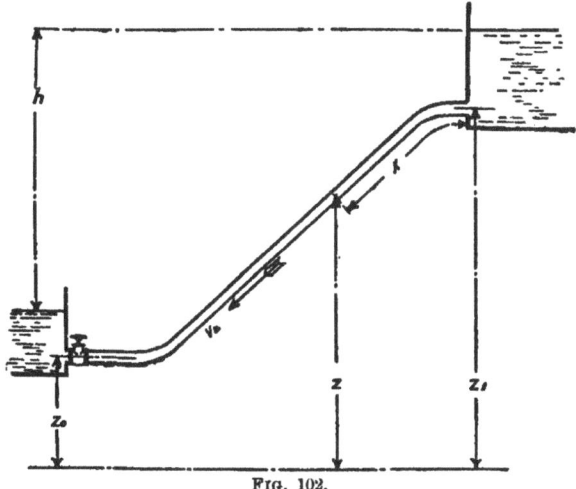

FIG. 102.

$\dfrac{f\,v^2}{2\,g\,m}$ per lb., per unit length of the pipe, as is usual, the equation as
finally modified for friction and for acceleration becomes

$$\frac{d}{dx}\left\{\frac{p}{w}+\frac{v^2}{2g}+z\right\}=-\left\{\frac{1}{g}\frac{dv}{dt}+\frac{fv^2}{2gm}\right\}\tag{2}$$

where z is the height of a given point in the fluid, above datum level, and x
is its distance from some abitrary point, measured in the direction of flow.
This equation is true even if the pipe line be not uniform in diameter.

Integrating both sides of (2) with respect to x we get

$$\frac{p}{w}+\frac{v^2}{2g}+z=-\frac{1}{g}\int_0^x\frac{dv}{dt}\cdot dx-\frac{f}{2gm}\int_0^x v^2 dx+c\tag{3}$$

Whenever the acceleration is a known function of the time or of the
distance travelled by a particle, equation (3) may be solved and the
pressure at any point obtained.

As an example, consider the uniformly retarded flow through a pipe of uniform cross-sectional area of and length l. Let $\dfrac{dv}{dt} = -a$, and let the suffixes v and $_1$ refer to the pipe immediately behind the valve and to the inlet at the top respectively. Let x be measured from the inlet (Fig. 102), and let v_a be the velocity in the pipe line.

Then at the inlet, where $x = 0$, we have $p = p_1$, $z = z_1$,

$$\int_0^x v^2 . dx = 0, \text{ so that } c = \frac{p_1}{w} + \frac{v_a^2}{2g} + z_1 \text{ from (3)}$$

When $x = l$, i.e., behind the valve, we have $p = p_v$, $z = z_v$,

$$\int_0^l v^2 dx = v_a^2 l, \int_0^l \frac{dv}{dt} dx = -a \int_0^l dx = -al;$$

$$\therefore \quad \frac{p_v}{w} + \frac{v_a^2}{2g} + z_v = \frac{a}{g}.l + \frac{p_1}{w} + \frac{v_a^2}{2g} + z_1 - \frac{fl v_a^2}{2gm} \quad (4)$$

But $\dfrac{p_1}{w} + z_1 + \dfrac{v_a^2}{2g} - z_v$ is the head equivalent of the statical pressure p_s at the valve with no flow through the pipe, so that we get

$$\frac{p_v}{w} = \frac{a}{g} l + \frac{p_s}{w} - \frac{v_a^2}{2g} \left\{ 1 + \frac{fl}{m} \right\} \text{ feet of water,} \quad (5)$$

or $\quad p_v = p_s + \dfrac{w}{g} \left\{ al - \dfrac{v_a^2}{2} \left(1 + \dfrac{fl}{m} \right) \right\}$ lbs. per square foot,

the result previously obtained from general considerations. Obviously this expression has its maximum value when $v_a = 0$, i.e., at the instant the valve reaches its seat.

In order to get uniform retardation of a column by closing a valve at its lower end, the rate of closure of this valve would, however, need to be somewhat complicated. If a is the pipe area, and a_0 the effective valve area at any instant (the effective valve area is the actual area multiplied by the coefficient of discharge), and if v_0 is the corresponding velocity of efflux, v_a being the corresponding velocity of pipe flow, we have $v_a = \dfrac{a_0 v_0}{a}$, so that

$$\frac{dv_a}{dt} = \frac{1}{a} \left\{ a_0 \frac{dv_0}{dt} + v_0 \frac{da_0}{dt} \right\}.$$

If a_1 is the effective valve area when the valve begins to close, and if v_1 is the corresponding velocity of pipe flow, the value of a_0 after t seconds is given by

$$a_0 = a \left\{ \frac{v_1 + at}{\sqrt{2al + 2gh - \frac{fl}{m}(v_1 + at)^2}} \right\}^1$$

See "Water Hammer in Hydraulic Pipe Lines," p. 8. Gibson. Constable & Co., 1908.

In an experiment carried out by Prof. I. P. Church,[1] on a pipe line 1 inch in diameter and 2,895 feet long, fitted with a nozzle 2 inches diameter at its lower end and discharging into the atmosphere, the nozzle was closed in 25 seconds, so as, it is stated, to give uniform retardation in the pipe. The statical head at the valve was 302 feet (131 lbs. per square inch), and the pressure at the nozzle during steady flow was 108 lbs. per square inch. The maximum pressure attained was 143 lbs. per square inch, so that $p_v - p_s = 12$ lbs. per square inch.

Here, assuming a coefficient of velocity of ·985, the velocity of efflux would be $·985 \sqrt{2\,g \times 108 \times 2·31} = 125$ feet per second, so that the velocity in the pipe would be 7·81 feet per second.

This makes—$a = ·312$ feet per sec., per sec., and makes

$$- \frac{w}{g} . a\,l = \frac{62·4 \times ·312 \times 2395}{32·2} = 1,455 \text{ lbs. per square foot,}$$

$$= 10·1 \text{ lbs. per square inch,}$$

as compared with the observed value 12 lbs. per square inch.

Uniform Closure of Valve.—Where the outlet valve is closed uniformly, the acceleration varies from instant to instant according to a complicated law.

Let the pipe line, of uniform area a square feet, discharge at its lower end through a valve into a chamber where the pressure is uniformly p_0 lbs. per square foot. Let times be measured *backward* from the instant the valve reaches its seat, so that, if the valve be closed uniformly in T seconds, using the same notation as before we have $a_0 = a_1 \frac{t}{T}$ as giving the valve opening at an instant t seconds *before closure is complete*. Let v_a be the velocity in the pipe line. Equation (3) now becomes

$$\frac{p}{w} + \frac{v^2}{2\,g} + z = \frac{1}{g} \int_0^x \frac{d\,v}{d\,t} . d\,x - \frac{f}{2\,g\,m} \int_0^x v^2\,d\,x + c \qquad (6)$$

δt being negative.

Also since, when $x = 0$, $\begin{cases} p = p_1,\ z = z_1,\ \int_0^z \frac{d\,v}{d\,t}\,d\,x = 0, \\ v = v_a,\ \int_0^x v^2\,d\,x = 0, \end{cases}$

$$\therefore \quad c = \frac{v_a^2}{2\,g} + z_1 + \frac{p_1}{w}.$$

Again, when $x = l$, *i.e.*, on the outlet side of the valve, neglecting losses in the valve, we have

$\begin{cases} p = p_0,\ z = z_0, \\ v = v_0,\ \int_0^l v^2\,d\,x = v_a^2\,l, \end{cases} \qquad \int_0^l \frac{d\,v}{d\,t} . d\,x = l \frac{d\,v}{d\,t} \ \Big\};$

[1] Journal of Franklin Institute, April and May, 1890.

H.A.   Q so that $\dfrac{v_0^2 - v_a^2}{2\,g} + \dfrac{p_0 - p_1}{w} + z_0 - z_1 = \dfrac{l}{g}\left\{ \dfrac{d\,v_a}{d\,t} - \dfrac{f\,v_a^2}{2\,m} \right\}$ $\qquad$ (7)

Writing $\dfrac{p_1}{w} + \dfrac{v_a^2}{2\,g} + z_1 - \dfrac{p_0}{w} - z_0 = h$ feet, where h is the difference of statical head on the two sides of the valve with no flow taking place, equation (7) becomes

$$\frac{v_0^2}{2\,g} - h = \frac{l}{g}\left\{ \frac{d\,v_a}{d\,t} - \frac{f\,v_a^2}{2\,m} \right\} \qquad (8)$$

On substituting for $\dfrac{d\,v_a}{d\,t}$, its value $\dfrac{1}{a}\left\{ a_0 \dfrac{d\,v_0}{d\,t} + v_0 \dfrac{d\,a_0}{d\,t} \right\}$ this becomes

$$a_0 \frac{d\,v_0}{d\,t} + v_0 \frac{d\,a_0}{d\,t} = \frac{a}{l}\left\{ \frac{v_0^2}{2}\left(1 + \frac{a_0^2}{a^2}\frac{fl}{m} \right) - g\,h \right\} \qquad (9)$$

and on dividing throughout by the coefficient of v_0^2, we get

$$k\,a_0 \frac{d\,v_0}{d\,t} = v_0^2 - b\,v_0 - c,$$

or $\qquad \displaystyle\int \frac{d\,v_0}{v_0^2 - b\,v_0 - c} + D = \frac{1}{k}\int\frac{d\,t}{a_0} = \frac{T}{k\,a_1}\int\frac{d\,t}{t}$ $\qquad$ (10)

where $b = \dfrac{\dfrac{2\,l}{a}\cdot\dfrac{d\,a_0}{d\,t}}{1 + \dfrac{fl}{m}\left(\dfrac{a_0}{a}\right)^2}$; $\;c = \dfrac{2\,g\,h}{1 + \dfrac{fl}{m}\left(\dfrac{a_0}{a}\right)^2}$; $\;k = \dfrac{2\,l}{a\left\{1 + \dfrac{fl}{m}\left(\dfrac{a_0}{a}\right)^2\right\}}$.

If a_0/a is small, so that the term $\dfrac{fl}{m}\left(\dfrac{a_0}{a}\right)^2$ is small in comparison with unity, and may therefore be neglected, b, c, and k become constants having the values

$$b = \frac{2\,l}{a}\cdot\frac{d\,a_0}{d\,t}; \;\; c = 2\,g\,h; \;\; k = \frac{2\,l}{a}.$$

This will always be the case as the valve gets close to its seat, and when in consequence the hammer effect is most noticeable. In such a case both sides of (10) become integrable. Writing this in the form

$$-\int \frac{d\,v_0}{\left(\sqrt{c + \dfrac{b^2}{4}}\right)^2 - \left(v_0 - \dfrac{b}{2}\right)^2} + D = \frac{T}{k\,a_1}\log_e t \qquad (11)$$

and determining D from the consideration that when $t = T$, v_0 has a known value $\bar{v}_0$, we have

$$\frac{1}{2\sqrt{c + \dfrac{b^2}{4}}}\log_e \left\{ \frac{\sqrt{c + \dfrac{b^2}{4}} - \dfrac{b}{2} + v_0}{\sqrt{c + \dfrac{b^2}{4}} + \dfrac{b}{2} - v_0} \cdot \frac{\sqrt{c + \dfrac{b^2}{4}} + \dfrac{b}{2} - \bar{v}_0}{\sqrt{c + \dfrac{b^2}{4}} - \dfrac{b}{2} + \bar{v}_0} \right\} =$$

$$\frac{T}{k\,a_1}\log_e \frac{T}{t}$$

$$\text{or } \frac{1}{m} \log_e \left\{ \frac{r+v_0}{q-v_0} \cdot \frac{q-v_0}{r+v_0} \right\} = \frac{T}{k\,a_1} \log_e \frac{T}{t} \qquad (12)$$

$$\therefore \quad v_0 = \frac{\dfrac{r+\bar{v}_0}{q-\bar{v}_0} \cdot q \cdot \left(\dfrac{T}{t}\right)^{\frac{mT}{ka_1}} - r}{1 + \dfrac{r+\bar{v}_0}{q-\bar{v}_0}\left(\dfrac{T}{t}\right)^{\frac{mT}{ka_1}}} \quad \text{feet per second} \qquad (13)$$

where $r = \sqrt{c + \dfrac{b^2}{4}} - \dfrac{b}{2}$; $\quad q = \sqrt{c + \dfrac{b^2}{4}} + \dfrac{b}{2}$; $\quad m = 2\sqrt{c + \dfrac{b^2}{4}}$

This gives the velocity of efflux, from which the velocity v_a at any instant within the range of valve opening over which $\dfrac{fl}{m}\left(\dfrac{a_0}{a}\right)^2$ is negligibly small, may be readily obtained.[1]

Writing p_v for the difference of pressure on the two sides of the valve at any instant during closure, we get, as in equation (5),

$$p_v = p_s + \frac{w}{g}\left\{ \frac{d\,v_a}{d\,t} \cdot l - \frac{v_a^2}{2}\left(1 + \frac{fl}{m}\right) \right\} \text{ lbs. per square foot,}$$

and on substituting for $\dfrac{d\,v_a}{d\,t}$ from (8) this becomes

$$p_v = p_s + \frac{w}{g}\left\{ \frac{v_0^2}{2} - \frac{v_a^2}{2} - g\,h \right\} \text{ lbs. per sq. ft.} \qquad (14)$$

Evidently this has its maximum value when v_0 is a maximum and therefore, from (13), when t vanishes, i.e., at the instant the valve reaches its seat. At this instant v_0 attains the limiting value q, while v_a becomes zero, so that we get

$$(p_v)_{max} = p_s + \frac{w}{g}\left\{ \frac{q^2}{2} - g\,h \right\} \text{ lbs. per sq. ft.}$$

$$\text{But } \frac{q^2}{2} - g\,h = \frac{c}{2} + \frac{b^2}{4} + \frac{b}{2}\sqrt{c + \frac{b^2}{4}} - g\,h \qquad .$$

$$= \left(\frac{l}{a} \cdot \frac{d\,a_0}{d\,t}\right)^2 + \frac{l}{a} \cdot \frac{d\,a_0}{d\,t} \cdot \sqrt{2\,g\,h + \left(\frac{l}{a} \cdot \frac{d\,a_0}{d\,t}\right)^2}$$

It follows that the rise in pressure behind the valve at the instant when closure is complete, above that obtaining with no flow through the pipe, is given by

$$r' = \frac{w}{g}\left[\left(\frac{l}{a} \cdot \frac{a_1}{T}\right)^2 + \frac{l}{a} \cdot \frac{a_1}{T}\sqrt{2\,g\,h + \left(\frac{l}{a} \cdot \frac{a_1}{T}\right)^2} \right] \text{ lbs. per sq. ft.} \qquad (15)$$

---

[1] Where $\frac{fl}{m}\left(\frac{a_0}{a}\right)^2$ is not negligible the treatment follows the lines outlined on p. 28. "Water Hammer," ante cit., p. 224. This case is, however, not of great practical importance, since the rise in pressure before the valve gets near to its seat, and hence before the state of affairs hypothecated obtains, is usually very small.

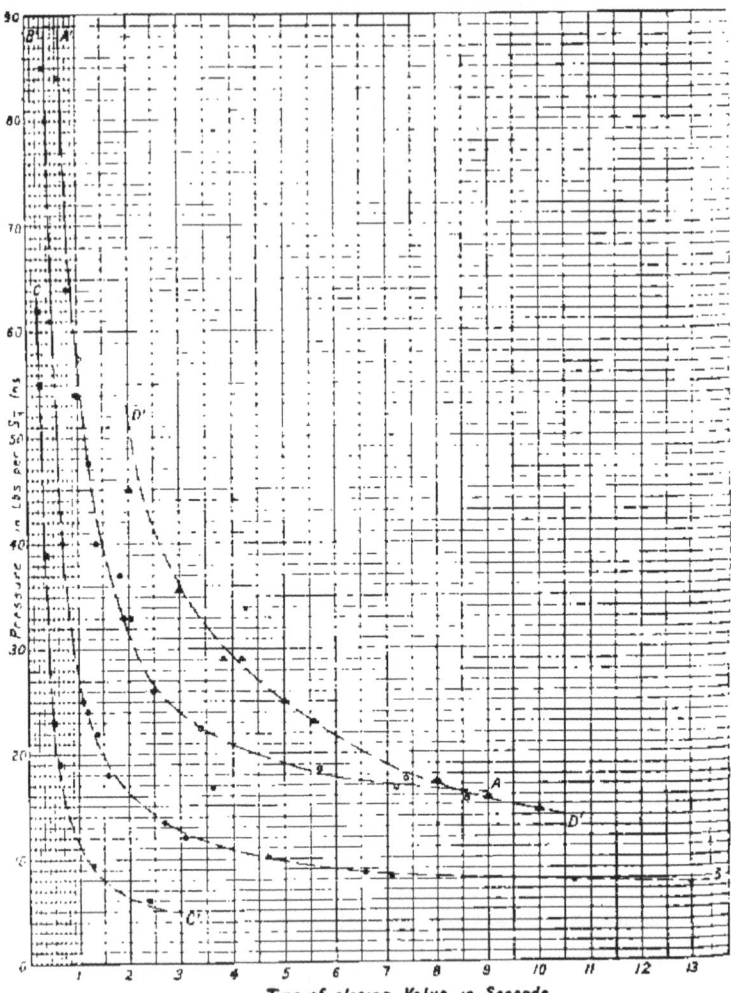

Fig. 103.—Pressures Attained Behind Valve in Excess of those Obtaining with Steady Flow with Valve Open.

Experiments by the author on a cast-iron pipe line 550 feet long and 3·75 inches diameter, with a range of values of the ratio $a : a_1$ from 9 to 79 and with values of T ranging from ·22 to 13 seconds, show results in close accordance with those calculated from this formula.   In Fig. 103 the

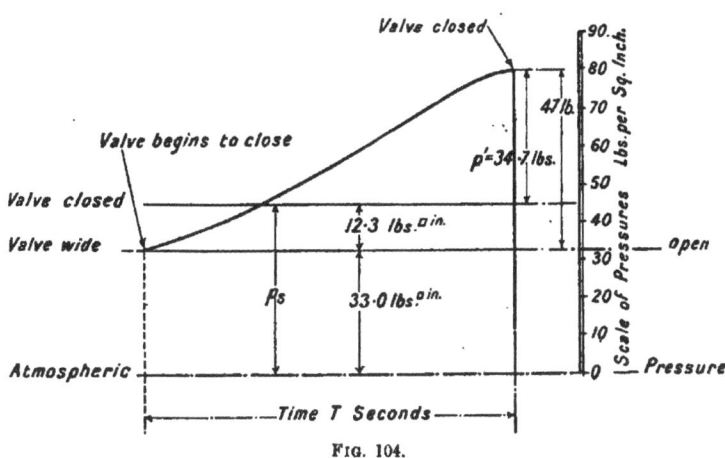

FIG. 104.

experimental results are plotted against the dotted curves which represent
the calculated results.

Series A. $a \div a_1 = 19\cdot5$ $h = 104\cdot6$ ft.

„   B.   „ $= 34\cdot7$ „ $= 104\cdot6$ „

„   C.   „ $= 72\cdot5$ „ $= 105\cdot5$ „

„   D.   „ $= 8\cdot6$ „ $= 104\cdot0$ „

Pressures were measured by an indicator whose drum received its
rotary motion directly
from the spindle of the
valve, and a typical
diagram under these
conditions is shown in
Fig. 104.

When the valve has
reached its seat the
pressure falls below that
corresponding to the
statical head, then rises
again, a wave of pres-

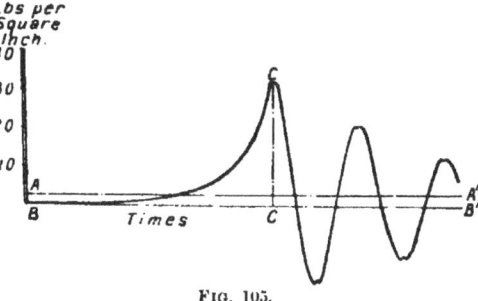

FIG. 105.

sure being reflected backwards and forwards along the pipe.   This portion
of the phenomenon, due solely to the elasticity of the water column, will

be explained later. If the indicator drum be rotated uniformly and independently of the valve spindle, a diagram similar to Fig. 105 is obtained. Here $A\ A'$ marks the pressure in the main before opening the valve, $B\ B'$ the pressure at the valve with steady flow, so that the distance from $A\ A'$ to $B\ B'$ represents $\dfrac{f\,l\,v^2}{2\,g\,m}$. C marks the instant of closing of the valve and $C\ C'$ indicates the excess pressure p' due to closure.

Both theory and practice emphasise the importance of a relatively slow motion of the valve as it approaches its seat, and particularly at the instant of closing.

Gradual Opening of Valve.—If the valve be gradually opened, so that both valve area and velocity of pipe flow increase with time, equation (6) becomes

$$\frac{p}{w} + \frac{v^2}{2\,g} + z = -\frac{1}{g}\int_0^x \frac{d\,v}{d\,t}\,d\,x - \frac{f}{2\,g\,m}\int_0^x v^2\,d\,x + C \qquad (6')$$

If the valve is opening uniformly, on proceeding as before (9) becomes

$$a_0\frac{d\,v_0}{d\,t} + v_0\frac{d\,a_0}{d\,t} = -\frac{a}{l}\left[\frac{v_0^2}{2}\left\{1 + \left(\frac{a_0}{a}\right)^2\frac{fl}{m}\right\} - g\,h\right] \qquad (9')$$

and on making the assumption that $\left(\dfrac{a_0}{a}\right)^2\dfrac{fl}{m}$ is small, this becomes

$$\int\frac{d\,v_0}{v_0^2 + b\,v_0 - c} + D = -\frac{1}{k}\int\frac{d\,t}{a_0}.$$

When $t = 0$, let $v_0 = \overline{v_0}$, the flow being steady, and let $a_0 = a_1$. Then $a_0 = a_1 + t\dfrac{d\,a_0}{d\,t} = a_1 + Kt$, where $K = \dfrac{d\,a_0}{d\,t}$.

$$\therefore\quad \left\{\frac{v_0 - r}{v_0 + q}\cdot\frac{\overline{v_0} + q}{\overline{v_0} - r}\right\} = \left(\frac{a_1}{a_1 + Kt}\right)^{\frac{m}{Kk}}$$

from which we get

$$v_0 = \frac{\dfrac{\overline{v_0} - r}{\overline{v_0} + q}\cdot q\left(\dfrac{a_1}{a_1 + Kt}\right)^{\frac{m}{Kk}} + r}{1 - \dfrac{\overline{v_0} - r}{\overline{v_0} + q}\left(\dfrac{a_1}{a_1 + Kt}\right)^{\frac{m}{Kk}}}\quad\text{ft. per second,}$$

where r, q, m and k have the meanings attached to them on p. 227, viz.,

$$r = \sqrt{c + \frac{b^2}{4}} - \frac{b}{2};\quad q = \sqrt{c + \frac{b^2}{4}} + \frac{b}{2};\quad m = 2\sqrt{c + \frac{b^2}{4}};\quad k = \frac{2\,l}{a}:\text{[1]}$$

This gives the velocity of efflux after an interval of t seconds from the commencement of the motion, in terms of the valve opening and velocity

---

[1] Here $b = \dfrac{2\,l}{a}\cdot\dfrac{d\,a_0}{d\,t}$ and $c = 2\,g\,h.$

of efflux at the latter instant. This only holds so long as the valve is opening. Suppose the valve to be stopped at an instant when its opening is a_0', the velocity of efflux at this instant being calculated to be v_0'. Let $a_0' \div a = n$.

From this time onwards $\dfrac{d\,v_a}{d\,t} = n \cdot \dfrac{d\,v_0}{d\,t}$, and equation (9') becomes

$$l\,n\,\frac{d\,v_0}{d\,t} = -\left[\frac{v_0^2}{2}\left\{1 + n^2\frac{fl}{m}\right\} - g\,h\right]$$

So that

$$\int \frac{d\,v_0}{c' - v_0^2} + D = \frac{1}{k'}\int d\,t$$

where $c' = \dfrac{2\,g\,h}{1 + n^2\dfrac{fl}{m}}$; $k' = \dfrac{2\,l\,n}{1 + n^2\dfrac{fl}{m}}$:

Integrating we get

$$\frac{1}{2\sqrt{c'}}\log\frac{\sqrt{c'} + v_0}{\sqrt{c'} - v_0} + D = \frac{t}{k'}.$$

When $t = 0$, i.e., immediately the valve comes to rest, $v_0 = v_0'$. Using this to determine D, we finally get

$$v_0 = \frac{\dfrac{\sqrt{c'} + v_0'}{\sqrt{c'} - v_0'} \cdot e^{\frac{2\sqrt{c'}}{k'}t} - 1}{\dfrac{\sqrt{c'} + v_0'}{\sqrt{c'} - v_0'} \cdot e^{\frac{2\sqrt{c'}}{k'}t} + 1} \quad \sqrt{c'} \text{ feet per second} \quad (16)$$

as the velocity of efflux after t seconds from the stoppage of the valve.

It will be noted that as t increases, this tends to the limit

$$\sqrt{c'} = \sqrt{\frac{2\,g\,h}{1 + n^2\dfrac{fl}{m}}}.$$

The method of treatment so far outlined, while giving results which are rigorously true for an incompressible fluid in a rigid pipe line fails to account for many of the phenomena actually observed during the stoppage of motion in a long column of water, since these are largely due to the elasticity of the water column. For example, an examination of equations (1) or (2) indicates that an instantaneous stoppage of motion, involving an infinite retardation, will necessitate an infinite retarding force, and hence an infinite pressure at the closed end of the pipe, a conclusion which is not at all borne out by the result of experiment.

Actually, when the column is brought instantaneously to rest, compression takes place; a wave of compression is reflected from the closed end of the pipe; and the initial kinetic energy of the water is transformed into resilient energy or energy of strain.

When the retardation is gradual, part of the kinetic energy is absorbed in doing work against the retarding force, and part in compressing the column, the latter factor becoming increasingly important as the rate of retardation is increased.

(b) Sudden Stoppage of Motion—Ideal Case.

If a column of water, flowing with velocity v along a uniform pipe (supposed rigid), have its motion checked by the instantaneous closure of a rigid valve, the phenomena experienced are due entirely to the elasticity of the column, and are analogous to those obtaining in the case of the longitudinal impact of an elastic bar against a rigid wall.

At the instant of impact, the motion of the layer in contact with the valve is suddenly stopped, and its kinetic energy is changed into resilience, or energy of strain, with a consequent sudden rise in pressure. This stoppage and rise in pressure is almost instantaneously transmitted to the adjacent layer, and so on, the state of zero velocity and maximum pressure (this at any point being p' above the pressure obtaining at that point with steady flow at velocity v) being propagated as a pressure-wave along the pipe, with velocity V_p. [V_p is the same as the velocity of sound through water, $i.e.$, about 4,700 ft. per second, depending slightly on temperature.]

This wave reaches the open end of the pipe after t seconds, where $t = l \div V_p$. At this instant the whole of the column is instantaneously at rest in a state of compression.

At the open end, however, a constant pressure p_1 is maintained, and in consequence the strain energy of the end layer is reconverted into kinetic energy, this (neglecting losses), rebounding with its original velocity v and with the normal pressure obtaining at this point under a state of steady flow towards the open end with this velocity.

This state of normal pressure and of velocity $(-v)$ is then propagated as a wave towards the valve, reaching the latter after a second interval $l \div V_p$ seconds. At this latter instant the whole of the column is unstrained and is moving towards the open end with velocity v. At the same instant the motion of the layer nearest the valve is stopped, and a wave of zero velocity and of pressure (p' below the pressure obtaining at the point at the instant before the stoppage of the motion, or p below the pressure at the point with no flow through the pipe) is transmitted along the pipe to be reflected from the open end as a wave of normal pressure and velocity v towards the valve. When this wave reaches the valve,

$4l \div V_p$ seconds after the latter is closed, the conditions are the same as at the beginning of the cycle and the whole is repeated.

Under such ideal conditions the state of affairs behind the valve, as regards pressure, would be represented by such a diagram as Fig. 106 A, the cycle, in the case of an elastic, non-viscous fluid, being repeated

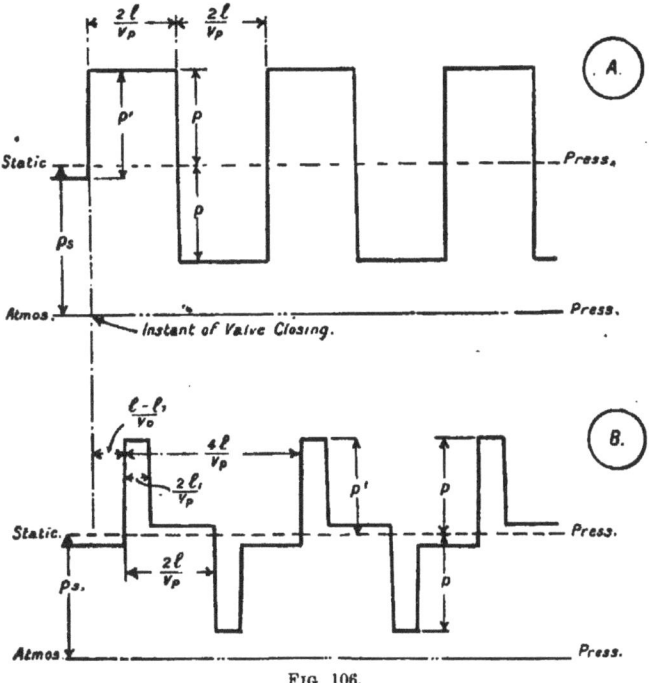

FIG. 106.

indefinitely. At any other point in the pipe, at a distance l_1 from the open end, the pressure-time diagram would appear as in Fig. 106 B.

Actually, because of the elasticity of the pipe walls and joints, part of the kinetic energy of the moving column is expended in stretching these, with a resultant reduction in the maximum pressure attained, this reduction depending entirely on the form, material, and construction of the pipe line. Obviously an air vessel or any such device near the closed end will considerably reduce the pressure, and its action may be considered as being due either to a reduction in the effective modulus of elasticity of the pipe as a whole, or to an increase in the time occupied in bringing the moving column to rest. Owing to this, and to the viscosity of the water, the motion gradually dies out.

The state of affairs is then as indicated in Fig. 107, of which *A* represents a diagram from behind the valve, and *B* from a point 15 feet from the open end of the pipe line experimented on by the author. In

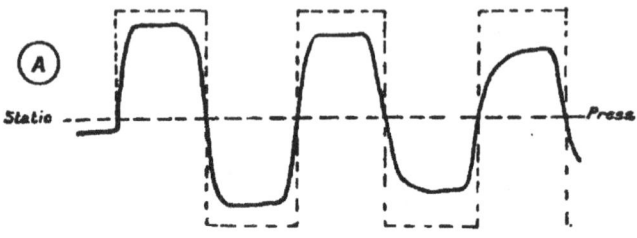

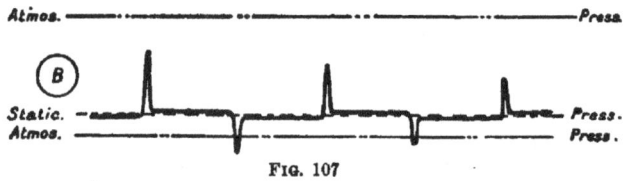

Fig. 107

this case the valve was closed in ·07 seconds, and the vibrations died out so that the motion of the pencil of the indicator became imperceptible, after about 30 complete oscillations.

Magnitude of Rise in Pressure following Sudden Closure of a Valve.

If p' be the rise in pressure in lbs. per square foot; if K be the modulus of cubical compressibility of the water; and if v be the velocity of flow at the instant of stoppage (supposed instantaneous), we have. assuming the pipe line rigid, on equating the loss of kinetic energy per lb. to the increase in resilience :—

$$\frac{v^2}{2\,g} = \frac{p'^2}{2\,K\,w'}$$

$$\therefore\ p' = v\,\sqrt{\frac{K\,w}{g}}\ . \qquad . \qquad . \qquad . \qquad . \ (1)$$

Putting $K = 300,000 \times 144$ lbs. per square foot; $w = 62\cdot4$; $g = 32\cdot2$; this becomes

$$p = 9160\,v \text{ lbs. per square foot.}$$
$$= 63\cdot7\ v \text{ lbs. per square inch.}$$

A closer approximation to the actual rise in pressure may be obtained by assuming that while the pipe line is rigid in that the motion is instantaneously stopped, yet the elasticity is felt in its effect on the value of K, this adopting the value K' where $\dfrac{1}{K'} = \dfrac{1}{K} + \dfrac{2\,r}{t\,E}$ approx.[1]

In the author's experimental pipe line this makes $K' = 251,000 \times 144$ lbs. per square foot, and makes $p' = 58\cdot4\ v$ lbs. per square inch.

The following demonstration shows how the elasticity of the pipe line and water column may be taken fully into account.

Let K' and E have the meaning already attached to them, and let w

[1] Suppose the pipe to be of radius r feet, and of comparatively small thickness t feet, and let the material of which it is composed have a modulus of elasticity E lbs. per square foot, and a Poisson's ratio $\dfrac{1}{\sigma}$.

Then if at any section of the pipe the increase in pressure due to retardation is p' lbs. per square foot, the increase in the circumferential stress in the pipe walls is $\dfrac{p'\,r}{t}$ and in the longitudinal stress is $\dfrac{p'\,r}{2\,t}$ lbs. per square foot.

It, then, $\delta\,x$ is the change in length of an element of the pipe at this point, whose original length was x, we have

$$\frac{\delta\,x}{x} = \frac{p'\,r}{2\,t\,E} - \frac{p'\,r}{\sigma\,t\,E} = \frac{p'\,r}{2\,t\,E}\left\{1 - \frac{2}{\sigma}\right\}$$

$$\text{Also}\ \frac{\delta\,r}{r} = \frac{p'\,r}{t\,E} - \frac{p'\,r}{2\,\sigma\,t\,E}$$

$$\therefore\ \delta\,r = r\,\frac{p'\,r}{t\,E}\left\{1 - \frac{1}{2\,\sigma}\right\}.$$

The change in the volume of this element is therefore given by

$$\pi\left\{(r + \delta\,r)^2\,(x + \delta\,x) - r^2 x\right\},$$

$$= \pi\left\{2\,r\,x\,\delta\,r + r^2\,\delta\,x\right\} \left.\begin{array}{l}\text{neglecting small quantities}\\ \text{of the second order.}\end{array}\right.$$

$$= \pi\,r^2\,x\left\{\frac{2\,p'\,r}{t\,E}\left(1 - \frac{1}{2\,\sigma}\right) + \frac{p'\,r}{2\,t\,E}\left(1 - \frac{2}{\sigma}\right)\right\}$$

$$= \pi\,r^2\,x \times \frac{p'\,r}{2\,t\,E}\left\{5 - \frac{4}{\sigma}\right\}$$

$$\therefore\ \frac{\delta\,V}{V} = \frac{p'\,r}{2\,t\,E}\left\{5 - \frac{4}{\sigma}\right\}.$$

But the actual new volume of the liquid $= \pi\,r^2\,x\left(1 - \dfrac{p'}{K}\right)$ while its apparent new volume $= \pi\,r^2\,x\left\{1 - \dfrac{p'}{K} - \dfrac{p'\,r}{2\,t\,E}\left(5 - \dfrac{4}{\sigma}\right)\right\}$, so that the effective value of K, which will be denoted by K', is given by the relation

$$\frac{1}{K'} = \frac{1}{K} + \frac{r}{2\,t\,E}\left(5 - \frac{4}{\sigma}\right).$$

For iron pipes σ may be taken as $3\cdot6$ approximately.

and w_m, V and V_m, a and a_m be the weights of unit volume of, the velocities of wave propagation in, and the sectional areas of the water column and metal of the pipe wall respectively.

Then, with instantaneous closure the ends of the water and metal columns move, at impact, with a common velocity u, and waves, respectively of compression and of extension, travel along the water column and the pipe wall.

Hence, after a very short interval of time δt, lengths $V \delta t$ and $V_m \delta t$ of the water column and of the pipe will be moving with velocity u, and the equation of momentum gives :—

$$\{ w\, a\, V + w_m\, a_m\, V_m \}\, u\, \delta t = w\, a\, V\, v\, \delta t$$

$$\therefore \quad u = v \left\{ \frac{1}{1 + \dfrac{w_m\, a_m\, V_m}{w\, a\, V}} \right\}$$

Each element of the column and of the pipe, as the wave passes it, takes suddenly the velocity u, while each element of the water column takes the compression $\dfrac{v - u}{V}$ and therefore the stress $(v - u) \sqrt{\dfrac{w\, K'}{g}}$, and each element of the pipe takes the extension $\dfrac{u}{V_m}$ and the stress $u \sqrt{\dfrac{w_m\, E}{g}}$.

Substituting for u we have the pressure rise in the water given by

$$p' = v \left\{ \frac{1}{1 + \dfrac{w\, a\, V}{w_m\, a_m\, V_m}} \right\} \sqrt{\frac{w\, K'}{g}} \ \text{lbs. per square foot.}$$

Since $V = \sqrt{\dfrac{K'\, g}{w}}$ and $V_m = \sqrt{\dfrac{E\, g}{w_m}}$,[1] this may be written

$$p' = v \left\{ \frac{1}{1 + \dfrac{a}{a_m} \sqrt{\dfrac{K'\, w}{E\, w_m}}} \right\} \sqrt{\frac{w\, K'}{g}}$$

$$= v \left\{ \frac{1}{\sqrt{\dfrac{g}{K'\, w}} + \dfrac{a}{a_m} \sqrt{\dfrac{g}{E\, w_m}}} \right\} \ \text{lbs. per square foot.} \quad (2$$

---

[1] Imagine a bar of unit cross-sectional area to impinge with velocity v in the direction of its axis, against a rigid wall. After a very short interval δt seconds, a mass $\dfrac{w_m\, V_m\, \delta t}{g}$ has been brought to rest, and, if p is the (uniform) pressure on the end of the bar during this interval we have, equating the force × time, to the change of momentum :—

$$p\, \delta t = \frac{w_m\, V_m\, \delta t}{g} . v \ \text{or} \ p = \frac{w_m}{g} . V_m . v \ \text{lbs.}$$

But $p = v \sqrt{\dfrac{E\, w_m}{g}}$, so that, equating these two expressions we get $V_m = \sqrt{\dfrac{E\, g}{w_m}}$ ft. per second.

The longitudinal stress f, produced in the pipe walls by hammer action, which equals $u \sqrt{\dfrac{u_m E}{g}}$, then becomes, on substitution,

$$f = r \left\{ \frac{1}{\sqrt{\dfrac{g}{E\, w_m}} + \dfrac{a_m}{a} \sqrt{\dfrac{g}{K'\, w}}} \right\} \text{ lbs. per square foot.}$$

Valve Shut Suddenly, but not Instantaneously.

As the time of closure of a valve becomes less and less, the maximum rise in pressure will evidently tend to the limit given by formula (2) p. 236.

Now if the time of closure is so short that $\dfrac{l}{V_p} > T = \dfrac{x}{V_p}$, the disturbance initiated at the valve has travelled a distance x, and has not arrived at the open end when the latter reaches its seat.

In this case if the retardation is uniform $(= -a)$, equation (1), p. 222, becomes $p' = \dfrac{w\,a\,x}{g}$ lbs.

But $a = \dfrac{v_a}{T} = \dfrac{v_a}{x} V_p$, so that

$$p' = \frac{w}{g} \cdot V_p,\ v_a = v_a \sqrt{\frac{K'\, w}{g}} \text{ lbs.}$$

this being the value obtained with instantaneous stoppage. It follows that whatever the law of valve closure, if this is completed in a less time than $l \div V_p$ the pressure rise will be the same as with instantaneous closure.

For values of T between $l \div V_p$ and $2l \div V_p$ the falling off in pressure will usually be comparatively small, so that it is in general sufficiently accurate for all practical purposes to count as "sudden," any stoppage occupying a shorter time than this.

For values of $T > 4l \div V_p$, formula (15), p. 227, may be used without serious error.

Experimental Results with Sudden Closure of Valve. In the author's experiments $l = 550.$ feet; $K' = 251,000 \times 144$; $E = 10^7 \times 144$ lbs. per square foot; $a : a_m = 1{\cdot}275$; formula (1) p. 234, gives

$$p' = 7780\ v \text{ lbs. per square foot,}$$
$$= 54{\cdot}0\ v \text{ lbs. per square inch.}$$

For comparison the observed results are shown in the following table, against those as obtained by using this formula.

Experiment.	Velocity before closing Valve.	Time of Closing.	Rise in pressure.	
			Calculated ($p = 54\ v$).	Experimental.
	feet per second.	seconds.	lbs. per square inch.	lbs. per square inch.
1	·3625	·070	19·5	19·5
2	,,	·090	,,	19·5
3	,,	·140	,,	18·7
4	,,	·270	,,	16·3
5	,,	·280	,,	14·7
6	·551	·065	29·7	29·3
7	,,	·090	,,	29·3
8	,,	·175	,,	29·3
9	,,	·255	,,	25·0
10	,,	·275	,,	24·4
11	,,	·275	,,	26·2
12	·720	·125	38·9	37·5
13	,,	·135	,,	38·1
14	,,	·150	,,	38·1
15	,,	·250	,,	37·0
16	,,	·270	,,	35·7
17	,,	·270	,,	35·7
18	1·094	·110	59·0	57·5
19	,,	·150	,,	58·7
20	,,	·245	,,	55·0
21	,,	·285	,,	46·3
22	1·444	·160	77·9	75·0
23	,,	·210	,,	73·7
24	,,	·215	,,	73·0
25	,,	·300	,,	62·5
26	,,	·370	,,	58·8

From these results it appears that so long as T is less than ·13 seconds $(l \div V_p = ·13)$ the calculated and observed pressures are in every case in close agreement. This agreement is substantially maintained until $T =$

about ·21 seconds, while when $T = \cdot 26$ seconds, the mean error involved in using the uncorrected formula in this case is about 14 per cent.

In a series of experiments carried out by M. Joukowsky[1] on cast-iron pipes of 4 inches and 6 inches diameter, having lengths of 1,050 and 1,066 feet respectively, the time of valve closing being ·08 seconds in each case, the observed rise in pressure agrees closely with the formula, $p = 57\, v$. The following are some of the results obtained by interpolation from the plotted results of these experiments.

4-INCH PIPE.

Velocity, feet per second	·5	2·0	3·0	4·0	9·0
Observed pressure—lbs. per square inch .	31	119	172	228	511
$p = 57\, v$	29	114	171	228	513

6-INCH PIPE.

Velocity, feet per second	·6	2·0	3·0	7·5
Observed pressure—lbs. per square inch .	43	113	173	426
$p = 57\, v$	34	114	171	427

The pressure in the last experiment, calculated on the assumption that the water is incompressible, is 3,585 lbs. per square inch, a result which sufficiently indicates the nature of the errors involved in extreme cases by neglecting the effect of elasticity.

These sudden increases of pressure, commonly known as water hammer, may evidently become most serious with large values of v, and in such cases the ill effects due to the too sudden closing of a valve

---

[1] *Stoss in Wasserleitungsröhren*, St. Petersburg, 1900. The author has been unable to ascertain the thickness of the walls of these pipes. Abstract by O. Simin in Trans. Am. Waterworks Ass., 1904.

should be guarded against by a relief valve or other similar device placed as near as convenient to the main valve. In the case of a pipe line for a power plant, where the head is not excessive it is usual to provide a stand pipe, or simple vertical pipe capable of taking the whole discharge of the main, and open at the top to the atmosphere. This should be coupled to the supply main just before its entrance to the power-house, and the height should be so arranged that when standing under the statical pressure of the supply reservoir, the water level is within a short distance of the top. Under these conditions, the maximum pressure which may occur in the pipe line is that due to the statical pressure in the stand pipe, together with that necessary to produce motion up this pipe.

It is usual in practice to make some allowance for possible water hammer by designing the pipes to withstand a pressure of 100 lbs. per square inch in excess of that due to the statical head, thus, in effect, allowing for an instantaneous stoppage at a velocity of 1·6 feet per second.

Sudden Opening of a Valve.

If the valve at the lower end of a pipe line be suddenly opened, the pressure behind the valve falls by an amount p lbs. per square inch, and a wave of velocity v towards the valve $\left\{ v = p \sqrt{\dfrac{g}{K'w}} \text{ (approx.) } \right\}$, and of pressure p below statical, is propagated towards the pipe inlet.

The magnitude of p depends on the speed and amount of opening of the valve, and if the latter could be thrown wide open instantaneously the pressure would fall to that obtaining on the discharge side. In the author's experiments, with the valve thrown open through ·5 of a complete turn the maximum drop in pressure was 40 lbs. per square inch, the statical pressure being 45 lbs. per square inch.

With the valve opened through ·10 of a complete turn the maximum drop was 20 lbs. per square inch, and with $\frac{1}{20}$ of a complete turn the drop was 11 lbs. per square inch. In each case the time of opening was less than ·13 seconds $(l \div V_p)$.

In the case of a horizontal pipe, or one which is so situated that the absolute statical pressure is everywhere greater than p, this pressure wave reaches the pipe inlet with approximately its original amplitude, and at this instant the whole column is moving towards the valve with velocity v and pressure p below normal.

The pressure at the inlet is, however, maintained normal, so that the wave returns from this end with normal pressure and with velocity $2v$.

At the valve this wave is reflected with a velocity which is the difference between $2v$ and the velocity of efflux at this instant, and with a corresponding pressure. As the velocity of efflux will now be greater than v, the wave velocity will be less than v, and the rise in pressure less than p above normal. This wave is reflected from the inlet to the valve, and here the cycle is repeated, the amplitude of the pressure wave diminishing rapidly until steady flow ensues.

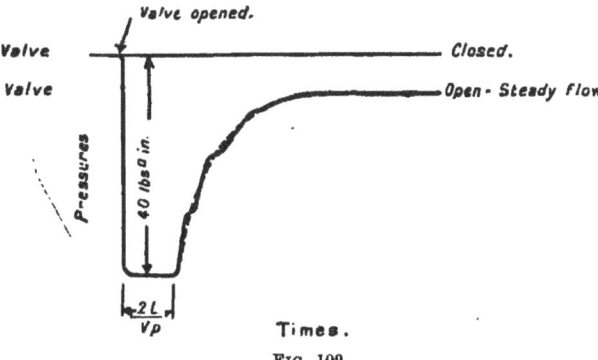

FIG. 108.

Fig. 108 shows the diagram obtained by the author from the experimental pipe line under these conditions.

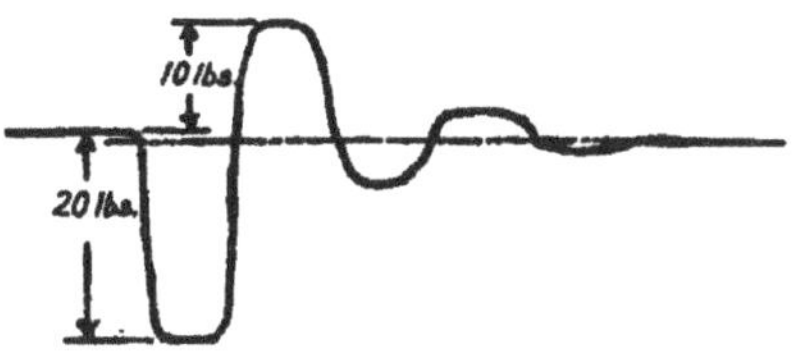

Where the pipe slopes upwards towards its inlet, so that, beyond a certain point in its length the absolute statical pressure is less than the drop in pressure caused at the valve by sudden opening, then on the passage of the first wave of negative pressure the wave motion becomes

FIG. 109.

partially discontinuous after this point is reached,[1] and the wave travels on to the inlet with a gradually diminishing amplitude. The amplitude with which it reaches the inlet, and which will be probably 2 or 3 lbs. per square inch less than the absolute statical pressure at inlet, decides the state of velocity of the reflected wave. This will evidently be less

[1] Actually before this, since water gives up its dissolved air rapidly when the pressure falls to within 2 or 3 lbs. of a complete vacuum.

than in the preceding case, and under such circumstances the wave motion dies out very quickly. As the valve opening becomes greater, the efficiency of the valve as a reflecting surface becomes less, so that with a moderate opening the pressure may never even attain the pressure due to the statical head.

This is shown in Fig. 109, which is a diagram obtained by the author from the experimental pipe line when the outlet valve was opened suddenly (time $<$ $\cdot$13 seconds) through half a complete turn.

Neglecting the effect of elasticity of the water column, the velocity of efflux accompanying a sudden valve opening may be obtained as follows:

Imagine the effective valve opening to assume instantaneously a value a_0 and to remain of this value, so that $\dfrac{dv_a}{dt} = \dfrac{a_0}{a} \cdot \dfrac{dv_0}{dt}$. Equation (6), (p. 225), now becomes

$$\frac{p}{w} + \frac{v^2}{2g} + z = -\frac{1}{g}\int_0^x \frac{dv}{dt}\,dx - \frac{f}{2gm}\int_0^x v^2 dx + c \qquad (6')$$

while equation (9) becomes

$$- a_0\frac{dv_0}{dt} = \frac{a}{l}\left\{ \frac{v_0^2}{2}\left(1 + \frac{fl}{m}\left(\frac{a_0}{a} \right)^2 \right) - gh \right\} \qquad (9')$$

$$\text{or } k\frac{dv_0}{dt} = c^2 - v_0^2$$

$$\text{where } \begin{cases} k = \dfrac{2\,la_0}{a} \cdot \dfrac{1}{1 + \dfrac{fla_0^2}{ma^2}} \\[4mm] c^2 = \dfrac{2\,gh}{1 + \dfrac{fl}{m} \cdot \dfrac{a_0^2}{a^2}} \end{cases}$$

$$\text{so that } \int \frac{dv_0}{c^2 - v_0^2} + D = \frac{1}{k}\int dt.$$

From this we get

$$\frac{1}{2c}\log\frac{c + v_0}{c - v_0} + D = \frac{t}{k}, \qquad (11')$$

while since $v_0 = 0$ when $t = 0$, we have $D = 0$.

$$\therefore \quad v_0 = c\left\{ \frac{1 - e^{\frac{2c}{k}\cdot t}}{1 + e^{\frac{2c}{k}\cdot t}} \right\} \text{ feet per second}[1] \qquad (12')$$

giving the velocity of efflux at an instant t seconds after the valve opens.

---

[1] "Water Hammer" ante cit., p. 51. This formula receives close experimental confirmation from the results of experiments on the velocity of flow down the drive pipe of a hydraulic ram, published in the Bulletin of the University of Wisconsin. No. 205, 1908, p. 143.

As t increases, this approximates to the value c or

$$\sqrt{\frac{2\,gh}{1 + \frac{fl}{m} \cdot \frac{a_0{}^2}{a^2}}}$$

By substitution in (9″) the value of $\frac{dv_0}{dt}$ at any instant and therefore of $\frac{dv}{dt}$ may be obtained, and knowing this the pressure behind the valve may be readily obtained.

EXAMPLES.

(1) Experiments by Dr. Lampe on the 16-inch asphalted pipes of the Dantzic main gave results which for velocites between 1·6 and 3·0 feet per second agree with the value as deduced from the formula $\frac{h}{l} = \cdot000371 \frac{v^{1.85}}{d^{1.15}}$. Determine the corresponding values of f in the formulae $h = \frac{f\,l\,v^2}{2\,g\,m}$ when $v = 1\cdot6$ and $3\cdot0$ feet per second.

Answer. $\begin{cases} \cdot00531. \\ \cdot00485. \end{cases}$

(2) Darcy's experiments on a cast-iron pipe ·617 feet diameter give the result $\frac{h}{l} = \cdot000380 \frac{v^{1.95}}{d^{1.06}}$ with fair accuracy. Determine the velocity of flow and the discharge per minute from a similar pipe 1,000 feet long under a head of 50 feet.

Answer. $\begin{cases} \text{Velocity} = 2\cdot893 \text{ feet per second.} \\ \text{Volume} = 51\cdot9 \text{ cubic feet per minute.} \end{cases}$

(3) The following is a convenient mnemonic for flow in clean cast-iron pipes of diameters between 2 and 6 inches with a velocity of 3 feet per second; $h = \frac{l}{25\,d}$, where h is in feet, d in inches. Taking Unwin's exponential formula as being correct, determine the percentage error for pipe diameters 3, 6, 9, and 12 inches.

Answer. $\begin{cases} 3 \text{ in. diameter. Error} - \quad\cdot62 \text{ per cent.} \\ 6 \text{ ,,} \qquad\text{,,} \qquad\qquad \text{,, } + \ 4\cdot0 \quad\text{,,} \\ 9 \text{ ,,} \qquad\text{,,} \qquad\qquad \text{,, } + \ 9\cdot9 \quad\text{,,} \\ 12 \text{ ,,} \qquad\text{,,} \qquad\qquad \text{,, } + 16\cdot4 \quad\text{,,} \end{cases}$

(4) W. Cox (*Engineering* (1892), p. 613) gives the following formula

R 2

for flow in clean C. I. pipes:—$h = \dfrac{C\,l}{d\ (\text{in.})}$, where C has the following values:—

Velocity (ft. per sec.)	1	2	3	4	5	6	7	8	9	10
C	·00583	·020	·0408	·0683	·1025	·143	·191	·245	·306	·373

Compare these with the values obtained by using Unwin's formula, and determine the per cent. difference for a 3 inch and 6 inch pipe at velocities of 2, 4, 6, and 10 feet per second.

Answer.

		Velocity f.s.			
		2	4	6	10
The per cent. error of the approximate formula is	3 in. pipe -	+ 10%	− 2·38%	− 7·13%	− 11·15%
	6 in. pipe -	+ 14·7%	+ 2·13%	− 2·6%	− 7·6%

(5) The jet of a Pelton wheel has an effective diameter of 2 inches. The supply pipe is 6,000 feet long and is an asphalted pipe 15 inches diameter, and the supply head is 800 feet. Determine the probable discharge in cubic feet per second, and the horse-power of the jet. Assume $c_v = \cdot972 : f = \cdot0050$.

> Answer. Velocity of jet = 218 f.s.; discharge = 4·75
> cubic feet per second; 396 horse-power.

(6) With a given slope, a clean cast-iron pipe 9 inches diameter, is found to give a discharge of 25,000 gallons per hour. Determine the necessary diameter of pipe, having twice the slope, to give a discharge of 50,000 gallons per hour. (Take Unwin's values for the index of d and of v, p. 202.)

> Answer. 10·3 inches.

(7) The outlet valve from a main 5,000 feet long is closed in 1 second. Determine the rise in pressure if the initial velocity of flow is 4 feet per second, and the pipe is rigid.

> Answer. 254·8 lbs. square inch.

(8) A uniform pipe, 200 feet long, is fitted with a plunger which, originally moving at 6 feet per second, is brought to rest uniformly in 1·5 second. Assuming the water to be incompressible, determine the pressure on the piston caused by the retardation.

Answer. 10·76 lbs. per square inch.

(9) If, in the above example, the plunger is driven from a crank 1 foot long, and making 100 revolutions per minute, and with S. H. motion, determine the pressure produced by retardation at the end of the stroke.

Answer. 295 lbs. per square inch.

CHAPTER IX.

Art. 71.—Pipe Line Losses.

In constructing a pipe line to connect two reservoirs, or to distribute the discharge from any reservoir, the problem which usually presents itself to the engineer is that of determining the minimum size of pipe which, under given conditions of head loss, shall be capable of discharging a given quantity of water per minute. In the construction of a supply pipe line for a power station, the problem is much the same, and in every case it is first of all necessary to determine the conditions involving loss of head, and the magnitude of these losses.

Commencing at the supply end of the pipe, we have

(1) Loss due to friction and eddy formation at the entrance to the pipe.

(2) Frictional losses in the pipe itself.

(3) Losses at valves, sluices, etc.

(4) Losses at all elbows, bends, or deviations from the straight.

(5) Losses at pipe junctions.

(6) Losses at sudden enlargements, or contractions in the area of the pipe.

(7) Loss at exit, due to the rejection of kinetic energy.

In every case these losses are approximately proportional to the square of the velocity, so that if v be the velocity we may write total loss of head $= {}_1H_7 = F' v^2$.

Where a pipe line connects two reservoirs, the difference of head between their free surfaces must then equal $F' v^2$, for the pipe to run full with velocity v.

If in Fig. 110 a horizontal A B be drawn through the upper free surface, and if a series of ordinates be drawn vertically downwards from A B representing on the vertical scale of the drawing the total loss of pressure energy per lb. from the pipe entrance to the particular point considered, the ends of all such ordinates being connected give a curve called the **hydraulic gradient** for the pipe line. If now any datum line CD be taken, such that the height CA represents the potential energy of the water at A, the height of any point on the gradient line, above CD, will evidently represent the head available for producing flow at that point, while the pressure energy at all points on the hydraulic gradient will be zero. It follows that if a series of open stand pipes are erected at various points on the pipe line the free surfaces in these pipes will lie on the gradient line, while the pressure in the pipe at any

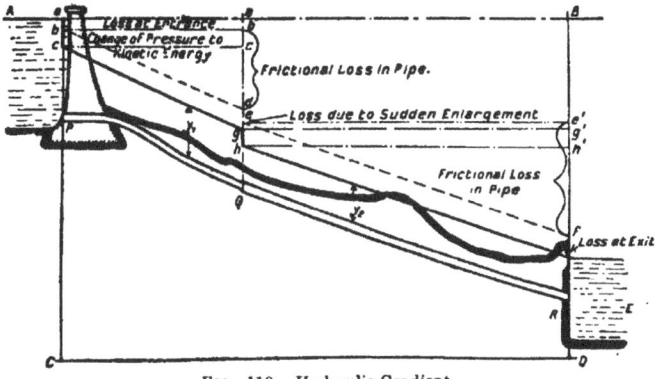

FIG. 110.—Hydraulic Gradient.

point will be measured by the vertical distance y_1, y_2, etc., of that point below the gradient.

The slope of the hydraulic gradient is termed the "**virtual slope**" of the pipe.

Fig. 110 represents the hydraulic gradient for the pipe line shown in elevation, which consists of a parallel pipe PQ, having a sudden enlargement of section at Q, remaining parallel from Q to R, and discharging at R into the service reservoir E.

Here $a\,b$ represents frictional and eddy loss at entrance: $b\,d$ represents frictional loss from P to $Q = \dfrac{f\,l_1\,v_1^2}{2\,g\,m_1}$ ft.-lbs. per lb.: $d\,e$ represents loss due to sudden enlargement of section $= \dfrac{(v_1 - v_2)^2}{2\,g}$ ft.-lbs. per lb.: $e'\,f$ represents loss due to friction between Q and $R = \dfrac{f\,l_2\,v_2^2}{2\,g\,m_2}$ ft.-lbs. per lb. : $f\,k$ represents loss due to rejection of kinetic energy at exit.

The vertical distance from the datum to the broken line $a\ b\ d\ e\ f\ k$, now represents the sum of the (kinetic + pressure + potential) energies at any point, and if $c\ g$ be drawn parallel to $b\ d$ at a vertical distance $b\ c$ below $b\ d$, equal to $\dfrac{v_1^2}{2\ g}$, the distance from the datum to the line $c\ g$ now gives the sum of the (pressure + potential) energies at any point from P to Q, If similarly a line $h\ k$ be drawn parallel to $e\ f$, at a vertical distance below this equal to $\dfrac{v_2^2}{2\ g}$, the whole line $a\ b\ c\ g\ h\ k$ now represents the hydraulic gradient for the pipe.

The pressure in the pipe line will be everywhere greater than that of the atmosphere, so long as the pipes nowhere rise above the hydraulic gradient. If part of the pipe line be laid above the gradient line, the pressure in this portion of the pipe will be less than atmospheric, and any leakage at a joint allows air to be drawn in with a possible stoppage of flow. If the pipe rises above the gradient line by a distance equivalent to the barometric height, 34 feet, the flow will of necessity stop completely. Owing to the discharge of dissolved air from water at low pressures, the maximum height practically attainable is however much less than this. The syphon (Art. 82) is an instance of the pipe line being above the hydraulic gradient.

If then the suffixes A and E refer to the surfaces in the two reservoirs and if Z_A and Z_E are the heights of these free surfaces above some datum, we have, if the pipe discharges below the surface in the lower reservoir

$$Z_A - Z_E = {}_A H_E = \text{losses at entrance + losses in pipe}$$
$$+ \text{ losses at exit.}$$

ART. 72.—DETAILED LOSSES IN PIPE LINE.

(1) **Losses at Entrance.**—These depend on the form of entrance adopted. Thus with a bell mouthpiece the loss of head is about $\cdot 05\ \dfrac{v^2}{2\ g}$ feet of water (p. 119), while with a pipe projecting into the reservoir and forming a re-entrant mouthpiece, the loss, when running full, is $\dfrac{v^2}{2\ g}$ feet of water (p. 113).

Where the pipe opens flush with the side or bottom of the reservoir the loss of head becomes about $\cdot 47\ \dfrac{v^2}{2\ g}$ feet (p. 117).

From what has already been said, it will be seen that this loss of energy occurs simply in getting the water into the pipe, due to the formation of a *vena contracta* and the subsequent re-enlargement of the stream to fill the pipe. This reduces the energy available for producing motion along the pipe and gives a reduced flow with the same total head.

(2) **Frictional Losses in the Pipe.**—These have been considered in pp. 195—210.

(3) **Losses at Valves, etc.**—The loss of energy caused by the presence of a valve or sluice in a pipe line may be looked upon as being due to the sinuous motion set up by the expansion of the stream to fill the pipe,

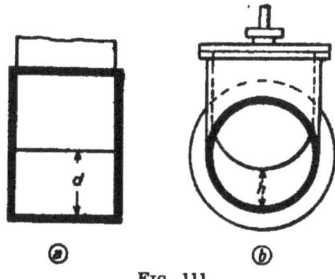

FIG. 111.

after its contraction in passing the valve and, by an application of the formulae deduced on pp. 88—94, this loss can, except for irregularities in design which themselves cause sinuous motion, and which may, even when the valve is wide open, cause a loss of head amounting to as much as from one to ten times $v^2 \div 2g$, be approximately determined.

Loss caused by Sluice in Rectangular Pipe (Fig. 111a).—Depth of pipe D. Depth of sluice opening d.[1]

$\frac{d}{D}$	·1	·2	·3	·4	·5	·6	·7	·8	·9	1·0
F	193	44·5	17·8	8·12	4·02	2·08	·95	·39	·09	·00

Here contraction is prevented in three directions, and for small openings the result of this is marked by the reduction in the value of F.

Gate Valve in Circular Pipe (Fig. 111 b).—Let h = ratio of height of opening to diameter of pipe.

h	$\frac{1}{8}$	$\frac{1}{4}$	$\frac{3}{8}$	$\frac{1}{2}$	$\frac{5}{8}$	$\frac{3}{4}$	$\frac{7}{8}$	1·0
F	97·8	17·00	5·52	2·06	·81	·26	·07	·00

[1] Loss = $F c^2 \div 2g$ feet. Results due to Weisbach.

Cock in Cylindrical Pipe (Fig. 112 a).—Here a = area of section through valve : A = area of pipe : θ = angle through which valve is turned.

θ	5°	10°	15°	20°	25°	30°	35°	40°	45°
$\dfrac{a}{A}$	·93	·85	·77	·69	·61	·535	·46	·385	·315
F	·05	·29	·75	1·56	3·1	5·47	9·68	17·3	31·2

θ	50°	55°	60°	65°	82°
$\dfrac{a}{A}$	·25	·19	·14	·09	Valve closed.
F	52·6	106	206	486	—

Throttle Valve in Cylindrical Pipe (Fig. 112 b).—These experiments

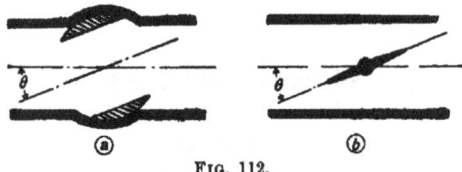

Fig. 112.

were carried out on pipes and valves of slightly under 2 inches diameter.

Experiments on a gate valve for a 24-inch pipe[1] gave values of F as

θ	5°	10°	20°	30°	40°	50°	60°	70°	90°
F	·24	·52	1·54	3·91	10·8	32·6	118	751	—

[1] Kuichling, "Transactions American Society Civil Engineers," 1892, vol. 26.

indicated in the following table :—

$\frac{h}{D}$	$\frac{2}{3}$	$\frac{1}{2}$	$\frac{3}{8}$	$\frac{1}{4}$	$\frac{1}{16}$
F	·8	1·6	3·3	22·7	41·2

This loss due to alteration in area and shape of section is serious in all hydraulic machinery when working at high velocities, and especially in machines of the piston type. Here, for efficiency of working, it is

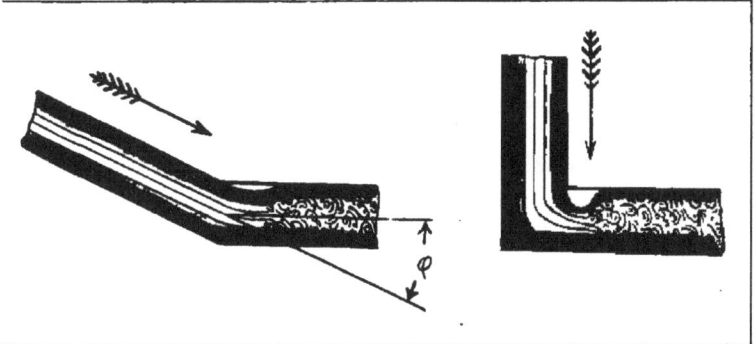

FIG. 113.

above all things important that the velocities should be kept as low as possible.

(4) **Losses at Bends and Elbows.**—Whenever the direction of motion of a stream is abruptly changed, as at a sharp bend or elbow, a loss of head is experienced which appears to be due to the formation of a *vena contracta* on passing the elbow and to the subsequent re-enlargement and shock which then takes place (Fig. 113). With an easy bend, recent experiments[1] by *Dr. Brightmore* show that the state of affairs is very different, the water flowing round the bend with a motion approximating to that in a free vortex, its velocity being greatest at the inside and least at the outside of the bend. In these experiments it was shown that in such a case the loss due to the bend does not occur so

[1] " Proceedings Institute Civil Engineers," 1906–7, vol. 169, p. 315.

much in the bend itself as in the portion of straight pipe immediately following, where the equalisation of velocities in the stream of water gives rise to eddy production. Using cast-iron pipes of 3" and 4" diameter, the loss in the bend itself was found to be almost identical with (sometimes less than) the loss in a corresponding length of straight pipe. From this point of view it is probable that the loss occurring with a bend of uniform curvature will be largely independent of the angle through which the bend is taken, and that a bend of say 45° will cause little less resistance than one of 90°. Also, as is confirmed by experiment, the resistance caused by a reflex bend will be much greater than

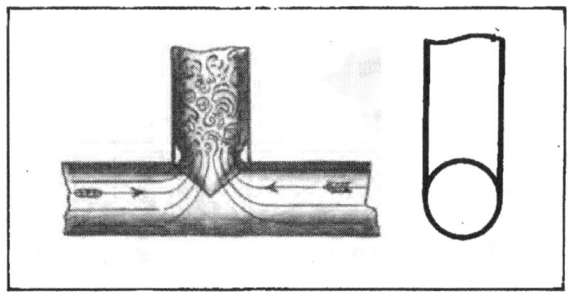

FIG. 114.

that caused by two similar bends having continuous curvature in one direction.

The first experiments of any note on the resistance of bends are due to *Weisbach*, who from experiments on pipes of 1¼ inches diameter, deduced the formula

$$h_B = \text{loss of head due to bend} = F\frac{v^2}{2\,g} \times \frac{\theta^\circ}{180^\circ} \text{ feet,}$$

where θ is the angle through which the bend is carried.

For circular pipes, F has the value $\left[\cdot131 + 1\cdot847 \left(\frac{r}{R}\right)^{\frac{7}{2}} \right]$ where r is the radius of the pipe, and R the radius of the bend.

For pipes of rectangular section, $F = \cdot124 + 3\cdot104 \left(\frac{S}{2\,R}\right)^{\frac{1}{2}}$ where S is the length of side of a section parallel to the radius of curvature of the bend.

These experiments were, however, not numerous and were only carried out on bends of small radius, so that not much reliance is to be placed in the results.

For sharp bends or elbows (Fig. 113), Weisbach deduced the formula

$$\text{Loss} = F \frac{v^2}{2\,g} \text{ feet}$$

where $F = \cdot946 \sin^2 \frac{\theta}{2} + 2\cdot05 \sin^4 \frac{\theta}{2}$,

θ being the angle of deviation of the elbow.

With a tee branch pipe (Fig. 114) the loss is rather greater than in a right-angled elbow (see p. 256).

Recent experiments by the author on elbows of rectangular section, $\frac{1}{2}$ in. $\times$ 1 in., showed the loss to be proportional to v^2 for all velocities up to 22 feet per second, and gave the following values for F:

θ	90°	60°	45°	30°	15°
F. (Author)	1·20	·492	·268	·111	·0240
F. (Weisbach)	·99	·365	·183	·0728	·0222

These correspond to the relationship $F = \cdot0000676\ \theta^{2\cdot17}$ where θ is in degrees. The values are considerably greater than those given by Weisbach's formula, and while the difference may be due to some extent to the difference in the shapes and sizes of the passages, recent experiments on elbows of circular cross section, see p. 254, tend rather to confirm the author's value when $\theta = 90°$.

Experiments by *Alexander*,[1] by *Williams*,[2] and by *Brightmore*,[3] the former using varnished wooden pipes of $1\frac{1}{4}$ inches diameter, Williams using asphalted pipes of 12, 16, and 30 inches diameter, and Brightmore using cast-iron pipes of 3 and 4 inches diameter, indicate that the additional loss due to the curvature of a pipe does not, as might be expected, diminish uniformly as the radius of curvature increases, but, after attaining a minimum value for a value of $R = 5\,r$ (Williams and Alexander), $R = 7\cdot5\,r$ (Brightmore), increases slightly to a point where

[1] " Proceedings Institute Civil Engineers," vol. 159, p. 341.

[2] " Proceedings American Society Civil Engineers," 1901, p. 314.

[3] " Proceedings Institute Civil Engineers," 1906–7, vol. 169, p. 315

$R =$ about 13 r, and afterwards diminishes to zero with a curve of infinite radius. The experiments further show that the power of r, to which the loss is proportional in a gradual bend, is the same for the bend as for the straight pipe. Alexander, as the result of his own and of Williams' experiments, concludes that the additional loss due to a bend of radius $R = 5\, r$, is equivalent to that offered by a length of straight pipe equal to 3·38 l, where l is the length of the curved portion of the pipe. Thus if the angle of the bend is 90° this makes the equivalent length equal to 13·3 d, where $d =$ pipe diameter in feet. This agrees with the results of a number of experiments made at the Yorkshire College,[1] from which it was concluded that the resistance of an easy right-angled bend is equivalent to that in a straight pipe 10 to 15 diameters in length, while for a sharp right-angled bend or elbow the equivalent length is from 30 to 36 diameters.

Brightmore's results point to the fact that for all curves of the best radius, for all diameters of cast-iron pipes and for all velocities, the additional loss of head due to the curvature in a right-angled bend is approximately equal to ·3 $\dfrac{v^2}{2\,g}$ feet.

The following values of F are deduced from Brightmore's results :—

Value of $R \div r$.

—	Vel. f.s.	Elbow.	4	8	12	16	20
Pipe, 3″ diam.	5·0	1·14	·43	·32	·37	·32	·26
,,	7·6	1·26	·43	·32	·40	·33	·19
,,	10·0	1·17	·42	·31	·39	·35	·19

Value of $R \div r$.

—	Vel. f.s.	Elbow.	4	8	12	16	20
Pipe, 4″ diam.	5·0	1·14	·37	·26	·37	·26	·26
,,	7·6	1·19	·38	·30	·31	·27	·21
,,	10·0	1·17	·39	·30	·32	·30	·21

[1] *Engineering*, September 25, 1896, p. 390.

Experiments by *E. W. Schoder*[1] on right-angled bends having radii from 1·34 to 20 pipe diameters, on a 6-inch wrought-iron pipe, give the following approximate values for F. The resistance curves appear to attain a minimum where $R = 10\,r$; rise to a maximum for $R = 14\,r$; attain a second and lower minimum for $R = 30\,r$; and afterwards show increased values as R increases within the limits of the experiments.

Vel. f.s.	$R \div r.$						
	2 68	5	10	15	20	30	40
5	·41	·36	·36	·39	·36	·34	·41
10	·45	·32	·27	·34	·27	·23	·37
16	·49	·36	·34	·38	·32	·28	·40

The general conclusion to be drawn from the foregoing results is that R should be about $30\,r$ for minimum loss of head, while if circumstances forbid the use of bends of such great radius, R should be between 5 and $10\,r$. Values of R less than $5\,r$, or between $10\,r$ and $20\,r$, should be avoided where possible.

Loss of Head in Commercial Screw Pipe Elbows and Tees.—Experiments

LOSS OF HEAD IN COMMERCIAL ELBOWS AND TEES.

(1) Experimenter.	(2) Fitting name and type.	(3) Velocity in pipe feet per second.	(4) Excess loss of head caused by fitting feet of water.	(5) (6) Length of straight pipe required to give same excess loss of head		(7) Value of F in loss of head $= F\,\dfrac{r^2}{2g}$
				(In feet)	(In pipe diameters)	
Rain. . .	¾-inch black mall. elbow (old)	2	0·051	1·54	23	0·82 ⎫
		5	0·29	,,	,,	0·76 ⎬
		10	1·10	,,	,,	0·72 ⎭
,, . . .	¾-inch galv. mall. elbow (new)	2	0·0355	1·08	16	0·57 ⎫
		5	0·206	,,	,,	0·53 ⎬
		10	0·78	,,	,,	0·50 ⎭
,, . . .	1-inch black mall. elbow (old)	2	0·047	1·90	23	0·76 ⎫
		5	0·27	,,	,,	0·70 ⎬
		10	1·02	,,	,,	0·67 ⎭

[1] "Proceedings American Society Civil Engineers," 1908, pp. 34, 416—445.

LOSS OF HEAD IN COMMERCIAL ELBOWS AND TEES (*continued*).

(1) Experimenter.	(2) Fitting name and type.	(3) Velocity in pipe feet per second.	(4) Excess loss of head caused by fitting feet of water.	(5) Length of straight pipe required to give same excess loss of head. (In feet)	(6) (In pipe diameters)	(7) Value of F in loss of head $= F\frac{v^2}{2g}$
Bain . . .	1-inch cast-iron elbow (old)	2 5 10	0·063 0·365 1·37	2·55 ,, ,,	31 ,, ,,	1·02 0·95 0·90
Davis . . .	2-inch mall. iron elbow	2 5 10	0·046 0·28 1·07	4·81 5·82 6·46	28 34 38	0·74 0·72 0·69
,, .	2-inch cast-iron elbow	2 5 10	0·080 0·52 2·04	8·37 10·8 12·3	49 63 72	1·29 1·34 1·32
Daley . . .	3-inch cast-iron elbow	1 5 10 25	0·0088 0·211 0·84 5·15	5·58 6·20 6·67 7·23	20 24 26 28	0·57 0·54 0·54 0·53
,, . . .	4-inch cast-iron elbow	1 5 10 25	0·0107 0·234 0·89 5·10	9·10 ,, ,, ,,	27 ,, ,, ,,	0·69 0·61 0·58 0·54
Schoder . .	6-inch cast-iron elbow	3 5 10 16	0·077 0·195 0·75 1·90	15·3 14·4 14·5 14·7	30 28 29 29	0·55 0·50 0·48 0·48
Davis . . .	2-inch cast-iron tee and plug (water leaving branch)	2 5 10	0·115 0·74 2·92	12·0 15·4 17·6	70 90 102	1·85 1·91 1·88
,, . . .	Same tee (water entering branch)	2 5 10	0·089 0·60 2·52	9·3 12·5 15·2	54 72 88	1·43 1·55 1·63
Daley . . .	3-inch cast-iron tee and plug (water entering branch)	1 5 10 25	0·0392 0·950 3·76 22·65	24·9 27·9 29·8 31·8	96 104 115 123	2·53 2·45 2·43 2·33
,, . . .	Same tee (water leaving branch)	1 5 10 25	0·0242 0·563 2·22 13·40	15·4 16·5 17·6 18·8	59 64 68 73	1·56 1·45 1·43 1·37
,, . . .	3-inch cast-iron tee and dead end (water entering branch)	1 5 10 25	0·0202 0·352 1·41 8·65	12·8 10·6 11·2 12·2	50 41 43 47	1·30 0·91 0·91 0·89

LOSS OF HEAD IN COMMERCIAL ELBOWS AND TEES (*continued*).

(1)	(2)	(3)	(4)	(5) (6) Length of straight pipe required to give same excess loss of head.		(7)
Experimenter.	Fitting name and type.	Velocity in pipe feet per second.	Excess loss of head caused by fitting feet of water.	(In feet)	(In pipe diameters)	Value of F in loss of head $= F \frac{v^2}{2g}$
Daley . . .	Same tee (water leaving branch)	1 5 10 25	0·0161 0·275 1·16 7·40	10·2 8·2 9·2 10·4	40 32 36 40	1·04 0·71 0·75 0·76
,, . .	4-inch cast-iron tee and plug (water entering branch)	1 5 10 25	0·0291 0·600 2·185 11·80	24·8 22·7 21·8 20·1	73 67 64 59	1·88 1·55 1·41 1·22
,, . .	Same tee (water leaving branch)	1 5 10 25	0·0223 0·483 1·82 10·70	18·9 18·3 18·3 19·2	55 54 54 54	1·44 1·24 1·17 1·10
,, . .	4-inch cast-iron tee and dead end (water entering branch)	1 5 10 25	0·0199 0·455 1·75 10·40	16·9 17·4 17·6 17·7	50 51 52 52	1·28 1·25 1·13 1·07
,, . .	Same tee (water leaving branch)	1 5 10 25	0·0175 0·378 1·50 9·20	14·9 14·3 15·1 15·7	44 42 44 46	1·13 0·97 0·97 0·95
,, . .	4-inch cast-iron tee filled in to make a square elbow	1 5 10 25	0·0173 0·427 1·66 10·40	14·7 16·2 16·7 17·7	43 48 49 52	1·12 1·10 1·07 1·07
,, . .	3-inch coupling			0·25	1·0	
,, . .	4-inch coupling			0·65	1·9	

by Professor *E. W. Schoder*, *Messrs. D. H. Daley, P. Bain*, and *G. J. Davis*,[1] on common cast-iron and malleable-iron short turn, screw end elbows and tees in wrought-iron pipe lines give the results shown in the following tables. The range of sizes is from ¾ inch to 6 inches diameter. In these fittings the inside "burr" at the ends of the pipes, caused by the wheel pipe cutter, had been reamed out. Two sets of experiments were carried out with each tee pipe. In the one, a short length of pipe with a

[1] The *Cornell Civil Engineer*, Vol. 20, No. 8, December, 1911.

cap was screwed on to the idle end forming a " dead end," while in the other the idle end of the tee was capped directly by a screw plug.

(5) **Losses at Sudden Changes in Section of the Pipe.**—These have been already considered in Art. 33.

(6) **Losses at the Exit from the Pipe.**—Where a pipe discharges below the surface, it is possible by using a diverging outlet, to convert a certain proportion, up to about $\frac{2}{3}$, of the kinetic energy of pipe flow, into pressure energy. With this exception the whole of the kinetic energy is dissipated in eddy production in the surrounding mass of water.

With a given difference of surface level in the two reservoirs, the depth of immersion of the pipe entrance or of its exit does not in the least affect the flow, since, although the difference of level between entrance and exit is increased by lowering the exit or by reducing the depth of immersion of the inlet, yet the pressure at which the water is discharged is increased, and that at which it enters the pipe line is reduced, by a corresponding amount, so that the effective head producing flow is unchanged.

Where discharge takes place above the free surface, the pressure at the exit is atmospheric, and the energy at this point exists solely in the potential and kinetic form. If h_e represents the height of the outlet above the free surface E, the equation of energy now becomes

$$Z_A - Z_E = {}_A H_E = F\frac{v^2}{2\,g} + h_e,$$

or $Z_A - [Z_E + h_e] = $ loss at entrance + losses in pipe $+ \dfrac{v^2}{2\,g}$, the whole of the kinetic energy being rejected in this case.

Where a pipe is composed of a series of lengths having different diameters, the total loss of head in the pipe will be given by $\Sigma\left(F\dfrac{v^2}{2\,g}\right)$, where $F\dfrac{v^2}{2\,g}$ represents the loss in any length of pipe having the velocity of flow v. Since the velocities in the different sections of the pipe are inversely as the areas of these sections, the whole series of losses can then be expressed in terms of a single velocity, and this having been determined the discharge may be calculated.

As an example of the application of this reasoning to the solution of a specific case consider the following.

EXAMPLE.

A 6-inch main takes water directly out of the side of a reservoir at a depth of 10 feet. At the end of the first mile, in the course of which here are six right-angled bends having a radius of curvature of 6 inches, t is suddenly contracted to 3 inches diameter, and remains of this diameter for 2 miles, until its exit directly into the side of a second reservoir at a point 2 feet below the surface. The difference of surface level in the two reservoirs is 220 feet. Determine the flow through the pipe per minute.

Taking the losses in the order in which they occur we have

(1) Loss at entrance $= \cdot 5 \ \dfrac{v^2{}_1}{2\,g}$ (in eddy formation) where $v_1 =$ velocity in 6-inch pipe.

(2) Frictional losses in one mile of 6-inch pipe. Taking

$f = \cdot 010$ this becomes $\dfrac{f\,l\,v_1{}^2}{2\,g\,m} = \dfrac{\cdot 010 \times 5280 \times v_1{}^2}{2\,g \times \left(\frac{1}{4} \right)}$ feet.

$$= 422 \cdot 4 \ \frac{v_1{}^2}{2\,g} \text{ feet.}$$

(3) Loss at six bends in 6-inch pipe.

$$= 6 \left[\cdot 36 \right] \frac{v_1{}^2}{2\,g} \text{ feet (p. } \cdot 255)$$

$$= 2 \cdot 16 \ \frac{v_1{}^2}{2\,g} \text{ feet.}$$

(4) Loss at sudden change of section.

Assuming a *vena contracta* to be formed of sectional area equal to $\cdot 66$ that of the 3-inch pipe, we have, if v_2 be the velocity in this pipe.

$$\text{Loss} = \frac{v_2{}^2}{2\,g} \left\{ \frac{1}{\cdot 66} - 1 \right\}^2 = \frac{\cdot 266 \ v_2{}^2}{2\,g} \text{ feet.}$$

Since $\dfrac{v_2}{v_1} = \dfrac{6^2}{3^2} = 4$, we have loss at change of section $= 4 \cdot 25 \ \dfrac{v_1{}^2}{2\,g}$ feet.

(5) Friction loss in 3-inch pipe.

This equals $\dfrac{f\,l\,v_2{}^2}{2\,g\,m} = \dfrac{16\,f\,l\,v_1{}^2}{2\,g\,m}$

$$= \frac{16 \times \cdot 01 \times 2 \times 5,280}{\left(\frac{1}{4} \right)} \cdot \frac{v_1{}^2}{2\,g} \text{ feet}$$

$$= 27,033 \cdot 6 \frac{v_1{}^2}{2\,g} \text{ feet.}$$

(6) Loss at exit.

Since the whole of the kinetic energy is thrown away, the loss will be

$$\frac{v_2{}^2}{2\,g} = 16 \ \frac{v_1{}^2}{2\,g} \text{ feet.}$$

s 2

$\therefore$ The total loss of head $\left.\right\} = \dfrac{v_1^2}{2\,g}\,\{\,\cdot 5 + 422\cdot 4 + 2\cdot 2 + 4\cdot 2 + 27,033\cdot 6 + 16\,\}$

$$= 27,479\,\dfrac{v_1^2}{2\,g}\ \text{feet.}$$

Since the pressures at the entrance B and exit D are those corresponding to their depths below the free surfaces, viz., 10 feet and 2 feet, we have, neglecting the velocity before and after leaving the pipe—

Head before entering pipe $= Z_B + 10 = Z_A$.

Head after leaving pipe $= Z_D + 2 = Z_E$.

$\therefore$ Loss of head in pipe $= Z_A - Z_E = 220$ feet.

$$\therefore\ \ 27,479\,\dfrac{v_1^2}{2\,g} = 220$$

$$\therefore\ \ v_1 = \sqrt{\dfrac{64\cdot 4 \times 220}{27,479}} = \cdot 717\ \text{feet per second,}$$

$$\therefore\ \ v_2 = 2\cdot 868\ \text{feet per second.}$$

$$\therefore\ \ \text{Quantity flowing per second} = \dfrac{\cdot 717 \times \pi}{16}\ \text{cubic feet,}$$

$$= \cdot 141\ \text{cubic feet per second.}$$

In gallons per minute this gives $\{\,\cdot 141 \times 6\cdot 24 \times 60\,\}$.

$$= 52\cdot 8\ \text{gallons per minute.}$$

If it be required to find the diameter of pipe necessary to give a certain discharge between two reservoirs, the difference of level in the two reservoirs being fixed, on expressing the fact that the total difference of head is equal to the sum of the pipe losses, we have, if

$l =$ length; $d =$ diameter of pipe; $v =$ velocity of flow;

$H =$ difference of head in reservoirs; $Q =$ quantity required per second in cubic feet.

$$H = \dfrac{K'\,v^2}{2\,g}\ \text{(at entrance)} + \dfrac{4\,f\,l\,v^2}{2\,g\,d}\ \text{(in friction)} + \dfrac{K''\,v^2}{2\,g}\ \text{(at exit).}$$

If we have any bends or obstructions in the pipe, the losses caused by these may all be expressed as $K'''\,\dfrac{v^2}{2\,g}$, so that if $K = (K' + K'' + K''')$ we have
d

$$H = \dfrac{v^2}{2\,g}\left\{K + \dfrac{4\,f\,l}{d}\right\}\ \text{feet.}$$

Also $Q = v \times$ area of pipe, $\therefore v = 4\,Q \div \pi\,d^2$

$$\therefore\ \ H = \dfrac{16\,Q^2}{2\,g\,\pi^2\,d^4}\left\{K + \dfrac{4\,f\,l}{d}\right\}\ \text{feet,}$$

an equation from which the value of d may be obtained by graphical solution, by trial, or by successive approximations.

Art. 73.—Flow in Long Pipes.

A consideration of the preceding example will show that in a long pipe the losses at bends, at entrance and exit, and at changes of section, are usually so small in comparison with the friction losses as to be negligible, so that for a long pipe connecting two reservoirs, the whole resistance may be taken to be given by

$$\Sigma \frac{f\,l\,v^2}{2\,g\,m} = \frac{f}{2\,g} \left\{ \frac{l_1\,r_1^2}{m_1} + \frac{l_2\,r_2^2}{m_2} + \frac{l_3\,r_3^2}{m_3} + - - - \right\} \text{ feet head}$$

r_1, r_2, etc., being the velocities, and m_1, m_2, etc., the hydraulic mean depths, in the lengths l_1, l_2, etc., of the pipe.

In short pipes the losses due to velocity changes become of greater importance as the length of pipe diminishes, and for pipes of lengths less than 100 diameters will, in general, be important.

Art. 74.—Time of Discharge Through an Uniform Pipe Line.

If two reservoirs of area A_1 and A_2 are connected by a single pipe of diameter d and length l, and if v be the velocity in the pipe when h is the difference in surface level in the two reservoirs, we have

$$h = \frac{v^2}{2\,g} \left\{ K + \frac{4\,f\,l}{d} \right\} \text{ feet.}$$

where $K =$ coefficient of loss at entrance and exit.

If the pipe is long this may be written

$$h = \frac{v^2}{2\,g} \left\{ \frac{4\,f\,l}{d} \right\} \text{ without sensible error.}$$

In this case $v = \sqrt{\dfrac{2\,g\,h\,d}{4\,f\,l}}$ feet per second.

Also $-\dfrac{d\,h}{d\,t} =$ relative velocity of surfaces A_1 and A_2

$$= v \cdot \frac{\pi\,d^2}{4} \left\{ \frac{1}{A_1} + \frac{1}{A_2} \right\}$$

$$\therefore \; -\frac{d\,h}{d\,t} = \sqrt{\frac{2\,g\,d}{4\,f\,l}} \cdot \frac{\pi\,d^2}{4} \cdot \left\{ \frac{1}{A_1} + \frac{1}{A_2} \right\} \sqrt{h.}$$

The time ($t_2 - t_1 = t$) necessary to reduce the difference in level from H_1 to H_2 is then got by integrating this expression between the given limits

$$\therefore \; t = \frac{8\,\sqrt{4\,f\,l}}{\pi\,d^2 \left\{ \dfrac{1}{A_1} + \dfrac{1}{A_2} \right\} \sqrt{2\,g\,d}} \left\{ H_1^{\frac{1}{2}} - H_2^{\frac{1}{2}} \right\} \text{ secs.}$$

$$= \frac{2\sqrt{fl}}{\pi \left\{ \dfrac{1}{A_1} + \dfrac{1}{A_2} \right\} d^{\frac{5}{2}}} \left\{ H_1^{\frac{1}{2}} - H_2^{\frac{1}{2}} \right\} \text{ secs.}$$

Thus the time of filling a reservoir A_2 from a second reservoir A_1, whose level remains constant, i.e., $A_1 = \infty$ is given by

$$t = \frac{2\sqrt{fl \cdot A_2}}{\pi d^{\frac{5}{2}}} \left\{ H_1^{\frac{1}{2}} - H_2^{\frac{1}{2}} \right\} \text{ secs.}$$

ART. 75.—Equivalent Diameter of an Uniform Main.

The diameter of an uniform pipe which will give the same discharge as that of a pipe of variable diameter when laid between the same points and under the same conditions as to head, may be determined by equating the resistances of the two pipes.

If l_1, l_2, l_3, etc., be the length of portions of the pipe having diameters d_1, d_2, d_3, etc., and velocities of flow, v_1, v_2, v_3, and if L, D, and V refer to the uniform pipe, we have for the same flow

$$\frac{fLV^2}{2gm} = \frac{f}{2g} \left\{ \frac{l_1 v_1^2}{m_1} + \frac{l_2 v_2^2}{m_2} + \frac{l_3 v_3^2}{m_3} + \text{etc.} \right\} \tag{1}$$

or

$$\frac{LV^2}{D} = \left\{ \frac{l_1 v_1^2}{d_1} + \frac{l_2 v_2^2}{d_2} + \frac{l_3 v_3^2}{d_3} + \text{etc.} \right\} \tag{2}$$

The discharge Q in cubic feet per second is given by

$$\frac{\pi D^2}{4} \cdot V = \frac{\pi d_1^2}{4} \cdot v_1 = \frac{\pi d_2^2}{4} \cdot v_2, \text{ etc.,}$$

$$\therefore V = \frac{4Q}{\pi D^2} : v_1 = \frac{4Q}{\pi d_1^2} : v_2 = \frac{4Q}{\pi d_2^2}, \text{ etc.}$$

So that equation (2) becomes

$$\frac{L}{D^5} = \left\{ \frac{l_1}{d_1^5} + \frac{l_2}{d_2^5} + \frac{l_3}{d_3^5} + \text{etc.} \right\}$$

$$\therefore D = \left\{ \frac{L}{\Sigma \left(\dfrac{l}{d^5} \right)} \right\}^{\frac{1}{5}}.$$

This neglects losses due to the changes of section between the lengths l_1, l_2, etc., and will only be true when the pipe is so long, and the number of changes of section so small or so gradual as to render this loss sensibly negligible.

With a pipe which has a large number of sudden enlargements in the direction of flow, we get

$$\frac{V^2}{2g} + \frac{fLV^2}{2gm} = \frac{f}{2g} \left\{ \frac{l_1 v_1^2}{m_1} + \frac{l_2 v_2^2}{m_2} + \frac{l_3 v_3^2}{m_3} + \text{etc.} \right\}$$

$$+\frac{1}{2\,g}\,\{\,(v_1-v_2)^2+(v_2-v_3)^2+\text{etc.}\,\}\,+\frac{v_1^2}{2\,g}.$$

The last two terms may be written as

$$\frac{1}{2\,g}\,\{\,2\,(v_1^2+v_2^2+\text{etc.}\,)-2\,(v_1\,v_2+v_2\,v_3+v_3\,v_4+\text{etc.})\,\}$$

$$\therefore\frac{V^2}{2\,g}\left\{1+\frac{fL}{m}\right\}=\frac{1}{2\,g}\left[\Sigma\frac{f\,l\,v^2}{m}+2\,\Sigma\,v^2-2\,(v_1\,v_2+v_2\,v_3+\text{etc.})\right]$$

$$\therefore\frac{1+\dfrac{4fL}{D}}{D^4}=\left[\Sigma\frac{4\,f\,l}{d^5}+2\,\Sigma\frac{1}{d^4}-2\left(\frac{1}{d_1^2\,d_2^2}+\frac{1}{d_2^2\,d_3^2}+\text{etc.}\right)\right]$$

from which, when d_1, d_2, d_3, etc., are known, the value of D may be determined.

ART. 76.—BRANCH MAINS.

Where a large main is divided into a number of branches, d_1, d_2, d_3, etc., of different lengths and discharging into reservoirs against different heads, the flow along each of these branches may be determined as follows. Let Fig. 114A represent the arrangement diagrammatically, the reservoir A supplying the pipe a, which in turn supplies the reservoirs B, C, and D through pipes b, c, and d. Let Z_A, Z_B, Z_C, Z_D represent the heights above some common datum,

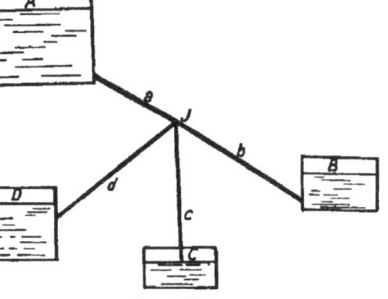

FIG. 114A.

of the free surfaces in the respective reservoirs, and let Z_J represent the height of the junction J. Let v_a, v_b, v_c, etc., represent the velocities in the various pipes, and let A_a, A_b, A_c, etc., represent their areas.

Then

$$Z_A=Z_J+\frac{p_J}{W}+\frac{v_a^2}{2\,g}+{}_AH_J \qquad \begin{cases}\text{where } {}_AH_J \text{ represents the}\\ \text{loss of head from } A \text{ to } J.\end{cases} \qquad (1)$$

Similarly

$$Z_J+\frac{p_J}{W}+\frac{v_b^2}{2\,g}=Z_b+{}_JH_B \qquad (2)$$

$$Z_J+\frac{p_J}{W}+\frac{v_c^2}{2\,g}=Z_c+{}_JH_C \qquad (3)$$

$$Z_J+\frac{p_J}{W}+\frac{v_d^2}{2\,g}=Z_D+{}_JH_D \qquad (4)$$

Also if all the pipes run full we have for continuity of flow

$$A_a \, v_a = A_b \, v_b + A_c \, v_c + A_d \, v_d. \tag{5}$$

Since, in these five equations, the only unknowns are the four velocities and the pressure at J (the losses $_AHj$, $_JII_B$, etc., being determinate in terms of the velocities), the equations are perfectly determinate and a solution will give the velocities in the various pipes in terms of known quantities. The quantities discharged through each pipe may then be determined.

EXAMPLE.

A reservoir A supplies three supplementary reservoirs B, C, D through a single 24-inch pipe divided at J into two 12-inch and one 18-inch pipe leading respectively to reservoirs B, C, and D. If the lengths of these pipes are $l_a = 500$ feet, $l_b = 1,000$ feet, $l_c = 1,500$ feet, $l_d = 3,000$ feet: and if $Z_A = 50$ feet, $Z_B = 30$ feet, $Z_C = 10$ feet, $Z_D = 20$ feet, $Z_J = 40$ feet, determine the velocities of flow in each pipe. Take $f = \cdot005$, and neglect all except friction losses.

Here $_AH_J$ in equation (1) above becomes

$$\frac{\cdot005 \times 500 \times 4 \, v_a^2}{2} \cdot \frac{}{2\,g} = \frac{5 \, v_a^2}{2 \, g}.$$

Determining all such values, and substituting, equations (1) to (5) above become

$$\frac{p_J}{W} + 6 \frac{v_a^2}{2\,g} = 10 \tag{1}$$

$$\frac{p_J}{W} - 19 \frac{v_b^2}{2\,g} = -10 \tag{2}$$

$$\frac{p_J}{W} - 29 \frac{v_c^2}{2\,g} = -30 \tag{3}$$

$$\frac{p_J}{W} - 39 \frac{v_d^2}{2\,g} = -20 \tag{4}$$

$$4 \, v_a = v_b + v_c + 2\cdot25 \, v_d. \tag{5}$$

Subtracting (2) from (1), (3) from (4), and (3) from (2) we eliminate $\frac{p_J}{W}$, and get

$$6 \, v_a^2 + 19 \, v_b^2 = 40 \, g \tag{6}$$

$$29 \, v_c^2 - 39 \, v_d^2 = 20 \, g \tag{7}$$

$$29 \, v_c^2 - 19 \, v_b^2 = 40 \, g \tag{8}$$

Determining v_b, v_c, and v_d in terms of v_a from equations (6), (7), and (8), and substituting these values in (5), this becomes, on writing $g = 32\cdot2$, and simplifying

$$4 \, v_a = \sqrt{67\cdot75 - \cdot316 \, v_a^2} + \sqrt{88\cdot8 - \cdot207 \, v_a^2} +$$
$$2\cdot25 \sqrt{49\cdot5 - \cdot154 \, v_a^2}. \tag{9}$$

Writing this as $4 v_a - \phi(v_a) = F(v_a)$ (where $\phi(v_a)$ is the right-hand side of this equation) and giving v_a the value

6·0 this makes $(F\ v_a) = -7·82$.

Putting $v_a = 6·5$,, ,, $F'(v_a) = -5·13$.

,, $v_a = 7·5$,, ,, $F'(v_a) = +·26$.

Plotting these values of v_a and $F'(v_a)$ we find that $v_a = 7·48$ makes $F'(v_a) = 0$, and therefore satisfies the above equation (9).

Substituting this value of v_a in equations (6), (7) and (8) gives $v_b = 7·08$, $v_c = 8·79$, $v_d = 6·39$, while from equation (1) we have

$$\frac{p_J}{W} = 10 - 6\frac{v_a^2}{2g} = 4·78 \text{ feet of water.}$$

Art. 77.—Multiple Supply.

Where more than one reservoir or source of supply feeds into one common pipe, the surfaces of the water in the supply reservoirs being at different levels, it becomes necessary to determine what share of the total flow each of these sources of supply contributes. *E.g.*, in the case illustrated in Fig. 115 the two reservoirs A and B, with surface levels Z_A and Z_B above datum, feed through pipes of areas A_a and A_b, into a common pipe of area A_c, at J, the joint flow passing into a reservoir at C, with its surface at a height Z_c above datum level.

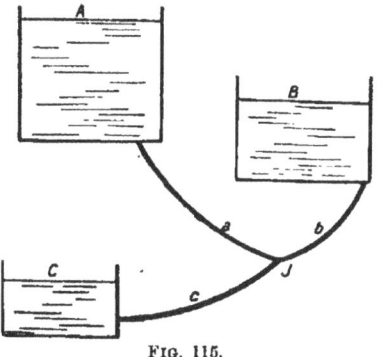

FIG. 115.

Here we have

$$Z_A = Z_J + \frac{p_J}{W} + \frac{v_a^2}{2g} + {}_AH_J \quad \begin{cases} {}_AH_J \text{ representing the} \\ \text{loss from } A \text{ to } J. \end{cases} \quad (1)$$

$$Z_B = Z_J + \frac{p_J}{W} + \frac{v_b^2}{2g} + {}_BH_J \quad (2)$$

$$Z_c + {}_JH_C = Z_J + \frac{p_J}{W} + \frac{v_c^2}{2g} \quad (3)$$

Also if all the pipes run full we have for continuity of flow

$$A_a v_a + A_b v_b = A_c v_c. \quad (4)$$

Then since ${}_AH_J$, ${}_BH_J$, ${}_JH_C$ are respectively proportional to v_a^2, v_b^2, v_c^2, and may be determined in terms of these velocities when the construction and sizes of pipes are known, the only unknowns are the three velocities v_a, v_b, v_c, and the pressure p_J. These equations may then be solved and the unknown factors determined. A similar method of solution will apply to any case of multiple supply, with any number n of sources of supply. Here we shall have $n + 2$ equations formed, from which the $(n + 1)$ velocities and the pressure at the junction may be determined.

ART. 78.—FLOW ALONG A BYE-PASS.

If p_1 and p_2 lbs. per square foot are the pressures in the main pipe at the entrance to and exit from the bye-pass pipe or diversion (Fig. 116), we have, putting V and v for the velocities in the large and small pipes respectively,

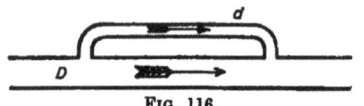

FIG. 116.

$$\frac{p_1 - p_2}{W} = \frac{4 f L V^2}{2 g D} = \frac{4 f l v^2}{2 g d} + K \frac{v^2}{2 g}$$

where $K \dfrac{v^2}{2 g}$ represents the loss in the bye-pass at entrance and exit and at any valves.

From this we have, assuming f to have the same value in the two pipes,

$$\frac{L V^2}{D} = \frac{l v^2}{d} + K' v^2 = \left\{ \frac{l}{d} + K' \right\} v^2$$

$$\therefore \frac{V^2}{v^2} = \frac{D}{L} \left\{ \frac{l}{d} + K' \right\}.$$

If Q and q are the quantities flowing along the two pipes

$$Q = \frac{V \cdot \pi D^2}{4} \qquad q = \frac{v \pi d^2}{4}$$

$$\therefore \frac{Q}{q} = \frac{V D^2}{v d^2} = \sqrt{\frac{D}{L} \left\{ \frac{l}{d} + K' \right\}} \cdot \frac{D^2}{d^2}$$

$$= \sqrt{\left(\frac{D}{d} \right)^5 \cdot \frac{l + K' d}{L}}$$

The proportion of the whole flow which passes along the diversion or $\dfrac{q}{Q + q}$ is given by

$$q = \frac{1}{1 + \sqrt{\left(\dfrac{D}{d} \right)^5 \cdot \dfrac{l + K' d}{L}}} (Q + q).$$

ART. 79.—FLOW THROUGH PIPES COUPLED UP IN PARALLEL (FIG. 117).

Here pipes d_1, d_2, etc., of length l_1, l_2, etc, couple up two vessels whose pressures at the points of exit and inlet are p_1 and p_2 lbs. per square foot. We now have

$$\frac{p_1 - p_2}{W} = 4f\frac{l_1\,r_1^2}{2\,g\,d_1} = 4f\frac{l_2\,r_2^2}{2\,g\,d_2} = 4f\frac{l_3\,r_3^2}{2\,g\,d_3} = \text{etc.,}$$

neglecting all losses except those due to friction.

If $Q =$ total flow through pipes in cubic feet per second, we have

$$Q = \frac{\pi}{4}\left\{r_1\,d_1^2 + r^2\,d_2^2 + r_3\,d_3^2 + \text{etc.}\right\}$$

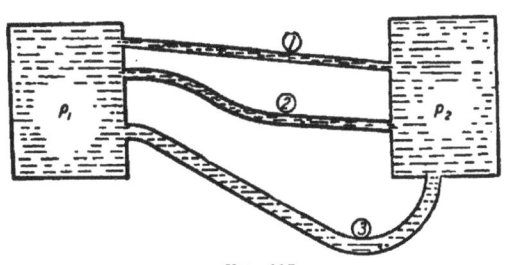

FIG. 117.

$\therefore$ Writing $r\,d^2 = \sqrt{\dfrac{l\,v^2}{d}} \cdot \dfrac{d^{\frac{5}{2}}}{l^{\frac{1}{2}}}$ we get

$$Q = \frac{\pi}{4}\sqrt{\frac{l_1\,r_1^2}{d_1}}\left\{\frac{d_1^{\frac{5}{2}}}{l_1^{\frac{1}{2}}} + \frac{d_2^{\frac{5}{2}}}{l_2^{\frac{1}{2}}} + \frac{d_3^{\frac{5}{2}}}{l_3^{\frac{1}{2}}} + \text{etc.}\right\}.$$

And since $\dfrac{p_1 - p_2}{W} = \dfrac{4f}{2g} \cdot \dfrac{l_1\,v_1^2}{d_1}$, this becomes

$$Q = \frac{\pi}{4}\sqrt{\frac{p_1 - p_2}{W} \cdot \frac{g}{2f}}\left\{\Sigma\frac{d^{\frac{5}{2}}}{l^{\frac{1}{2}}}\right\}.$$

EXAMPLE.

Determine the diameter of a pipe of length l, to give the same discharge as two parallel pipes of the same length and of diameter d.

Discharge from two small pipes $= \dfrac{\pi}{4} \sqrt{\dfrac{p_1 - p_2}{W} \cdot \dfrac{g}{2f}} \left\{ \dfrac{2\, d^{\frac{5}{2}}}{l^{\frac{1}{2}}} \right\}$

„ „ large pipe $= \dfrac{\pi}{4} \sqrt{\dfrac{p_1 - p_2}{W} \cdot \dfrac{g}{2f}} \left\{ \dfrac{D^{\frac{5}{2}}}{l^{\frac{1}{2}}} \right\}$

$\therefore$ For same discharge $D^{\frac{5}{2}} = 2\, d^{\frac{5}{2}}$

$$\therefore D = 2^{\frac{2}{5}}.d = 1\cdot 32\, d.$$

Thus, assuming the resistance to vary as v^2, one pipe 15·84 inches diameter would give the same discharge as two 12-inch pipes.

Assuming more correctly the results of the experiments quoted on p. 222, and taking

$$Q = C \left(\dfrac{H}{l} \right)^{\frac{1}{2}} d^{2\cdot 5\text{s}} = \dfrac{C}{l^{\frac{1}{2}}} \sqrt{\dfrac{p_1 - p_2}{W}}\, d^{2\cdot 5\text{s}},$$

we should have in the above example, $D^{2\cdot 5\text{s}} = 2\, d^{2\cdot 5\text{s}}$

$$\therefore D = 2^{\frac{1}{2\cdot 5\text{s}}} . d = 1\cdot 308\, d.$$

or one pipe 15·70 inches would now give the same discharge as the two 12 inch pipes.

This duplication in parallel of supply pipes is very common in large water supply systems, and is also of use where, in the case of a fire main, the pressure at the nozzle is insufficient to give the required velocity of flow. By coupling a second line of hose between the supply main and the hydrant box, the fall in pressure at the nozzle is much reduced and consequently a higher jet is obtained.

ART. 80.—MAIN OF UNIFORM DIAMETER IN WHICH THE DISCHARGE DIMINISHES AS THE LENGTH INCREASES.

In water mains for domestic supply, the main pipe is tapped at intervals by service pipes, so that the volume carried gradually diminishes. Let the rate of diminution be uniform and equal to q cubic feet per second per foot run of the pipe. Let l be the total length; H the total loss of head in the pipe; Q the initial supply; V the initial velocity of flow. Then the volume passing any point P distant x from the entrance, will be $Q - qx$ c. f. s. Let h_x be the loss of head up to this point.

Then since the loss of head in a length δx at P

$$= \dfrac{f\, l\, v^2}{2\, g\, m} \delta x = \dfrac{f \cdot \delta x \cdot V^2}{2\, g\, m} \left(\dfrac{Q - q\, x}{Q} \right)^2 \text{feet,}$$

the loss h_x, up to $P = \dfrac{f\,V^2}{2\,g\,m\,Q^2} \displaystyle\int_o^x (Q - q\,x)^2\,dx$

$$= \frac{f\,V^2}{2\,g\,m\,Q^2}\left[Q^2\,x - Q\,q\,x^2 + \tfrac{1}{3}\,q^2\,x^3\right]\text{ feet,}$$

and since, if Q_x is the flow at this point, $Q = Q_x + qx$, this can be written

$$h_x = \frac{f\,V^2}{2\,g\,m\,Q^2}\left[Q_x^2\,x - Q_x\,q\,x^2 + \tfrac{1}{3}\,q^2\,x^3\right]\text{ feet,}$$

At the discharge end of the pipe line $Q_x = o$; $q\,x = Q$; $x = l$.

$$\therefore H = \frac{f\,V^2}{2\,g\,m\,Q^2}\cdot\left[\tfrac{1}{3}\,Q^2\right]l = \tfrac{1}{3}\frac{f\,l\,V^2}{2\,g\,m},$$

or the loss of head is one third that occurring in the same pipe line if the flow were uniform instead of gradually diminishing.

Art. 81.—Distribution of Water.

The consumption of water for domestic and trade purposes varies largely from town to town. In Great Britain the domestic supply ranges from about 18 to 25 gallons per head per day, while in the United States the consumption ranges from about 40 to 200 gallons per day. During the summer months the consumption per day may be as much as 40 per cent. greater than the average for the whole year. The hourly fluctuation in demand necessitates a maximum rate of supply about 33 per cent. greater than the average daily rate taken over 24 hours, so that the supply pipes should be sufficiently large to give a temporary supply at least 85 per cent. greater than the yearly average. It is usual to allow for a maximum rate of flow equal to at least twice the mean rate to be anticipated when reasonable increases of population have been taken into account.

In order to render the fluctuating run-off from the catchment area, available for the fluctuating demand, a storage reservoir is necessary to catch and store the run-off when in excess of the temporary demand, and when the average monthly run-off and probable demand is known with fair accuracy, the necessary volume of this may be calculated. Usually the reservoir is at some considerable distance from the town to be supplied, and to avoid laying down a long pipe line to supply water at the maximum hourly rate demanded, and to minimise to some extent the inconvenience caused by a possible break in this line, a smaller "service" reservoir, capable of storing about three day's supply is constructed as near to the town as is convenient, and, if feasible, at a height to permit the service mains to be supplied with water under a pressure of from 100 to 150 feet. Where this is not possible it becomes necessary to adopt some pumping system and to pump water under pressure into the pipes as required.

Where the difference of level between the supply and service reservoirs is great, the whole of the supply pipe line may be put under considerable statical pressure if a valve is fitted at its outlet, and the cost of a pipe line designed to withstand such a pressure may be excessive. With a view of reducing the maximum pressures, the regulating valve may be fitted at the pipe entrance, or one or more small reservoirs—known as **break-pressure reservoirs**—may be provided at suitable intervals in the

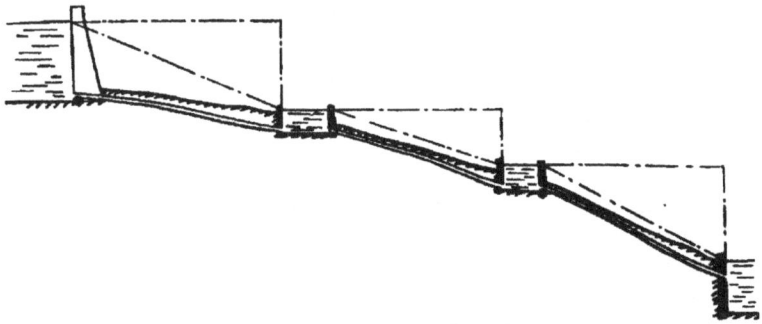

FIG. 118.—Break-Pressure Reservoirs.

line, as shown in Fig. 118. The service level in each of these reservoirs is in the gradient line for the system, and the hydrostatic pressure in any length of the pipe cannot now exceed that due to the next higher reservoir.

In order to reduce the risk of a total stoppage of the supply in case of accident to the supply main, the latter may be laid in duplicate, two pipes of smaller diameter taking the place of the single larger pipe. Where the lines are long, there should be cross connections with valves, so that in case of a break in either line a short section only need be cut out. This gives a greater discharge than would be possible with the line single throughout.

For pipes up to about 24 inches in diameter the cost of the pipe itself, the jointing, excavating, and laying, is roughly proportional to the pipe diameter, and the cost of a twin pipe with cross connections and valves is about 50 per cent. greater than that of a single pipe line. For larger pipes, up to 72 inches diameter, the cost increases more rapidly than the diameter, being roughly proportional to its 1·5th power, and the cost of a twin line is about 30 per cent. greater than that of a single line.

Pipe Line Accessories.—Where the summit of a pipe line approaches the gradient line, and generally at the highest point of each vertical bend, an air valve should be provided to discharge any air which might tend to accumulate. This valve usually takes the form of a ball float which falls as air accumulates and allows it to escape. Fig. 119a shows a small valve of this type, while Fig. 119b shows the type of valve fitted

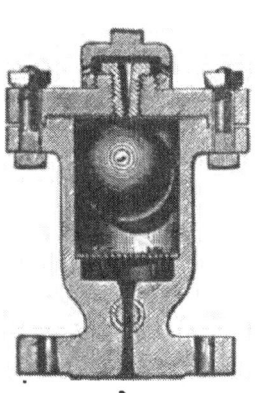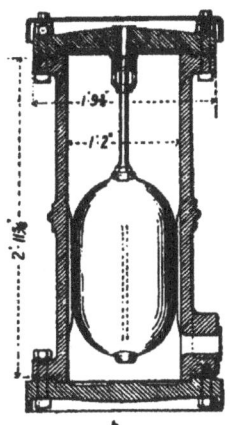

FIG. 119.—Air Valves.

to the 42-inch supply pipe lines of the Loch Leven power works.[1] In the latter case the float, working between guides, carries the air-valve spindle at its upper end, the upper portion of the valve casing serving as an air vessel to reduce shocks in the pipe.

Such valves also serve to admit air to the pipe line and to prevent the formation of a vacuum in case of a rapid eflux of water following a fracture at some lower point of the line. This is of importance in the case of large steel pipes which are usually too thin to withstand an external pressure of any magnitude without collapsing.

To guard against the discharge of water backwards from the main in the case of a fracture occurring in an inverted syphon below the level of the discharge reservoir, or in any similar position, a **reflux valve** is

[1] " Proc. Inst. C.E.," vol. 187., 1911-12, pt. 1, p. 28.

usually introduced at the inlet to a reservoir or near the outlet from such an inverted syphon. This consists of an enlargement in the pipe fitted with a diaphragm pierced with a series of valve openings. These are furnished with flap valves opening in the direction of normal flow, and automatically close if the direction of the current is reversed.

Where serious damage would follow fracture of a main it is usual to fit an **automatic stop valve**. Such a valve is placed, if possible, under comparatively light pressure, near a deep depression in the pipe line. In

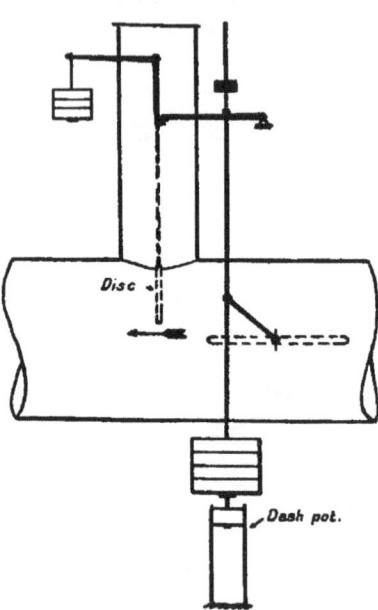

Disc

Dash pot.

FIG. 120.—Automatic Throttle Valve.

this type of valve a disc which is held by a lever, and projects into the water way, is thrown back when the velocity of flow exceeds a predetermined limit. This releases a trigger and an attached weight which closes the valve. The speed of closure may be regulated by means of a dashpot. Such an arrangement is shown diagrammatically in Fig. 120. In other valves of the same class the main valve is of the sluice type with parallel faces and is opened or closed by means of a loaded piston in a hydraulic cylinder surmounting the valve. Water under pressure is admitted to the under or upper side of this piston by a four way valve, actuated either by the release of a trigger as in the former type, or by the motion of a loaded piston in an auxiliary cylinder which is coupled to the main.

Where different parts of a town are at widely different elevations, the head necessary to supply the more elevated sections may lead to an excessive pressure in the more low lying portions of the supply system, and in such a case it is usual to divide the area into zones at respectively lower levels, each zone carrying an independent distribution system fed from the main. The lower zones are then supplied through a series of **reducing valves**, each set to maintain the required maximum pressure in its respective zone. In case of fire it is advisable that the full head be available, and for this purpose the type of reducing valve shown diagrammatically in Fig. 121 has been devised.[1] This consists essentially of a double-beat equilibrium valve whose opening is normally regulated by the pressure on its discharge side. In case of an abnormal draught on the main, such as might occur in case of fire, the pressure falls sufficiently low for the weight W to open the auxiliary valve V, and the under side of the plunger P is put into free communication with the atmosphere. This causes the weight, and the valve, to fall to its lowest limit, giving an uninterrupted flow past the main valve.

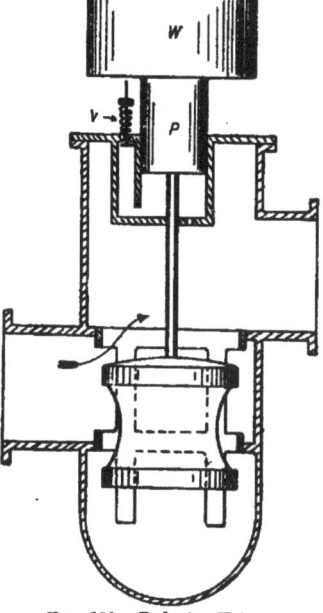

FIG. 121.—Reducing Valve.

Two methods of lay-out are common in the demand area of supply systems. In the first of these a large main is laid through the centre of the district with branch pipes extending from it to form a gridiron covering all parts of the district, the outer ends of these branches being connected by a small main so as to eliminate dead ends.

In the second system, commonly termed the "ring" system, a large main is laid to enclose the district, and from this main branch pipes are taken to form a grid covering the whole area.

If both systems are designed to give the same discharge at the same pressure at all points of the district, the former system usually costs considerably less than the latter, and is to be preferred.

ART. 82.—SYPHONS.

Where a pipe line is to be laid to connect two reservoirs at different levels, over ground which is higher than either water level, the cost of excavation is often so great as to preclude the use of a pipe line which

---

[1] By Mr. G. F. Deacon. This device is used on the distribution system of the Liverpool Water Works.

shall fall below the hydraulic gradient, and in such cases a syphon (Fig. 122) is commonly used.

In its simplest form this consists of an inverted U-tube (Fig. 123), both legs being full of water, and the flow is generally calculated by equating the total head producing flow, *i.e.*, the head due to the unbalanced column of water $Z_A - Z_C$, or the difference of heads in the two reservoirs, to the sum of the frictional and other losses in the pipe and of the velocity head produced.

Thus $Z_A - Z_C =$ loss at entrance and exit $+ \dfrac{f\,l\,v^2}{2\,g\,m}$, l being the total length of the syphon $A'\,B\,C'$.

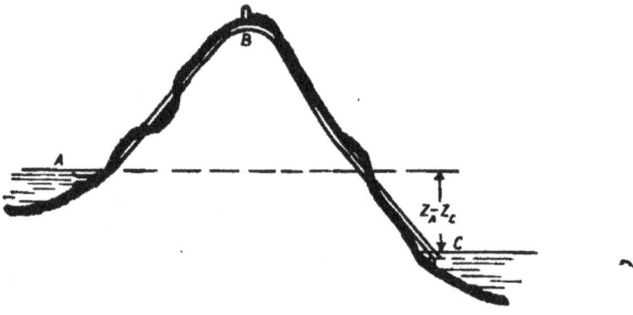

FIG. 122.

This may be seen by considering the flow along each leg of the syphon separately.

Along $A'\,B$, we have

$$\frac{p_{A'}}{W} + Z_{A'} = \frac{p_B}{W} + Z_B + \frac{v^2}{2g} + \frac{fl_{A'B}\,v^2}{2\,g\,m} + \text{loss at entrance,}$$

$$\frac{p_{A'}}{W} + Z_{A'} - Z_B - \frac{p_B}{W} = \frac{v^2}{2g}\left\{1 + \frac{fl_{A'B}}{m} + K\right\}. \tag{1}$$

Along $B\,C'$ we have

$$Z_B + \frac{v^2}{2g} + \frac{p_B}{W} = Z_{C'} + \frac{v^2}{2g} + \frac{p_{C'}}{W} + \frac{fl_{BC'}\,v^2}{2\,g\,m}.$$

$$\therefore Z_B - Z_{C'} + \frac{p_B}{W} = \frac{p_{C'}}{W} + \frac{fl_{BC'}\,v^2}{2g}. \tag{2}$$

$\therefore$ From (1) and (2) we get on adding

$$Z_{A'} - Z_{C'} = \frac{p_{C'} - p_{A'}}{W} + \frac{v^2}{2g}\left\{1 + \frac{fl}{m} + K\right\}$$

But

$$\begin{cases} Z_{A'} + \dfrac{p_{A'}}{W} = Z_A \\[2mm] Z_{C'} + \dfrac{p_{C'}}{W} = Z_C \end{cases}$$

$$\therefore Z_A - Z_C = \frac{v^2}{2\,g}\left\{1 + \frac{f\,l}{m} + K\right\}$$

= loss at exit + friction loss + loss at entrance.

The assumption that both legs of the syphon run full is one which is not always justified in practice. Evidently the height $B\,A$ must be less than the barometric height by an amount — $\dfrac{v^2}{2\,g}\left\{1 + \dfrac{f\,l_{A'B}}{m} + K\right\}$ or we should have an absolute vacuum formed at points below B, and the flow would cease. Theoretically, the limit of possible flow up the inlet leg is reached when the pressure at the summit B is absolute zero (-34 feet of water),[1] and is then given by the equation

$$34 + \frac{p_{A'}}{W} - (Z_B - Z_{A'}) =$$

$$\frac{v_1^2}{2\,g}\left\{1 + \frac{f\,l_1}{m} + K\right\}$$

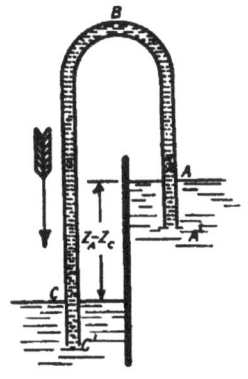

Fig. 123.

Or writing $K = \cdot 5$ and Z_A for $Z_A + \dfrac{p_{A'}}{W}$ we get

$$34 - (Z_B - Z_A) = \frac{v_1^2}{2\,g}\left\{1\cdot 5 + \frac{f\,l_1}{m}\right\}$$

the suffix (1) referring to the inlet leg.

If the actual flow is less than this, p_B is greater than zero, and we get an additional head aiding the flow down the outlet leg.

The velocity of flow down the outlet leg with maximum flow up the inlet is given by the equation

$$Z_B - Z_C - 34 = \frac{f\,l_2\,v_2^2}{2\,g\,m}$$

the suffix (2) referring to this leg.

If the syphon is to run full, we must have v_2 not greater than v_1

i.e.,
$$\frac{2\,g\,m}{f\,l_2}\left\{Z_B - Z_C - 34\right\} \not> \frac{2\,g\,m}{1\cdot 5\,m + f\,l_1}\left\{34 - (Z_B - Z_A)\right\}$$

[1] Actually less than this, because of liberation of air at low pressures.

or

$$\frac{(Z_B - Z_C) - 34}{34 - (Z_B - Z_A)} \not> \frac{f\, l_2}{1\cdot 5\, m + f\, l_1}$$

If the syphon be long, so that $1\cdot 5\, m$ may be neglected in comparison with $f\, l_1$ we have

$$\frac{(Z_B - Z_C) - 34}{34 - (Z_B - Z_A)} \not> \frac{l_2}{l_1}$$

or

$$\frac{Z_A - Z_C}{34 - (Z_B - Z_A)} \not> \frac{l_1 + l_2}{l_1}$$

$$\therefore \frac{l_1}{l} \not> \frac{34 - (Z_B - Z_A)}{(Z_A - Z_C)}$$

Example.

If
$$\begin{cases} Z_A - Z_C = & 50 \text{ ft.} \\ \qquad\quad l = 1{,}000 \text{ ft.} \\ Z_B - Z_A = & 10 \text{ ft.} \end{cases}$$

$$l_1 \not> \frac{1{,}000 \times 24}{50} = 480 \text{ ft.}$$

or the outlet leg will not run full if the inlet leg is more than 480 feet in length.

With a longer inlet and shorter outlet the flow up the inlet will not be able to keep pace with that down the outlet, and this will then run only partly full. Also the velocity up the inlet will not now be so great as with a shorter inlet, so that the discharge will be less. Evidently, then, the position of the apex of the syphon has a great influence on the discharge.

With a shorter inlet and a longer outlet, the total length being the same, the discharge will be unaltered, but the syphon will have the advantage of working under a greater absolute pressure at the apex, and is therefore less likely to be affected by air leakage at the joints.

In practice it is necessary to place an air chamber at the highest point of the syphon, into which air gradually accumulates during its working. This air is then removed at frequent intervals, either by some form of air pump, or by means of a steam ejector.

Where the syphon discharges into the atmosphere, any failure of the outlet leg to run full, by admitting air to the apex at once breaks the vacuum and stops the flow.

Figure 124 shows the hydraulic gradient for a syphon, the straight line $A\,C$ being the gradient line. In drawing this the only losses taken into account have been those due to friction. If a second line $A'\,C'$ be drawn parallel to and at a vertical distance from $A\,C$ equal to the barometric

eight, the distance of the syphon below A' C' will give the absolute
pressure at any point. In the sketch, syphons A B_1 C, A B_2 C, and
A B_3 C are shown connecting A and C, all rising to the same height h,
above the surface at A. Here, although B_2 is not nearly 34 feet above
A, an absolute vacuum would be attained before reaching B_2 and the
syphon will consequently not work. A comparison of ① and ③ shows
that there is a greater pressure in the air vessel at B_1 than at B_3, and
the syphon ① will thus run longer without removal of air from this

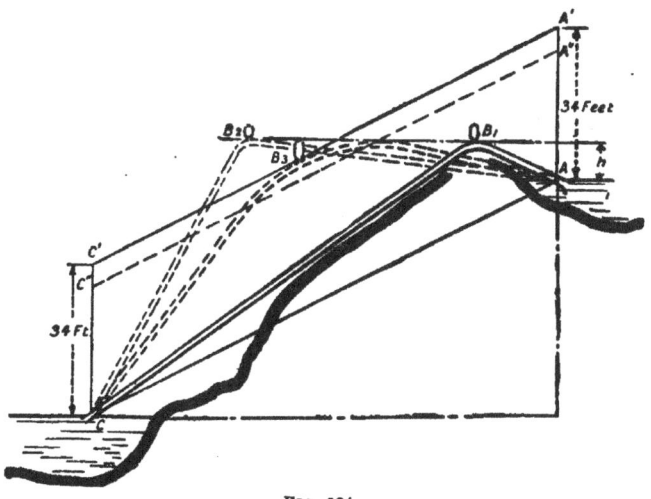

FIG. 124.

chamber than will ③. ' Leakage at joints is not likely to have so serious
an effect as with ③.

Any accumulation of air at the highest part of the pipe has the effect
of increasing the pressure, and hence of lowering the line A' B'. Directly
this line is lowered sufficiently to cut the pipe line the syphon ceases to
flow. The air vessel should always be placed at the point of least
pressure, $i.e.$, at the point nearest to the hydraulic gradient line A' C'.

If A' $A'' = C'$ $C'' = \dfrac{v^2}{2\,g}$, the line A'' C'' will give the hydraulic gradient

taking into account change of potential into kinetic energy at the
entrance to the pipe. The effect of this is to reduce the value of the
ratio A B : B C, for both branches of the syphon to run full with

maximum discharge, while the true pressure in the pipe is now measured by the vertical distance between A'' C'' and the pipe line.

Where a regulating valve is to be used on a syphon, this should always be placed on the outlet leg.

Art. 83.—Inverted Syphon.

Where the pipes connecting two reservoirs cross a deep valley it is usual to use an inverted syphon (Fig. 125). The main pipe line is led into a storage tank at A, and out of a second tank at C, the connection between A and C being made by means of the inverted syphon. This has the advantage of reducing the maximum pressure which may be

FIG. 125.

brought to bear on the pipe line by the sudden closing of a valve, since the pressure at A cannot now exceed that of the atmosphere.

Here, as in the case of the ordinary syphon, the velocity of flow is given by

$$Z_A - Z_C = \frac{v^2}{2\,g}\left\{1 + \frac{f\,l}{m} + K\right\}$$

or if $Z_A - Z_C = H$

$$v = \sqrt{\frac{2\,g\,H}{\left(1 + \frac{f\,l}{m} + K\right)}}.$$

With an inverted syphon, an automatic valve should always be placed at the entrance, so that if, due to the bursting of a pipe, the velocity of flow attains more than its normal value, water may be automatically cut off from the pipe line.

Art. 84.—Flow through Nozzle at end of Pipe Line.

Where a supply of water moving with a high velocity is required, as for fire extinguishing, or for the jets of an impulse turbine or Pelton wheel, a converging nozzle is fitted to the delivery end of the supply pipe. (See also Art. 126.)

The issuing jet now possesses high velocity and its store of energy is almost entirely in the kinetic form.

Theoretically, if pointed vertically upwards, and if no energy losses were experienced, the height of the jet would be the same as that of the free surface of the supply reservoir, or that corresponding to the pressure head inside the nozzle. The various frictional resistances, however, reduce the nozzle pressure and the issuing velocity, after which the resistance of the air and that due to the impact of falling particles of water tend to retard the upward motion of the rising particles, so that the height to which the jet rises is considerably less than that given by

$$h = \frac{v^2}{2\,g},$$ v being the velocity of efflux.

The following results are deduced from experiments carried out by *J. T. Fanning*[1] with ordinary converging fire nozzles and with a stream slightly inclined to the vertical, so that the effect of the falling particles would not be so great as with a vertical stream.

Nozzle diameter.	Pressure at Nozzle.	Measured Velocity of Efflux.	Velocity theoretically corresponding to Trajectory.	Percentage, Actual, of theoretical height.
1 inch	46·5 lbs. per sq. inch	83·1 ft. per sec.	67·0 ft. per sec.	81·0 %
1 ,,	130·0 ,, ,, ,,	127·1 ,, ,,	80·0 ,, ,,	63·0 %
1⅛ ,,	44·5 ,, ,, ,,	79·9 ,, ,,	67·0 ,, ,,	84·0 %
1⅛ ,,	103 0 ,, ,, ,,	120·8 ,, ,,	80·0 ,, ,,	66·3 %
1¼ ,,	43·0 ,, ,, ,,	80·0 ,, ,,	67·0 ,, ,,	84·0 %
1¼ ,,	93·3 ,, ,, ,,	120·0 ,, ,,	80·0 ,, ,,	66·6 %
1⅜ ,,	41·5 ,, ,, ,,	79·6 ,, ,,	67·0 ,, ,,	83·0 %
1⅜ ,,	88·0 ,, ,, ,,	116·9 ,, ,,	80·0 ,, ,,	66·6 %

Forms of Nozzle.—These are usually of circular section and may either converge uniformly to a short parallel neck at the orifice (Fig. 126a), or

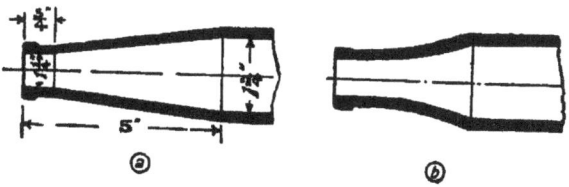

FIG. 126.

have a convergence which becomes more gradual as the outlet is approached (Fig. 126b).

[1] *Engineering News*, July 14, 1892.

In either case, the coefficient of contraction is unity, and the coefficient of discharge about ·98.

The following values of the latter coefficient are deduced from experiments by *Freeman*[1] on smooth conical nozzles.

Diameter of nozzle . .	¾ in.	⅞ in.	1 in.	1⅛ in.	1¼ in.
Value of C	·983	·982	·972	·976	·971

A form known as the ring nozzle is used to a less extent, and consists of a converging nozzle having a circular orifice, which is fitted with a short annular ring of square section (Fig. 126a). This, with a ring ⅛-inch square, gives a stream having a *vena contracta* of area about ·764 times that of the orifice. The value of C_v is about ·97, the coefficient of discharge being about ·74. Since the efficiency of a nozzle depends entirely on the value of its coefficient of velocity C_v the ring nozzle would appear to have no advantage over the ordinary smooth nozzle, and in practice, with the same pressure head and size of nozzle, throws a jet to a slightly less height. It has been proposed to use a small re-entrant mouthpiece, so as to form a Borda orifice in connection with this nozzle

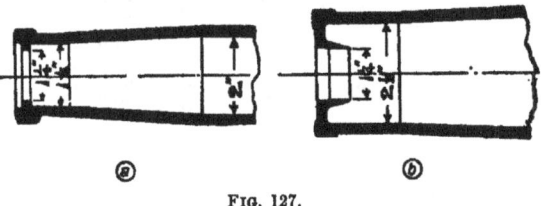

FIG. 127.

(Fig. 127b), and to use this as a standard nozzle to experimentally determine the horse-power of a pumping engine, by measuring the pressure inside a nozzle or series of nozzles supplied by the engine. The coefficient of discharge of such a nozzle as shown in Fig. 127b is given by Freeman as ·582. Since, however, the ordinary type of nozzle shown in Fig. 126 a and b may be relied upon to give discharges which are identical within the limits of practical measurement under given pressure con-

[1] Appendix, Table D.

ditions, certainly within 1 per cent., these nozzles are very satisfactory for such a purpose, this accuracy being quite as high as that attending the use of a standard weir for measuring purposes.

The form of nozzle used in connection with the Pelton wheel is discussed in Arts. 125 and 126.

Velocity of Flow through a Nozzle.

Let A, L, and v_A refer to the supply pipe, and a and v_a to the nozzle

Then $\dfrac{v_A}{v_a} = \dfrac{a}{A}$.

If H = supply head in feet we have

$$H = K\frac{v_A^2}{2g} + \frac{f\,l\,v_A^2}{2\,g\,m} + \frac{v_a^2}{2g} + k\,\frac{v_a^2}{2g}$$

where K and k represent the coefficients of loss at the entrance to the pipe and at the nozzle.

Putting $v_A = v_a \cdot \dfrac{a}{A}$ we get

$$H = \left\{ K\frac{a}{A} + \frac{f\,l\,a^2}{m\,A^2} + 1 + k \right\} \frac{v_a^2}{2g}$$

$$\therefore v_a = \sqrt{\frac{2\,g\,H}{1 + k + K\dfrac{a}{A} + \dfrac{f\,l\,a^2}{m\,A^2}}} \tag{1}$$

Since $k = {}\cdot05$ (approximately), while $K\dfrac{a}{A}$ is in general small, neglecting these terms we get

$$v_a = \sqrt{\frac{2\,g\,H}{1 + \dfrac{f\,l\,a^2}{m\,A^2}}} = \sqrt{\frac{2\,g\,H}{1 + \dfrac{4\,f\,l\,d^4}{D^5}}} \tag{2}$$

If p = pressure in pounds per square inch at the entrance to the nozzle and if $\dfrac{k\,v_a^2}{2g}$ = loss in nozzle

$$\frac{p \times 144}{W} + \frac{v_A^2}{2g} = \frac{v_a^2}{2g}(1 + k)$$

$$\therefore \ 2\cdot3\,p = \frac{v_a^2}{2g}\left\{ 1 + k - \frac{a^2}{A^2} \right\}$$

$$\therefore \ v_a = \sqrt{\frac{4\cdot6\,p\,g}{1 + k - \dfrac{a^2}{A^2}}} \tag{3}$$

This formula may be used to determine k, and hence the coefficient of velocity $\sqrt{(1 - k)}$, by measurement of p and of the quantity discharged.

With a ring nozzle the preceding formula becomes

$$v_a = \sqrt{\frac{4 \cdot 6 \, p \, g}{1 + k - \frac{a_c^2}{A^2}}} \qquad (4)$$

where a_c is now the area of the *vena contracta* of the issuing stream.

In any case, when k and the coefficient of contraction for any given nozzle are known, the value of v_a can be directly determined in terms of p. Then since the energy discharged at the nozzle per second

$$= \frac{W \, a_c \, v_a^3}{2 \, g} \text{ ft. lbs.,}$$

we have the horse-power delivered at the nozzle given by

$$\text{H. P.} = \frac{W \, a_c \, v_a^3}{2 \, g \times 550} = \frac{62 \cdot 4 \, a_c \, v_a^3}{1,100 \, g} = \cdot 00176 \, a_c \, v_a^3$$

$$= 3 \cdot 17 \, a_c \left\{ \frac{p}{1 + k - \frac{a_c^2}{A^2}} \right\}^{\frac{3}{2}}. \qquad (5)$$

EXAMPLE.

With a uniformly converging nozzle, $1\frac{1}{2}$ inch diameter, taking $k = \cdot 03$, and assuming a supply pipe of 3 inches diameter, we have $a_c = a = $ area of $1\frac{1}{2}$ inch pipe $= \cdot 01227$ square feet, while $\frac{a_c^2}{A^2} = \frac{1}{4}$. Thus if the pressure at the nozzle is 80 lbs. per square inch, we have

$$\text{H.P. at nozzle} = 3 \cdot 17 \times \cdot 01227 \left\{ \frac{80}{1 \cdot 03 - \cdot 25} \right\}^{\frac{3}{2}}$$

$$= \cdot 0389 \left\{ 102 \cdot 7 \right\}^{\frac{3}{2}}$$

$$= 40 \cdot 5 \text{ H. P.}$$

If water is supplied at the pipe entrance under a constant pressure P lbs. per square foot, neglecting the difference in head between pipe entrance and nozzle, we have $\frac{P}{W} = H$,

$$\therefore \quad v_a = \sqrt{\frac{2 \, g \, H}{\left(1 + \frac{4 \, f \, l \, d^4}{D^5} \right)}} \text{ ft. per sec.}$$

Without the nozzle we should have $a = A$, $v_a = v_A$,

and

$$v_A = \sqrt{\frac{2 \, g \, H}{1 + \frac{4 \, f \, l}{D}}} \text{ ft. per sec.}$$

so that the velocity with, is greater than without the nozzle.

The discharge per second without the nozzle is given by

$$v_A \times A = \sqrt{\frac{2 g H}{1 + \frac{4 f l}{D}}} \times A \text{ cub. ft.,}$$

and the kinetic energy by $\frac{v_A^2}{2 g}$. $A \times 62{\cdot}4$ ft. lbs.

$$= \left\{ \frac{2 g H}{1 + \frac{4 f l}{D}} \right\}^{\frac{3}{2}} \cdot \frac{62{\cdot}4}{2 g} A \text{ ft. lbs.}$$

With the nozzle, the quantity per second is

$$v_a \times a = \sqrt{\frac{2 g H}{1 + \frac{4 f l d^4}{D^5}}} \times a$$

$$\therefore \quad \frac{Q \text{ with nozzle}}{Q \text{ without nozzle}} = \sqrt{\frac{\dfrac{D^5}{(D^5 + 4 f l d^4)} \left\{ \dfrac{\pi^2 d^4}{16} \right\}}{\dfrac{D}{(D + 4 f l)} \left\{ \dfrac{\pi^2 D^4}{16} \right\}}}$$

$$= \sqrt{\frac{d^4 (D + 4 f l)}{(D^5 + 4 f l d^4)}} = \sqrt{\frac{D d^4 + 4 f l d^4}{D^5 + 4 f l d^4}}$$

or the quantity passing the pipe is always less with, than without the nozzle.

Since the kinetic energy varies as the product of two factors (the quantity and the (velocity)²), one of which increases, while the other diminishes as the nozzle area is increased, a maximum amount of kinetic energy will be delivered at the nozzle with some definite ratio of pipe and nozzle areas.

To obtain this ratio we have

K.E. with nozzle $= \dfrac{v_a^2}{2 g} \times 62{\cdot}4 \, a$ ft. lbs. per sec.

$$= \left\{ \frac{2 g H}{1 + \frac{4 f l d^4}{D^5}} \right\}^{\frac{3}{2}} \times \frac{62{\cdot}4 \, \pi \, d^2}{2 g \times 4}$$

$$= 395 \, d^2 \left\{ \frac{H}{1 + \frac{4 f l d^4}{D^5}} \right\}^{\frac{3}{2}} \text{ ft. lbs. per sec.} \qquad (6)$$

$$= 895 \frac{a}{A} D^2 \left\{ \frac{H}{1 + \frac{4 f l}{D} \cdot \frac{a^2}{A^2}} \right\}^{\frac{3}{2}} \text{ ft. lbs. per sec.} \qquad (7)$$

Differentiating this with respect to $\frac{a}{A}$, and equating the result to zero[1] we have the condition that the K. E. should be a maximum. This gives[1]

$$\left\{\frac{d}{D}\right\}^4 = \frac{D}{8 f l}$$

or

$$\frac{a}{A} = \sqrt{\frac{D}{8 f l}}$$

the dimensions being taken in feet.

If for example the pipe supplying the nozzle of a Pelton wheel be 1 foot in diameter and 500 feet long, the maximum K. E. is delivered when

$$\frac{a}{A} = \sqrt{\frac{1}{8 \times 500 f}}$$

and if $f = {\cdot}01$ this becomes

$$\frac{a}{A} = \sqrt{\frac{1}{40}} = {\cdot}158.$$

By substituting this value of $\frac{a}{A}$ or of $\frac{d^2}{D^2}$ in equation (7) above, the value of this K. E. is given.

Thus (K. E.)$_{max.}$

$$= 395 \times {\cdot}158 \left\{\frac{H}{1 + \frac{4 \times {\cdot}01 \times 500 \times ({\cdot}158)^2}{1}}\right\}^{\frac{3}{2}} \quad \text{ft. lbs. per sec.}$$

$$= 62{\cdot}4 \left\{\frac{H}{1{\cdot}50}\right\}^{\frac{3}{2}}$$

$$= 34 \, H^{\frac{3}{2}} \text{ ft. lbs. per second.}$$

If the Pelton wheel have an efficiency of 80 per cent. the work done by the wheel per second will be given by

$${\cdot}8 \times 34 \, H^{\frac{3}{2}} \text{ ft. lbs.}$$

$$= \frac{27{\cdot}2}{550} H^{\frac{3}{2}} \text{ horse-power}$$

$$= {\cdot}0495 \, H^{\frac{3}{2}} \text{ horse power.}$$

[1] $\dfrac{d\,(K\,E)}{d\left(\dfrac{a}{A}\right)} = \left(1 + \dfrac{4 f l}{D} \cdot \dfrac{a^2}{A^2}\right) - \dfrac{a}{A} \times \dfrac{3}{2} \sqrt{1 + \dfrac{4 f l}{D} \cdot \dfrac{a^2}{A^2}} \times 8 \dfrac{f l}{D} \cdot \dfrac{a}{A}.$

Equating this to zero we have

$$\frac{12 f l}{D} \cdot \frac{a^2}{A^2} = 1 + \frac{4 f l}{D} \frac{a^2}{A^2}$$

$$\therefore \quad \frac{a^2}{A^2} = \frac{D}{8 f l}.$$

With a circular nozzle this makes $d = \sqrt[4]{\dfrac{D^5}{8 f l}}$

Thus with a head of 100 feet the wheel would develop 49·5 horse-power.

As the nozzle area is increased, starting from zero, the power developed thus increases to a maximum of 49·5 H.P. with a nozzle opening $a = ·158 A$, and then again diminishes.

If in the above problem f be taken $= ·005$, we get the maximum K. E. when $\frac{a}{A} = ·224$. The value of this K. E. $= 48·1 H^{\frac{3}{2}}$ foot lbs. per second, so that with the same head and wheel efficiency the maximum power developed would be 70·0 H.P.

In a fire nozzle, the problem is to obtain a stream moving with as high a velocity as possible, and this is evidently to be obtained by making the expression $\left[1 + k + K\frac{a}{A} + \frac{f l a^2}{m A^2} \right]$, the denominator of the fraction expressing the velocity, as small as possible. This is done by increasing, as far as practicable, the ratio $\frac{A}{a}$.

In the case of the supply to a Pelton wheel, a stream carrying the maximum possible amount of kinetic energy is required, and as just demonstrated, this can only be obtained by having a correct ratio of pipe and nozzle area. With a smaller nozzle area the weight issuing per second is unduly restricted, while with a greater area the loss due to increased friction in the pipe, due to the greater velocity of flow, causes the velocity of efflux to be reduced to such an extent as to more than counterbalance the increased weight passing the nozzle.

This fact may be of importance in the regulation of a Pelton wheel, which regulates its supply of water by automatic opening or throttling at the nozzle (see Art. 125).

So long as this nozzle area has less than the critical value for the particular pipe, any further opening will admit more water and a greater supply of kinetic energy to the wheel. Above this point any further opening of the valve admits more water, but gives a smaller supply of kinetic energy to the wheel, which will consequently slow down. On the other hand, with a nozzle area greater than the critical value, throttling leads to an increased supply of energy being given to the wheel and to an increased speed.

For successful governing the maximum nozzle area should not exceed that corresponding to the critical value, so that everywhere within the range of opening $\frac{d(K E)}{d(a)}$ may be positive, and the supply of energy may increase with the nozzle opening. The curves (Fig. 128) derived from equation (6) of this article, show the kinetic energy (expressed as horse-power) delivered from pipes of diameters 1·0 and 2·0 feet, 1,000 feet long, under a head of 200 feet, with different values of the ratio $\frac{a}{A}$. The value of f has been taken at ·005. In each case the maximum nozzle opening for successful governing is that corresponding to the point E.[1] These

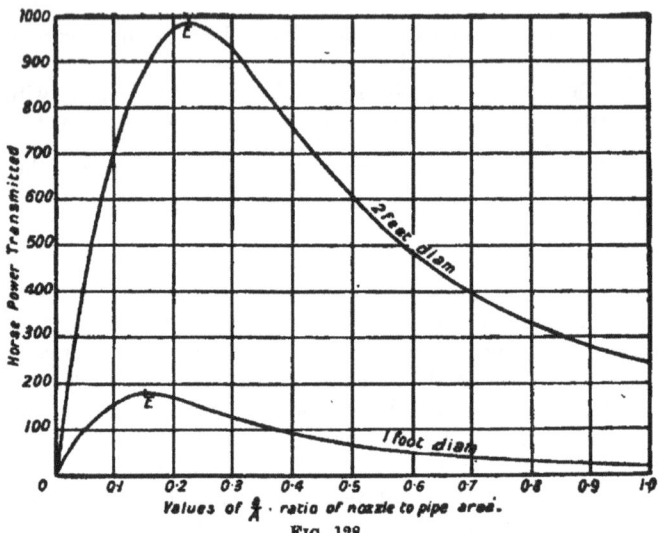

FIG. 128.

curves are worth study as denoting the great increase in available energy with the larger pipes.

While the above investigation is interesting, it is not usual, in a well-designed pipe line, to come across a case in which the nozzle area is greater than the maximum for successful governing since this would entail a velocity of flow in the main much greater in general than that (3 to 6 feet per second) adopted in practice.

EXAMPLES.

(1) Two reservoirs are connected by a pipe 500 yards long. For the first 250 yards its diameter is 4 inches, increasing for the second 250

---

[1] For a further consideration of this subject see an article by Professor John Goodman in *Engineering*, November 4, 1904.

yards to 8 inches. A re-entrant mouthpiece is fitted at the entrance, while discharge takes place directly into the side of the lower reservoir at a depth of 6 feet below the surface. If the difference in the surface level in the reservoirs is 10 feet, determine the discharge in gallons per minute. $f = \cdot005$.

Answer. 121 gallons per minute.

(2) A gate valve in a 12-inch cylindrical C. I. pipe is lifted through $\frac{2}{3}$ of its full opening. Determine the equivalent length of a straight pipe offering the same resistance. $f = \cdot005$.

Answer. $l = 276$ feet.

(3) Two reservoirs of 80,000 and 10,000 square feet area are connected by a 6-inch pipe, 500 feet long. Initially, the difference of surface level is 16 feet. Determine how soon the level in the two reservoirs will be the same. Take $f = \cdot0075$.

Answer. About 69 hours.

(4) Two reservoirs, surfaces 15 and 25 feet above a common datum feed through a 12-inch and an 18-inch pipe respectively, into a common 24-inch pipe at a height 5 feet above datum level, while this in turn feeds a reservoir whose surface level is taken as datum. If the lengths of the 12-inch, 18-inch, and 24-inch pipes are respectively 1,000 feet, 1,500 feet, and 2,000 feet, determine the velocity of flow in and the discharge through each pipe, neglecting all losses of head except those due to friction. Also determine the pressure at the junction of the three pipes. Take $f = \cdot005$.

Answer.
$$\begin{cases} \text{12 in. pipe.} & v = 4\cdot62 \text{ f.s.} & Q = 3\cdot62 \text{ c.f.s.} \\ \text{18 ,, ,,} & v = 7\cdot22 \text{ f.s.} & Q = 12\cdot76 \text{ c.f.s.} \\ \text{24 ,, ,,} & v = 5\cdot21 \text{ f.s.} & Q = 16\cdot38 \text{ c.f.s.} \\ \multicolumn{3}{c}{\text{Pressure at junction} = 3\cdot03 \text{ ft. of water.}} \end{cases}$$

(5) Assuming $Q \propto \sqrt{\dfrac{H}{l}}\, d^{2\cdot58}$ determine the discharge from a 12-inch pipe, if a similar 8-inch pipe of half the length gives a discharge of 10,000 gallons per hour under the same head.

Answer. 20,153 gallons per hour.

(6) A pumping engine supplies water at a pressure of 75 lbs. per square inch through a short pipe 20 inches diameter to a hydrant box, from which it is discharged by four parallel nozzles 2 inches in diameter. Taking the coefficient of loss in the nozzles to be $\cdot03$, determine the water horse-power of the engine.

Answer. 181 horse-power.

(7) The difference of surface level in two reservoirs which are connected

by a syphon is 25 feet. The length of the syphon is 2,000 feet and its diameter is 12 inches. Assuming $f = \cdot005$, and that the syphon runs full, determine the discharge. Also if the vertex of the pipe line is 16 feet above the surface level in the upper reservoir, determine the maximum length of inlet leg for the pipe to run full. Neglect all but friction losses.

Answer. $Q = 4 \cdot 99$ c.f.s.

$= 1,865$ gallons per minute.

Maximum length of inlet $= 1,440$ feet.

CHAPTER X.

ART. 85.—FLOW IN AN OPEN CHANNEL.

THE term "open channel" includes all rivers, artificial canals, aqueducts, and conduits, and, in addition, sewers and pipes of whatever section which run partially full, and which consequently do not present a solid boundary to every side of the contained liquid. The force producing flow cannot now be provided by any external head, but is solely due to the slope or gradient of the channel.

If a circular pipe be laid almost horizontally and if the surface level of water flowing through the pipe be allowed to rise, the change from the state in which the flow is governed by the laws appertaining to an open channel, to that in which the ordinary laws of pipe flow hold, is not abrupt, and it is to be inferred that a general formula is deducible which by satisfactory adjustment of constants shall fit either type of flow.

Still, the comparative simplicity of the conditions holding in the case of a circular pipe, the complications which must of necessity be introduced where water flows through a channel of uneven section, and the ease with which accurate observations are made in the one case and the difficulty with which even such a fundamental observation as the difference in level at points widely distant is accurately determined in the other, render it impossible that the laws governing the flow in open channels should be so definite and of such universal application as those already considered.

Assuming the resistance, R, to flow, to be proportional to the wetted perimeter P of the channel, this may be expressed as

$$R = f' \, S \, v^n,$$

where f' is a coefficient depending on the condition of the surface and probably, from analogy to pipe flow, also on the velocity v, while n is a number probably varying from 1·79 to 2·00, depending on the surface and on the velocity v, and $S = P \times l$, where $l =$ length of channel.

U

If A = sectional area of channel beneath water line, and if we assume the resistance to be equally divided over the area we have, if p = resistance per unit area of the stream

$$p = f' \cdot \frac{P}{A} \cdot l\, v^n.$$

Here $\frac{A}{P}$, or m is the hydraulic mean depth of the section.

If the channel be of uniform slope $\frac{h}{l}$, where $\frac{h}{l} = i = \sin\theta$ (θ being the angle of inclination), then the weight of water in this length l, per unit area of the channel, being $W\, l$ lbs., the resolved part of this weight in the direction of motion $= W\, l\, \frac{h}{l} = W\, h$ lbs.

∴ If the velocity is constant so that this force is entirely expended in overcoming friction and not in producing acceleration, we have

$$W\, h = f' \frac{P}{A}\, l\, v^n$$

$$h = \frac{f''\, l\, v^n}{m}$$

$$\text{or } h = \frac{f\, l\, v^n}{2\, g\, m}$$

In an open channel n may be taken as being approximately equal to 2, so that the formula becomes

$$h = \frac{f\, l\, v^2}{2\, g\, m} \tag{1}$$

This may be written in the form adopted by *Chezy,* viz.,

$$v = \sqrt{\frac{2\, g}{f} \cdot \frac{h}{l}\, m} = C\, \sqrt{m\, i} \tag{2}$$

where $$C^2 = \frac{2\, g}{f}$$

Many experiments have been devoted to determining the values of C or of f for channels having different physical characteristics, and the results of the more important of these are as follow, the numerical values of the coefficients obtained by the various observers being collected and tabulated on pp. 293—297.

Darcy and *Bazin* (1855—9), as the results of experiments carried out on the Bourgoyne Canal, gave C the value $\dfrac{1}{\sqrt{a + \dfrac{b}{m}}}$ where a and b

(p. 293) vary only with the material and condition of the bed and sides of the channel.

These channels were of many different forms and dimensions; were lined with different materials, and had slopes varying from ·001 to ·01.

Prony, from experiments by Chezy and Dubuat on earthen channels and on wooden channels of small section put

$$a v + b v^2 = m i$$

or

$$C = \sqrt{\frac{1}{b + \dfrac{a}{v}}}.$$

The corresponding value of $f = 2 g \left(b + \dfrac{a}{v} \right) = A + \dfrac{B}{v}.$

where
$$\begin{cases} \dfrac{1}{a} = 22{,}472. \quad A = ·00607. \\[2mm] \dfrac{1}{b} = 10{,}607. \quad B = ·00286. \end{cases}$$

Eytelwein, from experiments on the Rhine channel, gave the same type of formula, his coefficients being

$$\frac{1}{a} = 41{,}211. \quad A = ·00719.$$

$$\frac{1}{b} = 8{,}975. \quad B = ·00156.$$

In both these cases the unit of length is 1 foot. With moderate velocities $a v$ is small compared with $b v^2$ and may be neglected, when the formulae reduce to

Prony $\qquad v = \dfrac{1}{\sqrt{b}} \sqrt{mi} = 103 \sqrt{m\ i}. \quad f = ·00607.$

Eytelwein $\qquad v = - - - - = 95 \sqrt{m\ i}. \quad f = ·00714.$

These coefficients, being independent of the condition of the surface, are obviously only applicable to channels having the same physical characteristics as those experimented upon.

Bazin (1897), as the result of a very large number of experiments on canals and conduits of all sections and dimensions, deduced for C the value

$$\frac{157·6}{1 + \dfrac{N}{\sqrt{m}}} \text{ in foot units.}$$

N varying with the character of the surface.

Values of N for different types of surface are given on p. 293.

This gives a value of $f = ·000259 \left\{ 1 + \dfrac{2 N}{\sqrt{m}} + \dfrac{N^2}{m} \right\}.$

This form of equation is in common use in France, and has given good results with velocities not exceeding 4 feet per second.

Ganguillet and *Kutter* deduced the coefficient

$$C = \frac{41 \cdot 6 + \dfrac{\cdot 00281}{i} + \dfrac{1 \cdot 8112}{N}}{1 + \left(41 \cdot 6 + \dfrac{\cdot 00281}{i}\right) \dfrac{N}{\sqrt{m}}} \quad \text{in foot units.}$$

the equation being identical with that used for pipe flow. N depends on the character of the surface, and has values given on p. 298.

The complication of this formula is largely due to an attempt to make it conform to the results of experiments made on the Mississippi. In certain of these, however, the results should have been corrected for the error introduced by the use of double floats, while in others the slope of the water surface was too slight to be measured with any degree of accuracy.

More recent investigations render it extremely doubtful whether the value of C does depend on i as this formula indicates, and the simpler formula of *Bazin* would appear to give results at least as accurate, except possibly in the case of very large channels. The formula is, however, of very general application in Great Britain, India, Germany and the United States, and the inconveniences due to its complication are removed by the use of hydraulic tables which have been prepared giving the values of C for practically all values of i and of N.

By altering the value of i in this formula from ·001 to ·01, the value of C is altered by less than 1 per cent. For streams of fairly rapid slope the value of i may then be taken as sensibly equal to ·001, in which case the value of C simplifies to

$$C = \frac{44 \cdot 4 + \dfrac{1 \cdot 811}{N}}{1 + 44 \cdot 4 \dfrac{N}{\sqrt{m}}}$$

In very large rivers the flow is sensibly independent of the character of the bed, and for such a case *Manning*[1] gives C the value

$$C = 62 \left\{ 1 + \frac{\sqrt{m}}{7} - \frac{\cdot 05}{\sqrt{m}} \right\} \quad \text{in foot units.}$$

$$C = 34 \left\{ 1 + \frac{\sqrt{m}}{4} - \frac{\cdot 03}{\sqrt{m}} \right\} \quad \text{in metre units.}$$

From the nature of the case it would appear hopeless to obtain any

[1] Inst. Civil Engineers of Ireland, December 4, 1889.

strictly mathematical solution for flow in open channels and rivers of irregular section, and even to observe and record correctly the physical data required is almost impossible. An examination of the results given by an application of the various formulae shows that for abnormal sections or velocities a difference of 50 per cent. is not uncommon.

COEFFICIENTS FOR FLOW IN OPEN CHANNELS.

| Character of Surface. | Darcy. | | Bazin. | Kutter. |
	a	b	N.	N.
Smooth cement or planed timber	·000046	·0000045	·109	·009 to ·010
Unplaned timber, flumes, slightly tuberculated iron, ashlar and well-laid brickwork . .	·000058	·0000133	·290	·012 to ·013
Rubble masonry and brickwork in an inferior condition. Fine gravel well rammed . .	·000073	·000060	·833	·017
Rubble in inferior condition. Canals with earth beds in very good condition . . .				·020
Canals with earth beds in good condition			1·540	·0225
Ditto in moderate condition .	·000085	·00035		·025
Canals and rivers in rather bad order			2·355	·030
Ditto in very bad order . .	·00012	·00070	3·170	·035

Here a channel is said to be in very good order when it is free from boulders, hollows in its bed and banks, sharp bends, snags and weeds.

When badly choked with weeds the value of N in Kutter's formula may become much greater than ·035. The following values of N in the latter formula are taken from Jackson's tables, and are probably slightly more accurate than those given above.

$$N.$$

Planed timber accurately jointed—glazed or enamelled surfaces　.　·009
Smooth cement or plaster .　.　.　.　.　.　.　·010
Unplaned timber well jointed—new brickwork well laid　.　.　·012
Unglazed stonework—iron—brick and ashlar　.　.　.　.　·013
Wooden troughs with battens inside, ½ inch apart　.　.　.　·015
Rubble set in cement　.　.　.　.　.　.　.　·017

If any of these are in bad order the next higher value for N is to be taken.

For convenience in applying the results of these formulae the values of f in the formula $h = \dfrac{f\ l\ v^2}{2\ g\ m}$, and of C in the formula $v = C\sqrt{m\,i}$ have been calculated and are tabulated opposite.

The following table gives values of C in the formula $v = C\sqrt{m\,i}$, calculated from Bazin's formula in which $C = \dfrac{157\cdot6}{1 + \dfrac{N}{\sqrt{m}}}$.

Hydraulic mean Depth.	Values of N.					
m *ft.*	·109	·290	·833	1·54	2·35	3·17
·5	137	112	72	50	35	29
1·0	142	122	86	62	47	38
1·5	145	128	94	70	54	44
2·0	146	131	100	76	59	49
2·5	147	133	104	80	64	53
3·0	148	135	107	84	67	56
4·0	149	138	111	89	72	61
5·0	150	140	115	93	77	65
6·0	151	141	118	97	80	69
8·0	152	143	122	102	86	74
10·0	152	145	125	106	90	79
15·0	153	147	130	113	98	87
20·0	154	148	133	117	103	92
25·0	155	149	135	121	107	96
30·0	155	149	137	123	110	100
50·0	156	150	144	129	119	108

Character of Surface		Darcy			Bazin			Kutter $\left\{\frac{\text{Slope}}{1 \text{ in } 1,000.}\right.$		
		m = ·5	m = 1	m = 2	m = ·5	m = 1	m = 2	m = ·5	m = 1	m = 2
Smooth cement or planed timber	$f =$	·00354	·00325	·00310	·00345	·00318	·00300	·00334	·00264	·00219
	$c =$	135	141	144	136·7	142	146	139	156	171
Unplaned timber, flumes, slightly tuberculated iron, ashlar and well laid brickwork	$f =$	·00544	·00459	·00416	·00515	·00431	·00376	·00517	·00396	·00320
	$c =$	109	118·5	124·5	112	122	131	120·3	127·6	143·2
Rubble masonry and brickwork in an inferior condition—fine gravel well rammed	$f =$	·01241	·00856	·00663	·01227	·00870	·00653	·01208	·00865	·00663
	$c =$	72·0	86·7	98·5	72·5	86·0	99·4	73·1	86·4	98·5
Rubble in inferior condition. Canals with earth beds in perfect condition	$f =$							·01671	·01260	·00936
	$c =$							62·0	71·5	83·0
Canals with earth beds in good condition	$f =$				·02620	·01670	·01130	·02400	·01648	·01200
	$c =$				49·6	62·0	75·5	51·8	62·5	73·3
Canals with earth beds in moderate condition	$f =$	·0550	·0280	·0167	·0543			·0312	0·210	·0151
	$c =$	34·2	48·0	62·0	34·5			45·5	55·4	65·5
Canals and rivers in rather bad order, weeds on bottom	$f =$					·02916	·0184	·0190	·0318	·0221
	$c =$					47·0	59·1	36·2	45·0	54·0
Canals and rivers in very bad order—choked with boulders	$f =$	·0979	·0528	·0302	·0779	·0450	·0266	·0710	·0452	·0305
	$c =$	25·6	33·0	45·1	28·8	37·8	49·2	31·1	37·6	46·0

Rational Formula.

From analogy with pipe flow it would appear probable that a formula of the type

$$h = \frac{f\,l\,v^n}{\left(\dfrac{A}{P}\right)^x} = \frac{f\,l\,v^n}{m^x}$$

where, as in the case of a pipe, n is in general less than 2, would most nearly represent the law of channel flow.

Claxton Fidler[1] has determined the values of f, n, and x from many experimental results of Darcy, Bazin, Smith, Stearns, and other observers, and the following table is abridged from values given by him :—

Form of Section.	Material of Surface.	n	x	f
Circular	Smooth neat cement	1·75	1·167	·0000676
Rectangular.	,, ,, ,,			
Circular	Cement and sand	,,	,,	·0000787
,,	Smooth brick.			
Rectangular.	Smooth ashlar	,,	,,	·0000904
Circular	Bare metal pipes with rivetted joints.	1·77	1·18	·0000871
,,	Rough brickwork	1·80	1·20	·0000977
Rectangular.	Unplaned timber	,,	,,	·0000944
,,	Rough Brickwork or ashlar	,,	,,	·0001122
Circular	Lined with fine gravel	1·90	1·33	·0001202
Rectangular.	,, ,, ,, ,,	1·96	1·40	·0001521
,,	,, ,, coarse gravel	2·10	1·50	·0001862
,,	Rubble masonry	,,	,,	·0002240

While further investigation may slightly alter these values, it is extremely probable that the final solution of the problem of flow in regular channels will be found in this type of formula.

The pipe flow formula of *Thrupp*

$$h = \frac{C^m\,v^n\,l}{m^x}$$

where m is the hydraulic mean depth is also applicable to channel flow, the following being the values of the quantities C^m, n, and x. When m is small, $x + a\sqrt{\dfrac{b}{m}} - 1$ should be substituted for x.

[1] Fidler, "Calculations in Hydraulic Engineering," Part II. (Longmans & Co.), 1902.

Surface.	$n.$	$C^n.$	$x.$	$a.$	$b.$
Neat cement {semi-circular section . .	1·74	·0000680	1·165		
Neat cement {rectangular section . .	1·95	·0000494	1·190		
Brickwork, well laid	2·00	·0000600	1·220		
Unplaned plank	2·00	·0000714	1·230		
Brickwork, rough	2·00	·0000780	1·250	·0670	·50
Lined with fine gravel . . .	2·00	·0001399	1·320	·0245	·50
Chiselled masonry	2·00	·0001246	1·320	·0788	·60
Lined with coarse gravel . . .	2·00	·0002005	1·410	·1565	1·00
Earth in fair condition . . .	2·00	·0002360	1·440	·1518	1·00
Rough earth	2·00	·0002600	1·560		

The results obtained by this formula compare very well with those of Fidler, the latter probably on the whole giving the better results.

Prof. G. S. Williams, adopting this exponential formula, gives n and x constant values respectively equal to 1·9 and 1·25. The formula then becomes $h = \dfrac{K \, v^n \, l}{m^x}$, or $v = C \, m^{·67} \times i^{·54}$, where K and C have the following values :—

	$C.$	$K.$
Very smooth channels . . .	180 to 190	·00030 to ·00035
Unplaned plank	145 „ 165	·00045 „ ·00050
Sewer crock.	140 „ 160	·00050 „ ·00075
Brick sewers	130 „ 160	·00050 „ ·00080
Earth channels	60 „ 80	·0010 „ ·0020
Rough natural channels . .	40 „ 50	·0020 „ ·0050

ART. 86.—CRITICAL VELOCITY IN AN OPEN CHANNEL.

So far it has been assumed that in channel flow the resistance to motion is proportioned to some power of the mean velocity approximating to the second, but while this is undoubtedly true in all natural streams having a fairly rapid slope it is in all probability not the case where velocities are very low.

It might, in fact, be inferred from analogy with pipe flow that below some " critical " velocity the resistance will be proportional to the first power of the velocity. The clear glassy non-distortive reflecting surface observed in any long straight reach of a deep and sluggish stream tends to strengthen this inference, while the behaviour of small particles of suspended matter appears to show almost conclusively that at low speeds motion takes place in stream lines.

Experiments by *Mr. E. C. Thrupp*[1] on the Thames and the Kennet, the former having a mean depth of 7·6 feet and the latter of 2·4 feet, showed that velocities of ·665 feet per second in the former, and ·64 feet per second in the latter case, were below the critical, and that for all smaller values the velocity was practically proportional to the surface slope. The experiments did not, however, indicate the point at which the velocity-slope law changed.

Although, owing to the difficulty of measuring such small differences of head as are involved in flow at low velocities, accurate determinations are not practicable, yet the values quoted above show that this critical velocity is immensely high compared with that calculated from Reynold's formula (p. 55) for a cylindrical pipe of the same hydraulic mean depth. The existence of a critical velocity would at once explain the great discrepancy which in some cases exists between the results of experiments on channels having similar physical characteristics, but with very different velocities of flow.

ART. 87.—FORM OF CHANNEL.

Since for a channel of given sectional area A, the hydraulic mean depth $A \div P$ varies with the form of its section, while the resistance to flow increases as $A \div P$ diminishes, it becomes important to determine what form of channel will give the maximum value of $A \div P$ for a given value of A, since this will be the channel of maximum discharge for a given slope. Further, if this sectional area is a minimum, the cost of excavation is a minimum, and since in general the perimeter increases with the sectional area, the cost of pitching the faces of the channel is also a minimum. Theoretically, the best form of channel is one in which the bed is a circular arc, since this gives a minimum ratio of wetted perimeter to sectional area.

An investigation into the properties of different sections will be simplified if the coefficient C in the formula $v = C \sqrt{\dfrac{A}{P} . i}$, be assumed constant for a given surface. On this assumption we have:—

$$Q = A v = C \sqrt{\frac{A^3}{P} . i} \text{ cub ft. per sec.}$$

For v to be a maximum, $\dfrac{A}{P}$ must be a maximum, so that $d \left(\dfrac{A}{P} \right) = 0$

$$\therefore \quad P \, d A - A \, d P = 0. \tag{1}$$

---

[1] "Proc. Inst. C.E.," vol. 171, 1907–8, p. 316.

Again, for Q to be a maximum, $\dfrac{A^3}{P}$ is to be a maximum, so that $d\left(\dfrac{A^3}{P}\right) = 0.$

$$\therefore 3\, P\, A^2\, d\, A - A^3\, d\, P = 0. \tag{2}$$

Where A is fixed, $d\, A = 0$ and both conditions are satisfied if $d\, P = 0$.

Example.

(1) **Rectangular Channel.**—Breadth $2\, b$ — depth d.

Here $\qquad A = 2\, b\, d : P = 2\, b + 2\, d = \dfrac{A}{d} + 2\, d$

$$\therefore \quad \frac{d\, P}{d\, (d)} = -\frac{A}{d^2} + 2.$$

Putting $A = 2\, b\, d$ and equating $\dfrac{d\, P}{d\, (d)}$ to zero, we have $b = d$.

Putting the full breadth $= B$, we have $d = \dfrac{B}{2}$, i.e., for maximum flow the depth must equal one-half the breadth.

We then have $\qquad Q = C\sqrt{\dfrac{A^3}{P} \cdot i}$

$$= C\sqrt{\frac{8\, b^3\, d^3}{2\, b + 2\, d} \cdot i}$$

$$= C\sqrt{2\, i \cdot b^{\frac{5}{2}}}$$

$$= \frac{C}{4}\sqrt{i\, B^{\frac{5}{2}}} \tag{1}$$

(2) **Trapezoidal Channel.**—Fig. 129.

Let $b =$ half bottom breadth; $d =$ depth; $s =$ cotangent of angle of slope of sides.

Then $A = 2\, b\, d + s\, d^2$.

$P = 2\, (b + d\sqrt{1 + s^2})$.

For Q to be a maximum with a given area of channel or for the cost of construction to be a minimum, it is necessary that $\dfrac{d\, P}{d\, (d)} = 0$.

But $\qquad P = 2\left\{\dfrac{A}{2\, d} - \dfrac{s\, d}{2} + d\sqrt{1 + s^2}\right\}$

$$\therefore \qquad \frac{d\, P}{d\, (d)} = 2\left\{-\frac{A}{2\, d^2} - \frac{s}{2} + \sqrt{1 + s^2}\right\}$$

$\therefore$ For maximum value
of Q
$$\sqrt{1 + s^2} = \frac{2\,b\,d + s\,d^2}{2\,d^2} + \frac{s}{2}$$

$$= \frac{b}{d} + s$$

$\therefore$ $(1 + s^2)\,d^2 = (b + s\,d)^2$ (2)

But from the figure it will be seen that if a circle having its centre in

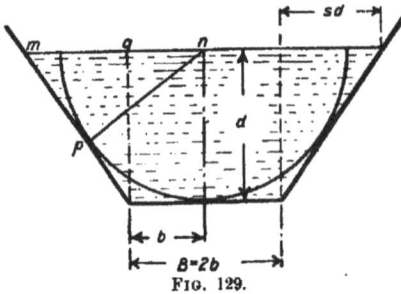

the surface of the water can be drawn to touch the sides and bottom, we have
$$m\,n = b + s\,d\,; \ m\,p = m\,q$$
$$= s\,d\,; \ n\,p = d,$$
and since $(m\,n)^2 = (m\,p)^2 + (n\,p)^2$, the above equation is satisfied. These proportions then give the best results.

Fig. 129.

The value of s depends largely on the material in which the channel is excavated. The following may be taken as the minimum permissible values.

Earthen canal with faced sides $s = 1\cdot0$.
      ,,   ,,   ,,   natural ,, $s = 1\cdot5$.
      ,,   ,,   in light soil $s = 2\cdot0$

The latter value is usually adopted for all unfaced earthern sides. Substituting this value of s in equation (2) we have
$$5\,d^2 = (b + 2d)^2$$
$$\therefore d = 4\cdot24\,b$$ (3)

$\therefore$ For maximum discharge $d = 2\cdot12\,B$, where B is the bottom breadth

We then have $Q = C\sqrt{\dfrac{A^3}{P} \cdot i}$

$$= C\sqrt{\frac{(2\,b\,d + s\,d^2)^3}{2\,(b + d\sqrt{1 + s^2})} \cdot i}$$

Substituting for d from (2) we have

$$Q = C\,b^{\frac{5}{2}}\frac{(2\sqrt{1 + s^2} - s)}{\sqrt{2}\,(\sqrt{1 + s^2} - s)^{\frac{5}{2}}} \cdot \sqrt{i}$$

and giving s the value 2

$$Q = 204\,C\,b^{\frac{5}{2}} \text{ cub. ft. per sec.}$$

if C and b are taken in foot units

or $Q = 36\cdot1\,C\,B^{\frac{5}{2}}.$

Whatever the slope of the sides, the trapezium of best shape will be hat in which the sides are made tangent to the circle of radius $= d$ laving its centre in the surface, and as may be readily shown, all such hannels have the same hydraulic mean depth $= \dfrac{d}{2}$. It follows then that the velocity of flow when the channel is full will be independent of he slope of the sides, and will depend solely on the gradient of the bed. The discharge of any two trapezoidal channels of the best form and of the same gradient and depths, will, when running full, be proportional o their respective mean widths.

The following table indicates how the top and bottom widths for a lection of this type, vary with the slope of the sides :—

Slope.	Angle of inclination of sides.	Width.	
		Top.	Bottom.
0 to 1	90°	2·000 d	2·000 d
·25 to 1	75° . 58′	2·062 d	1·562 d
·5 to 1	63° . 26′	2·236 d	1·236 d
·75 to 1	53° . 8′	2·500 d	1·000 d
1·0 to 1	45° . 0′	2·828 d	·828 d
1·5 to 1	33° . 41′	3·606 d	·606 d
2·0 to 1	26° . 34′	4·472 d	·472 d
2·5 to 1	21° . 48′	5·385 d	·385 d
3·0 to 1	18° . 26′	6·325 d	·325 d

Circular Section.—Fig. 130.

Let $d =$ diameter of circle.

„ $\theta =$ angle at centre subtended by wetted perimeter.

Then
$$A = \frac{d^2}{8}(\theta - \sin\theta) \; ; \; P = \frac{d^2}{2}\,\theta$$

$$\therefore \frac{A}{P} = \frac{d}{4}\left(1 - \frac{\sin\theta}{\theta}\right). \quad \text{Suppose } d \text{ fixed.}$$

For maximum velocity
$$\frac{d\left(\dfrac{A}{P}\right)}{d\theta} = 0$$

$$\therefore \theta = \tan\theta$$

$$\therefore \theta = 257\tfrac{1}{2}°.$$

For maximum discharge
$$\frac{d\left(\frac{A^3}{P}\right)}{d\,\theta} = 0$$

$$\therefore 3\,P\frac{d\,A}{d\,\theta} - A\frac{d\,P}{d\,\theta} = 0$$

$$\therefore 3\,\theta\,(1 - \cos\theta) = \theta - \sin\theta$$

$$\therefore 2\,\theta - 3\,\theta\cos\theta + \sin\theta = 0.$$

The value of θ which satisfies this equation is 308°, so that a circular conduit will give its maximum discharge when the depth of water is about ·95 of the diameter, the discharge then being about 5 per cent greater than when completely full.

The discharge corresponding to any depth of water is given by

$$Q = C\sqrt{\frac{A^3}{P}\cdot i}$$

$$= C\sqrt{\frac{d^5}{256}\,\frac{(\theta - \sin\theta)^3}{\theta}\cdot i}$$

$$= \frac{C}{16}\,d^{\frac{5}{2}}\,i^{\frac{1}{2}}\sqrt{\frac{(\theta - \sin\theta)^3}{\theta}}$$

when $\theta = 180° = \pi$

$$Q = \frac{C}{5\cdot1}\,d^{\frac{5}{2}}\sqrt{i.}\text{ cub. ft. per sec.}$$

The semi-circular section when running full has a hydraulic mean

FIG. 130.

depth of $\frac{d}{4}$, and since this is greater than that of any other form of channel of the same area. this section is well fitted for an open channel.

Where a polygonal channel is used, the hydraulic mean depth is greatest when the sides and bottom of the channel are designed so as to be tangent to a circle having its centre in the water line. The trapezoidal section and rectangular section of greatest flow, are particular cases of this. Where vertical sides are to be used the most suitable form of bottom consists of a circular arc, concave upwards.

Channel of Constant Mean Velocity.—Where the depth of water in a channel may vary within wide limits, it is in general desirable to design this so that the velocity of flow may be as nearly as possible independent of the depth. Otherwise, in an open canal, the velocity may become so great as to damage the sides and bottom by scouring (Art. 97), while in a sewer, with low heads, the velocity may become insufficient to produce the necessary flushing. On the assumption that $v = C \sqrt{m\, i}$, where $C =$ constant, the only essential condition to be satisfied for v to be independent of the depth is that the hydraulic mean depth shall also be independent of the depth of water.

Thus the required channel must have sides formed by a continuous curve such that the area bounded by the sides, and any two horizontals varies as the length of the arcs intercepted between these horizontals. No curve can be found to satisfy these conditions, though close approximations may be obtained.

Obviously, a rectangular section of great depth compared with its width would satisfy the conditions approximately, and especially if its

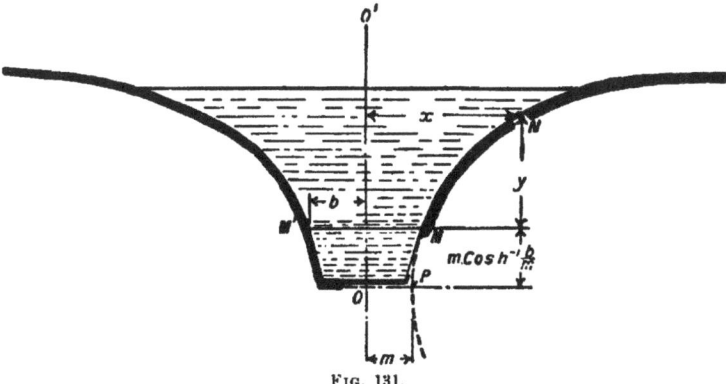

FIG. 131.

bottom were constructed so as to offer less resistance per unit area than its sides.

A construction which gives accurate results between certain limits may, however, be obtained as follows.

In Fig. 131 let x be the half breadth of the section at a height y above $M'\, M$ where the half breadth is b, and let s be the length of the arc $M\, N$

The position of the axis $M'\, M$ and the breadth b are usually fixed from a consideration of the minimum discharge to be expected through the channel, a trapezoidal channel having an upper breadth $M'\, M\ (= 2\, b)$ being designed to take this minimum discharge when running full. Let m be the hydraulic mean depth of this small channel, let p be its half perimeter, and a its half area. It is required to continue the sides of this channel so as to give a section for which the hydraulic mean depth $A \div P$ shall be equal to m for all depths of water.

Considering the section of the complete channel to one side of the axis $O\ O'$, we have

$$\frac{A}{P} = \frac{a + \int x\, d y}{p + s} = \text{constant} = m$$

$$\therefore\ a + \int x\, d y = m\,(p + s).$$

Differentiating, this gives $x = m\,\dfrac{d\,s}{d\,y}.$

But

$$\frac{d\,s}{d\,y} = \sqrt{1 + \left(\frac{d\,x}{d\,y}\right)^2}$$

$$\therefore\ x^2 = m^2 \left\{ 1 + \left(\frac{d\,x}{d\,y}\right)^2 \right\}$$

$$\therefore\ \frac{d\,y}{m} = \frac{d\,x}{\sqrt{x^2 - m^2}}.$$

Integrating this we have

$$y = m\,\cosh^{-1}\frac{x}{m} + D$$

$$= m\,\log_e \{ x + \sqrt{x^2 - m^2} \} + D'.$$

But $x = b$ when $y = 0$

$$\therefore\ D = -\,m\,\cosh^{-1}\frac{b}{m}$$

$$D' = -\,m\,\log_e \{ b + \sqrt{b^2 - m^2} \}$$

$$\therefore\ y = m\left(\cosh^{-1}\frac{x}{m} - \cosh^{-1}\frac{b}{m} \right) \tag{1}$$

$$= m\,\log_e \left\{ \frac{x + \sqrt{x^2 - m^2}}{b + \sqrt{b^2 - m^2}} \right\}. \tag{2}$$

From equation (2) the curve of the side may be plotted by calculating values of y, corresponding to a series of values of x.

Since $v = C\,\sqrt{m\,i}$ this velocity with any given gradient may be adjusted to any given value by designing the small channel so as to give the required value of m. The only restriction is that m cannot exceed $b \div 2$, this being its value when the lower channel is semicircular, or rectangular with a breadth equal to twice its depth.

EXAMPLE.

To design a channel to give an uniform velocity of flow of 4 feet per second, the half breadth b being 2·5 feet, and C having a value 90.

Here, assuming a rectangular section for the lower channel, of depth 2·5 feet, we have $m = 1·25$ feet.

$$\therefore\ 4 = 90\,\sqrt{1·25\,i}$$

$$\therefore\ i = ·00158.$$

Again when $x = 5$ we have

$$y = 1\cdot25 \log_e \left\{ \frac{5 + \sqrt{25 - 1\cdot5625}}{2\cdot5 + \sqrt{6\cdot25 - 1\cdot5625}} \right\}$$

$$= 1\cdot25 \log_e \left\{ \frac{5 + \sqrt{33\cdot4375}}{2\cdot5 + \sqrt{4\cdot6875}} \right\}$$

$$= 1\cdot25 \log_e 2\cdot108$$

$$= 1\cdot25 \times 2\cdot302 \log_{10} (2\cdot108)$$

$$= \cdot933 \text{ feet.}$$

Obtaining a series of such values of y, corresponding to definite values of x, the section may be constructed. For this particular example the following table shows how the half breadth of the section increases with the depth:—

x	2·5	5·0	10·0	15·0	20·0	30·0	50·0
y	0	·933	1·817	2·320	2·520	2·832	3·300

The curve is a portion of a catenary, and, writing its equation in the form $\dfrac{y - D}{m} = \cosh^{-1} \dfrac{x}{m}$,

or $$m \cosh\left(\frac{y - D}{m}\right) = x,$$

it will be seen that this catenary has its axis parallel to and at a distance $(-D) = m \cosh^{-1} \dfrac{b}{m}$ below the axis $M' M$, while its vertex P is at a horizontal distance m from the centre line $O\,O'$ (Fig. 131).

In a closed channel, or sewer, it is impossible to make the mean depth, and therefore the velocity, constant for all depths of water. To approximate to this as far as possible the egg shaped sewer (Fig. 132) is often used. In section this consists of two circular arcs centred at A and B, and connected by a second pair of circular arcs centred

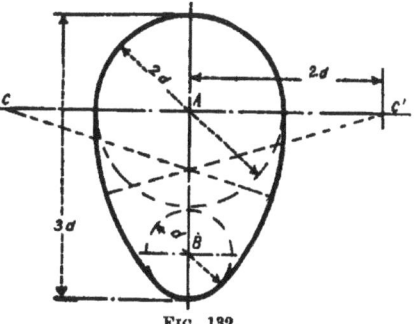

FIG. 132.

at C and C'. The proportions often adopted in practice are indicated in Fig. 132.

Figure 133 a and b shows sections which are sometimes adopted for large sewers to the same end, the hydraulic mean depth being fairly high even with a small discharge.

Effect of varying m or i.

Assuming

$$v = C \sqrt{m\,i}$$

we have

$$\frac{d\,v}{d\,m} = \frac{C}{2} \sqrt{\frac{i}{m}}$$

or

$$d\,v = \frac{C}{2} \sqrt{\frac{i}{m}} \cdot d\,m = \frac{v}{2\,m} \cdot d\,m$$

$$\therefore \quad \frac{d\,v}{v} = \frac{d\,m}{2\,m}.$$

Thus a small increase in m produces one-half its percentage increase in v.

Similarly it may be shown that $\dfrac{d\,v}{v} = \dfrac{d\,i}{2\,i}$, so that in calculating v, and therefore the discharge, from this formula, any error in the value

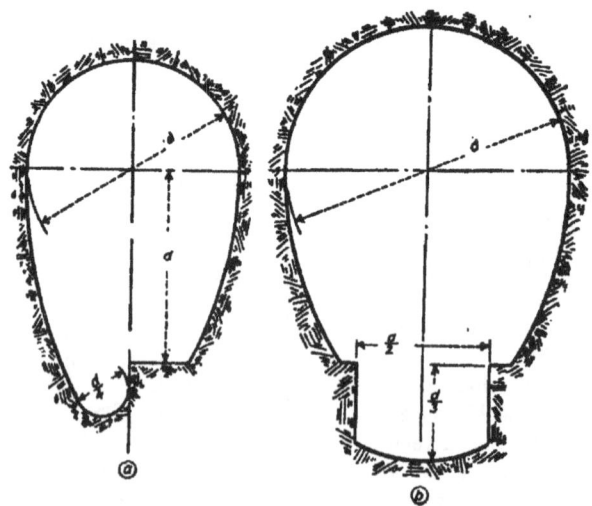

Fig. 133.

assumed for the slope will lead to one-half the proportional error in the estimated discharge.

Again, since
$$Q = C \sqrt{\frac{A^3}{P}} \cdot i$$

$$\frac{dQ}{dA} = \frac{3}{2} C \sqrt{\frac{i}{P}} \cdot A^{\frac{1}{2}}$$

$$\therefore \quad \frac{dQ}{Q} = \frac{3}{2} \frac{dA}{A},$$

so that, neglecting the small increase in the wetted perimeter accompanying an increase in depth, any small increase in the cross sectional area produced by such a change in depth will be accompanied by 1·5 times this proportional increase in the discharge.

Again assuming A to be known and a small error to be made in the estimated value of P, we have

$$\frac{dQ}{dP} = C \sqrt{i} \left(- \frac{1}{2} \frac{A^{\frac{3}{2}}}{P^{\frac{3}{2}}} \right)$$

$$\therefore \quad \frac{dQ}{Q} = - \frac{1}{2} \frac{dP}{P},$$

so that this error leads to one-half the proportional error in the estimation of Q.

Since these errors should be severally small and may all occur in the same direction, the total possible error will be equal to their sum.

Thus if the probable error in the estimation of $i = p$ per cent.

,,　　,,　　,,　　,,　　,,　　,,　　,, $A = q$ per cent.

,,　　,,　　,,　　,,　　,,　　,,　　,, $P = r$ per cent.

The possible area in the estimation of the discharge, assuming C to have its correct value, will be given by

$$\left\{ \frac{p + r}{2} + 1 \cdot 5\, q \right\} \text{ per cent.}$$

ART. 88.—GENERAL EQUATION OF FLOW IN AN OPEN CHANNEL.

Consider a steady stream of cross-sectional area A, flowing over a bed having an inclination θ to the horizontal, where $\sin \theta = $ slope $= i$.

Let $A\ B$ (Fig. 134) be any stream tube, the vertical depths of A and B below the surface being y_A and y_B.

FIG. 134.

Let $_A h_B$ be the loss of head in this stream tube from A to B, due to frictional resistances.

x 2

Then applying Bernoulli's equation of energy, we have

$$\frac{p_A}{W} + \frac{v_A^2}{2g} + z_A = \frac{p_B}{W} + \frac{v_B^2}{2g} + z_B + {}_A h_B.$$

Let the difference in the level of the water surface over the points A and B be r.

Then $z_A + y_A = z_B + y_B + r$

$$\therefore z_A - z_B = r + y_B - y_A$$

$$\therefore \frac{p_A}{W} + \frac{v_A^2}{2g} + r + y_B - y_A = \frac{p_B}{W} + \frac{v_B^2}{2g} + {}_A h_B.$$

If the stream is sensibly parallel over the length $A\ B$, as will be the case if θ is not large, we have

$$\frac{p_A}{W} = y_A \text{ and } \frac{p_B}{W} = y_B$$

$$\therefore \frac{v_A^2}{2g} + r = \frac{v_B^2}{2g} + {}_A h_B$$

$$\therefore r = \frac{v_B^2 - v_A^2}{2g} + {}_A h_B.$$

If now we imagine the area A divided into n elementary sections, each equal to $\frac{A}{n}$ we get, for each stream tube of area $\frac{A}{n}$:—

$$\frac{A}{n} \cdot r = \frac{A}{n} \cdot \frac{v_B^2 - v_A^2}{2g} + \frac{A}{n} \cdot {}_A h_B$$

and, summing these over the whole section,

$$\Sigma_0^n \left(\frac{A}{n} \cdot r \right) = \Sigma_0^n \left(\frac{A}{n} \cdot \frac{v_B^2 - v_A^2}{2g} \right) + \Sigma_0^n \left(\frac{A}{n} \cdot {}_A h_B \right).$$

If we assume that the velocity is constant over any cross section, the above equation reduces to

$$A\ r = A\ \frac{v_B^2 - v_A^2}{2g} + {}_A H_B$$

where ${}_A H_B$ is the total frictional loss between the cross sections at A and B.

This is still true of the whole mass of water in the stream if the velocity at a cross section is not uniform, provided that the distribution of velocity is such that the total kinetic energy at that section is equal to the mass of water multiplied by the square of the mean velocity at the section. In this case v_B and v_A become the mean velocities. Experiments by Messrs. Fteley and Stearns on the flow of water in the Sudbury conduit, 9 feet wide and 8 feet deep, in which the velocity was measured at 97 different points in a cross section, gave results showing that the error in assuming this to be true was less than 1 per cent. The error

rill be greater in a shallow channel having a rough bed, but in general
he results calculated on this assumption may be taken as substantially
orrect.

If P = wetted perimeter of section, and if $(\bar{v})^2$ = mean square of the
elocity from A to B

$$_AH_B = \frac{f\,(\bar{v})^2}{2\,g} \cdot P \cdot A\,B,$$

$$\therefore r = \frac{v_B{}^2 - v_A{}^2}{2\,g} + \frac{f\,(\bar{v})^2}{2\,g} \cdot \frac{P}{A} \cdot A\,B.$$

If $A\,B = \delta\,l$ we have $r = \dfrac{d\,r}{d\,l} \cdot \delta\,l$, while if $v_A = v,\ v_B = v + \dfrac{d\,v}{d\,l} \cdot \delta\,l$

nd $(\bar{v})^2 = \left(v + m\dfrac{d\,v}{d\,l}\,\delta\,l\right)^2$, where m is less than unity.

So that, neglecting small quantities of the second order

$$\frac{d\,r}{d\,l}\,\delta\,l = \frac{2\,v\,\dfrac{d\,v}{d\,l}\,\delta\,l}{2\,g} + \frac{f\,v^2}{2\,g} \cdot \frac{P}{A}\,\delta\,l$$

$$\frac{d\,r}{d\,l} = \frac{v}{g} \cdot \frac{d\,v}{d\,l} + \frac{f\,v^2}{2\,g} \cdot \frac{P}{A}. \tag{1}$$

This is the general equation of flow in an open channel, v being the
ıean velocity at a cross section, and though the assumptions made in its
ınception are not altogether justified by the result of experiment, yet it
ɔrms a useful guide and is capable of a wide range of application in the
eneral problems of channel flow.

If h is the depth of water at A (measured vertically from the surface),
he depth at B is given by

$$h - \frac{d\,r}{d\,l} \cdot \delta\,l + i \cdot \delta\,l\,\cdot$$

Again the depth at B is given by

$$h + \frac{d\,h}{d\,l} \cdot \delta\,l$$

$$\therefore i\,\delta\,l = \frac{d\,r}{d\,l} \cdot \delta\,l + \frac{d\,h}{d\,l} \cdot \delta\,l$$

$$\therefore \frac{d\,r}{d\,l} = i - \frac{d\,h}{d\,l}.$$

Substituting this value in (1) we get

$$i = \frac{d\,h}{d\,l} = \frac{v}{g}\frac{d\,r}{d\,l} + \frac{f\,v^2}{2\,g} \cdot \frac{P}{A}, \tag{2}$$

ving the general equation in terms of the slope of the bed.

The physical interpretation of this equation is that the total loss of
ɔtential and pressure) energy per unit length of the channel, due to the

fall in the level of the bed and in the depth of the water, is equal to the increase of kinetic energy together with the loss in friction per unit length of channel.

For uniform flow such as occurs in a culvert with slope, velocity, and depth of water constant, we have $\dfrac{d\,h}{d\,l} = 0, \dfrac{d\,v}{d\,l} = 0$

$$\therefore i = \frac{f\,v^2}{2\,g} \cdot \frac{P}{A}$$

or the total potential energy is absorbed in overcoming frictional resistances. This gives the relation between the slope and the velocity, or the discharge Q, for since $v = \sqrt{\dfrac{2\,g\,i\,A}{f\,P}}$

$$\therefore v\,A = Q = \sqrt{\frac{2\,g\,i\,A^3}{f\,P}},$$

so that for a given slope we can find the section for v to be a constant, and to give any required discharge.

With a rectangular section, breadth b, we get for either uniform or non-uniform flow, if b is constant and if Q is constant

$$Q = v\,b\,h = \text{const.}$$
$$\therefore v\,h = \text{const.}$$
$$\therefore h\,\frac{d\,v}{d\,l} + v\,\frac{d\,h}{d\,l} = 0$$
$$\therefore \frac{d\,v}{d\,l} = -\frac{v}{h} \cdot \frac{d\,h}{d\,l}.$$

Substituting this value, equation (2) becomes

$$i - \frac{d\,h}{d\,l} = -\frac{v^2}{g\,h}\,\frac{d\,h}{d\,l} + \frac{f\,v^2}{2\,g} \cdot \frac{P}{A}$$

$$\therefore \frac{d\,h}{d\,l} = \frac{i - \dfrac{f\,v^2}{2\,g} \cdot \dfrac{P}{A}}{1 - \dfrac{v^2}{g\,h}} \tag{3}$$

Here $-\dfrac{v^2}{g\,h} \cdot \dfrac{d\,h}{d\,l}$ still represents the rate of increase of kinetic energy with length, and shows that the K. E. increases when the depth diminishes, i.e., when $\dfrac{d\,h}{d\,l}$ is negative.

If b be great in comparison with h, we may write $\dfrac{P}{A} = \dfrac{b + 2\,h}{b\,h} = \dfrac{1}{h}$ (approximately), especially if, as is very usual in open channels, the bottom is rougher than the sides.

Substituting this value in equation (3) we have, for such a channel,

$$\frac{d\,h}{d\,l} = \frac{i - \dfrac{f\,r^2}{2\,g\,h}}{1 - \dfrac{v^2}{g\,h}} = i\left\{ \frac{1 - \dfrac{f\,v^2}{2\,g\,h\,i}}{1 - \dfrac{v^2}{g\,h}} \right\} \tag{4}$$

This gives the slope of the water surface, and from a solution of this equation, the profile of this surface may be determined.

Thus for steady uniform flow $\dfrac{d\,h}{d\,l} = 0$, *i.e.*, the depth is constant throughout.

$$\therefore\; 1 - \frac{f\,v^2}{2\,g\,h\,i} = 0$$

or
$$h = \frac{f\,v^2}{2\,g\,i} \tag{5}$$

ART. 89.—NON-UNIFORM FLOW.

If, as is usual, the motion while being constant at a point, varies from point to point in the length of the stream, so that $\dfrac{d\,v}{d\,l}$ and therefore $\dfrac{d\,h}{d\,l}$, is not zero, let H be the equivalent depth of an uniform stream of breadth b which would give the same discharge as the variable stream in unit time.

Then
$$H = \frac{f\,V^2}{2\,g\,i} \qquad\qquad \text{from (5)}$$

where
$$Q = V\,b\,H \text{ or } V = \frac{Q}{b\,H}$$

$$\therefore\; \frac{Q^2}{b^2\,H^2} = \frac{2\,g\,i\,H}{f} \text{ or } \frac{Q^2}{b^2\,h^2} = v^2 = \frac{2\,g\,i\,H^3}{h^2\,f}$$

Substituting $\dfrac{2\,g\,i\,H^3}{h^2\,f}$ for v^2 in (4), this becomes

$$\therefore\; \frac{d\,h}{d\,l} = i\left\{ \frac{1 - \dfrac{H^3}{h^3}}{1 - \dfrac{H^3}{h^3}\cdot\dfrac{2\,i}{f}} \right\} \tag{6}$$

This is the differential equation to the curve forming the longitudinal profile of the surface.

Since the value of $\dfrac{d\,h}{d\,l}$ depends both on the ratio $\dfrac{h}{H}$ which may be artificially adjusted in any stream, and on the ratio $\dfrac{2\,i}{f}$ which is fixed once the slope and physical condition of the bed is fixed, an investigation of any particular case of flow must take into account both these factors.

The surface curves corresponding to a few particular cases of flow will now be investigated.

First suppose $\frac{2\,i}{f}$ less than unity, the state of affairs existing in a channel of slope less than $\frac{f}{2}$.

The following may be taken as approximate values of f at such velocities as are common in practice (Bazin), the foot being the unit of length.

Smooth cemented surface	$f = \cdot 0030$
Ashlar or brickwork	$= \cdot 0037$
Rubble masonry	$= \cdot 0065$
Earth	$= \cdot 0120$

so that for $\frac{2\,i}{f}$ to be less than unity, with a rubble masonry channel the slope would not exceed $\cdot 00325$ feet per foot, or 1 in 310.

Case 1 (a). Let $\frac{2\,i}{f} < 1$ and also $h^3 < \frac{2\,i}{f}\,H^3$.

Both numerator and denominator of the right-hand side of equation (6) are now negative, so that $\frac{d\,h}{d\,l}$ is positive, i.e., the depth of water increases down stream.

Also as h increases it finally reaches the critical value $\sqrt[3]{\dfrac{2\,i}{f}}$. H.

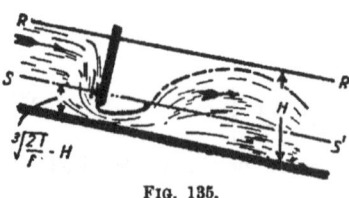

$\sqrt[3]{\frac{2i}{f}} \cdot H$

FIG. 135.

Here the denominator becomes equal to zero, and in consequence the value of $\frac{d\,h}{d\,l}$ becomes ∞, or the surface curve at this point becomes vertical (Fig. 135), and the phenomenon known as the standing wave is produced.

In the figure, suppose the dotted line $S\,S'$ to be drawn parallel to the bed, to represent a depth $\sqrt[3]{\dfrac{2\,i}{f}}$. H. If by means of a sluice we can get the water surface below this level, then on passing the sluice the depth of water increases as shown. Finally, when $h = \sqrt[3]{\dfrac{2\,i}{f}} \cdot H$, the curve should be vertical where it intersects this line. Before this limit is reached, however, the hypothesis that the stream lines are sensibly parallel ceases to be even approximately true, and the curve becomes modified as shown in the dotted lines. This is exemplified in the case of a sluice fitted in a channel having a very small slope.

If h_1 and h_2 be the depths of the stream before and after its sudden change of level, the value of h_2 may be calculated.

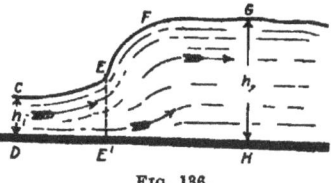

FIG. 136.

Let v_1 and v_2 be the velocities at sections h_1 and h_2.

It is not now legitimate to assume that the loss due to shock at the sudden change of section is $\dfrac{(v_1 - v_2)^2}{g}$ as in the case of pipe flow, since the pressure over the area $E'\ E$ (Fig. 136) is no longer uniform and equal to that from E to F but varies with the depth, and hence one of the fundamental assumptions made in deducing this formula is unjustified.

On applying the equation of momentum, however, to this particular case, we have

$$\left.\begin{array}{l}\text{Difference of forces acting in the direction of motion,}\\ \text{on the faces } C\,D \text{ and } G\,H\end{array}\right\} = p_1\,A_1 - p_2\,A_2,$$

where p_1 and p_2 are the mean pressures over the areas A_1 and A_2.

Then $\qquad p_1 = \dfrac{W\,h_1}{2} \qquad\qquad p_2 = \dfrac{W\,h_2}{2}.$

$$\left.\begin{array}{l}\text{The change of momentum per second, in}\\ \text{passing the sections } C\,D \text{ and } G\,H\end{array}\right\} = \dfrac{W}{g}\left\{A_2\,v_2{}^2 - A_1\,v_1{}^2\right\}.$$

Also $A_1\,v_1 = A_2\,v_2$, and if the section is rectangular, $h_1\,v_1 = h_2\,v_2$, so that on equating the momentum per second to the force producing it, we have

$$\frac{h_2}{2}\frac{v_1}{v_2} - \frac{h_1}{2} = \frac{v_1{}^2 - v_1\,v_2}{g}$$

$$\therefore\ \frac{h_2}{2}\cdot\frac{h_2}{h_1} - \frac{h_1}{2} = \frac{v_1{}^2}{g}\left\{1 - \frac{h_1}{h_2}\right\}$$

$$\therefore\ \frac{v_1{}^2}{g} = \frac{(h_2{}^2 - h_1{}^2)}{2\,h_1}\cdot\frac{h_2}{h_2 - h_1} = \frac{(h_2 + h_1)}{2\,h_1}\,h_2.$$

If $h_2 - h_1 = x$ this reduces to

$$\frac{v_1^2}{g} = \frac{(x + 2 h_1)(x + h_1)}{2 h_1}$$

$$\therefore x = \sqrt{\frac{h_1^2}{4} + \frac{2 h_1 v_1^2}{g}} - \frac{3}{2} h_1.$$

This gives the height of the standing wave.

An explanation of the production of the standing wave may be found as follows. An examination of equation (3) shows that $\frac{d h}{d l}$ can only be infinite and a standing wave formed when $v^2 = g h$, or when

$$\frac{v^2}{g h} \frac{d h}{d l} = \frac{d h}{d l}.$$

But

$$\frac{v^2}{g h} \cdot \frac{d h}{d l} = \frac{v}{g} \cdot \frac{v}{h} \cdot \frac{d h}{d l} = -\frac{v}{g} \frac{d v}{d l} = -\frac{d}{d l}\left(\frac{v^2}{2 g}\right)$$

so that the standing wave is produced when

$$-\frac{d}{d l}\left(\frac{v^2}{2 g}\right) = \frac{d h}{d l}$$

i.e., when the rate of decrease of kinetic energy is equal to the rate of increase of potential and pressure energy due to an increase in the depth, or vice versâ.

Until this point is reached the rate of decrease of kinetic energy is greater than that of increase of pressure and potential energy, the difference being due to energy expended in eddy formation. Assuming for the moment that the surface curve could be continued through the point, we should have the rate of increase of potential and pressure energy greater than that of decrease of kinetic energy, and hence should have an actual increase in total energy, a state of affairs which is manifestly impossible.

This can only be overcome by a sudden change in the distribution of pressure over the section of the stream, the effect being almost identical with that produced by the introduction of a solid obstacle in the path of the stream. As a consequence of the shock thus produced there is a sudden loss of energy in eddy production, the velocity of flow of necessity falls, and a corresponding rise of surface ensues.

After rising to the level, h_2, where $h_2 \begin{smallmatrix} > \\ < \end{smallmatrix} \begin{smallmatrix} \sqrt[3]{\frac{2 i}{f}} \cdot H \\ H \end{smallmatrix}$, we have the state of affairs considered in Case 1 (b).

Case 1 (b). Here $\dfrac{2\,i}{f} < 1$, while h is greater than $\sqrt[3]{\dfrac{2\,i}{f}}$. H and is less than H.

In equation (6) the numerator is now negative, while the denominator is positive, so that $\dfrac{d\,h}{d\,l}$ is negative, or the depth h diminishes down-stream.

As the velocity increases and h diminishes, the denominator of the fraction $\dfrac{h^3 - H^3}{h^3 - \dfrac{2\,i}{f}\,H^3}$ vanishes before the numerator, so that $\dfrac{d\,h}{d\,l}$ tends to a limiting value $-\infty$ where $h = \sqrt[3]{\dfrac{2\,i}{f}}\,.\,H$.

At this point the surface curve becomes vertical as shown in Fig. 137. If produced by a sudden drop in the bed of a stream, as shown in this figure, h increases up-stream, and approaches more nearly to H as this distance increases, the surface curve being asymptotic to the line $R\,R'$.

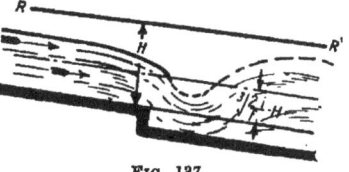

FIG. 137.

Such a drop in the bed may cause an appreciable increase in the velo-city of flow for a considerable dis-tance up-stream and may thus affect the foundations of structures (bridges, etc.) which may be placed up-stream, besides causing serious erosion of the bed.

In the case of the sluice (Fig. 135), the water after rising to the height h_2 is governed by this second set of conditions, so that the level again falls until $h = \sqrt[3]{\dfrac{2\,i}{f}}\,.\,H$. Inertia then causes the level to fall below this, when we have the conditions of Case 1 (a) repeated. Thus a series of stationary waves are produced, the level alternately rising and falling above and below that given by $h = \sqrt{\dfrac{2\,i}{f}}\,.\,H$. At each successive jump a loss of energy occurs, and the velocity energy after the jump is therefore diminished. It follows that the value of h_2 must be greater after each successive jump, and ultimately will become equal to H, after which steady flow occurs.

The same reasoning applies to the stream after passing the drop in the bed (Fig. 137) the depth ultimately settling down to H.

The state of affairs outlined in this second case may be met with where a flume having a slight inclination delivers water to a penstock from which one or more turbines or water wheels are fed. It then becomes important that the proportions of the flume should be such as to prevent the water level from falling below a certain minimum. This problem will afterwards be considered in detail (p. 324).

Case 1 (c).

$$\text{Let } \begin{cases} \dfrac{2\,i}{f} < 1. \\ h > H. \end{cases}$$

Here the surface is everywhere above the line $R\,R'$ (Fig. 138). Both the numerator and denominator in the fraction.

$$i \cdot \left\{ \frac{h^3 - H^3}{h^3 - \dfrac{2\,i}{f}\,H^3} \right\} \text{ (equation 6) are positive}$$

$$\therefore \quad \frac{d\,h}{d\,l} \text{ is positive.}$$

Down-stream then the depth increases, and $\dfrac{h^3 - H^3}{h^3 - \dfrac{2\,i}{f}\,H^3}$ ultimately

tends to the limit unity, *i.e.*, $\dfrac{d\,h}{d\,l}$ tends to the limit i, the slope of the

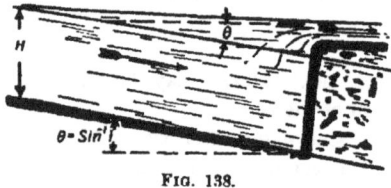

FIG. 138.

bed. It follows that the down-stream surface tends to become horizontal.

Up-stream h tends to the limit H, and $\dfrac{d\,h}{d\,l}$ to the limit zero, so that the curve tends to become asymptotic to the line $R\,R'$.

This is the form of surface curve produced by a weir or dam in a stream of small slope, and is of importance since the introduction of such a dam causes what may be a serious raising of the backwater level for some considerable distance up-stream.

Next let $\dfrac{2\,i}{f}$ be greater than unity, the state of affairs usually existing in artificial water supply channels.

Case 2 (a).

$$\text{Let } \begin{cases} \dfrac{2\,i}{f} > 1. \\ h < H. \end{cases}$$

$\frac{d\,h}{d\,l}$ (equation 6) is now positive and the depth increases down-stream.

Since, as h increases, the numerator vanishes before the denominator $\frac{d\,h}{d\,l} = 0$ in the limit, i.e., the surface curve tends to become asymptotic to the line $R\,R'$ (Fig. 139).

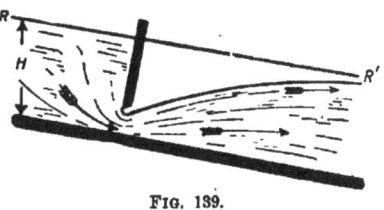

FIG. 139.

This state of affairs is attained at a sluice in a stream having a slope greater than $\frac{f}{2}$.

Case 2 (b).

Let $\frac{2\,i}{f} > 1$, and let h be greater than H and less than $\sqrt[3]{\frac{2\,i}{f}}$. H.

Here $\frac{d\,h}{d\,l}$ (equation 6) is negative and the depth diminishes downstream. As h diminishes the numerator vanishes before the denominator and in the limit $\frac{d\,h}{d\,l} = 0$, or the curve becomes asymptotic to the line $R\,R'$, and the stream settles down to the uniform depth H. This state of affairs is realised where an obstacle in a river bed may have caused the level to rise to within the required limits. The surface curve is then as shown in Fig. 140. Upstream, as h increases it finally

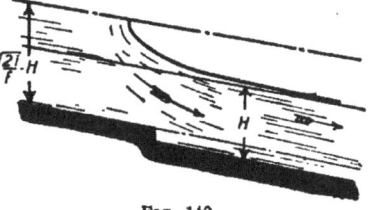

FIG. 140.

reaches the value $\sqrt[3]{\frac{2\,i}{f}}$. H. Here $\frac{d\,h}{d\,l}$ is $-\infty$, and the curve becomes perpendicular to the bed of the stream. As h increases still further the state of affairs considered in Case 2 (c) is attained. This vertical front is seen when a sudden rush of water, such as may be produced by the bursting of an embankment, is caused in a channel of fairly rapid slope. It is also seen in the bores which occur at certain states of the tide in the Seine between Havre and Rouen, and in various other rivers and contracted channels.

Case 2 (c).

Let $\begin{cases} \dfrac{2\,i}{f} > 1 \\[2mm] h > \sqrt[3]{\dfrac{2\,i}{f}}\,H. \end{cases}$

Here $\dfrac{d\,h}{d\,l}$ is positive $\therefore$ h increases down-stream.   Down-stream

$\dfrac{h - H^3}{h^3 - \dfrac{2\,i}{f}H^3}$ tends to the limiting value unity, so that in this direction

the limiting value of $\dfrac{d\,h}{d\,l}$ is i, or the surface tends to become horizontal
(Fig. 141).

Up-stream, as the depth diminishes, we reach a point where
$h = \sqrt[3]{\dfrac{2\,i}{f}}\,H$, and, for this value of h, $\dfrac{d\,h}{d\,l} = \infty$ or the surface curve
here becomes perpendicular to the bed of the stream, a standing wave
being produced.

This is the curve obtained where an under-water obstruction such as a
dam or broad-crested weir is placed across a stream of rapid slope.
Since the possibility of $\dfrac{d\,h}{d\,l}$ becoming infinite, depends on $\dfrac{2\,i}{f}$ being
greater than unity, the production of a standing wave under these

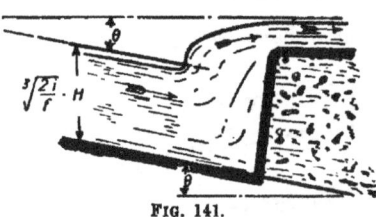

FIG. 141.

circumstances is only possible
where this latter condition is satisfied.

In practice the two most important cases are those represented
in 1 (b) and 1 (c).   In the first of
these, the effect of a sudden drop
in the bed of a stream may, as
already explained, be serious, while
the case of the reduction in level in a fore-bay feeding a power plant,
caused by the sudden demand for energy by the turbines also comes under
this heading.   In the second, the effect of a dam in increasing the surface
elevation at points further up-stream is important.   The investigation of
each of these cases resolves itself into determining, from a solution of
equation (6), the value of h corresponding to any point at a distance l
from some datum, since when this is known, the rise or fall from normal,
and consequently the change in velocity, can be determined.

To obtain a solution for the equation, we have

$$\frac{d\,h}{d\,l} = i\left\{\frac{\dfrac{h^3}{H^3} - 1}{\dfrac{h^3}{H^3} - \dfrac{2\,i}{f}}\right\}. \tag{6}$$

Writing $\dfrac{h}{H} = m$, so that $\dfrac{d\,h}{d\,m} = H$, this becomes

$$H\frac{d\,m}{d\,l} = i\left\{\frac{m^3 - 1}{m^3 - \dfrac{2\,i}{f}}\right\}$$

$$\therefore d\,m\left\{1 + \frac{1 - \dfrac{2\,i}{f}}{m^3 - 1}\right\} = \frac{i}{H}\,d\,l.$$

Integrating this expression,

$$\frac{i}{H}\,l = m + \left(1 - \frac{2\,i}{f}\right)\int\frac{d\,m}{m^3 - 1} + \text{const.} \qquad (7)$$

while

$$\int\frac{d\,m}{m^3 - 1} = \frac{1}{2}\int\left\{\frac{m+1}{(m^2 + m + 1)\,(m - 1)} - \frac{1}{m^2 + m + 1}\right\}d\,m$$

$$= -\frac{1}{2}\left\{\frac{1}{3}\log_e\frac{m^2 + m + 1}{(m - 1)^2} + \frac{2}{\sqrt{3}}\,\tan^{-1}\frac{2\,m + 1}{\sqrt{3}}\right\}$$

$$\therefore \frac{i}{H}\,l = \left[m - \left(1 - \frac{2\,i}{f}\right)\right.$$

$$\left.\left\{\frac{1}{6}\log_e\frac{m^2 + m + 1}{(m - 1)^2} + \frac{1}{\sqrt{3}}\,\tan^{-1}\frac{2\,m + 1}{\sqrt{3}}\right\}\right] + C. \quad (8)$$

The expression

$$\left\{\frac{1}{6}\log_e\frac{m^2 + m + 1}{(m - 1)^2} + \frac{1}{\sqrt{3}}\,\tan^{-1}\frac{2\,m + 1}{\sqrt{3}}\right\}$$

is often termed the "backwater function." Writing this as $\phi\,(m)$, the equation becomes

$$\frac{i}{H}\,l = m - \left(1 - \frac{2\,i}{f}\right)\phi\,(m) + C$$

$$\therefore i\,l = h - H\left(1 - \frac{2\,i}{f}\right)\phi\,(m) + C$$

$$\therefore h = i\,l + H\left(1 - \frac{2\,i}{f}\right)\phi\,(m) + C \qquad (9)$$

Thus if h_1 and h_2 are the depths at points distant l_1 and l_2 from the datum, we have

$$h_1 - h_2 = i\,(l_1 - l_2) + H\left(1 - \frac{2\,i}{f}\right)\left\{\phi\,(m_1) - \phi\,(m_2)\right\} \quad (10)$$

The following table gives values of $\phi\,(m)$ for different values of $\dfrac{h}{H}$ in the case of a dam, where h is always greater than H.

From these values a curve may be constructed if required for use, and intermediate values obtained by interpolation.

$\frac{h}{H}$	$\phi\,(m)$	$\frac{h}{H}$	$\phi\,(m)$	$\frac{h}{H}$	$\phi\,(m)$	$\frac{h}{H}$	$\phi\,(m)$
1·000	∞	1·020	2·098	1·10	1·587	2·20	1·015
1·001	3·090	1·025	2·025	1·15	1·468	2·50	·989
1·002	2·860	1·030	1·966	1·20	1·387	3·0	·963
1·003	2·725	1·036	1·908	1·30	1·280	4·0	·939
1·004	2·629	1·044	1·843	1·40	1·211	5·0	·927
1·005	2·555	1·050	1·803	1·50	1·162	7·0	·915
1·007	2·445	1·056	1·763	1·60	1·125	10·0	·911
1·010	2·326	1·060	1·745	1·70	1·096	15·0	·909
1·012	2·266	1·070	1·697	1·80	1·073	20·0	·908
1·015	2·192	1·080	1·656	2·00	1·039	50·0	·907

In the case of a fall down-stream, $\frac{h}{H}$ is always less than unity. The following table gives values of $(\psi\,m)$ for this case.

$\frac{h}{H}$	$\phi\,(m)$	$\frac{h}{H}$	$\phi\,(m)$	$\frac{h}{H}$	$\phi\,(m)$	$\frac{h}{H}$	$\phi\,(m)$
1·000	∞	·985	2·183	·850	1·367	·400	·709
·999	3·090	·980	2·085	·800	1·253	·350	·656
·998	2·859	·975	2·009	·750	1·159	·300	·605
·997	2·723	·970	1·946	·700	1·078	·250	·553
·996	2·628	·960	1·847	·650	1·006	·200	·503
·995	2·552	·950	1·769	·600	·939	·150	·453
·994	2·491	·940	1·705	·550	·877	·100	·402
·992	2·395	·920	1·602	·500	·819	·050	·352
·990	2·319	·900	1·522	·450	·763	·000	·302

As an example of the use of these tables, calculate the rise in level at a point $\frac{1}{2}$ mile up stream, produced by a dam arranged so as to raise the level at its crest through 8 feet. The original depth of the stream, supposed uniform, was 2 feet, the slope of the bed 1 in 500 ($=$·002), and the value of $f=$·006.

The necessary height of the dam may be calculated by an application of equation (1), p. 168. Assuming this to be done, we have, in the preceding formulae

$$II = 2. \quad 1 - \frac{2\,i}{f} = 1 - \frac{2}{3} = \frac{1}{3}.$$

Let the suffix (1) refer to a point just above the dam, and the suffix (2) to the given point. Then since the positive direction of l is down-stream, we have in equation (10), $h_1 = 10$; $l_1 = 0$; $l_2 = -2640$, and from the tables we get $\phi\,(m_1) = \phi\left(-\dfrac{10}{2}\right) = \cdot 927$, so that this equation becomes

$$10 - h_2 = \cdot 002\,(2640) + \cdot 6\dot{6}\left\{\cdot 927 - \phi\left(\frac{h_2}{2}\right)\right\}$$

$$\therefore\ h_2 - \frac{2}{3}\,\phi\left(\frac{h_2}{2}\right) = 4 \cdot 102.$$

This equation can only be solved by trial.

Let $\qquad\qquad h_2 - \dfrac{2}{3}\cdot\phi\left(\dfrac{h_2}{2}\right) - 4 \cdot 102 = y$

Then if $\qquad h_2 = 5, y = 5 - \cdot 6593 - 4 \cdot 102 = + \cdot 2387$

,, $\qquad\qquad h_2 = 4, y = 4 - \cdot 6927 - 4 \cdot 102 = - \cdot 7947$

For a solution of the equation, y must equal 0, and since the value of a continuous function such as y cannot change from $+$ to $-$ without passing through the value zero, it follows that for some value of h_2 between 4 and 5, $y = 0$.

Evidently, too, the correct value of h_2 is nearer 5 than 4. Try $h_2 = 4 \cdot 75$.

If $h_2 = 4 \cdot 75, y = 4 \cdot 75 - \cdot 6656 - 4 \cdot 102 = - \cdot 0176$. The value of h_2 is then between $4 \cdot 75$ and $5 \cdot 0$.

A close approximation to the correct result can then be obtained by drawing a curve connecting those values of y and of h_2 already found. Where this curve intersects the axis of h_2, we shall have the value of h_2 which makes $y = 0$, and therefore which satisfies the equation. In the problem, $h_2 = 4 \cdot 78$ provides a very close approximation to the correct value. At a distance up-stream equal to 4,000 feet the value of h, determined in the same way, is $2 \cdot 34$ feet. Since the slope is $\cdot 002$ the height of the bed at this latter point, above that at the dam, is $\cdot 002 \times 4,000 = 8 \cdot 0$ feet.

The surface at this latter point is therefore $\cdot 34$ feet higher than at the dam. With the dam removed and the flow per minute unchanged, the flow being uniform and the depth of channel equal to H, the difference of level instead of being $\cdot 34$ feet would be $8 \cdot 0$ feet.

Figure 142 illustrates the form of backwater curve observed by

D'Aubuisson on the Wesser. Here the mean slope of the bed was 2·33 feet per mile = ·000441, and the depth before introducing the dam was 2·46 feet. The effect of the dam in raising the surface level was apparent for 4·33 miles up-stream.

In a second series of observations on the Werra, the following results were obtained.

Mean depth $H = 1·7$ feet; width = 80 feet; fall = 3·88 feet per mile.

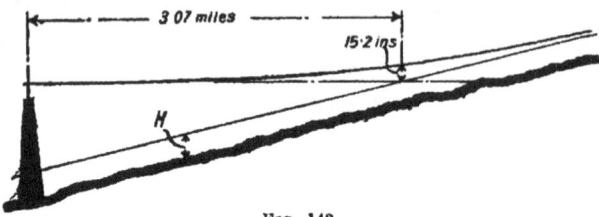

3 07 miles

15·2 ins

H

FIG. 142.

A dam 15·66 feet in height was placed across the stream, and the height of water over the sill was found to be 1·13 feet.

The following table indicates the observed and calculated depths, and rises in surface level at points above the dam.

Distance of observed point from Dam.		0.	·65 Miles.	1·5 Miles.	3·5 Miles.
Depth of water in feet .	observed	16·79	12·30	11·28	3·01
	calculated	—	13·50	11·35	3·20
Rise of level in feet .	observed	15·09	10·60	10·58	1·31
	calculated	—	11·80	10·65	1·50

In these calculations the value of f has been taken as ·02.

As an example of the effect of a drop in the bed of a stream in producing an increased velocity at points up stream, consider the same stream as before to have a fall at some point in its length (Case 1 (b)), and suppose that this causes a lowering of the surface just above the fall through a depth of 6 inches.

Then as before $H = 2$; $1 - \dfrac{2\,i}{f} = \dfrac{1}{3}$.

Also in equation (10), we have

$$h_1 = 1\cdot 5\; ;\; l_1 = 0\; ;\; \phi\,(m_1) = \phi\left(\frac{1\cdot 5}{2}\right) = 1\cdot 159 \text{ (from table).}$$

To determine the depth at a point 50 feet up stream we have $l_2 = -50$ feet, so that the equation becomes

$$1\cdot 50 - h_2 = \cdot002\,(50) + \frac{2}{3}\left\{ 1\cdot 159 - \phi\left(\frac{h_2}{2}\right) \right\}$$

$$\therefore\; h_2 - \frac{2}{3}\phi\left(\frac{h_2}{2}\right) - 1\cdot 50 - \cdot 10 - \cdot 773$$

$$= \cdot 627.$$

Putting $h_2 - \dfrac{2}{3}\,\phi\left(\dfrac{h_2}{2}\right) = \cdot 627 = y$ we get

if $h_2 = 1\cdot 8$, $y = 1\cdot 8\ -\ 1\cdot 0146 - \cdot 627 = +\ \cdot 1584$

„ $h_2 = 1\cdot 9$, $y = 1\cdot 9\ -\ 1\cdot 1793 - \cdot 627 = +\ \cdot 0937$

„ $h_2 = 1\cdot 95$, $y = 1\cdot 95 - 1\cdot 3393 - \cdot 627 = -\ \cdot 0163$

On plotting values of h_2 and y, the curve shows that y_2 is zero when $h_2 = 1\cdot 946$ (approximately), and this, therefore, gives the depth at the given point.

At a point 20 feet up stream we have

$$h_2 - \frac{2}{3}\,\phi\left(\frac{h_2}{2}\right) = \cdot 667$$

On solving this equation in the same way, we find that the depth here is $1\cdot 932$ feet (approximately). Since the breadth is constant, the mean velocity at any point is inversely proportional to the depth, so that at the two points 20 and 50 feet up stream the velocities are increased by the fall in the ratios $\dfrac{2}{1\cdot 932}$ and $\dfrac{2}{1\cdot 946}$ respectively.

This action becomes increasingly important as the slope is diminished. For example, in the previous case, if the slope were diminished to $\cdot 001$, the velocities at the same two points would be increased by the fall in the ratios $\dfrac{2}{1\cdot 56}$ and $\dfrac{2}{1\cdot 72}$ respectively.

As a further example of the use of these formulae, consider the case of a flume of rectangular section, feeding a forebay from which a turbine is to be supplied.

The breadth of flume is 20 feet, the slope 1 in 1,000, the length 1,000 yards, and the value of $f = \cdot 003$. The discharge required is 500 cubic feet per second.

The value of H, the uniform depth necessary to give this supply is given by

$$H = \sqrt[3]{\frac{f\,Q^2}{b^2\,2\,g\,i}} = \sqrt[3]{\frac{\cdot 003 \times 25 \times 10{,}000}{64\cdot 4 \times 400 \times \cdot 001}}$$

$$= 3\cdot 08 \text{ feet.}$$

If at the upper end the depth of water is greater than this, say 4 feet, we have (Case 1 (c)) and everywhere $h > H$. The depth of water thus increases down stream.

Applying equation (10), we now have

$$\begin{cases} h \text{ (at entrance to flume)} = 4\cdot 0\,;\ l_1 = 0 \\[6pt] H = 3\cdot 08\,;\ l_2 = 3{,}000 \text{ feet}\,;\ \dfrac{2\,i}{f} = \dfrac{\cdot 002}{\cdot 003} = \dfrac{2}{3} \\[6pt] \phi\left(\dfrac{h_1}{H}\right) = \phi\left(\dfrac{4}{3\cdot 08}\right) = \phi\,(1\cdot 3) = 1\cdot 280 \text{ (tables)} \end{cases}$$

$$\therefore\ 4 - h_2 = -\,\cdot 001\,(3{,}000) + \frac{3\cdot 08}{3}\left\{1\cdot 280 - \phi\left(\frac{h_2}{H}\right)\right\}.$$

$$\therefore\ 7 - 1\cdot 315 = h_2 - 1\cdot 027\ \phi\left(\frac{h_2}{H}\right)$$

$$\therefore\ h_2 - 1\cdot 027\ \phi\left(\frac{h_2}{H}\right) - 5\cdot 685 = y.$$

If $h_2 = 6\cdot 70$ $y = 1\cdot 015 - 1\cdot 027\,(1\cdot 017) = -\,\cdot 030$

,, $h_2 = 6\cdot 75$ $y = 1\cdot 065 - 1\cdot 027\,(1\cdot 015) = +\,\cdot 022.$

The correct value of h_2, the depth in the forebay, is approximately 6·73 feet. The depth of the water in the flume at different points in its length can be calculated in the same way, and the necessary height of side ascertained.

If, at the upper end, the depth of water is equal to H, this will remain constant throughout, while if less than H and greater than $\sqrt[3]{\dfrac{2\,i}{f}}\,H$ or ·871 H, i.e., between 3·08 feet and 2·68 feet, we get Case 1 (b). The height will now decrease down stream until it reaches the value $\sqrt{\dfrac{2\,i}{f}}$, after which a series of waves will be produced, and the depth will, as explained in Case 1 (b), finally settle down to 3·08 feet.

The critical point is found by putting $h_2 = \sqrt[3]{\dfrac{2\,i}{f}}\,H = 2\cdot 68$ in equation (10). Let $h_1 = 3\cdot 0$ feet.

Then we have at the critical point

$$3 - 2\cdot 68 = \cdot 001\,(-\,l_2) + \frac{3\cdot 08}{3}\left\{\ \phi\left(\frac{3\cdot 0}{3\cdot 08}\right) - \phi\left\{\frac{2\cdot 68}{3\cdot 08}\right\}\ \right\}$$

$$\therefore \quad \cdot 82 = \cdot 001 \, (- l_2) - 1 \cdot 027 \, \{ \, 1 \cdot 996 - 1 \cdot 429 \, \}$$
$$\therefore \quad \cdot 262 = \cdot 001 \, l_2$$
$$\therefore \quad l_2 = 262 \text{ feet.}$$

If, at the entrance, the depth is less than 2·68 feet, as might occur if this flume were fed from a sluice, we have Case 1 (a) repeated, and the depth would finally increase up to 3·08 feet. With an open channel leading directly out of a reservoir, the required discharge could only be obtained by having the depth at entrance equal to or greater than H.

ART. 90.—CHANNEL WITH HORIZONTAL BED.

Here i is zero, so that equation (6) of the last article ceases to apply. Making $i = o$ in equation (3), p. 310, we get

$$\frac{d\,h}{d\,l} = \frac{\dfrac{f\,v^2}{2\,g} \cdot \dfrac{P}{A}}{1 - \dfrac{v^2}{g\,h}} \tag{1}$$

Writing $v^2 = \dfrac{Q^2}{b^2\,h^2}$ we have, if the channel is rectangular and broad, so that $\dfrac{P}{A} = \dfrac{1}{h}$ (sensibly),

$$\frac{d\,h}{d\,l} = \frac{\dfrac{f\,Q^2}{2\,g\,b^2\,h^3}}{1 - \dfrac{Q^2}{g\,b^2\,h^3}}$$

$$\therefore \quad d\,h \left\{ \frac{2\,g\,b^2\,h^3}{f\,Q^2} - \frac{2}{f} \right\} = d\,l. \tag{2}$$

Integrating between the limits l_1 and l_2 we get

$$l_1 - l_2 = \frac{1}{f} \left\{ \frac{g\,b^2}{2\,Q^2} \, (h_1{}^4 - h_2{}^4) - 2\,(h_1 - h_2) \right\} \tag{3}$$

from which the difference in level $(h_1 - h_2)$ at any two points distant $l_1 - l_2$ from each other, may be calculated when a given quantity Q cubic feet per second is flowing along the channel.

Expressing (2) as

$$\frac{d\,h}{d\,l} = \frac{1}{\dfrac{2}{f} \left\{ \dfrac{g\,b^2\,h^3}{Q^2} - 1 \right\}} \tag{4}$$

we have, for $\dfrac{d\,h}{d\,l}$ to be infinite, the condition

$$g\,b^2\,h^3 = Q^2 = v^2\,b^2\,h^2$$
$$\therefore \quad v^2 = g\,h,$$

so that if by any means such as drawing off a considerable amount of water suddenly by opening a lock gate, the velocity can be made equal to $\sqrt{g\,h}$, a wave with vertical crest will be produced.

Art. 91.—Change of Level in a Stream Produced by Bridge, Piers, etc.

Where a series of piers are placed across the bed of a stream, the effect

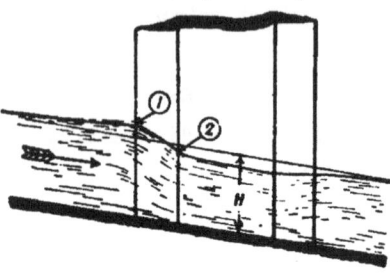
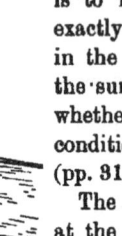

is to raise the up-stream level exactly as if a dam were placed in the stream, and the form of the surface curve will depend on whether the stream satisfies the conditions of Case 1 (c) or 2 (c) (pp. 316 and 317).

The height will be a maximum at the up-stream end of the pier. On arriving at the contracted section of the stream, the velocity will be increased, the increase in kinetic energy necessitating a corresponding loss of potential energy, and the depth is diminished. On again arriving at the open channel the velocity diminishes and the depth increases (Fig. 143).

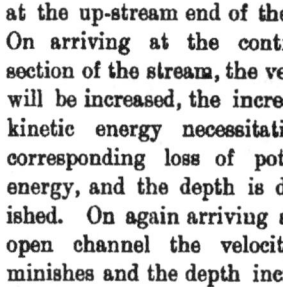
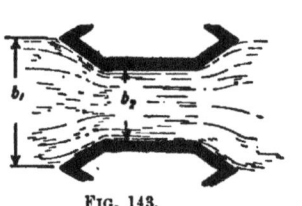

Fig. 143.

Neglecting losses by friction between the sections (1) and (2), if b_1 and b_2 are the effective breadths and h_1, h_2 the depths at these points, we have

$$h_1 + \frac{r_1^2}{2\,g} = h_2 + \frac{r_2^2}{2\,g}$$

assuming the kinetic energy to be that given by $\frac{r_1^2}{2\,g}$ and $\frac{r_2^2}{2\,g}$ where r_1 and r_2 are the mean velocities at the two sections, an assumption which within narrow limits is justified by experiment.

$$\therefore \quad r_2^2 = r_1^2 + 2\,g\,x, \text{ where } x = h_1 - h_2.$$

If the discharge through the contracted area at (2) is given by $c\,b_2\,h_2\,r_2$, we have

$$r_2 = \frac{Q}{c\,b_2\,h_2}$$

Also
$$v_1 = \frac{Q}{b_1\,h_1}$$

$$\therefore \quad \frac{Q^2}{(c\,b_2\,h_2)^2} = \frac{Q^2}{(b_1\,h_1)^2} + 2\,g\,x$$

$$\therefore \quad x = \frac{Q^2}{2\,g}\left\{\frac{1}{c^2\,b_2^2\,h_2^2} - \frac{1}{b_1^2\,h_1^2}\right\}$$

or
$$x = \frac{Q^2}{2\,g}\left\{\frac{1}{c^2\,b_2^2\,(h_1 - x)^2} - \frac{1}{b_1^2\,h_1^2}\right\}.$$

The value of c varies with the form of pier, but with pointed cutwaters is about ·95 (Eytelwein), diminishing to ·85 for a bridge having square or rectangular piers. By considering the problem as one of flow through a weir or notch having a submerged crest (this crest being level with the bed of the stream), and under an effective head x, we may obtain a second expression for Q in terms of x, and by equating these two expressions the value of h_1 may be obtained in terms of Q and of b_1 and b_2. From this, an application of equation (9) (p. 319) will give the depth at any point up stream, and the entire up-stream profile may then be plotted. On the down-stream side of the obstacle there is a gradual rise of the surface level as the depth increases to a uniform value H.

ART. 92.

With radial outward flow over a horizontal bed, such as occurs when a vertical stream impinges on such a surface, we have, if h is the depth at a radius r, Q the quantity per second, and v the velocity at radius r,

$$Q = v \times 2\,\pi\,r\,h = \text{const.}$$

$$\therefore \quad v\,r\,\frac{d\,h}{d\,r} + r\,h\,\frac{d\,v}{d\,r} + v\,h = 0$$

$$\therefore \quad \frac{d\,v}{d\,r} = -\left\{\frac{v\,d\,h}{h\,d\,r} + \frac{v}{r}\right\} \tag{1}$$

Substituting this value in equation (2) (p. 309), we have

$$i - \frac{d\,h}{d\,r} = -\left\{\frac{v^2}{g\,h}\frac{d\,h}{d\,l} + \frac{v^2}{g\,r}\right\} + \frac{f\,r^2}{2\,g}\cdot\frac{P}{A}. \tag{2}$$

But with a horizontal bed $i = o$.

Also
$$\frac{P}{A} = \frac{2\,\pi\,r}{2\,\pi\,r\,h} = \frac{1}{h}, \text{ and } l = r$$

$$\therefore \quad (2) \text{ becomes } \frac{d\,h}{d\,r} = \frac{\dfrac{v^2}{g\,r} - \dfrac{f\,v^2}{2\,g\,h}}{1 - \dfrac{v^2}{g\,h}} = \frac{\dfrac{v^2}{g}\left\{\dfrac{1}{r} - \dfrac{f}{2\,h}\right\}}{1 - \dfrac{v^2}{g\,h}}. \tag{3}$$

This becomes infinite if $v^2 = g\,h$,

i.e., if
$$\frac{Q^2}{4\,\pi^2\,r^2\,h^2} = g\,h$$

if
$$h^3 = \frac{Q^2}{4\,\pi^2\,g} \cdot \frac{1}{r^2}. \tag{4}$$

At the radius at which this relation holds, a standing wave will be formed.

The height of this wave may be estimated, as in the case of the wave produced in a rectangular channel.

If v_1 and v_2 are the velocities and h_1 and h_2 the depths immediately before and after the rise, so that $h_2 - h_1 = x$, we have, as on p. 313,

$$\frac{v_1^2}{g} = \frac{(h_2 + h_1)\,h_2}{2\,h_1}$$

from which

$$h_2 - h_1 = x = \sqrt{\frac{h_1^2}{4} + \frac{2\,h_1\,v_1^2}{g}} - \frac{3}{2}\,h_1.$$

ART. 93.—CHANGE OF LEVEL PRODUCED BY THE PASSAGE OF A BOAT THROUGH A NARROW CANAL WITH HORIZONTAL BED.

Let A = cross sectional area of canal.

„ a = sectional area of vessel amidships, beneath water line, by a plane perpendicular to its axis.

Let v = velocity of vessel.

Here the state of affairs may be simplified if we first consider the water to be a perfect fluid. As the vessel moves along through this fluid, the volume displaced by the forepart passes along backwards between the vessel and the sides and bottom of the canal to fill the space vacated in the rear. In this case we get a backward current extending from the prow to the stern of the boat, its velocity increasing as the effective area of the channel diminishes, and having a maximum value $v\left(\dfrac{a}{A-a}\right)$ at the amidships section.

To produce this current a surface gradient is necessary, the surface falling from its normal level at the prow to a minimum at the amidships section, and from this point rising to its normal level at the stern.

Due to the adhesion and viscosity of the fluid, however, a mass of water is dragged along with the boat, forming a current confined mainly to the centre and surface of the canal.

Since, for permanence of the *régime*, the backward flow across any section of the canal must equal the corresponding forward flow, the backward bottom current must now be sufficiently great to supply an additional mass of water equal to this, so that its velocity at the minimum section will be $\left(K + \dfrac{a'}{A - a'} \right) v$, its velocity at the bows being $K v$. Here $a' = a + a_1$ where a_1 is the area of the channel occupied by the forward current at the amidships section. $A - a'$ is then the effective area of the backward current.

But to produce a backward velocity of flow at the bows of the boat the surface level at the bows must be less than at some distance ahead, and will thus be below the normal. The result is that the water level in the canal falls as the boat approaches, has its minimum value near the amidships section, and then rises to attain its normal value. The effect of the bow waves in modifying the level at the bows is here neglected.

By applying equation (3) (p. 325), the difference of level at any two

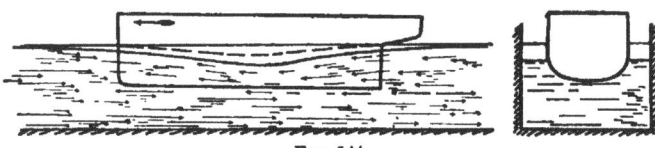

FIG. 144.

points in advance of the boat may be deduced in terms of $K v$, since $Q = K v b h_1$, where h_1 is the depth of water at the bows.

Fig. 144 shows the surface curves for a perfect fluid (dotted lines) and for water.[1]

If the boat is nearer to one side of the channel the velocities of flow are greater on this side of the boat, the pressures, particularly abaft its beam are consequently less, with the result that it tends to sheer off towards the further side.

ART. 93A.—SUCTION EFFECT BETWEEN PASSING SHIPS.

Even in open water, where one boat is overtaking another in moderately close proximity on a parallel path their mutual action, due to interference of currents between their hulls may have serious effects. The mass of water displaced by the forepart of the leading boat, returning to fill the space vacated by its stern causes a continual influx of water towards the

---

[1] For the further investigation of the change of level round a moving vessel, a paper in *The Engineer*, vol. 63, p. 252, may be consulted.

stern of the latter, and this is increased by the influx necessary to provide the water thrown astern by the propeller. Further astern the impact of the streams converging from the two sides of the hull produces a region of outflowing currents.

The bows of the overtaking boat first come within the influence of this region which tends to produce a slight outward sheer. As it creeps further ahead the bows come within the influence of the inflowing currents while the stern is still being repelled, with a resultant tendency to inward sheer which has often led to serious collisions. This effect is a maximum where the bows of the follower are about one-third of its length aft the bows of the leading ship. As the follower draws further ahead the tendency to sheer diminishes and is replaced by a tendency to bodily inward drift, while when almost abreast, the bows of the follower become exposed to the outflowing currents from the leader's bows while its stern is still being attracted, with a consequent tendency to an outward sheer.[1]

The effect depends largely on the sizes, speeds, and relative speeds of the vessels, increasing with the size of the leader, and with the common speed, and diminishing as the relative speed increases.

Art. 94.—Flow round River Bends.

A river flowing through an alluvial plain always tends to gradually increase any winding which may occur in its course, until finally a new channel is cut through the narrow neck of land thus formed. The following explanation of this scouring of the outer bank of a bend and the deposition of detritus on the inner bank has been given by Professor James Thompson.[2]

In consequence of the centrifugal force, the pressure at any level in a transverse section of the stream increases outwards, so that the level of the free surface is highest near the outer bank. Near the bottom, however, the resistance of the bed reduces the velocity and consequently the centrifugal force of the water, which now becomes insufficient to overcome the tendency to inward flow produced by the higher level of the free surface at the outside of the curve. The water near the bottom, then has a tendency to flow inwards and to carry with it gravel and other detritus which is left at the inner bank. Experiments in a model river

---

[1] For a full discussion of the phenomena of interaction an article in "Bedrock," Vol. I. No. 1, pp. 66—87, may be consulted.
[2] "Proceedings Royal Society," 1877, p. 356.

bend, in which the direction of flow was indicated by coloured stream lines and by the behaviour of threads tied to pins fixed in the bed of the stream, as well as by floating particles of matter, indicated a state of affairs as represented in Fig. 145. Here the dotted line A B indicates the path of a particle floating in the surface, while the curves shown in full represent the motion near the bed of the stream.

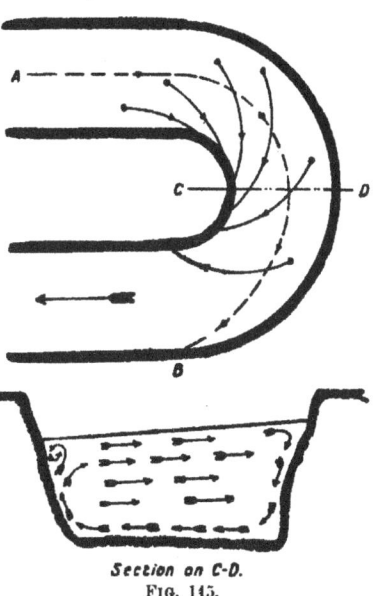

As indicated, a counter-current flows from inner to outer bank over the upper portion of the stream, but since the same volume of water is moved by the two currents, and since the sectional area of the outer current is comparatively very large, its effect in carrying suspended matter to the outer bank is negligible.

While this theory undoubtedly accounts for a portion of the erosion, and for the deposition of detritus at the inner bank, it is probable that the impact of the stream on the concave bank is a more potent factor in actually causing erosion, and more particularly is this the case when

Section on C-D.
Fig. 145.

the stream is in flood and when in consequence the erosive effects are most serious. Under such circumstances observation shows that the surface velocity is a maximum near the outer, and not the inner, bank.

Art. 94A.—Loss of Head Produced by Bends in an Open Channel.

Very little experimental evidence is available regarding the loss of head due to bends in an open channel. Experiments on a cement lined semicircular conduit, 9·8 feet in diameter, divided into four consecutive sections A B C D, showed the following results.[1]

Section A is a tangent 640 feet long.

   ,, B is 120 feet long and includes a curve of 100 feet radius.

[1] *Engineering Record*, Oct. 21st, 1911. By E. G. Hobson.

Section *C* is 220 feet long and includes two 50 feet radius reverse curves.

   „   *D* is 1075 feet long and is practically straight.

The horizontal curves were approximated to in construction by 10 foot tangents. The mean depth throughout was approximately 4 feet and the hydraulic mean radius 2·14 feet.

Section.	A	B	C	D
Mean velocity . .	7·10	6·86	6·94	7·15
Co-efficient *C* . .	129	114	90	119
Kutter's *n* . . .	·0132	·0149	·0189	·0142

The low value of the coefficient *C* in *D* as compared with that in *A* is doubtless due to the loss produced in this section during the redistribution of velocities produced by bend *C* and ought strictly to be debited to that bend, while similarly, a certain portion of the loss really due to bend *B* would appear due to the bends in the next section *C*.

Probably the following values of *C* would be more approximately correct.

	Value of *C*.
A. and *D*. Straight channel . .	128
B. Curve of 100 ft. radius . .	118
C. Reverse curves of 50 ft. radius .	88

ART. 95.—DISTRIBUTION OF VELOCITY IN AN OPEN CHANNEL.

Depression of the Filament of Maximum Velocity.

As in the case of a closed pipe, the resistance introduced by the solid boundaries causes the velocity to diminish in the neighbourhood of the ides and bottom of an open channel, and from analogy with pipe flow it night be expected that the maximum velocity in any cross section would e found in the surface and at the centre of the stream.

While this is commonly the case in a broad, rapid, and shallow stream

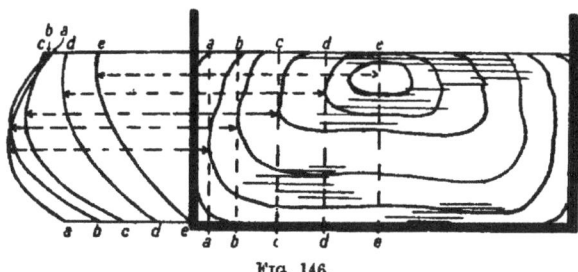

FIG. 146.

n any other case the filament of maximum velocity is usually found)elow the surface even with a down-stream wind. Its depth varies with he direction of the wind, with the depth and physical characteristics of he stream, and with the velocity of flow. On a calm day it usually lies it a depth between ·1 h and ·4 h (where h is the depth of the stream) and 'or depths above 5 feet, has a mean depth of about ·3 h.

Fig 146, taken from a gauging by Darcy of a rectangular channel ·25

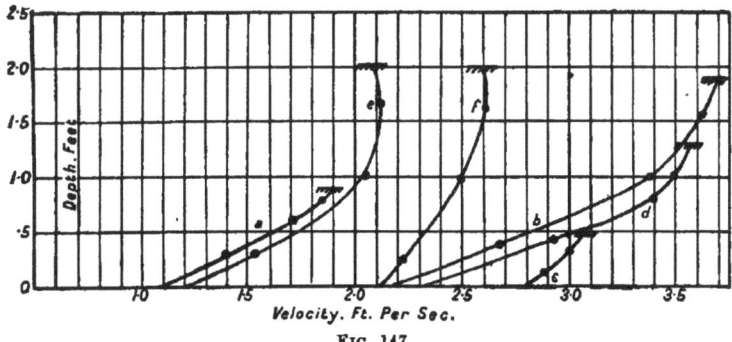

FIG. 147.

metre deep and ·8 metre wide, shows the general distribution of velocity \wer various vertical sections of a rectangular channel and also the equi-Velocity contours in a cross section, while Figs. 147 and 148, show the results of gaugings on the experimental channel of the Cornell University.[1]

This is of rectangular section, with concrete sides and bottom having a slope of 1 in 500, and has a width of 16 feet. Velocity measurements were made in eight verticals in a cross-section by means of current meters.

The curves in Figs. 147 and 148 show the variations of velocity in a vertical plane in typical of these experiments, each plotted point giving the mean of all eight observations at that depth in the cross-section.

The effect of a large ratio of width to depth in raising the filament of maximum velocity is evident from a comparison of the curves of Fig. 147

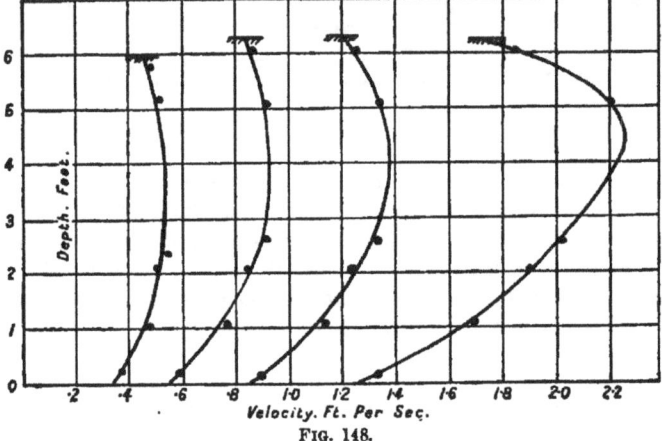

FIG. 148.

and of Fig. 148, while the effect of an increased velocity of flow in raising the filament is evident from a comparison of the several curves of Fig. 148.

The depression of this filament of maximum velocity is mainly due to the action of the sides of the channel. Frictional losses at the sides reduce the energy and thus the head of the water in their neighbourhood, with the result that the surface level at the sides is lower than near the centre of the stream, and the cross-sectional profile of the water surface is a curve concave to the bed. Owing to this super-elevation of the water near the centre and to its tendency to find its own level, transverse currents are set up which travel downwards near the centre of the stream; outwards along the bottom to either bank, upwards along the sides, and, for permanence of *régime*, inwards along and near the surface.

[1] U. S. Geological Survey. Water Supply and Irrigation Papers, No. 95, pp. 76 and 77.

Since the inward surface drifts consist of water which has travelled up the sides and has come from the region of minimum velocity, they will evidently have the effect of reducing the surface velocity and of depressing the filament of maximum velocity.

The sketches in Fig. 149 *a* and *b* show respectively the directions

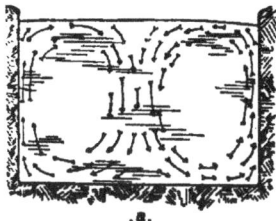 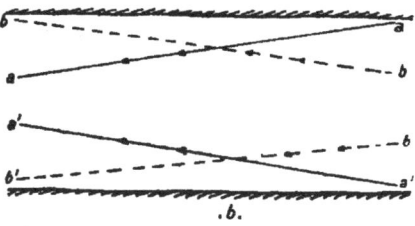

.a. .b.

FIG. 149.

of the transverse currents, and of the resultant motion of the stream, the full lines *a'a',· aa*, in Fig. 149 *b* representing the direction of the surface currents, and the dotted lines *b'b'*, *bb*, those of the bottom currents. The presence of such currents in channels of various sizes has been experimentally demonstrated by the author.[1]

In addition to this action of the sides, any retardation of the flow

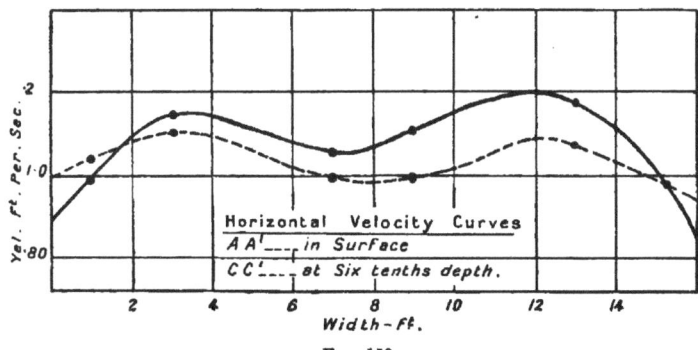

FIG. 150.

being more marked over the central and swifter portions of the stream tends to increase the super-elevation of the central surface and the formation of these transverse currents, while an acceleration of the flow

[1] Proc. Roy. Soc., A., Vol. LXXXII., 1909, pp. 149—159.

tends to reduce them. The author's experiments however indicate that for any such non-uniform flow as is likely to be experienced at a gauging station, the influence of the sides is the all-important factor.

This theory explains why, as is found in practice, the depth of the filament of maximum velocity, and, as will be seen later, also that of mean velocity in any vertical,

(a) is greater as the influence of the sides increases and hence as the ratio of depth to width of the stream increases.

(b) is less as the roughness of the bottom increases, since this rough-

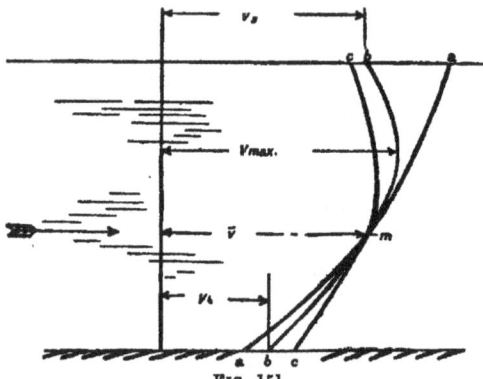

ness retards the transverse current without having any compensating effect.

(c) in the case of a rectangular channel, is greater nearer the sides.

It also explains why, on measuring the velocities across a horizontal in a stream, two points of maximum velocity are often found, these being one

FIG. 151.

on each side of the centre as shown in Fig. 150, which is taken from a gauging of the Cornell channel.[1]

The effect of the wind on the curve of velocities in a vertical is indicated in Fig. 151, which shows the curves

(a) with a strong up-stream wind.

(b) with no wind.

(c) with a strong down-stream wind.

It is found that although both the magnitude and position of the filament of maximum velocity is affected, that of the filament of mean velocity (m in Fig. 151) is sensibly independent of the state of the wind. The probable explanation of this is that an up-stream wind banks up the head waters and so increases the surface gradient of the stream, thereby increasing the velocity of flow over its lower portions to an extent which compensates for the reduced velocity of the surface layers.

[1] From U. S. Geol. Survey, Water Supply Papers, No. 95, pp. 73 and 74.

Mean Velocity in a Vertical.

Actually the position of the filament of maximum velocity in a vertical is not of great importance.   That of the filament of mean velocity, which is at a greater depth, is however very important in stream gauging, since, if it be known, the operation of gauging reduces itself to the measurement of a single velocity at this depth in each of a series of verticals distributed across the stream.

The depth of the latter filament varies from about ·5h to ·7h, having the former value in a wide and shallow stream of depth less than about 2·0 feet, and the latter value in a smooth wooden or cement channel whose depth is approximately one-half the width.   In the great majority of cases in practice it lies between ·55h and ·65h increasing with the depth and diminishing with the roughness of the channel.   An examination of a large number of river and canal gaugings by members of the U.S. Geological Survey [1] leads to the following as the most probable values of its depth.

Condition of bed.	Very rough with boulders.					Large gravel and small boulders.				
Depth of stream, feet . . .	0 to 2	2 to 4	4 to 6	6 to 10	above 10	0 to 2	2 to 4	4 to 6	6 to 10	above 10
Ratio $\dfrac{\text{depth of filament of mean vel.}}{\text{depth of stream.}}$	·50	·56	·59	·63	·67	·54	·58	·62	·66	·69

Condition of bed.	Small gravel and sand.					Very smooth wood or cement.				
Depth of stream, feet . . .	0 to 2	2 to 4	4 to 6	6 to 10	above 10	0 to 2	2 to 4	4 to 6	6 to 10	above 10
Ratio $\dfrac{\text{depth of filament of mean vel.}}{\text{depth of stream.}}$	·57	·60	·65	·69	·71	·61	·65	·68	·70	·72

Generally speaking, the velocity at six-tenths depth in any vertical will give the mean velocity in that vertical within 5 per cent. except in

---

[1] U. S. Geol. Survey, Water Supply and Irrigation Papers, No. 95.

abnormal cases, while the mean of the velocities at two-tenths and at eight-tenths of the depth may also be relied upon as giving the mean velocity within narrow limits.

The velocity in a vertical is least at the bottom, the ratio of bottom to mean velocity ranging from ·6 to ·9. It usually lies between ·75 and ·85, but varies widely in a short interval in the same stream.

The ratio of the mean to the surface velocity in a vertical also varies within somewhat wide limits and depends largely on the direction and force of the wind. On a calm day it lies between ·80 and ·90, diminishing with the velocity of flow, with the roughness of the channel, and with the ratio of breadth to depth. While usually inadvisable to use the surface velocity in computing the discharge of a stream, it is sometimes impossible, in time of flood to make any other measurements. Under such circumstances the surface velocity, multiplied by ·85 will give the mean velocity in a vertical with a fair degree of approximation.

The ratio of the mean velocity over the whole section to the maximum surface velocity varies considerably with the depth and state of the channel and with the direction of the wind. On a calm day it usually lies between ·60 and ·85, increasing with the depth of the stream. In a gauging of the Rhine—depth 6 to 19 feet—its value was ·73 while Harlacher obtained the same value in gauging the Elbe—depth 4—7 feet. Gaugings of the Eger at Falkenau (·62 to 1·1 feet deep) gave a value of ·58. The following values of this ratio are deduced from Bazin's formula (p. 342), by writing $v_{mean} = C \sqrt{m \sin. \theta}$ and by giving C its appropriate values.

Hydraulic Mean Depth of Section.	Material of Bed.			
	Planed Planks, Cement, etc.	Brickwork.	Rubble Masonry.	Earth.
1·0 feet	·85	·83	·77	·65
2·0 ,,	,,	,,	·79	·71
8·0 ,,	,,	,,	·80	·73
4·0 ,,	,,	,,	·81	·75
5·0 ,,	,,	,,	,,	·76
6·0 ,,	,,	·84	,,	·77
10·0 ,,	,,	,,	·82	·78
20·0 ,,	,,	,,	,,	·80

In a very shallow stream the vertical velocity curves approximate to straight lines, and in this case the means of surface and bottom velocities give a close approximation to the mean velocity.

The main results of a large number of river gaugings by members of the U.S. Geological Survey are given below.[1]

Here the symbol S means sandy; G gravelly; R rocky; B boulders.

River.	Approximate Width Feet.	Range of depth. Feet.	Coefficient for reducing to mean velocity in any vertical the vel. observed at following points.			Per cent. of depth at which thread of mean vel. is found.	Character of bottom.
			Six-tenths depth.	Mean of top and bottom.	Top.		
Appomattox, Va.	150	2·5 — 4·9	1·00	1·11	·81	61·5	S
James, Va.	850	3·0— 4·4	1·01	1·08	·88	59·6	S
Roanoke, Va	110	1·8— 3·3	·99	1·01	·81	60·9	R and S
Staunton, N.C.	400	2·0-- 6·0	·96	1·12	·95	65·7	G and S
Dan, N.C.	600	1·4— 3·7	·99	1·01	·86	61·6	S
Dan, Va.	350	3·5— 9·8	·98	1·09	·90	63·6	S
Reddie, N.C.	85	1·7— 2·5	1·02	·97	·88	57·7	S
Yadkin, N.C.	160	2·7— 6·3	·96	1·12	·91	66·5	S and B
Yadkin, N.C.	450	4·0—11·3	1·02	1·06	·81	59·2	S and R
Catauba, N.C.	200	1·8— 5·0	1·00	1·04	·82	60·6	S and G
Catauba, N.C.	200	6·3— 7·0	1·00	1·08	·88	58·5	M
Catauba, N.C.	110	3·5	1·01	1·05	·80	59·0	S
Wateree, S.C.	300	12·3—17·7	1·01	1·13	·90	58·4	M
Broad, S.C.	500	5·0— 8·9	·96	1·22	·89	65·4	M and S
Saluda, S.C.	800	3·0— 8·5	·97	1·03	·82	62·2	S
Little Tennessee, N.C.	660	3·6— 6·0	1·03	1·06	·83	58·7	B
Nolichucky, Tennessee	300	1·6— 5·1	1·02	1·02	·80	59·1	B
Fishkill, N.Y.	90	2— 5	1·036	—	·79	58·7	G
Wallkill, N.Y.	130	3—17	·98	—	·85	63·7	S
Farad Flume, Cal.	10·1	5·98	·95	1·25	1·09	76·0	Wood
Cornell Canal	16·0	7·2— 8·3	—	—	—	65·7	Concrete
,, ,,	16·0	·55— 1·9	—	—	—	54·3	,,

The ratio of the velocity at mid depth to the mean velocity in any vertical appears to vary very little, its usual value ranging from 1·02 to 1·06, increasing with the depth of the stream. A value of 1·04 may be relied upon as giving the mean velocity within 3 per cent. for all normal sections and velocities of flow.

ART. 96.—DISTRIBUTION OF VELOCITY OVER A VERTICAL THROUGH THE CENTRE OF THE STREAM.

In spite of very many experiments which have been carried out to determine the distribution of velocity, and of many attempts to formularise the results of such investigations, so many and so varied are the factors

[1] U. S. Geol. Survey, Water Supply and Irrigation Papers, No. 95, pp. 150—158.

which influence this distribution, that, as might be expected from the nature of the case, the formulae so far collected can only be considered as giving useful approximations to the required result, and this is more particularly the case where the flow in a natural channel of irregular section is under consideration.

By making one or two assumptions as to the circumstances governing the flow in an open channel, a theoretical formula may be deduced, which, while only applying so far as these assumptions are justified, may still serve as the rational basis of a more exact empirical formula, for giving the distribution of velocity. Such a formula will now be considered.

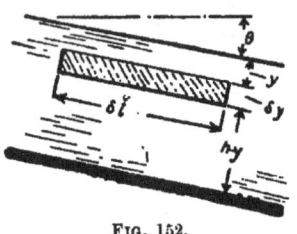

Suppose the stream to be sensibly parallel; of width which is great in comparison with its depth; flowing steadily; and that the resistance to flow is due entirely to simple viscous shear, a state of affairs never exactly realised in practice.

FIG. 152.

Let y be the vertical distance from the surface, of a stratum of the fluid, δy the thickness, δl the length, and b the breadth of the stratum (Fig. 152).

The weight of this element of fluid $= W b \, \delta y \, \delta l$.

The resolved part of this weight in the direction of motion $\left.\right\} = W b \, \delta y \, \delta l \cdot \sin \theta$.

The difference of tractive force on the upper and lower faces of the stratum $= \mu \dfrac{d^2 v}{d y^2} . b . \delta l . \delta y$, where μ is the coefficient of viscosity (p. 67) and where v is the velocity of flow in the direction of the stream. The pressures on the two ends of the stratum are equal since these are at the same depth and are of the same area. Also since the stream is wide, the variation of shear on the two vertical sides of the stratum may be neglected, as explained on p. 66.

$$\therefore \quad W b \, \delta y \, \delta l \sin \theta = - \mu \frac{d^2 v}{d y^2} . b \, \delta l . \delta y$$

$$\therefore \quad \frac{W \sin \theta}{\mu} = - \frac{d^2 v}{d y^2},$$

the negative sign denoting that the resultant shear force acting upon the element is in opposite direction to the force $W \sin \theta$.

Integrating this expression twice, we get

$$v = C + B y - \frac{W \sin \theta}{2 \mu} y^2 \qquad (1)$$

If r_s = surface velocity, *i.e.*, where $y = 0$, $C = v_s$

$$\therefore \ v = r_s + B y - \frac{W \sin \theta}{2 \mu} \cdot y^2 \tag{2}$$

$$= v_s - \frac{W \sin \theta}{2 \mu} \left(y - \frac{B \mu}{W \sin \theta} \right)^2 + \frac{B^2 \mu}{2 \, W \sin \theta}$$

$$\therefore \ v = v_s + \frac{B^2 \mu}{2 \, W \sin \theta} - \frac{W \sin \theta}{2 \mu} \left(y - \frac{B \mu}{W \sin \theta} \right)^2 \tag{3}$$

the equation to a parabola having a horizontal axis at a depth

$$\frac{B \mu}{W \sin \theta} = y_1.$$

Since
$$\frac{d v}{d y} = \frac{W \sin \theta}{\mu} \left\{ y - \frac{B \mu}{W \sin \theta} \right\}$$

we have $\dfrac{d v}{d y} = 0$, *i.e.*, the velocity is a maximum where

$$y = \frac{B \mu}{W \sin \theta}, \ \textit{i.e.,} \ \text{at a depth } y_1$$

$$\therefore \ r_{max} = v_s + \frac{B^2 \mu}{2 \, W \sin \theta}$$

$$= v_s + \frac{W \sin \theta}{2 \mu} \cdot y_1^2 \tag{4}$$

$\therefore$ from (2) and (4) we have $r_{max} - v = \dfrac{W \sin \theta}{2 \mu} (y_1 - y)^2$. (5)

If r_b = bottom velocity, where $y = h$

$$r_b = v_s + B h - \frac{W \sin \theta}{2 \mu} h^2 \text{ from (2)}$$

$$\therefore \ B = \frac{r_b - r_s}{h} + \frac{W \sin \theta}{2 \mu} h$$

$$\therefore \ v = v_s + \frac{v_b - v_s}{h} \cdot y + \frac{W \sin \theta}{2 \mu} (h y - y^2). \tag{6}$$

Also
$$v - v_b = B (y - h) + \frac{W \sin \theta}{2 \mu} (h^2 - y^2)$$

$$= \frac{W \sin \theta}{2 \mu} \left\{ 2 y_1 (y - h) + (h^2 - y^2) \right\}$$

$$\therefore \ r_{max} - v_b = \frac{W \sin \theta}{2 \mu} \{ h - y_1 \}^2. \tag{7}$$

While different observers have deduced different forms for the vertical velocity curve, the parabola with its vertex either in or below the surface appears to fit the majority of cases fairly well.

The foregoing analysis is therefore interesting, as giving the correct form of curve.

Bazin, experimenting on a stream having the maximum velocity in the surface, obtained

$$v_{s\,(max)} - v_{mean} = 25\cdot4 \ \sqrt{m \sin \theta}$$
$$v_{mean} - v_b \ \ = 10\cdot87 \sqrt{m \sin \theta}$$
$$v_{s\,(max)} - v_b \ \ = 36\cdot27 \sqrt{m \sin \theta}$$

the general equation being

$$v = (v_s)_{max} - 36\cdot27 \ \sqrt{m \sin \theta} \left(\frac{y}{h}\right)^2.$$

Here v_{mean} is the mean velocity over the whole section, and m is the hydraulic mean depth, the dimensions being taken in feet and the velocities in feet per second. He also states that wherever the position of maximum velocity, the relation

$$v_{max} - v_b = 36\cdot27 \ \sqrt{m \sin \theta}$$

holds true. In the vertical plane containing the filament of maximum velocity, we have from equation (7)

$$36\cdot27 \ \sqrt{m \sin \theta} = \frac{W \sin \theta}{2 \mu} \ \{h - y_1\}^2$$

Substituting the value of $\dfrac{W \sin \theta}{2 \mu}$ thus found, in equation (5), when the maximum velocity is below the surface

$$v_{max} - v = 36\cdot27 \ \sqrt{m \sin \theta} \left\{\frac{y - y_1}{h - y_1}\right\}^2 \tag{8}$$

a formula which gives fairly accurate results in practice.

Rankine states that the maximum, mean, and bottom velocities may be taken as being in the ratio 5 : 4 : 3 in ordinary cases, and in the ratio 4 : 3 : 2 in very slow currents, and these ratios may be taken as being approximately correct for streams and rivers of moderate size.

Velocity at Mid-depth.

From equation (5) of this article, we may obtain the mean velocity over any vertical by integrating the sum of such terms as $v \ \delta \ y$ over the vertical, and by dividing this sum by its length h. Thus

$$\bar{v} = \frac{\displaystyle\int_0^h \left\{v_{max} - \frac{W \sin \theta}{2 \mu} (y_1 - y)^2\right\} d \ y}{h}$$

$$= v_{max} - \frac{W \sin \theta}{2 \mu} \left\{\frac{h^2}{3} - h \ y_1 + y_1^2\right\} \tag{9}$$

while from (5) we may obtain the velocity at mid-depth, *i.e.*, where

$$y = \frac{h}{2}.$$

Thus
$$v_{\frac{h}{2}} = v_{max} - \frac{W \sin \theta}{2\,\mu} \left\{ \frac{h^2}{4} - h\,y_1 + y_1{}^2 \right\}$$
$$\therefore v_{\frac{h}{2}} - \bar{v} = \frac{W \sin \theta\, h^2}{24\,\mu}$$

from which, by determination of the mid-depth velocity, the mean velocity may be determined.

In general the mid-depth velocity is from 1·02 to 1·06 times the mean, and from ·94 to ·98 of the maximum.

If $\bar{y}$ be the depth at the point having a velocity equal to the mean, we have, from equations (5) and (9)

$$\frac{h^2}{3} - h\,y_1 + y_1{}^2 = \left\{ y_1 - \bar{y} \right\}^2$$
$$\therefore \bar{y} = y_1 \pm \sqrt{\frac{h^2}{3} - h\,y_1 + y_1{}^2}.$$

Putting $y_1 = ·2\,h$ this gives $\bar{y} = ·62\,h$.
   „ $y_1 = ·3\,h$ „   „ $\bar{y} = ·65\,h$.

ART. 97.—PERMISSIBLE VELOCITY IN OPEN CHANNELS; EROSION AND DEPOSITION OF SILT.

Water in motion exerts an erosive or scouring action on the bed and sides of the containing channel, and the maximum permissible velocity thus depends on the nature of the bed.

Particles of matter once disturbed, may be transported either by being rolled along the bed of the stream or by being carried in suspension, and for each material a certain critical velocity must be attained, depending on its size and specific gravity, before this is set in motion.   Once in motion, however, the velocity may be reduced somewhat below this critical value before the material is again deposited, as is indicated (p. 844) by the results of experiments by Dubuat[1] on transportation in small wooden channels.

While the erosive power of water varies as the square of its velocity, its transporting power, or the power to move boulders, etc., which may lie in its path, varies approximately as v^6.   This may be seen if we consider that the force exerted by the stream on any body is equal to the change of momentum produced in the stream passing the body, and since the area of that portion of the stream affected is proportional to the sectional area, a^2, of the body, this force will be equal to $K\,v^2\,a^2$ lbs. The force resisting motion is that of the friction of the body on the

[1] *Principes d'Hydraulique*, Dubuat, Paris, 1816.

bottom of the stream and is proportional to its weight, and therefore to its volume a^3.

Material.	Bottom Velocities, in ft. per sec., at which		
	Transportation Begins.	Material is in Equilibrium.	Deposition Begins.
Coarse sand	1·07	·71	·62
Gravel—			
Size of pea . . .	·71	·62	
,, small bean . .	1·56	1·07	·71
Shingle—rounded, one inch or more in diameter . .	3·2	2·14	1·56
Flints—Size of hen's egg .	4·0	3·2	2·14

Equating these forces, we have $K v^2 a^2 = c a^3$

$$\therefore a \propto v^2$$
$$\therefore a^3 \propto v^6$$

i.e., the weight of the solid moved is proportional to the sixth power of the velocity. Obviously this only holds so long as the bodies are similar, the velocity necessary to move a sphere being much less than that to move a cubical block of the same weight.

The size of particle moved by a stream over a smooth sandy bed is given approximately by $d = \dfrac{45 \, v^2}{w - 64}$ inches, where w is its density in lbs. per cubic foot, and v is the velocity in feet per second.[1]

A stream which carries a certain amount of fine material in suspension has a greater capacity for transporting larger material than one which carries only the larger material. Experiments show that a stream will carry more than four times the weight of sand of 4 to 5 mm. diameter in the presence of a certain weight of sand of ·3 mm. diameter than in its absence.[2]

While an excessive velocity of flow leads to erosion of the channel, a *too*

---

[1] Dr. G. S. Owens. *Engineer*, May, 15, 1908, p. 511.

[2] *Engineering News*, New York, vol. 63, 1910 (p. 580).

sluggish flow favours the growth of aquatic plants, while any change of velocity from high to low in a stream carrying material in suspension, causes a deposition of a portion of the material, and a consequent silting up of the channel. In order to prevent deposit in small sewers or drains, a mean velocity of not less than 3 feet per second is necessary. For sewers from 12 to 24 inches diameter the velocity should not be less than 2·5 feet per second, while with larger sizes than this the velocity may be reduced to 2 feet per second.

Mr. R. G. Kennedy,[1] from observations on a large number of Indian irrigation canals, concludes that there is a certain critical velocity at which a long canal will maintain its channel in silty equilibrium. This velocity is given by $v_o = c \, h^{·64}$ feet per second, where c has the following values :—

Light sandy soil	$c = ·82.$
Coarse sandy soil	·90.
Sandy loam	·99.
Coarse silt	1·07.

Where a main canal supplies or is supplied by feeders, the various depths and velocities of flow should be adjusted to suit this relationship in order that there may be no silting or erosion in the main or feeder canals.

If v be any other velocity, and if q_o and q be the amounts of silt carried respectively at v_o and v.

$$q = q_o \left(\frac{v}{v_o}\right)^{\frac{5}{2}} \text{ approximately.}$$

Taking $c = ·84$, the following table shows suitable mean velocities of maximum flow for equilibrium of such channels in sandy soil :—

Depth of channel (feet) . .	2	3	4	5	6	7	8
Mean velocity (feet per sec.) .	1·3	1·7	2·0	2·4	2·65	2·9	3·2

Ganguillet and Kutter give the following as the safe bottom and mean velocities, but state that these are probably too small rather than too large :—

[1] " Proc. Inst. C.E.," vol. 119, 1874-5, p. 281.

Material of Channel.	Safe Bottom Velocity. Feet per Second.	Safe Mean Velocity. Feet per Second.
Soft brown earth	·25	·33
Soft loam	·50	·66
Sand	1·00	1·32
Gravel.	2·00	2·64
Pebbles	3·00	3·94
Broken stone or flint . . .	4·00	5·58
Conglomerate	5·00	6·56
Stratified rock	6·00	8·20
Hard rock	10·00	13·13

Actually, as indicated by Kennedy, the safe mean velocity depends also upon the depth. More recent work shows that at medium depths through firm loamy soil a mean velocity of 3·0 to 3·5 feet per second is safe, while with fine well-rammed gravel or loose rock this may be increased to from 5 to 7 feet per second. In a concrete-lined channel faced with cement, the maximum safe velocity with water which carries solid material in suspension is about 9 feet per second. A higher velocity wears and roughens the bottom until the roughness thus produced reduces the velocity sufficiently to prevent further erosion. With an ordinary brick or heavy dry-laid rubble channel, the velocity should not exceed 15 feet per second, any higher velocity necessitating a carefully-laid facing of heavy masonry with cemented joints.

ART. 98.—GAUGING OF FLOW IN STREAMS AND OPEN CHANNELS.

Many methods are available for obtaining the discharge of a stream, these differing widely in the accuracy of their results and the cost and difficulty of their application. The method to be adopted in any case depends largely on the degree of accuracy required and on the size of the stream.

The accuracy of a discharge measurement, whatever be the method adopted, depends greatly on the physical characteristics of the stream at the point of measurement. If possible this should lie on a straight reach and away from the influence of a bend, the bed should be permanent and not strewn with boulders, and the slope and wetted perimeter such that at all stages of the stream the velocity at all parts of the section may be easily measurable. The banks should be sufficiently high to prevent overflow in times of flood, and the section should be outside the sphere of influence of bridge piers or mill dams.

Where a high degree of accuracy is demanded, as may be required in determining the flow of compensation water from the supply reservoir of a waterworks, the best method is to deflect the stream and catch the whole discharge for a given time in a graduated tank.

This can, however, only be carried out in small streams where a measuring tank of sufficient capacity to hold the discharge for about two minutes is available. In this case the error should not exceed 1 per cent.

For larger streams, the most accurate method is that of gauging the flow by placing a weir across the stream and allowing the whole flow to take place over this or over one or more triangular or rectangular notches, the former being used for small and the latter for fairly large streams. Where every precaution is taken as explained in Art. 59 this method gives results which may be relied upon as being accurate within about 5 per cent. As a temporary measuring contrivance, however, the weir is too cumbrous and costly to be applied to a river of even moderate dimensions, and where the discharge is great the only method of obtaining the discharge is to obtain as nearly as possible the mean velocity (v feet per second) of the stream, to multiply this by the cross sectional area (A square feet), and to get the discharge Q by the relation.

$$Q = v \, A \text{ cubic feet per second.}$$

The value of v may be approximated to in many ways.

(a) By using one or other of the formulae given in Art. 85, a suitable coefficient being applied to take into account the state of the channel. The slope of the stream must then be obtained by field observations. To do this a long straight reach of the river should be selected where possible, and the reduced levels of bench marks placed at each end of the reach should be obtained by levelling. The level of each bench mark should then be transferred to a hook gauge

FIG. 153.—
Hook Gauge.

(Fig. 153) or measuring staff placed in a gauge pit communicating with the bed of the stream through a pipe which opens out at a point away from any disturbing influences likely to lead to eddy formation. The difference of surface level at each end of the reach can then be obtained.

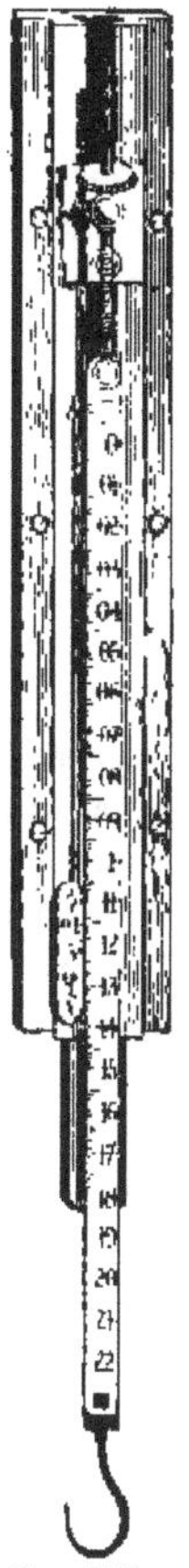

The distance from end to end of the reach may be obtained by chaining a line running as nearly as possible parallel to the centre line of the river. Soundings should then be taken at short distances apart at several cross sections of the stream, and these cross sections plotted. From these a mean value of the wetted perimeter and of the sectional area, and thus of the hydraulic mean depth, may be obtained, and the formula may then be applied. During the whole observation period the stream should be in a state of steady flow, and neither rising nor falling.

The method has the disadvantage that it is extremely difficult to measure the slope of a river accurately. Captain Cunningham as a result of some hundreds of slope measurements on the Ganges Canal,[1] found that the slope was very different at different points of a reach from one to two miles long, and varied by as much as 50 per cent. at different sides of the stream. An examination of the Mississippi[2] showed that with the main body of water flowing south with a velocity of four to five miles per hour, the water near the shore may be moving north at a speed of one or two miles per hour. It was in fact not unusual to find a slope towards the south on one bank and towards the north on the opposite bank. The slope then is so uncertain an element that no great accuracy is to be expected for any such formula, except possibly in the case of an artificial channel of uniform section. Under any other circumstances the results cannot be relied upon as being accurate within 25 per cent., and may under specially unfavourable circumstances, even with the most skilful observers, be in error by as much as 100 per cent.

Wherever possible, then, the mean velocity should be obtained in some other manner. This may be done

(b) By using a current meter or Pitot tube to give the velocity at a point or series of points in a cross section, and by deducing the mean velocity from such observations ;

(c) By using one or other type of float, and by measuring the time necessary for a series of these to traverse a given length of the channel.

Before considering these methods in detail, a few general observations as to their relative advantages and disadvantages may be made. Experiment shows that the motion at any point in an open channel is never steady and uniform, but suffers a series of pulsations, the periodic time of which may vary from a few seconds to two or three minutes. These are due to a variety of causes. Eddies formed at the sides and bottom

---

[1] "Proc. Inst. C. E.," vol. 71, p. 11.
[2] Report on the Mississippi, Humphreys and Abbot, p. 218.

drift away to every portion of the stream; snags and hollows in the bed, bends, and falls, all produce some (irregular) disturbance of the flow, with the result that the velocity at a point in the surface may vary by 20 per cent., and at a point near the bed by as much as 50 per cent. (Harlacher) in a short interval of time.

In experiments on the St. Clair River (1899) the velocity-time curves showed two sets of waves, small ones of 15 to 60 seconds amplitude and larger ones of 3 to 6 minutes amplitude. The range of velocities as found from the larger waves was in some cases 35 per cent. of the mean velocity shown by the meter reading taken over ten minutes. These experiments indicate that the pulsations are very limited in extent in a direction at right angles to the current. The whole depth of the river is affected by them, although their effect decreases from the bottom towards the surface.

It follows that a float, measuring as it does the velocity due to a single pulsation, may give results which are greatly in error, and the only chance of obtaining a fair estimate of the mean velocity over a single section of the stream is to take the mean of a large number—40 or 50—of the values given by floats. The complexity of the motion is very evident when floats are used. Of a series dropped into a stream at the same point, no two will trace out the same path, and as may be well understood when the multitude of observations necessary to give any pretensions to accuracy is remembered, this method though at first sight so simple, may easily prove the most expensive method of determining the discharge. With current meters, on the other hand, the mean velocity at any point may be obtained with great accuracy, provided the period of observation is sufficient to cover a series of the pulsations of velocity. Professor Unwin found that the mean time of successive 100 revolutions of such a meter in the Thames, when plotted, gave a very irregular curve, while the mean times of successive 500 revolutions gave an almost straight line. In general the time of a single observation should not be less than five minutes, a period of six to ten minutes being advisable.

This renders it essential that in order to avoid spending an excessive length of time in the field and thus running the risk of serious fluctuations in the water level, the discharge be found from single observations in comparatively few verticals, and that the ratio of the velocity at the depth chosen, to the mean velocity, be known from vertical velocity curves. This emphasises the importance of a thorough investigation of the relation between velocity and depth in a vertical longitudinal plane, and the change in this relation with any change in the state of a river.

<h2>ART. 99.—CURRENT METERS.</h2>

Meters in use at the present day may be divided into two classes: (1) those in which the revolving part carries a series of helicoidal vanes

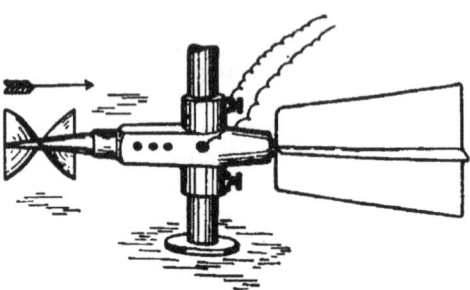

FIG. 154.—Amsler Current Meter.

mounted on a horizontal axis, and (2) those in which a series of conical or hemispherical cups is mounted on arms, as in an anemometer, on a vertical axis. The former type is illustrated in Fig. 154, which shows the Amsler meter and in Fig. 155, which shows the Haskell meter, while the latter is shown in Fig. 156, which illustrates the Price meter. The latter type of meter has some advantages over the former in that friction is usually less since it practically all comes on one point which is easily protected from any grit in the water, while in addition this type will start in a current of less velocity than will move the other, and yet will not revolve as rapidly under the same conditions of high velocity flow.

The meter is fitted with a guide vane which keeps its axis perpendicular to the direction of the current. The wheel may be either geared to a counter which records the revolutions direct and is put into and out

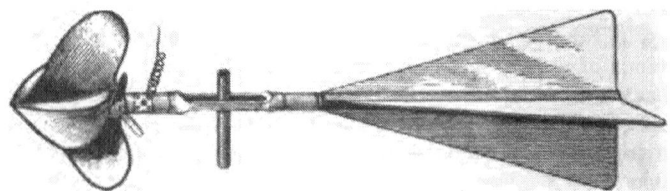

FIG. 155.—Haskell Current Meter.

of gear by means of a cord from the point of suspension of the meter, or may make and break the contact in an electrical circuit at each revolution, thus enabling the number of revolutions to be indicated by means of a counter or buzzer placed on shore or in a boat. The advantages of the latter method in reducing the resistance to rotation and the tendency to clog are obvious, and the mechanically operated meter is becoming obsolete.

The instrument is previously calibrated by towing at known velocities through still water, the number of revolutions corresponding to these velocities being recorded. It has the disadvantages that it cannot be used where floating grass or weed is prevalent, and that it requires rating at frequent intervals. Further, it cannot be used at very low velocities. The minimum permissible velocity depends on the type of meter, but in general varies from 3 to 6 inches per second.

There are two methods of using the meter. In the first, the "point"

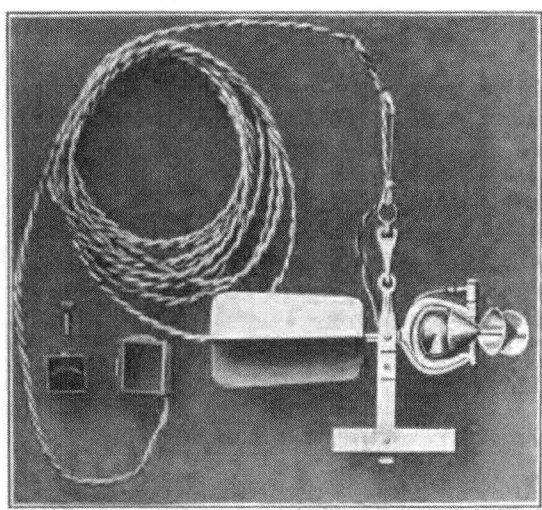

FIG. 156.—Price Current Meter.

method, it is held successively at certain points in a cross section. In a shallow stream this may be done by clamping it to a staff which is carried by an observer in waders, and which is held vertically at the required points, with one end resting on the bed of the stream. In deeper streams it is attached to a heavy sinker and is suspended from a convenient bridge or cable placed across the stream where possible, or from an outrigger fixed to an anchored boat where the width precludes this. When the "point" method is used, the meter may either be held, (1) at several equidistant points in certain equidistant verticals, the mean velocity being deduced from these readings as explained later : (2) at six-tenths, or at mid-depth in a series of equidistant verticals, the mean velocity in each of these verticals then being found by applying a factor ; (3) at the surface, bottom, and mid-depth in a series of verticals ; (4) at the surface and bottom only, or at two-tenths and eight-tenths of the depth in a series of verticals, in which case the mean of the two readings is taken as the mean velocity in the vertical. While the first method is likely to give the best results in a steady stream, yet, as previously indicated, the length of time necessary to obtain the many observations is a serious drawback in a stream of any considerable size.

In a large stream where it is impossible to see the bottom, owing to the impossibility of fixing the meter very near to the sides and bottom where the velocities are least, the results tend to be too high. To obviate this the meter should not be placed nearer to the surface than one foot.

The mid-depth point is used because the factor, about ·96, which is used to obtain the mean velocity is more constant for it than for any other point on the vertical ; while the six-tenths point gives very approximately the true mean velocity on the vertical. These factors are discussed at further length on pp. 337 and 339. Observations taken at either of these points are capable of giving excellent results.

Method (3) was adopted by Moore in his gauging of the Thames.[1] Assuming the vertical velocity curve to be a parabola, its area is given by the formula $A = \dfrac{h}{6} \{ v_s + 4 v_{\frac{h}{2}} + v_b \}$, h being the depth, v_s and v_b the surface and bottom velocities respectively. The discharge per second flowing between the two end verticals is given by

$$\text{Vol.} \doteq \frac{d}{3} \{ \Sigma (A_1 + A_n) + 4 \Sigma (A_2 + A_4 + \quad) + 2 \Sigma (A_3 + A_5 + \quad) \} \text{ c.f.s.}$$

where d is the breadth of the successive vertical strips ; the first term is the sum of the areas of the first and last velocity curves ; the second term is four times the sum of the even sections ; and the last term is twice the sum of the odd sections excluding the first and last. The total discharge is then obtained by adding the small volume flowing between each end section and the shore. On account of the large variation in bottom velocity with a given mean flow this method is, however, not to be recommended.

Method (4), in which the surface and bottom velocities are measured is only advisable for very shallow steams. Experiments at Cornell University show that the results thus obtained agree closely with those given by a weir if the bed is smooth or gravelly, the depth from ·4 to

[1] " Proc. Inst. C. E.," vol. 45, p. 220.

1·0 feet and the velocities from ·4 to 1·5 feet per second. For a gravelly bed the meter should be held with its centre from 3 to 4 inches above the bottom and about 2 inches below the surface, while with a smooth bed each distance should be about 2 inches. With depths between 5 and 10 feet, the mean of velocities ·5 feet above the bottom and ·5 feet below the surface gave results too low by as much as 30 per cent. In such cases the mean of readings at two-tenths and at eight-tenths the depth gives good results.

In the "integration" method, the meter is kept in motion during the whole period of its immersion. It may either be moved uniformly from the surface to the bottom of the stream in a series of vertical lines; diagonally across from one side to the other, at the same time being moved from the surface to the bottom several times; or across the stream at a given depth. The recorded velocity is then taken as the mean for the particular vertical or for the whole section as the case may be. Although an observation by this method can be carried out in considerably less time than by the point method, the results are not nearly so accurate. The velocity recorded being the resultant of the velocities of the meter and of the water is always higher than the true velocity, the error increasing with the speed of movement of the meter and also increasing as the velocity of flow diminishes. It is only to be recommended where a stream is rising or falling rapidly and where in consequence the speed with which the observations can be made is a great advantage.

Simultaneously with the velocity observations, soundings should be taken from which the cross section of the stream may be obtained. In a narrow stream these should be taken at intervals of from 2 to 5 feet, while where the breadth exceeds 100 feet, they should be taken at intervals of from 10 to 25 feet, depending on the roughness of the bed.

Field Notes.—The following shows the method adopted for entering up field observations and computing mean velocities in the case where velocities are measured at several points on a cross section.

[Gauging made January 23, 1904, by B.S.D.   Meter No. 349, on Dan River, Madison, N.C. Gauge height; beginning 2·10 feet.; end 2·26 feet; river rising.]

Distance from initial point.	Depth of stream.	Depth of observations.	Time in seconds.	Total number of revolutions.	Revolutions per second.	Velocity per second.	Per cent. of depth.
40	0·3	0·5	500	600	1·20	2·88	17
		1·0	500	580	1·16	2·78	33
		1·5	500	540	1·08	2·59	50
		2·0	500	470	·94	2·27	67
		2·5	500	380	·76	1·83	83

H.A.   A A

These observations are recorded for a series of verticals in the cross section. They are then plotted on squared paper, depths as ordinates and velocities as abscissæ, and a smooth curve is drawn through the plotted points, care being taken to give them as nearly as possible equal weight if they do not all fall on a smooth curve. From this curve velocities are read off at top and bottom and at equal intervals of, say, each ·5 foot, and are set down in order. Thus from the above curve we get—

$$0·0 \ldots v_s = 2·90 \qquad 2·0 \ldots v_4 = 2·25$$
$$0·5 \ldots v_1 = 2·88 \qquad 2·5 \ldots v_5 = 1·88$$
$$1·0 \ldots v_2 = 2·77 \qquad 3·0 \ldots v_b = 1·31$$
$$1·5 \ldots v_3 = 2·58$$

The mean velocity in this vertical is then computed from the prismoidal formula for seven abscissæ as follows :—

$$v_m = \tfrac{1}{18} \left\{ v_s + v_b + 4 \left(v_1 + v_3 + v_5 \right) + 2 \left(v_2 + v_4 \right) \right\}$$

In this case we have:—

$$v_s + v_b = 2·90 + 1·31 = 4·21$$
$$4 \left(v_1 + v_3 + v_5 \right) = 4 \left\{ 2·88 + 2·58 + 1·88 \right\}$$
$$= 29·36$$
$$2 \left(v_2 + v_4 \right) = 2 \left(2·77 + 2·25 \right)$$
$$= 10·04$$
$$\therefore v_m = \tfrac{1}{18} \left\{ 4·21 + 29·36 + 10·04 \right\}$$
$$= 2·42 \cdot \text{f.s.}$$

The cross section having been plotted, the areas of the various compartments having such verticals as their centre lines may be obtained, either by direct measurement by planimeter or by calculation, and the discharge calculated as follows :—

Compartment.	Area of section square feet.	Mean velocity. feet per second.	Discharge c.f.s.
1	15·1	1·32	19·9
2	28·2	1·97	55·6
3	36·5	2·12	88·3
4	32·1	2·56	82·1
5	23·7	1·99	47·2
6	13·5	1·33	17·9

Total ... 311·0 c.f.s.

When the vertical velocity curves have been obtained the discharge may be computed somewhat more accurately by considering the discharge between any two such verticals as being represented by the volume of the solid having these curves bounding opposite parallel sides as shown in Fig. 157. For example, the discharge between the verticals 2 and 3 in this figure is given by

$$\frac{{}_2d_3}{3}\left\{\ \bar{v}_2\,h_2 + \bar{v}_3\,h_3 + \sqrt{\bar{v}_2\,h_2\,\bar{v}_3\,h_3}\ \right\}\ \text{c.f.s.}$$

where $\bar{v}_2$ and $\bar{v}_3$ are mean velocities in the verticals 2 and 3, and where h_2 and h_3 are the corresponding soundings, ${}_2d_3$ being the distance between the verticals. The discharge between the two end soundings is then given by the sum of such terms as the above between these soundings

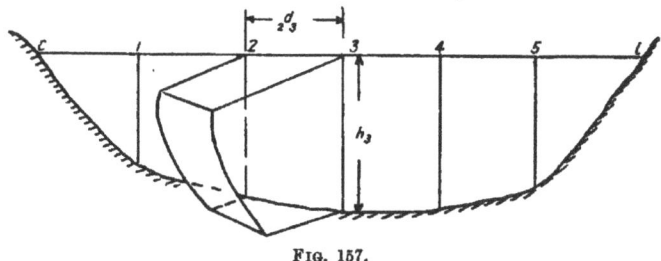

FIG. 157.

To this must be added the discharge over these sections outside the end soundings, which is given by

$$\tfrac{1}{3}\left\{\ \bar{v}_1\,h_1 \times {}_0d_1 + \bar{v}_6\,h_6 \times {}_5d_l\ \right\}\ \text{c.f.s.}$$

Calibration of Current Meters.—In rating a meter it is usually suspended from a car or a boat, and is towed with a uniform velocity through still water at a depth of 2 or 3 feet. The length of a run varies from 100 to 300 feet, with sufficient of a starting run to attain a steady velocity before entering the measured length. It is moved in either direction from end to end of the run to eliminate the effect of a current in either direction, and the time of the run and the number of revolutions of the meter are recorded by means of a chronograph.

The range of velocities employed in rating should be those for which the meter is to be used, and no attempt should be made to extend the rating table beyond its experimental limits.

When in use the meter may either be suspended from a cable, in which case its axis is free to move about both a vertical and a horizontal axis, or it may be fixed to a vertical rod in such a way as to remove the second degree of freedom. Experiments indicate that the same rating table is

A A 2

not strictly accurate for the two cases, and that with a given velocity of flow the revolutions increase as the freedom of motion decreases.[1] The difference depends on the type of meter, and for velocities of 1 foot per second is usually about 2 per cent.

A further source of inaccuracy, particularly with very low velocities of flow, is due to the fact that a rating carried out in still water is not quite accurate when applied to the same relative velocities in moving water.

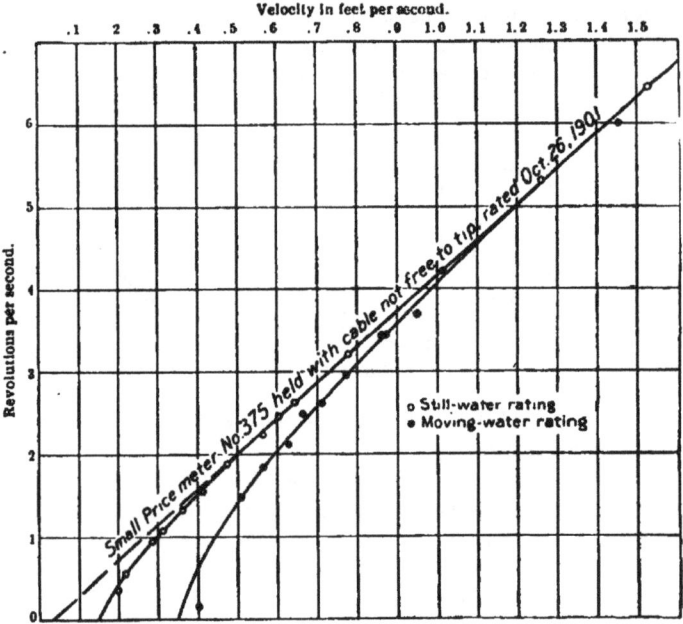

Velocity in feet per second.

Revolutions per second.

o Still-water rating
• Moving-water rating

FIG. 158.—Rating Curves of Price Current Meter.

Experiments[1] indicate that the meter, particularly of the cup type, does not indicate so high a velocity when dragged through still water as when held in a current, the difference varying from 1 to 4 per cent. at a velocity of 1 foot per second with different types of meter. The difference is about 1 per cent. at a velocity of 2 feet per second.

In calibrating a current meter it is usual to plot the curve connecting velocity of current and number of revolutions of meter per second. In

[1] U. S. Water Supply and Irrigation Paper, No. 95, pp. 83—89, also p. 81.

the majority of cases this is found to be of the form shown in Fig. 158. At very low speeds the friction of the instrument varies between fairly wide limits, but diminishes as the speed increases. This causes the plotted points to lie more or less on a curved line, but renders this portion of the calibration unreliable. At a certain critical speed of the instrument the friction takes a fairly constant value, and the curve becomes very approximately a straight line of the form

$$v = a\, n + b.$$

It is not advisable to use the meter to register speeds below the critical. This depends on the instrument, but is usually from 3 to 6 inches per second, and in general it may be taken that on this account the meter is not a suitable instrument for the measurement of the discharge of a stream if the velocity over more than 15 per cent. of its area is less than 6 inches per second.

A form of current meter which is occasionally used consists of a flat circular plate which is rigidly attached by means of a horizontal arm to one end of a vertical wire, the other end of which is fixed. The wire is supported in bearings, and the free end carries a pointer which, working over a graduated disc, enables the angle of twist to be ascertained. In using the instrument, the pointer is adjusted to zero with the plate out of water and normal to the direction of flow of the stream. The plate is then submerged and the angle of twist necessary to bring it once more normal to the direction of flow is noted.

Then if P = force on plate in lbs.

l = length of arm from centre of plate to centre of wire.

A = area of plate in square feet.

θ = angle of twist of wire.

v = velocity of flow of stream.

We have $P\,l = K\,\theta$, where K is a constant for any instrument and depends solely on the material, length, and radius of the wire.

Also $P = 1{\cdot}15\,A\,v^2$ (approx.) the constant depending on the size of the plate, from which $v^2 = \dfrac{K}{1{\cdot}15\,A\,l}\,.\,\theta.$

Even with a constant velocity of flow, however, eddy formation at the rear of the plate causes the value of P to undergo periodic fluctuations, and the difficulty in obtaining a true mean value for θ, and in keeping the plate normal to the direction of the stream, prevent this method from having any pretensions to great accuracy. The instrument is now practically obsolete.

Art. 100.—Estimation of Velocity by Floats.

These are liberated at a series of points in a long straight reach (Captain Cunningham, from experiments on the Ganges Canal[1] recommends that this length should not be less than 200 feet) and the time occupied in covering a measured distance is noted.

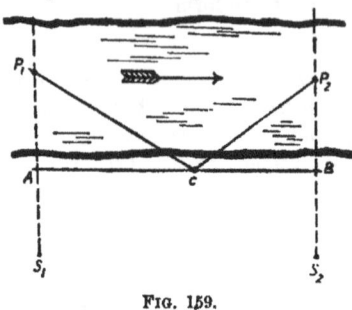

Floats may be divided into four classes :—

(1) Surface floats.

(2) Sub-surface floats.

(3) Twin floats.

(4) Velocity rods.

(1) **Surface Floats.**—These consist of any easily seen masses of light material, painted cork or discs of light wood for example, of small size so as to move along with, and register,

FIG. 159.

the velocity of the surface filaments. A series of trials are necessary to get the maximum surface velocity r_s of the stream, from which the mean velocity of flow may be estimated from Bazin's formula (p. 342). It is preferable, however, to deduce the mean velocity in each of a number of sections of the stream from repeated observations of the surface velocity in each of these sections. The sections may be marked in a stream of moderate dimensions by ropes hanging from a bridge or temporary support.

In a large river, observations with the theodolite are necessary to determine the track of the float. This may be satisfactorily carried out as follows :—A base line $A B$ (Fig. 159) is chained out parallel to the river for a length of about 250 feet, depending on the width of the river. At the two ends stakes are erected, while second stakes are erected in lines ranged perpendicularly to the base line, as at S_1, S_2. An observer with a theodolite is stationed near the centre of the base line at C, and an observer is stationed at each stake, S_1, S_2. The float being liberated up stream, the theodolite observer keeps the line of collimation of his instrument on this. As it passes the line of sight $S_1 A$, the observer at S_1 gives an audible signal and the theodolite observer notes the angle $A C P_1$. On passing the line $S_2 B$ a second signal is given at the angle $B C P_2$ noted. The line $P_1 P_2$ can then be plotted. With a stream of moderate velocity the same observer may give the signals both at

[1] "Proceedings Inst. Civil Engineers," 1882, vol. 71.

_A_ and _B_. The effect of wind on the surface velocity, however, together with the tendency of the floats to follow every variable cross current and to be affected by every surface eddy, renders the results obtained by this method unreliable except as approximations to the truth.

(2) **Sub-surface Floats.**—These consist of bodies having surfaces of large area, as illustrated for example in Fig. 160, attached to small surface floats for ease of observation, the length of connection being adjusted so as to allow the true float to remain at any given depth. The velocity of the float will then be approximately that of the current at the required depth. The figure shows the float used in the Connecticut River survey in 1874. The sub-surface float was a hollow annulus of tin $8\frac{1}{2}$ inches high, $8\frac{1}{2}$ inches outside diameter, and $7\frac{1}{2}$ inches inside diameter. This was weighted with 28 oz. of lead. The surface float was an ellipsoid of tin 6 inches in diameter and 1·5 inches deep, the connecting cord being ·036 inches in diameter. A series of such floats liberated at different points in the cross section of a stream and at different depths may be used to give by their mean velocity the mean of that of the stream, or by arranging a single row, the depth of each being $\frac{3}{8}$ that of the stream at the point of introduction, these may be taken as giving the mean velocities in their respective sections. While this type is more reliable than the surface float it suffers from the disadvantage that it is impossible to determine the exact position or depth of the lower float, for while the position of the upper float may be known, that of the lower float varies with the direction and velocity of the wind and with the length of cord connecting the two floats. Also the upper float may either drag or be dragged by the lower, and the upper is on this account likely to retard the lower where the latter is above the filament of maximum velocity, and to accelerate it when it is at a greater depth than this. As this latter effect extends over a greater proportion of the depth than the former, it would tend to make the velocities of flow recorded by the floats too high. Experiments made by T. G. Ellis, 1874, on the Connecticut River (mean velocity 2·1 ft. per sec.) with current meters and with

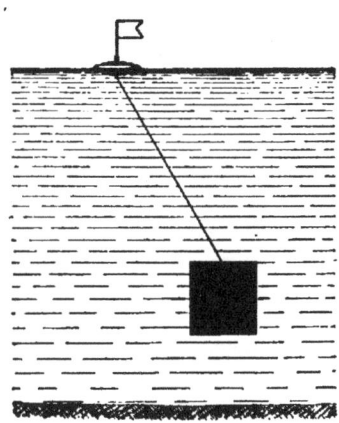

FIG. 160.

double floats [1] showed that the mean velocity as found by floats was from 6 to 26 per cent. greater than by meter, the difference increasing with the velocity. Marr—October, 1879, on the Mississippi,[2] the width being about 2,000 feet and the depth 16·4 feet (mean velocity 2·6 ft. per sec.) found the mean float velocity to be about 3·5 per cent. greater than the meter velocity, while Henry—1869—on the St. Clair River [3]—45 feet deep—and with a mean velocity of 3·4 feet per second, found the mean float velocity about 10 per cent. greater than the meter velocity. In this case the float velocity was less than the meter velocity to a depth of about 7 feet. Below that depth the float velocity was the greater, the difference increasing with the depth.

(3) **Twin Floats.**—These consist of two masses of equal size, usually spheres coupled together by means of a wire, the lower of which is weighted so as to remain vertically below the upper, which floats at the surface. The velocity of the float then gives the mean of the velocities at the surface and at the depth of the lower mass. If this is adjusted so as to just clear the bottom, the velocity of the float will be approximately the mean velocity for the vertical in which the instrument floats.

(4) **Velocity Rods.**—The velocity rod, or rod float, consists of a light wooden rod or tin tube about 1 inch in diameter, and made in adjustable lengths. The lower end of the bottom length is weighted and the length adjusted until the rod floats vertically with its lower end clearing the bottom by a few inches. In a large river and where these are not likely to interfere with navigation, logs of wood about 12 inches in diameter, having their lower ends weighted with iron and their upper ends painted white, may be used.

The velocity of the rod is approximately the same as the mean over its depth, and gives the mean velocity over the vertical in which it floats. The difficulty in using the rod lies in its tendency to drag over shoals and weeds, and to obviate this its lower end may be arranged to float at a height h^1 above the bed of the stream.

For such a case Francis gives the empirical formula

$$r_m = r_r \left(1 \cdot 012 - \cdot 116 \sqrt{\frac{h^1}{h}} \right)$$

giving the mean velocity in the vertical containing the rod in terms of the velocity of the rod (r_r), h^1, and h the depth of the stream. Here h^1 should be less than ·25 h.

---

[1] Report Chief Eng., U.S.A., 1878, Appendix B.
[2] McKenzie, A. Report on Current Meter Observations. Burlington, 1884.
[3] " Journal Franklin Inst.," vol. 62, p. 322.

Of all floats the velocity rod gives the best results, and for channels of moderate and uniform depth, encumbered with floating weeds and grass, this is probably the best method of obtaining the velocity. In a series of experiments on the Loch Katrine Aqueduct; concreted surface; concave bottom; width 9' 1"; radius of curvature 20' 10½"; hydraulic mean depth 2·87 feet; velocity rods 2' 2" long, gave results which agreed within ¾ of 1 per cent. with results as obtained by weir measurement, while the velocity as obtained from the maximum surface velocity, and an application of the formula $r = r_s - 25·4 \sqrt{m\,i}$, was 18 per cent. too low.

An elaborate series of experiments was carried out in 1856 by J. B. Francis on the Lowell Canal[1] to determine the relative accuracy of weir and rod float measurements, this canal being 27·75 feet wide where the first 68 experiments were made and 14 feet wide where the remaining 52 were made. The length of run was 70 feet, the floats being loaded tin tubes, 2 inches in diameter. From these it was found that the mean difference in the discharge as obtained by the two methods was less than 2 per cent. in all but three of the experiments, the mean difference being about 1 per cent. The mean velocity in these experiments varied from ·5 to 5 feet per second.

Experiments in 1900 at Cornell University[2] showed about the same degree of accuracy in the case of flow in a canal 16 feet wide and with depths of water ranging from 5 to 10 feet, and velocities of flow up to 2·07 feet per second. The immersed portions of the rods varied from 75 per cent. to 95 per cent. of the depth of the stream, and the length of measured run varied from 7 to 25 feet, depending on the velocity. In every case the float velocity was slightly less than that given by the weir.

Other Methods of Measuring the Velocity.

ART. 101.---RIPPLE FORMATION.

An ingenious method of obtaining the surface velocity at various points in the cross section of a stream was described by Mr. E. C. Thrupp ("Proc. Inst. C.E.," vol. 167, 1907, p. 217). This depends upon the fact that if a small obstruction cut the surface of a stream, ripples are formed if the velocity exceeds about 9 inches per second, while the angle of divergence of these ripples appears to bear a definite relation to the surface velocity. To overcome the difficulty of accurately measuring this angle Mr. Thrupp constructed a velocity meter consisting of two vertical

[1] Lowell, Hydraulic Experiments, p. 170.
[2] "Trans. Am. Soc. C.E.," vol. 12, p. 301.

pegs ($\frac{1}{8}$ iron nails) at a known distance d inches apart, with a scale for measuring the distance from the base line of the point of intersection of the ripples formed. Calling this distance l (Fig. 161), the following equations were found to give the surface velocity in feet per second.

$$\text{For } d = 6'', v = \cdot 40 + \cdot 206\, l.$$
$$\text{,, } d = 4'', v = \cdot 40 + \cdot 280\, l.$$

With $d = 6''$ and with a velocity of ·8 feet per second the value of l is about 2 inches, while with a velocity of 8·5 feet per second, l is 15 inches.

This method would appear to be capable of results at least as accurate as those obtained by the use of surface floats, and possibly more so because of the greater possibilities of accuracy in the determination of the area of the stream at one definite cross section.

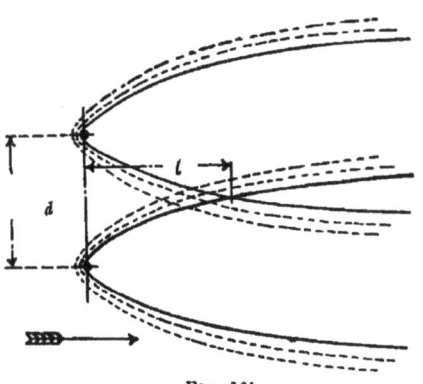

FIG. 161.

The Pitot Tube.—The velocity at any point in the cross section may also be estimated by means of the Pitot tube (Art. 68), p. 217.

This method is not so well adapted for measuring such low velocities as usually occur in open channels as for higher velocities such as are more common in pipe flow.

For small, shallow, and rapid streams it is, however, capable of giving fairly good results. Fig. 162 shows a tube, with positive and negative pressure openings as used for the rating of such streams by the United States Geological Survey. This tube was rated in still water in a reservoir and in moving water, being placed for the latter rating at about 80 points in the cross section of a channel 1 foot wide and ·6 feet deep. The former rating gave values of C in the formula $V = C \sqrt{2\, g\, h}$ ranging from ·855 to ·87, with a mean value of ·86. The velocities as found by this tube from the still water rating, were invariably greater than were given by the moving water rating the average difference being 6·4 per cent.[1] This great difference is, however, probably due partly to the comparatively large disturbing effect of the tube in such a small channel, and partly to the impossibility of taking measurements near the walls where the velocity is least.

[1] *Engineering News*, vol. 62, No. 7, p. 174.

The Hydrometric Pendulum.—Where flow takes place through an uniform channel of small dimensions, and where the velocity can be initially determined by some accurate method, as by a weir, the hydrometric pendulum may be calibrated so as to record this velocity at any future time. The instrument consists of a pendulum having a submerged spherical bob which is heavier than the water which it displaces, and which hangs vertically when the water is at rest. When in motion the pressure of the water causes the pendulum to take up an inclined position, the angle of inclination being a measure of the velocity, and from a previous calibration, this may be read off directly.

Measurement of Flow in a Parallel Conduit.—A method recently devised[1] for measuring the discharge from a parallel conduit consists in the provision of a light but rigid apron of canvas over a framework of angle iron, suspended vertically from a light carriage which runs on rails fixed on either side of the conduit. When lowered, the apron fills the conduit with very little clearance and is carried along with the same velocity as the stream. Its velocity is then measured by a chronometer and electrical contacts. This method necessitates a conduit of 80 to 100 feet in length, and has been applied to conduits up to 20 feet wide and 12 feet deep, for the measurement of the water supplied to turbines under test.

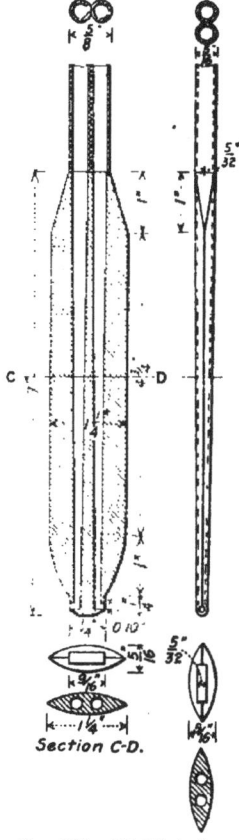

Section C-D.

FIG. 162.—Pitot Tube for Steam Rating.

ART. 102.—STREAM RATING TABLES.

The usual object of velocity measurements in a river is the construction of a rating table, which shall show the relation at a given point between the height of water, referred to some permanent bench mark, and the discharge of the river. In order to prepare such a table it is necessary to obtain the discharge at various stages of a stream, covering the usual

[1] By Prof. E. Andersson of Stockholm. See *Zeitschrift des Vereins Deutscher Ingenieur,* April 20, 1907.

range of fluctuation. Usually the data are embodied in the form of a rating curve, showing graphically the relationship between discharge and height of surface level. The length of time during which such a curve can be safely applied depends on the class of channel. Where the channel is constantly shifting it cannot be used for many months unless the soundings are frequently checked with reference to the original datum level.

ART. 103. GAUGING OF ICE-COVERED STREAMS.

When a river is ice bound its flow becomes somewhat similar to that in a closed flume, the water now flowing under pressure. A series of measurements of such streams by members of the U.S. Geol. Survey[1] lead to the following conclusions :

(1) The maximum velocity occurs at a point between 35 per cent. and 40 per cent. of the depth measured from the underside of the ice. The ratio of mean to maximum velocity ranges from about ·80 with a depth of 3 feet to ·92 with a depth of 16 feet, having a mean value of ·85.

(2) There are two points of mean velocity on a vertical, the first lying between ·08 and ·013 of the depth, and the second between ·68 and ·74 of the depth.

(3) The vertical velocity curve becomes more concave as the river rises, owing to the increased head.

(4) In making gaugings of such streams the vertical velocity curve method, or the integration method, should be adopted in preference to any of the single-point and co-efficient methods.

EXAMPLES.

(1) A canal whose depth is 4 feet, having slopes 2 to 1, has a bottom width of 10 feet. The bed is of earth (Kutter's $N = ·025$), and the gradient is 1 foot per mile. Determine the discharge in cubic feet per second.

Answer $\begin{cases} \text{Hydraulic mean depth} = 2·58 \text{ feet.} \\ C = 68·8. \\ \text{Discharge} = 109·5 \text{ cubic feet per second.} \end{cases}$

(2) A rectangular flume 4 feet wide and 2 feet deep is roughly constructed of unplaned timber, and is required to deliver 80 cubic feet of water per second. Determine the necessary gradient, and assuming it to supply water to a power station distant 5 miles from the supply reservoir,

---

[1] Water Supply and Irrigation Paper. No. 95, p. 158.

letermine the percentage loss in transmission if the difference of level ›etween the supply reservoir and tail race is 500 feet. $C = 127\cdot6$.

Answer. Gradient 1 in 162·9.

Loss of energy $= 32\cdot4$ per cent.

(3) A flat-bottomed channel is required to have a constant velocity of low for all depths of water. The bottom breadth is 5 feet. Determine he depth at a section where the breadth is 20 feet, if the hydraulic mean lepth is 1·25 feet. $C = 60$.

Answer. 4·35 feet.

(4) The original depth of a wide stream is 8 feet, and the slope of its ›ed is 1 in 1,000, the value of f being ·0131, $C = 70$. A dam 10 feet high s erected across the stream. Determine the rise in the water level mmediately behind the dam and at points $\frac{1}{2}$ and 1 mile up stream. Assume the coefficient of discharge for the dam to be ·560.)

Answer. Rise behind dam $= 9\cdot28$ feet.

,, $\frac{1}{2}$ mile up stream $= 6\cdot87$ feet.

,,   1 ,,   ,,   ,, $= 4\cdot04$.

(5) It is required to excavate a canal out of rock to be of rectangular ›ection and to bring 500 cubic feet of water per second from a distance of 1 miles with a velocity of $7\frac{1}{2}$ feet per second. Determine the gradient and he most suitable section for the canal. Take $C = 150$.

Answer. Section 11·54 feet wide, 5·77 feet deep.

Gradient 1 in 1,156.

(6) In carrying out field operations to determine the discharge of a river, a straight reach 500 feet long is available. The slope is approximately $\frac{1}{10000}$, and the levelling is possibly accurate within $\frac{1}{500}$ foot. The possible error in determining the wetted perimeter is 8 per cent., and in determining the mean sectional area is 5 per cent. To what degree of accuracy are the final results likely to approximate.

Answer. Within about $13\frac{1}{2}$ per cent.

(7) The value of f for a stream having a slope of $\frac{1}{1000}$ is ·0050. Normally, the stream is of depth 4 feet and breadth 60 feet, but is passed through a sluice having an opening $2\frac{1}{2}$ feet deep. Determine whether the conditions are such as to lead to the formation of a standing wave, and if so determine the probable height of the crest of this wave above the upper edge of the sluice.

Answer. Yes. ·93 feet.

CHAPTER XI.

ART. 104.—IMPACT OF JETS.

WHEN a steady jet of water impinges on any solid surface there is none of the rebound which follows the impact of two solid bodies. Instead of this, a thin stream is formed which glides along the surface until it reaches the boundaries, when it leaves approximately tangential to the surface.

In theoretical discussions it is usual to assume that the sheet of water leaves the surface tangentially. Actually the action is similar to that indicated in Fig. 163, where the dotted lines indicate the true path of the sheet.

This digression from a straight path is due to the force exerted by the surface tension of the film of water clinging to the outer periphery of the plate. It may be reduced by making the edges of the plate extremely thin, and is of less consequence as the velocity of the issuing stream is increased, and as the inertia of the water becomes, in consequence, of greater relative importance.

When the initial and final directions and velocities of an impinging jet are known, the pressure which it exerts on the surface in any direction may be calculated by equating this pressure to the total change of momentum of the jet per second in this direction.

It is important at this stage to differentiate between the "absolute" and "relative" velocities of a jet. Thus, if the jet be projected from a fixed nozzle and strike a moving surface, its velocity may be considered from the point of view of a person standing by the nozzle and who notes its velocity relatively to the earth, or from that of a person moving with the surface struck, and who notes the motion relative to this moving surface. The first person then notes the absolute, and the second the relative velocity of the jet.

In the case of impact on a fixed surface the change of relative velocity at impact is identical with the change of absolute velocity, and in applying the equation of momentum either may be considered. In any other case, however, the change of momentum must be measured by the change of *absolute* and not of relative velocity.

If friction be neglected and also losses due to shock, the velocity relative to the surface will be unaffected by the impact. Also, the pressure exerted on the surface at any point will be in the direction of the normal at that point. On these assumptions we may consider the following cases:—

(1) **Normal Impact on a Stationary Plane Surface** (Fig. 163).

Let A = sectional area of jet in square feet.

v = velocity of jet in feet per second.

Then the weight of water impinging on the plane per second = $W A v$ lbs., where W is the weight of 1 cubic foot of water.

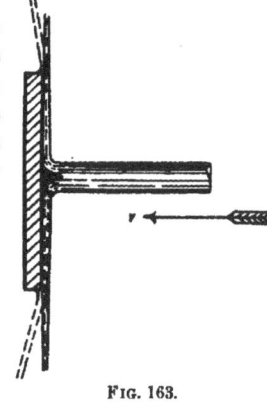

FIG. 163.

The initial momentum of this per second normal to the plane

$$= \frac{W A v^2}{g} \text{ ft. lb. units.}$$

Since the final velocity is tangential to the plane, the final momentum normal to the plane $=$ 0.

∴ Change of momentum per second normal to plane $= \dfrac{W A v^2}{g}$.

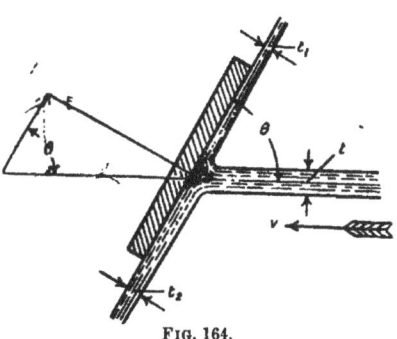

FIG. 164.

∴ Normal pressure on plane

$$= \frac{W A v^2}{g} \text{ lbs.}$$

If θ be the angle which the sheet of water makes with the plane of the surface on leaving, the final velocity per second normal to the plane $= v \sin \theta$, and the momentum in this direction

$$= \frac{W A v^2}{g} \sin \theta.$$

The change of momentum per second and therefore the pressure normal to the plane is now

$$\frac{W A v^2}{g} (1 - \sin \theta) \text{ lbs.}$$

(2) **Oblique Impact on a Stationary Plane Surface** (Fig. 164).

Assuming the jet to be of the same width as the plane and to be prevented from spreading sideways by flanges, part of the stream will escape
from each end of the plane. The sectional area of each of these streams
can be calculated by expressing the fact that the change of momentum
parallel to the plate is unchanged by impact if friction be neglected.

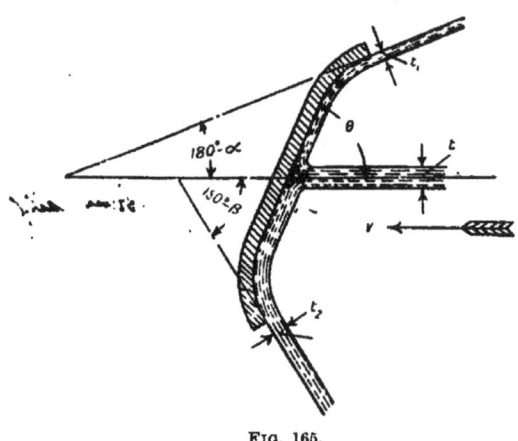

FIG. 165.

Suppose the jet of unit width and of area t, the thickness of the discharge
streams being t_1 and t_2.

Let θ be the (acute) angle between the direction of the jet and the
plane, v the velocity of the jet.

Then initial momentum parallel to plane $= \dfrac{W t v^2}{g} \cos \theta$

and final momentum parallel to plane $\quad = \dfrac{W v^2}{g} (t_2 - t_1)$

$$\therefore\ t \cos \theta = t_2 - t_1$$

But $\qquad\qquad t = t_2 + t_1$

$$\therefore\ \frac{t_1}{t_2} = \frac{1 - \cos \theta}{1 + \cos \theta},\ i.e.,\ t_2 > t_1.$$

Also $\qquad\qquad t_1 = t \left(\dfrac{1 - \cos \theta}{2} \right)$

$$t_2 = t \left(\dfrac{1 + \cos \theta}{2} \right).$$

Again, the initial momentum, in a direction perpendicular to the plane

$= \dfrac{W' t v^2}{g}$. $\sin \theta$, and the final momentum in this direction $= 0$.

$\therefore$ Normal pressure on plane $= \dfrac{W' t v^2}{g}$. $\sin \theta$ lbs.

$\therefore$ Pressure in direction of jet $= \dfrac{W' t v^2}{g}$. $\sin^2 \theta$ lbs.

Impact on Stationary Curved Vane (Fig. 165).

If the inclined plane of the previous case be fitted with ends curved so as to deflect the escaping streams into directions making angles a and β with that of the jet, the pressure on the vane in the direction of the jet will be increased or diminished according as a and β are greater or less than 90°.

As before $\qquad t_1 = t \left(\dfrac{1 - \cos \theta}{2} \right).$

$$t_2 = t \left(\dfrac{1 + \cos \theta}{2} \right).$$

The final momentum per sec. in the direction of the jet $\Big\} = \dfrac{W}{g} v \left\{ t_1 v \cos a + t_2 \cos \beta \right\}$

$$= \dfrac{W v^2}{g} \left\{ t_1 \cos a + t_2 \cos \beta \right\}$$

$\therefore$ Change of momentum per sec. in this direction, by impact $\Big\} = \dfrac{W v^2}{g} \left\{ t - t_1 \cos a - t_2 \cos \beta \right\}$

$\therefore$ Pressure on vane in direction of jet

$$= \dfrac{W}{g} v^2 t \left\{ 1 - \dfrac{\cos a + \cos \beta}{2} - \dfrac{\cos \theta (\cos \beta - \cos a)}{2} \right\} \text{ lbs.}$$

This is a maximum when $a = 180°$ and $\beta = 180°$, i.e., when the discharge is returned parallel to the jet, and then has the value $\dfrac{2 W}{g} v^2 t$ lbs. In this particular case, as whenever $a = \beta$, the pressure is independent of θ, the angle of impact.

(3) **Impact on a Surface of Revolution Symmetrical with respect to the Jet** (Fig. 166).

Here let $a =$ angle of deflection of jet.

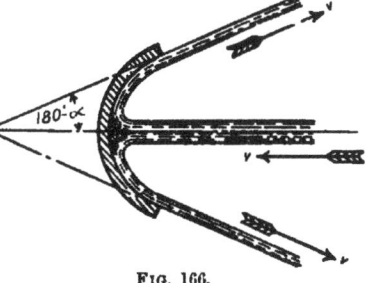

Fig. 166.

H.A.

Then the initial momentum per sec. in $\left.\begin{array}{l}\\\end{array}\right\} = \dfrac{W\,A\,v^2}{g}$
direction of jet

Final momentum per sec. in this direction $= \dfrac{W\,A\,v^2}{g}$. cos a

∴. Change of momentum per sec. $=\left.\begin{array}{l}\\\end{array}\right\} = \dfrac{W\,A\,v^2}{g}(1 - \cos a)$ lb :.
pressure on surface in this direction

This is a maximum when cos a is a minimum, *i.e.*, when $a = 180^\circ$, as in the case in a hemispherical cup.

Here the pressure $\dfrac{2\,W\,A\,v^2}{g}$ lbs.

ART. 105.—ACTUAL FORCE OF IMPACT.

In practice, with flat or recurved vanes, the pressure actually obtained is always slightly less than that given by the above formulae. With normal incidence on a flat plane, as previously explained, the discharging stream is always slightly inclined to the plane and possesses some undestroyed momentum in that direction. This, too, however large the plane (within practical limits). If the plane is too small so that the direction of the whole mass of water has not been completely changed before discharge, a further loss will occur. To obviate this the diameter of plate should be not less than three times the diameter of the jet.

In the case of a curved vane or of a plane with oblique impact, any change in the velocity of discharge affects the change of momentum and hence the force of impact. In every case the final velocity is reduced by surface friction and generally also by loss of energy due to eddy formation in the mass of dead water at the point of impact of an unsteady jet. This latter loss is obviated when the jet strikes the plane tangentially and also when the jet has stream line motion. The total effect depends largely on the size and form of the vanes. Where these are arranged to deflect the jet through less than 90° the actual should exceed the theoretical pressure since these losses reduce the final momentum and thus increase the change of momentum. Where the jet is deflected through more than 90° the actual pressure is less than the theoretical, while with normal incidence the velocity of discharge only affects the force of impact in that the effect of surface tension in affecting the angle of discharge, is more marked as this velocity diminishes. This latter effect is, of course, common to every form of vane, but becomes of less importance as the angle of deflection increases or decreases from 90°.

On the whole, the ratio of actual to theoretical pressure may be expected to become less as the angle of deflection is increased from 90° to

$180°$ and to have its minimum value for the latter angle, while its value may be expected to become more nearly equal to unity as the velocity of impact increases. For let r_1 and r_2 be the initial and final velocities of the jet relative to the vane. Then neglecting changes of level at impact and losses due to eddy formation, we have, per lb. of the water,

$$\frac{r_1^2}{2g} = \frac{r_2^2}{2g} + \frac{f l v^n}{2 g m}.$$

Where f = coefficient of friction between water and vane.

l = length of path of contact of jet in feet.

m = hydraulic mean depth of stream in contact with vane
    = thickness of stream,

and where n is less than 2 for any but very rough surfaces. For such surfaces as are commonly met with forming the vanes of impulse turbines, n may be taken as $1·83$ and f as $·005$.

Also if $r_1 - r_2$ is small, as is usually the case, v may be taken equal to r_1 without sensible error

$$\therefore \quad r_1^2 \left\{ 1 - \frac{f l}{m\, v_1^{2-n}} \right\} = r_2^2$$

and since the ratio $\dfrac{\text{actual pressure}}{\text{theoretical pressure}} = \dfrac{r_1 - r_2 \cos a}{r_1 - r_1 \cos a}$, where a = angle of deflection

this equals $\quad \dfrac{1 - \cos a \sqrt{\left(1 - 2\dfrac{f l}{m\, v^{2-n}} \right)}}{1 - \cos a}$ (approximately)

$$= 1 + \frac{\cos a}{1 - \cos a} \left(\frac{f l}{2\, m\, v^{2-n}} \right) \text{ (approximately)}$$

an expression which diminishes as a (Fig. 166) increases from $90°$ to $180°$, and which increases, for values of a between these limits, as v increases.

EXAMPLE.

A 1 inch circular jet strikes the bucket of a Pelton wheel with a relative velocity of 50 feet per second. The wetted surface is 20 square inches, the bucket being 4 inches wide and 3 inches broad, so that the escaping streams are each 3 inches wide. The length of path of contact is $3·33$ inches $= ·277$ feet.

$$m = \frac{\frac{·7854}{144}}{\frac{6}{12}} \text{ feet} = \frac{\text{sectional area of jet}}{\text{width of streams}} = ·0109 \text{ feet}$$

$$\therefore \frac{f l}{m\, v^{2-n}} = \frac{·005 \times ·277}{·0109 \times 50^{·17}} = \frac{·005 \times ·277}{·0109 \times 1·945} = ·0653$$

$$\therefore \ r_2 = r_1 \sqrt{1 - \cdot 0658} = \cdot 967\ r_1.$$

Also $\dfrac{\text{actual pressure}}{\text{theoretical pressure}} = \dfrac{1 - \cdot 967 \cos a}{1 - \cos a}$.

If $a = 160°$ ($\cos a = -\cdot 9897$) the ratio becomes $\cdot 984$, a value which would diminish as the velocity diminished. This demonstration has neglected any loss directly due to eddy formation. The actual ratio in the case of a Pelton wheel bucket, where such loss is small, would prob ably be about $\cdot 95$, and would be less than this in the case of a jet impinging normally at the centre of a hemispherical cup.

The following are the results of a series of experiments carried out b the author on an apparatus designed by Professor Osborne Reynolds determine the ratio of actual to theoretical force of impact, under varying conditions. In each case the surface to be acted upon was rigidly fixe to the end of a horizontal lever, which was then accurately balanced. vertical jet was allowed to impinge from below on this surface, and the flow was adjusted until the force of impact was sufficient to balance known weight resting on the lever vertically above the axis of the jet, and to cause the lever to float in its equilibrium position. The velocity of impact was measured by measuring the area of the discharge orifice and the weight of water discharged in a given time, and by taking into account the height h (small) between the orifice and the surface Thus if $r = $ velocity of impact and $r_0 = $ velocity at orifice, we have $v = \sqrt{r_0^2 - 2\,g\,h}$.

The surfaces experimented upon consisted of three flat circular bra plates of diameters respectively $\cdot 54$ inch, $1\cdot 15$ inches, and $2\cdot 0$ inche each $\frac{1}{16}$ inch thick and having edges perpendicular to the plane of the plate; a similar flat plate of 2 inches diameter, having its rear fac ground down until it formed a knife edge around the discharging periphery; and a plain hemispherical cup of 1 inch diameter. The diameter of the orifice was accurately $\cdot 200$ inch.

The results of these experiments are tabulated below.

(1) *Flat Plate $\cdot 54$ in. diameter, $\frac{1}{16}$ in. thick.*

Velocity v ft. per sec.	25·60	82·61	86·70	49·10	50·73	58·9
Ratio $\dfrac{\text{actual}}{\text{calculated}}$ pressures	·891	·940	·874	·858	·914	·917

(2) *Flat Plate* 1·15 *ins. diameter,* $\frac{1}{16}$ *in. thick.*

'elocity . . .	25·82	32·21	36·90	48·05	54·70
latio . . .	·874	·962	·865	·897	·877

(3) *Flat Plate* 2·0 *ins. diameter,* $\frac{1}{16}$ *in. thick.*

'elocity . .	25·94	31·92	37·85	48·05	50·78	57·15
latio . . .	·870	·978	·831	·897	·914	·955

(4) *Flat Plate* 2·0 *ins. diameter, ground to knife edge.*

elocity . .	25·8	33·6	36·15	41·90	46·55	52·50	57·80
atio . .	·901	·903	·906	·925	·944	·956	·962

(5) *Hemispherical cup,* 1 *in. diameter.*

elocity . .	18·19	22·66	33·45	43·15	51·15	54·50
atio . . .	·890	·968	·890	·853	·833	·834

In the first three of the flat-plate experiments, the most noteworthy atures are the remarkable increase in efficiency in each case with a locity of about 32 feet per second (an effect which is also marked in the se of the hemispherical cup at about 22 feet per second), and the disrbing effect of the capillary action at the periphery. This deflected the caping stream upward through an angle varying from 3° to 6°, the lue of $1 - \sin \theta$ varying between ·9477 and ·8955. With a sharpged periphery the effect of surface tension was less marked, particularly low velocities, the angle apparently varying steadily from about 5° to ($1 - \sin \theta$ from ·913 to ·965) as the velocity increased.

It will be noticed that, except at very high velocities and at the " critil " velocity, the smallest was quite as efficient as the two larger plates.

In the case of the hemispherical cup, the escaping stream, which eoretically should have been vertical, showed the effect of capillary traction by being inclined at 18° to the vertical. On taking this into count, the ratio of actual to theoretical pressure is increased by about

1 per cent. in each case. The reduction of efficiency at high as com
pared with low velocities, is here to be accounted for by the interferenc
of the descending stream with the ascending jet.

One interesting difference is to be noted between the behaviour of
steady jet and of an unsteady (sinuous) jet on impact. The forme
invariably impinges without any splashing. The latter, on the other han:

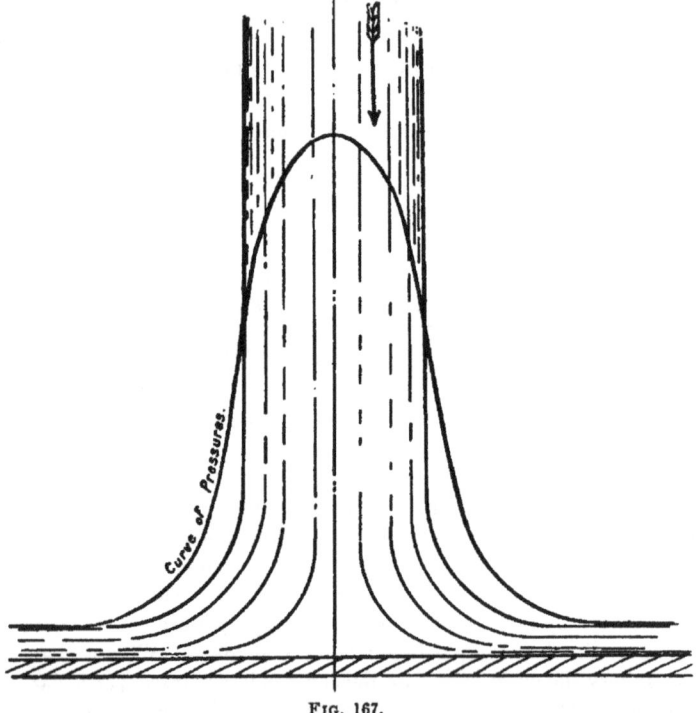

Curve of Pressures.

FIG. 167.

is always accompanied by considerable splash. With a steady jet ther
appears to be no formation of deadwater at the central point of impac
as is indicated in black in the sketches in Figs. 165 and 166.

ART. 106.—DISTRIBUTION OF PRESSURE OVER PLATE AT IMPACT.

In general, this is unimportant, the total pressure only being needed
Owing to the curvature of the stream in the neighbourhood of th
plate (Fig. 167), and to the centrifugal force caused thereby, the pressur

ncreases along the radius of curvature towards the surface of the
)late and the centre of the jet, the velocity suffering a corresponding
liminution.

Assuming no loss of energy before impact, the energy per lb. of water
will be $\dfrac{v^2}{2\,g} = h$ ft. lbs., where, in the case of a vertical jet, h is the height
)f the free surface of the supply reservoir above the plate. Thus, at the
.entre of the jet at the plate where the velocity is zero, the pressure
intensity will have its maximum value $W\,h = \dfrac{W}{2}\dfrac{v^2}{g}$ lbs. per square foot.
From this point the pressure intensity falls off radially as indicated in
the figure, the pressure curve being approximately as shown.

Experiments show that the pressure at the centre of the jet is
practically the same as (slightly less than) that corresponding to $\dfrac{v^2}{2\,g}$ feet
of water.

The following table, taken in abstract from the Roorkee Papers on
Indian Engineering ("Proc. Inst. C.E.," vol. 60, p. 436), shows the
pressure exerted at different radii by a vertical jet $1\frac{18}{}''$ diameter, when
impinging normally on a fixed plate.

Height from free surface in containing vessel to surface of plate in inches.	Radial distance from axis of jet in inches.	Pressure intensity on plate in inches of water.
27·125	·000	26·875
,,	·125	26·75
,,	·225	26·375
27	·325	26·125
,,	·425	25·50
,,	·525	24·50
,,	·625	23·25
,,	·725	21·75
,,	·825	20·25
,,	·925	18·00
26·5	1·125	13·50
,,	1·225	10·75
,,	1·325	8·00
,,	1·425	6·25
,,	1·525	4·50
,,	2·025	4·00
,,	2·075	3·50
,,	2·350	2·00

In general, with a plate having a diameter from two to three times that of the jet, the total pressure exerted will exceed 90 per cent. of the theoretical.

ART. 107. —IMPACT ON MOVING VANES.

Let v be the velocity of the jet in feet per second.

„ u be the velocity of the vane in the direction of motion of the jet.

Then the relative velocity of jet and vane $= v - u$.

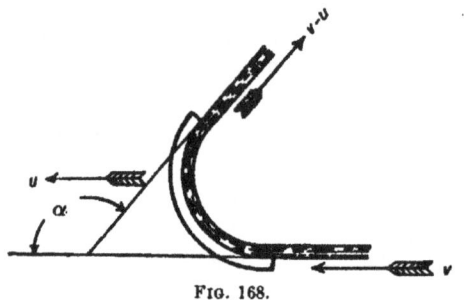

FIG. 168.

(1) **Impact on a single vane curved through an angle a, and moving in the direction of the jet (Fig. 168).**

$$\text{Here the weight of water striking the vane per sec.} = W A (v - u) \text{ lbs.}$$

$$\text{Initial momentum in direction of motion} = \frac{W A (v - u) v}{g}$$

$$\text{Final velocity in direction of motion} = u + (v - u) \cos a$$

$$\therefore \text{Final momentum in direction of motion} = \frac{W A}{g} \{ (v - u) u + (v - u)^2 \cos a \}$$

$$\therefore \text{Change of momentum in this direction} = \frac{W A}{g} \{ (v - u) [v - u - (v - u) \cos a] \}$$

$$= \frac{W A}{g} (v - u)^2 (1 - \cos a)$$

$$\therefore \text{Work done on vane} = \frac{W A}{g} (v - u)^2 (1 - \cos a) u \text{ ft. lbs. per sec.}$$

$$\text{Initial kinetic energy of jet} = \frac{W A v^3}{2 g} \text{ ft. lbs.}$$

$$\therefore \text{ Efficiency} = \frac{2 (v - u)^2 (1 - \cos a) u}{v^3} = \eta.$$

For maximum efficiency $\qquad \dfrac{d\,\eta}{d\,u} = 0$

$$\therefore \quad 2\,(v - u)^2 - 4\,(v - u)\,u = 0$$

$$\therefore \quad \text{either } v = u \quad \text{or } v - u = 2\,u$$

so that $\qquad\qquad\qquad\qquad\qquad v = 3\,u.$

In the first case the velocity of the jet is unchanged and the work done on the vane is zero. In the second case we have :—

$$\text{Work done on vane} = \frac{W\,A}{g}\left(\frac{2}{3}\,v\right)^2 \cdot \frac{v}{3}\,(1 - \cos a)\ \text{ft. lbs. per sec.}$$

$$= \frac{4}{27}\,\frac{W\,A}{g}\cdot v^3\,(1 - \cos a)\ \text{ft. lbs. per sec.}$$

$$\therefore \text{Efficiency (max.)} = \frac{8}{27}\,(1 - \cos a).$$

This has its greatest value when $a = 180°$, and then equals $\dfrac{16}{27}$.

When $a = 90°$, i.e., in the case of normal impact on a single flat plate, we have, as before, the maximum efficiency when $u = \dfrac{v}{3}$, and then

$$\text{efficiency (max.)} = \frac{8}{27}.$$

(2) Impact on a Series of Moving Vanes.

If, instead of a single vane, we have a series of vanes successively placed in the path of the jet at frequent intervals, the weight of water striking these vanes per second becomes $W\,A\,v$ lbs.

If the vanes form surfaces of revolution having their axes in the line of action of the jet, neglecting losses due to splash we have, if a be the angle through which the stream is deflected :—

$$\left.\begin{array}{l}\text{Change of momentum}\\ \text{per second in direction}\\ \text{of jet}\end{array}\right\} = \frac{W\,A\,v}{g}\,(v - u)\,(1 - \cos a)$$

$$\therefore \text{Total pressure on vanes} = \frac{W\,A\,v}{g}\,(v - u)\,(1 - \cos a)\ \text{lbs.}$$

$$\left.\begin{array}{l}\text{Work done on vanes per}\\ \text{second}\end{array}\right\} = \frac{W\,A\,v\,u}{g}\,(v - u)\,(1 - \cos a)\ \text{ft. lbs.}$$

$$\therefore \quad \text{Efficiency} = \frac{2\,(v\,u)\,(v - u)\,(1 - \cos a)}{v^3} = \eta$$

For maximum efficiency $\dfrac{d\,\eta}{d\,u} = 0$

$$\therefore \quad v\,(v - u) - v\,u = 0$$

or $$v = 2\,u$$

$$\therefore \ \text{Efficiency (max.)} = \frac{v^2 \times \dfrac{v}{2}\,(1 - \cos a)}{v^3}$$

$$= \frac{1 - \cos a}{2}$$

This is a maximum for $a = 180°$, *i.e.*, with a series of hemispherical cups and then equals unity. With a series of flat plates having normal incidence $a = 90°$ and the efficiency equals ·5.

Art. 108.—Impact on one of a Series of Recurved Vanes whose Direction of Motion makes an Angle with that of the Jet.

This problem is one of much importance in the design of impulse turbines. Let a be the angle between the directions of v and of u, and

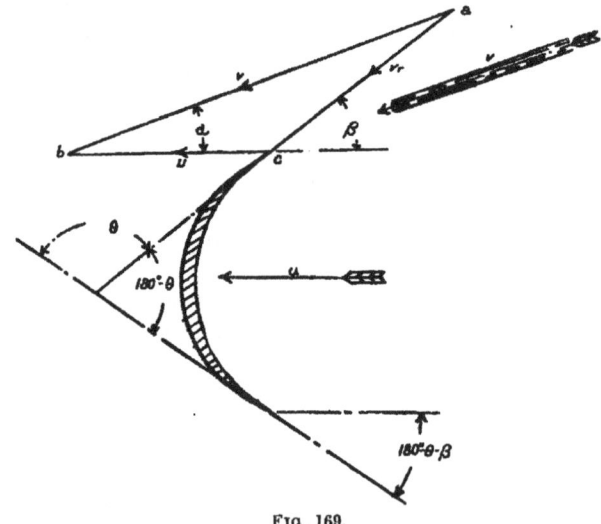

Fig. 169.

let θ be the total angle through which the vane is recurved (Fig. 169). Then if, as is usual, the incidence is tangential, the relative velocity v_r of jet and vane at impact is given by

$$v_r^2 = v^2 + u^2 - 2\,v\,u \cos a \text{ (triangle } a\,b\,c.)$$

and, neglecting friction and eddy losses, the relative velocity at discharge will be the same as this.

Also, for tangential incidence, the direction of the vane at incidence must be parallel to the direction of the jet relative to the vane, and must therefore make an angle β with the direction of motion of the vane where β is obtained from the relationship (triangle $a\ b\ c$).

$$\text{Sin } \beta = \frac{v}{v_r} \cdot \sin a.$$

The initial velocity of jet in the direction of motion of vane $= v \cos a$

,, final ,, ,, ,, ,, ,,
$$= u - v_r \cos (180° - \theta - \beta)$$
$$= u + v_r \cos (\theta + \beta)$$

∴ Change of momentum per sec. in direction of motion of vane $\left. \right\} = \dfrac{W\,Q}{g} \left\{ v \cos a - u - v_r \cos (\theta + \beta) \right\}$

∴ Press on vane $= \dfrac{W\,Q}{g} \left\{ v \cos a - u - v_r \cos (\theta + \beta) \right\}$ lbs.

ART. 109.—GRAPHICAL CONSTRUCTION TO DETERMINE THE PRESSURE EXERTED ON A VANE (Fig. 170).

(1) Impact on a Fixed Vane.

Let the vector $\overline{BA}$ represent the initial velocity of the jet in feet per second.

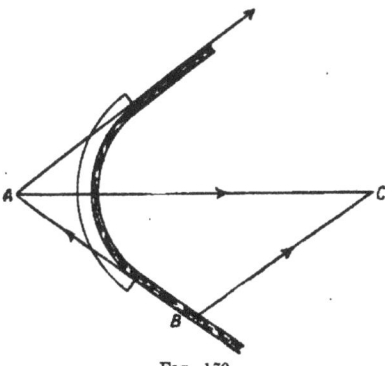

FIG. 170.

Let the vector $\overline{BC}$ represent its final velocity on leaving the vane.

Then ,, ,, $\overline{AC}$ represents the change of velocity, and therefore gives a measure of the resultant pressure on the vane, for if $W'\,Q$ lbs. of water strike the vane per second, the change of momentum in the direction AC per second $= W\,Q.\ A\ddot{C} \div g$.

∴ Resultant pressure on vane acts in the direction $C\,A$ and is of magnitude $\dfrac{W\,Q}{g}\cdot\overline{C\,A}$ lbs.

(2) Impact on One of a Series of Moving Vanes.

Let $\overline{BA}$ (Fig. 171 a and b) represent the initial velocity of the jet in magnitude and direction.

Let BC represent the velocity of the vane.

Then $\overline{CA}$ represents the relative velocity of the water over the surface of the vane.

Draw $E\,F = C\,A$ tangential to the vane at exit and make $F\,G$ equal and parallel to $B\,C$. The vector $\overline{EG}$, which represents the velocity com-

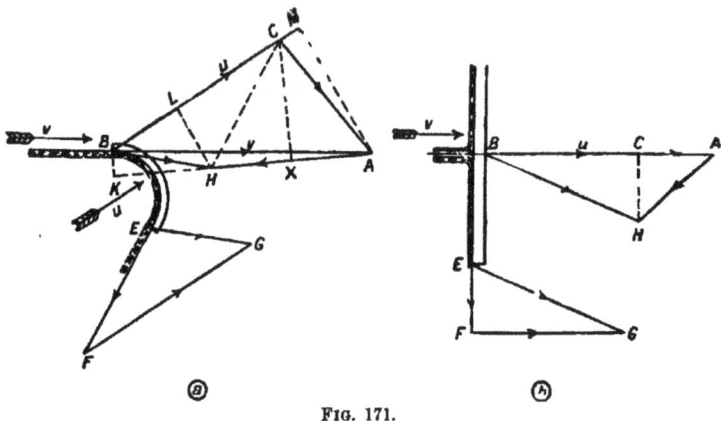

FIG. 171.

pounded of the velocity of the vane and of that of the water relative to the vane, now gives the absolute velocity of the discharge stream.

Drawing $B\,H$ equal and parallel to $E\,G$, the acceleration which is given to the water by the vane is represented by $\overline{A\,H}$, and the resultant pressure on the vane $P = \dfrac{W.\,Q}{g}\cdot\overline{HA}$ lbs. The line of action of this pressure is parallel to $H\,A$.

The effective pressure is the component of this in the direction of motion of the vane. Thus in Fig. 171 a, this is given by $\dfrac{W.\,Q}{g}\cdot\overline{LM}$ lbs., and the work done per second by $\dfrac{W.\,Q}{g}\cdot\overline{LM}\cdot\overline{BC}$ ft. lbs. In Fig. 171 b, the effective pressure $= \dfrac{W \cdot Q}{g} \cdot \overline{CA}$ lbs. and the work per second

$= \dfrac{W \cdot Q}{g} \cdot \overline{CA} \cdot \overline{BC}$ ft. lbs.

By producing $A\,H$ to K (Fig. 171 a) and dropping perpendiculars $B\,K$, $C\,X$, on to $A\,H$, we can prove that

$$\overline{BA^2} - \overline{BH^2} = \overline{H\,A}\,(\overline{H\,A} + 2\,\overline{K\,H}).$$

Also, since $\overline{CA}$ represents the initial relative velocity of jet and vane and $\overline{CH}$ their final relative velocity, we have—neglecting friction—$\overline{CH} = \overline{CA}. \quad \therefore \overline{HA} = 2\,\overline{HX}$

$$\therefore \quad K\,A = KH + 2\,H\,X$$
$$\therefore \quad K\,A + K\,H = H\,A + 2\,K\,H = 2\,(K\,H + H\,X)$$
$$\therefore \quad H\,A + 2\,K\,H = 2\,KX$$
$$\text{Also } \frac{2\,K\,X}{2\,B\,C} = \frac{L\,M}{A\,H}$$
$$\therefore \quad H\,A\,(H\,A + 2\,K\,H) = 2\,(L\,M \cdot B\,C)$$
$$\therefore \text{ Work done} = \frac{W \cdot Q}{2\,g}\,(\overline{B\,A^2} - \overline{B\,H^2})$$
$$= \frac{W \cdot Q}{2\,g}\,(v_1{}^2 - v_2{}^2)$$

where v_1 and v_2 are the initial and final absolute velocities of the water.

$$\therefore \text{ Efficiency} = \frac{\text{Work done on vane}}{\text{Total energy of jet}} \text{ per second}$$
$$= \frac{\dfrac{W \cdot Q}{2\,g}\,(v_1{}^2 - v_2{}^2)}{\dfrac{W \cdot Q}{2\,g}\,v_1{}^2}$$
$$= 1 - \left(\frac{v_2}{v_1}\right)^2$$

Centre of Pressure on Vane.—The position of the centre of pressure on any vane receiving a jet tangentially may be determined as follows. Consider any small arc $P\,Q$ (Fig. 172 a) of the vane. If the velocity is supposed unaltered by friction, $P\,A$ and $A\,Q$, tangents at P and Q represent to some scale the (equal) velocities at P and Q, while $R\,Q$, perpendicular to the chord $P\,Q$, represents to the same scale the change of velocity between P and Q. Normals $P\,C$ and $Q\,C$ to the curve intersect in C, the centre of curvature of the arc, and $\dfrac{R\,Q}{A\,Q} = \dfrac{P\,Q}{P\,C}$, so that if $P\,C$ represent the velocity v at P, the chord $P\,Q$ represents the change of velocity between P and Q and the resultant pressure on the arc PQ is given by $\dfrac{W \cdot Q}{g} \cdot \overline{PQ}$ lbs., if Q is the volume in cubic feet striking the vane per second.

Thus if a series of normals to the curve are drawn intersecting at C_1, C_2, C_3, etc. (Fig. 172 b), the pressure on the corresponding arcs will be given by $\dfrac{W \cdot Q}{g} \cdot \left\{ \dfrac{\text{arc}}{\text{radius}} \right\} v$ lbs., and these pressures act outwards through the middle points of their respective arcs. Drawing in the lines

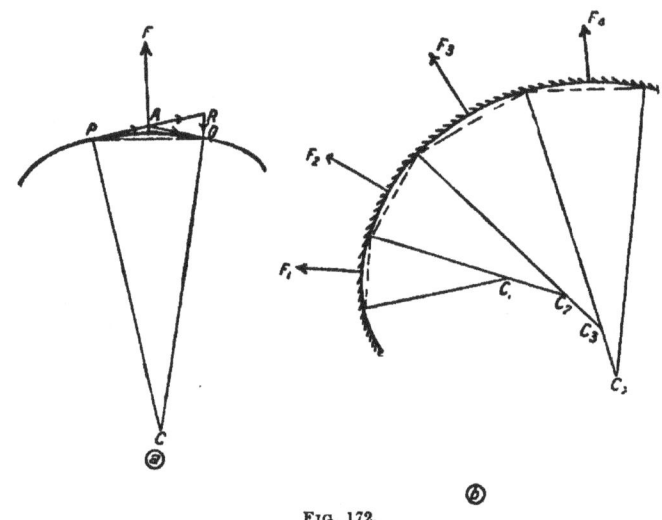

FIG. 172.

representing these pressures F_1, F_2, F_3, etc., the funicular polygon for these forces may be drawn, and the line of action of their resultant obtained as explained in any work on applied mechanics. The point of intersection of this line with the surface of the vane gives the centre of pressure on the vane.

If the velocity varies from point to point of the vane the same general principles apply except that now the velocity v in the expression—

pressure $= \dfrac{W \cdot Q}{g} \left\{ \dfrac{\text{arc}}{\text{radius}} \right\} v$. lbs.—varies from point to point. Where the law of its variation is known, the problem becomes perfectly determinate.

ART. 110.—COMPOUNDING OF JETS.

If two steady streams are allowed to impinge on each other under atmospheric pressure, they combine to form a single stream.

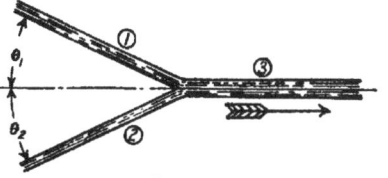

Let streams (1) and (2) combine to form stream (3) (Fig. 173). Then if a, v, and Q represent the sectional areas, velocities of flow, and quantity carried by each stream, we have, if θ be the angle

FIG. 173.

made by an impinging stream with the direction of the resultant stream :—

For continuity of flow, $v_1\, a_1 + v_2\, a_2, = v_3\, a_3$ (1)

The equations of momentum give :—

$$Q_1\, v_1 \sin\theta_1 - Q_2\, v_2 \sin\theta_2 = 0 \tag{2}$$

$$Q_1\, v_1 \cos\theta_1 + Q_2\, v_2 \cos\theta_2 = Q_3\, v_3 \tag{3}$$

while the equation of energy gives :—

$$\frac{W\,Q_1\,v_1^2}{2\,g} + \frac{W\,Q_2\,v_2^2}{2\,g} = \frac{W\,Q_3\,v_3^2}{2\,g} + \text{loss at impact.}$$

$$= \frac{W\,(Q_1 + Q_2)v_3^2}{2\,g} + H'$$

$$\therefore \;\; H' = \frac{W}{2\,g}\left\{\, Q_1\,v_1^2 + Q_2\,v_2^2 - (Q_1 + Q_2)\,v_3^2 \,\right\}$$

$$= \frac{W}{2\,g}\left\{\, Q_1\,(v_1^2 - v_3^2) + Q_2\,(v_2^2 - v_3^2) \,\right\} \tag{4}$$

By substitution from equations (2) and (3) above, this loss may be determined in terms of v_1, v_2, θ_1 and θ_2.

In two particular cases H' may be zero. In each of these it is necessary that $\left.\begin{array}{l} v_1^2 - v_3^2 = 0 \\ v_2^2 - v_3^2 = 0 \end{array}\right\}$ simultaneously, and therefore that $\pm v_1 = \pm v_2 = \pm v_3$.

The first case is found where $v_1 = v_2 = v_3$, i.e., where two parallel streams moving with the same velocity com-

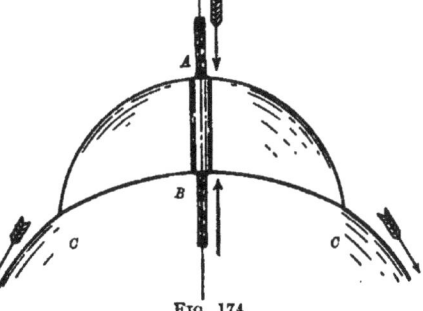

FIG. 174.

bine to form a single stream, with an area equal to the combined area of the two. The second case is found where $v_1 = -v_2$, each of these being

numerically equal to v_3, and corresponds to the direct impact of two
streams of equal velocity. A film of water is then formed, the velocity
of whose mass centre (v_3 in the equation of momentum) is zero, but
which has a velocity of outward flow equal to v_1 or v_2. Professor Osborne
Reynolds illustrated this by allowing two streams of equal velocity to
meet by direct impact, and noting the clear and glassy appearance of the
resultant film. If a cylindrical prism having plane and parallel ends be
placed in the path of the stream (Fig. 174), the films from A and B to
the point of contact C, are still perfectly clear. After C, however, the
frosted appearance of the film indicates eddy formation and the institution
of sinuous motion.

Art. 110a.—Compounding of Confined Streams.—Loss at Impact.

When the impinging streams are confined, the pressure is no longer
the same before and after impact and the available data is insufficient to
allow the equations of momentum to be applied. Experiments by the
author[1] on the loss following the impact of such streams, only one of
which is deviated by the impact, show that this is given by

$$\text{loss} = a\,\frac{v_1^2}{2\,g} + b\,\frac{v_2^2}{2\,g} \text{ ft. lbs. per lb. of the impinging jet} \tag{2}$$

By the impinging jet is meant that which suffers deviation. The
velocity of this jet is v_2 while the velocity of the primary or undeviated
stream is v_1. The values of the constants a and b depend on the angle
of impact θ, and on the ratio m of areas of the primary and impinging
streams. The values of θ in the experiments were varied from 5° to 90°,
while m was varied from 1 to 5. The area of the impinging stream was
$\frac{1}{2}'' \times 1''$ throughout, and the area of the primary stream was the same
before and after impact. The velocities ranged up to 23 ft. per sec.
Under these conditions the following are the values of a and of b.

θ	Values of m, i.e. ratio of area of primary and impinging streams.									
	1		2		3		4		5	
	a	b	a	b	a	b	a	b	a	b
90°	3·0	1·53	1·85	·97	1·57	·915	1·42	·921	1·33	·925
60°	2·0	·71	·49	·59	·38	·70	·33	·75	·31	·79
45°	1·5	·44	·32	·45	·22	·60	·19	·68	·17	·73
30°	1·0	·22	·20	·35	·12	·53	·10	·62	·083	·68
15°	·50	·060	·090	·28	·050	·48	·040	·58	·034	·652
5°	·17	·008	·030	·254	·013	·447	·011	·566	·009	·642
0°	·00	·00	·00	·250	·00	·444	·00	·568	·00	·640

[1] " Proc. Roy. Soc. Edinburgh," 1912–13.

It will be noted that when θ is large, and particularly where m is small, the r_1^2 term is all important, while for small values of θ and large values of m the r_2^2 term becomes the more important. With large values of m the value of b approximates, as would be anticipated, to unity for all values of θ. Where θ, and the volumes of streams (1) and (2) are known the above values of a and b enable the value of m for minimum loss to be calculated. Thus if $Q_1 = n\, Q_2$, $r_1 = \dfrac{n}{m} v_2$, and the loss is given by

$$\text{loss} = \left\{ a \left(\frac{n}{m} \right)^2 + b \right\} \frac{r_2^2}{2\,g} \text{ ft. lbs. per lb. of stream (2).}$$

e.g. If $\theta = 30$ and $Q_1 = 2\, Q_2$, *i.e.* $n = 2$

When $m = 1\cdot5$, $a = \cdot34$, $b = \cdot24$, ... loss $= \cdot843 \dfrac{r_2^2}{2\,g}$

,, $m = 2\cdot0$, $a = \cdot20$, $b = \cdot35$, ... loss $= \cdot550 \dfrac{r_2^2}{2\,g}$

,, $m = 2\cdot5$, $a = \cdot15$, $b = \cdot44$, ... loss $= \cdot536 \dfrac{r_2^2}{2\,g}$

,, $m = 3\cdot0$, $a = \cdot12$, $b = \cdot52$, ... loss $= \cdot573 \dfrac{r_2^2}{2\,g}$

On plotting these values of m against the loss it appears that this is minimum when $m = 2\cdot5$ and then amounts to $\cdot536 \dfrac{r_2^2}{2\,g}$ ft. lbs. per lb. of jet 2.

For values of θ between $0°$ and $45°$ and of m between 1 and 6, the value of m for minimum loss is given by

$$m = \left\{ 1 + \frac{2\,\theta}{100} + \frac{\sqrt{\theta}}{11\cdot4} \cdot \frac{Q_1}{Q_2} \right\}$$

The following table indicates how this best value of m varies with θ and with the ratio of Q_1 to Q_2,

θ	Value of $Q_1 \div Q_2$.						
	1	2	4	6	8	10	12
5°	1·31	1·50	1·85	2·25	2·65	3·05	3·45
10°	1·5	1·8	2·35	2·9	3·4	4·0	4·6
15°	1·65	1·95	2·65	3·45	4·05	4·75	5·35
20°	1·8	2·2	3·0	3·8	4·5	5·2	6·1
30°	2·1	2·55	3·5	4·5	5·4	6·4	7·3
45°	2·55	3·15	4·25	5·5	6·7	7·8	8·9

H.A.   C C

while the loss of energy expressed as a fraction of $\dfrac{v_2^2}{2\,g}$, experienced with the best value of m is as follows.

θ	Value of $Q_1 \div Q_2$						
	1	2	4	6	8	10	12
5°	·13	·18	·27	·35	·42	·47	·51
10°	·22	·29	·43	·53	·60	·67	·71
15°	·28	·36	·53	·64	·71	·78	·83
20°	·33	·43	·60	·71	·79	·85	·91
30°	·41	·53	·72	·82	·91	·97	1·02
45°	·53	·68	·88	·97	1·04	1·10	1·14

Art. 111.—Resistance of Submerged Plane Surfaces.

If an entirely submerged plane surface be moved normally or obliquely with uniform velocity through still water, the resistance to motion depends slightly on frictional resistances, but to a much larger extent on the change of momentum produced in the surrounding water during the passage of the plane, and on the eddy production in the rear of the plane.

Normal Motion of a Plane through Still Water.

Here, in front of the plane, stream line motion is set up, and if a be the area of the plate, and v its velocity, a column of water of sectional area a and of length v feet, is transferred from front to rear of the plane per second. The effect of this in producing resistance, may be seen by considering the flow of a steady stream past such a submerged plane. As before, up to the plane the motion is steady, and the stream line formation is as indicated in Fig. 175.[1] The plane, therefore, affects the momentum in a direction normal to its plane, of a mass of water of volume $a\,v$ cubic feet, per second. Since the velocity of the mass in this direction is initially v feet per second, if it were possible to destroy the whole of its momentum the total pressure on the front of the plane would be $\dfrac{W\,a\,v^2}{g}$ lbs. From a consideration of the stream line formation, it is, however, clear that it is only those stream lines at and near the centre of the plane which are actually diverted at right angles to their normal direction, the outer layers being diverted through a smaller angle depending on their distance from the centre, so that the change of

[1] From a paper by Professor Hele Shaw, "Trans. Inst. Naval Architects," 1898, vol. 85.

momentum in the direction of motion, and hence the pressure on the front of the plane, is less than $\dfrac{W\,a\,v^2}{g}$. At only one point, *i.e.*, the centre of the plane, is the momentum actually destroyed, and here the pressure intensity amounts to $\dfrac{W\,v^2}{2\,g}$, the head corresponding to the velocity of flow. Immediately after passing the plane the motion becomes sinuous, eddies are formed,[1] and since the energy of eddy production has to be supplied in the form of extra work done on the plate, this directly increases the resistance to motion. In other words, while the pressure on the front of the plane is unaffected, that on the rear face is reduced by this eddy production, and since the resistance to motion is equal to the difference of pressure on the two faces, this is increased. Plates of

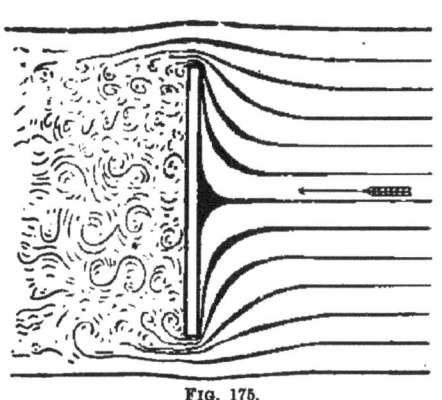

FIG. 175.

different shapes have different effects as regards eddy production, the circular shape giving least resistance for a given area, while generally the resistance increases slightly with the ratio of the length of periphery to the area of the plane. Also it would appear that as the size of plate increases, the proportional effect of the eddy production increases slightly. Experiments show that for the normal motion of a submerged plane through still water, where the boundaries are so remote as not to affect the resistance, this is given by $k\,\dfrac{W\,a\,v^2}{g}$ lbs., where k is a coefficient depending on the size and shape of the plate, and diminishing slightly as the speed increases.

With a circular plate, k varies from about ·560 in a plate of 1 inch diameter to ·650 with a diameter of 3 inches and ·720 with a diameter of 6 inches, afterwards increasing slightly with the diameter. Dubuat and Duchemin obtained a mean value of ·717 for a plate 1 foot square moving through still water, k being ·50 for the front of the plate and ·217 for the

[1] See Art. 15, p. 47.

o c 2

back. Experiment also tends to show that the resistance is somewhat greater when the plate is stationary in a moving current than when it is moved through still water. This is probably due to the fact that the water when in motion is in a much more unstable condition than when at rest, so that the sphere of influence of eddies projected from the boundaries of the plane is greater, and the consequent dissipation of energy is greater in the former than in the latter case.

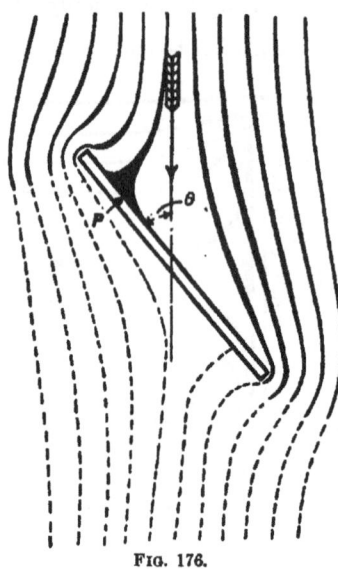

With a plate 1 inch square held in a moving current, Stanton[1] obtained a value of $k = \cdot 620$.

Submerged Plane in Pipe of Small Cross-Sectional Area.

The effect of placing the plane in a pipe of restricted area, is to increase the velocity with which the water escapes over the edge of the plane. This causes an increased eddy production, a consequent reduction of pressure on the rear of the plane, and hence an increased resistance.

FIG. 176.

Oblique Motion of Submerged Planes.

Where an oblique plane makes an angle θ, with its own direction of motion (Fig. 176), the velocity of the water normal to the plane $= v \sin \theta$.

The column of water whose momentum is affected, is now of sectional area $a \sin \theta$, so that the change of momentum produced by the passage of the plane is proportional to

$$\frac{W\,v\,a \sin \theta\,v \sin \theta}{g}, \; i.e., \; \text{to} \; \frac{W\,a}{g}\,v^2 \sin^2\theta.$$

It might then be expected that the resistance to the oblique motion of a plane would equal

$$\text{Direct resistance} \times \sin^2\theta.$$

Due, however, to the unequal eddy formation at the rear of the plate with the two kinds of motion, and to the fact that as θ is diminished,

[1] " Trans. Inst. N.A.," 1909.

frictional resistances form an increasingly large portion of the whole, this law does not hold. Lord Rayleigh,[1] indeed, showed that a rational expression for the normal pressure on the front face of the plane when moving through an infinite mass of fluid is given by

$$P = \frac{W}{g} \frac{a}{} \cdot \frac{\pi \sin \theta}{4 + \pi \sin \theta} \cdot v^2 \text{ lbs.}$$

this neglecting the effect of eddy formation.

From this we have, if P' = normal pressure on oblique plane, and if P = corresponding pressure on a normal plane,

$$P' = P \cdot \frac{(4 + \pi) \sin \theta}{4 + \pi \sin \theta} = P \frac{\sin \theta}{\cdot 56 + \cdot 44 \sin \theta}.$$

As the result of experiment M. Joessels, of the French Navy, deduced an empirical formula of this type, making

$$P' = P \frac{\sin \theta}{\cdot 39 + \cdot 61 \sin \theta}.$$

while Duchemin deduced the relationship

$$P' = P \cdot \frac{2 \sin \theta}{1 + \sin^2 \theta}.$$

The following table shows results experimentally obtained by Colonel Beaufoy and by Stanton, and also some results of experiments by Vince quoted by Rayleigh, together with corresponding values as calculated by the $\sin^2 \theta$ formula, and by those of Rayleigh, of Joessels, and of Duchemin.

Angle made by plane with direction of motion .		90°	80°	70°	60°	50°	40°	30°	20°	10°
Ratio $\frac{P'}{P}$ experimentally obtained	Vince .	1·00	—	·974	—	·873	—	·663	·458	·278
	Beaufoy	1·00	·915	·845	·828	·722	·579	—	·321	·272
	Stanton (square plane)	1·00	1·00	1·00	·97	·93	·915	·89	·59	·27
$\sin^2 \theta$		1·00	·97	·88	·75	·587	·413	·250	·117	·030
$\frac{\sin \theta}{\cdot 56 + \cdot 44 \sin \theta}$ (Rayleigh) .		1·00	·990	·965	·919	·854	·751	·641	·481	·273
$\frac{\sin \theta}{\cdot 39 + \cdot 61 \sin \theta}$ (Joessels) .		1·00	·994	·975	·914	·894	·821	·715	·571	·351
$\frac{2 \sin \theta}{1 + \sin^2 \theta}$ (Duchemin) .		1·00	1·00	1·00	·99	·965	·91	·80	·61	·34

[1] "Scientific Papers," I., p. 287, and III., p. 491 ; or see Lamb's "Hydrodynamics," p. 93.

The resistance in the direction of motion is given by $P' \sin \theta$. .

Probably the experiments by Stanton are the more reliable, and for values of θ greater than 15°, the agreement of these results with those calculated by the formula of Duchemin, is very close.

As in the case of the normal plane, there is only one point P, this in the median plane of the plate, at which the velocity is zero and at which the maximum pressure $\dfrac{W}{2}\dfrac{v^2}{g}$ is therefore attained. This is in advance of the centre of the plane, and its distance from the centre in terms of the length l of the plane, as obtained theoretically, is given in the following table.[1] The distance $\bar{x}$ of the centre of pressure from the centre of the plane, is theoretically given by the formula $\bar{x} = \dfrac{3}{4} \cdot \dfrac{\cos \theta}{4 + \pi \sin \theta} \cdot l$,[1] and values of $\bar{x}$ are also tabulated below.

θ	90°	70°	50°	30°	20°	10°
$\bar{x}$	·000	·037 l	·075 l	·117 l	·139 l	·163 l
Distance of point where stream divides, from centre of plane	·000	·232 l	·402 l	·483 l	·496 l	·500 l

It is found, moreover, that with a rectangular oblique plane the total pressure for a given value of θ depends largely on whether the long or short edges of the plane are perpendicular to the stream, the resistance being greatest when the long edges are so placed. The reason for this is explained by Lord Rayleigh as follows. Although there is only one point of maximum pressure whatever the manner of presentation of the plane, yet with the long edges perpendicular to the stream the motion is approximately in two dimensions, and a region of almost maximum pressure extends over the greater part of the length. The case is very different, however, when the short dimension is perpendicular to the stream, for then, along the greater part of the length the flow is rapid and the tressure in consequence low.

This is of importance in the design of oar blades, the floats of paddle-

---

[1] From Lamb's "Hydrodynamics," p. 94.

wheels, and the gliders of aeroplanes, since, area for area, a short (in the direction of motion) wide surface is considerably more efficient than a long narrow one, the total pressure approximating more nearly to $\dfrac{W\,a\,v^2}{2\,g}$ as the surface is made shorter and wider.[1]

As applied to the design of rudders it explains why a deep narrow rudder gives better results than one which, having the same area, is shallower and wider.

The following table shows the ratios of P' to P experimentally obtained by Stanton on rectangular planes.

Angle of inclination . .	90°	80°	70°	60°	50°	40°	30°	20°	10°
Rectangle length = 2 breadth	1·00	1·01	1·02	1·00	1·11	1·12	·80	·45	·165
Rectangle length = ½ breadth	1·00	1·01	1·00	·973	·91	·77	·71	·71	·50

The maximum ratio, 1·15, for the former plane was attained when θ was 44°, while with the latter plane the pressure curve had a characteristic hump (ratio = ·74) when θ was 25°.

ART. 112.—RUDDER ACTION.

The normal pressure which is produced on an oblique plane by its motion through water is taken advantage of in the ordinary rudder. Since the flow of water to the rudder is guided by the form of the stern of the vessel, the distribution of pressure is entirely different to that occurring in the cases previously considered. In any case, however, the effect of the motion is to produce a distribution of normal pressure over the rudder which has a single resultant tending to turn it about its point of attachment to the stern post. This action being resisted by the rudder chains, the nett effect is that of a single force P acting on the vessel at B in the direction $A\,B$ (Fig. 177 a).

This is equivalent to an equal and parallel force applied at the centre of gravity G of the vessel, altogether with a couple of moment $P \times A\,G$ tending to rotate the vessel about G. It is this moment which tends to turn the vessel. The single force simply tends to produce a bodily drift of

---

[1] For curves showing the effect of varying the manner of presentation of glider surfaces for aeroplanes, see Lord Rayleigh's paper, *ante loq.*

the vessel in a direction parallel to *A B*.   This explains why a constant
rudder angle will not enable a vessel to describe a circle.

The point in the rudder body, at which it is pivoted, does not affect this
force or the couple produced, and advantage has been taken of this to
mount the rudder on pivots near its centre.   Being then approximately
in balance, the moment necessary to rotate it is considerably reduced, and
a much greater proportion of the steering force is directly transmitted
through the pivots (Fig. 177 *b*), instead of through the rudder chains.

Experiments by Stanton[1] show that the divergence of the stream

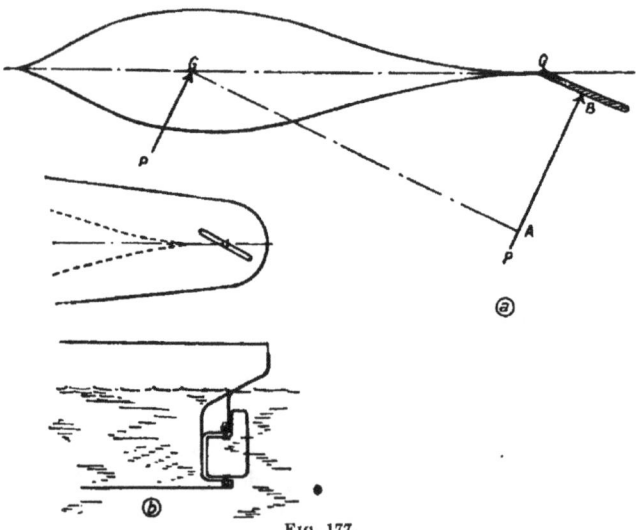

Fig. 177.

impinging on the rudder, produced by the hull of the boat, considerably
reduces the normal pressure on the rudder.   Where the lines of the stern
of the boat converged at an angle of 10°, the ratios of the pressures obtained,
to those obtained with the hull removed were as follows :

Angle of inclination of rudder .	10°	20°	30°	40°	50°
Ratio of pressures on rudder with and without hull in position .	·43	·57	·67	·61	·61

[1] "Trans. Inst. Naval Architects," 1909.

ART. 113.—RESISTANCE TO MOTION OF SUBMERGED BODIES.

If the plane already considered forms the end of a solid prism whose axis is parallel to the direction of motion and whose length is more than about three times the diameter of the plane, the directions of the stream lines are modified as shown in Fig. 178. Eddies are still formed at C, after which the motion becomes parallel to the axis of the prism, until at B a second formation of eddies takes place.

The total eddy formation at B and C is now less than at B alone with a plane surface, and this results in a higher pressure on the rear of the prism than on the plane and a consequent smaller resistance to motion. Even including skin friction, with a moderate ratio of length to diameter the resistance of the prism is less than that of the plane. Putting the resistance equal to $k \dfrac{W}{g} a v^2$, we have $k = \cdot 55$ with a prism having plane ends· and a length of about three times its diameter. If fitted with

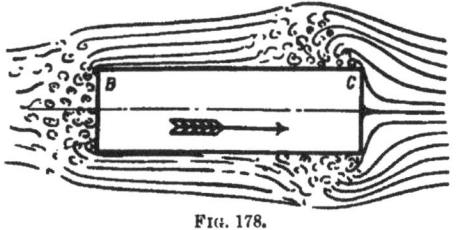

FIG. 178.

a tapering cutwater the production of eddies at C is obviated and the value of k becomes about $\cdot 40$. Fitted also with a tapering stern eddy formation is largely prevented at B, and k is reduced to about $\cdot 125$. The resistance is now largely due to skin friction and should be calculated on that assumption (p. 175).

Experiments by Dubuat, on a square prism, section $a \times a$, length l, gave resistances in the following ratios :

$l \div a$	$\cdot 03$	1	2	3	6
k	$\cdot 93$	$\cdot 73$	$\cdot 67$	$\cdot 66$	$\cdot 73$

ART. 114.—RESISTANCE OF SHIPS.

The resistance to the motion of a ship is due mainly to skin friction, but also to the formation of surface waves and of eddies (chiefly at the stern). Mr. Froude found that although the velocities of gliding vary largely at different points of the hull of a ship, no sensible error is involved if the frictional resistance be calculated on the assumption that the wetted surface is equivalent to that of a plane of equal area and length in the direction of motion, and moving at the same speed. The frictional resistance of the ship may thus be calculated from Froude's experimental results on the resistance of plane surfaces (Art. 61).

With an inviscid fluid, the particles displaced laterally by the prow would move over surrounding particles without any frictional losses and without any tendency to eddy formation, and would immediately return to exert a pressure on the stern equivalent to that on the bows. Thus the only resistance to uniform motion through such a fluid would be that due to wave formation, and, with a deeply immersed body, would be zero. A geometrical construction for the stream lines in a perfect fluid has been deduced by Professor Rankine, while Professor Hele-Shaw has verified the accuracy of this construction by experiments on a viscous fluid flowing past an obstacle, the motion taking place between parallel glass plates at a very small distance apart.[1] In this case the motion is governed almost entirely by viscosity, all eddy motion is prevented, and, as proved by Professor Sir G. G. Stokes,[1] the effect as regards stream-line formation is the same as in the case of a perfect fluid.

This may be shown as follows :[2]

At all points in the same horizontal plane in a perfect fluid we have, if u be the velocity of flow, $\dfrac{p}{W} + \dfrac{u^2}{2\,g} = \text{const.}$

$$\therefore \frac{d\,p}{W} + u\,\frac{d\,u}{g} = 0 \qquad (1)$$

If the stream lines are curved, and if $\delta\,p$ be the change in pressure, due to centrifugal action, across a stream tube of radial width $\delta\,r$, and of radius of curvature r, we have (p. 95)

$$\frac{d\,p}{d\,r} = \frac{W\,u^2}{g\,r}$$

and on substituting this value in (1),

$$\frac{u}{r} + \frac{d\,u}{d\,r} = 0 \qquad (2)$$

In the case of a viscous fluid flowing with stream line motion between two parallel plates, if s be the direction of flow at any instant, we have

(p. 67) $\dfrac{d\,p}{d\,y} = 0$; $\dfrac{d\,p}{d\,z} = 0$; $\dfrac{d\,p}{d\,s} = \mu\,\dfrac{d^2\,u}{d\,y^2}$; while if $\bar{u}$ be the mean velocity

[1] British Association Report, 1898 ; also " Transactions Inst. Naval Architects," 1898, vol. 85.

[2] Dunkerley, "Transactions Inst. Naval Architects," 1900, vol. 42, p. 227.

of flow this latter equation reduces to

$$\frac{d\,p}{d\,s} = -\,\frac{3\,\mu}{h^2}\,.\,\bar{u}\;.\;(\text{p. 68}).$$

The first two of these equations show that lines of equal pressure cut the stream lines at right angles. If then in Fig. 179, A and C, as also B and D, are points of equal pressure on two adjacent stream lines $A\,B$ and $C\,D$, over which the mean velocities are $u + \delta\,u$ and u, the corresponding values of $\delta\,s$ for equal values of $\delta\,p$ are $A\,B$ and $C\,D$, so that

$$\frac{A\,B}{C\,D} = \frac{u}{u + \delta u}.$$

But the centre of curvature of the stream lines is at the point of inter-section of $A\,C$ and $B\,D$ produced, so that $\dfrac{A\,B}{C\,D} = \dfrac{r + \delta\,r}{r}$

$$\therefore \frac{u}{u + \delta u} = \frac{r + \delta\,r}{r}$$

and, neglecting small quantities of the second order, this reduces to

$$\frac{u}{r} + \frac{d\,u}{d\,r} = 0$$

which is identical with equation (2) above.

Wave production is a very complicated phenomenon, and depends in magnitude and in form largely on the form and speed of the boat. In general it may be taken that the motion is accompanied by the formation of bow and stern waves, and by a fall of the water surface amidships (Fig. 180). The fact that outward stream-line flow must commence in front of the bows, and that the head necessary to produce this can only be obtained by a relative elevation of the surface level, accounts for the bow wave, while the reduction in velocity of the accompanying stream at the stern and the consequent increase in pressure accounts for the stern wave.[1] Also the increased velocity amidships is

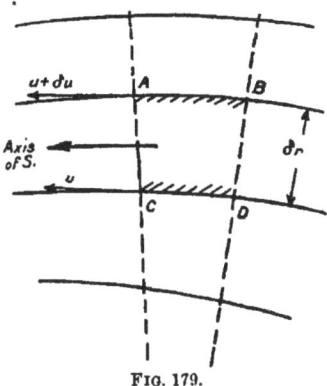

FIG. 179.

accompanied by a diminution in pressure, and accounts for the lowering of the surface level at this point. With a wholly submerged body the displacements produced on the surrounding mass of water are identical in

---

[1] For an article on the changes of level around a vessel, see the *Engineer*, vol. 63, p. 252.

form at all velocities, and are similar for similar bodies. Also, as pointed
out by Mr. Froude, and subsequently confirmed by experiment, this holds for
partially submerged bodies in spite of the effect of gravity on the vertical
displacements, if the similar bodies move with velocities proportional to
$\sqrt{D}$, where D is the ratio of their linear dimensions. Assuming then.
as appears to be approximately true, that the height of the waves is
proportional to v^2, and that their breadth is proportional to their height.
we have their mass proportional to v^4, and the energy of formation to
v^6. This energy is largely dependent on the form and relative length of
entrance and run of a ship, and every vessel would appear to have some
limiting speed beyond which any increase is accompanied by an altogether
disproportionate increase in wave-making resistance. Mr. Scott Russell
states that this limit is somewhat less than that corresponding to the
length of the wave which the ship tends to form, which length depends

Fig. 180.

on the length of entrance and run, and gives the following formula [1] for
the maximum velocity obtainable without abnormal resistance :—

$$V = 1.03 \sqrt{L_1 + L_2}.$$

Where V = velocity in knots; L_1 and L_2 are lengths of entrance and run
in feet.

He also states that L_1 should not be less than $.562\ V^2$
$$L_2 \quad\quad ,, \quad\quad\quad ,, \quad\quad\quad ,, \quad .375\ V^2.$$
Thus for a speed of 10 knots, $L_1 + L_2 > 93.7$ feet.
$$,, \quad ,, \quad ,, \quad 20 \quad ,, \quad L_1 + L_2 > 375 \quad ,,$$
$$,, \quad ,. \quad ,. \quad 30 \quad ,, \quad L_1 + L_2 > 843 \quad ,,$$

While agreeing fairly well with observed results, more recent investigations [2] point to the incompleteness of this rule, and indicate that the
length of the middle body of a ship also affects the wave resistance.

Eddy formation, apart from that due to skin friction, is largely confined

---

[1] " Transactions Inst. Naval Architects," vols. 1 and 2.

[2] " Transactions Inst. Naval Architects," 1881.

to the stern, and is due to flow in what is in effect a channel with diverging boundaries. Mr. Froude, in his experiments, found it necessary not only to use a cutwater, but also to taper off the stern of his planks in order to get a resistance — length curve, which should pass through the origin of co-ordinates, the effect being as indicated in Fig. 181.

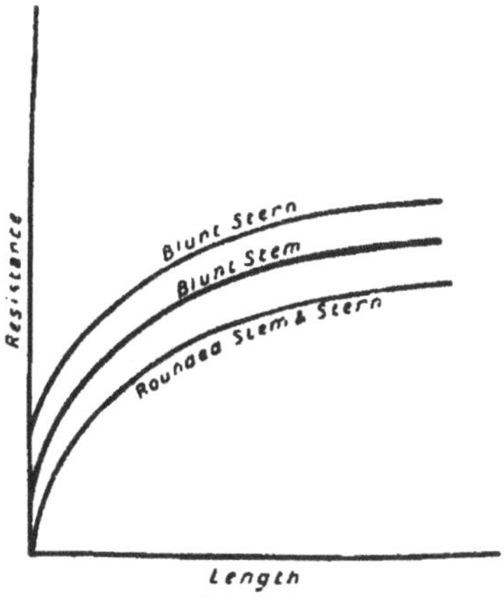

As a factor in reducing resistance in fact, a finely tapered stern or run is of much greater value in a ship-shaped body than is a fine stem. With a model as shown in Fig. 182, the directions of motion for least and greatest resistances are as indicated.

Experiments by Stanton [1] on the resistance of models having one end hemispherical and the other conical, give the following values of the relative resistance R.

Fig. 181.

Angle of convergence of conical end.	Method of application.	R.
12°	Hemispherical end first Conical ,, ,,	·51 ·69
20°	Hemispherical end first Conical ,, ,,	·59 ·76
40°	Hemispherical end first Conical ,, ,,	·99 1·00

Taking S to be the projected area of the stern, the reduction in

[1] " Transactions Inst. Naval Architects," 1909.

pressure, due to eddy production is approximately proportional to v^2, and the resistance thus produced proportional to $S\, v^2$.

In general, however, skin friction accounts for the greater part of the total resistance, varying from 80-90 per cent. of the total for speeds of 6 to 8 knots, to 50 or 60 per cent. at very high speeds—this with clean bottoms. Eddy production, in a well-formed ship, accounts for 8-10 per cent. of the total, and wave-making resistance for the remainder.

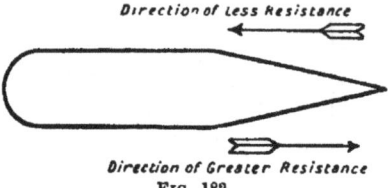

Direction of Less Resistance

Direction of Greater Resistance
FIG. 182.

The total resistance, at speeds up to about 10 knots, is approximately proportional to v^2, while Sir William White [1] states that as the speed increases further, the power of the velocity to which the resistance is proportional increases to a maximum value of about 8, owing to the increasing magnitude of the wave-making resistance, and then falls again to a value slightly below 2. Thus in the case of an 80-foot boat exampled by Sir William White

The resistance up to 10 knots was approximately $\propto v^2$
  ,, ,, at 13 ,, ,, ,, $\propto v^3$
  ,, ,, ,, 17-18 ,, ,, ,, $\propto v^{1.9}$

while with the Iris—300 feet long,

the resistance up to 13 knots was approximately $\propto v^2$.
  ,, ,, at 18 ,, ,, ,, $\propto v^{2.8}$.

The total resistance of a ship may be deduced from that of a scale model, and the skin friction alone from Froude's results, so that it becomes possible to deduce the eddy and wave-making resistances experimentally.

Before proceeding to describe Mr. Froude's methods of doing this, we may note that, if the relative scales of a ship and its model are as $D:1$, the relative wetted areas are as $D^2:1$, and if the suffix s refers to the ship and m to the model, the frictional resistances are given by

$$\left.\begin{aligned} R_m &= f_m\, S_m\, V_m{}^2 \\ R_s &= f_s\, S_s\, V_s{}^2 \end{aligned}\right\} \text{assuming resistance} \propto V^2,$$

and, neglecting for the time the difference between f_m and f_s, we have

$$\frac{R_s}{R_m} = \frac{S_s}{S_m}\left(\frac{V_s}{V_m}\right)^2 = D^2\left(\frac{V_s}{V_m}\right)^2 \tag{1}$$

[1] "Manual of Naval Architecture," by W. H. White, p. 466. London, John Murray.

Again, the ratio of the wave-making resistances is given by

$$\left(\frac{V_s}{V_m}\right)^6 \qquad (2)$$

while the ratio of eddy resistances

$$= \frac{S_s}{S_m}\left(\frac{V_s}{V_m}\right)^2 = D^2\left(\frac{V_s}{V_m}\right)^2. \qquad (3)$$

Putting $\left(\frac{V_s}{V_m}\right)^2 = D$, each of these resistances, and therefore the total becomes proportional to D^3, so that, to quote Mr. Froude, " If a ship be

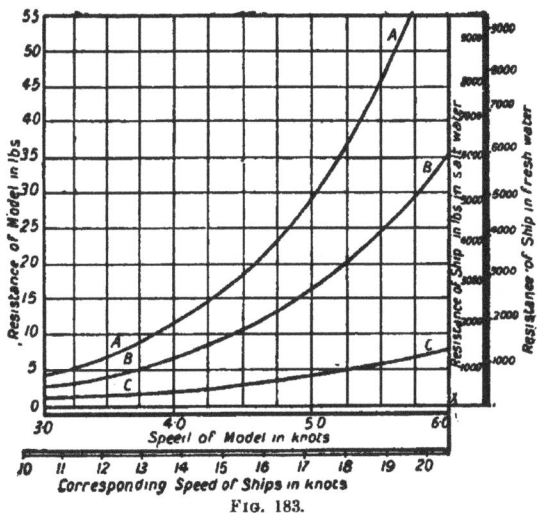

FIG. 183.

D times the dimensions of the model, and if at speeds V_1, V_2, V_3, the measured resistances of the model are R_1, R_2, R_3, then for speeds $V_1\sqrt{D}$, $V_2\sqrt{D}$, $V_3\sqrt{D}$, the resistances of the ship will be $D^3 R_1$, $D^3 R_2$, $D_3 R_3$. To the speeds of the model and ship thus related it is convenient to apply the term ' corresponding speeds.' "

In determining the resistance of any proposed ship, a scale model is made usually of paraffin wax, and is towed through still water, the resistance corresponding to any speed being noted. Thus in Fig. 183, $A A$ represents a resistance curve, the vertical ordinates from the line $O X$ representing to scale the total resistance of the model.

The area and length of the wetted surface being known, and the coefficient of friction determined, the frictional resistance can now be calculated for any speed, and the curve $B\,B$, of frictional resistances drawn.

If now the horizontal scale be increased in the ratio $\sqrt{D} : 1$, and the vertical scale in the ratio $D^3 : 1$, the curve $A\,A$ serves as the total resistance curve for the ship. Thus if the model is $\frac{1}{12}$ the size of the ship $D = 12$, the corresponding speeds of ship and model are in the ratio $\sqrt{12} : 1 = 3\cdot461 : 1$, and at this corresponding speed the resistances are in the ratio $12^3 : 1 = 1728 : 1$.

If fresh water is used in the experimental tank the vertical scale is to be increased again in the ratio of the densities of salt and fresh water, while a further final correction is necessary because of the different values of f for the ship and model. This is got over by calculating the actual frictional resistance of the ship for her true length at various speeds, and by setting the values thus obtained as ordinates downwards from the curve $B\,B$, to form the curve $C\,C$. The true resistance of the ship at any speed is then given by the corresponding vertical intercept between $A\,A$ and $C\,C$.

The resistance at any given speed V_s, is calculated from model observations at the corresponding speed V_m, as follows :—

Total resistance of model (observed) $= R_m$ lbs.

Frictional ,, ,, ,, (calculated) $= f_m\,S_m\,V_m{}^n$. lbs.

∴ Wave-making and eddy resistance of model $\Big\} = R_m - f_m\,S_m\,V_m{}^n . = E$ lbs.

∴ Wave-making and eddy resistance of ship in salt water $\Big\} = D^3\,E \times \dfrac{64}{62\cdot4}$. lbs.

$$\therefore \text{Total resistance of ship} = \frac{64}{62\cdot4}\,D^3\,E + f_s\,S_s\,V_s{}^n . \text{ lbs.}$$

A second method of carrying out tank experiments is due to Colonel English, and has certain advantages. Suppose the resistance of a ship in commission to be known at velocity V_1, that of another proposed ship to be determined at a velocity V_2. Make models of the two ships. Let suffix 1 refer to existing ship ; suffix 2 to that to be built, and let prefixes s and m refer to ship and model respectively.

Let $\quad \dfrac{_mV_1}{_sV_1} = \sqrt{\dfrac{_ml_1}{_sl_1}} \; ; \; \dfrac{_mV_2}{_sV_2} = \sqrt{\dfrac{_ml_2}{_sl_2}} \; ;$ and let $_mV_1 = {_mV_2}$

i.e., make $_ml_1$ and $_ml_2$ satisfy the conditions that

$$_sV_1 \sqrt{\frac{_ml_1}{_sl_1}} = {_sV_2}\sqrt{\frac{_ml_2}{_sl_2}} \text{ or } \frac{_ml_1}{_ml_2} = \left(\frac{_sV_2}{_sV_1}\right)^2 \frac{_sl_1}{_sl_2}.$$

If now the models be towed simultaneously, each attached to one of the ends of a horizontal lever with an adjustable fulcrum, the position of this fulcrum may be readily adjusted until the lever floats in its mid position, and the relative resistances of the two models are then in the ratio of the lengths of the arms of the lever. Let resistance of model (2) be n times that of model (1).

Let E represent wave-making and eddy resistances; E = skin friction. Thus resistance of model (2) = $_mE_2 + {}_mF_2 = n\{_mE_1 + {}_mF_1\}$

But
$$_mE_2 = {}_sE_2\left(\frac{_ml_2}{_sl_2}\right)^3$$

$$\therefore \quad {}_sE_2\left(\frac{_ml_2}{_sl_2}\right)^3 = n\left\{ {}_sE_1\left(\frac{_ml_1}{_sl_1}\right)^3 + {}_mF_1 \right\} - {}_mF_2$$

$\therefore$ Total resistance of new ship is given by

$$_sR_2 = {}_sE_2 + {}_sF_2 = {}_sF_2 + \left(\frac{_sl_2}{_ml_2}\right)^3\left[n\left\{ {}_sE_1\left(\frac{_ml_1}{_sl_1}\right)^3 + {}_mF_1 \right\} - {}_mF_2 \right]$$

Of the terms in this expression $_sF_2$, $_mF_1$, and $_mF_2$ can be readily calculated, while $_sE_1$ being equal to $_sR_1 - {}_sF_1$, can also be obtained, since the total resistance $_sR_1$ of ship (1) is known, while its frictional resistance $_sF_1$ can be readily calculated.

ART. 115.—THE PROPULSION OF SHIPS.

Of the many systems of mechanical propulsion which have from time to time been devised, only three have attained any measure of success. These respectively use the paddle wheel, the screw propeller, and the hydraulic jet as their propelling agents.

The principle underlying all these systems is the same, the propeller being devised so as to create a sternwards current of water, and the corresponding reaction on the propeller providing the propelling force on the ship. Thus, whatever system be adopted, if a mass of water of weight C lbs. per second have its sternward velocity increased by v feet per second by the action of the propeller, the change of momentum per second in this direction $= \dfrac{Cv}{g}$ foot-pound units, and the thrust on the propeller is of the same magnitude, $\dfrac{Cv}{g}$ lbs., and in the opposite direction.

Since the thrust varies as the product of C and v, any one of these factors may be changed without affecting the thrust if the other factor suffer a corresponding change, so that a given thrust may be obtained by the comparatively slow movement of a large mass of water, or by the quick movement of a smaller mass. Other things being equal, then, an increase in the area of the moving stream and a diminution in its velocity will tend to efficiency by reducing shock and kinetic losses.

While this conclusion is verified in practice, in the case of the paddle wheel and of the hydraulic jet (see Art. 116) practical considerations soon limit the maximum possible area (sooner in the case of the jet than of the paddle wheel). In the case of the screw propeller, moreover, frictional losses rapidly increase with the area of the screw, while an attempt to increase the area by increasing the radius, increases the centrifugal action of the water, and by reducing the pressure near the centre of the propeller, tends to reduce the effective thrust.

Paddle Wheels.—These give excellent results in smooth water, and where the draught and therefore the depth of immersion of the paddles is not likely to vary largely. They are well adapted for river navigation, particularly for shallow draught vessels, but are quite unfitted for use in any ocean-going boat which may be exposed to rough weather, and whose draught may differ by some feet on the outward-bound and homeward-bound journeys.

If R = mean foot radius,

     „ N = number of revolutions per second,

then $2 \pi R N = V_P$ = velocity of paddles relative to the ship in feet per second.

If V_s be the absolute velocity of the ship, $(V_P - V_s)$ is termed the slip, or more correctly the apparent slip, and $100 \dfrac{V_P - V_s}{V_P}$ is termed the percentage slip. This in general varies from 20 to 30 per cent. The chief losses are due to shock at entrance and exit from the water and are reduced as far as possible by the use of feathering floats arranged so as to enter the water without shock. Where, as is usual, the paddle wheels are placed amidships, the stream-line motion over the run of the ship is greatly affected, at least over those layers between the surface and the bottom of the wheel, and since the relative velocity of flow over this portion of the ship is largely increased, the effect is to augment the resistance as compared with the towing resistance with paddles removed.

The Screw Propeller is by far the most important of the three types. Its advantages consist in its possibilities of adoption to high speed prime movers; its depth of immersion, which makes its efficiency largely independent of a varying draught, and its reduced liability to accident, in virtue of its sheltered position.

If P = mean pitch of propeller blades, i.e., the distance the boat would travel per revolution if the screw were supposed to rotate in a fixed solid nut, and if V_P is the corresponding axial velocity so that $V_P = N\ P$, then $V_P - V_s$ is usually termed the slip, or more correctly the apparent slip of the screw, and, if this worked in still water, would give the stern-ward velocity in the propeller race relative to the surrounding water. The real slip is the change actually produced by the screw on the velocity of the water in the propeller race, and since the propeller works in an accompanying current of water which has an initial absolute velocity V_w in the direction of the ship, this is given by $(V_P - V_s + V_w)$.

Evidently the apparent is always less than the true slip, and may, if V_w is sufficiently great, become negative. In general, however, it is positive and, expressed as a percentage of V_P, has a value of about 20 per cent.

The real slip is always positive if the screw is to have any propelling effect, as will be evident if it be remembered that it measures the change in the sternward momentum of the water.

Owing to the centrifugal action of the water, the pressure over the front face of the propeller is negative, so that part of the total change of velocity occurs before the water actually reaches the propeller. There is thus a tendency to draw water from the stern of the vessel and to reduce the forward pressure over this portion of its surface, with the result that the resistance, as compared with the towing resistance, is considerably augmented.

The velocity with which water can be supplied to the screws is entirely dependent on the atmospheric pressure augmented by the head of water over the screw. Should this be insufficient to give the necessary velocity of inflow the column of water in front of the screw is broken and "cavitation" is caused, just as in a pump which is being driven at too high a speed. This may be prevented either by increasing the depth of immersion or by reducing the speed of the propeller.

The maximum efficiency of the propeller would appear to be about 75 per cent., the magnitude of the various losses then probably approximating to the following values:—

Friction losses . . . . . . 9 per cent.
Eddy losses . . . . 10 „
Losses by kinetic energy rejected in wake . 6 „

Assuming an efficiency for the engine and shafting of 80 per cent. this gives a combined efficiency of 60 per cent.

In spite of much experimental work and theoretical investigation, very little is actually known as to the best design of screw for any given conditions. Mr. Froude, after an extended series of experiments, concluded

D D 2

that the mean effective angle of the screw blade should be 45°, this making the pitch equal to about twice the extreme diameter, and that the true slip should be about $12\frac{1}{2}$ per cent. The blade area, projected on a plane perpendicular to the axis of the screw should then be equal to $\dfrac{8 \cdot 9\ R}{V_s^{\frac{3}{2}}}$ square feet, where R = resistance of ship in pounds at the maximum velocity V_s.[1]

Power Necessary for Propulsion.

If R = resistance of ship in lbs., and V_s its velocity in feet per second we have

Work done in propelling vessel = $R\,V_s$ foot-pounds per second.

∴ Horse-power to overcome resistance = $\dfrac{R\,V_s}{550}$.

The I.H.P. of the ship's engines will be considerably more than this, because of mechanical friction losses in the engine and propeller shaft and, to a still greater extent, because of the inefficiency of the propeller itself. In general it may be taken that from 45 per cent. to 60 per cent. of the energy developed in the engine cylinders is utilised in doing useful work.

Since R is approximately proportional to V_s^2, the horse-power will vary as V_s^3, except at very high speeds, where the wave-making resistance becomes abnormal.

ART. 116.—JET PROPULSION.

When a jet of water escapes from an orifice in the side of a vessel, the force necessary to produce this outflow is equal in magnitude to the flux of momentum per second across the *vena contracta* of the jet, and acts in the direction of flow of the jet. This force necessitates an otherwise unbalanced pressure or reaction on the side of the vessel opposite to the orifice (p. 110), which reaction tends to move the vessel in the opposite direction to that of the jet.

Advantage has been taken of this in a system which has been applied (though with only moderate success) to the propulsion of large vessels. Here a supply of water is drawn into the boat, usually through a vertical pipe opening amidships, by a centrifugal pump driven by the main

---

[1] For a further investigation into the action of the propeller the reader is referred to a paper on the action of propellers by Professor Rankine, " Transactions Inst. Naval Architects," vol. 6; also papers by Mr. Froude in vols. 6, 8, and 19 of the same Transactions, and to White's " Naval Architecture," p. 543. Also to papers in the " Proc. Inst. C.E.," vol. 102, p. 74; vol. 122, p. 51; vol. 165, p. 293; and in the " Transactions Inst. Naval Architects," 1897, p. 241.

engines, and is then discharged directly astern. The escaping stream, in virtue of its reaction on the vessel, does work in propulsion, while the theoretical efficiency of the system may be calculated as follows :—

Let A = sectional area of discharge orifices in square feet.

u = velocity of vessel in feet per second.

v = velocity of efflux of stream relative to boat.

Then $v - u$ = absolute velocity of efflux of stream, i.e., its velocity relative to the surrounding water.

$$\left.\begin{array}{l}\text{The initial velocity of the}\\\text{water before being drawn}\\\text{into the vessel}\end{array}\right\} = 0$$

$$\left.\begin{array}{l}\text{Its final velocity in the direc-}\\\text{tion of motion of the vessel}\end{array}\right\} = u - v \text{ ft. per sec.}$$

$$\left.\begin{array}{l}\text{The weight of water dis-}\\\text{charged per second}\end{array}\right\} = W A v \text{ lbs.}$$

$$\left.\begin{array}{l}\therefore \text{ The change of momen-}\\\text{tum of the water in the}\\\text{opposite direction to that of}\\\text{motion of the vessel}\end{array}\right\} = \frac{W A v}{g} (v - u) \text{ per sec.}$$

$$\therefore \text{ Propelling force on boat} = \frac{W A v}{g} (v - u) \text{ lbs.} \tag{1}$$

$$\left.\begin{array}{l}\text{Work done in propulsion}\\\text{per second}\end{array}\right\} = \frac{W A v \, u}{g} (v - u) \text{ ft. lbs.} \tag{2}$$

$$\left.\begin{array}{l}\text{Kinetic energy rejected per}\\\text{second in the discharge}\end{array}\right\} = \frac{W A v}{2 g} (v - u)^2 \text{ ft. lbs.} \tag{3}$$

$$\left.\begin{array}{l}\therefore \text{ Total energy given to}\\\text{water per second neglecting}\\\text{eddy and frictional losses}\end{array}\right\} = \frac{W A v}{2 g} \left\{ (v - u)^2 + 2 u (v - u) \right\} \text{ ft. lbs.}$$

$$= \frac{W A v}{2 g} (v^2 - u^2) \text{ ft. lbs.} \tag{4}$$

$$\left.\begin{array}{l}\therefore \text{ Theoretical efficiency of}\\\text{jet}\end{array}\right\} = \frac{\text{useful work done by jet}}{\text{energy given to jet}} = \frac{2 u (v - u)}{v^2 - u^2}$$

$$= \frac{2 u}{v + u}. \tag{5}$$

This has its maximum value, unity, when $v = u$.

An examination of equation (1) will, however, show that under these circumstances the propelling force is zero, and that with a large propelling force it is impossible to work under conditions which conduce to high efficiency.

Water may be taken into the pumps either through one or more vertical or horizontal pipes at right angles to the axis of the vessel, through pipes facing forwards in the direction of the axis, or through vertical or horizontal pipes fitted with a scoop facing in the direction of motion of the vessel.   In the latter case the effect is the same as with the inlet pipes facing forwards except that the scoop introduces a slight additional resistance to motion.   If h be the depth of the inlet, the head producing flow along the inlet pipe is given by $h + \dfrac{u^2}{g}$ feet in the two latter cases, and by h feet if the inlet opens flush with the sides or bottom of the boat, and since in every case the delivery pressure is that corresponding to the depth of immersion of the outlet, less energy is required of the pump per lb. of water to discharge at a given velocity with the inlet facing forwards than with a plain side or bottom inlet.   In any case the total change of momentum per second is the same provided the discharge velocities are the same.

Variation of Efficiency with Size of Orifices.

Assuming the energy of propulsion to be given by $k \, u^2$ ft. lbs. per second (p. 404), where k is constant for a given vessel,

$$k \, u^2 = \frac{A \, W}{g} \, u \, v \, (v - u)$$

$$\therefore \quad k \, u^2 + u \, . \, \frac{A \, W}{g} v - \frac{A \, W}{g} v^2 = 0$$

or

$$u = -\frac{A \, W}{2 \, g \, k} v \left\{ 1 - \sqrt{1 + \frac{4 \, g \, k}{A \, W}} \right\}.$$

Substituting this value of u in equation (5), we have

$$\text{Efficiency} = \frac{2 \, u}{u + v} = \frac{2 \left\{ 1 - \sqrt{1 + \dfrac{4 \, g \, k}{A \, W}} \right\}}{1 - \sqrt{1 + \dfrac{4 \, g \, k}{A \, W}} - \dfrac{2 \, g \, k}{A \, W}}$$

Multiplying numerator and denominator by $1 + \sqrt{1 + \dfrac{4 \, g \, k}{A \, W}}$ this finally gives

$$\text{Efficiency} = \frac{4}{3 + \sqrt{1 + \dfrac{4 \, g \, k}{A \, W}}},$$

so that the efficiency of propulsion increases as the ratio $\dfrac{A}{k}$ increases, i.e., in the case of any given boat, as the area of the orifices increases. But as the quantity discharged per minute, and also the size of pump necessary to give this discharge increase with A, the limit of efficiency in this direction is soon reached.

EXAMPLE.

If $k = 2\cdot4$ and if $A = 2$ square feet, we have efficiency of jet

$$= \frac{4}{3 + \sqrt{1 + \frac{4\cdot8}{2}}} = \frac{4}{4\cdot85} = 82\cdot5 \text{ per cent.}$$

Suppose the boat to travel at 15 miles per hour, $u = 22$ feet per second.

$$\text{Then efficiency} = \frac{2\,u}{u + v} = \cdot825$$

$$\therefore \quad 1\cdot175\,u = \cdot825\,v$$

$$\therefore \quad v = \frac{1\cdot175 \times 22}{\cdot825} = 31\cdot33 \text{ feet per second.}$$

$$Q = 31\cdot33 \times 2 = 62\cdot66 \text{ cubic feet per second.}$$

Assuming the combined efficiency of engine, pump, and jet to be $\cdot80 \times \cdot60 \times \cdot825 = \cdot396$, we have :—

$$\text{I.H.P. of engine} = \frac{k\,u^3}{550} \times \frac{1}{\cdot396}$$

$$= \frac{2\cdot4 \times 22^3}{550 \times \cdot396} = 117 \text{ I.H.P.}$$

The most noteworthy experiments on hydraulic propulsion have been carried out by the British Government. In 1866 the Admiralty built two almost similar gunboats, the *Waterwitch* and the *Viper*, the former being fitted with jet propulsion and the latter with a screw propeller. Their displacements were, *Waterwitch* 1,161 tons, *Viper* 1,180 tons. The *Waterwitch* took water in through a vertical opening amidships, passed it through a 14-foot centrifugal pump, and discharged astern through two 24-inch nozzles. When discharging 5·2 tons of water per second with a relative velocity of 29 feet per second, the engines indicated 760 I.H.P., and gave a speed of 9·3 knots (15·71 feet per second) with a jet efficiency of 70 per cent. The *Viper*, with 696 I.H.P., gave 9·58 knots. This comparison is, however, rather unfair to the *Viper*, as its speed suffered from the provision of a double bilge keel, and from its slightly fuller run.

In 1878, the Swedish Government built two torpedo boats, 58 feet long —10' 9" beam—and with 20 and 21 tons displacement, the heavier machinery of the hydraulic boat necessitating the larger displacement. The latter boat took in water vertically, and with 78 I.H.P. gave a speed of 8·12 knots. The screw boat with 90 I.H.P. gave 10 knots.

In 1882, the Admiralty had one of a batch of torpedo boats fitted with hydraulic propulsion.

The details of the boats were as follows :—

	Length.	Beam.	Draught.	Displacement.	I.H.P.	Speed.
Screw	63·0 ft.	7' 6"	3' 8½"	12·89 tons	170	17·3 knots
Hydraulic	66·4 ft.	7' 6"	2' 6"	14·4 tons	167	12·6 knots

The hydraulic boat was fitted with a centrifugal pump 2' 6" diameter, running at 428 revolutions per minute, and discharged astern through two 9-inch outlets. The pump delivered approximately one ton of water per second at a velocity of 37·25 feet per second (as against 21·28 feet per second of the boat), and was fitted with a vertical inlet pipe, provided with a scoop facing forward.

In each case the efficiency of the pump was approximately 48 per cent. The last-mentioned torpedo boats gave the highest jet efficiency, viz., 72·8 per cent. The combined efficiency of jet and pump was then 34·9 per cent. as compared with an average efficiency of about 65 per cent. in the case of a screw propeller. Taking an efficiency of 80 per cent. for the engine and shafting in each case, though this would be slightly greater in the case of the pump, we have the combined efficiency of propelling mechanism

Hydraulic.	Screw.
27·9 %	52·0 %

The low efficiency of the centrifugal pump has, in the past, prevented the adoption of the system of jet propulsion on any large scale. As a propeller, the jet itself is more efficient than the screw, and there would appear to be no valid reason why, with the more efficient modern types of pump, the combination should not be made as efficient as the screw propeller.

It should be noted that the system works equally well with the discharge either above or below water level, except that in the former case energy is wasted in lifting the water to the level of the discharge orifice. The advantages of the system are

(1) No racing of propellers in rough weather ;
(2) No under water obstacles to become entangled in wreckage ;
(3) Ease of control from some central station on the bridge ;
(4) Great facilities for manœuvring.

ART. 117.—HYDRAULIC MINING.

The fact that a high velocity jet of water carries an immense amount of destructive energy, was first taken advantage of to any large extent on the Pacific Coast of North America. Here, owing to the configuration of the country, the only available water supply is to be found in comparatively small streams, at considerable elevations. The construction of a small dam and a flume or ditch to bring the supply to the nearest suitable point on the mountain side, and the further construction of a pipe line leading the supply under pressure down the mountain side, renders available a comparatively small quantity of water under great pressure. In the process known as Hydraulicing, chiefly applied to gold mining, this supply is led into a pressure box securely bolted to the ground at a distance of from 100 to 200 feet from the face of the cliff to be mined. From the pressure box one or two jets, of diameters ranging from 4 inches to 11 inches are led by means of nozzles mounted on ball-and-socket joints, and are played on to the face of the cliff, the *débris* being carried away by sluices on which the process of washing and amalgamating is completed.

EXAMPLES.

(1) A horizontal jet issuing from an orifice 1 inch in diameter discharges 2 gallons per second and impinges normally on a large fixed plane. Determine the force exerted on the plane and also, neglecting losses, the maximum pressure intensity likely to be attained.

Answer. $\begin{cases} 36\cdot5 \text{ lbs.} \\ 23\cdot25 \text{ lbs. per square inch.} \end{cases}$

(2) If the above plate has edges curved so as to deflect the stream through a total angle of 150°, determine the pressure on the plate.

Answer. 68 lbs.

(3) A jet from a rectangular orifice 6″ wide × 1″ deep impinges on a curved vane 6″ wide, with a velocity of 60 feet per second. On incidence the jet makes an angle of 30° with the plane of the vane, and the portions into which it is divided are deflected through total angles of 120° (the smaller portion) and 90° (the larger portion). Determine the pressure on the plane in the direction of the jet.

Answer. 300 lbs.

(4) Assuming a series of vanes similar to that in question (3) to move

in the direction of the jet with a velocity of 80 feet per second, determine the efficiency of the arrangement.

(5) Two free jets of sectional area 2 square inches and 1 square inch, and of velocities 20 f.s. and 30 f.s., are inclined to each other at an angle of 60°, and combine to form a single stream. Determine the direction and velocity of this stream and the loss of energy at impact.

Answer. $\begin{cases} \text{Resultant stream makes an angle of 31° 58' with} \\ \quad \text{direction of first stream.} \\ \text{Velocity} = 21\cdot06 \text{ feet per second.} \\ \text{Loss of head} = 80\cdot3 \text{ feet lbs. per second.} \end{cases}$

(6) A jet propelled vessel has a wetted surface area of 800 square feet, and a coefficient of resistance of ·004. If the area of the nozzle openings is 3·0 square feet, determine the maximum theoretical efficiency of the jet considered as a propeller. Also, assuming the pump efficiency to be 50 per cent. and the mechanical efficiency of the engines to be 85 per cent., determine the efficiency of propulsion.

Answer. $\begin{cases} \text{Efficiency} \quad = \cdot 836. \\ \text{Total efficiency} = \cdot 355. \end{cases}$

(7) If the boat of the preceding example is travelling at 12 miles per hour, determine the necessary jet velocity and the discharge per second, for maximum efficiency.

Answer. $\begin{cases} \text{Velocity} \quad = 24\cdot56 \text{ feet per second.} \\ \text{Discharge} = 2\cdot05 \text{ tons per second.} \end{cases}$

(8) Water flows at 20 feet per second through a 6″ pipe forming a right-angled bend. Find the magnitude of the resultant force tending to move the pipe.

Answer. 215 lbs.

(9) A jet delivering 3 cubic feet of water per second at 100 feet per second impinges tangentially on one of a series of vanes moving at 50 feet per second in a direction inclined at 20° to that of the jet. If the vanes deflect the jet backwards so that its final direction of motion is the same as that of the vane, and if the final relative velocity of jet and vane is ·8 times the initial relative velocity, determine the pressure on the vane in its direction of motion.

Answer. 515 lbs.

(10) In the *Greyhound*, length 160 feet; breadth 33½ feet; draught 13¾ feet; displacement, 1,160 tons; the wetted area is 7,540 square feet. The

following corresponding values of resistance and speed were experimentally obtained :—

Speed (knots).	4	6	8	10	12
Resistance (tons)	·6	1·4.	2·5	4·7	9·0

Taking $f = ·00935$ (the unit of velocity being 1 knot), and assuming eddy making resistance to form 8 per cent. of the whole, determine the magnitude of the frictional, eddy, and wave-making resistances, and express these as a percentage of the whole.

Answer.

	4 knots.		8 knots.		12 knots.	
	Lbs.	%	Lbs.	%	Lbs.	%
Frictional resistances . .	891	66·3	3169	56·6	6655	33·0
Eddy resistances . . .	107	8·0	448	8·0	1618	8·0
Wave-making resistances .	346	25·7	1983	35·4	11892	59·0

(11) In the previous example, determine the energy actually absorbed in propulsion, and assuming that 45 per cent. of the I.H.P. of the engine is utilised, determine the I.H.P. at speeds of 4, 8, and 12 knots.

Answer.

	4 knots.	8 knots.	12 knots.
Useful horse power .	16·5	198	744
I.H.P.	86·7	807	1651

(12) In the _Merkara_, length 360 feet; breadth 37·2 feet; draught 16·25;

displacement 3,980 tons, the wetted area is 18,660 feet. The following are experimental results:—

Speed (knots). .	4	6	8	10	12	13
Resistance (tons) .	1·0	2·3	3·9	6·0	9·0	11·5

Taking $f = $ ·00917, determine the percentage resistance due to frictions and to eddy and wave-making resistances, at 4, 8, and 12 knots. Also, assuming 42 per cent. of energy developed in the engines to be utilised in propulsion,. determine the I.H.P. at these speeds.

Answer.

	4 knots.	8 knots.	12 knots.
Frictional resistance. .	96·6 %	87·8 %	80·1 %
Eddy and wave-making .	3·4 %	12·2 %	19·9 %
I.H.P. of engines . .	65·6	511	1770

(13) In the *Greyhound* the length of entrance and of run are each 75 feet; in the *Merkara* they are each 144 feet. Determine the " limiting " speed in each case.

Answer. $\begin{cases} \textit{Greyhound, } 1·08 \sqrt{150} = 12·63 \text{ knots.} \\ \textit{Merkara, } \quad 1·08 \sqrt{288} = 17·5 \text{ knots.} \end{cases}$

Note how these values bear out the abnormal increase in wave-making resistance at the limiting speed as determined in the preceding examples. In the *Merkara* the wave-making resistance at 19 knots was found to be over 60 per cent. of the total.

(14) Experiments on a 20-feet model are carried out to determine the probable horse-power required in a ship 600 feet long when doing 24 knots. Determine the corresponding speed of the model, and, assuming the value of f for the ship to be ·00910 and that for the model to be ·00935.

determine the probable horse-power of the engines if the resistance of the model at the corresponding speed is 9·54 lbs. Assume 60 per cent. of the I.H.P. to do useful work at the propeller, and assume wetted area of ship = 48,000 square feet; n for ship = 1·83 ; for model 1·85.

Answer. $\begin{cases} \text{Corresponding speed} = 4\text{·}38 \text{ knots.} \\ \text{I.H.P.} = 25{,}600. \end{cases}$

CHAPTER XII

Art. 118.—Waves.

WAVES may be divided into three main classes according as they are
(a) Waves of Transmission.
(b) Waves of Oscillation.
(c) Ripples.

In a **Wave of Transmission**, not only does the wave form advance, but each particle of water over which the wave passes is translated forward during its passage and is finally left at some distance ahead of its original

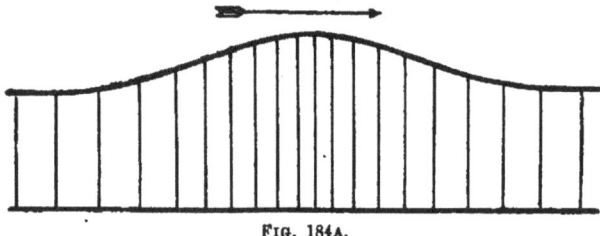

FIG. 184A.

position. Perfect waves of this type are solitary and the wave itself is either wholly raised above or wholly depressed below the general surface of the fluid. In the former case it is termed a positive; in the latter case a negative, wave. Such positive waves are formed by the sudden opening of a sluice gate admitting a body of water into a long, level canal, or may be formed in a long trough by the sudden immersion at one end. of a solid body of volume equal to that of the required wave. The negative wave of transmission is very unstable, and always gives rise to a train of waves of oscillation.

Method of Transmission.—If the water when at rest be supposed subdivided by a series of equidistant vertical planes, perpendicular to the direction of the wave's transmission, the columns which they enclose suffer the distortion shown in Fig. 184A, during the passage of the wave. As the front of the wave approaches one of these columns the pressure on the plane forming its rear face is increased, and under this pressure the plane moves forwards, heaping up the water ahead of it. When the column has been raised to its greatest height, at the crest of the wave, it presses equally on both front and rear planes, accelerating the velocity of the column ahead, retarding that behind, and so increasing its own width until it finally comes to rest at its original level. Each successive column is in turn displaced forward in the direction of transmission, and the result is that a volume of water equal to that of the wave is displaced in this direction. The motion of each particle is very approximately a semi-ellipse, with its major axis horizontal, horizontal displacements being uniform, and vertical displacements proportional to the distance above the bottom of the channel.

Velocity of Propagation.—Imagine the wave propagated in a stream

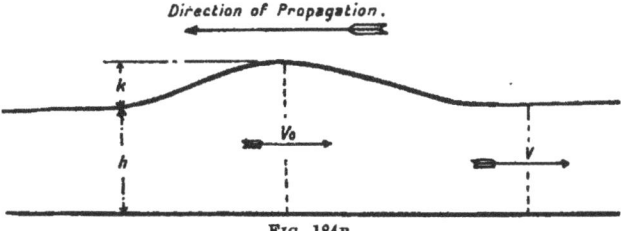

Direction of Propagation.

FIG. 184B.

running in the opposite direction with such uniform velocity V as to keep the wave form stationary relative to the banks.

Then if h be the original depth of water; k the height of wave; V_o the velocity at the crest of the wave (Fig. 184B)

we have
$$V_o = V \frac{h}{h+k}$$

Applying Bernoulli's equation to the surface filaments where the pressure is constant

$$h + k + \frac{V_o^2}{2g} = h + \frac{V^2}{2g}$$

$$\therefore \frac{V^2}{2g}\left\{1 - \left(\frac{h}{h+k}\right)^2\right\} = k$$

$$V^2 = 2g\frac{(h+k)^2}{2h+k} = 2g \cdot \frac{h+k}{1 + \frac{h}{h+k}}$$

Usually k is small compared with h, in which case
$$V = \sqrt{g\,(h + k)} \text{ (approx.)}$$
and if k is comparatively very small, this approximates to
$$V = \sqrt{g\,h}$$
Since the distribution of pressure or motion is not altered by the

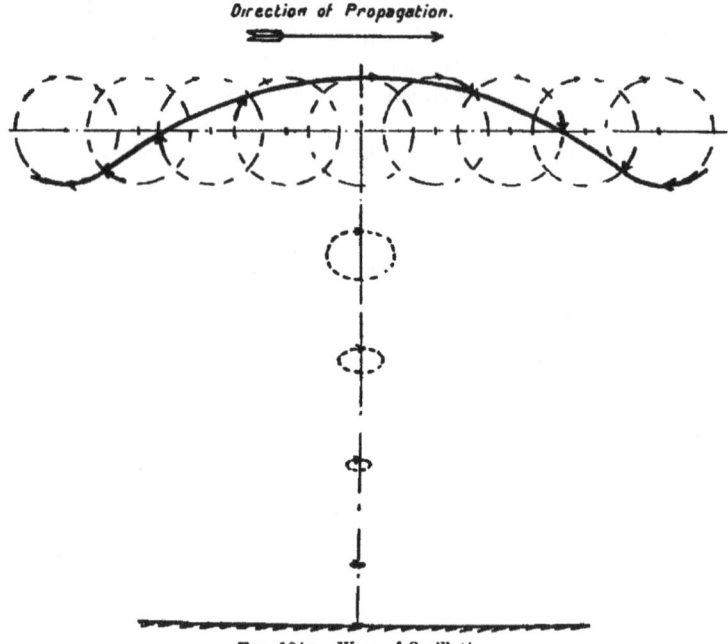

FIG. 184c.—Wave of Oscillation.

motion of the stream, V is the same as the velocity of propagation of the wave form in still water.

The maximum velocity of horizontal translation of the particles forming the wave is given by $V - V_0$, *i.e.*, by $V \dfrac{k}{h + k}$.

Experiment shows that as k approaches h in value, the wave breaks at the crest.

ART. 118A.—WAVES OF OSCILLATION.

In waves of oscillation, as exemplified in the ordinary deep sea wave, the particles involved in the motion are not transported in the direction of propagation, but oscillate with uniform angular velocity about a mean position, in a vertical plane parallel to that direction. In deep water the orbit of a particle near the surface is sensibly circular, and the wave form is trochoidal. In shallower water the orbit becomes approximately elliptical with the major axis horizontal. In either case the particles in the surface have the largest orbits, the extent of the motion diminishing as the depth below the surface increases. The vertical motion diminishes more rapidly than the horizontal motion, so that the deeper a particle the flatter is its orbit. In deep water the maximum diameter of the orbit diminishes in geometrical progression as the depth below the surface increases in arithmetical progression. The following table[1] gives the maximum horizontal and vertical displacements of the particles at different depths for waves whose lengths are respectively equal to, and ten times as great as the depth of the water they are traversing, the greatest horizontal displacement of the particles at the bottom being represented by unity.

Depth below surface.	Length of wave = depth of water.		Length of wave = 10 times depth.	
	Horizontal displacement.	Vertical displacement.	Horizontal displacement.	Vertical displacement.
At surface . .	267·7	267·7	1·204	·670
·10 depth . .	142·8	142·8	1·164	·596
·20 ,, . .	76·2	76·2	1·129	·524
·30 ,, . .	40·6	40·6	1·098	·454
·40 ,, . .	21·7	21·2	1·072	·886
·60 ,, . .	6·2	6·1	1·031	·254
·80 ,, . .	1·9	1·6	1·008	·126
At bottom . .	1·0	0·0	1·000	·000

The motion of the particles in a wave of oscillation in fairly deep water is shown in Fig. 184c. Those particles in the crest of the wave move forward in the direction of propagation; those in the trough move backwards; while those at the mean level have simply vertical motion.

Velocity, Length, and Height of Waves of Oscillation in Deep Water.— Taking the surface particles to describe circular orbits of radius r with

Airy, "Tides and Waves," Table IV.

angular velocity ω, the height of the wave is $2\,r$. Let l be its length. measured from crest to crest. Imagine the wave form brought to rest by imposing on it a velocity equal and opposite at every point to that of its normal motion, *i.e.*, imagine the orbital circle concentric with a circle of radius R, where $2\,\pi\,R = l$, rolling, as shown in Fig. 184D, on a horizontal plane with angular velocity ω, and with a linear velocity V equal to that of propagation. Then $V = \omega\,R = \dfrac{\omega\,l}{2\,\pi}$.

Under these conditions the velocity of a particle at Q is compounded of a velocity ω. $O\,K$ perpendicular to $O\,K$, and ω. $O\,Q$ perpendicular to $O\,Q$,

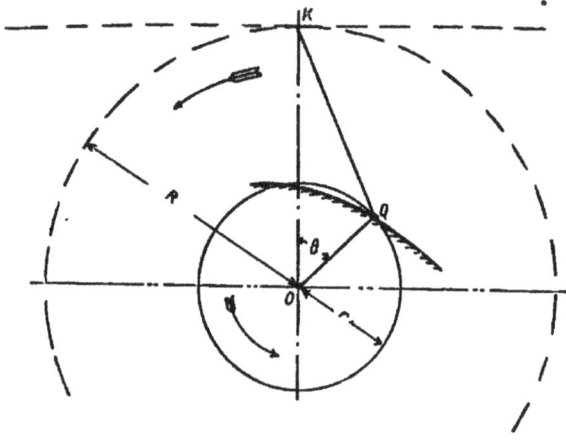

FIG. 184D.

and so equals ω. $K\,Q$ perpendicular to $K\,Q$, so that $K\,Q$ is normal to the surface at Q. If now v_c be the velocity of a particle in the crest, and v the velocity at any other point Q in the free surface, and therefore at the same pressure,

$$\therefore \quad \frac{v^2}{2\,g} + r\cos\theta = \frac{v_c^{\,2}}{2\,g} + r$$

$$\therefore \quad \frac{\omega^2}{2\,g}\,\{\,\overline{Q\,K}^2 - (R - r)^2\,\} = r\,(1 - \cos\theta).$$

But $$\overline{Q\,K}^2 = (R - r\cos\theta)^2 + (r\sin\theta)^2$$
$$= R^2 - 2\,R\,r\cos\theta + r^2$$

ınd on substituting this value and simplifying we have—

$$\left\{ \frac{\omega^2 R}{g} - 1 \right\} r (1 - \cos \theta) = 0 \qquad (1)$$

$$\therefore \ \omega = \sqrt{\frac{g}{R}}$$

$$\therefore \ V = \omega R = \sqrt{g R}$$

$$= \sqrt{\frac{g l}{2 \pi}}$$

ı.e., in deep water the velocity is independent of the height of wave and cf ıhe depth of water, and depends only on the length of wave. This is true, within small limits, so long as the depth of water is greater than one-half the length of the wave.

In shallow water the velocity of propagation becomes equal to $\sqrt{\frac{g l}{2 \pi} \cdot \frac{b}{a}}$ where a and b are the horizontal and vertical axes of the elliptical orbit, and vary with the depth of water. In waves which are very long compared with the depth, the velocity approximates to $\sqrt{g h}$, where h is the depth, so that as the water becomes shallower and shallower the velocity approximates more nearly to that of the wave of translation. The wave of oscillation in shallow water is indeed intermediate between the true wave of oscillation and the wave of translation.

There is no definite relationship between the length and height of waves. Both depend largely on the velocity of the wind which has raised them, and on the distance travelled under its influence. Where this distance is great the velocity is practically identical with the mean velocity of the wind.[1] For short "fetches," such as are usual in reservoirs, Stevenson gives the formula.

$$k = 1\cdot5 \sqrt{D} + 2\cdot5 - \sqrt[4]{D}$$

where k is the height of wave in feet, and D is the "fetch" in miles. As deep sea waves approach a shallowing beach, the orbital motion of their lower particles is checked, they partake to an increasing extent of the nature of waves of translation, and finally usually break when the depth of water is little more than the height of the wave.

Art. 118b.—Ripples.

So far it has been assumed that the only forces involved in wave formation and propagation are those due to the masses of the particles of

---

[1] Dr. Vaughan Cornish, "Cantor Lecture," 1912.

water. In large waves this is sensibly true, but in small waves, the curvature of whose surface is comparatively great, the modifying effect of the forces called into play by surface tension becomes appreciable, and in very small waves becomes the predominating factor. The effect of surface tension is to increase the sub-surface pressure under the crests and to reduce that under the troughs of the waves. If T be the surface tension in lbs. per linear foot of surface, and if ρ be the radius of curvature at any point, the resultant increase or diminution of pressure in feet of water is given by $\dfrac{T}{W\,\rho}$ feet.

Assuming the wave to be of trochoidal form, the horizontal and vertical displacements of a particle since leaving the crest are given by—

$$x = R\,\theta \text{ (approx.)}: \quad y = r\,(1 - \cos\theta).$$
$$\therefore \quad \frac{1}{\rho} = \frac{d^2\,y}{d\,x^2}\text{(approx.)} = \frac{r}{R^2}\cos\theta.$$

If the pressures at the crest and at any other point Q (Fig. 184D) are not equal, but are respectively p_c and p lbs. per square foot, we have :—

$$\frac{v^2}{2\,g} + r\cos\theta - \frac{v_c^2}{2\,g} - r = \frac{p_c - p}{W}$$
$$= \frac{T}{W}\left(\frac{1}{\rho_c} - \frac{1}{\rho}\right)$$
$$= \frac{T}{W}\frac{r}{R^2}(1 - \cos\theta)$$

But $\dfrac{r^2}{2\,g} + r\cos\theta - \dfrac{v_c^2}{2\,g} - r = \left(\dfrac{\omega^2}{g}R - 1\right)r\,(1 - \cos\theta)$ (1) p. 419.

$$\therefore \quad \omega^2 = \frac{g}{R} + \frac{T\,g}{W\,R^3}$$
$$\therefore \quad V^2 = g\,R + \frac{T\,g}{W\,R}$$
$$= \frac{g\,l}{2\,\pi} + \frac{2\,\pi\,g}{W}\frac{T}{l}.$$

For water at 60° F, $T = \cdot005$ lbs. per foot (approx.), and on substituting this value, the quadratic becomes

$$l = \cdot0975\,V^2 \pm \sqrt{\cdot0095\,V^4 - \cdot00324}.$$

For this to have real roots V^4 must be not less than $\cdot342$, and V not less than $\cdot765$ f.s., or 9·2 inches per second. When V has this value, $l = \cdot67$ inches.

For higher values of V, l has two values, one less and one greater than $\cdot67$. The greater value represents the length of the ordinary wave of oscillation in which surface tension plays a comparatively small part, while the smaller value represents the length of the wave in which surface tension is the predominating factor.   Such waves are called ripples.   No wave or ripple can be produced by a moving object whose velocity is less than this critical value of 9·2 inches per second, and a breeze of velocity less than this has no power to ruffle the surface of a still pool.

SECTION III

CHAPTER XIII

Hydraulic Prime Movers—Water-Wheels—The Overshot—Breast—Side—Undershot and Poncelet Wheels—The Pelton Wheel—Losses—Form and Number of Buckets—Speed Regulation—Jets from Needle-nozzles—Typical Installations—Summary.

ART. 119.—HYDRAULIC PRIME MOVERS, WATER-WHEELS.

ALTHOUGH the question of the utilization of natural water powers has always been one of great economic importance, the introduction and perfection of electrical manufacturing processes, and the possibility of transmitting electrical energy without great loss or expense to a great distance from the place of its generation, has of recent years made it practicable to take advantage of many water powers far remote from large centres of industry and has raised the whole question to an altogether higher plane of importance, while the consequent demand for hydraulic prime movers capable of developing large powers in single units, and of satisfying the exhaustive demands of such installations in the way of speed regulation and efficiency, has led to a great transformation in the design of such motors.

The first hydraulic prime mover consisted of a wooden paddle waterwheel dipping into the current of a stream, and as such a motor was only required to do the work previously performed by an animate agency, the power required was small and the efficiency of only secondary importance.

The construction was at first of the most primitive type, but was gradually improved ; iron took the place of wood ; improvements in design led to increased efficiency ; the demand for greater powers led to the necessity for utilizing larger falls and the consequent development of the breast and overshot wheels, until a type of wheel was evolved, which within its limitations was as efficient as the most modern of turbines. Its chief disadvantages lay in its slow speed of rotation, the impossibility of close speed regulation, and in the large size of wheel required for even small powers ; and while for the purposes for which the motor was first required these were not serious, the introduction of more modern machinery, more particularly for textile purposes, involved the necessity for a motor which, having a fairly high speed of rotation in order to avoid excessive loss in gearing, should be capable of close speed regulation and of taking advantage of higher falls and of large quantities of water. For such purposes the water-wheel was almost entirely superseded by one or other type of turbine.

The introduction of electric driving with its large and almost instantaneous changes of load, while giving an additional fillip to the manufacture of high-speed turbines, had its greatest effect in modifying and perfecting the methods of speed regulation, and in increasing the size of the unit, while at the same time rendering it imperative to design a motor which should be highly efficient under a wide range of loads.

The success which has attended the attempt to satisfy these onerous conditions may be inferred when it is remembered that many manufacturers will now guarantee to construct a turbine which shall give an efficiency of over 80 per cent. over a range of loads of 50 per cent., and which shall respond to an increased demand for power of 33 per cent. with less than 3 5 per cent. variation in speed. With smaller load variations the speed variation is almost infinitesimal, and it becomes easy to run a series of alternating current machines in step with such motors.

The design of hydraulic motors has thus proceeded by well-defined stages, the size and efficiency steadily increasing until at the present time a single unit developing 15,000 H.P. and giving an efficiency of 85 per cent. is not at all uncommon, while further development promises to proceed in the direction of still larger units. So far, indeed, as mechanical difficulties affect the question, there appears to be no reason why units developing up to at least 25,000 H.P. should not be constructed directly the demand arises.

Wherever a continuous supply of water at a sufficient elevation, or in motion as in a stream, is available, the potential or kinetic energy which this possesses may be turned into useful work.

Before embarking on any power scheme for utilizing such energy, it is however of the highest importance that the true possibilities of the scheme should be ascertained, for as the usefulness of the supply depends in most cases on its uniformity over long periods of time, the maximum available power is strictly regulated by the least power which is available after the longest probable period of drought.

This minimum supply can only be satisfactorily ascertained by investigation of past records extending over many years. Where such records are not available, every attempt should be made by a close investigation of the rainfall records for the particular districts over a long period of years, and of the character, condition, and area of the gathering ground, to estimate the minimum supply likely to be available under the worst probable combination of circumstances, and the scheme may then, and not until then, be developed.

The method of utilizing the supply depends largely on its magnitude. form, and locality. Where, though comparatively small, it is continuous. the available horse-power may be largely increased by the formation of a storage reservoir capable of impounding at least a 24 hours' inflow. By this means energy may be utilized for the eight hours or so comprising a working day at a rate greatly in excess of the mean rate of inflow.

Where the natural configuration of the country necessitates the power plant being placed at some distance from the storage reservoir, the supply is usually led through an open canal or ditch having a slight gradient, into a smaller storage reservoir termed the forebay, which is placed as near to the power plant as possible. From the forebay the supply is then taken to the prime mover by means of a closed pipe termed the penstock.

In the case of a water-wheel installation the penstock may consist of an open channel.

The supply of water to the prime mover is regulated by means of sluices or gates, which may either form an integral part of the machine, as in the case of most turbines, or may be fitted in the supply pipe or channel.

After doing work, the water is rejected into a discharge channel termed the tail-race.

The most suitable type of prime mover for any particular case depends on—

(1) The quantity of water available.
(2) The supply head.
(3) The regulritay of flow.
(4) The possibility of floods.
(5) The purpose for which power is required.

Those types in general use consist of—

(1) Water-wheels.
(2) Turbines.
(3) Piston engines.

Each has its own sphere of usefulness, and in determining the type to be adopted each installation demands special consideration, guided by the circumstances peculiar to the case.

In general, the water-wheel is only suitable for small powers and for comparatively low heads and where close speed regulation is not essential. Its efficiency is greatly affected by a variation in the supply and in the head or tail-race levels. It is of great size and weight in proportion to the power developed, and has a low rotative speed. On the other hand, its construction is simple, its repair inexpensive and easy, and the construction of the supply channel, tail-race, and housing in general inexpensive, while for heads of less than 1 foot it forms the only suitable type of motor.

For all heads above 1 foot, where large power is desired, one or other type of turbine becomes suitable, while in certain cases for comparatively small powers, and where a high head is available and a slow rate of rotation is required, the piston engine is most satisfactory.

In passing through a prime mover, water may do work either by changing potential energy or kinetic energy or pressure energy into work ; or by a combination of these processes.

In the overshot water-wheel, for example (Art. 120), rotation is produced almost entirely by the weight of the water ; in impulse wheels deriving their motive force from the impact of a high velocity jet of water, work is done solely in virtue of the kinetic energy of the jet ; in turbines of the reaction type the pressure energy of the water is partly changed into kinetic energy in the wheel itself, this being absorbed in producing rotation of the wheel ; while in a piston engine the water does work in virtue of its pressure, its velocity being so small as to be negligible.

In designing any type of hydraulic prime mover, certain general principles should be borne in mind.

(a) All shock, whether of water on moving or stationary surfaces, or on water moving with a low velocity, should be avoided as being productive of loss of energy in eddy formation.

This may be prevented by arranging that as far as possible any stream of water on meeting a solid surface is moving tangentially to the surface, and that passages conveying the working fluid are not subject to abrupt changes of sectional area or of form.

(b) Abrupt changes in the direction of motion are productive of eddy formation and should be avoided by designing passages and channels with as far as possible an uniform or gradually changing curvature.

(c) Frictional losses should be reduced to a minimum by reducing the area of the wetted surfaces to a minimum compatible with easy curves of flow, and by reducing the relative velocity of flow over such surfaces to a minimum.

(d) As far as possible, the motive fluid should be rejected devoid of energy, and therefore moving with as low an absolute velocity as will suffice to carry it out of the motor.

The possibility of conforming to these general principles varies with the type of motor. In general, apart from mechanical friction, water-wheels suffer chiefly from the causes outlined in sections (a), (b), and (d); turbines from those in sections (a), (c), and (d); while losses due to shock and eddy production, (a) and (b), are all-important in piston engines.

These types of prime mover will now be considered somewhat in detail.

ART. 120.—THE OVERSHOT WATER-WHEEL (FIG. 185).

In this type of wheel water is supplied near the highest point of the

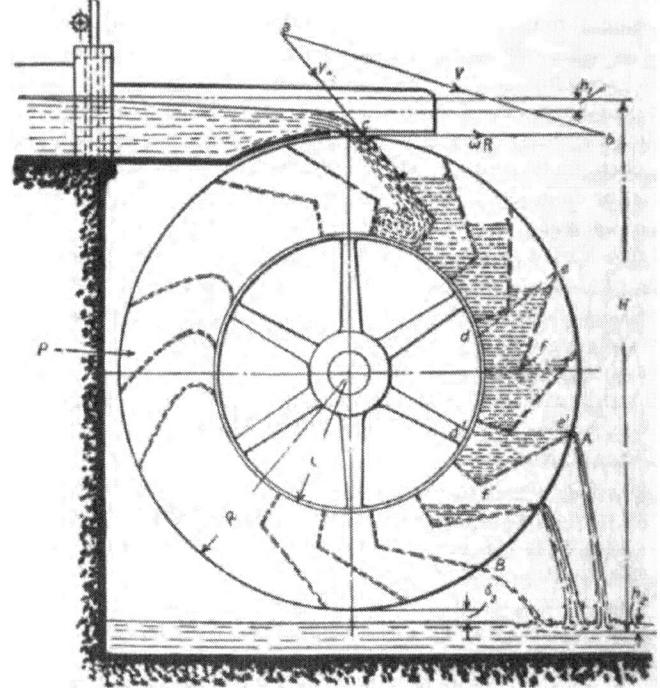

FIG. 185.—Overshot Water-Wheel.

circumference to a series of buckets formed by vanes connected at each end to circular shrouds, the bottoms of the buckets being formed by the inner circumference of the wheel. For convenience of construction the vanes are often made of wood and in two parts, the inner part being radial and the outer inclined to this at an angle depending on the speed of the wheel and the velocity of the supply stream.

A preferable form of bucket is that indicated at P (Fig. 185). Here the vanes, usually of metal, are made in a single piece, and have a continuous curvature throughout.

Theory of Action.—Let H be the total head available. A certain proportion of this head must first be utilized in giving the supply water sufficient velocity to carry it into the wheel buckets. If h_1 is this head, the velocity will then be given by $v = \sqrt{2gh_1}$.

A small clearance must be allowed between the highest point of the wheel and the bottom of the inlet channel, this clearance δ_1 being usually about 1 inch.

A rather larger clearance δ_2 must in general be allowed between the lowest point of the wheel and the level in the tail-race, so as to prevent submergence of the wheel buckets in time of flood.

In general δ_2 is about 6 inches, but depends largely on the special circumstances of the plant.

Finally, a certain proportion h_2 of the head must be devoted to producing velocity of flow along the tail-race, so as to give a free discharge from the wheel.

The outer diameter of the wheel buckets is thus limited to $H - (h_1 + h_2) - (\delta_1 + \delta_2)$.

Let R = outer radius of wheel.

„ r = inner „ „

Then $2R = H - (h_1 + h_2) - (\delta_1 + \delta_2)$.

The depth of buckets depends on the diameter, breadth and velocity of wheel, and on the quantity of water to be utilized.

Let Q = quantity of water per second in cubic feet.

„ ω = angular velocity of wheel in radians per second.

„ b = breadth of wheel,

and since the buckets are never completely filled with water, let x = fraction of bucket volume occupied by water. Generally x lies between $\frac{1}{3}$ and $\frac{2}{3}$.

Then we have, neglecting the volume occupied by the wheel vanes,

Bucket volume passing inlet per second $\left.\right\} = \pi (R^2 - r^2) \times \dfrac{\omega}{2\pi} \times b$ cubic feet.

$$\therefore \quad Q = \frac{x (R^2 - r^2) \omega b}{2} \text{ cubic feet per second.}$$

$$\therefore \quad r = \sqrt{R^2 - \frac{2Q}{\omega b x}}$$

giving r, and therefore $R - r$, the depth of the buckets.

To avoid excessive loss under low heads this should be as small as practicable.

Efficiency of Wheel.—Soon after the buckets pass the centre line of the wheel they begin to empty, at A (Fig. 185), while they are completely emptied by the time they reach the position B, where the outer part of the bucket is horizontal. If then h is the mean vertical distance through which the water is carried before being discharged, the work done in virtue of its weight $= W Q h$ foot lbs. per second.

It may readily be shown that the efficiency is a maximum when the peripheral velocity is one half that of the inflowing stream. A considerable increase in speed has, however, very little effect on the efficiency. The most important effect of such an increase is due to the tendency to a premature emptying of the buckets by increased centrifugal action.

To prevent loss by splash and shock at entrance to the buckets, the

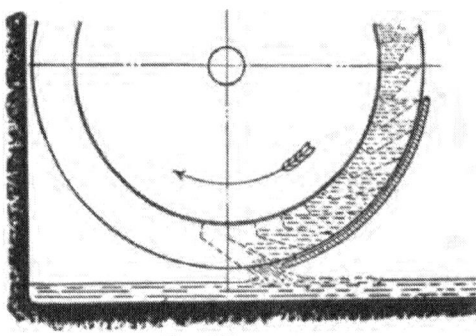

vane angles should be so arranged that the relative motion of water and vane at entrance is parallel to the tip of the vane. Thus if $a b$ (Fig. 185) represents the velocity v in direction and magnitude, and if $c b$ represents the linear velocity, ωR of the vane, then $a c$ represents the velocity of the water

FIG. 185A.

relative to the vane, and for the water to enter by sliding along the vane this should be parallel to $a c$ at entrance.

The general practice is to form the bucket tips so as to make an angle of 25° to 30° with the tangent to the circumference at the tip. This gives a bucket which retains the water for a vertical distance equal to about ·8 of the wheel diameter.

If this angle be β, the bucket is not completely emptied until the wheel has turned through $180° - \beta$.

Having drawn in the profile of the buckets, if a straight line $d e$ (Fig. 185) be drawn through the bucket tip so as to enclose an area $d e f = (x \times$ bucket area), the water will begin to escape from the bucket when $e d$ becomes horizontal. When $f e$ becomes horizontal the bucket is completely emptied. Thus with radial vanes the water is entirely emptied from a bucket by the time it has fallen to the level of the wheel axle.

Water may be retained in the buckets until these are near the lowest point of the wheel, by enclosing the discharge side of the wheel below A in a closely fitting shrouding, with as small a clearance as possible (Fig. 185A), and by this means the efficiency may be increased.   This method has the further advantage that the relative velocity of discharge is now increased by the head of water in the buckets, and as the direction of this motion is opposite to that of the wheel, the absolute velocity of discharge, and therefore the kinetic energy rejected, is reduced.

Effect of Varying the Tail-Race Level.—If the tail-race level rises so that the wheel is partially submerged, considerable resistance to rotation is caused if the vanes move in the opposite direction to that of flow in the tail-race.   By reversing the direction of inflow, however (Fig. 186), the direction of the tail-race flow becomes the same as that of the buckets, and these may now become partially submerged without serious loss of efficiency.

Further advantage may be taken of the fall by arranging a masonry breast-

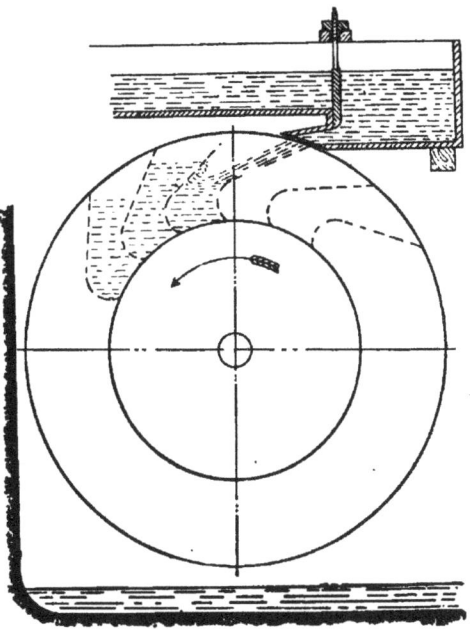

FIG. 186.—Overshot Wheel with Reversed Inflow.

work A (Fig. 187) to fit the wheel closely, the tail-race level being now slightly below the level at which each bucket finally empties itself.   The compartment B is kept dry either by draining into a sump where practicable, or by means of a small pump driven by the wheel.

To avoid running at inconveniently low speeds either of two expedients may be adopted.   The first is to run the wheel at a speed from 50 to 100 per cent. in excess of that giving maximum efficiency, when, since velocities are small, the amount of energy wasted by shock at entrance is not considerable.

The second expedient consists in giving h_1 a larger value, and in taking the supply by means of a closed guide passage of suitable depth out of the bottom of an open forebay (Fig. 188).

The velocity of efflux is then increased, and the velocity of rotation may

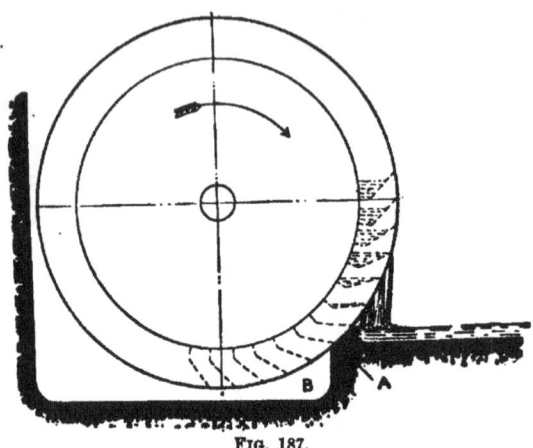

FIG. 187.

be increased proportionately. The diameter of the wheel is reduced, and also its width for a given volume of water. A cheaper wheel, and one rotating at a more convenient speed for transmission purposes is thus obtained. The efficiency is, however, slightly reduced, since losses due to shock and friction are increased by the higher velocities, as are the losses due to rejection of kinetic energy in the tail water, while in addition, the increased centrifugal action tends to empty the buckets sooner. The latter action,

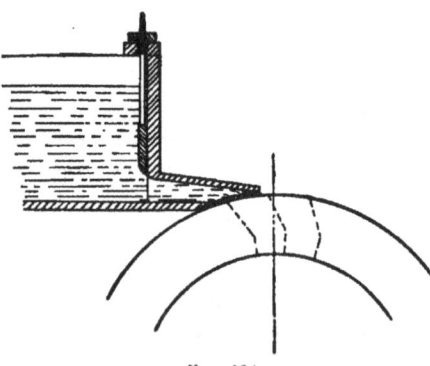

FIG. 188.

however, while reducing the efficiency of the wheel, tends to make it, to a certain extent self-governing under variable loads, since a diminution in load, followed by an increase in speed, tends to empty the buckets.

The following results of experiments by Smeaton indicate to what extent the efficiency is lowered by increasing the proportion of the total head absorbed in giving velocity energy to the supply water.

Diameter of Wheel. Total Head H	Proportion of Total Head absorbed in giving Velocity to supply Water.	Efficiency.
·90	·10	·73
·84	·16	·69
·80	·20	·66
·73	·27	·62
·68	·32	·59

Regulation is usually performed by a sluice governing the discharge from the penstock.

The overshot wheel is well suited for small powers and heads ranging from about 15 to 50 feet, and when working under suitable conditions gives efficiencies up to about 80 per cent. As the head diminishes, the larger proportional loss of head necessitated by the depth of the buckets and by the clearances δ_1 and δ_2 renders the wheel less efficient, and for heads between 15 feet and 6 feet the breast wheel becomes more suitable.

ART. 121.—THE BREAST WHEEL (FIG. 189).

Here the wheel itself is almost identical with the overshot. The principles of its construction and of the design of its buckets are the same, but water is now admitted to the buckets at some point in the breast of the wheel.

As before, the supply may be brought to the wheel either in an open supply channel under a comparatively low head not exceeding 1 foot, in which case the supply is led on below the wheel centre, or by means of a closed supply pipe under a greater head, when the supply is led on above the centre. The general arrangement in each case is indicated in Fig. 189 a and b. The water is prevented from escaping from the buckets before reaching the bottom of the wheel by means of a breastwork of masonry, the clearance between the wheel and masonry being reduced to the minimum possible, usually about $\frac{3}{16}$ inch. The necessity for this breast-work renders the wheel more expensive than the overshot. Regulation is performed by throttling the supply by means of sluices arranged as indicated in Figs. 189 a and b.

As in the case of the overshot wheel, the maximum efficiency is obtained when the bucket angles are arranged so as to give entry without shock and when the peripheral speed of the wheel is one half $v \cos \alpha$.   Here α is the angle which the direction of the inflowing stream makes with the tangent to the wheel at the point of entry.

For maximum efficiency the level in the tail-race should be the same as that in the buckets at discharge.   In this type of wheel, on account of the

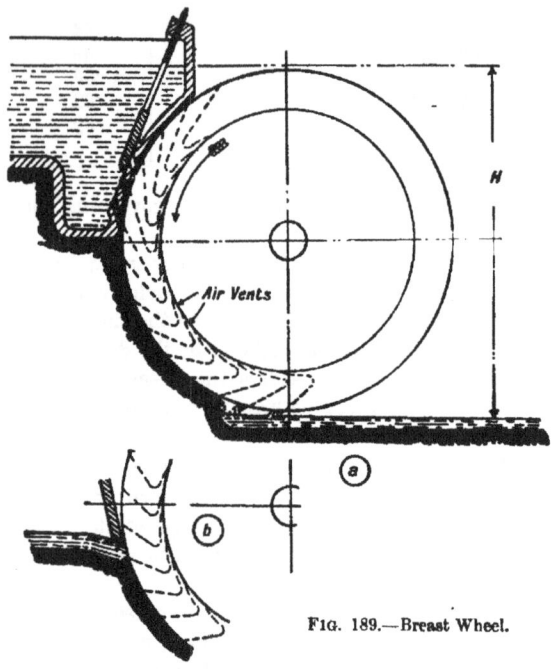

Fig. 189.—Breast Wheel.

manner of filling the buckets, special provision must be made for letting air out as the water rushes in.   To this end air vents are usually formed in the inner circumference of the buckets.   The wheel is capable of more accurate speed regulation under varying heads than is the overshot, and its efficiency under favourable circumstances may be as high as 65 per cent.

Art. 122.—The Side Wheel.

Where the fall is between 3 feet and 6 feet, the breast wheel becomes unsuitable because of the smallness of its diameter, and in such a case the

Sagebien wheel may be adopted. This wheel (Fig. 190) has buckets formed by a series of flat vanes, which are tangential to a circle concentric with the wheel itself. The buckets are open top and bottom, and are of comparatively great depth. The water enters the buckets with a velocity sensibly the same as that in the approach channel, the vane angles being determined as indicated in the figure, so that the vanes enter the water without shock.

A circular casing is provided in which the wheel works with little clearance, and which connects the head and tail-race. Then, neglecting leakage between this casing and the vanes, each bucket retains its supply until it passes its lowest point of the wheel, after which communication is

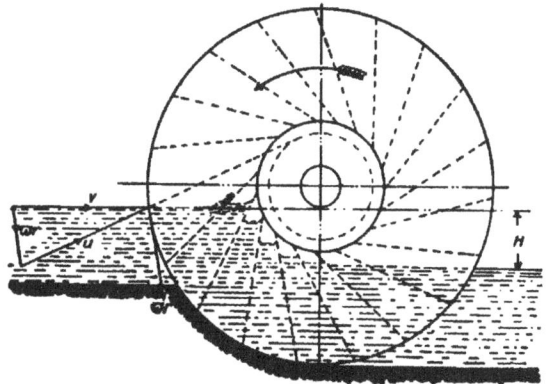

Fig. 190.—Sagebien Wheel.

made with the tail-race, and the level in the bucket falls to that of the tail-race water. For maximum efficiency the wheel should be designed so that the level in the bucket on reaching the bottom of the wheel is the same as that in the tail-race.

If v_r represents the relative velocity of water and bucket at entrance, the water will rise initially to a height in the bucket above that in the head-race, this height being given by $\frac{v_r^2}{2g}$, and the depth of bucket should be such that in time of flood this does not cause flow to take place over the inner end of the buckets.

In this wheel the velocity of rotation is proportional to the flow, and the wheel is thus capable of dealing with large quantities of water. It is however, unfitted for driving a variable load, since an increase in load, by

causing a diminution in speed, reduces the flow through the wheel, and
thus reduces the energy supply when it is most needed. Its peripheral
velocity is low, and on that account it is well adapted for driving a
pumping plant or milling machinery where the load is uniform and where
high velocities are not required.

The chief losses occur during the emergence of the vanes from the tail-
race. Owing, however, to the slow speed of the wheel, all hydraulic losses
are low and an efficiency of up to 80 per cent. may be obtained under
favourable circumstances, though the large size of the wheel and its
comparatively costly construction very largely counterbalance the
advantages of high efficiency.

Art. 123.—The Undershot Wheel.

For heads below 3 feet the undershot wheel is preferable. In its

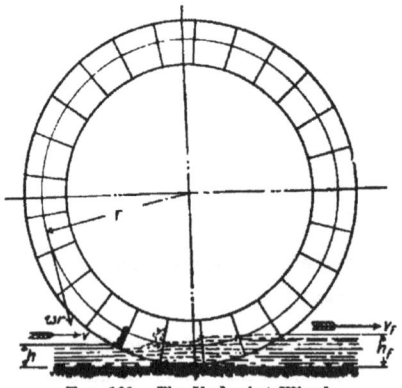

FIG. 191.—The Undershot Wheel.

simplest form this consists of a
wheel carrying a series of flat
radial vanes around its circumference (Fig. 191). These dip
into the water flowing either
through an open channel or
through a penstock of slightly
greater width than the wheel,
and are arranged so as to clear
the bottom of the penstock by
about $\frac{1}{4}$ inch. In some cases
the penstock itself is curved to
fit the wheel, and leakage past
the buckets, in the interval between successive buckets arriv-
ing at the lowest point of their path, is then largely prevented.

In this wheel, work is done solely in virtue of the kinetic energy of the
moving stream, the force on the moving vanes being due to the change of
momentum produced in the stream by their presence.

For maximum work the peripheral velocity should be one half the
velocity of flow of the stream, in which case the theoretical efficiency
is ·5.

Owing to mechanical friction and hydraulic losses this efficiency is,
however, reduced to about 35 per cent., and the maximum efficiency is
obtained with a value of v_f, slightly less than $\frac{1}{2} v$ (Fig. 191).

Art. 124.—The Poncelet Wheel.

If the vanes of an undershot wheel, instead of being radial, are inclined backward so as to make an angle β at the tips with the tangent to the circumference, and if α be the angle between the direction of the approach stream and this tangent, then by suitable adjustment of α, β, and the speed of rotation, the loss due to shock at entrance may be prevented, and at the same time the discharge water may be given a backward velocity

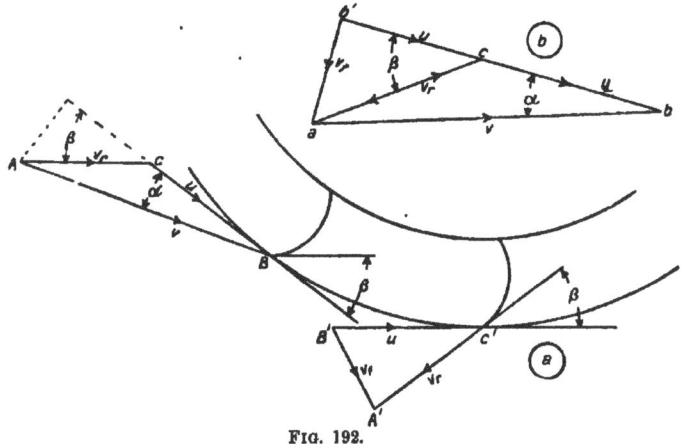

Fig. 192.

relative to the wheel, thus reducing the absolute velocity of discharge and the loss by rejection of kinetic energy to the tail-race.

With flat vanes the best results are obtained when β is about 30°, and efficiencies of up to 55 per cent. may then be obtained.

In the Poncelet wheel (Fig. 193) these vanes, instead of being flat, form arcs of circles, and with this type of wheel efficiencies of from 60 to 70 per cent. are usual.

To determine the correct vane angles, let

AB (Fig. 192 a) represent the absolute velocity of water at entrance.

CB represent the absolute velocity of vanes.

Then AC represents the velocity of water relative to vanes, and to avoid shock, the vane tips should be parallel to AC.

Again, at the discharge point, let

$B'C'' =$ velocity of vanes.

$C'A' =$ velocity of water relative to the vanes.

Then $B'A' =$ absolute velocity of discharge.

F F 2

Let v = initial velocity of water.

,, v_f = final   ,,   ,,   ,,

,, v_r = relative ,,   ,,   ,,   and wheel.

,, u = velocity of buckets.

On entering the buckets the relative velocity is v_r, and in virtue of this the water will rise to a height approximately equal to $\dfrac{v_r^2}{2\,g}$ feet above its normal level.

It then falls through this height relative to the wheel under the action of gravity, so that on leaving the wheel its relative velocity will again be approximately equal to v_r. This assumption neglects the effect of friction and of eddy formation in the buckets, both of which tend to make the final less than the initial relative velocity. Assuming, however, for simplicity that v_r is the same at inlet and at discharge, we have

$$AC = C'A' = v_r$$
$$CB = B'C' = u.$$

For v_f to be as small as possible with a given value of v_r, evidently $A'B'$ should be perpendicular to $B'C'$.

The two diagrams may now be combined graphically so as to give the most suitable angles a and β by making $A'C''$ coincide with AC.

Thus, draw $c\,b$ (Fig. 192 b) $= u$ and produce $b\,c$ to b', making $b'\,c = c\,b$. From b' draw a perpendicular to $b\,b'$, and with b as centre describe an arc of a circle with v as radius to cut this at a. Join $a\,c$. Then $ac = v_r$; $\widehat{a\,b\,c} = a$; $\widehat{a\,c\,b'} = \beta$.

From the figure it is evident that for minimum loss of kinetic energy at discharge we must have $v \cos a = 2\,u.$

$$\therefore\quad u = \frac{v}{2} \cdot \cos a.$$

In practice a is usually made about $15°$.

$$\therefore\quad \cos a = \cdot 966. \quad \therefore \quad u = \cdot 488\,v.$$

The theoretical efficiency is given by

$$\eta = \frac{\dfrac{W\,Q}{g}\,\{v^2 - v_f^2\}}{\dfrac{W\,Q}{g}\,\{v^2\}}$$

$$\therefore\quad \eta = \frac{v^2 - v_f^2}{v^2}$$

But from the figure we have

$$v^2 - v_f^2 = 4\,u^2$$

$$\therefore\quad \eta = \frac{4\,u^2}{v^2} = \cos{}^2 a$$

$\therefore$ With $a = 15°$, the maximum theoretical efficiency is ·93.
Again (Fig. 192),

$$u \sin \beta = v \sin (\beta - a)$$

$$\therefore \; \frac{v}{2} \cos a \sin \beta = v \sin (\beta - a)$$

$$\therefore \; \cot \beta \tan a = \frac{1}{2}$$

$$\therefore \; \tan \beta = 2 \tan a$$

If
$$a = 15°, \tan \beta = ·5358$$

$$\therefore \; \beta = 28·2°.$$

Actually, because of hydraulic losses caused by relative motion of the mass of water in the buckets, and which are proportional to v_r^2, it is found advisable to diminish the relative velocity slightly by giving the vanes a velocity varying from ·5 to ·6 v. Under these circumstances the maximum working efficiency is obtained.

The construction of the wheel is substantially as shown (Fig. 193). The buckets are open both at their inner and outer circumferences, and to prevent water at impact from flowing into the inner part of the wheel, the depth of buckets should be not less than $h + \frac{v_r^2}{2g}$, where $h =$ thickness of stream. In practice h should not exceed 9 inches.

But
$$r_r = \frac{u \sin a}{\sin (\beta - a)}$$

$\therefore$ taking $a = 15°$, $\beta = 30°$ (approx.), we have $v_r = u = ·55 v$ (approx.), and taking $v^2 = 2gH$, where H is the supply head, we have

$$\text{Depth of buckets} = ·3 \frac{r^2}{2g} + h$$

$$= ·3 H + h.$$

In practice the depth is usually taken as $\frac{H}{3} + h$.

The spacing varies so as to give about forty-eight buckets in the circumference, the maximum spacing being about 16 inches. The most suitable arc of water contact is about 80°. Since at all points of this arc the direction of the approach stream should make an angle β with the tangent to the circumference, the approach channel is not straight but has a bed curved so as to fulfil this condition.

To draw this curve, let K and M (Fig. 193) be the extremities of the arc of contact, and from K and M draw KO and MO perpendicular to the required directions of the stream, i.e., making an angle a with the normals at K and M, and intersecting in O. Then an approach bed, having as profile the arc described with centre O, and passing through M. will give the required inclination at K and M, and approximately for all points between.

Regulation is performed by an adjustable sluice S, whose position is regulated by some form of centrifugal or float governor. In order to prevent loss by leakage past the vane tips the supply bed is extended to form a circular lip closely fitting the wheel. This should be no longer than is necessary to give contact with two vanes at once. If made too long, the water on flowing down the vanes, instead of freely escaping with relative velocity r_r, meets this lip, its relative velocity is destroyed, and on.

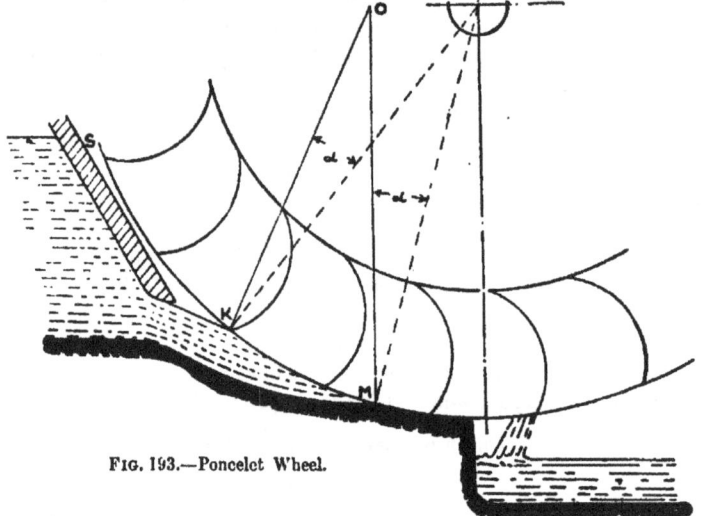

Fig. 193.—Poncelet Wheel.

emerging from the lip it escapes with the forward velocity of the vane as in the ordinary type of undershot wheel.

In common with all impulse wheels, for efficient working the vanes must not be submerged, and the level of the supply bed must be sufficiently above that of the tail-race to obviate any flooding. This wheel is well adapted for heads between 4 and 7 feet. Its speed is fairly high, and the consequent fly-wheel effect renders it easy of regulation under variable loads.

Its part-gate efficiency is high if the head be kept fairly constant, but with very variable heads, owing to the variation in velocity of approach, its efficiency is not so good.

ART. 125.—THE PELTON WHEEL.

The Pelton wheel (Fig. 194[1]) is the only form of water-wheel which is adopted for use with high heads, and where a limited supply of water under such a head is available it often forms the most suitable type of prime mover. In such a case the turbine proper, with the exception of the Girard type (Art. 129), is unsuitable, as will be seen later (Art. 128), while where the supply water is charged with sand or similar matter in suspension, as is not unusual, the Pelton wheel, on account of the simplicity of its construction and of the ease with which its buckets can be renewed, has manifest advantages over the Girard turbine. The

FIG. 194.—Pelton Wheel.

pressure water is supplied through a pipe line terminating in one or more nozzles which play on to a series of buckets fixed around the periphery of the wheel.

The latter is a development of the old hurdy-gurdy of the Pacific Slope. This consisted of a wheel having a rim to which a series of flat plates were fixed radially, the jets from one or more nozzles impinging freely on these and causing rotation. Under these conditions, the theoretical efficiency cannot exceed 50 per cent. (p. 378), while in practice loss by splashing, friction, etc., reduces this to about 30 per cent.

[1] By courtesy of Messrs. Gilbert, Gilkes & Co., Ltd., Kendal.

The first important improvement in the machine was made about 1870, when the flat plates were replaced by hemispherical cups fixed alternately on each side of the centre line of the wheel with their concave sides to the jet. This was

known as the Cascade wheel (Fig. 195). By this means the jet was deflected backwards, and the theoretical possibilities of the wheel were at once doubled (see p. 378), the maximum theoretical efficiency becoming unity.

FIG. 195.

The next step was to replace these cups by a series of concave buckets mounted on the centre line of the wheel, fitted with knife-edged ridges to split the jet and having surfaces curved so as to give the jet its backward deflection as smoothly and uniformly as possible. Several types of bucket have been designed with this end in view and some of the more successful are illustrated in Fig. 196 (a, b, and c) and in Fig. 197 (a and b).

While the type of bucket fitted with a lip, as shown in Fig. 196 (b) and in Fig. 197 (a), is common in practice, it does not satisfy the conditions necessary for high efficiency so well as the bucket which omits that portion of the lip in the line of the jet as shown in Figs. 196 (a and c) and 197 (b). The lip and ridge of the bucket deflect the jet in two planes, approximately at right angles, and as the paths of the

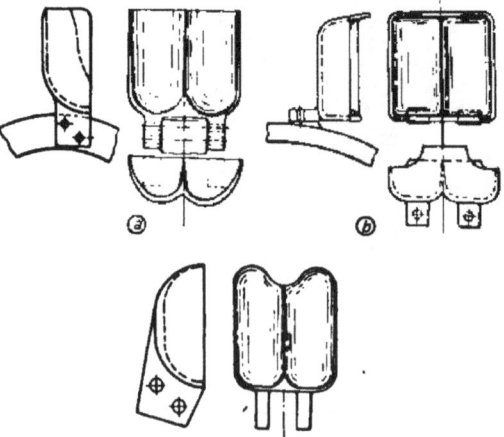

FIG. 196.

streams thus formed cross, a certain amount of energy is dissipated by their impact. Futhermore, the lip tends to deflect the jet radially inwards towards the rim of the wheel, in which case some fouling of the succeeding bucket is inevitable. Relative tests of buckets (Fig. 197, a and b) fitted to a wheel developing 375 B.H.P. under 860 feet head, and having a 2-inch jet on a 35-inch pitch circle, showed an efficiency about 6 per cent. greater with bucket *b* than with bucket *a*.[1]

In practice an efficiency of unity is impossible of attainment for several reasons.

(1) In order that the discharge from one shall clear the back of the following bucket, the jet cannot be deflected through the full 180°, the actual deflection usually being 160°. Thus kinetic energy is rejected in virtue of the motion of the water parallel to the axis of the wheel at discharge. To prevent this loss becoming large, the buckets should not be spaced too closely together.

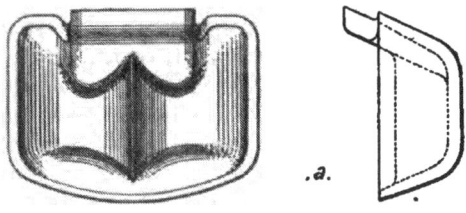

(2) The relative velocity of water and bucket at discharge is less than at the point of impact because of skin friction, while windage causes the actual velocity of impact to be less than that theoretically equivalent to the head at the nozzle. Both these causes have the effect of

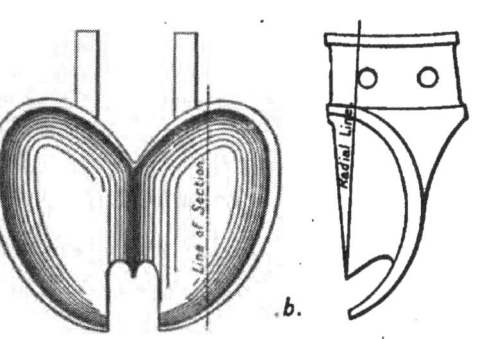

FIG. 197.

reducing the pressure on the bucket, and to obviate this loss as far as possible the wetted surface of the buckets should be a minimum, and therefore the number of buckets should be as small as is consistent with continuous impact, while they should be made no larger than is necessary to give the required change of direction with easy curves and without shock. Also the surface should be as smooth and well finished as possible.

To reduce windage the jet should be circular in section, since this gives the minimum perimeter per unit area of cross section, while it has the further advantage of being the most stable form of jet. Other forms

[1] "Proceedings Inst. Civil Engineers," 1907, vol. 170, p. 51.

ultimately tend to the circular, and in doing so tend to becom: unsteady.

(3) Sharp corners and uneven curves in the buckets cause loss of energy by eddy formation.

(4) Splash on entering buckets, if unsuitably designed (reduced by reducing the number of buckets).

(5) The jet, being placed tangential to the pitch circle of the buckets, meets and remains in contact with each bucket in turn through some appreciable angle of rotation. The angle at which the jet meets the bucket, and also the angle of discharge, will in consequence vary as the wheel rotates, and it follows that unless the buckets are designed so as to give normal impact on the ridge and a discharge which is tangential to the wheel, and unless the speed of the wheel is regulated so that the backward velocity of discharge is equal to the forward velocity of the buckets, an excess of kinetic energy will be rejected to the tail-race.

Theoretically, assuming the angle of deflection to be 180° and neglecting the effect of friction, the most efficient speed of the buckets is one half that of the jet (p. 378). When allowance is made for the effect of friction, as on p. 371, the most efficient bucket speed is seen to be slightly less than this. In practice the most efficient bucket speed is found to be from ·44 to ·48 times that of the jet, the higher ratio being possible with the more efficient buckets.

Efficiency of Pelton Wheel.

Let u = peripheral speed of buckets at pitch circle.

$\qquad = \dfrac{2 \pi r N}{60}$ where r = perpendicular distance from axis of jet to centre of wheel; N = revs. per minute.

Let v = initial velocity of jet.

Let v_2 = final absolute velocity.

Let $_1v_r$ = relative velocity of jet and bucket at entrance.

Let $_2v_r$ = relative velocity at discharge.

Let a = mean angle between jet and tangent at point of contact.

Let γ = total angle of deflection of jet.

Then initial velocity of jet in direction of tangent $\left.\begin{array}{c}\\ \\\end{array}\right\}$ = $v \cos a$. at point of impact

Component, parallel to tangent at discharge, of $\left.\begin{array}{c}\\ \\\end{array}\right\}$ = $_2v_r \cos \gamma$. final velocity relative to bucket

$\therefore$ Absolute velocity in this direction at discharge = $u + _2v_r \cos \gamma$.

$\therefore$ Change of tangential momentum per second, per lb.

$$= \frac{1}{g} \{ v \cos a - u - {}_2r_r \cos \gamma \}.$$

$\therefore$ Work done per lb. of water per second

$$= \frac{u}{g} \{ v \cos a - u - {}_2r_r \cos \gamma \} \text{ ft. lbs.}$$

$\therefore$ Efficiency $= \frac{u}{g\,h} \{ v \cos a - u - {}_2r_r \cos \gamma \} \text{ ft. lbs.}$

The loss due to friction and eddies in buckets $= \frac{{}_1r_r{}^2 - {}_2r_r{}^2}{2\,g}$ ft. lbs. per lb.

where ${}_1r_r = \sqrt{v^2 + u^2 - 2\,v\,u \cos a}$ (Fig. 199).

The loss due to rejection of kinetic energy $= \frac{r_2{}^2}{2\,g}$ ft. lbs. per lb.

where $r_2{}^2 = u^2 + {}_2r_r{}^2 + 2\,u\,{}_2r_r \cos \gamma$.

Experiments indicate that in the average wheel ${}_2r_r$ may be as low as from ·5 to ·6 times ${}_1r_r$. It is certain, however, that in a well-designed bucket, having a ratio of bucket width to jet diameter not less than about 3·3, this ratio is greater, and approximates to ·75.

Taking $a = 10°$; $\gamma = 160°$; $u = ·46\ v$; ${}_2r_r = ·75\ {}_1r_r$; this makes ${}_1r_r = ·55\ v$; ${}_2r_r = ·41\ v$; and the hydraulic efficiency $= ·84$, a value agreeing closely with the results of the best modern practice.

Test Number.	1.	2.	3.	4.
Revolutions per minute	302	300	301	299
Output in kilowatts . . .	962	1724	2296	2527
Diam. of jet, ins.	4·36	5·61	6·56	6·80
Mean velocity of jet, f.s. . .	221·4	222·8	224·2	227·4
Ratio of bucket to jet velocity . .	·406	·401	·400	·399
Discharge, c.f.s.	22·9	38·2	52·9	57·6
Nozzle efficiency, per cent. . . .	95·8	96·8	98·2	98·6
Relative velocity of jet entering bucket .	132·1	134·0	135·1	138·9
,, ,, ,, leaving ,, .	77·5	79·2	65·1	63·9
Distribution of Energy of Jet.				
Useful work, per cent. . . .	74·4	74·2	70·4	68·1
Bucket friction and eddies, per cent. .	23·0	23·2	27·7	29·2
Kinetic energy in discharge, per cent. .	1·1	1·0	1·8	1·9
Other hydraulic losses, due to splash at entrance, changing angle of application of jet, etc.	1·5	1·6	1·1	0·8

The above table shows the distribution of energy as obtained in a series of tests on a wheel of which the following are the details [1] :—

Number of buckets . . 15; angle $a = 4° 41·5'$.
Width ,, ,, . . 19·5 inches; angle $\gamma = 166°$.
Projected area ,, . . 252 square inches; head, 810 feet.
Radius of pitch circle . . 33·5 inches.
,, outside tip of buckets . 40·5 ,,
Revolutions per minute . . 300.
Nozzle—needle nozzle, with tip 7·5 inches diameter.

The large value of the bucket losses, particularly in trials 3 and 4, is undoubtedly due partly to the comparatively small ratio of width of

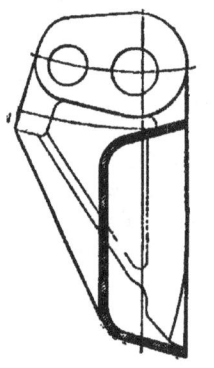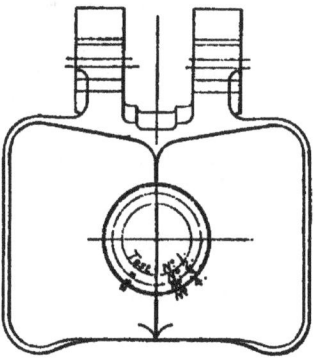

FIG. 198.

bucket to diameter of jet, and partly to the design of bucket, which is shown in Fig. 198.

The following table, showing results obtained in recent tests of Pelton wheels,[2] well illustrates the extent to which the high efficiency is maintained at part loads in a well-designed wheel.

No.	Number of Nozzles.	Fall in Metres.	Revolutions per Minute.	Efficient Horse-power at Full Gate.	a = per cent. of Full Load. b = per cent. Efficiency of the Turbine.											
					a	b	a	b	a	b	a	b	a	b	a	b
X.	2	90	355	326	100·0	76·0	89·?	79·7	86·5	81·6	71·4	83·6	39·6	84·2	—	—
XI.	1	100	180	300	100·0	88·9	85·4	89·3	72·7	87·8	56·0	86·0	42·0	87·8	24·0	77·4
XII.	2	850	376	6,050	100·0	83·5	89·9	81·0	75·8	82·8	55·1	83·8	27·1	80·5	14·2	75·0
XIII.	1	850	630	3,710	100·0	86·2	89·4	86·9	59·2	85·2	71·2	85·1	46·7	82·9	22·3	75·0

[1] " Proceedings Inst. Mechanical Engineers," January, 1910.
[2] By Professor F. Prazil. " Proceedings Inst. Mechanical Engineers," 1910-11.

Form of Buckets.—Where the dividing ridges of the buckets are straight in profile, these are not fixed radially but are inclined backwards from the direction of rotation at such an angle as to give normal incidence on the first impact of the jet. If placed radially the jet would be deflected into the rim of the wheel during the first half of the period of impact and would tend to produce serious inefficiency.

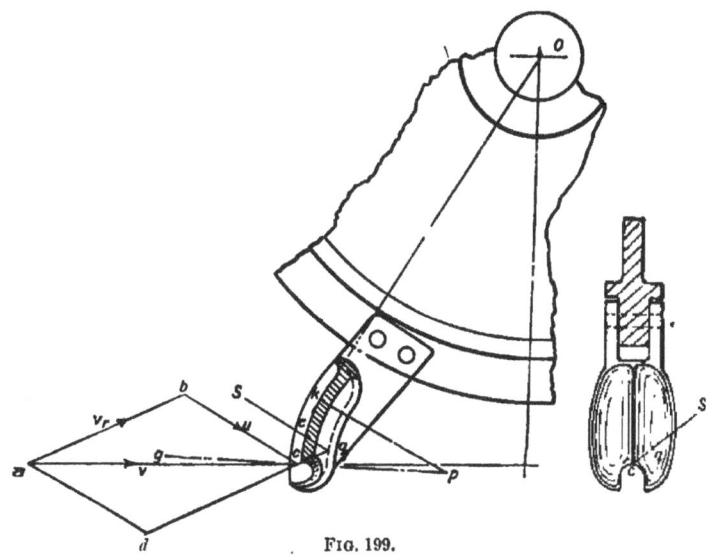

FIG. 199.

A type of construction which is more theoretically correct, and which is found to give better results in practice, is indicated in Fig. 199.

Let $\overline{ac} = v$ = velocity of jet.

Let $\overline{bc} = u$ = velocity of bucket.

Then $\overline{ab}$ = relative velocity of jet and bucket.

If ω = angular velocity of wheel, and if r = radius at the point of impact, we have $u = \omega r$ and $\overline{bc}$ is perpendicular to $\overline{oc}$.

Draw dc parallel to ab. Then dc represents the direction of the jet relative to the moving bucket.

For the jet to leave the bucket with zero absolute tangential velocity, its final direction must be parallel to, and the component parallel to the plane of the wheel of its final relative velocity must be equal to $\overline{cb}$. If then $\overline{gc}$, the bisector of the angle $\overline{b\,c\,d}$, be a normal to the surface of impact at c, the required conditions will be fulfilled, the jet striking the vane in the direction $\overline{d\,c}$ and leaving (relatively to the wheel) in the direction of $\overline{c\,b}$. The direction and magnitude of $\overline{ac}$, and the direction of $b\,c$ being fixed, if the final relative velocity be approximately known, the magnitude of $\overline{bc}$ and therefore the most efficient speed of rotation may be determined. In a well-designed bucket the final relative velocity may be taken as ·75 of the initial. If c and k be the first and last points at which the jet impinges on the ridge and if a third point l be taken midway between c and k, the directions of such normals as $c\,g$ may be determined for these three points, and a smooth curve drawn through these points and having the required normals will give the correct curve for a longitudinal section of the receiving edge of the bucket. In general, a circular arc with centre at p, the intersection of the normals through c and k will give a very close approximation to the curve.

Strictly, since the path of the mid particles of the jet relative to the bucket is given by $c\,q\,s$, the normal at q should bisect this angle. If, however, the curve through q be made parallel to $c\,l\,k$, the approximation to the correct curve will be sufficiently near.

A close approximation may also be obtained by determining graphically the points of intersection of the bucket with the axis of the jet for different positions of the bucket, and by drawing a smooth curve such that the axis of the jet is normal to the curve in every position of the bucket.

To prevent the jet striking the back of the bucket, this should be everywhere above the line $d\,c$, while to reduce splash on passing through the jet the edge at c should be as sharp as possible.

In modern practice the width of the buckets is between three and five times the diameter of the jet, the ratio diminishing as the size of jet increases, while the wheel diameter should not be less than about ten times the jet diameter. If, on settling the number of revolutions and peripheral speed, and hence the diameter of a wheel, this is less than the required multiple of the diameter of a single jet to give the required power, duplicate jets should be used.

Number of Buckets.—For minimum loss these must be as few as is consistent with the jet being wholly intercepted for all bucket positions, so that the entering bucket may entirely intercept the jet before the leaving bucket begins to free itself. From this consideration, a simple geometrical construction shows that if n be the minimum possible number of buckets, R the extreme outer radius over the receiving edges of the buckets, r the pitch circle radius, and t the thickness or diameter of the jet, n is given very approximately by the relationship

$$n = \frac{\pi}{\sqrt{1 - \frac{\left(r + \frac{t}{2}\right)^2}{R^2}}}$$

If $R = r + s$, so that s is that portion of the bucket projecting beyond the pitch circle, we have

$$n = \frac{\pi}{\sqrt{1 - \left(\frac{r + \frac{t}{2}}{r + s}\right)^2}}$$

Giving s a value ranging from ·60 t in the case of a wheel of less than 3 feet diameter to ·565 t where the wheel is upwards of 6 feet in diameter, values of n in close accord with modern practice are obtained. Generally, values of n given by the formula $n = k \sqrt{\frac{r}{t}}$, where k ranges from 7·0 to 8·0 as the wheel diameter decreases from 6 feet to 3 feet, will be found to give results which are sufficiently near for all practical purposes. The theoretical value of s thus being obtained, a little additional overlap is usually given to allow for any slight variation in the axial position of the jet.

Speed Regulation.—Since the efficiency of a Pelton wheel, or other impulse wheel, depends on the maintenance of the correct ratio of peripheral velocity of bucket and velocity of jet, if high efficiency is to be expected at all loads the method of governing must be such as to keep the latter velocity as nearly as possible constant. Where this is the case, there is no reason, except for the greater proportional effect of windage and mechanical friction at part loads, why the efficiency should not be independent of the load. Where, however, the jet velocity is variable, the efficiency falls off considerably as this departs from its theoretically correct value, and for this reason the impulse wheel, while giving excellent part-load efficiencies under a constant supply head, is unfitted for situations in which the percentage variation of head is likely to be great. Since this is more likely to be the case under a low supply head, it affords one reason why the impulse wheel is not in general advisable under such conditions.

The Speed Regulation of a Pelton wheel is usually performed in one of four ways.

(1) The stream may be deflected so as to partially miss the buckets at part load, either by swivelling the nozzle, which is then carried on a ball-and-socket joint, or by a stream deflector placed between the nozzle and the wheel. In the former case, owing to the friction at the swivelling joint a considerable force is required to deflect the nozzle, and in consequence the governor must be fitted with a hydraulic relay cylinder, as at C (Fig. 207). The piston rod of this cylinder carries the nozzle, and the governor by regulating the supply of pressure water to one side or other of this piston, also regulates the position of the nozzle.

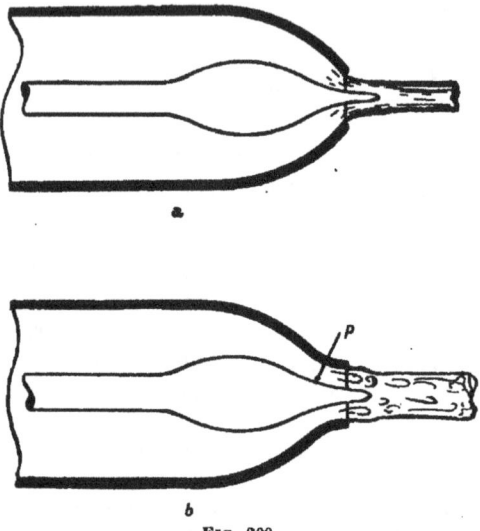

FIG. 200.

This method of regulation has the disadvantage of being wasteful of energy at part load, while the nuisance caused by the discharge of the jet directly into the wheel pit may be very great.

On the Pacific slopes, however, many of the water companies require that a constant flow through the pipes be maintained, in order that a constant supply may be delivered over a weir to a ditch of lower level, and in this case the deflecting nozzle affords the most suitable means of speed regulation. The method possesses a further advantage in that it avoids all action of the nature of water ram in the pipes.

(2) The velocity of the jet may be reduced by means of a throttle valve placed behind the nozzle. This is not to be recommended, since the contraction and subsequent enlargement of the stream which occurs at the valve is wasteful of energy, while the variation in the velocity of the jet tends to inefficiency in working.

Further, since the sudden closing of the valve causes a corresponding increase of pressure throughout the pipe due to water hammer (p. 222), this method of governing should never be adopted without the addition of some suitable protecting device, such as a stand pipe, relief valve, or pressure regulator, to the pipe line, this being placed as near to the valve as possible.

(3) A portion of the jet may be cut off at the nozzle by means of a sharp-edged sluice sliding across the orifice, or the section of the jet may be reduced by means of a needle regulator (Figs. 200—202). This consists of a cylindrical needle of tapering section fitted inside the nozzle axially with the jet. The water flows through the annulus between the needle and the nozzle, forming a solid cylindrical jet on

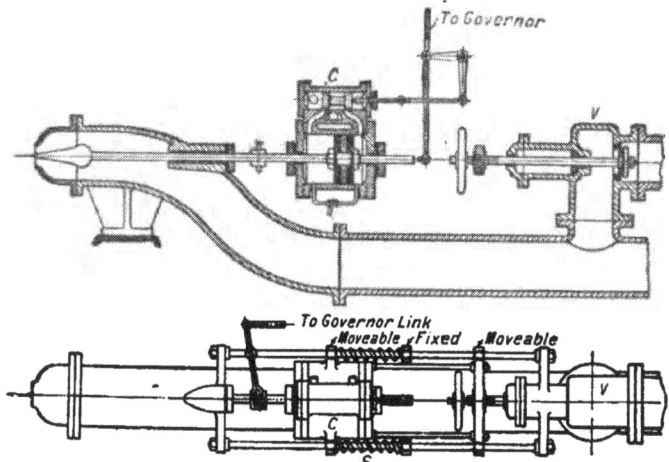

FIG. 201.—Needle Regulator and Pressure Regulating Device for Pelton Wheel.

leaving the needle. By axial regulation, the latter may be adjusted so as to fill the orifice either partially or wholly.

While giving a slightly greater loss by friction than the sluice regulation, a more stable jet is obtained, and on the whole needle regulation is to be preferred.

It is highly important, however, that the position of the needle in the nozzle should be perfectly central, or the form and efficiency of the jet may be seriously affected. Also the needle must be supported so as to prevent all vibration and consequent distortion of the jet. A further point to be noted is that the minimum section of the discharge channel should occur exactly at the tip of the nozzle for all positions of the needle. This may be illustrated by reference to Figs. 200 a and b. In a this condition is satisfied. In b this minimum cross section occurs at some point "*p*." After passing this point the area increases, with consequent tendency to unsteadiness of the jet and to loss of energy in

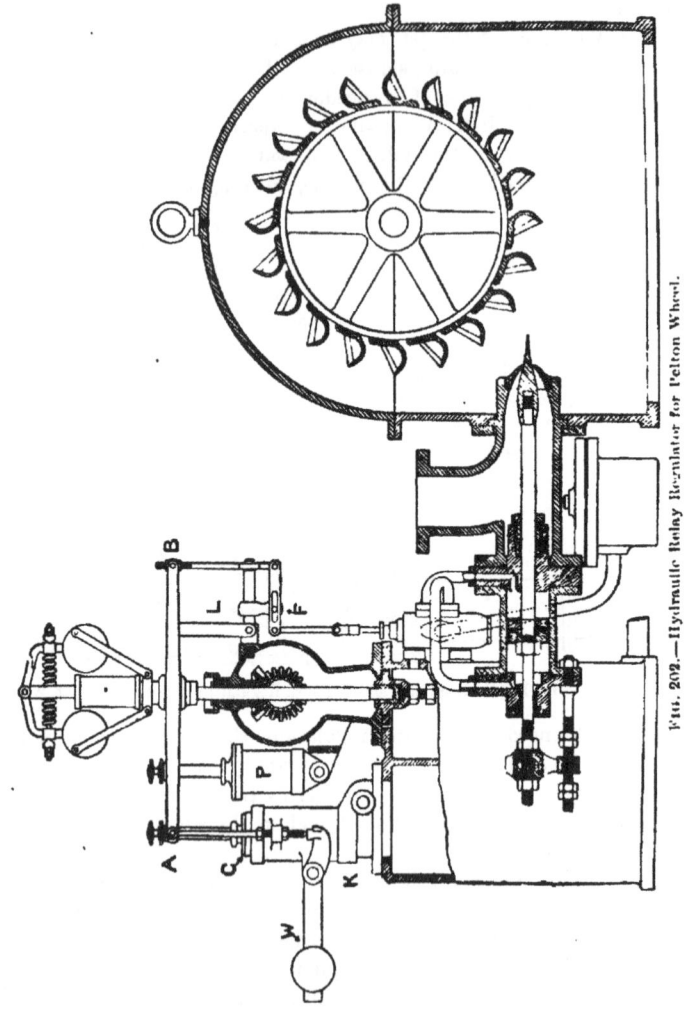

FIG. 202.—Hydraulic Relay Regulator for Pelton Wheel.

eddy formation.   Further details as to the properties of such jets are given on p. 459.

By either method of regulation the velocity of efflux is maintained approximately constant, and the efficiency is therefore only slightly affected at low loads, the quantity of water used being approximately proportional to the load.

On the other hand, the inertia of the supply column tends to prevent close governing unless a relief valve, or some such device, is fitted near to the nozzle, while care should always be taken, as explained on p. 285, that the closing of the nozzle actually does diminish the supply of energy to the wheel.

One device which prevents a rise in pressure following any sudden closing of the regulating nozzle is shown in Fig. 201. Here the relay cylinder C is supplied with oil or water under pressure, this supply being regulated by a valve operated by the governor link. Any increase in speed is then accompanied by the admission of pressure water to the right-hand side of the piston. This forces the needle over to the left, reducing the supply of water to the wheel, and at the same time moves the cylinder itself to the right against the resistance of the springs at S, and so opens the byepass valve V. In this it is aided by the pressure on the valve itself, so that the pressure is quickly relieved. The motion of the cylinder relatively to its valve moreover tends to cut off the supply of pressure water to the right-hand side of the piston, while the motion of the needle is utilized to bring the governor link back into its central position. This equalizes the pressure on the two sides of the piston, and the cylinder itself, under the action of the side springs S, returns to its central position, at the same time closing the byepass valve. The whole apparatus is now ready to respond to a further change of speed in either direction. Some relay returning device of this nature is indispensable if hunting is to be prevented (Art. 139).

An extremely neat device for the same purpose is illustrated in Fig. 202,[1] and is shown in Fig. 203 [1] as fitted to a twin Pelton wheel.

Here the horizontal governor lever A B is not connected to any fixed fulcrum, but is pivoted at A on the end of a plunger working in the dashpot C. At B it is connected to the spindle of the regulating valve, F being a fixed fulcrum. A subsidiary lever connects the end of the plunger working in the dashpot P with the anchor link L and with the governor collar, this being solely for the purpose of steadying the motion of the governor.

On a sudden increase in speed, following a reduction in load, the governor collar lifts and the valve spindle is depressed, admitting water

[1] By courtesy of Messrs. Gilbert Gilkes & Co., Ltd., Kendal.

behind the relay piston and forcing the spear rod into the nozzle.   This
spear rod is connected with the dashpot C, which itself works in the outer
fixed casing K, by a series of links and a bell-crank lever not shown in the
sketch, and as the spear rod moves to the right the dashpot is lifted,
raising at the same time the fulcrum A.   During this portion of the
motion, there is a slight downward motion of the dashpot plunger and
fulcrum relative to the cylinder.   As the motion of the latter ceases, however, the plunger is gradually lifted by the weighted lever W, bringing

FIG. 203.—Twin Pelton Wheel with Hydraulic Relay Governor.

down the pin at B, and returning the valve to its central position with the
governor lever also in its central position.

Any further motion of the spear rod is thus stopped until the wheel
has had time to readjust itself to the changed conditions, when the whole
arrangement is again ready to adjust itself to any fresh change of speed.

Water ram on closing the nozzle may, if necessary, be prevented by a
special automatic device of the makers.   In this the spear rod is directly
connected through a link with a dashpot plunger, the cylinder of which is
vertical, is capable of axial movement, and which is itself connected to a
small needle valve which is opened by any upward motion of the
cylinder.   The main relief valve is slightly overbalanced hydraulically so

as to remain closed whatever the pressure in the main. If, however, the spear rod closes the nozzle rapidly, the sudden motion of the dashpot plunger sucks up the dashpot cylinder and with it the small needle valve. This allows water to escape from above the main relief valve, which is then lifted by the excess pressure on its under side and permits of free discharge from the body of the nozzle.

The dashpot cylinder now begins to fall by its own weight, closing the needle valve and thus the relief valve, the time of closing being adjusted

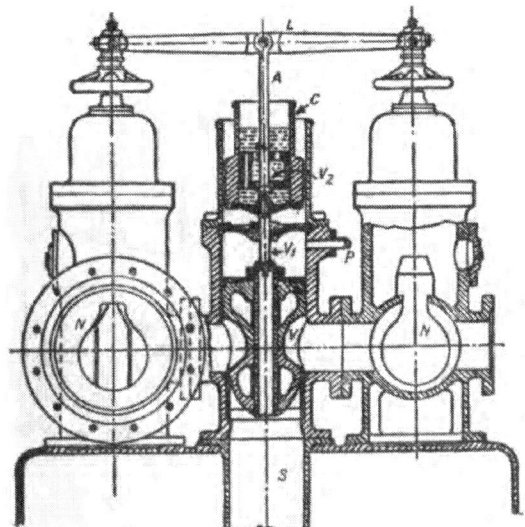

FIG. 204.—Pressure Regulator for Pelton Wheel.

by regulation of the dashpot orifices to suit the length of the supply pipe line.

This system has the great advantage that its working is quite independent of any rise in pressure in the main, but rather anticipates any such possible rise.

Fig. 204 shows details of a device working on exactly the same principle, and applied in this case to the twin Pelton wheel shown in Fig. 205. Here the cross lever L is connected to the piston rods of the two relay cylinders, and carries the dashpot rod A. Its connected plunger works in the weighted dashpot C, which itself carries the needle valve V_1. Pressure water supplied through the small pipe P keeps the main escape valve V closed so long as the valve V_1 is closed. If this valve is opened, however. by a sudden upward motion of L, the pressure above the main valve is relieved, and the valve opens, relieving the pressure at the nozzles $N N$.

The valve V_2 permits of a sudden depression of L, without unduly stressing the dashpot rod A.

A modification of the needle method of regulation is indicated in

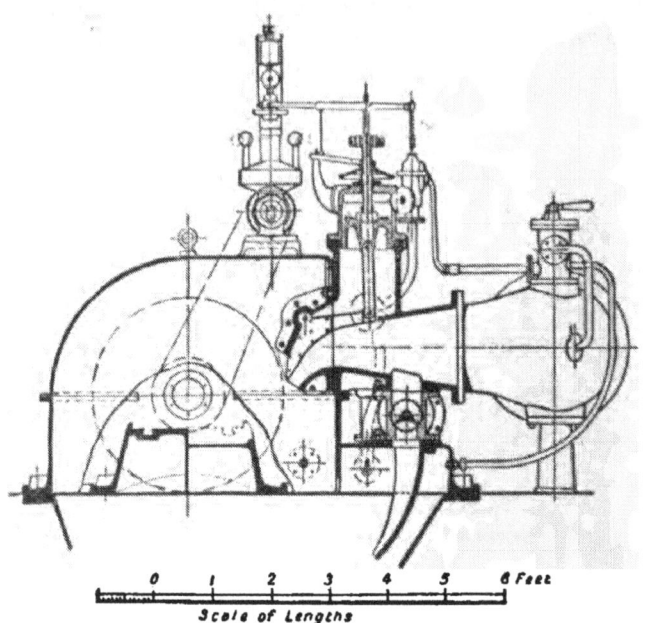

FIG. 205.—Double Tangential Impulse Wheel, 500 H.P. at 375 Revolutions under 262 feet head; wheel diameter 3·28 feet. The Kubel Electric Power Plant, St. Gall.

Fig. 205,[1] which shows a section of a double tangential wheel of 3·28 feet diameter developing 500 H.P. under a head of 262 feet. Here the nozzle is rectangular in section, while its upper side is formed by a pivoted flap whose position is regulated by that of the piston of a relay cylinder actuated by the governor. The area of this piston is so large that when its upper side is relieved of pressure, the upward pressure on its lower

---

[1] By courtesy of Messrs. Escher, Wyss & Cie., Zurich.

face, which is in communication with the nozzle, is sufficient to close the flap. Pressure water from the nozzle is supplied to the regulating valve V (Fig. 206) which regulates the pressure on the top of piston P. If the speed of the wheel increases the governor sleeve rises and the lever $A\ C$ turns about the fulcrum B, depressing valve V and putting the upper side of piston P into communication with the exhaust. This piston rises, closing the nozzle, and also lifting the point of attachment F of the link $F\ B$. This raises B and also C and brings the valve V into a new position of equilibrium, in which it is prepared to take control of any fresh change of speed. A striking feature of this installation is that it is fitted with a draught tube (Art. 184), and works under a suction head of 22 feet.

(4) A modern and very common method of regulation is illustrated in Fig. 207. Here a combination needle and deflecting nozzle is used, the needle being set by hand, so as to take the maximum load likely to occur during any hour, while the deflection takes care of any variation of load up to this peak. With a very variable load, such as occurs in electric lighting plants, considerable

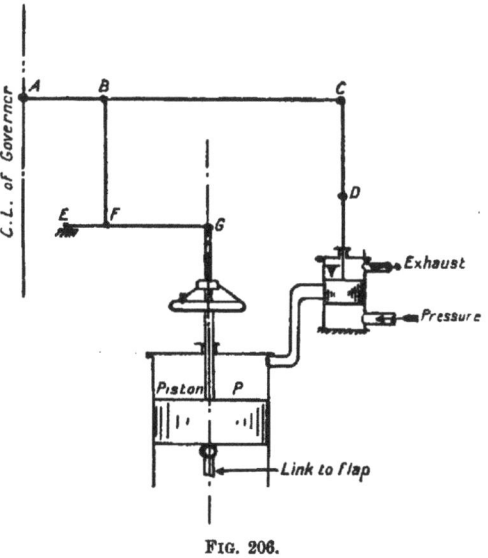

FIG. 206.

economy may thus be effected, while the possibility of water ram is eliminated.

A self-regulating wheel which has been tried with good results as regards speed regulation consists of two discs mounted side by side on the same shaft and capable of relative sidelong motion. These are kept in position by springs, and each carries a series of half buckets which fit together when the discs are close together and then form ordinary Pelton buckets. An increase in speed, by the consequent increased centrifugal force on masses mounted on bell-crank levers connected to the wheel, produces a relative sidelong motion of the discs, which part in the middle and allow a portion of the jet to pass through to waste.

The complication introduced by this device, together with the waste of energy common to any such method of governing, form the chief drawbacks to the scheme.

The table on the opposite page gives some details of typical Pelton wheel installations of comparatively recent date.

If desired, two or three jets may be arranged so as to play on a single wheel, and the power obtained is then practically proportional to the

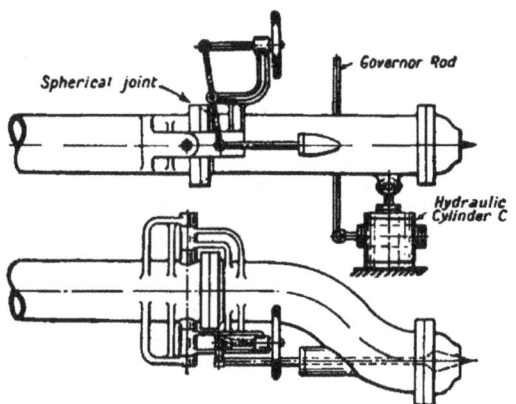

FIG. 207.—Combined Needle and Deflecting Nozzle.

number of jets. In such a case the sliding hood provides the most convenient method of speed regulation.

For heads above 400 feet, and for powers in single units up to about 2,000 B.H.P., the Pelton wheel is by far the most suitable type of prime mover, while for units up to 15,000 H.P. and with heads ranging from 100 to 400 feet, it is for many purposes to be preferred to its only serious rival, the inward radial flow or Francis turbine. In view of its combined simplicity, efficiency, and ease of regulation, it is probably the most perfect of all hydraulic prime movers, and this may be the more readily granted when the difficult conditions under which it works are remembered. Taking a jet of water to all intents and appearances as rigid as a rod of glass, and, in virtue of its enormous velocity, possessing almost infinite destructive possibilities ; dropping it almost without splash into the tail-race divested of practically the whole of its kinetic

Locality.	Head at nozzle in feet	Number and Diameter of Wheels—Details of Governing Device, etc.	Number and size of nozzles on each wheel.	Revolutions per minute.	Speed of Buckets.	Velocity of Jets f.s.	Horse Power of each wheel.	Efficiency.
Cauvery Falls	382·5	4 wheels, 4' 6" diam., 24 buckets to each wheel. Nozzle throttling valves. With 25% load variation speed varies 3%; " 50% " " " 5%; " 100% " " " 10%	2 nozzles, each 5" × 4"	300	70·7 f.s.	154·7 f.s.	1,015	75% guaranteed, 70% at half gate.
Pike's Peak Power Company, Colorado	1,160	1 wheel, 68" diam.	1 nozzle, 1" diam.	450	132 f.s.	270 f.s.	236	83%
Los Angeles, 1907	810	4 wheels, 10' diam.; 18 buckets, each 28" wide; combined needle and deflecting nozzles	1 nozzle, 7¼" diam.	250	131 f.s.	225·5 f.s.	5,800 (approx.)	?
University of California, 1884	50 8	1 wheel, 15" diam.	1—⅞" nozzle, 1—⅝" nozzle, 1—⅞" nozzle					82·6%, 82·5%, 73·0%
McGill University, 1895	235	1 wheel, 18" diam.	1—·55" nozzle, 1—·75" nozzle	276, 750	21·72 f.s., 59·5 f.s.	121·4 f.s.		87·9%, 70·8%
Grass Valley	380·5	1 wheel, 72" diam.	1—1·89" nozzle	225·5	70·8 f.s.	155·7 f.s.		87·3%
Cerro Anos, 1906	98	1 wheel, 20' 0" diam., governed by throttle valve placed behind nozzles. 48 buckets	2 nozzles, 4½" and 4¾" diam.	36	37·7 f.s.	78·3 f.s.	140	?
Pike's Peak Hydro-Electric Company, Manitou	2,170	3 wheels, each 7' 4" diam. on pitch circle, 7' 9" diam over all. Pressure at nozzles when operating 940 lbs. sq. inch; stat. pressure 1,047 lbs. sq. inch; regulation by combined needle and deflecting nozzles. 36 buckets	1 nozzle, 2¼" diam.	450	173 f.s.	368·2 f.s.	2,000 (approx.)	?
Plant No. 5 San Joaquin Light and Power Company, 1908, Doble wheels	385	2 wheels, each delivering 1,750 H.P., governing by Doble needle regulating nozzles. 55" diam.	1 nozzle, 6" diam.	380	72·0 f.s.	155·0 f.s.	353, 484, 715, 1,730, 1,780	77·8%, 79·5%, 81·4%, 83·0%, 83·9%
Cornell University	134	2 main wheels of 280 B.H.P., Doble needle regulating nozzles. 6' 0" diam.	1 nozzle, 7" diam.	124	42·2 f.s.	91·5 f.s.	70, 140, 210, 280, 370	70·8%, 75·5%, 79·3%, 80·7%, 82·1%
Cornell University	134	2 Exciter wheels of 50 B.H.P., Doble needle regulating nozzles. 3' 1" diam.	1 nozzle, 3" diam.	260	42·0 f.s.	91·5 f.s.	12·5, 25·0, 37·5, 70·0, 62·5	77·8%, 82·6%, 84·4%, 84·3%, 84·4%

In each case the velocity at the nozzle has been calculated from the formula $v = c_v \sqrt{2gh}$, where $c_v = ·965$.

energy; the whole affords an unique example of the possibilities of engineering science.

Design of Pelton Wheel.

EXAMPLE.

To design a Pelton wheel to work under an effective head of 500 feet and to develop 800 H.P. at 360 revolutions per minute.

Assuming a coefficient of velocity = ·985, the velocity of efflux of the jet = ·985 × $\sqrt{500 \times 64\cdot4}$

= 177 feet per second.

Taking the velocity of the pitch circle of the wheel as ·46 times that of the jet, we have

Peripheral velocity of wheel = 81·3 feet per second.

∴   Radius of pitch circle = $\dfrac{81\cdot3 \times 60}{2\,\pi \times 360}$ = 2·158 feet.

∴   Diameter of pitch circle = 4 feet 3¾ inches.

Next assuming an efficiency of 85 per cent., we have the energy passing the nozzle per second given by $\dfrac{800 \times 550}{\cdot85}$ ft. lbs. = 518,000 ft. lbs., and

since each cubic foot of water contains $\dfrac{62\cdot4 \times (177)^2}{2\,g}$ ft. lbs. = 30,380

ft. lbs. in the form of kinetic energy, this requires $\dfrac{518,000}{30,380}$ = 17·06 cubic feet per second.

The required area of the nozzle is thus $\dfrac{17\cdot06}{177}$ = ·0964 sq. ft.

= 13·89 sq. ins.

giving a jet diameter of 4·20 inches.

Taking $n = 7\cdot5 \sqrt{\dfrac{r}{t}}$, this gives the number of buckets as equal to

$7\cdot5 \sqrt{\dfrac{25\cdot9}{4\cdot22}}$ = 18·6, or say 20 for convenience in balancing.

Next applying the formula $n = \dfrac{\pi}{\sqrt{1 - \left(\dfrac{r + \dfrac{t}{2}}{r + s} \right)}}$, we get, on

substituting for n, r and t, on reduction $s = 2\cdot5$ inches, giving the amount by which the buckets must project beyond the pitch circle for continuous impact.   For safety it is usual to increase this slightly, say to 2·75 inches, giving an extreme wheel diameter of 4 feet 9¼ inches.

The buckets would in this case be about 21 inches wide.

ART. 126.—JETS FROM NEEDLE-NOZZLE.

The presence of the central needle in a nozzle provided with needle regulation causes a reduction in the velocity of the central filament,

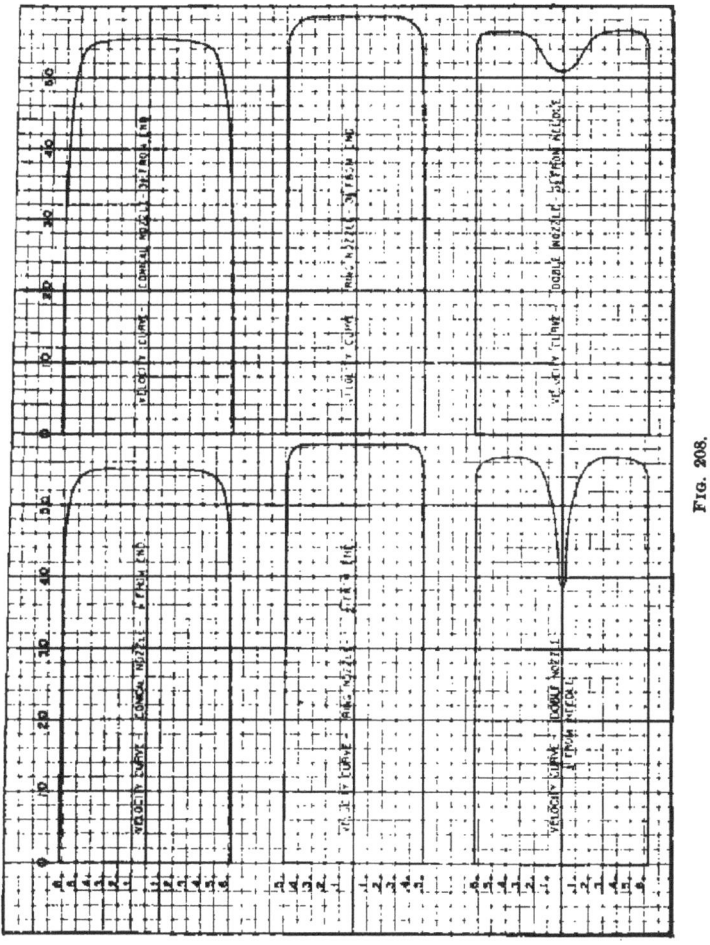

FIG. 208.

.nd to this extent tends to reduce the efficiency of the jet. Fig. 208 .hows the velocity obtained at different points in the cross section of . jet obtained respectively from a plain conical nozzle, a ring nozzle

and a Pelton wheel nozzle with needle regulator.[1]   From these it appears
that the central velocity at a point distant $\frac{1}{2}$ inch from the tip of the needle
is only ·68 of the maximum velocity.   At a section 3½ inches from the tip
this ratio becomes ·90, while when the distance is 9½ inches it becomes ·96.

At mid opening (diameter 1·25 inches) the coefficient of velocity diminishes slightly as the head increases, from about ·992 with 23 feet head to
·978 with 120 feet head.   With a given head the velocity was slightly the

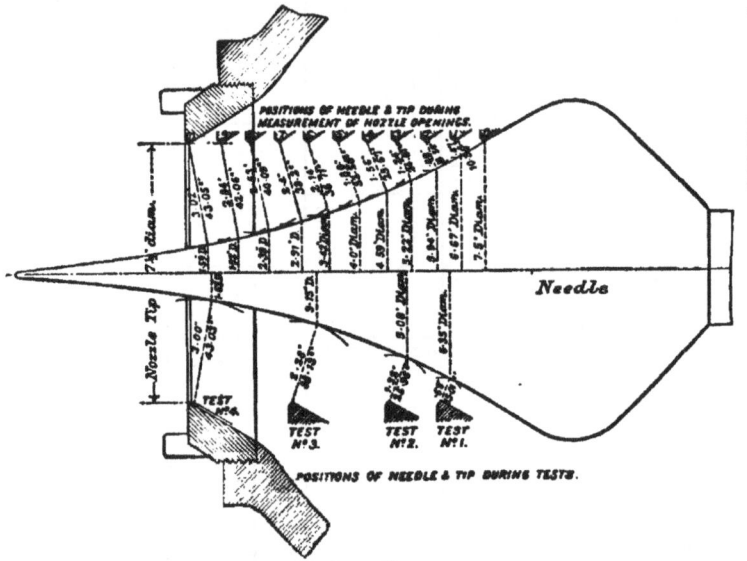

Fig. 209.

greatest with the nozzle half open.   The efficiencies in these experiments
varied from ·964 to ·998.   The maximum jet diameter was 1·50 inches.

Experiments on a larger nozzle, giving a jet up to 7 inches diameter
under heads up to 850 feet,[2] showed the following results :

Distance from centre of jet (inches).	0·0	·5	1·0	2·0	3·0
Velocity (feet per second)	212·7	228·7	229·3	229·9	227·8

[1] From a Thesis by H. C. Crowell and G. C. Lenthe (Massachusetts Institute of
Technology. 1903).
[2] W. R. Eckhart, Inst. Mech. Engineers, January, 1910.

The coefficient of velocity increased from ·971 to ·989 as the nozzle area was increased, the coefficient of discharge diminishing at the same time from ·965 to ·838, and the efficiency increasing from ·958 to ·986. Fig. 209 shows the shape of needle and tip used in these experiments.

EXAMPLES.

(1) A Pelton wheel working under an effective head of 2,100 feet is 36″ diameter and is supplied through a single $\frac{1}{4}$″ nozzle. Determine the necessary number of revolutions of the wheel for approximately maximum efficiency and the probable horse-power, assuming an efficiency of 83 per cent.

$$\text{Answer.} \quad \begin{cases} 1,060 \text{ revolutions per minute.} \\ 97·5 \text{ H.P.} \end{cases}$$

(2) A Pelton wheel develops 140 B.H.P. under a head of 98 feet. The wheel is 20′ 0″ in diameter, and is supplied by two nozzles. Determine the number of revolutions per minute and the necessary nozzle diameter, if the efficiency is 80 per cent.

$$\text{Answer.} \quad \begin{cases} 35 \text{ revolutions per minute.} \\ \text{Diam.} = 4·3 \text{ ins.} \end{cases}$$

(3) Show that the efficiency of a Pelton wheel is theoretically equal to

$$\frac{2\,\pi\,r\,N}{60\,g\,h} \left\{ C_v \sqrt{2\,g\,h} - \frac{2\,\pi\,r\,N}{60} \right\} \left\{ 1 - k \cos a \right\}$$

Where r = mean radius of bucket circle.

$\quad N$ = revolutions per minute.

$\quad h$ = effective head at nozzle.

$\quad C_v$ = coefficient of velocity at nozzle.

$\quad k$ = ratio of relative velocity at exit from and entrance to buckets.

$\quad a$ = total angle through which jet is deflected.

CHAPTER XIV

ART. 127.—TURBINES.

IN general, by a turbine is meant a water-wheel which is so arranged as to allow of water being admitted simultaneously at all points on its circumference, thus enabling a greatly increased power to be obtained with the same wheel diameter.

Turbines may be divided into two main classes, known respectively as *Impulse* turbines and as *Pressure or Reaction* turbines, according to the manner in which they abstract energy from the supply water.

In an impulse turbine, the whole head of the supply water is converted into kinetic energy before the wheel is reached, the water issuing from the nozzles or guide passages in a series of streams or jets moving with high velocity and exposed to the pressure (usually atmospheric) obtaining in the turbine casing. It then enters a series of buckets formed by curved vanes in the turbine wheel, and in virtue of the change of direction, and hence of tangential momentum produced by these vanes, exerts a driving force, and so does work on the turbine shaft. Its surface pressure remains uniform throughout the turbine if this is correctly designed, and its direction is freely deviated by the vanes. For this reason, this is sometimes termed a turbine of free deviation.

For the pressure to remain uniform throughout the wheel it is essential that the stream should not fill the space between any two moving vanes, and to prevent this occurring the buckets are usually ventilated as shown in Fig. 210, which represents a part section through the wheel and guides of a Girard turbine.

In a *Pressure or Reaction* turbine, the water on leaving the guide vanes and entering the wheel is under pressure, and thus supplies energy partly in the kinetic and partly in the pressure form. In its passage through the wheel this pressure energy is gradually converted into kinetic energy, and the water finally leaves the wheel at a pressure not sensibly greater than that of the atmosphere. The change of momentum accompanying this change from pressure head to velocity head necessitates an equivalent reaction on the moving vanes, and work is thus done on the turbine shaft. This turbine, as well as the impulse type, therefore owes its propelling force not to statical pressure, but to changes of momentum, the pressure difference over the concave and convex faces of a bucket being produced, as in the impulse wheel, by the change of momentum in the stream passing the bucket. In the case of a wheel having vertical downward flow the weight of the water also adds to this propelling force.

Since the turbine works under pressure the buckets should always

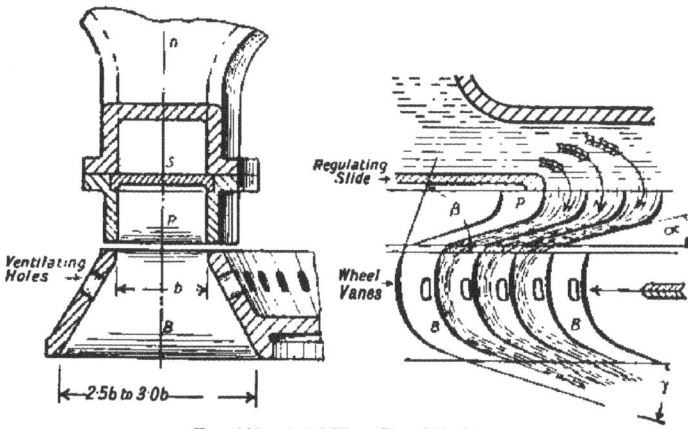

FIG. 210.—Axial Flow Girard Turbine.

remain full of water, and to this end admission should take place continuously all around the circumference of the wheel. If not, those buckets which happen to be idle will either be empty, having discharged their contents into the discharge pipe, or will contain dead water. In the first case the buckets must be refilled before the pressure at the circumference can be utilised, while in the second case the necessity for imparting momentum to this dead water causes loss of energy by impact. In either case the loss of energy may be considerable. In the impulse wheel, on the other hand, the supply may be admitted either wholly or partially around the circumference without loss of energy.

These two main types of turbine may be subdivided, according as the general direction of flow through the wheel is radial and perpendicular

to the axis, parallel to the axis, or is a combination of these, these sul-
types being designated respectively as

Radial flow
Axial or parallel flow } turbines.
Mixed flow

Radial flow turbines may again be subdivided into inward flow
machines, when flow takes place from the circumference to the centre of
the wheel, and outward flow when the flow is in the opposite direction.

The chief turbines in the various classes are :—

(1) **Impulse Turbines.**

Axial or radial flow   .   .   Girard turbine.
Mixed flow   .   .   .   .   Pelton wheel.

(2) **Pressure or Reaction Turbines.**

Radial flow {
    (a) *Inward.*—Thomson vortex turbine and the original
        Francis turbine.
    (b) *Outward.*—Fourneyron turbine.

Axial flow   .   .   Borda turbine, Henschel-Jonval turbine.
Mixed flow   .   .   Hercules, Victor, and other turbines of the Ameri-
                can type.   All modern Francis turbines are to
                a certain extent of the mixed flow type.

One special type of turbine, the Haenel, may work either as an impulse
or pressure wheel.

ART. 128.—THE IMPULSE TURBINE.

All impulse turbines may be considered as modifications of the
tangential or Pelton wheel, in which the jet is unconfined laterally.

Where the supply head is very great the necessary peripheral speed of
a turbine to take full advantage of this is also great, while, as will be
shown later, the necessary speed is greater in the case of a pressure
turbine than with one of the impulse type.   This peripheral speed may
be obtained either by having a wheel of large diameter with low angular
velocity, or with a small wheel making a large number of revolutions per
minute, and for a pressure turbine, where it is necessary to admit water
all around the circumference, it is imperative that the periphery, and
therefore the diameter, be comparatively small, and the angular velocity
in consequence high.   For many purposes the necessary speed of rotation
under very high heads then becomes too great, while the hydraulic resistances inside the turbine casing become excessive.

In such a case the pressure turbine suffers from the further disadvantage that the ports and passages are of necessity small and constricted in

area, and are in consequence liable to be choked by any floating matter which may escape the strainers in the head-race.

For very high falls, then, the most suitable turbine is one in which the wheel itself is not submerged; in which the supply may be admitted to as much of the circumference as is necessary to develop the required power; and such that any particular diameter may be adopted which will best suit the desired speed of rotation.

The impulse turbine in the form of the tangential water-wheel or of the Girard turbine satisfies these conditions within wide limits, and for heads between 100 and 300 feet will often, and for heads above 300 feet will generally be the most suitable type of prime mover for all but the largest powers. Since with suitable means of regulation the jet velocity

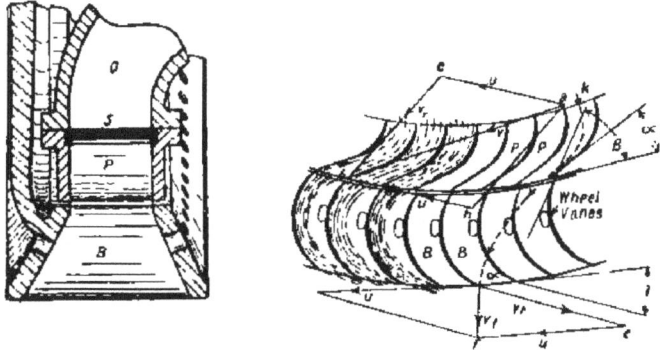

Fig. 211.—Girard Turbine with Outward Radial Flow.

s constant under a constant supply head for all loads, under these circumstances the efficiency of an impulse turbine is approximately ndependent of the load, the variation in efficiency being chiefly due to he proportionately greater effect of mechanical friction and of air resistance or windage at low loads.

Art. 129.—The Girard Turbine.

This turbine may be constructed either as an axial flow machine Fig. 210), in which case the axis is usually vertical, or with inward or more commonly outward radial flow (Figs. 211 and 212). With radial ow the axis may be either vertical or horizontal. The axial flow type s more suitable for large powers under comparatively low heads, where ill circumferential injection is required.

H.A.   H H

Pressure water supplied through the pipe Q is guided by the converging passages $P\ P$, its pressure diminishing as its velocity increases and is discharged at atmospheric pressure into the moving buckets $B\ B$. These are ventilated to prevent the jet expanding to touch the rear vane, and since the width of bucket diminishes with the angle of inclination of the vanes, they are also splayed out from the inlet to the discharge side, the breadth at discharge usually varying from 2·5 to 3 times that at inlet. The outward deviation produced by this splaying of the buckets, while slightly diminishing the efficiency of working, cannot be avoided. The guide and vane angles at entry and exit are so designed that water

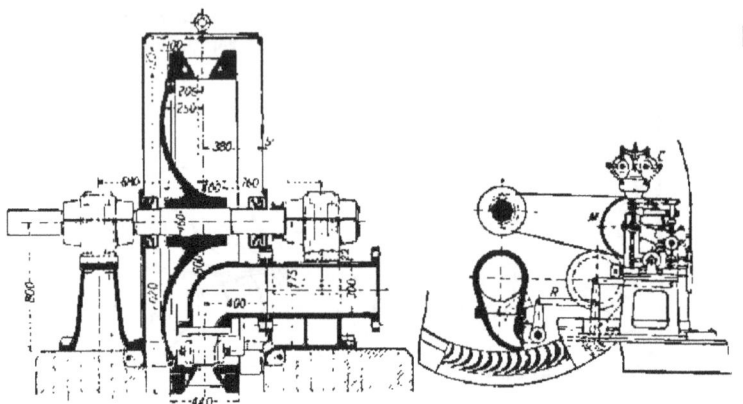

FIG. 212.—Partial Admission Girard Turbine.　1,000 H.P. at 500 revolutions per minute under 1,640 ft. head.

enters the buckets without shock, and is discharged with an absolute velocity which is only sufficiently great to ensure its ready removal from the wheel.

When less power is required one or more of the inlet passages may be cut off by means of the slide S, the motion being regulated either by hand or by a governor. By the provision of a series of supply ports which may be completely cut out of action one by one, the loss of energy which is inevitable through contraction and re-enlargement of section whenever a stream is throttled, is reduced to a minimum. Where only one admission port is used, the supply should be regulated by means of a sluice or hood working between the port and the entrance to the buckets. By this means the velocity of efflux is unaltered, and the only loss introduced is that which may be caused by any alteration in the angle of impact of the jet.

Fig. 212 shows such a turbine, built by Messrs. Piccard, Pictet & Co., of Geneva, and developing 1,000 H.P. at 500 revolutions per minute, under a head of 1,640 feet.

In a radial flow machine having full circumferential admission, a cylindrical sluice or gate is often used, this partially cutting off the supply to each bucket.

While specially well fitted for heads of 100 feet and upwards, this turbine, with full circumferential injection, gives good results with heads from 10 to 50 feet, and has indeed been used with a head as low as 16½ inches. Under the latter head an efficiency of about 55 per cent. may be attained. With low heads and full injection the wheel must be horizontal, since with a vertical wheel the jet velocity at the highest and lowest points would be very different, while at the same time the loss of head due to the difference in level of the guide vanes at exit and the tail-race would become serious. To avoid the latter loss as far as possible in the case of a vertical wheel with partial injection, the guides are placed as near the bottom of the wheel as practicable. The horizontal wheel offers the further advantage for large volumes of water, in that it affords greater facilities for getting rid of a complete circumferential discharge.

In common with all impulse turbines, the part gate efficiency is high, while under suitable conditions the full load efficiency may amount to 80 per cent. In the case of an outward flow Girard turbine described in the "Proceedings of the Institution of Civil Engineers,"[1] and giving 400 H.P. under 594 feet head, the outer diameter of the wheel was 8' 11", inside diameter 7' 10¼", the vanes, 110 in number, were 4·7 inches wide at the entrance, and were splayed out to 15¾ inches. A single inlet passage was used 4·81 inches in width. Under this head the jet velocity was 181·6 feet per second, and the efficiencies were as follows :—

B.H.P.	Revolutions.	Efficiency.
82·5	211	59·5 %
341	210	76·4 %
400	209	79·0 %

In this type of impulse wheel the impossibility of making the

[1] 1881-2, Part 4.

tangential to the wheel at entrance, and the necessity for the escaping stream to clear the discharge from the following bucket render it impossible to deflect the jet through 180°. If a is the angle which the incoming jet makes with the plane of the wheel in an axial flow turbine and with the tangent plane to the wheel at the point of impact in a radial flow machine, and if γ be the angle which the discharge tips of the vanes make with the same plane (Figs. 210 and 211), a is generally made about 24° and γ about 21°. These values, however, depend upon the head increasing from about 12° and 13° respectively, with large heads and small volumes of water, to about 30° and 28° with low heads and large volumes. β, the angle of inclination of the vanes at entrance is then made so that the entering stream slides along the vanes without shock.

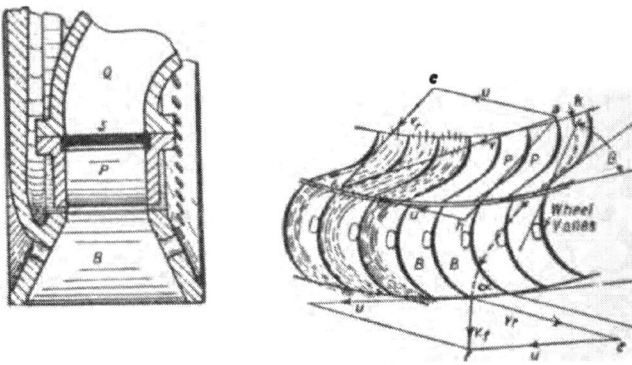

FIG. 211.

The construction for determining the vane angles is shown in Fig. 211. Here $a\,b$ represents v, the velocity of the stream leaving the guide vanes, in magnitude and direction, while $h\,b = a\,c$ represents u, the velocity of the wheel buckets at the point of entry. $c\,b = a\,h$ then represents the relative velocity at entrance to the buckets, and marks the correct inclination of the bucket tips.

In order to take advantage of the full head any impulse turbine working under atmospheric pressure should be located at as small an elevation above the tail-race as is possible. While keeping this in view, however, it is highly important that the situation of the wheel be such that it is not liable to become submerged by a raising of the tail-race level in time of flood. If this should occur the buckets run full, the wheel works as a pressure turbine, the conditions for which it is designed are entirely violated and efficient working becomes impossible.

This often necessitates the sacrificing of a portion of the available head, and, with a low fall, renders the use of such a turbine inadvisable. With a high fall such proportional loss is in general so small as to be negligible.

Attempts have been made to remove this drawback to the impulse turbine. Thus Girard, in his system of Hydro-pneumatization, placed the whole turbine in an air-tight casing, the lower end of which opened out beneath the surface in the tail-race (Fig. 213). By means of an air pump driven by the turbine the air in this casing was maintained at such a pressure as to keep the water level inside the casing below that of the turbine wheel, whatever the tail-race level. The complication and expense thus introduced, however, together with the fact that power is required to work the air pump, prevented the general adoption of this idea.

By mounting the wheel in an air-tight casing at some distance above the tail-race and coupling this to a discharge pipe or draught tube (Art. 184), delivering below the surface of the tail-race, the difficulty may be overcome. On starting up the turbine the escaping water ejects the air from the casing and creates a partial vacuum. An air valve, actuated by a float in a chamber connected with both casing and draught tube, then admits sufficient air to prevent the water level from rising as high as the

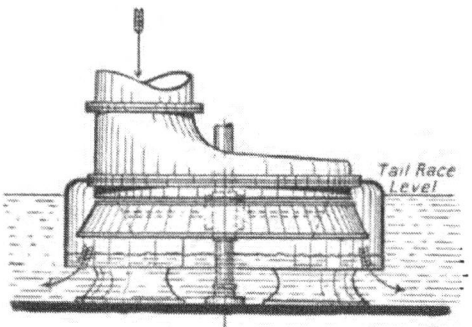

Fig. 213.—Axial Flow Girard Turbine with Full Circumferential Injection and with Girard's System of Hydropneumatization.

wheel. Fig. 205 shows one of a series of double Pelton wheels of 500 H.P. which work perfectly well under a suction head of 20 feet.

An older device, due to Meunier, consisted in regulating the discharge by means of a sluice automatically regulated by a float. The required level in the turbine casing was thus maintained, and the addition of a draught tube rendered possible.

In the *Haenel* "limit" turbine, which is essentially the same as the Girard, the buckets are so designed that they run full when working as an impulse turbine, the areas of the wheel passages being approximately the same throughout. The flooding of the turbine does not then affect its efficiency except in so far as it affects the available head, since the machine then acts as a pressure turbine. It is fairly good for low falls with a head which does not vary greatly, while its efficiency varies from about 60 per cent. at half gate to a maximum of about 72 per cent. It is seldom met with in modern practice.

Whether a horizontal or a vertical shaft machine is to be preferred depends largely on the location of the plant.

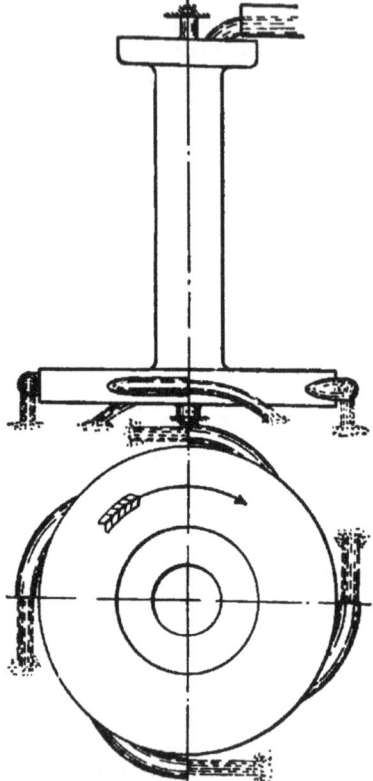

FIG. 214.—Barker's Mill.

The horizontal shaft design gives a motor which is very accessible, and which is conveniently situated for gearing by means of belting to other machinery, and where the power-house is situated near the tail-race level, the supply being conveyed from the head-race by pipes, this design will in general be adopted, the turbines being placed directly on the floor of the power-house. Where the more convenient site for the power-house is near the head-race, a well must be sunk down to tail-race level, connected to the tail-race by means of a tunnel or pipe, and the turbines erected at the bottom of this well. A vertical shaft machine is now almost essential, this shaft being carried vertically upwards into the power-house and supported at intervals by suitable bearings. When driving an electrical generator this forms a convenient arrangement. The armature is mounted directly on the rotating shaft, and the arrangement has the further advantage that since all the electrical machinery may be placed well above the head-race level it is not likely to be affected by floods. This arrangement is, however, in general not to be recommended where it is possible to place the power station near the tail-race level. Not only is the turbine well costly to construct, but the cost of construction of the discharge tunnel or pipe line is much greater than that of the

corresponding length of the supply pipe line in the latter scheme. In fact, in all turbine schemes, it may be taken as a general principle that the cost per unit length of tail-race is greater than that of head-race or supply pipe. Also the necessity for a long and heavy vertical shaft increases the first cost of the turbine, renders it less accessible, and involves the use of expensive and complicated bearings for dealing with the end thrust thus set up.[1]

ART. 130.—PRESSURE OR RE-
ACTION TURBINES.

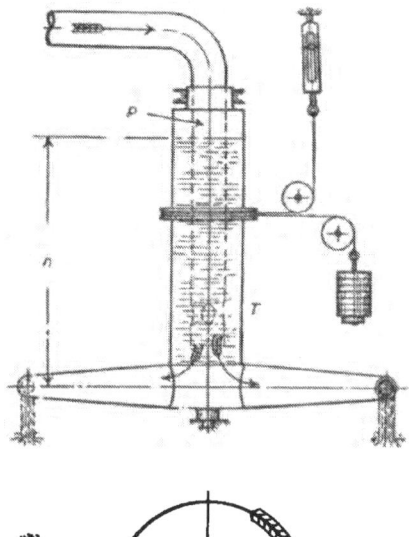

All pressure turbines of the radial outward flow type may be considered as modifications of the old Scotch turbine—Re-action wheel, Barker's mill, or Segner's turbine, as it is variously called. In this turbine (Figs. 214 and 215), water is admitted through a vertical supply pipe, flows outwards through straight or curved horizontal arms, and escapes through orifices so placed in these arms as to give a series of horizontal jets perpendicular to the diameters containing the orifices. The reaction of the jets then produces rotation of

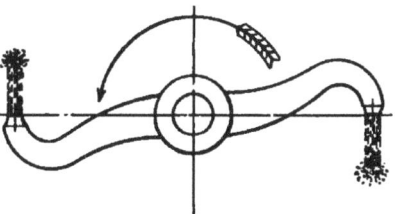

FIG. 215.—Barker's Mill.

the wheel. This is, however, only made in small sizes and is not of practical importance.

Theory of the Barker's Mill.

Let v = velocity of water issuing from each nozzle relatively to the nozzle, in feet per second.

Let u = velocity of nozzle relatively to the ground.

Then $v - u$ = absolute velocity of discharge.

[1] For a description of such bearings see Arts. 133 and 135, and Figs. 225 and 234D.

Let Q = volume of water discharged per second in cubic feet.

„ h = head of water above the orifice in feet.

Then the horizontal reaction of the jets, i.e., the momentum generated per second $\Big\}$ = $\dfrac{Q\,W}{g}(v - u)$ lbs.

∴ Work done by this reaction per second $\Big\}$ = $U = \dfrac{Q\,W}{g}(v - u)\,u$ ft. lbs.

The energy given to the wheel per second $\Big\}$ = $Q\,W\,h$.

$$\therefore \text{ Efficiency} = \frac{(v - u)\,u}{g\,h} = \eta.$$

Again, the total head at the orifice is the sum of the pressure due to the head h and of the kinetic head due to the velocity of whirl u, so that, neglecting friction,

$$\frac{v^2}{2\,g} = h + \frac{u^2}{2\,g}.$$

Substituting this value of v in the expression for the efficiency, we get

$$\eta = \frac{u^2}{g\,h}\left\{\sqrt{1 + \frac{2\,g\,h}{u^2}} - 1\right\}$$

Differentiating this with respect to u and equating the result to zero, we finally get for maximum efficiency $\dfrac{g\,h}{u^2} = 0$, a result which can only be true when u is infinitely large. It follows that with a frictionless wheel the efficiency would increase with the speed and would become unity when the speed was infinite. Actually, however, frictional losses, which increase with the speed, cause a maximum efficiency to be obtained at some definite speed with any given wheel.

Taking frictional resistances inside the wheel into account, and assuming these to be proportional to v^2 and to equal $F\,\dfrac{v^2}{2\,g}$ we have :—

Total head behind orifice = $h + \dfrac{u^2}{2\,g}$.

This must equal the kinetic energy at the orifice together with the loss by friction

$$\therefore\; h + \frac{u^2}{2\,g} = \frac{v^2}{2\,g} + F\,\frac{v^2}{2\,g} = \frac{v^2}{2\,g}(1 + F)$$

$$\therefore\; v^2(1 + F) - u^2 = 2\,g\,h.$$

Substituting this value of v in the expression for the efficiency, this now becomes

$$\eta = \frac{u}{g\,h}\left\{\sqrt{\frac{2\,g\,h + u^2}{1 + F}} - u\right\}$$

and on differentiating and equating the result to zero we get, for maximum efficiency

$$u^2 = \left\{ \sqrt{1 + \frac{1}{F}} - 1 \right\} g\,h.$$

In general the maximum hydraulic efficiency of the wheel does not

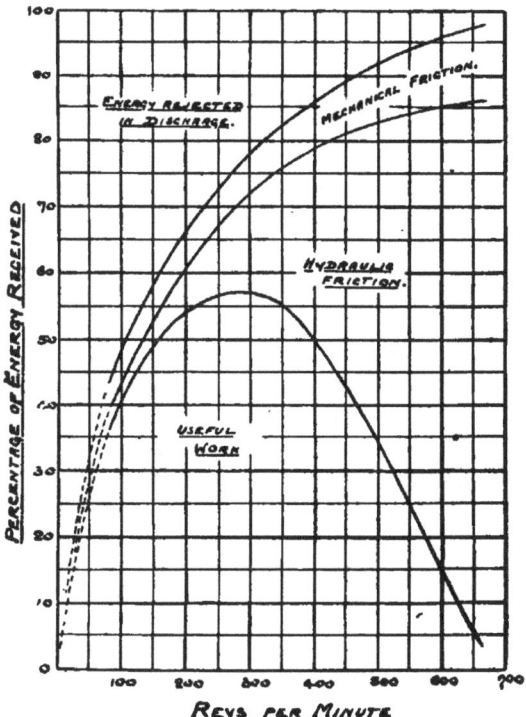

Fig. 216.—Curves showing Distribution of Energy in a Barker's Mill.

exceed 66·0 per cent., while the mechanical friction losses bring this down to about 60 per cent.

If the wheel is loaded by means of a brake, the magnitude of the various transformations of energy may be determined as follows :—

Let L = nett brake moment in foot pounds.

N = number of revolutions of wheel per second.

Then useful work per second $= 2\,\pi\,L\,N$ ft. lbs. $= U$, while the energy rejected in the discharge

$$= \frac{Q W (v - u)^2}{2 g} \text{ ft. lbs.} = E_W.$$

From this we have :—

Energy lost inside the wheel by hydraulic friction, etc.

= Energy given to wheel, — Energy accounted for per second

$$= Q W \left[h - \frac{(v - u)^2}{2 g} - \frac{(v - u)}{g} u \right] = E_F.$$

Energy lost per second in overcoming friction of bearings

$$= E_B = \frac{Q W (v - u) u}{g} - 2 \pi L N, \text{giving } E_F + E_B + E_W + U = Q W h$$

The distribution of energy may be shown graphically as in Fig. 216, which records the results of a series of trials by the author on such a wheel. The details of the wheel were as follows :—

Diameter of nozzles	·253 inches.
Number of nozzles	2.
Radius of nozzle path	5·875 inches.
Head of water above nozzles	3·20 feet.

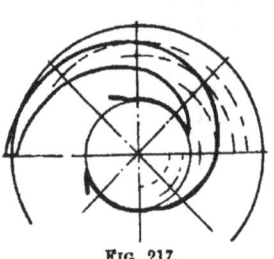

FIG. 217.

In these trials the power was absorbed by means of a Prony brake applied to a horizontal drum. Water is admitted by means of a vertical down pipe P (Fig. 215) open at the bottom, and concentric with the rotating tube T, and trouble caused by the entrainment of air bubbles in the down-coming stream is thus avoided. The maximum brake efficiency of this machine, as determined from the results of a large number of tests is 60·6 per cent.

The maximum efficiency was obtained with a speed of 295 revolutions per minute, giving a nozzle velocity of 14·75 f.s.

In this case, for maximum efficiency $u = 1·49 \sqrt{g h}$

$$= 1·052 \sqrt{2 g h}.$$

From this we have $\sqrt{1 + \frac{1}{F}} - 1 = 1·49^2 = 2·22.$

$$\therefore F = \frac{1}{9·38} = ·1065.$$

Substituting these values in the expression for the theoretical hydraulic efficiency we get $\eta = 69·2$ per cent., as against the value, 64 per cent., actually obtained.

One form of this wheel, Whitelaw's mill, was constructed with arms in the form of an equiangular spiral (Fig. 217), the idea being that when in motion the water would flow outwards from the centre to the jet in radial lines, and that any loss due to eddy formation would be avoided. A little consideration will, however, show that this can only be the case when $v = u$, and when in consequence no work is being done by the wheel.

ART. 131.

The **Borda** wheel was in all probability the first practical pressure turbine to be constructed. This consists of a couple of concentric cylindrical casings (Fig. 218) mounted on a vertical shaft, the space between these being provided with a series of inclined vanes. The casing is usually of some considerable depth and the mean radius of the vanes large. Water is led into the casing in a direction almost normal to the vanes and acts partly by impact. The pressure produced by its weight is, however, the chief factor in producing rotation. Strictly speaking, the wheel is a pressure or impulse turbine according as the buckets run wholly or partially full, this depending on the distance between consecutive vanes. In the Borda, in common with all other axial flow turbines, since the direction of

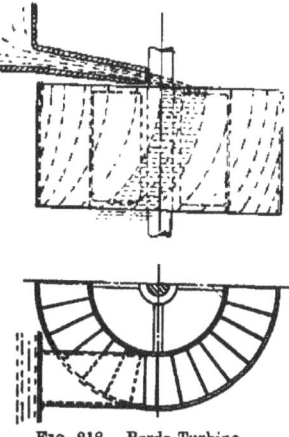

FIG. 218.—Borda Turbine.

the flow is parallel to the axis, the effect of centrifugal force on the flow may be neglected. In spite of its crudity, efficiencies of up to 70 per cent. have been obtained with this, which is the origin of all modern turbines of the parallel flow type.

ART. 132.—THE FOURNEYRON TURBINE.

The first highly efficient pressure turbine was, however, a development of the reaction wheel by *Fourneyron* (1827). The **Fourneyron** turbine is an outward radial flow reaction wheel (Fig. 219). Water is supplied through the pipe S which is closed at the bottom and terminates in an inverted cone, the outside of the pipe forming the entrance to a series of guide passages P. Guided by these passages, the water enters the wheel moving in the same direction as the wheel buckets, impinges on the curved vanes *B*, has its direction of motion changed, and finally escapes around the periphery of the wheel.

This type of turbine has been used with heads from 1 foot to 350 feet, and with moderate heads is capable of an efficiency of about 75 per cent. at full power. With high heads the speed is, however, inconveniently high, and the size of buckets and guide passages consequently small, rendering these very apt to be choked. Speed regulation is usually performed either by throttling the supply at its entrance to the wheel by means of a sliding cylindrical or ring gate, or sluice, fitting between the fixed and moving vanes (Fig. 220) and actuated by means of a governor or by throttling the discharge by means of a similar ring gate fitting outside the moving vanes (Fig. 221). This, by increasing the pressure in the wheel reduces the effective head producing rotation.

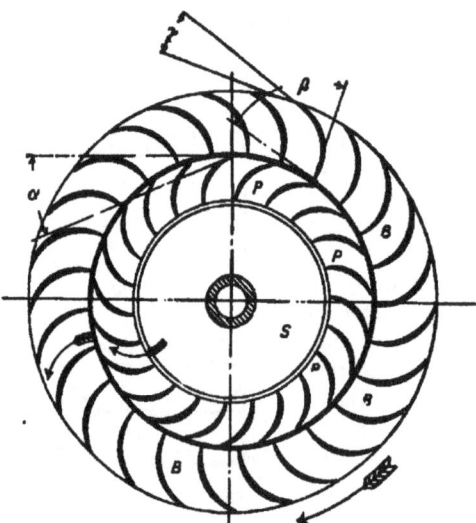

FIG. 219.—Section through Guides and Runner of Fourneyron Turbine.

The former method has the disadvantage that the entering streams of water, after their contraction in escaping past the edge of the ring gate, re-expand to fill the moving buckets, with consequent loss of energy. On account of this the efficiency at part gate is low. It may be improved if the turbine wheel be divided by parallel diaphragms as indicated in Figs. 220 and 221, into what is in effect a series of wheels in parallel.

In such a wheel this enlargement of section after cut off can only affect one chamber, and the part gate efficiency is in consequence increased. The method has the drawback, however, that the areas of the apertures are reduced and also that frictional resistances to flow are increased by the diaphragms, so that the full gate efficiency suffers. In spite of this, it forms the most general and satisfactory method of governing turbines of this type.

The second method, by increasing the pressure at exit, diminishes the effective head and increases the loss of kinetic energy at exit, and is hence very inefficient at part gate. In the first turbines erected at Niagara Falls, which were of the Fourneyron type, and of 5,500 H.P., this method of governing was adopted with satisfactory results as regards speed regulation.[1]

Outward flow turbines are in general difficult to govern, because an increase in speed caused by a reduction in load increases the centrifugal pressure of the water in the turbine wheel, and thus causes an increased outward flow which tends to increase the speed

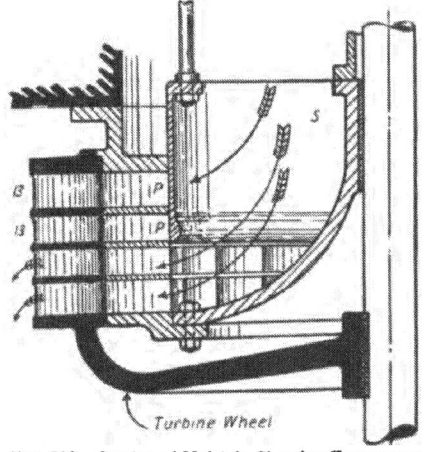

FIG. 220.—Section of Multiple Chamber Fourneyron Turbine Runner and Guides, with Inside Cylinder Gate.

still further. Governing by throttling the discharge has the advantage that it does to some extent tend to counterbalance this action.

The fact that centrifugal force tends to increase the velocity of flow through the wheel also explains to some extent why the speed of the wheel is of necessity so high under high heads.

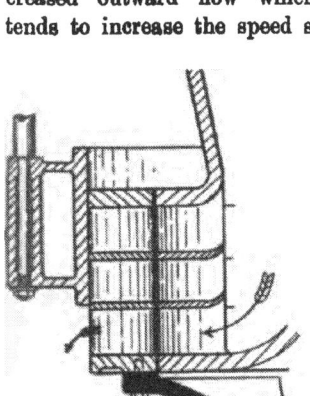

FIG. 221.—Outside Cylinder Gate.

The efficiency of the Fourneyron turbine may be increased by the addition of the diffuser, probably invented by Boyden (1844).

This consists of a fixed annular casing (Fig. 222), surrounding the wheel and fitting closely to the outer periphery of the moving vanes. The sides of this casing diverge gradually, its depth increasing from that of the buckets to about

[1] These turbines were designed by Messrs. Faesch and Piccard (1895), and work under 132 feet head. A full load efficiency of 82·5 per cent. is said to have been obtained. In this

twice this, and its width being about four times that of the wheel. By this means, part of the kinetic energy of the discharge is converted into pressure energy, and since the pressure at the outside of the diffuser is that corresponding to the depth of immersion, the pressure at the inside and at the exit from the turbine wheel is less than this, so that the effective head is increased. In this manner the efficiency may be increased by about 6 per cent. in a well-designed turbine under moderate head, the proportional increase being less as the head increases. The device is, however, now practically obsolete.

The outward flow turbine suffers in efficiency from the fact that its passages are of necessity divergent and that flow through these diverging passages is always accompanied by loss of energy in eddy production. It is, moreover, an expensive machine, not easy to govern well, and has

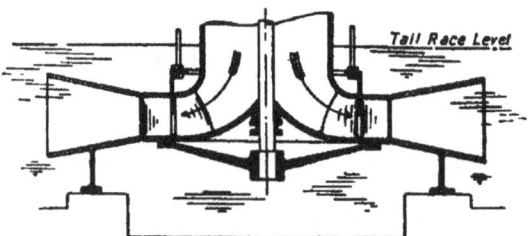

FIG. 222.—Outward Radial Flow Turbine with Diffuser.

been generally replaced by turbines of the Francis or some other more modern type.

The following results of tests on a Fourneyron turbine fitted with an internal cylinder gate, are given by Unwin,—

first series of turbines the ring gates are arranged to open downwards, the idea being that it is safer to allow the gates to open suddenly in case of accident to the coupling rods than to close suddenly, because of the probable effect of water ram in the latter case. The fact that the lower section of both wheels is not opened for the escape of water except at full load, and the possibility of a dangerous accumulation of detritus taking place in these sections, along with the nuisance caused by the violent upward escape of water against the turbine deck, led to the gates in the second series of turbines being designed to shut downwards. The gates are regulated by a mechanical relay governor having the gearing, which moves the gates, operated by clutches put in motion by changes of speed, the motion of the governor balls allowing one or another pawl to gear with a ratchet wheel, which gives motion through the clutche · and gearing to a rack coupled to a lever on the lay shaft from which the gates are directly worked.

A counterbalance v eight is used to balance the weight of the gates and coupling rods.

While these turbines have given satisfactory results, the whole of the later series of 5,000 H.P. and 10,000 H.P. turbines are of the inward radial flow type.

Gate opening . .	1·0	·875	·625	·375
Efficiency . . .	·62	·60	·43	·30

Art. 133.—The Jonval Turbine.

By shortening the casing of the Borda turbine, and adding suitable guide vanes to direct the water under pressure into the wheel, Jonval (1843) devised a form of turbine which had many advantages over and largely displaced the Fourneyron turbines then in use. In this, which is an axial flow turbine, water is directed by means of radial guides into a series of radial buckets (Fig. 223). Since each particle of water in its motion through the wheel remains at approximately the same distance from the axis, the effect of centrifugal force on the flow becomes negligible, and the difficulty in governing which is so pronounced in the Fourneyron turbine is thus removed.

In all axial flow turbines, however, whether of the pressure or impulse

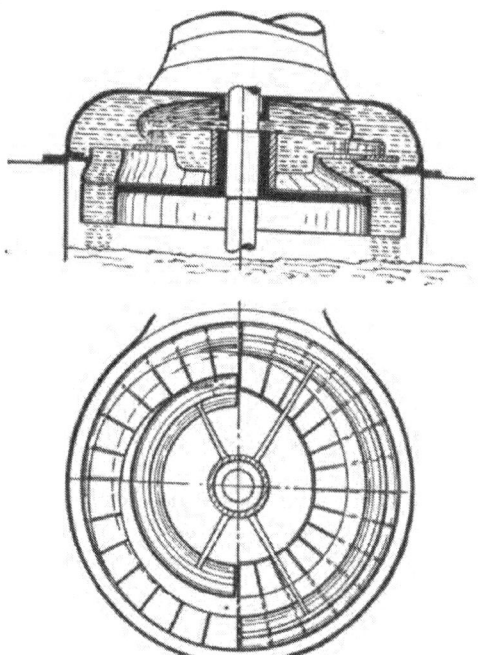

Fig. 223.—Jonval Turbine.

type, the linear velocity of points at the entrance to the buckets varies with the radius, and as the velocity of efflux from the guide passages is approximately uniform, there is, with radial vanes, only one particular radius at which the ratio between the velocities of the wheel and of efflux is suited to any given blade angles. For efficient working, and to

avoid undue shock at entrance, the radial width of the buckets must then
be small compared with the radius of the wheel, and in general should
not exceed one-fifth of the latter.

Governing is usually performed by cutting off the supply to one or
more guide passages by a circular slide (Fig. 224), or by a scroll gate,
and this greatly reduces the efficiency at part gate. Thus a turbine
which has an efficiency of, say, 82 per cent. at full gate, will probably not
exceed 66 per cent. at half gate.

The most important improvement in the design of the Jonval turbine

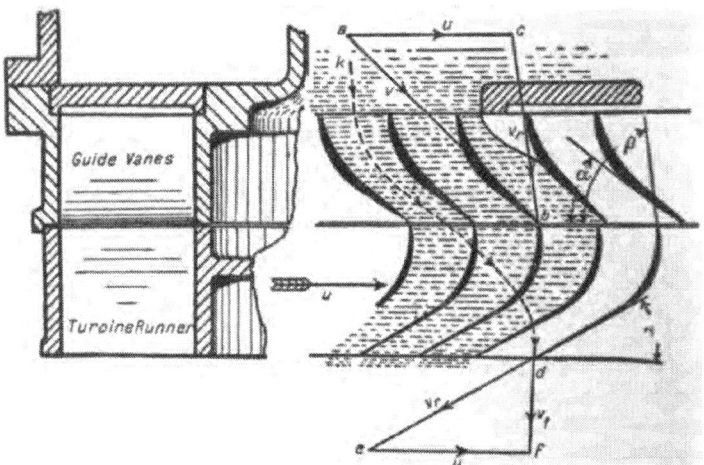

FIG. 224.—Section through Runner and Guides of Downward Flow Jonval Turbine.

consisted in the subdivision of the wheel into concentric compartments,
each forming a complete turbine.

Then by regulating the water supply to each compartment in turn, and,
if necessary, completely cutting off the supply to one or more compartments, the wheel may be utilized with fairly high efficiencies, and, by
supplying compartments at different distances from the axis, may be
given a constant speed under varying heads. Thus with a double turbine
the outer compartment, having a higher velocity, would be used with a
minimum supply and a maximum head, while the outer and inner compartments together would be designed to give the same power with a
reduced head and an increased supply. The vane angles should be
different in the two compartments.

In practice, the turbine is regulated by opening the necessary number of guide buckets in one compartment after another, and while causing loss by shock, this is probably the best method of regulation.

In the case of a Jonval turbine, built for the Zurich Waterworks, to work under a head which varies from 4′ 9″ to 10′ 6″, the number of compartments was three. The turbine was designed for 90 H.P., and the outer compartment alone gave this power under the full head, when using 6,300 cubic feet per minute. The outer and middle compartments together gave 90 H.P., under a head of 7′ 10″, using 8,400 cubic feet per minute, while the three together gave 90 H.P. with a head of 4′ 9″ using 10,000 cubic feet per minute. The speed throughout was 25 revolutions, and official tests gave the following results :—

	Head.	Efficiency.
Outer compartment alone	10′ 6″	73·71 per cent.
Outer and middle together	7′ 0″	75·39 per cent.
All three compartments	4′ 9″	80·70 per cent.

This type of turbine combines the advantages of fairly high efficiency at part gate and of constant speed under variable head in a manner which is unequalled by any but the radial inward flow or Francis turbine, and is therefore suitable for variable conditions of working. It may be applied to heads from 2 feet to 180 feet, and for speeds from 20 to 400 revolutions per minute, but is more particularly fitted for low and medium heads with large quantities of water, the large area of the water passages enabling it to pass large volumes of water. Since European users are in general compelled to take advantage of such sources of power, this largely accounts for the favour with which the Jonval turbine was received and for its large development in Europe. Of late years, however, it has been largely displaced by the inward radial flow turbine, and is not at the present time manufactured to any large extent.

One of its chief disadvantages is, that with a downward flow machine the whole water pressure is transmitted to the step bearing unless prevented by some special device. One method of doing this is to allow the water to flow upwards through the wheel, while in a second method a balance piston is fitted to the turbine shaft as shown in Fig. 226, one side of this piston being exposed to the supply pressure, and any leakage past it being drained to the tail-race. By suitably proportioning the area of this piston, it then becomes possible to balance not only the water pressure on the runner, but also the weight of the rotating parts.

H.A.   I I

In either case a thrust bearing must be provided to take care of any unbalanced pressure. This consists either of an ordinary submerged step bearing with the shaft running in a lignum-vitæ bush, or preferably of a suspension bearing placed above tail-water level. The latter method provides obvious advantages in the way of accessibility, ease of examination, and freedom from grit, and enables forced lubrication to be applied. One type of suspension bearing is illustrated in Fig. 225.[1] Here the turbine

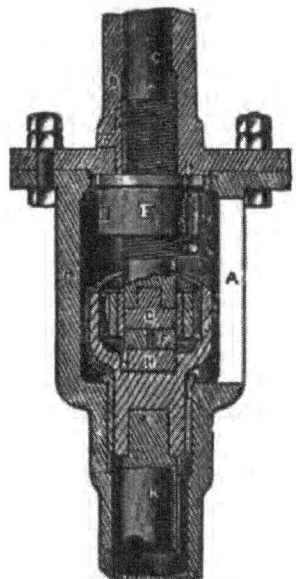

Fig. 225.—Suspension Bearing for Vertical Turbine Shaft.

wheel is keyed to a hollow shaft which terminates at its upper end in the lantern *A*. This lantern is connected by the feather key *D* to the steel shaft *C*, which is fitted with a lock-nut *E*, by which the vertical adjustment of the wheel may be altered.

A gun-metal washer *F* works between the hardened steel discs *G* and *H*, of which *G* is rigidly fixed to the bottom of the shaft *C*, and *H* to the oil cup *J*, which in its turn is cottered on to the shaft *K*. This latter shaft is continued downwards and is firmly fixed in a cast-iron socket on the tail-race floor. The bottom end of the shaft *C* is prevented from moving laterally by the gun-metal bush *O*, and a series of radial grooves on each face of the washer *F* enable oil to reach every part of the bearing surfaces.

The comparative ease of regulation by cylindrical gates, together with the large passage areas possible with the axial flow type of wheel, led to the design, for fairly large powers under low heads, of the cone turbine.

Here, as indicated in the sketch (Fig. 226),[2] the flow is diagonal from the entrance to the exit from the wheel, and the turbine becomes intermediate between the inward radial and the axial flow type. As shown, the wheel may be subdivided into several complete wheels of different diameters, each of which may be regulated by a cylindrical gate. This

---

[1] By kind permission of Messrs. Gilbert Gilkes & Co., Ltd., Kendal.
[2] By permission of Messrs. Escher, Wyss & Cie., Zurich.

type, which has only been manufactured to a limited extent, is thus more

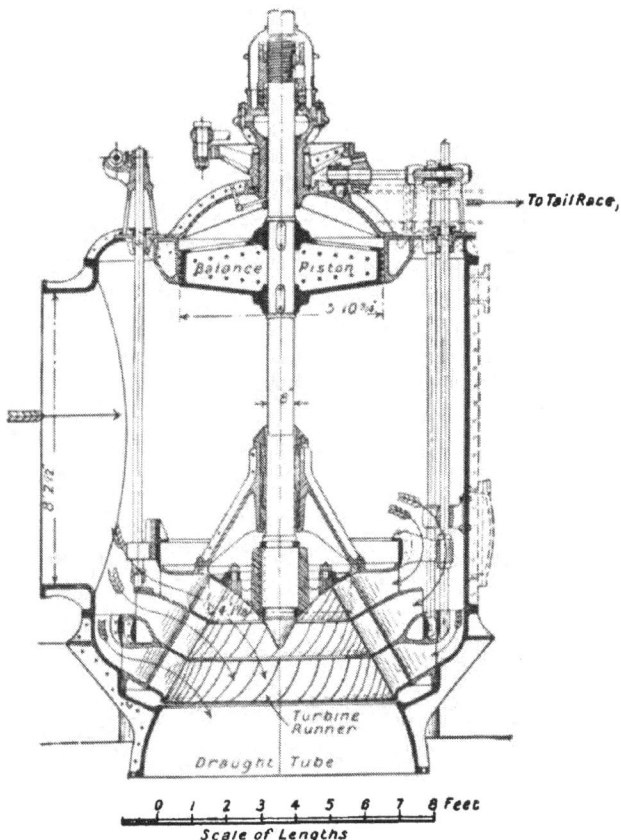

FIG. 226.—Cone Turbine, 1,250 H.P., Head 26 ft. to 33 ft., 120 Revolutions, with Water Balance Piston.

suitable where a constant speed is required under a low head which may suffer considerable percentage variation.

ART. 134.—THE SUCTION TUBE.

An invention of Jonval (1843) greatly increased the possibility of adapting the pressure turbine to suit local conditions. This consists in lengthening the vertical discharge pipe until its lower end always discharges below the surface level in the tail-race, thus forming what is termed a **Suction** or **Draught** tube. By this means the turbine may be placed at any level, up to about 25 feet[1] above the tail-race without any loss of head. The truth of this statement may be seen if it be considered that since the pressure in the draught tube at the tail-race level is approximately equal to that of the atmosphere (neglecting the kinetic head in the tube), the pressure at the turbine will be less than this by an amount equivalent to the difference of statical head at turbine and tail-race, so that the available head at the turbine is equal to the difference of level between turbine and head-race, together with the difference between turbine and tail-race, i.e., to the difference between head-race and tail-race. Expressed symbolically, if suffixes (1) and (2) refer respectively to turbine and tail-race (Fig. 227),

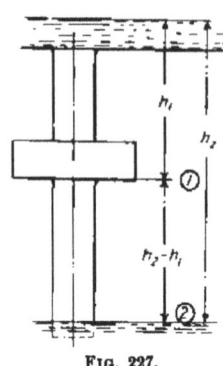

FIG. 227.

$$\frac{p_1}{W} = \frac{p_2}{W} - (h_2 - h_1) \text{ feet.}$$

∴ (Pressure + potential) head at exit from turbine, which equals $\frac{p_1}{W} + h_2 - h_1$ feet.

$$= \frac{p_2}{W} - (h_2 - h_1) + h_2 - h_1 = \frac{p_2}{W} = 0.$$

∴ Available head for driving turbine $= h_2 - \frac{p_2}{W}$ feet.

$$= h_2 \text{ feet.}$$

In order that on starting a turbine the air may be carried out of the draught tube, the velocity of flow through the tube should be greater

[1] The maximum elevation depends largely on the diameter of the draught tube, the following values, adapted from those given by Meissner, showing the maximum values to be used with a given diameter of tube.

Diameter of suction tube in feet	·5	1·0	1·5	2·0	2·5	3·0	4·0	6·0	8·0	10·0
Maximum possible elevation in feet	31·1	29·8	28·0	26·4	24·8	23·4	21·0	17·0	14·0	12·0

From these values, however, should be subtracted the head $\frac{v^2}{2g}$, corresponding to the velocity of flow, v feet per second, down the tube.

than 2 feet per second. Also the area of the tube at its point of connection to the turbine, should be as nearly as possible equal to the discharge area of the runner so as to avoid loss by shock at the sudden change of section. The area should then increase gradually to the open end of the tube, the angle of flare not exceeding about 15° and decreasing as the length of tube increases. This serves two useful purposes, since, in addition to changing part of the kinetic energy of discharge into useful pressure energy, it usually improves the speed regulation of the plant. With quick regulation and a sudden closing of the turbine gates, the momentum of the suction column may break the column and cause a vacuum at the turbine.[1] Immediately this action is overcome, atmospheric pressure forces water up the tube again, and this may strike the runner with great force. Even a small change of load may set up such pulsations, which are detrimental to steady running and are reduced by the use of a conical draught tube.

When fitted to a pressure turbine, water will, in general, enter the draught tube with a not inconsiderable velocity of whirl, and with a tube of large diameter when working at part gate, an air core may be formed in the tube when starting up the plant, and may exist for some considerable time before being expelled. The turbine then loses the advantage of the tube to some extent. To obviate this, gates for throttling the lower end of the tube have sometimes been used. While advantageous when starting the turbine, they are, however, not often fitted on account of the expense.

The lower end of a draught tube should always be bell-mouthed to facilitate the escape of water.

The draught tube is applicable to any type of pressure turbine, but

---

[1] Let the suction tube be parallel; l feet long; dipping h_d feet below the surface in the tail-race, and suppose air leakage increases the pressure at the top of the tube by the equivalent of h_a feet of water.

Thus for separation due to downward momentum we must have

$$34 - (l - h_d) - h_a = \frac{l}{g} a$$

$$\therefore a = \frac{32}{l} (34 + h_d - h_a) - 32 \text{ feet per second per second.}$$

EXAMPLE.

$p_a = 2$ lbs. per square inch, $h_a = 4\cdot6$ feet, $l = 28$ feet, $h_d = 8$ feet.

Thus $a = \frac{32}{28} (37 - 4\cdot6) - 32 = 5$ feet per second per second.

If $v = 8$ feet per second, separation would take place if the gates were shut in less time than 1·6 seconds. Actually since the retardation is not uniform during a uniform closing of the gates, but increases to a maximum at the instant of closing, this retardation would probably be attained if the time of closing were less than three seconds.

FIG. 228.— Single Mixed-Flow Turbine with Cylinder Gate, mounted horizontally in Steel Housing with Quarter Turn Discharge and Draught Tube.

more particularly, for mechanical reasons, to the inward flow type. It is not commonly used with impulse turbines, though it may be fitted if desired.

The pressure turbine thus fitted possesses many advantages over the submerged type. The turbine is dry when the head water is cut off, and is easily accessible: a horizontal shaft machine may frequently be adopted where otherwise this would be impossible, and the general accessibility for examination and repairs is greatly increased, while the risk of damage to machinery by floods is diminished.

With a single horizontal shaft turbine, or with two horizontal turbines on the same shaft if these discharge outwards, it is necessary for the wheel shaft to pass through the draught tube as in Fig. 228, and a stuffing box becomes necessary to prevent leakage of air into the tube. Tightness is commonly assured by means of a water seal, consisting of a chamber C surrounding the shaft (Fig. 229), and supplied with pressure water from the penstock by means of a small pipe P. Any slackness at the gland then allows this pressure water to escape outwards, or into the draught tube, and does not lead to air leakage.

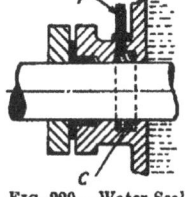

Fig. 229.—Water Seal for Draught Tube Stuffing Box.

While the draught tube often discharges vertically into the tail-race, it is advantageous to fit a right-angled bend beneath the water level at exit, and to discharge in the direction of flow of the tail-race. By so doing the kinetic energy of discharge is not entirely wasted, a fair proportion being utilized in producing this flow. A still further proportion may be utilized if the section of the tube be gradually increased towards its exit.

Art. 185.—The Francis Turbine.

The next important step in turbine development was due to J. B. Francis (1849), who, placing the guide vanes outside the wheel, and reversing the direction of flow of the Fourneyron turbine so as to discharge at the centre, obtained the inward radial flow turbine bearing his name (Fig. 230).

Several important advantages accompanied this change in design.

(1) The inlet ports and wheel passages now being convergent, steady flow became possible throughout the wheel.

(2) The increased accessibility of the guide passages and vanes made it possible to use improved methods of regulating the flow of water to the runner.

(3) Any increase in the speed of rotation, by increasing the centrifugal pressure at the outside of the wheel and at the outlet from the guide passages, tends to check the flow through and the supply of energy to the wheel, which now becomes to a certain extent self-regulating.

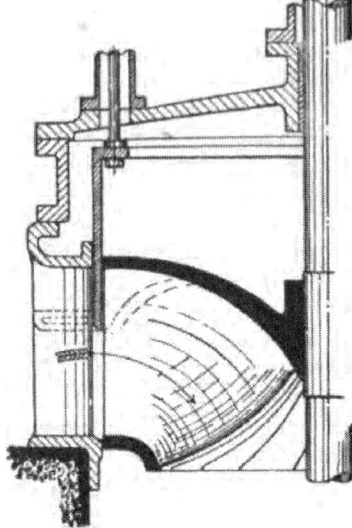

FIG. 230.—Francis Turbine with Inside Cylinder Gate Regulation.

(4) The centrifugal pressure of the water also balances the pressure due to a portion—in practice generally about one-half—of the supply head, so that only one-half of the pressure head at entrance is absorbed in producing velocity of influx, the other half remaining as pressure head and being gradually absorbed in its passage through the wheel. The velocity of influx is thus never greater than about $\sqrt{g\,h}$, and hydraulic friction losses are thereby much reduced, while the corresponding reduction in the peripheral speed of the wheel enables this to be applied successfully to very high heads, up to about 500 feet. Since the mean velocity of flow in an inward flow turbine is less under

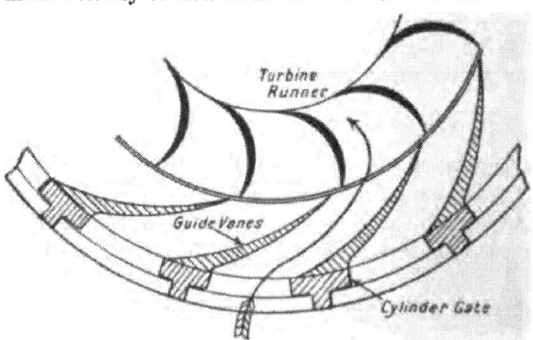

FIG. 231.—Outside Register Gate.

a given head than in an outward flow, or axial flow machine, the size of wheel is greater for a given power. As the size is usually increased axially, the extra cost is, however, only small.

(5) In this type of turbine the supply water when moving with its maximum velocity (at entrance) is admitted to the wheel at its outer circumference, and consequently at its most rapidly moving part. It thus becomes practicable to design the guide passages and inlet vanes so that even for the highest heads water may be admitted to the wheel without shock, while since the water leaves at the centre, which is the most slowly moving part of the wheel, it is more easily discharged without excessive loss of kinetic energy.

The wheel was improved by constructing its vanes so as to give a combined radial and axial discharge, and to this end these vanes at exit are given a curvature in a direction parallel to that of the disc (see Fig. 230). This largely increases the available discharge area and enables a greater volume of water to be handled with a given size of wheel.

Regulation is usually performed by throttling the supply of water to the wheel either by slid-

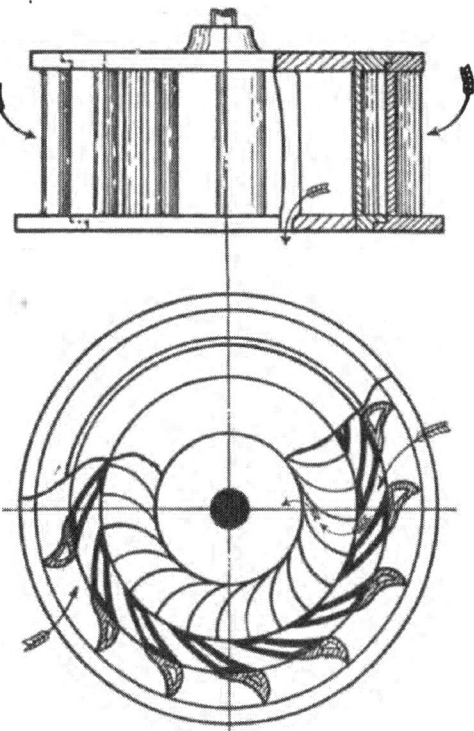

FIG. 232.—Inside Register Gate for Francis Turbine.

ing cylindrical gates, register gates, or wicket gates. The cylindrical gate usually consists of a plain cylinder throttling the supply at the entrance to the wheel buckets (Fig. 230). In some instances these gates have been fitted with fingers fitting between the guide vanes, as indicated in dotted lines in Fig. 230, with the idea of diminishing the contraction in section of the entrant stream, and thus the loss by shock at part gate. While this object is realized to a limited extent, yet the introduction of the fingers, as will be explained later (p. 525), renders close speed regulation almost impossible.

The register gate, which consists of a rotating cylinder gate, and of which two types are illustrated in Figs. 231 and 232, has the advantage that the travel necessary to cut off the supply is small, and therefore tends to more rapid regulation. On the other hand, it is very liable to get out of order where floating material in the water may jam between gate and guide or wheel vanes, and is less efficient than the plain cylinder gate at part load. In view of these disadvantages, these gates are now practically obsolete. The latter remark also applies to the original form of wicket gate, which, as its name suggests, consisted of a series of plates

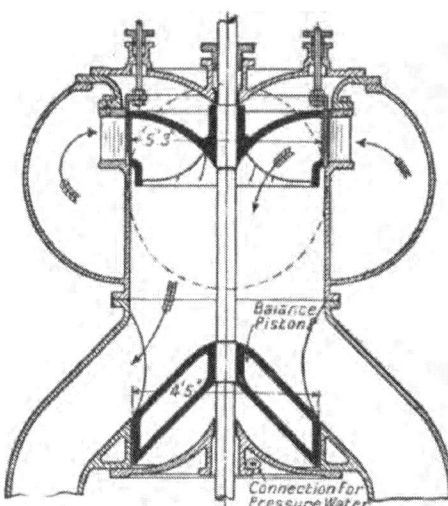

pivoted either at their ends or preferably at their centres, and which throttled the supply by closing the guide passages as the plates were rotated. As modified by Professor Thomson and by Fink and others, the wicket gate, however, gives very close and efficient regulation under widely varying conditions. It will be considered in further detail in Art. 136.

Where a draught tube is fitted, regulation may be performed by means of a butterfly valve placed in the tube so as to throttle the discharge. The drawback to this system is that

FIG. 233.—Francis Turbine with Cylinder Gate Regulation developing 5,500 H.P. at 250 revs. per min. under 146 feet head. Penstock 7' 6" diam.

the valve is large and heavy, possesses considerable inertia, and requires a large force to move it, while part gate efficiency is low. This method of governing has been adopted with success as regards speed regulation in the case of Francis turbines of 6,000 H.P. working under 135 feet head at the Shawinigan Falls.[1] Here the penstocks are of considerable length, and the method promised to give better results than gates on the pressure side of the turbine runner.

Figs. 233 and 234 illustrate noteworthy examples of Francis turbines with cylinder gate regulation. Fig. 233 shows one of a series of turbines

[1] For a description of the plant see *Cassier's Magazine*, June, 1904.

alled in 1900 in Power-house No. 2 of the Niagara Falls Power Comy.[1] These are single Francis turbines with vertical shaft direct-

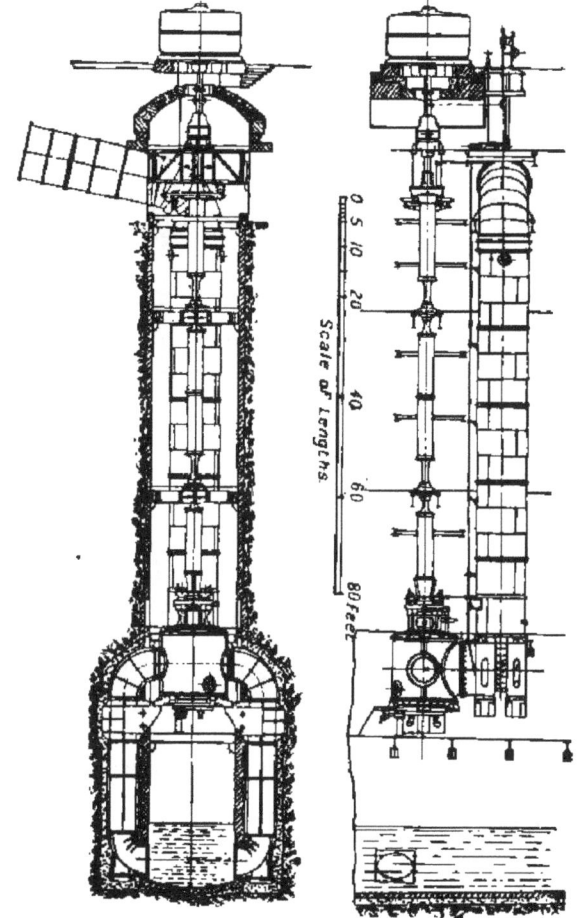

ь. 231ᴀ.—General arrangement of Double Francis Turbine developing 10,250 H.P. at 250 revs. per min. under 133 feet head. Canadian Niagara Power Co.

ipled to a dynamo, and developing 5,550 H.P. at 250 revolutions per inute under a head of 146 feet. The turbine runner is 5′ 3″ outside

[1] By Messrs. Escher, Wyss & Cie., Zurich.

diameter, and regulation is performed by an annular bronze ring operat
by an oil pressure relay governor (see Art. 139), and arranged so as
close by its own weight.

Power is transmitted through a tubular steel shaft 38 inches in diamet
the weight of this shaft, which is 120 feet long and weighs 71 tons, bea

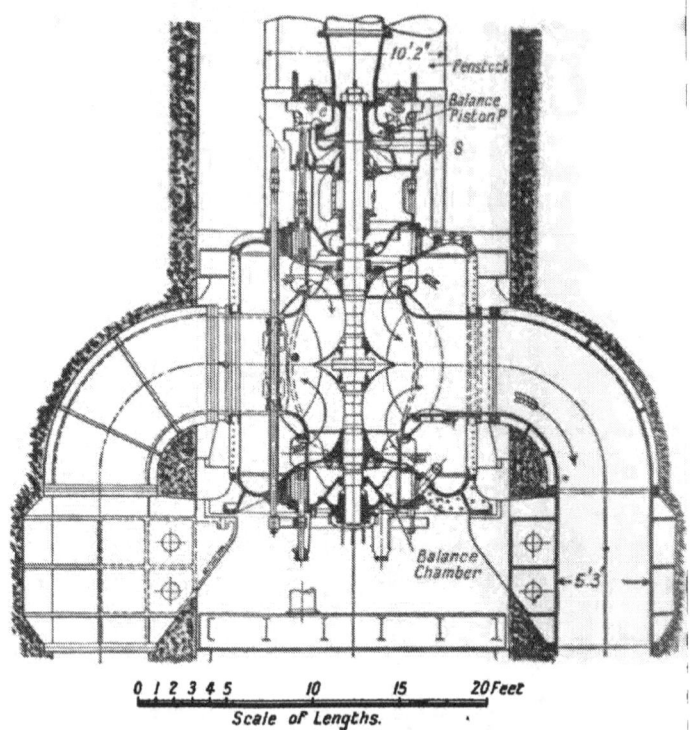

FIG. 234B.—Sectional Elevation of Double Francis Turbine for 10,250 H.P. Canali
Niagara Power Co.

balanced by the upward pressure on the balance piston P, which is 4'
diameter. The under side of this piston is exposed to the full suppl
head by means of a pipe not shown in the sketch, and any leakage pa
the piston escapes directly into the tail-race. Any unbalanced end thru
on the shaft is taken up by means of a thrust bearing on the top de
The draught tube is forked to keep the tail-race free, and is arranged
as to give 22 feet of suction head.

'igs. 234[1] A, B, C, D and E, illustrate one of a series of double Francis
)ines installed (1903) in the power-house of the Canadian Niagara
ver Company. These are vertical shaft machines, each direct-coupled
ι generator and developing 10,250 H.P. at 250 revolutions under a
d of 133 feet.

'ower is transmitted through a tubular steel shaft 40 inches diameter
l ·582 inch thick. The weight of the rotating parts is about 120 tons

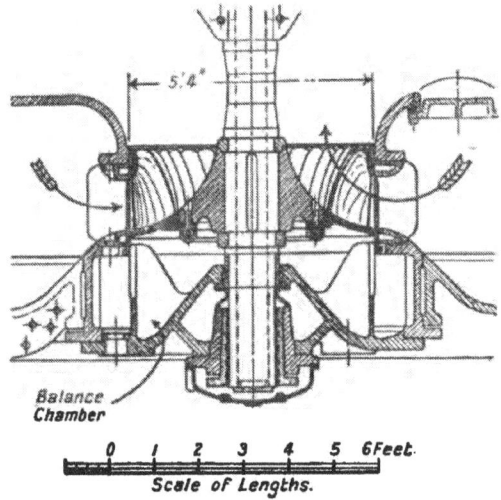

IG. 234C.—Section through Lower Runner and Balance Chamber of 10,250 H.P. Turbine.

l is balanced, partly by the upward pressure on the bottom face of the
ier runner, water under the full pressure of the supply head being
nitted to a balance chamber (Fig. 234c), beneath this runner, and
tly by the upward pressure on the rotating balancing piston P
g. 234B), which is mounted on the turbine shaft, and which is
)osed over its under side to the full pressure of the supply head.
akage past this piston is drained away to the tail-race, and by adjusting
ι valve on the pipe S which supplies pressure water, the upward pressure
the piston may be regulated with great nicety. Any unbalanced load
supported by the suspension bearing (Fig. 234D), which is placed on
ι upper deck. In this bearing, oil under a pressure of 375 lbs. per

[1] By courtesy of Messrs. Escher, Wyss & Cie.

square inch is supplied to the annular chamber C surrounding
bush B, and escapes outwards between the fixed and rotating discs

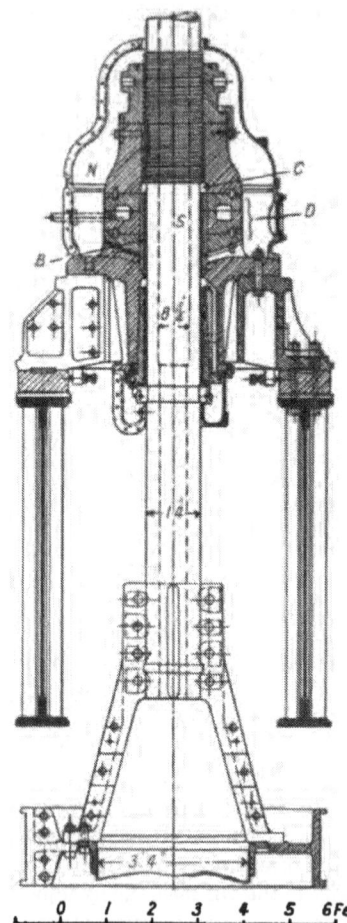

Scale of Lengths.
Fig. 234D.—Main Footstep Bearing for
10,250 H.P. Turbine.

These discs have an outside diame
of 36 inches and a bearing are
about 780 square inches, the u
thus floating on a film of oil
giving a very frictionless beari
The hollowed screwed spindle S
14″ outside and $8\frac{3}{4}″$ inside diame
and is provided with two locknu
at N, by means of which the turb
shaft may be adjusted vertical
Any slight swing or lateral wear
the shaft is permitted by the sphe
cal bearing surface of the low
disc.

Speed regulation is performed
a centrifugal governor (Fig. 234
operating a regulating valve whi
regulates the supply of oil (mai
tained at a pressure of 1,120 lbs. p
square inch) to the upper side
relay cylinder C, the downward pre
sure on this piston overbalancin
the weight of the gate mechanis
and thus operating the cylindric
speed gates. Adjustment of t
speed while the turbines are runni
may be performed by the hand reg
lating wheel H.

The turbine runners have a
ameter of 64 inches and a bla
depth of 11·8 inches, while ea
carries twenty-one vanes. T
guide vanes are twenty-two in nu
ber. The tail-race which takes
discharge from the whole batt
of turbines is 2,590 feet in leng

and has a gradient of 7 in 100, being designed to discharge, at full lo
8,800 cubic feet of water per second. As the sectional area of the u

·ace tunnel is 866 square feet, this gives a velocity of efflux of 24 feet per
second.

With the Francis turbine and cylindrical gate regulation, the full-load
efficiency may be as high as 88 per cent., but this efficiency falls rather

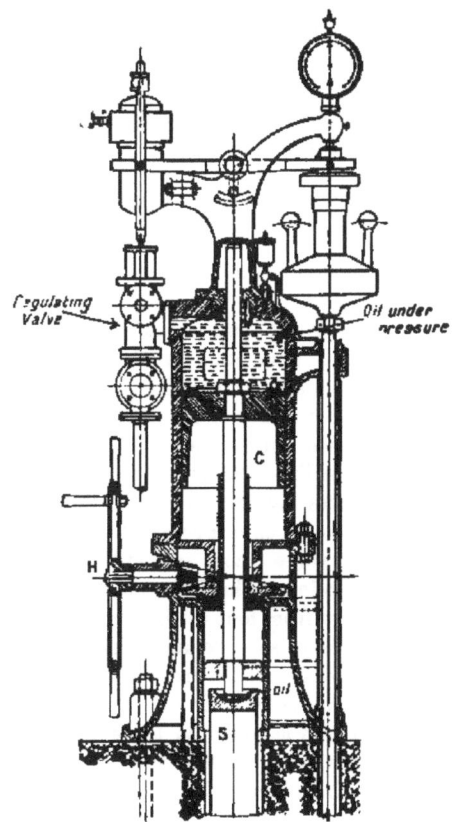

Fig. 234ɛ.—Oil Pressure Relay Governor for 10,250 H.P. Turbine.

rapidly as the gate opening is diminished, and does not in general
exceed 75 per cent. at half gate. Two Francis turbines installed at
Schaffhausen in an open water chamber, and developing at full load
434 H.P. at 169 revolutions and under 13·6 feet head, gave the following
efficiencies :—

Gate opening . .	$\frac{1}{2}$	$\frac{3}{4}$	Full.
Efficiency . . .	77 %	82·6 %	86·6 %

Where an ample water supply is available this falling off in efficiency is unimportant, and as this turbine admits of a simple and fairly cheap construction, and is capable of close speed regulation, it often forms the most suitable type to use. Where, however, high part-gate efficiency is more important than low first cost, one form or other of the turbine invented by Professor James Thomson becomes advisable.

ART. 136.—THE THOMSON VORTEX TURBINE (FIG. 235).[1]

The special features of this turbine, which is an inward radial flow machine, consists in the form of chamber in which the runner is mounted called the vortex chamber, and in the type of guide vane adopted. The runner, which is similar to that of the Francis turbine, is mounted inside a spiral casing. Water enters tangentially at the largest part of the spiral (as shown in Fig. 236), and sweeps around the casing, the area of which is so arranged that the linear velocity of the supply water is the same at all points of the circumference. A common, but less correct type of construction, is that indicated in Figs. 235 and 237, in which the water enters the casing radially and divides into two streams flowing along either side of the wheel. In either case the entering water is directed into the wheel buckets by a series of guide vanes placed around the outer circumference these being designed so as to follow the lines of flow in a spiral vortex These guides vary in number from four to eight and are movable, being pivoted near their inner ends, so as to be approximately in balance. They are coupled together by a series of bell-crank levers and links as indicated in Fig. 236,[2] so as to rotate together and shut off water equally from all parts of the wheel. Motion is given to these guide vanes either by hand or by an automatic governor. Where the load and the supply head are constant the guide blades may be fixed, the ports then being designed so as to give the full-power flow. This gives a much cheaper machine, and where a battery of turbines is in use, it is in general preferable to give fixed blades to all but one or two, regulation for small load variations being performed by those machines having movable guides, and for large variations by cutting out one or more of the machines with fixed guides.

[1] By courtesy of Messrs. G. Gilkes & Co., Ltd., Kendal.
[2] By courtesy of the Platt Iron Works, Dayton, Ohio.

This turbine may be constructed either as a double or single vortex heel. In the double wheel a series of vanes is fixed on either side of the inner disc, which is keyed to the turbine shaft. Discharge takes place

FIG. 235.—Thomson Vortex Turbine.

radially at the centre, and the water is then diverted axially through two discharge pipes, or draught tubes, placed one on each side of the wheel. This gives a wheel which is perfectly in balance as regards end thrust. To facilitate the discharge, the wheel vanes are usually curved at their outlet edges so as to direct the discharge water in the direction of the axis,

H.A.   K K

I

while for the same reason only alternate wheel vanes are carried to the centre. This has the further advantage of reducing friction losses. This

FIG. 286. Single Vortex Turbine with Hydraulic Relay Governor.

double vaned wheel with pivoted guide vanes is very suitable for medium and fairly high falls where the load is very variable, and where an economical use of the supply water at all loads is essential. The full-load efficiency is high, up to 87 per cent. under favourable conditions, while the part-load efficiency is also high, half-load efficiencies of as much as 82 per cent. being on record. The turbine may be constructed with either horizontal or vertical shaft, mechanical considerations rendering the former construction preferable.

In the single vaned wheel the vanes are fixed on one side of the rotating disc, and discharge takes place on one side only. The disc is therefore subject to end thrust, which must either be hydraulically balanced or taken up by means of a suitable thrust bearing. This disadvantage, which is common to all single discharge pressure turbines, may be over-

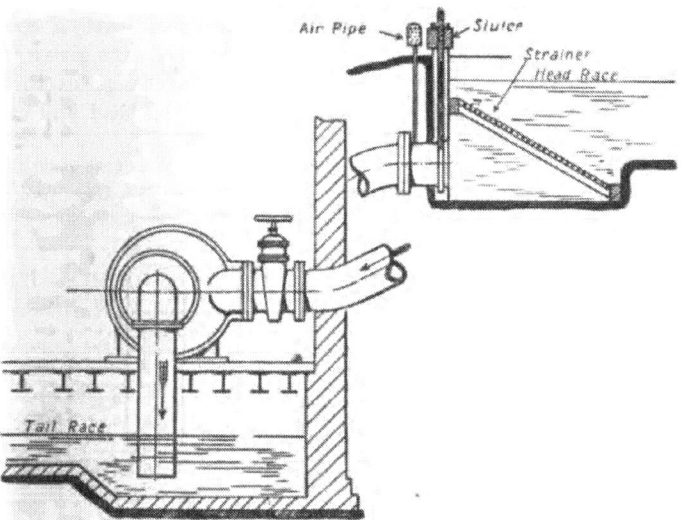

FIG. 237.—Arrangement of Vortex Turbine with Horizontal Shaft and Draught Tube.

come by mounting a pair of similar wheels on the same shaft, the flow being in opposite directions through the two wheels. The two end thrusts thus balance each other, while the arrangement has the further advantage for electric driving, that with a given head, since two smaller wheels are used instead by a single larger one, and since the peripheral speed of the wheel depends solely on the head, the speed of rotation is higher with the twin wheel. The single vaned wheel with vertical shaft is well fitted for low or medium falls and where the quantity of water available is large and the head is variable. Its efficiency is practically the same as that of the double wheel.

K K 2

The method of regulation by pivoted guides has many advantages. Of these the following are the more important :—

(1) At all gates the guide passages are of a gradually convergent form and offer easy curves to the supply water.

(2) Water is admitted (with the spiral casing) evenly all around the circumference.

(3) The guide vanes are easily moved, and an easy and rapid regulation of speed under sudden load variations is possible (specially important in electric driving).

(4) The guides may be arranged to give a small difference in the inclination of the stream entering the wheel buckets, together with a large difference in flow, and therefore to give a constant speed with a constant head and under a variable load, or may be so arranged as to give a greater change in inclination of the guides with a medium change in the flow. and thus to give a fairly constant speed under a variable head and variable load.

(5) The efficiency at part gate is high. The following test results have been chosen as showing how the efficiency varies with gate opening in this type of machine.

(a)[1] 45" diameter, single wheel. 128¼' head, 1,000 H.P., at 286 revolutions.	Gate opening . .	·2	·4	·6	·8	·9
	Efficiency . . .	70·9	77·4	78·4	78·4	78·3
	H.P. . . .	209	469	712	950	1,040
	Quantity of water, cubic feet per minute .	783·3	1,615	2,424	3,195	3,640

	H.P.	Head feet.	Revolutions.	Efficiency.	
(b)[2]	200	21·8	186	½ gate ¾ ,, full ,,	86·0 85·2 85·4
(c)[3]	1,050	322	500	½ gate ¾ ,, full ,,	80·0 85·0 79·0

[1] By the Platt Iron Works, Dayton, Ohio, at the Quebec Railway Light and Power Company's Plant, Montmorency, Quebec.

[2] By Messrs. Escher, Wyss & Cie., at Sihl Paper Mill, Zurich.

[3] By Messrs. Escher, Wyss & Cie., at Reutte, Austria.

Strictly speaking, the spiral casing forms an essential part of the Thomson wheel, though this may be replaced by an ordinary cylindrical casing (Fig. 237), or the turbine be submerged in the open penstock with free approach from all sides (Fig. 238), without seriously affecting the efficiency.

Where, however, it is required to take off power below head-water level a casing is essential, while in any case it is advisable for heads exceeding 10 feet. For medium falls above 10 feet, the horizontal shaft machine is, in general, to be preferred.

As modified by Fink and others, the pivoted guide vane devised by Thomson is largely fitted to modern turbines of the Francis type, these

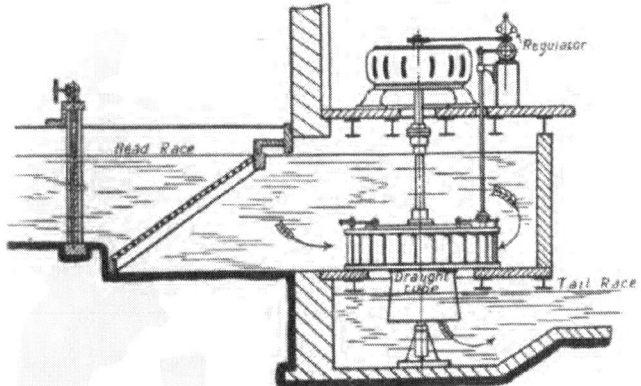

FIG. 238.—Arrangement of Vertical Shaft Single Vortex or Combined Flow Turbine working under Low Head in Open Forebay.

turbines only differing from the former type in that the guide vanes are shorter, while their number is increased until approximately equal to the number of wheel vanes.

The machine as thus constructed is better fitted for dealing with large volumes of water, and may be taken as being at present the most perfect type of pressure turbine.

Figs. 239 A, B, C, D, E,[1] illustrate with some detail what is one of the largest single wheel turbines of this type yet built. This wheel, which has inward radial flow and combined radial and axial discharge, is designed to give 10,000 B.H.P. at 300 revolutions per minute, under an

[1] At Snoqualmie Falls; reproduced by courtesy of the makers, the Platt Iron Works, Dayton, Ohio.

effective head of 260 feet. The runner is mounted in a spiral casing and is
66 inches outside diameter and 9½ inches wide through the vanes, which
are thirty-four in number. The guide vanes, thirty-two in number, are

FIG. 239A.—Front Elevation of Single Wheel Horizontal Shaft Francis Turbine for
Snoqualmie Falls, developing 10,000 H.P. at 300 revs. per min. under 260 ft. head.

of the pivoted type and are connected by means of arms projecting
radially inward, as shown in Fig. 239B, to a movable ring concentric with
the turbine shaft. This ring is rotated by means of a pinion actuated by
the governor, which gears into a rack mounted at the extremity of a
rocking lever. This lever transmits its motion to the ring by means of

vo links coupled to the ring by pins set at 180°. To prevent end thrust
n the guide spindles due to leakage of pressure water behind these,

FIG. 239B.—Rear Elevation of Francis Turbine for Snoqualmie Falls.

drainage passages are arranged to carry away any such water into the
space behind the wheel.

In order to tie the two sides of the housing together, a series of tie
diaphragms are provided outside the swivel guides and are so formed as
to act as preliminary guides. The turbine proper has only one bearing,
the direct-coupled generator having two bearings, making the whole unit

a three-bearing machine. The turbine runner is a steel casting whose radial depth is very slightly greater than the vanes, the shaft being enlarged into a disc of sufficient diameter to permit of bolting the vane ring directly to it. The vanes are finished smooth by filing.

Owing to the large diameter of the wheel and the high statical pressure at entrance, special means were necessary to balance the considerable end

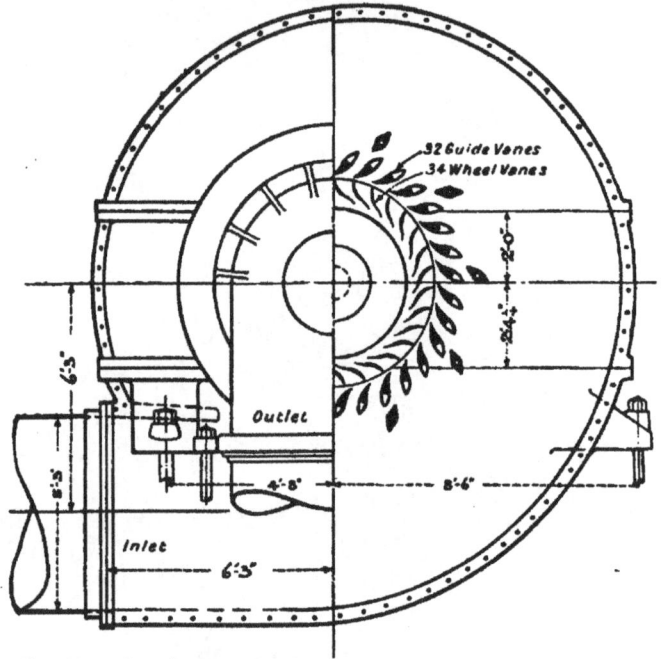

32 Guide Vanes
34 Wheel Vanes

Outlet

Inlet

Fig. 239c.—Cross Section and End Elevation of Turbine for Snoqualmie Falls.

thrust on the shaft. Owing to the leakage of pressure water into the space behind the wheel, the rear face is subject to a pressure substantially equal to that at entrance, while the front face is subject to a pressure varying from that at entrance to that in the draught tube. This produces a large excess of pressure towards the draught tube, and although the axial discharge, by producing a change of momentum in an axial direction, calls for a reaction on the wheel in the opposite direction yet the effect of this is small in comparison with that previously considered.

The greater part of the pressure thrust is eliminated by venting the space behind the wheel into the draught tube through six holes in the wheel disc, while a series of radial vanes cast on the back head of the wheel casing and almost touching the wheel prevent the formation of a forced vortex behind the wheel. The increase in pressure outwards, due

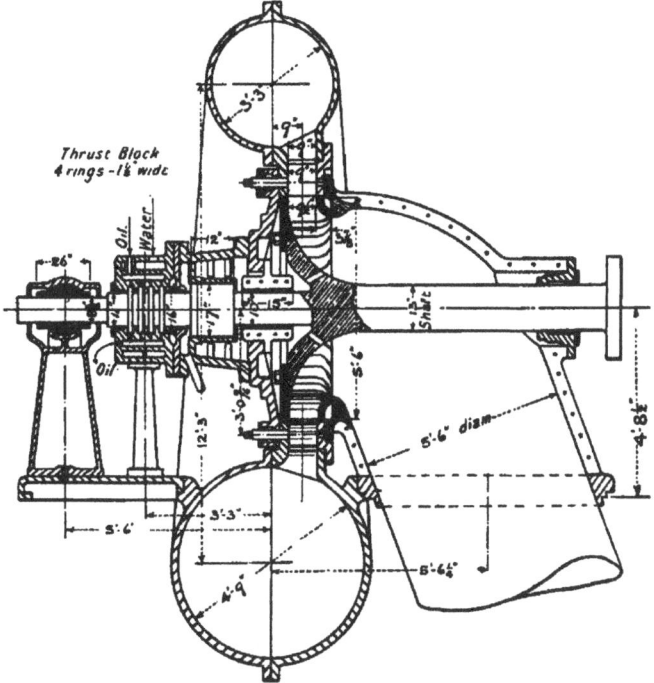

FIG. 239D.—Longitudinal Section of Single Wheel Horizontal Shaft Francis Turbine developing 10,000 H.P. at 300 R.P.M. under 260 ft. effective head. Outer diameter of runner 66 ins.

to centrifugal action, is thus prevented to a large extent, and the mean pressure reduced. There is, however, a resultant thrust towards the draught tube, which increases with the gate opening, and a closer balance is obtained by means of a balancing piston behind the back head of the wheel casing. This is a forged enlargement of the shaft, 17 inches in diameter, and works in a water-packed brass sleeve as shown in Fig. 239D.

The chamber in front of the piston is supplied with pressure water from the supply pipe through a strainer, while the space behind the piston is drained into the draught tube. A constant thrust towards the left is thus produced, and since there is a small leakage past the piston this thrust may be very accurately adjusted to suit the conditions of running, by adjustment of the supply valve. Any remaining thrust due

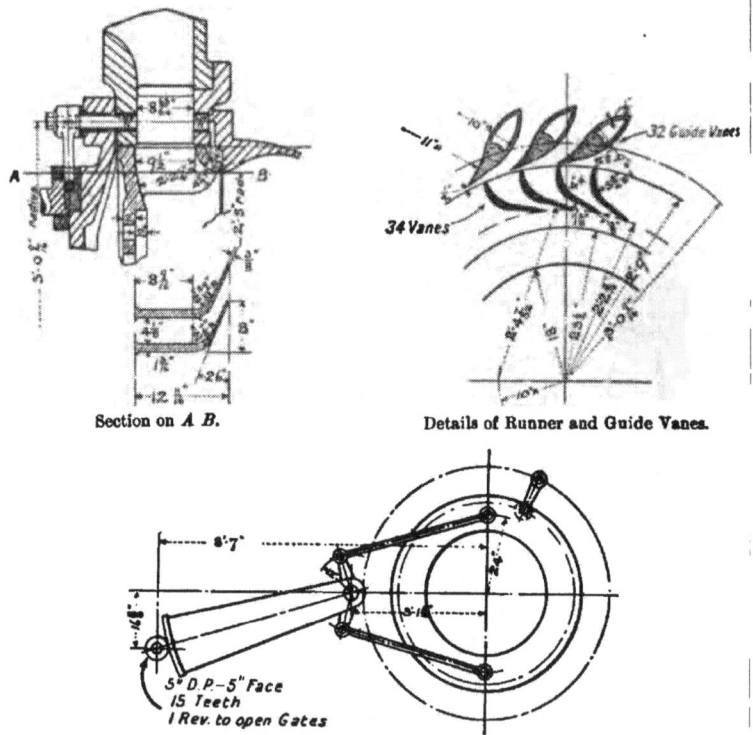

Section on *A B.*

Details of Runner and Guide Vanes.

Details of Gate Connections.

FIG. 289E.—Details of Turbine for Snoqualmie Falls.

to change of load is taken up by a collar thrust bearing situated behind the balance piston. An adjustment of the balance piston supply valve to give balance at ⅝ full load renders the thrust bearing liable to a possible thrust of about 25,000 lbs. at maximum, or very low loads. The collars, four in number and of 18½ inches mean diameter, have a total bearing area of 418 square inches. All bearing surfaces are babbited. The

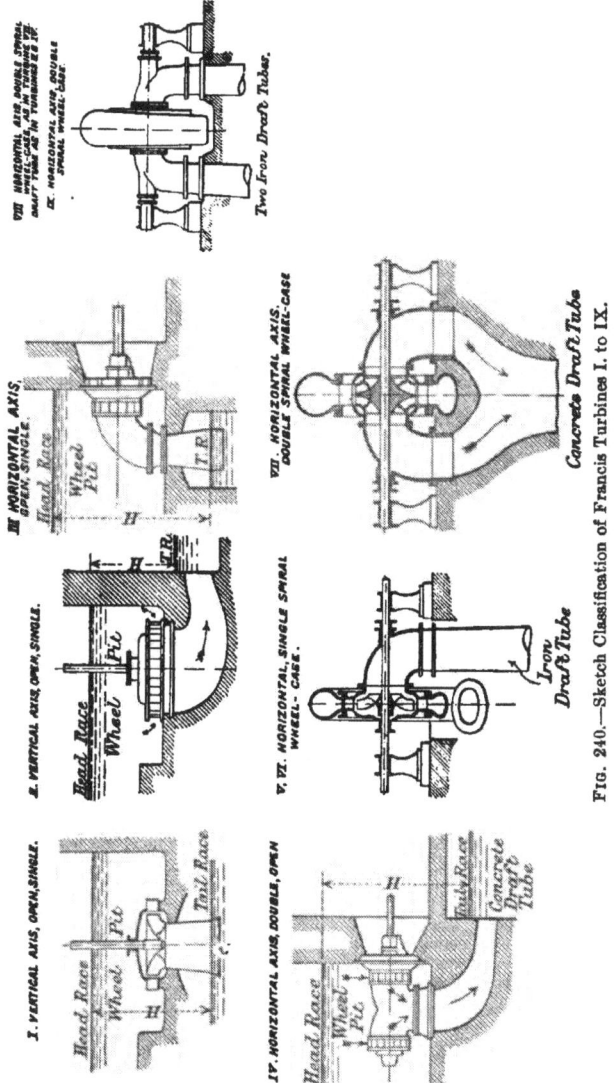

Fig. 240.—Sketch Classification of Francis Turbines I. to IX.

DIMENSIONS AND TEST RESULTS OF FRANCIS TURBINES.

No. of Turbine	System	Base Data: Fall in Metres	Water Flow, Cubic Metres per Second	Revolutions per Minute	H.P. Full Load	Inlet Dia. D, Metres	Inlet Breadth B, Metres	Number of Blades	Peripheral Speed, Revolutions Due to Velocity $u = \pi n/60$	Velocity Due to Fall $C = \sqrt{2gH}$	Velocity Co-efficient $K_u = u/C$	Fall in Metres	Revolutions per Minute	Full Load H.P.	100	90	80	70	60	50	40
I.	Single	4·6	3·000	100	148	1·25	0·300	17	6·30	9·5	0·67	4·6	100	158·3	88·1	88·5	87·5	85·5	82·2	78·0	...
II.	Open	4·4	4·940	100	220	1·30	0·435	17	6·82	9·3	0·72	4·4	100	260	82·5	87·0	87·2	87·0	84·0	80·5	...
III.	Single	6·6	5·400	127	572	1·30	0·495	16	8·70	11·35	0·78	7·0	128	434·5	76·9	83·5	85·0	83·5	79·7	74·5	...
IV.	Double	10·4	11·28	172	1250	1·30	2×0·325	16	11·7	14·2	0·81	10·4	160	1220	81·3	84·5	86·5	86·5	85·0	88·5	79·5
V.	Single	42·6	1·300	428	550	0·80	0·100	15	17·8	28·5	0·615	42·0	411	550	81·5	82·0	81·5	90·0	78·9	75·0	70·5
VI.		62·0	5·000	400	3200	1·10	0·220	17	23·1	34·8	0·67	64·0	400	4000	...	...	...	87·5	86·5	84·5	81·3
VII.		60·0	4·000	500	2500	0·90	2×0·0075	19	23·4	34·2	0·68	100·0	496	2096	78·6	87·5	87·5	84·5	78·9	...	...
VIII.		87·0	2·875	500	2500	0·95	2×0·110	...	25·0	41·2	0·60	87·0	490	2020	83·5	83·5	84·5	83·0	80·5	77·7	...
IX.	Double	148·0	2·000	600	3000	1·10	2×0·0400	...	34·2	52·8	0·65	147·0	601	3468	77·2	79·5	78·5	77·0	74·5	71·8	...

I. & II. vertical axis; III. & IV. horizontal axis. — V., VI., VII., VIII., IX. Horizontal axis, spiral wheel-case.

DETAILS OF DESIGN. — TEST RESULTS. — RUNNER DIMENSIONS. — PERCENTAGE OF FULL GATE EFFECTIVE H.P. — PERCENTAGE EFFICIENCY.

supply pipe is 5 feet 3 inches and the discharge 5 feet 6 inches diameter. A test of this wheel when driving 10,000 H.P. is stated to have given 84 per cent. efficiency, though the figure is subject to the inaccuracy of the method used for measuring the water consumption. This was deduced from the fall in pressure across the head gate, whose opening was accurately known.

A number of test results of typical modern Francis turbines are given in the table opposite,[1] the general arrangement of each turbine being shown in Fig. 240.

ART. 137.—COMPOUND TURBINES.

One possible method of getting over the difficulty of adapting pressure turbines of small power to very high heads consists in compounding two

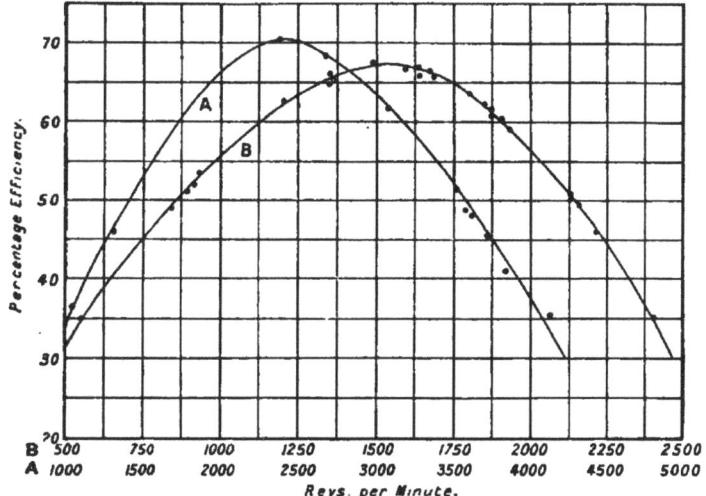

FIG. 241.—Efficiency Curves for Single and for Quadruple Compound Turbine.

or more runners in series on the same shaft, the fall in pressure and the work done then taking place in stages. As will be shown later, the peripheral speed of a pressure turbine for maximum efficiency is proportional to $\sqrt{H}$, where H is the working head, so that by doubling the number of runners the rotative speed is reduced in the ratio $1 : \sqrt{2} = \cdot 707$.

This reduction in speed has the effect of reducing disc friction, and the

[1] By Professor F. Prašil, "Proc. Inst. Mech. Engineers," 1910–11.

hydraulic resistances in each chamber will be less than in the single chamber of the larger wheel.

Since, however, these losses are duplicated in each successive chamber, and since in addition there is a loss of head due to the resistance of the connecting passages, it is not to be expected that the efficiency of the compound will be so high as that of the single chamber turbine.

Experiments carried out by the author on a small inward radial flow

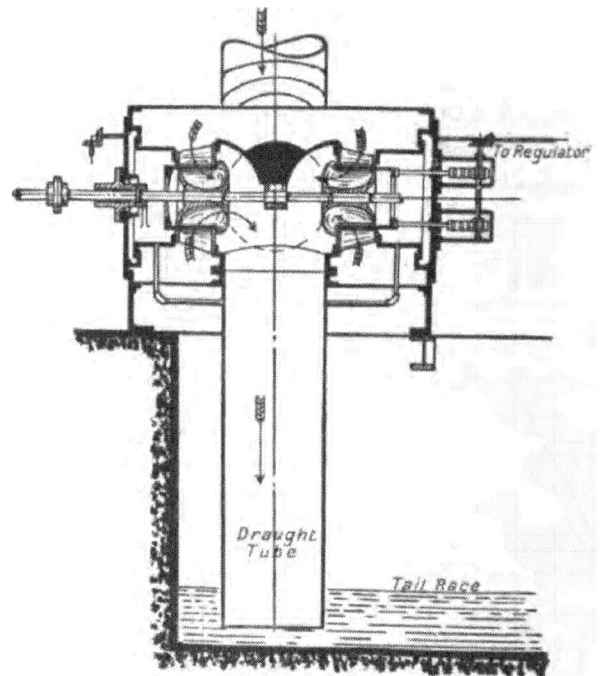

FIG. 242.—General Arrangement of Twin Mixed-Flow Turbine with Horizontal Shaft.

and axial discharge turbine fitted with four similar runners in series, and which could also be worked as a single turbine, showed that for this machine at all events this conclusion is correct. Fig. 241 shows the efficiency curves obtained from the two turbines; A when working with a single runner; B with four runners in series, under approximately the same head.

Here the outer diameter of the runner $= 3.35$ inches.

    ,,   ,, inner   ,, (mean) ,,   ,, $= 1.675$,,

Vanes radial at inlet.   Head $=$ (approx.) 85 feet.

Art. 138.—The "American" Type or "Mixed Flow" Turbine.
While the improved Francis or Thomson turbine is undoubtedly the

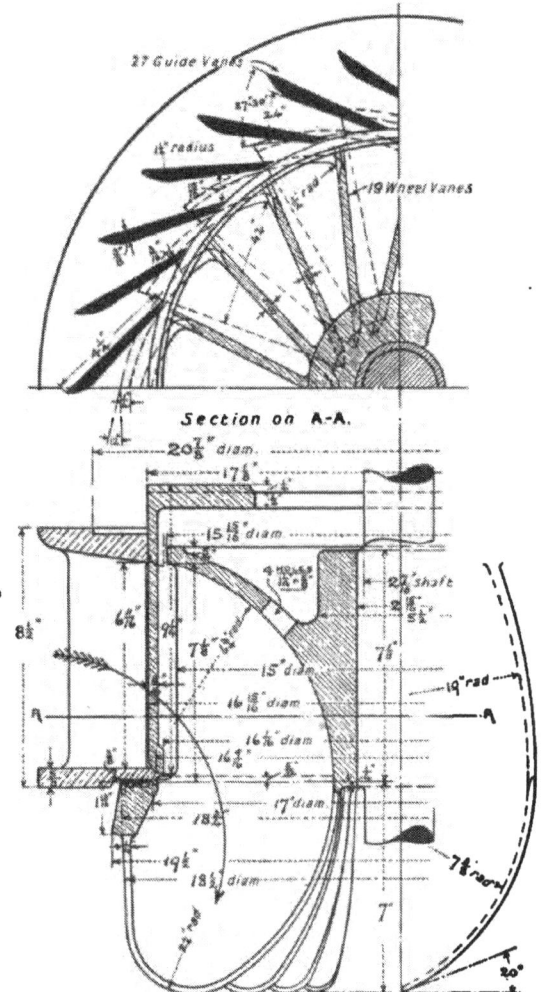

Fig. 243.—Section through Guides and Runners of Victor Mixed-Flow Turbine with Cylinder-Gate; 179 H.P. at 664 revs. under 50 ft. head.

most efficient and offers advantages in respect of ease of regulation and

high part-gate efficiency which are unequalled by any other type, th-
high first cost prohibits its use in many instances. The demand, particularly in the United States, for a turbine suitable for low and medium
falls, which must above all things be cheap, and in which the efficiency
need not necessarily be very high, has led to the development of a type
of machine which, although for many years confined to the United States,
is at present being manufactured in some numbers in Great Britain and
to a less extent on the Continent. The Hercules and Victor low-pressure
turbines may be taken as representative of this class.

These machines, which are almost invariably fitted with fixed guide-

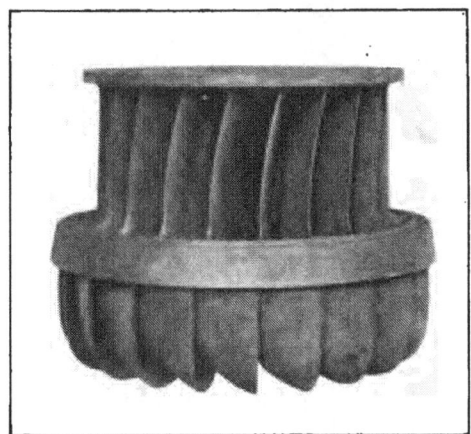

Fig. 244.—Runner for 15 in. Mixed-Flow Victor Turbine.

vanes and regulated by means of the cylindrical gate or ring sluice, have
inward radial flow as in the Francis turbine. After the inlet the wheel
buckets are curved both laterally and vertically, the water in its
passage through the wheel tracing out a path which is approximately a
quadrant of a circle, and being finally discharged partly in an axial and
partly in an outward radial direction.

Fig. 242 shows the general arrangement of an enclosed double horizontal shaft turbine of this type, while Figs. 243 and 244 show details of
the guide vanes and runner of a Victor turbine,[1] as designed to develop
180 H.P. when running at 665 revolutions per minute under a head of
50 feet. The vanes at the outlet are spoon-shaped. By this type of

[1] By courtesy of the makers, the Platt Iron Works, Dayton, Ohio.

onstruction an extremely large discharge area is ensured, while by
naking the wheel deep at inlet,
he inlet area is corresponding-
y increased. The wheel thus
becomes of very compact construction and is capable of deal-
ng with a large volume of
vater, but has the grave defect
hat in virtue of this great
lepth its efficiency at part gate
s comparatively low.

In the turbine illustrated,
he wheel diameter is 15 inches
and the depth 7½ inches at
entrance, while at exit the diameter is 18½ inches, the over-
ll depth of the vanes being
4⅛ inches. The guide vanes,
wenty-seven in number, are
ixed, and give a mean inlet
angle of about 26°. The wheel
vanes, nineteen in number, are
lat at entrance, and are in-
lined forwards towards the
irection of rotation, making
n angle of about 110° with
he tangent to the inlet
ircle.

The vane angle at exit varies
rom 12° to 20°, the minimum
alue being that affecting the
adial outward discharge. As
nay be readily understood, the
ifficulty of designing these
it edges so as to give the
orrect inclination at each ra-
ius is almost insuperable, and
xperiment proves the only

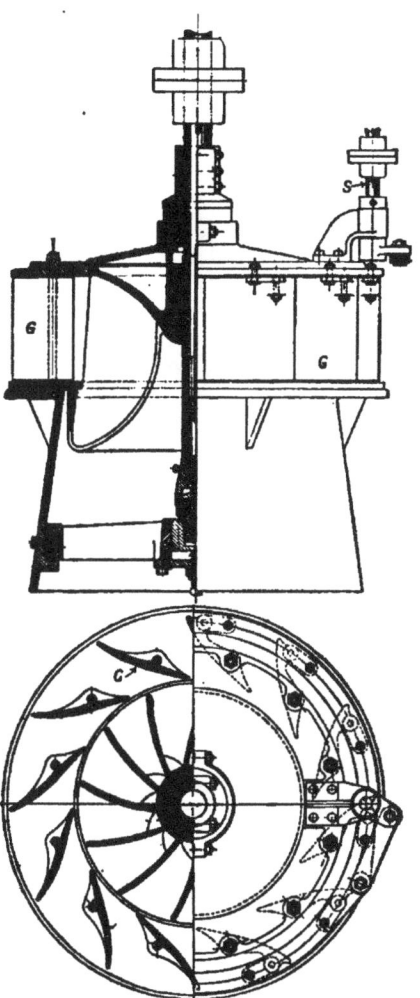

FIG. 245.—"New American" Turbine.

fe guide as to the precise curvature to give to the vanes. Governing is
erformed by means of a cylinder gate set between guide vanes and wheel,

H.A.   L L

sliding axially and receiving its motion from two draw-bars which carry racks gearing with pinions which are actuated either by an automatic governor or by hand (Figs. 228 and 242).

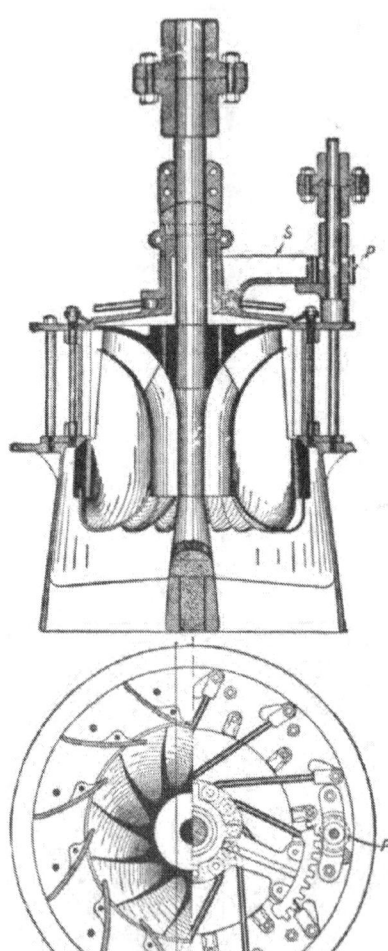

As thus constructed the turbine is capable of a full-load efficiency of about 82 per cent., falling to about 65 per cent. at half gate.

In the Hercules turbine the wheel vanes are provided with a series of horizontal wings or projections, which to some extent serve the purpose of separate compartments in confining the effect of throttling to one portion of the wheel and thus increasing the part-gate efficiency, at the expense, however, of that at full gate.

Fig. 245 shows the general arrangement of a vertical New American turbine, in which the admission of water is controlled by the wicket gates G. These are operated through a ring which is moved by a link connected with the governor through the shaft S.

Fig. 246 illustrates the Samson-Leffel turbine, which combines a radial inflow runner of the Francis type with an inward radial admission and axial discharge runner of the typical American type of turbine. Here again the gates are of the wicket type and are operated from the governor through the pinion P and geared sector S.

FIG. 246.—Samson-Leffel Turbine.

If specially designed for the particular head, flow, and speed of rotation, his class of wheel is well adapted for moderate powers and for medium eads up to about 35 feet where the head is fairly constant, and where art-gate efficiency is unimportant as compared with low first cost. The eneral practice of manufacturing it in stock sizes, and of supplying that ize which most nearly meets the requirements of the purchaser instead f designing the machine to suit its location, together with the fact that ach American machinery has in the past been characterized by a imsiness of construction unusual in English and Continental practice, as, however, had the effect of discrediting this class of turbine among uropean engineers to an extent greater than its inherent disadvantages eserve. Evolution in this type of machine would appear to be tending i the direction of fewer and deeper buckets with wider openings to avoid bstruction.

ART. 139.—GOVERNING OF TURBINE PLANTS.

The difficulties in the way of the efficient speed regulation of a water heel or turbine are many and peculiar to this form of motor, and the oblem is much more complicated than in the case of a steam engine or irbine. In either type of motor, when running at a uniform speed there an exact balance between the energy given up by the motive fluid per nit time in its passage through the motor and the energy absorbed in eful work and in overcoming friction. If more load is thrown on, in ther case the speed diminishes until the work done against the increased sistance is again equal to the energy given up by the fluid.

In the case of a steam engine or turbine, directly the speed diminishes e governor alters the admission valves, admits more steam to the linders, and in a very short interval of time an exact balance is again t up between the supply of and the demand for energy, so that the gine again runs at a uniform, though slightly lower, speed. The mission valves being light and easily moved, the governor itself is in neral quite capable of adjusting these rapidly and accurately, while, ice the steam is an elastic fluid and in a state of high compression, any ght opening of the valves is accompanied by an instantaneous rush of am at high velocity.

Also, since the amount of available energy per pound of high pressure am is very great, the mass and inertia of the column of motive fluid are nparatively small, so that its velocity may be rapidly changed without y appreciable change in the pressure in the steam chest. Thus, in an iciently governed steam engine, fitted with a flywheel of fair size, it is possible to throw the whole external load off with an instantaneous increase in speed not exceeding 2 per cent. of the normal and with a final increase of less than 1 per cent., the time to attain this normal speed not exceeding 5 seconds. This, then, is the ideal to be aimed at in the governing of a water-power plant, and while such close regulation as this is practically impossible, an examination of the special difficulties to be overcome in this case will indicate in what direction their most satisfactory solution is to be found.

In the first place, the motive fluid (water) is almost incompressible,

FIG. 247.—Governor with Mechanical Relay as fitted to Girard Turbine.

and contains a much smaller store of energy per unit weight than in the case of steam, so that a similar demand for energy must be followed by a largely increased mass flow. The only force available to give the water this increased velocity is that of gravity, and it follows that even in the most favourable circumstances, i.e., when the turbine is set directly in an open forebay of ample dimensions, this velocity cannot exceed that due to the supply head. Where the turbine is supplied through a long pipe line of small slope the state of affairs is much worse, since the force of gravity has now not only to produce increased mass flow and hence to give increased kinetic energy to the moving column of water, but has also to overcome the pipe resistance, with the result that the possible acceleration of the supply column is reduced.

Next consider the action of the governor. In reply to a demand for energy, denoted by a reduction in the speed of rotation, the governor attempts to open the turbine gates. These may be very massive, possessing considerable inertia, and may in addition, through working submerged in water containing solid matter in suspension, offer considerable frictional resistance to rotation.

The governor itself is thus quite incapable of giving the required motion, and some form of relay becomes necessary. A device which was often adopted in the earlier days, but which is now practically obsolete, consisted in a system of fast and loose pulleys, mounted on one shaft and driven from a countershaft by means of two belts, one open and the other crossed.

The position of these belts, one of which is always riding on the loose pulley, is regulated by the governor, and as in consequence the open or crossed belt comes to ride on one of the fixed pulleys, the direction of rotation of this shaft changes. Its rotation causes the turbine gates to open or close and thus regulates the speed of the wheel.

Two types of a more modern mechanical relay device are shown in Figs. 228 and 247. In the latter,[1] a double ratchet is worked by a link, as shown, from a lay shaft belt-driven from the turbine shaft. A ratchet wheel, which is mounted on a second lay shaft by which the turbine gate is directly operated, is wholly or partially masked by a plate whose position depends on the height of the governor. Thus, under normal conditions of working, the plate covers the wheel so as to put both pawls out of gear. Any increase in speed then raises the governor, rotates the guard plate, and allows one pawl to gear with the ratchet wheel, rotating the lay shaft and closing the turbine gates. A decrease in speed causes the second pawl to be put into gear, and thus produces an opposite rotation of the lay shaft and an opening of the gates.

With any such type of mechanical device, however, some considerable time is required to open a sluice gate, and while for such a purpose as driving textile machinery, where the changes of load are relatively small, this type fulfils the requirements, yet for electric driving for lighting and power transmission, where a constant speed is required with very large and sudden variations in load, the mechanical relay, except in combination with a large and costly flywheel, is unsatisfactory.

In such a case the hydraulic relay provides the only satisfactory

---

[1] By courtesy of Messrs. Gilbert Gilkes & Co., Ltd., Kendal.

solution. Here the centrifugal governor operates a regulating valve
which admits either water or oil under pressure to one side or other of a
piston in a relay cylinder, this piston being connected with and operating
the turbine gate mechanism.

Types of this relay mechanism are illustrated in Figs. 201 to 205, 234,
236, 239A, 248 and 249.

Even with this relay accurate speed regulation under difficult circumstances cannot be obtained without the provision of what is termed a

FIG. 248.—Thomson Vortex Turbine fitted with Hydraulic Relay Governor,
Compensating Device, and Automatic Pressure Regulator.

relay return or compensating device. The reason for this is evident if we
consider that as the speed falls, the gates are opened and the supply
column is accelerated, this opening going on until the supply of energy
per unit time is equal to the demand. But the acceleration of the water
column goes on for an appreciable time after the gate opening has ceased,
and in consequence the supply now becomes too great for the requirements of the wheel, the speed rises, and the governor commences to close
the gates. This suddenly checks the motion of the supply column, and in
virtue of its inertia produces an increased pressure at the valve and

ı temporarily increased velocity of flow through the gates. The speed of
ıhe wheel thus increases still further, and the gates are closed until an

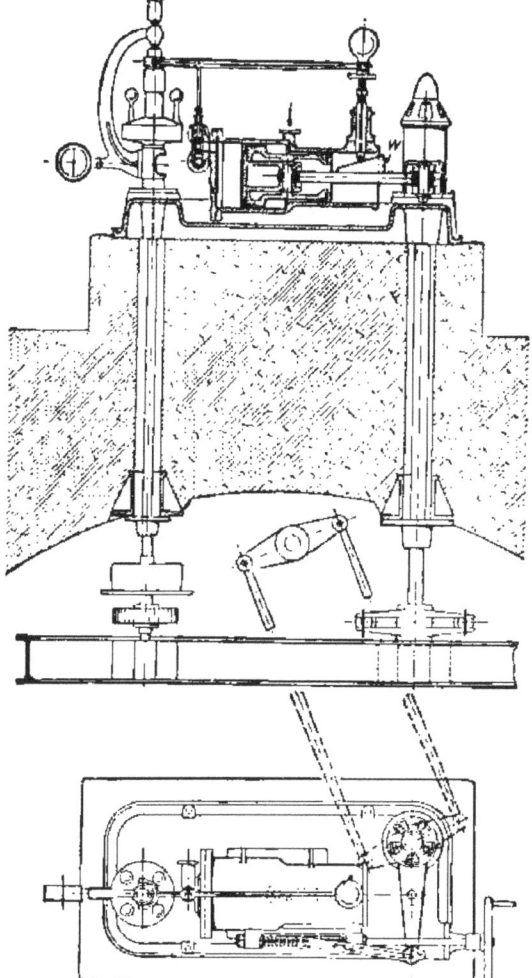

Fig. 249.—Hydraulic Relay and Compensating Device.

instantaneous balance is set up between supply and demand. As the
inertia pressure falls the supply now becomes less than the demand, the

speed falls, the gates commence to reopen, and the state of hunting, whi.l is here outlined, may not die out for some considerable time. To preven: this some form of relay return device should be fitted, this being s arranged that all parts of the governor connections, including the regulating valve, return to a normal mid position as soon as the action of the governor ceases. This tends to prevent over-regulation and hunting. Where, in the case of a long penstock, the quick closing of the turbine gates may lead to excessive water hammer, a pressure regulator shou.: also be fitted, this consisting of an automatic relief valve which is throw: open by the closing of the turbine gates, and which is then slow.; returned to its seat. One such pressure regulator is shown in Fig. 20 while a second type, as described on p. 451, is shown applied at P to Thomson vortex turbine in Fig. 248.

Types of relay return devices are shown in Figs. 202 and 206, and a further type, similar in general principle to those fitted to the Niagara turbines (Art. 135), is illustrated in Fig. 249. Here a force of 50 ton is available on the relay piston for operating the governing mechanism. and gates. Hunting is prevented by the wedge W, which, as the pistor moves out, lowers the fulcrum of the governor lever, and thus closes the relay valve until a fresh movement of the governor reopens it.

Two other devices which also give considerable assistance in specia cases are the stand pipe and the relief valve.

The **stand pipe** (Art. 152) consists of a vertical open pipe, its lower end being connected to the penstock near to its connection with the turbines, and of such a height that when exposed to the statical head in the supply reservoir the water level is within a short distance of the top. Any increase in pressure at the turbine, due to a sudden closing of the gates, then produces a flow up the stand pipe, the water escaping at the top, and the maximum possible pressure in the penstock becomes that due to the statical head in the supply reservoir together with that necessary to produce flow up the stand pipe. Obviously the stand pipe cannot be applied where the supply head is very great, although in one modern plant[1] such an open pipe 235 feet in height has been fitted.

A sudden demand for power is also responded to more easily where a stand pipe is provided, the level in the pipe falling, and energy thus being supplied to the wheel while the supply column is being accelerated (Art. 152).

The **relief valve**, as its name implies, consists simply of a valve placed on the penstock near to the turbine casing and arranged so as to open outwards. This is adjusted so as to open directly the pressure exceeds

---

[1] At the St. Louis Hydro-Electric Plant. See *The Engineer*, February 15, 1907.

he normal by a few pounds per square inch, and its area should be such
hat, if the gates are closed suddenly due to a throwing-off of the entire
oad, it is capable of taking the whole discharge.   If A be the minimum
:otal cross sectional area of the guide passages when these are wide open,

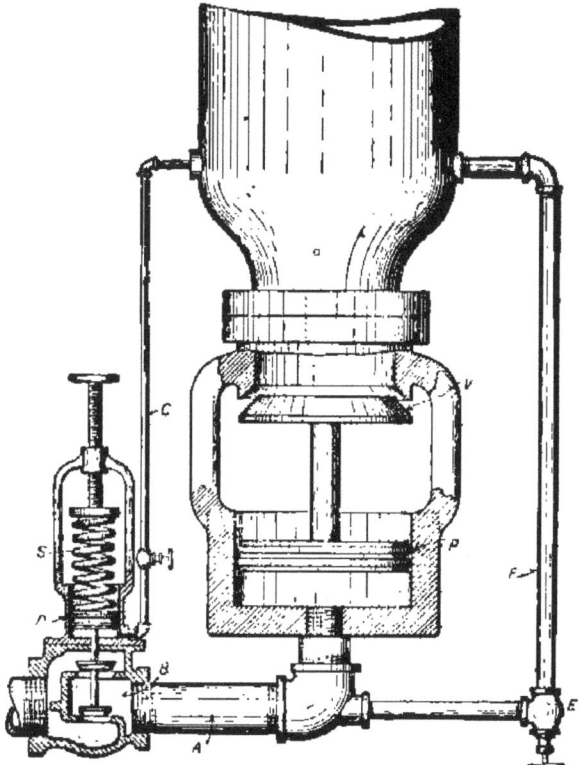

FIG. 250.—Lombard Relief Valve.

in order to allow for exceptional circumstances the total relief valve area
should not be less than ·7 A.

The ordinary spring-loaded relief valve is not usually very successful on
a large plant, one or other type of hydraulically operated valve being
commonly fitted.   Such a one is the Lombard valve, illustrated diagrammatically in Fig. 250.   Here P is the penstock, with its relief valve V,
which is held up to its seat by the water pressure on the piston P.   The

space behind this piston is connected through the pipe A to the waste valve B. This is a balanced valve held closed by means of the spring S against the pressure of the penstock water which acts through the pipe C on the piston D. When the pressure in the penstock becomes greater than normal the waste valve B is forced open, allowing water to escape and relieving the pressure behind the piston P. The relief valve V then opens, relieving the pressure in the main. When this pressure falls below normal the valve B again closes, and the pressure behind the piston P gradually increases to that in the penstock, and again closes the valve V. The rate of closing can be regulated to prevent surging by suitable adjustment of the throttle valve E on the connecting pipe F.

Special consideration of the circumstances of each installation is necessary to determine which of these regulating devices is likely to give the best results.

Dealing firstly with pressure turbines, the easiest type of plant to govern is one in which the turbine is placed in a forebay of ample dimensions fed directly from the supply canal (Fig. 238). Here a demand for power is instantly met by an increased flow, at the velocity corresponding to the supply head, while, when the gates are closed, inertia effects are unimportant. Under these circumstances the speed may be regulated with great nicety, and in general the more nearly the arrangement of any power plant approximates to this the easier does it become to get good regulation. Both head and tail-race should be of ample size, so that any fluctuation in flow may not cause an appreciable difference in either level, while all approach channels and passages should have easy curves and well-finished surfaces so that the production of any periodic wave motion may be prevented.

Wherever possible the use of a long penstock should be avoided, and the water brought as near as possible to its work in an open channel of ample area, for it may be laid down as a general principle that the easiest plants to govern are those in which the slope from open head-water to open tail-water is as steep as possible, and in which the ratio of kinetic energy to total energy is as small as possible.

A few specific types of plant will now be considered in more detail, with respect to their possibilities in the way of speed regulation.

(a) Turbine fed by a Supply Pipe which is almost vertical, i.e., with a slope of 60° or over.

Here a demand for energy on an increasing load receives an immediate response, and speed regulation in this direction, with a supply pipe of

connected by levers to a central ring, which is rotated by means of the relay. In either case the gearing is usually placed inside the casing, and while accurate speed regulation is possible with either design, the submerged gearing needs to be designed on more substantial lines to compensate for its inaccessibility for examination.

Sliding cylinder gates are commonly moved through a couple of parallel drawbars terminating in racks, which gear with pinions on a shaft perpendicular to the wheel axis, this latter shaft deriving its motion from the relay mechanism by one or other of the devices shown in Figs. 228, 234A, and 249. Where this type of gate is fitted to a vertical shaft machine, it often becomes advisable to balance the weight of the gate and

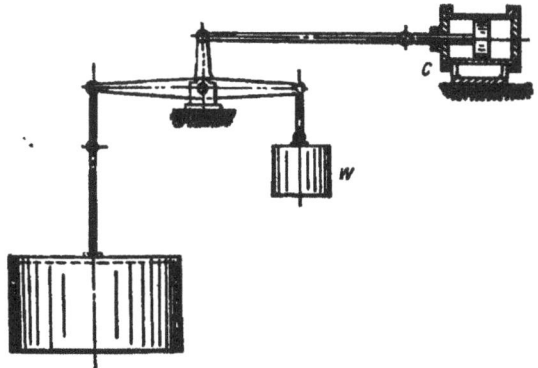

FIG. 251.—Direct Relay Governing Mechanism for Sliding Cylinder Gate.

its drawbars by means of a counterbalance weight, in which case a suitable type of connection is shown in Fig. 251.

For successful governing, the gate should consist of a plain cylinder. If provided with fingers, as indicated by the dotted lines in Fig. 230, the water pressure on the upper side of these is largely in excess of that on their lower face. This necessitates a very heavy counterbalance weight, possessing considerable inertia, and increases the force necessary to start and stop the motion of the gate, while the weight and cost of the connecting links necessary to withstand the stress become excessive. Without the balance weight the steady resistance produced by the unbalanced pressure produces an excessive stress on the gate connections. In either case the very slight addition to part-gate efficiency is totally insufficient to compensate for the increased difficulty in governing.

Governing of Impulse Wheels —The preceding considerations also apply,

The governing of both turbines is by oil-pressure Servo-motor (relay motor).
The diagrams show the maximum change of speed with sudden charge or discharge. Observations to the left of each vertical line represent charge in kilowatts; those to the right, discharge in kilowatts.

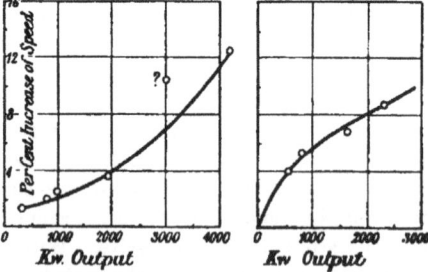

TURBINE VII
Normal 500 Revs per Min
Fly-wheel Moment of Inertia
gD². 56000 Kgm²
Head H · 60 m
These are fitted with heavy Fly-wheel
Kw Load 2000 1000
Kw Load 1000 2000
% Increase of Speed
% Decrease of Speed
Cut off Period at 1800 Kw Load ·16 Sec
Pressure Variation 13%
Length of Supply Pipe · 200 m
Diameter · 2·0 m

TURBINE IX
Normal 600 Revs per Min
Fly wheel Moment of Inertia
gD². 10500 Kgm²
Head H · 147 m
Total Load Variation
Kw Load 2000 1000
Kw Load 1000 2000
Cut off Period at 2150 Kw Load ·25 Sec
These had no separate Fly-wheel
Pressure Variation 10%
Length of Supply Pipe · 400 m
Diameter · 2·0 m—1·8 m

-------- Partial Load Variation
———— Total " ,— "

FIGS. 252, 253.—Governing Tests of Pressure Turbines.

so far as cases *a* and *b* are concerned, to the governing of impulse turbines.

Both turbines are governed by oil-pressure Servo-motor.

Turbine XII
The turbine is fitted with automatic pressure regulation.
Normal 375 revs. per minute
Head H = 350 m.
Fly-wheel moment of inertia g D² = 55,000 sq. kg.-m.
Max. pressure variation, 1.8 per cent.
Length of supply-pipe - 925 m.
Diameter = 1.35 m. - 1.05 m.

Turbine XIII
The turbine is fitted with jet cut-off gear.
Normal 630 revs. per minute
Head H = 850 m.
Fly-wheel moment of inertia g D² = 13,000 sq. kg.-m.
Max. pressure variation, 3.9 per cent.
Length of supply pipe = 2130 m.
Diameter = 0.5 m.

Per Cent Increase of Speed
Kw. Output
Kw Output

FIG. 254.—Governing Tests of Pelton Wheel.

except where, as in the case of a Pelton wheel fitted with deflecting nozzle, the velocity of flow through the supply main is maintained uniform for all loads. Although in this case inertia effects are not to be feared in the governing of the turbine, yet the occasional necessity for quickly shutting off the supply renders the provision of a relief valve near the lower end of the pipe essential.

Owing to the absence of any cyclical variation of turning moment in a pressure turbine, a special flywheel is not usually necessary for close governing, sufficient flywheel effect in general being obtained from the turbine runner and shaft itself, and from the electric motor when such is used.

In the Pelton wheel, however, the turning moment undergoes a slight periodic variation, the period depending on the number of buckets and on the speed of the wheel. On account of this and on account of the comparatively small weight of the wheel for a given power, a flywheel is in general essential for such close governing as is necessary for the driving of alternators in parallel.

Figs. 252 and 253[1] show the results of governing tests on turbines VII. and IX. (pressure turbines) of p. 508 and Fig. 254 the results of similar tests on turbines XII. and XIII. (Pelton wheels) of p. 444. Each of the latter turbines is fitted with Doble needle regulators, while turbine XII. is also provided with an automatic pressure regulator. In turbine XIII. a decrease in load is followed by the automatic interposition of a shutter between nozzle and wheel. This shutter is then gradually withdrawn by the action of the relay returning device, and the needle is at the same time gradually moved forward in the nozzle, the operation taking place so slowly that no appreciable increase of pressure takes place.

ART. 140.—DESIGN OF HEAD AND TAIL-RACES.

The construction of the head and tail-races for a turbine plant requires careful consideration. The forebay should be free from sharp turns and sudden changes of section, the velocity of flow not exceeding from 3 to 4 feet per second. The tail-race should be of the same capacity and should be formed with a well under the turbine outlet, which should contain from 2 to 4 feet of dead water when the turbines are idle. If this be not attended to, a serious loss of head may be caused.

Where a draught tube is fitted this should be submerged from 3 to 6 inches in the standing tail-water, while it is preferably bent at its lower end, so as to discharge in the direction of flow in the tail-race.

Where a long penstock is installed, this should be supplied with an air pipe (Fig. 237) at its highest point and also at the highest point of any vertical bends in its length, to permit the escape of accumulated air, and also to prevent the collapse of the pipe due to the formation of a vacuum should the turbine gates be opened with the head gates closed. (See p. 271.)

A strainer is always fitted at the exit from the forebay, or supply canal,

[1] "Proc. Inst. Mech. Engineers," 1910–11.

and consists of a series of wooden or metal grids. These are usually spaced about 1 inch apart, and in order to reduce the loss due to the contraction and subsequent expansion of sections of the stream, should be as narrow as is consistent with strength. The angle of inclination of the strainer should be not less than 45°, in order to give a large area of waterway.

Effect of Ice Formation.—Although the hydraulic power plant is not greatly hampered by ice formation in Great Britain and the western portion of the continent of Europe, ice troubles may become serious in such climates as are found in Canada and the northern portion of the United States, and may necessitate some modification in the design of the head-race.

The trouble which is often experienced, particularly with frazil ice (Art. 2, p. 5) due to its tendency to adhere to the racks, strainers and gates of a turbine, can, however, be prevented by a slight heating of the racks or turbine gates. At the Ottawa Electric Company's Power House No. 1 a line of steam pipes laid above water level and against the face of the rack was found to answer perfectly. In the same installation, consisting of three 39-inch wheels, 30 feet head, using 100,000 cubic feet of water per minute, steam was supplied by a small pipe to each of the wheel housings when the unit began to lose capacity. To supply this, 20 tons of coal were used during four months of winter, with eleven days on which frazil was bad, only occasional injection of steam being found to be necessary. Electric heating of the same racks has also been tried successfully, 600 amperes at ·3 volts removing the ice at once from a single rack bar with the air temperature at 15° Fahr.[1] These bars were $1\frac{5}{8}$ inches thick and 18 feet long.

In a power plant it is usually advisable that the water at the intake should be covered with surface ice, as being the most effective preventative of the formation of both frazil and anchor ice. If there are large stretches of open water above the surface ice, however, frazil is formed and adheres to the lower surface, and may result in a stoppage of the channel. In such a case, or when located at the foot of rapids, it is better to construct a head-race of sufficient size to serve as a settling basin for the ice drawn in. Even then it may sometimes be necessary to blast a channel in the surface sheet. Where a long narrow canal is fed from a stretch of open water the ice difficulty becomes very great. A surface covering is then harmful, as encouraging the adherence of frazil.

[1] These results have been taken from "Ice Formation," by Barnes, Wiley & Son, N.Y. 1907. Here the whole subject is considered in detail.

EXAMPLES.

1. Discuss the relative advantages and disadvantages of the impulse and pressure turbine as regards—

(a) Applicability to high, medium, or low heads.

(b) Applicability to suit local conditions.

(c) Efficiency.

(d) Speed regulation.

(e) Speed of rotation.

2. Sketch any device suitable for the speed regulation of—

(a) A Pelton wheel.

(b) A Girard turbine.

(c) An inward radial flow turbine.

(d) An outward radial flow turbine.

3. The nozzle circle of a Barker's mill has a diameter of 2 feet. The nozzles, two in number, are ¾″ diameter, and when working under a head of 1 foot the wheel makes 240 revolutions per minute. Determine its hydraulic efficiency, neglecting the effect of friction.

Answer ·982.

4. In the wheel of the previous example, the weight of water used at 240 revolutions per minute, working head 6 feet, was 670 lbs. The brake horse power was ·056.

Determine the coefficient of frictional resistance inside the wheel; the hydraulic efficiency, the total efficiency, the speed for maximum possible hydraulic efficiency, and this efficiency.

Answer :—

$$F = ·2.$$

Hydraulic efficiency   = ·522.

Total efficiency   = ·46.

Speed for maximum efficiency = 160 revolutions.

Maximum efficiency   = ·598.

CHAPTER XV

Theory of Turbine Design—Design of Stand Pipes.

ART. 141.—THEORY OF TURBINE DESIGN.

THE turbine system, as a whole, may be divided into the supply pipe, the turbine itself, and the discharge pipe. Losses of head are experienced in each branch of the system, so that if H be the total difference of level between open head and tail-race, the head available for doing work on the turbine will be less than H by the amount necessary to overcome the frictional and other losses in the supply and discharge pipes.

The loss due to this cause is approximately proportional to the lengths of the pipes and to the square of the velocity of flow, and its relative importance diminishes as the gradient of the pipe line and its sectional area are increased. Theoretically, by making the pipes of sufficiently large area the loss may be made quite negligible. This increase in area is, however, accompanied by a corresponding increase in the first cost, and it appears to be fairly well agreed that in practice it does not pay to reduce the pipe line velocity below from 6 to 8 feet per second, the value to be adopted increasing with the gradient and with the head.

In a large power plant where the head is high and the penstock direct. this velocity may be increased without serious proportional loss of head up to a maximum of about 16 feet per second. .

If, in any type of turbine, v be the velocity of the supply water at its exit from the guide vanes, and if a be the angle between the guide vanes and the direction of motion of the wheel at the point of entry, v may be resolved into two components ; $v \sin a$, perpendicular to the direction of motion of the vanes, which is usually termed the velocity of flow, and $v \cos a$ parallel to this direction, which is termed the velocity of whirl. Throughout the following discussion the velocity of flow will be denoted by f, and that of whirl by w. Thus in a radial-flow turbine f is radial and w tangential to the wheel, while in an axial-flow machine f is parallel to the turbine axis and w is in the plane of the wheel.

In virtue of the velocity of whirl, the supply water possesses momentum in the plane of the wheel, and it is the change in the moment of this momentum about the axis of the wheel during the passage of the water through the wheel buckets which provides the turning moment on the shaft. For this turning moment to be a maximum with a given value of v and a given quantity of water, it follows that the value of w should be a maximum, and therefore that a should be as nearly as possible zero.

On the other hand, the volume of water which a given wheel is capable of handling per second depends on f, since it is in virtue of this component of velocity that water is carried into the turbine buckets. As a is diminished, therefore, the size of turbine for a given power, and the first cost, increases, and the problem before the designer is to determine at what point the diminution in efficiency due to an increase in a becomes of more importance than the corresponding diminution in first cost. A similar state of affairs holds at exit. For maximum hydraulic efficiency the energy rejected in the discharge should be reduced to a minimum. This requires the absolute velocity of discharge from the wheel to be as small as possible. The minimum permissible velocity of discharge is, however, governed by the necessity for getting a given volume of water per second through the limited sectional area of the buckets at this point, and here also an increase in the velocity of flow at the expense of the velocity of whirl will enable a larger volume of water to be dealt with and a greater power to be obtained, but with a sacrifice of the hydraulic, though possibly not of the economic, efficiency.

Where an abundant supply of water is available at all times, the efficiency of the turbine may become quite a secondary consideration as compared with its prime cost, and a cheap but comparatively inefficient turbine may be preferable on all counts. In such a case high efficiency at part loads is a minor consideration and may be entirely subordinated to considerations of cheapness and of ease of governing. Here, however, it must be remembered that where a long supply pipe or channel is necessary, a decrease in the efficiency of the turbine, particularly at full load, necessitating as it does an increased water supply, may cause the initial cost of construction of such channels or pipes to more than counterbalance the decreased prime cost of the motor.

Again, where the supply is variable and where in times of drought barely sufficient water is available, it is highly important that high efficiency at all gates be the first consideration.

Thus the turbine designer must keep many conflicting possibilities in view, each of which has its own effect on the most suitable design to be adopted, and no hard and fast rules can be formulated for the design of any type of machine. Certain broad principles may, however, be laid down, to which the design must conform if the turbine is to be efficient and these will now be briefly indicated.

In the following demonstrations :—

Let ω = angular velocity of the wheel in radians per second.

r = radius in feet at any point indicated by a suffix.

v = velocity of supply stream at its exit from the guide vanes. in feet per second.

$u = \omega r$ = velocity of wheel at point indicated by a suffix.

f = velocity of flow.

w = velocity of whirl.

a = angle between guide vanes and direction of motion of wheel at entrance.

β = angle between lip of moving vanes and direction of motion of wheel.

γ = angle between discharge edges of moving vanes and direction of motion of wheel.

Q = flow in cubic feet per second.

W = weight of 1 cubic foot of water = 62·4 lbs.

ART. 142.—GENERAL CASE OF INWARD RADIAL FLOW TURBINE (FIG. 255).

Let the suffix (a) refer to the state of affairs in the supply pipe.

(b) refer to the state of affairs in the discharge pipe.

(1) refer to the state of affairs at the exit from guide vanes.

(2) refer to the state of affairs at the inlet to wheel vanes.

(3) refer to the state of affairs at the exit from wheel vanes.

Then a consideration of the diagram shows that if the vane angles are proportioned so as to avoid shock at entrance :

$$\begin{cases} f_2 = w_2 \tan a = (w_2 - u_2) \tan \beta, \therefore u_2 = w_2 \left(1 - \dfrac{\tan a}{\tan \beta} \right); \\ f_3 = (u_3 - w_3) \tan \gamma; \; _2 v_r = f_2 \operatorname{cosec} \beta; \; _3 v_r = f_3 \operatorname{cosec} \gamma. \end{cases}$$

The moment of momentum of the water leaving the guide vanes per sec. about the axis of rotation $\Big\} = \dfrac{W Q}{g} w_1 r_1$ ft. lb. units, and since.

if losses at the exit from the guide vanes are neglected, $w_1 = w_2$ while.

neglecting clearance, $r_1 = r_2$, this becomes $\dfrac{W Q}{g} w_2 r_2$ ft. lb. units.

The final moment of momentum $= \dfrac{W'Q}{g} \, w_3 \, r_3$ ft. lb. units.

∴ Change of moment of momentum = turning moment $\Big\} = \dfrac{W'Q}{g} \{ \, w_2 \, r_2 - w_3 \, r_3 \, \}$ ft. lbs.

∴ Work done by this moment per second $\Big\} = \dfrac{W'Q}{g} \{ \, w_2 \, r_2 - w_3 \, r_3 \, \} \, \omega$ ft. lbs.

$$= \frac{W'Q}{g} \{ w_2 \, u_2 - w_3 \, u_3 \} \text{ ft. lbs.} \quad (1)$$

Evidently this has its maximum value when $w_3 = 0$, and then the work done per second $= U = \dfrac{W \, Q}{g} \{ \, w_2 \, u_2 \, \}$ ft. lbs. $\quad (2)$

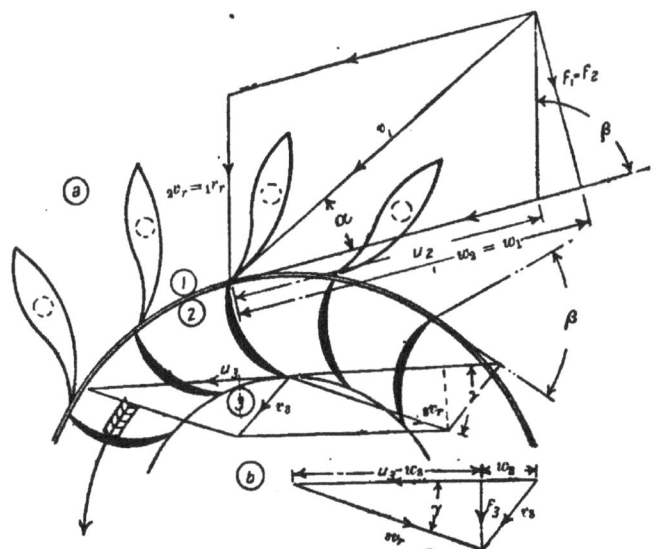

FIG. 255. – Guide and Vane Angles for Inward Radial Flow Turbine.

If w_3 is not zero, we have, on substituting its value $w_3 = u_3 - f_3 \cot \gamma$ in (1):—

$$U = \frac{W \, Q}{g} \{ w_2 \, u_2 - u_3^2 + u_3 f_3 \cot \gamma \} \text{ ft. lbs. per second.} \quad (2a)$$

If the vane angles are correctly proportioned as indicated in Fig. 255 so as to avoid shock at entrance, we have:—

$$u_2 = w_2 \left(1 - \frac{\tan a}{\tan \beta} \right) ;$$

while if b_2 and b_3 are the effective breadths of the wheel passages at entrance and exit, so that $2 \pi b_2 r_2$ and $2 \pi b_3 r_3$ are the effective passage areas, we have, for continuity of flow, $f_3 = f_2 \dfrac{b_2 r_2}{b_3 r_3}$. Also $\dfrac{u_3}{u_2} = \dfrac{r_3}{r_2}$, so that

$$U = \frac{W}{g} Q \left[w_2^2 \left(1 - \frac{\tan a}{\tan \beta} \right) \left\{ \begin{array}{l} 1 - \left(\dfrac{r_3}{r_2} \right)^2 \left(1 - \dfrac{\tan a}{\tan \beta} \right) \\ + \dfrac{b_2}{b_3} \dfrac{\tan a}{\tan \gamma} \end{array} \right\} \right] \quad (2)$$

Assuming the turbine to be designed, however, so that $w_3 = 0$, we get from (2)

$$U = \frac{W}{g} Q\, w_2^2 \left(1 - \frac{\tan a}{\tan \cdot \beta} \right). \quad (3)$$

If the wheel is horizontal, or if in a vertical wheel we neglect the differences of level at the highest and lowest points and also neglect losses at entrance, we have :—

$$\frac{p_2}{W} + \frac{r_2^2}{2g} = \frac{p_3}{W} + \frac{r_3^2}{2g} + \begin{array}{c} \text{work done by} \\ \text{water per lb.} \end{array} + \begin{array}{c} \text{losses per lb. be-} \\ \text{tween (2) and (3).} \end{array} \quad (4)$$

If then $H' = H - \dfrac{F\, L\, v^2}{2\, g\, m}$ = head available for producing flow through the wheel, i.e., the total head minus that necessary to overcome pipe line losses, we must have :—

$$H' = \frac{p_2}{W} + \frac{r_2^2}{2g} - \frac{p_3}{W} \quad (5)$$

so that, substituting in (4) and putting $\left\{ \begin{array}{l} v_2^2 = w_2^2 + f_2^2 \\ r_3^2 = w_3^2 + f_3^2 \\ \quad = f_3^2 \text{ if } w_3 = 0. \end{array} \right.$

we have

$$H' = \frac{f_3^2}{2g} + \frac{w_2^2}{g} \left(1 - \frac{\tan a}{\tan \beta} \right)^1 \quad (6)$$

from which, writing $f_3 = f_2 \dfrac{b_2 r_2}{b_3 r_3} = w_2 \tan a \dfrac{b_2 r_2}{b_3 r_3}$ we get :—

$$H' = \frac{w_2^2}{2g} \left\{ 2 + \left(\frac{b_2 r_2}{b_3 r_3} \tan a \right)^2 - 2 \frac{\tan a}{\tan \beta} \right\} \quad (7)$$

$$\therefore\ w_2 = \sqrt{ \frac{2\, g\, H'}{2 + \left(\dfrac{b_2 r_2}{b_3 r_3} \tan a \right)^2 - 2 \dfrac{\tan a}{\tan \beta}} } \quad (8)$$

$$\therefore\ u_2 = \left(1 - \frac{\tan a}{\tan \beta} \right) \sqrt{ \frac{2\, g\, H'}{2 + \left(\dfrac{b_2 r_2}{b_3 r_3} \tan a \right)^2 - 2 \dfrac{\tan a}{\tan \beta}} }. \quad (9)$$

---

[1] This neglects losses due to friction, etc., in the wheel.

This gives the velocity of whirl, and the peripheral speed of the wheel for maximum efficiency, in terms of the available head H'.

The effect of any variation in a or β, on the peripheral speed for maximum efficiency, is shown in the following table, which gives the theoretical values of k (where $u_2 = k \sqrt{2\,g\,H'}$) in the case where $f_2 = f_3$.

Values of β.	Values of a.							
	0°	5°	10°	12½°	15°	20°	25°	30°
60°			·658		·636	·604	·564	·516
75°			·685		·669	·648	·625	·596
90°	·707	·705	·702	·698	·695	·685	·672	·655
105°			·724		·729	·732	·733	·730
120°			·741		·748	·756	·764	·770

On the assumption that $w_3 = o$ and that the loss at entrance is zero, the maximum theoretical efficiency η of a turbine is given by

$$\eta = \frac{\text{work done per second by water}}{\text{energy supplied per second}} = \frac{\dfrac{W\,Q}{g} \cdot w_2^2 \left(1 - \dfrac{\tan a}{\tan \beta}\right)}{W\,Q\,H'}$$

$$= \frac{2\left(1 - \dfrac{\tan a}{\tan \beta}\right)}{2\left(1 - \dfrac{\tan a}{\tan \beta}\right) + \dfrac{b_2^2\,r_2^2}{b_3^2\,r_3^2}\tan^2 a}$$

$$= \frac{1}{1 + \frac{1}{2}\left(\dfrac{b_2\,r_2}{b_3\,r_3}\right)^2 \dfrac{\tan^2 a}{1 - \dfrac{\tan a}{\tan \beta}}} \qquad (10)$$

This gives the hydraulic efficiency of the machine, and does not take into account losses due to mechanical friction in the turbine. The actual efficiency of the machine is the ratio of the useful work delivered at the turbine shaft to the energy supplied at the wheel inlet, and is given by the ratio

$\dfrac{2 \pi N M}{W Q H'}$ where N = revolutions per second
           M = turning moment on shaft in foot lbs.

Here M is less than the hydraulic turning moment $\dfrac{W Q}{g} (w_2 r_2 - w_3 r_3)$ foot lbs. by an amount depending on the frictional resistances of the turbine bearings and on the hydraulic frictional losses in the wheel itself.

From (10) it appears that the efficiency should theoretically increase as the ratio $\dfrac{b_2 r_2}{b_3 r_3}$ diminishes, i.e., as the breadth of the turbine is more rapidly increased towards the centre. Even theoretically, however, this possible increase is only small because of the smallness of tan $^2 a$, while such a construction, by giving wheel passages which have a sectional area increasing in the direction of flow, tends to produce unsteady motion with a consequent loss of energy in eddy production.

Again from equation (10) it appears that the efficiency increases as β increases, and diminishes with an increase in a, the following table giving values of η corresponding to different values of these angles, in the case where $\dfrac{b_2 r_2}{b_3 r_3} = 1$, and where in consequence $f_2 = f_3$.

Values of β.	Values of a.				
	10°	15°	20°	25°	30°
60°	·981	·959	·922	·871	·800
75°	·983	·962	·931	·888	·835
90°	·984	·964	·936	·902	·857
105°	·985	·966	·941	·910	·874
120°	·986	·968	·946	·920	·889

From this it would appear that it is an advantage to make β as large as possible. But since we have $f_2 = w_2 \tan a = u_2 \left\{ \dfrac{\tan a}{1 - \dfrac{\tan a}{\tan \beta}} \right\}$, the velocity of flow for a given peripheral wheel speed diminishes as β increases, so that an increase in β necessitates either a larger and more expensive turbine or a higher peripheral speed. In the latter case frictional losses are increased, and in view of these facts it has become usual to make $\beta = 90°$ for all medium heads. For very high heads β may range from 60° to 90°, and for very low heads from 90° to 135°.

In the case where $\beta = 90°$ the hydraulic efficiency is given by

$$\eta = \frac{2}{2 + \left(\dfrac{b_2 \, r_2}{b_3 \, r_3} \tan a \right)^2}. \tag{10a}$$

Similarly, although the hydraulic efficiency decreases as a increases, yet the volume passing through the turbine, and consequently its horse power, also increases, the maximum power being obtained when the product of Q and η is a maximum. It follows that the most satisfactory value of a depends on the purpose for which the turbine is desired. In a high-class turbine, a will be as small as mechanical considerations permit—generally between 10° and 15°, and the turbine will gain in efficiency at the expense of a higher prime cost. Where a cheap turbine is required a may have any value up to about 35°.

The **volume of water** passing through the turbine per second is given by $Q = 2 \pi r_2 b_2 f_2 = 2 \pi r_2 b_2 w_2 \tan a$ cubic feet,[1] and when the turbine is working under conditions of maximum efficiency this becomes

$$Q = 2 \pi r_2 b_2 \tan a \sqrt{\frac{2 \, g \, H'}{2 + \left(\dfrac{b_2 \, r_2}{b_3 \, r_3} \tan a \right)^2 - 2 \, \dfrac{\tan a}{\tan \beta}}} \tag{11}$$

so that both the velocity of the turbine for maximum efficiency and the volume of water passed through the wheel vary as $\sqrt{H'}$.

---

[1] This assumes that the passages run full, and neglects the effect of the thickness of the vanes. The latter factor may readily be allowed for, and is considered later (Art. 144). The construction of the vanes may, however (p. 543), cause some contraction of the stream as indicated in Fig. 257 c, in which case the actual area over which flow takes place is less than that of the passages. We then get

$$Q = k \times 2 \pi r_2 b_2 f_2 = k \times 2 \pi r_2 b_2 w_2 \tan a \text{ cubic feet,}$$

where k equals the coefficient of discharge of the passages. This, which includes both the coefficient of velocity and of contraction, is usually taken as about ·95 and must be introduced in the application of these formulæ to any specific example.

Since for maximum efficiency, the work done

$$U = \frac{W\,Q}{g}\,w_2^2 \left(1 - \frac{\tan a}{\tan \beta}\right) \text{ foot lbs. per second.}$$

$$\therefore \quad U = \frac{W \times 2\,\pi\,r_2\,b_2 \tan a}{g} \left(1 - \frac{\tan a}{\tan \beta}\right) \times$$

$$\left\{ \frac{2\,g\,H'}{2 + \left(\frac{b_2\,r_2}{b_3\,r_3}\tan a\right)^2 - 2\frac{\tan a}{\tan \beta}} \right\}^{\frac{3}{2}} \text{ foot lbs. per second.} \quad (12$$

$\therefore$ the work done is proportional to $H^{\frac{3}{2}}$.

An examination of equation (10) shows that the hydraulic efficiency diminishes with an increase in the ratio $\frac{r_2}{r_3} (= n,)$ except where $b_2\,r_2 = b_3\,r_3$ and therefore where the velocity of flow is the same at inlet and outlet. Apart from this, an increase in n, by increasing the length of wheel passages, reduces the efficiency by increasing frictional losses. This disadvantage is, however, counterbalanced by the increased regulating effect of the centrifugal pressure.

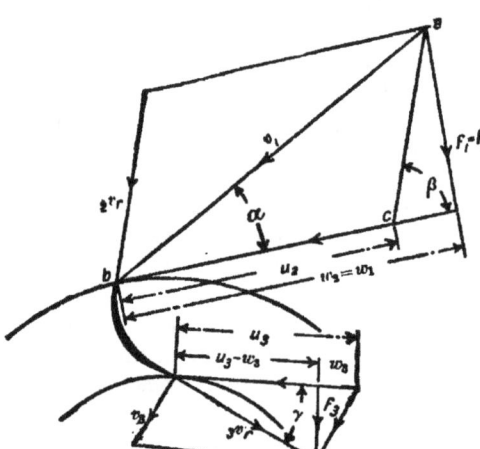

FIG. 256.—Vane Angles for Inward Radial Flow Turbine.

sure. It follows that as the efficiency of the governing mechanism is improved, it becomes advisable to reduce the value of n, and this explains why the value adopted in practice has been gradually reduced of recent years from 2 to as low as 1·25. Its usual value is about 1·5.

The discharge angle γ of the vanes (Fig. 256) may be determined from the consideration that, if $w_3 = 0$,

$$\tan \gamma = \frac{f_3}{u_3} = \frac{f_2}{u_3}\frac{b_2\,r_2}{b_3\,r_3}$$

$$= \frac{w_2}{u_3}\tan a \frac{b_2\,r_2}{b_3\,r_3}$$

If $\beta = 90°$, $w_2 = u_2$, and since $\dfrac{v_2}{u_3} = \dfrac{r_2}{r_3}$

$$\therefore \quad \tan \gamma = \frac{b_2\, r_2^2}{b_3\, r_3^2} \tan a. \tag{13}$$

If f is constant this gives :—

$$\tan \gamma = \frac{r_2}{r_3} \tan a. \tag{14}$$

And if $\dfrac{r_2}{r_3} = n$,

$$\tan \gamma = n \tan a. \tag{15}$$

Change of Pressure through Wheel.—Since the motion of a particle of water at any point in the wheel may be compounded of its motion in a forced vortex with angular velocity ω, and of its motion parallel to the wheel vanes with (variable) velocity v_r, the difference of pressure at any two points in the wheel will be the algebraic sum of the differences necessary to produce these motions.

Thus, due to the vortex motion,

$$\frac{p_2' - p_3'}{W} = \frac{u_2^2 - u_3^2}{2\,g} \text{ feet,}$$

while due to the flow between the vanes,

$$\frac{p_2'' - p_3''}{W} = \frac{{}_3v_r^2 - {}_2v_r^2}{2\,g} \text{ feet.}$$

Summing these we have :—

Total difference of pressure at inlet and outlet. $\left.\right\} = \dfrac{p_2 - p_3}{W} = \dfrac{u_2^2 - u_3^2}{2\,g} + \dfrac{{}_3v_r^2 - {}_2v_r^2}{2\,g}.$

But ${}_3v_r = f_3 \operatorname{cosec} \gamma$, and ${}_2v_r = f_2 \operatorname{cosec} \beta$, while $u_3 = \dfrac{u_2}{n}$,

$$\therefore \quad \frac{p_2 - p_3}{W} = \frac{u_2^2}{2\,g}\left(1 - \frac{1}{n^2}\right) + \frac{f_3^2 \operatorname{cosec}{}^2\gamma - f_2^2 \operatorname{cosec}{}^2\beta}{2\,g}. \tag{16}$$

The pressure p, at any radius r between inlet and outlet may be obtained if the angle θ made by the vanes at this radius with the tangent to the corresponding circle, and the velocity of flow, f, be known.

Here, if u be the velocity of the wheel at r,

$$u = \frac{u_2\, r}{r_2}, \text{ while } v_r = f \operatorname{cosec} \theta,$$

$$\therefore \quad \frac{p_2 - p}{W} = \frac{u_2^2}{2\,g}\left\{1 - \left(\frac{r}{r_2}\right)^2\right\} + \frac{f^2 \operatorname{cosec}{}^2\theta - f_2^2 \operatorname{cosec}{}^2\beta}{2\,g}$$

$$\text{or} \quad p = p_2 - W\left[\frac{u_2^2}{2\,g}\left\{1 - \left(\frac{r}{r_2}\right)^2\right\} + \frac{f^2 \operatorname{cosec}{}^2\theta - f^2 \operatorname{cosec}{}^2\beta}{2\,g}\right]$$

lbs. per square foot. $\tag{17}$

If the velocity of flow is constant $f_2 = f$, and this expression simplifies to :—

$$p = p_2 - \frac{W}{2\,g} \left[u_2^2 \left\{ 1 - \left(\frac{r}{r_2} \right)^2 \right\} + f^2 \left(\operatorname{cosec}{}^2\theta - \operatorname{cosec}{}^2\beta \right) \right].$$

As every term in this expression is known, the pressure at any point and therefore the whole pressure on that portion of the runner which carries the vanes, may be determined.

An easier graphical method is, however, indicated in Art. 145.

The pressure over the face of the runner inside the vanes $= p_3$ lbs. per square foot, so that the total pressure over this face may be determined. Owing to leakage past the outer periphery of the runner the pressure on the rear face may, however, amount to as much as p_2 lbs. per square foot, and owing to the large difference of pressure thus produced on the two faces the end thrust on the shaft may become excessive. Various methods of balancing this end-thrust have been adopted, and have been illustrated in the preceding chapter.

Further consideration of these methods will be postponed to Art. 183, where the similar problem of balancing the end thrust on the spindle of a centrifugal pump is considered in some detail.

Summary.—Collecting the more important of the results so far obtained we have in the case of an inward radial flow turbine, working without shock at entrance and rejecting its discharge water without any tangential velocity, and therefore (neglecting the effect of other losses) working at its maximum efficiency,

$(1)_a$
$$u_2 = \left(1 - \frac{\tan a}{\tan \beta} \right) w_2$$

$$= \left(1 - \frac{\tan a}{\tan \beta} \right) \sqrt{ \frac{2\,g\,H'}{2 - 2\frac{\tan a}{\tan \beta} + \left(\frac{n\,b_2}{b_3}\,\tan a \right)^2} }$$

$(2)_a$
$$f_2 = w_2 \tan a \text{ feet per second.}$$

$(3)_a$
$$\tan \gamma = n\,\frac{w_2\,b_2}{u_3\,b_3}\,\tan a$$

$(4)_a$
$$f_3 = n\,\frac{b_2}{b_3}\,f_2 \text{ feet per second.}$$

$(5)_a$
$$p = p_2 - \frac{W}{2\,g} \left[u_2^2 \left\{ 1 - \left(\frac{r}{r_2} \right)^2 \right\} + f^2 \operatorname{cosec}{}^2\theta - f_2^2 \operatorname{cosec}{}^2\beta \right]$$

lbs. per square foot.

$(6)_a$ Hydraulic efficiency
$$\eta = \frac{2}{2 + \left(\frac{b_2}{b_3}\,n\,\tan a \right)^2} \times \frac{1}{1 - \frac{\tan a}{\tan \beta}}$$

$(7)_a$ $$\text{Revolutions} = \frac{u_2 \times 60}{2\,\pi\,r_2} \text{ per minute.}$$

Radial Inward Flow Turbine with Radial Vane Tips.

In practice the vanes are very commonly made radial at the tips. In this case, putting $\beta = 90°$, $\tan \beta = \infty$, we now have, for no shock at entrance, the velocity of whirl w_2 equal to the peripheral velocity u_2 of the wheel. Making these substitutions in the general expressions already obtained we get :—

$(1)_b$ $$u_2 = w_2 = \sqrt{\frac{2\,g\,H'}{2 + \left(n\,\frac{b_2}{b_3}\,\tan a\right)^2}} \text{ feet per second.}$$

$(2)_b$ $$f_2 = w_2 \tan a \text{ feet per second.}$$

$(3)_b$ $$\tan \gamma = n^2\,\frac{b_2}{b_3}\,\tan a$$

$(4)_b$ $$f_3 = n\,\frac{b_2}{b_3}\,f_2 \text{ feet per second.}$$

$(5)_b$ $$p = p_2 - \frac{W}{2\,g}\left[u_2^2\left\{1 - \left(\frac{r}{r_2}\right)^2\right\} + f^2 \operatorname{cosec}^2\theta - f_2^2 \right]$$
$$\text{lbs. per square foot.}$$

$(6)_b$ $$\eta = \frac{2}{2 + \left(n\,\frac{b_2}{b_3}\,\tan a\right)^2}.$$

In some cases the velocity of flow is kept constant by increasing the breadth of the turbine as the radius diminishes so as to keep $b\,r$ constant. In this case $f_2 = f_3$, $b_2\,r_2 = b_3\,r_3$, and therefore $n\,\dfrac{b_2}{b_3} = 1$, and the foregoing results are modified as follows :—

$(1)'$ $$u_2 = w_2 = \sqrt{\frac{2\,g\,H'}{2 + \tan^2 a}} \text{ feet per second.}$$

$(3)'$ $$\tan \gamma = n \tan a$$

$(4)'$ $$f_3 = f_2 \text{ feet per second.}$$

$(5)'$ $$p = p_2 - \frac{W}{2\,g}\left[u_2^2\left\{1 - \left(\frac{r}{r_2}\right)^2\right\} + f_2^2\,(\operatorname{cosec}^2\theta - 1) \right]$$
$$\text{lbs. per square foot.}$$

$(6)'$ $$\eta = \frac{2}{2 + \tan^2 a}$$

Since a is always small, the peripheral velocity of the wheel for maximum velocity is very approximately given $(1)'$ by

$$u_2 = w_2 = \sqrt{\frac{2\,g\,H'}{2}} = \cdot 707\,\sqrt{2\,g\,H'},$$

so that with radial tips the peripheral velocity at entrance is nearly that due to a fall through a height $\frac{H'}{2}$, while the supply water at this point has changed only approximately one half of its total store into kinetic energy.

From the foregoing analysis, or from a consideration of the triangle of velocities $a\,b\,c$ of Fig. 256, it is evident that the speed of the wheel is a function solely of the velocity due to the head, and of the angle a.

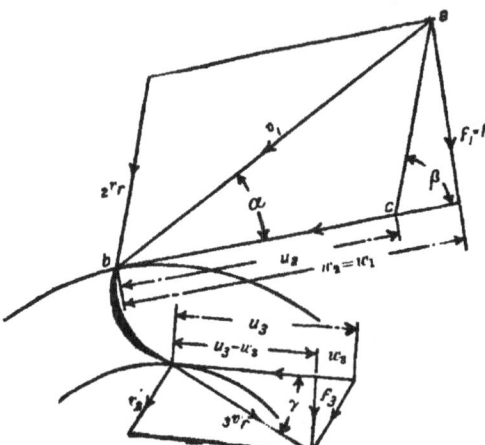

FIG. 256.—Vane Angles for Inward Radial Flow Turbine.

This being so, it remains to decide upon some relation between the velocities of flow and of whirl before this angle, and the wheel speed, can be settled. The precise relations between these two velocities, which shall conduce to the highest economic efficiency, can only be deduced from experiment, and the following table shows the relationships which modern practice has shown to be most successful :—

Type	f_2.	w_2.	a.	$n = \frac{2}{3}$
Inward radial flow turbine—				
Thomson type . . .	About ·125 $\sqrt{2gH'}$	About ·66 $\sqrt{2gH'}$	About 11°	·2
Francis type	From ·125 $\sqrt{2gH'}$ to ·175 $\sqrt{2gH'}$	From ·66 $\sqrt{2gH'}$ to ·72 $\sqrt{2gH'}$	From 11° to 14°	From 1·2 to 1·30
Mixed flow turbine of the American type	From ·35 $\sqrt{2gH'}$ to ·40 $\sqrt{2gH'}$	From ·72 $\sqrt{2gH'}$ to ·80 $\sqrt{2gH'}$	From 22° to 28°	
Outward radial flow turbine .	About ·25 $\sqrt{2gH'}$	From ·56 $\sqrt{2gH'}$ to ·62 $\sqrt{2gH'}$	From 20 to 25	From 20 to 2°
Axial flow turbine . . .	From ·175 $\sqrt{2gH'}$ to ·235 $\sqrt{2gH'}$	From ·62 $\sqrt{2gH'}$ to ·68 $\sqrt{2gH'}$	From 16° to 22°	1·0

Remarks on the Theory of Turbine Design.

Although the preceding theory is extremely valuable, its limitations
re important and must be kept in view. In the first place, even with
anes designed so as (theoretically) to prevent shock at entrance, experi-
ient shows that a certain contraction of section of the stream, as
idicated in Fig. 257 *a* and *b*, takes place, and also indicates that this con-

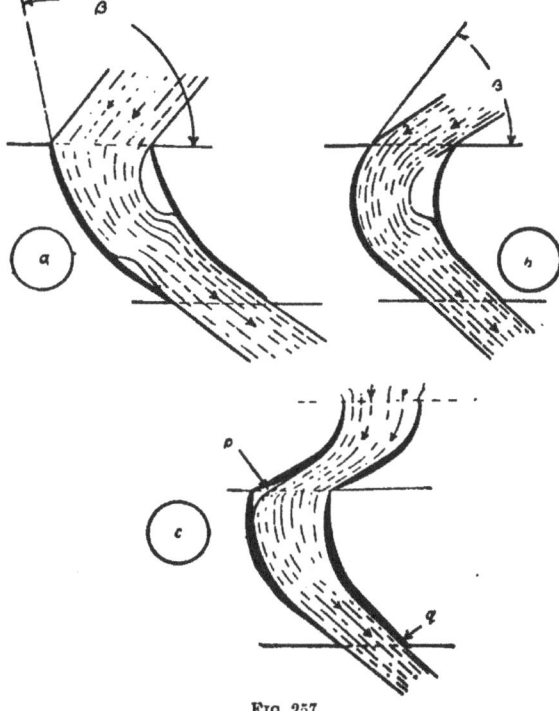

FIG. 257.

raction and the subsequent re-expansion is greater with the theoretically
orrect entrant angle than with one slightly different. When working at
art gate the ingoing stream may, if sufficiently reduced in width, not fill
he buckets at all, in which case the wheel runs as an impulse turbine,
he pressure at the exit from the guides falls to that in the discharge pipe,
and the outflow per unit area is largely increased. Since the wheel
speed is now altogether unsuited to the velocity of influx, the efficiency is

low. Even though the stream may re-expand to fill the buckets and the wheel act as a pressure turbine, yet with the same pressure at exit from the wheel, the pressure at the exit from the guides will be greater than when running full, though not to the same extent as before, so that in either case the volume of water passing the wheel is larger than might be expected from a consideration of the gate opening.

This action is well illustrated by the following results of tests carried out by Mr. J. B. Francis on a mixed flow turbine, of which the following are the leading dimensions[1] :—

Outer diameter of runner, 6 feet. $a = 25°$.
Least diameter of runner, 2 feet 8 inches. $\beta = 90°$.
Width of guide passages, 13·1 inches. γ from 22° to 26°.
Width of buckets, b_2, 13·3 inches.   Number of guide vanes = 24.
Measured area of outflow from guides,   Number of bucket vanes = 25.
    9·88 square feet. $t_1 = 0·4$ inches.
Measured area of outflow from buckets, 9·56 square feet.

H feet.	Gate Opening.	Q cubic feet per second.	Percentage of Flow.	Revolutions.	Efficiency.
14·3	·153	51·2	31·0	60·5	47·4 °/₀
13·7	·306	83·9	50·8	60·1	66·6 °/₀
13·1	·459	110·1	66·6	66·4	76·1 °/₀
13·0	·612	130·2	78·9	64·0	80·1 °/₀
12·7	·765	144·8	87·5	62·7	83·6 °/₀
12·7	1·00	165·1	100·0	66·6	82·8 °/₀

Again, friction losses in the wheel increase continuously with the speed, and do not attain a minimum value simultaneously with the minimum values of the losses by shock and by rejection of kinetic energy, so that, although the expressions previously obtained for the efficiency by neglecting these losses, indicate that this is independent of the speed of rotation, there will, in actual working, be one particular speed for any turbine working under a given head—that speed at which the sum of the various losses forms the least proportion of the energy supplied by the water—for which the efficiency will be a maximum.

Experiments by Professor Fliegner, of Zurich,[2] indicate that the loss at entrance diminishes as the working head increases, and that its minimum value does not occur for inflow without shock, but when the angle β has a value differing from the theoretical, the best angle being greater than the theoretical for values of β less than about 105°, and less than the theoretical for values of β greater than this.

[1] Journal Franklin Institute, vol. 99, p. 249.
[2] *Zeitschrift des Vereines Deutscher Ingenieure*, vol. 23, p. 459.

The following table gives some of Fliegner's results :—

Value of discharge angle γ	$15°$	$30°$	$15°$	$30°$	$15°$	$30°$
Value of β for no shock at entrance	$120°$	$120°$	$90°$	$90°$	$60°$	$60°$
Experimental value of β for maximum efficiency	$111°$	$109°$	$105°$	$102°$	$88\frac{1}{2}°$	$85°$

It follows that with angles designed for entry without shock, the most efficient speed will be less than the theoretical for values of β less than $105°$, and will be greater for greater values of β, a conclusion which is verified by the results of experiment, and which is indicated by the values of u_2 given in the table on p. 542.

Fliegner's results led him to the conclusion that the best value for β is given by the formula $\beta' = 90° + \dfrac{\beta - \gamma}{5} - 30 \dfrac{b_3 - b_2}{b_2}$, where β and γ are the values of inlet and discharge angles calculated in the usual way for maximum efficiency, and where b_2 and b_3 are the bucket widths at entrance and exit.

Again, in the pressure turbine, the assumption that the water is completely guided by the vanes is probably not even approximately true, only a small proportion of the water being directly guided, and that only on one side of the stream. Other parts of the stream may follow very different paths. Moreover, unless the guide passages are parallel for some short distance before the point of exit, the issuing stream may (as at p in Fig. 257 c) fail to occupy the total exit area, so that, even apart from the effect of the vane thickness, which will be considered later, the effective area of flow is less than $2 \pi r_2 b_2$.

It is usual to allow for this effect approximately by making the calculations on the assumption that the coefficient of contraction is ·95. The same reasoning applies at the point of discharge.

Further, we have the impossibility of taking full account of the various frictional and eddy formation losses in the turbine, except when guided by the results of experiment on the particular type of wheel under consideration.

The true value of the theory thus lies in its power of indicating the relative influence of the different details of design on the efficiency, and in its possibility of giving a preliminary design which may afterwards be slightly modified by the results of experiment on some similar type of machine, so as to approximate more nearly to that of the perfect turbine.

Example of Design.—As an application of the results of the foregoing analysis, consider the design of an inward radial flow turbine of the Francis swivelling gate type, to give 10,000 H.P. at 300 revolutions per minute under a total head of 260 feet. The wheel vanes to have radial tips, the velocity of flow to be kept constant, and the wheel to be supplied through a steel penstock whose length is 450 feet.

Assuming a probable full-load efficiency of 84 per cent., the capacity of the penstock must be sufficient to allow of a supply of $\dfrac{10,000 \times 550}{\cdot 84 \times 260 \times 62}$

$= 404$ cubic feet per second.

Allowing a mean velocity under maximum load of 12 feet per second in the penstock, the area of this becomes $33\frac{2}{3}$ square feet, corresponding to a diameter of approximately 6 feet 6 inches.

In such a turbine it is usual to arrange the design so as to give a maximum efficiency at about $\frac{3}{4}$ full-load. At this load the velocity of pipe flow is approximately 8 feet per second, and if the coefficient of friction be taken as $\cdot 005$, the loss of head due to friction and to the velocity of flow (assuming the kinetic energy due to the latter to be entirely lost) may be written as equal to

$$\frac{v^2}{2\,g}\left(\frac{f\,l}{m}+1\right) \text{ feet} = \frac{64}{64\cdot4}\left\{\frac{\cdot 005 \times 450 \times 4}{6\cdot 5}+1\right\} \text{ feet} = 2\cdot 37 \text{ feet.}$$

The effective head H' is thus $257\cdot 6$ feet, so that $\sqrt{2\,g\,H'} = 129$ feet per second.

Taking $a = 13°$, $\tan a = \cdot 231$, $\tan{}^2 a = \cdot 053$, while from (1) we have

$$w_2 = u_2 = \frac{129}{\sqrt{2\cdot 053}} = 90\cdot 1 \text{ feet per second.}$$

The outer radius of the runner is then given by the relation

$$\frac{2\,\pi\,r_2\,N}{60} = 90\cdot 1. \qquad \therefore \quad r_2 = \frac{60 \times 90\cdot 1}{2\,\pi \times 300} = 2\cdot 87 \text{ feet.}$$

$\therefore$ Outer diameter of runner $= 5\cdot 74$ feet $= 5'\ 9''$.

Assuming an efficiency of 86 per cent. at $\frac{3}{4}$ load, we have:—
$Q = 296$ cubic feet per second, so that from the expression
$Q = 2\,\pi\,r_2\,b_2\,\tan a\ w_2$, we get:—

$$b_2 = \frac{Q}{2\,\pi\,r_2\,w_2\,\tan a} = \frac{296}{2\,\pi \times 2\cdot 87 \times 90\cdot 1 \times \cdot 231} \text{ feet}$$

$= \cdot 79$ feet $= 9\cdot 5$ inches (approximately).

Taking $n = 1\cdot 30$, we have $r_3 = \dfrac{2\cdot 87}{1\cdot 30} = 2\cdot 21$ feet, so that the inner diameter of the runner is $4'\ 5''$, while $b_3 = \cdot 79 \times 1\cdot 30 = 12\frac{5}{16}$ inches.

Also, since $\tan \gamma = n \tan a$, this makes $\tan \gamma = \cdot 300$, giving γ the value $16° \, 42'$.

The theoretical hydraulic efficiency $\dfrac{2}{2 + \tan {}^2a}$ now equals $\dfrac{2}{2 \cdot 053}$ $= 97 \cdot 4$ per cent.

Applying Fliegner's correction, it appears that for maximum efficiency t this speed of rotation β should be increased from $90°$ to a value β' where

$$\begin{aligned} \beta' &= 90° + \frac{90° - 16 \cdot 7°}{5} - 30 \; \frac{\cdot 79 \, (1 \cdot 30 - 1)°}{\cdot 79} \\ &= 90° + 14 \cdot 7° - 9° \\ &= 95 \cdot 7°. \end{aligned}$$

As will be seen later, these results, however, need further correction or the thickness of the vanes at their inlet and outlet edges.

ART. 143.—SOURCES AND MAGNITUDE OF LOSSES IN THE PRESSURE TURBINE.

So far the various losses in the turbine and its appendages have been ieglected, and while it is impossible to take these fully into account in a

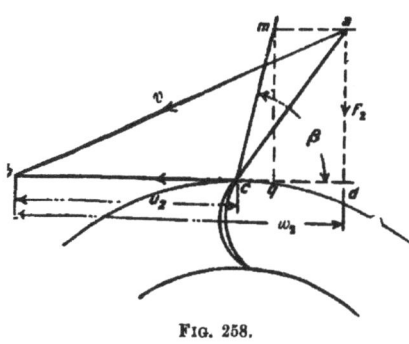

FIG. 258.

theoretical discussion, yet a more detailed examination will be of value as indicating their relative importance. In general, these losses consist of :—

(1) Frictional losses in supply and discharge pipes.

(2) Loss by leakage between guides and wheel.

(3) Losses due to shock at entrance if the vane angles are not adapted to the speed if the wheel, and to contraction and subsequent expansion of section of he stream.

(4) Frictional losses due to motion of the water over the vanes and rown of the wheel.

(5) Eddy losses caused by any sudden curvature of the vanes by sudden hanges of section or divergence of the passages.

(6) Losses due to shock caused by sudden enlargement of the stream ection on entering the buckets at part gate.

N N 2

(7) Loss due to rejection of kinetic energy in the discharge.

(8) Loss due to mechanical friction at bearings.

(1) Of these losses, that due to the friction of the pipe line may be readily estimated, and depends on the length, diameter and velocity of flow through the pipes.

(2) **Loss by Leakage,** H_L.—This loss being proportional to the possible area through which leakage may take place and to the velocity of efflux over this area, is proportional to the product of the periphery of the wheel and the radial clearance at entrance, and to the square root of the head at entrance. Its magnitude is greatest in turbines of the inward flow type and may amount to from 2 to 4 per cent. of the total energy supplied.

(3) **Loss due to Shock at Entrance,** H_E.—if angle β is not correctly proportioned.

Let $\overline{a\,b} = v$ (Fig. 258) represent the velocity at the exit from guides.

Let $\overline{c\,b} = u_2$ represent the velocity of vane tips.

Then before entering the buckets the relative velocity of water and of wheel in the direction of the tangent at $c = \overline{c\,d}$.

Also if $\widehat{m\,c\,q} = \beta$, the relative velocity in the same direction on entering the buckets $= \overline{c\,q}$.

$\therefore$ Loss of head due to shock at entrance $= \dfrac{(\overline{c\,d} - \overline{c\,q})^2}{2\,g}$ feet of water.

But $\overline{c\,d} = w_2 - u_2$

And $\overline{c\,q} = \overline{m\,q}\cot\beta = f_2\cot\beta.$

$\therefore$ Loss of head $H_E = \dfrac{\{w_2 - u_2 - f_2\cot\beta\}^2}{2\,g}$ feet

$$= \frac{w_2^2}{2\,g}\left\{1 - \frac{u_2}{w_2} - \frac{\tan a}{\tan \beta}\right\}^2 \text{ feet.} \qquad (1$$

The actual loss due to shock is in general less than that calculated. since only a portion of the whole supply stream suffers the extreme change of velocity.

(4) **Frictional Losses in the Wheel,** H_F.—These may be divided into the losses caused by (a) Flow over the surfaces of the vanes and crowns: (b) Disc friction due to rotation of the turbine crown or crowns through the surrounding water.

(a) If $r_r =$ mean relative velocity of flow through turbine, m the hydraulic mean depth of turbine passages, l the effective length of passages, F the coefficient of friction, this loss is given by

$$H_F = \frac{F\,l\,v_r^2}{2\,g\,m} \text{ feet of water.}$$

(b) The disc friction due to rotation of the turbine crowns has been considered in detail in Art. 62, p. 179.

Its magnitude depends considerably on the type of turbine. In a single wheel radial flow turbine the whole of the rear face of the runner will, in general, be subject to this resistance, as will that portion of the front face which lies between the shaft and the inner tips of the vanes, while in the case of a double discharge turbine of the Thomson vortex type, this rubbing area is almost doubled. A large increase ·in disc friction is also experienced in the case of a turbine balanced by the addition of a rotating balance piston.

In a wheel of the parallel flow type the design may be such as to cause a similar resistance at the outer circumference whose radius is r_2 and breadth b_2, the loss of energy in this case being given by $f \, \omega^3 \, r_2{}^4 \, b_2$ foot lbs. per second.

In any case this loss of energy per second is proportional to ω^3, and the loss per lb. to ω^2, since Q is proportional to ω. The magnitude of the loss may be from 3 to 6 per cent.

(5) and (6) **Eddy Losses.** H_G.—These losses, due to eddy formation at changes of curvature and to shock at entrance at part gate, do not admit of even approximate calculation. They may, however, be minimised by designing all passages to have as easy a curvature as possible, and by the adoption of gates of the swivel type. With this type of gate these losses may account for between 1 and 8 per cent. of the total head, while with cylinder regulation they may amount to as much as 20 per cent. at half gate.

(7) **Loss due to Rejection of Kinetic Energy in the Discharge,** H_K.— Assuming the whole of the kinetic energy of discharge from the buckets to be lost, this loss is given by—

$$\frac{f_3{}^2 + w_3{}^2}{2\,g} \text{ foot lbs. per lb.}$$

In an inward radial flow turbine, where $n = \dfrac{r_2}{r_3}$, we have

$$w_3 = u_3 - f_3 \cot \gamma = \frac{u_2}{n} - f_3 \cot \gamma, \text{ and if } f_3 = f_2, \text{ the loss becomes—}$$

$$\frac{f_2{}^2 + (\frac{u_2}{n} - f_2 \cot \gamma)^2}{2\,g} \text{ foot lbs. per lb.} \qquad (2)$$

Expressed in terms of w_2, this becomes—

$$\frac{w_2{}^2}{2\,g} \left[\tan^2 a + \left\{ n \left(1 - \frac{\tan a}{\tan \beta} \right) - \frac{\tan a}{\tan \gamma} \right\}^2 \right] \text{ foot lbs.}$$

This loss becomes a minimum when w_3, *i.e.*, the velocity of whirl exit $= 0$, and then has the value $\dfrac{f_3^2}{2\,g}$.

Practically the whole of this energy is lost where the turbine discharges either directly into the tail-race or into a parallel suction tube whose area is equal to that of the vanes at discharge. If, however, the suction tube has an area which gradually increases towards its outlet, a portion up to about 25 per cent., of this may be converted into pressure energy, with a consequent gain of efficiency by the wheel.

In general this source of loss accounts for between 3 and 8 per cent. of the total energy supplied, being greatest in turbines of the outward flow type and least in those of the axial flow type.

(8) **Mechanical Friction, H_B.** — This generally accounts for between 2 and 4 per cent. of the total energy, its magnitude depending largely on the type of machine (whether hydraulically balanced or not).

Taking these losses into account, if H is the total supply head, $H = H' +$ loss in pipe friction.

The hydraulic efficiency η of the turbine is given by $\left.\right\}$ $\dfrac{U}{H - \text{loss in pipe friction}} = \dfrac{U}{H'}$

The work done on the turbine shaft $\left.\right\}$ $= U - H_{L+E+F+G}$ ft. lbs. per sec.

$\therefore$ Gross efficiency of turbine wheel $\left.\right\}$ $= \dfrac{U - H_{L+E+F+G}}{H'}$

Useful work delivered at turbine shaft $\left.\right\}$ $= U - H_{L+E+F+G+B}$ ft. lbs. per sec.

$\therefore$ Nett efficiency of turbine $\left.\right\}$ $= \dfrac{U - H_{L+E+F+G+B}}{H'}$

While the gross efficiency of the plant, including supply and discharge pipes $\left.\right\}$ $= \dfrac{U - H_{L+E+F+G+B}}{H}$.

ART. 144.—THICKNESS OF VANES.

So far no account has been taken of the fact that the vanes must be made of a certain thickness, and therefore reduce the effective area of the guide and wheel passages. The necessary corrections for this in the case of an inward flow turbine may be made as follows :—

Let t be the vane thickness, and n the number of vanes which cut the circumference under consideration.

At inlet, the area of guide vane circle occupied by these vanes $= b_1\, n_1\, t_1$

:osec a (approx.), while the area of bucket vane circle $= b_2\, n_2\, t_2$ cosec β (approx.).

At outlet the area of bucket vane circle $= b_3\, n_2\, t_3$ cosec γ (approx.), where a, β, and γ, are the angles as calculated when neglecting the blade thickness.

Thus the outlet area is reduced in the ratio

$$\frac{2\,\pi\,r_3\,b_3 - n_2\,t_3\,b_3 \text{ cosec } \gamma}{2\,\pi\,r_3\,b_3}, \text{ so that---}$$

$$f_3 \text{ (true)} = f_3 \text{ (approx.)} \left\{ 1 - \frac{n_2\,t_3 \text{ cosec } \gamma}{2\,\pi\,r_3} \right\}.$$

For f_3 to be kept the same we must then either have $\dfrac{\tan \gamma \text{ (true)}}{\tan \gamma \text{ (approx.)}}$

$$= \frac{1}{1 - \dfrac{n_2\,t_3 \text{ cosec } \gamma}{2\,\pi\,r_3}}, \text{ or the breadth } b_3 \text{ must be increased in the same}$$

ratio.

Similar corrections may be applied at the inlet to the buckets and the outlet from the guides.

Allowance should be made for the difference in radii between the guide and wheel vane circles, and in order to keep the velocity of flow constant where the water leaves the guides and enters the wheel, the breadth b of the guides may be made slightly different to that of the vanes, so as to keep the area through which radial flow takes place, constant. We then have---

$$b_1 = \left\{ \frac{2\,\pi\,r_2 - n_2\,t_2 \text{ cosec } \beta}{2\,\pi\,r_1 - n_1\,t_1 \text{ cosec } a} \right\} b_2.$$

This is only approximate since the passage of the wheel vanes before the guide passages tends to diminish the effective area of the latter, while the effective area of the wheel at inlet is similarly diminished by the presence of the guide vanes. Sufficient data are not available to fix the best number of wheel vanes in any particular case; the greater the number, the more perfect is the guidance given to the water, although at the same time frictional losses are increased. The longer the water passages the fewer the vanes necessary to give sufficient guidance. In the case of a number of modern inward radial flow turbines examined by the author, and of sizes ranging from 3 inches diameter to 66 inches diameter, the number of vanes was given with fair accuracy by the relation $n = k \sqrt[3]{d}$, where $d =$ diameter in inches and where k is a coefficient varying from about 7·7 in the smaller to 8·4 in the larger wheels and having a mean value $= 8$.

In general, with swivelling vanes, the number of guide vanes is made slightly less than the number of wheel vanes, while with stationary guides the number is usually slightly greater. The thickness t varies from $\frac{1}{4}$ inch in a small turbine with steel plate vanes to about $\frac{1}{2}$ inch in a large turbine with cast vanes. In high-class turbines the vanes have rounded edges at entrance and exit, so that the effective value of t generally varies from about $\frac{1}{16}$ inch to $\frac{5}{16}$ inch.

Art. 145.—Curvature of Vanes.

So long as the inlet and outlet angles of the vanes are correctly proportioned, the shape of the vane between these points only affects the efficiency in so far as it tends to give steady or unsteady motion in the stream. To this end the design should be such that the passages are nowhere divergent, and that any changes of curvature are as gradual as possible. The first of these requirements is more easily satisfied in the inward flow than in the outward flow turbine. With this requirement fulfilled, the most efficient vane curve will be that with which the change in curvature of the path of the stream is most gradual, and to determine this it is advisable to set out a diagram showing for any proposed vane the true path of the particles of water in passing through the wheel. Two such diagrams are shown in Fig. 259, in which (a) shows the true path where the velocity of flow is uniform, and (b) where the velocity of flow varies inversely as the radius. To construct diagram (a), a series of equidistant circles are set out between the inner and outer vane circles. If s be the radial distance between each pair of these, the time for a particle to pass from one to the other $= \dfrac{s}{f}$ seconds. Next set out the same number of equidistant vanes, the distance apart on the outer vane circle being $\omega\, r_2\, \dfrac{s}{f}$ feet. A particle leaving the intersection of the first circle and first vane will then be at the intersection of the second circle and vane after an interval of time $\dfrac{s}{f}$ seconds and so on, so that the path of the particle can be sketched in, as at $l\, m$.

Where the velocity of flow is not uniform, the only difference in the construction is that the intermediate circles are not equidistant but are so spaced that the particle travels radially from one to the other in equal intervals of time. Thus in case (b) a radius $o\, a$ being drawn, a right-angled triangle $o\, a\, b$ is constructed on this and lines $c\, d$, $c_1\, d_1$, etc., drawn.

cutting off equal areas $c_2 d_1$, $c_1 d$, etc., from the triangle. Circles drawn through c_1, c_2, etc., will now, by their intersections with the equidistant vanes, give points on the path l' m' of a particle.

These curves may be utilized to obtain the absolute velocity of the water and the relative velocity of water and vane at any radius, for if at any point P of radius r, $P q$ be drawn perpendicular to $O P$ and equal to ωr, and if $q k$ be drawn parallel to the tangent to the vane at

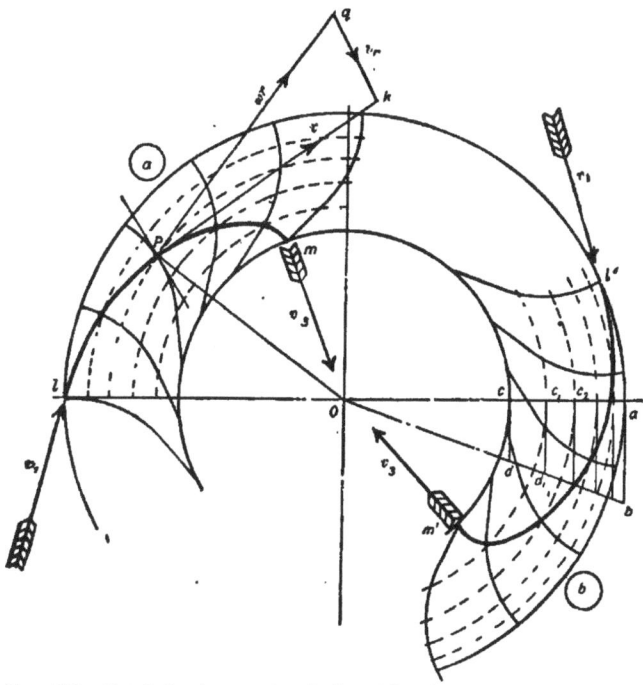

FIG. 259.—Sketch showing actual path of particles of water through an Inward Radial Flow Turbine.

P and $P k$ be drawn tangential to the curve at P, then since the actual velocity of the particle at P is compounded of the velocity of the vane at P, i.e., of ωr, and of its velocity relative to the vane, and since its actual velocity is tangential to the curve at P and its relative velocity is parallel to the vane, $P q k$ serves as the triangle of velocities at P, and $\overline{P k} =$

the absolute velocity v, while $\overline{q\,k}$ = the relative velocity r_r of water and vane.

By obtaining r_r in this way the pressure "p" at any radius r may be easily obtained by an application of the formula

$$p = p_2 - \frac{W}{2\,g} \left\{ u_2{}^2 - u^2 + r_r{}^2 - {}_2r_r{}^2 \right\} \text{ lbs. per square foot,}$$

where u and v_r refer to a point at radius r.

EXAMPLE.

A turbine runner has an outer diameter of 5 feet 6 inches and an inner diameter 4 feet 3 inches. It makes 800 revolutions per minute. The space occupied by the blades being divided into five concentric strips, each $1\frac{1}{2}$ inches wide, it is found graphically that the relative velocities at the centres of these strips, commencing at the outside are,

26 ; 24 ; 26 ; 40 ; 65 feet per second.

The relative velocity at entrance is 27 feet per second and at exit is 76 feet per second. The pressure head at inlet is 125·5 feet.

Denoting these strips by a, b, c, d, e, we have :—

$$p_a = p_2 - \frac{62\cdot4}{64\cdot4} \left\{ (86\cdot5)^2 - (84\cdot5)^2 + (26)^2 - (27)^2 \right\}$$
$$= p_2 - 280.$$

$$p_b = p_2 - \frac{62\cdot4}{64\cdot4} \left\{ (86\cdot5)^2 - (80\cdot5)^2 + (24)^2 - (27)^2 \right\}$$
$$= p_2 - 820.$$

$$p_c = p_2 - \frac{62\cdot4}{64\cdot4} \left\{ (86\cdot5)^2 - (76\cdot5)^2 + (26)^2 - (27)^2 \right\}$$
$$= p_2 - 1,510.$$

$$p_d = p_2 - \frac{62\cdot4}{64\cdot4} \left\{ (86\cdot5)^2 - (72\cdot6)^2 + (40)^2 - (27^2) \right\}$$
$$= p_2 - 3,010.$$

$$p_e = p_2 - \frac{62\cdot4}{64\cdot4} \left\{ (86\cdot5)^2 - (68\cdot8)^2 + (65)^2 - (27)^2 \right\}$$
$$= p_2 - 6,040.$$

At exit $p_3 = p_2 - \dfrac{62\cdot4}{64\cdot4} \left\{ (86\cdot5)^2 - (66\cdot8)^2 + (76)^2 - (27)^2 \right\}$

$$= p_2 - 7,810.$$

$$\therefore \ \frac{p_2 - p_3}{W} = \frac{7,810}{62\cdot4} = 125\cdot3 \text{ feet.}$$

This affords a check as to the accuracy of the construction. Assuming the pressure over the corresponding portion of the back face of the disc o be p_2 lbs. per square foot, the total unbalanced pressure over this portion, in the direction of the suction tube is equal to

$$\frac{2\pi \times 1\cdot5}{12} \left[\left(\frac{32\cdot25}{12} \times 280\right) + \left(\frac{30\cdot75}{12} \times 820\right) + \left(\frac{29\cdot25}{12} \times 1{,}510\right) \right.$$

$$\left. + \left(\frac{27\cdot75}{12} \times 3{,}010\right) + \left(\frac{26\cdot25}{12} \times 6{,}040\right) \right] \text{ lbs.}$$

$$= \cdot7854 \{ 752 + 2{,}105 + 3{,}680 + 6{,}960 + 13{,}210 \}$$

$$= 21{,}000 \text{ lbs.}$$

ART. 146.—THE OUTWARD RADIAL FLOW PRESSURE TURBINE.

The general details of design of the outward flow turbine are exactly the same as for the inward flow type, and the same symbols and equations apply throughout.

Now, however, $n = \dfrac{r_2}{r_3}$ is less than unity, so that in equation (16), p. 539,

$$\frac{p_2 - p_3}{W} = \frac{u_2^2}{2g}\left(1 - \frac{1}{n^2}\right) + \frac{f_3^2 \operatorname{cosec}^2\gamma - f_2^2 \operatorname{cosec}^2\beta}{2g}$$

the term $\dfrac{u_2^2}{2g}\left(1 - \dfrac{1}{n^2}\right)$ is negative, while, strictly speaking, the second term of the equation ceases to apply, since the flow now takes place through a series of diverging channels, and eddy formation is in consequence set up.

Centrifugal force now aids the flow through the turbine, and an increase in speed, by increasing the term $\dfrac{u_2^2\left(\dfrac{1}{n^2} - 1\right)}{2g}$, decreases the inlet pressure, and causes an increased flow through the wheel. This turbine is in consequence difficult to govern satisfactorily. To reduce this effect as far as possible the term $\left(\dfrac{1}{n^2} - 1\right)$ should be small. This necessitates n or $\dfrac{r_2}{r_3}$ being made as nearly unity as practicable, and necessitates a bucket depth as small as is compatible with easy curves connecting inlet and outlet lips. In general r_3 is made from $1\cdot20$ to $1\cdot25$ times r_2.

Owing to the high peripheral velocity at exit, it is now impracticable to design the exit angles so as to make the velocity of whirl at exit equal to zero. The losses due to rejection of kinetic energy are thus in general higher with this than with the inward flow type.

In this type of turbine f_2 is generally given a value about $\cdot 25 \sqrt{2 g H}$. while u_2 varies from $[\cdot 56$ to $\cdot 62] \sqrt{2 g H'}$. In general γ lies between $20°$ and $30°$, and in high-class turbines a lies between $20°$ and $25°$.

Art. 147.—Axial Flow Pressure Turbine.

Here the general theory is the same as for the inward and outward radial flow types of turbine, and the same demonstrations hold good if it be remembered that $r_2 = r_3 = r$; $u_2 = u_3 = \omega r$; $n = 1$.

If, as assumed in the previous cases, the plane of the wheel is horizontal, the equation of energy now becomes :—

$$\frac{p_2}{W} + \frac{r_2^2}{2 g} = \frac{p_3}{W} + \frac{f_3^2}{2 g} + \{ \text{work done in wheel} + \text{losses from (2) to}$$

$$(3) - h \} \text{ per lb.}$$

where $h = $ depth of wheel.

This assumes no velocity of whirl at exit, so that $f_3 = r_3$.

Also, from equation (16), p. 589,

$$\frac{p_2 - p_3}{W} = \frac{f_3^2 \operatorname{cosec}{}^2\gamma - f_2^2 \operatorname{cosec}{}^2\beta}{2 g} - h$$

the term $\frac{u_2^2}{2 g}\left(1 - \frac{1}{n^2}\right)$ expressing the centrifugal effect, now vanishing.

Here f_2 generally equals from $[\cdot 175$ to $\cdot 225] \sqrt{2 g (H' - h)}$, while u_2 varies from $[\cdot 62$ to $\cdot 68] \sqrt{2 g (H' - h)}$. a varies from $16°$ to $22°$, while γ varies from $15°$ to $25°$.

Evidently with a given value of a and of β, at only one point in the radius of the wheel for any given speed, will the conditions be suitable for entrance without shock. For entrance without shock at all radii, the value of β should change continuously, so as to suit the corresponding peripheral speed. This construction is seldom carried out in practice, it being usual to have helical vanes, with radial inlet and outlet edges, both for guides and wheel, and to give a and β their correct values at the mean radius. With such vanes, having a constant pitch, the angle of inclination diminishes as the radius increases, and while this is an advantage in the case of the guides, it is the reverse in the case of the wheel, where the value of β for no shock should increase with the peripheral velocity and therefore with the radius. Better results would be obtained by giving the wheel vanes the same angle at all radii, although if the width of the buckets is small—not exceeding $\frac{1}{10}$ the wheel diameter—the loss from shock is trifling.

ART. 148.—AMERICAN TYPE: COMBINED RADIAL INWARD FLOW AND AXIAL DISCHARGE PRESSURE TURBINES.

Here, as in the inward flow type of wheel, the turbine is to a certain extent self-regulating. The design of the vanes at inlet is regulated by the laws governing the design of the inward flow wheel and at outlet by the laws governing that of the axial flow type. In general, a higher peripheral velocity is adopted for this type, this varying from ·7 to ·75 $\sqrt{2\,g\,h}$ for maximum efficiency at full gate. Where regulated by cylinder gates, the speed for maximum efficiency falls to from ·57 to ·61 $\sqrt{2\,g\,H}$ at half gate, the efficiency under these conditions varying from about 80 per cent. at full gate to 65 per cent. at half gate.

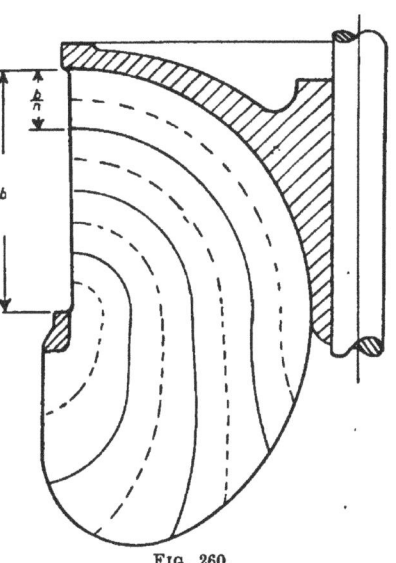

FIG. 260.

With the better makes of this class of machine, having inlet angles of about the same magnitude as those of the Francis and Thomson turbines, the full load efficiency would appear to be almost, if not quite, as high as is attainable with either of the latter types.

The correct inclination of the tangent plane to the vane at discharge, at any radius, may be determined on the assumption that when the wheel runs full there is no relative radial interchange of the particles of water. The turbine may then be imagined as subdivided into a series of n elements each having a depth at inlet $= b \div n$, and a width at outlet $= l \div n$, where b is the depth of the wheel at inlet and l is the length of the discharging periphery of each bucket (Fig. 260). It then becomes easy to calculate the respective angles of inclination to the horizontal and the vertical at the mid point of each element at outlet in order that the discharge may be as nearly as possible axial, and so to obtain the contours of the vane.

This method cannot, however, be relied upon to give very accurate results, since the velocity of flow across the whole outlet area will not be equal. This follows because of the reduced resistance to flow through those elements which offer the shorter path to the water, and in which at the same time, because of their shorter radial length, the resistance to inward flow caused by the centrifugal action of the water, is least. Thus the velocity of flow will be greater in those elements of the discharge area which are at a greater distance from the centre.

It thus becomes necessary for accurate results to treat each section as a separate turbine with given inlet and outlet pressures, and so to calculate the relative flow per unit area across each section.

This involves very elaborate calculations,[1] and the more usual method in practice is to determine the correct mean angle for the outflow at the point of mean radius on the assumption that this outflow is uniform over the whole section.

Art. 149.—Impulse Turbine of the Girard Type.

Here the pressure remains constant throughout the turbine, being either atmospheric or that corresponding to the air pressure inside the turbine casing, so that $p_2 = p_3$.

As in the pressure turbine, the work done by the water, assuming the vanes designed to give no velocity of whirl at exit, is given by

$$U = \frac{W\,Q}{g}\,w_2\,u_2 \text{ foot lbs. per second.}$$

The equation of energy—

$$\frac{p_2}{W} + \frac{w_2^2 + f_2^2}{2\,g} = \frac{p_3}{W} + \frac{f_3^2}{2\,g} + \frac{w_2\,u_2}{g}$$

now simplifies to

$$w_2^2 + f_2^2 - f_3^2 = 2\,w_2\,u_2. \tag{1}$$

Writing $f_3 = k\,f_2$, this becomes—

$$w_2^2 + (1 - k^2)\,f_2^2 = 2\,w_2\,u_2. \tag{2}$$

If $f_2 = f_3$, i.e., $k = 1$, this reduces to $u_2 = \frac{w_2}{2}$, and since $\sqrt{w_2^2 + f_2^2}$

$= C_v\,\sqrt{2\,g\,H'}$, where $C_v = \cdot97$ (approximately)

$$u_2 = \frac{\sqrt{C_v^2 \times 2\,g\,H' - f_2^2}}{2}$$

$$= \frac{C_v\,\sqrt{2\,g\,H'}}{2} \text{ (approx.).}$$

---

[1] For a mathematical investigation into this matter the reader may consult an article by Professor Lorenz, *Zeitschrift des Vereines Deutscher Ingenieure*, October, 1905 (p. 1670), or *Zur Theorie der Francis Turbinen*, Fritz Oestarien. Berlin. Julius Springer.

so that the peripheral speed for maximum efficiency is approximately half that due to the supply lead.

Since the kinetic energy rejected at discharge increases with an increase in f_3, it is necessary to keep this as small as possible, so that in practice the vanes are usually designed to give k a value between $\frac{1}{2}$ and $\frac{1}{3}$, while f_2 is given a value about $\cdot 40 \sqrt{2 g H'}$. On this assumption, we have—

$$w_2{}^2 = C_v{}^2 \times 2 g H' - f_2{}^2$$
$$= 2 g H' \{ C_v{}^2 - \cdot 16 \}$$
$$= \cdot 781 \times 2 g H'$$
$$\therefore \quad w_2 = \cdot 884 \sqrt{2 g H'}.$$

Again,
$$\frac{f_2}{w_2} = \tan a$$
$$\therefore \quad \tan a = \frac{\cdot 40}{\cdot 884} = \cdot 453$$
$$a = 24° 24' \text{ (approximately)}.$$

Assuming $k = \frac{1}{2}$, and writing (2) in the form

$$u_2 = \frac{w_2}{2} + \frac{(1 - k^2) f_2{}^2}{2 w_2}$$

this becomes on substituting

$$u_2 = \frac{w_2}{2} \{ 1 + \tfrac{3}{4} \tan{}^2 a \}$$
$$= \cdot 577 \, w_2 = \cdot 525 \, C_v \sqrt{2 g H'};$$

so that the peripheral speed of the wheel is slightly greater than half that corresponding to the supply head.

Again, since
$$f_2 \cot \beta = w_2 - u_2$$
$$= w_2 (1 - \cdot 577)$$
we have
$$\cot \beta = \cdot 423 \cot a$$
$$= \frac{\cdot 423}{\cdot 453} = \cdot 934$$
$$\therefore \quad \beta = 47° \text{ (approximately)}.$$

Again,
$$f_3 = u_3 \tan \gamma$$
$$= u_2 \cdot \frac{r_3}{r_2} \tan \gamma.$$

In the case of an axial flow turbine $r_3 = r_2$, so that

$$f_3 = u_2 \tan \gamma$$
$$\therefore \quad \tan \gamma = \frac{k f_2}{u_2} = \frac{k w_2 \tan a}{\cdot 577 \, w_2}$$
$$= \frac{\cdot 5}{\cdot 577} \tan a = \cdot 393$$
$$\therefore \quad \gamma = 21° 30' \text{ (approximately)}.$$

Evidently the whole series of angles depends entirely on the value t be given to f_2.

If the relative velocity of water and vane is unaltered by its passage through the wheel, we have

$$f_2 \cosec \beta = f_3 \cosec \gamma \qquad \therefore \ \frac{\sin \beta}{\sin \gamma} = \frac{f_2}{f_3} = \frac{1}{k}.$$

Again, the effective sectional area of the wheel passages at inlet $= 2 \pi r_2 b_2 \sin \beta$, and at outlet $= 2 \pi r_3 b_3 \sin \gamma$ (neglecting the thickness of the vanes), and since the effective area should increase rather

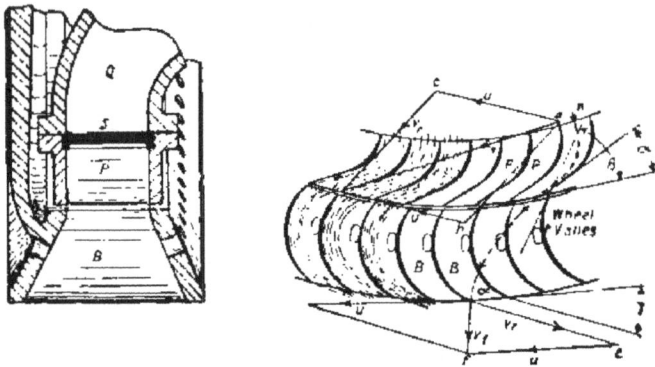

FIG. 261.—Girard Turbine with Outward Radial Flow.

than diminish towards the outlet, in order to give free deviation of the jet, we must have

$$\frac{2 \pi r_3 b_3 \sin \gamma}{2 \pi r_2 b_2 \sin \beta} > 1.$$

In an axial flow machine this makes $\dfrac{b_3 \sin \gamma}{b_2 \sin \beta} \left(= k \dfrac{b_3}{b_2} \right)$ equal to or greater than 1, so that b_3 must be equal to or greater than $\dfrac{b_2}{k}$. This necessitates the buckets being splayed out towards the exit as illustrated in Fig. 261.

The buckets should not be more than ·9 full at entrance, and ·75 full at outlet. The pitch of the guides should then be less than that of the wheel vanes, the breadth b_2 being calculated to give the necessary proportion full at entrance.

The pitch of the vanes should be small to avoid excessive loss by shock at entrance when the tip of the wheel vanes has passed the corresponding guide vane.

The actual path, $k\,d$, of a particle through the wheel may be drawn as in the case of the pressure turbine, except that now, in the case of an axial flow turbine, the relative velocity of water and vane is fixed,[1] while the velocity of flow varies. In this case, then, a series of equidistant points on the curve of the vane being taken from entrance to exit, the points in which concentric circles through these points cut corresponding equidistant vane positions will give points on the true path of the particle, the time required for the particle to travel from point to point along the vane being equal to the time required for the vane to travel from one position to the next.

Once a and γ have been determined, the peripheral speed for maximum efficiency may readily be obtained graphically.

Thus, with the usual notation, $a\,b\,c$ and $d\,e\,f$ (Fig. 263) represent the triangles of velocity for the inlet and outlet edges of an impulse turbine. In an axial flow turbine the relative velocity $d\,f$ at exit will be equal to that of $a\,c$ at inlet. In an outward flow turbine $d\,f$ will be greater, but, as previously explained, may be determined graphically.

Also for maximum efficiency the velocity of the water on leaving the

---

[1] Except as modified by the influence of gravity. Neglecting frictional resistances and windage, this is true so long as every portion of the vane over which a given filament passes is moving at the same speed, as is the case in an axial flow machine where the path of each particle is presumably parallel to the axis. If, however, different portions of the surface with which a particle comes in contact have different velocities as in the case of a radial flow turbine, the relative velocity is no longer constant. It may, however, be determined graphically, since it will be the resultant of the relative velocity at inlet, and of the component in the direction of the vane at the required point, of the relative velocity of the vane at that point and at inlet. Thus, if in Fig. 262,

$$n\,a = \text{relative velocity at inlet}$$
$$a\,b = \text{velocity of vane at inlet}$$
$$c\,d = \text{velocity of vane at outlet}$$
$$\widehat{n\,c\,p} = \gamma.$$

Then $d\,e = $ relative velocity of vane at outlet and at inlet, and $e\,f$, drawn parallel to $c\,m$, represents the component of this in the direction of the vane at outlet. If then $c\,k = n\,a$, and if $c\,k$ be produced to m where $k\,m = e\,f$, the relative velocity at out-

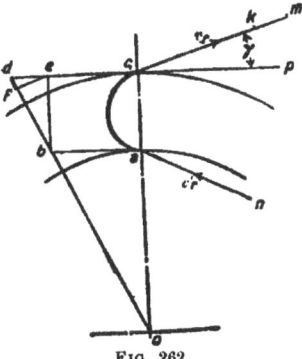

FIG. 262.

let is represented by $e\,m$. Where, in the case of a Girard turbine, the ratio of outer and inner radii $= 1\cdot25$ with a value of $\gamma = 21°$ the actual relative velocity at outlet is approximately $1\cdot23$ times that at inlet. Frictional resistance will, however, reduce this by some unknown amount, and will probably bring the ratio down to about $1\cdot10$. In any case, the effect on the value of γ for maximum efficiency will be slight, the effect being to reduce this value, and this should be taken into account in arranging the design (see Fig. 261).

buckets must have a minimum value so that ef must be perpendicular to de.

If then a straight line, $b'\ a'$, be drawn to represent v, and if a right-angled triangle, $b'\ a'\ e'$, be described on $b'\ a'$, the angle $\widehat{b'\ a'\ e'}$ being equal to a, the side $a'\ e'$ will represent $2\ u$. In the case of a radial flow

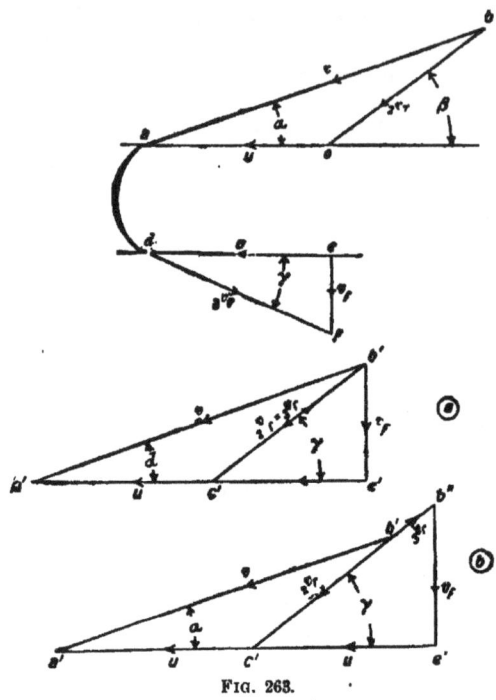

Fig. 263.

turbine the construction is modified as shown in Fig. 263 b, where $c'\ b''$ represents the relative velocity at exit.

Art. 150.—Effect of Centrifugal Action.

In an axial flow impulse turbine with radial vanes, centrifugal action tends to heap up the water towards the outside of the buckets and so to cause an unevenness of flow which militates against efficient working.

Thus in Fig. 264 a particle of water entering at P (in plan) tends to follow a path $P\ A$ instead of its actual path $P\ B$. The outer particles are prevented from following the path PA by the action of the outer walls of the bucket, but at points nearer the centre of rotation this constraint is absent and the particles tend to follow their natural paths. The relative motion which then takes place may be prevented by designing the buckets so that the actual path of each particle, in plan, is a straight line perpendicular to the radius. In this case, if Q is the middle point of the bucket at inlet, R will be its middle point at outlet, and the bucket will be splayed out symmetrically about R instead of B'.

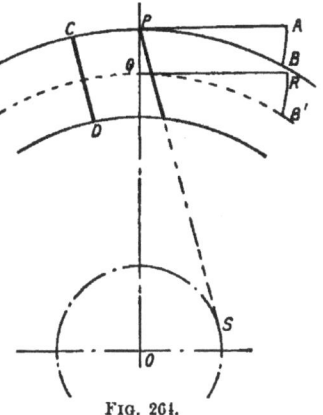

Fig. 264.

A second method which has been adopted consists in making the outlet edge at P, parallel to $P S$, instead of being radial, where $\widehat{S P O} = \widehat{A P B}$. The inlet edge $C D$ is then made parallel to this, with the result that the length of path traversed by the various particles becomes more nearly equal and the relative motion is largely prevented.

ART. 151.—GENERAL COMPARISON OF IMPULSE AND PRESSURE TURBINES.

The impulse wheel, having a peripheral velocity of approximately $\frac{1}{2} \sqrt{2 g H}$, as against about ·7 $\sqrt{2 g H}$ for the pressure turbine, is well fitted for very high falls. For the same reason its velocity becomes low under low heads, and this renders it unsuitable for driving electric generating machinery under such conditions. Further, with low falls the percentage variation in head is generally comparatively large, and the difficulty of maintaining the speed approximately constant, and of maintaining the efficiency under such head variations, is great. On the other hand, the part gate efficiency is high where the head is constant and where the load or supply is variable. Either type may be used for any head up to 500 feet, though the impulse type is preferable for heads above about 200 feet, except for very large powers. Also with either type full load efficiencies of about 85 per cent. may be obtained under favourable circumstances, the more modern type of Francis turbines with swivel guides having a slight advantage in th'·-

respect. Either type may be used in connection with a suction tube, though the pressure turbine lends itself more readily to this construction and has the further advantage that it may be drowned without loss of efficiency. The efficiency of the pressure wheel is not so sensitive to changes of supply pressure as that of the impulse wheel, and therefore this type is better fitted for work under a variable head. On the other hand, except when fitted with swivelling guide blades, its part gate efficiency is low. Apart from the conditions outlined, the possibilities of accurate speed regulation are about equal in the two types.

While the cost of the machine depends largely on the type and form of construction, the capital costs of a pressure and an impulse turbine to give equally good results as regards efficiency and speed regulation are practically equal for a head of about 175 feet. For greater heads the pressure turbine, and for lower heads the impulse turbine, becomes the more expensive.

Art. 152.—The Stand Pipe.

The advantages of a stand pipe in increasing the possibilities of accurate speed regulation on an increasing load have already been indicated, and, as will be readily understood, the larger the area of this pipe the more satisfactory are the results likely to be. Mechanical difficulties, as well as considerations of first cost, however, limit the maximum permissible size, and it becomes important to determine what minimum size of pipe will enable satisfactory speed regulation to be performed.

The following investigation, though only approximate, gives results which are sufficiently near to enable the necessary size to be estimated with fair accuracy.

In this investigation, which will take the form of a specific example, the horse power of the turbine, its efficiency, the diameter of the penstock, its length, and the working head, are assumed as being known, as is the maximum increase in load likely to occur at any one time. This enables the necessary velocity of flow along the penstock to be determined both before the increase in load and after the velocity has again become constant after this increase. By applying the equation of energy in the two cases, the pressure at the stand pipe, and thus the free level may be obtained, from which the fall in level, and hence the volume of water leaving the stand pipe during the change, may be obtained in terms of the area. The energy entering the wheel from the stand pipe may then be calculated, and, if it be assumed that the acceleration in the penstock is sensibly uniform, the energy entering the wheel from the supply reservoir during the change may also be calculated, so that the total energy supplied to the wheel during the period of transition may be obtained. Equating this to the energy required to develop the required horse power, the time necessary to produce the required change in the velocity of flow, and hence the acceleration may be calculated in terms of the stand pipe area. Having obtained this, it only remains to equate to the maximum acceleration consistent with good speed regulation.

The value of the latter factor depends largely on the exact requirements of the plant as regards speed regulation. Where this is to be very close, as in a plant for electric driving, the acceleration should not exceed that given by the formula

$$a = \frac{\cdot075 \, g \, h}{l} \text{ ft. per sec. per sec.}$$

$$= 2\cdot4 \, \frac{h}{l} \text{ ft. per sec. per sec.}$$

Example.

Consider a turbine, supplied under a head of 60 feet, through a penstock 4 feet diameter and 200 feet long, and working under a normal load of 300 B.H.P. Assuming the efficiency of the turbine to be ·80, this necessitates a supply of energy $= \dfrac{300 \times 550}{\cdot8} = 206,000$ foot lbs. per second.

And since the energy entering the wheel casing per second $\left. \right\} = 62\cdot4 \, a \, v \left\{ h - \dfrac{v^2}{2 \, g} \dfrac{f \, l}{m} \right\}$

Where a = area of penstock $\qquad$ = 12·57 square feet.

$\quad\;\; h$ = supply head $\qquad\qquad$ = 60 feet.

$\quad\;\; f$ = coefficient of friction $\quad$ = ·005 (say).

This gives on substitution and reduction—

$$v = 4\cdot4 \text{ feet per second}$$

as the velocity of flow along the penstock.

Similarly, if the maximum increase in load is one of 50 per cent. up to 450 H.P., the new velocity, when steady flow is once more attained, will be 6·64 feet per second.

Now, if h_j is the head at the entrance to the turbine casing, and therefore at the stand pipe, we have, in the first case—

$$h_j = h - \frac{v^2}{2 \, g} \left(1 + \frac{f \, l}{m} \right)$$

$$= 60 - \cdot3 \, (1 + 1)$$

$$= 59\cdot4 \text{ feet.}$$

While in the second case, when $v = 6\cdot64$, we have—

$$h_j = 60 - \cdot685 \times 2$$
$$= 58\cdot63 \text{ feet.}$$

$\therefore$ Fall in level at stand pipe $= \cdot77$ feet.

The mean height in stand pipe $= 59\cdot0$ feet, so that if A is its area, the energy leaving during the transition

$$= \cdot81 \times 59 \times 62\cdot4 \times A \text{ foot lbs.}$$
$$= 2,830\ A \text{ foot lbs.}$$

The energy entering the casing from the penstock in the same interval of time, t_1 seconds, is given by

$$\int_o^{t_1} 62\cdot4\ a\ v \left\{ h - \frac{v^2}{2\ g} \frac{f\ l}{m} \right\} d\ t$$

and, assuming uniform acceleration so that $\dfrac{6\cdot64 - 4\cdot4}{t_1} = a$, and writing

$$v = v_1 + a\ t = 4\cdot4 + \frac{2\cdot24}{t_1} \cdot t, \text{ this becomes}$$

$$62\cdot4\ a \int_o^{t_1} \left\{ h\ (v_1 + a\ t) - \frac{f\ l}{2\ g\ m} (v_1 + a\ t)^3 \right\} d\ t$$

$$= 784\ t_1 \left[(60 \times 4\cdot4) + (30 \times 2\cdot24) \right.$$

$$\left. - \frac{1}{64\cdot4} \left\{ (4\cdot4^3) + \left(\frac{3}{2} \times 4\cdot4^2 \times 2\cdot24 \right) + (4\cdot4 \times 2\cdot24^2) + \frac{2\cdot24^3}{4} \right\} \right]$$

$$= 784\ t_1 \left\{ 264 + 67\cdot2 - 2\cdot7 \right\}$$
$$= 257,500\ t_1 \text{ foot lbs.}$$

$\therefore$ For speed to be maintained with the increased load, we must have :—

$$2,830\ A + 257,500\ t_1 = \frac{450 \times 550}{\cdot8} \times t_1 \qquad (1)$$

$$= 309,000\ t_1$$

$$\therefore A = \frac{51,500}{2,830}\ t_1 = 18\cdot20\ t_1$$

$$\text{or } t_1 = \cdot055\ A.$$

Thus the acceleration of the supply column, corresponding to any increase in load, varies inversely as the area of the stand pipe.

With a 4 foot stand pipe $a = \dfrac{2\cdot24}{t_1} = \dfrac{2\cdot24}{12\cdot87 \times \cdot055}$

$$= 3\cdot16 \text{ f.s.s.}$$

Applying the rule $a = 2\cdot 4\,\dfrac{h}{l} = \dfrac{2\cdot 4 \times 60}{200} = \cdot 72$ f.s.s., this gives us

$$\cdot 72 = \frac{2\cdot 24}{\cdot 055\,A}$$

$\therefore\ A = 56\cdot 5$ square feet,

corresponding to a diameter at the top of $8\cdot 48$ feet.

The stand pipe would in this case take the form of a vertical pipe about 3 feet in diameter, and carrying a circular cistern 8 feet 6 inches in diameter at the top, the top of this cistern being about 62 feet above the centre line of the turbine and its depth about 8 feet 3 inches, thus leaving a depth of water equal to $3\cdot 25 - 2\cdot 0 - \cdot 81 = \cdot 44$ feet, when working under full over-load.

The stand pipe is not usually fitted where the supply head is above 200 feet. In the power plant of the St. Louis Hydro-Electric Company,[1] the total head is 380 feet, developed on a pipe line about 5,000 feet long. When finally completed there are to be eight parallel pipes, each 7 feet in diameter, coupled to a transverse receiver 500 feet back from the power house, which receiver is itself at an elevation of 145 feet. From the receiver, an open stand pipe 235 feet long and 6 feet diameter, carrying at the top a circular tank 30 feet in diameter, is erected.

The whole plant is intended to consist of eight units of 13,000 B.H.P. each, the stand pipe being designed to supply sufficient energy for an additional sudden demand of 10,000 B.H.P.

In the Wenatchee River Power Plant[2] three 4,000 K.W. Francis turbines are supplied under a head of 200 feet through a pipe line $8\cdot 5$ feet diameter and $2\cdot 5$ miles long. In this plant a surge pipe 8 feet diameter is provided, the overflow level being 7 feet above the crest of the dam.

ART. 153.—FLYWHEEL EFFECT.

So far, the effect of any flywheel which may be fitted to the turbine shaft has been neglected, the rules already given applying where no special flywheel is fitted.

To consider the effect of such a wheel it must be remembered that the total store of kinetic energy in a wheel of weight W lbs. and of effective radius r feet when rotating at a speed of ω radians per second $\left(N \text{ revolutions per minute, where } \omega = \dfrac{2\,\pi\,N}{60}\right)$, is equal to $\dfrac{1}{2}\,\dfrac{W\,r^2}{g}\,\omega^2$ foot lbs. $= \dfrac{1}{2}\,I\,\omega^2$, where $I =$ moment of inertia of wheel. If then

---

[1] *The Engineer*, February 15, 1907, p. 155.

[2] *The Engineer*, February 18, 1910, p. 166.

the speed of such a wheel is reduced from ω_1 to ω_2, the store of energy

given out $= \frac{1}{2} I (\omega_1{}^2 - \omega_2{}^2) = \frac{1}{2} I (\omega_1 + \omega_2)(\omega_1 - \omega_2) = \delta E$,

and if ω is the mean angular velocity, this may be written :—

$$\frac{1}{2} I \omega \, \delta \omega = \frac{\delta E}{2}.$$
$$\therefore \frac{1}{2} I \omega^2 \frac{\delta \omega}{\omega} = \frac{\delta E}{2}.$$

Putting $\frac{1}{2} I \omega^2 = E$, this becomes

$$\frac{\delta \omega}{\omega} = \frac{\delta E}{2 E}$$

i.e., the proportional change in the store of energy in the wheel is twice as great as the proportional change in velocity.

Suppose, for instance, in the numerical example just considered (p. 565), the turbine, rotating at a mean speed of 240 revolutions per minute ($\omega = 8 \pi$), to be fitted with a flywheel weighing 5 tons and having an effective radius of 2·5 feet. The value of $E = \frac{1}{2} I \omega^2$ now becomes

$$\frac{1}{2} \cdot \frac{5 \times 2{,}240}{32 \cdot 2} \times \frac{25}{\cdot 4} \times 64 \pi^2$$
$$= 687{,}000 \text{ foot lbs.}$$

If the maximum speed variation on throwing on the excess load is to be 4 per cent. of the mean, so that $\frac{\delta \omega}{\omega} = \cdot 04$, we have δE, the energy given out by the wheel during its retardation, given by

$$\delta E = 2 \times \cdot 04 \times 687{,}000 \text{ foot lbs.}$$
$$= 55{,}000 \text{ foot lbs.}$$

If the same acceleration in the penstock be assumed, the amount of energy required from the stand pipe during the transition may be reduced by this amount, and since each square foot of stand pipe area gives up 2,830 foot lbs. of energy, this area may be reduced by $\frac{55.000}{2{,}830}$ square feet $= 19 \cdot 4$ square feet.

This gives an area $= 53 \cdot 6 - 19 \cdot 4 = 34 \cdot 2$ square feet, and a diameter of 6 feet 6 inches, as against 8 feet 6 inches without the wheel.

Evidently with a sufficiently heavy flywheel it would be possible to eliminate the upper cistern altogether.

For further information on this subject, Papers by R. D. Johnson[1] and by Professor Irving P. Church[2] should be consulted.

[1] Am. Soc. C.E., June, 1908, p. 443.
[2] *Cornell Civil Engineer*, December, 1911, p. 114.

EXAMPLES.

(1) Show that in a reaction turbine working under conditions of maximum efficiency, the efficiency is given by

$$\eta = 2 (1 - e) \cos^2 a \left(1 - \frac{\tan a}{\tan \beta}\right)$$

where e measures the proportion of energy existing in the form of pressure energy, in the water at entrance to the wheel.

(2) The angle of the guide blades in an I.F. reaction turbine is 12°, the peripheral speed is 32 feet per second, and the velocity of the water at inlet is 36 feet per second. Determine theoretical vane angles at inlet and outlet, the inner being $\frac{2}{3}$ the outer diameter and the velocity of flow constant.

Answer. $\begin{cases} \text{Inlet angle} & = 67°. \\ \text{Outlet angle} & = 17° 20'. \end{cases}$

(3) If in the previous example the head is 36 feet, the B.H.P. 50, the gross efficiency 82 per cent., what must be the effective area of the wheel inlet, assuming a coefficient of contraction of ·95.

Answer. 2·10 square feet.

(4) The external and internal diameters of an I.F. reaction turbine are 4 feet and 2 feet 3 inches, the vanes are radial at inlet, the velocity of flow through the wheel is $= \frac{1}{8} \sqrt{2 g H'}$, and the peripheral velocity is that due to a fall through $\frac{H'}{2}$. Determine the vane angle at outlet for the water to be discharged without any tangential velocity.

Answer. 17° 27'.

(5) If in the turbine of the preceding question the vanes at outlet make an angle of 20° with the circumference, determine the speed at which the wheel should run; the velocity of flow; and the pressure and kinetic heads in the supply chamber, in terms of the available head H', and also determine the angle which the guide blades make with the circumference.

Answer.

Revolutions per minute $= 4·71 \sqrt{g H'}$ $a = 10° 11'.$
Velocity of flow, f $= ·7 \sqrt{g H'}$
Pressure head $= ·492 H'$
Kinetic head $= ·508 H'.$

(6) A Jonval turbine works under a head of 13·5 feet. The mean diameter is 8 feet, the width of buckets = $17\frac{3}{4}$ inches, the number of revolutions 46 per minute, and the turbine develops 266 horse power with an efficiency of 86 per cent. The number of vanes is thirty-eight, these being $\frac{3}{16}$ inch thick. Assuming guide angles of 18°, and a coefficient of discharge of ·9, determine the velocity of exit from the guides, and the inlet and outlet angles of the wheel vanes for entry without shock and for rejection of water without velocity of whirl. Assume a coefficient of discharge of ·9 for the discharge orifices.

(7) The following are details of an outward flow reaction turbine :—

$a = 28°$; $\beta = 90°$; $\gamma = 22°$;

$r_2 = 3·875$ feet; $r_3 = 4·146$ feet;

$b_1 = ·971$ feet; $b_2 = ·937$ feet; $b_3 = ·932$ feet;

$n_1 = 33$; $n_2 = 44$; $t_1 = ·0083$ feet; $t_2 = ·0117$ feet.

Measured outflow area of guide passages = 6·537 square feet.

　　　　　,,　　　　,,　　　,,　　　buckets　　　= 7·687　　,,

The available head is 13 feet. Determine the number of revolutions for maximum efficiency, and determine the hydraulic efficiency under such conditions.

(8) The following are details of a 800 H.P. outward radial flow Girard turbine :—

$a = 20°$; $\beta = 36°$; $\gamma = 30°$; $r_2 = 4·1$ feet; $r_3 = 4·71$ feet; $b_1 = b_2 = 4·91$ inches; $b_3 = 16·14$ inches. The effective head is 595·5 feet, and the coefficient of discharge from the guide passages is found to be ·85, the coefficient of velocity being ·92. Calculate the speed of rotation (actually 200 per minute) for maximum efficiency.

CHAPTER XVI

ART. 154.—THE HYDRAULIC ENGINE.

WHERE a supply of high pressure water is available, and where intermittent rotary motion at a moderate speed is desired, the reciprocating
piston engine has certain advantages, particularly where it is able to work
at or near full load, and where the speed variation may be excessive, as
occurs, for example, in the working of a capstan. For such work the
rotary motor is out of the question, both on account of the necessity
for gearing to reduce its necessarily high speed, and of the great
reduction in its efficiency under variable speed conditions. The reciprocating engine, however, having an efficiency which is approximately
independent of its speed, and being compact, is particularly well adapted
for such work. For small powers, too, where the load is fairly constant,
such as for driving ventilating fans, organ bellows, etc., its high
efficiency and the absence of noise connected with its use often render
it, in the absence of an electric supply, the most suitable motor to
use.

One of the most widely used types of engine is the Brotherhood
(Fig. 265), which is designed to work with pressures from 60 lbs. to
1,050 lbs. per square inch.

Here three single acting cylinders fitted with trunk pistons are fixed
radially at 120° to an external cylindrical casing, the three connecting
rods working on a single crank pin. Each cylinder is fitted with a
single inlet and outlet port, the opening of this to supply and exhaust
being regulated by the rotary valve shown at D in Fig. 265.

This valve is rotated by the crank shaft, and carries passages connecting with the pressure supply and the exhaust which are alternately
presented before the port of each cylinder in turn. The method of
keeping the rotating joints tight against such high pressures is indicated
in the sketch. Here A is a leather joint washer, on which the back nut B
rotates, the play due to wear on the joint being taken up by the expansion of the rubber ring C, which rotates with the valve and back nut. The

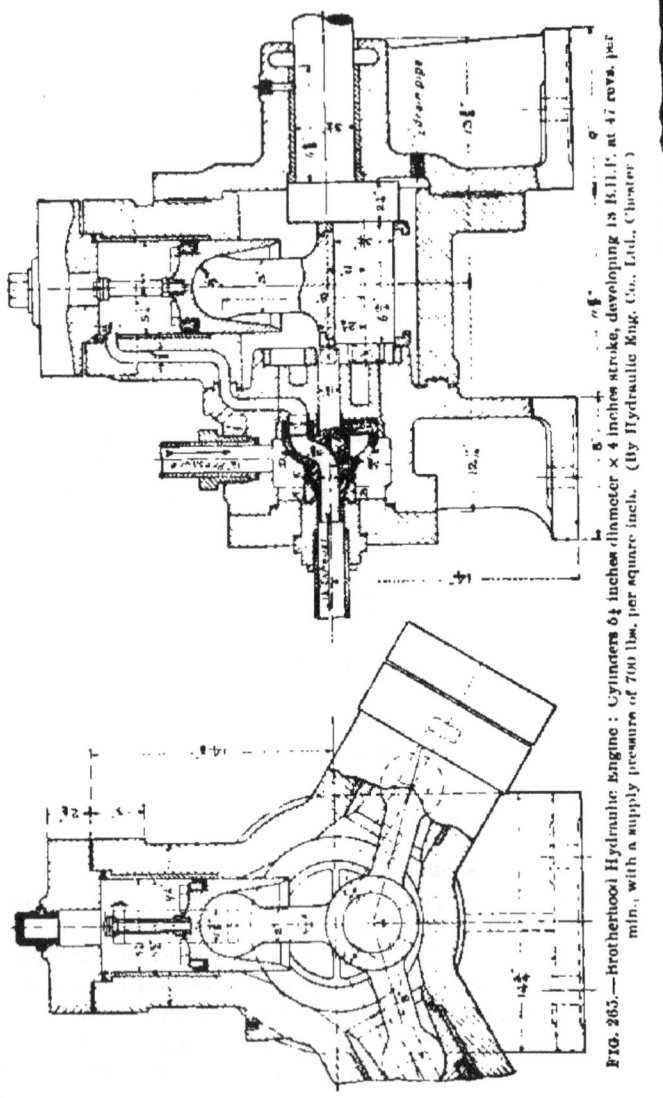

FIG. 265.—Brotherhood Hydraulic Engine : Cylinders 6¼ inches diameter × 4 inches stroke, developing 13 B.H.P. at 47 revs. per min., with a supply pressure of 700 lbs. per square inch. (By Hydraulic Eng. Co., Ltd., Chester.)

1 ve itself bears against a lignum-vitæ seat. All pistons are packed with L " leathers, and the cylinders and all working parts are lined with ass.

The engine as thus constructed forms a compact and serviceable motor, .s no dead centre, and is built in sizes up to about 30 B.H.P. The ston speed is about 30 feet per minute for all sizes, the engine shown in g. 265 having cylinders 5¼ inches diameter × 4-inch stroke and veloping 13 B.H.P. at forty-seven revolutions per minute when supplied ith water at 700 lbs. pressure.

The full power efficiency, as measured on the brake horse power, varies ith the working pressure from about 52 per cent. with 60 lbs. pressure, 65 per cent. at 1,050 lbs. This is equivalent to an hydraulic efficiency from 61 per cent. to 76 per cent. These values are probably too low ther than too high.

All constant stroke engines, however, suffer from the fact that water nnot be used expansively, and since, to avoid shock, it is necessary to ɔp the cylinders full of water, the same energy is used whatever the load a the engine, causing the efficiency to be low at light or variable loads. has been attempted to overcome this difficulty, but without great ɪccess, by cutting off the pressure supply before the end of the stroke nd admitting low pressure water from an auxiliary supply for the rest f the stroke.

A device due to Meyer consists in providing an air chamber at each nd of the (double acting) cylinder. Cut-off may then take place before ɪe end of the stroke, the air afterwards expanding and driving the iston. No gain in efficiency is to be anticipated from this method of orking.

The more usual device is to reduce the stroke and piston displacement ɔ suit the varying demands for power. In the Brotherhood engine this as been accomplished by the Hastie regulating device.

As thus constructed, power is transmitted through a hollow crank shaft ɔ the driving pulley by means of a volute spring, an increase in the load roducing a further coiling of this spring. The inner end of the spring is xed to the hollow crank shaft, while the driving pulley carries a disc eyed to a cam shaft working inside the crank shaft. Any variation in he load then produces a relative rotation of the crank and cam shaft. A am keyed to the latter shaft utilizes this relative rotation to increase or iminish the crank radius, and thus to adapt the volume of piston dis- lacement to the demand for power. This device is, however, seldom ɪow fitted to the engine.

Of all variable power engines, that of Mr. R. Rigg [1] has achieved the greatest success in practice.

This engine is provided with three cylinders, fitted with plungers which are pivoted at their outer ends to an external cylindrical ring, which is itself keyed to the driving shaft. The cylinders face radially outwards at 120°, are single acting, and are rigidly fixed at their inner ends to a ring which rotates on a fixed hollow shaft forming the supply pipe, eccentric with the external casing, and carrying the inlet and outlet ports. The rotation of the outer ring is thus accompanied by a reciprocating motion of the pistons in their cylinders, the stroke of each being twice the eccentricity of the two rings. There are three ports, one to each cylinder, and as these rotate each in turn is presented before an inlet and an outlet port in the central hollow shaft. Regulation of power at constant speed is obtained by altering the eccentricity, and therefore the stroke of the engine, by means of an hydraulic relay governed by a centrifugal governor. The reduction in water consumption is thus proportional to the reduction in the stroke. When regulating the eccentricity by hand at constant power, a decrease in stroke will be accompanied by a corresponding increase in speed, the work done per second then being approximately the same. This method of working may be adopted for capstans and the like, where when hauling in slack, etc., a rapid rotation with very short stroke is required, while when the full pull is to be exerted by the rope, a long stroke and slow rate of rotation is essential. By reversing the relative position of the centre the direction of rotation is reversed.

The speed of the engine may be anything up to about 500 revolutions per minute, though probably 250 revolutions marks the limit of its really efficient performance. At the latter speed the inventor claims to obtain efficiencies up to 80 per cent., though this value would appear to be improbably high.

In the Armstrong type of engine, oscillating cylinders mounted side by side and driving on to a common crank shaft are adopted. Three cylinders driving cranks at 120° are usual, and are fitted, either with externally packed rams forming a single acting engine, or with differential rams having areas in the ratio 2 : 1. The smaller of these is exposed to a constant pressure head, and the engine becomes double acting with equal efforts on each stroke. The single acting engine is more commonly used. Admission and discharge take place through a circular slide valve working within the hollow trunnions which carry the cylinders. This engine is made to develop up to about 70 B.H.P.

[1] See *Engineering*, vol. 45, p. 61.

Art. 155.—Theory of the Hydraulic Engine.—Horse Power.

If K = number of cylinders—supposed single acting.

p = mean effective pressure in lbs. per square inch in each cylinder.

N = number of revolutions per minute.

l = length of stroke in feet.

A = ram area in square inches.

Then I.H.P. $= K \cdot \dfrac{p\, l\, A\, N}{33,000}$.

The mechanical efficiency varies with the size and type of engine, and with its condition, but will be generally about 85 per cent.

If Q = volume of water used per minute in cubic feet.

H = supply head in feet.

The hydraulic efficiency

$$= \frac{\text{indicated work on piston}}{\text{energy in supply water}} = \frac{K \cdot p\, l\, A\, N}{62 \cdot 4\, Q\, H},$$

or writing $\qquad Q = K\, l\, A\, N \div 144,$

we have the hydraulic efficiency $= \dfrac{144\, p}{62 \cdot 4\, H} = \dfrac{2 \cdot 31\, p}{H}.$

The total efficiency of the system $= \dfrac{33,000\ (\text{B.H.P.})}{62 \cdot 4\, Q\, H}$

$=$ hydraulic efficiency $\times$ mechanical efficiency.

Pressure on Piston.—As in the reciprocating pump, the pressure on the piston at any point of the stroke is affected by the inertia of the supply column. The engine may in fact be considered as a reversed pump with mechanically operated valves, and the investigation into pressure conditions in the cylinder proceeds on exactly similar lines to that in the case of the pump. For a further investigation of these pressure effects the reader is referred to Art. 163. It may be noted, however, that at any point of the stroke, where a is the piston acceleration and v its velocity, a_s is the area and l_s the length of the supply pipe, m being its hydraulic mean depth, we have:—

$$\left. \begin{array}{c} \text{Head on piston} \\ \text{in feet} \end{array} \right\} = \left[\begin{array}{c} \text{supply head} \\ \text{in feet} \end{array} - \frac{A}{a_s} \cdot \frac{l_s}{g} \cdot \left\{ a + \frac{f\, v^2\, A}{2\, m\, a_s} \right\} \text{ft.} \right].$$

Here a is positive during the first, and negative during the last part of the stroke.

A weighted accumulator feeding the supply pipe line has the effect of increasing acceleration pressures as explained in Art. 193. The provision of an air vessel on the supply side of the engine materially improves the smoothness of running, and by maintaining an approximately uniform flow in the supply main, reduces frictional and shock losses and so increases the efficiency of the motor. The necessary dimensions of the air vessel depend on the number and arrangement of the cylinders; on the speed and dimensions of the engine; and on the length of supply pipe. If more than one cylinder is used, the cranks being placed at equal angles round the shaft, the velocity of flow through the supply pipe is considerably steadied, and indeed with the usual type of three-cylinder engine having cranks at 120°, becomes so nearly uniform that it becomes possible to dispense with the air vessel.

For a further consideration of the questions deciding the size of the air vessel in any particular case reference should be made to Art. 163. With the high pressures usually adopted in these engines it becomes imperative either to provide some mechanical device for maintaining the charge of air in the vessel, or to make the vessel of ample area to maintain its mean working level approximately constant over long periods of working. Thus the necessary size of air vessel for the engine will in general be slightly greater than that for the corresponding pump.

Losses in the Hydraulic Engine.—Port Areas.—These losses are due partly to friction but more particularly to shock produced at sudden changes of section, and are therefore approximately proportional to the square of the velocity. To reduce these, all throttling is to be prevented as far as possible, inlet and outlet ports are to be short, direct, and of ample area, with easy curves and with few changes in sectional area or shape.

Where, as in some instances, the inlet ports are emptied at the end of each exhaust stroke, to be refilled before the commencement of the next working stroke, this is productive of a direct loss of energy, since owing to the fact that the fluid is inexpansive, no work is done on the piston until these ports are completely filled. This loss increases with the area of the ports, while friction losses and those due to the loss of the kinetic energy of entrance decrease as this area increases, so that in any particular case there will be some one port area for which the total loss is a minimum. In the case of a single acting engine:—

The loss of energy per revolution due to water necessary to fill inlet ports of area a square feet and length l feet, at a pressure p lbs. per square inch $= 2 \cdot 31 \, p \cdot l \cdot a$ foot lbs.

Loss by friction per stroke $= 62 \cdot 4 \, L \, A \times \dfrac{f \, l \, \bar{v}^2}{2 \, g \, m}$ foot lbs.

loss of kinetic energy per stroke
(assuming all this to be lost) $\Bigg\} = 62\!\cdot\!4 \ L \ A \ \dfrac{\bar{v}^2}{2\,g}$ foot lbs.

here L = length of stroke of piston

$\quad D$ = diameter, A = area of piston in square feet

$\quad \bar{v}^2$ = mean square of velocity of flow through ports

$\quad = v^2 \dfrac{A^2}{a^2}$, where v^2 = mean square of piston velocities throughout

a stroke. In general v may be taken as $1\!\cdot\!25$ times the mean piston velocity v_m with sufficient accuracy for practical calculations.[1]

Since the losses of head included under the two latter headings serve both to diminish the effective pressure on the working stroke and to increase the back pressure on the discharge, we have the total loss of energy per working stroke

$$= 2\!\cdot\!31 \ p \ l \ a + 195 \ \frac{L \, A^3}{a^2} \cdot \frac{v^2_m}{2\,g} \left\{ \frac{f\,l}{m} + 1 \right\} \text{ foot lbs.}$$

Substituting for A and a in terms of D and d, and writing $m = \dfrac{d}{4}$, this becomes

$$\frac{\pi}{4} \left[\ 2\!\cdot\!31 \ p \ l \ d^2 + \frac{195 \ D^6}{d^4} \ L \ \frac{v^2_m}{2\,g} \left\{ \frac{4\,f\,l}{d} + 1 \right\} \ \right].$$

Differentiating this with respect to d and equating the result to zero, we have :—

$$d^6 = D^6 \times \frac{2\!\cdot\!62 \ L \ v^2_m \left\{ 1 + \dfrac{5\,f\,l}{d} \right\}}{p \ l}.$$

from which, by successive approximations, or by graphical solution, we can find d, the diameter of inlet ports for the total loss to be a minimum. If the inlet passages are rectangular in section it is sufficiently near for practical purposes to make their sectional area equal to that of this circle.

---

[1] Here $v_m = L \div$ time to complete one stroke.

If a curve be plotted having the squares of the piston velocities as ordinates on a displacement base, the mean height of the curve will equal $v^2 \left(\dfrac{a}{A} \right)^2$. In the case of an oscillating cylinder with a connecting rod equal to three cranks in length, the ratio $\dfrac{\bar{v}}{v_m}$ is approximately equal to $1\!\cdot\!27$, so that $\left(\dfrac{\bar{v}}{v_m} \right)^2 = 1\!\cdot\!61$. With a longer connecting rod this will be reduced, so that in general $\left(\dfrac{\bar{v}}{v_m} \right)^2$ will approximately equal $1\!\cdot\!56 = (1\!\cdot\!25)^2$.

EXAMPLE.

Hydraulic engine, 12 inches diameter, 12 inches stroke.

$p = 750$ lbs. per square inch, mean piston velocity 8 feet per second, length of ports 2 feet ; $f = \cdot 01$. Here $L = 1$; $D = 1$; $l = 2$:

We now have $\qquad d^6 = \dfrac{2 \cdot 62 \times 9}{750 \times 2} \times \left\{ 1 \times \dfrac{\cdot 1}{d} \right\}.$

Neglecting the $\dfrac{\cdot 1}{d}$ in the last factor, we get $d^6 = \cdot 0157$ as a first approximation, from which $d = \cdot 50$ feet.

Substituting this value of d in the factor $1 + \dfrac{\cdot 1}{d}$, we now get as a second approximation—

$$d^6 = \cdot 0157 \times 1 \cdot 2 = \cdot 0189,$$
$$\text{giving } d = \cdot 515 \text{ foot} = 6\tfrac{3}{16} \text{ inches.}$$

If this value were adopted for d in the last factor of the above equation, and a solution obtained as before, a still closer approximation to the true value would be obtained. Generally, however, a second approximation gives results which are sufficiently close for any practical purpose.

If this method be applied to the design of the Brotherhood engine (Fig. 265), having a $5\frac{1}{4}$-inch cylinder with 4-inch stroke, working at forty-seven revolutions per minute ($r_{(mean)} = \cdot 52$ feet per second) and having a port length of 18 inches, taking $f = \cdot 010$ we have :—

$$d^6 = \frac{2 \cdot 62 \times (\cdot 52)^3 \times 7^6}{1 \cdot 5 \times 3 \times 16^6 \times 750} \left\{ 1 + \frac{\cdot 075}{d} \right\}$$

From which we finally get $d = \cdot 116$ foot $= 1 \cdot 39$ inches.

The area of this corresponds to that of a rectangular port $1\frac{3}{4}$ inches wide by $\frac{32}{32}$ inch deep, as compared with the actual dimensions, $1\frac{3}{4}$ inches $\times \frac{5}{8}$ inch.

This investigation shows the importance of having as far as possible separate inlet and outlet ports for these engines, or, where using a single port, of designing this so as to remain full until readmission takes place. Where this design is carried out the port area may be arranged to give a mean velocity of flow of from 2·5 to 3·5 feet per second. In the alternative case a smaller port area will in general give better results, the velocity being increased up to a maximum of about 8 feet per second.

CHAPTER XVII

ART. 156.—PUMPS.

Most hydraulic prime movers are, with slight modifications, capable of being reversed, and when driven by an external agency provide a means of raising water from a lower to a higher level.

Thus the overshot water wheel corresponds to the chain and bucket pump; the breast or Sagebien wheel to the scoop wheel; the reversed pressure turbine gives the centrifugal pump, and the reversed reciprocating engine the reciprocating pump. The capacity of each of these machines as a prime mover also to a large extent indicates its capacity, when reversed, as a pump, and just as the reciprocating engine and turbine are the most important types of prime mover, so the reciprocating piston pump and the centrifugal pump are the most important types of pump.

In addition to those already mentioned, we have a series of special types of pump, each of which is specially adapted to some particular combination of circumstances. Of these, the Archimedean screw, the jet pump, the positive rotary pump, the hydraulic ram, and the air lift pump, are interesting examples and will be considered in due course.

ART. 157.—THE SCOOP WHEEL.

This has in the past been largely applied to the drainage of fen districts, and simply consists of a Sagebien wheel reversed and driven usually by steam power, the water then being lifted in the buckets from the lower to the higher level. It is fitted for lifts up to about 6 feet and may be constructed to deliver up to about 400 tons per minute, giving an efficiency under favourable conditions of upwards of 75 per cent. Its chief advantages appear in cases where a large quantity of *débris* is encountered. As in the Sagebien wheel, the inclination of the floats should be such as to prevent shock at entrance and losses at exit as far as possible. It is found that the best results are obtained when the angles which the vanes make with the water surface at entrance and exit are equal. If any variation is made from this design, it is better to increase the angle of egress, since this reduces the loss due to lifting the water above head-race level. While increasing the loss at entrance due to shock, and to driving the water back from the floats, this is in general less serious than the former source of loss. In some cases the angle of egress is made equal to twice the angle of ingress. The floats are found

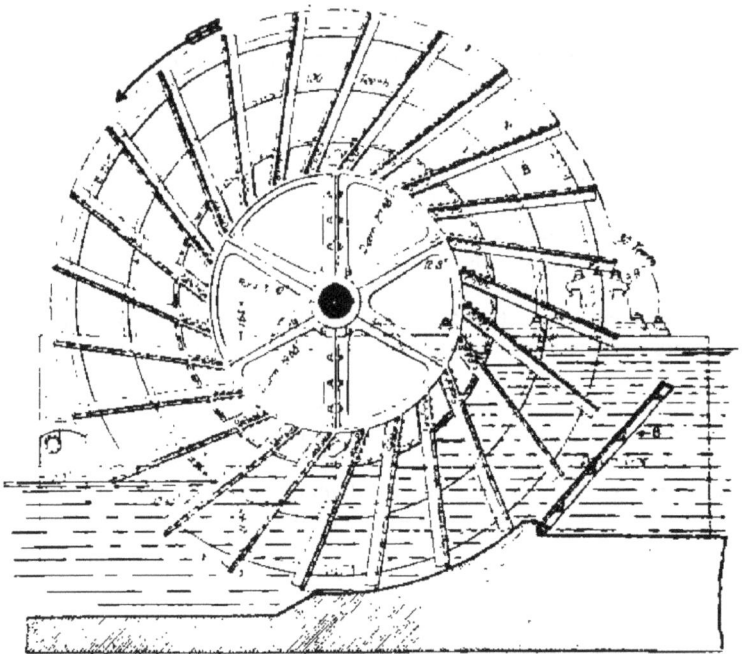

FIG. 266.—Scoop Wheel with movable breast.

to give better results when flat than when curved, and are arranged to make an angle of from 20° to 40° with the radial line. Since any variation in the head or tail-race level militates against efficient working. it is advisable to regulate the supply level at the wheel by means of an adjustable sluice, so as to keep this constant. As usually constructed, the diameter of the wheel lies between $9 \sqrt{H}$ and $10 \sqrt{H}$, where H is the lift in feet. The peripheral speed is usually about 8 feet per second.

Fig. 266 shows one of a set of six wheels installed in 1901 at Schellingwoude for the purpose of maintaining the level of the Amsterdam Canal. The plant is required to lift over a range of heads varying from ·5 foot to 8 feet, and to discharge 1,500 cubic feet per second against a normal head of 1·8 feet at 4·5 revolutions per minute.

Under normal conditions the vane angle at entrance is 24°, and at exit 48°. The diameter is 28 feet, the diameter of the circle to which the vanes are tangent being 5·5 feet. An important feature of the installation is the movable breast float B which is fitted in front of each wheel. This breast is pivoted on a horizontal axis at its lower end, and is free to take up a natural and unrestrained position in the current of discharging water. It is constructed of heavy planking and angle iron, and the comparatively high efficiency of the plant is attributed largely to the action of this float. The overall efficiency varies from 40 per cent. under 1·6 feet head to 74 per cent. under 6·6 feet head.

ART. 158.—THE SCREW PUMP OR ARCHIMEDEAN SCREW

has in the past been largely used in Holland, and works with advantage against heads not exceeding 10 feet, having an efficiency equal to that of the scoop wheel. The pump consists of an inclined shaft carrying one or more helices of considerable diameter, which rotate with small clearance in a closely-fitting tube or open semi-circular channel connecting head and tail-water.

The angle of inclination of the shaft to the horizontal is so arranged

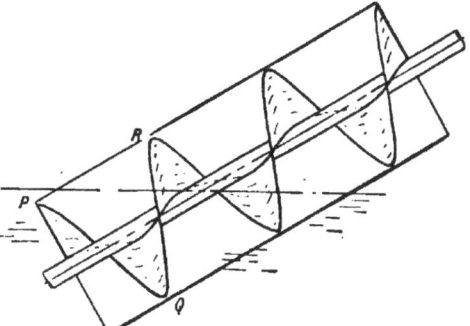

FIG. 267.—Archimedean Screw.

as to be less than that of the helical surface, so that water on being admitted to the bottom of the tube always tends to run down this surface. Thus (Fig. 267), a particle of water admitted at P tends to flow to the point Q. By a rotation of the axis portions of the helix from Q to R successively adopt the same position as Q relative to the axis. As they do so the water tends to flow into these positions and is thus passed along the screw, finally emerging at the top into the head-water. The most advantageous angle for the helix is found to be between 30° and 40°.

In the more modern form of screw pump the screw itself is similar to a screw propeller, but usually carries about six blades. This is carried on a horizontal or vertical axis and works with small radial clearance in a cylindrical chamber through which flow takes place. In such a pump. installed some few years ago in connection with the Chicago main drainage scheme, the screw has a diameter of 13 feet 6 inches, and when rotating at fifty-two revolutions per minute, has a capacity of 23,000 gallons per minute against 3·5 feet head.[1]

Although both screw pumps and scoop wheels are capable of high efficiencies they are cumbrous, and run at inconveniently low speeds, and are in almost every case being replaced by the centrifugal pump.

ART. 159.—THE RECIPROCATING PUMP.

The oldest type of reciprocating pump is the bucket pump illustrated diagrammatically in Fig. 268. Originally devised as a lift pump, it was fitted with a hollow bucket or piston surmounted by a valve, and with a foot valve to prevent escape of water on the down stroke.

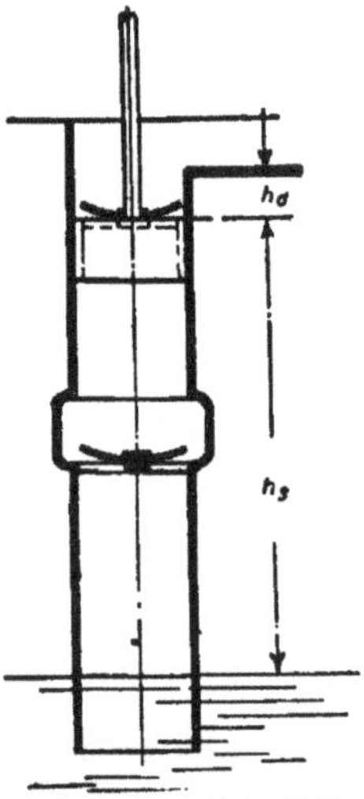

FIG. 268.—Bucket or Lift Pump.

On the up stroke of the pump a partial vacuum is produced below the bucket, and the pressure of the atmosphere acting on the free surface in the supply reservoir produces a flow up the suction tube in virtue of this difference of pressure.

If h_s = suction head in feet of water for any given position of the bucket.

π_a = atmospheric pressure (in feet of water). Then, neglecting frictional losses and the effect of acceleration, the pressure head on the under side of bucket = $\pi_a - h_s$ feet. This has its minimum theoretical value when $\pi_a - h_s = 0$, i.e.. when an absolute vacuum is produced below the bucket, and the maximum possible suction head is thus equal to π_a, or 34 feet approximately. Practically, owing to the resistance of the suction valve, leakage at joints and past the bucket, and to the liberation of dissolved air at low pressures. this head is impossible of attainment, a suction head of 24 feet being only maintained with difficulty, and the maximum value of the suction head,

---

[1] For a sketch of this pump see the *Mechanical Engineer*, March 20, 1908, p. 367.

i.e., the distance from supply level to level of bucket valve with the bucket in its highest position should not exceed this value.

If h_d = delivery head on pump in feet, *i.e.*, height between bucket and

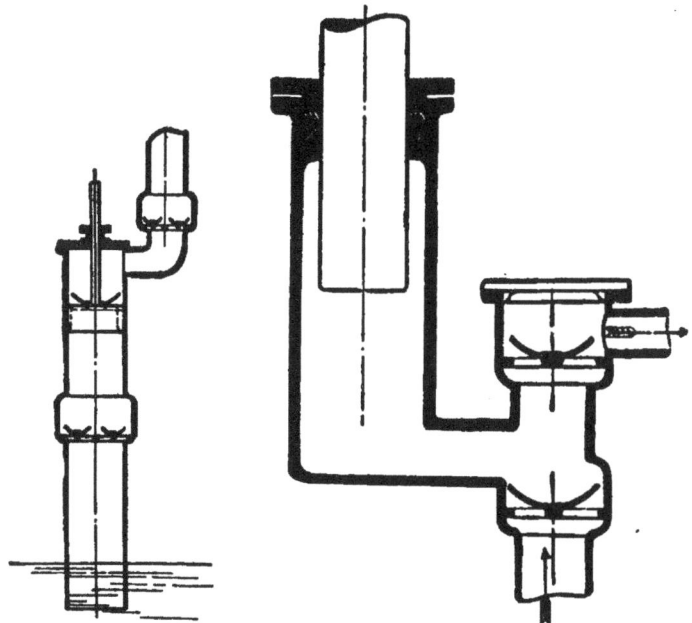

FIG. 269.—Single-acting Force Pump. FIG. 270.—Single-acting Plunger Pump.

outlet, the pressure head on upper side of bucket = $\pi_a + h_d$ feet.

∴ Total head on bucket

$$= \pi_a + h_d - (\pi_a - h_s) \text{ feet}$$
$$= h_d + h_s = H \text{ feet,}$$

where H = total lift of pump.

On the up stroke, then, water is lifted out at the top of the pump and the tension of the pump rod is given by $W H A$ lbs., where

A = area of bucket in square feet.

W = weight of 1 cubic foot of water = 62·4 lbs.

(This neglects the resistance of valves and passages.) On the down stroke water escapes through the valve, from the under to the upper side of the bucket, so that all the work is done on the up stroke.

By the addition of a closed top fitted with a stuffing box through which

the bucket rod works, the machine becomes a force pump for delivering
water under pressure (Fig. 269).   The provision of a back pressure valve
on the delivery side of the pump is now necessary to prevent the backward escape of the water on the down or idle stroke.   As thus arranged
the pump may be either vertical or horizontal.

As pressures are increased, the bucket type of pump is found to be
unsatisfactory on account of the difficulty in keeping the bucket and its
valves tight and of detecting any leakage, and this led to the adoption of
the *Plunger Pump* (Fig. 270).   Here the bucket is replaced by a plunger of

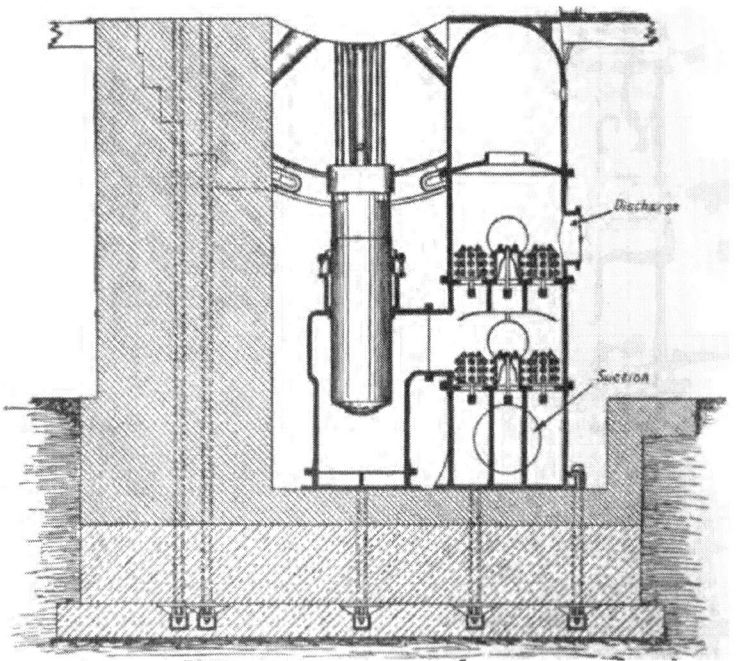

FIG. 271.—Steam Driven Single-acting Plunger Pump.

uniform section, all the packing being supplied from the outside and
being easily replaced and examined.   In this type of pump, which may be
either vertical or horizontal, work is done on both strokes, suction taking
place on the out-stroke of the plunger, and delivery by plunger displacement on the in-stroke.   The latter in general necessitates the greater

work, and as will be noted the ram or plunger is in compression during this stroke.

If L = length of stroke we have :—

Work done on suction stroke = $A \{\pi_a - (\pi_a - h_s)\}\ W\ L$ foot lbs.

$\qquad\qquad\qquad = W\ h_s\ A\ L$ foot lbs.

Work done on delivery stroke = $W\ h_d\ A\ L$ foot lbs.

A separate valve box may now contain both suction and delivery valves, and these become more accessible for examination and repairs.

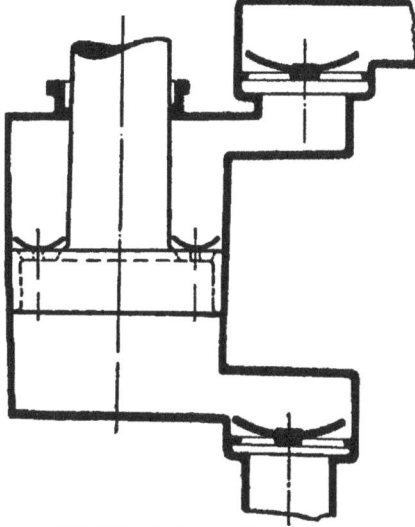

FIG. 272.—Bucket and Plunger Pump.

Fig. 271 shows a section of such a pump having a plunger diameter of 32 inches, and a stroke of 5 feet. The valves for this pump are situated on the sides and top of small hexagonal prisms instead of being arranged on a single plane surface. The pump is directly driven by a steam engine and makes 40 strokes per minute against 153 feet head.

So far, each type considered has suffered from the disadvantage that it only delivers water on alternate strokes. This difficulty is, however, overcome in the "Bucket and Plunger" pump (Fig. 272). Here the piston rod of the ordinary bucket pump is enlarged to form a plunger of about half the area of the bucket which it carries.

Suction now takes place on the up stroke, and, if a and A are the areas of plunger and bucket, a volume of water = $A\ L$ is drawn into the pump, while a volume $(A - a)\ L$ is displaced through the delivery valves. On the down stroke the plunger displaces a volume $A\ L$, and in consequence this volume passes to the upper side of the bucket. Of this the volume $(A - a)\ L$ remains in the annular space between the barrel and the plunger, while the remaining volume $a\ L$ is displaced through the delivery valves.

Thus for equal deliveries on the two strokes :—

$$(A - a)\ L = a\ L$$
$$\therefore A = 2\ a.$$

But if h_s and h_d are the mean suction and delivery heads, we have:—

Work on up stroke $= W \{ (A - a) h_d + A h_s \} L$ foot lbs.

Work on down stroke $= W \{a h_d\} L$ foot lbs.

∴ For equality :—

$$(A - a) h_d + A h = a h_d$$
$$\therefore A (h_d + h_s) = 2 a h_d$$
$$\therefore \frac{a}{A} = \frac{h_d + h_s}{2 h_d},$$

which approximates to $\frac{1}{2}$ as h_d becomes large compared with h_s.

Where the pump is vertical, and the weight of plunger line great, this requires modification if the forces acting at the upper end of the plunger are

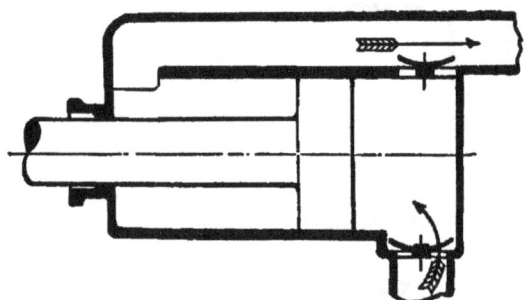

FIG. 273.—Piston and Plunger Pump.

to be equal on both strokes. In this case, if $W_P =$ weight of plunger line :—

Force to be exerted on up stroke $\Big\} = W \{ (A - a) h_d + A h_s \} + W_P$ lbs.

Force to be exerted on down stroke $\Big\} = W \{ a h_d \} - W_P$ lbs.

$$\therefore \text{ For equality, } 2 W_P = W \{ (2 a - A) h_d - A h_s \}$$
$$= W \{ 2 a h_d - A (h_d + h_s) \}$$
$$\therefore a = \frac{W_P}{W h_d} + \frac{A (h_d + h_s)}{2 h_d}.$$

The bucket valves may be eliminated while retaining the advantage of uniform delivery or uniform work on both strokes, by the type of construction indicated in Fig. 273 and known as the *Piston and Plunger* pump. Here a solid piston is used instead of the hollow bucket. Suction takes place on the out-stroke, while at the same time a volume $(A - a)$ L is delivered. On the in-stroke, a volume $L A$ is discharged through the delivery valve, but of this a volume $= (A - a) L$ finds its way to the other side of the piston, and the volume actually delivered $= a L$. As before, for equality of delivery on the two strokes, $\dfrac{A}{a} = 2$. In addition to an equal delivery on each stroke, the further advantage of an equal suction on each stroke may be obtained by duplicating the suction and delivery valves at each end of the barrel as indicated in Fig. 274, each end becoming in effect a separate displacement pump.

This, the *Double Acting* type, may be fitted either as a piston pump, having a packed piston and sleeve, or with a turned plunger working in an unpacked ring, both types being shown in Fig. 274.

For fairly low pressures, up to about 75 lbs. per square inch, either type is good, the piston pump giving a slightly larger displacement for the same floor space. Where clean water is to be pumped, the unpacked plunger type, however, is advantageous on the ground of its reduced friction.

A short fitting ring is used, easily renewable, and the ease of refitting such a

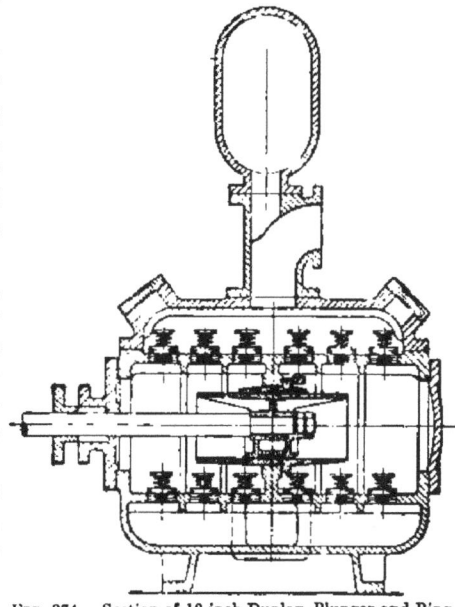

FIG. 274.—Section of 12-inch Duplex Plunger and Ring, or Piston Pump : 10-inch suction ; 8-inch delivery ; 12-inch stroke. For pressures up to 100 lbs. per square inch.

ring compared with that of re-boring a piston barrel renders its use advisable, where the condition of the liquid to be pumped permits. In either case the work done on the two strokes is practically the same.

For very high pressures, or where the water contains gritty matter in suspension, the piston, bucket, or internally packed plunger pump is unsatisfactory, and the type known as the *Double-Acting Outside Packed Plunger* pump becomes more suitable.

Here again the pump discharges a volume $A L$ from one end of the barrel and admits an equal volume (neglecting the volume of the plunger rod if this is used) at the other end of each stroke. Fig. 275 shows a direct steam-driven pump of this type having centre-packed plungers,[1]

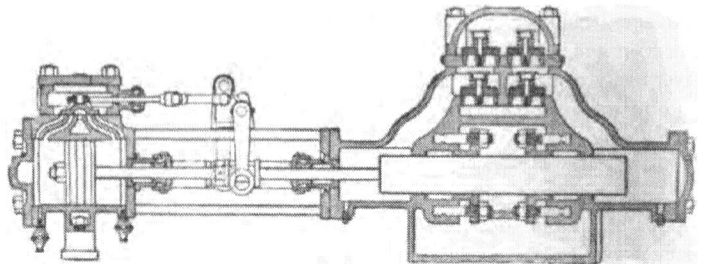

FIG. 275.—Central-Packed Double-Acting Plunger Pump.

and designed for 80 strokes per minute, with 10-inch plunger; 12-inch stroke; 18-inch steam cylinder; 10-inch suction and 7-inch discharge pipes.

Fig. 276 shows an outside end-packed plunger pump of this type, suitable for moderately high pressures, the two plungers carrying crossheads which are connected by side rods, while Fig. 277 shows a similar

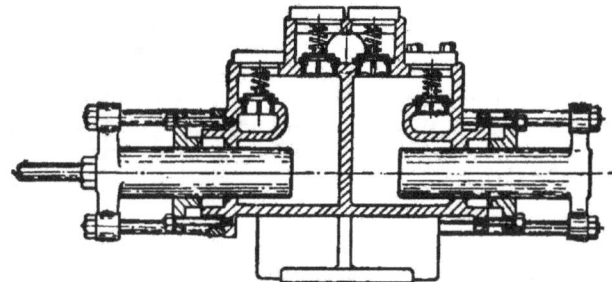

FIG. 276.—Double-Acting Duplex Outside End-Packed Plunger Pump : 6-inch plunger; 12-inch steam cylinder; 12-inch stroke; 5-inch suction; 4-inch delivery; 80 strokes per minute; up to 300 lbs. per square inch.

pump as constructed for the highest pressures. This latter pump has a separate valve box for each end of the cylinder, the construction of the valves (which are 1 inch in diameter) and of the valve box, being shown in Fig. 278.[2]

[1] By courtesy of the Buffalo Steam Pump Company.
[2] Figs. 277 and 278 are inserted by courtesy of the makers Messrs. Henry Berry & Co., Leeds.

FIG. 277.—Outside End-packed Plunger Pump for pressures up to 1,120 lbs. per square inch.

This type of pump has the advantage that only two glands need packing as against three in the centre-packed type, although the latter type lends itself to a more compact construction.

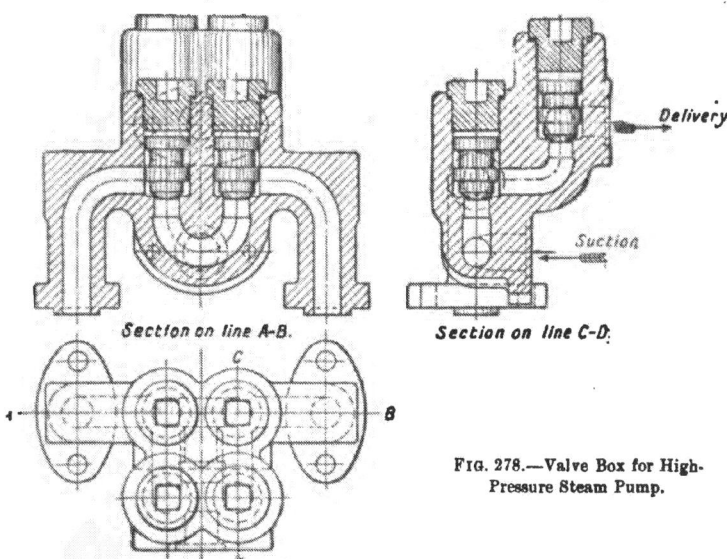

Section on line A-B.

Section on line C-D.

FIG. 278.—Valve Box for High-Pressure Steam Pump.

Deep Well Pumps.—Where pumping operations are necessary in a deep well or bore hole of small diameter, the ordinary lift pump with separate

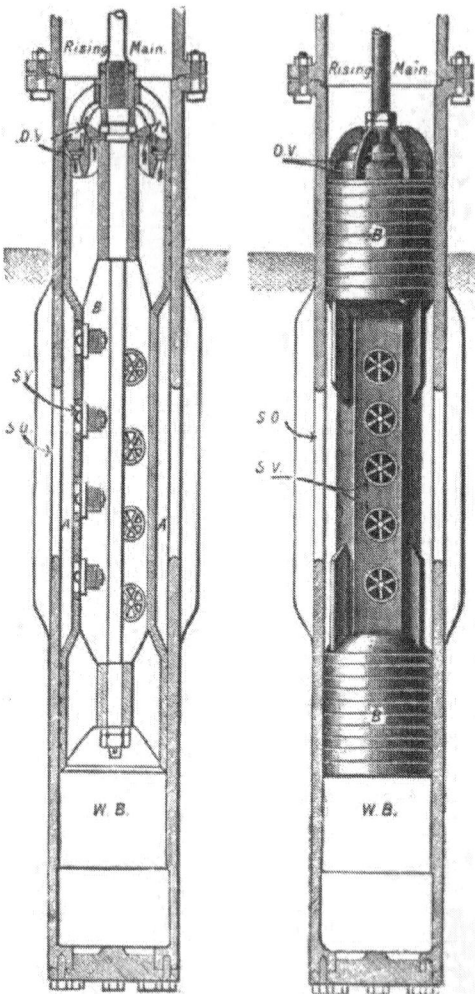

foot valve is at a disadvantage because of the great difficulty which is experienced in raising and replacing this foot valve should it become choked or in any way out of order. To obviate this difficulty the "Ashley" pump, Fig. 279, carries both suction and delivery valves in its bucket, this being readily withdrawn for examination through the rising main.

The bucket B, which is open at its lower end, reciprocates in the working barrel $W.B.$, which is closed at the bottom. The sides of this barrel are pierced by orifices $S.O.$ through which the surrounding fluid is admitted to the under side of the suction valves $S.V.$ On the upward stroke of the pump a partial vacuum is formed inside the bucket, and water is drawn through these valves to fill the space inside and below

FIG. 279.—Single-Acting "Ashley" Bore-Hole Pump.

the bucket, while the water above the bucket is forced up the rising main. On the downward stroke the delivery valves $D.V.$ open, and the water in the body of the bucket is transferred to its upper side to be pumped to the surface on the succeeding stroke. A double-acting pump of this type is also on the market.

ART. 160.—PUMP VALVES.

The valve area should be so designed as to allow of a mean velocity not exceeding 4 feet per second. For low pressures these valves usually consist of rubber or composition discs (Figs. 274, 275, 280 a and b),

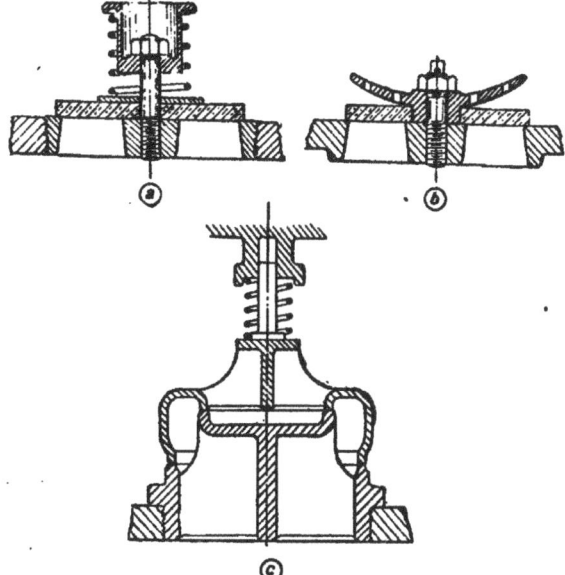

FIG. 280.—Types of Pump Valve.

working against a perforated grid, and are either spring loaded or automatically return to their seats in virtue of their own elasticity, together with the pressure of water above them. For moderate speeds and pressures these are very satisfactory.

At high pressures, however, the discs quickly become indented, and some form of metallic valve becomes essential. Fig. 280 c shows a double-beat valve of this type. These valves may be spring loaded, or may return to their seats by their own weight, and so long as the speed is moderate are satisfactory.

The ordinary disc or double-beat valve suffers from the drawback that the kinetic energy of the discharging streams is of necessity dissipated in the shock accompanying the sudden change in the direction of flow. The Haste and the Gutermuth valves are interesting examples of designs intended to obviate this source of loss. The action of the former is obvious from the sketch Fig. 281.

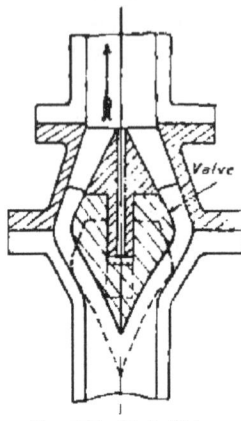

FIG. 281.—Haste Valve.

The Gutermuth valve (Fig. 282) is formed from a single sheet of special bronze, either of the same thickness throughout or, in large valves, having the end forming the valve thickened. The sheets are slightly wider at the coiled end to prevent fouling, and are slipped on to a grooved spindle and clamped to the valve seat cones at the required tension.

The valve is always placed at an angle with the port opening, and the latter thus becomes uncovered with a very small movement of the valve itself, while no such abrupt changes in the direction of the escaping stream are necessitated as in the case of disc or mushroom valves.

The automatic or self-closing valve, while simple and satisfactory for low velocities, possesses several disadvantages which tend to reduce its suitability for high speed work.

In the first place, with automatic suction valves, the difference of

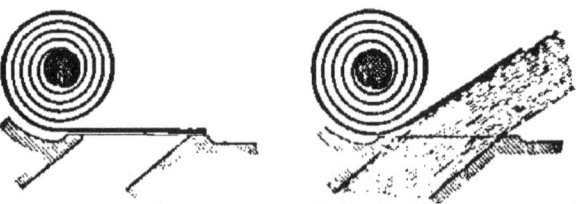

FIG. 282.—The Gutermuth Valve.

pressure below and above must be sufficient to lift the valve, and with a heavy valve this appreciably diminishes the possible suction lift. A light valve, by coming slowly to its seat at the end of the stroke, enables water to leak back into the suction pipe, since, although theoretically the valve is on its seat when the piston is at rest, actually this is not by any means the case except at slow speeds. The same thing applies on the delivery side. Also considerable shock takes place when these valves close, this shock being due, not only to the valve itself dropping suddenly to its seat, but also to the fact that a large mass of water partakes of the return motion.

The violence of the shock depends on the kinetic energy possessed by the valve and accompanying water at the instant of closing, and will therefore increase with the weight of the valve, with the mass of the accompanying water, and with the maximum distance of the valve from its seat, since the latter factor will determine the velocity of closing.

The mass of water accompanying the valve is found to be proportional to the mass included between the valve and the water level in the corresponding air vessel, so that to minimise this effect, the difference in level between valve and air vessel should be reduced as far as possible, while the lift of the valve should be as small as is consistent with ample inlet and outlet areas.

With self-closing valves, the lift may be reduced either—

(1) by increasing the weight of the valve ;
(2) by increasing the spring loading of a light valve ;
(3) by limiting the lift by stops ;
(4) by increasing the number or diameter of the valves.

The first method, while reducing the lift and giving a quicker closing effect, increases the hydraulic resistance; while the increased weight of the valve is in itself productive of shock. On the other hand, a light valve is more subject to vibration while opening or closing, and this may cause large oscillations of pressure in the pipe line. This tendency to vibration increases with the speed of the pump, and diminishes with an increase in the delivery pressure. On the whole, however, the balance of advantage lies with the fairly light spring-loaded valve.

The method of limiting the lift by stops is decidedly unsatisfactory, as giving rise to oscillations of the valve, and hence of the pressure in the pipe line.

The best method is to increase the effective valve area by an increase in the number or diameter of the valves. In the ordinary disc valve (Fig. 280 a and b),

$$\text{If } r = \text{radius and } l = \text{lift of valve,}$$

the area of valve seat $= \pi r^2$ (neglecting the effect of guides, etc.).

But the effective valve area is the area of the cylindrical surface generated by the perimeter of the valve during its lift $= 2 \pi r l$.

The most effective lift is thus obtained when these values are identical, i.e., when—

H.A.   Q Q

$$2 \pi r l = \pi r^2$$
$$\therefore l = \frac{r}{2}.$$

It follows that, in order to take advantage of the available valve seat area, it is impracticable to use very large valves, since for a given lift the effective discharge area varies as the diameter of the valves, while the valve weight varies more nearly as $d^{\frac{5}{2}}$. Also if the lift were made equal to $\frac{r}{2}$, this would soon become excessive. Because of this, small valves should be used, with a lift giving a discharge area approaching that of the valve seat, and for high speed pumps modern practice is opposed to the use of disc valves of more than about 3 inches diameter. Where double beat valves are used this may be increased, but in no case should the valve have a lift exceeding $\frac{3}{4}$ inch.

Valve Leakage and Slip.—A further point to be noted is that slip, or leakage past the valves while closing, is proportional to the mean effective opening of the valve; to $\sqrt{h}$, where h is the head on the valve; and to the time of closing, t. Generally we may take t as proportional to $\sqrt{l}$.

If, then, a number of small valves replace a single large valve of the same effective discharge area, the slip will be reduced, since to get the maximum discharge effect the lifts of the valves must in every case be proportional to their diameters, and this lift, and therefore the time of closing, will be greater with the larger single valve.

Thus, whereas the slip past n valves of diameter d is proportional to $n\, h^{\frac{1}{2}} d^{\frac{5}{2}}$, that past a single valve of the same effective discharge area, and, therefore, of diameter D where $D = d \sqrt{n}$, is proportional to $h^{\frac{1}{2}} d^{\frac{5}{2}} n^{\frac{5}{4}}$, so that by increasing the number of valves to n, the leakage is reduced in the ratio $\dfrac{n}{n^{\frac{5}{4}}} = \dfrac{1}{n^{\frac{1}{4}}}$.

E.g., where $n = 4$, the leakage is equal to $\dfrac{1}{4^{\frac{1}{4}}} = \cdot 707$ times that found with a single large valve.

ART. 161.—HIGH SPEED RECIPROCATING PUMPS.

Owing to the length of time necessary for an automatic disc valve to close, and to the irregularities in its action produced by inertia effects of the water in the supply and delivery pipes, a high rotative speed is impossible with a reciprocating pump fitted with this type of valve, and it becomes necessary to use a long stroke, slow rotation pump, giving ample time for the valves to come to rest at the end of each stroke. With

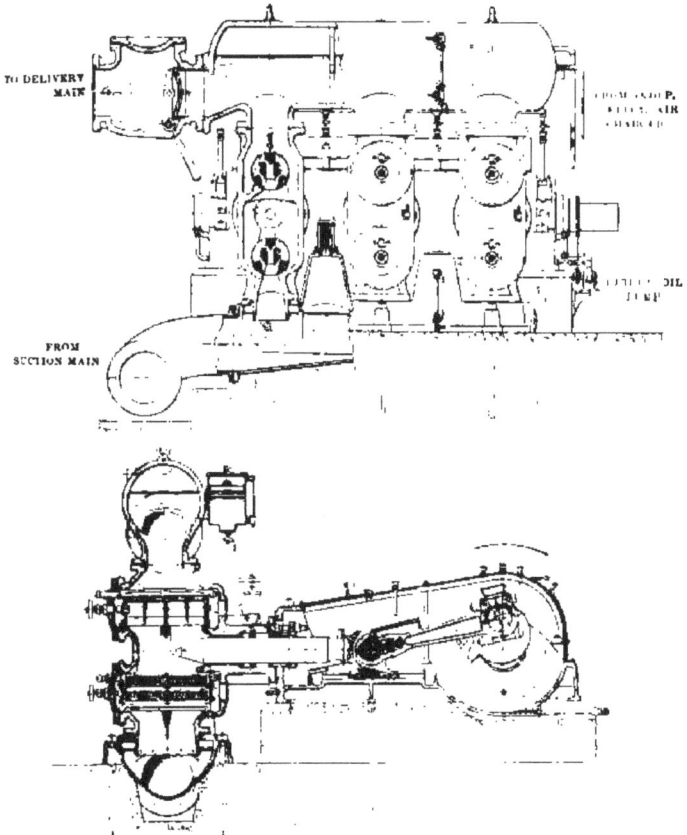

FIG. 283.—Gutermuth 3-Throw Pump ; 6¾-inch diameter ; × 16-inch stroke ;
× 180 revs. per min. ; 1,000 gallons per min. ; 750 ft. head.

this type of pump, and until comparatively recently, the maximum attainable piston speed was about 100 feet per minute at about sixty revolutions per minute.

By paying special attention to the design of valves and water passages

Q Q 2

it has, however, become possible to adopt much higher speeds, even with automatic valves.

One modern type of high-speed pump which has proved itself capable of excellent results is the Gutermuth (Fig. 283).[1] The illustrations show a sectional plan and elevation of one of a pair of three-throw pumps of this type, having plungers 6¾ inches diameter by 16 inches stroke and delivering 1,000 gallons per minute against 750 feet head at 180 revolutions per minute. Each pump is driven from a 275 H.P. three-phase motor through a flexible coupling. The design is very compact, the pump bodies being mounted on a suction air vessel of cylindrical form, which also acts as a bedplate. On this air vessel is cast a branch flange for connecting up to the suction main. On top of one of the pump bodies is bolted a delivery air vessel, having flanged branches to connect to the pump bodies, and with the end flanged to connect to the retaining valve on the delivery main.

The connecting rods are of cast steel with marine type babbited ends or the crank pin, and gun-metal wedge adjustment boxes for the cross-head end. The plungers are of gun-metal, and are supported in gun-metal bushed glands and neck rings.

Forced lubrication is fitted throughout, while the two delivery air vessels are supplied by an independent electrically-driven two-stage air charger of the Reavel type, the compressor being capable of compressing 5 cubic feet of free air per minute to a pressure of 350 lbs. per square inch.

The valves, which are of the Gutermuth type and are perhaps the most interesting part of these pumps, are contained in cylindrical bronze valve seats, each pump having one set for suction and one for delivery. These are held in place and tightened by means of wedges which are readily accessible when the valve covers are removed.

The sectional end view of Fig. 283 shows very clearly the straight and unobstructed passages offered to the water in this type of pump.

Frictional losses are thus low; the lightness of the valve and its small opening tend to reduce shock on closing; and the possible speed of rotation is correspondingly increased.

The high speed at which these pumps can be run, as a direct result of the valve action, permits of a design which takes up considerably less floor space than the ordinary slow running pump, the actual overall length being, in this case, 11 feet 8 inches × 8 feet 6 inches. It also allows the pump to be direct connected to the motor, which, though adding somewhat to the expense of the latter, does away with transmission gears which are

[1] By courtesy of the manufacturers, Messrs. Fraser & Chalmers, Ltd.

usually noisy and troublesome, and which, under the most favourable circumstances, in a pump of this size, would reduce the efficiency by from 3 per cent. to 4 per cent.

For very high speeds, however, the automatic valve, even though well designed, becomes unsatisfactory, and mechanically operated valves are necessary.

By their substitution uncertainty as to the exact time of closing is avoided, more uniform closing is effected with less accompanying shock, and by this means, and by careful design of the valves, the speed has been increased until piston velocities of 600 feet per minute at 300 revolutions per minute are now easily obtained with almost entire absence of shock

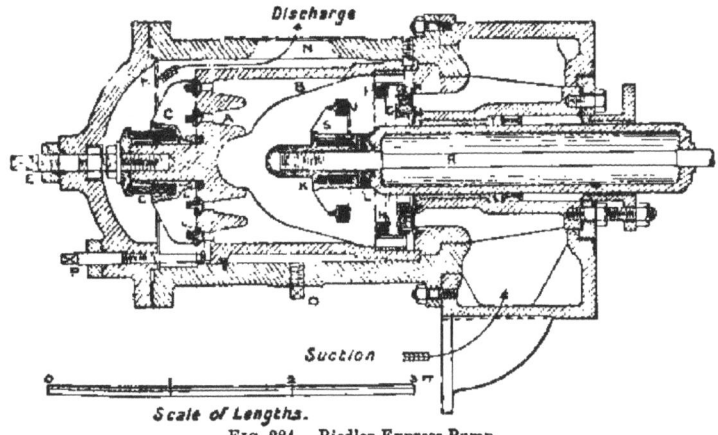

Fig. 284.—Riedler Express Pump

This increase in speed permits of the pump dimensions being reduced for the same duty; gives a smaller delivery per stroke, and hence reduces the liability to shock; while the possibility of a more uniform flow in both supply and discharge pipes tends to the same end.

Fig. 284 shows the construction of the pump barrels, rams and valves of a type of high-speed pump designed by Professor Riedler, this particular pump being designed to deliver 375 gallons per minute against a head of 500 feet. It is a two-throw pump having rams $6\frac{3}{4}$ inches diameter by 9 inches stroke; running at 200 revolutions per minute and driven by an electric motor of 75 B.H.P. running at 500 revolutions per minute.

The outer end A of the working cylinder B forms the seating of the delivery valve, which consists of two annular brass rings, C_1 and C_2, let into a gun-metal frame C. This valve is kept up to its seat by means of the cylindrical indiarubber spring D, the compression of which may be adjusted by means of the bolt E, while leather sealing rings are also provided to ensure its efficient action.

The inner end of the working cylinder carries a gun-metal guide ring F, in which works the annular suction valve G. This valve is constructed with a wooden face let into a channel section annular brass ring, and its range of opening is limited by the rubber ring H, let into the guide ring F.

The ram R passes through the suction valve, and at its inner end carries a buffer stop S, which mechanically closes the suction valve at the end of the outer or suction stroke. Shock at impact is minimised by the provision of cylindrical rubber springs at J and K. A series of removable brass liners L between the ram and the buffer permit of the latter being adjusted so as to take up any wear in the buffer itself or in the suction valve.

The delivery valve is thus automatically regulated, while the suction valve is mechanically operated only so far as affects its closing at the end of the suction stroke, this valve being both opened and closed on the outstroke of the ram. On the in-stroke, water is delivered against the resistance of the delivery valve into the annular chamber M, from which it flows away through the pipe N into an air vessel and away to the discharge. The chamber M is fitted with a starting valve at O, 2 inches in diameter, so that in starting the pump the pressure may be relieved and the pump started light. The small spindle valve P allows of water passing from the chamber M into the working barrel, so that if for any cause sufficient water cannot enter through the suction valves, more water may be allowed to enter through the valve P, so as to enable the pump to run without shock.

A small compound air pump, having a high pressure plunger $1\frac{1}{2}$ inches diameter by 1·8 inches stroke and a low-pressure plunger 3 inches diameter by 2·7 inches stroke is provided, and is worked directly from the crank shaft of the main pump, exhausting air from the suction air vessel and discharging it into the delivery air vessel.

Should the air supply in the suction air vessel be insufficient, more may be admitted through a small valve; while should the air pump deliver too great a supply, the surplus air can be let out of the delivery air vessel.

Tests carried out on such a pump as described,[1] showed a combined

[1] By Mr. John Morris. See a paper on the " Unwatering of the Achddu Colliery." Trans. Inst. of Mining Engineers, Vol. 30, part 2, p. 131.

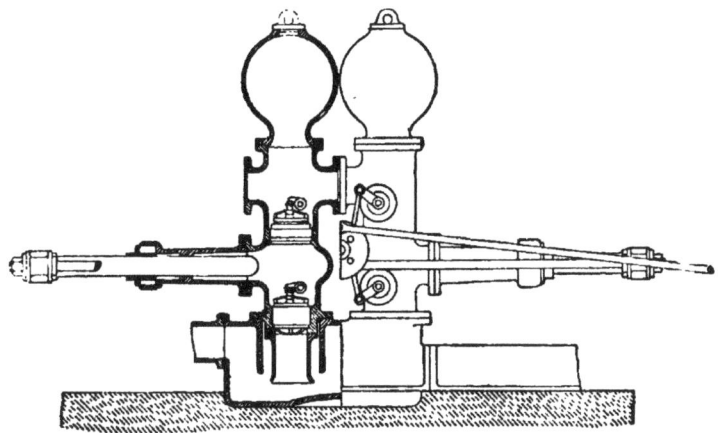

FIG. 285.—Riedler Express Pump.

efficiency of pump and motor of about 85 per cent., with a discharge coefficient of ·92.

For still higher speeds, the pump is designed with suction and delivery

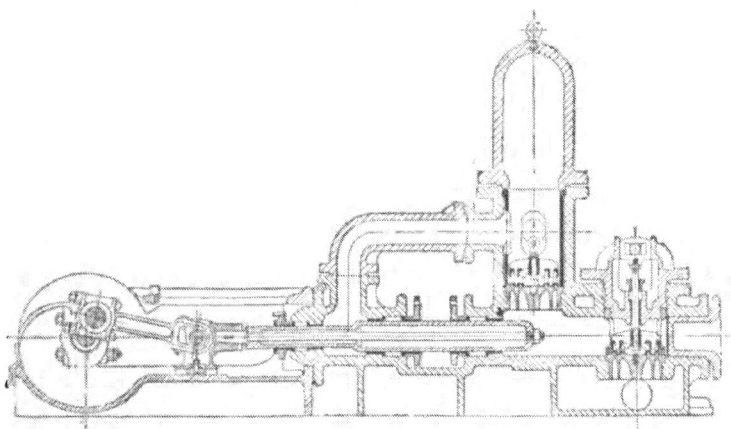

FIG. 286.—Oddie-Barclay High Speed Ram Pump.

valves mechanically operated from a wrist-plate driven by an eccentric on the main shaft, as shown in Fig. 285.

Fig. 286 shows a section through an Oddie-Barclay high speed ram pump, having mechanical control to both valves. Tests of such a pump, having a differential ram 5 inches and $7\frac{1}{16}$ inches diameter by 9 inches stroke, when running at 150 revolutions per minute showed a mechanical efficiency ranging from 82 to 86 per cènt. as the head increased from 620 to 1,050 feet, with a discharge coefficient of ·96.

ART. 161A.—HYDRAULIC RECIPROCATING PUMPS.

Where a high pressure water supply is available, the hydraulically operated reciprocating pump has been extensively adopted for pumping water for domestic or other purposes and for pumping sewage. Such a pump is illustrated in Fig. 287.[2] This is driven by two double-acting hydraulic cylinders placed one on each side of the pump body casting to which they are attached, the two plungers PP and the pump rod R being connected to the same crosshead. The pump is operated by means of a piston valve in the valve chest V, this valve being worked from the crosshead by means of the tappet rod T and lever L shown.

ART. 162.—DISPLACEMENT CURVES.

Discharge Coefficient.—In the theoretically perfect pump the action would be simple. On the suction stroke the delivery valves would be tightly closed while the suction valves would open, admitting sufficient water to entirely fill the barrel. At the commencement of the delivery stroke these valves would immediately close, while the delivery valves would open, and a volume of water equal to the plunger displacement would be discharged. In practice, however, owing to the fact that the valves do not instantaneously close, and because of leakage past the plunger, etc., the volume delivered is not in general equal to the plunger displacement. The ratio $\dfrac{\text{actual}}{\text{theoretical}}$ discharge, termed the **discharge coefficient,** varies with the type, speed, and condition of the pump, but with moderate speed pumps in good condition and of good design lies between ·94 and ·99. With high-speed pumps the modifying effects of the inertia of the suction column may be such as to give a discharge greater in volume than the piston displacement, the excess amounting in exceptional cases to as much as 50 per cent. This effect will be considered in further detail at a later stage.

If a curve, having piston velocities as ordinates be plotted on a time

[1] *Mechanical Engineer.* June 26, 1908, p. 811.
[2] By courtesy of the Hydraulic Engineering Co., Ltd., Chester.

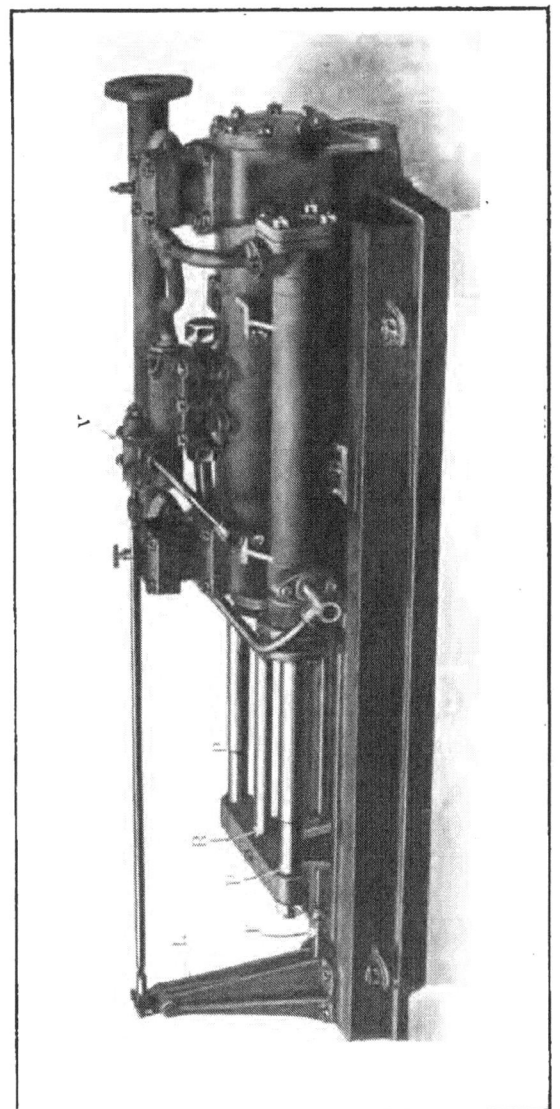

Fig. 287.—Hydraulically operated Reciprocating Pump.

base, the area included between the curve, the base line, and any two ordinates, will measure to some scale the volume displaced by the piston in the corresponding interval of time. The curve so obtained is termed a displacement curve. Thus, if $O\,Q$ and $Q\,P$ represent the crank and

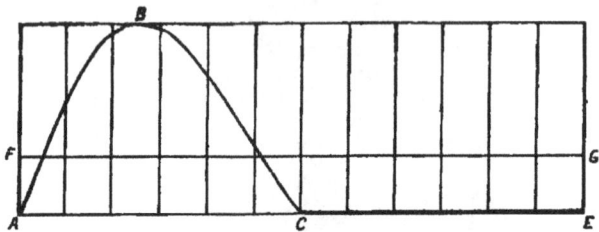

Fig. 288A.—Displacement Curve for Single-Cylinder Single-acting Pump.

connecting rod of a pump for a given piston position, and if $P\,Q$ be produced to meet the perpendicular $O\,C$ to the line of centres in C, then $O\,C$ represents the corresponding piston velocity to the scale on which $O\,Q$ represents $\omega\,r$ the velocity of the crank pin. If a series of such points as Q are taken at equidistant intervals on the crank circle, and the corresponding values of $O\,C$ found, the displacement curve may then be plotted as in Figs. 288A–D. Here Fig. 288A represents the curve for a

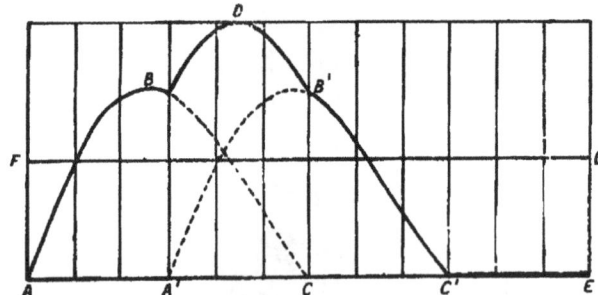

Fig. 288C.—Curve for Pair of Single-acting Cylinders with Cranks at Right Angles.

single-barrel single-acting pump having a connecting rod four cranks in length, $A\,C$ representing the time to perform half, and $A\,E$ to complete a revolution.

The area $A\,B\,C$ now represents the displacement of the pump per revolution, while $C\,E$ represents the idle stroke.

If $F\ G$ be drawn parallel to $A\ E$, so that $A\ F$ represents the mean velocity of the piston, the area $A\ F\ G\ E =$ area $A\ B\ C$.

Similarly, Fig. 288B represents the displacement curve $A\ B\ D\ B'\ C'\ E$, for a pair of single-acting pumps having cranks at right angles and

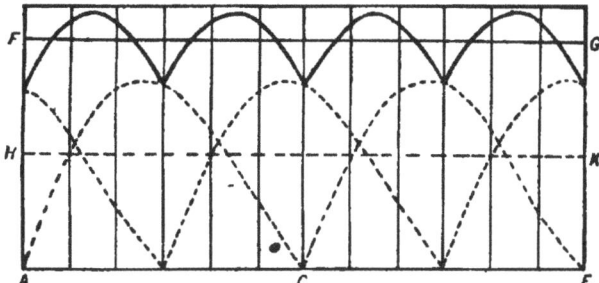

FIG. 288c.—Curve for Pair of Double-Acting Pumps with Cranks at Right Angles.

drawing from and delivering into a common main. Here $A\ B\ C$ and $A'\ B'\ C'$ are the respective curves for each piston, and these are compounded by adding ordinates so as to give the displacement curve. The area $A\ F\ G\ E$ is now equal to the sum of the areas $A\ B\ C$ and $A'\ B'\ C'$, or to the whole area $A\ B\ D\ B'\ C'$.

Again, Fig. 288c, obtained in a similar manner, shows the curve for a pair of double-acting pumps having cranks at right angles, $F\ G$ again

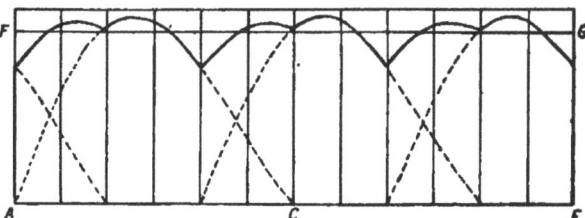

FIG. 288D.—Displacement Curve for Three-Throw Single-Acting Pump with Cranks at 120°.

representing the mean velocity line. Here $H\ K$ represents what would be the mean velocity line for a single double-acting pump.

Similarly, Fig. 288D represents the curve for a three-throw pump having cranks at intervals of 120°.

It will be noted that as the frequency with which the pumps discharge per revolution increases, the range of velocities in the discharge and suction pipes decreases, and also the rate of change of this velocity, i.e., the acceleration, and the smoothness of working in consequence increases.

The following table indicates how this velocity changes :—

Type of Pump.	Ratio of Maximum to Mean Velocity in Discharge Pipes.
Single cylinder, single-acting	3·24
Two single-acting cylinders, cranks at right angles .	2·17
Single cylinder, double-acting	1·62
Two double-acting cylinders, cranks at right angles .	1·11
Three-throw pump, crank at 120° { single-acting .	1·09
double-acting .	1·05

As will be readily understood, the varying velocity and acceleration in the supply and discharge pipes—particularly in the supply pipes—produce a tendency to water hammer.

So long as this hammer is prevented, either by suitably enlarging the pipes ; by reducing the maximum piston velocity or acceleration ; or by the provision of air vessels on suction and delivery pipes, the action of a pump may be predicted very accurately from theoretical considerations. Once water hammer is set up so many factors combine to influence the result, and the subject presents such difficulties of treatment that, except in simple cases, no satisfactory attempt can be made to deal with the matter analytically.   This is, however, less important, in that water hammer is not, under any conditions, admissible in a pump, and while its effect may be impossible to predict with any degree of accuracy, save in the most simple cases, the steps necessary to prevent its occurrence are well understood.

The following demonstration may be relied upon as giving results which are substantially correct so long as the pump is working without shock.

ART. 168.—VARIATIONS OF PRESSURE IN THE CYLINDER OF A SINGLE CYLINDER PUMP WITHOUT AIR VESSELS.

For the water in the suction pipe to follow and maintain contact with the piston throughout the suction stroke, this column of water must

receive an acceleration at the commencement of the stroke, the magnitude
of the acceleration being given by—

$$a \, \frac{A}{a_s} \text{ f.s.s.}$$

where a = piston acceleration in f.s.s.
               A = piston area in square feet.
               a_s = area of suction pipe in square feet.

The force necessary to give this acceleration can only be produced by a
difference in pressure at the two ends of the suction pipe, and varies as
the mass of water in the pipe and as its acceleration. Expressed symbolically we have—

Force necessary to produce acceleration $= \dfrac{W}{g} \, l_s \, a_s \, . \, \dfrac{A}{a_s} \, a$ lbs.

If the pressure difference at the two ends of the pipe corresponding to
this force is p' lbs. per square foot—

$$p' \, a_s = \frac{W}{g} \, l_s \, A \, a \text{ lbs.}$$

$$\therefore \quad p' = \frac{W}{g} \, l_s \, \frac{A}{a_s} \, a \text{ lbs. per square foot.}$$

If at the same instant the piston velocity is v f.s., for continuity of
flow we have $v_s = v \dfrac{A}{a_s}$; and the loss of pressure due to friction in the
supply pipe corresponding to this is given by :—

$$p'' = \frac{W f l_s \, v_s^2}{2 \, g \, m} = \frac{W f l_s \, A^2}{2 \, g \, m \, a_s^2} \, v^2 \text{ lbs. per square foot.}$$

$\therefore$ Total difference of pressure at the inlet and outlet of the suction
pipe is given by :—

$$p' + p'' = p = \frac{W}{g} \, \frac{A}{a_s} \, l_s \left\{ a + \frac{f A}{2 \, m \, a_s} \, v^2 \right\} \text{ lbs. per square foot.}$$

Or, expressed as a head " h " in feet of water,

$$h = \frac{A \, l_s}{g \, a_s} \left\{ a + \frac{f A}{2 \, m \, a_s} \, . \, v^2 \right\} \text{ feet,}$$

where a is positive or negative according as the piston is being accelerated
or retarded.

Now the head actually available to produce this flow is strictly limited,
the higher pressure—at the pipe inlet—being that corresponding to its
depth of immersion together with that of the atmosphere, while the lower
limit of pressure is theoretically that corresponding to an absolute
vacuum, although in practice it is impossible to obtain this degree

of exhaustion in the pump. If the level of the pump is above that of the suction reservoir so as to give a suction lift of h_s feet (Fig. 289), the available head is correspondingly reduced, and has a maximum theoretical value of $(\pi_a - h_s)$ feet, where π_a is the height of the water barometer.

Thus, for continuity of contact between piston and water on the suction stroke, we must have :—

$$\pi_a - h_s > \frac{A\,l_s}{g\,a_s}\left\{ a + \frac{f A}{2\,m\,a_s}\,r^2 \right\}\ \text{feet}. \tag{1}$$

Should this condition not be satisfied the piston leaves the water at some point—usually at the beginning of the stroke, since here a has its

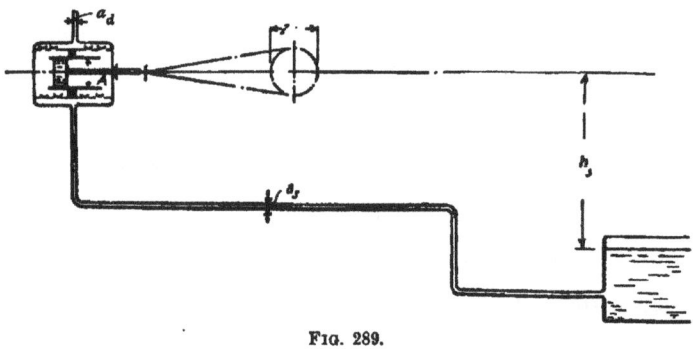

Fig. 289.

maximum value—the action being termed **Separation** or **Cavitation**. So long as this state of affairs exists, the pressure behind the piston is uniform, being that of water vapour at suction temperature, and in consequence the water flows along the pipe with an acceleration which is uniform, except for the increasing effect of friction as its velocity increases. The piston acceleration is, however, continuously diminishing, so that the water overtakes the latter at some point before the completion of the stroke, the meeting being usually accompanied by considerable shock, while pressures considerably in excess of those corresponding to the statical head are produced.

Separation may also occur between the delivery column and the piston during the second half of the delivery stroke, when the piston is being retarded. Thus if $-a$ is the magnitude of this retardation, the head necessary to produce the retardation in the delivery column is given by

$- \dfrac{A}{a_d} \dfrac{l_d}{g} a$ feet, so that to prevent separation during this stroke we must have:—

$$\pi_a + h_d > \frac{A}{a_d} \frac{l_d}{g} \left\{ -a - \frac{f A}{2 \, m \, a_d} r^2 \right\} \tag{2}$$

Note.—Since during the latter half of the stroke the piston is being retarded $(-a)$ is a positive quantity.

Where the pump is driven from a shaft rotating with uniform angular velocity ω radians per second, by means of a crank of radius r, assuming the connecting rod to be of infinite length:—

$$\begin{cases} a = \omega^2 \, r \cos \theta \quad \text{f.s.s.} \\ v = \omega \; r \sin \theta \quad \text{f.s.} \end{cases}$$

where θ is the crank angle, measured from the inner dead centre, while with a connecting rod of length l these expressions become :—

$$\begin{cases} a = \omega^2 \, r \left\{ \cos \theta + \dfrac{r \, l^2 \cos 2 \, \theta + r^3 \sin^4 \theta}{(l^2 - r^2 \sin^2 \theta)^{\frac{3}{2}}} \right\} \text{ f.s.s.} \\ v = \omega \, r \left\{ \sin \theta + \dfrac{r \sin 2 \, \theta}{2 \sqrt{l^2 - r^2 \sin^2 \theta}} \right\} \text{ f.s.} \end{cases}$$

giving a the maximum value $\omega^2 \, r \left\{ 1 \pm \dfrac{r}{l} \right\}$ according as the crank is on the inner or outer dead centres respectively (*i.e.*, according as $\theta = 0°$ or $180°$).

Neglecting, for simplicity, the effect of the obliquity of the connecting rod, and therefore assuming the piston to have simple harmonic motion, the maximum velocity is given by $\omega \, r$, while the maximum acceleration $= \omega^2 \, r$, and therefore for a given displacement the acceleration is comparatively reduced by making the stroke of the pump large and the angular velocity of the crank, or the number of strokes per minute, low. This enables a higher piston speed to be adopted, since frictional effects are usually small compared with those due to acceleration.

Substituting for a and r in terms of the crank angle θ, equation (1) becomes :—

$$\pi_a - h_s > \frac{A}{a_s} \frac{l_s}{g} \left\{ \omega^2 \, r \cos \theta + \frac{f \, \omega^2 \, r^2 \sin^2 \theta \, A}{2 \, m \, a_s} \right\}$$

$$> \omega^2 \, r \frac{A}{a_s} \frac{l_s}{g} \left\{ \cos \theta + \frac{f \, r \sin^2 \theta \, A}{2 \, m \, a_s} \right\}$$

giving $\qquad \omega = \sqrt{\dfrac{\dfrac{g \, a_s}{r \, A \, l_s} \{ \pi_a - h_s \}}{\cos \theta + \dfrac{f \, r \sin^2 \theta \, A}{2 \, m \, a_s}}} \tag{8}$

as the critical velocity, above which separation will occur on the suction stroke.

Similarly, substituting in equation (2) we obtain :—

$$\omega = \sqrt{\dfrac{\dfrac{g\,a_d}{r\,A\,l_d}\{\pi_a + h_d\}}{-\cos\theta - \dfrac{f\,r\,\sin^2\theta\;A}{2\,m\,a_d}}} \qquad (4$$

as the velocity, above which separation occurs on the delivery stroke.

Here θ is in every case measured from the beginning of the stroke, so that $\cos\theta$ in the latter expression is negative.

Putting $\pi_a = 34$ feet, and writing $\theta = 0$ in equation (3):—

$$\omega = \sqrt{\dfrac{g\,a_s}{r\,A\,l_s}\{34 - h_s\}} \qquad (5$$

is the limiting speed at which separation will occur at the commencement of the suction stroke. Since $\omega = \dfrac{2\,\pi\,N}{60}$ (where N = revolutions per minute), this becomes :—

$$N = \dfrac{30}{\pi}\sqrt{\dfrac{g\,a_s}{r\,A\,l_s}(34 - h_s)}. \qquad (6$$

With a finite connecting rod of length l, we have :—

$$N = \dfrac{30}{\pi}\sqrt{\dfrac{g\,a_s}{r\,A\,l_s}\cdot\dfrac{\{34 - h_s\}}{\left\{1 + \dfrac{r}{l}\right\}}}. \qquad (7$$

The action may be shown graphically as follows :—

In Fig. 290, $O\,O'$ represents the atmospheric pressure line, and, assuming simple harmonic motion, ordinates drawn to the straight line $A\,H\,A'$ represent the head necessary to accelerate the water column in the suction pipe. Then $O\,A = O'\,A' = \dfrac{\omega^2\,r\,l_s}{g}\cdot\dfrac{A}{a_s}$. Vertical ordinates, set off from $A\,H\,A'$ as base line, to the curve $A\,B\,A'$, represent the heads necessary to overcome frictional resistance, zero at the ends, and having a maximum value $= \dfrac{f\,l_s\,A^2}{2\,g\,a_s^2}\cdot\dfrac{\omega^2\,r^2}{m}$, at the middle of the stroke.

The vertical ordinates of the shaded area then give the differences of head between the two ends of the suction pipe due to friction and inertia, these being negative or positive, according as ordinates are measured below or above $O\,O'$.

If now $C\,C'$ be drawn at a distance below $O\,O'$, representing the available head $(34 - h_s)$ feet, the ordinates of the curve $A\,B\,A'$, measured from $C\ C'$ as base line, give the effective pressures in the suction chamber, expressed in feet of water.

If the suction head be increased so that $O\ D$ represents $84 - h_s$ feet, separation will occur at the commencement of the stroke, since the available head is now insufficient to give the necessary acceleration. At D'' the head becomes sufficient both for this purpose and to overcome frictional losses, while at some point X, the acceleration of the water remaining approximately constant while that of the piston is continually diminishing, the water overtakes the piston and knocking occurs. Up to

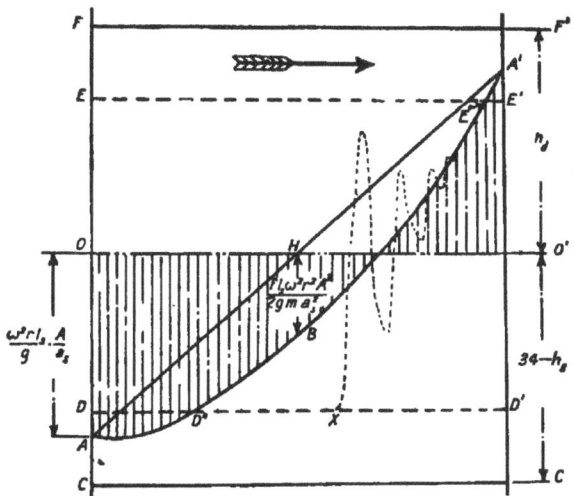

FIG. 290.—Theoretical Diagram of Piston Pressure during Suction Stroke of Reciprocating Pump.

this point the pressure behind the piston is constant, and has a negative value equal to $O\ D$ in feet of water. At the shock, violent oscillations of pressure are set up as represented by the dotted lines and the most that theory can do in this case is to indicate the maximum pressure to be expected and the means of reducing this.

Under normal conditions of working, the maximum pressure attained on the suction stroke is less than the delivery pressure $O\ F$.

If, however, this latter pressure be reduced, as for example to $O\ E$, the suction pressure becomes equal to this at the point E'', and for the remainder of the stroke discharge takes place through the delivery valves, the pressure remaining constant and following the line $E'''\ E'$.

The coefficient of discharge now becomes greater than unity. Its value may be deduced since the area $A'\ E''\ E'$ represents the work done in pumping a volume of water v cubic feet against a head $h_d (= OE$ feet.

The area $A\ E''\ E'$ thus represents $62.4\ v\ h_d$ foot lbs. $\therefore\ v = \dfrac{\text{area } A\ E''\ E'}{62.4\ h_d}$

The scale to which this area is to be measured is given by the product of

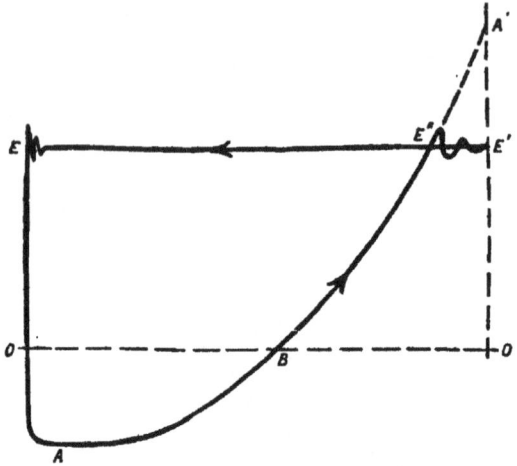

FIG. 290A.—Pump Diagram showing delivery during Suction Stroke.

the scales to which ordinates of the diagram represent heads in feet and abscissæ represent pounds of water.

The Coefficient of discharge $C_d = 1 + \dfrac{v}{V}$ where V is the piston displacement per stroke.

Assuming simple harmonic motion, the area $A'\ E''\ E'$ may be calculated analytically. In more complicated cases, it is preferable to measure it by planimeter.

Where an actual diagram is to be estimated (Fig. 290A), the suction head curve $A\ B\ E''$ may be produced by hand with fair accuracy to A' and the area then measured.

Since, at the speed at which separation occurs, water hammer raises the pressure towards the end of the suction stroke by an abnormal amount, it is to be inferred that about this speed a sudden increase in the discharge coefficient will take place. This inference is justified by the results of experiments by Professor John Goodman, the increase in this coefficient at the knocking speed in his pump, varying from 58 per cent. with a delivery pressure of 10 lbs. per square inch to 5 per cent. with a pressure of 70 lbs. per square inch.

Although this increases the capacity of the pump, yet, as might be expected, its efficiency is lowered, due to the increased losses by shock. The experiments showed that in this particular pump an increase in the

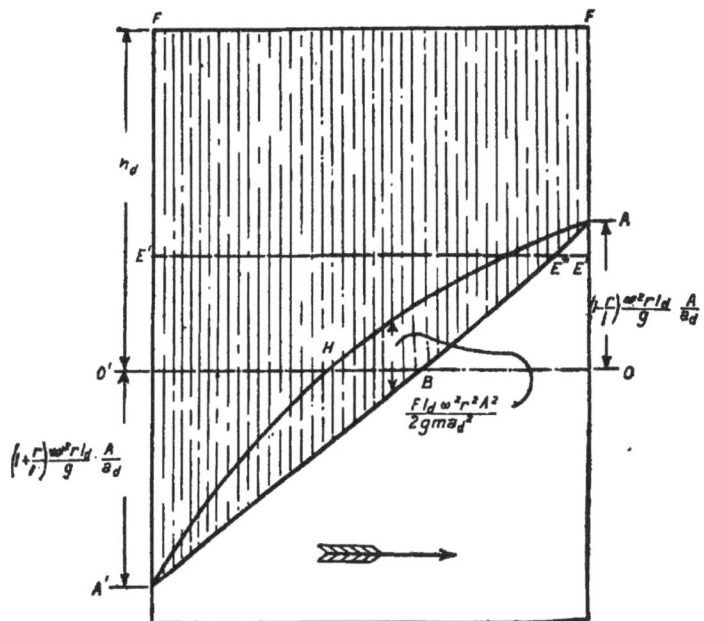

FIG. 291.—Theoretical Diagram of Piston Pressures during Delivery Stroke of Reciprocating Pump.

discharge coefficient from 1·059 to 1·517, was accompanied by a decrease of 10 per cent. in the efficiency.

A theoretical pressure diagram for the delivery side of the pump is shown in Fig. 291, where, however, the line $A' H A$, representing the acceleration pressure, has been drawn to take into account the effect of the obliquity of the connecting rod.

Also, since frictional resistances now increase the head on the piston, the friction line $A' B A$ is drawn below the acceleration line.

R R 2

If $O F$ represents the delivery head h_d, the total head on the piston is given by the ordinates of the curve $A E'' B A'$, measured from $F F'$ as datum.

If $O E$ were to represent the delivery head, the pressure would become negative on passing the point E'' and the suction valve would open, giving suction on the delivery side of the pump. At high speeds, and with self closing valves, this valve action becomes very irregular, delivery often occurring during the major part of the suction stroke and suction during the delivery stroke.[1]

Art. 164.—Rise in Pressure following Separation in a Pump.

During separation the accelerating force on the suction column $= W a_s \{\pi_a - h_s - h_f - h_t\}$ lbs., where h_f is the head necessary to overcome friction and therefore depends on the velocity, and h_t is the pressure in the cylinder due to vapour tension and to air leakage.

Neglecting the effect of friction, the acceleration in pipe line

$$= \frac{g \ W \ a_s \ \{\pi - h_s - h_t\}}{W' \ l_s \ a_s} = \frac{g \ (\pi_a - h_s - h_t)}{l_s} \text{ f.s.s.}$$

$\therefore$ Acceleration of water sur-
face in cylinder $\left. \begin{array}{c} \\ \end{array} \right\} = g \ \frac{(\pi_a - h_s - h_t)}{l_s} \cdot \frac{a_s}{A}$ f.s.s.

If the water overtakes the piston at a distance x feet from the beginning of the stroke, the time taken by the water surface to cover this distance under its constant accelerating force must equal that taken by the piston to cover the same space.

The former of these times is given by $T = \sqrt{\dfrac{2 \ x \ l_s \ A}{g \ \{\pi_a - h_s - h_t\} \ a}}$

since, with uniform acceleration, $T = \sqrt{\dfrac{2 \text{ space}}{\text{acceleration}}}.$

Assuming $S.H.$ motion, the time occupied by the piston to cover the same space is given by $\dfrac{\theta}{\omega}$ seconds,

where $x = r \ (1 - \cos \theta)$ (Fig. 292)

or $\theta = \cos^{-1} \left(1 - \dfrac{x}{r} \right).$

$\therefore$ Equating these times :—

$$\frac{1}{\omega} \cos^{-1} \left(1 - \frac{x}{r} \right) = \sqrt{\frac{2 \ x \ l_s \ A}{g \ \{\pi_a - h_s - h_t\} \ a_s}}$$

[1] For a series of diagrams showing this action reference may be made to Professor Goodman's paper. "Proc. Inst. Mech. Engineers," 1903.

$$\therefore \quad 1 - \frac{x}{r} = \cos \omega \sqrt{\frac{2\,x\,l_s\,A}{g\,(\pi_a - h_s - h_t)\,a_s}},$$

an equation from which x may be obtained by trial. For purposes of calculation h_t may be taken as zero. An attempt to include the effects of friction and of a finite connecting rod greatly complicates the result unless h_f be taken to be constant and to have a value corresponding to the mean velocity during the period of separation. By this means a close agreement with experimental results is obtained.

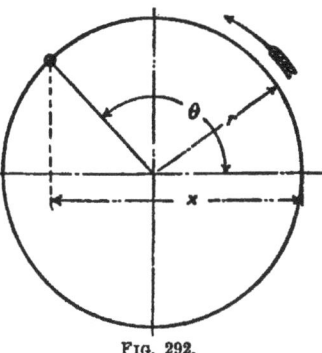

FIG. 292.

The above formula has been applied to the case of a pump described by Professor John Goodman[1] and having the following dimensions :—

$\dfrac{A}{a_s} = 1\cdot83$; $l_s = 63$ feet; $r = \cdot25$ feet.

In this particular experiment the pressure in the suction valve chamber was measured, the loss of head due to height of suction, to friction, and to air tension, being approximately 8·0 feet, making—

$$(\pi_a - h_s - h_f - h_t) = 26\cdot0.$$

The revolutions per minute were 70, making $\omega = \dfrac{2\,\pi \times 70}{60} = 7\cdot33.$

The equation then becomes :—

$$\cos 7\cdot33\,\sqrt{\frac{126 \times 1\cdot83}{32 \times 26}}\,.\,x = 1 - 4\,x$$

or $\qquad\qquad \cos 8\cdot86\,\sqrt{x} = 1 - 4\,x$

giving a value of $x = \cdot47$ feet ;

i.e., knock takes place at $\dfrac{\cdot47}{\cdot50} = \cdot94$ of the stroke.

The indicator diagram, of which Fig. 293 is a copy, shows this to occur at about ·95 of the stroke.

The velocity of the water column immediately before impact may be deduced from the equation

$$\text{velocity} = \sqrt{\frac{2 \times \text{acceleration} \times \text{space covered under this}}{\text{acceleration}}}\ \text{f.s.}$$

[1] " Proc. Inst. Mech. Engineers," 1903, part 1 (p. 143).

And since, this effective space $= x \cdot \dfrac{A}{a_s}$, this gives

$$\text{velocity} = \sqrt{\frac{2\,g\,(\pi_a - h_s - h_f - h_t)}{l_s}} \cdot x\,\frac{A}{a_s} \text{ feet per second.}$$

while the piston velocity $= \omega\, r \sin \theta$

$$= \omega\, r \sqrt{1 - \cos^2\theta}$$

$$= \omega \sqrt{\left(2 - \frac{x}{r}\right) x\, r} \text{ feet per second.}$$

After impact the mean velocity of the supply column becomes equal to that of the piston multiplied by $\dfrac{A}{a_s}$.

$\therefore$ Change of velocity at impact $= \Bigg\{ \sqrt{\dfrac{2\,g\,(\pi_a - h_s - h_f - h_t)}{l_s}} \cdot \dfrac{x\,A}{a_s}$

$$- \frac{A}{a_s}\, \omega \sqrt{x\, r \left(2 - \frac{x}{r}\right)} \Bigg\}$$

$$= r_x \text{ feet per second.}$$

If this change of velocity be assumed to take place instantaneously, the increase of pressure due to water hammer is given by $63\cdot7\ r_x$ lbs. per square inch (p. 235). In the example previously considered, taking $x = \cdot47$, we have :—

Change of velocity at impact

$$= \sqrt{\frac{64 \times 26 \times \cdot 86}{63}} - 1\cdot83 \times 7\cdot33 \times \sqrt{\cdot12 \times \cdot12}$$

$$= 4\cdot76 - 1\cdot61$$

$$= 3\cdot15 \text{ feet per second.}$$

$\therefore$ Water hammer pressure $= 3\cdot15 \times 63\cdot7$ lbs. per square inch
$$= 201 \text{ lbs. per square inch.}$$

In addition to this we have the pressure necessary to produce a retardation $\omega^2\, r \cos \theta\ \dfrac{A}{a_s}$ feet per second per second in the supply column.

This pressure $= - \dfrac{\omega^2\, r\, A \left(1 - \dfrac{x}{r}\right) \times W\, a_s\, L}{a_s \times g \times 144\, a_s}$ lbs. per square inch

$$= \frac{(7\cdot33)^2 \times \cdot25 \times 1\cdot83 \times \cdot88 \times 62\cdot4 \times 63}{32 \times 144}$$

$$= 18\cdot5 \text{ lbs. per square inch.}$$

On taking into account the obliquity of the connecting rod, this becomes 23 lbs. per square inch.

The total pressure which may be attained at impact (provided this pressure is not sufficiently great to lift the delivery valve), is then given by the sum of the water hammer and the retardation pressures, and is 219 lbs. per square inch.

By exterpolation from the curves showing the results of the experiments under consideration, the actual pressure at this speed would apparently vary from about 115 lbs. per square inch with a delivery pressure of 20 lbs. per square inch, to about 195 lbs. per square inch with a delivery pressure of 60 lbs. per square inch. This is a result which might have been inferred, since directly the delivery pressure is exceeded, the delivery valve opens, and the maximum pressure is reduced by an amount which cannot be deduced quantitatively.

It is, however, to be expected—and this is verified in practice—that this reduction will be greater as the delivery valve area is increased, and

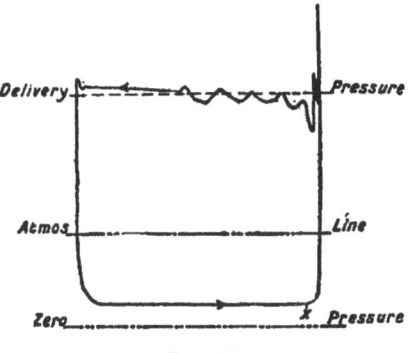

FIG. 293.

as the delivery pressure is reduced, since the latter reduces the pressure necessary to produce flow through the valves, while the former ensures a more easy delivery.

ART. 165.—EFFECT OF THE ELASTICITY OF THE SUCTION COLUMN.

While the formulae already obtained enable the pressure on the piston to be calculated with fair accuracy for the greater part of the stroke, it is found that the pressures actually obtained towards the end of the suction stroke, even when separation does not take place, are usually much greater than those calculated in this manner. So far, it will be noted, any effect which the elasticity of the water column may have in modifying this pressure has been neglected. Because of this elasticity, however, the change of velocity and of pressure at the open end of the pipe will lag behind that at the piston by the time necessary for a pressure wave to traverse the pipe, i.e., by a time $\frac{l}{4,700}$ seconds, and if the acceleration at the plunger end at a given instant be a, the difference in velocity at the two ends will be $a \times \frac{l}{4,700}$ f.s.

Thus, assuming S.H. motion, when the piston comes to rest the velocity at the open end will still be $\frac{\omega^2 \, r \, l}{4,700} \cdot \frac{A}{a_s}$ f.s., while the mean velocity in the pipe will be half this.   In virtue of this velocity the column possesses a store of kinetic energy which, on stoppage of the piston, is transformed into energy of strain, and which in consequence gives rise to a rapid rise in pressure, of the nature of water hammer.

Actually this occurs before the end of the stroke at a point where the retardation due to the piston becomes equal to $\frac{4,700 \, v}{l}$, v being the velocity of flow in the pipe at this instant, and the resultant rise in pressure, assuming a rigid pipe line, will equal $63 \cdot 7 \, v$ lbs. per square inch.   As the retardation and velocity can both be calculated in terms of θ, the position

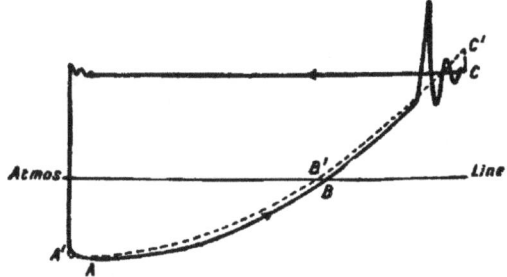

FIG. 294.—Pump Diagram showing the effect of the elasticity of Suction Column.   Air Vessel on Delivery side only.

of the piston when this occurs, and the magnitude of the shock, can be readily calculated.

The effect of the elasticity of the suction column is therefore to modify the shape of the diagram as shown in Fig. 294, where the dotted line $A' \, B' \, C'$ represents the theoretical curve, neglecting the effect of elasticity, and $A \, B \, C$ is the actual curve.

In the preceding investigations, the effect of loss of energy due to the sudden enlargement of section of the stream on entering the pump barrel, and to valve resistances, has been neglected.   In general, however, this will be comparatively small, except where the suction pipe is very short, in which case the difficulties already outlined cease to exist.

Even with a long suction pipe these may be considerably minimised, if not entirely removed, by the provision of an air vessel—or vacuum vessel as it is sometimes termed, since the pressure of the contained air is less than that of the atmosphere—on the suction side of the pump. The effect of such an air vessel will now be considered. Its action is as follows:—During the first part of the stroke the pressure behind the piston is reduced and water flows out of the air vessel. The flow along the suction pipe is thus reduced, as is the acceleration of the whole mass of water. This reduces the frictional resistance in the suction pipe, while the pressure behind the piston is increased both on this account and because of the reduced acceleration. At the same time tendency to separation and to water hammer at the end of the stroke is reduced, if not entirely eliminated; the discharge coefficient becomes unity, or slightly less than unity; and the pump diagram approximates

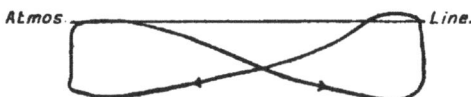

FIG. 295.—Pressure Diagram from Suction Air Vessel of
Reciprocating Pump.

more and more nearly to the rectangle given by a perfect pump, as the sizes of the air vessels are increased.

A typical indicator diagram taken from the suction air vessel of a double-acting pump is shown in Fig. 295.

ART. 166.—AIR VESSEL APPLIED TO A SINGLE OR DOUBLE-ACTING SINGLE CYLINDER PUMP.

Effect of Air Vessel placed on Suction Side of Pump.

Let a_s, v_s, and a_s represent the area of suction pipe between supply reservoir and air vessel, the velocity and the acceleration in this pipe respectively.

a_v, v_v, a_v represent ditto, in the air vessel itself.

A, V, a represent ditto, in the pump cylinder.

h_a represent the pressure of air in air vessel, in feet of water.

π represent the atmospheric pressure, in feet of water.

$h_v =$ height in feet, of water level in air vessel above centre line of pump.

During the first part of suction stroke water will flow out of air vessel into pump, and for continuity of flow:—

$$v_s \, a_s + v_v \, a_v = V \, A$$

∴ Differentiating, we have $a_s \, a_s + a_v \, a_v = A \, a$ \qquad (1)

If, as is usual, the air vessel is placed near to the pump, so that the pressure at the junction of air vessel and suction pipe may be taken as substantially equal to that in the suction chamber we have, denoting the pressure by h_j feet of water, neglecting frictional losses in the supply pipe, and simply considering the acceleration effect :—

$$(\pi - h_s - h_j)\, a_s\, W = \frac{a_s\, W\, l_s\, a_s}{g}$$

$$\therefore \quad h_j = \pi - h_s - \frac{l_s\, a_s}{g} \qquad (2$$

Also, considering the flow down the air vessel :—

$$h_a + h_v - h_j = \frac{h_v\, a_v}{g}\ ^1$$

$$\therefore \quad h_j = h_a + h_v - \frac{h_v\, a_v}{g} \qquad (3)$$

Substituting for a_v in terms of a_s from (1) we get :—

$$h_j = h_a + h_v - \frac{h_v}{g} \left\{ \frac{A\, a - a_s\, a_s}{a_v} \right\} \qquad (4)$$

Substituting for h_j from (2), this becomes :—

$$\pi - h_s - \frac{l_s\, a_s}{g} = h_a + h_v - \frac{h_v}{g} \left\{ \frac{A\, a - a_s\, a_s}{a_v} \right\} \qquad (5)$$

$$\therefore \quad a_s \left\{ \frac{a_s}{a_v} \cdot \frac{h_v}{g} + \frac{l_s}{g} \right\} = \pi - h_s - h_a - h_v + \frac{h_v}{g} \frac{A\, a}{a_v}$$

$$\therefore \quad a_s = g\, \frac{\left\{ \pi - (h_s + h_a) + h_v \left(\frac{A\, a}{g\, a_v} - 1 \right) \right\}}{\frac{a_s\, h_v}{a_v} + l_s} \qquad (6)$$

as compared with its value $\frac{A\, a}{a_s}$, without air vessel.

Neglecting, for the time being, the variation in h_a and h_v with a variation in the piston acceleration a, it is evident from (6) that for a_s to be affected as little as possible by a variation in a, the term involving a must be as small as possible. This indicates that a_v, the sectional area of the vessel, should be as large, and h_v as small as possible—a deduction which is verified in practice.

When the pump is working, the water surface h_v undergoes cyclical variations in height, h_a assuming corresponding values. The connection between the two may be obtained on the assumption that the air follows

---

[1] This assumes the air vessel to be of uniform diameter to its junction with the suction pipe. If, as is more usual, the junction is made through a smaller pipe of area a_1, this formula becomes $h_a + h_v - h_j = \frac{h_v\, a_1}{g}$, where $a_1 = a_v \frac{a_v}{a_1}$.

e law (pressure $\times$ volume $=$ constant), for if $H_v =$ height of top of
: vessel above centre line of pump:—

$$h_a \left\{ H_v - h_r \right\} = \text{constant} = K$$

$$\therefore \quad h_v = H_v - \frac{K}{h_a} \tag{7}$$

$$\text{or } h_a = \frac{K}{H_v - h_r} \tag{8}$$

The mean height h_v may be adjusted by admitting more or less air
to the air vessel, and this adjustment should be made until h_v is as low
is consistent with no air being drawn over into the suction chamber as
e level varies.

With a single-acting pump, the total cyclical variation in volume in
ie air chamber is about ·56 of the piston displacement per stroke.

Since the fluctuation in level diminishes with an increase in cross-
ctional area, an increase in a_v has the further advantage that it permits
ie mean working value of h_v to be reduced.

Again, substituting in (6) from (8), it appears that while the fluctuation
. a_s corresponding to a given variation in h_v, diminishes as H_v increases
et this effect is small compared with that of an increase in a_v. In effect
ien, the area of the vessel is of much greater importance than its length,

id for a given volume, the ratio $\dfrac{\text{area}}{\text{length}}$ should be as large as possible.

EXAMPLE.

$A = 1\cdot0$ square foot. $l_s = 30$ feet.
$a_s = \cdot25$ square foot. $h_s = 9\cdot5$ feet.
$a_v = 1\cdot00$ square foot. $H_v = 4$ feet.
Length of stroke $= 1\cdot0$ foot.   No. of revolutions $= 100$ per min.

When the pump is standing let $h_v = 6$ inches. We then have $h_a =$
$34 - 10) = 24$ feet absolute head,

$$\text{so that } 24 \left\{ 4 - \tfrac{1}{2} \right\} = \text{constant} = K$$

$$\therefore \quad K = 84.$$

Assuming the total fluctuation of volume in the air vessel to be equal
o ·56 times the delivery per stroke, this gives a total fluctuation equal to
56 cubic feet, and therefore a fluctuation in level of ·56 feet.

The acceleration in the supply pipe corresponding to any value of the
iston acceleration may now be obtained from equation (6).

$$\text{Thus } a_s = \frac{32\cdot2 \left\{ 34 - 9\cdot5 - \dfrac{84}{4 - h_v} + h_v \left(\dfrac{a}{32\cdot2} - 1 \right) \right\}}{\cdot25\,h_s + 30} \text{ f.s.s.}$$

It only remains to substitute for h_v, and if, as indicator diagrams show to be usually the case, we assume that this has its minimum value shortly after the piston begins its suction stroke, we may obtain the acceleration at this point by putting $h_v = [\cdot 5 - \cdot 28] = \cdot 22$ feet in the above expression, and by writing

$$a = \frac{4 \pi^2 \times 100^2}{3,600} \times \tfrac{1}{2} = 54 \cdot 8 \text{ f.s.s.}$$

$$\text{Then } a_s = \frac{32 \cdot 2 \left\{ 24 \cdot 5 - \frac{84}{3 \cdot 78} + \cdot 22 \left(\frac{54 \cdot 8}{32 \cdot 2} - 1 \right) \right\}}{30 \cdot 055}$$

$$= 2 \cdot 62 \text{ f.s.s.}$$

as compared with its value $\omega^2 r \times 4 = 219 \cdot 3$ f.s.s. without air vessel.

The maximum acceleration will in general be found to occur at about $\frac{1}{4}$ of the suction stroke.

Evidently a further increase in the size of air vessel, or an increase in the length of suction pipe will reduce the value of a_s still further, and with a suction pipe of any considerable length its value approximates very sensibly to zero. In such a case the flow along the pipe is sensibly constant, and the velocity is equal to the discharge in cubic feet per second divided by the area of the pipe. If this assumption be made, calculations relating to the necessary size, etc., of the air vessel are considerably simplified, as will be shown later.

Modifying Effect of Friction and Kinetic Losses in Suction Pipe.—Taking the total difference of head between supply reservoir and piston as being given by

$$\frac{v_s^2}{2 g} \left(1 + \frac{f l_s}{m} \right) + \frac{l_s a_s}{g} \text{ feet,}$$

this may be written as:—

$$\frac{a_s}{g} \left\{ \frac{r}{2} \frac{\sin^2 \theta}{\cos \theta} \cdot \frac{A}{a_s} \left(1 + \frac{f l_s}{m} \right) + l_s \right\} \text{ feet.}$$

$$\left(\begin{array}{l} \text{Since } a_s = \omega^2 r \cos \theta \, \dfrac{A}{a_s} \\[2mm] \text{and } v_s^2 = \omega^2 r^2 \sin^2 \theta \, \dfrac{A^2}{a_s^2} = a_s r \, \dfrac{\sin^2 \theta}{\cos \theta} \cdot \dfrac{A}{a_s} \end{array} \right)$$

$$\therefore \quad \pi - h_s - h_j = \frac{a_s}{g} \left\{ l_s + B \frac{\sin^2 \theta}{\cos \theta} \right\} \text{ feet.}$$

The preceding equations now become:—

$$h_j = \pi - h_s - \frac{a_s}{g} \left\{ l_s + B \frac{\sin^2 \theta}{\cos \theta} \right\} \qquad (2'$$

$$h_j = h_a + h_v - \frac{h_r\, a_v}{g} \tag{3'}$$

eglecting frictional losses in air vessel as being comparatively small).

On substituting for a_v in (3') in terms of a_s from (1), as before, we have,
uation (4) :—

$$h_j = h_a + h_v - \frac{h_r}{g}\left\{\frac{A\,a - a_s a_s}{a_v}\right\} \tag{4'}$$

id substituting in this equation for h_j from (2'), on reduction :—

$$a_s = \frac{g\left\{\pi - (h_s + h_a) + h_v\left(\dfrac{A\,a}{g\,a_v} - 1\right)\right\}}{l_s + \dfrac{a_s\,h_v}{a_v} + B\,\dfrac{\sin^2\theta}{\cos\theta}} \tag{6'}$$

By substituting in (4') for a_s from (2') we get, on reduction :—

$$h_j = \frac{\pi - h_s + \dfrac{a_v\left(l_s + B\dfrac{\sin^2\theta}{\cos\theta}\right)}{h_r\,a_s}\left[h_a + h_v - \dfrac{h_r\,A\,a}{a_r\,g}\right]}{1 + \dfrac{a_v}{h_r\,a_s}\left\{l_s + B\dfrac{\sin^2\theta}{\cos\theta}\right\}} \text{ feet,}$$

om which, on assuming values for h_v, a curve similar to Fig. 290,
iowing the pressure on the piston for a series of values of θ may
e plotted.

In practice, with single-barrel double-acting pumps, suction air vessels
: from 1·0 to 3·0 times the capacity of the pump per revolution are
·und to give good results, the necessary volume increasing with the
itative speed of the pump and with the length of suction pipe.

ART. 167.—AIR VESSEL ON DELIVERY SIDE OF PUMP.

Here exactly the same reasoning applies, except that now flow into the
ir vessel will take place during the first half of the delivery stroke, and
ow out of the vessel during the second half when the water column in
ie delivery pipe is being retarded.

Considering the latter part of the stroke, for continuity of flow :—

$$a_d v_d - a_v v_v = A\,V$$
$$\therefore\quad a_d a_d - a_v a_v = A\,a.$$

Also h_d now corresponds to $(h_s - \pi)$ in the case of the suction vessel.
$\therefore$ Equation (2) becomes :—

$$h = h_d + \frac{l_d a_d}{g} \text{ (neglecting friction);}$$

while (3) becomes :—

$$h_j - h_v - h_a = \frac{h_r\, a_v}{g}$$

$$\therefore \quad h_d + \frac{l_d\, a_d}{g} = h_v + h_a + \frac{h_r\, a_r}{g}$$

$$= h_v + h_a + \frac{h_v}{g} \left\{ \frac{A\, a - a_d\, a_d}{a_v} \right\}$$

$$\therefore \quad a_d = \frac{g \left\{ h_v + h_a - h_d + \dfrac{h_v}{g} \dfrac{A\, a}{a_v} \right\}}{\left\{ l_d + \dfrac{a_d\, h_v}{a_v} \right\}}$$

But without air vessel, so long as separation does not occur :—

$$a'_d = a\, \frac{A}{a_d}$$

$$\therefore \quad a'_d - a_d = \frac{1}{l_d + \dfrac{a_d}{a}\, h_v} \left\{ \frac{A\, a\, l_d}{a_d} - g\, (h_d - h_a - h_v) \right\}$$

An examination of this equation indicates that the change in the retardation in the delivery pipe, and therefore in the pressure in the pump, due to the provision of the chamber, increases with an increase in a_v, and since h_v is in general small compared with h_d, diminishes with an increase in h_v. It follows that the mean level in the air vessel should be reduced to the lowest practicable limit, and that h_a should be as large as practicable, i.e., the air supply should be maintained so as to keep the water-level as low as is consistent with the air vessel still containing some water at the end of the delivery stroke.

The modifying effect of frictional resistances may be examined as in the case of the suction air vessel. In general, owing to the fact that the delivery head is much greater than the suction head, and that the water at high pressure is able to dissolve an increased volume of air, the air in the vessel is gradually absorbed, so that either some device must be fitted for renewing the supply, or an air vessel of such dimensions must be fitted as will enable the mean level to be maintained fairly constant over long periods of working. In practice, with a single-barrel double-acting pump, the delivery air vessel usually has a volume equal to from six to nine times the pump displacement per revolution, depending on (increasing with) the speed of rotation and the length of delivery pipe. Here, again, an increase in the area of the vessel is of greater advantage than an increase in its length.

Art. 168.

If it be assumed that the velocity of flow along the suction and delivery pipes is sensibly uniform, and equal to the mean velocity of the pump plunger, multiplied by the ratio of areas of plunger and pipe, the volume of water entering the air chamber per stroke may be determined with fair accuracy. Thus, if the ordinates of the displacement curves $A B C D E$ (Fig. 296) represent piston velocities, and if $A F$ represent the mean

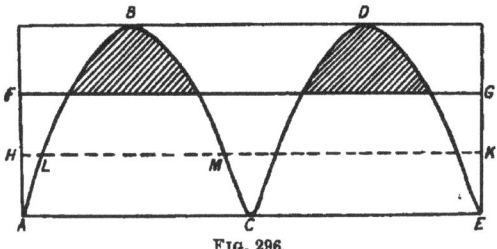

FIG. 296.

piston velocity, on multiplying the vertical scale by $\dfrac{A}{a_d}$ the curve would give the velocities of flow along the delivery pipe if no air vessel were fitted, $A F$ measuring the mean velocity.

Thus the ratio of each of the sectional areas to the whole area $A F G E$

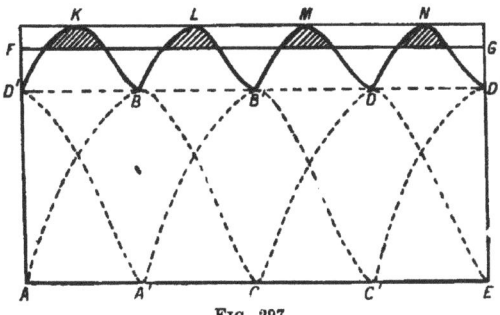

FIG. 297.

gives the ratio of the volume entering the air vessel per cycle to the total discharge per revolution. This applies to a double-acting pump. In a single-acting pump the volume discharged will be given by the area $A H K E$, where $A H = \frac{1}{2} A F$, while the volume entering the air vessel will be given by the area $L B M$. In the case of a double-acting duplex pump, having cranks at right angles, Fig. 297 represents the state of affairs.

Here the curve D' K B L B', etc., formed by adding the ordinates of the two single velocity curves A B C, A' B' C', etc., gives the velocity of the combined discharge, without air vessel. The area A E G F represents the discharge per revolution, and each of the sectioned areas represents to the same scale the volume entering and leaving the air vessel per cycle.

These areas may be calculated or measured by planimeter. The following table gives the proportion of the whole discharge per revolution which enters and leaves the air vessel per cycle.

Type of Pump.	Proportion of Water entering the Air Vessel per Cycle.	
	Assuming an infinitely Long Connecting Rod.	Ratio $\dfrac{\text{Connecting Rod}}{\text{Crank}}$ = 4 : 1.
Single-acting pump . . .	·55	·562
Two single-acting pumps with cranks at right angles.	·35	·365
Double-acting pump . . .	·105	·115
Two double-acting pumps with cranks at right angles.	·0105	·0106
Three-throw pump with cranks at 120° { Single-acting	·0109	·0111
Double-acting }	·0029	·003

For satisfactory working the volume of the delivery air vessel should be from forty to sixty times the volume of water entering it per cycle, this proportion increasing with the speed of rotation and the length of delivery pipe.

On the suction side the volume should be from ten to thirty times the volume entering per cycle, this proportion also increasing with the speed and with the length of suction pipe.

To Summarise.—An air vessel on the suction side of a pump reduces the maximum acceleration and the range of velocities in the supply pipe, and thus, besides reducing friction losses, reduces the fluctuations of pressure in the suction chamber, and therefore the liability to water hammer or separation. The steadying effect becomes more pronounced as A, a, l, are increased and less pronounced as a_s is increased. The larger the volume of the chamber the greater is its effect, an increase of sectional area being of more value than an increase in length. Also, for efficient working, the water-level in the air vessel should be adjusted by adjusting the air pressure, until as low as is consistent with water remaining in the vessel during the first part of the suction stroke. For the air vessel to be as effective as possible in preventing shock it should be so situated as to provide an effective air cushion to the entrant water. Fig. 298 *a, b,* and *c,*

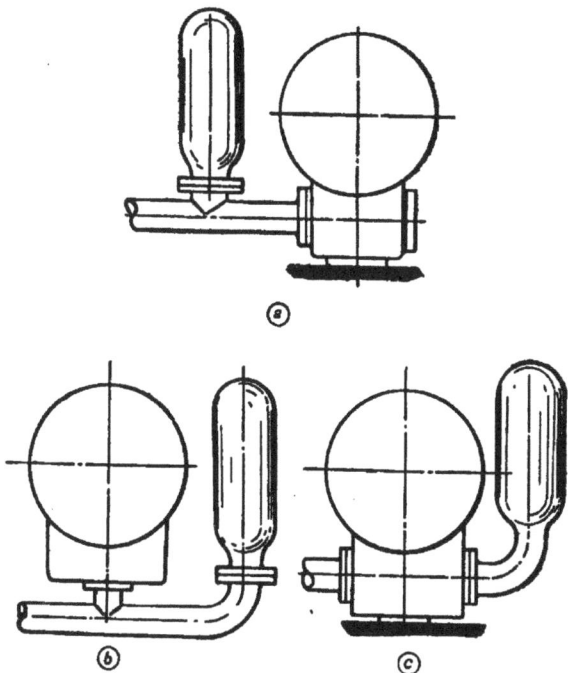

FIG. 298.—Suction Air Vessels for Reciprocating Pumps.

shows various methods of applying the air vessel. Of these (*a*) is very little good in preventing shock. (*b*) is good except that the provision of a right-angled bend at the entry to the suction chamber is inadvisable. The best method is that illustrated at (*c*), since here the air vessel is in a direct line with the suction pipe, while discharge either from the air vessel or supply pipe takes place directly into the suction chamber without the intervention of bends or elbows of any description. It may be premised that the air vessel should always be placed so that a sudden

H.A.   S S retardation of the suction column may produce a direct flow into the vessel, without the intervention of any acute bends or contracted passages.

Precisely the same reasoning applies to the delivery air vessel, and here again, for efficient working, the water-level should be adjusted by adjusting the air pressure, until as low as is consistent with water remaining in the vessel throughout the whole cycle.

ART. 169.—AIR-CHARGING DEVICES.

One of the simplest devices for maintaining the level in an air vessel is the air injector of Messrs. Wippermann and Lewis. In this apparatus,

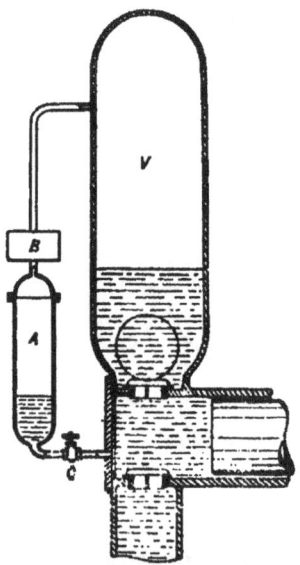

FIG. 299.—Wippermann Air Injector.

which is represented diagrammatically in Fig. 299, the small cylindrical chamber A is connected to the pump barrel by means of a small pipe with regulating cock, and at its upper end carries a valve-box B containing air inlet and outlet valves, which is in turn connected to the air space of the air vessel V.

On the suction stroke in the main pump this chamber is partially emptied, the air is drawn in through the inlet valve. On the delivery stroke of the pump, water is forced into the chamber A and its contained air is driven through its outlet valve into the air vessel V.

The amount of water entering and leaving A per cycle, and therefore the air entering V, may be accurately adjusted by means of the regulating cock C.

Another simple device consists of a small compound air pump, worked by the main pump shaft, which draws air out of the suction chamber, where it tends to accumulate, and pumps it into the delivery chamber.

ART. 170.—EFFICIENCY OF THE RECIPROCATING PUMP.

When dealing with considerable pressures, the reciprocating pump if well designed and working at a fairly slow speed is capable of an efficiency of up to about 90 per cent.

Since a large proportion of the loss is due to mechanical friction and is therefore approximately independent of the pressure, this efficiency falls off rapidly as the working head is reduced, so that in general, for heads below about 100 feet, the centrifugal pump becomes the more efficient. The piston pump, however, has the advantage of being positive in action, is not so liable as the centrifugal pump to lose its water, and has an efficiency which, to a larger extent than in the case of the latter type, is independent of speed.

ART. 171.—POSITIVE ROTARY PUMPS.

This type of pump forms the connecting link between the centrifugal and the reciprocating piston pump.   Like the former, its motion is rotary

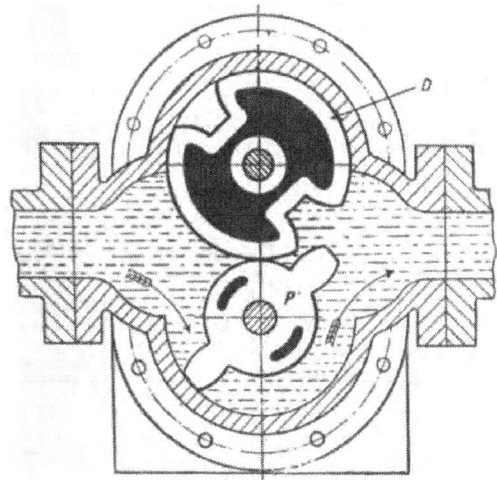

FIG. 300.—Drum Pump.

and its delivery practically continuous and free from vibration, while, like the latter, its action is positive and it will work well over a large range of speeds.   Its great drawback lies in the difficulty of keeping the rotating pistons tight against each other and against the pump casing, the wear which invariably occurs leading to considerable leakage and loss of efficiency.

In spite of this, the convenience of the method of driving, the fact that no valves are required, and the steadiness of working, render the pump valuable in many instances, and more particularly where viscid liquid is

s s 2

to be handled. One of the best of this type, the Drum **Pump**, is illustrated in section in Fig. 300.[1] Here P is the revolving piston, which carries two projecting ribs, these gearing into suitable slots on the revolving drum D. The piston and drum are geared together by external gear wheels, and at each rotation of the piston a volume of liquid $= 2 \pi R A$ cubic feet is delivered, where $R =$ mean radius of the projecting rib and $A =$ its projected area on a diametrical plane. The pump is built in sizes to deliver up to about 700 gallons per minute.

EXAMPLES.

(1) Sketch the displacement curve for a five-cylinder single-acting pump having cranks at 72° and, assuming zero acceleration in the pipe line, determine the proportion of the delivery per revolution which enters the air vessel per cycle.

Answer. ·0013.

(2) Assuming no air vessels, determine the critical speeds at which separation will occur on the suction and delivery sides respectively of the following pump :—

Cylinder diameter	= 10 inches.	Length of connecting rod =	3 feet.
Cylinder stroke	= 18 inches.	Length of suction pipe =	40 feet.
Diameter of suction pipe =	5 inches.	Length of delivery pipe =	250 feet.
Diameter of delivery pipe =	4 inches.	Suction lift =	10 feet.
		Delivery lift =	180 feet.

Answer. { On suction stroke 21·7 revolutions per minute.
{ On delivery stroke 20·7 revolutions per minute.

(3) Assuming the pump of example (2) to run at forty revolutions per minute, determine at what point in the stroke shock will take place, and assuming all connections, etc., to be rigid, and neglecting the effect of the opening of the delivery valves, determine the maximum hammer pressure then produced.

Answer. 99·3 per cent. of stroke.
Hammer pressure 834 lbs. per square inch.

(4) Determine the discharge coefficients for a pump of 6-inch stroke, having a ratio $\dfrac{\text{connecting rod}}{\text{crank length}} = \dfrac{4}{1}$; a ratio $\dfrac{\text{piston area}}{\text{suction pipe area}} = 1\cdot89$; length of suction pipe = 63 feet, when running at fifty revolutions per minute, and when the delivery pressure is respectively

(a) 5 lbs. per square inch.
(b) 10 lbs. per square inch.

[1] By courtesy of the Drum Engineering Company, Bradford.

Also (c) for the same pump when fitted with a suction pipe 36 feet long and when running at sixty revolutions per minute against a head of 11·5 feet.

Answer. (a) . . 1·15.
(b) . . 1·01.
(c) . . 1·10.

(5) A double-acting pump, cylinder diameter 10 inches, stroke 18 inches, is fitted with an air vessel on the suction side 15 inches diameter, and 4 feet 6 inches long measured from its point of junction with the suction chamber. The length of suction pipe is 150 feet, its diameter is 5 inches, the suction lift, measured to the level of the suction chamber, is 10 feet, and air is admitted to the vessel until the mean working level is 4 feet from the top, the fluctuation in level being 2 inches. Determine the acceleration in the suction column at the beginning of the out-stroke—ratio of connecting rod to crank length being 4 : 1—when running at eighty revolutions per minute.

Answer $\begin{cases} h_a = 23\cdot5 \text{ feet.} \\ a_s = \cdot32 \text{ f.s.s.} \end{cases}$

CHAPTER XVIII

Centrifugal Pumps—Types and Construction—Theory—Balancing of End Thrust.

ART. 172.—CENTRIFUGAL PUMPS.

UNDER low heads the efficiency of the reciprocating pump falls off considerably, and when in addition very large quantities of water are to be handled its excessive dimensions render it expensive to construct and to instal. When working against a variable head, it also suffers from the disadvantage that its speed cannot be increased to any large extent to enable it to deliver a larger quantity of water as the head is reduced.

Under such conditions, with heads ranging from about 6 feet to 100 feet, the centrifugal pump having a single impeller is on all accounts most suitable, giving as it does a good efficiency—up to about 75 per cent. in the modern type of pump—along with moderate dimensions, simple construction, ease of installation and maintained high efficiency under continuous working conditions.

In the latter respect its freedom from valves gives it an advantage over the reciprocator, whose valves, glands, and packing rings need to be frequently overhauled if the efficiency is to be maintained, this advantage being still more pronounced where the liquid pumped contains gritty matter in suspension.

A further advantage is involved in its continuous and even discharge and the consequent freedom from shock in the delivery pipe line.

The invention, in 1875, by Professor Osborne Reynolds, of the modern form of high lift pump, having an efficiency equal to that of the old type of low lift pump, opened out a new field of application for the centrifugal pump, and of recent years this has been to an increasing extent invading the province of the reciprocator, its efficiency increasing with improvements in design, until at the present time heads of upwards of 1,500 feet may be overcome with efficiencies of from 75 to 80 per cent. In a pump designed for such work the water passes through a sequence of impellers mounted in series on the same shaft, the increase in head taking place in stages.

A further advantage of the centrifugal pump consists in the possibility of adapting it to the high speeds of rotation common in the case of the electric motor or steam turbine, its even torque rendering it particularly well fitted for such a purpose, and the general tendency towards the extended use of such motors has of recent years given a great impetus to the development of the pump.

The extent of this adaptability may be realised from experiments by M. Rateau,[1] who, using a pump having a single impeller of 3·15 inches diameter, and rotating at 18,000 revolutions per minute, obtained an efficiency of approximately 60 per cent. when pumping against 863 feet head.

Indeed, to such an extent have the possibilities in design responded to the demands made upon them in recent years, that the centrifugal pump promises to replace the reciprocator to an ever-increasing extent in every class of work, except where the volume of water to be handled is very small in comparison with the working head.

For mine drainage, the motor-driven centrifugal has the advantage of requiring no expensive emplacements ; while for elevator work this motor-driven pump, with an automatically controlled rheostat to regulate the discharge, has an advantage in that since the delivery pressure cannot increase to any large extent, no bye-pass is required. With a reciprocating pump this bye-pass is essential and involves a loss of energy by leakage.

Applied to dredging operations, the centrifugal pump is capable of removing sand, gravel, or clay broken up by a water jet or mechanical agitator, the amount of solid varying up to 40 per cent. of the volume handled. With a mixture containing 15 per cent. of gravel or 35 per cent. of fine sand, efficiencies of about 45 per cent. may be attained.

In its essentials the pump may be looked upon as a reversed inward radial or mixed flow turbine, having the wheel vanes driven in the opposite direction to that of rotation in the case of the turbine, and discharging outwards.

If the pump be filled, the rotation of the wheel produces a forced vortex in the contained water, with a consequent increase of pressure in an outward radial direction and a tendency to outward flow. If the speed of rotation is sufficiently high, this increase in pressure becomes more than sufficient to balance the statical pressure of the delivery head and flow takes place. A partial vacuum is thus produced at the centre of the wheel and water is forced up through the supply pipe by atmospheric pressure to take the place of that discharged outwards by centrifugal action.

[1] *Engineer*, March 7, 1902 (p. 23).

The whole object of a centrifugal pump, as indeed of any pump, is to increase the pressure of the water which it handles, and where, as in the case of a centrifugal pump, the water is delivered from the impeller with a considerable velocity, the degree of efficiency to which the machine may attain depends very largely on the extent to which the kinetic energy of

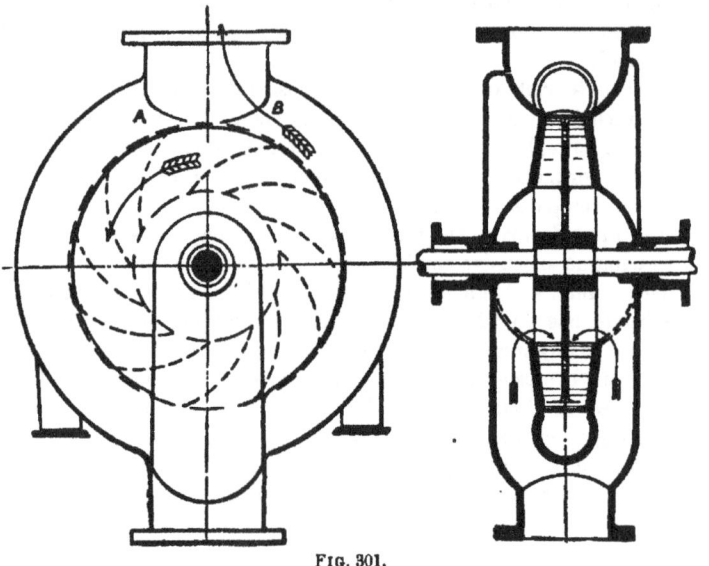

FIG. 301.

discharge from the impeller may be converted into pressure energy in the pump casing.

Any device having this end in view should be designed so as to reduce the velocity of discharge from the impeller gradually and without shock or eddy formation, to that of flow along the discharge pipe.

In some pumps no attempt is made to do this, and the water is simply allowed to discharge into a small chamber surrounding, and concentric with the wheel, out of which chamber the discharge pipe is led (Fig. 301). Since each of the vanes is continuously discharging, the quantity passing a section of the collecting chamber will increase continuously from a section at A just past the discharge pipe, to be a maximum at the section

B just before reaching this pipe. The velocity of whirl in this chamber will thus vary from A to B, and can only at one particular section correspond with that at discharge. The result is, that practically the whole of the kinetic energy at discharge is dissipated in shock and eddy production.

This may be avoided to a certain extent by designing the chamber so as to have a sectional area which increases uniformly from A to B, a cutwater being placed as shown at A (Fig. 302), so as to ensure the whole flow being at once discharged from the chamber.[1] This is termed a volute chamber and is usually so designed as to give a uniform velocity of whirl in the chamber, equal to about ·4 times the velocity of whirl on leaving the impeller.

Here again, however, the velocity of whirl on leaving the wheel is always much greater than that of flow in the volute, so that there is still a loss

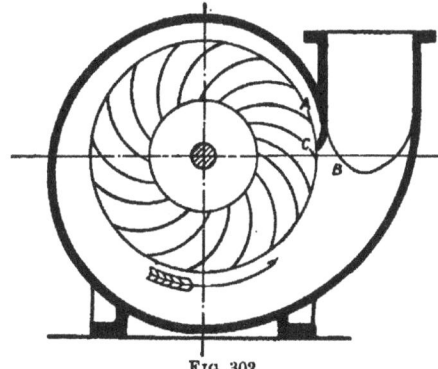

FIG. 302.

by shock due to the impact of the high velocity water leaving the vanes, on the more slowly moving water in the volute chamber.

Practically the efficiency of the chamber as usually designed is very low, experiments by Dr. Stanton[2] indicating that it often does not exceed about 10 per cent., and that the volute chamber in itself is only slightly more efficient than the concentric chamber.[3]

---

[1] This cutwater, if designed so as almost to touch the impeller, tends to cause considerable vibration when the pump is working. Generally the working is found to improve, and the efficiency not to suffer unduly, by the provision of a generous amount of clearance at this point.

[2] " Proceedings Institute Mechanical Engineers," 1903 (p. 715).

[3] When correctly designed, the chamber, however, is capable of converting some 60 per cent. of the kinetic energy of discharge into pressure energy. For a rational design of such chambers a paper to be read by the Author before the Institution of Mechanical Engineers during the session 1912–13 should be consulted.

Whirlpool Chamber.—In the arrangement of collecting chamber suggested by Professor James Thomson and known as the vortex or whirlpool chamber, the impeller is surrounded by a casing which may be looked upon as a volute chamber of uniformly increasing area superposed upon a circular chamber concentric with and of considerably larger diameter than the wheel. Fig. 303 shows such a vortex chamber. In the concentric portion of the casing, the water on leaving the wheel is free to adopt its own manner of motion which approximates to that of a free vortex. In this vortex the pressure increases outwards, theoretically following the

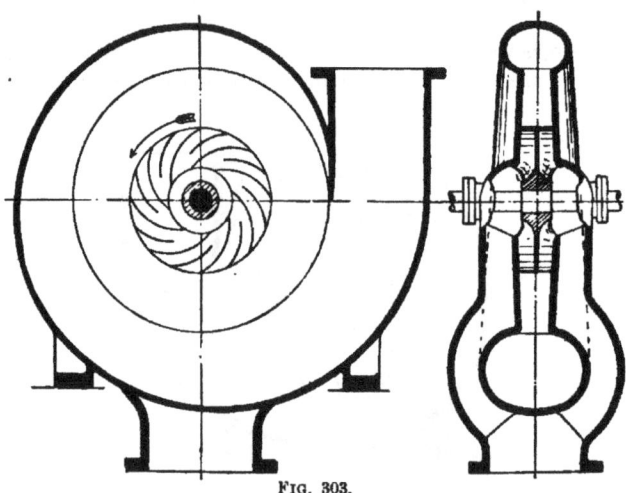

Fig. 303.

ordinary free vortex law. Uniform discharge then takes place around the circumference of the vortex chamber, through the gradually increasing volute passage. The great drawback to this device is that to get a very efficient chamber, the dimensions become excessive—the efficiency increasing with the radius—and, in consequence, it is seldom adopted save in a modified form. In this form it is very general.

Even with this chamber, however, the efficiency of transformation is greatly diminished owing to the instability of diverging motion and the consequent loss of head in eddy formation, and the efficiency actually obtained does not in general exceed about 40 per cent. of the theoretical.

Guide Vanes.—The tendency to instability of motion and the heavy losses due to shock may be largely prevented by the introduction of fixed

guide vanes around the impeller, as shown in Fig. 304,[1] having angles so
designed as to receive the water without shock on leaving the wheel, and to
direct this by gradually diverging passages, either into a vortex chamber,
or directly into the collecting volute from which it is taken by the discharge pipe.   In the latter case the pressure change takes place entirely
in the guide passages themselves.   The angle *a* which the guide vanes make
with the circumference of the discharge circle is calculated exactly as in the
case of the inlet vanes of a turbine, and, where the pump is required to

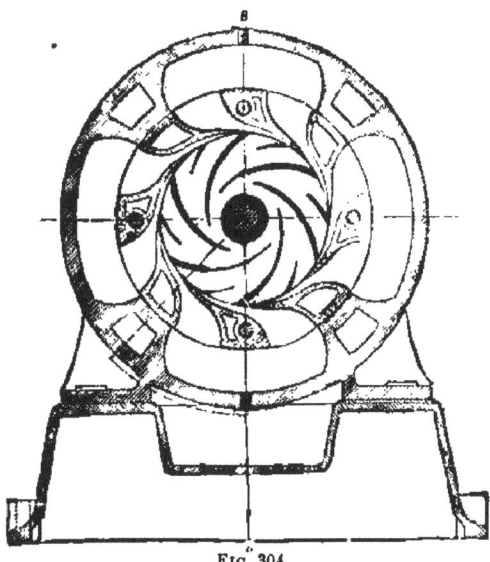

Fig. 304.

work under variable conditions, should be suited to the discharge at which
the maximum efficiency is desired.   Thus fitted, the pump becomes in
every essential a reversed turbine, and is commonly known as a " turbine "
pump.   Where the guides deliver into a vortex chamber they should be
designed so as to follow the curvature of the stream lines in free vortex
flow with the discharge, and with the tangential velocity at the entrance
to the guides, obtaining under normal conditions of working.   The ring
of guide vanes in such a pump is known as the *diffuser ring*.   Under
favourable circumstances such an arrangement is capable of converting
up to 75 per cent. of the kinetic energy at discharge into pressure energy.

[1] By courtesy of the Buffalo Steam Pump Company.

Where the conditions are very variable, however, the guide—or diffuser ring—may easily prove an actual source of loss by shock rather than of efficiency. Under such circumstances the guides are preferably omitted, the most suitable type of pump being one fitted with a moderate vortex chamber and volute, this both on account of its greater adaptability to varying circumstances, and of its cheaper construction.

Types of Centrifugal Pump.

Centrifugal pumps may be divided into three classes :—

(1) Pumps having a single impeller with open vanes, and discharging directly into a volute casing or vortex chamber.

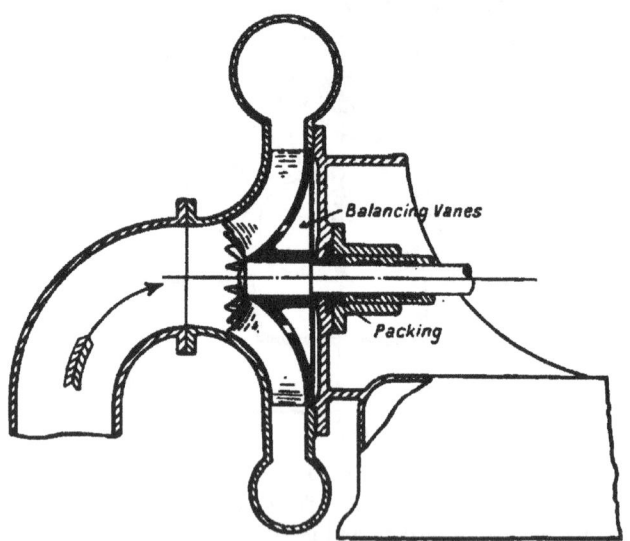

Fig. 305.—Open Vaned Centrifugal Pump with Balancing Vanes.

(2) Pumps having a single impeller with encased vanes, and either discharging as above, or fitted with a diffuser ring between impeller and vortex chamber.

(3) Compound pumps, which are invariably fitted with encased vanes and with diffuser rings with or without the addition of a vortex chamber.

Fig. 305 shows an example of the first type, having an axial inlet on one side only of the impeller. Here the water is deflected into a radial direction by the conical disc on which the vanes are formed.

Fig. 301 shows a pump having vanes open on both sides, with a suction ilet on each side of the wheel. This type has the advantage of being rfectly in balance as regards axial thrust on the shaft, while the single let type necessitates provision being made for balancing any such thrust. n the other hand, the single inlet pump is particularly convenient for tuations where a vertical shaft is permissible, and, as denoted in the gure, lends itself to a very compact and simple type of construction.

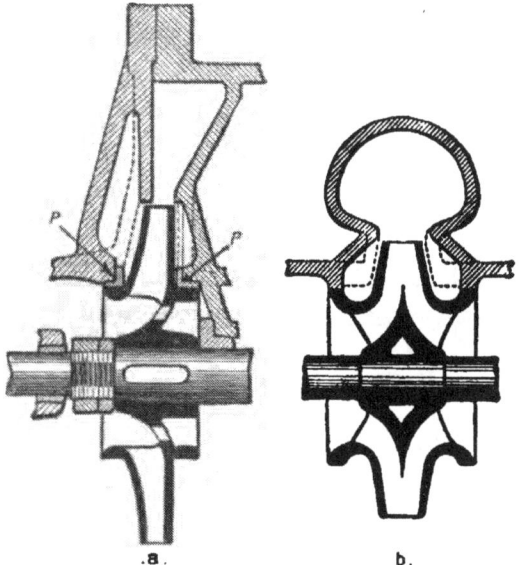

.a.   b.

FIG. 306.—Single and Double Inlet Encased Impellers with Vortex Chamber and Volute.

The open vane pump is, however, subject to considerable and incalculable)ss by slip or leakage of water between the pump casing and impeller lades, and while this may be reduced by making the clearance at these ooints as small as possible, the presence of gritty matter in suspension in he water causes rapid wear, and the slip may then become excessive. 'urthermore, the disc friction accompanying the rotation of such open anes over the surface of the casing is considerably greater than when he vanes are enclosed at the sides by discs or shroudings, so that on very count the latter encased type of pump is preferable. Such a pump, 'ig. 306 a and b, may have either single or double suction inlet, and will thus require balancing for end thrust or not, just as does the open vaned pump. The possibilities in this direction are somewhat greater than with the latter type.

It is very suitable for heads between 30 and 80 feet, but must, for high efficiency under high heads, be fitted with guide vanes outside the impeller ring. As thus constructed, efficiencies up to about 80 per cent. may be obtained. Free circulation of water behind the impeller and into the suction space is usually prevented by the introduction of a brass packing ring at P (Fig. 306).

Where the working head exceeds about 100 feet, the single impeller

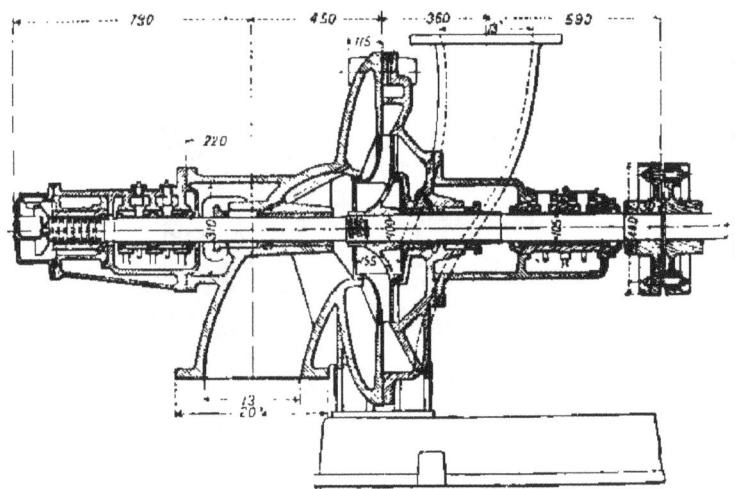

FIG. 307.—Worthington Single Impeller High Lift Pump.

pump as usually constructed falls off rapidly in efficiency owing to the necessary high speed of rotation and the consequent excessive frictional and eddy losses. It may be compounded, and so made suitable for such work by mounting a number of impellers in series in separate chambers and on the same shaft, each taking the discharge from its predecessor and raising it through a fraction of the whole head depending on the number of impellers used. For this to be done with fair efficiency, it is essential that as far as possible the kinetic energy of discharge from each wheel be converted into pressure energy before entering the next chamber, and this renders the use of efficient volute chambers or of guide or diffuser vanes on the discharge side essential.

Where the water to be pumped contains grit, as is usual for example in
olliery workings, the leading edges of such vanes are apt to be badly worn
r bent from their original position, in which case the efficiency of working
s seriously affected. To obviate this difficulty a design of single impeller
iigh-lift pump, in which these multiple vanes are absent, has been evolved

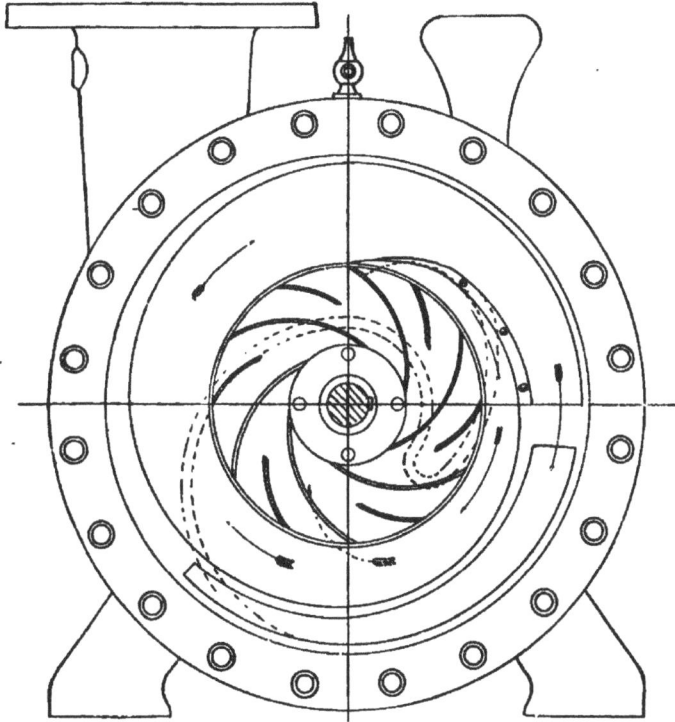

FIG. 308.—Worthington Single Impeller High Lift Pump.

>y the Worthington Pump Co., and is illustrated in Figs. 307 and
}08. In this pump, designed to deliver 2,500 gallons per minute at
l,170 revolutions per minute against 300 feet head, the combined efficiency
>f pump and motor attained, on test, a maximum value of 73·8 per cent.
;he corresponding pump efficiency being approximately 80 per cent.[1]

[1] *Engineering*, Feb. 5, 1909. By courtesy of Messrs. The Worthington Pump Co.

Some modern types of construction of the compound high-lift pump are indicated in Figs. 309 to 317.

Fig. 309 shows the construction adopted by Messrs. Sulzer Bros. Here the impellers are mounted in pairs back to back, the flow through these

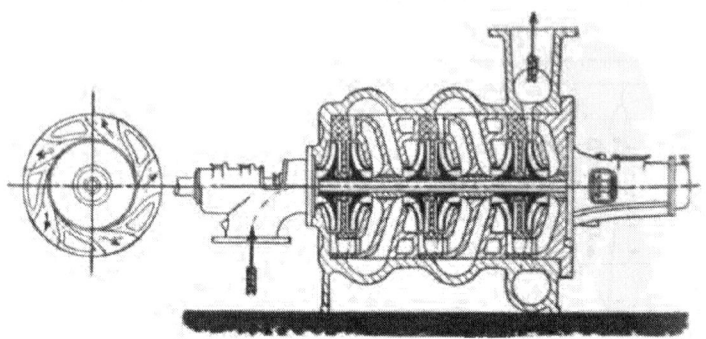

FIG. 309.—Sulzer Sextuple Compound High Lift Pump.

being in opposite directions. By this construction each pair of impellers is in balance as regards end thrust. The pump is fitted with diverging guide passages, curved vanes, and a vortex chamber, while Fig. 310 shows the type of water-sealed stuffing box and water-cooled bearing adopted by the makers.

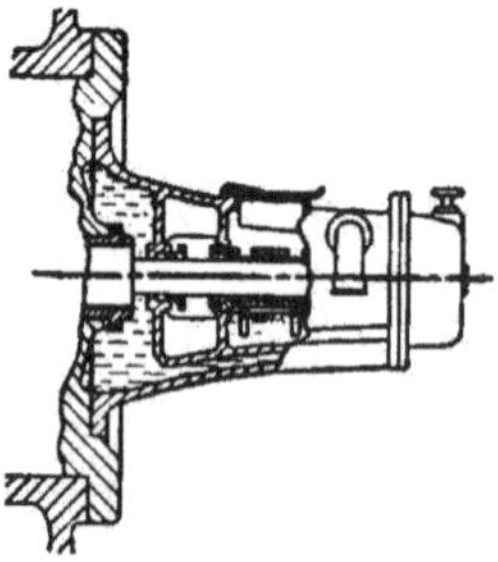

The Buffalo high-lift pump (Figs. 311 and 312) is built on somewhat similar lines also having impellers mounted in pairs. while in the Mather-Reynolds pump (Fig. 313), constructed with a double inlet to each propeller, the guide passages and curved vanes are retained, while the vortex chamber is omitted. The construction is thus simplified without seriously affecting the efficiency, a quadruple pump of this type giving efficiencies up to 75 per cent. when delivering 1,000 gallons per minute against 320 feet head.

FIG. 310.—Water-Sealed Stuffing-box for Sulzer Pump.

The foregoing arrangement of impeller, however, necessitates complicated and tortuous connecting passages, and a simpler construction is obtained where, as shown in Figs. 314 to 318, impellers, each having a single inlet, are used. This system has the further advantage that any odd number of impellers may be used. On the other hand, with the single

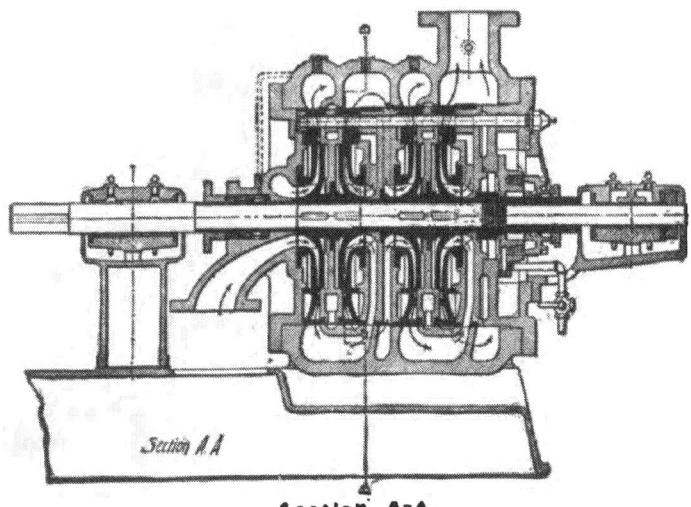

Section A-A.

FIG. 311.—Sectional Elevation of Quadruple Compound Buffalo High-Lift Pump.

Section B-B.

FIG. 312.—Sectional End Elevation of Buffalo High-Lift Pump.

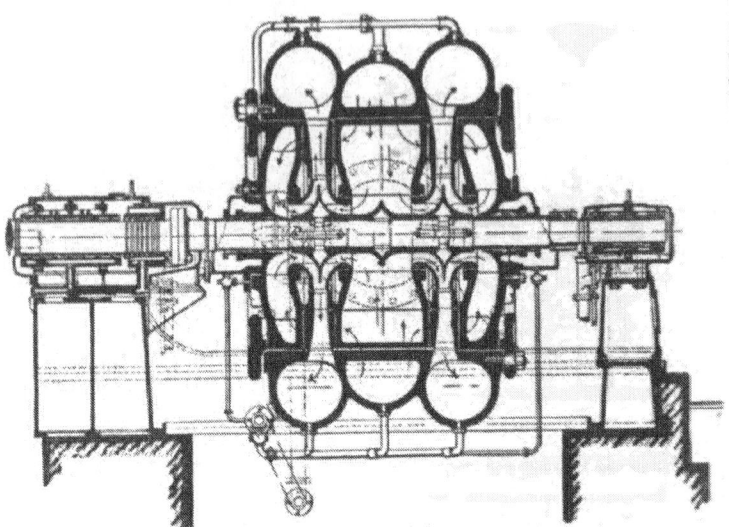

FIG. 313.—Mather-Reynolds High-Lift Pump with Double Inlet.

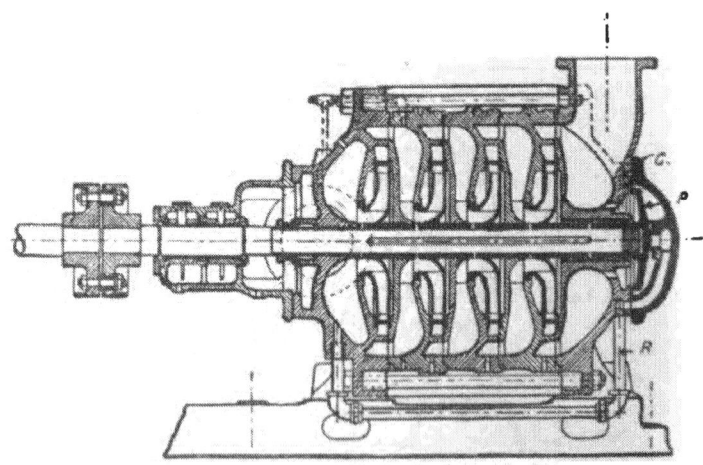

FIG. 314.—Mather-Reynolds Quadruple Turbine Pump.

inlet, end thrust becomes serious and special devices must be adopted to overcome this difficulty. These will be considered in detail in Art. 183. With any of these types of pump, efficiencies of between 72 and 80 per

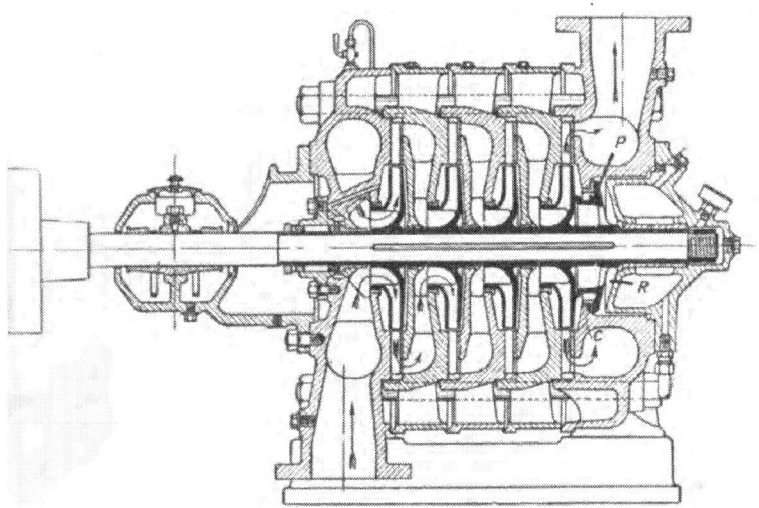

FIG. 315.—Holden and Brooke Quadruple High-Lift Pump.

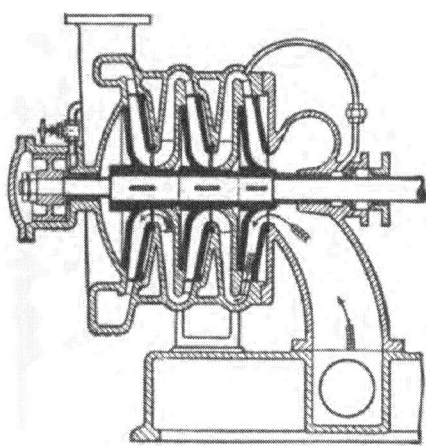

FIG. 316.—Rateau Triple High-Lift Pump.

cent. may be obtained, while they are all capable of being constructed so as to deal with heads up to about 600 feet, the head in each chamber usually varying from 60 to 100 feet.

T T 2

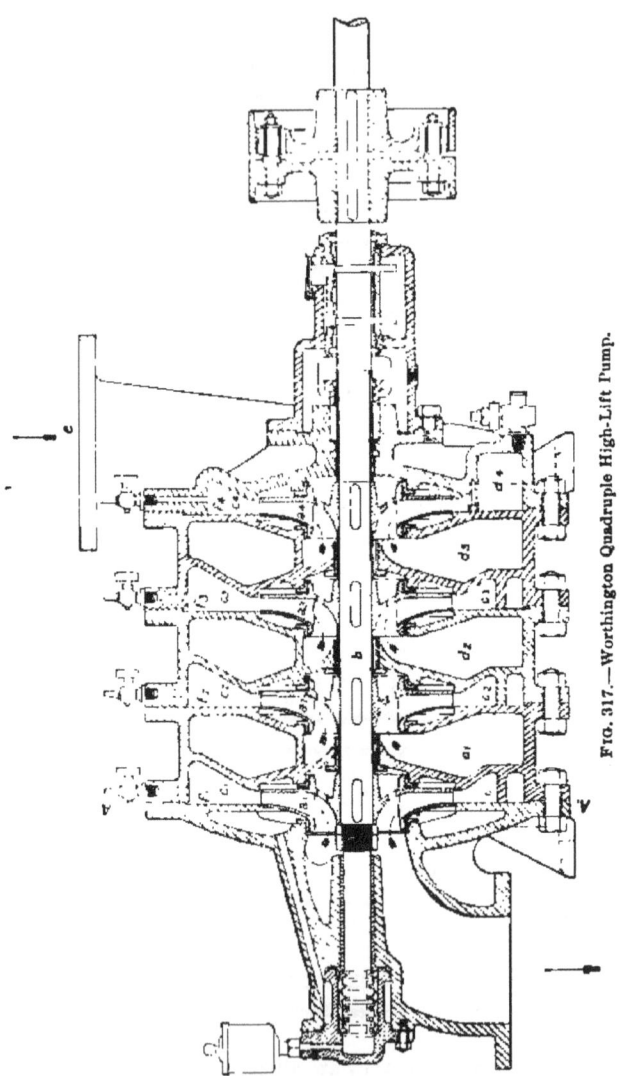

FIG. 317.—Worthington Quadruple High-Lift Pump.

The maximum speed of the impeller is limited by the fact that at extreme speeds cavitation is set up, and the pump will not fill itself.

Leakage from stage to stage of a high-lift pump is prevented by brass packing rings surrounding the shaft between each pair of chambers, while to prevent corrosion of the pump spindle this is usually protected by a brass sleeve.

Admission of air on the suction side of such a pump is to be guarded against with the greatest care, as being productive of inefficiency and of considerable shock in the pump casing and delivery pipes.

ART. 174.—SUCTION AND DELIVERY PIPES.

The area of the suction pipe is commonly made equal to the discharge area of the impeller. A foot valve and strainer should always be fitted to this pipe, the area through the valve being not less than half that of the pipe. No part of the pipe should be above the pump inlet in order that the formation of air pockets may be prevented, while when the pump is circulating water through a pipe line forming a syphon, an ejector or air pump should be fitted to the highest point of the pipe, for priming the pump and for the removal of any accumulation of air.

The suction lift should be as small and as direct as practicable, and should never, if possible, exceed 20 feet. Where hot liquids are to be handled, the vapour pressure reduces the possible suction lift, the effect of temperature in the case of water being as follows :—

Temperature of water, degrees Fahr. .	60°	100°	140°	180°	212°
Maximum theoretical suction lift . .	33·0 ft.	31·4 ft.	26·7 ft.	16·7 ft.	0

Practically the limit is reached much before this because of the liberation of air when the pressure is reduced nearly to that corresponding to the saturation temperature, and because of the increasing importance of slight air leakage at joints, and at the stuffing boxes of the pump spindle at these low pressures. In no case should the suction lift exceed two-thirds of the values given above, while where hot liquids are to be lifted it is advisable to place the pump below the supply level.

The above remarks may be taken as applying with equal force to the reciprocating pump.

When parallel, the area of the discharge pipe should, in general, be not less than that of the suction pipe, and may with advantage be increased to three times this area where the working head is high. It is, moreover, advantageous to have a main discharge pipe of greater area than the outlet from the collecting chamber of the pump, the connecting pipe having a gradual divergence.   By this means a partial conversion of kinetic into pressure energy is obtained in this connecting pipe.

With heads exceeding about 100 feet, a non-return valve should be fitted on the delivery side, while when delivering into a rising main of great length an air vessel should be fitted on the same side of the pump to avoid shock on starting and stopping.

This is specially advisable with a belt-driven pump, where the vibration of the belting may produce variations of considerable magnitude in the angular velocity of the shaft under normal working conditions.   In a belt-driven quadruple high-lift pump under the author's observation, making 1,400 revolutions per minute and discharging through 600 feet of 4-inch piping, against a total head of 143 feet, the pressure in the last collecting chamber varied from 122 to 164 feet.   One successful combination of non-return valve and air vessel is illustrated in Fig. 318.

Self-charging Device.—Since a centrifugal pump will not begin to lift unless first charged with water, if fixed above supply water level provision must be made for priming or flooding the pump casing from an auxiliary pressure supply or for withdrawing the air by means of an ejector or auxiliary air pump.

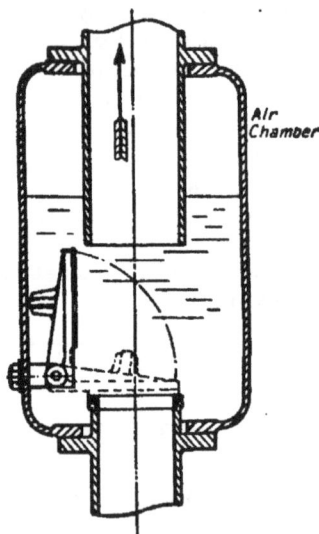

Air Chamber

FIG. 318.—Delivery Valve with Air Vessel for High-Lift Centrifugal Pump.

ART. 175.—GENERAL THEORY OF CENTRIFUGAL PUMP.

In the following discussion of the theoretical considerations governing the design of the centrifugal pump, the symbols used are the same and have the same meaning as in the case of the turbine (p. 532).

Thus the suffix (1) refers to the water just before entering the impeller.

(2) refers to the water just after entering the impeller.

(3) refers to the water discharging from the impeller.

while u_2 = peripheral velocity of impeller at entrance.

$\quad u_3$ = peripheral velocity of impeller at exit.

$\quad \beta$ = vane angle at entrance.

$\quad \gamma$ = vane angle at exit. (Fig. 319.)

In this discussion it is assumed throughout that the pump runs full at all speeds within its working limits, the theory ceasing to apply if any action of the nature of cavitation take place. The further assumptions are made that each particle of water, immediately before entering the wheel, is moving radially, and that its initial velocity of whirl w_2 is zero, and also that all particles of water on leaving the impellers have the same velocity and are moving in directions which make the same angle with the tangent to the periphery at the point of discharge.

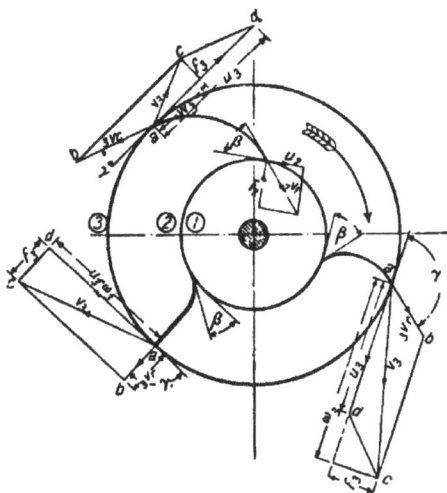

FIG. 319.—Velocity Diagram for Vanes of a Centrifugal Pump.

Form of Vanes.—Just as in the case of the turbine all shock at entrance to the vanes is to be avoided, and, assuming radial flow at the entrance, this gives as a necessary condition for entry without shock. (Fig. 319.)

$$f_2 = u_2 \tan \beta.$$

The relative velocity of water and vane at entrance is then given by

$$_2v_r = f_2 \operatorname{cosec} \beta = \sqrt{f_2^2 + u_2^2}.$$

If the angle β does not satisfy the above condition, there will be loss by shock at entry. The magnitude of this may be approximately calculated, for the relative velocity of water and vane in the direction of rotation before entering the wheel is u_2, while the relative velocity in the same direction after entry is $f_2 \cot \beta$. The loss of head due to this change in relative velocity is then approximately equal to

$$\frac{(u_2 - f_2 \cot \beta)^2}{2\,g} \text{ feet.} \quad \text{(p. 83).}$$

The greatest source of loss in the pump, as compared with the turbine is, however, due to rejection of kinetic energy in the discharge from the impeller, for while this is comparatively unimportant in the turbine, it becomes of the greatest importance in the pump, since it is when leaving the wheel that the water is moving with its maximum velocity. At the best, only a portion of this energy of discharge can be recovered by means of a vortex chamber or guide vanes, and it is therefore advisable to reduce the velocity of discharge to as low a point as is compatible with efficiency in other directions. This may be done by curving the vanes backward at their tips, so as to make the discharge angle γ (Fig. 320) less than 90°. The relative velocity of water and vane at discharge then has a tangential component in the opposite direction to that of the wheel's rotation. this component increasing as γ is reduced, the result being that the absolute velocity of discharge is reduced. Thus, for example, in Fig. 320 the triangles of velocity are drawn for the cases in which the vanes are respectively radial, curved forward at exit, and curved backward at exit. In each

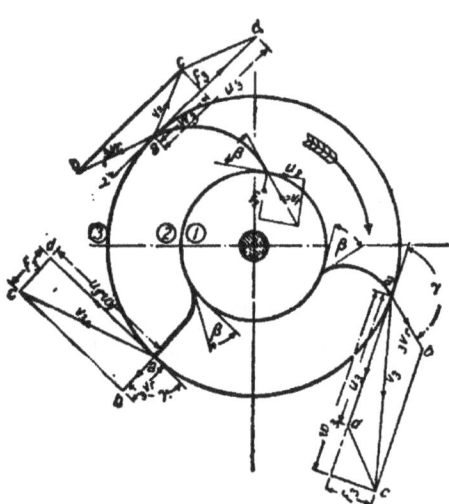

FIG. 320.—Velocity Diagram for Vanes of a Centrifugal Pump.

case the same value has been adopted for f_3, the velocity of flow at exit, and for u_3 the peripheral velocity of the vanes, while $\overline{a\ c}$ represents the direction and the absolute velocity of discharge.

A comparison of the diagrams will indicate how this diminishes as the angle of backward inclination of the vane tips increases.

As will be seen later, however, the necessary peripheral speed of the wheel for pumping against a given head increases as γ is reduced, and this causes the frictional losses, which vary approximately as u^3, to increase.

This backward curvature of the vanes offers a further advantage in that it gives passages of more uniform cross section. This reduces the diver-

;ence, and thus the tendency to instability of flow, which is one of the mportant factors in reducing the efficiency of the pump as compared with he inward flow turbine. Since the relative velocity of·flow increases ·utwards, the passages would in all probability be most effective if designed ·o as to be convergent outwards to suit this increased relative velocity. This view is borne out by the results of a series of experiments carried out)y Mr. J. A. Smith, of Melbourne,[1] in which instantaneous photographs)f the flow through the impeller of a pump model while freely discharging .nto the atmosphere, indicate that at a certain velocity the water tends to :eave the leading face of a passage as indicated in Fig. 321, which is reproduced from his paper. If discharging under pressure it is evident that the empty space shown in these passages would be occupied by dead water and would be the source of considerable loss in eddy production. The successive curves 1, 2, and 3, mark the boundaries of the stream with increasing velocities.

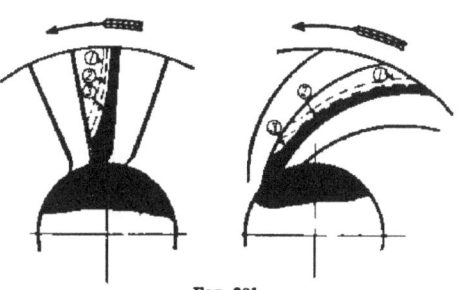

Fig. 321.

In practice, the purpose for which the pump is designed. determines the value of γ, which may have any value from 15° to 90°, so that in general the water on leaving the vanes has a comparatively high absolute velocity.

As is apparent from Fig. 320, at discharge,

$$f_3 \cot \gamma = u_3 - w_3,$$

while the relative velocity of water and vane is given by

$$_3 v_r = f_3 \operatorname{cosec} \gamma.$$

Work done on Pump.—The turning moment on the shaft, equivalent to the change per second in the angular momentum of the water passing through the wheel

$$= \frac{W Q}{g} \left\{ w_3 r_3 - w_2 r_2 \right\} \text{ foot lbs.}$$

∴ Work done on water per second $= \dfrac{W Q}{g} \left\{ w_3 r_3 - w_2 r_2 \right\} \omega$ foot lbs.

[1] See *Engineering*, December 5, 1902. This view is also borne out by the results of experiments by C. B. Stewart, Bulletin of University of Wisconsin. No. 173, 1907.

And since the initial tangential velocity of the water, before coming under the influence of the impeller is zero, this becomes

$$U = \frac{W\,Q}{g} \cdot w_3\, r_3\, \omega = \frac{W\,Q}{g}\, w_3\, u_3 \text{ foot lbs. per second.}$$

$$= \frac{w_3\, u_3}{g} \text{ foot lbs. per lb.}$$

This is quite independent of all losses in eddy formation, shock, and friction in the wheel passages, and if to it be added the work done against the friction of the impeller on the surrounding water, against the mechanical friction of the bearings, and that absorbed in pumping water which may leak from the discharge side to the suction side of the impeller,

the result will give the power required to drive the pump. The work done against these resistances may be experimentally obtained by driving the pump at the required speed of rotation with the discharge valve closed so as not to deliver any water, and by noting the power then absorbed. This will, however, be somewhat high owing to the fact that leakage round the impeller will be greater than under normal running conditions, and also that power will be absorbed, owing to the viscosity of the water, in maintaining a rotation of the water in the

FIG. 322.

eye of the pump and in the collecting chamber surrounding the wheel. Also, in all probability, in maintaining such a series of currents as indicated in Fig. 322.

Energy obtained from Pump.—The useful work done by a pump is the product of the weight of water handled and the height through which this would be lifted provided there were no losses of head in suction and delivery pipes.

If H is the difference of level between suction and discharge reservoirs, H_f the friction loss in suction and delivery pipes, and $\bar{v}$ the velocity of flow along the discharge pipe, the energy obtained from the pump per lb. of water $= H + H_f + \dfrac{\bar{v}^2}{2\,g}$ foot lbs.

If pressure gauge or manometer readings be taken on the suction and delivery pipes at the same level immediately before and behind the pump he suction reading will be $- \left(H_s + H_{f_s} + \dfrac{\bar{v}_s{}^2}{2\,g} \right)$ feet, and the delivery

eading will be $H_d + H_{fd} - \dfrac{\bar{v}_d{}^2}{2\,g} + \dfrac{\bar{v}^2}{2\,g}$ if the section of the pipe is

ncreased after passing the manometer, and will be $H_d + H_{fd}$ if it emains of the same cross section. In either case if $\bar{v}_s = \bar{v}_d$ the " mano-

netric head " will be given by $H + H_f + \dfrac{\bar{v}^2}{2\,g}$ foot $= H_m$.

It is worth noting that this is greater than the head H' obtained by idding the dead lift H and the friction head H_f. In the average pump $\bar{v}$ nay range up to 8 feet per second, so that in a low lift pump the term $\dfrac{\bar{v}^2}{2\,g}$ should not be neglected.

Efficiency of Pump.—Manometric Efficiency.—Neglecting losses due to lisc friction, mechanical friction, and slip, we have seen that the work lone on the water per lb. is $\dfrac{w_3\,u_3}{g}$ foot lbs. The ratio of the energy H_m

obtained from the pump per lb. of water, to $\dfrac{w_3\,u_3}{g}$ is sometimes termed the hydraulic efficiency, but more correctly the **theoretical manometric efficiency** η'.

$$\therefore \; \eta' = \frac{g\,H_m}{u_3\,w_3} = \frac{g\,H_m}{u_3\,(u_3 - f_3\,\cot \gamma)}$$

Hydraulic Efficiency.—The work actually done on the water per lb. is given by $\dfrac{u_3\,w_3}{g} + \dfrac{L_h}{W\,Q}$, where L_h represents the total loss of energy in foot lbs. expended in overcoming hydraulic resistances in the pump itself, and the ratio

$$\eta_h = \frac{H_m}{\dfrac{w_3\,u_3}{g} + L_h}$$

is more correctly termed the hydraulic efficiency.

Actual Working Efficiency.—The actual working efficiency is the ratio of the energy obtained from the pump to the work done on the pump shaft per lb. of water. If N be the number of revolutions per second ; Q the volume per second in cubic feet; and T the turning moment on the shaft in feet and lbs.,

$$\eta = \frac{Q\,W\,H_m}{2\,\pi\,N\,T} = \frac{H_m}{\dfrac{w_3\,u_3}{g} + \dfrac{L_h + L_m}{W\,Q}}$$

where L_h and L_m are respectively the hydraulic and mechanical losses in the pump. From this result it appears that as the discharge Q is diminished the actual efficiency diminishes more rapidly than the mano metric efficiency $\dfrac{g\,H_m}{u_3\,u_3}$ which indeed has a value usually about ·5 when the discharge Q and therefore the actual efficiency is zero. Under normal conditions as to head, speed, and discharge, the calculated manometric efficiency is, however, not widely different from the true working efficiency, the ratio of the latter to the former ranging from about ·85 in a pump with recurved vanes and an inefficient collecting chamber, to about 1·0 in a pump with radial vanes and an efficient vortex chamber or diffuser, so that a knowledge of the probable manometric efficiency guided by a knowledge of the performance of somewhat similar pumps, enables the working efficiency to be predetermined with a fair degree of accuracy.

Change of Pressure in Passing through Pump.—As will be clear from what has already been said, the increase in pressure during the passage of the water through the pump must be such as to balance the statical head together with the head necessary to overcome frictional resistances and that equivalent to the kinetic energy of flow along the suction or discharge pipes.

Where the water, on leaving the wheel, is allowed to make the best of its way to the discharge pipe without the provision of a volute, vortex chamber, or guide vanes, the K.E. of discharge is entirely dissipated in shock, and the full pressure change takes place in the impeller. Where provision is made for gradually reducing the velocity of the discharging water by one of these devices, a further increase in pressure takes place after leaving the impeller but before leaving the pump casing, while if a diverging discharge pipe is used, as is often the case a further increase in pressure takes place in this pipe.

The magnitude of these changes in pressure will now be considered.

(a) **Change of Pressure in Passing through the Wheel.**—The absolute velocity of a particle of water at any point in the wheel may be resolved into two components, one of whirl with the wheel with a velocity ωr, and the second of flow parallel to the vanes with relative velocity r_r. This latter velocity is evidently that which the water would have if the same volume were passing with the wheel at rest. The total difference of pressure at any two different radii is thus compounded of the differences due to—

(1) Rotation in a forced vortex with angular velocity ω.
(2) Outward flow parallel to the vanes with velocity v_r.

In the forced vortex we have, considering the points (2) and (3):—

$$\frac{p'_2}{W} - \frac{\omega^2 r_2^2}{2\,g} = \frac{p'_3}{W} - \frac{\omega^2 r_3^2}{2\,g}$$

$$\therefore \quad \frac{p'_3 - p'_2}{W} = \frac{\omega^2 (r_3^2 - r_2^2)}{2\,g} = \frac{u_3^2 - u_2^2}{2\,g}; \qquad (1)$$

while due to relative outward flow we have—

$$\frac{p''_2}{W} + \frac{v_r^2}{2\,g} = \frac{p''_3}{W} + \frac{v_r^2}{2\,g}$$

$$\therefore \quad \frac{p''_3 - p''_2}{W} = \frac{v_r^2 - v_r^2}{2\,g}$$

$$= \frac{f_2^2 + u_2^2 - f_3^2 \operatorname{cosec}^2 \gamma}{2\,g}. \qquad (2)$$

Summing these and writing $p_3 = p'_3 + p''_3$, etc., we get the total difference in pressure between the inlet and discharge edges of the vanes, i.e.,

$$\frac{p_3 - p_2}{W} = \frac{u_3^2 + f_2^2 - f_3^2 \operatorname{cosec}^2 \gamma}{2\,g}. \qquad (3)$$

EXAMPLE.

A pump, 1 foot diameter at inlet, 2 feet diameter at outlet, 6 inches broad at inlet, 4 inches at outlet, discharges 5·0 cubic feet per second, when making 200 revolutions per minute. Determine the rise in pressure in passing through the wheel, and hence, neglecting all frictional losses, the head pumped against. Assume $\gamma = 25°$ and neglect the effect of the vane thickness.

Here $Q = f_2 \times \pi \times \frac{1}{2} = f_3 \times 2\,\pi \times \frac{1}{3}$

$$\therefore \quad f_2 = \frac{10}{\pi} = 3·18 \text{ f.s.} \qquad f_3 = \frac{15}{2\,\pi} = 2·386 \text{ f.s.}$$

Again, $u_3 = \dfrac{2\,\pi \times 1 \times 200}{60} = 20·96 \text{ f.s.}$

and $\operatorname{cosec}^2 \gamma = 5·6$

$$\therefore \quad \frac{p_2 - p_3}{W} = \frac{(20·96)^2 + (3·18)^2 - (2·386)^2 \times 5·6}{64·4} = 6·48 \text{ feet.}$$

∴ rise in pressure, $p_2 - p_3 = 6·48 \times 62·4 = 404$ lbs. per square foot. Head pumped against $= 6·48$ feet.

(b) **Change of Pressure in Volute Chamber.**—Writing the gain of head in this chamber as $\dfrac{k}{2\,g} (w_3^2 + f_3^2)$ feet $= \dfrac{k\,v_3^2}{2\,g}$ feet we have

$$\left. \begin{array}{c} \text{Total gain of pressure} \\ \text{in pump} \end{array} \right\} = \frac{1}{2\,g} \left\{ k\,v_3^2 + u_3^2 + f_2^2 - f_3^2 \operatorname{cosec}^2 \gamma \right\} \text{ ft.} \quad (4)$$

Experiments show that K has a value often as low as ·10. With a well-designed volute chamber, however, experiments show that K may be increased to about ·60 (see p. 633, footnote).

(c) **Volute provided with Divergent Discharge Pipe.**—If the discharge from the volute take place into a pipe of gradually increasing sectional area, the gain of pressure in this pipe may be readily estimated in terms of the velocities of flow from the data of Art. 34, p. 84, when the angle of divergence of the sides is known.

(d) **Change of Pressure in Vortex Chamber.**—Here the water on leaving the vanes forms approximately a free vortex; the pressure increases as the velocity diminishes towards the outside of the chamber, and part of the kinetic energy of discharge may thus be recovered as pressure energy.

If the suffix (3') now refers to the outside of the vortex, we have, neglecting changes of level between (3) and (3'):—

$$\frac{p_{3'} - p_3}{W} = \frac{v_3^2 - v_3'^2}{2\,g},\qquad (5)$$

giving the gain of pressure head in the chamber on the assumption of true vortex motion, with no eddy losses.

But if r_3 and r'_3 are the inner and outer radii of the chamber we have $\dfrac{v_3'}{v_3} = \dfrac{r_3}{r_{3'}} = c$ (say)

$$\therefore \quad \frac{p_{3'} - p_3}{W} = \frac{v_3^2\,(1 - c^2)}{2\,g} = \frac{(w_3^2 + f_3^2)\,(1 - c^2)}{2\,g}\ \text{feet of water.}\qquad (6)$$

The theoretical efficiency of the vortex chamber may be taken as $(1-c^2)$, the following table indicating how this varies with an increase in the radius of the chamber.

Value of $\frac{r_{3'}}{r_3}$	1·00	1·25	1·50	1·75	2·00	2·50	3·00
Theoretical efficiency of vortex chamber	0	·36	·556	·673	·750	·840	·889

Experiments by Stanton[1] on a pump having a vortex chamber 18 inches in diameter, showed a chamber efficiency of about 39 per cent. with either a 7-inch or an 11-inch wheel.

The actual gain in pressure is thus considerably less than that obtained in the ideal case, and is given more nearly by—

$$\frac{K\,(w_3^2 + f_3^2)\,(1 - c^2)}{2\,g}\ \text{feet}\qquad (7)$$

where K varies probably from ·4 to ·55, depending on the form of the

[1] Proc. Inst. Mech., Eng., 1903 (p. 715).

vortex chamber. On adding this gain of head to that previously obtained in passing through the wheel we have :—

$$\frac{p_{3'} - p_3 + p_3 - p_2}{W} = \frac{K\,(w_3{}^2 + f_3{}^2)\,(1 - c^2)}{2\,g}$$
$$+ \frac{u_3{}^2 + f_2{}^2 - f_3{}^2\,\text{cosec }^2\gamma}{2\,g} \qquad (8)$$

= total gain of pressure head in pump.

(*e*) **Change of Pressure in Guide Vanes.**—In Stanton's experiments on a pump fitted with guide vanes and radial impeller vanes, the guide efficiency varied from 59 per cent. to 70 per cent., while with back curved vanes this efficiency varied from 47 per cent. to 52 per cent. With a third wheel of 12 inches diameter having curved vanes and working under a head of 65 feet, the guide passages had an efficiency of 75 per cent.

In each case, with curved vanes, the vane angle at inlet was 15°, at outlet 30°, guide angle $a = 3°$. Vane thickness ·05 inch. Four guides were fitted, and the number of impeller vanes was

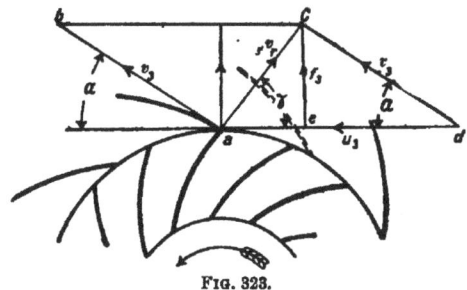

FIG. 323.

varied from twelve to twenty-two without any appreciable effect on the efficiency.

An examination of Fig. 323 shows that the correct value of *a* is given by—

$$\tan a = \frac{c\,e}{e\,d} = \frac{c\,e}{a\,d - a\,e}$$
$$= \frac{f_3}{u_3 - f_3 \cot \gamma}.$$

Since the guide passages are rectangular in section the guide vanes should diverge at an angle of about 11° (p. 87) for maximum efficiency. Under these conditions, with *a* designed so as to prevent shock at entry to the guide vanes as far as possible, about 75 per cent. of the kinetic energy of discharge is converted into pressure energy.

The total gain of pressure head in the pump is then equal to:

$$\frac{k\,v_3{}^2 + u_3{}^2 + f_2{}^2 - f_3{}^2\,\text{cosec }^2\gamma}{2\,g}\ \text{feet}$$

where k has a maximum value of about ·75.

The general effect of the curvature, length, and dimensions of entrance of the guide passages, and of the curvature and angle of delivery of the return passages to the eye of the impeller, are shown in the curves of Fig. 324.[1]

Head and efficiency curves are given for four different designs of guide and return passages, the same impeller of standard shrouded type being

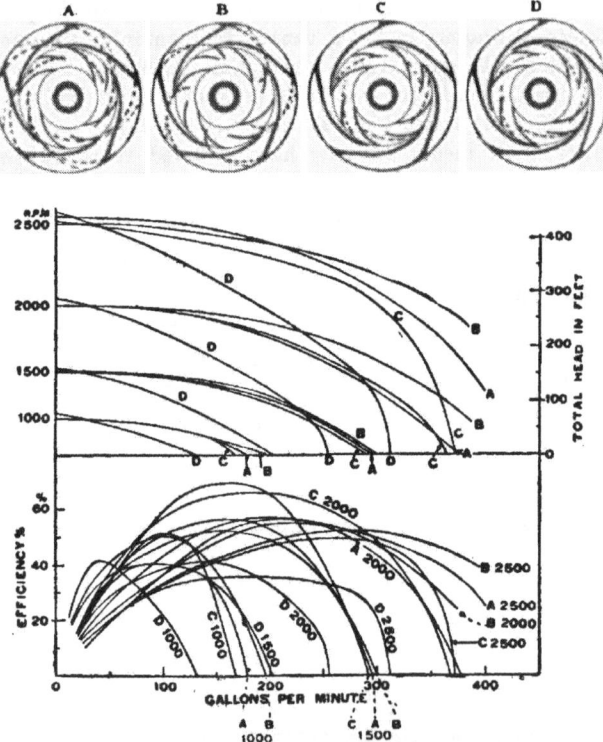

FIG. 324.—Effect of Guide and Return Passages of Different Form.

used in each case. Design A has short guide vanes with wide opening on the radial line. The return passages are of similar curvature. Design B has similar guide vanes, but the return passages have a short curve becoming radial near the eye of the impeller. Design C also has similar guide vanes and the return passages are similar in curvature

[1] Proc. Inst. Mech. Eng., 1912, No. 1, p. 18.

to those of A, but are not extended to the outer periphery of the return chamber. In design D the opening on the radial line is only one-half that in A, B, and C. The return passages are similar to those in C. The head and efficiency curves are given for speeds of 1,000, 1,500 and 2,000 revolutions per minute, and show that design D is much inferior due to throttling at the throat of the guide passages. B is superior to both A and C in generation of head, and superior .to A in efficiency especially at low speeds, but is inferior to C in efficiency except at high speeds. At these speeds great loss of energy results on the eddying which takes place in the collecting chamber of C which is prevented by the guides forming the continuous passages of design B. Design B is most usually adopted as best meeting average conditions. Design C, which approaches more nearly to the conditions of a single chamber pump, gives considerably higher maximum efficiency at speeds of 1,500 and 2,000 revs., due to less power being absorbed by friction against the walls of the guide passages, and also to tangential motion imparted to the water as it enters the subsequent impeller by the tangential curvature of the return passages.

Art. 176.—Manometric Efficiency under different Working Conditions.

If there were no losses in the pump other than those already considered, the expressions just obtained would give the manometric head H_m. Actually, frictional losses and leakage in the impeller itself along with losses due to shock at entrance to impeller vanes and to guide vanes at any other than normal speed and discharge, make the true manometric head less than that calculated. The ratio of the calculated manometric head —neglecting these losses—to the head $\dfrac{w_3\,u_3}{g}$ is termed the theoretical manometric efficiency and will be denoted by η'.

If the sum of the dead lift, H, and of the friction loss H_f in suction and delivery pipes be called H', the total gain of pressure in the pump must be $H' + \dfrac{\bar{v}^2}{2\,g}$ feet, where $\bar{v}$ is the velocity of flow along the discharge pipe. Thus, neglecting hydraulic losses in the impeller:—

$$\frac{u_3{}^2 + f_2{}^2 - f_3{}^2 \operatorname{cosec}{}^2\gamma}{2\,g} + \left\{ \begin{array}{l}\text{increase in pressure}\\ \text{after leaving impeller}\end{array} \right\} = H' + \frac{\bar{v}^2}{2\,g}\ \text{feet} \quad (9)$$

and we have :—

$$\eta' = \frac{u_3{}^2 + f_2{}^2 - f_3{}^2 \operatorname{cosec}{}^2\gamma + k\,v_3{}^2}{2\,w_3\,u_3}$$

$$= \frac{u_3{}^2 + f_2{}^2 - f_3{}^2 \cosec {}^2\gamma + k\, v_3{}^2}{2\, u_3\, (u_3 - f_3 \cot \gamma)} \qquad (10)$$

where k has the value indicated in the preceding article for the type of pump under consideration.

The various cases will now be considered in greater detail, and as, except for very low lifts, $\dfrac{\bar{v}^2}{2\,g}$ is small in comparison with H' while $\bar{v}$ is approximately equal to f_3, the foregoing expressions will be simplified by writing

$$\frac{u_3{}^2 - f_3{}^2 \cosec {}^2\gamma}{2\,g} + \left\{ \begin{array}{c} \text{increase of pressure} \\ \text{after leaving impeller} \end{array} \right\} = H' \text{ feet} \qquad (11)$$

and
$$\eta' = \frac{u_3{}^2 - f_3{}^2 \cosec {}^2\gamma + k\, v_3{}^2}{2\, u_3\, (u_3 - f_3 \cot \gamma)} \qquad (12)$$

(1) **Pump without Special Provision for Utilizing the Kinetic Energy of Discharge from the Impeller.**—Here $k = o$, and if the pump be working so that water enters without shock,

$$\eta' = \tfrac{1}{2} \cdot \frac{u_3{}^2 - f_3{}^2 \cosec {}^2\gamma}{u_3\, (u_3 - f_3 \cot \gamma)} \qquad (13)$$

while
$$2\, g\, H' = u_3{}^2 - f_3{}^2 \cosec {}^2\gamma \qquad (14)$$

so that
$$u_3 = \sqrt{2\, g\, H' + f_3{}^2 \cosec {}^2\gamma} \qquad (15)$$

If $\gamma = 90°$, i.e. with radial vane tips.

$$\eta' = \cdot 5 - \frac{f_3{}^2}{2\, u_3{}^2}$$

a value which is always less than 50 per cent.

If γ is very small $\cosec \gamma = \cot \gamma$ (approx.) and we have

$$\eta' = \frac{u_3 + f_3 \cot \gamma}{2\, u_3} \text{ (approx.).}$$

Since $f_3 \cot \gamma$ or $f_3 \cosec \gamma$ approximates more nearly to u_3 as γ diminishes, the theoretical efficiency in this case approximates to a value unity.

Usually f_3 is taken as some definite fraction, commonly from $\tfrac{1}{4}$ to $\tfrac{1}{5}$ of $\sqrt{2\, g\, H'}$, and the following table shows how η' varies with γ for these values of f_3.

γ	90°		60°		30°		15°	
	$f_3 = \tfrac{1}{4}\sqrt{2\,g\,H'}$	$f_3 = \tfrac{1}{5}\sqrt{2\,g\,H'}$	$\tfrac{1}{4}\sqrt{2\,g\,H'}$	$\tfrac{1}{5}\sqrt{2\,g\,H'}$	$\tfrac{1}{4}\sqrt{2\,g\,H'}$	$\tfrac{1}{5}\sqrt{2\,g\,H'}$	$\tfrac{1}{4}\sqrt{2\,g\,H'}$	$\tfrac{1}{5}\sqrt{2\,g\,H'}$
$u_3 \div \sqrt{2\,g\,H'}$	1·03	1·008	1·04	1·01	1·12	1·03	1·39	1·11
η' . . .	·47	·49	·53	·53	·65	·61	·79	·70

Effect of a Variation in γ.—Equation (12) indicates that as γ is diminished the efficiency is increased, and this is in general borne out by the results of experiment. As previously pointed out, however, this gain in theoretical efficiency is to a certain extent counterbalanced by the fact that since a diminution in γ necessitates an increased speed of rotation for pumping against a given head, this involves increased frictional losses.

Thus experiments by Parsons[1] on two 14 inch impellers, one having $\gamma = 90°$ and the other $\gamma = 25°$ (approx.), showed that the second was about 1·16 times as efficient as the first. In each case $f_3 = \frac{1}{2} \sqrt{2 g H'}$, and an examination of the table on p. 658 shows that the theoretical manometric efficiencies in the two cases would be approximately ·49 and ·63, the ratio of these being 1·28.

Again, since :—

$$H' = \frac{1}{2 g} \left\{ u_3{}^2 - f_3{}^2 \operatorname{cosec}{}^2 \gamma \right\}$$

it follows that the necessary peripheral speed increases with the working head, so that, because of increased frictional losses at these high speeds, it might be inferred that the higher efficiencies are to be expected with comparatively low working heads—a view which, in the ordinary type of single impeller pump, is borne out in practice. The minimum permissible value of γ increases with the working head, and while for heads of about 10 feet it may be as low as 15°, it increases to about 25° with 30 feet head, and for heads of upwards of 60 feet is not generally less than 35°. In the modern types of high-lift pump, however, great care is taken to polish every part of the impeller so as to reduce friction losses to a minimum, and under such circumstances γ may be reduced to as low as 20° against heads of from 90 to 120 feet with excellent results as regards efficiency.

Although a high efficiency is to be aimed at in the design of a pump, this is not the only factor which may affect the most suitable value of γ. From (15) we have

$$f_3 = \sin \gamma \sqrt{u_3{}^2 - 2 g H'}, \tag{16}$$

and if b_3 feet is the width of the impeller at the discharging periphery, and n the number of vanes each of effective thickness t feet, the area of the wheel passages at the periphery is

$$A_3 = 2 \pi r_3 b_3 - n t b_3 \operatorname{cosec} \gamma,$$

while

$$Q = f_3 A_3 = A_3 \sin \gamma \sqrt{u_3{}^2 - 2 g H'}. \tag{17}$$

---

[1] " P roc. Inst. C. E.," Vol. xlvii., 1876–77, p. 267.

On differentiating equation (17) with respect to H', we finally get :—

$$\frac{d Q}{d H'} = - \frac{g}{Q} A_3{}^2 \sin {}^2\gamma$$

and, therefore, other things being equal, $\frac{d H'}{d Q}$ will have its least value when $\sin \gamma$ has its greatest value, *i.e.*, when $\gamma = 90°$; that is to say, the change in delivery head corresponding to a change in the volume delivered by the pump, will be least when radial tipped vanes are used.

This is of importance in the case of a high-lift pump used for boiler feed purposes where the quantity pumped may be varied, but where the delivery pressure is required to remain approximately constant, and for this purpose radial vanes are most suitable. The same reasoning applies to the case of pumps for elevator work, where the delivery pressure is to be approximately constant.

Also, where a pump is required for dry dock or similar work, the possibility of obtaining a large increase in Q as H diminishes with the emptying of the dock, renders the radial vane type most suitable, for although the increased volume necessitates a largely increased power, this is in general unimportant as compared with the reduction in the time necessary to empty the dock.

Where a pump is electrically driven, however, this large increase in power with a reduced head involves the danger of overloading the motor, and this is more particularly the case when induction motors are used and where speed variation is in consequence impossible. In such a case backward curved vanes are essential, for, since the horse power is proportional to $H' Q$ and therefore to

$$H' A_3 \sin \gamma \sqrt{u_3{}^2 - 2 g H'}$$

we get, on differentiating,

$$\frac{d (H' Q)}{d H'} = A_3 \sin \gamma \left\{ \frac{u_3{}^2 - 3 g H'}{\sqrt{u_3{}^2 - 2 g H'}} \right\}$$

This expression diminishes with γ, and indicates that the rate of increase of the horse-power with a diminution of head is less the smaller the value of γ.

Again, with a pump initially designed to work against a certain head, if the vanes are radial, the possible diminution in speed is very small, but increases as the backward curvature of the vanes increases. With radial vanes, indeed, the pump ceases to lift altogether when the speed falls slightly below that corresponding to normal working. It follows that where the working head cannot be accurately predetermined, the pump

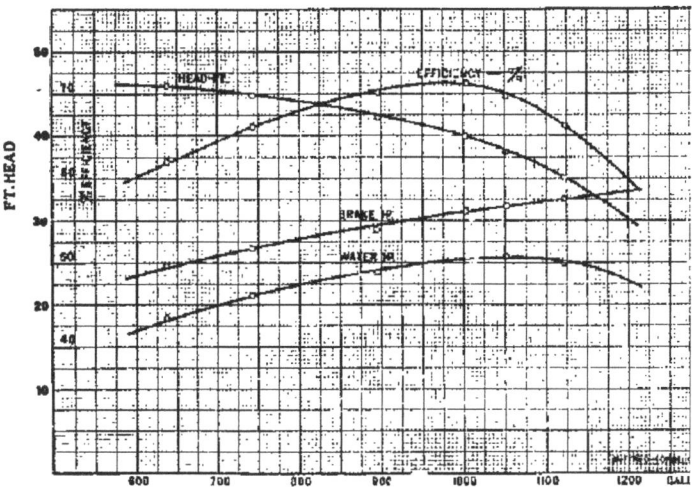

FIG. 325.—Characteristic Curves for Single Low-Lift Centrifugal Pump w
Recurved Vanes.

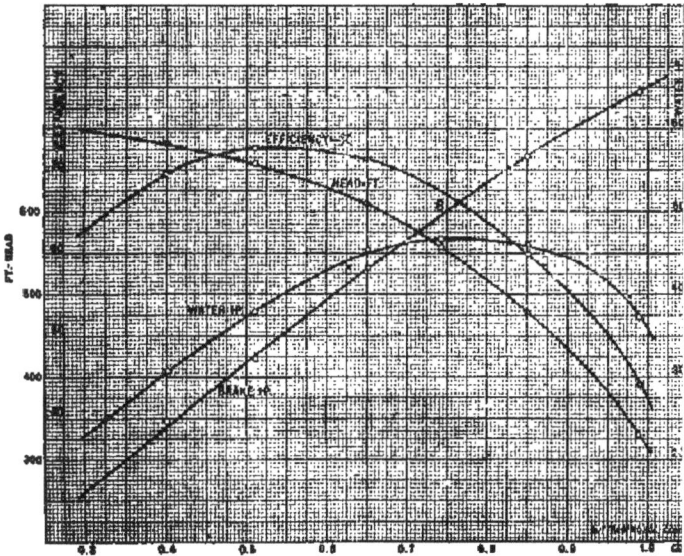

FIG. 326.—Characteristic Curves from 4-Stage Quadruple High-Lift Pump
Radial Vanes.

with recurved vanes has a great advantage in virtue of its greater adaptability to suit varying conditions without serious loss of efficiency.

If, on installing a pump, the head is greater than that for which the vanes were designed, less than the rated quantity will be delivered, or in an extreme case the pump will not lift at all. Generally a slight increase in speed will rectify this.

If, on the other hand, the designed head is greater than the actual, the delivery will be increased, and the engine or motor may be overloaded. This may be rectified either by reducing the speed or, and in general preferably, by slightly throttling the discharge, so as to increase the head artificially. In either case, the possibilities of perfect adjustment are much greater with recurved vanes.

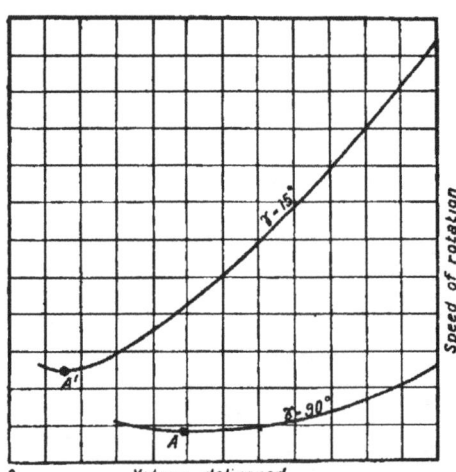

FIG. 327.—Curves showing the influence of the discharge angle γ on the volume delivered under constant head.

These points are well brought out by a comparison of Figs. 325[1] and 326,[1] which show the characteristic curves from a low-lift pump having recurved vanes with an angle γ approximately 30°, and a high-lift quadruple pump with radial vanes, the speed being constant in both cases

Thus, in the pump with radial vanes, a 10 per cent. diminution in head about the point of maximum efficiency is accompanied by a 23 per cent. increase in B.H.P., while the same percentage decrease in the second pump only involves a 7½ per cent. increase in B.H.P.

On the other hand, the corresponding increase in the volume delivered is 31·3 per cent. with radial vanes as against only 11·7 per cent. in the other pump. A glance at the two curves shows that the efficiency falls off much more rapidly with varying conditions when the vanes are radial.

Fig. 327 indicates approximately the effect of a variation in γ on the speed (angular velocity) required to deliver a given volume of water,

[1] By courtesy of the Buffalo Forge Company.

where the head is constant. Here the lowest points A and A' of each curve indicate the minimum volume the pump will lift, and the speed below which pumping will not take place. Obviously the minimum speed is increased and the minimum quantity diminished by any recurvature of the vanes.

Pump used for Circulating Purposes.—Where a centrifugal pump is used for circulating water through the tubes of a surface condenser or of a cooler, and where the actual height of lift is small, the resistance to flow, and therefore the head against which the pump works, varies approximately as the square of the velocity of flow. In such a case the suction and delivery pipe line is often arranged so as to form a syphon, in which case the whole work of the pump consists in overcoming frictional resistances.

Here, putting $H' = \dfrac{f L \bar{v}^2}{m}$ in equation (17), p. 659, we get :—

$$f_3 = \sin \gamma \sqrt{u_3^2 - \frac{f L \bar{v}^2}{m}}$$

and since $\bar{v}$ is proportioned to f_3 for all speeds,

$$\therefore \quad f_3 \propto u_3 = B u_3 \text{ for all speeds.}$$

Equation (13) now becomes :—

$$\eta' = \frac{1 - B^2 \operatorname{cosec}^2 \gamma}{2 (1 - B \cot \gamma)},$$

so that the hydraulic efficiency is independent of the speed of rotation. Since this discussion neglects frictional losses in the wheel which increase with the speed, the actual efficiency will then diminish as the speed increases.

(2) **Pump with Whirlpool Chamber.**—The same general considerations apply to the case of the pump fitted with vortex chamber or guide vanes, as to the simple pump, though modified to some extent quantitatively.

Where a whirlpool chamber is fitted we have, from (9) on equating the gain of pressure head in the pump to the head pumped against, and assuming $\bar{v} = f_2$:—

$$K (w_3^2 + f_3^2) (1 - c^2) + u_3^2 - f_3^2 \operatorname{cosec}^2 \gamma = 2 g H'.$$

Putting $w_3 = u_3 - f_3 \cot \gamma$, we get

$$K (u_3 - f_3 \cot \gamma)^2 (1 - c^2) + u_3^2 - f_3^2 \operatorname{cosec}^2 \gamma + K f_3^2 (1 - c^2)$$
$$= 2 g H', \tag{18}$$

from which f_3 may be found in terms of the peripheral speed and the head.

The efficiency η' is thus equal to—

$$\frac{\left[\begin{array}{c} u_3^2 \{ K (1 - c^2) + 1 \} + f_3^2 \operatorname{cosec}^2 \gamma \{ K (1 - c^2) - 1 \} \\ - 2 K u_3 f_3 \cot \gamma (1 - c^2) \end{array} \right]}{2 u_3 (u_3 - f_3 \cot \gamma)} \tag{19}$$

Putting $K = 1$, *i.e.*, neglecting losses in the whirlpool chamber, this reduces to—

$$\eta' = \frac{u_3^2 (2 - c^2) - f_3^2 c^2 \operatorname{cosec}^2 \gamma - 2 u_3 f_3 \cot \gamma (1 - c^2)}{2 (u_3^2 - u_3 f_3 \cot \gamma)}.$$

Assuming $f_3 = \frac{1}{4} u_3$, the following table traces the variation in this efficiency with a change in γ in the ideal cases when $K = 1$, and when $K = \cdot 5$.

$\dfrac{r_3{'}}{r_3}$	Efficiency.							
	$\gamma = 90°$.		$\gamma = 60°$.		$\gamma = 45°$.		$\gamma = 30°$.	
	$K = 1$.	$K = \cdot 5$.	$K = \cdot 1$.	$K = \cdot 5$.	$K = 1$.	$K = \cdot 5$.	$K = 1$.	$K = \cdot 5$
1·00[1]	·469	·469	·535	·535	·584	·584	·661	·661[1]
1·25	·660	·564	·695	·618	·734	·658	·783	·737
1·50	·764	·615	·793	·663	·815	·698	·852	·772
1·75	·826	·647	·848	·694	·863	·724	·890	·795
2·00	·867	·670	·883	·710	·895	·733	·915	·806
3·00	·941	·700	·943	·745	·955	·769	·963	·830

From these results it is evident that with an efficient whirlpool chamber there is very little advantage to be gained by giving the vanes any considerable backward curvature. Moreover, as these efficiencies do not take into account friction losses which increase as γ diminishes, the actual advantage is less than appears from the table.

(3) Pump with Guide Vanes or Diffuser Ring.—As previously mentioned, experiments tend to show that with well designed guide vanes on the discharge side of the wheel, up to 75 per cent. of the kinetic energy of discharge may be converted into pressure energy, so that the gain of energy per pound in the guide passages will be given by $\dfrac{k (w_3^2 + f_3^2)}{2 g}$ where k has a maximum value of about ·75.

The total gain of pressure head in the pump is now equal to

$$\frac{k (w_3^2 + f_3^2)}{2 g} + \frac{u_3^2 + f_3^2 - f_3^2 \operatorname{cosec}^2 \gamma}{2 g} = H' + \frac{\bar{v}^2}{2 g}.$$

Assuming $\bar{v} = f_3$ and putting $w_3 = u_3 - f_3 \cot \gamma$, we get :—

$$k (u_3 - f_3 \cot \gamma)^2 + u_3^2 - f_3^2 \operatorname{cosec}^2 \gamma + k f_3^2 = 2 g H' \qquad (20)$$

or $2 g H' = u_3^2 (k + 1) + f_3^2 \operatorname{cosec}^2 \gamma (k - 1) - 2 k u_3 f_3 \cot \gamma.$

[1] No whirlpool chamber.

The efficiency η' of the pump is thus given by—

$$\eta' = \frac{u_3{}^2\,(k+1) + f_3{}^2\,\text{cosec}\,{}^2\gamma\,(k-1) - 2\,k\,u_3 f_3 \cot \gamma}{2\,u_3\,(u_3 - f_3 \cot \gamma)} \quad (21)$$

Giving k the value ·75 and taking $f_3 = \frac{1}{4}\,u_3$, we get the following values of η' :—

γ	$90°$	$75°$	$60°$	$45°$	$30°$
η'	·867	·875	·884	·896	·921

Here again, any large reduction in the value of γ, by necessitating an increased speed of rotation, is likely to reduce rather than increase the overall efficiency.

For the guides to be efficient it is essential that their angle of divergence be about 11°; that the vane angle a be so designed as to take the water without shock, on leaving the wheel; that a sufficient number of guide vanes be used to efficiently direct the mass of water, four being about the minimum; that the areas of the guide passages at the exit from the wheel should be proportioned so as to keep the velocity at entrance, the same as on leaving the wheel, and that all guide curves should be smooth and gradual.

Since the whole object of the guides is to neutralise the evil effects of a high velocity of discharge, their relative effect will be greatest where this velocity is greatest, i.e., with radial pump vanes when delivering against a high head, and will be least with recurved vanes and a low head. For this reason, and since large percentage variations of head are more likely to occur where this is low, the diffuser ring is seldom fitted for heads under about 80 feet.

The gain in overall efficiency attainable by its use naturally varies considerably, but may be taken as between 10 per cent. and 20 per cent.

ART. 177.—COMPOUND MULTIPLE CHAMBER PUMP.

Where a number "n" of impellers mounted on the same shaft are used in series so as to form a compound high-lift pump, the impeller diameters, and vane angles are made the same for each chamber, so that each impeller gives a total head $= \dfrac{H'}{n}$ feet. If, in the foregoing theory then,

H' be replaced by $\dfrac{H'}{n}$, the deductions also apply to the compound pump.

The work done on the shaft per lb. of water, neglecting frictional losses, is now given by $\left.\right\}$ $\dfrac{n\,w_3\,u_3}{g}$ foot lbs. and the manometric efficiency η' by $\dfrac{g\,H'}{n\,w_3\,u_3}$.

while neglecting friction the power required to drive the pump $\left.\right\}$ $= \dfrac{W}{550}\dfrac{Q}{\eta'}\dfrac{H'}{\eta'}$ B.H.P.

$$= \frac{W}{550}\frac{Q}{g}\cdot n\,w_3\,u_3 \text{ B.H.P.}$$

ART. 178.—General Equation for Pump.

From equation (11), p. 658, we have
$$2\,g\,H' = u_3^2 + kv_3^2 - f_3^2\,\text{cosec}^2\,\gamma$$
for any pump, and since $v_3^2 = w_3^2 + f_3^2$
$$= (u_3 - f_3\cot\gamma)^2 + f_3^2$$
the foregoing relationship can be written—
$$2g\,H' = A\,u_3^2 + B\,u_3 f_3 + C\,f_3^2$$
$$= a\,N^2 + b\,N\,Q + c\,Q^2.$$

Where N = revs. per min.; Q = discharge; and where A, B, C, a, b, c, are constants for any particular pump. It follows that if the speed, the discharge, and the head be measured for three different speeds, discharges, or heads, the values of these constants may be obtained and the discharge calculated for any other speed or head and *vice versâ*.

ART. 179.—Peripheral Speed of a Pump.

If H' = total head pumped against, including friction head, we have
$$\eta' = \frac{g\,H'}{u_3\,(u_3 - f_3\cot\gamma)},$$
so that with a perfect pump in which all losses were negligible, the peripheral velocity of the vanes at discharge would be given by
$$u_3\,(u_3 - f_3\cot\gamma) = g\,H'.$$
and with radial vanes we should have $u_3 = \sqrt{g\,H'}$. As γ diminishes the peripheral speed increases, while any diminution in efficiency naturally necessitates a higher peripheral speed again, so that actually we have $u_3 = k\,\sqrt{g\,H'}$, where k depends upon γ; upon the value adopted for f_3; and upon the type of pump. In practice it is usual to make f_3 from [·2 to ·3] u_3, the co-efficient increasing from about ·21 when $\gamma = 15°$ to ·29 when $\gamma = 90°$, while k is given a value between 1·2 and

1·8, increasing from about 1·2 in the case of a well designed pump with whirlpool chamber or guides and with a value of $\gamma = 90°$, to about 1·8 in the case of a pump having a volute chamber only, and a value of $\gamma = 15°$.

This makes $f_3 = \frac{1}{4} \sqrt{2 g H'}$ (approx.). In the case of a pump dealing with a large head in a single chamber this, however, gives an excessive value of f_3, and in such a case the value may be reduced to as little as $\frac{1}{8} \sqrt{2 g H'}$.

ART. 180.—Speed at which Pumping Commences.

Even if a centrifugal pump be primed, there will be no flow through the delivery pipe until the pressure difference through the wheel, which depends entirely on the speed of rotation, is sufficiently great to overcome the total head of lift, the pump until then merely sustaining a stationary column of water in this pipe.

If the suction lift is H_s feet, the pump will not maintain its charge without a foot valve on the suction pipe, unless the speed is sufficiently great to cause a pressure difference of more than H_s feet between the pump inlet and outlet.

Assuming uniform rotation with no flow through the pump, the pressure difference in the forced vortex becomes—

$$\frac{p_3 - p_2}{W} = \frac{u_3^2 - u_2^2}{2 g} \text{ feet, } f_2 \text{ and } f_3 \text{ being zero.}$$

∴ For the pump to remain charged when once filled we must have—

$$\frac{\omega^2 (r_3^2 - r_2^2)}{2 g} > H \text{ feet,}$$

while for delivery to take place we must have—

$$\frac{\omega^2 (r_3^2 - r_2^2)}{2 g} > H \text{ feet.}$$

Once free flow is established, the state of affairs changes. A further increase of pressure is now necessary to overcome frictional resistances, and in the case of a pump not fitted with vortex chamber or guides this necessitates the speed for free delivery being slightly greater than is given above. A reduction of the speed below this limit will cause pumping to cease.

With a whirlpool chamber, or guide ring, however, once flow is instituted part of the kinetic energy of flow through the wheel is converted into pressure energy, so that the speed may be reduced below that necessary to initiate flow, without pumping being stopped.

Owing to viscosity moreover, even though the pump be not actually discharging, the water in the vortex chamber will be affected by the rotation of the impeller, and will, to a certain extent, form a free vortex with the pressure greatest and the velocity least at the outside. This reduces the speed for impending delivery by an amount which depends on the design and construction of the vortex chamber, and for the calculation of which insufficient experimental evidence is available. Experiments[1] on a series of pumps having radial vanes with impellers 8·813″ outside and 5·375″ inside diameter, and with a vortex chamber 11·375″ diameter, showed that when on the point of impending delivery this served as a true vortex chamber, the value of K (p. 654) being about ·5.

In all probability this effect would not be so pronounced in a pump having a proportionately larger vortex chamber.

Art. 181.—Size of Pump for a Given Discharge—Similar Pumps - Proportions of Pumps.

For a given speed of rotation and a given radius r_3, the difference in pressure between inlet and outlet, and therefore the head pumped against, increases with the difference between the inner and outer radii of the impeller r_2 and r_3. Since, too, the proportional effect of disc friction ($\propto r^5$, see p. 180), diminishes rapidly as the radius diminishes, the inner radius should, for efficiency, be made small. This may be accomplished, keeping the discharge constant, by increasing the velocity of flow f_2, but with a large suction head a limit to this maximum velocity is soon reached, and in practice it is usual to make the inner radius from $\frac{1}{3}$ to $\frac{1}{2}$ the outer ($r_3 = 3\ r_2$ to $2\ r_2$), the former value being preferable.

Again, since the head pumped against is approximately proportional to u_3^2, i.e., to $\omega^2\ r_3^2$, a given head may be obtained either by an increase in ω or in r. But $Q \propto f_3\ r_3\ b_3$, and assuming f_3 to be proportional to u_3, we have :—

$$Q \propto u_3\ r_3\ b_3,$$
$$\propto \omega\ r_3^2\ b_3,$$
$$\therefore \quad \frac{H'}{Q} \propto \frac{\omega}{b_3}.$$

It follows that for large values of H', in order to avoid excessive values of ω, the value of b_3 should be comparatively small. This is borne out in practice, where the breadth b_3 of the impeller at the rim is usually

[1] "Bulletin of the University of Wisconsin," No. 173. Vol. III. No. 6, p. 447. By C. B. Stewart.

roportional to the radius and has a value ranging from $\frac{1}{8}$ r_3 to $\frac{1}{10}$ r_3, the ormer value applying to low-lift, and the latter to high-lift pumps.

Putting $b_3 \propto r_3$, we have $Q \propto \omega r_3^3$

$$\therefore \quad \frac{H'}{Q} \propto \frac{\omega}{r_3} \propto \frac{u_3}{r_3^2} \propto \frac{u_3^2}{r_3^2 u_3}.$$

While this is not strictly true in the case of an actual pump, yet it hows that in every case for a given value of H' and of Q, there is definite value of r for maximum efficiency, this value, however, epending on the relative magnitude of the frictional losses.

Since, in a perfect pump, with radial vane tips, we have $g H' = u_3^2$, ;hile $Q \propto u_3 r_3^2$, if the ratios $\dfrac{g H'}{u_3^2}$, and $\dfrac{Q}{u_3 r_3^2}$ be plotted this enables a omparison to be made between the performances of different pumps.

Professor Rateau terms the ratio $\dfrac{g H'}{u_3^2}$ the manometric efficiency; the atio $\dfrac{Q}{u_3 r_3^2}$ the volumetric efficiency; and the ratio of the product of hese, viz., $\dfrac{g H'}{u_3^2} \cdot \dfrac{Q}{u_3 r_3^2}$ to the mechanical efficiency $\dfrac{W Q H'}{U}$, the o-efficient of transmission to the pump shaft. The latter thus equals—

$$\frac{g H'}{u_3^2} \cdot \frac{Q}{u_3 r_3^2} \cdot \frac{U}{W Q H'} = \frac{g U}{W u_3^3 r_3^2}.$$

The three curves showing the mechanical efficiency, the manometric efficiency, and the co-efficient of transmission, on a base of volumetric efficiencies, are then termed the characteristics of the pump, and if drawn for a given pump apply to any similar pump of different size, so long as the previous relationships hold, and therefore so long as

(1) The peripheral speeds are proportional to $\sqrt{H'}$;

(2) The revolutions are proportional to $\dfrac{\sqrt{H'}}{S}$;

(3) The quantity discharged is proportional to $S^2 \sqrt{H'}$;

where S is the ratio of similar linear dimensions of the two pumps.

The same conditions hold for identical results to be obtained from two similar pressure turbines.

ART. 182.—REMARKS ON THEORY OF PUMP DESIGN.

None of the fundamental assumptions made in the foregoing discussion, are accurately true. Thus the assumption of radial motion immediately before entering the impeller is certainly incorrect since viscosity must cause a deflection of the lines of flow in the direction of rotation before the wheel is reached. This has the effect of increasing the value of the inlet angle β for entry without shock at any given speed of rotation. though experimental results are too scanty to allow of the magnitude of this effect being calculated.

The assumption that all particles of water on leaving the impeller have the same velocity v_3 and are moving in paths making an angle γ with the tangent to the periphery, or that $w_3 = u_3 - f_3 \cot \gamma$ for all particles. is also incorrect as appears from the results of experiment. A measure of the error involved may be obtained by comparing the actual and theoretical manometric efficiencies, for if from the energy expended in driving a pump, that necessary to overcome disc and mechanical friction be deducted, the remainder should equal $u_3 w_3 \div g$ foot lbs. per lb. of water. If the ratio of the measured manometric head H_m to this quantity be termed the experimental manometric efficiency, the ratio of the theoretical and experimental manometric efficiencies will be a measure of the ratio of the true w_3 to that given by the foregoing formula.

The following results from tests of a pump by Mr. Parsons [1] have been chosen to illustrate this point. The details of the pump are as follow :— $r_3 = 9\cdot25$ inches ; $r_2 = 4\cdot625$ inches ; $b_2 = b_3 = 5\cdot75$ inches ; $\gamma = 15°$: $\beta = 40°$; 8 vanes, assumed $\frac{3}{8}$ inch thick for purposes of calculation.

Experiment.	H_m ft.	Q c.f.s.	Revs. per min.	H.P. less Disc and Mech. Friction.	H.P. Output.	Manometric Efficiency.		Calculated Observed	E'.
						Experimental.	Calculated.		
1	14·67	2·70	392	7·68	4·50	·586	·561	·958	
7	14·70	4·01	402	10·43	6·69	·642	·586	·915	
11	14·80	4·68	406	11·83	7·85	·664	·609	·917	
14	17·20	3·20	427	10·88	6·24	·573	·564	·983	
18	17·40	4·01	432	12·90	7·90	·625	·590	·945	
22	17·60	4·68	436	13·61	9·35	·687	·615	·895	

Mean ... ·933

In these experiments the mean power necessary to overcome the friction of the pump bearings and driving belt and the disc friction of the pump was found to be 1·37 H.P., and this value has been used in deducing the values in column 5.

Again experiments on an experimental pump, $r_3 = 4\cdot41$ inches ; $r_2 = 2\cdot188$ inches ; $b_2 = b_3 = 1\cdot125$ inches ; $\gamma = 90°$; $\beta = 18° 50'$, at the

[1] " Proc. Inst. C. E.," Vol. 53, p. 271.

adison University [1] give the following values for the ratio of calculated
observed manometric efficiency.

Series 1. 24 vanes, area of waterways increasing . . ·910
Series 2. 24 „ „ „ constant . . ·910
Series 8. 12 „ „ „ increasing . . ·875
Series 4. 12 „ „ „ constant . . ·845
Series 5. 6 „ „ „ increasing . . ·75
Series 6. 6 „ „ „ constant . . ·68

From these and similar results it appears that w_3 is always less than
given by the formula $w_3 = u_3 - f_3 \cot \gamma$. This is probably due partly
the fact that a dead water space which is not utilised for discharge is
rmed on the rear side of each vane, thus increasing the radial com-
onent f_3, and partly to the fact that only those layers of water near to
he driving edge of the vane are discharged parallel to its tip. Thus the
rue mean values of f_3 and of cot γ are both greater than the apparent
alues. It also appears that the ratio of the true to the calculated value
f w_3 increases with the number of vanes and hence as the guidance of
he water becomes more perfect, but diminishes as the width of the
assages is reduced, probably because the dead water space then forms a
roportionately larger part of the whole discharging area.

It also diminishes slightly as the discharge increases, and as the angle
increases.

The following may be taken as approximate values of the ratio, in
umps of normal design :—

$\dfrac{w_3 \text{ experimental.}}{w_3 \text{ calculated.}}$

Pump upwards of 20 in. diameter ; 12 or more vanes—
γ from 15° to 30° . ·97
„ 30° to 60° . ·95
„ 60° to 90° . ·92

Pump 10 in. to 20 in. diameter ; 12 vanes—
γ from 15° to 30° . . ·93
„ 30° to 60° . . ·90
„ 60° to 90° . . ·87

„ „ „ „ 8 to 12 vanes—
γ from 15° to 30° . . ·90
„ 30° to 60° . . ·87
„ 60° to 90° . . ·84

[1] "Bulletin of the University of Wisconsin," No. 178. 1907.

Pump 10 in. to 20 in. diameter ; 6 vanes—

γ from 15° to 30° . . ·81
„ 30° to 60° . . ·78
„ 60° to 90° . . ·75

The values point to the absolute necessity for providing a sufficient number of wheel vanes where a diffuser ring is fitted, and where, in consequence, serious loss by shock may occur if the guide vane angle is designed to suit what may be a fictitious direction of outflow from the impeller.

ART. 183.—BALANCING OF END THRUST.

End thrust on a pump shaft having one or more impellers with single axial inlets is due to a number of causes.

(a) To the difference of pressure at a given radius on the two sides of the vane shrouding, due to the fact that while the water in the impeller is rotating in a forced vortex, that outside the shrouding is in a state of comparative rest, and therefore exists under different pressure conditions. This is by far the most important factor in producing end thrust.

(b) To the fact that if the discharge diameters of the shroudings in a double cased pump are equal, there is an unbalanced pressure on the portion of the shrouding opposite to the inlet opening. This produces a thrust in the direction of inflow and so tends to balance (a).

(c) Since the water is taken in axially and diverted radially, it suffers a change of momentum in an axial direction, and this change of momentum can only be produced by an axial force transmitted through the shaft to the impellers.

Thus if $\bar{v}$ is the velocity of axial flow through the supply passages; Q the discharge per second; and n the number of impellers, this change of momentum takes place n times in the pump, and the total end thrust on the shaft due to this cause is given by—

$$n \cdot \frac{62 \cdot 4 \, Q}{g} \cdot \bar{v} \text{ lbs.}$$

This thrust also acts in the direction of inflow.

Apart from the system of arranging the impellers in pairs placed back to back, each pair thus being in balance, four methods of balancing are in use :—

(a) By radial balancing vanes mounted on the rear face of the shrouding (Fig. 805).

(b) By making the diameter of shrouding on the entrant side greater than that on the exit side, the difference of area being just sufficient to balance the pressure difference (Fig. 316).

(c) By a rotary balance piston or disc keyed to the pump shaft, one side being exposed to delivery pressure, and the other to the pressure on the suction side of the pump (Figs. 314, 315, 316).

(d) By relieving the pressure over a certain area behind the shrouding by means of a rotating balance ring (Figs. 306A, 307, and 317).

Whichever of these methods is adopted, with the exception of (c), the wheel will only be in perfect balance at one speed and with one rate of delivery, and in such cases it is necessary to arrange a thrust block to take the end thrust caused at starting or stopping and in the case of a variable load.

These methods of balancing will now be considered in further detail :—

(a) **Radial Balancing Vanes.**—Since it is impossible to keep the joint between the outer periphery of the shrouding and casing tight, the space behind the shrouding will be full of water normally at delivery pressure, and since the mean pressure in the wheel is considerably less than this, the resultant effect in a single shrouded wheel (Fig. 305) will be an axial thrust of considerable magnitude, in the opposite direction to that of axial flow.

If a series of holes be made through the disc, as indicated in Fig. 305, the pressure at this radius on both sides of the shrouding will be equalised, and there will be a constant circulation of water past the rim of the impeller, behind the shrouding to the zone of low pressure, and out to the working side of the shrouding.

While the axial thrust is then largely balanced, this leakage is productive of inefficient working, and the method, though often adopted in turbine practice, is inadvisable.

If, however, shallow radial vanes are fitted to the rear face of the shrouding, the water in the clearance space is forced to rotate with vortex motion, and in consequence its pressure diminishes from the outside, where it has a definite value, to the inside, following approximately the forced vortex law. The degree to which it deviates from this law depends on the amount of side clearance between the balance vanes and the pump casing, any increase in this clearance, by reducing the mean angular velocity, tending to increase the mean pressure behind the shrouding. By suitably regulating the clearance and the radial length of the balance vanes, the whole, or any portion of the axial thrust, may thus be balanced.

H.A.   X X

For example, in the wheel shown in Fig. 305, the pressure in the wheel itself varies at different radii owing, firstly, to the production of a force vortex, and secondly, to the necessity of maintaining an outward flow. In the clearance space to the right this outward flow is absent, so that the difference of pressure on the two sides of the shrouding at a radius r is given by the pressure necessary to maintain this flow, and if p_r represent this pressure intensity in pounds per square foot

$$\frac{p_r}{W} = \frac{p_2}{W} + \frac{{}_2v_r^2 - {}_rv_r^2}{2\,g}. \tag{1}$$

This assumes the law of pressure variation in outward flow to be the same as in inward flow, i.e., neglects losses of energy due to eddy formation, and since this loss varies with the form and number of the blades (i.e., with the rate of their divergence), becoming less as the number and curvature of the vanes is increased, the theory is to this extent unsatisfactory. Allowing for this, we have :—

$$\frac{p_r}{W} = K\,\frac{p_2}{W} + \frac{K\,{}_2v_r^2 - {}_rv_r^2}{2\,g}, \tag{2}$$

where K is a co-efficient, varying probably from about ·7 in the case of radial vanes to ·85 with vanes having a delivery angle of $30°$.

Now $\qquad\qquad {}_2v_r = \sqrt{f_2^2 + u_2^2}$

And $_rv_r = f_r$ cosec θ, where θ = angle made by the vanes at this radius with the tangent to the corresponding circle.

$$\therefore\quad \frac{p_r}{W} = K\left\{\frac{p_2}{W} + \frac{f_2^2 + u_2^2}{2\,g}\right\} - \frac{f_r^2 \text{ cosec }^2\theta}{2\,g}. \tag{3}$$

The axial force F may be obtained by dividing the disc into a series of concentric elements, and by obtaining the relative velocity at the mean radius of each element by this method or by the graphical construction of p. 553. The unbalanced force on each element may then be calculated by an application of equation (2) above, as shown on p. 554, and the sum of these, taken over the whole area, gives the resultant axial force.

Equating this to the unbalanced pressure on the inlet side of the shrouding produced by the axial change of momentum of the water, and to the unbalanced pressure on the remaining annulus of width $r_3 - R_0$, on fixing R_1 the required outer radius R_0 may be determined.

Where balancing vanes are fitted they should not be too deep and ιould work with the minimum possible clearance over the face of the ιsing, which should be machined and painted. It is probable that vanes ιout $\frac{1}{4}$ inch deep and with a side clearance not exceeding $\frac{1}{16}$ inch would ιve good results. Balancing vanes, however, in any case greatly increase iction losses (p. 190), and in view of this and of the impossibility of ιtaining exact balancing by their use, are seldom fitted on modern ιmps.

(b) Here (Fig. 316) the diameter of the shrouding on the side remote ιom the entrance is reduced so as to make the total area of the ιroudings approximately equal.

The clearance space pressures are thus balanced, and the excess of ιressure on the inlet shrouding due to the greater pressure at the outer ιdius of the runner tends to balance the pressure in the opposite ιirection due to momentum changes. This method also is impossible of ιxact calculation, and is therefore only suitable when used in conjunction ιith a thrust block or balance piston to take up any minor unbalanced ιhrust.

(c) Where a balance piston is used (Fig. 316), leakage past this piston ι slight, and by adjustment of a valve on the pressure pipe P, which ιdjustment may be automatic, the pressure may be very accurately ιdjusted while running, to suit any condition of working.

In the pumps shown in Figs. 314 and 315, the shrouding area ιhich is exposed to the discharge pressure from each impeller is con-ιiderably greater on the side removed from the inlet, and consequently ιhe nett pressure is from right to left. To counterbalance this a balance ιiston or disc P is fitted, exposed to pressure water from the last impeller ιn its left hand face. This works normally with small clearance over the ιixed casing at C. When the pressure to the right becomes equal to the ιull discharge pressure it is more than sufficient to counterbalance the ιnd thrust on the impellers, the spindle moves to the right, the clearance ιetween piston or disc and casing is increased, and the pressure water ιscapes into the low pressure chamber R, relieving the end thrust on the ιiston. The regulation is perfectly automatic, the spindle taking up a ιosition in which the clearance is just sufficient to maintain the necessary ιressure in the space to the left of the balance disc. In view of the ιimplicity and automatic nature of this device it promises to become ιeneral on all modern high speed pumps.

(d) In this method of balancing (Figs. 306A, 307, and 317) the outer ιiameter of the balance ring is made slightly less than that of the ιmpeller at the packing ring P, while a series of holes through the shrouding equalises the pressure in the interior of the balance ring and of the impeller.

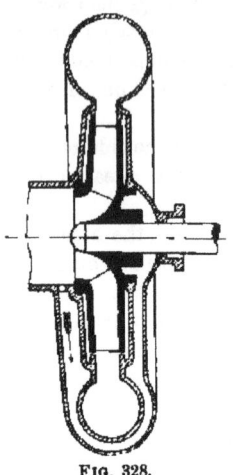

FIG. 328.

This is then approximately in balance, the slight reduction in the diameter of the balance ring creating an excess pressure towards the inlet, which counterbalances the change of axial momentum of the supply water.

Brass packing rings are fitted at P (306A) to prevent leakage of pressure water from the clearance space into the balance ring.

A somewhat analogous method of balancing a single impeller is shown in Fig. 328. .

Where a centrifugal pump is fitted with a vertical shaft, the whole weight of the pump and driving shaft may usually be balanced by an application of the preceding principles ; while exactly the same reasoning applies to the balancing of the axial thrust on a turbine shaft.

ART. 184.—EXAMPLES OF THE DESIGN OF CENTRIFUGAL PUMPS.

As an example of the application of the foregoing formulae, the main points in the theoretical design of one or two types of pump will now be considered.

(1) Low-lift pump—12 feet working head—to deliver 6,000 gallons per minute at 220 revolutions.

$$\text{Assume} \begin{cases} f_3 = \frac{1}{4} \sqrt{2\,g\,H'} = \frac{8 \cdot 02}{4} \sqrt{1 \bar{2}} = 6 \cdot 95 \text{ f.s.} \\ \gamma = 30°. \\ u_3 = 1 \cdot 6 \sqrt{g\,H'} = 31 \cdot 5 \text{ f.s.} \end{cases}$$

Then $\qquad A_3 = \dfrac{Q}{f_3} = \dfrac{1,000}{62 \cdot 4 \times 6 \cdot 95} = 2 \cdot 31$ square feet.

$$= 332 \text{ square inches.}$$

while $\qquad r_3 = \dfrac{31 \cdot 5 \times 60}{2\,\pi \times 220} = 1 \cdot 367$ feet $= 16 \cdot 4$ inches.

$\therefore \quad b_3 = \dfrac{A_3}{2\,\pi\,r_3} = \dfrac{332}{2\,\pi \times 16 \cdot 4} = 3 \cdot 22$ inches.

Assuming a ratio $\dfrac{r_3}{r_2} = \dfrac{2 \cdot 25}{1}$, this makes $r_2 = 7 \cdot 3$ inches, and if the vane breadth at inlet be increased to 4·5 inches so as to reduce the velocity of flow at this point, this makes :—

$$f_2 = f_3 \times \frac{3 \cdot 22}{4 \cdot 5} \times 2 \cdot 25 = \frac{6 \cdot 95 \times 3 \cdot 22 \times 2 \cdot 25}{4 \cdot 5} = 11 \cdot 20 \text{ f.s.}$$

Since $f_2 = u_2 \tan \beta$, we have :—

$$\tan \beta = \frac{f_2}{u_2} = \frac{11 \cdot 20}{31 \cdot 5} = \frac{11 \cdot 20 \times 2 \cdot 25}{31 \cdot 5} = \cdot 800,$$
$$2 \cdot 25$$
$$\beta = 38° 39'$$

giving the inlet angle for the vanes.

(2) A pump—50 feet working head—is fitted with a whirlpool chamber whose radius is twice that of the impeller, and whose efficiency is 50 per cent. The pump is to deliver 5 cubic feet per second. Determine its leading dimensions—its speed of rotation—its hydraulic efficiency, and the probable H.P. necessary to drive it.

To begin with, we will assume that since the whirlpool chamber is fairly efficient and the head high, the value of γ may be taken as fairly high—say 60°—so as to keep down the speed and friction losses. Also assume $f_3 = \frac{1}{8} \sqrt{2 g H'}$.

Then $f_3 = \frac{8 \cdot 02}{8} \sqrt{50} = 7 \cdot 09$ f.s.

Now substituting ·5 for c and ·5 for K in equation (18), (p. 663), we get—

$$\cdot 5 (u_3 - 7 \cdot 09 \cot 60°)^2 \times \tfrac{3}{4} + u_3^2 - 50 \cdot 2 \operatorname{cosec}^2 60° + 25 \cdot 1 \times \tfrac{3}{4}$$
$$= 100 \, g = 3{,}220$$
$$\therefore \quad u_3^2 - 2 \cdot 232 \, u_3 - 2{,}878 = 0,$$
$$\text{or } u_3 = 49 \cdot 9 \text{ feet per second.}$$

Since $\quad \sqrt{g \, H'} = 40 \cdot 1$, this makes $u_3 = 1 \cdot 245 \sqrt{g \, H'}$.

Next taking $\quad b_3 = \frac{r_3}{10}$ we have $A_3 = 2 \pi r_3 b_3 = \frac{\pi r_3^2}{5}$,

and since $\quad Q = A_3 f_3 = \frac{\pi r_3^2}{5} \times 7 \cdot 09,$

we have $\quad r_3^2 = \frac{25}{7 \cdot 09 \, \pi} = 1 \cdot 122.$

$$\therefore \quad r_3 = 1 \cdot 06 \text{ feet} = 12\tfrac{3}{4} \text{ inches.}$$
$$\therefore \quad b_3 = 1 \cdot 275 \text{ inches.}$$

This neglects the effect of the vane thickness. Since the vanes reduce the effective discharge area by $b_3 \, n \, t_3 \operatorname{cosec} \gamma$, when the number and thickness of vanes has been decided upon the above value of b_3 must be increased in the ratio

$$\frac{2 \pi r_3}{2 \pi r_3 - n t_3 \cosec 60°}$$

Thus, taking eighteen vanes, each having a thickness at the tips of $\frac{1}{4}$ inch, this ratio becomes

$$\frac{2 \pi \times 12.75}{2 \pi \times 12.75 - \dfrac{18}{4 \times .8660}} = \frac{80.1}{74.9} = 1.07$$

and the true breadth $b_3 = 1.275 \times 1.07 = 1.365$ inches.

Again $\omega = \dfrac{49.9}{1.06} = 47.0$ radians per second.

$\therefore N = \dfrac{60}{2 \pi} \omega = 449$ revolutions per minute.

Assuming $r_3 = 2.5 \ r_2$, this makes $u_2 = \dfrac{49.9}{2.5} = 19.95$ f.s., while if the vanes be broadened out towards the centre so as to keep the velocity of flow down to say 10 feet per second, this makes $\tan \beta = \dfrac{f_2}{u_2} = \dfrac{10}{19.95} = .5012$.

$$\therefore \ \beta = 26° 37'$$

The manometric efficiency, $\dfrac{g H'}{u_3 (u_3 - f_3 \cot \gamma)}$, is equal to

$$\frac{1,610}{49.9 (49.9 - 7.09 \times .5774)} = \frac{1,610}{2,282} = .705.$$

Probably mechanical and hydraulic frictional resistances will combine to reduce this efficiency to about .65.

Taking this value, the work done on the pump shaft per second

$$= \frac{62.4 \ Q \ H'}{.65} \text{ foot lbs.}$$

$$\therefore \ \text{H.P.} = \frac{62.4 \ Q \ H'}{550 \times .65} = \frac{62.4 \times 5 \times 50}{550 \times .65} = 43.6.$$

The speed at which the pump begins to lift is given by

$$u_3{}^2 - u_2{}^2 = 2 \ g \ H = 3,220$$

or

$$\omega^2 (r_3{}^2 - r_2{}^2) = 3,220$$

$$\therefore \ \omega^2 = \frac{3,220}{1.06^2 - .425^2} = 3,420$$

$$\therefore \ \omega = 58.5$$

$$\therefore \ N = \frac{60 \times 58.5}{2 \pi} = 558.$$

Thus the speed necessary to institute pumping is considerably higher han that necessary for working once delivery has commenced. This .ssumes that until flow takes place the whirlpool chamber has no effect n converting kinetic into pressure energy. Actually, however, owing to ʋiscosity, the actual speed for lifting to commence is somewhat less than .hat indicated above.

(3) Compound high-lift pump, fitted with guide vanes and vortex ɔhambers having a pressure conversion efficiency of 75 per cent., to deliver 5 cubic feet per second under 300 feet head. Assuming a lift of 50 feet in each of six chambers; $\gamma = 60°$, $f_3 = \frac{1}{3} \sqrt{2 g H'}$; and considering each chamber as a separate pump, we have, as in example (2), $f_3 = 7·09$ f.s. Then, taking $b_3 = \frac{r_3}{10}$, we get, as before, $b_3 = 1·275$ inches, or, allowing for the same vanes, $b_3 = 1·365$ inches, while $r_3 = 1·06$ feet. We now have the factor k of equation (20) (p. 664) equal to ·75, and this equation becomes :—

$$·75 \, (u_3 - 4·09)^2 + u_3^2 - 66·95 + 87·6 = 3,220.$$
$$\therefore u_3^2 - 3·51 \, u_3 - 1,850 = 0.$$
$$\therefore u_3 = 44·76 \text{ f.s.}$$

This makes $u_3 = 1·116 \sqrt{g H'}$.

Also $N = \dfrac{60 \, u_3}{2 \pi r_3} = \dfrac{60 \times 44·76}{2 \pi \times 1·06} = 403$ revolutions per minute, while since $\tan a = \dfrac{f_3}{u_3 - f_3 \cot \gamma} = \dfrac{7·09}{44·76 - 4·09} = ·1744$, this gives a guide vane angle $a = 9° 54'$.

Assuming $u_3 - f_3 \cot \gamma$ or w_3 to have ·95 times its theoretical value, p. 671, this makes $\tan a = ·1834$ and $a = 10° 24'$.

In this case the manometric efficiency $\dfrac{g H'}{u_3 \, (u_3 - f_3 \cot \gamma)}$

$$= \dfrac{1,610}{44·76 \times 40·67} = \dfrac{1,610}{1,822} = ·884.$$

Frictional losses would probably reduce this to about ·80, so that the H.P. would be equal to

$$\dfrac{62·4 \times Q \times n \, H'}{550 \times ·80} = \dfrac{62·4 \times 5 \times 300}{550 \times ·80} = 213.$$

EXAMPLES.

(1) A centrifugal pump is 4 feet in diameter and makes 200 revolutions per minute, delivering 64·8 cubic feet of sea water per second, against a

head of 20 feet. The discharge area $= 8\cdot33$ square feet, and the discharge angle $\gamma = 26°$. The ratio $\dfrac{r_3}{r_2} = \dfrac{2}{1}$.

Determine the manometric efficiency, and, assuming a loss of 10 per cent. in friction, the H.P. to drive the pump, and the speed at which lifting commences.

Answer.
$\begin{cases}
\text{Manometric efficiency} = \cdot592. \\
\text{Mechanical efficiency} = \cdot492. \\
\text{H.P.} \qquad\qquad\quad = 306. \\
\text{Lifting commences at 198 revolutions.}
\end{cases}$

(2) The following are results obtained from tests of a centrifugal pump, having the following dimensions : $r_3 = 15\cdot25$ inches ; $r_2 = 7\cdot675$ inches; $b_3 = 3\cdot0$ inches; $b_2 = 4\cdot0$ inches ; $\gamma = 30°$

Revolutions per minute	.	188·3	202·7	213·7
Gallons per minute .	.	1,895	1,705	1,976
Lift in feet. H'	.	12·33	12·58	13·0
Water H.P.	.	5·22	6·51	7·81
Dynamometric H.P.	.	8·11	10·74	11·02
Efficiency	.	64·5	60·74	55·72

Determine from this the value of u_3 for maximum efficiency in terms of $\sqrt{g\,H'}$, and determine the hydraulic efficiency in each case.

(3) A pump delivers 3 cubic feet per second against 60 feet head, and is required to rotate at 500 revolutions per minute. Making $f = \frac{1}{6}\sqrt{2\,g\,H'}$, and giving the vanes radial tips, settle the leading features of the design, on the assumption that guides are fitted with a conversion efficiency of 65 per cent.

(4) A pump has an inner radius of 1 foot, and an outer radius of 2 feet. It is not fitted with vortex chamber or guide vanes.

Determine the speed at which lifting will commence against heads of 10, 20, 40 and 60 feet respectively.

Answer. 99; 140; 198; 242 revolutions per minute.

(5) A pump is intended to lift 25 cubic feet per second against a head

of 16 feet. A model is made and delivers 1 cubic foot per second against 16 feet head when making 1,450 revolutions per minute, then giving its maximum efficiency. The radius of the model impeller is 4·5 inches. Determine the speed and radius of the large pump for maximum efficiency.

$$\text{Answer.} \quad \begin{cases} \text{Radius} = 22\cdot5 \text{ inches.} \\ \text{Speed} = 290 \text{ revolutions.} \end{cases}$$

(6) The peripheral speed of a centrifugal pump = 30 f.s. The vanes are curved backward so that the discharge angle $\gamma = 35°$, while the water leaves the wheel with a radial velocity of 5 f.s. If 120 cubic feet of water pass through the pump per minute, determine the hydraulic turning moment on the shaft if the radius of the wheel is 2 feet.

Answer. 177 foot pounds.

CHAPTER XIX.

Other Types of Pumping Machinery—Water Hoisting—The Hydraulic Ram—Hydraulic Air Compressor—The Jet Pump—The Injector Hydrant—The Air Lift Pump—Reversed Air Lift Pump as Air Compressor—Humphrey's Gas Pump.

ART. 185.—WATER HOISTING FROM MINES.[1]

THE method of direct hoisting of water in large tanks has come very rapidly into favour of recent years in the anthracite region of Pennsylvania for mine drainage purposes.

The system has the advantages that in general, with the exception of the tanks, and the guides used for keeping these vertical while hoisting, no new machinery is needed, the only cost being that due to extra wear and tear of the hoisting engines and to the steam used while hoisting. Further, the whole of the operating machinery is on the surface and free from the danger of being flooded, while no underground steam pipes, with the accompanying losses by condensation and the danger of damage by a slip of the roof, are necessary.

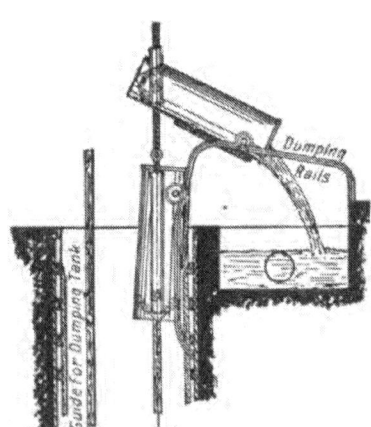

FIG. 329.—Method of End Dumping in direct Water-hoisting Plant.

Cylindrical hoisting tanks are now general, these having a couple of butterfly valves in the bottom placed at an angle of 45° (Fig. 329).

The tanks may discharge at the top of the shaft either by overturning or by automatic opening of the bottom valves. The former method is preferable as rendering more rapid manipulation possible. With tanks of

[1] For a descriptive article on this method of mine drainage, see a paper by R. V. Norris before the American Inst. of Mining Engineers, 1903, or an abstract of this paper in "Cassier's Magazine," for May, 1904.

,500 gallons capacity, the capacity of such a plant ranges up to about 50,000 gallons per day of twelve hours.

ART. 186.—THE HYDRAULIC RAM.

The hydraulic ram, which owes its conception as a practical machine o Montgolfier (about the end of the eighteenth century), is an apparatus levised to utilize the kinetic energy of a moving column of water to pump up part of this water to a height greater than that of the supply lead. In its simplest form, the ram consists of an inclined supply pipe

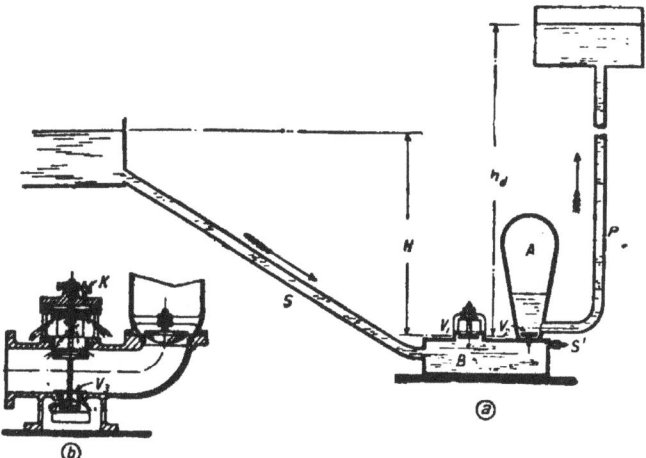

FIG. 330.—Types of Hydraulic Ram.

S (Fig. 330 a), terminating in a valve box B. This valve box is fitted with a waste valve V_1, opening inwards, and a discharge valve V_2 opening outwards and delivering pressure water into an air vessel A, from which it is delivered in a steady stream by the discharge pipe P.

The action of the ram is as follows : The waste valve being opened, water is free to escape, and flow is set up along the supply pipe. The velocity of flow increases under the influence of the supply head until the dynamic pressure on the under side of the valve becomes sufficiently great to overcome its weight. The valve now closes rapidly and the supply column suffers a consequent retardation which gives rise to a rapid increase of pressure in the valve box until this pressure becomes sufficiently great to open the delivery valve.

Water then escapes through this valve into the air vessel, compresses the air, and flows away along the rising main.

As soon as the momentum of the supply column is destroyed the delivery valve closes, the water below the valve partaking of the backward motion thus instituted. This motion, once set up, can only be checked by a reduction of pressure in the valve box below that corresponding to the statical head and consequently the pressure in the valve box is reduced rapidly until at some instant the waste valve reopens, and the whole cycle of operations is repeated. Fig. 331 shows a typical pressure diagram from the valve box of such a ram throughout one complete cycle of operations.

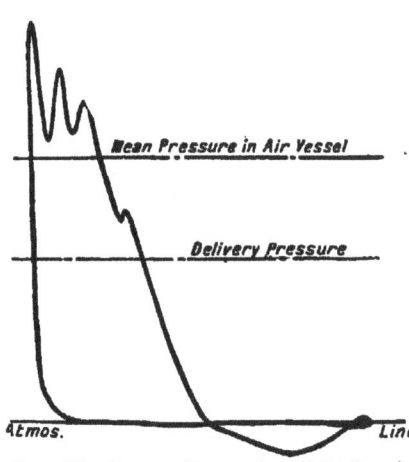

FIG. 331.—Pressure Diagram from Valve Box of Hydraulic Ram.

The idea that the waste valve reopens because the pressure due to the statical head of the supply column is insufficient to keep it to its seat is quite erroneous. In general, the valve will open however light it may be, since the pressure in the valve box is reduced below that of the atmosphere by the reflux action of the water on its rebound. In practice the waste valve is usually made to weigh from ·30 lbs. to ·45 lbs. per square inch of area, so that a statical pressure corresponding to 1 foot head would be sufficient to prevent any opening.

Advantage is taken of this reduction of pressure to keep the air vessel charged, by the introduction of a snifting valve at S_1 (Fig. 330 a), air being drawn through this valve into the valve box B when the pressure falls below that of the atmosphere.

The whole cycle, which may only take a fraction of a second to complete, may be divided into four periods, during which the waste valve is respectively opening, wide open, closing, and closed.

Since the force tending to open the valve is equal to its weight together with a much larger force due to pressure differences on its two faces, and since the acceleration of the valve will therefore diminish as its weight increases, the time of opening will tend to increase slightly as the weight increases, and will also increase with the travel of the valve. For all practical purposes, however, the opening may be considered as instantaneous.

The period during which the valve is full open depends entirely on the time necessary to produce the required velocity of flow along the supply pipe, and will therefore increase with the weight of the valve, and with the ratio of length of supply pipe to supply head.

Thus let :—

H = supply head in feet.
h_d = delivery.
l = length of supply pipe.

a = area of supply pipe in square feet.
a_v = effective discharge area of waste valve.
= actual discharge area multiplied by the co-efficient of discharge.

Then on the assumption of instantaneous opening of the waste valve, the velocity of flow in the supply pipe after t seconds is given by

$$v = c \, \frac{a}{a_v} \left\{ \frac{1 - e^{-\frac{2c}{k} \cdot t}}{1 + e^{-\frac{2c}{k} \cdot t}} \right\} \text{ ft. per sec.}$$

(equation 12″, p. 242).

where $c = \sqrt{\dfrac{2gH}{1 + \dfrac{fl}{m} \cdot \dfrac{a_v^2}{a^2}}}$; and $k = 2l \dfrac{a_v}{a} \cdot \dfrac{1}{1 + \dfrac{fl}{m} \cdot \dfrac{a_v^2}{a^2}}$:

Experiments [1] show that this formula gives results in close agreement with those obtained in practice.

The weight of the valve is then adjusted so as to give v a value which, for most efficient working, is approximately $\cdot 4 \sqrt{h_d}$ feet per second.

The time which the valve takes to close cannot be calculated with any pretension to accuracy. It will evidently depend largely on the form of the valve body and of the valve box, and will increase as the lift of the valve, and its weight, increase.

The total time during which it remains off its seat will thus increase with the delivery head and with the length of supply pipe, and will diminish as the ratio $H \div l$ increases, also increasing with its weight and lift.

The time during which it is on its seat increases with the distance from valve seat to delivery air chamber, and increases as the delivery head increases, since the first of these factors regulates the time taken by the reflex pressure wave to reach the waste valve, and the second regulates the time at which the delivery valve closes, and hence the time of initiation of this reflex wave.

[1] Harza. Bulletin of the University of Wisconsin. No. 205, p. 211.

Experiments on a ram having a drive pipe 85·3 feet long with a supply head of 8·15 feet, show the following approximate results:—

h_d ft.	Proportion of cycle during which valve is		
	Wide open.	Closing.	Closed.
10·3	·58	·11	·31
19·3	·78	·09	·13
50·5	·88	·07	·05

Efficiency of Ram.

The efficiency of the ram may be considered from two points of view. If q is the volume delivered by the ram, and Q that escaping through the waste valve, H being the effective supply head, and h_d the effective delivery head measured from the level of the waste valve and including the friction in the delivery pipe line, the total input of energy to the ram is $(Q+q) H$, and the total output is $q h_d$. The ratio

$$\frac{q h_d}{(Q + q) H},$$

known as D'Aubuisson's efficiency ratio, then gives the efficiency of the ram as a machine.

The ram may, however, be looked upon as a hydraulically-operated pump, actuated by a volume Q under head H and utilising the energy of this supply to lift a volume q. As this q is initially at a height H, the additional energy given to it in the ram is simply $(h_d - H)$ foot lbs. per lb., and from this point of view the ratio

$$\frac{q (h_d - H)}{Q H}$$

gives the efficiency of the plant as a whole. This expression is known as Rankine's formula for efficiency.

Although it is difficult to justify the idea of entire separation of the water pumped from the operating water, yet, for the sake of comparison with other types of pump, the latter formula, which gives results consistently lower than the former, will be adopted in this connection.

Whenever the efficiency of a ram is given, it should be stated which formula is used.

Sources of Loss.—These are due to :—

(1) Leakage at waste valve.

(2) Resistance of valves and of supply pipe.

(3) Eddy production due to sudden changes of section.

(4) Loss of resilient energy.

Leakage from the waste valve increases with the time during which it s off its seat; with the lift and area of the valve; and with the velocity of efflux; all of which, with the exception of the valve area, must be increased with an increase in the delivery head.

The area of the valve is usually made from two to four times that of the supply pipe, an increased area with a correspondingly reduced lift tending to efficiency in working.

This is the most serious of all the sources of loss, and usually accounts for between 15 and 25 per cent. of the total energy received.

To enable it to be reduced as far as possible, the weight and travel of the waste valve should be adjustable to suit any given conditions of working. It should be noted that this loss is not necessarily least when the time during which the valve is open is reduced to a minimum, for with a given supply and delivery head there is a certain valve travel below which the pressure will not exceed the delivery head. Increasing the travel increases the velocity of efflux and the time of opening, and therefore the leakage, but at the same time increases the pressure and therefore the proportion of energy entering the air chamber. This goes on up to a certain point, which can only be determined experimentally, where the increased leakage losses counterbalance the proportional gain of energy, and which gives the most efficient working lift.

This point is brought out in Fig. 332 which shows a series of efficiency curves obtained by the author from a small hydraulic ram of the type shown in Fig. 330 a, having a supply pipe 4 feet 6 inches long and 1¼ inches diameter, and working under a uniform head of 4 feet 6 inches, the waste valve being 1½ inches diameter. From these curves it is evident that although with low delivery heads the efficiency increased with an increase in the number of beats of the waste valve per minute, as the delivery head was increased the speed for maximum efficiency rapidly diminished.

(2) and (3) Valve resistances are approximately independent of head, while loss by shock and frictional losses in supply and delivery pipes increase as the velocity, and therefore as the delivery head, increases.

(4) The loss of energy due to resilience, being proportional to the square of the pressure of the water at the instant of closing the delivery valve, will vary as the square of the delivery head, and also with the mass of water affected, and will therefore increase with the length of the supply pipe and with the ratio $l \div H$.

Evidently, then, the most economical working is to be expected with a ram in which the delivery head is low and in which the ratio $l \div H$ is small. While the latter factor is not essential for fairly efficient working,

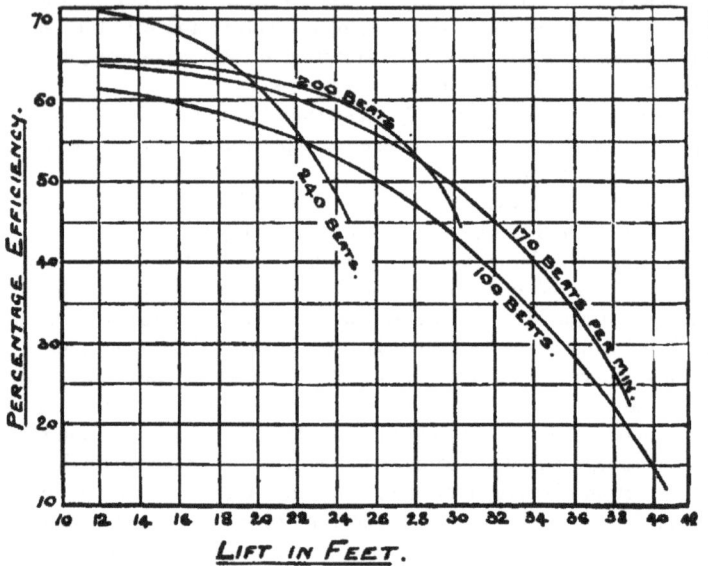

FIG. 332.—Efficiency Curves for Hydraulic Ram working under a constant head of 4·5 feet.

it is advisable where possible that this ratio should not exceed 2·5. However, where necessary this may be largely exceeded, and a supply pipe length of 1,000 feet with a ratio $l \div H = 25$ is well within the limits of everyday practice.

The delivery head may be anything up to about 250 feet and the supply head anything above 18 inches, but the ram becomes very inefficient as the ratio of delivery to supply head becomes great.

The ram will work with this ratio as great as 30 to 1, but under such circumstances has an efficiency not exceeding about 20 per cent. With lower delivery heads, up to about four times that of the supply, the ram will transform up to 75 per cent. of the energy in the supply reservoir into useful work.

Rankine gives the efficiency in terms of the ratio $\dfrac{h_d - H}{H}$ as being equal to

$$1\cdot12 - \cdot2\ \sqrt{\frac{h_d - H}{H}},$$

and while this cannot be looked upon as being generally true, it indicates how rapidly the efficiency falls off as $\dfrac{h_d}{H}$ increases. The curves of Fig. 332 also bring out this fact very clearly.

The simple type of ram already described gives excellent results where the diameter of supply pipe does not exceed about 4 inches. With larger sizes the shock caused by the sudden closing of the waste valve becomes excessive, and though various devices have been adopted to prevent this, none of them have proved satisfactory as applied to the ordinary ram. One such device is illustrated in Fig. 330 b. Here an air cushion, regulated by the air-cock K, is provided for the waste valve, but although this effectively prevents shock, it also prevents any high degree of efficiency being obtained. This is clear if it is remem-

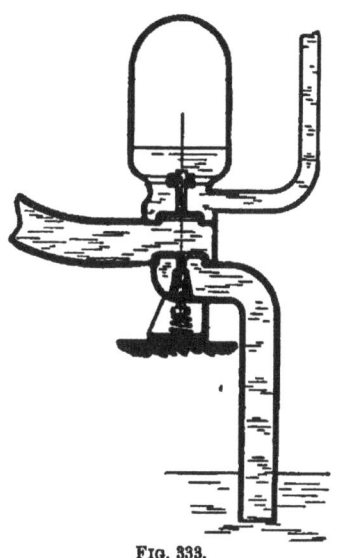

FIG. 333.

bered that the velocity of efflux of the waste water is increasing the whole of the time that the valve is closing and has its maximum value immediately before the valve comes to its seat, so that leakage during this portion of the cycle is more important than at any other time. Slowness of closing is thus particularly detrimental as the valve approaches its seat, and in fact the more quickly the valve reaches its seat after once beginning to close, the less will be the consequent loss of energy in the waste water expressed as a proportion of the whole kinetic energy of the column. A further drawback to the device lies in the fact that because of this leakage it becomes impossible to pump against a head greater than about six times the supply head.

In the above example the upward pressure of the water on the valve while closing is increased by the provision of a deflector attached to the valve spindle, this deflector also serving as the piston of the air buffer. An auxiliary waste valve V_3, mounted on the main valve spindle as shown, opens with the main valve, and allows any gritty material or pebbles to escape.

If necessary, the hydraulic ram may be situated well above the tail water level, the waste valve then discharging into a closed chamber which communicates with the tail water by means of a suction tube. The suction head produced in this discharge pipe then helps to increase the velocity of flow on opening the waste valve. The valve must now, however, be aided by means of a spring so as to be approximately balanced under this suction head. Fig. 333 shows diagrammatically an

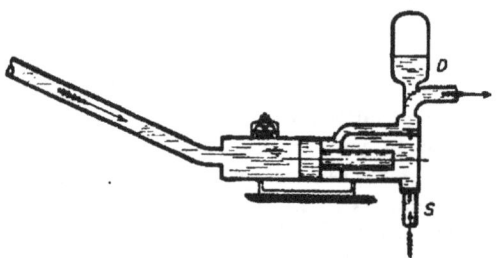

Fig. 334.—Hydraulic Ram for pumping clean water by means of a larger supply of dirty water under a lower head.

arrangement of this type devised by Decœurs, which has given very good results.

Fig. 334 shows the hydraulic ram as arranged for utilizing a large supply of impure water for pumping a smaller supply of clean water. Here S and D indicate the clean water suction and delivery pipes.

In place of the differential plunger pump shown, a flexible diaphragm is sometimes used to divide the waste valve box from the clean water supply and delivery valve box, the vibration of this diaphragm under the action of the ram serving the same purpose as that of the plunger in the previous sketch. As thus constructed, the clean water may be lifted against practically any head though the efficiency is only low.

A simpler device, but one not so certain in its action, consists in the provision of a pipe leading the clean water under a head about ⅓ that of the supply head into that part of the valve box remote from the supply pipe. A check valve prevents flow out of the valve box along this pipe, and a charge of clean water is drawn into the valve box as the pressure falls at each beat. The action may be regulated with considerable nicety by the provision of a regulating valve on this secondary supply pipe.

It was not until the invention of the hydraulic engine of Mr. Pearsall that the ram attained its highest development and became a really efficient machine for successfully handling large volumes of water. In general terms, this only differs from the ordinary ram in that its valve is opened and closed by mechanical means, this enabling a cylindrical balanced valve to be used, and the periods of the various portions of a cycle to be regulated to suit any given conditions of working.

Fig. 335 shows the general arrangement of the machine. Here A is the supply pipe and B the cylindrical waste valve, which is operated by the valve rod D, and which allows water to escape by the ports C. On closing this valve water enters the chamber E without shock and drives out before it the contained air, through a valve regulated by the wooden float F. When the water reaches a certain height the valve at F closes, and the pressure in E rises until sufficient to lift the delivery valves at G. The small remaining volume of compressed air and the water then enter the air vessel H, from which the water is led away along the delivery pipe T. A second air chamber S is sometimes fitted, but is not essential. The valve B is now opened, the rush

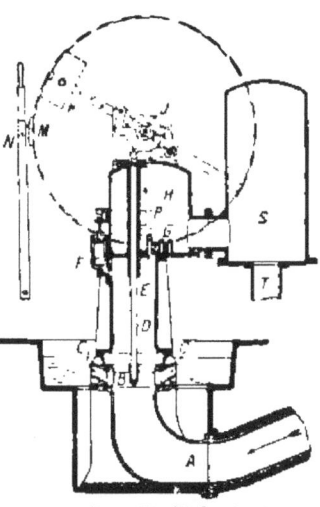

FIG. 335.—Pearsall's Hydraulic Engine or Ram.

of water out of E and down the supply pipe is followed by its closure, and the cycle of operations is repeated as before.

The method of working this valve is ingenious. The shaft J carries a pendulum K, which swings through an arc of about 240°, and also a cam so proportioned as to divide the time of a swing of the pendulum into two parts suitable for the flow and delivery parts of the cycle. This cam regulates the motion of the valve rod.

In order to maintain the swing of the pendulum against friction, a crank on J is coupled to a piston in the small single-acting cylinder P, into which air is admitted from the air vessel at each double stroke, so as to give a slight impetus to the pendulum at the middle of its swing.

The engine is stopped and started by the bar N, which, when held against the pendulum, engages with the rachet M when this begins to descend. This stopping takes place immediately before the end of a working stroke, when the main valve is closed and when the flow of water in the main pump has for the moment ceased. On releasing the rachet, the ram at once engages on a normal stroke.

As thus constructed, the machine is capable of dealing with practically any quantity of water, and works as noiselessly as a pumping engine. The smoothness of its working as compared with that of the ordinary type of ram may be inferred from Fig. 336, which shows a diagram taken from the valve box of a ram of this type.

The simplicity of the mechanism of the hydraulic ram, its high

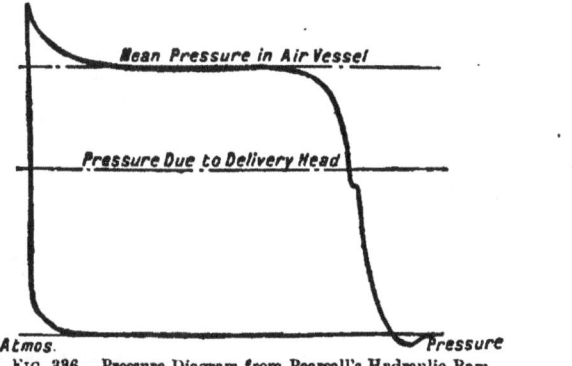

FIG. 336.—Pressure Diagram from Pearsall's Hydraulic Ram.

efficiency, and the fact that it is capable of working for very long periods without attention, render it specially well fitted for use in a private pumping plant, and there is every indication that at the present time its many advantages are being to an increasing extent realized.

Hydraulic Ram for Air Compression.—With slight modifications the hydraulic ram may be adapted for use as an air compressor. Thus in the Pearsall ram the chamber E is enlarged so as to hold the whole volume of air compressed in a single stroke, while the valve at F is modified so as to confine this air, and the delivery valves at G are slightly modified. The cylinder P is also now worked by pressure water from the air vessel E instead of by compressed air. As thus constructed, efficiencies of upwards of 80 per cent. may be obtained.

Fig. 337 shows a type of air compressor on somewhat similar lines

esigned by M. Sommellier and used in the work on the Mont Cenis
!unnel. Here the inlet valve V_1 and the waste valve V_2 are mechanically,
.riven, and are coupled together. When the valve V_2 is opened the water
n the compressor finds its own level and air at atmospheric pressure is
lrawn in through the air valve V_4. V_2 is then closed and V_1 opened,
.llowing pressure water to flow along the pipe A, and in virtue of its
)ressure and momentum to compress the air in the chamber B, whence
t passes through the delivery valve V_3 into the air reservoir. V_1 is then
:losed, V_2 opened, and the cycle of operations repeated as before. Work-
ng under a head of 85 feet, this compressor delivers air at a pressure of

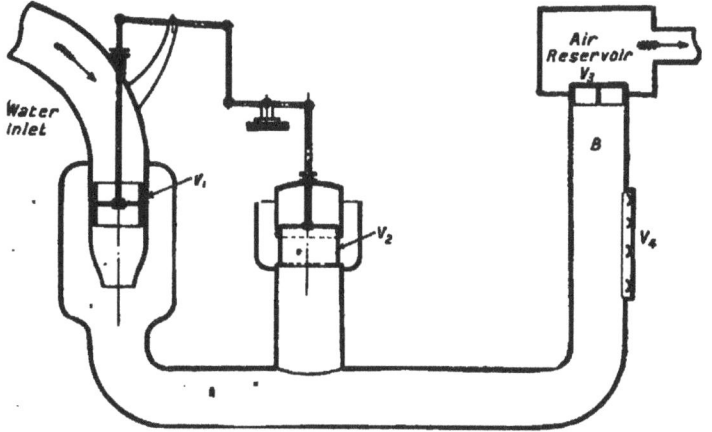

FIG. 337.—Hydraulic Air Compressor.

75 lbs. per square inch. The machine is, however, somewhat cumbrous
for the amount of work which it is capable of performing.

ART. 187.—THE JET PUMP.

The fact that the pressure energy of a water supply may be converted
into kinetic energy, with a consequent reduction of pressure, is taken
advantage of in the type of jet pump devised by Professor James Thomson
(about 1852). The pump, as usually constructed, is illustrated in Fig. 338.
Here water from the source of supply is led through the converging
passage P, its pressure diminishing as its velocity increases, and is
finally discharged into the delivery pipe through the diverging passage D
It follows that at the section J, where its velocity is greatest, its pressure

may become considerably less than that of the atmosphere. A chamber surrounding J is connected to the supply of water to be pumped, by the suction pipe S. The reduction of pressure in this chamber is then accompanied by a flow of water along the suction pipe, which, meeting the high pressure jet, is carried forward as a combined stream into the diverging discharge pipe D. Here its kinetic energy is partially reconverted into pressure energy, which is utilized in overcoming the head to be pumped against.

Let h_1 = height of supply head above jet in feet.

„ h_s = height of jet above suction supply   „

„ H_d = height of delivery head above jet   „

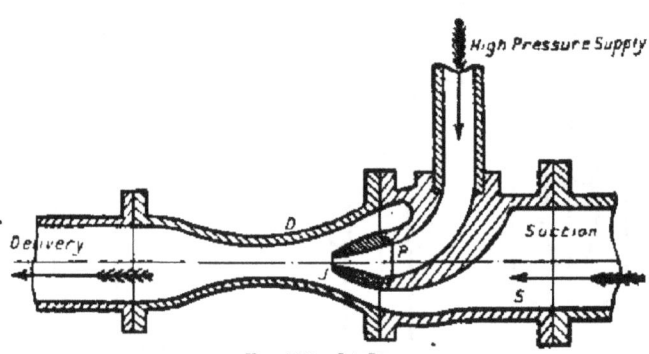

FIG. 338.—Jet Pump.

Let $h_d = \left\{ \dfrac{p_d}{W} + \dfrac{v_d{}^2}{2g} \right\} = H_d + $ losses between point D and delivery.

„ a_1 = area of nozzle in square feet.

„ a_s = area of annular suction pipe in plane of nozzle, square feet.

„ a_d = area of mixing chamber at throat, square feet.

„ Q = volume passing per second, v = velocity, and p the pressure in lbs. per square foot at the point denoted by a suffix.

On the assumption that the sides of the mixing chamber are sensibly parallel from the nozzle until the jets have attained a common velocity and pressure at D, so that, neglecting friction, the sides of the chamber exert no force on the water, we may apply the equation of momentum, which now becomes :—

$$\frac{Q_d v_d}{g} - \left\{ \frac{Q_s v_s}{g} + \frac{Q_1 v_1}{g} \right\} = \frac{p_1 a_1 + p_s a_s - p_d a_d}{W}$$

$$\therefore \quad \frac{a_d\, v_d^2 - a_s\, v_s^2 - a_1\, v_1^2}{g} = \frac{p_1\, a_1 + p_s\, a_s - p_d\, a_d}{W}$$

$$\therefore \quad a_1\left(\frac{p_1}{W} + \frac{v_1^2}{2\,g}\right) + a_s\left(\frac{p_s}{W} + \frac{v_s^2}{2\,g}\right) - a_d\left(\frac{p_d}{W} + \frac{v_d^2}{2\,g}\right)$$

$$= \frac{1}{2\,g}\left\{a_d\, v_d^2 - a_s\, v_s^2 - a_1\, v_1^2\right\}$$

or $\quad a_1\, h_1 -^1 a_s\, h_s - a_d\, h_d = \dfrac{1}{2\,g}\left\{a_d\, v_d^2 - a_s\, v_s^2 - a_1\, v_1^2\right\}$ (1)

Again, for continuity of flow, we have:—

$$\left.\begin{array}{c} a_1\, v_1 + a_s\, v_s = a_d\, v_d \\ \text{or} \quad Q_1 + Q_s \quad = Q_d \end{array}\right\} \tag{2}$$

From these equations, when the dimensions of the pump and the heads are given, any two unknown velocities, and hence quantities, may be determined. For example, if Q is given, Q_s and Q_d may be determined. If, in addition, we assume that the pressure across the mixing chamber immediately in front of the nozzle is uniform, and equal to p_j (an assumption which is only true so long as both streams are parallel), we have

$$\left\{\begin{array}{l} h_1 = \dfrac{v_1^2}{2\,g} + \dfrac{p_j}{W} \\[2mm] - h_s = \dfrac{v_s^2}{2\,g} + \dfrac{p_j}{W} \end{array}\right.$$

$$\therefore \quad \frac{v_1^2}{2\,g} - h_1 = \frac{v_s^2}{2\,g} + h_s$$

or $\quad v_s^2 = v_1^2 - 2\,g\,(h_1 + h_s)$. (3)

Introducing this value of v_s in (1) we get:—

$$a_1\, h_1 - a_s\, h_s - a_d\, h_d = \frac{1}{2\,g}\left\{a_d\, v_d^2 - (a_1 + a_s)\, v_1^2\right\} + a_s\,(h_1 + h_s)$$

or $\quad (a_1 - a_s)\, h_1 - 2\, a_s\, h_s - a_d\, h_d = \dfrac{1}{2\,g}\left\{a_d\, v_d^2 - (a_1 + a_s)\, v_1^2\right\}$. (4)

While, by substitution in (2):—

$$a_1\, v_1 + a_s\, \sqrt{v_1^2 - 2\,g\,(h_1 + h_s)} = a_d\, v_d. \tag{5}$$

From equations (3), (4) and (5), if the areas of the passages and the various heads are given, the velocities v_1, v_s and v_d, and thus the quantities Q_1, $Q_s + Q_d$, may be determined.

EXAMPLE.

Thomson's Jet Pump.

$h_1 = 40$ feet. $a_1 = \cdot2$ square feet.

$h_s = 15$ feet. $a_s = \cdot4$ square feet.

$h_d = 10$ feet. $a_d = \cdot6$ square feet.

---

[1] Negative sign because $\left(\dfrac{p_s}{W} + \dfrac{v_s^2}{2\,g}\right)$ is negative if h_s is positive.

Determine Q_1, Q_s and Q_d, and also the pressure $\frac{p_d}{W}$ at the throat of the mixing cone and $\frac{p_j}{W}$ in the plane of the orifices.

From equation (4) we have :—

$$- \{ \cdot 2 \times 40 + \cdot 8 \times 15 + \cdot 6 \times 10 \} \frac{64 \cdot 4}{\cdot 6} = v_d{}^2 - v_1{}^2;$$

$$\therefore v_1{}^2 - v_d{}^2 = 2,790. \quad \text{(i)}$$

Again, from (5),

$$(\cdot 6 \, v_d - \cdot 2 v_1)^2 = \cdot 16 \, \{ v_1{}^2 - 64 \cdot 4 \times 55 \}$$

$$\therefore v_1{}^2 + 2 \, v_1 \, v_d - 3 \, v_d{}^2 = 4,718. \quad \text{(ii)}$$

Substituting for $v_d{}^2$ in (ii) from (i) :—

$$v_1{}^2 + 2 \, v_1 \sqrt{v_1{}^2 - 2,790} - 3 \, (v_1{}^2 - 2,790) = 4,718.$$

$$\therefore v_1{}^2 - 1,826 = v_1 \sqrt{v_1{}^2 - 2,790}.$$

Squaring both sides, we get, on reduction :—

$$862 \, v_1{}^2 = 3,333,000$$

$$\text{or } v_1{}^2 = 3,866$$

$$\therefore v_1 = 62 \cdot 2 \text{ feet per second.}$$

Substituting this value in (i) :—

$$v_d = \sqrt{3,866 - 2,790} = 32 \cdot 8 \text{ feet per second ;}$$

while from equation (3) :—

$$v_s = \sqrt{3,866 - 3,542} = 18 \cdot 0 \text{ feet per second.}$$

$$\therefore Q_1 = \cdot 2 \, v_1 = 12 \cdot 4 \text{ cubic feet per second.}$$

$$\bullet \quad Q_d = \cdot 6 \, v_d = 19 \cdot 7 \text{ cubic feet per second.}$$

$$Q_s = \cdot 4 \, v_s = 7 \cdot 2 \text{ cubic feet per second.}$$

Again, since $\frac{p_j}{W} + \frac{v_1{}^2}{2 \, g} = h_1$, :—

$$\frac{p_j}{W} = 40 - 60 \cdot 1 = - \ 20 \cdot 1 \text{ feet of water.}$$

while since $\qquad h_d = \frac{p_d}{W} + \frac{v_d{}^2}{2 \, g}$:—

$$\therefore \frac{p_d}{W} = 10 - 16 \cdot 7 = - \ 6 \cdot 7 \text{ feet of water.}$$

The actual height through which the water may be forced by the pump is less than the value h_d given by $\left\{ \frac{p_d}{W} + \frac{v_d{}^2}{2 \, g} \right\}$ feet, because of the loss of energy by eddy formation in the diverging discharge pipe, and may amount to between $\cdot 6$ and $\cdot 7 \, h_d$.

This loss of energy is proportional to $v_d{}^2$, and will therefore increase— since the necessary value for v_d increases—as h_d increases. Consequently,

,ince the total work done in pumping is proportional to $h_d + h_s$, while this loss depends only on h_d, the efficiency will increase as h_s is increased at the expense of h_d.

It follows that with a given total lift, the suction head should be increased as far as possible—up to about 22 feet—at the expense of the delivery head. This conclusion is borne out in practice.

The efficiency of the pump is given by—

$$\eta = \frac{Q_s (H_d + h_s)}{Q_1 (h_1 - H_d)}.$$

This efficiency is of necessity low, since the action depends on the mixing of two streams moving with different velocities, and hence involves considerable loss by shock. E.g., in the numerical example considered on p. 696, the efficiency (assuming $H_d = \cdot 7\, h_d$) is given by—

$$\eta = \frac{7 \cdot 2\, (7 + 15)}{12 \cdot 4 \times 33} = \cdot 387.$$

Actually, frictional losses reduce the efficiency still further, and the maximum efficiency attained in practice, even with a pump placed at delivery level, is about 25 per cent. This is increased to about 30 per cent. where, as when used for delivering a high velocity jet of water for fire purposes, the necessity for converting the kinetic energy of the jet into pressure energy is absent.

For continuous pumping and drainage operations where a fair pressure supply is obtainable, and where the volume to be lifted and the working head are small, the method offers the advantages of simplicity and low first cost, while practically no attention is required. Unless the supply head is large compared with the lift, the ratio $\dfrac{Q_s}{Q}$ is, however, very small—often so low as $\frac{1}{5}$.

The principle of the steam injector, as fitted for boiler feed purposes is identical with that of the jet pump. The preceding equations, however, need to be modified, since the streams of fluid on impinging are not of equal density, although they become so on condensation of the high velocity steam jet.

The principle of the jet pump has been applied in an intensifier for raising the pressure of a large quantity of low pressure water by means of a small supply at high pressure, the delivery pipe D leading directly into the cylinder of the intensifier. While not economical from an energy standpoint, the simplicity and low first cost of the apparatus render it very suitable for such work where its use is only occasional.

Art. 188.—The Injector Hydrant.

Since the chief loss of energy in the ordinary jet pump is due to shock at the collision of the two jets, it would appear that the total loss might be diminished by diminishing the velocity of the high pressure, or increasing that of the low pressure jet in stages, instead of at a single impact.

This method has been applied with success by Mr. Greathead in the

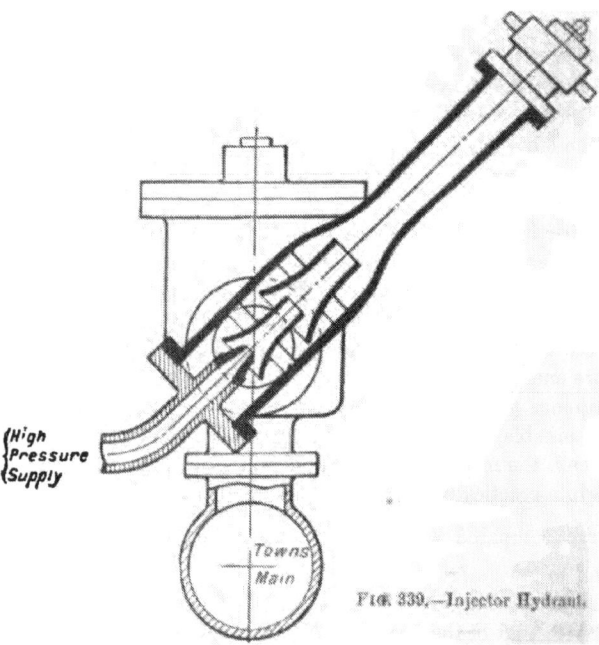

Fig. 339.—Injector Hydrant.

construction of his injector hydrant (Fig. 339), which is adapted for fire extinguishing purposes where a continuous supply of high pressure water is available, as is the case near the pipe line from an hydraulic power station. By itself, the water in the power main is of insufficient volume to have any appreciable effect on a fire, but when used with an injector hydrant in connection with a low pressure main the advantages of the system are very great. As exemplifying the effect of a small jet of high pressure water in increasing the height of the main jet, it is stated that while an ordinary 1½-inch hydrant supplied from a main at 40 lbs. pressure will

ve a stream about 50 feet high, the same when reinforced by a ⅜-inch
t of water at 750 lbs. per square inch will lift a slightly greater (about
; per cent.) volume of water from the main and will deliver this as a jet
; feet high.

The efficiency of the hydrant from an energy point of view ranges from
₃ per cent. to 33 per cent.

The following table, given by Mr. Greathead[1], shows the quantity
: high pressure water, at 700 lbs. per square inch, required to deliver a
;t of 150 gallons per minute through a 1-inch nozzle, through a height
ariously estimated to be from 75 to 84 feet, and requiring a head at the
ozzle of 100 feet. Here allowance is made for 200 feet of 2½-inch hose,
ie resistance of which is equivalent to 50 feet head.

Low Pressure Supply.		High Pressure Supply.
Lbs. per square inch.	Feet.	Gallons per minute.
60	139	3·7
50	115	10·9
40	92	18·1
30	69	25·2
20	46	32·4
10	23	39·6

ART. 189.—THE AIR LIFT PUMP.

Among other devices for pumping liquids against a large head, that
known as the air lift pump is worthy of notice. Invented probably by
Carl Löscher about 1797, the system fell into comparative desuetude for
many years, and has only recently been revived and improved. In view
of its increasing use, and of its adaptability to many difficult cases of
pumping, it is worth while considering the system somewhat in detail.
Briefly, the method consists in sinking an open vertical pipe with its
lower end submerged in the liquid to be raised, and having its upper end
arranged to discharge into a reservoir at the required height. Air from
a compressor is then forced through a smaller air pipe into the submerged
opening of the lift pipe or rising main. The air bubbles, rising through
the water in the lift tube, so reduce the specific gravity of the mixture,
and therefore the weight of the column, that the excess pressure at the

1 " Proceedings Institute Mechanical Engineers," 1879, p. 364.

base of the column, due to the external water pressure, becomes sufficiently
great to force the mixture above the supply level and out of the top of the

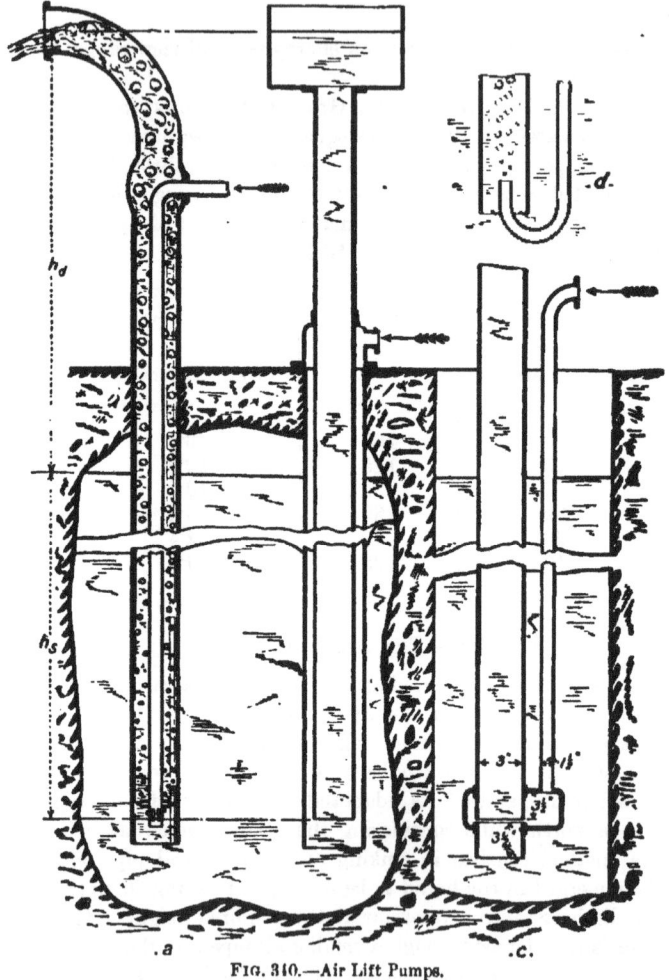

FIG. 310.—Air Lift Pumps.

pipe.   This excess pressure increases with the depth of submersion of the
pipe, and the latter must therefore be regulated to suit the height to
which water is to be lifted.

In general, the depth of submersion h_s (Fig. 340) is made from (1·5 to 2) mes the lift h_d, so that the total length of lift pipe $= (2·5$ to 3) h_d. As e depth of immersion is reduced, the relative air consumption increases id the efficiency diminishes. As will be shown later, a further increase ι h_s tends to more efficient working, and is advisable where this may be ptained without great expense in deepening the bore hole.

To keep down frictional losses, the velocity in the lift tube, calculated a the volume of water discharged, should not exceed 5 feet per second. he efficiency of the system, as calculated from the ratio of the work done ι lifting water through a height h_d, to the indicated work in the air pmpressor engine cylinder, is generally between 25 and 30 per cent.—this llowing for a compressor efficiency of 75 per cent.—but under favourable onditions may rise to 45 per cent.

There are three methods of arranging the pipe lines in a well or pre hole.

(1) The central air tube system (Fig. 340 a), in which the air pipe is iuspended in the centre of the lift tube.

(2) The annular air tube system, in which the space between the lift ιube and the bore hole is used as the air line (Fig. 340 b).

(3) The side-by-side system, in which the air and lift tubes are carried lown the well side by side (Fig. 340 c).

The first of these systems has the disadvantage that the hydraulic mean iepth of the water passage in the lift tube is reduced by the air tube, being given by—

$$\frac{\pi (R^2 - r^2)}{2 \pi (R + r)} = \frac{R - r}{2} = \frac{D - d}{4},$$

where D and d are the internal diameter of the lift tube and the external liameter of the air tube respectively.[1]

This leads to increased frictional losses and so to diminished efficiency. The system is, however, very suitable for application to a small bore hole pf suitable dimensions, since the only additional expense is the provision pf the comparatively small air pipe, while any alteration in the length of this, to suit different conditions of working, is a simple matter. In general this will be found more advantageous than the second system, the chief advantage of the latter lying in its possibilities of more effective air distribution.

Where the well or bore hole is of large diameter, the side-by-side system has many advantages in virtue of its accessibility, simplicity, and flexibility.

[1] With a plain tube of the same sectional area the hydraulic mean depth is given by $\frac{D_1}{4}$, where $D_1 = \sqrt{D^2 - d^2}$.

In every case provision must be made for distributing the air evenly and in small bubbles among the water in the lift tube, since experiment shows that the system is then much more effective than where the air bubbles are so large as to fill the tube. The diameter of the bubbles at their initiation should be about $\frac{1}{4}$ inch. Some such arrangement of foot box, as shown in Fig. 340 c, is essential for efficient working. Comparative tests show that this type, in which air enters all around the circumference of the lift tube gives efficiencies 20 per cent. greater than that shown in Fig. 340 d, in which the air is supplied in a single central jet.

Theory of the Air Lift Pump.

Let　　　V_w = volume of water raised in cubic feet per second.

,,　　　V_m = mean volume of air used, in cubic feet per second, during its passage through the rising main.

,,　　　V_a = volume used in cubic feet per second, at atmospheric pressure, p_a.

,,　　　p_1 = pressure at base of rising main.

,,　　　$h_d + h_s = l$ feet.

Then, assuming isothermal expansion of the air in the lift tube, we have:—

$$V_m = \frac{p_a}{p_1 - p_a}\left(\log_e \frac{p_1}{p_a}\right) V_a \tag{1}$$

The mean specific gravity of the mixture in the tube $= \dfrac{V_w}{V_w + V_m}$.

$\therefore$ Head producing flow $= h_s - (h_d + h_s)\dfrac{V_w}{V_w + V_m}$ feet of water,

$$= h_s\left(\frac{V_w + V_m}{V_w}\right) - (h_d + h_s) \text{ feet of mixture in}$$
the lift tube.

$$= \frac{V_m}{V_w} h_s - h_d \text{ feet of mixture.}$$

Equating this to the sum of the friction head h_f, and the kinetic head h_v, we have, on reduction :—

$$V_m = V_w \frac{h_d + h_f + h_v}{h_s},$$

$$\therefore V_a = V_w \frac{p_1 - p_a}{p_a \log_e \frac{p_1}{p_a}} \cdot \frac{h_d + h_f + h_v}{h},$$

$$= \frac{V_w(h_d + h_f + h_v)}{34 \log_e \frac{p_1}{p_a}} \cdot \left(\text{since } \frac{p_1 - p_a}{p_a} = \frac{34 + h_s - 34}{34} = \frac{h_s}{34}\right).$$

This relation enables the volume of free air per cubic foot of water to e determined in terms of h_f and h_v. Writing $h_v = \dfrac{1}{2g} \left\{ \dfrac{V_a + V_w}{A} \right\}^2$, and

putting $h_f = \dfrac{f(h_d + h_s) v^2}{2 g m}$ (where v^2 is the mean square of the velocity

in the tube) this latter term may be taken as approximately equal to

$\dfrac{(h_s + h_d)}{2 g m} \left\{ \dfrac{V_a + 2 V_w}{2 A} \right\}^2$, in which case the ratio $V_a \div V_w$ may be directly

obtained in terms of h_d, h_s, A and f.

The author has determined the values of f for a mixture of air and water the friction head being expressed in feet of a column of the mixture in the tube) from the published data of a large number of trials on such pumps.

Making the above assumption as to the value of r, the value of f varies from ·033 in the case of a 3-inch pipe with $r = 12\cdot16$ f.s. to ·023 in a 12-inch pipe with $v = 6\cdot5$ f.s. In every case f has a value very approximately six times that obtaining for the flow of water alone at the same velocity.

In practice the following approximate values of $V_a \div V_w$ are found to give the best results :—

h_d (feet)	10	20	30	50	100
$V_a \div V_w$	1·0	1·5	2·0	2·5	3·0

Efficiency of the Air Lift Pump.—Assuming isothermal compression, the work done on the air during compression from p_a to p_1 $= p_a V_a \log_e \dfrac{p_1}{p_a}$ foot lbs.

The useful work done by the air in raising V_w cubic feet of water through a height h_d feet $= 62\cdot4 \, V_w \, h_d$ foot lbs.

$\therefore$ Efficiency—

$$\eta = \frac{62\cdot4 \, V_w \, h_d}{p_a V_a \log_e \dfrac{p_1}{p_a}} = \frac{62\cdot4 \, V_w \, h_d \times 34 \log_e \dfrac{p_1}{p_a}}{p_a \log_e \dfrac{p_1}{p_a} \times V_w (h_d + h_f + h_v)}$$

$$= \frac{h_d}{h_d + h_f + h_v} \qquad (2)$$

On the assumption of adiabatic compression from p_a to p_1, the work done on the air $= 3\cdot463 \, p_a \, V_a \left\{ \left(\dfrac{p_1}{p_a}\right)^{\cdot29} - 1 \right\}$ foot lbs., so that the efficiency

$$= \frac{h_d \log_e \frac{p_1}{p_a}}{3 \cdot 468 \left\{ \left(\frac{p_1}{p_a}\right)^{\cdot 29} - 1\right\} \{h_d + h_f + h_v\}} \tag{3}$$

From expression (2) it appears that as h_d is increased from zero (keeping h_s constant) the efficiency will increase until some point is reached at which the (velocity of flow)^2 increases more rapidly than does h_d. This gives the value of h_d for maximum efficiency. In practice it is found that the ratio $h_s \div h_d$ then lies between 1·5 and 2·5, the larger values of the ratio being used with low values of h_d.

The following table gives the results of tests on a plant of the type illustrated in Fig. 340 c, carried out by Professor Jossè at Charlottenburg :—

Diameter of lift tube, inches	$3\frac{7}{16}$	$3\frac{7}{16}$	$3\frac{7}{16}$	$3\frac{7}{16}$	$3\frac{7}{16}$	$7\frac{1}{2}$	$2\frac{3}{4}$	$2\frac{3}{4}$	$2\frac{3}{4}$
Diameter of air pipe, inches.	$1\frac{9}{16}$	$1\frac{9}{16}$	$1\frac{9}{16}$	$1\frac{9}{16}$	$1\frac{9}{16}$	5	—	—	—
Diameter of bore hole, inches	$6\frac{1}{2}$	$6\frac{1}{2}$	$6\frac{1}{2}$	$6\frac{1}{2}$	$6\frac{1}{2}$	—	—	—	—
Depth of immersion, h_s feet	49·2	49·2	49·2	49·2	49·2	63	69·2	72·9	62·0
Height of lift, h_d feet .	24·6	24·6	24·6	24·6	24·6	43·5	50·5	46·7	57·8
V_w {Gallons per minute .	24·2	68·3	94·0	96·8	94·8	800	47·5	51·1	39·2
{Cubic feet per second .	·065	·177	·251	·259	·253	2·35	·127	·137	·105
V_a cub. ft. at atmospheric pressure	·127	·309	·739	·842	1·766	6·46	·316	·334	·346
$\frac{V_a}{V_w}$ = volume of air per cub. ft. of water .	1·96	1·75	2·94	3·68	7·50	2·75	2·49	2·45	3·30
Velocity of flow at entrance, f.s.	2·54	3·46	4·90	5·07	4·61	7·65	—	—	—
Mean velocity of mixture in tube	5·16	6·64	12·46	14·87	22·80	20·8	—	—	—
Efficiency {Water H.P. / I.H.P. in compressor cylinder.	39·8%	44·9%	26·7%	21·3%	10·6%	38·4%	44·5%	32·9%	13·3%

A very extensive series of experiments carried out by the Westinghouse Air Brake Company in a 6-inch well, 174 feet deep, at Wilderning, Pa., lead to the following general conclusions:—

(1) The rate of delivery of water, and the air consumption per gallon, with fixed size of discharge pipe, are practically constant for all lifts, provided the ratio of lift to submergence is maintained constant.

(2) With a discharge pipe of given diameter, the delivery decreases and the air consumption per gallon increases as the ratio of lift to submergence increases.

(3) With a fixed ratio of lift to submergence, the air consumption per gallon decreases as the size of discharge pipe increases.

(4) The least air pressure that will give continuous flow is the proper pressure to use. A slightly lower pressure gives intermittent delivery and the amount delivered is much decreased, though the air consumption per gallon is slightly lower than with continuous flow. With pressure higher than just enough to give continuous flow, the delivery is increased somewhat, but the air consumption per gallon delivered is increased in greater ratio; and with further increase in air pressure a point of maximum delivery is reached, beyond which the delivery is decreased in amount. The sound of the discharge is a reliable guide to proper regulation of the air supply.

(5) It appears from (2) that by increasing the submergence, i.e. locating the foot piece deeper down in the water, for a given lift, the air consumption is progressively reduced. But as the required air pressure is increased with the greater depth, a cubic foot of air represents greater power. A curve representing the variation of horse-power required per gallon of water delivered, with depth varying, shows that the power first decreases with increasing depth, then reaches a minimum and thence increases. The ratio of lift to submergence at this minimum point may be called the " economical ratio."

(6) For a given size of discharge pipe the economic ratio decreases as the lift increases; i.e., the submergence should be increased in greater ratio than the lift. For a given lift, the economical ratio increases (submergence decreases) as the size of discharge pipe increases.

(7) A tail piece, or projection of the discharge pipe below the air inlet, is essential in starting, as it tends to prevent the air from backing down into the well and rising in the casing outside the discharge pipe.

(8) Anything in the shape of a jet or pipe introduced into the discharge pipe to serve as air inlet has no value, and is, in fact, detrimental by forming an obstacle to the free passage of water.

H.A.   Z Z

(9) In starting the pumping the air should be admitted slowly. Pumping will not commence immediately, but after several seconds, perhaps even a minute, water will come with a rush. This is followed by a lull, after which the operation becomes more uniform. The valve can then be opened until continuous flow is obtained.

For deep well pumping, the air lift pump is very suitable, since it can be used in any bore hole of sufficient diameter to admit the necessary pipe-lines, and can take advantage of the whole discharging capacity of the hole.

In addition, the absence of moving parts below the surface, the possibility of installing the compressing plant at practically any distance from the bore hole, and of pumping corrosive liquid or water carrying solid matter in suspension, together with the certainty of operation, give the system very obvious advantages, and in many instances greatly outweigh the disadvantage of moderate efficiency.

With hot liquids, too, the efficiency is augmented, since the volume of air in the rising main is increased by the rise in the temperature, while in many instances the aerating effect of the air is an advantage.[1]

Art. 190.—Hydraulic Air Compressor.

By reversing the action of the air lift pump, and allowing water, under a head h_d, to flow down a vertical pipe of length $(h_d + h_s)$, which has a length h_s submerged in the tail race (Fig. 341) a type of air compressor is obtained which is fairly efficient, and has obtained some success from its simplicity of construction.

Water entering at the upper end of the down pipe induces a series of small air jets through suitably placed openings, and, if the velocity is sufficiently great, carries the entrained air to the bottom of the pipe, where its pressure $= 2·3\ h_s$ lbs. per square inch approximately. The water is then allowed to escape, while the air is collected in an air chamber surrounding the falling main.

The pressure to which the air may be compressed is thus independent of the supply head and depends solely on h_s. Since, however, the head required to maintain the required velocity of flow increases with h_s, this limits the pressure attainable.

---

[1] Further information on this subject may be obtained from the following papers :—
" Proceedings Institute Civil Engineers," vol. 140, p. 323.
" Proceedings Institute Civil Engineers," vol. 163, 1905–6, part I., p. 353.
" British Association of Waterworks Engineers," 1903.
Engineer, January 10, 1908, p. 26.

The velocity with which fine bubbles rise through still water is pproximately 9 inches per second, and it is essential that the velocity of ow be greater than this. Experiments show that velocities of from 2 to 16 feet per second give the best results.

The volume of air compressed per cubic foot of water used, may be eternrined as in the case of the air lift pump.

Recently published tests of such a plant as here described are said

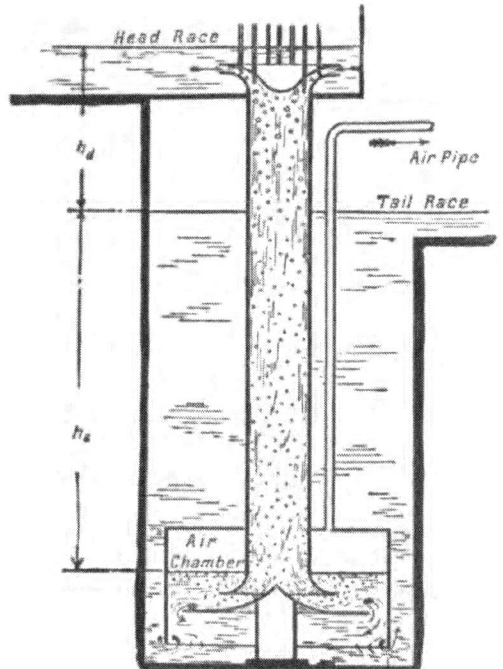

FIG. 341.—Hydraulic Air Compressor.

to have given an efficiency of 82 per cent.[1] Here $h_d = 71$ feet and $h_s = 261$ feet. Three vertical shafts are used, each 5 feet in diameter, and the plant is capable of developing 4000 H.P., compressing the air to a pressure of 117 lbs. per square inch above the atmosphere.

[1] *Engineering and Mining Journal*, New York, January 19, 1907, p. 125. See also an abstract in "Proceedings Institute Civil Engineers," vol. 169, p. 500. This value is probably high. See also *Engineer*, Nov. 10, 1911, p. 482.

Art. 191.—The Humphrey Gas Pump.

In the Humphrey pump the expansive force following the ignition of an explosive mixture of gas and air is directly utilised to pump water. In its simplest form the pump consists of a combustion chamber C (Fig. 342), fitted with valves A and E for the admission of gas and air and for the exhaustion of the waste products of combustion. A continuation of the combustion chamber forms a suction chamber W with its suction valves V and the delivery main D, which discharges into the elevated tank $E\,T$. The action of the pump is as follows:—A compressed charge of gas and air in C is ignited by an electric spark and expands,

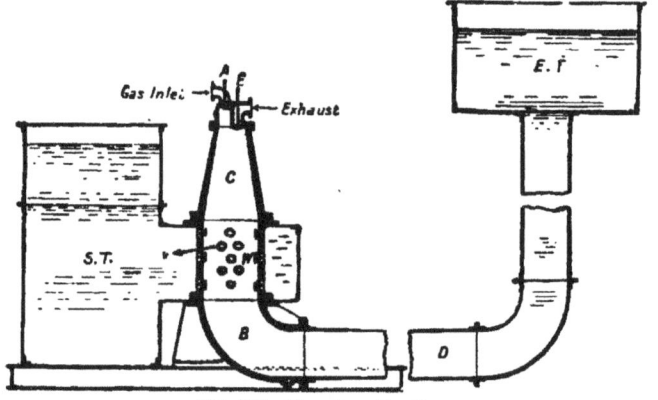

Fig. 342.—Humphrey Gas Pump.

driving forwards the column of water in the delivery pipe. Expansion proceeds until the pressure falls to or below atmospheric, when the suction valves V and the exhaust valve E open. In virtue of its momentum the delivery column maintains its motion for some appreciable time, during which water is drawn through the suction valves, part of this joining in the motion of the column and part entering the combustion chamber. After a short time the momentum is destroyed and the column, acted upon by the pressure due to the delivery head, begins to return, closing the suction valves and forcing the waste products out through the valve E. This action is continued until the water level rises to that of this valve, which is closed by the impact, and the remaining products are compressed into the space F. This compression continues until the column is brought to rest, when a second outward motion of the column ensues and the pressure in F falls to atmospheric. At this instant the inlet valves are opened, and the further motion of the column draws in a fresh charge of air and gas. Again the column returns under the elevated tank pressure compressing this charge which is then ignited to start a fresh cycle of operations. The cycle is thus identical with that of the four-cycle gas engine. By a comparatively simple modification of the combustion chamber and its valves the cycle may, however, be made to correspond with the two-cycle engine.[1]

EXAMPLES.

(1) A hydraulic ram uses 50 gallons of water per minute under a supply head of 4 feet, and pumps 5 gallons of this against an effective head of 30 feet. Determine the efficiency of the ram.

Answer. 72·25 per cent.

(2) A ram uses 900 gallons of water per minute under 10 feet head, and pumps 50 gallons of this through 500 feet of 2½-inch piping into a reservoir at a height of 80 feet above the ram. Determine the efficiency, taking $f = ·014$.

Answer. 60 per cent.

(3) The waste valve of a hydraulic ram is 4 inches diameter and is required to begin to close when the velocity of flow past the valve itself is 6 feet per second. Assuming the dynamic pressure on the valve per unit area to be given by $1·35 \dfrac{W v^2}{2 g}$ lbs., where $W =$ weight per cubic foot of water, determine the necessary weight of the valve.

Answer. ·328 lbs. per square inch.
Total weight $= 4·12$ lbs.

(4) A jet pump placed 8 feet above the suction reservoir and 60 feet below the supply reservoir, lifts its water through a total height of 8 feet 9 inches. Determine its efficiency when delivering 100 gallons per minute and when using 36·5 gallons per minute from the supply reservoir.

Answer. ·257.

(5) An injector hydrant takes 25·2 gallons per minute of high pressure water at 700 lbs. per square inch and delivers 150 gallons per minute at a pressure of 65 lbs. per square inch, the low pressure supply being at 30 lbs. per square inch. Determine the efficiency.

Answer. ·273.

[1] Details of the mechanical construction of these pumps are given in *Proceedings Institute Mechanical Engineers*, 1909, p. 1075. A set of five recently constructed for the Metropolitan Water Board pump 180 millions of gallons per day, with a lift of 25 to 30 feet.

main steam pipe are automatically closed as the ram reaches the extreme limit of its upward stroke. The engines under steam are thus brought to a standstill, and remain so until the tappet is released by the descent of the ram. Each accumulator is fitted with an electric bell, which gives warning when the ram is about 10 feet from the bottom of its stroke.

The pressure water is led into the streets by four 6-inch cast-iron pipes, after which the branch pipes vary in diameter by even inches from 6 inches down to 2 inches.

The joint flanges are oval, the joint consisting of a bevelled spigot and

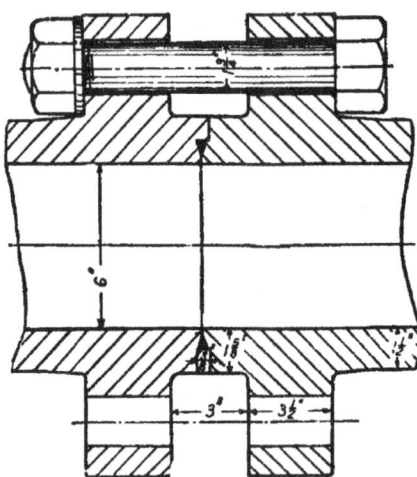

faucet union securing a $\frac{3}{8}$-inch gutta-percha ring by two bolts. Fig. 343 illustrates the type of pipe joint as adopted for a 6-inch pipe, and as invented by Mr. E. B. Ellington, the maximum and minimum diameter of the flange being 19 inches and 10$\frac{1}{2}$ inches respectively. These pipes are laid with the longer axis of the flange horizontal for facility in getting at the bolts.

The main stop valves are balanced both ways by the insertion of a small valve 1$\frac{1}{4}$ inch in diameter inside the main valve, the effort required to open the latter only being that necessary to overcome its dead weight. A spring-loaded momentum valve, having a ram 1$\frac{1}{4}$ inch diameter, is fitted on either side of every stop valve to minimise any shocks that may occur in the main.

FIG. 343.—Joint for 6-in. Pipe, 1,100 lbs. per square inch.

To indicate the condition of the mains and valves, a daily record of the minimum flow during the time the demand is at its lowest (between 11 p.m. and 4 a.m.) is kept by means of an automatic electrical recorder. Should this show an abnormal increase in the output for several consecutive nights the mains are tested. For this purpose certain of the stop valves on the trunk mains are kept closed so that the several circuits are connected only at the power station. Here they can be separated into four sections, and the section in which the abnormal flow is occurring is indicated by the behaviour of the pressure gauge connected with that circuit. The stop valves of this main are then shut down in succession until the defect is discovered, either by the aid of an iron rod which conveys the sound of the escaping water to the ear, or by applying a pressure gauge. Usually the former method is adopted.

All the pressure water is metered by Kent's high pressure rotary motors before reaching the consumer, some 97 per cent of the water delivered by the pumps being registered in these meters.

The following abbreviated scale of charges, which came into force at the end of 1907, may be of interest, as indicating the probable cost of such power.[1]

Quantity of water used in gallons per quarter	2,000	5,000	10,000	20,000	50,000	100,000	200,000	300,000
Charge per 1,000 gallons in shillings	12·5	8·6	6·4	5·2	4·5	3·7	3·10	9·4

Power water taken in excess of 300,000 gallons per quarter is charged 2s. per 1,000 gallons for the excess quantity so taken, and where the consumer agrees to take a minimum quantity of 500,000 gallons, the price attains a minimum of 1s. 3d. per 1,000 gallons for a minimum of 3,000,000 gallons per quarter.

Assuming an efficiency of 75 per cent for the consumers' machinery, this gives a cost per B.H.P. hour varying from 1·562 shillings, in the case of the smallest consumers, to ·156 shillings or 1·875 pence in the case of the largest. Power water for motors running on an average 9 hours per day is charged at 1s. 6d. per 1,000 gallons.

The following list of costs of buildings and plant of this station may be of interest :—

	£	s.	d.
Buildings, tanks, girders, columns, etc. . .	16,405	8	0
Boilers, stokers, economisers, elevators, etc. .	4,093	0	0
Engines, pipes, valves, etc. . . .	20,614	2	0
Total	£41,172	10	0

In the London installation the water is taken from the river or from

---

[1] For these particulars the author is indebted to Mr. L. Holme Lewis, the chief engineer to the Corporation Power Supply Department.

wells, and as it is essential that all deposit should be removed before use, it is allowed to stand for some time in storage tanks. The greater part of the solid matter is deposited here, and the water is then passed through the surface condensers of the engines to a series of filters, in which it is passed first through a layer of broken sponge 18 inches thick, and afterwards through a bed of charcoal. After leaving the filters it is pumped into the clean water tank, from which the main pumps derive their supply.

Among other advantages of hydraulic transmission it may be noted that power is always immediately available; that gearing in the machine is in general unnecessary, the force being transmitted directly from the hydraulic piston; that perfect regulation is easy; that when applied to the direct working of lifts and of hoists a brake is unnecessary, and that so long as the velocity of flow is kept low the transmission losses are small—with well designed pipe lines this loss should not exceed 10 lbs. per square inch per mile.

As compared with electric transmission, it has the advantage that fire risks are eliminated, while for slowly moving machinery, intermediate gearing is largely eliminated. Compared with transmission by compressed air, it has the advantage that any leakage is easily detected, while under suitable conditions the hydraulic transmission losses are much the lesser. Each of the three systems of course has its own particular sphere of application. For long-distance work the necessary cost of, and losses in the pipe line, would effectively militate against the application of hydraulic transmission, and a radius of 15 miles from the central station would appear to mark the limit of its effective use.

The various losses occur—

(1) At the power station—roughly about 15 per cent.;

(2) In transmission—about 5 per cent.;

(3) In use—about 8 per cent.;

leaving a percentage to be utilized of about 72 per cent.

The last two items, however, vary considerably with the type of machinery, and the energy utilized may vary from 30 to 95 per cent., the latter percentage being obtained with such machines as direct acting coal shoots, where the load, during its descent, may be made to pump pressure water back into the mains.

Losses.—The losses at the power station are those incidental to the use of reciprocating pumps and accumulators, and are considered in detail in that connection.

Transmission Losses.

Let p = pressure at pipe inlet in lbs. per square inch.

„ d = pipe diameter (supposed uniform) in feet.

„ a = „ area in square feet.

„ l = length of pipe in feet.

„ v = velocity of flow in feet per second.

Then the energy at entrance, per lb. $= \dfrac{144 \, p}{62\cdot4} = 2\cdot31 \, p$ ft. lbs.

$\therefore$ Energy entering pipe per second $= H = 2\cdot31 \, p \times 62\cdot4 \, a \, v.$

$$= 144 \, p \, a \, v \text{ foot lbs.}$$

$$= \frac{144}{550} p \, a \, v \text{ H.P.}$$

$$= \cdot262 \, p \, a \, v \text{ H.P.}[1]$$

Again the loss of energy in friction per lb. $= \dfrac{f \, l \, v^2}{2 \, g \, m}$ foot lbs.

$\therefore$ loss of energy per second $= H_f = \dfrac{f \, l \, v^2}{2 \, g \, m} \times \dfrac{62\cdot4 \, a \, v}{550}$ H.P.

Substituting for v in terms of H we get—

$$H_f = \frac{62\cdot4 \, a \, f \, l}{2 \, g \, m \times 550} \left\{ \frac{H}{\cdot262 \, p \, a} \right\}^3 \text{ H.P.}$$

and putting $m = \dfrac{d}{4}$; $g = 32\cdot2$ this becomes—

$$H_f = \cdot635 f \, l \, \frac{H^3}{p^3 \, d^5} \text{ H.P.} \tag{1}$$

The energy delivered per second-U—

$$= H - H_f = H \left\{ 1 - \cdot635 f \, l \, \frac{H^2}{p^3 \, d^5} \right\} \tag{2}$$

$\therefore$ Efficiency of transmission—

$$= \frac{U}{H} = 1 - \cdot635 f \, l \, \frac{H^2}{p^3 \, d^5} \tag{3}$$

Differentiating U with respect to H, and equating the result to zero, we get the condition that the maximum horse power may be transmitted.

Expressed algebraically this gives—

$$H^2 = \frac{1}{3} \frac{d^5 \, p^3}{\cdot635 f \, l} = \frac{d^5 \, p^3}{1\cdot90 f \, l},$$

or $$H = \cdot725 \sqrt{\frac{d^5 \, p^3}{f \, l}}, \tag{4}$$

---

[1] If $p = 750$ lbs. per square inch we thus get the approximate rule that two gallons of water per minute is equivalent to one horse power.

from which, by substitution in equation (2), we have the energy delivered

through the pipe, or $U = \cdot488 \sqrt{\dfrac{d^5 \, p^3}{f \, l}}$ H.P.

$$= \cdot138 \sqrt{\dfrac{d^5 \, h^3}{f \, l}} \text{ H.P.}$$

of h = head in feet at entrance to pipe.

Substituting the value of H from (4) in equation (3), we see that under circumstances of maximum transmission, the efficiency is $\frac{2}{3}$, and that $\frac{1}{3}$ of the energy entering the pipe is absorbed in overcoming friction.   On the other hand it is evident that maximum efficiency is obtained when H is as small, and p and d as large as practicable.

The point at which it ceases to pay to still further increase the diameter of the pipe line for a given horse power, depends on the relative cost per yard of the pipe line, including excavation, jointing and laying, and of the power production per horse power.[1]   In general, however, a size of pipe which allows of a pressure drop of about 10 lbs. per square inch per mile will be found to give most economical results in practice.   In modern practice the largest pipes are about 6 inches diameter, the pipe lines being duplicated for large powers.

EXAMPLE.

Let H = 100 H.P.

  „ p = 750 lbs. per square inch.

Assume $f = \cdot006$ (this varies with the diameter, velocity of flow, and condition of pipe).

Then allowing for a drop of 10 lbs. per mile we have

Efficiency of transmission $= 1 - \dfrac{10}{750} \cdot \dfrac{l}{5,280}$

$$= 1 - \dfrac{\cdot635 \, f \, l \, H^2}{p^3 \, d^5},$$

$\therefore d^5 = \dfrac{\cdot635 \times \cdot006 \times 5,280 \times 10,000 \times 750}{750 \times 750 \times 750 \times 10}$ feet

$$= \cdot0358 \text{ feet,}$$

$\therefore \; d = \cdot514$ feet $= 6\cdot17$ inches.

The loss per mile $H_f = \dfrac{10}{750} \times 100 = 1\cdot33$ H.P.

---

[1] See "Proceedings Institute Mechanical Engineers," 1895, p. 353 ; also *Engineering* May 22nd and June 5th, 1891.

The efficiency of transmission is then given by :—

Length of pipe in miles . .	1	2	5	10
Efficiency of transmission . .	·987	·973	·933	·867

Also
$$v = \frac{H.P. \times 550}{144\, p \times a} \text{ f.s.}$$
$$= \frac{55,000 \times 4}{750 \times \pi \times 144 \times \cdot2642} \text{ f.s.}$$
$$= 2\cdot45 \text{ feet per second.}$$

If $p = 1,120$, then for the same fall in pressure per mile we have, for 100 H.P. :—

$$d = \cdot4377 \text{ feet} = 5\cdot25 \text{ inches}$$
while $v = 2\cdot27$ feet per second.

The following table then gives the efficiency for various lengths of pipe line :—

Length in miles . .	1	2	5	10	20
Efficiency . . .	·991	·982	·955	·911	·821

The velocity of flow through the pipe should not exceed 4 feet per second, velocities ranging from 2·5 to 4·0 feet per second being usual.

While an increase in the working pressure increases the efficiency of transmission, it also necessitates an increase in the thickness of the pipe walls, which counterbalances the advantages of the reduced internal diameter. Also the difficulty of preventing leakage at joints increases with the pressure, so that in practice it has not been found advisable to adopt pressures much in excess of 1,100 lbs. per square inch.

Losses in Use.—These are due partly to friction, but, in the majority of hydraulic machines, more particularly to shock at sudden changes of section in valve boxes and supply ports and pipes, and to the necessity in many machines for filling the inlet passages with pressure water before the commencement of each working stroke. The latter loss may be prevented by having separate inlet and outlet passages to the working cylinder, while to prevent the former losses becoming excessive all working velocities must be kept low.

A further loss of energy occurs in some such machines as presses and riveters, where the maximum force which the plunger can exert is only needed for a short portion of its stroke, but where the expenditure of energy is the same as if this were needed for the whole stroke. Also, in the case of a hydraulic crane, if only one lifting cylinder is provided without any special regulating device, the expenditure of energy is the same whatever load, up to the maximum capacity of the crane, be lifted. Certain devices which have been invented to overcome this difficulty will be considered later.

ART. 193.—ACCUMULATORS.

Since the delivery from a reciprocating pump is not uniform and since it is necessary to have some reserve of energy to meet a sudden or abnormal demand, some means of storing pressure energy is a necessary adjunct to the hydraulic power station.

With the high pressures in common use the elevated storage tank is out of the question and the accumulator, devised by Sir W. G. Armstrong, takes its place.

Pressure water from the pumps, then, is not led directly into the supply mains, but first into an accumulator from which it is taken to feed the pipe line.

Stripped of unessentials, the accumulator consists of a vertical cylinder fitted with a weighted ram, the weight and area of this being adjusted so as to give the required pressure in the mains.

Thus, if A = area of ram in square inches,

W = weight of ram in lbs.,

we have $p\,A = W$.

The energy storage capacity of the accumulator is evidently simply equal to the potential energy of the lifted ram and weight, and if L is the length of its travel in feet, is given by $L\,W$ foot lbs.

From another point of view, the storage capacity is given by

$$2 \cdot 8\,p \times \frac{62 \cdot 4 \times A\,L}{144} = p\,A\,L,$$

i.e., by the pressure energy in the volume of water stored in the cylinder, and since $p\,A = W$, this leads to the same result as before.

EXAMPLE.

Let p = 1,120 lbs. per square inch, L = 23 feet, $A = \pi \times 9^2 = 81\,\pi$.

Storage capacity $= 1,120 \times 81\ \pi = 23$ foot lbs.

$= 6,554,000$ foot lbs.

$= \dfrac{6,554,000}{33,000 \times 60} = 3\cdot31$ horse power hours.

The accumulator is therefore capable of giving out energy at the rate of 3·31 H.P. for one hour, or 39·7 H.P. for five minutes.

From this example it is evident that the storage capacity is not large and that the main function of an accumulator is not so much to store energy, in the sense that an electric accumulator stores it, as to permit of momentary fluctuations in the rates of supply and demand, or in other words, to act as a flywheel does to a steam or gas engine. It also serves to regulate the delivery pressure, and is usually made to control the motive power automatically. Its efficiency is high, up to 98 per cent. of the energy expended in charging being returned during delivery.

In its most common form, the accumulator consists of a vertical cylinder, fitted with a ram carrying a platform which is weighted with some heavy material, usually pig iron or iron slag.[1] Fig. 344 shows this type, the weight here being carried in a wrought iron cistern suspended from the ram platform.

FIG. 344.—Accumulator.

Inlet and outlet passages are provided in the base of the cylinder, and an air valve is fitted in the top of the cylinder for convenience in first filling. The ram is guided in its travel by a framework not shown in the figure. If the pumps are delivering

[1] The following table shows the approximate volume occupied per ton of weighting material :—

Substance.	Cubic Feet per Ton.
Pig iron or wrought iron scrap . . .	6·25
Broken stone . . .	17·2
Clay or earth	18·5
Bricks	22·2

more water than the motors require the ram rises, and on reaching
the upper limit of its travel moves a stop which, by suitable link
connection, causes steam to be shut off from the pumping engines.
When the ram falls steam is again admitted to the engines, and so on.

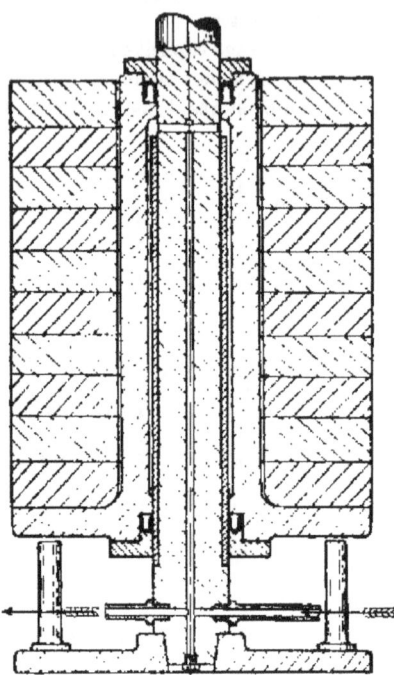

FIG. 345.—Tweddell's Differential Accumulator.

Various modifications of this
type have been adopted, the ram
in some cases being inverted,
fixed and fitted with suitable
inlet and outlet orifices, and
the loaded cylinder moving
vertically.

The differential accumulator
of Mr. Tweddell may also be
noted. As indicated in the
sketch (Fig. 345), this consists
of a fixed ram of area A, surrounded over the lower portion
of its length by a closely fitting
bush of area a.

This bush terminates below
the inlet and outlet holes. The
ram passes through both ends
of the storage cylinder, through
glands of area $(A + a)$ and A,
and the effective cylinder area
exposed to upward pressure
is a.

Thus $p\ a = W$, and by
making the bush of small
thickness, a very large pres-
sure may be maintained by a comparatively small weight.

EXAMPLE.

If the ram diameter = 6 inches and the bush is $\frac{1}{4}$ inch thick, we have
$a = 4\cdot91$ square inches.
$$\therefore \text{If } p = 1,120 \text{ lbs. per square inch,}$$
$$W = p\ a = 1,120 \times 4\cdot91 = 5,500 \text{ lbs.}$$

Since the storage of energy is only small, this type of accumulator is
more suitable for use with single machines of the riveter type.

On board ship, and especially for naval purposes, the use of hydraulic machinery for training the heavy guns, rotating turrets, etc., is very general, but here, for obvious reasons, the accumulator loaded with a mass of pig iron weighing many tons is quite inadmissible.

In its place the steam accumulator (Fig. 346) is used. This consists of a steam cylinder fitted with a piston and its piston rod or ram, which takes the place of the weight-loaded ram of the ordinary type. Steam

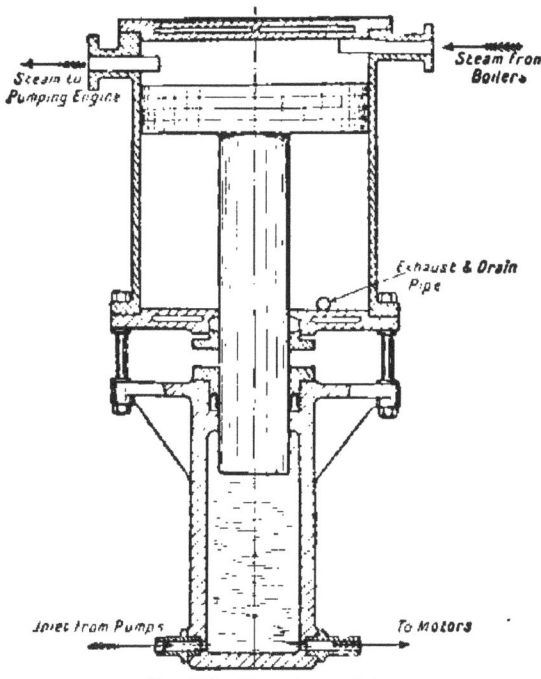

FIG. 346.—Steam Accumulator.

from the boiler is admitted to the upper side of the piston, first passing through a reducing valve which ensures a constant pressure, and with a given steam pressure P, a suitable adjustment of the areas A_s and A of the steam piston and ram, will enable any required hydraulic pressure,

$p = P \dfrac{A_s}{A}$ lbs. per square inch, to be maintained. The steam supply to the pumping engines is taken through the steam cylinder, and the accumulator piston automatically cuts off this supply on reaching a given height, and thus stops pumping until the ram descends. The steam port is usually designed so that steam may be cut off gradually and the speed of the pumps gradually reduced as the piston approaches the upper limit of its travel.

A drain pipe is arranged to carry away any water or steam leaking past the piston. The storage capacity is $P A, L$ foot lbs., and this type has the advantage that the ram may be placed either horizontally or vertically.

Effect of Accumulator on Working Pressure in Motor Cylinder.—If the motor, piston-area a square inches, derives its supply from the accumulator cylinder alone, then if A square inches = area of ram; a = acceleration of motor piston; a' = acceleration of ram, we have $a' = a\frac{a}{A}$.

The force necessary to produce this acceleration is given by

$$F = \frac{W}{g} a' = \frac{W}{g} \cdot \frac{a}{A} \cdot a, \text{ lbs.}$$

$\therefore$ Equivalent pressure in lbs. per square inch on ram $= \frac{W}{g} \cdot \frac{a}{A^2} \cdot a$.

$\therefore$ Pressure at entrance to delivery pipe $= \frac{W}{A} \left\{ 1 - \frac{a}{g A} a \right\}$ lbs. per square inch.

If a_s = area of this pipe, then $a_s = a \frac{a}{a_s}$, and if l is its length, we have putting v = velocity of piston:—

Pressure on piston

$$= \frac{W}{A} \left\{ 1 - \frac{a}{g A} a \right\} - \frac{62 \cdot 4}{144} \frac{l a}{g a_s} a - \frac{62 \cdot 4}{144} \cdot \frac{a^2}{a_s^2} \frac{f l v^2}{2 g m}$$

$$= \frac{W}{A} - \frac{a a}{g} \left\{ \frac{W}{A^2} + \frac{62 \cdot 4 l}{144 a_s} \right\} - \frac{62 \cdot 4}{144} \cdot \frac{a^2}{a_s^2} \cdot \frac{f l v^2}{2 g m} \text{ lbs. per square inch.}$$

With a steam accumulator this becomes :—

$$\frac{P A_s}{A} - \frac{a a}{g} \left\{ \frac{W}{A^2} + \frac{62 \cdot 4 l}{144 a_s} \right\} - \frac{62 \cdot 4}{144} \cdot \frac{a^2}{a_s^2} \cdot \frac{f l v^2}{2 g m} \text{ lbs. per square inch,}$$

and since W is now comparatively small, the term $\frac{a a}{g} \cdot \frac{W}{A^2}$, which represents the effect of the inertia of the ram, becomes negligible. For this reason the steam accumulator is not subject to the shocks and jars to which the weighted accumulator is subjected in virtue of the great inertia of its moving parts.

To prevent inertia shocks becoming dangerous, a relief valve is sometimes placed on the outlet pipe, this being set to blow off at 10 per cent. above normal pressure. The loss due to the leakage which this necessitates may be avoided by the provision, in the place of the relief valve, of a spring-loaded plunger, in which case the kinetic energy of the moving ram is expended in compressing the spring.

Its inertia is, however, an advantage in some cases, as, for example, where fitted to a hydraulic riveter or similar machine. Here the inertia is utilized to increase the pressure at the end of the stroke, the final and sudden impact thus produced causing the rivet to fill up its hole effectively.

Fig. 346A. shows a spring loaded plunger with relief valve arranged to open when the rise in pressure exceeds a certain limit. The necessary dimensions of this may be calculated when the size of accumulator and circumstances involved in its use are known. If, for example, the weight of accumulator ram and load is 160 tons; the maximum velocity of fall 10 ft. per minute = ·166 ft. per second; the diameter of ram 9 inches; the normal working pressure 2·5 tons per square inch; the energy of the falling weight to be absorbed by the spring loaded plunger with a 10 per cent increase in pressure.

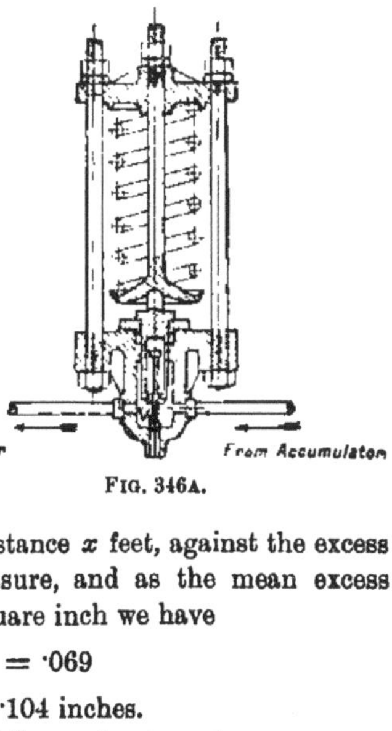

Kinetic energy of falling weight

$$= \frac{160}{36 \times 64\cdot4} = ·069 \text{ ft. tons.}$$

To Motor From Accumulator

FIG. 346A.

To absorb this amount of energy the ram must fall through a further distance x feet, against the excess resistance due to this increase in pressure, and as the mean excess resistance is 5 per cent. of 2·5 tons per square inch we have

$$·125 \times 81 \frac{\pi}{4} \times x = ·069$$

$$\therefore x = ·0087 \text{ feet} = ·104 \text{ inches.}$$

$$\therefore \text{ vol. of water displaced while coming to rest}$$

$$= ·104 \times \frac{81\,\pi}{4} = 6·61 \text{ cub. in.}$$

Making the plunger of the valve 2 inches diameter, the spring would require to be so designed as to allow of a displacement of $\frac{6·61}{\pi}$ = 2·1 inches under an increase of pressure from 2·5 to 2·75 tons per square inch. With any greater displacement the under side of the plunger would engage with and would lift the small escape valve V.

3 A 2

ART. 194.—The Hydraulic Intensifier.

Where the main pressure supply is of less intensity than is required to work the hydraulic machinery an intensifier is used. In its simplest form, this consists of a ram of area a, carrying a piston of larger area A (Fig. 347). Water from the pressure mains, at pressure p, is admitted behind the piston and compresses the water in the ram cylinder to an increased pressure P where $P = p\dfrac{A}{a}$.

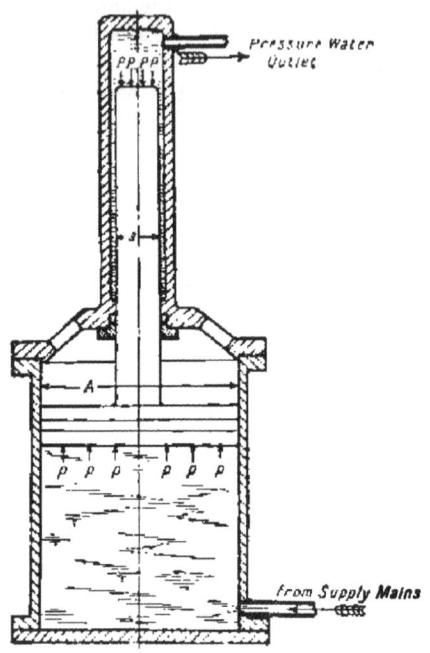

FIG. 347.—Hydraulic Pressure Intensifier.

Example.

$\begin{cases} p = 40 \text{ lbs. per square inch.} \\ \text{Piston diameter} = 48 \text{ inches.} \\ \text{Ram diameter} = 8 \text{ inches.} \end{cases}$

$$\frac{A}{a} = 36.$$

$\therefore P = 40 \times 36 = 1,440 \text{ lbs.}$ per square inch.

This neglects the friction of the packings, and also the weight of the ram and piston. Including these we have

$$p\,A - (w + F) = P\,a$$
$$\therefore P = p\,\frac{A}{a} - \frac{w + F}{a} \text{ lbs.}$$

per square inch. Where $w =$ weight of ram and piston in lbs. $F =$ frictional resistance in lbs.

If on the down stroke communication be made between the under side of the piston and the upper side of the ram, the pressure p' below the piston becomes

$$p' = \frac{w - F}{A - a} \text{ lbs. per square inch.}$$

Various modifications of this type of intensifier are in use, one of these being illustrated in Fig. 348. Here low pressure water is admitted above the hollow ram A, while the intensified water is led away through the small stationary ram of area a.

If w is the weight of the outer ram, we now have

$$P = p \frac{A}{a} + \frac{w - F}{a} \text{ lbs. per square inch.}$$

With a single intensifier the supply of high pressure water cannot be made continuous, and delivery only takes place on the in stroke. At the end of this stroke water is admitted to the ram cylinder from the supply mains, while the water below the piston is allowed to escape. This type of intensifier is often fitted to testing machines deriving their pressure supply from towns' mains at a comparatively low pressure.

Where a continuous supply of high pressure water is required, this may be obtained by using two intensifiers placed side by side, each automatically working the valves of the other.

When applied to the working of a hydraulic press, the water escaping from beneath the piston during the down stroke may be utilised to bring the press platform up to its work, and to perform the first part of the compression.[1]

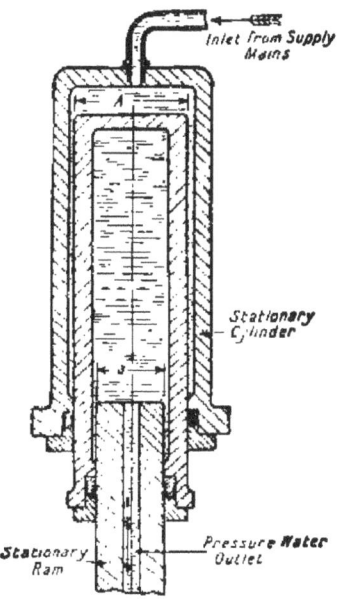

FIG. 348.—Hydraulic Pressure Intensifier.

ART. 195.—FRICTION OF LEATHER COLLARS FOR RAMS.

One or other of the types of packing illustrated in Fig. 349 is commonly used for hydraulic rams or plungers. The material used is leather, and, since the pressure of the water itself forces the packing against the ram, this pressure, and the friction produced, become proportional to the pressure intensity of the water. A very complete series of experiments carried out by Mr. John Hicks on rams ½ inch, 4 inches, and 8 inches diameter, and with pressures up to 6,400 lbs. per square inch, indicate that—

(1) For pressures above 400 lbs. per square inch, friction is directly proportional to pressure intensity.

[1] For further details of valve arrangements, etc., the reader may refer to Blaine's "Hydraulic Machinery," p. 345.

(2) For rams of different diameters exposed to the same pressure intensity, the friction in lbs. is directly proportional to the diameter, and therefore to the square root of the gross load.

(3) The depth of the collar does not affect the friction. In several of the experiments the depth was reduced from $\frac{7}{8}$ inch to $\frac{3}{8}$ inch without any appreciable effect on the friction.

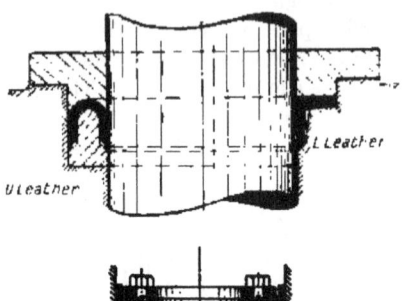

FIG. 349.—Leather Collars for Hydraulic Rams and Pistons.

The following approximate formulae were deduced from the results of these experiments :

Friction in lbs. = C × diameter in inches × pressure in lbs. per square inch.

where $\begin{cases} C = \cdot0471 \text{ for new or badly lubricated collars,} \\ C = \cdot0314 \text{ for collars in good condition and well lubricated.} \end{cases}$

The annexed table gives the frictional resistance expressed as a percentage of the total pressure on the piston, for rams from 2 inches to 20 inches diameter and for pressures exceeding 400 lbs. per square inch :

Diameter in inches	2	3	4	5	6	7	8	10	12	14	16	18	20
Friction, % of total pressure on ram. Well lubricated	2·00	1·33	1·00	·80	·66	·57	·50	·40	·33	·28	·25	·22	·20
New or badly lubricated .	3·00	2·00	1·50	1·20	·99	·85	·75	·60	·50	·42	·37	·33	·30

For lower pressures, the formulae

$$F \text{ (lbs.)} = p\,d \left\{ \cdot0467 - \cdot0000139\,p \right\}$$

gives more accurate results, the coefficients here applying to leathers in good condition and well lubricated.

Where the loading is eccentric, as is often the case in hydraulic jacks, etc., these values may however be increased by as much as 100 per cent.

Recent experiments by Prof. Martens, of Berlin,[1] on the packings

[1] *Mechanical Engineer*, Sept. 7th, 1907.

fitted to the rams of 5 testing machines showed the following friction losses :

Pressure (Atmospheres).	Per cent. Loss per Packing.
50	2 — 5
100	1·8 — 3·0
200	1·0 — 1·6

Experiments by S. L. Davis[1] on a 5 inch testing machine ram carrying a U leather at its lower end and working in a copper lined cylinder showed that after a fair amount of service the friction, with increasing loads, varied irregularly from about 5 per cent to zero, with a mean value of 1·3 per cent., the pressure meanwhile increasing from 500 to 4,500 lbs. per square inch. With diminishing loads the friction had a maximum value of 3·6 per cent. at the lowest pressure, with a mean value of ·2 per cent. over the whole range.

For satisfactory working the U leather should have a ring of metal or other material inserted between the flaps, and should as far as possible have a metal backing over its curved portion.

Experience shows that a narrow fitting strip—not above ½ inch wide—is preferable to one which is wider, since, owing to the reduced tendency to bending at the bottom of the U with a shallow collar, the leather is not so liable to crack.

Hemp packing is also used to a limited extent for hydraulic glands. Here the percentage loss in friction decreases with an increasing load, but since the packing must be tightened so as to prevent leakage at the highest pressures to which it may be subjected, the loss at low pressure is probably three to four times that of a leather collar.

ART. 196.—WATER METERS.

It is usually important that the volume of water supplied for domestic or power purposes should be accurately measured, and various meters have been devised for this purpose.

These may be divided into the following classes :—

(1) Low pressure meters.

(2) Inferential meters.

(8) Positive meters.

[1] *Engineering News*, Feb. 11th, 1909. p. 167.

(4) Meters for waste detection.

(5) Venturi meters.

(1) This type suffers from the disadvantage that all the pressure head of the supply is lost, and that when used for domestic supply it must therefore be placed at the top of the building. It is, however, well fitted for the measurement of small flows. The "Parkinson" meter, which is of this type, is illustrated in Fig. 350, and has given excellent results in measuring the power water delivered by the City of London Hydraulic Supply Company. In this case the meter is applied to measuring the

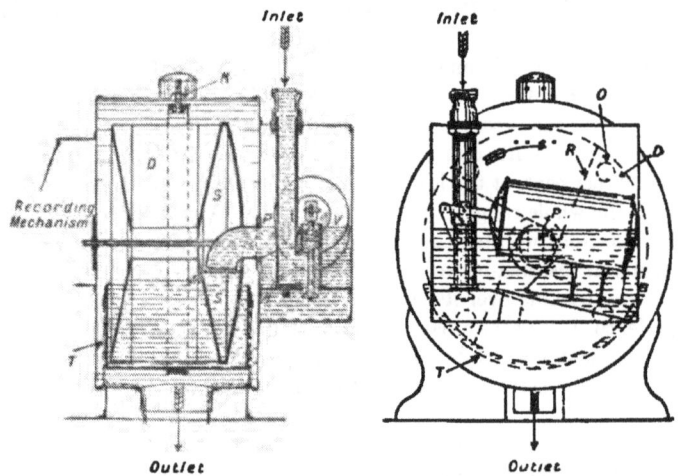

FIG. 350.—"Parkinson's" Low Pressure Water Meter.

exhaust water from the various machines. Here water from the inlet pipe is maintained at a uniform level in the inlet chamber by means of a float and valve V. This valve is constructed as shown so as to be balanced whatever the pressure in the supply pipe. On leaving this chamber by the pipe P, the water flows into the annular space S formed in the drum D. This drum is hollow and contains four compartments formed by oblique radiating plates R, which overlap each other to the extent of about 90°. Each compartment opens at its inner periphery into the space S, and in turn receives a supply of water. The centre of gravity of the water in the compartment being, on account of its position, to one side of the axis of the drum, this produces a rotation about the axis and brings the next compartment into communication with the space S. At the same time the outlet O, from the first compartment, which is on the opposite side of the drum to S, is brought by the rotation below the water level in the compartment, and discharges the water into the trough T in which the drum rotates, and from which it flows away to the discharge pipe. The height of the trough may be adjusted as required, and as the volume discharged per revolution depends on the depth of the immersion of the drum, this enables the discharge per revolution to be adjusted. The number of revolutions of the drum, and hence the volume passing the meter, may then be recorded on a suitably engraved dial.

When used for domestic supply purposes, discharge takes place into a cistern from which the water is led over the building. An inlet valve on

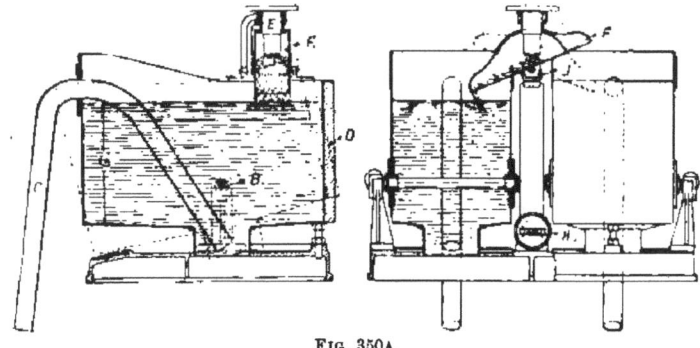

FIG. 350A.

the supply pipe—not shown in the sketch—is then opened by a ball valve when the water level in this cistern is lowered.

Another meter of this general type is shown in Fig. 350A. The apparatus consists of two tanks of equal size carried on knife edges at B. Each tank is fitted at one end with a syphon pipe C, and at the other with a weight D. The liquid to be measured flows through the inlet pipe E along the movable guide channel F into whichever tank happens to be in operation.

The weights D are so adjusted that until the tanks are full up to the height marked G, they remain in a horizontal position, but as the weight of liquid increases by the continued flow, the tanks come into the position shown by the dotted line, when the liquid flows through the syphon pipe. After the syphon has been started and the level of the liquid in the tank has fallen sufficiently, the tank tilts back again to its original position, by the influence of the weight D, the syphon continuing in action until the tank is emptied.   As each tank assumes the position indicated by the dotted lines, it suddenly tilts the guide F over, so that the new liquid to be measured falls into the other tank, when the same operation is repeated.   It will thus be seen that both tanks are filled automatically with fresh liquid, while the measured liquid runs away into a reservoir or other receptacle as required.

The number of times each tank is filled and emptied is registered by the indicator H, which is connected with both tanks.   When either tank is in a horizontal position, the guide F rests on the support J, which is of saddle form, so that when the tank is in the act of tipping no influence is exercised either by the weight of the guide or by the pressure of the liquid in the guide, or by the resistance of the counter.

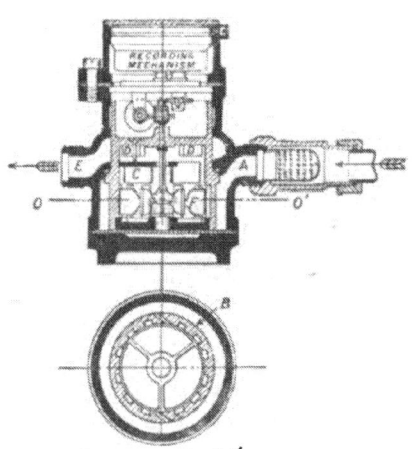

Section on Line OO'

FIG. 351.—Tylor's Inferential Water Meter.

(2) The inferential meter consists simply of a small turbine, through which the whole supply is passed, which drives the recording apparatus.   The water is not actually measured, but its volume is inferred from the number of revolutions of the turbine runner or fan, which is the only moving part. The meter must be calibrated by allowing it to pass a known volume of water per minute, and has the advantage of being small, light, and cheap, and fairly accurate for good speeds of flow.   Since, however, there is a limiting velocity of flow, below which the reaction on the runner vanes is insufficient to overcome the friction of the bearings and recording mechanism, it is unsuitable for recording small flows.   Moreover, the runner tends to keep on rotating for some short time after the flow of water has ceased, and thus to over-record the flow.   Where taps are opened and closed frequently, this action, unless guarded against, may lead to the flow registered being largely in excess of that actually taking place.

Tylor's Inferential Meter (Fig. 351) is of this type.   Here water enters at *A*, and surrounds the inner casing shown in section at *B*. It then finds its way through two inclined ports in this casing, and, impinging on the vanes of the fan *F*, drives this around with a velocity which depends on the flow of water, and which is recorded on the dial worked by its spindle and worm gear, afterwards escaping through the ports *D* and pipe *E*. To prevent overrunning, eddy formation is fostered by a series of recesses formed around the inside of the inner casing, and by baffles above the fan at *C*. To reduce friction at the lower footstep bearing an oil reservoir is provided in the hollow spindle of the fan.

(3) The Positive Meter consists of a small hydraulic engine, either of the rotary or reciprocating piston type. All the water to be measured passes through the cylinder or cylinders of this engine, and its volume is taken as that of the piston displacement.

The number of revolutions or strokes of the piston being registered on a recording apparatus, this is easily arranged to record the volume passed.

The rotary type is common in the United States of America, and, as usually made, consists of a casing of gun-metal or vulcanite, in which works a rotary vulcanite piston. This has no means of compensating for wear, and, as thus constructed, is very unreliable for small flows, even when new. After being in use for some time the increased leakage past the piston renders it still less reliable.

The Kent "Uniform" meter (Fig. 352) is one of the best of this type, and here compensation is made for the effect of wear of the rotary piston *P* by an adjustable metal tongue *S*. In this meter water is admitted at *A* and fills the casing around the working chamber *B*. The vulcanite piston *P*, elliptical in section, rotates and slides freely, but without play, on the fixed hub *Q*, which is itself eccentric with respect to the working chamber. The piston carries a central pin which describes a circular path as rotation takes place, and which actuates the recording mechanism.

The bottom ports at *C* are in free communication with the chamber *B*, and the action of the meter is as follows :—

Assuming the piston to be in the position shown in dotted lines, water is admitted through these ports and the upper port *D*, to the space between the chamber, the piston, and the tongue *S*, and to the interior of the hollow piston, thus exerting a pressure between the hub and the inside of the inner end of the piston, as well as on the outside of the piston from *C* to *S*, and driving the latter round in a clockwise direction. At the end of half a revolution the other end of the piston becomes the driver and so on.

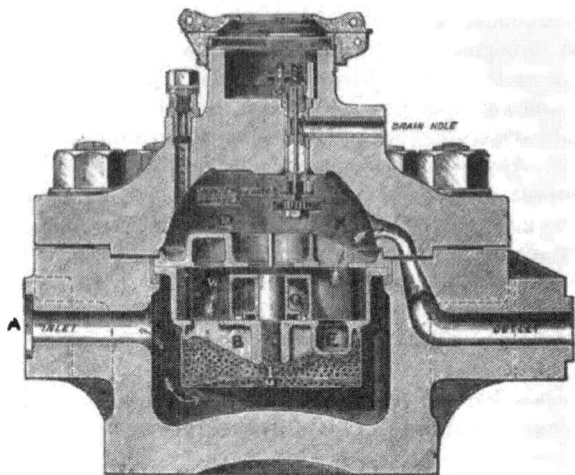

SECTION THROUGH A.A.

PLAN WITH TOP COVER REMOVED

FIG. 352.—" Kent " Positive Water Meter.

In the meantime water has been filling the space to the left of the
piston until the position shown in full lines is reached, when the supply
is cut off from the space F, this space is put into communication with the

lischarge port K by way of the lower port E and the hollow piston, and or the remaining half revolution the water in this space and in the outer md of the piston is discharged through K, the whole cycle of operations hen being repeated. The action

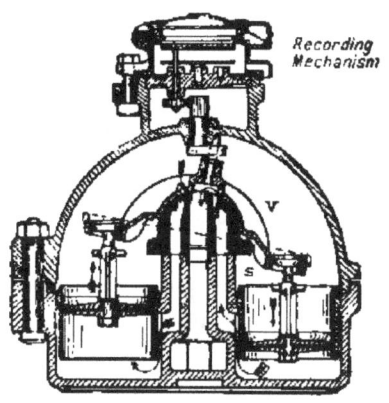

becomes much more evident if a racing showing the piston be otated, keeping its correct relative position, through a whole cycle. This meter is used exclusively in connection with the measurement of pressure water from the power station of the Manchester Corporation, and has given excellent results. For such a purpose this type has the advantage that in case of a breakdown the flow of water is not stopped, the wastage of water thus entailed being of small consequence when compared with the inconvenience caused by a stoppage of the power supply.

Many types of the reciprocating piston meter have been made, but space forbids the mention of more than one example. The "Imperial" meter of Mr. Schönheyder (Fig. 353) consists of three single-acting cylinders fitted with a single hemispherical gun-metal distributing valve V bearing on a vulcanite seat S. The upper side of each piston is exposed

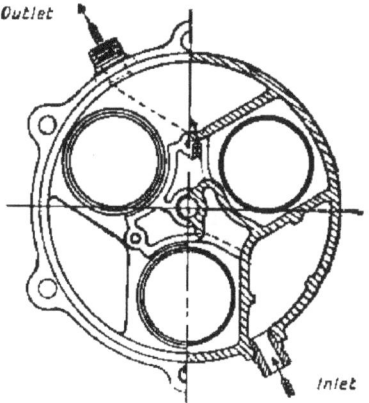

Fig. 353.—Schönheyder Positive Water Meter.

to inlet pressure, and according to the position of the valve the lower side of each in succession is put into communication with the outlet passage. The pistons are thus successively forced down and their contents discharged into the outlet. At the same time one or both of the other cylinders is having its piston raised, water being admitted below the piston.

Discharge is then practically continuous and the machine has no dea
centre, while the smallest flow is registered. The positive type has the hi
advantage over the inferential meter that whereas the correct registration o
the former is unaffected by an increase in the friction of the moving part:
such an increase in friction may seriously affect the speed of the latte
for a given flow. Its chief drawbacks consist in its liability to wate
hammer unless worked at a very low speed, and its consequent larg
dimensions and high first cost.

(4) One of the best types of meter for the determination of the varyin
flow in a pipe, and hence of leakage, is that of Mr. Deacon (Fig. 354
Here the water flows through a conical tube containing an axial rc
which carries a circular disc D. Any axial movement of this disc
resisted by a spring, and is recorde
on the registering apparatus. Th
varying pressure on the disc, pro
duced by any variation in the rat
of flow, may then be registered, an
by suitably calibrating the recordir
mechanism the position of the rc
may be arranged to indicate tl
flow in gallons per minute.

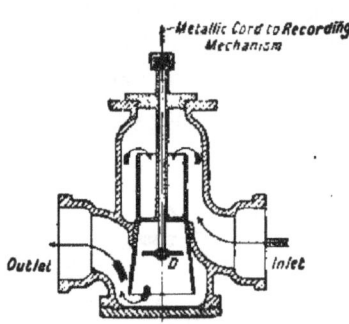

FIG. 354.—" Deacon " Meter.

(5) The **Venturi** water meter, in
vented by Herschel in 1881, an
called by him after Venturi becaus
of the experimental work of the latte
on the physical properties of diverg

ing tubes, depends in its principles on the truth of Bernoulli's theoren

It is at once the simplest, and for large quantities of water the mo
satisfactory meter yet designed, and simply consists (Fig. 355) of a pir
passing the whole quantity of water to be measured, and fitted with
portion BC, uniformly converging to a short parallel throat CD. At
the pipe again diverges to its full diameter at E. The usual proportior
of the meter are indicated in the figure in terms of the pipe diamete
experiments showing that an angle of divergence of $5° 6'$ gives the be
results in the reconversion of kinetic to pressure energy from D to I
If the pipe be horizontal, and if A and a be the areas of main pipe and
throat, then, as shown onp 80, with a perfect fluid

$$V_A = \sqrt{\frac{2g(p_A - p_a)}{W\left\{\left(\frac{A}{a}\right)^2 - 1\right\}}}$$

Owing to viscosity, the true velocity accompanying a given fall of pressure ($p_A - p_a$) is less than this, being given by

$$V_A = c \sqrt{\frac{2 g (p_A - p_a)}{W \left\{ \left(\frac{A}{a}\right)^2 - 1 \right\}}}$$

Where c is a coefficient of velocity which depends slightly on the diameter and material of the pipes and on the velocity of flow, increasing with the diameter and velocity of flow and diminishing as the surface roughness increases.

Experiments by Herschel show that c varies from ·94 to unity, the great majority of tests giving values between ·96 and ·99. In a 48″ meter c had the value ·995.

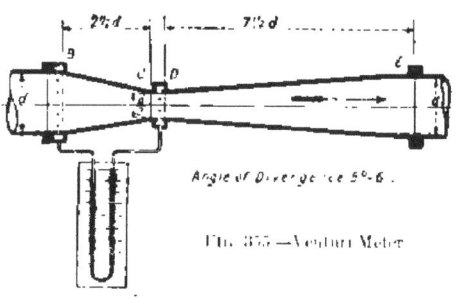

Angle of Divergence 5°·6.

Fig. 355.—Venturi Meter

For any meter $\left(\dfrac{A}{a}\right)$ is fixed, the ratio commonly being 9 : 1, so that

$$\sqrt{\frac{2 g}{\left(\frac{A}{a}\right)^2 - 1}} \text{ is constant} = k.$$

Taking $\dfrac{A}{a} = 9$, then $k = \sqrt{\dfrac{2 g}{80}} = ·8972.$

Then the volume in cubic feet per second through meter

$$\left.\begin{matrix} \\ \end{matrix}\right\} = V_A A = c k A \sqrt{\frac{p_A - p_a}{W}}$$

$$= c k' \sqrt{\frac{p_A - p_a}{W}} \tag{1}$$

Here $\dfrac{p_A - p_a}{W}$ or $h_A - h_a$ is the difference in pressure at the throat (1) and entrance (2) expressed as a head in feet of water, and is directly measured in the meter. The constants c and k being determined for the instrument, the volume passing per second may be directly inferred.

This meter has the advantage of registering at almost any velocity, the permissible range of velocities depending on the permissible loss of head in passing the meter. Generally, a maximum velocity of up to sixteen times the minimum is permissible. It will register with velocities so low

as ·2 foot per second, and is exceedingly accurate when fitted to large
mains, but is not suitable without careful calibration for use in small
pipes below about 2″ diameter, because of the greater proportional effect of
viscosity in such pipes. It is, moreover, not well adapted for use in pipes
where the water is subjected to periodic pulsations, as, for example, in the
discharge pipe from a reciprocating pump, since this is likely to set up
oscillations in the recording mechanism.

Prof. C. M. Allen ("Am. Soc. Mech. Engineers," December 1909), on tests
of a 2″ Venturi used for boiler feed, found a factor " C " varying from ·935
at 40 lbs. per sq. in. to ·962 at 200 lbs. With steady flow errors were less
than 1 per cent.; with pulsating flow, within 2½ per cent.

For measuring the difference of head $h_A - h_a$, a differential gauge

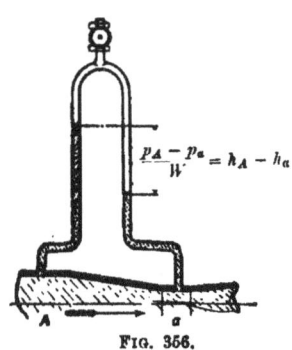

FIG. 356.

consisting of a U-tube containing mercury,
may be used (Fig. 355),[1] though where
small differences of pressure are to be
measured a preferable device is that shown
in Fig. 356, where the difference of pressure head is directly measured in feet of
water. Here compressed air must be supplied to the higher portion of the inverted
U-tube.

If the meter tube be not horizontal, and
if z be the difference in level at the entrance
and throat, so that we have

$$\frac{p_A}{W} + \frac{V_A^2}{2g} = \frac{p_a}{W} + \frac{V_a^2}{2g} + z$$

it is easily shown that equation (1) becomes :—

$$\text{Volume per second} = c\, k' \sqrt{(h_A - h_a) - z,}$$

If the connecting tubes be shut off from the main, and connection be
made so that the water may attain a common level in the two tubes, and
if now the pencil of the recorder be put to zero, the effect is to add z
automatically to the observed head, and on cutting off the connection
between the tubes and coupling up to the mains, true readings will be
given on the ordinary record sheet.

It should be noted that the converging portion of the main is the only
part really essential to the meter action. The diverging cone simply
ensures that the reconversion of kinetic into potential energy shall take

[1] Where a mercury gauge is used having the connecting pipes full of water, it is easily
shown that the effective gauge reading is less than the apparent in the ratio $\dfrac{13\cdot6 - 1}{13\cdot6} = \cdot926$.

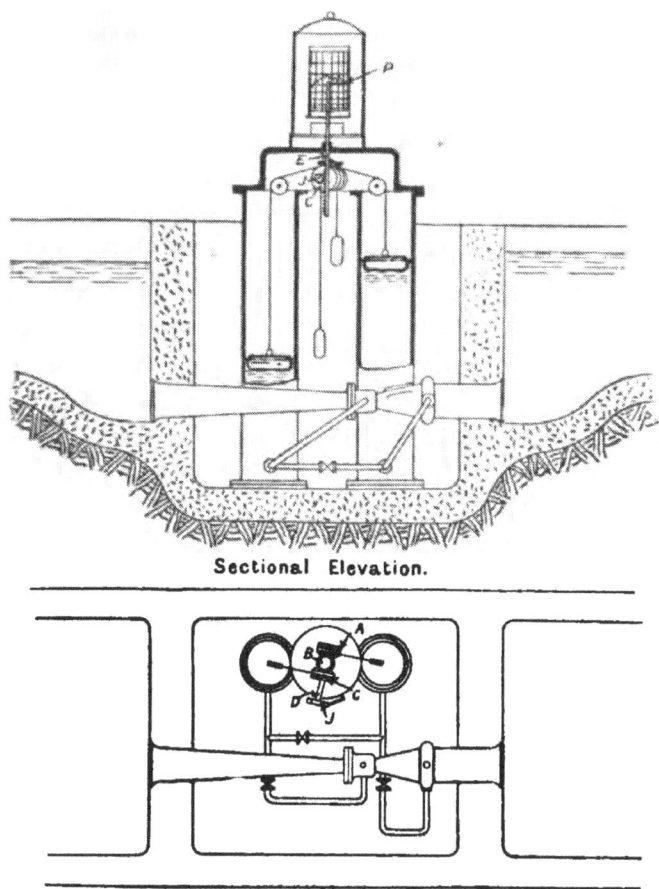

Sectional Elevation.

Plan

FIG. 357.—Recording Device for Venturi Meter.

place without undue loss. Where the meter is required to measure the flow in either direction, the angles of convergence and divergence are each made equal to 5° 6′.

The Venturi meter is often used with a registering device giving an automatic record of the velocity or discharge. One form of such a recorder is shown in Fig. 357. Here two float pipes are connected

Z.A.   3 B

respectively to the upstream and throat chambers of the tube. Each
contains a float, and these are connected by means of wire cords to a
differential gear consisting essentially of three bevel wheels A, B, and C
of which the motions of the two equal wheels A and C are controlled by
the floats, while B is carried on an axis attached to a loose sleeve.
Evidently if the wheels A and C revolve in opposite directions owing to

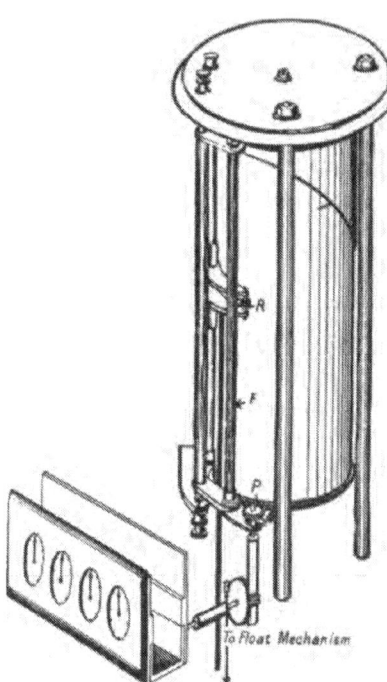

the water columns rising or
falling together, the wheel B
will simply revolve on its axis.
Any alteration in the relative
level, however, causes the wheel
B and the sleeve on which it is
mounted to rotate about the
axis D, and thereby to produce
a vertical movement of the rack
E, which gears with a pinion J
mounted on the outer end of
the sleeve, and which carries
the recording pencil P at its
upper end. The recorder may
be arranged to indicate either
the velocity of flow and therefore the discharge at any
instant, or the total discharge
of the meter. In the former
case the pencil traces out a
curve on a sheet carried by a
vertical drum driven at a constant rate by clockwork, this
paper being ruled with horizontal lines the distances of
which (representing equal increment of velocity) from the

FIG. 858.—Integrating Mechanism for Venturi
Meter.

zero line, are proportional to $\sqrt{h}$. Where it is required to have an
automatic record of the discharge as well as a record of the rate
of flow, an ingenious integrating device is used. This consists of an
additional drum concentric with the recording drum and rotated uniformly
—usually once in 10 minutes—by clockwork. The surface of this drum
is in two planes ; one of the full diameter of the drum, and the other of a
reduced diameter forming a recessed surface. The boundary curve of the

raised surface is a portion of a parabola. The arrangement is shown diagrammatically in Fig. 358. A roller R receives vertical motion from the float mechanism, and is pressed against the drum by a rocking frame F. This frame carries a pinion P which actuates the counter mechanism, and which does, or does not, gear with the teeth of a spur wheel carried by the drum according as the roller is on the recessed or the raised portion of its surface.

Thus when the roller is at the highest point it engages only with the raised surface, so that in this position—corresponding to no flow—the counter is not actuated. At the lowest position the roller is entirely upon the recessed surface, and the counter is actuated continuously. In any intermediate position the counter revolves only while the roller is in contact with the recessed surface, so that the fraction of the period of revolution of the drums during which the counter rotates is proportional to $\sqrt{h}$. Thus since the velocity of flow is also proportional to $\sqrt{h}$, the discharge is summed or integrated, and can be read directly from the counter.

Another type of velocity recorder is shown in Fig. 359, while where a combined velocity and discharge recorder is required, a modification of this in which a cast-iron U, having both legs of the same area and containing mercury, may be used. These contain iron floats which carry light racks gearing with pinions, which convey their motion to corresponding racks placed outside the tubes. The racks carry light rods which pass up to the recording mechanism. That connected to the float in the throat chamber regulates the amount of registration by the counter, while the second carries the pencil of the velocity recorder.

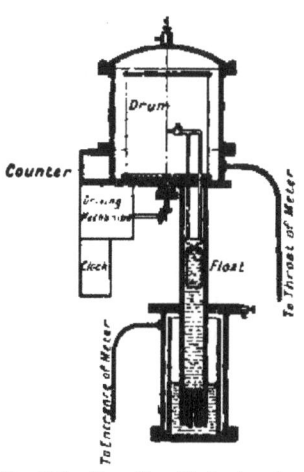

FIG. 359.—Recording Mechanism for Venturi Meter.

EXAMPLES.

(1) Determine the H.P. transmitted through a 6-inch pipe if the velocity of flow is 3 feet per second, and the delivery pressure 1,000 lbs. per square inch.

Answer. 154 H.P.

(2) If in the preceding question the pressure at the station is 1,120 lbs. per square inch, determine the efficiency of transmission, and also, taking $f = \cdot 01$, the length of the supply pipe line.

Answer. Efficiency = 89·2 per cent.
Length   = 4·7 miles.

(3) 100 B.H.P. is required from a hydraulic motor having an efficiency of 75 per cent. The motor is two miles from the generating station and only a single 6-inch pipe line is available. The pressure at the station being 1,120 lbs. per square inch, determine the pressure at the motor, the efficiency of transmission, and the velocity of flow.

Answer. Pressure = 1,088 lbs. per sq. inch.
Efficiency = 97·0 per cent.
Velocity = 2·392 f.s.

(4) Two branch pipes, respectively 4 inches and 3 inches diameter, are supplied from a 6-inch pipe. The pressure at the delivery end of the 4-inch pipe is 700 lbs. per square inch ; that at the end of the 3-inch pipe is 710 lbs. per square inch. These pipes are respectively 500 and 700 feet long. The 6-inch pipe is 880 feet long. Take f throughout as being $= \cdot 01$ and determine the pressure at the inlet to the latter pipe.

(5) Determine the maximum H.P. which can be transmitted through a 4-inch pipe two miles long—$f = \cdot 012$—if the inlet pressure = 750 lbs. per square inch. Also determine the pressure at the outlet, and the velocity of flow when this power is being transmitted.

Answer. 56·4 H.P.
Pressure = 500 lbs. per square inch.
Velocity = 4·94 feet per second.

(6) An accumulator has an 18-inch ram and 23 feet lift, and is loaded with 129 tons total weight. Taking friction to account for ·25 per cent. of the total pressure on the ram, determine the H.P. given into the mains if the accumulator falls steadily in three minutes, the pumps delivering 500 gallons per minute in the meantime.

Answer. Total H.P. = 67 + 396 = 463.

(7) A steam accumulator is placed horizontally and has a 48-inch steam piston coupled to a 6-inch ram. The steam piston packings, etc., exert a frictional force of 500 lbs., while the hydraulic packings account for 1 per cent. of the total pressure exerted on the ram. Determine this pressure if the steam pressure is 150 lbs. per square inch.

Answer. 9,486 lbs. per square inch.

(8) The ram of a differential accumulator is 4 inches diameter, and the surrounding bush is $\frac{1}{2}$ inch thick. Determine the accumulator pressure if the supported weight is 10 tons, neglecting the effect of friction.

Answer. 3,168 lbs. per square inch.

(9) The accumulator of the preceding question feeds a riveter, whose ram, at the end of its working stroke, suffers a retardation of 5 feet per second per second. The riveter ram is 5 inches diameter. Determine the pressure on the rivet head at the end of the stroke.

Answer. 32·1 tons.

CHAPTER XXI

Hydraulic Appliances—Lifts and Hoists—The Hydraulic Jigger—Cranes—Coal Tips—Crane Valves—The Hydraulic Jack—Press—Forging Press—Riveters—Lock Gate Machinery—Sluice Gates—Capstans—Hydraulic Transmission Gear—The Hydraulic Brake—The Hydraulic Dynamometer.

HYDRAULIC APPLIANCES.

ART. 197.—HYDRAULIC LIFTS AND HOISTS.

PROBABLY in the aggregate more power is used by lifts and hoists than by any other class of hydraulic machinery, and for such work as this, hydraulic transmission is particularly suitable.

Several types of lift are in use, these consisting of modifications of the simple direct-acting or of the suspended type. The former consists of a hydraulic cylinder sunk vertically in the ground; of length slightly greater than the maximum travel of the lift; and fitted with a ram which carries the lift cage as shown in Fig. 360.[1]

Pressure water is admitted below the ram, and thus raises the cage. It follows that the ram, considered as a loaded column, must be of sufficiently large sectional area to support the weight without buckling, and this prevents the use of very high pressures in the ram cylinder.

EXAMPLE.

If the gross weight to be lifted = 2 tons.

  ,,   pressure in cylinder   = 750 lbs. per square inch.

  ,,   lift travel   = 80 feet.

We have the area necessary to $\Big\}$ raise the weight $= \dfrac{4,480}{750} = 6$ square inches.

∴ Ram diameter   = $2\frac{3}{4}$ inches.

a diameter which is obviously too small for a column 80 feet long, to support 2 tons without buckling.

Actually, however, the area of the ram would need to be greater than this in order to overcome friction and to give the necessary acceleration at starting.

---

[1] By kind permission of the makers.

Thus, if a = acceleration of ram and cage in feet per second per second we have.

$$\left.\begin{array}{l}\text{Force necessary to produce}\\\text{this acceleration}\end{array}\right\} = \frac{2 \times 2{,}240}{g} \times a \text{ lbs.}$$

FIG. 860.—Direct-Acting Hydraulic Hoist.

And if F = force in lbs. necessary to overcome friction of ram we have

$$\text{area of ram} = \frac{4{,}480 \left\{ 1 + \dfrac{a}{g} \right\} + F}{750}.$$

Thus if $a = 2$ feet per second per second, while $F = 10$ per cent. of the total force on ram, we have

$$\text{area of ram} \quad = \frac{4,480}{750} \left\{ 1\tfrac{1}{16} \right\} 1\cdot1$$

$$= 1\cdot17 \times \frac{4,480}{750} = 7 \text{ square inches.}$$

In practice it is usual to make allowance for friction and acceleration

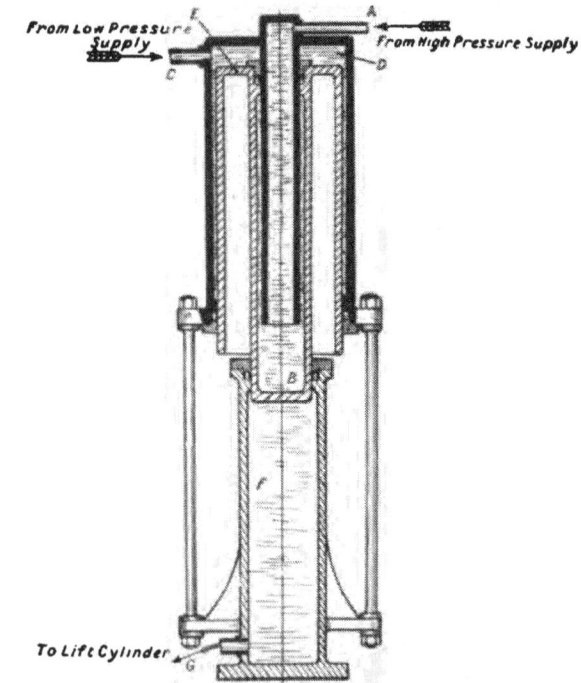

From Low Pressure Supply

From High Pressure Supply

To Lift Cylinder

FIG. 361.—Balance Cylinder for Hydraulic Lift.

by making calculations for a load about 25 per cent. in excess of the nominal.

If the area of the ram be increased, the working pressure must be reduced to suit, and for this purpose some form of pressure reducer—in effect a reversed intensifier—is used. Also, since the weight of ram and cage forms a large proportion of the whole load to be lifted, this must be balanced for efficient working.

Since the volume of water displaced by the ram diminishes as the lift rises, the effective weight of the ram, which is its own weight less that of the water displaced, increases. In lifts for large powers the effect of this variation is in general unimportant, and becomes of less importance as the working pressure increases.

EXAMPLE.

Pressure = 250 lbs. per square inch.

W = 5 tons.

Lift = 60 ft.

$$\text{Area of ram} = \frac{5 \times 2,240}{250} = 44 \cdot 8 \text{ square inches.}$$

∴ Difference in apparent weight of ram at top and bottom of its stroke $\left.\begin{array}{l}\\\\\\\\\end{array}\right\} = \left\{\begin{array}{l}\text{Weight of a column of} \\ \text{water 60 feet long and} \\ 44 \cdot 8 \text{ square inches sec-} \\ \text{tional area,}\end{array}\right.$

$$= \frac{60 \times 44 \cdot 8}{144} \times 62 \cdot 4$$

$$= 1,164 \text{ lbs.}$$

If working pressure = 500 lbs. per square inch, the area of ram = 22·4 square inches and its difference of weight = 583 lbs., a value which is small in comparison with the weight of five tons.

Various devices have been adopted to overcome these difficulties.

The weight of the ram and cage may be balanced by a counterbalance weight attached to the cage by chains passing over a series of pulleys at the top of the lift shaft, and since, as the lift rises, the length of chain on the balance-weight side of the pulleys increases,

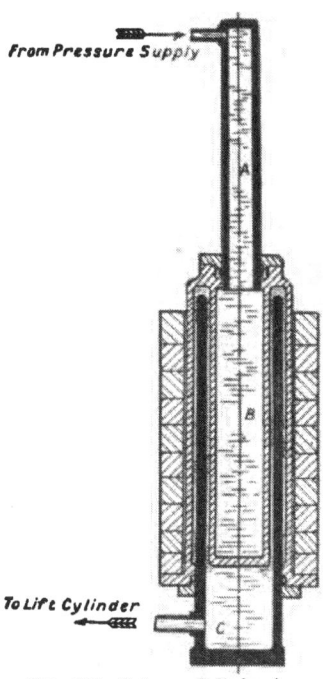

From Pressure Supply

To Lift Cylinder

Fig. 362.—Balance Cylinder for Hydraulic Lift.

this may be made to counterbalance the increasing effective weight of the ram by making the chain of such dimensions that its weight per foot run is half that per foot run of the column of water displaced by the ram. This method suffers from the disadvantage that the upper part of the ram is in tension, and a fracture would cause the cage to be dashed against the top of the shaft. It thus detracts from the otherwise essentially safety features of this type of lift, and also increases the mass to be accelerated at the beginning of the travel.

A second device, which is more common in high-class work, is that of the balance cylinder, one type of which is illustrated in Fig. 361. Here pressure water is admitted to the interior of the hollow ram B. The cylinder D is in communication with an auxiliary low pressure supply, through the pipe C, and a downward pressure on the annulus at E is thus produced, which, together with the weight of this ram, produces a

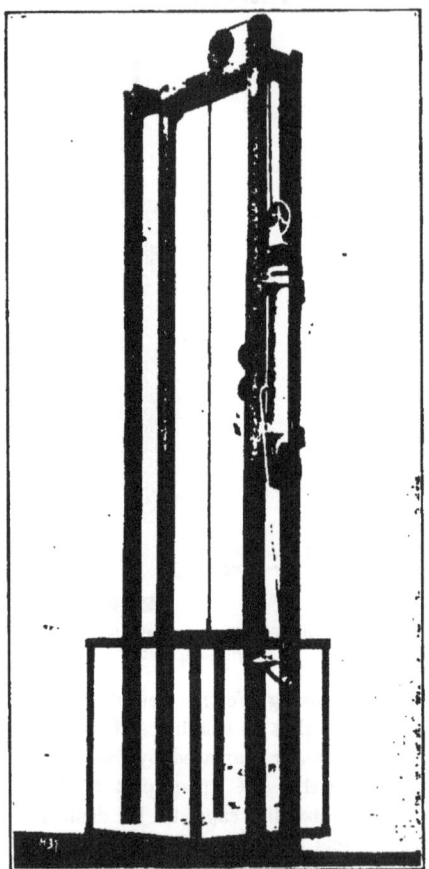

pressure in the cylinder F sufficiently great to balance any required proportion of the weight of the lift ram and cage. The total pressure transmitted to the water in the cylinder F is then the sum of the weight of the ram B and of the pressures on E and on ram B, the former performing the balancing, and the latter lifting the load.

A suitable area of lift ram being assigned, the external diameter of B is calculated so as to give the required intensity of pressure in the cylinder F. The lift cylinder is supplied from F through the pipe G. On the down stroke of the lift, the ram B rises, the balance water is returned to its own supply tank, and the only water rejected is that originally filling the high-pressure ram B. In a lift of this type mentioned by Mr. Ellington, the lift ram was $4\frac{1}{4}$ inches diameter, the lift carrying 7 cwts. with a 70 feet rise. The volume of pressure water at 700 lbs. per square inch was $10\frac{1}{2}$ gallons per trip,

Fig. 363.—Suspended Hoist.

as against 43 gallons when working direct-acting and without the balance cylinder.

It will be observed that as the balance ram falls, the pressure on the annulus E increases, due to the increasing head to which it is subjected,

l this to a certain extent counterbalances the difference in effective
ight of the lift ram.

A second type of balance cylinder, which has the advantage that all
:kings are external, is illustrated in Fig. 362. Here pressure water is
:nitted through the hollow ram A to the movable cylinder B, and forces
ter at a reduced pressure out of the fixed cylinder C into the lift cylinder.
e cylinder B is weighted, this weight being proportioned so as to pro-
ce a pressure in C sufficient to approximately balance the weight of the
. ram and cage. No attempt is made to allow for the varying effective
ight of the lift ram. Sufficient of the weight is left unbalanced to
ase the lift to descend with sufficient rapidity on the down stroke
en with an empty cage. A lift of this type, to lift 20 cwt. through a
tance of 90 feet, carries a six-inch ram and uses 24½ gallons of water
700 lbs. pressure per trip, as against 109 gallons without balance
linder. With the direct-acting or ram-supported lift, hoisting speeds
to 180 feet per minute are common, 240 feet per minute being about
e maximum.

The second type of lift—the suspension type—is manipulated from a
draulic ram having a comparatively short stroke. The requisite travel
the wire rope or ropes by which the cage is suspended, is obtained by
altiplying this by means of a jigger.

The weight of the cage may be balanced by hanging weights, the vary-
g immersion of the ram in this case being unimportant. A hoist on
is principle, but with unbalanced cage, is shown in Fig. 363, while a
lanced lift is shown in Fig. 364. Here two wire ropes are employed
: lifting and two for carrying weights which partly counterbalance the
ge. As the cage of a suspended lift rises, a portion of the weight of the
spending rope is transferred to the plunger side of the supporting
lley, and the effective weight transferred to the plunger consequently
ries throughout the whole of its stroke. Fig. 365 shows one, and
g. 366 a second method of compensating for this rope variation. In
e former a double-balance chain is suspended from the cage as shown,
that if R be the travel of the cage, the length of each chain is $R \div 2$.
t m be the multiplying factor for the jigger; W the weight of
lbalanced portion of cage; w the weight of the suspending cable per
ot run; w' the weight of each balance chain per foot run.

Then with cage at bottom, the pull on plunger $= m \{ W + w R \}$

,,　　　,,　　,, top,　　　　,,　　　,,　　$= m \{ W + w' R \} - w R$

And for these to be equal, $w' = w \left(1 + \dfrac{1}{m} \right).$

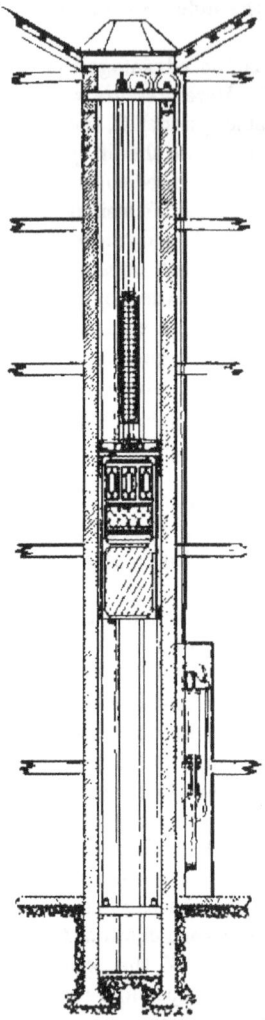

In the second method, the lower side
the plunger is in free communication w
an open standpipe of height h feet conta
ing water. Let d and D be the diametei
standpipe and of plunger, in feet. Tl
if $h = \dfrac{R}{m} \cdot \dfrac{D^2}{d^2}$, the difference of upw

pressure on the plunger at the top ɛ

bottom of its stroke is $62 \cdot 4 \, \dfrac{\pi D^2}{4} \left(h + \right.$

lbs.

For this difference of pressure to count
balance the difference in the effective wei₍
of cable, *i.e.*, $wR \left(1 + \dfrac{1}{m}\right)$, we must have

$$w R \left(1 + \frac{1}{m} \right) = 62 \cdot 4 \, \frac{\pi D^2}{4} \left(h + \frac{R}{m} \right.$$

$$\therefore h = \frac{R}{m} \left\{ \frac{4w \, (m + 1)}{62 \cdot 4 \, \pi \, D^2} - 1 \right\}$$

$$\text{while} \qquad d = \sqrt{\dfrac{D}{\dfrac{4w \, (m + 1)}{62 \cdot 4 \, \pi \, D^2} - 1}}$$

The suspension system has certain advɛ
tages in virtue of the cheapness of constr
tion of the shorter ram and cylinder, ɛ
does not necessitate the provision of a dᴇ
well below the lift shaft to contain
cylinder, which may be fixed horizontall;
required. Its drawbacks are due to
inefficiency of the multiplying jigger, and
the serious effects which may follow
rupture of a wire rope. If carefully design
and frequently examined, the latter cᴇ
tingency should, however, be very remᴇ
while the provision of adequate safety catcl
and brakes renders this almost as safe as t
direct-acting system. The speed of hoisti
may be made as great as is convenient. For passenger hoists thiʰ
usually about 2 feet per second, and for warehouse hoists up to abᴇ

FIG. 364. — Multiple Wire Suspended Lift with Counter-
balance Weights.

eet per second. In modern American practice, express passenger lifts occasionally run at speeds of 8 to 10 feet per second.

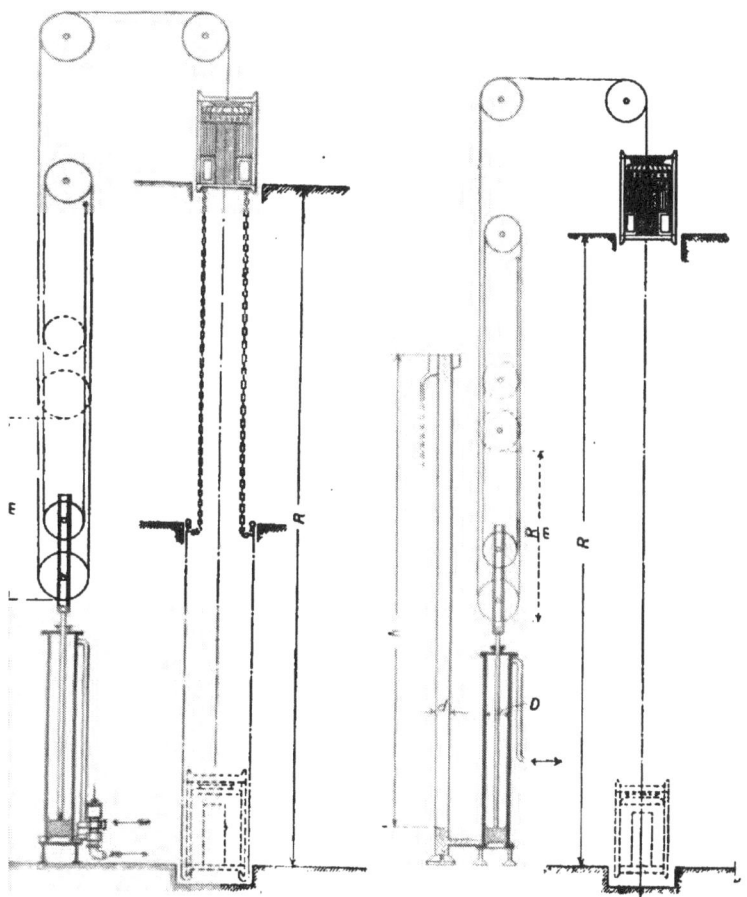

FIG. 365.—Elevator with Chain Compensation for Rope Variation.

FIG. 366.—Hydraulic Elevator with Water Column Compensation.

For very heavy lifting, such as is necessary in canal lifts, etc., where ads up to 1,000 tons may be carried on a single ram, the direct-acting is e only suitable type.

Art. 198.—Efficiency of the Hydraulic Jigger.

The chain, or wire rope, and pulley multiplying gear known as (
hydraulic jigger which is used to multiply the motion of a short str
hydraulic ram for crane or hoist, as illustrated in Figs. 364 to 3(
diminishes the mechanical efficiency of the system to a fairly large exte

The loss thus introduced increases with the number of multiplicatio
and its magnitude varies so largely with the size and condition of sheav
bearings, and rope or chain, that no definite law can be expected to co
each case even approximately.

With ordinary well-designed gearing, having large pulleys, sm
bearings, and wire ropes in good condition and well lubricated, t
efficiency of the jigger may be taken as being approximately giv
by the following formula (H. Adams)—

$$\eta = \cdot906 - \cdot021\,m$$

where m is the number of multiplications of the stroke.

If, then, the friction of packing leathers = 5 per cent. of the total fo
on the ram, the efficiency of ram and jigger is equal to

$$\cdot95\left\{\cdot906 - \cdot021\,m\right\}$$
$$= \cdot86 - \cdot02\,m$$

This gives the following values of the efficiency :—

m	2	4	6	8	10	15	20
Eff.	·82	·78	·74	·70	·66	·56	·46

Art. 199.—Hydraulic Cranes.

Where high-pressure water is available it provides a most convenie
means of operating power cranes, and in its safety, adaptability to s
varying conditions, and steadiness of operation, offers many advantag
over its rivals—compressed air and electricity.

Such cranes are usually operated by hydraulic jiggers, the vario
operations of lifting, racking, and slewing being often performed l
separate rams and cylinders, each regulated by its own separate valve.

Where the load to be lifted may vary within wide limits, some device
usually adopted to economise water at light loads. For small cranes, t
to about two tons, a differential or telescopic ram may be used, the small

working inside the larger, which itself works in the pressure cylinder. For light loads the larger is held stationary by locking gear, the smaller ram then doing the lifting. For heavy loads the two rams work together as one.

Such an arrangement is shown in Fig. 367, R_1 and R_2 being the two

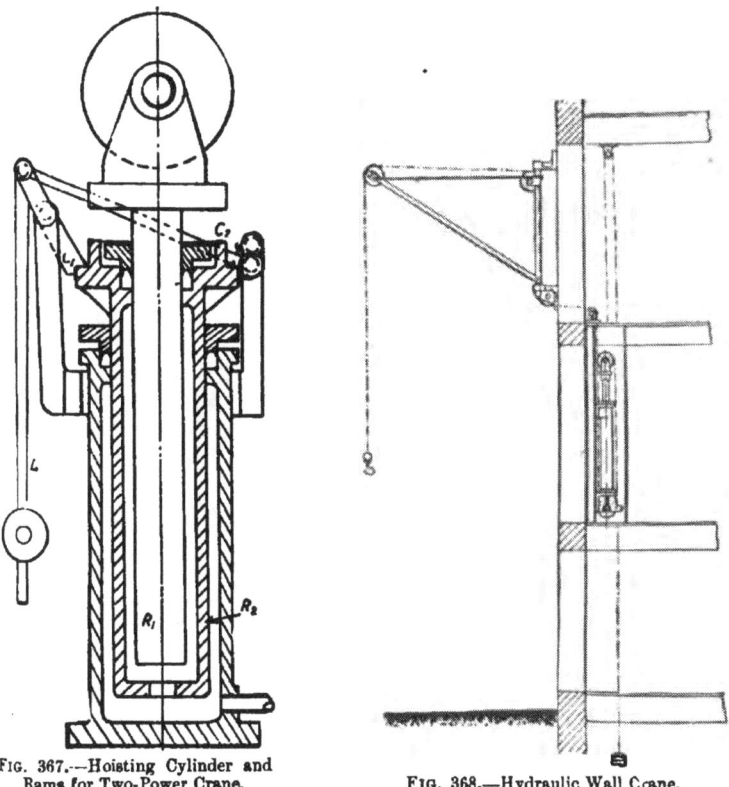

FIG. 367.—Hoisting Cylinder and Rams for Two-Power Crane.

FIG. 368.—Hydraulic Wall Crane.

rams. Under light loads the ram R_2 is held by means of the catches C_1 and C_2 which are actuated by the lever L.

A second arrangement consists of a single ram d carrying a plunger of somewhat larger diameter D. For heavy loads water is admitted only to the larger plunger, while for lighter loads both sides of the plunger are put into free communication with the pressure supply. The forces exerted in the two cases are then in the ratio of $D^2 : D^2 - d^2$, while the volumes of water used per stroke are in the same ratio.

For loads much above two tons, two distinct cylinders, each having its own valves, pipes, chains, and jib-head sleeves, offer many advantages. Thus for a 10-ton crane, one cylinder to lift $6\frac{1}{2}$ tons and a second to lift $3\frac{1}{2}$ tons would be suitable, the two working in conjunction for loads above $6\frac{1}{2}$ tons.

In Fig. 368 a simple type of hydraulic wall crane, suitable for a ware-

FIG. 369.—Self-contained Hydraulic Crane with separate Racking, Hoisting and Slewing Cylinders.

house, is illustrated. Here hydraulic power is used for lifting only. The jigger may be placed against the wall as shown, or horizontally if preferable, and the controlling valve worked from a hand rope on any floor of the building.

In Fig. 369, a type of hydraulic crane much used in steel works, for removing ingots from the soaking pit to the rolling mill, is illustrated.[1] The crane is self-contained, hoisting, lowering, racking in and out, and slewing being performed by hydraulic power. The latter operation is

[1] By kind permission of the makers.

performed by means of chains gearing with a chain wheel fixed on the foundation plate.

There are two racking cylinders R, with a six-fold multiplying motion, one hoisting cylinder H, with an eight-fold multiplication, and two slewing cylinders S, with a two-fold multiplication, the valves being so placed that one man has full control over the whole crane.

The illustration shows details fairly well, and is self-explanatory.

For comparatively small powers and lifts these cranes may be direct-acting, such an one, suitable for loads up to two tons, and for lifts up to about 6 feet, being illustrated in Fig. 370.[1] Here the lifting hook is attached directly to a carriage running along the jib, which is itself raised and lowered by a direct-acting hydraulic cylinder sliding between the cheeks of the mast and working upon a hollow steel ram forming the bottom centre of the crane. For smaller loads and lifts the lifting cylinder may itself be suspended from the travelling carriage, the

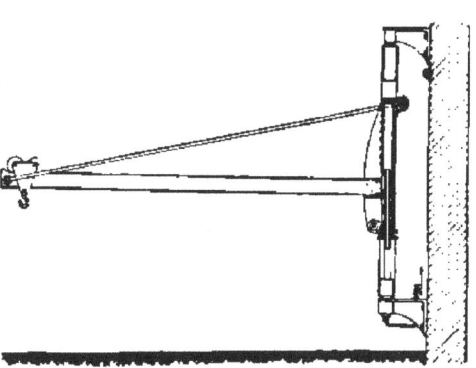

FIG. 370.—Direct-acting Wall Crane.

hook being attached to the ram, and pressure water being conveyed to the cylinder by a walking pipe.

With the hydraulic crane the speed of the lifting hook may be adjusted up to about 6 feet per second.

Dock Cranes.—Fig. 371[2] shows the general arrangement of a movable hydraulic luffing crane having a lower power of 15 tons and a maximum power of 30 tons. This crane has a lift of 66 feet and the jib has 39 feet maximum and 20 feet minimum rake.

Fig. 372 shows a type of balanced jib luffing crane,[3] as built for coaling purposes. The jib has an extended end to which are attached the counterbalance weights and tie rods. The lower ends of the tie rods are attached to a travelling crosshead actuated by the rams of the luffing cylinders and

---

[1] By Messrs. The Hydraulic Engineering Co., Ltd., Chester.
[2] By courtesy of Messrs. Sir W. G. Armstrong, Whitworth & Co., Ltd.
[3] By courtesy of Mr. Arthur Musker, M.I.C.E.

FIG. 871.—30-Ton Hydraulic Lifting Crane.

also carry a compensating pulley. The lifting rope or chain passes
over this pulley as shown in the sketch, with the result that when the jib

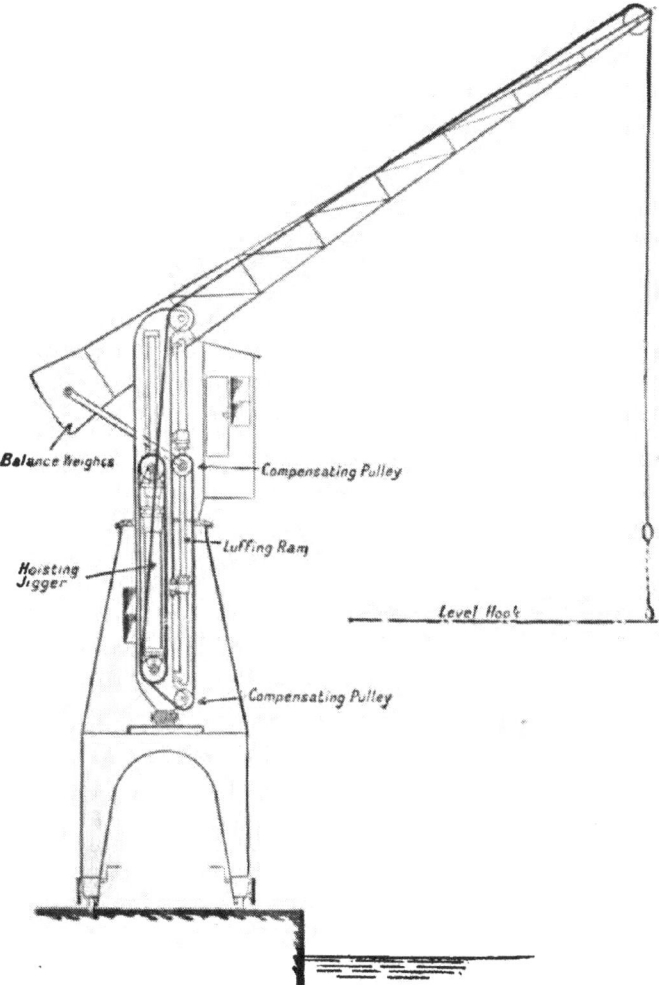

Balance Weights

Compensating Pulley

Luffing Ram

Hoisting Jigger

Level Hook

Compensating Pulley

FIG. 372.—Hydraulic Balanced-Jib Luffing Crane.

is luffed inwards the hoisting rope is paid out to compensate for the rise at the point of the jib. By suitably adjusting the stroke of the luffing ram and the inclination of the rods the level of the lifting hook may be maintained constant for all radial positions of the weight.

3 c 2

ART. 200.—HYDRAULIC COAL TIPS.

Fig. 373 shows one of a series of hydraulic coal tips designed to lift a
waggon of ten tons through a height of 45 feet and to discharge this
through the shoot S into the hold of a vessel. The lifting cradle C
is actuated by four rams, one small and one large one on each side. The
smaller rams are for the purpose of partially balancing the weight of
the cradle, and are in constant communication with the high-pressure
mains. These four rams are each 45 feet long, and press against
a cross girder above the cradle, which travels in vertical guides. The
cradle is suspended from this cross girder by adjustable bolts, and the
tipping cradle rests upon the main cradle and is hinged on the end
nearest the dock. The shore end of the cradle for tipping purposes is
actuated by means of wire ropes which pass up from the shore end
of the cradle on either side to near the top of the tip framing, thence
over sheaves. The bight of the rope is carried over guide pulleys and
up to the side of the main cradle, where it is passed over a sheave
attached to the framing of this cradle. The tipping ropes from each side
of the cradle are by this means made out of one rope, and any inequality
in the stretch of either end of the rope is adjusted by the bight of
the rope traversing over this sheave upon the tip cradle; this rope, which
acts the part of two ropes for the tipping cradle, is free to run round the
sheaves of the tipping ram and cylinder, as the main cradle lifts or
lowers, carrying the tipping cradle with it.

The main cradles are fitted with cross girders above the ordinary
height of the top of a wagon, and should the tipping cradle be very
rapidly lifted, these girders act as a stop to prevent the wagon being
thrown off. There are two cranes on each tip, one capable of working
four tons and the other eight tons. All movements of the various
appliances are controlled from the elevated cabin on the side of the tip.
The point of the shoot can also be lifted or lowered from the same place.

The butt of the shoot is lifted or lowered by means of the main
cradle, upon which there are a pair of sliding dogs, which may be pushed
out to engage in the shaft which carries the butt. The latter is
held, when the proper position is obtained, by means of chains, each
attached to one end of the shoot shaft and carried up to the top of
the tip framing, thence over sheaves and back down alongside the
middle frame of the tip, where there are suitable cleats arranged into
which these chains are placed, and there secured by bolts. The point of
the shoot is moved by means of wire ropes which pass up to the top

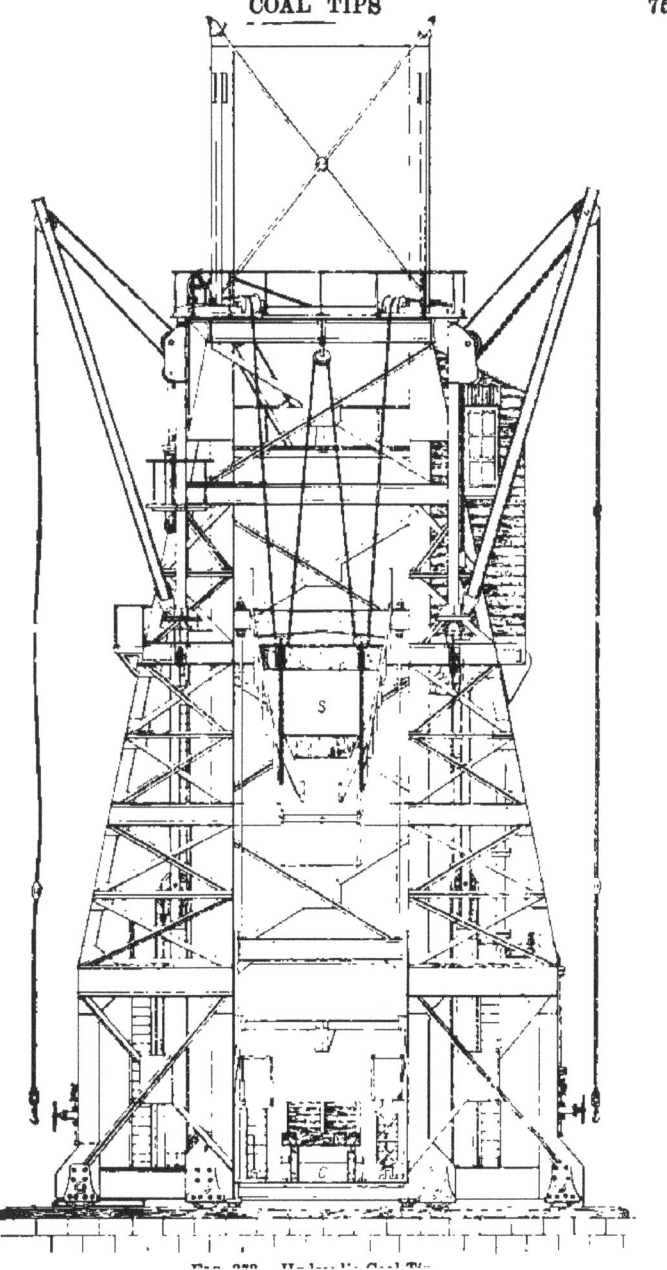

Fig. 272.— Heslop's Coal Tip.

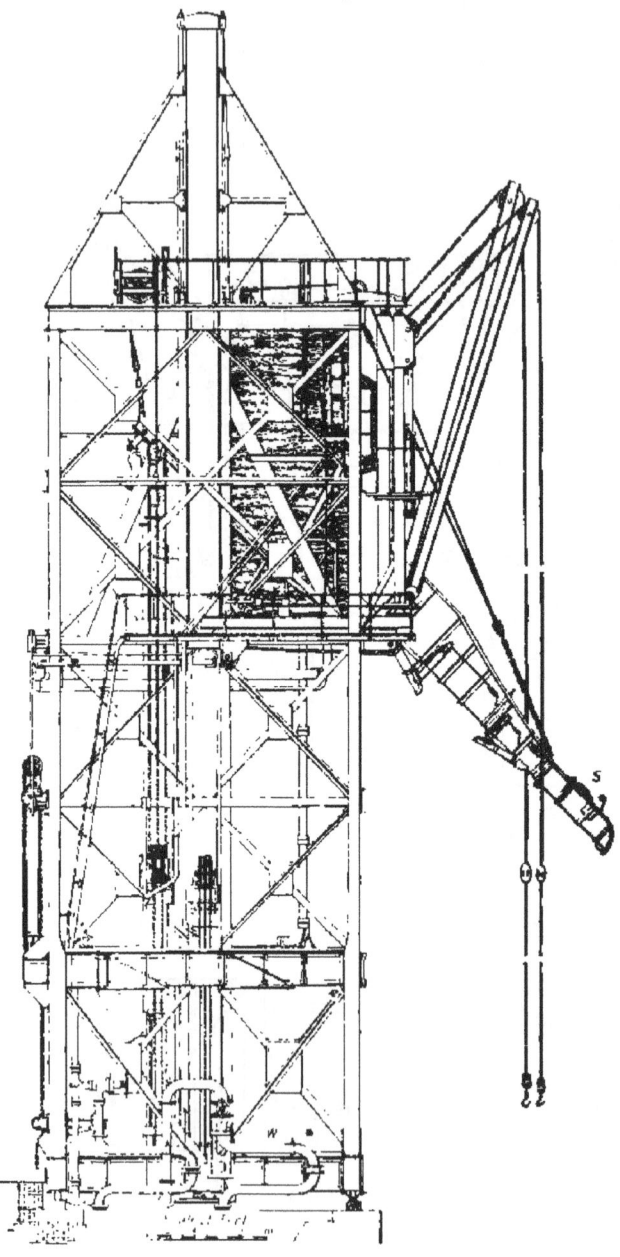

FIG. 374.—30-Ton Hydraulic Coal Tip.

of the tip and thence to a crab winch actuated by three-cylind
hydraulic engines and fitted with brakes for adjusting the shoot poi
where required.

The pressure water is brought by two tiers of 8-inch mains in a trenc
beneath the tips. To enable the tips to be moved laterally witho
uncoupling the pipes, these are fitted with walking pipes, shown at

in the illustration, which have a range of 15 feet, and as the shoots themselves are pivoted and may be radiated in either direction 5 feet from the centre of the tip, this gives an extreme range of 25 feet without changing any water connections.

The capacity of each tip is about 500 tons per hour. Fig. 374 shows one of a series of more recent tips erected by the same makers[1] at Newport, Mon. These are designed for wagons of 30 tons gross weight. the total lift being 50 feet. Hoisting is performed by wire ropes, two hoisting cylinders being provided. The walking pipes for supplying the cylinders are shown on the left hand of the sketch.

The main hoisting cylinder has a ram of 18 inches diameter, with a 25-foot stroke. The auxiliary ram is 9 inches in diameter, and has also a 25-foot stroke, while the tipping ram is 9 inches in diameter, with a stroke of 18 feet. Two cranes, one of 3 tons, and one of 5 tons capacity. are provided for handling anti-coal-breaking gear, having each a lift of 500 feet. They are provided with $10\frac{1}{2}$-inch and $12\frac{3}{4}$-inch rams respectively, both of 25-foot stroke. The slewing-gear of each crane is driven by a ram $6\frac{1}{2}$-inch in diameter and 2-foot stroke. The hoist may be worked anywhere within a range of 200 feet, the traverser gear for working the trucks extending over this distance. The cylinders for operating the traverser gear are fixed in pits beneath the track.[2]

Art. 201.—Hydraulic Crane Valves.

The supply and discharge of water to and from the cylinder of a crane may be adjusted by means of a simple or compound slide or piston valve. as shown in Fig. 375, or by poppet valves directly manipulated by hand. Where pressures are very high and the volume of water large the effort required to actuate such valves becomes excessive and some other arrangement becomes desirable. Such an arrangement[3] is shown in Fig. 376. Here A marks the pressure water inlet, D the connection to hydraulic cylinder, and E the exhaust.

The valves are operated by handle F, connected to rock-shaft G. Throwing F in one direction opens the inlet valve at A; throwing it in the other allows the water to escape from D through outlet at E.

---

[1] Messrs. Fielding & Platt, Ltd., Gloucester, by whose courtesy the foregoing sketches are available.

[2] These hoists were illustrated and described in a paper read before the Institution of Mechanical Engineers at their summer meeting held at Cardiff in 1906, and for further details of working and for drawings, &c., reference may be made to the proceedings of this Institution.

[3] Messrs. Dewhursts' Engineering Co., Ltd., Sheffield.

The valve stem H is raised by a cam surface cut in the upper side of rock-shaft G. The stem does not directly open the main valve; the upper end of a stem passes through main valve L in a clearance hole as shown, and when raised, it strikes against the bottom of pilot valve K, which it lifts against the pressure of the spring above and against the pressure of the water in chamber B. Chamber B is filled with water leaking from inlet space A, past the easy fit of the piston portion of valve L. As soon as K is raised, the pressure in B drops to that in service

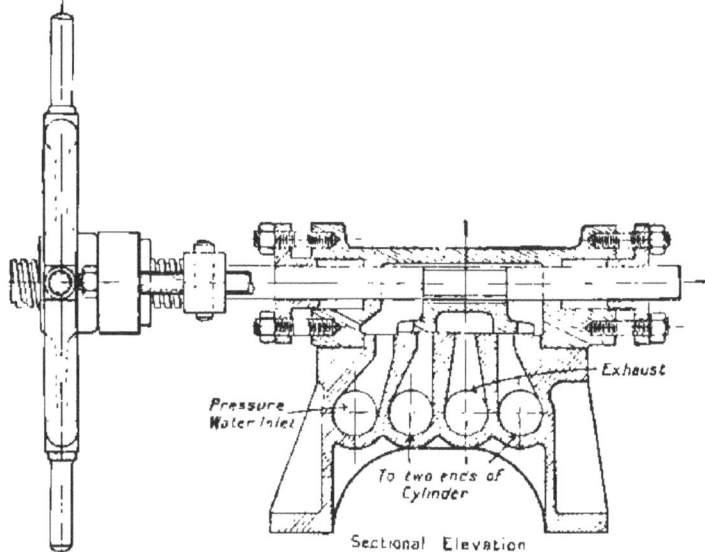

FIG. 375.—Slide Valve for Heavy Hydraulic Machinery.

connection D, since the outlet through the centre of the main valve is much larger than the area through which the leakage escapes from A. Under these circumstances there is an unbalanced pressure on valve L from the water in A, which forces it from its seat on ring C, this unbalanced pressure being due to the fact that the piston portion of main valve L is much larger in diameter than the seat on which it rests in ring C.

In closing, the reverse of this action takes place. Handle F being brought back to its central position, valve stem H, and with it pilot valve K, are lowered until the latter reaches its seat in valve L. Connection between B and D being thus closed, the leakage from A into B allows the pressure in the latter space to rise until it balances that in A, when the coil spring has sufficient pressure to force valve L down against its seat.

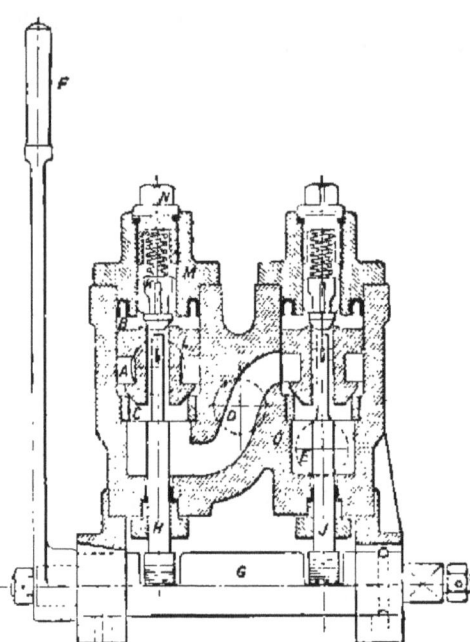

FIG. 376.—Hydraulic Operating Valves with Pilot Valves.

This construction evidently has a number of advantages. The use of the small pilot valve, the only member which has to be lifted against the full pressure of the water, makes the apparatus more easy to handle than would be the case if the whole main valve L had to be raised from its seat against the full pressure. Also there are no sliding movements to be effected through packings under heavy pressure, as the valve stem H is not under pressure until the valve is opened.

There would appear, also, to be little danger of shock from sudden closing of the valves, since the lowering of main valve L to its seat on C is effected by the leakage from A to B, which can be made as gradual as seems advisable, being regulated by the fit of L in its cylindrical chamber in the main casting O.

ART. 202.—THE HYDRAULIC JACK.

For the manipulation of heavy weights by hand the hydraulic jack is of the greatest value. In principle it consists of a Bramah's press on a small scale, and one type of its construction is illustrated in Fig. 377. Here the reciprocation of the hand lever pumps water from the cistern A, through the hollow plunger B, past the suction and delivery valves

V, and V_D, into the space C below the lifting ram, and raises the latter. The weight to be lifted is carried either on the ram table T, or on a side shoe projecting from the ram casing. Screws are provided for supplying the cistern A with water and for allowing of the inlet of air, while a lowering screw permits of the escape of pressure water from the space below the lifting ram into the supply cistern when it is required to lower the load. The lifting ram is usually packed by means of a cup leather, and the pump plunger by means of a single leather ring.

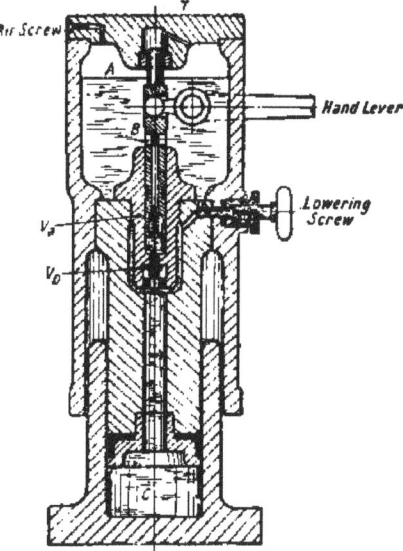

FIG. 377.—Hydraulic Jack.

If m = ratio of travels of lever handle and of pump plunger, and if a and A are the areas of plunger and ram, the theoretical mechanical advantage of the jack = $m\dfrac{A}{a}$, so that, neglecting friction, the force P to be applied at the lever handle to support a weight W on the ram table is given by $P = W\dfrac{a}{m\,A}$ lbs.

Thus if
$$m = \frac{24}{1\cdot25} = 19\cdot2.$$

" diameter of ram $= 5\frac{1}{2}$ inches $\left.\begin{array}{c}\\ \\\end{array}\right\}\dfrac{A}{a} = 30\cdot25.$
" diameter of plunger $= 1$ inch

if $P = 50$ lbs., $W = \dfrac{50 \times 19\cdot2 \times 30\cdot25}{2,240} = 13$ tons.

Actually the weight lifted is less than this because of friction losses. The efficiency of the jack, or the ratio $\dfrac{\text{actual}}{\text{theoretical}}$ weight lifted by the ram, can only be determined experimentally, and varies largely with the condition and size of the apparatus, as well as with the magnitude and position of the load.

Friction losses are proportionately less as the size of the machine increases, and, owing to the fact that the friction is partly mechanical and independent of the load, the losses diminish proportionately as the load increases.

Eccentric loading largely increases the mechanical friction, and may double the friction losses.

The efficiency of a jack in fairly good order may be taken as varying from about 66 per cent. in the case of a small 3-ton jack, with eccentric loading to about 93 per cent. with a 100-ton jack and central loading, and is approximately constant for loads greater than one-fifth of the nominal capacity of the jack.

ART. 203.—THE HYDRAULIC PRESS.

Reference has already been made in Art. 8 to the Bramah's press. Its modifications, as applied to such work as cotton baling, boiler-plate flanging, cartridge-case drawing, and heavy forging, are too numerous for detailed mention, and only one or two of such applications will be considered in detail in the present treatise.[1] Fig. 378[2] illustrates a form of press used for flanging operations, &c., and capable of exerting a pressure of 420 tons. In this machine two small rams are installed for lifting the head on the up stroke, while the pressure is applied by one central and two side rams, pressure water being supplied to these in succession as additional force is required. During the idle part of the down stroke, water from the exhaust is allowed to fill the space vacated by the rams. The arrangement of valves by which this is rendered possible is simple and worthy of notice, and is shown in detail in Fig. 379. The main pressure and exhaust valves V_P and V_E each carry a closely fitting piston of greater area than the valve itself, so that if the pressure above the piston and below the valve is equalised the effect of the pressure between the piston and valve is to lift the latter from its seat. A small orifice is provided in each piston, so that under normal conditions the pressure above and below the piston is equal, and pressure keeps the valve on its seat. The auxiliary valves V_1 and V_2 are worked directly from the operating lever, and when open give free communication between the under side of the corresponding main valve and the upper side of its piston.

[1] For further applications of the press the reader is referred to Blaine's "Hydraulics."
[2] By courtesy of the makers, Messrs. Henry Berry & Co., Leeds.

The opening of the auxiliary valve thus leads indirectly to the opening of the corresponding main valve. During the idle part of the down stroke both auxiliary valves are closed, a partial vacuum is produced

FIG. 378.—Hydraulic Flanging Press. Maximum pressure 420 tons.

above the exhaust valve, which opens, and water is drawn from the exhaust into the cylinder. When pressure is required, a quarter-turn of the operating lever raises the valve V_1 and thus the pressure valve, and admits pressure water through the passage P_1 to the cylinder. On the working stroke being completed, a half turn of the lever closes V_1 and opens V_2, thus opening the exhaust valve V_R and putting the cylinder into communication with the exhaust, while a second lever and valve admit

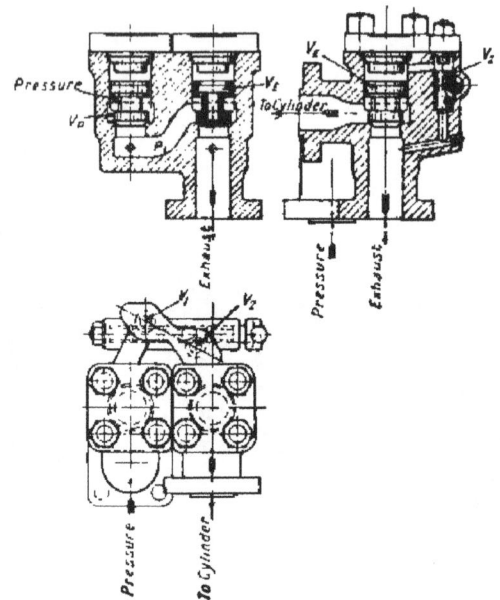

FIG. 379.—Details of 2¼-inch Operating Valve for 420 tons Press.

pressure water to the return cylinders. A smaller press for similar work is illustrated in Fig. 380.

ART. 204.—THE HYDRAULIC FORGING PRESS.

In the production of heavy forgings for large ingots of mild steel, it is essential that every part of the ingot should be equally worked if the resultant forging is to be homogeneous in structure. Where a steam hammer is used, the energy of the blow is absorbed in producing distortion of the outer layers, while the interior is practically unaffected. This disadvantage is overcome by the use of the hydraulic forging press, with its slow and powerful compression, and this is gradually supplanting the steam hammer for the production of very heavy forgings. The principle of the press is the same as that of the ordinary flanging press,

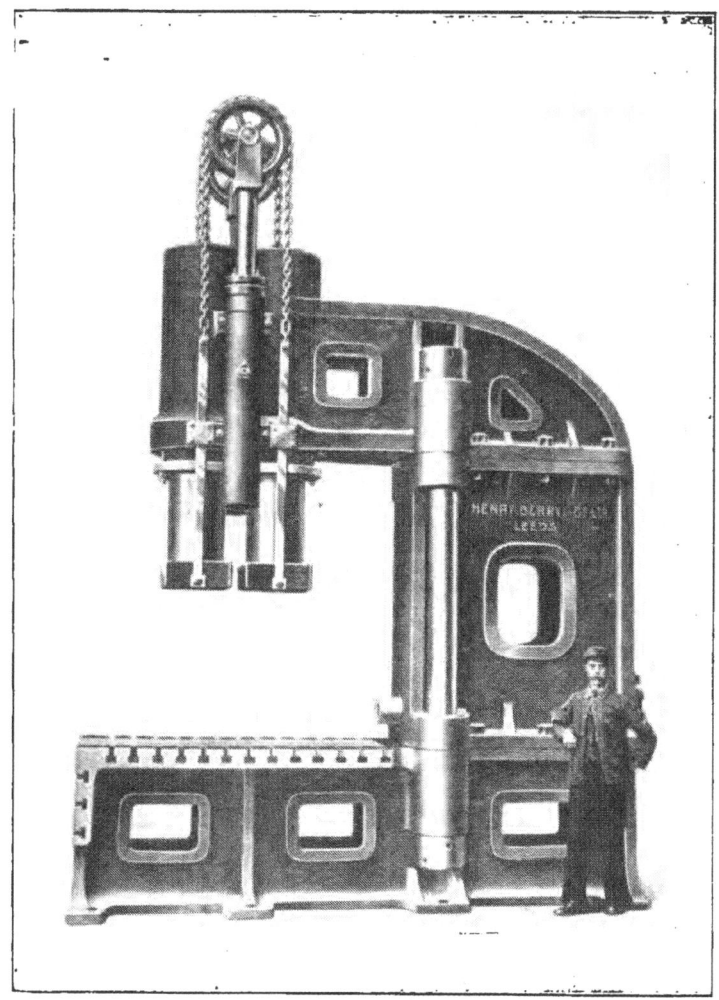

FIG. 380.—Hydraulic Flanging Press.

and for a very complete account of its development and for details of its design, the reader is referred to a paper by R. H. Tweddell.[1]

[1] "Proceedings Institute of Civil Engineers," vol. 117, 1893–4, p. 1.

The Allen press works on a very ingenious principle and is illustrated diagrammatically in Fig. 381.   Here a pressure accumulator is unnecessary, as are valves in the high-pressure water column.   For its operation a low-pressure water supply, at about 200—300 lbs. per square inch, is necessary, and during the idle part of the stroke this follows up the ram, the high-pressure connecting pipe being kept full in the meantime.

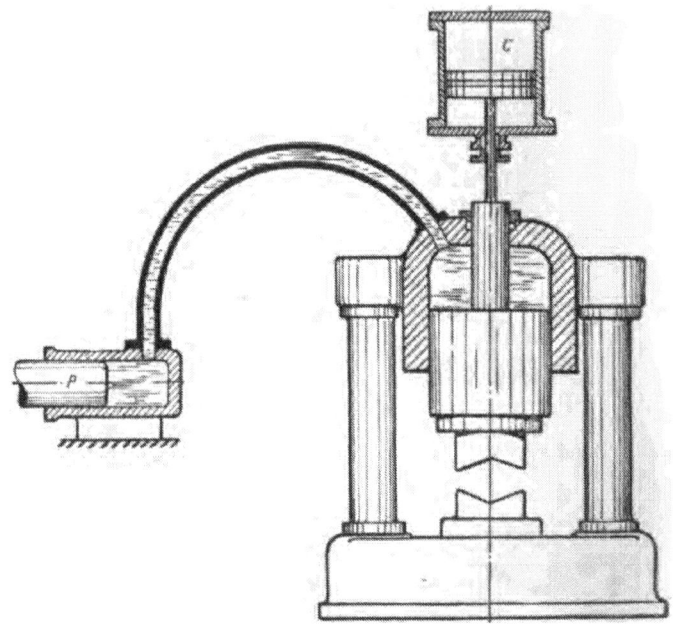

FIG. 381.—Allen's Hydraulic Forging Press.

When pressure is required this supply is cut off and communication is made with the high-pressure pump P.   This has no valves, so that the ram has a continuous up-and-down motion, the water column simply following the motion of the pump plunger.   The inertia of this column thus has a useful effect in increasing the pressure on the ram at the end of the working stroke.   A steam cylinder C is usually provided for lifting the ram.

\ type of forging press to be worked in connection with an accumulator and intensifier is illustrated in Fig. 382.   This press is fitted with a differential ram having diameters of 21 inches and 36 inches and supplied with pressure water at 600 atmospheres. By using each cylinder separately, or the two in combination, three powers having the ratio 1 : 2 : 3 may be obtained, the effective force varying from 1,300 tons with the small ram to 4,040 tons with the two in combination. Two lifting cylinders, using water at 50 atmospheres pressure, exert a constant upward

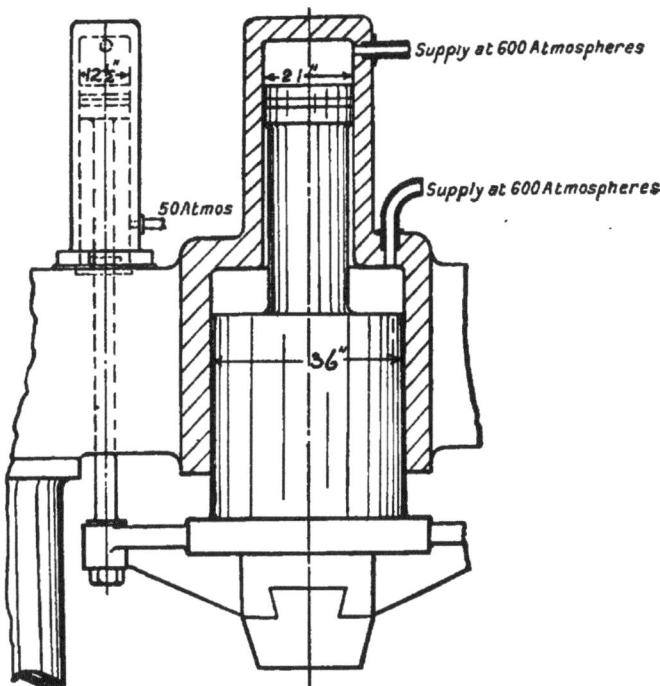

Fig. 382.—Cylinders of 3-power Hydraulic Forging Press for a maximum effort of 4,000 tons.

force of 70 tons, which has been taken into account in obtaining the above values.

As, during the working portion of the stroke of a hydraulic press or similar machine, the ram velocity is required to be only very slow, the diameters of the supply pipes may be very small without appreciable loss of head. A ratio of ram diameter to pipe diameter of about 12 to 1 is usually adopted.

ART. 204A.—STEAM-HYDRAULIC FORGING PRESS.

By combining a steam accumulator or intensifier with the hydraulic cylinders of a forging press and arranging steam actuated drawback cylinders to the main ram, a type of forging press is obtained which has been largely adopted of recent years on account of its flexibility, simplicity, and speed of working. Such a machine is illustrated in Fig. 383, which shows a press designed for a full working power of 1,200 tons, and a maximum stroke of 48 inches. At full power the stroke is about 6 inches, and the machine is capable of making from 70 to 80 short strokes per minute.

The press as shown is in direct communication with the steam intensifier S and a water reservoir R shown behind the steam intensifier. The main cylinder C of the press is supplied with water during the idle portion of the stroke from the reservoir through a large filling valve V bolted directly on the top of the cylinder. The water is returned to the reservoir after the pressing operation through the exhaust valve P secured to the top cylinder of the steam intensifier and connected directly to the reservoir.

The movements of the press are controlled by means of a main hand lever carried on a bracket on the steam intensifier, the movement of the press head corresponding with the movement of the main hand lever. The downward movement of the hand lever first of all exhausts the steam from the under side of the drawback pistons contained in the drawback cylinders DD secured to the tops of the columns of the press, thus allowing the press head to fall until the top die reaches the work. During this portion of the stroke of the main ram, the cylinder is filled with water from the reservoir through the filling valve. A further downward movement of the main hand lever raises the main steam admission valve of the steam intensifier which forces high-pressure water from the top cylinder of the intensifier into the main cylinder of the press thus exerting full power on the work. The upward movement of the main hand lever first opens the main exhaust valve of the steam intensifier, allowing the intensifier piston to descend by gravity, and thus releasing the high pressure on the main ram. The continued upward movement of the main hand lever then opens the exhaust valve on the top of the steam intensifier and allows the water to return from the main cylinder to the reservoir, the upward movement of the press head being effected by the re-admission of steam to the drawback cylinders, thereby completing the cycle of operations of the press and steam intensifier.

An auxiliary hand lever close to the main hand lever operates a small

FIG. 383.—1,200-ton Steam-Hydraulic Forging Press.

steam slide valve which admits constant pressure steam to the drawh
cylinders on the press for working the press with short quick strokes
planishing.

A small lever-worked valve at the foot of the steam intensifier controls the movements of a hydraulic turning cylinder T secured to the top table of the press.

ART. 205.—HYDRAULIC RIVETERS.

The hydraulic riveter provides another good illustration of the adaptability of the hydraulic machine to workshop processes. Here the problem is to get a fairly large pressure on the rivet during the first portion of the ram stroke, so as to form the rivet head and to clinch the plates, and a final larger pressure of the nature of an impact to cause the rivet to expand and fully fill its hole. The extent to which this is attained in the riveter will be evident from Fig. 384, which represents a typical pressure diagram taken from the cylinder of such a machine, supplied from an accumulator under a pressure of 1,100 lbs. per square inch. Here $A\,B$ represents the idle part of the stroke during which the ram is being brought up to its work, $B\,C$ the setting up the rivet and the formation of the head, $C\,D$ the clinching of the rivet and the closing of the plates, while the sudden stoppage of the heavy accumulator ram is responsible for a further rise in pressure $D\,E$ above the accumulator pressure, which is depended upon to fill up the rivet hole.

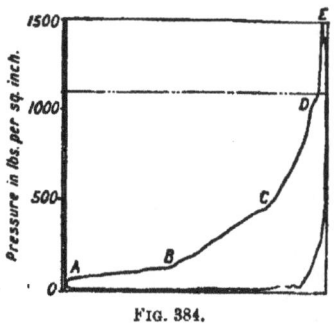

FIG. 384.

Pressure Diagram from Cylinder of Hydraulic Riveter. Accumulator pressure 1,100 lbs. per square inch.

One type of portable riveter is shown in Fig. 385.[1] Here the ram is situated at one end and the riveting is performed at the other end of a lever hinged at C. As thus arranged the machine offers some advantages over the more ordinary type of bear riveter shown in Fig. 386,[1] for work in restricted spaces. In the latter type the operation of riveting is directly performed by the hydraulic ram, the riveter jaws being formed as a single steel casting. In Fig. 387[2] a section of the cylinder and valves of a riveter of the hinged type is shown. Here water is admitted to or discharged from the ram cylinder by the arrangement of valves shown.

---

[1] By courtesy of the makers.
[2] By the courtesy of the makers, Messrs. Henry Berry & Co., Ltd., Leeds.

Thus a quarter-turn of the regulating lever raises the valve V_S and puts the cylinder into communication with the pressure supply. On the com-

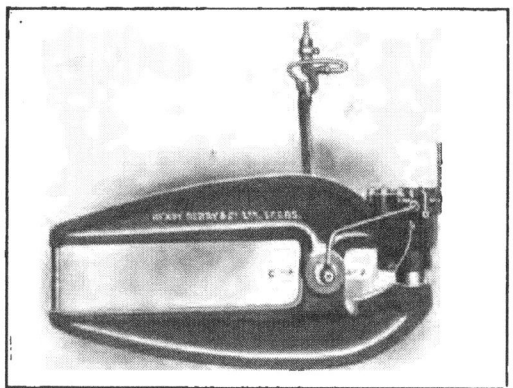

FIG. 385.—Portable Riveter. Hinged Type.

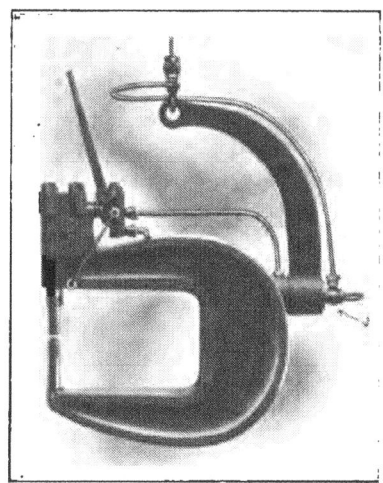

FIG. 386.—Portable Bear Riveter.

pletion of the working stroke a half-turn in the opposite direction closes the valve V_S and opens valve V_D, putting the cylinder into communication with the discharge passages. The main ram is drawn back on its idle stroke

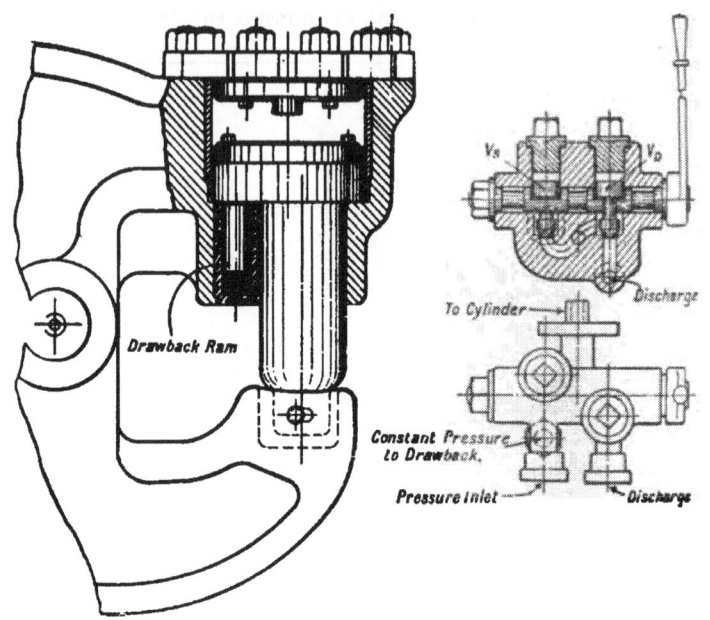

FIG. 387.—Section of Cylinder and Valves of Hinged Type Riveter.

by means of a special drawback ram which is always exposed to supply pressure. The method of packing the rams and the general construction is sufficiently well indicated in the figure.

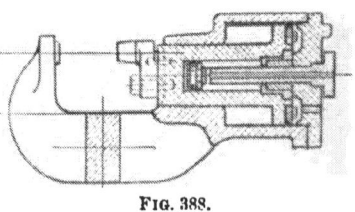

FIG. 388.

In these portable machines pressure water is supplied to the suspending hook by means of a walking pipe, and provision is made for working at a rivet at any inclination, by means of a watertight swivel joint at J (Fig. 385).

Fig. 388 shows a design of fixed-jaw portable riveter which has the advantages of a central drawback ram and a main ram with central guide.

Fig. 389 illustrates a form of fixed riveter suitable for the circumferential joints of large boiler shells. Here both jaws of the bear are fitted with rams, that to the right of the illustration being adjusted to suit the length of rivet to be handled. The working cylinder, to the left, is fitted with a differential ram so as to allow a larger range of work to

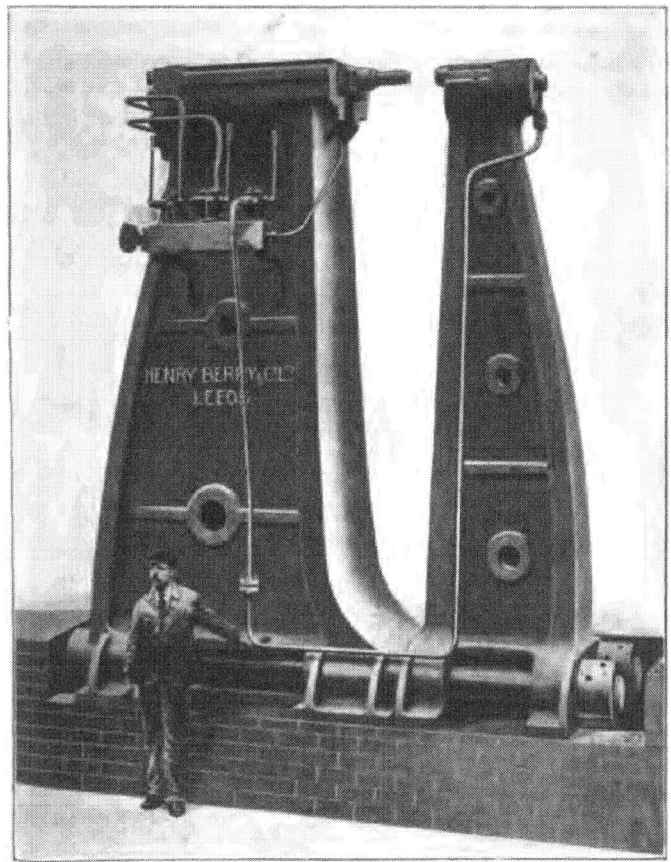

Fig. 389.—Fixed Hydraulic Riveter.

be handled with economy. In this case the pressure supply to each ram is regulated by a separate valve.

Art. 206.—Hydraulic Lock-Gate Machinery.

In the majority of modern docks the lock gates or caissons are actuated by hydraulic machinery. In the new "Royal Edward" Dock at

Avonmouth, for example, each leaf of the entrance lock gates is actuated by a direct-acting hydraulic cylinder with piston and rod, the stroke being 12 feet 9 inches.

The cylinder of each machine is placed in a pit at the side of the lock. The piston-rod is attached to a steel crosshead frame faced with gun-metal and working between steel guides. The connecting-rod is of steel plate of box section, and is fitted with a gimbal attachment at each end, so that a certain amount of vertical movement can take place in the gate

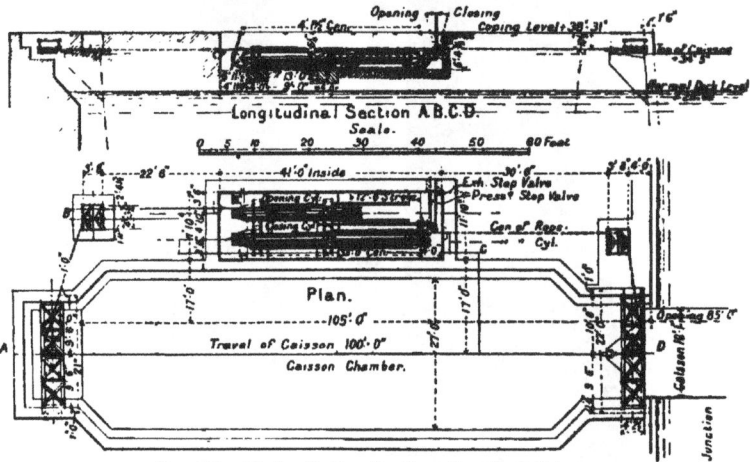

FIG. 390.—Hydraulic Gear for Operating Dock Caisson.

without interfering with the action of the machinery. Control is effected by valves which are operated from quay level.

The hauling machinery for operating each of the caissons installed in connection with the same dock is shown in Fig. 390,[1] and consists of two cast-iron hydraulic cylinders placed side by side. The working pressure is 750 lbs. per square inch. The multiplying ratio is 8 to 1, and the rams give a travel of the hauling rope of 66 feet per minute. One ram is used for opening, and the other for closing the passage. The hauling ropes are of steel wire fixed to an adjustable fast end on each cylinder, carried along the centre line of the caisson under the recess cover, and attached to a bracket projecting from the inner end of the caisson. Automatic cut-off gear is provided to prevent over-winding at either end of the travel.

Hydraulic Sluice Gates and Penstocks.—The sluice gates, 54 inches

[1] Figs. 390 and 391 are by courtesy of the Editor of " Engineering."

diameter, in connection with these caissons are also operated by direct-
acting hydraulic rams working under the same pressure, the details of

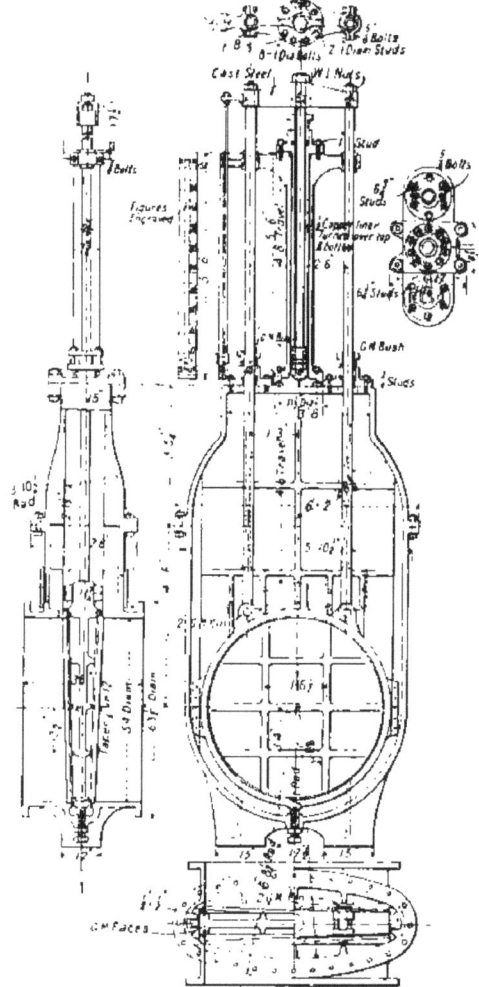

FIG. 391.—Hydraulically Operated Sluice Valve.

construction being shown in Fig. 391. The motion of the rams is
regulated from a valve chest with slide valves of gun-metal.

Art. 207.—Hydraulic Capstans.

Fig. 392, A, B, and C, shows a type of hydraulic capstan driven by a three-cylinder Brotherhood engine.[1] The supply and discharge pipes are led to the engine through trunnions $T\ T$, about which, on releasing the catch C, the whole machine, capstan and engine, may be rotated, thus bringing the engine upwards for inspection or repairs without breaking any

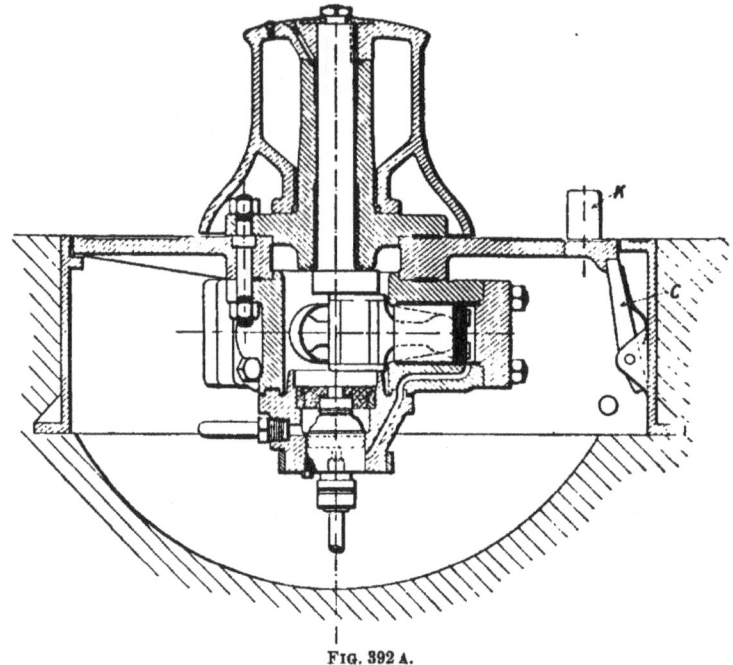

FIG. 392 A.

joïnts. The water supply is regulated by means of the treadle K which operates the admission valve. With a capstan head 1 foot 6 inches in diameter the hauling speed of such a machine is about 180 feet per minute.

Where the capstan is intended for very heavy work the engine may be connected to the capstan head by speed-reducing gear wheels, and Fig. 393 shows such a machine designed for two speeds exerting a pull of 7 tons

---

[1] By courtesy of the Hydraulic Engineering Co., Ltd., Chester.

51 feet per minute and 14 tons at 26½ feet per minute, the working
essure being 700 lbs. per square inch and the diameter of the capstan
ad 3 feet.

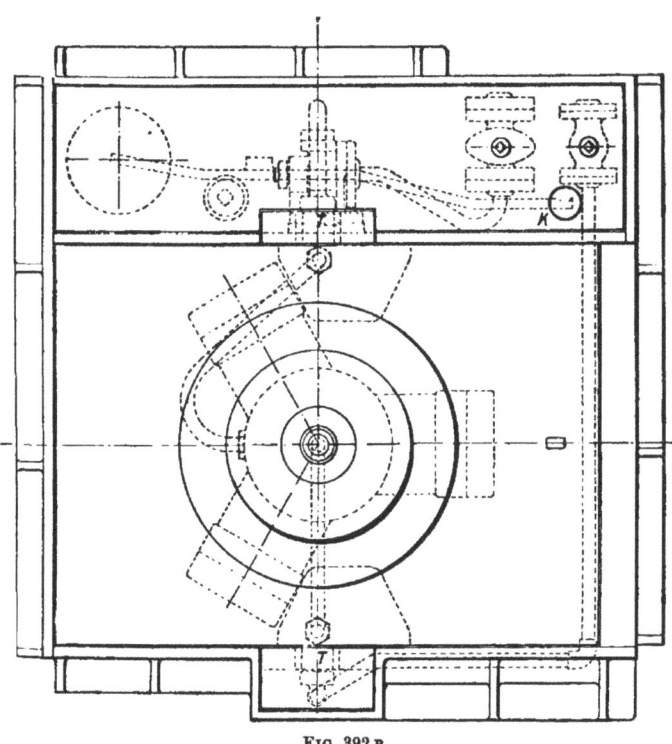

FIG. 392 B.

ART. 208.—HYDRAULIC TRANSMISSION GEAR.

Several devices for transmitting the torque developed at the crank shaft
f the engine of a motor car to the driving wheels by hydraulic means
ave been patented recently. All shock due to changes of gear wheels is
hus avoided, while the ratio of speeds of the driving and driven shafts
nay be regulated with a much greater degree of flexibility than is
possible with a mechanical drive. One such device, due to Dr. Hele Shaw,
s illustrated in Fig. 394. In this a ring R mounted on ball bearings
nd fixed as regards rotation, carries the crank pins of four pistons

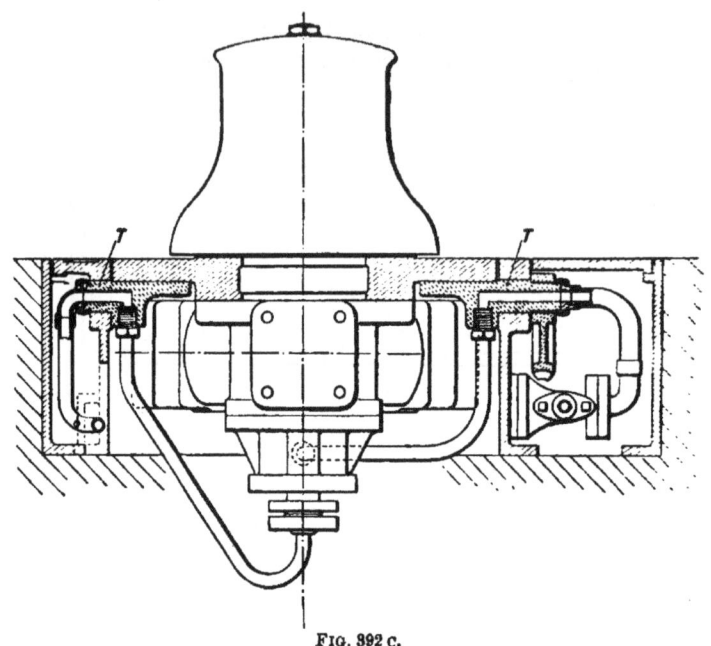

FIG. 392 c.

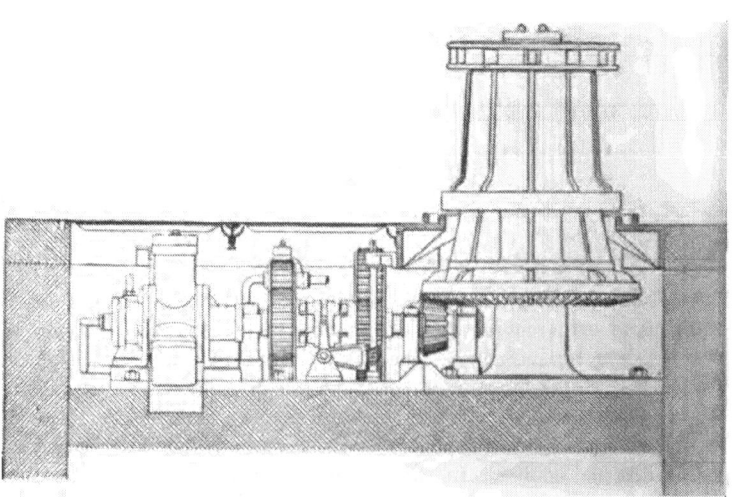

FIG. 393.—Double Power Hydraulic Capstan.

rking in cylinders A. The ring is eccentric with respect to the centre
e of the gear, its eccentricity being capable of regulation as desired.
ie cylinders A form a single casting keyed to the jaw clutch K which
coupled directly to the engine shaft. The supply of fluid to or from
з cylinders is regulated by means of a circular rotary valve V with
pply and discharge ports. The eccentricity of the ring R determines
e stroke of the pistons in these cylinders and thus the volume of fluid
splaced by them per revolution of the engine.

A second set of four cylinders B, of the same size as A, are keyed to
e jaw clutch N which is coupled direet to the driving wheels. The

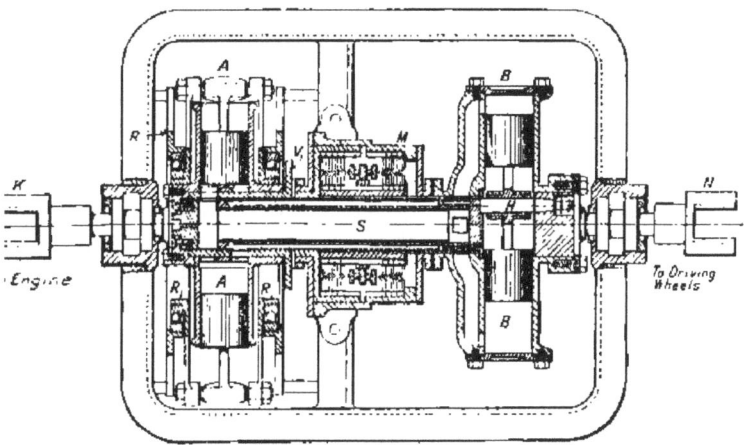

FIG. 394.—Hydraulic Transmission Gear.

onnecting rods of these pistons are coupled to a single crank pin H with
xed throw and thus have a constant stroke, while the crank shaft H is
eyed to one half of the cone clutch M but is otherwise free to rotate
зlatively to the frame of the motor. The compound clutch M consists
f three parts, one of which is fixed to the frame, one to the shaft H, and
ne to the cylinders A, and by suitable manipulation the shaft H may be
ither clutched to the frame or to the cylinder A. Assuming these
ylinders to be rotating continuously in one direction with the engine, the
ction of the apparatus is as follows.

(1.) **Cylinders A and Crank Shaft H both declutched.**—Liquid pumped by
iistons A is circulated freely through the system along the pipe S and
hrough cylinders B, causing shaft H to rotate idly in its bearings, with

a speed which is equal to or less than that of the engine according as tl
eccentricity of the ring R is equal to or less than the throw of tl
crank H.

(2.) **Shaft H Clutched to Frame.**—This shaft being fixed, the cylinders
are now constrained to rotate, the speed depending on the eccentricity
ring R, and the direction of flow, and therefore that of rotation, beir
regulated by the position of the rotary valve V.

(3.) **Shaft H clutched to Cylinders A.**—If now the eccentricity of R l
reduced to zero, no circulation of fluid takes place, and the cylinders
and B are in effect directly coupled together through the medium of $\imath$
incompressible column of liquid and rotate at the same speed. As tl
eccentricity of R is increased, the valve V remaining in the rever
position, circulation takes place and cylinders B are driven backwar
relative to A to an extent which depends on the eccentricity. Whe
this eccentricity is the same as the throw of H the backward speed of
is equal to the forward speed of A, and the actual speed of B relative
the frame is zero, while by suitably regulating the eccentricity betwee
these two limits any speed lower than that of the engine may be given
B and hence to the driving wheels.

By the use of such a device the full power of the engine is availab
for work on the driving wheels at all speeds of transmission, except in
far as this is reduced by hydraulic friction losses produced by the circt
lation of the working fluid. On the direct drive this is of course zer
and it is only at lower speeds that it becomes important. At lo
speeds it is not likely that the efficiency of transmission will be high
while the difficulties consequent on any leakage of the working fluid a
obvious. The chief advantage of the system lies in its extreme flexibili
and in the absence of shock on changing speeds.

Art. 209.—The Hydraulic Brake.

The necessity for some braking apparatus by which the kinetic energ
of a heavy body—such as a moving train or of a gun during recoil-
might be quickly and safely absorbed without the recoil effect obtainé
by the use of spring buffers, led to the invention of the hydraulic brake.

In its simplest form this consists of a cylinder fitted with piston an
rod and filled with some liquid, usually oil, water, or glycerine. The tw
ends of the cylinder are connected, either by one or more small passag\
formed by holes in the body of the piston itself, or by a bye-pass pipe fitte
with a spring-loaded valve or with a throttling valve by which the are

may be adjusted. In its simplest form the brake is extensively used as a dashpot for damping the vibrations of governing mechanism and the like.

When used as a buffer stop, the body whose kinetic energy is to be absorbed forces in the piston rod and produces a flow of liquid at high velocity through the connecting orifices. The energy of the body is thus partly transformed into kinetic energy of the liquid, which is dissipated in eddy formation, and partly expended in overcoming the frictional resistances of the connecting passages, together with the mechanical friction of the brake. The whole of the energy is thus ultimately transformed into heat. Since the energy absorbed by the brake is constant for a given mass moving with a given velocity, and is equal to the mean resistance of the brake multiplied by the length of its stroke, it is evident that the pressure in the brake cylinder will have its least maximum value when this pressure, and therefore the resistance, is uniform throughout the stroke, and when in consequence the pressure-displacement diagram forms a rectangle. The brake is therefore preferably designed so as to give as nearly as possible uniform resistance, and since the resistance varies as the square of the velocity of the liquid through the connecting orifices (very nearly), while the velocity of the moving body, and therefore of the piston, varies from a maximum at the instant of impact to zero at the end of the stroke, it is necessary either to make the connecting passages of diminishing area towards the end of the stroke so that the velocity of efflux may remain constant, or to discharge from one side of the piston to the other through a spring-loaded valve set to open at the required pressure.

Where passages of constant area are used it is evident that the resistance falls off very rapidly as the velocity diminishes and, e.g., has only one-quarter of its initial value when the velocity is reduced to one-half. In fact, if the resistance were solely measured by the production of kinetic energy in the contained fluid, the body would never be brought absolutely to rest. Actually, however, the additional resistance in the shape of solid friction at the cup leathers, &c., together with that of returning springs or balance weights, prevent this state of affairs being realised in practice.

The area of the connecting passage may be varied by forming it as a circular orifice through the piston, and allowing this to work over a taper circular spindle fixed longitudinally in the cylinder, the available passage area varying with the diameter of the spindle. A somewhat similar device is applied to a type of buffer stop adopted by Mr. Langley, two rectangular longitudinal slots cut in the piston body working over two

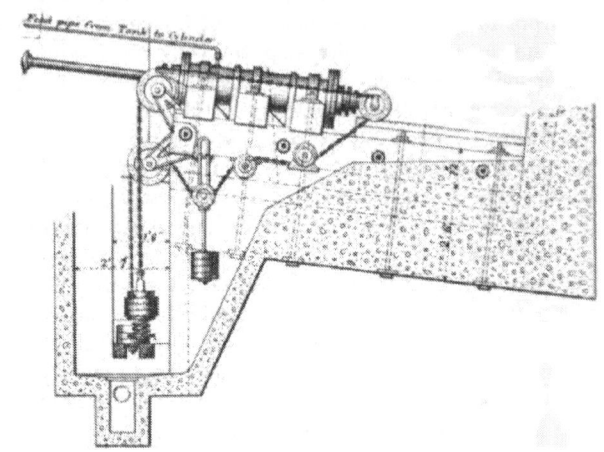

LONGITUDINAL SECTION OF TERMINAL PIT.

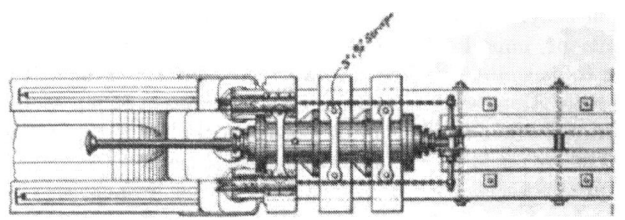

PLAN OF HYDRAULIC BUFFER.

SECTIONAL ELEVATIONS OF CYLINDER.   SECTIONAL PLAN OF CYLINDER.   DETAILS OF PISTON.

FIG. 395.—Hydraulic Buffer Stop.

rectangular longitudinal strips which are fixed inside the cylinder, have the same width as the slots, and vary in depth from end to end.

A buffer stop on these lines[1] is illustrated in Fig. 395. The cylinder, of cast iron, is 10 inches diameter and 4 feet long, its thickness varying from $1\frac{1}{2}$ inches at the front to $1\frac{1}{4}$ inches at the back end. The piston

---

[1] Described by Mr. P. W. Shaw ("Proc. Inst. C. E.," vol. 165, p. 290)

has a travel of 3 feet 6 inches, and is a plain disc, $9\frac{33}{64}$ inches diameter, with two waterways 3 inches wide by $1\frac{1}{2}$ inches deep working over two feathers running from end to end of the cylinder. These feathers are 3 inches wide, and are $1\frac{1}{4}$ inches thick at the back tapering to $\frac{1}{2}$ inch at the front end, the area of the waterways varying from 6 square inches at the back to zero at the front end of the cylinder. The clearance between cylinder and piston is equivalent to a further constant area of ·25 square inch. The covers are provided with two screwed glands, the inside gland of cast iron holding the hat leathers in position, while the outer glands of brass, which are merely intended as a stand-by, are packed slackly with hemp. A rubber pad $1\frac{1}{2}$ inches thick is inserted at the back end of the cylinder as a final cushion.

To bring the buffer forward after being pushed in a series of three counter weights are attached to the tail rod of the piston through chains working over pulleys at the front end. These weights must be put in motion gradually to prevent breakage of the chains by shock, and to this end the centre weight is divided into a main weight and a jockey weight, the latter being suspended from a 6-inch pulley working in guides and riding on the centre chain. The jockey weight is then supported on the slack of the chain when the buffer is in the forward position, and when the buffer is driven in is lifted before the main weight, thus taking up the first shock on the chain. For the same reason the side weights are mounted on spring hangers.

The cylinder is automatically fed with water by gravitation through a small pipe fitted with a non-return valve, while a small valve attached to the top of the cylinder is provided for the escape of any air which may accumulate, and for convenience in filling.

A similar brake, described by Mr. Langley, has a $8\frac{3}{4}$-inch piston rod and a piston 12-inch diameter and 4-feet stroke.

The total area of the connecting passages varies from 7·18 square inches at the front to ·38 square inch at the back end. After being driven home the piston is returned by means of counterweights. With this brake a maximum pressure of 800 lbs. per square inch was obtained when stopping a train weighing about 200 tons, and moving at 8 miles per hour.[1]

In a somewhat similar brake at Strasbourg[2] the piston diameter is 16 inches, and its travel 8·2 feet. A train of 200 tons moving at 8 miles per

[1] "Proc. Inst. Mech. Eng.," 1886, p. 105.
[2] "Proc. Inst. C. E.," vol. 119, p. 449.

hour is brought to rest with a pressure of 580 lbs. per square inch, giving an uniform resistance of 52 tons. An automatic valve is fitted to a pipe connecting the two ends of the cylinder so that this may open if the pressure becomes excessive. As an additional precaution against the production of a dangerous cylinder pressure the links supporting the whole stop are designed so as to break under an excessive load.

It will be noted in Fig. 394 that the piston rod passes through both ends of the cylinder, the reason being that where the rod is in compression during the working stroke, if no tail rod is fitted the displacement of rod plus piston increases throughout the stroke, and if the cylinder were originally full of liquid no motion of the piston would be possible. The difficulty can be avoided by the provision of an air space inside the cylinder of volume slightly greater than that of the portion of the rod entering the cylinder during the stroke. Owing to this air space, however, the piston during the first portion of its stroke is engaged in compressing air, with the result that the pressure rises more slowly and the necessary maximum pressure for a given weight and velocity is increased by about 15 per cent. Where the piston rod is in tension during the working stroke the above difficulty is entirely obviated. The cylinder is filled with liquid with the piston run in, and the resistance is now increased by the formation of a partial vacuum behind the piston on its outward stroke.

In a more recent type of compression buffer stop without tail rod,[1] the difficulty is overcome by an escape valve set to blow off at 50 lbs. per square inch, at the front end of the cylinder. A volume of water equal to the displacement of the piston rod is then discharged through this valve to waste per working stroke. The piston is returned automatically to the front of the cylinder by means of pressure water from the town's mains which is supplied to the cylinder through a small back-pressure valve. This does away with all necessity for springs or counterbalance weights and gives a very neat and compact arrangement, the only drawback being due to the fact that town's water is used and that effective lubrication of the working surfaces must be relied upon to prevent corrosion. In this buffer stop the connecting passages are formed by two longitudinal taper grooves cut in the body of the cylinder 1½ inches wide and varying in depth from ¾ inches at the front to zero at the back end of the cylinder, while in addition there are twelve ⅜-inch holes bored through the body of the piston, which is 12 inches diameter and has a travel of

---

[1] By the Hydraulic Engineering Company, of Chester.

5 feet. Protection against excessive load is provided by a relief valve loaded to 1,000 lbs. per square inch at the back end of the cylinder.

Recoil Cylinders for Guns.—In the case of a 6-inch quick-firing gun having a weight of recoiling parts equal to 14,800 lbs., when firing a cordite charge of $13\frac{1}{4}$ lbs. and giving a muzzle velocity of 2,150 feet per second to a projectile weighing 100 lbs., the velocity of recoil is found to be approximately equal to 17·5 feet per second. The energy of recoil is about 70,500 foot lbs., and is absorbed by a buffer of 12-inch stroke and $7\frac{1}{2}$ inches internal diameter.

For such a purpose a tension buffer is commonly used, and Fig. 396 illustrates such an one as fitted to a 6-inch gun. The liquid, escaping from left to right through the valve V on the working stroke, passes

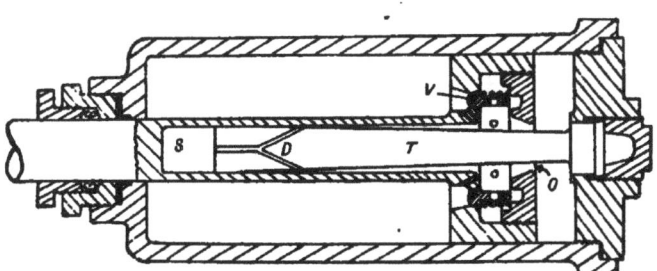

Fig. 396.—Tension Recoil Cylinder for 6-in. Gun.

through the annular passage O, whose area depends on the position of the piston relative to the central taper spindle T. The piston is returned by springs, whose action is buffered near the end of the stroke by the resistance to the flow of liquid from the space S through the holes at D.

Fig. 397 shows a type of compression buffer without tail rod, as fitted to the Canet quick-firing guns. Here the fact that the displacement increases throughout the stroke has been utilized to give a return device. In this buffer, when the piston A is pressed home, the displaced fluid passes through the pipe P and forces home the piston S, in the auxiliary cylinder B, against the resistance of the spring T. When the recoil has been absorbed this spring forces back the piston S, and increases the pressure in the main cylinder to an extent which depends on the strength of this spring. This pressure, acting on the unbalanced area of the piston rod, forces the main piston forward to the end of the cylinder. In this buffer the orifices are of constant area.

3 B 2

Where communication between the two ends of the cylinder is made through a spring-loaded valve, in order that the pressure should be approximately constant throughout the stroke it is necessary that the lift of the valve should be small, its weight small, and the resistance offered by the spring as constant as possible over the range of lift of the valve.

As a liquid for use in recoil cylinders, Castor oil or Rangoon oil is good and keeps the leathers in good condition. A mixture of four parts of glycerine to one of water is also good, as is a mixture of methylated spirits

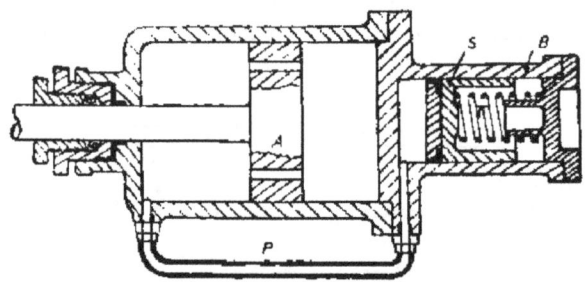

FIG. 397.—Recoil Cylinder for Canet Gun.

66 per cent, water 31 per cent., mineral oil 3 per cent., with 25 grains of carbonate of soda per gallon.

Theory of the Hydraulic Brake.—Suppose the piston rod to be in compression,

Let A = effective area of piston in square feet, *i.e.*, area of piston minus that of rod and of connecting orifices, if these are through the piston.

a = effective area of connecting orifices.

L = length of piston travel in feet.

l = length of connecting passages.

R = resistance of brake in lbs.

p = excess pressure behind piston in lbs. per square foot.

W = weight of moving body in lbs.

V = velocity of moving body, and of piston if brake is in operation.

v = velocity of fluid through orifices.

If the fluid is water we now have

$$\frac{p}{62\cdot4} = \frac{v^2}{2\,g}\left(1+\frac{f\,l}{m}\right) = \frac{V^2}{2\,g}\cdot\frac{A^2}{a^2}\left\{1+\frac{f\,l}{m}\right\} \qquad (1$$

while if F = resistance in lbs. due to mechanical friction and to effect of counterweights, &c.,

$$R = p A + F = \frac{62 \cdot 4\, V^2}{2\, g}\left\{1 + \frac{f\, l}{m}\right\}\frac{A^3}{a^2} + F. \qquad (2)$$

Brake with Uniform Resistance.—With uniform resistance the retardation of the moving body is uniform, and will be given by $\frac{V_1^2}{2\, L}$ feet per second per second, where V_1 is the velocity at impact, so that the velocity at any point distant x feet from the beginning of the stroke is given by

$$V^2 = V_1^2 - \frac{V_1^2}{L}\, x,$$
$$= V_1^2\left(1 - \frac{x}{L}\right).$$

By equating the work done on the brake to the loss of K. E. by the moving body we get

$$R\, L = \frac{W\, V_1^2}{2\, g}$$
$$\therefore \quad V_1^2 = \frac{2\, R\, L\, g}{W}, \qquad (3)$$

and

$$V^2 = \frac{2\, R\, L\, g\left(1 - \frac{x}{L}\right)}{W}.$$

Inserting this value in (2) above, we get

$$p A + F = \frac{62 \cdot 4\, L}{W}(p A + F)\left(1 - \frac{x}{L}\right)\left(1 + \frac{f\, l}{m}\right)\frac{A^3}{a^2} + F,$$

which finally reduces to

$$a^2 = \frac{62 \cdot 4\, L\, A^2\left(1 + \frac{f\, l}{m}\right)\left(A + \frac{F}{p}\right)}{W}\left(1 - \frac{x}{L}\right) \qquad (4)$$

giving the passage area for any value of x, when the form of the orifice is known.

If it be assumed that mechanical friction is equivalent to 5 per cent. of the force on the piston, and if the term $\left(1 + \frac{f\, l}{m}\right)$ be taken as unity (i.e., if fluid friction be neglected), this simplifies to

$$a^2 = \frac{65 \cdot 7\, L\, A^3}{W}\left(1 - \frac{x}{L}\right) \qquad (5)$$

EXAMPLE.

Buffer stop—piston, $12\frac{1}{4}$ inches diameter, provided with two slots of total area 4·75 square inches—$3\frac{1}{4}$-inch rod—length of stroke 4 feet. Weight of train = 100 tons.

$$A = \frac{105}{144} = \cdot728 \text{ square foot}; \quad W = 224{,}000 \text{ lbs.}$$

Equation (5) now becomes

$$a^2 = \frac{65\cdot7 \times 4 \times \cdot386}{224{,}000}\left(1 - \frac{x}{4}\right)$$

$$= \cdot000453\left(1 - \frac{x}{4}\right)$$

$$\therefore \quad a = \cdot02127\sqrt{\left(1 - \frac{x}{4}\right)} \text{ square feet.}$$

$$= 3\cdot06\sqrt{\left(1 - \frac{x}{4}\right)} \text{ square inches.}$$

Thus when $x = 0$, *i.e.*, at the beginning of the stroke, $a = 3\cdot06$ square inches. This gives the effective area of the orifice, and, when the entrant edges are well rounded so as to prevent the formation of a *vena contracta*, this will be the true area. With sharp-edged orifices, however, the orifice area will need to be greater than this in the ratio $\dfrac{1}{\text{coefficient of contraction,}}$ and this will depend upon the form and situation of the orifice.

To avoid errors in the preliminary calculation it is advisable to form the orifices with rounded entrant edges.

Assuming, in the example above, that $C_c = \cdot65$, we get the following values for a_1, where $C_c a_1 = a$:—

x feet	0	1·0	2·0	3·0	4·0
a_1 square inches . .	4·71	4·09	3·34	2·35	0

It is worthy of note that since both the hydraulic resistance and the kinetic energy of the moving body vary as the velocity squared, their relative value is independent of the velocity, so that the piston travel is approximately independent of the initial velocity of the moving body, and depends only on its weight.[1]

---

[1] In a buffer stop described by Mr. P. W. Shaw ("Proc. Inst. C. E.," 1905–6, Part iii., vol. 163, p. 290), the piston came to dead slow at about 9 inches from the end of its stroke, when resisting a mass of 11 tons, for all speeds of collision from 4 to 12 miles per hour. The details of the brake are as follow :—Cylinder, 10 inches diameter, 3 feet 6 inches stroke piston, 9⅞ inches diameter, with two rectangular slots 3 inches wide × 1½ inches deep, working over strips 3 inches wide × 1½ inches tapering to ¼ inch.

Brake with Passages of Constant Area.—In this case we have, neglecting mechanical friction,

$$p \times A = R = \frac{62\cdot4\, V^2}{2\,g} \left\{1 + \frac{fl}{m}\right\} \frac{A^3}{a^3}$$

$$= k\, V^2 \text{ where } k = \frac{62\cdot4}{2\,g} \left\{1 + \frac{fl}{m}\right\} \frac{A^3}{a^3}$$

Since this measures the mass × acceleration of the moving body

$$k\, V^2 = -\frac{W}{g}\frac{d\,V}{d\,t} = -\frac{W}{g}\, V \frac{d\,V}{d\,x}$$

the negative sign indicating that the motion is being retarded.

$$\therefore \quad k\, V = -\frac{W}{g}\frac{d\,V}{d\,x}$$

or

$$\int_V^{V_1} \frac{d\,V}{V} = -\int_x^{x_1} \frac{k\,g}{W}\, d\,x$$

The solution of this equation gives :—

$$\log_e \frac{V_1}{V} = -\frac{k\,g}{W}(x_1 - x) = \frac{k\,g}{W}(x - x_1).$$

Writing $x_1 = 0$, so that V_1 is the velocity at the instant of impact, we have

$$\log_e \frac{V}{V_1} = -\frac{k\,g}{W}\, x,$$

or

$$V = V_1\, e^{-\frac{k\,g}{W}\, x}.$$

giving the velocity corresponding to any position x of the piston. Since $e^{-\frac{k\,g}{W}\, x}$ never becomes equal to zero, no matter how large the value of x, the velocity cannot become zero until a change takes place in the law of resistance, either on account of the effect of solid friction, or because of the motion of the fluid becoming so slow that the resistance becomes approximately proportional to the first power of the velocity.

On taking mechanical friction into account we have, assuming this to be constant,

$$R = k\, V^2 + F = -\frac{W}{g}\, V \frac{d\,V}{d\,x} = -\frac{W}{2\,g}\frac{d\,(V^2)}{d\,x},$$

$$\therefore \quad \frac{d\,(V^2)}{d\,x} + \frac{2\,g\,k}{W}\, V^2 + \frac{2\,g\,F}{W} = 0,$$

or $\dfrac{d\,V^2}{d\,x} + b\, V^2 = c,$ where $\begin{cases} b = \dfrac{62\cdot4}{W}\dfrac{A^3}{a^3}\left(1 + \dfrac{fl}{m}\right). \\ c = -\dfrac{2\,g\,F}{W} \end{cases}$

The solution of this equation is

$$V^2 = \frac{c}{b} + D\, e^{-bx} \text{ where } D \text{ is a constant.}$$

Putting $V = V_1$ when $x = 0$ we have $V_1^2 = \frac{c}{b} + D$,

$$\therefore \quad V^2 = \frac{c}{b} + \left(V_1^2 - \frac{c}{b}\right) e^{-bx}$$

giving the velocity after a piston displacement x feet.

This may be written

$$e^{bx} = \frac{V_1^2 - \frac{c}{b}}{V^2 - \frac{c}{b}}$$

or

$$x = \frac{1}{b} \log_e \left\{ \frac{V_1^2 - \frac{c}{b}}{V^2 - \frac{c}{b}} \right\} = \frac{2 \cdot 302}{b} \log_{10} \left\{ \frac{V_1^2 - \frac{c}{b}}{V^2 - \frac{c}{b}} \right\} \text{feet.}$$

giving the position of the piston when the velocity has been reduced from V_1 to V feet per second.

Fig. 398 indicates the variation of pressure intensity inside the cylinder with piston displacement in the cases (a) where the resistance is uniform ; (b) where a compression buffer without tail rod, having passages of uniform area and with air compression is used ; and (c) with a tension buffer with passages of uniform area.

With constant pressure and resistance, the maximum pressure attained is about one-third that in the case of the tension buffer with passages of uniform area.

Art. 210.—The Hydraulic Dynamometer

is certainly the most perfect of all mechanical devices for measuring and absorbing the energy developed by a prime mover at a rotating shaft.

In its modern form it owes its conception—in all but one essential—to the late Mr. William Froude ; but the addition of the one detail which made the brake a practical success was due to Professor Osborne Reynolds.

The Reynolds—or Mather-Reynolds—Dynamometer shown in Fig. 399 consists of a double disc D, fixed to the power shaft by set screws or keys and carrying on its outer faces a series of narrow pockets.

These latter are semicircular in section, their plane is inclined at 45° to the axis of the shaft, and they face forwards in the direction of motion.

A casing C, carrying a double series of pockets similar to those on the disc, in the same planes but facing in the opposite direction, surrounds the disc and carries a graduated lever L from which are suspended the weights comprising the brake load.

The shaft passes through bushed openings in the casing which it fits closely so as to prevent undue leakage.

In the case of an 18-inch brake wheel the wheel itself carries twenty-four pockets on each face, while the casing carries twenty-five similar pockets. These are $4\frac{1}{2}$ inches in radial depth and have an axial width of $1\frac{1}{2}$ inch, the dividing vanes or partitions being $\frac{1}{4}$ inch thick.

Provision is made for supplying the pockets with water, and for allowing this to escape after having work done on it in the dynamometer, while a small air vent is provided in the thickness of each vane to admit air from an annular chamber K in the casing to the centre of the circle formed when two of the pockets on disc and casing directly face each other. It is to this detail that the

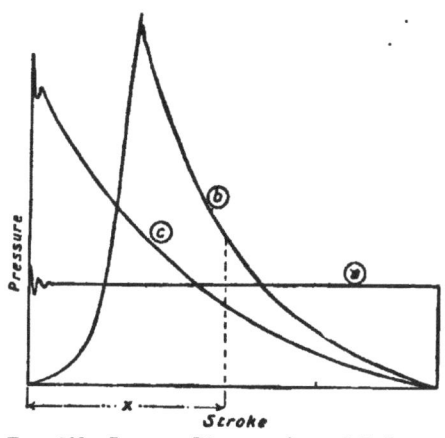

FIG. 398.—Pressure Diagrams from Cylinders of Hydraulic Brakes.

brake owes its successful action. As originally designed by Mr. Froude these air vents were absent.

The action of the dynamometer is as follows:—Water admitted to the casing through the flexible rubber tube at T finds its way through a series of four holes in the boss B into the chamber E between the discs, and thence through a series of small holes F F, formed in the thickness of the wheel vanes, into the pockets.

To prevent the water being projected into the air holes the radius of the inlet hole circle is made rather greater than that of the air vent circle.

Considering one of the pockets, its contained water is thrown outwards by centrifugal action, and, guided by the circular boundary of the pocket, is projected forwards into a stationary pocket in the casing.

Guided back by this pocket it enters a second moving pocket with increased velocity, is thrown outwards and projected forwards with still greater velocity into a second stationary pocket, and so on. Theo

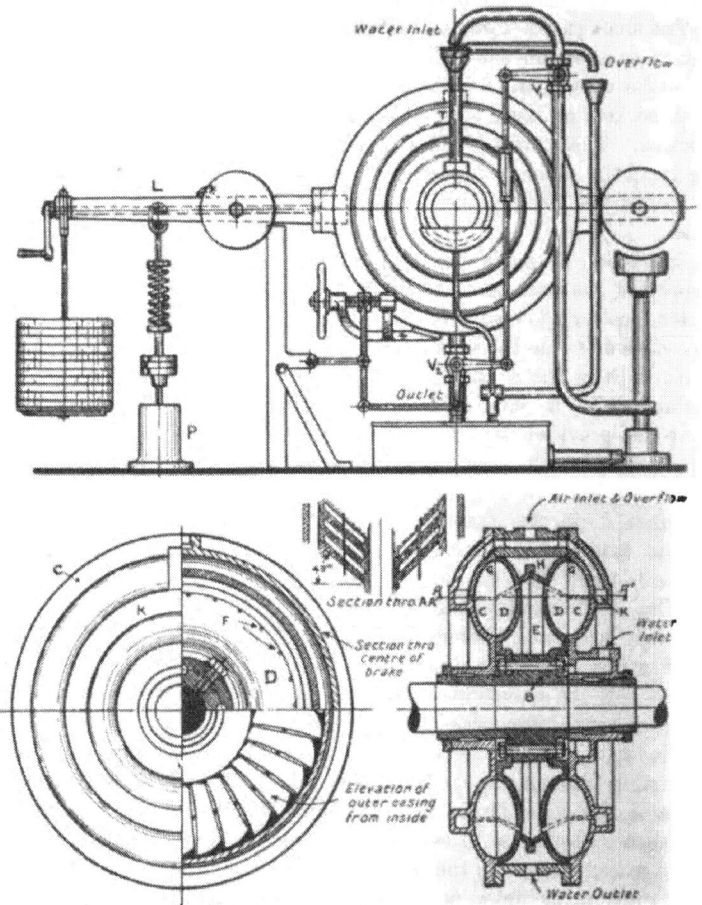

FIG. 399.—Reynolds' Hydraulic Dynamometer.

retically, but for the effect of friction, eddy losses, and the introduction of fresh water, this velocity would increase indefinitely. To produce the change in the moment of momentum about the shaft which occurs at each reversal of each stream, an equal moment must be applied to the disc and to the casing, and since the friction moment of the side glands also reacts equally on the casing and on the shaft, there is, so long as the shaft is rotating uniformly, an exact balance between the driving moment on the shaft and the resisting moment on the casing. The latter is provided and measured by the resisting moment of the brake load.

A slight side clearance between the outer circumference of the wheel and of the casing at G G permits of the escape of water into the concentric chamber H, which is always full when the brake is working. It escapes from this chamber through the automatically regulated valve V_2.

Since the change of momentum varies directly as the quantity of water in motion, and directly as its velocity, the brake resistance may be varied by varying either the inflow or outflow, a system of levers being arranged as indicated so as to do this if the brake lever rises or falls, and thus to prevent over or under loading. An oil dashpot at P serves to prevent hunting.

The object of the air vents may now be noted. The water in motion in each pair of pockets forms a vortex, and in consequence is at a greater pressure at the outside than at the centre of the pocket. The pressure at the centre may, in fact, in a closed pocket, become less than atmospheric, while in any case there is a tendency for air to accumulate at the points of least pressure, so that in the original type the dynamometer gradually emptied itself of water and became air charged. Further, since with a given speed of rotation the pressure from the inside to the outside of the vortices increases at a fixed rate, any change in the internal pressure is accompanied by a corresponding change in the pressure on the pockets of the wheel and casing, and hence affects the resistance.

By the provision of air vents, however, a constant pressure, equal to that of the atmosphere, is maintained at the centre of the vortices under all normal conditions of working; the brake need not, as in its original form, be full of water for satisfactory working; and for a given speed and water supply the resistance remains uniform.

This type of dynamometer has many advantages in view of its safety, its accuracy, ease of adjustment, and moderate dimensions.

The resisting moment varies as A v^2 r, where A is the combined cross-sectional area of the streams suffering change of direction, v is their mean velocity which is proportional to the angular velocity of the brake and to its radius, and r is the radius of the centre line of the brake pockets.

It follows that in two similar dynamometers rotating with the same angular velocity, and having corresponding linear dimensions in the ratio $s : 1$, if both brakes are running full we shall have :—

$$A_2 = s^2 A_1; \quad v_2 = s\, v_1; \quad r_2 = s\, r_1;$$
$$\therefore \quad A_2\, v_2^2\, r_2 = s^5\, (A_1\, v_1^2\, r_1),$$

so that the resisting moment, and, therefore the horse-power absorbed varies as the fifth power of the linear dimensions.

Experiments show that such a brake as illustrated will absorb a maximum of 29·5 H.P. at 100 revolutions, the disc diameter being 18 inches.

It follows that a brake having a disc 24 inches in diameter will absorb 1,100 H.P. at 300 revolutions, while by mounting two or more discs on one shaft the power which may be absorbed is practically unlimited.

The resistance with a given quantity of water varies approximately as the square of the brake speed, so that the brake is specially well adapted for high-speed work. Also, since the resisting moment at the instant of starting is zero and gradually increases with the speed, the brake is well adapted for the testing of internal-combustion engines or steam turbines of the pressure type, while once having been adjusted it requires no further attention no matter how the speed or power of the prime mover may vary within wide limits. The only drawback is the somewhat large first cost of the apparatus.

A dynamometer to absorb 6,000 H.P. at 300 r.p.m., built on almost exactly the same lines as the Parsons steam turbine, with circulation of water through the various rings of fixed and moving vanes is illustrated and described in *Engineering News*, December 30, 1909, p. 726.

For such high speeds as are common in steam turbines of the impulse type, and for small powers, a simpler type of hydraulic dynamometer gives good results. This consists simply of a series of parallel discs keyed to the power shaft, and rotating with small side clearance between a similar series of stationary discs fixed to the outer casing. As in the previous type of brake, with an uniform speed of rotation the resistance varies with the quantity of water in use, and may therefore be regulated by the opening or closing of the inlet or outlet valve. With a constant quantity of water in the brake the resistance depends on the wetted area, and varies approximately as the 1.8th power of the angular velocity. Assuming it to vary as the square of the velocity, the work done on each

face of each disc is given by $2\,\pi f\, \omega^3 \displaystyle\int_{R_2}^{R_1} r^4\, d\, r$, where f is a coefficient of

resistance, probably having a value of about ·0040 with roughened metal surfaces; ω = angular velocity in radians per second; and R_1 and R_2 are the outer and inner radii of the submerged portion of the rotating disc in feet.

On integrating this gives $\dfrac{2\,\pi f\,\omega^3}{5}\,(R_1{}^5 - R_2{}^5)$ foot lbs.

With n discs the work done against the resistance per second (neglecting the effect of the edges of the discs) is then given by

$$2\,n \times \frac{2\,\pi f\,\omega^3}{5}\,(R_1{}^5 - R_2{}^5) \text{ foot lbs.}$$

$$= \frac{4\,n\,\pi f\,\omega^3}{5 \times 550}\,(R_1{}^5 - R_2{}^5) \text{ H.P.}$$

EXAMPLE.

Brake provided with three rotating discs enclosed on both faces. Outer diameter 9 inches, submerged to an inner diameter of 6 inches. Assuming $f = \cdot004$, determine the B.H.P. absorbed at 10,000 revolutions per minute.

Here
$$\omega = \frac{2\,\pi \times 10,000}{60}$$

$$R_1{}^5 = (\cdot375)^5 = \cdot007413$$
$$R_2{}^5 = (\cdot25)^5 = \cdot000976$$

$$\therefore \text{ B.H.P.} = \frac{12 \times \pi \times \cdot004 \times 8\,\pi^3 \times 10^9 \times \cdot006437}{5 \times 216 \times 550}$$

$$= 405.$$

EXAMPLES.

(1) A direct acting hydraulic lift has a travel of 40 feet. The cage and ram weigh four tons, and are counterbalanced to the extent of three tons, by hanging weights. The lift is to take a load of three tons, with a maximum acceleration of 2 feet per second per second. The diameter of ram is decided on as being 5 inches. Determine the working pressure in the cylinder, assuming ram friction to account for 5 per cent. of this. If the pressure supply is 750 lbs. per square inch, this being reduced by means of a reversed intensifier of the ordinary type and having a stroke of 4 feet, determine the necessary size of this cylinder and of its ram, assuming friction to cause a loss of 5 per cent. Also determine the relative gain in efficiency of this system as compared with supplying the lift cylinder directly with pressure water throttled down to the required pressure.

N.B.—The total weight to be accelerated in this case $= 4 + 3 + 3 =$ 10 tons.

Answer.
$\begin{cases} \text{Working pressure 554 lbs. per square inch.} \\ \text{Diameter of reducer cylinder} = 15\cdot8 \text{ inches.} \\ \text{Diameter of reducer ram} = 13\cdot95 \text{ inches.} \\ \text{Gain in efficiency} = 35\cdot4 \text{ per cent.} \end{cases}$

(2) A direct acting hydraulic lift has a travel of 40 feet. The cage and ram weigh four tons, and the lift takes a weight of three tons, with an acceleration of 2 f.s.s. Assuming a ram diameter of 5 inches, and a hydraulic balance cylinder of the type shown in Fig. 361 to be fitted, this being designed so as to balance three-quarters of the weight of the cage and ram when the latter is at the upper limit of its travel, determine the leading dimensions of this balance cylinder, given that the stroke of its ram is 6 feet; that the ram B weighs one ton; and that the annular space D is supplied from a tank whose level is such as to produce a pressure of 30 lbs. per square inch on the annulus E when this ram is at the bottom of its stroke. The supply pressure at A is 1,100 lbs. per square inch.

Answer.
$\begin{cases} \text{Outer diameter of ram } B = 12\cdot95 \text{ inches.} \\ \text{Outer diameter of stationary inlet ram} = 9\cdot0 \text{ inches.} \\ \text{Outer diameter of annulus } E = 44 \text{ inches.} \end{cases}$

(3) If in the lift of the preceding example the type of balance cylinder of Fig. 362 is used, determine the necessary diameters of A, B, and C, and the necessary weight of ram B. Take into account the acceleration of B.

Answer.
$\begin{cases} \text{Outer diameter of ram } C = 12\cdot95 \text{ inches.} \\ \text{Outer diameter of ram } A = 9\cdot0 \text{ inches.} \\ \text{Weight of } B = 20\cdot2 \text{ tons.} \end{cases}$

(4) If in example (1) the cage and ram form part of a suspended lift, counterbalanced to the same extent as in that question, and operated through a jigger giving a multiplying ratio of 6 : 1, determine the necessary diameter of the cylinder of the jigger if the working pressure $=$ 750 lbs. per square inch; the efficiency of the multiplying mechanism $=$ 75 per cent.; and frictional losses account for 10 per cent. of the pressure on the ram.

Answer.   12·8 inches diameter.

(5) A direct acting crane of the type shown in Fig. 370 is to lift two tons, with a maximum acceleration of 4 f.s.s. The supply pressure is

500 lbs. per square inch. Assuming an efficiency of 75 per cent. determine the necessary size of ram.

Answer. 3·5 inches diameter.

(6) A hydraulic jack has an efficiency of 80 per cent. The diameter of the ram is 8 inches, of the plunger ¾ inch. The leverage of the operating lever is 20 : 1. Determine the pressure on the handle when lifting forty tons.

Answer. 49·2 lbs.

(7) A buffer stop is to be designed to stop a train weighing 150 tons when going at ten miles per hour, in 8 feet. The cylinder diameter is 16½ inches, the piston rod being 5$\frac{9}{16}$ inches diameter. The thickness of the piston is 4 inches, but the entrant edges of the orifices are rounded so as to make their effective length equal to 2 inches. There are two rectangular orifices, each 8 inches wide by 2·10 inches deep. Determine their effective depth at points where the piston travel is respectively 0, 2, 4, 6 and 8 feet, in order that the resistance may be uniform throughout the stroke. Also determine the magnitude of this resistance and the pressure in the cylinder, assuming that counterbalance weights and friction exert a constant resistance of one ton.

Answer. Resistance 140, 300 lbs. = 62·65 tons.

Pressure in cylinder   = 781 lbs. per square inch.

Stroke	0	2 ft.	4 ft.	6 ft.	8 ft.
Effective depth . .	1·30 ins.	1·13 ins.	·92 ins.	·65 ins.	0

(8) If the buffer stop of the preceding example has the same effective piston area with two rectangular connecting orifices each 8 inches wide which together have a combined area of 6 square inches, this remaining uniform throughout the stroke, determine the maximum pressure attained in the cylinder and the length of stroke which would be necessary for the piston to come to rest without touching the end of the cylinder.

Answer. Maximum pressure = 1,320 lbs. per square inch.

Stroke   = 22·45 feet.

(9) If the area of the passages in Example 8 were 8 square inches, determine the maximum pressure attained, and the length of stroke before coming to rest.

Answer. Pressure = 5,275 lbs. per square inch.

Stroke = 7·53 feet.

APPENDIX.

——•——

USEFUL DATA FOR HYDRAULIC CALCULATIONS.

Multiplier for converting logarithms :—

$\left\{\begin{array}{l}\text{Common to hyperbolic (to base } e) \text{ } 2\cdot30258.} \\ \text{Hyperbolic to common} \qquad \cdot43429.\end{array}\right.$

One radian $= 57\cdot296°$.

$g \qquad = 32\cdot1908$ at Greenwich.

One knot $= 6,080$ feet per hour.

One metre $= 39\cdot37$ inches $= 3\cdot28$ feet.

Standard atmosphere $= 29\cdot95$ inches $= 760$ millimetres of mercury
$\qquad\qquad\qquad = 33\cdot9$ feet of water.
$\qquad\qquad\qquad = 14\cdot7$ lbs. per square inch.

Inches of mercury $\times \cdot4907 =$ lbs. per square inch.

Feet of water $\qquad \times \cdot4331 =$ lbs. per square inch.

A pressure of 1 lb. per square inch is equivalent to a column of water
$2\cdot309$ feet high $\qquad = 27\cdot7$ inches high.

One imperial gallon $= \cdot1605$ cubic feet.
$\qquad\qquad\qquad = 277\cdot27$ cubic inches.
$\qquad\qquad\qquad = 10$ lbs.

One U.S. gallon $\quad = 231$ cubic inches.
$\qquad\qquad\qquad = \cdot83254$ imperial gallons.

One cubic foot of fresh water $\quad = 62\cdot4$ lbs.

One cubic metre of fresh water $= 35\cdot32$ cubic feet $= 2,200$ lbs.

One litre of fresh water $\qquad = 2\cdot2$ lbs.

One ton of fresh water $\qquad = 35\cdot9$ cubic feet.

One cubic foot of sea water $\quad = 64\cdot0$ lbs.

APPENDIX

Table A.

Pressure of Water.

The pressure of water in pounds per square inch for every foot in height to 270 feet.

Feet Head	Pressure per Square Inch.	Feet Head	Pressure per Square Inch.	Feet Head	Pressure per Square Inch.	Feet Head	Pressure per Square Inch.	Feet Head	Pressure per Square Inch.	Feet Head	Pressure per Square Inch.
1	0·433	46	19·92	91	39·42	136	58·91	181	78·40	226	98·1(
2	0·866	47	20·35	92	39·85	137	59·34	182	78·84	227	98·3
3	1·299	48	20·79	93	40·28	138	59·77	183	79·27	228	98·7(
4	1·733	49	21·22	94	40·72	139	60·21	184	79·70	229	99·2(
5	2·165	50	21·65	95	41·15	140	60·64	185	80·14	230	99·6
6	2·599	51	22·09	96	41·58	141	61·07	186	80·57	231	100·0
7	3·032	52	22·52	97	42·01	142	61·51	187	81·00	232	100·4
8	3·465	53	22·95	98	42·45	143	61·94	188	81·43	233	100·9
9	3·898	54	23·39	99	42·88	144	62·37	189	81·87	234	101·3
10	4·331	55	23·82	100	43·31	145	62·81	190	82·30	235	101·7
11	4·764	56	24·26	101	43·75	146	63·24	191	82·73	236	102·2
12	5·20	57	24·69	102	44·18	147	63·67	192	83·17	237	102·6
13	5·63	58	25·12	103	44·61	148	64·10	193	83·60	238	103·0
14	6·06	59	25·55	104	45·05	149	64·54	194	84·03	239	103·5
15	6·49	60	25·99	105	45·48	150	64·97	195	84·47	240	103·9
16	6·93	61	26·42	106	45·91	151	65·49	196	84·90	241	104·3
17	7·36	62	26·85	107	46·34	152	65·84	197	85·33	242	104·8
18	7·79	63	27·29	108	46·78	153	66·27	198	85·76	243	105·2
19	8·22	64	27·72	109	47·21	154	66·70	199	86·20	244	105·6
20	8·66	65	28·15	110	47·64	155	67·14	200	86·63	245	106·1
21	9·09	66	28·58	111	48·08	156	67·57	201	87·07	246	106·5
22	9·53	67	29·02	112	48·51	157	68·00	202	87·50	247	106·9
23	9·96	68	29·45	113	48·94	158	68·43	203	87·93	248	107·4
24	10·39	69	29·88	114	49·38	159	68·87	204	88·36	249	107·8
25	10·82	70	30·32	115	49·81	160	69·31	205	88·80	250	108·2
26	11·26	71	30·75	116	50·24	161	69·74	206	89·23	251	108·7
27	11·69	72	31·18	117	50·68	162	70·17	207	89·66	252	109·1
28	12·12	73	31·62	118	51·11	163	70·61	208	90·10	253	109·5
29	12·55	74	32·05	119	51·54	164	71·04	209	90·53	254	110·0
30	12·99	75	32·48	120	51·98	165	71·47	210	90·96	255	110·4
31	13·42	76	32·92	121	52·41	166	71·91	211	91·39	256	110·8
32	13·86	77	33·35	122	52·84	167	72·34	212	91·83	257	111·3
33	14·29	78	33·78	123	53·28	168	72·77	213	92·26	258	111·7
34	14·72	79	34·21	124	53·71	169	73·20	214	92·69	259	112·1
35	15·16	80	34·65	125	54·15	170	73·64	215	93·13	260	112·6
36	15·59	81	35·08	126	54·58	171	74·07	216	93·56	261	113·0
37	16·02	82	35·52	127	55·01	172	74·50	217	93·99	262	113·4
38	16·45	83	35·95	128	55·44	173	74·94	218	94·43	263	113·9
39	16·89	84	36·39	129	55·88	174	75·37	219	94·86	264	114·3
40	17·32	85	36·82	130	56·31	175	75·80	220	95·30	265	114·7
41	17·75	86	37·25	131	56·74	176	76·23	221	95·73	266	115·2
42	18·19	87	37·68	132	57·18	177	76·67	222	96·16	267	115·6
43	18·62	88	38·12	133	57·61	178	77·10	223	96·60	268	116·0
44	19·05	89	38·55	134	58·04	179	77·53	224	97·03	269	116·5
45	19·49	90	38·98	135	58·48	180	77·97	225	97·46	270	116·9

Table B.

Areas of Circles.

Diameter Inches.	Area. Square inches.	Diameter. Inches.	Area. Square Inches.	Diameter. Inches.	Area. Square inches.
⅛	·0122	16½	213·82	38	1134·1
¼	·0490	17	226·98	38½	1164·2
⅜	·1104	17½	240·53	39	1194·6
½	·1963	18	254·47	39½	1225·4
¾	·4417	18½	268·80	40	1256·6
1	·7854	19	283·53	40½	1288·2
1⅛	·9940	19½	298·65	41	1320·3
1¼	1·227	20	314·16	41½	1352·7
1½	1·767	20½	330·06	42	1385·4
1¾	2·405	21	346·36	42½	1418·6
2	3·141	21½	363·05	43	1452·2
2¼	3·976	22	380·13	43½	1486·2
2½	4·908	22½	397·61	44	1520·5
2¾	5·939	23	415·48	44½	1555·3
3	7·068	23½	433·74	45	1590·4
3¼	8·295	24	452·39	45½	1626·0
3½	9·621	24½	471·44	46	1661·9
3¾	11·04	25	490·87	46½	1698·2
4	12·56	25½	510·71	47	1734·9
4½	15·90	26	530·93	47½	1772·1
5	19·63	26½	551·55	48	1808·6
5½	23·75	27	572·5	48½	1847·5
6	28·27	27½	593·9	49	1885·7
6½	33·18	28	615·7	49½	1924·4
7	38·48	28½	637·9	50	1963·5
7½	44·17	29	660·5	50½	2003·0
8	50·26	29½	683·4	51	2042·8
8½	56·74	30	706·8	51½	2083·1
9	63·61	30½	730·6	52	2123·7
9½	70·88	31	754·7	52½	2164·8
10	78·54	31½	779·3	53	2206·2
10½	86·59	32	804·2	53½	2248·0
11	95·03	32½	829·5	54	2290·2
11½	103·87	33	855·3	54½	2332·8
12	113·10	33½	881·4	55	2375·8
12½	122·72	34	907·9	55½	2419·2
13	132·73	34½	934·8	56	2463·0
13½	143·14	35	962·1	56	2507·2
14	153·94	35½	989·8	57	2551·8
14½	165·13	36	1017·9	57	2596·7
15	176·71	36½	1046·3	58	2642·1
15½	188·69	37	1075·2	59	2734·0
16	201·06	37½	1104·5	60	2827·4

TABLE C.

Theoretical Velocities of Water, $v = \sqrt{2\,g\,h}$, in Feet per Second, due Heads from One-tenth to One Hundred Feet.

Head in feet.	Velocity in feet per sec.	Head in feet.	Velocity in feet per sec.	Head in feet.	Velocity in feet per sec.	Head in feet.	Velocity in feet per sec.	Head in feet.	Velocity in feet per sec.
0·0	0·000	·8	17·571	28·	42·43	52·	57·83	76·	69·81
·1	2·536	·9	17·753	28·5	42·81	52·5	58·06	76·5	70·14
·2	3·587	5·	17·93	29·	43·19	53·	58·38	77·	70·35
·3	4·393	5·5	18·80	29·5	43·56	53·5	58·65	77·5	70·69
·4	5·072	6·	19·64	30·	43·92	54·	58·93	78·	70·83
·5	5·671	6·5	20·44	30·5	44·29	54·5	59·20	78·5	71·05
·6	6·212	7·	21·21	31·	44·65	55·	59·48	79·	71·28
·7	6·710	7·5	21·96	31·5	45·01	55·5	59·74	79·5	71·51
·8	7·137	8·	22·68	32·	45·36	56·	60·01	80·	71·73
·9	7·609	8·5	23·38	32·5	45·72	56·5	60·28	80·5	71·96
1·0	8·020	9·	24·06	33·	46·07	57·	60·55	81·	72·18
1	8·412	9·5	24·92	33·5	46·42	57·5	60·79	81·5	72·40
2	8.786	10·	25·36	34·	46·76	58·	61·08	82·	72·60
·3	9·144	10·5	25·98	34·5	47·10	58·5	61·34	82·5	72·84
·4	9·490	11·	26·60	35·	47·44	59·	61·60	83·	73·06
·5	9·823	11·5	27·19	35·5	47·78	59·5	61·81	83·5	73·28
·6	10·143	12·	27·78	36·	48·12	60·	62·12	84·	73·51
·7	10·457	12·5	28·35	36·5	48·4D	60·5	62·38	84·5	73·72
·8	10·760	13·	28·91	37·	48·78	61·	62·64	85·	73·94
·9	11·055	13·5	29·46	37·5	49·11	61·5	62·84	85·5	74·16
2·0	11·342	14·	30·00	38·	49·44	62·	63·15	86·	74·37
·1	11·622	14·5	30·54	38·5	49·76	62·5	63·40	86·5	74·54
·2	11·896	15·	31·06	39·	50·08	63·	63·65	87·	74·80
·3	12·163	15·5	31·57	39·5	50·40	63·5	63·90	87·5	75·02
·4	12·425	16·	32·08	40·	50·72	64·	64·16	88·	75·23
·5	12·681	16·5	32·57	40·5	51·04	64·5	64·41	88·5	75·45
·6	12·932	17·	33·06	41·	51·35	65·	64·66	89·	75·66
·7	13·179	17·5	33·55	41·5	51·66	65·5	64·90	89·5	75·87
·8	13·420	18·	34·02	42·	51·97	66·	65·15	90·	76·08
·9	13·658	18·5	34·49	42·5	52·28	66·5	65·39	90·5	76·29
3 0	13·891	19·	34·95	43·	52·59	67·	65·64	91·	76·51
·1	14·121	19·5	35·41	43·5	52·89	67·5	65·89	91·5	76·71
·2	14·347	20·	35·86	44·	53·20	68·	66·15	92·	76·92
·3	14·569	20·5	36·31	44·5	53·55	68·5	66·38	92·5	77·16
·4	14·789	21·	36·75	45·	53·80	69·	66·62	93·	77·34
·5	15·004	21·5	37·18	45·5	54·09	69·5	66·86	93·5	77·53
·6	15·217	22·	37·61	46·	54·39	70·	67·10	94·	77·82
·7	15·427	22·5	38·04	46·5	54·69	70·5	67·34	94·5	77·90
·8	15·634	23·	38·46	47·	54·98	71·	67·58	95·	78·11
·9	15·839	23·5	38·87	47·5	55·27	71·5	67·81	95·5	78·37
4·0	16·040	24·	39·29	48·	55·56	72·	68·05	96·	78·??
·1	16·240	24·5	39·69	48·5	55·85	72·5	68·28	96·5	78·7?
·2	16·437	25·	40·10	49·	56·14	73·	68·52	97·	78·99
·3	16·631	25·5	40·50	49·5	56·42	73·5	68·75	97·5	79·1?
·4	16·823	26·	40·89	50·	56·71	74·	68·99	98·	79·2?
·5	17·018	26·5	41·28	50·5	56·99	74·5	69·22	98·5	79·5?
·6	17·201	27·	41·61	51·	57·27	75·	69·45	99·	79·8?
·7	17·337	27·5	42·05	51·5	57·55	75·5	69·68	99·5	79·??

TABLE D.

Fire Streams.

Pressure required at nozzle and at pump, with quantity and pressure necessary to throw of effective streams various distances through different size nozzles, using 100 feet of dinary 2½-inch rubber-lined hose and smooth nozzles.

J. R. FREEMAN.

SIZE OF NOZZLE, ¾ INCH.

ressure at Nozzle, in lbs. per sq. in.	40	50	60	70	80	90	100
ressure at Pump, „ „ „	46	57	68	80	91	102	114
mperial Gallons per Minute . .	86	96	105	114	122	129	136
istance thrown Horizontal, in feet .	44	50	54	58	62	65	68
istance thrown Vertical, „ .	60	67	72	76	79	81	83

SIZE OF NOZZLE. ⅞ INCH.

ressure at Nozzle, in lbs. per sq. in.	40	50	60	70	80	90	100
ressure at Pump, „ „ „	50	63	75	88	101	113	126
mperial Gallons per Minute . .	118	132	144	156	167	177	186
istance thrown Horizontal, in feet.	49	55	61	66	70	74	76
istance thrown Vertical, „ .	62	71	77	81	85	88	90

SIZE OF NOZZLE, 1 INCH.

ressure at Nozzle, in lbs, per sq. in.	40	50	60	70	80	90	100
ressure at Pump, „ „ „	58	72	87	101	115	130	144
mperial Gallons per Minute . .	154	173	189	204	218	232	245
istance thrown Horizontal, in feet .	55	61	67	72	76	80	83
istance thrown Vertical, . .	64	73	79	85	89	92	96

SIZE OF NOZZLE, 1⅛ INCHES.

ressure at Nozzle, in lbs. per sq. in.	40	50	60	70	80	90	100
ressure at Pump, „ „ „	69	86	103	120	138	155	172
mperial Gallons per Minute . .	127	221	241	260	279	295	312
istance thrown Horizontal, in feet .	59	66	72	77	81	85	89
istance thrown Vertical, „	65	75	83	88	92	96	99

SIZE OF NOZZLE. 1¼ INCHES.

ressure at Nozzle, in lbs. per sq. in.	40	50	60	70	80	90	100
ressure at Pump, „ „ „	84	106	127	148	169	190	211
mperial Gallons per Minute . .	246	275	301	325	348	368	388
istance thrown Horizontal, in feet .	63	70	76	81	85	90	93
istance thrown Vertical, „ .	67	77	85	91	95	99	101

SIZE OF NOZZLE, 1⅜ INCHES.

ressure at Nozzle, in lbs. per sq. in.	40	50	60	70	80	90	100
ressure at Pump, „ „ „	107	134	160	187	214	240	268
mperial Gallons per Minute . .	301	337	369	398	426	452	476
istance thrown Horizontal, in feet .	66	73	79	84	88	92	96
istance thrown Vertical, „ .	69	79	87	92	97	100	103

The above pressures are based on the supposition that the hose is coupled direct to the delivery of the pump ; if, however, the hose is coupled to a hydrant which is supplied direct from the pump, then the corresponding fire pump pressure must be greater than the hydrant pressure by an amount equal to friction loss, and difference of head between hydrant and pump.

The distances given are for *effective* fire *streams* adapted for fire purposes, and are not for the isolated drops.

INDEX.

The Numerals refer to Pages.

THE WHITEFRIARS PRESS, LTD., LONDON AND TONBRIDGE.